CORPORATE FINANCE LAW

Corporate Finance is an area of law which is obviously of significant practical importance, but the academic analysis of this area of law has also been increasingly recognised. This book provides a discussion of the most interesting theoretical and policy issues in Corporate Finance law. It covers both the equity and debt sides of Corporate Finance law, and seeks, where possible, to compare the two, considering the desirability of each in various circumstances and pointing to areas of convergence and overlap. The topics covered include: an overview of the financing options available to companies; the relationship between debt and equity; legal capital; contractual protection for creditors; proprietary protection for creditors; single and multiple lenders; transferred debt; public offers of shares; the ongoing regulation of the capital market; the regulation of debt; takeovers; schemes of arrangement and private equity. Each chapter analyses the issues so as to enable the reader to understand the difficulties, risks and tensions inherent in this area of law, and the attempts made by the legislature and the courts, as well as the parties involved, to deal with them. This book discusses areas where the law is uncertain, including some difficult conceptual problems, and considers the present law critically, including options for possible reform. It will be of interest to practitioners, academics and students engaged in the practice and study of corporate finance law.

Corporate Finance Law

Principles and Policy

Louise Gullifer

and

Jennifer Payne

·H A R T·
PUBLISHING

OXFORD AND PORTLAND, OREGON
2011

Published in the United Kingdom by Hart Publishing Ltd
16C Worcester Place, Oxford, OX1 2JW
Telephone: +44 (0)1865 517530
Fax: +44 (0)1865 510710
E-mail: mail@hartpub.co.uk
Website: http://www.hartpub.co.uk
Published in North America (US and Canada) by
Hart Publishing
c/o International Specialized Book Services
920 NE 58th Avenue, Suite 300
Portland, OR 97213–3786
USA
Tel: +1 503 287 3093 or toll-free: (1) 800 944 6190
Fax: +1 503 280 8832
E-mail: orders@isbs.com
Website: http://www.isbs.com

British Library Cataloguing in Publication Data

Data Available

ISBN: 978-1-84946-004-0

Typeset by Columns Design XML Ltd, Reading
Printed and bound in Great Britain by
TJ International Ltd, Padstow, Cornwall

Preface and Acknowledgements

This book deals with UK Corporate Finance law, and aims to discuss both the substance of the law, and the policy issues underlying it. This book has arisen out of the Corporate Finance law course which we have taught in Oxford for the last few years. The shape and structure of this book have been formed by our experience in teaching the course. The process of creating an integrated course, and dealing with the debt and equity aspects of corporate finance, have been key in shaping this book. Many of the issues examined here were first raised and discussed around the seminar table and we would like to acknowledge and thank those alongside whom we have taught the course, and argued these points, namely John Armour, Paul Davies, Roy Goode, Roger McCormick, Dan Prentice and John Vella. Special thanks are also due to Chris Hale and Emma Watford who have taught the students (and us) about Private Equity. We would also like to thank the BCL/MJur students who have taken the course. In particular, we would like to acknowledge the students of 2008–09 and 2009–10 who saw draft chapters of this book and whose comments on various issues have helped to shape some of the discussions in the text.

This book aims to state the law and major policy developments as at 1 September 2010. However, no area of the law is static and inevitably in the period between finishing writing this book, and the proofs being finalised, the law on a number of issues has moved on. We note the following significant developments: the Alternative Investment Fund Managers directive (the text of which was finally voted through by the European Parliament in November 2010); the third Basel accord (Basel III) (agreed in outline in September 2010); two new papers in October 2010 dealing with the regulation of takeover bids, one produced by the Takeover Panel (*Review of certain Aspects of the Regulation of Takeover Bids* 2010/22) and one by the Government (BIS, *A long Term focus for Corporate Britain, A call for evidence*, URN 10/1225, 31–34) although this latter paper also raises issues of broader corporate importance; the public consultation launched by the EU in November 2010 on credit rating agencies; *Fearns v Anglo-Dutch Paint and Chemical Ltd* [2010] EWHC 2366 (Ch), which throws further doubt on the proposition (discussed in 5.2.4.3) that transaction set-off operates as a substantive defence; the decision by Briggs J in *Lomas v JRB Firth Rixson Inc* [2010] EWHC 3372 (Ch) that a 'flawed asset' type provision in the Master ISDA agreement did not contravene the anti-deprivation principle (this is the case mentioned in footnote 203 on page 176); the decision of the Court of Appeal in *Springwell Navigation Co v JP Morgan* [2010] EWCA Civ 1221, which confirms the points made about 'no representation' clauses in 7.4.4; the decision in *Habibson's Bank Ltd v Standard Chartered Bank (Hong Kong) Ltd* [2010] EWHC 702 (Comm) confirming that consent to novation can be given effectively in advance; the decision in *Pearson v Lehman Brothers Finance SA* [2010] EWHC 2914 (Ch) which addresses the identification of property issue in relation to securities held in a fungible account; the draft amendments to the Financial Collateral Arrangements (No. 2) Regulations which were issued by HM Treasury on 22 December 2010 and which deal with many of the technical problems with the Regulations mentioned in 3.3.1.2, 6.4.1.1 and 6.5.1.2; and the Supreme Court's decision in *Progress Property Co Ltd v Moorgarth Group Ltd* [2010] UKSC 55 which is interesting for the light it casts on the issue of distributions to shareholders.

In writing this book we have been assisted by a great many people. We are lucky enough to have friends and colleagues in Oxford and beyond with whom we have been able to discuss corporate law generally and the issues arising out of this book more particularly, and we would like to acknowledge their advice and assistance. Particular thanks are due to Hugh Beale, Michael Bridge, Roy Goode, Sandra Frisby and Niamh Moloney who have variously discussed points, answered queries and read and commented on draft chapters with unfailing patience, as well as providing more general (much appreciated) advice and support. Help on specific points has also been provided by Kate Sharp, Stephen Chait, Tim Cleary, Allen Jones, Woo-Jung Jon and Paul Lindsell. We have also been assisted by a number of excellent research assistants: Victoria Barns-Graham, Bernd Delahaye, Murray Cox and Emma Gullifer. Special thanks should go to Murray whose assistance with chapter 11, in particular, has been invaluable.

We would like to thank Hart Publishing, and in particular Richard Hart, for overseeing the production of this book through its various stages with great care and skill.

We would also like to thank our families for their unfailing patience and support during the writing of this book, and in particular to thank Robert and Nick (respectively) who have been sources of inspiration and encouragement and without whom this project could not have been completed. This book is dedicated to them.

Louise Gullifer and Jennifer Payne
Oxford, December 2010

Contents

Table of Cases

United Kingdom

Australia

British Virgin Islands

Canada

Table of Legislation

United Kingdom

Statutory Instruments

Other

European Union

Directives

Regulations

Australia

Canada

Portugal

Spain

United States

Table of Conventions, Treaties, etc

1

Introduction

The purpose of this book is to consider and analyse UK corporate finance law. We consider the principles and policy behind the law in this area, and examine the substantive provisions in light of that discussion. In particular we aim to consider both the debt and equity aspects of corporate finance law, and the interrelationship between the two. Before stating in more detail what we aim to achieve, it might also be helpful to set out some of the things we don't seek to achieve. First, although we hope that this book will be read by practitioners, as well as academics, students and policy-makers, and that practitioners will find it interesting and useful, this is not predominantly a how-to guide for practitioners. We don't aim to put the reader in a position to be able to carry out in practice the corporate finance transactions described here. By way of example, the chapter dealing with takeovers (chapter twelve) does not provide a step by step guide as to how to conduct a takeover in the UK. Rather it considers why jurisdictions generally regulate takeovers, why different jurisdictions regulate this issue in different ways, how the UK system compares to other jurisdictions (principally, in that chapter, the US) and then, once the aims of the UK regulation have been established, assesses the UK regulations against that background.

This raises another point, namely that while the book's focus is UK corporate finance law, other regimes are considered, and this comparative analysis can have one of two purposes. Some aspects of UK corporate finance law can only be understood if other regimes are discussed. For example, in a number of areas UK law is very heavily influenced by European developments. An obvious example of this are the disclosure requirements for prospectuses, discussed in chapters nine and eleven. The Prospectus Directive,[1] a maximum harmonisation directive, and its accompanying Regulation,[2] provide the substance of the UK's disclosure requirements. At other points we examine other jurisdictions as a comparison with the UK provisions in order to provide fresh insight as to the suitability and utility of the UK provisions. This is not intended as a comparative text, but examining other jurisdictions can help us better understand domestic provisions. For example, much of the jurisprudence on the policy issues relating to security interests comes from the US, and notice filing schemes such as the ones in Canada and New Zealand are discussed in the context of reform of the UK law on secured transactions.

Although we have said that the purpose of this book is to consider and analyse UK corporate finance law, it must be remembered that the UK consists of four countries: England, Wales, Scotland and Northern Ireland. While the law of England and Wales is the same for all relevant purposes, there are often significant differences between English and Scots law, and some between Northern Irish law and English law. The differences are most

---

[1] 2003/71/EC.
[2] Commission Regulation (EC) No 809/2004.

notable with regard to non-statutory law, such as property law and contract. Scots law, especially, comes from a different origin (the civilian tradition) and resembles, in some respects, the law in some European countries, although in other respects it resembles the English common law.[3] However, virtually all company law which is statute based is the same for the whole of the UK.[4] The same is true of most of the regulation discussed in this book, particularly securities regulation, much of which is now derived from European legislation. Other statutory provisions, though, are different as regards English law and Scots law.[5] The reader therefore needs to be aware of this issue. In general, in the debt sections of the book, the law discussed is that of England and Wales, while in the equity sections generally what is said is true for the whole of the UK.

Another general point is that this book is not intended to be comprehensive in any sense. The term 'corporate finance' is not a term of art, and can mean very different things to different people. In deciding what to include we have started from our own conception of what 'corporate finance' means and what it includes, which may well be different from that of others. In part we have also been guided by our interests, but, having taught this subject for a number of years, we have also been guided by what interests and stimulates others about this topic. We will no doubt have included some topics that others do not consider need to be present in a book dealing with corporate finance law, and left out other topics that others would have wished to see included.

It might be helpful, therefore, to explain what our conception of corporate finance entails. Our starting point is that corporate finance primarily concerns how a company can obtain money to finance its operations, and therefore corporate finance law consists of the legal rules that govern these issues. However, the term 'corporate finance law' is misleading to some extent since it is not one single body of law. Indeed, as will be clear on reading this book, the law described here includes, variously, general contract law, property law, company law and corporate insolvency law as well as more specialist regulatory law dealing with securities, takeovers and other issues. We restrict our analysis to the financing of companies limited by shares. We don't consider unlimited companies or companies limited by guarantee.[6] Neither do we cover the financing of limited liability partnerships, partnerships more generally, sole traders, charities, mutual funds, trusts or other similar structures.

In relation to the financing of companies, there are three basic sources of finance: share issues, debt and retained profits. To a large extent therefore we concentrate in this book on the mechanisms by which companies can raise equity capital, and what use they can make of that capital once it has been raised, and on the different methods by which they can raise debt financing. Debt financing is broadly defined, so as to include both loans and debt securities, and also other forms of credit such as trade credit extended to a company by other companies. However, it does not include all the money of which the company

---

[3]   See P Wood, *Law and Practice of International Finance* (London, Sweet & Maxwell, 2008) 3–24–3–26.

[4]   The Companies Act 2006 creates a single company law regime for the whole of the UK for the first time (see Companies Act 2006, Part 45) although some differences are preserved within the Act, such as the different regimes regarding derivative actions (Companies Act 2006, ss 260–264 for England, Wales and Northern Ireland and ss 265–269 for Scotland).

[5]   For example, the provisions on registration of company charges are found in Part 25, chapter 1 of the Companies Act 2006 with regard to England, Wales and Northern Ireland, and in Part 25, chapter 2 with regard to Scotland.

[6]   Companies Act 2006, s 3.

makes use, for example money which is owed by the company to a third party and which the company uses to finance its operations in the interim. One example of this might be a third party who has a tort claim against the company, another is someone who has a claim in respect of defective goods purchased from a company.

Thus, for the purposes of this book, we concentrate on the category of creditors who lend money or extend credit to the company and whose intention is to finance the company's activities, rather than on those who are not intending to become creditors, even though they may have chosen to contract, or otherwise deal, with the company. The additional category of creditors (not lenders) highlighted here, such as tort claimants, are not our predominant concern. This does not mean that they will be ignored in this book. They are of importance in policy discussions, since the contractual arrangements entered into between creditor-lenders and the company can impact on them. In general they are in a weak position to protect themselves (for example if they are involuntary creditors) and so the question arises whether the law should step in to protect them. The term 'lender' is used throughout the book generically to include all those who consciously lend to or extend credit to a company. In this context, the company is called the 'borrower'.[7] However, when wider issues about the protection of all those to whom the company owes money are discussed, the term 'creditor' is used to include both lenders and others such as tort and breach of contract claimants.

Any regulation imposed by the law will impact on those groups that are within the contemplation of this book, that is, those who buy shares or consciously lend or extend credit to a company. Generally speaking, investors in shares are protected primarily by regulatory law, although their contractual relationships, in particular with the company or with other shareholders, can be important. By contrast, those who lend or extend credit to a company are protected largely by contractual or proprietary rights for which they bargain, and only by regulatory law in certain specific circumstances.

It follows from this that this book concentrates on companies who are raising finance via equity and debt financing. There are companies (banks and other finance companies) whose business is predominantly to lend money to others. We are not concerned with those types of companies and the topic of banking regulation falls outside the remit of this book. However, the financing of companies who extend credit to other companies is discussed at various points.

As regards the companies that do fall within the ambit of this book, it is clear that there is considerable variety both as regards the size of companies, and the business of those companies, and this necessarily impacts on their financing needs and options. One point, which we want to make clear from the outset, is that there is not a one size fits all approach to financing which will suit all companies in all situations.

The business in which a company engages will have a significant impact on its financing choices. Companies may be categorised in terms of what they do, for example, financial companies, real property companies, construction companies, manufacturing companies, retail companies, services companies, investment companies or as special purpose vehicles (SPVs), engaged, for example, in project finance or in securitisation. The type of business conducted by the company will be crucial in determining, for example, whether it has assets over which security can be taken, whether it will depend on trade credit, or whether

---

[7] These terms are used even when the transaction is structured somewhat differently, for example, where receivables are sold to a receivables financier.

lenders can make use of some of the quasi-security devices such as retention of title clauses. There is likely to be all the difference in the world between the financing profile of the archetypal company manufacturing and supplying widgets, a large listed pension fund company whose main business is investing in other companies, and an SPV set up to carry out a project finance operation. So, for example, a manufacturing company will have to raise finance to buy equipment and stock, as well as to meet employment and other running expenses. Its main assets will be tangible (land, equipment, stock) and intangible (receivables, maybe intellectual property and goodwill). It could be financed through loan finance, secured on its assets, but alternatively by asset-based finance, including receivables financing and retention of title finance in relation to the acquisition of equipment and stock. The listed pension fund company's assets will be equity and debt securities issued by other companies, and it will look to borrow in transactions using these as financial collateral. The project finance SPV will typically only have one asset, the revenue-generating contract, on the strength of which it will raise loan or bond finance. It may also be significant whether the company operates within a group of companies and, if so, what role within the group that company performs.

As regards the size of companies, significant differences emerge according to whether the company in question is a private company or a publicly traded company, whether it has a small group of shareholders who are heavily involved in the management of the company or a wide and dispersed shareholding profile. Consider, for example, a small private company which is effectively an incorporated sole trader. The shareholders and directors are likely to be the same people. As regards financing it is likely that the director/shareholders will put in a relatively small amount of equity, and that the majority of the financing will be via loans either from the shareholder/directors and/or a bank. The primary purpose of shares in such a company is likely to be their control function rather than any capital raising device. Given the significant risk of insolvency for such a business the bank will be very keen to protect against this eventuality. It is unlikely that the business itself will have significant assets and usually the debts will be guaranteed by the director/shareholders personally and/or secured on their personal assets. In this situation, the relationship between the bank and the company is very important, and the bank will monitor the affairs of the company closely for signs of financial distress.

By contrast, in a somewhat larger private company, with some division between the shareholders and directors, shares become useful as finance raising devices. However, the illiquidity of private company shares can make them unattractive as an investment, and therefore it may not be straightforward to persuade external investors to invest by way of share capital. One model is to seek a significant injection of equity capital from venture capital (discussed in chapter fourteen). The company is likely to still depend heavily on bank lending (an overdraft and maybe also a longer term loan) and again the bank will be keen to protect itself against the risk of insolvency by taking security (both fixed and floating charges) over the company's assets. The bank would decide to lend based on the previous and projected cash flow of the company, and there would still be an ongoing relationship between the bank and company, involving monitoring as above. However, such a company may also borrow using asset-based finance, where the amount lent is directly related to the amount of assets the company has. The assets may be sold to the lender (as in the case of receivables) or the lender will take a charge, fixed if possible, over available assets. Depending on the nature of the company's business it may rely on financing supplied via trade creditors, customers etc.

Ultimately, for companies looking to increase significantly their levels of external equity finance, there is the option of issuing the company's shares to the public (discussed in chapter nine). An offer of shares to the public allows the company to have access to outside investors who can participate substantially in the company. This access to significantly increased levels of equity capital is one of the major advantages of offering shares to the public especially when combined with a listing. Obtaining a listing for the shares creates liquidity. Not only is there a ready market for the shares, but they must be freely transferable.[8] Larger companies, whether public or private, will raise debt finance from a number of lenders. Thus loan finance may come from a syndicate of banks, and the company may decide to issue debt securities to a selected number of financial institutions or, in rare instances, to the public. Both these techniques, which enable the risk of non-payment to be spread across many parties and therefore enable more debt finance to be raised, are discussed in chapter seven. Liquidity is available from the free transferability of debt securities, and, to a more limited extent, from the ability of the lender to novate a syndicated loan or to transfer the risk by other techniques. Transfer of debt is discussed in chapter eight.

A final, general point, regarding the aims of this book relates to tax. We recognise that tax law is an important driver in many of the decisions which a company may take about its financing choices, and indeed in the investment decisions taken by investors. We seek to highlight those instances in which tax has a particular impact on these issues, but this is not a book about tax law, and specialist books should be consulted in this regard.[9]

In terms of the scheme of the book, and following on for this discussion, in chapter two we provide an overview of the financing options which are available to companies, which operates to some extent as a menu of financing options for companies. We consider the options for equity financing, debt financing, and financing via retained profits. Those options are then considered in more detail in later chapters of the book. One of the strengths of this book, we hope, is the fact that we consider both the debt and the equity side of the equation for companies, including the interrelationship of these forms of financing, and the mix of debt and equity financing which a company may choose, and these issues are explored in chapter two, and throughout this book. In chapter three we continue to look at both debt and equity financing side by side, but this time from the perspective of the providers of the finance. In particular, chapter three examines the role that shareholders and lenders play in both solvent and insolvent companies.

Chapter four then considers the issue of legal capital. This can be regarded as an aspect of equity financing, ie how companies can raise finance from the shareholders and what they can then do with the capital that has been raised. It can also be regarded as a creditor protection issue, namely as a mechanism for providing a fund of capital available to creditors in certain circumstances. In this latter sense, chapter four links naturally with chapters five and six which also deal with creditor protection issues. When creditors lend to the company they are exposed to the risk that the company will not pay ongoing obligations of interest, or, even more seriously, that the company will be unable to pay the entire capital sum advanced. Chapter four relates to creditor protection by rules relating to the share capital, chapter five to creditor protection by contractual means (relating both to

---

8   FSA Handbook, Listing Rules, LR 2.2.4(1).
9   See eg GK Morse and D Williams, *Principles of Tax Law* (London, Sweet & Maxwell, 2008); J Tiley, *Revenue Law*, 6th edn (Oxford, Hart Publishing, 2008).

contracts with the borrowing company and to contracts with third parties) and chapter six to creditor protection by proprietary means (including both absolute and security interests). As mentioned above, creditors receive little protection from regulation. One exception is where there is a conflict between the interests of shareholders and creditors: thus the preservation of share capital is heavily regulated by company law rules, although the utility of this regulation is doubtful, as chapter four explains. On the other hand, creditors can bargain for considerable protection by contract, limited only by the general rules of contract law, as explained in chapter five. 'Regulation' in this area is largely to protect third parties, such as other creditors (who receive some protection by the insolvency rules as discussed in chapter three) and third parties who themselves give contractual protection, such as guarantors, who are protected to some extent by common law principles. The ability of creditors to bargain for proprietary protection is also fairly unlimited as explained in chapter six: such regulation as there is relates largely to the protection of other creditors, and includes the requirement to register security interests, some protection from insolvency law (discussed in chapters three and six) and rules relating to general property law.

Chapters seven and eight discuss more specific aspects of debt financing. Chapter seven discusses the problems that arise when there are multiple lenders, both in terms of organisational structure and in terms of decision-making procedures. The various techniques used to transfer debt, such as novation and assignment, and also to transfer the risk of debt, such as securitisation and loan participation, are discussed in chapter eight, and, by way of comparison, the transfer of shares is also discussed.

Chapters nine and ten then return to equity financing issues. Chapter nine considers the issue of initial public offers for shares, discussing why companies might wish to float their shares on a public market, and why and how the law regulates this issue, both in terms of ex ante disclosure requirements and ex post enforcement mechanisms. Chapter ten considers the next stage: once a company's shares have been listed, what ongoing regulation is put in place, and why is such regulation thought necessary? The purpose of this ongoing regulation is different to, and more complex than, the regulatory aims of prospectus regulation in chapter nine. Both disclosure requirements and market abuse rules are considered, and again both the ex ante and the ex post aspects of the regulatory regime are considered. Chapter eleven returns to debt financing, but continues the themes of chapters nine and ten by examining the regulation of the debt markets.

Chapters twelve and thirteen consider a slightly different aspect of equity financing. Equity capital, as discussed in chapters four, nine and ten (and to some extent chapter fourteen) is an important mechanism for raising finance, but holding shares in a company, particularly ordinary shares, provides the holder with voting rights, in addition to income and capital rights. As a result holding shares is an important mechanism for exercising control within the company. Transferring shares can effect a change of control within a company. In these chapters we therefore consider two mechanisms for transferring control in a company via a transfer of shares. Takeovers are considered in chapter twelve and schemes of arrangement in chapter thirteen. These mechanisms are often used to achieve the same ends, and are seen as alternatives, but they operate in quite different ways. A scheme of arrangement is an act of the company, and therefore stands in contrast to takeovers, discussed in the previous chapter. Takeovers do not involve the target company, but are an arrangement between the bidder and the target shareholders first and foremost. These differences have important implications, as discussed in these chapters.

Finally, in chapter fourteen, private equity transactions are examined. The growth of private equity as a mechanism for financing companies is examined, as is the content of a typical private equity transaction. Private equity grew enormously in the UK in the period until 2008, to the point where it was said to rival the public markets as a source of financing in the UK. A comparison of private equity-backed companies and public companies is undertaken in this chapter with a view to understanding this phenomenon. The different debt-equity profile of private equity-backed companies as compared to public companies, in particular, allows us an opportunity to draw together many of the discussions from earlier chapters regarding the utility of these different financing tools, including as a corporate governance tool.

It would be impossible to write a book on corporate finance law in 2010 without considering the effects of the global financial crisis that began with the credit crunch in 2007. However, the causes of the financial crisis lay in financing structures that repackaged debts due to financial institutions (such as mortgage loans and credit card receivables as well as corporate loans) that were invested in by banks and other financial institutions. Its effect on the financing of non-financial companies has been significant, but secondary to its profound effect on the financial system. As stated, this is not a book about banking regulation and therefore the effect of the financial crisis on the financial system, and the financing of financial companies falls outside the remit of this book. However, its effect on the financing of non-financial companies will be considered. First, it has had an impact on the way in which such companies raise finance. In particular, the crisis led to a severe reduction of available bank finance for all sorts of companies. In relation to small and medium sized enterprises, this has led to an increase in other sorts of finance (such as asset-based lending) and it has led larger companies to resort to more equity financing and bond issues. Second, it has led to an increase in regulation designed to ameliorate the systemic risk that led to the crisis. While not directed at corporate borrowing, such regulation may make the cost of borrowing more expensive,[10] or may affect the operation of institutions which are crucial to corporate financing, such as credit rating agencies.[11]

---

[10] An example is the proposal to make all credit derivatives only tradable on a market; this will increase the costs of those non-financial companies who use derivatives for hedging.

[11] See chapter 11.

2

Overview of Financing Options

2.1 Introduction

There are three basic sources of finance with which a company can finance its operations: share issues, debt and retained profits. This chapter will provide an overview of these techniques.[1] This is intended to provide an introduction to the issues which will be discussed in more detail in subsequent chapters. In particular this chapter will assess the different debt and equity financing options that are available to companies. However, it is possible, and indeed common, for hybrid instruments to be created that combine elements of both debt and equity and that blur the distinctions between the two. These are discussed at 2.4 below. Finally this chapter will assess the issue of the mix of financing options that a company should undertake.

2.2 Equity Financing

A company limited by shares, whether public or private, must have at least one issued share.[2] Although it is possible to set up both unlimited companies and companies limited by guarantee in the UK,[3] these types of companies are not commonly chosen by individuals setting up profit-making organisations. In the case of companies limited by guarantee, they do not provide a simple mechanism for the sharing of profits[4] and, in the case of unlimited companies, they forego the benefit that is often regarded as providing the greatest advantage to the corporate form, namely limited liability.[5] This book will therefore concentrate on companies limited by shares.

Every such company *must* therefore have at least some equity capital. By contrast there is no requirement that a company must have any debt, although in practice very few companies will be able to operate without some form of debt financing. As regards the share capital requirement, the levels may be very low. There is no minimum capital requirement for private companies in the UK and the minimum capital requirement for

---

[1] See, eg, BIS, *Financing a Private Sector Recovery*, Cm 7923, July 2010, ch 3.

[2] A company limited by shares is formed by one or more persons subscribing their names to the memorandum of association and complying with the registration requirements of the Companies Act 2006: Companies Act 2006, s 7.

[3] Companies Act 2006, s 3.

[4] Consequently, companies limited by guarantee are generally used for not-for-profit companies.

[5] P Davies (ed), *Gower and Davies: Principles of Modern Company Law*, 8th edn (London, Sweet & Maxwell, 2008) ch 1.

public companies is just £50,000.[6] It is common for small private companies to operate with very low levels of share capital indeed – perhaps just a £1 share held by each of the founder members – and for the majority of the financing to be via bank loans, often secured on the founder shareholders' personal assets. In such circumstances the effect of equity financing on the company's operations will be very slight.

The options available for companies raising money via equity financing are more limited than those available for debt financing, discussed at 2.3 below. The company only has the option of issuing shares. The main variables are the type of shares issued and the sources of the company's equity finance. On the first point, the company has considerable flexibility as to the rights that attach to its shares, and many different types of shares can be created. This will be discussed in the next section. On the second point, distinctions need to be drawn between companies which receive equity finance only from internal sources, predominantly the founder shareholder-directors of the company, those that have a mixture of internal and external equity funding (such as in private equity-backed companies) and those that are predominantly externally funded, and look to the public markets for the vast majority of their equity capital. These are obviously not watertight categorisations. Companies may well occupy midpoints between these categories. Neither are these categories static. Companies may well transition between these categories during their life cycle. The different sources of equity funding will be discussed at 2.2.2 below.

Before moving on to these sections however one important point needs to be made about equity financing via share issues, namely who, within the company, has control of this process. Before directors can allot new shares they must have the authority to allot them. For directors of private companies with only one class of shares the directors will have authority, unless the articles prohibit them from doing so.[7] For all other companies directors can allot shares if they are authorised to do so by the company's articles or by ordinary resolution.[8] In addition, any proposed allotment of equity securities must first be offered to existing shareholders pro rata based on the size of their existing holding (pre-emption rights).[9] This will be problematic if the directors wish to issue shares to anyone other than the existing shareholders. Pre-emption rights can be disapplied. In general this is achieved by a special resolution of the shareholders.[10]

As a consequence shareholders have the opportunity to exert control over directors in relation to the issue of new shares. This is less likely to be an issue in the small 'quasi-partnership' companies where the directors and shareholders are likely to be the same individuals. However, once a differentiation between the directors and the shareholders in a company arises, these issues can become significant. In public companies the operation of the Statement of Principles drawn up by the Pre-Emption Group means that

---

[6]   Companies Act 2006, s 763(1), implementing the Second Company Law Directive (EC) 77/91 [1977] OJ L26/1, art 6 (although the Second Directive requires a minimum capital level of just €25,000).

[7]   Companies Act 2006, s 550.

[8]   Ibid, s 551.

[9]   Ibid, s 561. Pre-emption rights are discussed in detail at 4.3.1.

[10]   Ibid, ss 569–571. Directors of private companies with only one class of shares can also be given this power by the articles: s 569(1). Additional constraints are placed on disapplications of pre-emption rights in public companies via a Statement of Principles drawn up by the Pre-Emption Group, which represents institutional investors: See Pre-Emption Group, *Statement of Principles: Disapplying Pre-emption Rights*, July 2008 available at www.pre-emptiongroup.org.uk/principles/index.htm. Although not technically binding this Statement has an important effect on the ability of public companies to raise new equity finance in practice. For discussion see 4.3.1.

if the directors want to raise new capital via a rights issue they must first engage in a dialogue with existing shareholders. This provides the shareholders, particularly the institutional investors, with an opportunity to engage with the company and potentially to perform a monitoring role. Indeed a positive relation between UK rights issues and managerial change has been found to exist.[11] For these reasons, financing the company with retained profits or debt finance may be a more attractive option to directors in some circumstances.

2.2.1   Different Types of Shares

Companies have a significant amount of flexibility as to the rights that they can attach to their shares. The rights are generally laid down in the articles of the company.[12] To a large extent these rights are a matter of contract, although a contract of a peculiar kind.[13] The articles are a contract binding the company and its members and the members inter se as a result of section 33 of the Companies Act 2006. The binding force of this contract arises from the terms of the statute rather than any actual bargain struck between the parties. The rights attached to the shares may not be specifically negotiated or agreed to by a particular shareholder. When an investor buys a share in a company he or she becomes bound by the terms of the articles then in existence, and these terms can subsequently be altered without the shareholders' permission in some circumstances, by a special resolution of the shareholders, ie a 75 per cent majority vote.[14] This contract is therefore quite unlike that between a creditor and the company which complies with the usual rules of contract law and thus, for example, cannot be altered without the creditor's agreement. Shareholders can enter into a separate, additional, contractual arrangement with the other shareholders: a shareholders' agreement. This is an agreement which operates separate to and outside the articles of association and operates as a conventional contract. It can be used by the shareholders as an additional method to order their relationship: a provision

---

[11]   J Franks, C Mayer and L Renneboog, 'Who Disciplines Management in Poorly Performing Companies?' (2001) 10 *Journal of Financial Intermediation* 209; D Hillier, SC Linn and P McColgan, 'Equity Issuance, CEO turnover and Corporate Governance' (2005) 11 *European Financial Management* 515. For further discussion see 4.3.1.

[12]   Some rights might also be included in a shareholders' agreement. In order to enforce these rights against the company, the company will need to be a party to this agreement. There has been some concern about whether the provisions of a shareholders' agreement could be enforced against a company who was a party to that agreement (*Russell v Northern Bank Development Corp Ltd* [1992] 1 WLR 588 discussed in E Ferran, 'The Decision of the House of Lords in *Russell v Northern Bank Limited*' (1994) 53 *Cambridge Law Journal* 343) on the basis that a company cannot contract out of its statutory power to alter its articles by special resolution (Companies Act 2006, s 21). However, the ability of shareholders to entrench provisions in the articles seems to undermine this argument.

[13]   *Bratton Seymour Service Co Ltd v Oxborough* [1992] BCC 471, 475 per Steyn LJ (in relation to Companies Act 1985, s 14, the similarly-worded predecessor to Companies Act 2006, s 33); *AG of Belize v Belize Telecom Ltd* [2009] UKPC 10.

[14]   Articles can be altered by a special resolution of the company (Companies Act 2006, s 21). This is subject to two provisos. If the right comprises a class right, and the class right is being varied (see *White v Bristol Aeroplane Co* [1953] Ch 65) then the statute creates additional protections for the shareholder (Companies Act 2006, ss 630–635). More generally the courts have determined that for an alteration to be valid the shareholders must vote bona fide in the best interests of the company on an alteration of articles (*Allen v Gold Reefs of West Africa Ltd* [1900] 1 Ch 656; *Citco Banking Corp NV v Pusser's Ltd* [2007] UKPC 13; [2007] BCC 205).

in a shareholders' agreement can have an effect similar to a provision in the articles.[15] A shareholders' agreement has an advantage over the articles in that it need not be registered at Companies House and therefore remains private. However, it has the disadvantage that new members of the company will not be automatically bound by its provisions unless they specifically assent to it. Unless the terms of the shareholder's agreement provide otherwise, the terms of the agreement will only be able to be altered by the agreement of all parties. Shareholders' agreements tend to be used in companies with relatively few shareholders, for example, small quasi-partnership companies, joint venture companies and venture capital companies.

In addition, however, statute has intervened to prevent companies having complete freedom as to how and when it may issue new shares,[16] and to determine the rights that may attach to those shares. For instance, even if the articles specify that certain shares will have a guaranteed right to a specified dividend, this will be subject to the statutory requirement that dividends can only be paid if the company has distributable profits.[17] These protections are sometimes put in place to protect the existing shareholders of the company[18] and sometimes to protect the creditors of the company.[19] These restrictions contrast with the position regarding debt, where the parties are in principle free to make their own bargain.

There are three main rights that tend to be specified in relation to shares: income rights, capital rights and voting rights.[20] Beyond these rights, however, there are a wide range of other rights and entitlements which could be attached to the share, a common one being the right to appoint one or more directors of the company.[21] The two most common forms of shares that are issued by companies are ordinary shares and preference shares.[22]

2.2.1.1   Ordinary Shares

Ordinary shares are the default shares of companies: if a company has only one class of share then they will be ordinary shares. In general, ordinary shares have no rights to

---

[15]   Shareholders' agreements are included within the definition of the constitution of the company for the purposes of Companies Act 2006, s 40 (s 40(3)(b)).

[16]   Eg new issues of shares are subject to pre-emption rights. If pre-emption rights are in place a fresh issue of shares must be offered pro rata to existing shareholders (see generally Companies Act 2006, ss 561–566) although these rights may be excluded or disapplied by the shareholders in certain circumstances (Companies Act 2006, ss 567–573, although in relation to public companies see also the Statement of Principles published by the Pre-Emption Group at www.pre-emptiongroup.org.uk/principles/index.htm).

[17]   Companies Act 2006, ss 830–831(for discussion see 4.4.1). In addition, the payment of the dividend will be subject to the dividend being declared by directors or by shareholders on the directors' recommendation (*Bond v Barrow Haematite Steel Co* [1902] 1 Ch 353) although it is possible – if rare – for articles to dispense with the need for dividends to be declared (*Evling v Israel & Oppenheimer Ltd* [1918] 1 Ch 101). It is obviously not possible for the articles to dispense with the need for the company to have made distributable profits. It is also possible for dividend distribution to be limited by debt covenants, although such covenants are quite rare in the UK, see pages 157–58 below.

[18]   Eg, pre-emption rights (see discussion at 4.3.1).

[19]   Eg, the minimum capital rules and maintenance of capital rules, discussed at 4.3.2 and 4.4.

[20]   For discussion see 3.2.1.1 and 3.2.1.2.

[21]   A right to appoint a director could in theory be a class right (for the definition of a class of shares see Companies Act 2006, s 629) if that right is attached to the shares (eg the right to appoint a director passes with the shares when they are sold) rather than attaching to the shareholder personally: see *Cumbrian Newspapers Group Ltd v Cumberland & Westmorland Herald Newspapers & Printing Co Ltd* [1987] Ch 1 per Scott J for a discussion of the definition of class rights in this context. For discussion see 3.2.1.1 and 3.2.1.2.

[22]   See 3.2.1.1 and 3.2.1.2. It is also common for these to be issued as redeemable ordinary shares or redeemable preference shares.

receive any fixed returns from the company. They usually have no entitlement to receive dividends from the company.[23] Their rights to participate in the capital of the company are generally limited to their entitlement to any surplus left over after all the liabilities have been paid, ie they have no guarantee of any return on a winding up. They are the residual claimants of the company. They take the lion's share of the risk, but, in the good times, they will take the lion's share of the rewards. Indeed, investors in ordinary shares will generally expect a return that is adequate to compensate them for the risk that they will not be repaid in the event of a winding up. In terms of voting rights, they usually have one vote per share. They are generally the decision-makers of the company, to the extent that decisions need to be taken by the general meeting.[24]

There may be a number of reasons for issuing ordinary shares in a company, unlike the issue of preference shares which is first and foremost a capital raising device. In some companies, particularly very small companies, the purpose of issuing shares may simply be to give the shareholders control of the company. It is very common for shareholders to use their voting rights to appoint themselves directors of the company, or to appoint their representatives to that position. The amount of capital injected via the ordinary shares may be negligible, with most of the financing in the form of a bank loan and/or overdraft secured on the personal assets of the shareholder-directors.[25] In such circumstances the ordinary shares issued will have little or no financing role. However, in larger companies, even though the control aspect of ordinary shares remains important, the use of ordinary shares as a capital-raising device cannot be ignored.[26]

Ordinary shares are a particularly flexible form of finance for companies. As long as the company is a going concern, the ordinary shareholders are not entitled to any particular level of return by way of dividend. In order to exit the company, shareholders may be able to sell their shares, but this depends upon finding a buyer. This will generally be difficult for shareholders in private companies since, in contrast to the shareholders in public companies, there is no ready market for their shares. Transfers of shares generally are discussed in chapter eight.[27] Otherwise, shareholders cannot withdraw the contribution they have made in exchange for their shares without the company's consent. This consent may be given at the time of issue, as is the case where the company issues redeemable shares to the shareholder,[28] or may be given later, in the event that the company offers to repurchase its shares.[29] The capital provided by the shareholder is therefore locked into the company to this extent.

---

[23] For discussion see 3.2.1.1.

[24] For discussion see 3.2.1.1.

[25] See, eg, BIS, *Financing a Private Sector Recovery*, n 1, ch 3.7 which states that a number of very small companies do not use formal sources of external finance at all, relying instead on retained earnings or personal finance to fund investment and growth.

[26] In private equity-backed companies, for example, the amount of equity financing (generally, today, all by way of ordinary shares) is by no means negligible, although the highly leveraged nature of these companies means that it is still significantly outweighed by the amount of debt finance (for further discussion see chapter 14).

[27] See 8.2.7.

[28] Companies Act 2006, ss 684–689 (for discussion see 4.4.2).

[29] Ibid, ss 690–723 (for discussion see 4.4.2).

2.2.1.2 Preference Shares

Ordinary shares can vary in form,[30] but the description set out above will be accurate for most purposes. By contrast preference shares can exist in much greater variety. However, a reasonably common form of preference share is one which is preferential as to a return of dividend[31] and preferential as to a return of capital, but does not give the preference shareholder the right to participate in surplus. In addition, it is usual for preference shareholders to have a right to vote only in certain limited circumstances, such as where the preferential dividend has been in arrears for a specified period. These issues are discussed in detail in chapter three.[32] Consequently, preference shares are primarily an instrument of corporate finance, unlike ordinary shares which may perform other significant roles within the company, such as decision-making (acting as the company in a general meeting) or monitoring the directors. However, this latter function is of less significance in a small private company where the directors and shareholders are effectively the same people.

However, there is no standard package of rights that attach to all preference shares. Preference shares can be placed at numerous points on the continuum which has the 'pure equity' of the ordinary shares at one end and debt at the other.[33] It is possible for a company to create a class of preferred ordinary shares, having a right to vote and to receive priority as to fixed income payments, but no priority as to the return of capital. Thus preference shareholders could be entitled to share in the surplus assets on a winding up, vote in a general meeting on all issues, but have a preference as to dividends and/or capital repayment. This form of preference share is rare.[34] It is more common for preference shares to be issued as a form of fixed interest security akin to debt.[35]

When debt is expensive, preference shares may be issued with a sufficiently attractive preferential dividend to tempt an investor, but with no rights to participate in the surplus and with only minimal rights to vote (generally only when the preferential dividend payments are in arrears). From the company's point of view this is attractive since the preference shareholder has no guaranteed right to the dividend,[36] unlike creditors who have a contractual right to receive interest payments, and often have a strong armoury of

---

[30] Eg non-voting ordinary shares are possible, though rare (particularly in public companies as they are unpopular with institutional investors: see generally Institutional Shareholder Services, Shearman & Sterling and European Corporate Governance Institute, 'Report on the Proportionality Principle in the European Union' (May 2007) available at www.ecgi.org/osov/documents/final_report_en.pdf). More common are multiple voting rights in small quasi-partnership companies designed to entrench the shareholder-directors in their position on the board (eg, *Bushell v Faith* [1970] AC 1099).

[31] The dividend will still be subject to the company having distributable profits (Companies Act 2006, ss 830–831) and, generally, subject to the dividend having been declared (*Bond v Barrow Haematite Steel Co* [1902] 1 Ch 353). For discussion see 3.2.1.2.

[32] See 3.2.1.2.

[33] Discussed at 3.2.1.2.

[34] However, a variation on the standard preference share model that sometimes occurs is a convertible preference share that entitles the holder of the preference share, at some point in the future, to convert it into another security of the company, commonly an ordinary share. This can allow the benefits of a preference share to be combined with the advantages of an ordinary share including, crucially in this instance, capital growth.

[35] For a discussion of preference shares as a form of hybrid security see pages 44–45.

[36] The preferential dividend entitlement is not a debt until declared, and therefore cannot be guaranteed: *Bond v Barrow Haematite Steel Co* [1902] 1 Ch 353. Even if the articles specify that the dividend does not need to be declared and specify the date on which the dividend payment is due, the payment will still not be guaranteed, since it will still be conditional on distributable profits being available: see Companies Act 2006, ss 830–831. If no such profits are available then at best the right to payment will be suspended until there are sufficient

weapons if they are unpaid.[37] The company therefore has maximum flexibility about how to manage its business, without interference from these capital-providers. However, the company may need to offer an attractive rate of preferential dividend to tempt a potential investor. Therefore, once debt becomes cheaper (usually when interest rates go down) it is usual for companies to then reduce their capital, repay the preference shares (possibly at par, depending on the rights attaching to those shares), and to refinance the company using debt.[38]

One point to note at this stage, therefore, is that the shareholders in a company, particularly the ordinary shareholders, will often be more than merely finance providers in a company. This is in contrast to creditors who are first and foremost providers of finance. Shareholders, via the right to vote, have a role as decision-makers in the company both directly, via their vote in the general meeting, and indirectly, via their control of the board. They also have a role as monitors of the directors. Creditors can have a monitoring role, as a result of their contractual relationship with the company.[39] It is important to understand the relationship between shareholders and creditors in order to understand the dynamics of company financing decisions. This relationship is discussed in chapter three, both in a solvent and an insolvent scenario. Broadly, shareholders' interests dominate in the solvent company whereas creditors' interests dominate in insolvency and in the twilight zone before insolvency actually commences.

One consequence of the dominance of shareholders in the solvent company is the fact that shareholders are in a position to benefit themselves at the expense of the creditors in a number of ways, such as by making distributions to themselves, or by manipulating the investment profile of the company in a way which advantages them and disadvantages the creditors, for example by taking on riskier projects than creditors contemplated when they extended credit.[40] Of course, creditors have a number of mechanisms in place whereby they can protect themselves by contractual and proprietary means. These are discussed in chapters three, five and six. However, in addition the law has created a number of rules the predominant purpose of which is to resolve this perceived conflict between the shareholders and creditors in favour of the creditors. These are the legal capital rules and the rules themselves, as well as their efficacy and desirability, are discussed in chapter four.

2.2.2   Sources of Equity Finance

As discussed, for very small companies, it is possible that issuing shares does not predominantly perform a financing role at all. In sole shareholder companies, or in so called quasi-partnership companies,[41] it may well be that the amount of issued share

---

distributable profits. This is the position in Australia (*Marra Developments Ltd v BW Rofe Pty Ltd* (1977) 2 NSWLR 616 (Sup Ct NSW)) and probably represents the English position, though there is no authority on this point.

[37] Eg the creditors may be able to petition to wind up the company if the debt remains unpaid: *Cornhill Insurance plc v Improvement Services Ltd* [1986] 1 WLR 114. They are likely also to have contractual weapons, such as the right to accelerate the loan and terminate the contract, see 5.2.3 below.

[38] See eg *Re Hunting plc* [2004] EWHC 2591 (Ch); [2005] 2 BCLC 211 as an example of this in practice. For a discussion of the cost of debt see 2.6.

[39] For discussion see 3.2.2.4.

[40] For discussion see 3.2.2.2.

[41] The existence of these forms of companies does not appear in companies legislation, but is well-recognised by the courts, see, eg, *O' Neill v Phillips* [1999] 1 WLR 1092.

capital is tiny. In such companies most of the financing will come from debt finance, often guaranteed by the director/shareholders and secured over their personal assets.[42] In these companies the primary value of the shares may be their control function, and in particular the ability of the shareholders to appoint themselves as directors and to protect themselves in that position. It will be shares with voting rights attached (generally ordinary shares) that will be most valuable for this purpose. Many small companies continue to rely on internal equity finance and bank finance. External equity finance plays only a small role in the financing of small businesses generally.[43]

This point raises an interesting contrast between debt and equity. It is possible for a single creditor to finance a company (for example a single bank) or for multiple lenders to finance a company. Financing by multiple lenders raises a number of distinct issues, which are dealt with in chapter seven. By contrast, although it is possible for companies to have a single shareholder and therefore, technically, to be financed by a single shareholder, in practice, as discussed, in single member companies the primary value of that share is not as a financing tool. In practice, to the extent that companies are financed by equity, they are financed by multiple shareholders. It is an assumption of the equity financing issues discussed in this book that the financing is being provided by multiple shareholders.

However, as companies become larger equity financing as a source of capital is likely to become more significant, and for most companies there will come a point in time where they cannot satisfy their equity financing needs purely from the original shareholders. Of course, even for larger companies, one option is to continue to rely on debt rather than equity. However this may not always be possible or desirable. Bank debt typically requires businesses to make regular interest and principal payments. For some types of investment the expected stream of revenues may be uncertain and only available far into the future. Internet companies, for example, including companies such as Amazon, will fall into this category. Such companies will simply not generate adequate revenue to make the necessary interest and principal payments in the first few years after the loan is made. Banks also generally impose numerous covenants designed to protect their debt investment,[44] which may be undesirable to the company. There may also be good reasons for having a more balanced debt:equity ratio within the company, an issue which is discussed further in 2.6.

At some point, therefore, many businesses will seek additional capital in the form of equity. Equity financing has some benefits compared to debt, especially for companies that only expect to be profitable in the future, as discussed above. However, there are downsides too. From the perspective of the existing shareholders, bringing in more equity owners will dilute the potential upside return from the business, unless non-participating shares are issued, but these are unlikely to be attractive to potential investors. These issues were discussed in 2.2.1. If the company wishes to increase its equity base in order to fund business expansion plans, to introduce new products or to reduce borrowings, it will need to consider how to attract additional equity investors (ie equity investors other than the original shareholders) and persuade them to put money into the company.

[42]   For discussion of guarantees see 5.3.1.3.
[43]   M Lund and J Wright, 'The Financing of Small Firms in the United Kingdom' [May 1999] *Bank of England Quarterly Bulletin* 195. See also BIS, *Financing a Private Sector Recovery*, n 1, 3.7.
[44]   See 3.2.2.3 and 5.2.

One possibility for such companies is to seek a significant injection of equity capital from a venture capital fund or a 'Business Angel' ie a high net worth individual who provides early stage venture capital to companies either alone or as part of a syndicate.[45] This option involves the founder shareholders potentially giving up a significant slice of their share ownership to the external investor. It avoids the need to go to the public markets, at least in the short-term, although an offering of shares to the public may be the mechanism whereby the external investor exits the company in the future. The availability of this form of equity capital does not appear to be spread evenly across the market, and external equity finance of this kind appears to be more readily available in some sectors of the economy, and for companies of a certain size and stage of development, than others.[46] This form of finance has been affected by the recent financial crisis.[47] A variation on this model is the management buy-out or leveraged buy-out model, which usually occurs when the company is significantly larger, and indeed can occur when the company is publicly listed. These involve a significant injection of capital from the management of the company and from a private equity fund, together with substantial debt financing. Private equity is discussed in detail in chapter fourteen.

An alternative model for an expanding company looking for additional equity financing is to look for funding from 'external' shareholders, ie those who will not be involved in the management of the company. This form of financing can be problematic. The problem is not the fact that the shareholders are not engaged in management. Limited liability allows shareholders to take no role in management and indeed, should they choose, not to monitor the management at all, secure in the knowledge that they know the full extent of their financial exposure to the company.[48] Without limited liability it is unlikely that a prudent investor would be prepared to invest in such a situation, or if they were prepared to invest they would expect a very high return to compensate them for the risks involved.

Rather, the problem is that investors' contributions to private companies are locked in. Selling shares in a private company is not straightforward. Finding a buyer for the shares in the majority of private companies will often be very difficult. The existing shareholders[49] may not be interested in increasing their stake in the company, or may not have the resources to do so, and any new external investors will generally be hard to find. There is a potential liquidity problem for external investors in such companies.[50] As discussed, in the absence of a buyer, they cannot withdraw the contribution they have made in exchange for their shares without the company's consent.[51] Redeemable shares, in particular, can be a

---

[45]   BIS, *Financing a Private Sector Recovery*, n 1, 3.46–3.48.

[46]   DTI, *A Mapping Study of Venture Capital Provision to SMEs in England* (DTI, Small Business Service, October 2005).

[47]   BIS, *Financing a Private Sector Recovery*, n 1, 3.49.

[48]   See SB Presser, 'Thwarting the Killing of the Corporation: Limited Liability, Democracy and Economics' (1992) 87 *Northwestern University Law Review* 148. Of course limited liability is a myth for the shareholders in quasi-partnership companies who may well give personal guarantees to the company's creditors (certainly the bank), and will often use their personal assets to secure the company's debts.

[49]   Pre-emption rights will generally mean, of course, that the existing shareholders have to be offered the shares first: Companies Act 2006, ss 561–577. For discussion see 4.3.1.

[50]   As far as venture capital investors, or private equity investors generally, are concerned, they tend to invest for a significant period of time (eg 3–5 years) and will generally have a clear exit strategy in mind, which might be a sale of the company or a flotation on the public markets. This is discussed in chapter 14. Generally such investors will not invest unless they are comfortable that a viable exit strategy exists at the end of their anticipated hold period.

[51]   See page 12.

valuable tool for a small to medium sized company which wishes to attract external investors as it may give them some comfort.[52] However, the future redemption of those shares is not guaranteed and will only occur if the company has available funds at the time of the redemption. For these reasons the ability to transfer the shares may be the shareholder's only option of exiting the company and realising its investment. However, shareholders wishing to transfer shares in small private companies often face a number of hurdles: finding a purchaser for this illiquid investment can be difficult as can agreeing a price, and if these difficulties are surmounted, the articles of such companies often contain restrictions on transferability.[53]

Ultimately, for companies looking to increase significantly their levels of external equity finance, there is the option of issuing the company's shares to the public.[54] The advantages of this course are clear. An offer of shares to the public allows the company to have access to outside investors who can participate substantially in the company. This access to significantly increased levels of equity capital is one of the major advantages of offering shares to the public especially when combined with a listing. Obtaining a listing for the shares creates liquidity. Not only is there a ready market for the shares, but they must be freely transferable.[55] Once shares are freely transferable they are no longer predominantly about a relationship between the shareholder and the company, but become items of property just like any other. Listed shares also become valuable in other ways, both to investors[56] and for the issuing company.[57] These are not the only advantages of an offer of shares to the public[58] but the access to significant levels of external equity finance that flow from an offer of shares to the public is the primary driver in most if not all such offers.

However, an offer of shares to the public is not something to be undertaken lightly. In order to offer shares to the public the company must be a public company.[59] Public companies face greater administrative burdens than private companies and the legal capital regime that they face is more burdensome.[60] In addition, in order to secure the liquidity gains involved in offering shares to the public, most offers will be accompanied by an admission of the company's shares to trading on a public market.[61] Companies are generally able to raise money more easily and to obtain a better price if after the initial issue of shares there is a healthy secondary market available to investors on which they can sell their shares and realise their investment, if they so choose. There are a number of options available for this listing. In the UK the London Stock Exchange offers the Main

---

[52]   For further discussion of redeemable shares see page 135.

[53]   For discussion of the transfer of shares see 8.2.7.

[54]   It may be possible for the company to issue its shares to 'external' investors while avoiding the need for a full IPO prospectus if the offer is not a public offer and if the securities are not admitted to listing on a regulated exchange (eg an admission to AIM combined with a non-public offer, although even here the company would have to comply with the disclosure obligations of the London Stock Exchange). Detailed discussion of these issues fall outside the scope of this book. For discussion see Davies, *Principles of Modern Company Law*, n 5, 872–77. Non-public offers of debt securities are more common, see chapter 11.

[55]   FSA Handbook, Listing Rules, LR 2.2.4(1).

[56]   Eg investors may find that banks will accept listed shares as security for loans.

[57]   Listed shares can be used as a form of payment, for example as consideration in share-for-share acquisitions, thereby widening the company's financing options when compared to unlisted companies. The liquidity associated with listed shares also provides greater scope for the company to offer remuneration packages that include shares and options.

[58]   For a fuller discussion, see 9.2.1.

[59]   Companies Act 2006, s 755.

[60]   See 9.2.2.

[61]   See 9.2.2.

Market, for well-established companies and the Alternative Investment Market (AIM) for less well-established companies. The London Stock Exchange has no monopoly on the operation of public markets for securities within the UK and a number of alternatives now exist, some intended to compete with the Main Market, or with AIM, and some that are aimed at companies involved in specialist areas.[62] However, there is no obligation on UK companies to list their shares on a UK market, and a UK company has complete freedom to list its shares elsewhere, either as a primary listing or, more commonly, as a secondary listing.[63] The initial public offer of shares is discussed in detail in chapter nine and the regulation of securities, once they have been listed on a UK public market, is discussed in chapter ten.

Once a company has its shares publicly listed then it can raise further equity capital via a fresh issue of shares. These may have to be offered first to the existing shareholders of the company in proportion to their existing shareholding in the company, in accordance with pre-emption rights.[64] However, pre-emption rights can be disapplied by special resolution[65] and if this occurs the shares can be offered to external investors. However, in publicly listed companies there is a further constraint on the directors' ability to issue shares to external investors. The Pre-Emption Group, an association representing institutional investors, has published a Statement of Principles providing guidance on the considerations which shareholders in such companies should take into account when deciding whether to vote in favour of a disapplication of pre-emption rights.[66] For example, requests by a company to issue not more than five per cent of its issued share capital non-preemptively in any given year are likely to be regarded as 'routine' but requests in excess of that figure are likely to require considerable justification from the directors before they will be approved. In practice these Principles have a significant impact as they tend to be followed by the institutional investors. Consequently, publicly listed companies obtain the vast majority of their equity capital by offering shares to existing shareholders (a rights issue). This process whereby the directors must justify any non-routine disapplication of pre-emption rights to the shareholders, if they want to raise new equity financing, has also been found to have potentially significant corporate governance implications, which are discussed in chapter four.[67]

So, equity capital is an important mechanism for raising finance, but it is also important for other reasons. As already discussed, holding shares in a company, particularly ordinary shares, provides its holder with voting rights as well as income and capital rights, and therefore holding shares is an important mechanism for exercising control within the company. Transferring shares can therefore effect a change of control within a company. Further, control can pass to new shareholders in a company as a result of the company issuing or re-purchasing shares, which is one reason why pre-emption rights are regarded as so valuable by shareholders.

---

[62] See page 412.
[63] See pages 412–13.
[64] Companies Act 2006, s 561, for discussion see 4.3.1.
[65] Ibid, ss 570–571 cf private companies with only one class of shares where directors can be given power by the articles or by special resolution to allot shares without complying with the statutory pre-emption provisions: s 569.
[66] See www.pre-emptiongroup.org.uk/principles/index.htm.
[67] See 4.3.1.

However, changes of control within a company can be effected in other ways. One way to transfer a company, or to merge one company with another, is via a transfer of the undertaking, ie a transfer of the assets and liabilities of the company. For example, one company can absorb all of the assets and liabilities of the other which is then dissolved, or a new company is formed and both companies transfer all of their assets etc to that new company, with the shareholders receiving shares in the new company. One way to effect this is via a scheme of arrangement, discussed in chapter thirteen (see 13.2.2). Schemes of arrangement can also be used to effect a division or demerger of one company into two or more companies. The assets and liabilities are divided up between them. However, it is relatively rare for a transfer of the control of a company to be carried out in this way. A transfer of the undertaking has consequences for third parties who deal with a company. As a starting point, those who contract with company A whose assets and liabilities are then transferred by way of a scheme to company B will still retain their relationship with company A. The terms of the contract may give the third party the right to terminate the contract or to insist on different terms in these circumstances.

More common is to effect the change of control via a transfer of shares, in which case this issue of third party rights does not arise from the structure of the transaction, though restrictions in the contract between company A and the third party can mimic the situation regarding a transfer of the undertaking. The two primary mechanisms for effecting a transfer of shares are takeovers and schemes of arrangement. Takeovers are discussed in detail in chapter twelve, with schemes of arrangement discussed in chapter thirteen. Takeovers involve an offer by a bidder for the shares in a company (the target) in exchange for cash, or for shares in the bidder (if the bidder is a company) or a mixture of the two. The offer is therefore made to the target shareholders, not to the directors of the target. Although the core transaction is between the bidder and the target shareholders, a takeover will have implications for others within the company, including the shareholders who do not agree to sell, the directors and other stakeholders, such as employees. These issues are explored in chapter twelve. Schemes of arrangement, by contrast, are corporate actions whereby the target directors ask the target shareholders to vote in favour of the change of control. There are other important differences between schemes and takeovers which are discussed in detail in 13.2.1.

2.3   Debt Financing

Very few companies have sufficient cash from equity capital or retained profits to meet every obligation as it falls due. Further, it would not be good business practice to do so. The operations of the company would be unduly restricted and the business would fail to grow. The company needs to borrow to expand its business, to invest in capital expenditure which will result in future income streams and to enable it to meet current expenditure which is necessary in order to achieve future income. It will be seen that the need for debt finance is therefore, at least in part, a question of cash flow. The company may have expectations of future profit (and in many cases these are more than expectations: money is actually due to the company in the future) but needs money up front to meet its immediate obligations. This type of financing can only be achieved by debt financing. It is relatively short-term so that the capital circulates: equity financing is therefore unsuitable. However, in relation to long-term financing the question of whether a company should finance by means of debt or equity becomes important. This question will arise in various forms throughout the discussion of debt financing, especially where the distinction between debt and equity becomes blurred.

Before discussing debt financing in more detail, it is worth noting some of the differences which exist between debt and equity financing. First, and most obviously, there is far more variety in the debt finance available to most companies, as compared to the equity financing options on offer. For equity financing there is only the issue of shares, the variety arising only as to the types of shares (which in practice tend to arise in a limited number of well understood variations on the ordinary and preference share theme) and the source of the finance (broadly whether the finance is provided by existing shareholders, new shareholders who then take part in management or external shareholders who do not participate in the management of the company). Debt financing is far more variable, as will appear from the discussion in this section. Because more variety is available, far more thought therefore needs to be given as to how the selection of the most appropriate forms of debt financing for each company is made. As this section will indicate, the process of selecting the most appropriate debt financing will depend on a number of factors, including the size and nature of the company, its current financial position, the nature of its assets, the reason the finance is needed, and the nature and requirements of the lender. In contrast to equity financing where the shareholders have a significant role, since they have the opportunity to exert control over directors in relation to the issue of new shares,[68] debt financing is a corporate decision taken solely by the directors.

2.3.1 General

2.3.1.1 *Choice of Debt Financing Transaction*

The term 'borrowing' is generally used to mean either borrowing by way of loan (usually from a bank) or by way of debt securities.[69] However, debt in a wider sense can also include credit extended by those whom the company would otherwise have to pay immediately. Thus when a company buys goods with payment due 30 days after delivery, or obtains services with payment due two months after the services have been supplied, the economic effect is the same as if the company had borrowed from the seller or supplier. Even closer in effect are situations where a company obtains equipment from a finance company on hire purchase or finance lease terms. The equipment is obtained immediately, yet the 'price' is paid in instalments over a long period. To understand how small and medium sized companies are financed it is important to realise both that this type of borrowing is widespread, and that the companies selling the goods, supplying the services or financing hire purchase agreements or finance leases themselves need finance. In order to meet the market requirements of giving credit, these companies need cash up front in order to meet the expenditure they have to make to provide the goods, the services or the equipment to the company which receives them. Even banks need to be financed by debt, as ultimately they cannot meet the cost of all the loans they make through equity

---

[68]   Discussed further at 4.3.1.
[69]   Such as bonds, notes or commercial paper. See 2.3.3 below.

financing, deposits (if they take them) and profits. Those who provide credit usually use the repayment obligations owed to them to enable them to obtain debt finance, either by borrowing on the security of those obligations or by transferring them outright for a price.[70] Banks obtain much of their finance on the money markets, either by issuing short-term debt securities (commercial paper)[71] or by using repos (structurally sale and repurchase but economically the same as short-term borrowing). The detail of these is beyond the scope of this book.

The type of debt financing used by any one company will depend on a number of factors. One very important factor is the size of the company: most small and medium sized companies are not in a position to issue debt securities, for example, and very large and credit-worthy companies usually only borrow unsecured.[72] Another will be the purpose for which credit is needed. If it is for a one-off project, such as a new building, a company taking a loan is likely to want a term loan, while for recurrent expenditure it is likely to want a revolving facility such as an overdraft. The cost of finance is also very important: this will be determined partly by outside factors such as interest rates and partly by the type of finance required. Generally, finance which is riskier for the lender is more expensive than less risky finance; thus, secured borrowing is (at least in theory) cheaper than unsecured, and shorter term finance is cheaper than long-term finance.[73]

The availability of types of finance will affect both the price and the choice of financial structure. For example, in a market where supply of goods on credit is common, no supplier can afford not to give credit and the credit is usually interest-free (though, of course, reflected in the overall price of the goods). Where credit is freely available, loans may be made and bonds issued with very few covenants[74] as a result of the competition between lenders to lend, but when credit becomes restricted such borrowing as there is will be on much harsher terms. A borrower also has to weigh up the advantages of flexibility, for example, from an overdraft or other revolving facility[75] or by issuing short-term debt securities, against the security of long-term finance, for example, a term loan or longer term securities. The flexibility of a revolving facility means that the company only borrows when it needs to, and this keeps the costs of financing down. However, where the company needs a fairly continuous level of borrowing, short-term financing may not be so suitable. This is because it requires constant refinancing which may be difficult if the company is in (temporary) difficulties, or if the market has changed so that finance is more expensive or no longer available. Paradoxically, taking short-term financing may be seen as a sign of confidence in the company's prospects since it shows that refinancing is viewed as likely to happen.

---

[70]   This is broadly called receivables financing. See 2.3.4.1.

[71]   See page 30.

[72]   BIS, *Financing a Private Sector Recovery* n 1, 3.5–3.17.

[73]   This is a generalisation, and in fact sometimes the opposite is true, for example because of outside factors such as interest rates set to achieve a particular government policy, see S Valdez, *An Introduction to Global Financial Markets*, 5th edn (Basingstoke, Palgrave Macmillan, 2007) 110.

[74]   Covenants are contractual obligations owed by the borrower to the lender, for the protection of the lender. See pages 23, 78–80 and 156–70 which contain detailed discussion of loan covenants. Loans and bonds with few covenants were called 'covenant-lite'. Another reason for this may be that the lender is selling on the loan, or at least the credit risk (using derivatives), so that it is less concerned about the credit risk for the borrower, see pages 86–87.

[75]   Whereby the borrower can draw down finance when it needs it and repay it when it does not. See pages 28–29.

Another relevant factor may be whether the company has any restrictions on its ability to borrow (or to borrow in a certain way) in its articles or in its contracts with other lenders.[76] For example, this might lead to a company selling its receivables rather than taking out a loan secured on the receivables.[77] Finally, in many situations the regulatory and tax implications of certain types of financing will be critical factors.

2.3.1.2   *Protection of Creditors: Contractual and Proprietary*

It is also necessary to consider what protection a creditor requires when lending or advancing credit, and how this affects the structure of the transaction. The first main concern of the creditor is credit risk, that is, the risk of non-payment.[78] This risk can be mitigated in a number of ways, mainly by the creditor obtaining rights as a result of its agreement with the borrower. These rights can be either contractual or proprietary. The main distinction between the two relates to the situation where the borrower is insolvent: a creditor with proprietary rights will have priority over the general class of unsecured creditors, while a creditor with merely contractual rights falls into the latter class. There are limited exceptions to this, such as set-off, which in many cases is effective on insolvency.[79]

Proprietary rights can be either absolute or security interests. The distinction between these two is discussed in detail in chapter six. If the creditor has an absolute interest, it becomes, or remains, the absolute owner of the relevant asset. A security interest, by contrast, is a proprietary interest in an asset securing the obligation to repay. It extends only to the amount of that obligation, so that on enforcement there is an obligation to account to the borrower for any surplus value in the asset. Security interests vary in form: pledges and liens are possessory interests (and are not discussed in detail in this book). One type of non-possessory security interest is a mortgage. Here, the title to the asset passes to the lender, who is obliged to retransfer the asset when the secured obligation is repaid. Another type is the charge, which entails no transfer of title but is an encumbrance on the asset. Charges can be fixed or floating. If a lender has a fixed charge, the borrower cannot dispose of the charged asset without the lender's consent. If the lender's charge is floating, the borrower can make such a disposition. Floating charges, therefore, are often taken over circulating assets and enable a lender to take security over all the assets of a company. These interests are discussed in more detail in chapter six.

Contractual rights are more varied. They can be divided into contractual rights against the borrower itself, and contractual rights against third parties. Both are discussed in detail in chapter five. Rights against a third party are obviously more valuable than rights against a borrower if the borrower becomes insolvent (unless the third party also becomes insolvent). Such rights include 'credit enhancement' transactions such as guarantees, insurance and credit default swaps. Broadly speaking, these transactions involve a promise by the third party to pay the lender if the borrower defaults, although the actual structures vary considerably.[80] The third party may be someone with a strong interest in the

---

[76]   Such restrictions in contracts include negative pledge clauses and are discussed at 5.2.1.
[77]   *Welsh Development Agency v Export Finance Co Ltd* [1992] BCC 270. Most recently drafted negative pledge clauses, however, extend to sales as well as charges over receivables.
[78]   For a more detailed discussion of the credit risk of creditors, see page 73.
[79]   5.2.4.
[80]   The details of the different structures are discussed at 5.3 below.

operation of the borrower, such as another company in the same group. Where the borrower is a small private company it is likely to be a director. In these cases the form of the transaction is likely to be a guarantee, and the third party takes on the liability without remuneration, although it would have a right to be indemnified by the borrower. Alternatively, the third party may be someone providing credit protection commercially for a fee: in this case the transaction is more likely to be an indemnity, a performance bond, credit insurance or a credit default swap.[81]

Rights against third parties also include an agreement made with another creditor to subordinate its claim to that of the protected creditor,[82] so that the subordinated creditor is not paid until the protected creditor has been paid in full. This has the effect of making it more likely that the protected creditor will be paid on the insolvency of the borrower, although, where the creditors are unsecured, it does not give priority over any creditor with a proprietary right. It is also very common for certain creditors to be subordinated to all other creditors, for example, where there are different tranches of loans or bond issues[83] or where hybrid securities are issued.[84] The indemnification rights of group companies and directors who give guarantees are usually subordinated to all other creditors.[85]

Contractual rights against the borrower (many of which are known as covenants) protect the position of the creditor in a number of different ways. Some covenants restrict activities of the borrower which may damage the creditors. Thus dividend distribution may be limited, or the dissipation of assets or the grant of security.[86] Other covenants seek to ensure that the creditor is properly informed about the credit risk it is undertaking: these include representations and warranties about the state of the company (or the assets transferred or given as security) at the time of the advance, and financial reporting covenants which oblige the company to give ongoing information and to maintain certain financial ratios.[87] Other types of clauses, such as acceleration or termination clauses on default, are often present to give the creditor the ability to force a restructuring, to terminate the lender's obligation (if there is one) to make further advances and, in the last resort, to enable the creditor to enforce the entire loan.[88] Where credit is extended on retention of title terms to enable the borrower to acquire tangible assets, a termination clause enables the lender to repossess the asset.[89] Secured loans will include provisions enabling enforcement of security, although this is now often done in the context of the insolvency procedure of administration.[90]

Another type of provision gives rights based on set-off.[91] Set-off operates outside insolvency to prevent circularity of action and to enable transactions to be settled without transferring large sums. It operates under the general law, but is usually provided for in a

---

[81] See 5.3.1.4, 5.3.2 and 5.3.3.
[82] 5.3.4.
[83] For example in a securitisation structure (see 8.3.3) or leveraged buyouts (14.4.3).
[84] See below 2.4.
[85] See, for example, *Re SSSL Realisations* [2006] EWCA Civ 7 and *Flightlease Holdings (Guernsey) v Flightlease (Ireland)* (Judgment 3/2009, unreported 14 January 2009, Royal Court of Guernsey).
[86] See 5.2.1.
[87] See 5.2.2.
[88] See 5.2.3.
[89] See below 2.3.4.3 and 6.5.2.1.
[90] See 6.5.3 below.
[91] See 5.2.4.

contract to avoid any uncertainty as to when it applies. On insolvency, set-off, where there are mutual parties, is compulsory.[92] Its operation enables a creditor to be paid pound for pound, thus giving an equivalent protection to that of a security interest. Thus, it is provisions which give rise to set-off on insolvency (such as netting and close-out provisions or flawed asset provisions) which provide significant credit risk protection.

These main contractual provisions for reducing credit risk are discussed in chapter five. Not all financing agreements include all these provisions, and some may include others. This will depend on many factors, including the type of transaction in question (for example, whether it is an issue of securities or a loan), the market conditions and the bargaining power of the parties.[93] Many loans are made on standard terms, such as those of the Loan Market Association for use in syndicated loans, or those used by particular banks or financiers. The creditor may also wish to protect itself against risks other than credit risk, such as the risk of the transaction turning out to be less profitable than it hoped because it has to pay more for the money it borrows to fund the transaction, for market reasons or because of changes in tax or regulatory rules. Clauses dealing with such a situation are common in syndicated loan transactions.[94] Debt securities usually contain fewer covenants included by the issuer (and its advisers) as a result of what is seen as necessary to make the securities attractive to potential investors. Investors buy debt securities on a 'take it or leave it' basis as there is no opportunity for negotiation of terms.[95]

The protection required by a creditor can, of course, have a profound effect on what types of financing are available to a particular borrower. For example, if a lender requires security in order to be persuaded to lend, a borrower who cannot give security will not be able to borrow (conversely, the provision of security may persuade a lender to lend who would not otherwise do so). It should, however, be borne in mind that most of the structures discussed in this book are, to some extent, standard in form with creditor protection already built in, so that the borrower will be choosing between different options rather than negotiating from scratch, although the detail of the documentation is usually negotiated except in small scale transactions. New forms of financing are developed all the time, of course, but this is largely in relation to very large transactions, often involving financial institutions who are repeat players, and they usually develop out of and use structures and concepts already in existence. With this in mind, this book will discuss the various legal issues which arise in the more common forms of debt corporate finance and will largely focus on devices which are for the protection of the creditor, although some benefit both parties, such as the appointment of a trustee in a bond issue.

2.3.1.3 *Protection of Creditors: Regulation*

Another way in which creditors can be protected is by regulation, that is, statutory provisions which impose conditions which have to be fulfilled before certain transactions can be entered into. These therefore limit the ability of borrowers and creditors to enter

---

[92]   See page 183.
[93]   See 3.2.2.3.
[94]   M Hughes, *Legal Principles in Banking and Structured Finance*, 2nd edn (Hayward's Heath, Tottel Publishing Ltd, 2006) 2.13; G Fuller, *Corporate Borrowing: Law and Practice*, 4th edn (Bristol, Jordan Publishing Ltd, 2009) 2.15.
[95]   See 7.3.1.

into whatever transactions they wish. Some areas of debt finance are more heavily regulated than others: in theory this is because they involve more risk to creditors, or more systemic risk to the market, although that is not entirely the case in practice. The issue of debt securities to the public is regulated in broadly the same way as an issue of equity securities.[96] This is to ensure that those buying the debt securities both on the primary and the secondary market have accurate and detailed information about the credit risk they are taking on. However, an issue of bonds to professionals is more lightly regulated,[97] and the syndicated loan market is completely unregulated except by contract. Another form of regulation is the requirement to register certain security interests so that other creditors know that they have been granted when they are considering lending to the borrower.[98] Sometimes particular transaction types are regulated, such as covered bonds.[99] Of course, another purpose of regulation is to protect all participants in the financial markets from systemic collapse, and much of the regulation of banks and other financial institutions[100] is to this effect. This specific type of regulation is a specialist area, and is not covered in detail in this book.

However, one aspect of financial regulation which can be conveniently explained at this point is the requirement that banks and other financial institutions[101] retain a certain level of capital in order to cover the risk that their debtors will not repay. This is an ongoing requirement, and is in addition to the legal capital requirements discussed in chapter four. The capital adequacy requirement[102] balances the amount of credit risk against the amount of capital which needs to be held. Broadly speaking, the firm must retain capital amounting to eight per cent of its risk exposure:[103] as this is an ongoing obligation, the firm must monitor constantly to ensure it is complying.[104] There are thus two separate calculations to decide whether a firm is complying: the risk exposure of the firm, and the amount of capital it holds. Both are the subject of detailed regulation in the FSA handbook, and only a very brief summary is given here. Capital adequacy requirements

---

[96] For discussion see chapters 9 and 11.

[97] See chapter 11.

[98] 6.4 below.

[99] See pages 36 and 534. The application of regulatory legislation to a particular credit product is a new departure, see C Oakley, 'Regulated Covered Bond Regulations: Issues arising from Interpretation of the UCITS Directive' (2008) 23 *Journal of International Banking and Financial Law* 240.

[100] Such as the capital adequacy requirements and the 'soft law' promulgated by the Financial Services Authority.

[101] In the interests of brevity, these will be called 'firms' in this section as this is the terminology used in the FSA handbook.

[102] Now found in the Capital Requirements Directive, which is the collective name for the Capital Adequacy Directive 2006/49/EC and the Banking and Consolidation Directive 2006/48/EC. These in turn implement Basel II, which is an agreement among the regulators from many countries around the world. Basel II was agreed in 2004 and amended the original agreement, Basel I, inter alia, to take account of risk-mitigation devices such as securitisation, credit derivatives, the use of security and netting. Basel II came into force in January 2008. The Capital Requirements Directive is implemented in the UK by the Financial Services and Markets Act 2000 and in the FSA Handbook. The relevant parts are the General Prudential Sourcebook (GENPRU) and the Prudential Sourcebook for Banks, Building Societies and Investment Firms (BIPRU). Both the Basel rules and the CRD are under constant review, especially in the aftermath of the financial crisis of 2007. In December 2009 the FSA published a consultation paper (CP09/29) discussing implementation of changes to the CRD included in CRD2 and CRD3 packages. A further consultation paper discussing the responses to CP09/29 has now been published (CP10/17).

[103] BIPRU 3.1.5. The FSA may require a higher ratio from particular firms (GENPRU 2.1.11).

[104] GENPRU 2.1.9. A firm must ensure that it can demonstrate its capital resources at any time if required to do so by the FSA (GENPRU 2.1.10).

are significant since the design of many transactions, particularly securities, has been heavily influenced by capital adequacy requirements.

The risk exposure of the firm depends on the amount of money owed to that firm and the risk weighting of each obligation. The risk weighting will be calculated on the basis of the credit-worthiness of the debtor (which may depend on the type of debtor and also on its rating[105]), any credit enhancement which makes it more likely that the debt will be repaid (such as a guarantee) and any collateral held against the debt.[106] A standardised approach based on these factors is used for unsophisticated firms; the more sophisticated are permitted to use an internal approach whereby they determine the risk levels themselves. Capital is also required to be held against some forms of operational risk, the measurement of which depends on the type of firm involved and its gross income.

The kind of capital a firm can hold is divided into three tiers, comprising equity and subordinated debt. Tier one is permanent capital, that is, capital that only has to be repaid on a winding up and includes ordinary shares and retained capital, as well as certain types of hybrid instruments designed to achieve tier one status.[107] It can be used against any form of risk exposure, while there are limits as to the use of tier two and, particularly, tier three capital. Tier two capital comprises hybrid instruments which are structured like debt but have some of the loss absorbency of equity, for example, by being deeply subordinated.[108] It is divided into upper tier two capital (permanent instruments) and lower tier two capital (dated instruments).[109] Tier three capital is short-term subordinated debt.[110]

2.3.1.4   *Multiple Lenders and Transfer of Debt*

Where the amount of debt financing required is large, a borrower will often seek funds from more than one lender. The loans may be consecutive, in which case issues of priority between lenders may arise.[111] However, in many cases a borrower will seek to raise funds from a number of lenders at once, such as in a syndicated loan[112] or bond issue.[113] Although there are great advantages to a borrower in accessing funds from a number of sources, there are also practical difficulties. For example, it is necessary to have some form of structure to enable decisions to be made in relation to the conduct of the borrowing relationship, such as whether modifications should be made to the terms of the loan, or whether the loan should be accelerated if a default has occurred. More prosaically, it is necessary to have one person who actually does the work required to administer the relationship, such as collecting payments from the borrower and distributing these to the lenders. There are two legal concepts that are used to overcome this problem: that of

---

[105]   By a rating agency, see below pages 32–33.

[106]   Note that even 'off balance sheet' transactions such as securitisations (see below page 35) may be taken into account if the firm is still at some risk, (BIPRU 9).

[107]   See below 2.4. Tier 1 capital can only contain 15% 'innovative' tier 1 capital, such as hybrids (GENPRU 2.2.30) and innovative tier 1 capital can only be included in tier 1 capital if the firm has a legal opinion as to its loss absorbency (GENPRU 2.2.118). Core tier 1 capital, such as ordinary shares, must make up at least 50% of tier 1 capital (GENPRU 2.2.29. This is to make sure that most of the tier 1 capital of a firm is of the highest quality, that is, capable of maximum loss absorption (GENPRU 2.2.31).

[108]   GENPRU 2.2.158. See pages 45–46.

[109]   GENPRU 2.2.157. Note that tier two instruments cannot contain any covenants which could lead to early repayment, such as a negative pledge clause or a cross-default clause, GENPRU 2.2.165.

[110]   GENPRU 2.2.242.

[111]   Priority questions between secured lenders are discussed at 6.4.3.

[112]   See page 29.

[113]   See 2.3.3.

agency and that of trust. The main difference is that where there is an agent, he may act for the borrower or for the lenders, depending on context, whereas a trustee holds the obligation to repay, and any security on trust for the lenders. Although an agent or trustee may have certain powers to make decisions, any important decisions have to be taken by the lenders, either unanimously, which may be hard to achieve, or by a majority. The structures arising from use of agents or trustees, and the complex questions of the extent of their rights and obligations are discussed in chapter seven.

While a creditor may wish to retain a relationship with the borrower, and may be content to fund the loan or other credit from its own resources until it is repaid, in many cases a creditor will wish to divest itself of the asset represented by the debt, for a number of reasons. It may just be that it wishes to use the debt as collateral for a loan to itself, either by creating a security interest over it, or by title transfer. In that case, the immediate credit risk of non-payment will be retained by the original lender. The lender may, however, wish to transfer the debt completely, so that the transferee takes on all risks in relation to the loan, including credit risk, in return for a price. A creditor may wish to do this to improve cash flow: it gets money up front for a debt due in the future (for example, by securitisation or by discounting a bill of exchange). Alternatively, the creditor may be concerned about the ability of the debtor to pay in the future, and hopes to get some money now rather than risk receiving nothing on the insolvency of the debtor (for example, by selling bonds). Or it may just be that there is a developed market for such debts and the sophisticated creditor can profit from movements in the market which are unrelated, or only loosely related, to the credit risk of the borrower. This is particularly true in relation to the most easily traded debt, that is, debt securities, where transfer is an integral part of the form of transaction. While most other debts can be sold, transfer may be less straightforward for a number of reasons, such as the presence of an anti-assignment clause in the original contract, or the fact that the lender is still obliged to make further advances. These problems have to a large extent been overcome by legal ingenuity, so that there is now a well-developed market in syndicated loans, and also in distressed debt, as well as extensive use of securitisation and receivables financing, both of which involve a sale of debts. Issues relating to the transfer of debts are discussed in chapter eight.

The following sections explain in outline the main types of debt financing, as defined above to include the provision of credit. Detailed consideration of relevant legal issues follow in the subsequent chapters.

2.3.2   Loans[114]

Loans are usually made to companies by banks, either by one bank or a number of banks.[115] It is, of course, possible for a company to borrow from other parties, such as individuals (for example, directors) or from other companies (for example, parent

---

[114]   See Fuller, *Corporate Borrowing*, n 94, ch 2; Tolley Company Law Service B5021-B5027; J Benjamin, *Financial Law* (Oxford, Oxford University Press, 2007) 8.1.2.2; P Cresswell (ed), *Encyclopedia of Banking Law* (London, Boston, Butterworths, 1982) chs C13, F3150–F3210. For the critical importance of bank lending in corporate finance see BIS, Financing a Private Sector Recovery, n 1, 3.18–3.28.

[115]   This would be a syndicated loan, which is discussed below at page 29 and 7.4.

companies or others in the same group). Such loans are quite likely to be subordinated[116] but will still contain both contractual and maybe proprietary protection for the lender, as discussed below in relation to bank loans.

One main distinction to be made in relation to loans to companies is between committed and on demand lending.[117] The most common example of on-demand lending is an overdraft, which is one of the most common forms of debt finance for small and medium sized companies.[118] Once agreed between the bank and the customer,[119] the customer can draw more money from its current account with the bank than it has paid in, up to the agreed limit. Normally, an overdraft is repayable on demand, although this can be varied by contrary agreement. Whether there is contrary agreement depends on the interpretation of the particular facility letter: the mere fact that the overdraft is available for a period of time does not mean that a provision that it is repayable on demand is ineffective.[120] This means that, unless the company takes specific steps to ensure appropriate wording in the overdraft documentation, it is in danger of the finance being withdrawn without notice when it itself is not in breach.[121] In theory this makes an overdraft a risky form of financing for a company, despite its popularity among small businesses.[122] There are, however, two ameliorating factors. First, generally a bank will not demand repayment of an overdraft without reason, and is, in fact, usually keen to continue the lending relationship with a company that is able to service its debts, since the interest payable on the overdrawn account is a source of income for the bank.[123] Second, the bank is obliged to honour cheques drawn on the account before demand.[124]

A committed facility is where the bank is committed to lend throughout a certain period, usually subject to the fulfilment of certain conditions.[125] It could be a term loan, where the amount lent is advanced all at once, or in successive tranches. It could be repayable in a single ('bullet') repayment or according to a payment schedule ('amortising'). It could have more flexibility, as in a revolving facility, which is similar to an

---

[116]   See below 5.3.4.

[117]   Tolley Company Law Service B5021.

[118]   A Cosh, A Hughes, A Bullock and I Milner, 'SME Finance and Innovation in the Current Economic Climate' (Centre for Business Research, University of Cambridge, 2007) This is confirmed by the 'Financial Risk Outlook 2010' (Financial Services Authority) 16, where the rising cost and lack of availability of bank finance for SMEs is noted. However, to some extent the gap has been filled by the growth of invoice discounting and asset-based lending, see 2.3.4 below and Asset Based Finance Association (ABFA) 'Asset Based Lending Backed Firms Show Increase In Sales' (7 September 2009) available at www.abfa.org.uk.

[119]   Prior agreement is essential; *Cunliffe Brooks & Co v Blackburn & District Benefit Building Society* (1884) LR 9 App Cas 857, but can be implied: *Cumming v Shand* (1860) 5 H & N 95.

[120]   *Williams & Glyn's Bank Ltd v Barnes* [1981] Com LR 205; *Lloyds Bank plc v Lampert* [1999] 1 All ER 161, 167–68; *Bank of Ireland v AMCD (Property Holdings) Ltd* [2001] 2 All ER 894, [15]–[17]. There are also other cases where an express obligation on the bank to provide the facility for a period of time has been held to rebut the presumption that the overdraft is repayable on demand, see *Titford Property Co Ltd v Cannon Street Acceptances Ltd* (25 May 1975, unreported) and *Crimpfil v Barclays Bank plc* (20 April 1994, unreported). However, these authorities may be unreliable in the light of the later cases, or at least, only explicable on the wording of the particular documentation.

[121]   It also appears that, at least in the absence of very special circumstances, a bank does not owe a duty of care to a borrower when demanding repayment of an overdraft, see *Chapman v Barclays Bank plc* [1997] 6 Bank LR 315 and *Hall v Royal Bank of Scotland plc* [2009] EWHC B36 (Mercantile).

[122]   See Benjamin, *Financial Law*, n 114, 8.17, citing R Cranston, *Principles of Banking Law*, 2nd edn (Oxford, Oxford University Press, 2002) 299.

[123]   See page 73.

[124]   *Rouse v Bradford Banking Co Ltd* [1894] AC 586, 596; *Williams & Glyn's Bank v Barnes* [1981] Com LR 205.

[125]   These are likely to be both conditions precedent and warranties, see discussion in chapter 5.2.2.

overdraft in that the company can draw down, repay, and draw down again, up to the date when the facility ends, when the borrowings have to be repaid. A company is more likely to use a term loan for a one-off purchase, such as land, or in an acquisition, and a revolving facility to raise working capital.[126] An even more flexible loan is a standby credit[127] or 'swingline'[128] which is often used to support an issue of commercial paper.[129] This is a short-term advance which may not be used at all, but can be used to tide the company over if it has to repay some commercial paper but does not want to issue another batch immediately because of market conditions.

The loan can be made in cash, but another method is where a bank agrees to accept bills of exchange drawn on it by the company.[130] The company then sells the bill in the market (or the bank will do so and reimburse the company) so that the company obtains money immediately. On the bill's maturity the bank, as acceptor, pays the person to whom the bill has been sold (the holder) and the company will then reimburse the bank for doing so.

All types of loans will include protection for the lender against the credit risk of the borrower. This may be just contractual rights (as against the borrower or also against third parties), but may also be proprietary. The proprietary protection in relation to a loan will be the provision of security by the borrower. The possible types of security and the policy issues relating to the taking of security are discussed below in chapter six.

Where the loan required is large, the risk of making it is usually spread among a number of lenders, through syndication and/or through the use of subordination. Syndication is where one bank, mandated by the company to arrange the loan, prepares an information memorandum about the company and solicits other banks to join in making the loan. Each bank in fact makes a separate loan to the company, so that their liability is several. This has the effect that no bank is liable if another bank fails to lend or becomes insolvent,[131] and also enables individual banks to exercise set-off rights against individual borrowers. This also means that each bank can enforce the debt due to it itself. As mentioned above, the administrative duties of the syndicated loan are carried out by an agent (usually one of the banks making the loan). Syndicated loans are discussed in detail in 7.4 below.

In an acquisition or leveraged buy-out it is usual for the amount of finance available to be increased by using subordination.[132] Under the subordination structure, the junior creditor agrees that it will not recover until the senior creditor has been paid in full, or that it will hold any recoveries on trust for the senior creditor.[133] The senior creditor is encouraged to lend more, as the junior debt provides a 'cushion' which will be lost first in the event of the insolvency of the borrower, and the junior creditors obtain a much higher

---

[126] Tolley Company Law Service B5024.
[127] S Valdez, *An Introduction to Global Financial Markets*, n 73, 84.
[128] See Fuller, *Corporate Borrowing*, n 94, 2.6.
[129] See below page 30.
[130] See Fuller, *Corporate Borrowing*, n 94, 2.5.
[131] P Wood, *International Loans, Bonds, Guarantees, Legal Opinions*, 2nd edn (London, Sweet & Maxwell, 2007), 3–006; Fuller, *Corporate Borrowing*, n 94, 2.17; M Hughes, *Legal Principles in Banking and Structured Finance*, 2nd edn (Hayward's Heath, Tottel Publishing Ltd, 2006) 9.2.
[132] See 14.4.3.
[133] 5.3.4.1.

interest rate, which compensates them for the extra risk they carry.[134] Sometimes the subordination is structural.[135] The junior debt layer may also be financed by the issuing of high yield bonds.[136]

It should be remembered that all debt can be sold, and so the banks making the loans described above can, if they wish, pass on the credit risk of the loans they make by transferring the debts which the loans represent. As mentioned above, there is a strong market in syndicated loans, and other loans can be disposed of by securitisation.[137] By transferring the loans they make, banks can obtain more capital to make more loans, and can reduce the amount of capital they have to hold under the capital adequacy requirements of Basel II.[138]

2.3.3   Debt Securities

2.3.3.1   General

Debt securities are tradable instruments which a company can issue in order to raise money from a variety of lenders. Such lenders will be more numerous and more varied in type than the single bank or syndicate of banks who would otherwise make a loan to the company. In theory, anyone can buy debt securities, although in most cases the target and actual investors are much more limited for a number of reasons.[139] Debt securities are issued, usually to a limited group of investors, in what is known as the primary market. The process of issuance is described in chapter seven.[140] Once issued, they can be traded in what is called the secondary market. Not all debt securities are traded: some are kept by the original owners until maturity.. Loan notes issued as part of a private equity transaction fall within this category.[141] However, many are, and anything which adds to their tradability (liquidity) adds to their value.[142]

In this book we will consider only debt securities issued by companies. However, it should be realised that a vast amount of debt securities are issued by Governments: these are usually the most highly rated (though it does depend on the credit standing of the relevant Government),[143] and the pricing of debt securities issued by companies is often tied to that of Government securities.[144] It should also be remembered that the term 'debt securities' covers a number of different kinds of instruments. Companies, or banks, needing short-term finance can raise it by issuing commercial paper, a term meaning short-term securities (with a term up to 364 days) or, if the company is authorised to carry on deposit taking, certificates of deposit, which can have a term of up to five years. Longer

---

[134]   P Wood, *Project Finance, Securitisations and Subordinated Debt,* 2nd edn (London, Sweet & Maxwell, 2007) 10–008.
[135]   See 5.3.4.1.4. Structural subordination is particularly important in private equity transactions, as discussed at 14.4.
[136]   See below page 33.
[137]   See chapter 8, especially 8.2.1 (novation of syndicated loans) and 8.3.3 (securitisation).
[138]   Above pages 25–26.
[139]   The regulatory issues are discussed in chapter 11 below.
[140]   7.3.1.
[141]   14.4.2.
[142]   M Choudhry, *Corporate Bonds and Structured Financial Products* (Amsterdam, London, Elsevier Butterworth-Heinemann, 2005) 59.
[143]   See, for example, the weak position of Greek government bonds during 2010.
[144]   See Choudhry, *Corporate Bonds and Structured Financial Products,* n 142, 5.3, 128.

term debt securities are called bonds or notes. Originally, notes were securities with a shorter term than bonds, but the terminology has now become more interchangeable, especially in the European markets. However, the term 'notes' is generally used where the interest rate is floating, and also where securities are issued as part of a programme.[145]

It needs to be remembered when considering different types of securities (and different varieties of terms within the documentation) that these are dictated by the requirements of two people: the issuer and the potential investors. The potential investors are often not in a position to negotiate terms, and so it is usually the lead manager[146] who will advise the issuer what sort of bonds and what terms will be marketable at an interest rate the issuer wishes to pay. This will include the level of covenants.[147] The issuer also will want to make sure that the issue fulfils its requirements, for example, as to the term of the financing (bearing in mind that the company will normally want to refinance on the maturity of the bond), the flexibility of the term (for example, whether the company has a call option[148]) and so on. When assessing the variety of the types of bonds available and the terms within the documentation, it is important to consider what features are for the protection of the lenders and what features are for the benefit of the issuer. In some cases, such as the use of a trustee, there are benefits for both parties.[149]

2.3.3.2 Securities Versus Loan

As a general rule, it is cheaper for a company to raise money by issuing debt securities than by taking a loan. However, once they are issued the company cannot usually pay back the debt represented by the securities until the end of the term of the issue, so it is a less flexible form of financing than a revolving facility or overdraft. Accordingly it is probably more accurate to compare the merits of an issue of securities to those of a term loan. Why is this form of raising finance cheaper? The rate of interest payable on securities is determined by a combination of features, including market rates. However, it does not have to cover as many costs as that set by a bank in relation to a loan, such as the carrying out of due diligence and the costs of monitoring.[150] Further, bondholders are generally less risk averse than banks, and so charge less interest. However, the best mix of financing (from the point of view of the borrower) may well be to include some bank financing in addition to the issue of bonds. Bank financing indicates that the bank has, after due diligence enquiries, decided that the company is a good credit risk. On the basis of this signalling, the bond issue can be at an even lower rate of interest.[151]

Another attractive feature of issuing debt securities for a company is that money is raised from a wider pool of lenders than is possible with a loan, even a syndicated loan, where the lenders are only banks. Holders of debt securities may include institutional investors, such as pension funds, other companies, including insurance companies, and

---

[145] See page 324.
[146] See page 324–25.
[147] See page 24.
[148] See page 34.
[149] For discussion of these, see 7.3.2.3.1.
[150] Very little monitoring is done by the trustee of a bond issue, see page 344.
[151] A Morrison, 'Credit Derivatives, Disintermediation and Investment Decisions' (May 2001). Oxford Financial Research Centre Working Paper 2001-FE-01, available at SSRN: www.ssrn.com/abstract=270269.

even private individuals.[152] The wide pool of lenders not only taps sources of finance for the borrower which would be unavailable in the context of a loan, but corporate borrowers see individual bondholders as less likely to cause trouble on default than bank lenders, particularly if there is a bond trustee.[153] Further, finance by means of a bond issue may be available even when bank funds are limited, as has been the case in the recent financial crisis.[154] Debt securities are attractive to investors in that not only do they provide a steady stream of income[155] but they are tradable on recognised markets. This means that the investor can easily realise its capital assets without waiting for the bond to mature and can offload the risk of default onto someone else (although this will be reflected in the price at which the bond is sold). Some bonds are more liquid (that is, more easily traded on the capital markets) than others, and this is reflected in the price. It should be noted, however, that in recent years the transfer of loans, or the transfer of risk of loans, using sub-participation, has become very common.[156]

2.3.3.3   *Who Issues Bonds?*

Although it might seem to make sense for most companies to raise money by issuing debt securities, many cannot. First, there may be restrictions in the nature of the company itself, for example, a private company cannot offer debentures to the public.[157] Second, the company may not have a good enough credit rating for the securities to be marketable. A credit rating, which is given to a company by a credit rating agency,[158] is based on the likelihood that the company will default on its securities and is important in the bond market for several reasons. Investors are much more likely to buy bonds with a high credit rating. However, because the demand will be high, the issuer can offer a lower rate of interest than on a riskier bond with a lower credit rating.[159] The ratings (in theory at least) allow investors to match the amount of risk they are prepared to take with the amount of yield on bonds that they purchase. Certain investors, mainly financial institutions, are only permitted to buy bonds with an 'investment grade' rating. Thus the market for investment grade rated bonds is much larger than for those with a lower rating. In fact, until relatively recently companies without such a rating could not issue bonds as no one would buy

---

[152]   There is very limited direct investment in corporate bonds by non-high worth individuals in the UK (see Trading Transparency in the UK bond markets, FSA discussion paper 05/5 September 2005), although many individuals will have exposure to the bond market through pensions and other investments. However, the London Stock Exchange has launched a new online market for retail bonds, which is encouraging the launch of issues aimed at a retail market. See www.londonstockexchange.com/specialist-issuers/retail-bonds/retail-bonds.htm.

[153]   D Petkovic, 'New Structures: "Whole Business" Securitisations of Project Cash Flows' [2000] *Journal of International Banking Law* 187.

[154]   This has led to larger companies fulfilling their borrowing requirements by issuing bonds rather than from bank loans, see 'Financial Risk Outlook 2010' (Financial Services Authority) 16. See BIS, *Financing a Private Sector Recovery*, n 1, 3.40.

[155]   Unless they are zero coupon bonds or commercial paper, where interest is not payable.

[156]   See chapter 8.

[157]   Companies Act 2006, s 755. See below pages 539–40.

[158]   The rating agencies are private companies who operate both in the domestic and international markets. The main agencies in the international markets are Moody's, Fitch and Standard & Poor's. Moody's grades are in the form Aaa to Baa3 (investment grade) and Ba1 to D (non-investment grade); the other two have grades in the form AAA to BBB (investment grade) and BB+ to D (non-investment grade). For a discussion on the regulation of rating agencies see 11.7.

[159]   M Doran, D Howe and R Pogrel, 'Debt Capital Markets, an Introduction' (2005) 16 *Practical Law Company* 21, 26.

them. However, in the 1970s a phenomenon grew up in the US called 'junk bonds' (or, more respectably, 'high yield' bonds)[160] which are very risky bonds issued by companies without an investment grade rating.[161] High Yield Bonds are often used for the mezzanine finance in leveraged buy-outs.[162] Even so, bond issues are not appropriate for small and medium sized enterprises, which are much more likely to be looking at bank or asset-based lending as their main source of debt finance.

2.3.3.4 Debt Securities Versus Equity

Whether a company which needs money issues equity or debt securities depends on a number of factors.[163] One particular advantage of debt securities over equity securities is that the interest paid on debt securities is tax deductible for the company, unlike dividends, which cannot be deducted.[164] This makes debt a much cheaper option than equity, at least up to a certain point.[165]

In one sense, the tradability of debt securities makes them similar, from an investor's point of view, to equity securities. Debt securities are traded on the secondary market and are frequently listed on a stock market, although much of the trading takes place over the counter (this is often abbreviated to 'OTC'). The big difference is that the owner of equity securities has a stake in the company and shares its profits and its losses. The owner of debt securities does not share in the profits, and, as a creditor, ranks above shareholders if the company is insolvent. These issues are discussed further in chapter three. The exact priority of the owner of debt securities will depend on various matters such as whether the securities are backed by security over other assets and whether they are the subject of a subordination agreement. There is also a twilight zone occupied by what are known as 'hybrid' instruments.[166] These are securities which have some characteristics of debt and some of equity, and are an attempt to give investors part of the best of both worlds, although, of course, they end up without the full benefits of either. For example, securities may be deeply subordinated, or perpetual,[167] or convertible into equity.[168]

2.3.3.5 Varieties of Bonds

Bonds in particular, as opposed to money market instruments such as commercial paper, come in all sorts of varieties, like ice cream. This similarity is reflected in the name given to a typical unadorned bond: plain vanilla. A plain vanilla bond is basically a promise by the issuer to pay both interest and, at maturity, the principal debt. The promise can be made

---

[160] The polite term is now used much more frequently as such bonds have become more widespread.

[161] For accounts of the history of junk bonds, see S Valdez, *An Introduction to Global Financial Markets*, n 73, 140–41 and G Fuller, *The Law and Practice of International Capital Markets* (London, LexisNexis Butterworths, 2007) 108–09. The high yield market is very susceptible to market conditions, so that during the credit crunch of 2007 and 2008 hardly any high yield bonds were issued (see A Sakoui, 'Junk Bond Hiatus Shows the Depth of Credit Squeeze' *Financial Times*, 23 July 2008). With the economic recovery in 2009 the market for high yield bonds is beginning to look up A van Duyn and N Bullock, 'High-yield Bonds Feel Thaw', *Financial Times*, 27 April 2009 and D Oakley, 'Total Returns on High-yield Bonds Rise 20%', *Financial Times*, 11 May 2009.

[162] See Wood, *International Loans*, n 131, 2–015.

[163] For a general discussion of the debt/equity mix in a company's capital structure, see 2.6 below.

[164] Discussed further in 2.6.

[165] For more discussion about the cost of capital, see 2.6 below.

[166] 2.4 below.

[167] See page 46.

[168] See page 45.

to the bondholders or to a trustee acting on their behalf.[169] The documentation will, of course, include more than just the promise: it will include details of the interest rate payable (which is usually fixed but can be floating and can also be linked to an index), the details of payment and redemption and other administrative details, and covenants to protect the interests of the bondholders.

One variation is a 'zero coupon' bond. The terminology originated when bonds were bearer bonds, so that whoever held them owned them. The issuer would not necessarily know who the holders were, and so each bond had a number of detachable 'coupons' which related to each interest payment. When an interest payment was due, the holder at the time detached the relevant coupon, sent it to the issuer and claimed the interest. This is no longer the practice (as we shall see, very few bondholders actually hold bearer bonds now)[170] but the term 'coupon' for interest still remains. If a bond is 'zero coupon', this means that there is no interest payable. Instead, it is issued at a discount to its face value, that is, to the amount that is payable on maturity. The 'interest payments' are therefore paid at the end, when the bond matures. This used to have certain tax advantages, since the gain was seen as capital rather than income, but many jurisdictions have changed their tax legislation so that the gain is now seen as interest. There are, however, other advantages to such a bond. For a UK corporate issuer, it can still deduct a notional amount as expenditure even though it is not paying interest.[171] Also, the regulations on withholding tax do not apply to these sorts of bonds.[172]

Another variation relates to the time of payment and the possibility of prepayment. The issuer may be given the option to buy back or redeem some or all of the bonds before maturity. This is called a 'call' option;[173] an issuer would wish to exercise this if interest rates fell below the rate payable on the bond, so that it could issue another bond at a lower rate, that is, refinance. Conversely, the holders could have an option to require early redemption: this is called a 'put' option. Debt securities cannot be redeemed early unless this is specifically provided for in the terms of the issue.[174] Securities also may be only repayable after a very long time or even be perpetual. These are seen as akin to equity for various purposes and are a type of hybrid security which is discussed below.[175]

Yet another variation is whether the securities are domestic or international. Domestic stock[176] is issued by a UK issuer in sterling and is aimed at UK investors. Eurobonds are aimed at the international markets, and can be issued in any country, though they are often denominated in a currency other than that of the country in which they are issued. Domestic securities are also now often issued in the form of eurobonds. The main structural difference between the two is that stock is one single debt which is either held for the stockholders by a trustee, or contained in a deed poll for the benefit of all the stockholders,[177] which can be divided up into holdings of any size represented by one

---

[169]   See chapter 7.
[170]   See page 335.
[171]   Tolley's Company Law Service, B5042.
[172]   Ibid.
[173]   M Choudhry, *Corporate Bonds and Structured Financial Products* (Amsterdam, London, Elsevier Butterworth-Heinemann, 2005) 126.
[174]   *Hooper v Western Counties and South Wales Telephone Co Ltd* (1892) 68 LT 78.
[175]   2.4.
[176]   See Fuller, *Corporate Borrowing*, n 94, 3.3.
[177]   See Fuller, *Corporate Borrowing*, n 94, 3.6 – 3.10. For further discussion see 7.3.2.2.

certificate (or CREST entry).[178] Eurobonds, on the other hand, are denominated in fixed amounts, and each bond is an agreement between the bondholder and the company, although often there is a trustee who holds the benefit of the covenant to pay for the bondholders.[179] Both stock and eurobonds can be, and often are, listed on the London Stock Exchange.[180] Eurobonds are rarely issued to the public,[181] but rather to sophisticated institutional investors, and most trading is OTC ('over the counter'), that is, away from the market and conducted between parties privately (usually over the telephone). The regulatory framework that governs listed debt issues is discussed below at chapter eleven.

So far we have considered bonds which are issued by a company which is obliged to pay back the amount due from its trading income and, on maturity, from its own assets (or by reborrowing). The rating of the bond therefore depends on the creditworthiness of the company (plus any credit enhancement). However, it is also possible for bonds to be issued on the basis that repayment comes from a pool of income-producing assets, such as receivables. This is the basic idea behind securities known as 'asset-backed securities' or 'ABS', where the bonds are issued, not by the original owner of the receivables, but by a special purpose vehicle ('SPV') which has bought the receivables from the original owner.[182] The original owner thus gets immediate cash in return for debts which are due in the future (and also, usually, acts as service provider for the SPV, that is, collects in the receivables and pays out proceeds to the bondholders, for which it receives a fee). It can be seen that this form of financing, known as securitisation, is therefore an alternative, for the owner of the receivables, to some forms of sale of the receivables to a financier (such as in invoice discounting)[183] or to taking a loan from a bank secured on the receivables (such as a term loan or overdraft secured by a floating or fixed charge).[184] It is usually only suitable where there is a steady stream of receivables, often where the owner is itself a lender, such as a bank or a credit card company, and is owed regular payments on, for example, home mortgage loans or credit card loans.[185] However, it should also be remembered that securitisation is a way for a bank to get off its balance sheet loans that it has itself made to companies, or for a finance company to do the same for finance provided by way of hire purchase or asset leasing. Thus finance provided to small companies is, at one remove, finance by securitisation.

The basic structure has been developed in various ways. First, where it is not possible or desirable to sell receivables to an SPV (for example, where they arise from diverse contracts or where contracts generate cash revenues[186]) the SPV can instead make a loan to the company secured on those assets, and issue securities to fund the loan. This is known as a whole business securitisation. The assets remain on the issuer's balance sheet, and so it is a way of shifting credit risk, and raising immediate cash against later receipts, but it does not assist with taking assets off the borrower's balance sheet. It is used

---

[178] For a discussion of the CREST system see page 328.
[179] For further discussion of the structure of bonds and the position of the trustee, see 7.3.2.3.
[180] 11.2.1.2.
[181] See Benjamin, *Financial Law*, n 114, 8.70. Note that retail bonds are becoming more common, with the launch of the London Stock Exchange Order book for Retail Bonds (see fn [148] above).
[182] See *Paragon Finance Plc v Pender* [2005] EWCA Civ 760 [13] and [14] and *MBNA Europe Bank Ltd v Revenue and Customs Commissioners* [2006] EWHC 2326 (Ch) [46]–[48]. For more detailed discussion, see 8.3.3.
[183] 2.3.4.1.
[184] 2.3.2.
[185] Less consistent receivables are often the subject of a whole business securitisation, see below.
[186] See Petkovic, 'New Structures', n 153, 188.

particularly in acquisition finance and project finance.[187] It is critical to this structure that the secured lender (the SPV) is able to enforce the security easily. This was the case before 2002 as the SPV, as a floating charge holder, could appoint an administrative receiver. When administrative receivership was abolished by the Enterprise Act 2002, whole business securitisations were exempted from this provision providing the debt was over £50 million[188] so that the appointment of an administrative receiver is still possible.[189] A concept similar to whole business securitisations is used in covered bonds, which are issued by the company itself but which are secured on a ringfenced pool of assets belonging to the company, so that the rating of the bonds depends on the quality of those assets rather than the overall credit rating of the company.

Where the motive behind securitising is removal of credit risk from the originator, another possibility is to transfer this synthetically to the SPV by means of a credit default swap or other derivative,[190] whereby the SPV agrees to pay the originator if there is default on the receivables, in return for a fee. The SPV issues securities in the same way as before, and invests the proceeds in some sort of safe investment. The payments that the SPV has to make on the securities are made partly from the interest from the safe investment and partly from the fee. Any payments that the SPV has to make to the originator under the credit default swap are made from the safe investment, thus reducing the amount available to pay the holders of the securities, who thus take the eventual credit risk on the receivables.[191]

So far the structures described have been relatively simple, in that they only involve the originator, the SPV and the bondholders in one transaction and one allocation of risk. However, in the years leading up to 2008, the transactions became far more complex, and involved the layering of securitisations on top of each other. These structures, which on any view contributed to the global financial crisis, are unlikely to become popular again, and are not discussed further in this book.

2.3.4   Finance Based on Assets

This section considers a number of financing structures which are largely used for small and medium sized businesses.[192] Unlike securitisation, which predominantly relates to companies whose business is in some way providing finance for others,[193] these structures concern the financing of manufacturing, trade and service-providing companies. The common feature in all these structures is that the finance is given on the basis of specific collateral provided by the company. The financier has either an absolute interest (by way of sale or retention of title) or (in the case of some asset-based lending) a security

---

[187]   See Petkovic, ibid, 187; M Brailsford, 'Securitisation-Creating Securities' (2004) 725 *Tax Journal* 15. Examples of businesses financed by whole business securitisations are London City Airport (1999), several pub companies such as Punch Taverns (2007), British Airports Authority (2007) and Thames Water (2006).

[188]   Insolvency Act 1986, s 72B (capital market transactions) defined in Sch 2A, para 1. Project finance transactions were also exempted, see ss 72C and 72D.

[189]   For further discussion of enforcement by a receiver, see 6.5.1.4.

[190]   For a discussion of credit default swaps see 5.3.3.

[191]   See Fuller, *Corporate Borrowing*, n 94, 4.75; Wood, *International Loans*, n 131, 28–23; S Henderson, 'Synthetic Securitisation, Part 1: The Elements' (2001) 9 *Journal of International Banking and Financial Law* 402.

[192]   BIS, *Financing a Private Sectory Recovery*, n 1, 3.29–3.32.

[193]   Although not totally, for example, car hire companies often securitise their receivables.

interest.[194] It can be seen that there are some similarities with securitisation structures and covered bonds, but here the finance is not provided by the issue of securities but by the lender itself (who, of course, may well securitise its receivables from the financing). The use of finance based on assets (especially invoice discounting and asset-based lending) has increased greatly in recent times,[195] and is particularly popular when traditional bank lending is not available, either because of global conditions (as in the financial crisis) or when a company has already borrowed as much as the bank will permit.

2.3.4.1   Receivables Financing

Receivables financing provides upfront cash for a company which is owed money in the future. To that extent, it has the same economic effect as a loan which is paid back as and when the receivables are paid. In its pure financing form, the credit risk of the receivables is borne by the 'borrowing' company, so that if the receivables do not generate enough to 'repay' the loan, the company is liable for the rest.[196] The logical corollary of this would be that if the receivables generate more than is required to 'repay' then the company retains the excess, and this characteristic is also found in this form of receivables financing.[197] This structure is usually called 'invoice discounting' and is achieved usually by a sale (an absolute assignment) of the receivables to the financier,[198] without notice to the debtors, so that the company continues to collect in the debts and holds the proceeds of sale on trust for the financier.[199] The transaction is said to be 'with recourse' which means that the credit risk of the receivables is retained by the company: this is usually achieved by a contractual obligation on the company to repurchase receivables which are not paid.[200]

---

[194] For further discussion of the distinction between the two, see 6.2.

[195] It is clear from the statistics produced by the Asset Based Finance Association ('ABFA') at www.abfa.org.uk/public/statistics.asp that invoice discounting has risen reasonably steadily over the last 15 years (although the figures plateau in the last two years because of the financial crisis). Asset-based lending has also become more popular, although ABFA have only begun keeping statistics for this kind of lending since the first quarter of 2009, and the statistics are still not very reliable because of the difficult of defining this kind of lending. We are grateful to Kate Sharp of ABFA for information on these statistics and also on asset-based lending generally. Asset finance (leasing or hire purchase) also increased during the first part of the credit crunch (ie 2007 and the first part of 2008) and only dropped back a little at the end of 2008 because of the difficulties the financiers had in obtaining finance, (Finance Leasing Association (FLA) Annual review 2009, page 8). It is a very widespread funding method for small and medium sized enterprises, see FLA Annual Review 2009, page 4 (A third of businesses with turnover below £50 million which needed external funding relied on asset finance).

[196] As we shall see, this could be said to be one of the indicia of a charge (below 6.2.5.2).

[197] See *In re George Inglefield Ltd* [1933] Ch 1, 20; *Olds Discount Co Ltd v John Playfair Ltd* [1938] 3 All ER 275, 276–277.

[198] Despite the presence of the indicia of a charge, the courts have repeatedly held that this can be structured as a sale, and have refused to recharacterise the transaction, see pages 233–34.

[199] Even where the receivables are transferred by absolute sale, the financier usually takes a charge over other assets of the borrower. This is, in part, to catch any receivables which are not within the sale agreement. One reason might be that the receivable contains an anti-assignment clause (see 8.2.2.2 below). Although it depends on the construction of the clause, it is possible that some clauses will prohibit outright assignments but not charges, see N Ruddy, S Mills, N Davidson (eds), *Salinger on Factoring*, 4th edn (London, Sweet & Maxwell, 2006) 13.12. A charge may also (particularly in the case of factoring) be security for any fees and other charges which may accrue from the borrower to the financier. This may include liability for any shortfall in the value of the receivables, for example, because of non-payment or breach of contract by the borrower. See S Frisby, 'Report on Insolvency Outcomes', (Report to Insolvency Service), 26 June 2006, 36.

[200] The borrower will also warrant that the amounts are due, so that it would be liable for the full amount if it were not paid by the account debtor, for example, because there was a breach of the agreement giving rise to the receivable. For detailed discussion of these contractual rights, see H Beale, M Bridge, L Gullifer and E Lomnicka, *The Law of Personal Property Security* (Oxford, Oxford University Press, 2007) 16.96 and for an

A receivables financing package can also include other services provided by the financier (for which, of course, the company pays). These include the transfer of the credit risk to the financier (as in securitisation) and the provision of a debt collecting service by the financier. Such a package is usually called 'factoring'. The company will sell the receivables to the financier by a statutory assignment, which means that the debtors are given notice and the financier can sue a non-paying debtor in its own name.[201]

As can be seen, from the company's point of view, receivables financing is very similar to a traditional securitisation, especially where the credit risk is transferred to the financier. A securitisation structure will generally be cheaper for a company large enough to use it. This is because the company only needs to pay fees to the bank which sets it up, rather than paying the bank both interest for accepting the credit risk and fees for arranging the transaction. Further, usually, the cost of borrowing from the market by way of securities is cheaper than borrowing from a bank.[202] The company also obtains a service charge for collecting in the receivables. However, normal receivables financing is more suitable for small or medium sized companies and for companies whose flow of receivables is less predictable or less consistent. The cost of setting up an invoice discounting agreement is lower than setting up a securitisation, and although more has to be paid for the actual financing, it is much more flexible as the company only needs to 'borrow' what it requires.

The other alternative to receivables financing, for small and medium sized companies, is straight secured borrowing from a bank, either by way of term loan or, more usually, by way of overdraft. In the past this has been very common, and banks have taken fixed charges over all assets it could, including receivables. However, as we shall see, the possibility of taking a fixed charge over receivables has been greatly reduced by the *Spectrum* decision[203] and this appears to be one of the factors which has led to a marked increase in invoice discounting (though not factoring).[204] Another reason may be the increase in flexibility of invoice discounting which has come from more sophisticated computerised methods of monitoring receivables and cash flow on the part of the financiers, which makes this form of financing a real alternative to an overdraft.

2.3.4.2   Asset-based Lending[205]

Asset-based lending originated in the US, and has only recently become popular in the UK. The term 'asset-based lending' is usually applied to financing against a wide variety of assets, including both revolving and fixed assets. The revolving assets include receivables,

---

example of a receivables financing agreement including such provisions, see E McKendrick (ed), *Goode on Commercial Law*, 4th edn (London, Penguin/LexisNexis, 2009) 849.

[201]   See page 290.

[202]   See page 31.

[203]   6.3.3.3.2.

[204]   The figures published by ABFA show that the sale volume of clients using invoice discounting rose from £4 billion in 1995 to £40 billion in 2007. Since then the figures have been roughly level. Comparable figures for factoring are £1.85 billion in 1995 and £5 billion in 2007, but the growth is much slower and the figures have been between £4 billion and £5 billion since 1999. See also J Armour, 'Should we Redistribute on Insolvency?' in J Getzler and J Payne (eds), *Company Charges: Spectrum and Beyond* (Oxford, Oxford University Press, 2006).

[205]   See C Swillman and A Cropley, 'Asset Based Lenders: Beneficiaries of the Credit Crunch?' (2007) 22 Journal of International Banking and Financial Law 629 and D Nash, 'ABL and Distressed Companies' (2008) 1(3) *Corporate Rescue and Insolvency* 104. We are very grateful to Steven Chait of Burdale Financial Ltd and Kate Sharp of ABFA for discussion on the structure and scope of asset-based lending.

intellectual property and stock. The fixed assets include plant and machinery, and land. The whole transaction will include different techniques for different assets, so that the financier will usually buy any receivables outright, but will take fixed charges over other assets if possible and if not, floating charges.[206] The difference between this sort of financing and ordinary bank lending is that the asset-based financier assesses the credit risk purely in relation to the assets available as collateral, whereas the bank will look at the profitability of the business as a whole, and the cash flow of the company in particular. Thus the asset-based financier will only lend the amount it can be sure to obtain from enforcing its security and absolute interests if the company becomes insolvent, taking into account any other creditors which might have priority over it, such as suppliers on retention of title (where stock is taken as collateral), and the likely size of the prescribed part and liability to preferential creditors,[207] where its security is a floating charge. This method of financing often means that a company can raise more finance than it can through the traditional bank lending route.

Where there are already other secured creditors, the asset-based lender will not lend unless it can obtain an agreement whereby it has priority over them. The significant proprietary protection for the financier means that there are likely to be fewer financial covenants than with a traditional bank loan. It also means that this financing is likely to be available in situations where banks will not lend, or where bank lending would be more expensive. This includes situations where companies appear to be failing but have substantial assets, where companies are refinancing, and in management buy-outs or buy-ins.[208] Asset-based lending has also proved popular in the recent financial crisis, growing steadily through 2007 and 2008, when other forms of lending were becoming scarcer.[209] It can be used to provide finance to very large companies, and where the amounts are large the deal is often syndicated. In fact, since it is now very difficult for providers of syndicated loans to securitise their loan portfolio, asset-based lending is becoming a popular alternative.

2.3.4.3 Devices Based on Retention of Title

The receivables financier has proprietary protection against the credit risk of the company being financed, either by a security interest over the receivables or, more usually by becoming the absolute owner of them. Another, similar, device for achieving proprietary protection is for the financier to have an absolute interest in tangible assets. The company can raise money on the basis of assets it already owns on this basis. The traditional method was by selling the assets to the financier and then leasing or buying them back.[210]

---

[206] The asset-based lender is likely to want a floating charge anyway, so that it can appoint an administrator, see page 286. Fixed charges over stock are not uncommon, since the lender may use warehousing techniques or other information technology mechanisms to achieve the necessary degree of control. For discussion of the level of control required see 6.3.3.3.2.

[207] 3.3.1.2.2 and 3.3.1.2.3.

[208] Often the asset-based lending financing is only part of the total debt package.

[209] See ABFA Quarterly statistics for December 2007 and December 2008. £17 billion was advanced by means of asset-based finance (including receivables financing) in 2008. The amount declined a little during the recession of 2009 (to £14 billion). The recent asset-based lending statistics (see footnote 204 above) show that 17% of this was asset-based lending (see ABFA Quarterly statistics for March 2010, page 4). For a list of asset-based lending deals done by ABFA members see www.abfa.org.uk/abl/abl.asp.

[210] 2.3.4.3.1.

Companies can also acquire assets using this device, either from a financier, by way of a hire purchase, conditional sale or finance lease agreement,[211] or from a trader, by use of retention of title.[212]

In all these structures, except for sales on retention of title, the company obtains cash or the use of the item upfront, and makes periodic payments to the financier. In a sale on retention of title, the credit is short-term: the seller, of course, then needs to obtain finance from elsewhere in order to fund the extension of credit. This could be by an overdraft, or by some form of receivables financing.

2.3.4.3.1   Sale and Leaseback

This structure can be used if a company has fixed assets (land, plant or machinery) and wishes to raise cash while retaining and using the asset. Of course, the company could just take out a loan secured on the asset, either from a bank or by way of asset-based lending. However, a sale and leaseback may allow the company to borrow on cheaper terms, especially if there are tax advantages.[213] If the assets are plant or machinery, the lease can be either a finance lease or an operating lease: this will depend on whether the risks and rewards of the assets are with the financier or the company. It is also possible to have a sale and saleback, where the assets are 'bought' back by the company by way of hire purchase or, less likely, a conditional sale.[214]

2.3.4.3.2   Asset Finance[215]

If a company wishes to acquire machinery or vehicles or other large pieces of equipment, there are a number of options available to it other than having to pay for it out of existing assets. The company could borrow the price from a bank (unsecured or secured on all its assets or on the acquired item only), and buy the asset outright. It could hire the item under an operating lease, usually from a financier to whom the item has been sold by the seller. Such a lease could be for any period of time, which means that the item could be hired just for the period when it is needed, and can be updated very easily. The company never acquires ownership of the asset, which means that this structure is 'off-balance sheet'.[216] The rental payments reflect the fact that the asset will eventually be returned to the financier. In between these two possibilities are the options of hire purchase and finance leasing.

---

[211]   2.3.4.3.2.

[212]   2.3.4.3.4.

[213]   This is likely to be the case where the leaseback is a finance lease (see below) or where land is sold to Real Estate Investment Trust (a tax transparent property holding company set up by Part 4 of the Finance Act 2006) and leased back to the company. In both cases the tax advantages to the financier are shared with the company in the form of lower rental payments.

[214]   For a discussion of the characterisation of these transactions see 6.2.5.1.

[215]   This is the term used in the industry to cover the acquisition of assets. See www.assetfinanceuk.com/af_introduction.htm. This is a significant form of finance, for example in 2009 almost £30 billion of finance was provided this way for businesses: BIS, Financing a Private Sector Recovery, n 1, 3.31.

[216]   See Inland Revenue Leasing Manual BLM0060, BLM000725. The International Accounting Standards Board is considering whether this is consistent with accounting standards and looking at ways to recognise the economic status of an operating lease on a balance sheet, see 'Leases – Preliminary Views' IASB Discussion Paper DP/2009/1.

A finance lease is similar to an operating lease in that the company never acquires ownership of the asset,[217] but the lease is for a fixed period of time, and the periodic payments made by the company include the capital cost of the asset, spread out over that period of time, as well as payments for hire. At the end of the period, there is a second period during which the company can hire the item for just the hire cost. At any time after the end of the first period, the company can sell the item as agent for the financier and is usually allowed to retain a very high proportion (usually over 90 per cent) of the proceeds.[218] The chief advantage of a finance lease, as opposed to a hire purchase agreement, used to be the very favourable tax treatment it received, in that the financier (the lessor) could claim capital allowance for the asset, some of which benefit could be passed on to the company (the lessee) and the lessee could deduct the hire payments as revenue expenses.[219] This benefit has been changed, in relation to long-term finance leases (called 'long-funded leases' in the legislation) by the Finance Act 2006,[220] so that such leases are now taxed according to their economic substance, in a way very similar to loans.[221]

Finance leases, while they can be used for any sort of tangible asset, are often used for 'big ticket' items, such as aeroplanes and large vehicles. An alternative, though similar, structure is hire purchase. Here the financier retains ownership of the item, but, as with a finance lease, all the risks and rewards are transferred to the company. The company (the 'hirer') makes periodic payments which in part reflect the hire charge and in part reflect the capital value of the item. At the end of the hire period the hirer has the option to purchase the item for a nominal fee. This structure does not attract the favourable tax and accounting treatment of a finance lease: the financier cannot claim capital allowance, and the payments made by the hirer are treated as partly rent (which is deductible from profits) and partly capital expenditure (on which capital allowance can be claimed).[222]

A similar structure, less used in the commercial sector than the consumer sector, is a conditional sale, where the owner agrees to sell at the beginning, but title is not transferred until the instalment payments have been made at the end of the agreed period.[223]

---

[217] The distinction between the two sorts of leases can be important for tax purposes, see IR Leasing Manual BLM00044. Basically, a finance lease is defined as a lease which transfers all the risks and rewards of ownership to the lessee, while an operating lease is a lease which does not. Generally speaking, a financier who leases on an operating lease is concerned with the inherent value of the item leased as it has an 'equity stake' in the item, while a financier leasing on a finance lease is only concerned with the creditworthiness of the lessee (although this is not true where the last payment is to be funded by the proceeds from the sale of the item). See also UK GAAP, paragraph 15 SSAP 21 and IFRS IAS 17.

[218] This is because in a finance lease, the lessee has all the risks and rewards of the item, but cannot acquire it itself, as this would turn it into a hire purchase agreement.

[219] This is in reality a timing rather than an absolute advantage, but depending on the tax position of both parties, the timing can be very significant. See BLM00710. There are also a large number of anti-avoidance provisions, see BLM01030.

[220] Finance Act 2006, s 81(1) which inserted ss 70A to 70YI Capital Allowances Act 2001. The rules relating to long-funded leases only apply to leases of plant and machinery, see Capital Allowances Act 2001, s 70G.

[221] Thus capital allowances are available to the lessee not the lessor, but the amount of rental payments that can be deducted is reduced accordingly. BLM20015, BLM42005.

[222] Capital Allowances Act 2001, s 67. BLM39010.

[223] One drawback of conditional sale, in the commercial context, is that if the buyer (in possession of the goods) makes an unauthorised sale to a third party, that party, if in good faith and without notice of the conditional sale agreement, can obtain good title under Sale of Goods Act, s 25(1). Conditional sales regulated by the Consumer Credit Act 1974 are excepted from this provision (s 25(2)) but this only includes sales to individuals and very small partnerships (Consumer Credit Act, s 8). Hire purchase agreements do not fall under the Sale of Goods Act, s 25, although in relation to vehicles, the Hire Purchase Act 1964, s 27 has a similar effect

2.3.4.3.3   Stock Finance[224]

Stock finance is a term that can cover a number of different structures based on the concepts already discussed. One, which is a variant of acquisition finance, involves the company entering into a hire purchase or conditional sale agreement as a temporary measure in order to fund the period between obtaining the item to display to potential customers and selling the item to a customer, rather than in order to own the item. This form of finance is usually provided in relation to motor vehicles, and the financier is likely to be a company associated with the manufacturer of the vehicles.

Another possible model is that, in order to 'lend' money against stock already owned by the company, the financier buys the stock from the company and the company sells it to customers as the undisclosed agent of the financier.[225] The company then holds the proceeds of sale on trust for the financier: in a similar way as in an invoice discounting arrangement. Both the arrangements discussed in this section are alternatives to a lender taking a charge over stock; while this would normally be floating, it could be fixed if sufficient control methods were put in place.[226]

2.3.4.3.4   Sales on Retention of Title Terms

The funding of the period between acquisition of raw materials or stock, and when these goods are disposed of (in their original state or after manufacture into something else), can be achieved, at least partly, by credit extended to the buyer by the seller. The seller is then exposed to the credit risk of the buyer. To protect itself the seller will usually retain title to the goods in the sale agreement.[227] While the goods are in the possession of the buyer, if the buyer does not pay, the seller has the right to retake the goods, and, since the seller has a proprietary right, this will survive the buyer's insolvency. However, this form of protection has its limitations. Any attempt by a seller to gain proprietary protection in the products of the raw materials supplied,[228] or in the proceeds of sale[229] of the stock supplied, is very likely to be characterised as a charge and therefore be registrable. Since it is impractical to register every sale agreement, this registrability means that the seller's proprietary protection is limited to an interest in the goods themselves.

---

where the sub-sale is to a private purchaser. This difference may account for the preference for hire purchase agreements over conditional sales in the commercial context.

[224]   See M Nield, 'Protecting Title in Stock Finance' (2007) 22 *Journal of International Banking and Financial Law* 638.

[225]   *Welsh Development Agency v Export Finance Co Ltd* [1992] BCLC 148.

[226]   See L Gullifer (ed), *Goode on Legal Problems of Credit and Security*, 4th edn (London, Sweet & Maxwell 2008) 4–17.

[227]   In relation to the goods themselves, this is easily done as the Sale of Goods Act, s 17 provides that property in the goods passes when the parties intend it to pass.

[228]   See, for example, *Borden (UK) Ltd v Scottish Timber Products Ltd* [1981] 1 Ch 25; *Re Peachdart Ltd* [1984] Ch 131; *Clough Mill Ltd v Martin* [1985] 1 WLR 111; *Modelboard Ltd v Outer Box Ltd* [1992] BCC 945; *Ian Chisholm Textiles Ltd v Griffiths* [1994] BCC 96.

[229]   *E Pfeiffer Weinkellerei-Weinein-kauf GmbH & Co v Arbuthnot Factors Ltd* [1988] 1 WLR 150; *Tatung (UK) Ltd v Galex Telesure Ltd* (1989) 5 BCC 325; *Compaq Computer Ltd v Abercorn Ltd* [1993] BCLC 602.

2.3.5   Specialised Forms of Finance

2.3.5.1   Project Finance

Project finance is a structure used to finance infrastructure projects, such as roads, pipelines, prisons or hospitals, whereby the lenders are paid out of the income generated by the project. The debt finance (which may be provided by way of loans or securities or a mixture of both) is made available to a special purpose vehicle (owned by one or more 'sponsors') which is a party to a concession agreement with the relevant government entitling it to build the infrastructure. The special purpose vehicle (SPV) contracts out the construction work (which is paid for by the borrowings) and, when the project is built, receives the revenues from its operation, which may come in the form of tolls (in the case of roads) or government payments, in the case of prisons or hospitals. The revenues are distributed according to a contractual clause, known as a waterfall clause, which provides for scheduled repayment of the debt finance. The SPV is usually highly leveraged, so that the debt to equity ratio is high, and the lenders take upon themselves a certain amount of the risk that the project will not be completed, or will not make money. Although the lenders will take what security they can, this will often largely consist of a charge over the revenue-generating contract, since the SPV will normally not own the item built, nor will the item have much independent value aside from its revenue-generating value.

2.3.5.2   Financing of Group Companies

Lending to a company which is part of a group presents special problems for a lender, which may lead to complicated financing structures involving guarantees and also, maybe set-offs or charge-backs.[230] Despite being part of a group, each company is treated as a separate entity by the law, and each has limited liability,[231] so that in order to have access to the assets of the group a lender will need to put in place contractual and proprietary protection by agreement. It will often be the case that the company which needs to borrow money does not have significant assets, since these are held by a parent company or another company in the group. In this situation, the lender may lend to the company which needs the money, and take a guarantee and security from the company with the assets (and probably all the other companies in the group). Alternatively, it may be another company in the group which has the ability to raise funds, for example, by a bond issue or a loan, rather than the company which actually needs the funds. Here the company who can raise the money will on-lend the money to the other company, who will give a guarantee of the repayment obligations under the bonds or loan.[232] Quite often the company who gives the guarantee will have a credit balance with the lender. The lender will seek to make sure that, if necessary, the obligation under the guarantee can be enforced by set-off, both outside and within insolvency, but may also seek to protect itself by taking a charge-back or using a flawed asset structure.[233] Group companies may also lend to each other, or extend credit to each other, and external lenders usually insist that

---

[230]   These issues are discussed in chapter 5.
[231]   For discussion see 3.3.3.1.
[232]   See, for example, the structure in *Re Polly Peck International plc (in administration)* [1996] 2 All ER 433.
[233]   See 5.2.4.1.

inter-group liabilities are subordinated to the debts to external lenders.[234] It will be seen that the financing structure of a group can be very complicated, and can cause significant problems on insolvency. Further, the business is likely to be structured as a group for tax or other cross-border purpose, in which case these issues will also impact on the financing structure.

2.3.5.3 Trade Finance

When goods are bought and sold internationally there is a considerable period of time between when the goods are shipped and when they are received. The seller may well extend credit to the buyer, on retention of title terms, or the buyer may need to borrow in order to pay the seller, using the goods as security by way of a pledge of documents of title to the goods. The financing of international trade is a specialist area of the law, and is not dealt with further in this book.[235]

2.4 Hybrids

A hybrid security combines some of the features generally associated with equity capital with some of those associated with debt capital. The idea behind hybrids is to obtain the best of all worlds, by designing a security which is treated as equity for some purposes and treated as debt for others. Hybrids come in a number of forms. Some are regarded as hybrid because their very nature contains elements associated with debt and equity (such as preference shares), others have both those elements by design (such as deeply subordinated debt securities) and others are regarded as hybrids because they start life as one type of capital (eg debt) but have the ability to be converted into the other (eg convertible securities). Some forms of hybrids have existed for some considerable time, such as preference shares, others have been developed more recently in response to particular issues, such as the regulatory capital requirements discussed in this section. This category of hybrids therefore contains a variety of different devices, which may be utilised for a variety of reasons, the uniting feature being that these securities combine both debt and equity features.

Preference shares are one form of hybrid security. A typical preference shareholder will be entitled to a fixed dividend[236] and a fixed return on capital, both generally payable in preference to the return on ordinary shares. Unlike ordinary shares, preference shares generally have no right to participate in the surplus, ie they are not residual claimants, and have no, or very limited, voting rights. The inclusion of rights to fixed returns on income and capital ahead of the ordinary shareholders means that preference shares to some extent resemble loan capital, although, as discussed, the rights of the preference shareholders are generally weaker than those of creditors, and continue to rank behind creditors in

---

[234] 5.3.4.

[235] For a detailed discussion, see E McKendrick (ed), *Goode on Commercial Law*, n 200, chapter 35 and H Beale, M Bridge, L Gullifer and E Lomnicka, *The Law of Personal Property Security*, n 200, 3.26–32 concerning pledges of documents of title to goods.

[236] Subject to the company having the necessary distributable profits and subject to the directors declaring the dividend – see pages 13–14.

the order of payment on a winding up.[237] Preference shares remain, at law, shares, although for accounting purposes they may be classified as either equity or debt, depending on their precise terms. Preference shares, then, are equity securities which have debt-like features.

The attraction of preference shares from the company's point of view (or, more particularly, that of the existing shareholders) over equity securities is that they rarely contain general voting rights and therefore they do not tend to disturb existing control rights. Their advantage over debt is that the return, though often expressed to be fixed, is not fixed in the same way as debt, and need not be paid in certain circumstances.[238] The advantage of preference shares to the holder is that they rank ahead of the ordinary shares for various purposes,[239] and that the preferential dividend should promise a higher return than the interest payment that could otherwise be obtained by that investor.

In contrast, many other effective hybrids are basically debt securities which have equity-like features. This is because this structure is generally more tax effective. For tax purposes it is advantageous for the security to be treated as debt, so that payments made on it will be tax deductible.[240] It is also because the cost of issuing debt is considerably less than the cost of equity.[241] However, equity-like features are attractive for two reasons. One is that equity features enable the investor to share in the benefit if the company does well. This is often the reason why securities are convertible or exchangeable, since it makes them more attractive to investors. Another reason, which is relevant to financial institutions, is that equity-like features enable the security to be treated favourably from a regulatory capital point of view.[242]

As mentioned above, one form of debt securities which overlap between debt and equity are those which include an option to convert them into full equity ('convertible securities'), or to exchange them for equity securities in a third party held by the issuer ('exchangeable securities'), or to buy shares in the issuer at a particular price ('equity warrants'). From the point of view of the holder, a debt security with the addition of a right to convert it into an equity security gives it the best of both worlds, as it can take advantage of improvements in the company's performance without taking the initial risk of holding equity, and, until conversion, it gets a guaranteed fixed income from the security.[243]

Another form of debt securities which overlap between debt and equity are hybrids designed to assist a financial institution meet its capital adequacy requirements.[244] An issuer who is a financial institution will benefit from a hybrid being treated as equity by qualifying for Tier 1 regulatory capital. However, more generally, all issuers will benefit from the treatment of hybrids as equity in the rating agencies' assessment of the

---

[237] See discussion at 2.3.2.

[238] See 3.2.1.2.

[239] Ibid.

[240] This is most advantageous if the holder of the security is receiving the payments in a jurisdiction where they are treated as dividends, see S Luder, 'Hybrid Financing' (2005) 810 *Tax Journal* 9.

[241] 'The Rise of the Hybrid' (April 2006) 37 *Euromoney* 2. For discussion of the different costs of capital, see 2.6 below.

[242] Discussed below.

[243] See Fuller, *The Law and Practice of International Capital Markets*, n 161, 1.24.

[244] See pages 25–26 above.

company's credit-worthiness,[245] and also if securities are treated as equity rather than debt in their balance sheets, as this makes it easier to comply with covenants which require a certain debt to equity ratio.[246] Convertible securities may be hybrids in the sense used above, if the other features apply, but the convertibility itself does not give the securities the required equity rating: this would only happen if the holder is obliged to convert.[247] However, in terms of regulatory capital requirements, the fact that debt securities are subordinated is enough for them to rank as Lower Tier 2 or Upper Tier 3 capital,[248] and such securities may be convertible so as to be attractive to investors.[249]

One important feature from the point of view of the rating agencies and the regulatory capital requirements is that the security has a long maturity date. However, to gain tax treatment as debt, maturity has to be 'within the foreseeable future'. Many hybrid securities now have two maturity dates: a shorter 'scheduled' date of, for example, thirty years and a longer 'final' maturity date of, for example, eighty years.[250] Another feature which makes such securities more 'equity-like' is an option, or, better still, an obligation on the issuer to repay by issuing equity securities, thus retaining or improving its equity to debt ratio.[251] A further feature is that the issuer has the ability to defer interest payments: this makes them similar to dividends, which the issuer has no obligation to pay.[252] The securities will also have to be deeply subordinated. As explained above, on the insolvency of a company, the unsecured creditors rank equally with equity holders ranking behind them. Unsecured creditors can, however, agree to rank behind other unsecured creditors, in other words, to be subordinated, and this is very common in various contexts. The more 'deeply' subordinated an issue of debt securities is, that is, the fewer creditors who rank below it, the more like equity it seems. It might be asked why investors would buy such debt securities, since the features set out so far would seem to make them very unattractive. The answer largely lies in the price, since the holders are compensated for the greater risk of hybrid securities by a much larger return.[253]

---

[245]   The rating agencies' willingness to do this was confirmed in February 2005 by Moody's, which published its 'Refinements to Moody's Tool Kit' which set out the precise criteria on which it would take into account the equity-like characteristics of hybrids. Standard and Poors and Fitch followed later in 2005, see 'Hybrid Capital goes from Strength to Strength' (April 2006) 37 *Euromoney* 4.

[246]   See 'The Rise of the Hybrid', (April 2006) 37 *Euromoney* 2. For discussion of such covenants, see page 169.

[247]   A Pinedo, 'Degree of Difficulty, 9; Style Points, 5 (or Understanding Hybrids)' (2007) 22 *Journal of International Banking and Financial Law* 203. Financial institutions have recently begun to issue debt securities which convert into equity on certain stress triggers, so as to provide an 'equity cushion' when needed; these are called contingent capital (for example, these were issued by Lloyds Bank and the Royal Bank of Scotland in 2009), see T Humphreys and A Pinedo, 'Is it a Bird? A Plane? Exploring Contingent Capital' (2010) 25 *Journal of International Banking and Financial Law* 67.

[248]   See above page 26. See Fuller, *The Law and Practice of International Capital Markets,* n 161, 10.27.

[249]   Ibid, 10.09.

[250]   A Pinedo, 'Degree of difficulty, 9; style points, 5 (or understanding hybrids)' (2007) 22 *Journal of International Banking and Financial Law* 203.

[251]   Ibid. See also A Pinedo, 'Exceptionally Intelligent Design' (2008) 23 *Journal of International Banking and Financial Law* 193.

[252]   A Pinedo, 'Degree of difficulty, 9; style points, 5 (or understanding hybrids)' (2007) 22 *Journal of International Banking and Financial Law* 203.

[253]   The same is also true of high yield bonds, which are often subordinated to other debt, see above page 33.

2.5   Retained Profits

Retained profits are an internal source of finance for the company, the availability of which will depend upon the profitability of the company, and the decisions taken by the company's directors as to whether to retain those profits or to return them to the shareholders, commonly by way of dividend payment or repurchases of the company's own shares. The ability of directors to distribute profits to the shareholders in this way is discussed in chapter four.[254] The capital maintenance rules discussed in that chapter impose some constraints on the circumstances in which returns can be made to shareholders, but where the company has distributable profits, these rules will cause little difficulty. Dividends can be paid as long as profits are available for the purpose,[255] and share repurchases can be made providing a shareholder resolution is obtained.[256] It is predominantly a matter for the directors, acting in accordance with their directors' duties, whether the company will be best served by retaining its profits to finance its operations or returning some of those profits to its shareholders.

Benefits to the company can flow from returning profits to the shareholders. A distinction again needs to be drawn between small owner-managed firms and larger companies with more widely dispersed shareholders. In small quasi-partnership firms share repurchase is unlikely to be a valuable option, since the shares at this point give the shareholders control over the business. The exception is where one of the shareholders wishes to leave the business. There is unlikely to be a ready market for the shares. If the other shareholders do not want to buy out the exiting shareholder, but there are funds available for the company to do so,[257] then a repurchase of the shares by the company may be a useful tool. Dividend payments are one way for the owner-managers to extract income from the company, but others are also available. Shareholders in quasi-partnership companies are often employed by the company, and so will be able to receive income by way of salary. They may also have lent money to the company, so that profits could be used to repay any capital sums outstanding. The decision as to which of these methods to use to return the company's profits to the shareholders, if any, will be determined by a variety of factors, and the decision will often be tax driven.

The external funding options for a small quasi-partnership company are generally more limited than those for larger companies.[258] Their primary form of external funding is likely to be a bank loan secured on their personal assets. Profits are likely to be a key source of financing for the business. However, this is first and foremost a decision for the directors. Once external shareholders become involved this is likely to change and the external shareholders will usually have expectations about the dividends they should

---

[254]   For discussion of these options see 4.4.1 and 4.4.2. Other methods of returning value to shareholders, which are less commonly used, include formal reductions of capital and schemes of arrangement.

[255]   Distributions to shareholders can only be made out of profits available for the purpose: Companies Act 2006, s 830 (and s 831 for public companies). For discussion see 4.4.

[256]   A special resolution is required for an 'off-market' purchase (Companies Act 2006, s 694) but only an ordinary resolution for an 'on-market' purchase (s 701). In addition, where a buy back is funded wholly out of the company's profits the amount by which the capital of the company is reduced must be transferred to a capital redemption reserve (s 733(2)) and this reserve is treated for most purposes as though it were share capital.

[257]   A private company can fund a repurchase of shares out of distributable profits, a fresh issue of shares or, in some circumstances, out of capital: Companies Act 2006, ss 690–723 discussed below at 4.4.2.

[258]   See BIS, *Financing a Private Sector Recovery*, n 1, 3.7 discussed above at 2.2.

receive. Shareholders are not per se in a strong position to demand dividend payments. In general these are subject to the company having distributable profits and the dividends having been declared.[259] However, it may be that a failure to pay dividends could amount to unfairly prejudicial conduct and thus allow a shareholder to bring a petition under section 996 of the Companies Act 2006.[260] This would require the shareholder to demonstrate that the failure to pay the dividends involved a breach of an agreement or understanding between the parties which it would be unfair to ignore.[261] This will often be an agreement arising, formally or informally, outside the constitutional documents of a company. This type of agreement is far more likely to arise in the context of small companies than public companies.[262]

The position is quite different in widely-owned companies, and here we are particularly focusing on publicly traded companies. In such companies, shareholders generally expect to receive regular dividends in respect of their shares. In general the dividends received by shareholders in public companies are kept at a fairly constant level, smoothed over time, and any increases in the dividend payments tend to reflect the underlying long-term prospects for the business.[263] As a result directors in publicly listed companies tend to be conservative about their dividend policy. Dividends are kept low and (hopefully) steady, and any increases are contemplated only if the directors are confident about the sustained growth of the company.[264]

Corporate finance theory posits that in frictionless markets dividend policy should not affect the overall market value of the company's shares.[265] This is based on the idea that where the company retains profits and invests them in new profitable ventures then the shares will have a higher capital value than they would have if the company had paid a dividend and then had to raise further finance to fund the new venture. A shareholder can then realise this (capital) gain by selling the shares in the market rather than relying on the company to pay the dividend. This suggests that companies should only pay dividends after all investment decisions have been made. However, this theory does not match the reality that is observable in the market. Markets are not frictionless and there is a cost involved in buying and selling shares. There is also a different tax treatment of dividends (taxed as income) and the capital gains made on the disposal of shares. In addition,

---

[259]   It is common for the articles to provide that final dividends are declared by the shareholders in general meeting (see Model Articles for Private Companies Limited by Shares, Art 30; Model Articles for Public Companies, Art 70: The Companies (Model Articles) Regulations 2008 (SI 3229/2008), Sch 1 and Sch 3) but subject to the recommendation of the directors. Since the shareholders generally cannot increase the level of dividend, and it is rare for them to declare less than recommended by the directors, this is largely a rubber stamping exercise.

[260]   The courts have accepted that dividend policy can amount to unfairly prejudicial conduct eg *Re Sam Weller & Sons Ltd* [1990] 1 Ch 682.

[261]   *O'Neill v Phillips* [1999] 1 WLR 1092. It is also possible to found a section 994 petition in other circumstances, in particular where there has been a breach of a legal right held by the petitioner, but this is unlikely to be helpful in the context of dividends (since any 'right' to receive a dividend will be dependent on other factors, such as the fact that the company has made distributable profits).

[262]   *Re Astec (BSR) plc* [1998] 2 BCLC 556.

[263]   J Lintner, 'Distribution of Incomes of Corporations Among Dividends, Retained Earnings, and Taxes' (1956) 46(2) *American Economic Review* 97; A Brav et al, 'Payout Policy in the 21st Century' (2005) 77 *Journal of Financial Economics* 483; F Bancel, UR Mittoo and N Bhattacharyya, 'Cross-country Determinants in Payout Policy: A Survey of European Firms' (2004) 33 *Financial Management* 103.

[264]   See A Brav et al, 'Payout Policy in the 21st Century', ibid.

[265]   MH Miller and F Modigliani, 'Dividend Policy, Growth and the Valuation of Shares' (1961) 34 *Journal of Business* 411.

investors may view the future gains to be made from new projects as more risky than dividends payable today, and so may undervalue shares in a company that pays low dividends,[266] or may simply prefer to receive steady dividends rather than to sell their shareholdings.[267] In practice directors do not conform to the model posited by this corporate finance theory. They tend to forego positive investment opportunities or borrow to fund dividends rather than reducing the existing levels of dividend payment. However, they do not generally *increase* levels of dividend payment until all investment decisions have been made.[268]

Dividend policy in publicly traded companies can therefore perform a signalling function about the state of the company. Paying healthy consistent dividends is a way for managers to signal to the market that they have long-term confidence in the business.[269] In the environment of conservative dividend payments detailed above, a dividend increase makes a strong statement about the expected future profitability of the company whereas a dividend cut may be taken as an indicator of a long-term problem within the company. A failure to meet shareholders' expectations is likely to have a negative effect on share price. However, any benefits obtained by using dividend policy to signal to the market have to be weighed against the need for companies to finance their existing and future operations, and returning retained profits to shareholders may well mean that companies have to access external finance in order to fund these operations.[270]

In the UK, dividend conservatism is prevalent in publicly traded companies, so that in general retained profits will be used to fund relatively low levels of dividends which remain fairly constant, and which increase only where the directors are confident about the company's future sustained growth.[271] As a result where directors have retained profits that they wish to return to the shareholders over and above existing dividend levels they may well do so via a repurchase of shares[272] as these do not raise expectations about future payouts. Returning profits to shareholders via a share buy-back can be very beneficial in circumstances where the company itself is unable to invest efficiently in profitable

---

[266] MJ Gordon, 'Dividends, Earnings and Stock Prices' (1959) 41 *Review of Economics and Statistics* 99.

[267] Ie investors may behave irrationally.

[268] A Brav et al, 'Payout Policy in the 21st Century', (2005) 77 *Journal of Financial Economics* 483.

[269] It has been suggested that directors can use dividend policy to make other signals to the market, for example in order to distinguish a company from its competitors (see eg MH Miller and K Rock, 'Dividend Policy under Asymmetric Information' (1985) 40 *Journal of Finance* 1031), but empirical evidence does not support this view: A Brav et al, ibid.

[270] Some commentators suggest that it is good for shareholders if directors pay high dividends precisely because directors will then have to expose their business record and future plans for the company to the scrutiny of lenders in the market and may have to submit to restrictive covenants in order to secure funds ie that it can precipitate monitoring by lenders that can be beneficial to shareholders: M Jensen, 'Agency Costs of Free Cash Flow, Corporate Finance and Takeovers' (1986) 76 *American Economic Review* 323; FH Easterbrook, 'Two Agency-Cost Explanations of Dividends' (1984) 74 *American Economic Review* 650. However, managers do not appear to regard dividend policy as imposing discipline on themselves: A Brav et al, 'Payout Policy in the 21st Century', (2005) 77 *Journal of Financial Economics* 483.

[271] Some scholarship has associated dividend policy with levels of shareholder protection within a jurisdiction (R La Porta, F Lopez de Silanes, A Schleifer and R Vishny, 'Agency Problems and Dividend Policies Around the World' (2000) 55 *Journal of Finance* 1) but this is controversial (eg F Bancel, UR Mittoo and N Bhattacharyya, 'Cross-country Determinants in Payout Policy: A Survey of European Firms' (2004) 33 *Financial Management* 103).

[272] Companies are also influenced by tax considerations: J Tiley, 'The Purchase by a Company of its Own Shares' [1992] *British Tax Review* 21.

investment projects.[273] This can be a particularly valuable way to return profits to the shareholders as it can have a positive impact on the company's performance ratios (earnings per share and net assets per share) that are used to assess corporate performance, since these ratios assess the figures (earning or net profits) by reference to the number of equity shares in issue.[274]

2.6   The Debt/Equity Mix

A company's capital structure comprises its mix of debt and equity. The question then arises whether an optimal capital structure exists for all companies, that maximises the company's value. It should be pointed out at this stage that, looking at the position from the point of view of the company, the cost of debt[275] is less than the cost of equity.[276] This is for two main reasons. First, although shareholders benefit from the upside when the company does well, they lose out before the creditors when the company becomes insolvent,[277] so they will charge more for the increased risk. Further, creditors are able to protect themselves from credit risk by the contractual and proprietary means discussed later in the book.[278] Second, companies can deduct the interest payable on debt from their profits for the purpose of assessing corporation tax: dividends are not so deductible.

It is, however, suggested by financial economists that a company's cost of capital, ie the total return expected by the providers of its debt and equity finance, is unaffected by its debt to equity ratio.[279] The Modigliani-Miller propositions suggest that no combination of debt and equity is better than any other and that a company's overall market value is independent of its capital structure. Although borrowing increases the expected rate of return on shareholders' investments, adding debt to a company's capital structure increases the risk of insolvency, and shareholders, whose investment will be wiped out first in the event, require compensation for this risk. According to Modigliani and Miller the additional return expected by equity investors exactly offsets the advantage of debt financing as a prior ranking in insolvency, and therefore cheaper, sources of finance. If this

---

[273]   Of course there is a danger that directors will decide to retain profits to expand the company's business into new ventures for reasons that are less to do with the growth to the company that may result and more to do with enhancing their personal reputation (eg V Brudney, 'Dividends, Discretion and Disclosure' (1980) 66 *Virginia Law Review* 85; DR Fischel, 'The Law and Economics of Dividend Policy' (1981) 67 *Virginia Law Review* 699; MC Jensen, 'Eclipse of the Public Corporation' [1989] *Harvard Business Review* 61). If this is correct, there may be some doubt as to the assessment of the company's ability to invest in profitable investment projects in this context.

[274]   For a general discussion of share buy-backs, including some of the other reasons why directors may want to consider them, see 4.4.2.

[275]   This is what the company has to pay to borrow, broadly, the interest rate of the loan and/or securities.

[276]   This is the rate of dividends which have to be paid to prevent the shareholders selling the shares and lowering the share price.

[277]   For discussion see below chapter 3.

[278]   Proprietary protection protects the secured creditors from unsecured creditors, and one can argue that the lowering of the cost of debt as a result of such protection is balanced out by an increase in the cost of unsecured debt. For a discussion of this debate, see 6.6.2 below.

[279]   F Modigliani and MH Miller, 'The Cost of Capital, Corporation Finance and the Theory of Investment' (1958) 48 *American Economic Review* 433; MH Miller, 'The Modigliani-Miller Propositions After Thirty Years' (1988) 2 *Journal of Economic Perspectives* 99; RA Brealey, SC Myers and F Allen, *Principles of Corporate Finance*, 9th edn (London, McGraw-Hill Higher Education, 2008) chs 17–18.

is correct then the amount of debt entered into by a company should be irrelevant and debt ratios should vary randomly from company to company and from industry to industry. Yet this is not what is observed in practice. Almost all utilities and banks, for example, rely heavily on debt, whereas in other sectors such as pharmaceuticals and advertising, almost all companies have traditionally been predominantly equity financed.[280] Clearly the original Modigliani-Miller propositions do not explain these circumstances.

In part this is because the Modigliani-Miller model was developed on the basis of certain restrictive assumptions, including the existence of well functioning capital markets[281] and the absence of taxes and insolvency costs. Once such assumptions are relaxed, in particular to take account of the tax deductible status of interest charges, it becomes clear that some debt can be added to a company's capital structure without affecting the return expected by its shareholders.[282] However, as the proportion of debt in the company increases, it becomes more likely that the company will default and enter into insolvency. Financial distress and insolvency is costly, in terms of the direct costs of lawyers, courts and insolvency practitioners, as well as the reduction in the value of the company associated with insolvency. There are also the indirect costs attached to the difficulties of running a company while going through insolvency.[283] Even if the company avoids insolvency it will still face the costs of financial distress, for example, the suppliers may demand more protection, creditors may charge more and employees may leave and look for other jobs. When considering the costs of distress it is also important to have regard to the nature of the company's assets. If the assets are 'real', for example property, then there will be reduced distress costs because this will provide some of the creditors at least with the assurance that even if the company is distressed there are assets available which can be used to repay their debts. By contrast, in companies such as high tech companies where the principal assets are ideas and people it is much more difficult on insolvency to cash in by selling off the assets. In order to understand the debt to equity ratio adopted by companies it is therefore relevant to consider not only the likelihood of insolvency but also the value of the company that is likely to be realisable if insolvency occurs.

The trade off theory of capital structure recognises that investors will look for an enhanced return to compensate them for the increased risk of having to absorb these costs of financial distress. The addition of debt to a company's capital structure is beneficial, but only up to the point where the tax savings resulting from the debt are outweighed by the insolvency costs. The theoretical optimum is reached when the present value of the tax saving is just offset by increases in the value of the costs of financial distress. As a result the

---

[280] SC Myers, 'Capital Structure' (2001) 15 *Journal of Economic Perspectives* 81. Some country-by-country differences are also observable: F Degeorge and EG Maug, 'Corporate Finance in Europe: A Survey' *ECGI – Finance Working Paper No 121/2006* (23 March 2006).

[281] For capital markets to be 'well functioning' for the purposes of this model, investors must be able to trade securities without restrictions and borrow and lend on the same terms as the company.

[282] F Modigliani and MH Miller, 'Corporate Income Taxes and the Cost of Capital: a Correction' (1963) 53 *American Economic Review* 261; H DeAngelo and RW Masulis, 'Optimal Capital Structure under Corporate and Personal Taxation' (1980) 8 *Journal of Financial Economics* 3.

[283] JB Warner, 'Bankruptcy Costs: Some Evidence' (1977) 26 *Journal of Finance* 337–48; LA Weiss, 'Bankruptcy Resolution: Direct Costs and Violation of Priority of Claims' (1990) 27 *Journal of Financial Economics* 285; EI Altman, 'A Further Investigation of the Bankruptcy Cost Question' (1984) 39 *Journal of Finance* 1067; G Andrade and SN Kaplan, 'How Costly is Financial (Not Economic) Distress? Evidence from Highly Leveraged Transactions that Became Distressed' (1998) 53 *Journal of Finance* 1443.

trade off theory recognises that debt equity ratios may vary from firm to firm. On this analysis companies with safe, tangible assets and plenty of taxable income ought to have a lot of debt, whereas unprofitable companies with risky intangible assets ought to rely primarily on equity financing. In practice this theory can explain some industry differences in capital structure, but it does not explain everything. It does not explain, for example, why some very successful companies thrive with very little debt. In fact some of the most profitable companies borrow the least whereas the trade off theory predicts the reverse.[284]

An alternative theory suggests that companies prefer to issue debt rather than equity only if internal finance is insufficient.[285] Internal finance is effectively retained profits, ie funds which could be paid out as dividends but which are instead retained by the company to finance its projects. Retained profits can therefore be viewed as additional capital invested by the shareholders. Since internal finance does not send any adverse signals which may lower the share price, this is the first choice for companies. If external finance is required, firms will issue debt, because this is less likely to be interpreted by investors as a bad omen, and external equity financing is regarded as a last resort. As a result there is no optimum debt to equity mix because there are two kinds of equity: internal equity, which is top of the 'pecking order', and external finance, which comes last. This analysis explains why the most profitable companies borrow less: they have access to the most internal finance and therefore do not need to rely heavily on outside finance. Indeed, the pecking order theory works best for large mature companies that have access to bond markets. These firms rarely issue new equity when they need to raise finance. They prefer internal financing but will turn to debt markets if necessary. However, this analysis is not without its difficulties either. In particular some studies suggest that companies do not always exhaust all sources of internal finance before turning to external sources[286] and others suggest that some smaller, growth companies seem to rely on equity (in the form of venture capital) rather than debt when external financing is required.[287]

Other theories of capital structure have developed as variations or refinements on these models which try to explain the structures that are observable in practice.[288] It seems that capital structure does matter, but that there is no single optimal structure for all companies. It is necessary to consider the size and type of the company, the nature of its underlying assets, and the availability of internal finance. For individual companies these considerations will be important, but more specific details about the nature of the financing on offer will often be determinative of the issue. For instance issues such as the identity of the lender (trade credit, institutional lenders etc) and the contractual features

---

[284]   JK Wald, 'How Firm Characteristics Affect Capital Structure: An International Comparison' (1999) 22 *Journal of Financial Research* 161.

[285]   SC Myers, 'The Capital Structure Puzzle' (1984) 39 *Journal of Finance* 575; L Shyam-Sunder and SC Myers, 'Testing Static Trade-off Against Pecking-Order Models of Capital Structure' (1999) 51 *Journal of Financial Economics* 219; EF Fama and KR French, 'Testing Trade-off and Pecking – Order Predictions about Dividends and Debt' (2002) 15 *Review of Financial Studies*; M Frank and V Goyal, 'Testing the Pecking Order Theory of Capital Structure' (2002) 67 *Journal of Financial Economics* 217.

[286]   C Mayer and O Sussman, 'A New Test of Capital Structure' available at www.ssrn.com/abstract=509022.

[287]   Eg L Shyam-Sunder and S C Myers, 'Testing Static Trade-off against Pecking-Order Models of Capital Structure' (1999) 51 *Journal of Financial Economics* 219.

[288]   Eg M Jensen and W Meckling, 'Theory of the Firm: Managerial behaviour, Agency Costs and Ownership Structure' (1976) 3 *Journal of Financial Economics* 305; M Baker and J Wurgler, 'Market Timing and Capital Structure' (2002) 57 *Journal of Finance* 1.

of the debt, such as maturity, conversion rights, collateral, events of default and guarantees will be important in determining the attractiveness of debt financing in a given scenario. Whereas on the equity side, the nature of the shares being issued (ordinary or preference, and whether or not they are redeemable), the rights attached to those shares, the price at which they are issued and whether pre-emption rights have been set aside, will all be of importance. Further, general market conditions may well determine how much debt can be raised, and also the means of raising it. This has been made clear by the recent financial crisis, when bank financing became difficult to obtain. Larger companies turned to the bond and equity markets,[289] while smaller companies suffered from lack of debt, although some turned to asset-based lending.[290]

2.7 Conclusion

There are, therefore, a huge number of options for a company to use to finance its operations. Almost all companies will utilise a mixture of equity and debt finance, and this chapter has sought to explore the factors which influence this mix in different situations. The basic advantage of equity to a company is that the capital is less likely to be withdrawn, and that dividends can only be paid when the company makes distributable profits and, even then, shareholders rarely have the right to demand payment. Interest on debt, conversely, has to be paid whatever the state of the company's profits, and usually the capital has to be repaid at some stage. The two forms of finance are also treated differently for tax purposes. The extent to which these considerations influence companies' choice of financing is discussed above.

Further, within the categories of equity and debt there are a number of variations and this chapter has sought to explore the factors which lead companies to choose between them. Equity options are more limited than debt options, consisting largely of ordinary shares and different types of preference shares. The range of options of sources of equity finance depends largely on the size of the company. Even where a company is large, the private equity structure is a significant alternative to offering shares to the public. The advantages and disadvantages of private equity will be discussed further in chapter fourteen. The options for debt financing are very wide, although most can be divided into either loans or issues of securities. The provision of trade credit is also significant, and itself requires financing. Small and medium sized companies tend to rely on bank loans, though nowadays these are often supplemented or replaced by some sort of financing based on assets. Large companies will look to borrow from a number of banks or other lenders, or to issue securities to tap into the wider bond markets. Financial companies, and those with a steady stream of receivables, are likely still to consider securitisation, although the more exotic forms of this type of financing are unlikely to reappear in the near future.

---

[289] FSA Financial Risk Outlook 2010 p.6; BIS, *Financing a Private Sector Recovery*, n 1, 3.40, 3.44.
[290] 2.3.4 above.

3

The Relationship between Equity and Debt

3.1 Introduction

All companies need capital in order to function. As discussed in chapter two, companies can finance their operations via share issues, debt, retained profits or, more likely, a combination of these options. These options were examined from the company's point of view in the previous chapter. This chapter will examine debt and equity financing from the point of view of those putting money in to the company: the shareholders and creditors. There are certain fundamental differences between a shareholder's interest in a company and that of a creditor which will be explored in this chapter, although it is accepted that both concepts can be manipulated in order to make the contrast less stark in practice. Hybrid arrangements were discussed in the last chapter, at 2.4.

We need to understand the respective roles that creditors and shareholders perform, the rights that they hold and therefore the risks that they undertake, in both solvent and insolvent companies. Broadly, shareholders' interests dominate in the solvent company whereas creditors' interests dominate in insolvency and in the twilight zone before insolvency actually commences. Determining the reasons for this dichotomy between the solvent and insolvent company scenario is important in order to understand the dynamics of company financing decisions and also to understand the rationale for the law's regulation of these issues. The discussion in this chapter will also form the basis for the more specific discussions regarding equity and debt financing that will be undertaken in the remaining chapters of this book.

The thesis of this chapter is that shareholders are pre-eminent within the solvent company because they are the residuary claimants of the company, and all of the risks and rewards of the company at this point fall on the shareholders rather than the creditors. The creditors' returns are fixed. They do not share proportionately in the upside of corporate decisions and they only share in the downside if the company becomes insolvent. Their downside risk is different to that of the shareholders, as discussed later in this chapter. It is particularly notable that the directors' general fiduciary duty to act in the best interests of the company is fundamentally shareholder-regarding while the company is solvent.[1] Whilst the company has significant shareholder funds, the creditors will normally favour projects which do not endanger this situation, even if a riskier project has a higher present value, because the creditors' position will not be materially enhanced by the higher value project. The danger of imposing creditor-focused duties on the directors

---

[1] Companies Act 2006, s 172(1), discussed below at 3.2.1.3.1.

while a company is a profitable going concern is that the creditors will be primarily interested in excessively low risk projects.[2] However companies are vehicles for taking entrepreneurial risks. Creditors' incentives are misaligned from maximising the firm's value when the company is solvent. Since the losses are borne by the shareholders first, when assessing strategic decisions directors should have paramount consideration to the risk profile of that group. An excessively risky project will impact most heavily on them, but they will share in the upside of any decision too.

In order to make these arguments, in section 3.2.1 below the position of shareholders in a solvent company is assessed. After an analysis of the rights that are typically held by shareholders, this section examines the main arguments in favour of the pre-eminence of shareholders. In line with the thesis set out above, it will be suggested that these arguments are stronger for certain shareholders than for others. In particular the argument is stronger for those with a residuary claim on the company, typically the ordinary shareholders. In section 3.2.2 the position of creditors in a solvent company is examined. The risks faced by creditors in a solvent company are assessed. This section examines the features that are common to all creditors in a solvent company. In general, the creditors' relationship in this period is left to contract law.[3] This chapter will suggest that most creditors are able to protect themselves through contract while the company remains solvent. The one group of creditors who may not be able to do so are the non-adjusting creditors, discussed below at 3.2.2.1.

By contrast, when the company is insolvent, or nearing insolvency, it is the creditors' interests that dominate. It is notable that at this point the directors' general fiduciary duty to the company becomes creditor-focused rather than shareholder-focused.[4] This is also explicable by understanding where the risks fall at this point. Section 3.3.1 will set out the order of payment out on a winding up or a distribution by an administrator. This analysis makes it very clear that at this point creditors rank ahead of shareholders, but also that there is a distinct order of distribution in which some creditors rank ahead of others, either because they have bargained for proprietary protection, or because they fall into a category of creditors given limited protection by statute. Creditors are also protected by statute and the common law, which, in certain circumstances before and after insolvency, prevents the diminution of the asset pool available for creditors and the uneven distribution of assets. These issues are discussed in section 3.3.2.

The pre-eminence of creditors as opposed to shareholders at this point in time is entirely appropriate. Once the shareholders' funds in the company have been dissipated entirely, or at least reduced to a very low level, it is in the interests of the shareholders to encourage excessively risky projects.[5] This is because the shareholders will be interested entirely in the upside of the decision. The extent to which shareholders take any downside risk of business decisions once their funds in the company have evaporated will depend

---

[2]   MC Jensen and WH Meckling, 'Theory of the Firm: Managerial Behaviour, Agency Costs and Ownership Structure' (1976) 3 *Journal of Financial Economics* 305.

[3]   The legal capital rules discussed in chapter 4 also have the predominant aim of creditor protection, though the value of these rules as a creditor-protection device is questionable.

[4]   *West Mercia Safetywear Ltd v Dodd* [1988] BCLC 250, discussed below at pages 105–107.

[5]   If the company is operating profitably, but its profits are fully distributed each year, the amount of shareholder funds in the company will be low, but the incentives for the directors to take on excessively risky projects will be weak, because the company's profit-making potential could be destroyed.

upon the extent to which the principle of limited liability is upheld within a jurisdiction.[6] As section 3.3.3.1 examines, in the UK the principle of limited liability is upheld almost in its entirety at common law, and although statutory exceptions do exist, most notably sections 213 and 214 of the Insolvency Act 1986, the levels of enforcement of these actions is extremely low.

If the directors are acting in the shareholders' interests at this point,[7] therefore, this would create an incentive structure for directors which would positively favour excessively risky projects. By contrast with the solvent scenario, creditors cannot at this point rely on the 'shareholders first' rule in relation to losses to protect their interests, because shareholder-regarding directors can focus exclusively on the upside of potential projects however remote the possibility of success might be. When comparing potential projects directors would be able to ignore the chances of a negative outcome. Shareholders at this point have little to lose from the downside of potential projects but stand to gain enormously from the potential upside. It is therefore appropriate that the law protects the creditors at this point.

3.2   The Relationship between Equity and Debt in a Solvent Company

In this section the rights and roles of shareholders and creditors in a solvent company will be compared and contrasted. It is important to separate the solvent and insolvent scenarios because, as will become apparent, the positions of shareholders and of creditors in these two periods change markedly.

For these purposes a slightly more constrained view of solvency is adopted than is required if the strict legal definition is applied. A company is insolvent for the purposes of the law if it becomes unable to pay its debts.[8] However there are two different approaches that can be adopted to determine when a company becomes unable to pay its debts. The first is the balance sheet test. This test measures the excess of liabilities over assets and considers whether the company's assets are insufficient to discharge its liabilities 'taking into account its contingent and prospective liabilities'.[9] The second is the cash flow test which assesses the ability of the company to meet its debts and liabilities as they become due.[10] Both tests operate in the UK.[11] Nevertheless, it is recognised that there is likely to be a period prior to formal insolvency when the roles of creditors and shareholders begin to

---

   [6]   DD Prentice, 'Creditor's Interests and Director's Duties' (1990) 10 *Oxford Journal of Legal Studies* 265.
   [7]   For a discussion of the point in time at which the company shifts from being shareholder-focused to being creditor-focused see pages 88–89.
   [8]   R Goode, *Principles of Corporate Insolvency Law*, 3rd edn (London, Sweet & Maxwell, 2005) ch 4.
   [9]   Insolvency Act 1986, s 123(2).
   [10]   Insolvency Act 1986, s 123(1)(e). However, this test seems to involve an element of futurity: *Re Cheyne Finance plc* [2007] EWHC 2402 (Ch); [2008] 1 BCLC 741; *BNY Corporate Trustee Services Limited v Eurosail-Uk 2007–3bl Plc* [2010] EWHC 2005 (Ch).
   [11]   In systems which do not demand any significant minimum legal capital levels, such as the UK, the cash flow test may be more appropriate. This is because many companies without significant legal capital are often balance sheet insolvent from the moment they begin to trade, since they will usually have exchanged cash for business-specific assets whose market value may immediately begin to depreciate, or they may have borrowed more than the value of their current assets on the basis of their future cash flow.

change and when the analysis entered into in this section will not necessarily be appropriate. A discussion of this twilight period prior to insolvency, and when that twilight period can be said to begin, is undertaken in the following section, 3.3. In this section, then, the concept of solvency is intended to encompass the scenario outside insolvency (as strictly defined) but also outside this twilight period, ie for the purposes of this section solvency encompasses the scenario in which there remain significant shareholder funds within the company and the company remains a profitable going concern.

3.2.1   The Position of Shareholders in a Solvent Company

In order to determine the position of shareholders in a solvent company, it is first necessary to understand the rights that are typically held by shareholders in such a company. The rights attaching to shares in a company are laid down in the company's constitution, in case law and in statute. Of course it is common for a company's share capital to comprise different classes of shares,[12] the most common being ordinary shares and preference shares.[13] However, a company under English law has practically unlimited freedom to create the capital structure it wishes for itself and the line between these different classes may not always be easy to define.

3.2.1.1   Ordinary Shares

An ordinary share is a default share, in the sense that the rights enjoyed by ordinary shares are those which attach to all shares unless contrary provision is made when the shares are issued or by subsequent variation of the rights attaching to the shares.[14] If a company's shares are all one class then these are necessarily ordinary shares and if a company has share capital it must have at least one ordinary share. However, the power to issue shares with different rights now usually appears in the articles of association.[15]

In some companies, particularly very small companies, the purpose of issuing shares may simply be to give the shareholders control of the company, for it is likely that the shareholders will use their voting rights as shareholders to appoint themselves directors of the company. The amount of capital injected via the ordinary shares may be negligible,[16] with most of the financing in the form of a bank loan secured on the personal assets of the shareholder/directors. However, in larger companies, even though the control aspect of ordinary shares remains important, the use of ordinary shares as a capital-raising device cannot be ignored.[17]

The rights attached to shares can usefully be divided into three types: rights to income, rights to capital and voting rights. As regards capital rights the default rule is that the

---

[12]   See 2.2.1.

[13]   Another common class of shares is redeemable shares. All classes of shares may be issued as redeemable at the option of the company: Companies Act 2006, ss 684–689.

[14]   A company that wants to issue shares with different rights must have the power to that effect in its constitution so as to displace the presumption that all shareholders are to be treated equally: *Campbell v Rofe* [1933] AC 98; *British and American Trustee and Finance Corporation v Couper* [1894] AC 399, 416.

[15]   See Model Articles for Private Companies Limited by Shares, Art 22; Model Articles for Public Companies, Art 43: The Companies (Model Articles) Regulations 2008 (SI 3229/2008), Sch 1 and Sch 3.

[16]   There are no minimum capital levels for private companies. For a discussion of minimum capital requirements see 4.3.2.

[17]   For a discussion of the advantages of issuing ordinary shares, from the company's point of view, see 2.2.1.1.

surplus left after the paid up capital has been repaid is distributable equally amongst the ordinary shareholders in proportion to the nominal value of their shares.[18] This principle can be modified by the company in its articles, but neither the Model Articles for Private Companies limited by shares nor the Model Articles for Public companies amend this default principle.[19]

The holder of an ordinary share does not have an absolute right to claim dividends.[20] The extent of any right to receive dividends will be set out in the company's articles, but shareholders only become entitled to receive a final dividend once that dividend has been declared,[21] at which point a debt is created.[22] By contrast an interim dividend remains at the discretion of the board, so that a resolution to pay such a dividend does not create an immediate debt.[23] Dividends must be paid in cash unless the articles provide otherwise,[24] although it is very common for articles to authorise the payment of dividends in kind.[25] The articles will also set out the procedural aspects of dividend payments.[26] As amongst themselves the holders of the fully paid up ordinary shares are entitled to share equally in dividends.[27]

A shareholder is a creditor in respect of any dividend that has been declared but not paid by the due date for payment.[28] However, when the company is in liquidation any sum due to a member of the company by way of dividend will only be paid after all of the creditors' debts are paid in full.[29] The order of payment out on a winding up or distribution by an administrator ranks creditors' claims ahead of shareholders' claims.[30] This principle is not undermined to the extent of any debts due to members in their capacity as members, which sums clearly include unpaid dividends. A distinction can be drawn between these sums and sums due to the member in some other capacity.[31]

---

[18]   *Birch v Cropper* (1889) 14 App Cas 525.
[19]   See Model Articles for Private Companies Limited by Shares; Model Articles for Public Companies: The Companies (Model Articles) Regulations 2008 (SI 3229/2008), Sch 1 and Sch 3.
[20]   For a discussion of dividend policy generally see 2.5.
[21]   *Bond v Barrow Haematite Steel Co* [1902] 1 Ch 353.
[22]   The debt is immediate if no date of payment is stipulated (*Re Severn and Wye and Severn Bridge Railway Co* [1896] 1 Ch 559) but the date when the dividend is due can also be specified in which case the shareholder cannot enforce payment until that date arrives (*Re Kidner* [1929] 2 Ch 121). The six year limitation period in respect of an unpaid dividend runs from the date when it is declared or any later date for payment: *Re Compania de Electricidad de la Provincia de Buenos Aires* [1980] 1 Ch 146.
[23]   *Lagunas Nitrate Co Ltd v Schroeder & Co and Schmidt* (1901) 85 LT 22. If the directors resolve to pay an interim dividend at a future date, a shareholder has no enforceable right to demand payment prior to that date.
[24]   *Wood v Odessa Waterworks Co* (1889) 42 Ch D 636.
[25]   See eg Model Articles for Private Companies Limited by Shares, art 34; Model Articles for Public Companies, art 76: The Companies (Model Articles) Regulations 2008 (SI 3229/2008), Sch 1 and Sch 3.
[26]   Model Articles for Private Companies Limited by Shares, art 30; Model Articles for Public Companies, art 70: The Companies (Model Articles) Regulations 2008 (SI 3229/2008), Sch 1 and Sch 3. It is common for articles to provide that final dividends are declared by the shareholders in general meeting, but subject to the recommendation of the directors. Since the shareholders cannot increase the level of dividend, and it is rare for them to declare less than the amount recommended by the directors, this is largely a rubber stamping exercise.
[27]   Where the shares are partly paid the position may be more complicated. It will depend on whether the return available is calculated according to the nominal value or the amounts paid up on them.
[28]   *Re Compania de Electricidad de la Provincia de Buenos Aires* [1980] 1 Ch 146.
[29]   Insolvency Act 1986, s 74(2)(f).
[30]   For discussion see 3.3.1.2.5.
[31]   *Soden v British & Commonwealth Holdings plc* [1998] AC 298. For discussion see 3.3.1.2.5.

The distinctive feature of the income and capital rights attaching to ordinary shares is that the returns are not fixed.[32] It is also in contrast to preference shares where, commonly, the rights in respect of dividends and/or capital may be in priority to the ordinary shares, but only for a fixed amount.[33] The definition of equity share capital within the Companies Act 2006 'means its issued share capital excluding any part of that capital that, neither as respects dividends nor as respects capital, carries any right to participate beyond a specified amount in a distribution'.[34] The ordinary shares are therefore the purest form of equity within the company.[35] They are the residual claimants in the company, with no guarantee of any dividend payment, and no guarantee of any return on a winding up. Their entitlement to the surplus of the company means that although the ordinary shareholders take the lion's share of the rewards, they also take the lion's share of the risk. In the event of winding up or administration the rights of the shareholders to be repaid is subject to the rights of the creditors, who get repaid in full ahead of the shareholders, so that the shareholders' right to repayment at that point will generally be worthless. This level of economic exposure explains the law's traditional willingness to give the shareholders control rights over the management of the company, at least while the company remains a going concern.

As regards voting rights, the default position is one vote per share unless the articles make alternative provision.[36] Ordinary shares usually follow the default position, although different configurations can be created. It is possible to create different classes of ordinary shares with different voting rights and it is possible to have non-voting ordinary shares, although these are rare.[37] The ordinary shareholders, then, are the decision-makers in the company to the extent that matters need to be resolved by the general meeting.

3.2.1.2 Preference Shares

A preference share is a share which in respect of dividend and/or capital enjoys priority, for a limited amount, over the company's ordinary shares. The precise extent of the priority will depend upon the rights attached to the shares, primarily by way of provisions in the company's articles, although the courts do also play a part in determining the extent of the rights, through the application of a series of presumptions.

The position regarding the default rights of the preference shareholders is set out below. These legal rights will generally be class rights. What amounts to a right attaching to a share is a matter for the articles, any shareholder agreements and the courts to decide.[38]

---

[32] In a company with deferred or founders shares, the ordinary shareholders get a fixed return and the deferred or founders shares get the balance. However, deferred shares and founders shares are rarely encountered in practice. This is in contrast to the returns to creditors, discussed below at pages 73–74.

[33] Preference shares are discussed further below at 3.2.1.2.

[34] Companies Act 2006, s 548.

[35] It is possible to create participating preference shares with a right to share in the surplus (and a preferential return on dividends and/or capital) which would normally fall within the definition of equity capital, although such shares are rare.

[36] Companies Act 2006, s 284.

[37] Non-voting shares are not prohibited by the UK Listing rules, but they are strongly discouraged by the London Stock Exchange and by the investment community and as a result they are rare: J Franks, C Mayer and S Rossi, 'Spending Less Time with the Family: The Decline of Family Ownership in the UK' in RK Morck (ed), *A History of Corporate Governance Around the World: Family Business Groups to Professional Managers* (Chicago, University of Chicago Press, 2005) 582–83.

[38] *Cumbrian Newspapers Group Ltd v Cumberland & Westmorland Herald Newspaper & Printing Co Ltd* [1987] Ch 1; *Harman v BML Group Ltd* [1994] 1 WLR 893.

Creditors of a company can also be divided into different classes. These may include secured and unsecured creditors and tranches of creditors in a structured transaction where the classes are determined by subordination. The extent of these rights is determined predominantly by the contractual arrangements between the creditors and the company but there may also be a role for the court in determining the classes of creditors, for example in relation to schemes of arrangement, discussed in chapter thirteen.

It is clear that preference shares carrying different rights to dividend and/or to capital will be treated as being in a different class of shares from the ordinary shares.[39] The significance of this is that there is a statutory procedure which needs to be followed where class rights are varied.[40] A class right found in the articles, for example, can only be changed by at least a 75 per cent majority of the class concerned. Any other right found in the articles can prima facie be altered by a 75 per cent majority of all members.[41] This appears to provide significant protection to the holders of class rights. However, this potential protection is diminished as a result of the extremely restrictive interpretation of the concept of 'variation' adopted by the courts for this purpose. Issuing new preference shares *pari passu* to existing preference shareholders might vary the enjoyment of the rights of the existing shareholders, but does not vary the right itself, and so the statutory procedure need not be followed.[42]

As regards capital rights there is a presumption that all shares rank equally with regard to the return of capital.[43] Any priority intended to be attached to preference shares regarding the return of capital must be expressly stated. The fact that preference shares have priority as to dividends does not mean that the shares are presumed to have priority as to a return of capital.[44] The sum repaid may be the par value of the shares, or the articles may provide for a higher sum. It is common to attach a Spens formula to preference shares which provides that on a repayment of capital the holders of the share capital are expressly entitled to a premium if, during a defined period prior to repayment, the shares have been standing in the market at a figure in excess of their par value.[45]

As regards the right to share in the surplus capital of the company, where a share carries a preferential right to capital on a winding up, this displaces the principle of equality and it is presumed that the express preferential right to capital is the sum total of the entitlement.[46] It is for the preference shareholders to demonstrate that a provision in the company's constitution or in the terms of issue of the shares confers an entitlement to share in any surplus assets.

---

[39]   See Companies Act 2006, s 629 for the definition of classes of shares. There was no such definition in the Companies Act 1985.

[40]   Now contained in Companies Act 2006, ss 630–635.

[41]   Companies Act 2006, s 21, subject, now, to the ability of shareholders to entrench rights in articles and to require a higher than 75% majority to alter those rights (Companies Act 2006, s 22). This general right to alter the articles by special resolution is also subject to the constraint that in order to be valid the alteration must be bona fide in the best interests of the company (*Allen v Gold Reefs of West Africa Ltd* [1900] 1 Ch 656).

[42]   *White v Bristol Aeroplane Co* [1953] 1 Ch 65.

[43]   *Welton v Saffery* [1897] AC 299, 309 per Lord Watson.

[44]   *Birch v Cropper* (1889) 14 App Cas 525.

[45]   For a discussion of par value see 4.3.2.2. The premium is usually ascertained by reference to the middle-market quotation in excess of par during the relevant period subject to adjustments to take account of any accrued arrears of dividend which is reflected in the market price of the shares.

[46]   *Scottish Insurance Corporation v Wilsons & Clyde Coal Co Ltd* [1949] AC 462, criticising the earlier suggestion (*Birch v Cropper* (1889) 14 App Cas 525, 546 per Lord Macnaghten) that preference shares were entitled to share in the surplus assets unless their terms contained an express and specific renunciation of the right.

The other occasion on which capital can be returned to the preference shareholders is on a reduction of capital. The articles may provide expressly for whether the preference shareholders are to be repaid in priority on a reduction, or the articles may be silent on this point. Where the articles provide that the shares have priority to capital on a winding up, but are silent regarding the position on a reduction, the courts have held that the rights on a reduction mirror those on a winding up.[47]

In relation to dividend rights, again any rights to a preferential dividend need to be set out expressly in the articles. The mere fact that the share carries a right to priority in respect of capital does not mean that the courts will imply a priority as to the payment of a dividend.[48] It is common, however, for preference shares to carry preferential rights in respect of both income and capital. Indeed, almost invariably the preferential rights attached to preference shares are income rights.

It is common for preferential dividends to be expressed as a specified percentage of the nominal value of the share, although other formulations are possible.[49] Preferential dividends are usually expressed to be payable only when declared,[50] but if no dividend is declared in a given year, or if the full entitlement is not paid, it is presumed that the unpaid amount is carried forward into subsequent years, unless the articles provide otherwise.[51] If the company goes into liquidation with the dividends still undeclared, there is a general presumption that the undeclared preferential dividends are not payable. However, the articles can, and often do, provide that on a liquidation or a reduction of capital a sum equal to the unpaid dividends (whether declared or not) be paid to the preference shareholders in priority to any payment to the ordinary shareholders.[52]

The preference shareholders are also at the mercy of the directors to the extent that the shareholders cannot declare a dividend in excess of the amount recommended by the directors.[53] If the directors do not recommend the full dividend in circumstances where the company has the necessary distributable profits the preference shareholders' options for redress are rather limited. They may be able to petition for relief under section 994 of the Companies Act 2006, on the basis that the company's affairs are being managed in a way which is unfairly prejudicial to them, or they could possibly be able to petition for a just and equitable winding up under section 122(1)(g) of the Insolvency Act 1986,[54] but neither option is guaranteed to produce the required result.

The default position on voting rights attaching to shares in a company is one vote per share unless the articles make alternative provision.[55] Preference shares normally carry only limited voting rights. Typically the right to vote will only arise where the preferential dividend has been in arrears for longer than a specified period. This may include the

---

[47]   *Re Saltdean Estate Co Ltd* [1968] 1 WLR 1844, approved by the House of Lords in *House of Fraser plc v ACGE Investments Ltd* [1987] AC 387 (though in that case the rights of preference shareholders on a reduction were expressly dealt with in the articles).

[48]   *Birch v Cropper* (1889) 14 App Cas 525.

[49]   Eg, the preferential dividend can be expressed as a percentage of the amount paid up on the share.

[50]   *Bond v Barrow Haematite Steel Co* [1902] 1 Ch 353.

[51]   *Webb v Earle* (1875) LR 20 Eq 556.

[52]   *Re Wharfedale Brewery Co Ltd* [1952] Ch 913.

[53]   Model Articles for Private Companies Limited by Shares, art 30(2); Model Articles for Public Companies, art 70(2): The Companies (Model Articles) Regulations 2008 (SI 3229/2008), Sch 1 and Sch 3.

[54]   *Re a Company ex p Glossop* [1988] 1 WLR 1068. It has also been suggested that the shareholders could bring an action against the directors for breach of the statutory contract under s 33 Companies Act 2006: *Re a Company* [1987] BCLC 82.

[55]   Companies Act 2006, s 284.

position where the company has insufficient distributable profits to pay the dividend, if the articles provide a payment date and the date has passed.[56]

There is no standard package of rights that attaches to all preference shares. Preference shares can be placed at numerous points on the continuum which has the 'pure equity' of the ordinary shares at one end and the creditors of the company at the other. It is possible for a company to create preference shares having a right to vote and to receive a priority as to fixed income payments, but no priority as to the return of capital. This would be unusual. More likely are convertible preference shares which start life as preference shares of the more usual variety (fixed rights to income and capital in priority to the ordinary shares, limited voting rights and no entitlement to surplus), which are subsequently convertible into another form of security in the company, such as ordinary shares, giving the holder the opportunity to participate in capital growth in the future.

However, more common still is the issue of preference shares as a form of fixed interest security akin to debt:

> In relation to the commercial requirements of the modern company the preference share cannot now be said to have any unique and essential function. It is probable that the great majority of companies find, in principle, little to choose between preference or debenture securities as instruments of corporate finance.[57]

This statement, although more than forty years old, remains accurate today.[58] However, the position of a preference shareholder will be inferior to that of the company's creditors in certain crucial respects. Unlike interest payments, the preferential dividend entitlement is not a debt until declared, and cannot be guaranteed. Even if the articles specify that the dividend does not need to be declared and the articles specify the due date of the dividend, the payment will still be conditional upon distributable profits being available.[59] The preference shareholder has less security of capital than the company's creditors, who may have a charge on the assets of the company, and, on a winding up or administration, any sums due to preference shareholders (by way of unpaid dividends or capital repayment) will continue to rank behind the creditors in order of payment out.[60] As regards voting rights, which might be considered to counterbalance, to some extent, the greater capital and dividend rights of the creditors, such rights are generally only provided to preference shareholders when the preferential dividend payments are in arrears. The membership advantages conferred on most preference shareholders are extremely limited.

---

[56]   *Re Bradford Investments plc* [1990] BCC 740.

[57]   M Pickering, 'The Problem of the Preference Share' (1963) 26 *Modern Law Review* 499, 517.

[58]   For a fuller discussion of the circumstances in which a company might make use of preference shares as a form of equity finance see 2.2.1.2. Because preference shares contain many of the same features of debt, they are often regarded as hybrid securities, as discussed at 2.4.

[59]   If no such profits are available then at best the right to payment will be suspended until there are sufficient distributable profits. This is the position in Australia (*Marra Developments Ltd v BW Rofe Pty Ltd* (1977) 2 NSWLR 616 (Sup Ct NSW)) and probably represents the English position, though there is no authority on this point.

[60]   Insolvency Act 1986, s 74(2)(f). For further discussion see 3.3.1.2.5.

3.2.1.3   The Role of Shareholders in a Solvent Company

3.2.1.3.1   Section 172 of the Companies Act 2006

When the company is solvent, it is the shareholders, rather than the creditors, who dominate UK company law. In a solvent company directors have traditionally owed their duties to the shareholders as a whole.[61] Section 172 of the Companies Act 2006 now provides that a director must 'act in a way he considers, in good faith, would be most likely to promote the success of the company for the benefit of its members as a whole', ie a subjectively assessed obligation to operate the company in the interests of the shareholders as a whole, in line with the pre-existing common law obligation. However, section 172 then potentially departs from the common law position by requiring that, in doing so, the director must have regard to a number of other stakeholder interests, such as the company's employees, suppliers, customers etc.

The introduction of this provision into the Companies Act 2006 has caused some concern. It is felt that section 172 might give rise to significant additional duties for directors. In particular, the concern is that when coupled with the new statutory derivative action,[62] directors might face actions from minority shareholders unhappy with decisions taken by them, either because the directors appear to have preferred the interests of other stakeholders over and above those of the shareholders, or possibly (if the minority shareholder in question is also representing the interests of the other stakeholders in some way) because the directors have not taken sufficient notice of the interests of one of the other stakeholder groups. The question arises whether it is possible for the directors to prefer the interests of those other stakeholders over and above those of the shareholders.

The preferable analysis of section 172 is that it requires directors to have regard to the long-term interests of the shareholders, and that in doing so the directors may have to take account of other stakeholder groups in order to determine what best ensures the long-term growth of the company. So, in a solvent company it is the long-term interests of the shareholders which remain the dominant concern, and the interests of other stakeholders are relevant only to the extent that they help to inform the directors' views of the long-term interests of the shareholders and the company. Notably, the interests of the creditors do not feature in this analysis at all. The extent of the *law's* protection of creditors in a solvent company is the capital maintenance regime, discussed in chapter four. Otherwise, creditors must protect themselves via contract, and other mechanisms, discussed in 3.2.2.

One point is worth noting here, concerning the preference shareholders. The directors' role under section 172 is to assess what 'would be most likely to promote the success of the company for the benefit of its members as a whole'. A differentiation can be made between different kinds of members in this regard The group most interested in the long-term success of the company will be those taking the lion's share of the risks and rewards, namely the residual claimants. As discussed, the preference shareholders may be given the right to participate in the residuary profits (and losses) of the company, but more likely they will be fixed claimants in a position akin to (but worse than) that of the creditors. To

---

[61] Eg *Re Smith and Fawcett Ltd* [1942] Ch 304, 306 per Lord Greene MR. As a rule directors do not owe duties to individual shareholders although they may do so in specific factual circumstances: *Peskin v Anderson* [2001] 1 BCC 874.

[62] Companies Act 2006, ss 260–264 (England, Wales and Northern Ireland), ss 265–269 (Scotland).

the extent that they are fixed claimants their interests may be only marginally more relevant than the interests of the creditors when assessing what is in the long-term interest of the company. Other types of hybrid instruments could also be considered in this context, particularly convertible instruments which allow the holder to convert their securities from debt to equity in specified circumstances.[63]

3.2.1.3.2   Explaining the Pre-eminence of Shareholders

The pre-eminence of the shareholders in this regard requires some thought. The conventional explanation is based on the shareholders' property rights as 'owners' of the company. There are two ways in which shareholders could be regarded as the 'owners' of the company, first by virtue of having something fundamental in their possession, and second in the sense of having control over the company's business. The second of these can be dealt with relatively quickly, the first is rather more complex.

Can shareholders be regarded as the owners of the company via their ability to control the company? Some incidents of being a shareholder appear to provide support for this view. For example, it is the exclusive power of the shareholders to form a company. A company must have subscribers holding at least one share each,[64] whereas there is no equivalent requirement for the company to have creditors. Likewise only shareholders can disband a company.[65] Unpaid creditors can only force a company into liquidation with the assistance of the court.[66] However, these differences do not seem to justify the pre-eminence of shareholders, and so we turn to the next possible explanation, namely whether shareholders can be said to be the owners of the company in some fundamental sense.

This view was certainly prevalent at an earlier point in the history of the company. In the early nineteenth century there were two principal vehicles for the conduct of large scale business ventures: the corporation and the joint stock company. The corporation owed its existence to either a Royal Charter or an Act of Parliament and had separate legal existence. The more important business vehicle however was the joint stock company which was nothing more than a large partnership.[67] The joint stock company did not have a separate legal identity from its members. In regulating this vehicle the courts, not surprisingly, employed the principles of partnership law.[68] The members, as partners, owned the assets, were jointly and severally liable for the debts incurred by the business and had all the rights and powers that ownership implies.

However, over the intervening period, much has occurred to alter this view of the nature of shareholders' rights in a company. Most importantly, the concept of the company as a separate legal entity has been developed. The Companies Act 1844 was the first to grant separate legal existence to any venture which complied with the statutory

---

[63]   For discussion see pages 45–46.

[64]   Companies Act 2006, s 8(1)(b).

[65]   Insolvency Act 1986, s 84(1)(b) and (c).

[66]   Insolvency Act 1986, s 122. Note however that certain creditors (notably the floating charge holder) can appoint an administrator out of court. See chapter 6.

[67]   L Sealy, 'Perception and Policy in Company Law Reform' in D Feldman and F Meisel (eds), *Corporate and Commercial Law: Modern Developments* (London, Lloyd's of London Press, 1996) 11–13.

[68]   Eg P Ireland, 'The Triumph of the Company Legal Form 1856–1914' in J Adams (ed), *Essays for Clive Schmitthoff* (Abingdon, Professional Books, 1983) 31.

machinery in the Companies Act,[69] although for much of the remainder of the nineteenth century the company remained, in the eyes of the law, a peculiar kind of partnership, and the shareholders its collective owners.[70] However in 1897 the decision of the House of Lords in *Salomon v A Salomon & Co Ltd*[71] recognised that the separate legal personality of the company meant that a new person was being created to which the debts and liabilities of the company attached. Crucially, this new legal person was also in a position to hold the property of the company.

Following on from this analysis, originally the idea of a share in a company meant the members' share in the common property of the business. However, by the beginning of the twentieth century the idea that shareholders had no direct interest in the company assets had become established. The most famous formulation of this concept is that of Farwell J in *Borland's Trustees v Steel Brothers & Co Ltd*:

> A share is the interest of a shareholder in the company measured by a sum of money, for the purpose of liability in the first place, and of interest in the second, but also consisting of a series of mutual covenants entered into by all the shareholders inter se...[72]

This makes it clear that shareholders do not share in the assets of the company. Instead, the company holds the legal title to its assets and it is the absolute owner of all the property vested in it. As a matter of course companies do not hold the beneficial title to their assets on trust for another, and neither do others hold the company's property on trust for it.

So, it is clear that shareholders hold no interest in the assets of the company, but we must then enquire as to what they do own. The quotation from Farwell J, above, suggests that while shareholders do not own the assets of the company, they can nevertheless be said to own a share in the company itself. On this view the company is not merely a person, and the subject of rights and duties, but also a res, and thereby the object of rights and duties. A contrasting view, which arose during the twentieth century, was that shares are merely a piece of property conferring rights in relation to the income and capital of the company, and not a proportionate share in the company itself: 'A share...forms...a separate right of property. The capital is the property of the corporation. The share...is the property of the corporator'.[73]

A good illustration of the practical difference between these two views can be seen from the facts of *Short v Treasury Commissioners*.[74] The entire share capital of the company was being compulsorily acquired by the Crown. In assessing the compensation payable it was suggested that, as all of the shares were being acquired, the shareholders were entitled to the entire value of the company, which was greater than the aggregate value of the shares. The Court of Appeal rejected this suggestion. The shareholders were not entitled to compensation for the value of the company, but only for what was being expropriated,

---

[69]   See Companies Act 2006, s 16(2).
[70]   Concepts of partnership law were used to resolve company law problems even in to the twentieth century: *Re Yenidje Tobacco Co Ltd* [1916] 2 Ch 426.
[71]   [1897] AC 22.
[72]   [1901] 1 Ch 279, 288.
[73]   *Bradbury v English Sewing Cotton Co Ltd* [1923] AC 744, 767 per Lord Wrenbury.
[74]   [1948] 1 KB 116.

namely their shares: 'Shareholders are not, in the eyes of the law, part owners of the undertaking. The undertaking is something different from the totality of the share-holdings'.[75]

In some circumstances shareholders will be able to obtain more than just the market value of his individual shares at any given time, for instance where the number of shares held gives that shareholder effective control over the company's affairs. However, in that case the shareholder is regarded as selling more than merely his parcel of shares. He is also selling that element of control, which has value. This does not interfere with the premise set out in *Short v Treasury Commissioners*. The holder of a block of shares in a company is in no real sense the owner of a proportionate part of the undertaking.

It seems clear, then, that shareholders do not own the assets of the company, nor do they hold a proportionate share of the company. What they do own are the shares themselves.[76] Once allotted the shares in a company become the assets of the sharehold-ers.[77] In many ways the proprietary nature of the ownership of shares is like the proprietary nature of debt securities,[78] in that shares can be transferred by the legal owner, they can be held on trust, and they survive the insolvency of a trustee or authorised transferee.[79]

Shares are a bundle of intangible property rights which shareholders receive from the company in return for their contribution of cash or non-cash assets to the company. The issue is to define the nature of this bundle of rights. One of the starting points for defining the rights attached to the shares is the company's constitution, primarily its articles. By virtue of section 33 of the Companies Act 2006[80] the articles form a contractual relationship between a company and its members,[81] and also between the members inter se. This is a peculiar form of contract.[82] Its binding force is derived from the terms of the statute, not from any bargain struck by the parties;[83] it is binding only so far as it affects the qua member interests of the members;[84] it can be altered by special resolution without

---

[75]   Ibid, 122 per Evershed LJ.

[76]   Indeed there is Australian authority that a company has no proprietary rights in its own shares: *Pilmer v Duke Group Ltd (in liquidation)* (2001) 75 ALJR 1067; (2001) 38 ACSR 121; [2001] 2 BCLC 773 (High Court of Australia) discussed in DD Prentice and R Nolan, 'The issue of shares – compensating the company for loss' [2002] *Law Quarterly Review* 180. This point is discussed at pages 130–32.

[77]   Shares are treated as personal property despite the ownership of land by the company: Companies Act 2006, s 541.

[78]   See page 315.

[79]   See generally the discussion at pages 320–21.

[80]   Previously Companies Act 1985, s 14. Section 33 of the Companies Act 2006 actually refers to the 'provisions of a company's constitution' binding the various parties, ie it includes provisions in the articles and in other constitutional documents (Companies Act 2006, s 17).

[81]   The members are the original subscribers to the memorandum and those persons who subsequently agree to become members and whose names are entered on the register of members: Companies Act 2006, s 112.

[82]   *Bratton Seymour Service Company Ltd v Oxborough* [1992] BCC 471, 475 per Steyn LJ.

[83]   The shareholder may seek to enforce it by seeking a declaration or injunction against the company for breach of the statutory contract. It may be possible for a shareholder to obtain damages from the company (Companies Act 2006, s 655 which reverses *Houldsworth v Glasgow City Bank* (1879–80) LR 5 App Cas 317) although there is no clear authority that a damages claim would be allowed by the courts, given the special nature of the statutory contract. Breach of the provisions of the company's constitution may also give rise to an unfair prejudice claim under Companies Act 2006, s 994.

[84]   *Hickman v Kent or Romney Marsh Sheepbreeders Association* [1915] 1 Ch 881, thus if an article purports to give someone the right to hold a position such as company solicitor or director those articles are not enforceable under the statutory contract cf *Quin & Axtens Ltd v Salmon* [1909] AC 442 which suggests that members should be able to enforce all the articles of the company, but the courts have tended to adopt the more restrictive approach.

the consent of all of the contracting parties;[85] it is not defeasible on the grounds of misrepresentation, common law mistake in equity, undue influence or duress; and it cannot be rectified on the grounds of mistake.

In addition to rights which may be specifically set out in the articles, or other constitutional documents, the interests of shareholders are also governed by statute and case law. For example, as we have seen, even if the articles state that the shareholders are entitled to a seven per cent dividend per annum, this right will be subject to the provisions of the Companies Act 2006 which provide that dividends may only be paid out of 'accumulated, realised profits…less its accumulated, realised losses'.[86] If that pot of money is not available in any given year, then no dividend can be declared. Likewise, the courts have created a number of presumptions which govern the rights attaching to shares, which will apply unless specifically disapplied by the articles. An example is the presumption that all shareholders are entitled to share equally in any surplus assets of the company which remain after all the debts and liabilities have been discharged and the nominal amount of the share capital has been repaid to shareholders.[87] These presumptions can be particularly important when new classes of shares are created.

So the nature of the rights attached to shares can be found by examining the company's constitutional documents, and the general law governing companies. However, the question of the content of those rights is still unanswered. Returning to the Farwell J quotation above, it is clear that the primary interest of a shareholder in a company is as an investor: a share is 'is an interest measured by a sum of money'. The shareholder pays a sum of money in the hope of earning a return. The primary interest of a shareholder in a company is therefore financial: a shareholder expects to earn a return on the investment in the form of dividends and capital growth. Of course there may be other rights attached to the share as well, such as the right to vote, or the right to appoint a director. The question arises, however, whether these latter interests are core to a shareholder's rights in the company, ie part of the default rights which form an intrinsic part of holding a share in a company, or whether shares can be regarded as merely a contractual entitlement to a portion of the income stream of the company.[88]

The idea that ownership of a share only gives the holder an entitlement to the capitalised income stream flowing from that share has been rejected by the High Court of Australia in *Gambotto v WCP Ltd*.[89] The question for the High Court of Australia in that case was whether it was lawful for the majority shareholders to alter the articles of the company in order to acquire compulsorily the shares of the minority shareholders. The High Court held the expropriation to be unlawful on the basis that it was oppressive to the minority shareholder even though the price offered was fair taking account not only of the current market value of the shares but also the dividends and future prospects of the

---

[85]   Eg the articles can be amended by special resolution (Companies Act 2006, s 21) subject only to the requirement that the power be exercised bona fide in the best interests of the company (*Allen v Gold Reefs of West Africa Ltd* [1900] 1 Ch 656).

[86]   Companies Act 2006, s 830(2).

[87]   *Birch v Cropper* (1889) 14 App Cas 525.

[88]   HG Manne, 'Our Two Corporation Systems: Law and Economics' (1967) 53 *Virginia Law Review* 259; RM Buxbaum, 'Corporate Legitimacy, Economic Theory, and Legal Doctrine' (1984) 45 *Ohio State Law Journal* 515.

[89]   (1995) 182 CLR 432, 447 (HC Aust).

company. It was also accepted that there were considerable tax and administrative advantages for the company if the expropriation was allowed to proceed. It is notable that the complainant in this case held just 0.2 per cent of the shares of the company. However, according to the court, to allow the expropriation would be to tilt the balance 'too far in favour of commercial expediency'. The High Court stated that '[a] share is liable to modification or destruction in appropriate circumstances, but is more than a "capitalised dividend stream": it is a form of investment that confers proprietary rights on the investor'.[90]

This does not seem to be the correct approach. Although there may be additional rights and interests which shareholders regard as being an incident of their relationship with a company, especially in a small company, such as the right to be involved in the management of the company, or the right to have a voice in setting company policy, these are rights and interests which are not protected by reason of holding a share in the company. They are not a part of the default package involved in being a shareholder in a company. Those rights need to be protected in other ways, for example via a separate contract, either a shareholders agreement, or a service contract, depending on the nature of the rights to be protected. They can also be protected via bargained-for amendments to the articles of association, and of course rights placed in the articles of association can now be entrenched.[91] Even if the agreement is informal, the minority shareholder may be able to rely upon it to demonstrate that she has been unfairly prejudiced if the rights are subsequently removed.[92] Of course minority protection of this kind will, in general, reduce the flexibility and freedom of the majority to run the company as they see fit, in accordance with the usual majority rule principle, and so is likely to have cost consequences. If minority shareholders want to bargain for these additional protections they are likely to have to pay for them. The more appropriate way to regard the default rights of a shareholder is as a capitalised income stream.

English law has not adopted the approach favoured by the High Court of Australia in *Gambotto*. In relation to alterations of articles cases the English courts apply the *Allen v Gold Reefs of West Africa Ltd*[93] test, ie whether the alteration is bona fide in the best interests of the company. They have adopted a subjective test of bona fides,[94] with the burden of proof on the person challenging the alteration.[95] It has been stated by Lord Hoffmann that the approach in *Gambotto* 'has no support in English authority'.[96] In practical terms as long as 'there are grounds on which reasonable men could come to the same decision' as the majority shareholders, the minority will not succeed in overturning

---

[90]   Ibid, 447.

[91]   Companies Act 2006, s 22 cf *Russell v Northern Bank Development Corp Ltd* [1992] 1 WLR 588.

[92]   Companies Act 2006, s 994. See *O'Neill v Phillips* [1999] 1 WLR 1092.

[93]   [1900] 1 Ch 656.

[94]   *Citco Banking Corp NV v Pusser's Ltd* [2007] UKPC 13; [2007] BCC 205, approving Scrutton LJ in *Shuttleworth v Cox Brothers and Co (Maidenhead) Ltd* [1927] 2 KB 9, 23.

[95]   Ibid, [18] endorsing *Peters' American Delicacy Company Ltd v Heath* (1939) 61 CLR 457, 482 per Latham CJ (HC Aust).

[96]   Ibid, [20].

alterations of articles endorsed by the majority.[97] The more obvious, and possibly more appropriate, route for disgruntled minorities will often be via an unfair prejudice petition.[98]

However, in the leading case on unfair prejudice, the House of Lords' decision in *O'Neill v Phillips*,[99] Lord Hoffmann made it clear that if the majority make an offer to buy out the minority at a fair price[100] any exclusion of the minority shareholder would not be unfair and the respondent would be entitled to have the petition struck out as showing no reasonable cause of action.[101] Given that the most common remedy awarded by the courts is an order that the petitioner's shares be bought out at a fair price this is a sensible approach designed to reduce the costs of such petitions, which are notoriously large. However, this approach is in accordance with the view that a share in a company comprises a sum of money and nothing more per se. Provided adequate compensation is offered for the removal of those shares (and of course that process of valuation is not straightforward in private companies) no wrong is done to the shareholder. A similar approach is followed in takeover situations. It is well accepted that once the offeror reaches the 90 per cent threshold then the remaining minority shareholder(s) can be required to sell their shares to the offeror on the same terms and therefore at the same price as the offer made for all the shares of the company, which will inevitably be at a premium to the market price (squeeze-out rights).[102]

The starting point for this discussion was the view that the pre-eminent position of shareholders in a solvent company can be justified by their ownership of the company. However, shareholders do not own the assets of the company, or a part share of the company itself. They own their shares, which entitles them to a bundle of intangible property rights in return for their cash or non-cash contribution to the company. Further, these intangible rights primarily consist of rights to a capitalised income stream from the company, ie can be measured in terms of cash. Any further rights, such as the right to be involved in management, need to be protected in other ways. This is not to suggest that shareholders do not have proprietary rights of some kind, clearly they do, albeit that those rights can be expropriated in certain circumstances. However, at least as a default position, what they appear to 'own' is a right to a sum of money (the capitalised income stream from their shares) in return for the payment of consideration for their shares. However, on this basis, they do not look dissimilar to creditors of the company. In one sense they

---

[97]   *Shuttleworth v Cox Brothers and Co (Maidenhead) Ltd* [1927] 2 KB 9, 23 per Scrutton LJ. Interestingly, that majority decision can include the votes of the shareholders who are advantaged by the alteration (see *Citco Banking Corp NV v Pusser's Ltd* [2007] UKPC 13; [2007] BCC 205, [27] cf the suggestion made in *Rights & Issues Investment Trust v Stylo Shoes Ltd* [1965] Ch 250 that these shares might have to be discounted). In this area of company law the general principle that a shareholder's vote is a piece of property that can be used as he or she sees fit remains good law (*Pender v Lushington* (1877) LR 6 Ch D 70) despite amendments to this principle introduced in relation to other aspects of company law (see Companies Act 2006, s 239 regarding voting to ratify a director's breach of duty).

[98]   Companies Act 2006, s 994.

[99]   [1999] 1 WLR 1092.

[100]   Lord Hoffmann provides guidance in *O'Neill* as to what this fair price includes in the context of an unfair prejudice petition (ibid, 1107). It will generally not be discounted for a minority holding, and where litigation has been commenced the reasonable offer would include on offer of costs as well.

[101]   [1999] 1 WLR 1092, 1107.

[102]   Companies Act 2006, ss 979–982. Squeeze-out rights are discussed in detail in 12.3.1.3.

therefore become just the providers of one form of the company's capital,[103] although the fact that their entitlement is not fixed remains a key difference.

One theoretical model has been developed in recent years which denies the 'ownership' model of company law. This is the nexus of contracts theory of company law[104] which treats the company as predominantly a web of contracts that link the various participants. On this analysis the function of company law is the facilitation of parties' bargains, and corporate personality is no more than convenient shorthand for the complex arrangements worked out between the various participants in the company. This theory reduces the company to the rights and duties of individuals, rights which require no further justification than that which already inheres in the notion of private rights.

However, this theory is problematic in a number of ways, and in particular it struggles to explain convincingly either the considerable amount of mandatory legislation that attaches to companies,[105] or indeed the basic fact of separate legal personality.[106] This theory also relies on an idea of contract (in which the parties have personal autonomy and can fix their bargain as they please) which does not seem an accurate description of many typical relationships within a company. For example, as discussed, while technically a contract, the articles of association are heavily overlaid by statute and cannot be regarded as a contract in any normal sense. In particular, the constitution of the vast majority of companies does not result from any real bargaining between the participants.[107] However, the shortcomings of the nexus of contracts theory does not mean that contract is not important as a doctrinal explanation of the rights of shareholders in a company. Clearly contract has played, and continues to play, an important role in UK company law, which provides the company's constitution, primarily the company's articles following the Companies Act 2006,[108] with contractual status.

The argument advanced here does not depend on the adoption of the nexus of contracts approach. What this discussion has sought to demonstrate, however, is that the

---

[103]   EF Fama, 'Agency Problems and the Theory of the Firm' (1980) 88 *Journal of Political Economy* 288.

[104]   See FH Easterbrook and DR Fischel, *The Economic Structure of Corporate Law* (Cambridge MA, Harvard University Press, 1991) and 'The Corporate Contract' (1989) 89 *Columbia Law Review* 1416; MC Jensen and WH Meckling, 'Theory of the Firm: Managerial Behaviour, Agency Costs and Ownership Structure' [1976] *Journal of Financial Economics* 305 and B Cheffins, *Company Law: Theory Structure and Operation* (Oxford, Clarendon Press, 1997).

[105]   MA Eisenberg, 'The Structure of Corporation Law' (1989) 89 *Columbia Law Review* 1461, 1486. Proponents of the contractual approach tend to accept that some mandatory legislation may be justifiable but suggest that it should be kept to a minimum and where possible parties should be able to make their own bargain in accordance with prevailing market forces see eg Easterbrook and Fischel, *The Economic Structure of Corporate Law,* ibid, 21–2 and B Cheffins, *Company Law: Theory, Structure and Operation* (Oxford, Clarendon Press, 1997) chs 3–4 where he considers the arguments for and against state intervention.

[106]   Eg Cheffins concedes that the contractual characterisation is 'at odds with the legal conceptualization of a company': see Cheffins, *Theory Structure and Operation* ibid, 32. This theory also fails to explain the processes by which company law is developed. It is clear that the courts and Parliament are motivated by considerations other than what, ex ante, the parties would have agreed to, when developing the law.

[107]   MA Eisenberg, 'The Structure of Corporation Law' (1989) 89 *Columbia Law Review* 1461; V Brudney, 'Corporate Governance, Agency Costs and the Rhetoric of Contract' (1985) 85 *Columbia Law Review* 1403. Private equity companies are an exception: see chapter 14.

[108]   Companies Act 2006, s 17. Under the Companies Act 1985 the company's constitutional documents comprised the memorandum and articles of association. However, the role of the memorandum has been substantially diminished by the 2006 Act (see Companies Act 2006, s 8) in response to a recommendation that companies should have a single constitutional document (Company Law Review, *Modern Company Law for a Competitive Economy: Final Report*, URN 01/942, July 2001, para 9.4).

shareholders cannot be said to own the company in any meaningful sense and that, further, ownership cannot provide a satisfactory explanation for their pre-eminent position in a solvent company.

The shareholders' pre-eminent position in the solvent company needs to be explained on another basis, namely that they are the residual claimants to the firm's income. As we have seen, the definition of equity share capital within the Companies Act 2006 is founded on the notion of residual claimants.[109] It is they, rather than the creditors, who will benefit from the capital gains that flow from the company's success but also they that will lose first should the enterprise fail. It is important to appreciate that the risk which the shareholders take is not merely the possibility that they will lose their initial stake, ie the price paid for their securities. In a successful company with undistributed reserves, the market value of the shares is likely to be higher than the price paid for the shares and it is the risk of this loss which the shareholders face if things go wrong. These factors give the shareholders (in particular, the ordinary shareholders) the incentive to monitor management, and it is for this reason that company law gives the shareholders a significant corporate governance role.

3.2.1.3.3   The Corporate Governance Role of Shareholders

The actual division of powers between the board and the shareholders is a matter for the articles,[110] but by far the most common scenario is the one in which substantial authority to manage the company is given to the board.[111] Nevertheless shareholders have a number of important governance entitlements by which they can monitor the performance of the board. In very small companies where the shareholders and directors are effectively the same people, these governance rights are largely meaningless, and any monitoring of the directors will need to be achieved by other means, such as monitoring by the company's creditors, discussed at 3.2.2.4. Once there is a difference in identity between the directors and shareholders then monitoring of the board by the shareholders becomes possible. If there is a single large shareholder that is not on the board then it is possible to introduce provisions into the articles giving substantial management powers (and perhaps veto rights) to that shareholder. In private equity companies, discussed in chapter fourteen, the private equity fund is likely to have representation on the board of the company, but is also likely to strengthen its oversight of management via provisions in the articles.

One of the most significant governance rights held by the shareholders is the right to remove the directors at any time by an ordinary resolution.[112] This provision expressly applies notwithstanding anything to the contrary in any agreement between the company and the director,[113] and potentially gives the shareholders significant influence in the

---

[109]   Companies Act 2006, s 548.

[110]   *Automatic Self-Cleansing Filter Syndicate Co Ltd v Cuninghame* [1906] 2 Ch 34. This is subject to a limited range of matters where statute requires the participation of shareholders in the decisions, for example alterations to the company's articles can only be made by a special resolution of the shareholders: Companies Act 2006, s 21.

[111]   For both public and private companies the default provisions, stated in the model sets of articles give substantial authority to the board: See Model Articles for Private Companies Limited by Shares, art 3; Model Articles for Public Companies, art 3: The Companies (Model Articles) Regulations 2008 (SI 3229/2008), Sch 1 and Sch 3. Despite these provisions, the general meeting retains default powers in the event that the board cannot exercise its powers for some reason, such as where there is a deadlock on the board (*Barron v Potter* [1914] 1 Ch 895) or where an effective quorum cannot be obtained (*Foster v Foster* [1916] 1 Ch 532).

[112]   Companies Act 2006, s 168.

[113]   Ibid, s 168(1).

affairs of the company. However a number of points need to be made. First, the section itself acknowledges that the director can protect himself by requiring compensation to be paid in the event of the termination of the service contract. While this will not per se prevent removal, if the compensation is substantial enough it may help to entrench the director in practice. Second, in relation to private companies, the courts have authorised provisions which provide an indirect way around this section. The House of Lords has held that the object of this section can be frustrated by a provision in the articles attaching increased votes to a director's shares on a resolution to remove him, thus enabling him to defeat the resolution.[114] It has also been recognised by the courts that the removal of a director in a 'quasi-partnership' company, ie a small private company that is a joint venture company, or possibly a company operating in effect an incorporated partnership, might constitute unfair prejudice justifying a buy-out of shares,[115] or possibly even a compulsory winding up of the company.[116] Third, once shareholdings become very dispersed it may be difficult for the shareholders to co-ordinate sufficiently to make this mechanism very valuable. In public companies there is also a problem of shareholder apathy which might mean that shareholders do not exercise this governance right in any meaningful way. The corporate governance role of shareholders in public companies is discussed in detail at 10.2.2.

In addition to the right to remove directors, shareholders have other important governance rights. In a solvent company, as we have seen, directors owe their duties to the company and the company for this purpose is regarded as comprising the long-term interests of the shareholders.[117] The shareholders have the right to ratify directors' wrongdoing[118] and to litigate on behalf of the company in certain circumstances.[119] Shareholders also have substantial control rights in relation to a number of corporate transactions. Company law requires transactions to which the counterparty is a director or a connected party[120] to be approved by the shareholders.[121] These include substantial property transactions[122] and corporate loans.[123] Additional governance rights are given to the shareholders in public companies; these are discussed further at 10.2.2. These rights are potentially very significant, although in the very smallest companies, where the directors and shareholders are the same people, the rights are meaningless, and in the very largest companies with dispersed share ownership, shareholder engagement in these issues

---

[114]   *Bushell v Faith* [1970] AC 1099.

[115]   Companies Act 2006, s 994. For discussion of the circumstances in which this section may be applied see *O'Neill v Phillips* [1999] 1 WLR 1092.

[116]   Ie a compulsory winding up on the just and equitable ground under Insolvency Act 1986, s 122(1)(g): *Ebrahimi v Westbourne Galleries Ltd* [1973] AC 360.

[117]   Companies Act 2006, s 172(1), discussed at 3.2.1.3.1.

[118]   *North-West Transportation Co Ltd v Beatty* (1887) LR 12 App Cas 589 and see now Companies Act 2006, s 239.

[119]   It is generally the board that takes the decision to litigate, but the majority can prima facie control this decision via their control of the board. The minority may be able to make use of the derivative action procedure: Companies Act 2006, ss 260–264 (England, Wales and Northern Ireland), ss 265–269 (Scotland). There is also the possibility of a using an unfair prejudice petition (Companies Act 2006, s 994) for this purpose (*Clark v Cutland* [2003] EWCA Civ 810; [2004] 1 WLR 783) although the extent of that option is far from clear (eg J Payne, 'Sections 459–461 Companies Act 1985: The Future of Shareholder Protection' [2005] *Cambridge Law Journal* 647).

[120]   Companies Act 2006, ss 252, 254.

[121]   Ibid, ss 177, 180.

[122]   Ibid, ss 190–196.

[123]   Ibid, ss 197–214.

may be limited. As discussed in 3.2.2.4 below the corporate governance role of debt may in some circumstances be more significant than that of equity.

3.2.2   The Position of the Creditors in a Solvent Company

As will be seen from the discussion in chapter two, there are many different types of creditors, who advance money to the company based on different contractual and proprietary structures. All creditors, however, have one thing in common: they are owed money by the company to which they have a legal right to payment at some time.[124] This right is usually, but not always, based on a pre-existing contract. Some creditors, such as trade creditors and tort claimants, have a right to a single payment, which they would like to be paid as soon as possible. However, most lenders who are in the business of providing finance do so in order to obtain an income stream, which, depending on the terms of the loan, will comprise interest or repayment of capital or a combination of both. In a sense, then, this contractual right to periodic payments can be compared and contrasted with the shareholders' right to a dividend, which is not contractually enforceable until the dividend is declared.[125]

Further, the payments to which the lender has a right are fixed, at least in the sense that they do not depend upon whether the company has made profits, although they may depend on other variables such as the current rate of interest. This means that, in relation to the lenders' right to income, they have no incentive for the company to engage in risky activity which increases profits, provided that sufficient profits are generated to meet the company's contractual obligations. In most financing structures, the profit which the lenders make comes from these periodic payments (loosely called 'interest' here), and so the lenders' incentive while the company is solvent is to keep the capital part of the loan outstanding for as long as possible so that they can make as much profit as possible. However, the lenders also have an incentive to ensure that the company remains solvent, since on insolvency it will lose not only the future profit of interest payments, but may lose the capital repayment, as discussed in the next paragraph.

Many lenders will also have a longer term contractual right to repayment of capital. This may be deeply subordinated or have a very long maturity date, as in a hybrid security.[126] Conversely, capital may be repaid totally through periodic payments, but the lender will usually have the right to accelerate repayment of the whole amount due if the borrower company defaults.[127] If the company remains solvent, this capital debt will eventually have to be repaid (unlike the capital contributed by the shareholders). This will often be by refinancing, so that the company just rolls over the debt with the same lenders or takes out new debt with different lenders. As mentioned above, most lenders do not have an incentive to seek early repayment, and would wish the lending relationship to go on for as long as possible if the company is solvent. However, the risk of losing the capital repayment if the company becomes insolvent is severe, and it is largely the protection

---

[124]   Even this is not entirely true. Those lenders who finance a company by purchasing its receivables (see 2.3.4.1) are actually owed nothing by the company so long as the proceeds from the assets are sufficient to cover the price. However, there is usually a contractual obligation for the company to make up any shortfall (see pages 233–34).

[125]   See page 58.

[126]   See 2.4.

[127]   See 5.2.3.

against this risk which is discussed below. It is a risk which all creditors bear equally although their claims rank ahead of all shareholders. Creditors are not, on the whole, protected by the general law, although the legal capital rules, discussed in chapter four, are one significant exception to that principle. Creditors generally have the ability to protect themselves by a variety of means, which are discussed above in chapter two, in the discussion following and in more detail in chapters five and six.

Proprietary means of protection, discussed in chapter six, improve a creditor's ranking when assets of an insolvent company are distributed,[128] and certain classes of creditors are given improved ranking by the general law.[129] It is, of course, only when the company is insolvent that the ranking of claims really matters, and, as discussed below, on insolvency not all creditors rank equally. When a company is solvent, ranking per se does not matter. We can see that from the two tests for insolvency under English law mentioned earlier.[130] If a company is balance sheet solvent its assets are greater than its liabilities, so that (in theory) all creditors could be paid, and if it is cash flow solvent it can pay its debts as they fall due so again creditors can be paid in due course. If we exclude the twilight period before insolvency from our consideration of a solvent company,[131] it might be thought that creditors have no concerns about repayment while the company is solvent. However, as this section will discuss, this view is not entirely accurate.

As well as improving their ranking on insolvency by taking proprietary protection, creditors can protect themselves by various contractual means, which are discussed in chapter five, and can also adjust to the dangers of insolvency by other means, such as increasing their price or refusing to contract. The ability of creditors to adjust has meant that there is little protection for creditors from the general law. However, there are some creditors who are said to be unable to adjust and who therefore might need statutory or other protection.

3.2.2.1   Non-adjusting Creditors[132]

To see who these non-adjusting creditors are, it is instructive to consider the types of creditor that exist. One could see creditors as falling into three categories: those who consciously extend credit to the company (whether in the form of loans or trade credit or otherwise), those who deal with the company without intending to extend credit, but who become creditors because the company becomes liable to them for breach of contract or otherwise (such as customers of goods or services), and those who have no prior contact with the company before becoming creditors (this category is mainly tort victims and the tax authorities).

The ability of some of the first category (lenders, investors and other financiers) to protect themselves and to influence the company's activities is discussed extensively throughout this book. Two categories of lenders other than financiers or suppliers may also be present. Directors may extend loans to the company, particularly when it is in

---

[128]   See 3.3.1.1.
[129]   See 3.3.1.2.
[130]   See page 56.
[131]   See pages 56–57.
[132]   The terminology 'adjusting' and 'non-adjusting' was first used in this context by L Bebchuk and J Fried, 'The Uneasy Case for the Priority of Secured Claims in Bankruptcy' (1996) 105 *Yale Law Journal* 857. For further discussion in the context of whether non-adjusting creditors should have some priority over secured creditors, see 6.6.2.3.

difficulties. Such loans are usually unsecured. Other companies in the same group may also lend to the company, and often this lending will be unsecured and, maybe, subordinated.[133] It should be remembered that directors and group companies may also guarantee loans to the company, and so will be unsecured creditors in any insolvency through their right of subrogation.[134]

Trade creditors also have means of protection at their disposal, although they may not be able to use them fully because of market pressure.[135] First, they can reflect the credit risks they face in the prices that they charge, either generally for all customers or in relation to a particular customer.[136] If they supply goods, they can protect themselves by the use of retention of title clauses, which are effective in relation to the goods themselves though not as regards the products of the goods or the proceeds of sale.[137] Certain protection is also afforded by the general law: under the Sale of Goods Act an unpaid seller has a lien on the goods before delivery,[138] and a right to stop the goods in transit if the buyer becomes insolvent.[139] These devices are not available to those who supply services, and they have to rely on more general measures (which are also available to those supplying goods). These include requiring payment in advance (if the market will bear this), spreading the risk of customer default by contracting with a wide number and variety of customers and monitoring the credit of customers so that they can refuse to supply to a customer in difficulties. This latter device depends on the terms of the original contract: either the supplier has to protect itself with a term enabling it to terminate the contract if the customer gets into difficulties, or it has to operate on the basis of separate contracts for each supply, which involves the risk of losing the business for reasons other than the customer's financial position.

Those in the second category will find it much harder to protect themselves. A pre-paying customer could protect itself against non-delivery of goods by providing that property in the goods passes on payment rather than on delivery.[140] More contentiously, it is possible to ensure that payments in advance are held on trust for customers until the goods or services are provided.[141] Ongoing customers may be able to negotiate a retention fund, so that not all the price is paid until they are satisfied that the goods or services are of a certain quality. Further, customers who have not paid, or who have a running account with the company, may be protected by set-off.[142] Otherwise, customers just have to rely on diversification, so that they are exposed to the risk of non-payment by each contractual partner only to a small extent. They can also refuse to contract if they discover that the company is in difficulties, although, of course, they are not in a position to monitor and would have to rely on signals from lender creditors or possibly from the market.

---

[133] We are indebted to Sandra Frisby for this information, which she drew from her extensive empirical research on insolvency.

[134] See 5.3.1.3.3.

[135] V Finch, 'Security, Insolvency and Risk: Who Pays the Price?' (1999) 62 *Modern Law Review* 633, 644.

[136] The latter may be difficult as it depends on expensive information gathering which may not be economic for small creditors. However, it is possible that information may be obtained by free-riding on the monitoring activities of other lenders.

[137] See 6.2.5.3.

[138] Sale of Goods Act 1979, s 41.

[139] Ibid, s 44.

[140] Ibid, s 17.

[141] *Re Kayford Ltd* [1975] 1 WLR 279; *Barclays Bank Ltd v Quistclose Investments Ltd* [1970] AC 567.

[142] See 5.2.4.

Employees are even less able to protect themselves, since they cannot diversify and are not usually in a position to change jobs quickly. Those providing services as an independent contractor fall, at least in theory, into the first category.

Those in the third category are truly non-adjusting creditors and cannot protect themselves at all. The tax authorities are, however, in a slightly different position, since although they cannot refuse to 'do business' with the company, they can be pro-active in enforcing the debt, or at least come to an arrangement with the company in relation to outstanding indebtedness. Tort victims are the least able to adjust, but they have some protection in the UK from the Third Party (Rights against Insurers) Act 2010.[143]

3.2.2.2   The Risks to Creditors from the Operation of a Solvent Company

The operations of a solvent company can create risk to a creditor. As discussed above, there is the risk that the company will in the future be unable to continue borrowing from the creditor and therefore cease to be a source of valuable profit. However, the more serious risk is that the company will, in the future but before the creditor is paid, become unable to pay the creditor's whole debt. These risks can be manifested in a number of ways. Some risks come from outside sources, such as an economic downturn which reduces the market for the company's products, or a sudden change in government policy. Other risks come from the conduct of the directors, who are managing the company. The directors may be fraudulent (and operating for their own gain) or incompetent. They can fail to react effectively to external events and forces, in a way which has a deleterious effect on the value of the company.[144] Alternatively, they may be acting in the way suggested in the previous section: in the best interests of the shareholders, but in situations where the interests of the shareholders and the creditors diverge, thus creating what are called 'agency problems'.

In many ways, when the company is solvent, the interests of the creditors and the shareholders are broadly similar. However, because the shareholders benefit from any rise in the value of the company, they are likely to favour riskier projects which may increase that value, while creditors would be happier with lower risk projects which merely retain the status quo.[145] What the general law's response to this divergence of interest should be is discussed in chapter four; this section will discuss the responses that creditors can have by way of individual adjustment.

These risks could manifest themselves in a number of ways.[146] First, the company might, after borrowing from a creditor, incur further debts to others which do not result

---

[143]   For further discussion see pages 297–98.

[144]   GG Triantis and RJ Daniels, 'The Role of Debt in Interactive Corporate Governance' (1995) 83 *California Law Review* 1073, 1075.

[145]   See pages 54–56 This view, while representing orthodox finance theory, is not universally held, even in relation to the run-up to insolvency. See DG Baird and RK Rasmussen, 'Private Debt and the Missing Lever of Corporate Governance' (2006) 154 *University of Pennsylvania Law Review* 1209, 1246, F Tung, 'Leverage in the Board Room: The Unsung Influence of Private Lenders in Corporate Governance' (2009) 57 *UCLA Law Review* 115 and JM Shepherd, F Tung and AH Yoon, 'What Else Matters for Corporate Governance?: The Case of Bank Monitoring' (2008) 88 *Boston University Law Review* 991.

[146]   See CW Smith and JB Warner, 'On Financial Contracting: An Analysis of Bond Covenants' (1979) 7 *Journal of Financial Economics* 117; J Day and P Taylor, 'Bankers' Perspectives on the Role of Covenants in Debt Contracts' [1996] *Journal of International Banking Law* 201, 202; W Bratton, 'Bond Covenants and Creditor Protection: Economics and Law, Theory and Practice, Substance and Process' (2006) 7 *European Business Organization Law Review* 39.

in an equivalent increase in assets. Supposing A Ltd borrows £100,000 from B and has £200,000 worth of assets. B at this point can be sure that it will be paid back. However, if A Ltd then borrows £100,000 from C, which it uses to pay its ongoing wages bill, B's position begins to look much more precarious. It is less of a problem if the money A Ltd borrows from C is used to buy a new machine worth £100,000, as A Ltd's assets rise to £300,000. However, even then, B's position is made worse as it will have to share the £100,000 'cushion' with C whereas before it had it all to itself. This problem is called 'claim dilution'.[147]

Second, the company might withdraw assets from the pool available to the creditors for repayment. Certain withdrawals are obviously necessary for the operation of the company (such as those for the payment of debts) but others may be less obviously in the interests of the creditors. This is particularly true where the recipients of the assets are the shareholders. One such withdrawal would be the payment of dividends, another the return of capital. Even if the withdrawn assets do not go to the shareholders, they may go to fund risky projects, which, if they fail, mean that the asset pool is reduced. Third, the company might substitute the assets which it had when the creditor made the loan for other, more risky assets, which potentially benefit the shareholders if the risk pays off and the company increases in value, but will be detrimental to the creditors if the risk does not pay off.

It is also sometimes said that there is a risk of underinvestment, where some of the benefits of more investment would accrue to the creditors rather than the shareholders. This would mean that the shareholders do not have enough incentive to invest and maximise the potential gains.[148] Benefits from investment would accrue to the creditors where the debt is risky on the basis that investment makes the debt less risky and therefore more valuable. This would be likely to occur either where the company is balance sheet insolvent (in that it has borrowed more than its assets) or near balance sheet insolvent, so that a growth in the value of the company is of real benefit to the creditors, but gives no benefit to the shareholders. If there is underinvestment, the creditors lose out on this benefit, and the shareholders have an incentive to divert value from the company to themselves so that they can use it for projects for which they will obtain all the benefit. However, the danger of underinvestment appears to recede the more solvent the company is.

Can the general law protect creditors against the risks identified above in any way? One possible method is by requiring a company to have a certain amount of capital. English law requires this in relation to public companies, and these rules are discussed below in chapter four. Certain types of financial companies are required to have particular amounts and types of capital under the capital adequacy rules: these are described briefly in chapter

---

[147]   CW Smith and JB Warner, 'On Financial Contracting: An Analysis of Bond Covenants' (1979) 7 *Journal of Financial Economics* 117, 118

[148]   SC Myers, 'Determinants of Corporate Borrowing' (1977) *Journal of Financial Economics* 147; CW Smith and JB Warner, 'On Financial Contracting: An Analysis of Bond Covenants' (1979) 7 *Journal of Financial Economics* 117, 199; R Scott 'A Relational Theory of Secured Financing' (1986) 86 *Columbia Law Review* 901, 920; W Bratton, 'Bond Covenants and Creditor Protection: Economics and Law, Theory and Practice, Substance and Process' (2006) 7 *European Business Organization Law Review* 39, 47.

two.[149] However, generally it is left to creditors to protect themselves, either by taking proprietary interests, discussed in chapter six, or by the contractual means described below and in chapter five.

One very simple way in which creditors can protect themselves against these risks is by pricing the cost of debt in a way which reflects them. If it were possible to do this accurately, creditors would be indifferent to the risks and would take no steps to reduce them. There are, however, various reasons why this does not happen. The first is that companies would rather agree to restrictions on their activity than have to pay the full cost of the risks generated by their unrestricted activity. Another is that neither creditors nor companies can foresee everything that is going to happen and therefore pricing of risk can never be wholly accurate: it is much safer for creditors to agree to contractual or proprietary ways to mitigate at least some risks so that the degree of adjustment of price to mitigate risk is limited.[150] Further, insolvency is costly to the company as well as to the creditors, so even if the creditors could be protected against a strong risk of insolvency by an adjustment in price, there is still a loss of overall value. This gives the company an incentive to agree to restrictions.[151] Another reason is that at least some creditors are not in a position to adjust the price or to impose restrictions on the company. The extent to which creditors can or cannot adjust is discussed elsewhere.[152]

3.2.2.3   Restrictions on the Company's Activities

Restrictions on the company's activities by creditors take the form of terms ('covenants') in the borrower/lender contract. The actual content and operation of them is discussed in detail in chapter five. The grant of security by the company also has a restrictive effect, and this is discussed in detail in chapter six. Certain important points about covenants can, however, be made here. Although the terms themselves are reasonably standard, the extent to which they are included in any given contract is a matter of the bargaining power of the parties, and what each party is able to, and wants to, achieve. Lenders will want as much protection from restrictions as possible, while borrowers will want maximum flexibility of operation, and therefore as few restrictions as possible. In theory the level of restriction could be a direct trade off against the price paid for the loan, so that the most expensive loan would be covenant-free, and the cheapest would include total restriction. In practice, other factors also play a part.[153]

The credit risk of the borrower is critical, so that a borrower who is a poor credit risk will only be able to borrow on reasonably tight covenants, and lenders will not lend to such a borrower below a certain level of covenant protection, at whatever price. Conversely, a strongly credit-worthy borrower will be able to borrow on the basis of few restrictions, and is likely to value flexibility of operation above the benefits of a very low interest rate.[154]

---

[149]   See page 26.
[150]   A Keay, 'A Theoretical Analysis of The Director's Duty to Consider Creditor Interests: The Progressive School's Approach' [2004] *Journal of Corporate Law Studies* 307, 321.
[151]   K Schmidt, 'The Economics of Covenants as a Means of Efficient Creditor Protection' (2006) 7 *European Business Organization Law Review* 89.
[152]   See 3.2.2.1 and 6.6.2.3.
[153]   W Bratton, 'Bond Covenants and Creditor Protection: Economics and Law, Theory and Practice, Substance and Process' (2006) 7 *European Business Organization Law Review* 39, 74–75.
[154]   Ibid, 75.

The number of lenders is also important. Where there is one lender (such as in a bank loan), covenants tend to be much stronger than where there are large numbers of lenders, such as in a bond issue. This is partly because the bank is in a position to negotiate firm covenants from the start, while in a bond issue, the level of protection is set by the issuer at the level it thinks (or is advised) the market will bear.[155] It is also partly because the bank is in a better position to monitor and react to breaches of covenant, and can use such breaches as a trigger for renegotiation. This process is much more cumbersome where there are multiple lenders, especially where their identity is not known to the issuer, as in a bond issue.[156] Another relevant reason is that bonds are tradable, and so the holders are able to exit more easily; they often would prefer to do this, rather than go through the process of enforcing covenants and renegotiating.[157] Further, bond investors can diversify their holdings and spread their risk, so they are less affected by the financial distress of one issuer.[158] In fact, an important function of bond covenants is to protect the value of the bond, rather than (directly) against the risk of non-payment.[159] However, where the issuer also has a considerable amount of loan debt, bondholders may not wish to be at a disadvantage compared to the lenders, and the bond covenants may go some way to reflect those in the loan agreements, at least to the extent that this is practicable.[160] It might be thought that as syndicated loans became more easily traded, this would lead to a reduction in covenants: this, however, does not appear to have been the case. Such evidence as there is suggests that covenants have been kept reasonably strict,[161] partly because the lead bank often retains its stake, partly to reassure purchasers of the quality of the loan purchased and partly to enable purchasers either to monitor themselves or to rely on the lead bank's continued monitoring.

[155] This point is made forcefully by R Youard in 'Default in International Loan Agreements' (Part 2) [1986] *Journal of Business Law* 378, 382–3.

[156] J Markland, 'Cov-lite – the New Cutting Edge in Acquisition Finance' (2007) 22 *Journal of International Banking and Financial Law* 379. The use of a bond trustee may assist in the process of waiver of breach and renegotiation, but the costs are still considerable.

[157] It should be pointed out, however, that not all the bondholders can exit: the more holders who sell the more the price will drop and in the end there may be no buyers at all on the market.

[158] A bank lender, of course, will also diversify to some extent, by lending to a large number of borrowers, and by limiting the amount lent to any one borrower by taking part in syndicated loans. Now that bank debt is more easily tradable, the ability of a bank to protect itself through diversification has increased, see CK Whitehead, 'The Evolution of Debt: Covenants, the Credit Market, and Corporate Governance' (2009) 34 *Journal of Corporation Law* 641, 653.

[159] This can be seen, for example, by the structure of the negative pledge covenant in a Eurobond issue, see pages 160–61. The position is different where there is a significant credit risk, for example, in high yield bond issues, where covenants are likely to be stricter (for the distinction between investment grade bonds and high yield bonds, see pages 32–33).

[160] M Hartley, 'Bondholder Protections Revisited' (2010) 25 *Journal of International Banking and Financial Law* 219.

[161] S Drucker and M Puri, 'On Loan Sales, Loan Contracting, and Lending Relationships' (2008) 21 *Review of Financial Studies* 1, cited in F Tung, 'Leverage in the Board Room: The unsung influence of private lenders in corporate governance' (2009) 57 *UCLA Law Review* 115, 166; CK Whitehead, 'The Evolution of Debt: Covenants, The Credit Market, and Corporate Governance' (2009) 34 *Journal of Corporation Law* 641, 664.

The state of the market is also relevant to the strictness of the covenants. During the mid 2000s, when credit was very plentiful and borrowers were in a position to dictate terms, there was a growth in covenant-lite deals.[162] This situation has now changed considerably.[163]

3.2.2.4   The Corporate Governance Role of Debt

It is well recognised that corporate law faces a fundamental difficulty in giving broad discretion to the directors to run the company effectively, and yet constraining them from exercising that discretion in their own interests rather than in the interests of the shareholders and other stakeholders. In very small companies where the shareholders and the directors are effectively the same people, there is no danger of the directors abusing shareholder interests, although other stakeholders will not necessarily be protected. Once companies get larger, however, the separation of ownership and control means that the possibility of abuse does arise. The law has traditionally regarded shareholders as having an important monitoring role.[164] Whether shareholders operate as effective corporate monitors once the shareholding becomes very dispersed, for example in a public company context, is discussed at 10.2.2.[165] Other possible forms of corporate governance, once the company reaches this size, are the presence of non-executive directors,[166] and the role of takeovers to create a market for corporate control.[167] What has been less well recognised in the past is the possibility of a corporate governance role for creditors in a company.

Recently, however, more attention has focused on the role of creditors in influencing, and even controlling, the activities of the directors. Much of the literature in this area is from the US, and care has to be taken in transplanting the arguments into a UK context. However, much of it appears to be relevant to the operation of UK debt financing in the present market. The creditors have a close interest in how the company operates in the run-up to insolvency, when their financial interests are clearly prejudiced, and will seek to exercise their contractual and proprietary protection at that stage. What is examined here, however, is the extent to which creditors can influence the operation of a company when the company is solvent, as defined above. It should be remembered, of course, that only adjusting creditors who are in the first category discussed above[168] (lenders) are in a position to impose covenants and to have a significant role in corporate governance.[169] Comparisons will be made to the corporate governance role of both shareholders[170] and

---

[162]   J Markland, 'Cov-lite – the New Cutting Edge in Acquisition Finance' (2007) 22 *Journal of International Banking and Financial Law* 379. These forms of covenants were used particularly in the context of private equity transactions prior to the financial crisis, for discussion see 14.4.3.1.

[163]   See, for example, M Hartley, 'Bondholder Protections Revisited', (2010) 25 *Journal of International and Financial Law* 219.

[164]   See 3.2.1.3.3.

[165]   Whether the private equity companies operate as a more successful corporate governance model than publicly traded companies is assessed in 14.6.

[166]   An obligation is placed on companies with a premium listing in the UK to disclose in their annual report and the extent to which they have complied with the UK Corporate Governance Code. The Code sets out standards of good practice including the existence and role of non-executive directors within a company: Financial Reporting Council, *UK Corporate Governance Code*, June 2010.

[167]   Discussed further in 12.3.2.2.2.

[168]   See pages 74–75.

[169]   Those making loans are in a stronger position than bondholders, see pages 81–82.

[170]   Discussed at 3.2.1.3.3 in relation to companies generally and 10.2.2 in the context of publicly listed companies.

non-executive directors.[171] It should also be remembered that the mere existence of debt in a company's financial structure has a corporate governance function, since the directors have to run the company in such a way that the debt repayments can be made. Risky activity jeopardises the ability to make these payments, even though it may have potential benefits for shareholders.[172]

In order to protect a creditor from the agency conflicts discussed above, the covenants included in a typical debt contract will do a number of things.[173] First, certain activities will be prohibited, or prohibited under certain circumstances.[174] Thus a negative pledge will prohibit the grant of security over the borrower's assets,[175] and further borrowing may be prohibited if the borrower's debt/equity ratio rises beyond a certain prescribed level. Disposal of assets except in the ordinary course of business is likely to be prohibited, as is the declaration of dividends or other distributions to the shareholders beyond a certain percentage of net profits, and also substantial changes of business and mergers without the consent of the lender. There may also be limits on capital expenditure, or covenants which require repayment of debt on the occurrence of certain specified events. Secondly, the agreement will require the company to meet certain financial ratios in relation to cash flow and net worth.[176] Thirdly, it will require the company to furnish the lender with information about its financial position.[177] Fourthly, it will include a number of warranties of the company's financial and legal position at the time of the agreement, which continue throughout the life of the loan.[178]

The agreement will specify events of default, which will include breaches of the terms of the agreement, but are likely also to include non-breach events such as default in relation to another agreement, the onset of any sort of insolvency or enforcement proceedings, and other events which might affect the borrower's ability to repay the loan. The lender will have the right to accelerate the loan and terminate the agreement if an event of default occurs.[179]

These provisions put the lender in a strong position both to monitor the company's operations and to influence them. Let us first consider monitoring.[180] The borrower's obligation in the loan agreement to furnish financial and other information will vary according to the type of lender, as will the lender's ability to use information to monitor effectively. The lender in the best position to monitor is the single bank, who has a relationship with the borrower, and who is able to impose obligations on the borrower to provide financial information at very regular intervals.[181] Further, a bank may well also control the borrower's current account, and therefore be in a position to monitor its cash

---

[171] See page 80.
[172] See MC Jensen and WH Meckling, 'Theory of the Firm: Managerial Behaviour, Agency Costs and Ownership Structure' (1976) 3 *Journal of Financial Economics* 305, and see also the discussion at page 683.
[173] See 5.2.
[174] See 5.2.1.
[175] Ibid.
[176] See pages 168–69.
[177] See page 170.
[178] See 5.2.2.2.
[179] See 5.2.3.
[180] As pointed out by Triantis and Daniels, governance can be divided into two parts: monitoring and reaction. G Triantis and R Daniels, 'The Role of Debt in Interactive Corporate Governance' (1995) 83 *California Law Review* 1073, 1079.
[181] For a clear statement of the use made of monitoring by banks lending to small and medium sized businesses in the UK, see British Bankers Association, Statement of Principles (2009) 8–10.

flow on a daily basis.[182] In some cases, the bank may also have the right to appoint a director of the borrowing company.[183] Thus, in many ways, it can be argued that a bank is in a better position to monitor than non-executive directors.[184] Bondholders, however, are less able to monitor effectively, because they are numerous and diverse. Even where there is a bond trustee, the terms of the trust deed normally exclude all active obligations to monitor and the trustee is only obliged to receive certificates of compliance from the issuer.[185] A single bank is therefore the most effective and the lowest cost monitor. Where a company raises finance from both bonds and from a bank, it is usually more efficient for the bank to do the primary monitoring and for the bondholders (and other creditors) to rely on the signals generated by the bank's monitoring and its reaction to it.[186]

Although the fact that the state of the company is being monitored is likely to make a difference to the behaviour of directors, monitoring by itself will not enable a lender to have a significant role in corporate governance. It is the restrictions contained in the covenants which restrain certain types of behaviour on the part of the directors and encourage other types of behaviour. Directors will, in general, wish to comply with the obligations and to avoid breach. This is partly in order to improve the company's reputation as a 'good' borrower, which may improve its ability to obtain cheaper finance in the future or finance with less restrictive covenants.[187] It is also partly to avoid the consequences of breach, which are discussed in the next paragraph.

The main way in which a lender can influence how a company is run is through the dialogue that arises if a covenant is breached. It may seem strange to see a breach as giving rise to a dialogue, since in theory it gives the lender power to accelerate the loan and terminate the contract.[188] This, however, is the 'nuclear weapon' which could well send the borrower into insolvency, and would at the very least terminate the relationship between the lender and the borrower. As pointed out above,[189] a lender does not wish to lose the profit resulting from the lending relationship, and will therefore wish to keep it going so long as its recovery of capital is not jeopardised by the risk of insolvency. Thus, although the threat of acceleration is always there in the background, and is used by lenders to give them 'leverage' over the borrower,[190] the actual influence is achieved by the renegotiation

---

[182]   F Tung, 'Leverage in the Board Room: The unsung influence of private lenders in corporate governance' (2009) *UCLA Law Review* 115, 140.

[183]   This is rare in the UK (E Ferran, *Principles of Corporate Finance Law* (Oxford, Oxford University Press, 2008) 344, but appears to be common in the US (F Tung, 'Leverage in the Board Room: The unsung influence of private lenders in corporate governance'(2009) *UCLA Law Review* 115, 139 citing RS Krozner and PE Strahan, 'Bankers on Boards: Monitoring, Conflicts of Interest, and Lender Liability' (2001) 62 *Journal of Financial Economics* 415, 436 who found that a third of large US firms have a banker on the board of directors).

[184]   See Tung, ibid, 132.

[185]   See page 344.

[186]   G Triantis and R Daniels, 'The Role of Debt in Interactive Corporate Governance' (1995) 83 *California Law Review* 1073, 1089.

[187]   CK Whitehead, 'The Evolution of Debt: Covenants, the Credit Market, and Corporate Governance' (2009) 34 *Journal of Corporation Law* 641, 666.

[188]   See 5.2.3. Triantis and Daniels explain that 'reaction' can be divided into exit and voice. Exit, in the present context, would be acceleration and termination of the loan, while voice involves attempting to correct, rather than escape from, a state of affairs, see G Triantis and R Daniels, 'The Role of Debt in Interactive Corporate Governance' (1995) 83 *California Law Review* 1073, 1079, citing AO Hirschman, *Exit, Voice, and Loyalty: Responses to Decline in Firms, Organizations, and States* (Harvard University Press, Cambridge MA, 1970) 10–15 as the origin of the ideas of exit and voice.

[189]   See page 73.

[190]   F Tung, 'Leverage in the Board Room: The unsung influence of private lenders in corporate govern-ance'(2009) *UCLA Law Review* 115, 216. 'Leverage' here is used in the sense of 'pulling the levers', a synonym for

which follows a covenant breach, and the terms on which the lender agrees to waive the breach. Another similar way of exercising influence is where the finance is provided by a series of short-term loans, where the terms are renegotiated at regular intervals.[191] Where the loan is a revolving facility, the threat of a refusal to extend any further credit is often enough for the borrower to comply with the wishes of the lender.[192]

The influence exerted by a lender through these means can have a number of effects on the operations of the company. It can affect the level of a company's borrowing,[193] and also from whom it borrows. It can also affect the level and direction of a company's investment. Thus the covenants which restrict the directors' activities in this regard can be seen as a default position against which the directors and the lenders bargain. If the bargaining were costless, and each party were fully informed, this should lead to the company pursuing the most efficient projects from the point of view of both the shareholders (for whom the directors act) and the creditors. Of course, this ideal world does not exist, and in the real world there has to be a compromise between the strength of the restrictions imposed by the covenants, and the costs of renegotiation. The stronger the covenants, the more the directors have to ask for permission for waiver, and the greater the ability of the lenders to demand changes as the 'price' of waiver. However, this can give rise to two problems.[194] One is that there is little incentive for the directors to investigate risky projects, even though these might enhance the value of the company, if these are going to be blocked by the lender. Secondly, if the lender's response to breach is always renegotiation, the borrower has less incentive to avoid breach.

There are other costs of renegotiation as well. For example the business routine is disrupted while the renegotiation is taking place, and the directors' time, which could, perhaps, be more profitably spent on other tasks, is lost.[195] Further, renegotiation is problematic when there are multiple lenders, particularly in bond issues: much will depend on the power of the trustee to deal with minor breaches and to negotiate on behalf of the bondholders.[196] The relative weakness of the renegotiation mechanism is another reason why covenants are usually weaker in bond issues than in bank loans, although even in the latter it will be seen that it is important to get right the balance between meaningful restriction which gives the bank some leverage and too much restriction, which can be costly.

The actual effects of lender influence, therefore, can be either the prevention of actions which the directors would otherwise take, such as further borrowing or the disposal or

---

effective governance much used in the US literature (for example, DG Baird and RK Rasmussen, 'Private Debt and the Missing Lever of Corporate Governance' (2006) 154 *University of Pennsylvania Law Review* 1209).

[191]   F Tung, 'Leverage in the Board Room: The unsung influence of private lenders in corporate governance' (2009) *UCLA Law Review* 115, 140.

[192]   DG Baird and RK Rasmussen, 'Private Debt and the Missing Lever of Corporate Governance' (2006) 154 *University of Pennsylvania Law Review* 1209.

[193]   See F Tung, 'Leverage in the Board Room: The unsung influence of private lenders in corporate governance' (2009) *UCLA Law Review* 115, 153 citing MR Roberts and A Sufi, 'Control Rights and Capital Structure: An Empirical Investigation' (2009) 64 *Journal of Finance* 1657 for evidence that a company's borrowing decreases after a covenant violation.

[194]   K Schmidt, 'The Economics of Covenants as a Means of Efficient Creditor Protection' (2006) 7 *European Business Organization Law Review* 89.

[195]   F Tung, 'Leverage in the Board Room: The unsung influence of private lenders in corporate governance' (2009) *UCLA Law Review* 115, 146.

[196]   K Schmidt, 'The Economics of Covenants as a Means of Efficient Creditor Protection' (2006) 7 *European Business Organization Law Review* 89 and see below, 7.3.3.

acquisition of assets, or the instigation of the adjustments which the lender insists on as the 'price' for waiving a breach of covenant. It should be noticed that this 'price' could be achieved whether the breach consists of a prohibited activity, or the failure to meet a financial ratio (that is, an early warning sign of financial distress). Thus the 'price' could be a change in strategy by the directors, but it could also be extra protection for the lender, such as the grant of additional security, a partial repayment of indebtedness, an increase in the cost of the loan or the imposition of more restrictive covenants.[197] It is harder to see these protective concessions as a form of corporate governance, or as externally valuable except to the extent that they send signals to other creditors of the possible weakness in the financial state of the company. Concessions which effect a change in corporate strategy, however, can realistically be described as a form of corporate governance.

One particularly significant effect that lender influence can have on corporate operations is the replacement of the top management of the company, for example, the managing director. A lender is unlikely to insist on this unless the company is in financial distress, but a combination of the threat of acceleration of the existing indebtedness and the threat of refusal to extent fresh credit (particularly under a revolving facility) may give a lender sufficient leverage to effect this change if it considers it necessary.[198]

It should be pointed out that if a lender becomes too involved in the operation of a company, it risks liability for the decisions it makes and implements. The lender could be classified as a de facto director or as a shadow director. A de facto director is someone who undertakes the functions of a director, even though not formally appointed as such.[199] Once someone is a de facto director then there is little doubt that the full range of directors' duties attach to them, including all of the general statutory duties now found in Part 10 of the Companies Act 2006. However, the risk of a lender becoming a de facto director is slight. Even if a bank is responsible for replacing a managing director, the bank, as nominator of the new incumbent, will not be responsible for that individual's actions, nor is it responsible for ensuring that the individual properly discharges his or her director's duties.[200]

By contrast, a shadow director is a person in accordance with whose directions or instructions the directors are accustomed to act.[201] A shadow director is someone who has real influence over the affairs of the company.[202] On the whole the case law on this issue requires that the lender must step outside the usual lender-borrower relationship before

---

[197]   G Triantis and R Daniels, 'The Role of Debt in Interactive Corporate Governance' (1995) 83 *California Law Review* 1073, 1098.

[198]   DG Baird and RK Rasmussen, 'Private Debt and the Missing Lever of Corporate Governance' (2006) 154 *University of Pennsylvania Law Review* 1209; F Tung, 'Leverage in the Board Room: the unsung influence of private lenders in corporate governance' (2009) *UCLA Law Review* 115 157 citing S Ozelge, 'The Role of Banks and Private Lenders in Forced CEO Turnovers' 5 (Jan 15, 2008) available at www.ssrn.com/abstract=1031814 and MS Weisbach, 'Outside Directors and CEO Turnover' (1988) 20 *Journal of Financial Economics* 431 as evidence that the turnover of Chief Executive Officers is higher in companies which have bank debt than in other companies, and that the influence of lenders in this regard is stronger even than that of independent boards.

[199]   See eg *S/St for Trade and Industry v Tjolle* [1998] 1 BCLC 333; *Ultraframe (Uk) Ltd v Fielding* [2005] EWHC 1638 (Ch), [1254].

[200]   *Kuwait Asia Bank v National Mutual Life Nominees Ltd* [1991] 1 AC 187.

[201]   Companies Act 2006, s 251; Insolvency Act 1986, s 251. The two concepts of de facto director and shadow director are not necessarily mutually exclusive: *Secretary of State for Trade and Industry v Aviss* [2006] EWHC 1846 (Ch); [2007] BCC 288, although they will not overlap extensively (see eg *Re Hydrodan (Corby) Ltd* [1994] 2 BCLC 180, 183 per Millett J).

[202]   *S/St for Trade and Industry v Deverell* [2001] Ch 340.

they are likely to be held to be a shadow director.[203] It is clear that a bank is entitled to keep a close eye on what is done with its money, and to impose conditions on its support of the company, without being found to be a shadow director.[204] If a lender became a shadow director this could, for example, give rise to liability for wrongful trading under section 214 of the Insolvency Act.[205] It remains unclear whether a shadow director is subject to the full range of directors' duties, or just to those, such as section 214, where the statute specifically extends liability to shadow directors. The Companies Act 2006 is unclear on this point,[206] and there is little judicial discussion of this issue. Lewison J in *Ultraframe (UK) Ltd v Fielding*[207] took the view that shadow directors do not owe the full range of directors' duties, in part because he thought they did not assume a duty of loyalty to the company. However, this seems an unfortunate decision. Given the extent of control necessary for a person to become a shadow director, it seems odd if a shadow director is not subject to the full range of directors' duties.

Much of the literature in this area considers the question of whether lender governance is efficient, in the sense that it improves the value of the company.[208] There are various ways in which this could be the case. First, creditors for whom monitoring and influence would be costly can 'free-ride' on the actions of a lender who can do this cheaper.[209] Thus the reaction of the lender to early warnings of distress can signal that distress to the other creditors, who can then adjust or act accordingly. Secondly, if the lender's influence helps to overcome the agency conflicts between the shareholders and the creditors, this is also to the benefit of the other creditors. Thirdly, to the extent that the lender's influence prevents managerial incompetence, fraud, self-interest or failure to react to external changes, it enures for the benefit of the shareholders as well as other creditors.[210] Empirical studies carried out in the US seem to show that the prospect of bank monitoring adds value to a company's shares, and conclude that this means that lender influence adds value to the company.[211]

It is also clear from the foregoing discussion that the most effective and economically efficient monitoring and influence is exercised by a single bank lender, as compared with the situation where finance is provided to a company by many creditors,[212] such as where a number of creditors lend, each on the security of separate assets, or where a loan is syndicated or where finance is provided by a bond issue (or a combination of these). The

---

[203]   *Ultraframe (Uk) Ltd v Fielding* [2005] EWHC 1638 (Ch); *Re PTZFM Ltd* [1995] 2 BCLC 354.

[204]   *Ultraframe (Uk) Ltd v Fielding* [2005] EWHC 1638 (Ch), [1268].

[205]   Insolvency Act 1986, s 214(7). See 3.3.3.

[206]   Companies Act 2006, s 170(5).

[207]   [2005] EWHC 1638 (Ch), [1279] et seq. Cf Toulson J, obiter, in *Yukong Line Ltd v Rendsburg Investments Corp of Liberia* [1998] 1 WLR 294.

[208]   CW Smith and JB Warner, 'On Financial Contracting: An Analysis of Bond Covenants' (1979) 7 *Journal of Financial Economics* 117; DG Baird and RK Rasmussen, 'Private Debt and the Missing Lever of Corporate Governance' (2006) 154 *University of Pennsylvania Law Review* 1209; JM Shepherd, F Tung and AH Yoon, 'What Else Matters for Corporate Governance?: The Case of Bank Monitoring' (2008) 88 *Boston University Law Review* 991.

[209]   S Levmore, 'Monitors and Freeriders in Commercial and Corporate Settings' (1982) 92 *Yale Law Journal* 49.

[210]   G Triantis and R Daniels, 'The Role of Debt in Interactive Corporate Governance' (1995) 83 *California Law Review* 1073, 1078.

[211]   JM Shepherd, F Tung and AH Yoon, 'What Else Matters for Corporate Governance?: The Case of Bank Monitoring' (2008) 88 *Boston University Law Review* 991.

[212]   For discussion of this argument in relation to secured lending see R Scott 'A Relational Theory of Secured Financing' (1986) 876 *Columbia Law Review* 901 and see pages 294–95.

single bank lender is most common in the case of small or medium sized enterprises. In the UK, banks make it clear to borrowers that they will monitor carefully and will expect to have a dialogue with the company throughout the course of the relationship, although especially at any time of financial distress.[213] Even where finance is provided from a number of sources, however, it appears that the influence of a bank lender is still significant.[214]

The conclusion reached by many commentators is that, both as a matter of theory and as a description of fact, lenders contribute significantly to corporate governance. Some have then gone on to consider whether such creditors should owe fiduciary or similar duties to the company.[215] However, creditors do not act as fiduciaries, but in their own interest and it is by acting in accordance with their own interests that they act most efficiently. Further, if a creditor does step over the line and exercises the same degree of control as a manager, it may be liable under English law either as a de facto director or as a shadow director.[216] This there is no need to impose extra duties on them.

As discussed in chapter two, there has been a move in recent years for those who make loans to divest themselves of some or all of the credit risk. This can happen through the transfer of syndicated loans,[217] through loan participation (which transfers the risk but not the loan itself),[218] through securitisation,[219] or through the use of credit derivatives.[220] Such practices potentially weaken the role of debt in corporate governance, as the person with the right to pull the levers of governance may not be the person who is exposed to the risk which incentivises the monitoring and governance. This can occur at several stages. First, the bank or other entity who makes the loan may have less incentive to perform strict due diligence if it is going to pass the risk on as soon as the loan is made. Second, banks which are no longer at risk have little incentive to monitor corporate activity, or to intervene to control mismanagement.[221] Third, and perhaps most disturbingly, a lender may over hedge[222] its credit risk in respect of a loan, using a credit default swap, so that it is better off if the borrower defaults than if it pays. The lender then has the perverse incentive not to waive any breaches or to rescue the company,[223] and, in fact, could even take steps to acquire shares in the company, in order to use the voting rights to put the company into default.[224]

---

[213]   British Bankers Association, Statement of Principles (2009).

[214]   G Triantis and R Daniels, 'The Role of Debt in Interactive Corporate Governance' (1995) 83 *California Law Review* 1073, 1080.

[215]   F Tung, 'Leverage in the Board Room: The unsung influence of private lenders in corporate governance' (2009) *UCLA Law Review* 115 170–73; M Hamer, 'Corporate Control and the Need for Meaningful Board Accountability' (2010) 94 *Minnesota Law Review* 541. This point has also arisen because 'activist' financiers (such as hedge funds) may hold hybrid instruments, so that the line between bondholders and shareholders is blurred.

[216]   See pages 84–85.

[217]   Discussed in chapter 8 at page 368 et seq.

[218]   8.3.1.

[219]   8.3.3.

[220]   5.3.2 and 8.3.2.

[221]   For evidence of this, see the account of the role of credit derivatives in the banks' lack of activity in relation to Enron, F Partnoy and DA Skeel Jnr, 'The Promise and Perils of Credit Derivatives' (2007) 75 *University of Cincinnati Law Review* 1019, 1032.

[222]   For a discussion of credit default swaps and of hedging more specifically see 5.3.3.

[223]   F Tung, 'Leverage in the Board Room: The unsung influence of private lenders in corporate governance' [2009] *UCLA Law Review* 115, 167–8; H Hu and B Black, 'Debt and Hybrid Decoupling: An Overview' [2008] *M&A Lawyer* 1, 7; V Finch, 'Corporate Rescue in a World of Debt' (2008) 8 *Journal of Business Law* 756, 764–5.

[224]   See Hu and Black, 'Debt and Hybrid Decoupling' [2008] ibid, 4 using the example of Bear Sterns.

Commentators have suggested several ways forward as a result of these concerns. First, it is pointed out that the dangers discussed in the last paragraph are rare in the market in syndicated loans. Banks making loans which are to be transferred still investigate extensively before making the loan and monitor before transfer, so as to assure buyers that the loans are worth buying, and also to secure their own reputation as a seller of good quality loans.[225] Lead banks of syndicates also wish to keep a reputation as an arranger, and will often not sell their stake, or at least will retain part of it.[226]

The main danger comes from the use of credit derivatives.[227] This market is not transparent, so it is not clear when a bank has hedged its exposure on a loan, and so the disincentives to governance are not apparent to other creditors. Reforms of the credit default swap market, suggested for reasons of systemic risk, such as greater transparency and the use of a central clearing house, could thus also improve the situation in relation to lender corporate governance.[228] It would also make the credit default swap market a better signal in relation to the credit risk of borrowers: if it were public that a lender had hedged its exposure, this would send a negative signal about the borrower. It might also damage the lender's reputation, and thus transparency could act as a disincentive to hedging, which could mitigate some of the dangers discussed above. A more radical view is that the market in loans and credit derivatives could itself act as a means of corporate governance complementary to that of the actions of lenders.[229]

It is important to remember that the position of creditors changes extensively in the twilight period before insolvency. There is a far greater incentive for a creditor to protect its own interests in this period, and this can often involve using its rights to accelerate and terminate a loan, or to enforce security. However, there is considerable evidence that lenders attempt, at the first signs of distress, to help a company pull out of its difficulties, by using the governance strategies discussed above. For many years the banks in the UK have operated a system called the 'London approach' which involves an agreement between the lending banks not to enforce their loans while investigations are made into the problem, and then the implementation of an agreed restructuring.[230] The operation of this approach is threatened by the fragmentation of debt which is described above, and also, to some extent, by the changes in the administration procedure, which are described below.[231] The London approach developed because the UK did not have a corporate rescue procedure such as Chapter 11 of the Bankruptcy Code in the US, and to the extent

---

[225]   F Tung, 'Leverage in the Board Room: The unsung influence of private lenders in corporate governance' [2009] *UCLA Law Review* 115, 163–6; CK Whitehead, 'The Evolution of Debt: Covenants, the Credit Market, and Corporate Governance' (2009) 34 *Journal of Corporation Law* 641, 662 et seq.

[226]   DG Baird and RK Rasmussen, 'Private Debt and the Missing Lever of Corporate Governance' (2006) 154 *University of Pennsylvania Law Review* 1209, 1244.

[227]   See 5.3.3.

[228]   F Tung, 'Leverage in the Board Room: The unsung influence of private lenders in corporate governance' [2009] *UCLA Law Review* 115, 176–8; H Hu and B Black, 'Debt and Hybrid Decoupling: An Overview' [2008] *M&A Lawyer* 1, 9; CK Whitehead, 'The Evolution of Debt: Covenants, the Credit Market, and Corporate Governance' (2009) 34 *Journal of Corporation Law* 641. See discussion at pages 208–209.

[229]   CK Whitehead, 'The Evolution of Debt: Covenants, the Credit Market, and Corporate Governance' (2009) 34 *Journal of Corporation Law* 641.

[230]   For a good description of the London Approach, see J Armour and S Deakin, 'Norms in Private Insolvency: The "London Approach" to the Resolution of Financial Distress' [2001] *Journal of Corporate Law Studies* 21, 34 et seq; British Bankers Association, The London Approach (2004) available at http://www.bba.org.uk/media/article/london-approach.

[231]   V Finch, 'Corporate Rescue in a World of Debt', (2008) 8 *Journal of Business Law* 756.

that administration performs this role, the demise of the approach is probably foreseeable. However, there is clearly a place for informal restructuring when a company falls into financial difficulties. This issue is discussed further in the context of schemes of arrangement in chapter thirteen.[232]

3.3   The Relationship between Debt and Equity in an Insolvent Company

This section of the chapter examines the respective positions of shareholders and creditors when a company is insolvent or nearing insolvency. The focus of the law's protection at this point is on the creditors. The first two parts of the section discuss the ways in which some creditors can obtain protection by being paid ahead of other creditors, and also from legal rules providing redress where the pool of assets is reduced or unevenly distributed in the run-up to insolvency. The duties of the directors to creditors in the run-up to insolvency are then considered. Whether the creditors (through the liquidator or administrator) can make any claims against the directors or the shareholders is considered in the final section.

First, though, a number of general points need to be made about the term 'insolvency'. This is a term which can be used in a number of different ways. One could say that insolvency commences when formal insolvency proceedings commence. For the purposes of the transaction avoidance provisions, this is defined in section 240(3) of the Insolvency Act 1986.[233] The label used is the 'onset of insolvency'. It is at this moment that formal collectivity occurs, and from which the order of distribution discussed below applies (although if the company goes into administration, there will be no actual distribution until the administrator decides to distribute or to put the company into liquidation). Further, once insolvency proceedings have commenced the directors are dispossessed and no longer run the company. The 'onset of insolvency', used in this sense, will be a fixed point in time which is clearly identifiable, but it may arise relatively late in the day. A company can be described as being insolvent at an earlier stage, sometimes a much earlier stage.

The line between a company being solvent or insolvent is not a fixed, clear point in time, unlike the commencement of insolvency proceedings, and the line between solvency and insolvency in this sense can be hard to define. As noted above,[234] a company is said to be insolvent when it is unable to pay its debts within the meaning of section 123 of the Insolvency Act 1986 ('section 123 insolvency'). This can be either through balance sheet insolvency or cash flow insolvency.[235] It is possible for a company to be balance sheet insolvent and not cash flow insolvent: in fact, many highly leveraged companies are in this position all the time. Such a company has borrowed more than its assets are worth, but

---

[232]   See 13.2.4.
[233]   The exact moment differs depending on whether the company is wound up or put into administration, and the process by which this occurs.
[234]   See pages 56–57.
[235]   These terms are defined at pages 56–57.

because the repayment of the borrowing is long-term, it is not cash flow insolvent.[236] It is much less likely that a company will be cash flow insolvent but not balance sheet insolvent, since a company with assets will usually be able to borrow funds to pay its debts. The protections for creditors described in this section are generally only activated once the company is in formal insolvency proceedings, and the actions are brought by an administrator or liquidator, but the protections arise (and liability is triggered) at an earlier point in time. One might think that the start of section 123 insolvency would be the moment when the general law started protecting creditors. However, the position is rather complex. For example, the protection given to creditors from the reduction of the pool of assets or from uneven distribution starts on either balance sheet or cash flow insolvency.[237] However, the triggering of potential liability under section 214 for wrongful trading appears to commence once companies are both balance sheet insolvent and cash flow insolvent.[238] In many ways this latter approach seems more appropriate since, as discussed, many companies are balance sheet insolvent from day one.

The term 'insolvency' can therefore be used to mean both when a company is within formal insolvency proceedings and when it is section 123 insolvent. It is used in both senses in this section. However, in this section we also use the term 'insolvency' to include another situation that can arise even earlier in time. As discussed above[239] section 3.2 dealt with solvent companies and solvency was defined to exclude both section 123 insolvent companies and those which while technically still solvent are nevertheless on the verge of insolvency. This section therefore considers the position of shareholders and creditors in these latter two situations. Some of the issues discussed here, such as the common law duty on directors to consider the interests of creditors, arise when the company is on the verge of insolvency, although it is likely that in practice the concept of near insolvency will be interpreted to arise very late in the day, when the company is practically section 123 insolvent[240]. When reading this section, therefore, the reader should be aware that the precise meaning of the term 'insolvency' at any point may depend on the particular context.

3.3.1 The Order of Payment Out on a Winding Up or Distribution by an Administrator

The following discussion briefly explains what happens when a company becomes insolvent. This is not a book on corporate insolvency, and so no attempt is made to give a comprehensive account of the law. However, in order to appreciate the issues that arise both in connection with how creditors of companies can protect themselves, and whether they should be protected in any way by the general law, it is necessary to understand how

---

[236] Certain short-term future liabilities may be taken into accounting when determining cash flow insolvency, see *Re Cheyne Finance plc* [2007] EWHC 2402 (Ch).

[237] This is because, in order for such transactions to be set aside, the company must be section 123 insolvent, or rendered such by the relevant transaction. See pages 99 and 104. Of course, the transaction will only be set aside if formal insolvency proceedings are commenced.

[238] The requirement of balance sheet insolvency arises from the statute (Insolvency Act 1986, s 214(6)) but the interpretation placed by the courts on the phrase 'no reasonable prospect that the company would avoid going into insolvent liquidation' in s 214(3) suggests that liability under the section will not be triggered unless the company is also cash flow insolvent, see eg *Re Purpoint Ltd* [1991] BCLC 491, discussed at pages 110–11.

[239] See pages 56–57.

[240] See page 107.

a company's assets are distributed on its insolvency. It is in the shadow of this order of distribution that creditors bargain for protection, both contractual and proprietary. If a corporate debtor is insolvent, an unsecured creditor will generally rank *pari passu* with other such creditors,[241] and usually this means that such a creditor obtains only a very small proportion of its claim. Creditors can avoid being in this position by obtaining proprietary protection, or, in certain cases, by being in a class of creditors which are raised up the order of distribution by statute. The order of distribution is described in the following paragraphs, which can then act as a reference point for discussion of the principles and policy relating to proprietary creditor protection, which follows in chapter six.

There are two formal insolvency procedures in English law: administration and winding up. There are also other possible responses to insolvency. One is administrative receivership or receivership, which is a process for the enforcement of security by a secured creditor,[242] and which is usually followed by a winding up. There are also statutory compromises, such as company voluntary arrangements and schemes of arrangement,[243] and contractual compromises with creditors.[244] A winding up, or liquidation, leads to the dissolution of the company, and involves the collection in of all the company's assets by the liquidator, which are then distributed to the company's creditors and shareholders. The order of distribution is discussed below.

In many insolvency situations, however, it is hoped that the company, or at least the business, can be rescued. The statutory or contractual compromises mentioned above can lead to rescue, but are basically private deals, and do not provide a mechanism for an outsider to manage the company in an attempt to save the business and increase the returns for unsecured creditors, nor do such mechanisms provide for a moratorium on enforcement by creditors while a rescue is attempted.[245] For this reason, the procedure of administration was introduced in 1986, and modified in 2002. The philosophy of corporate rescue is statutorily made clear by the hierarchy of objectives which an administrator must pursue.[246] The first objective is to rescue the company as a going concern, the second is to achieve a better result for the creditors as a whole than if the company were wound up, and the third is to realise property in order to make a distribution to one or more secured or preferential creditors. The administrator must pursue the first objective unless it is not reasonably practical, in which case he can move on to the second and so on. In pursuing the second and third objectives, the administrator will seek to realise the assets of the company, so that they can be distributed to creditors.

In order that the administrator can carry out these objectives, he is given extensive powers to do anything necessary or expedient for the management of the affairs, business or property of the company.[247] While the administration is in progress, there is a moratorium on legal process,[248] such as the enforcement of security and quasi-security,[249]

---

[241]   See below 3.3.1.2.4 for discussion of '*pari passu*'.
[242]   6.5.1.4. Security is also, now, enforced in some administrations, see pages 286–87.
[243]   See chapter 13, especially 13.2.4.
[244]   V Finch, *Corporate Insolvency Law: Perspectives and Principles* (Cambridge, Cambridge University Press, 2002) ch 7.
[245]   See Goode, *Principles of Corporate Insolvency Law*, n 8, 1–22.
[246]   Insolvency Act 1986, Para 3 Sch B1 (Sch B1 was added to the Insolvency Act by the Enterprise Act 2002).
[247]   Ibid, Para 59.
[248]   Ibid, Para 43.
[249]   6.5.3.

and any execution,[250] and the company cannot be wound up.[251] An administrator can distribute assets to creditors,[252] although he requires leave to distribute to unsecured non-preferential creditors. Such distribution follows the same order as a distribution in a liquidation.[253] An administration is often followed either by a company voluntary arrangement (CVA) or scheme of arrangement (if the company is to continue trading) or a liquidation (if it is not),[254] within which the distribution to unsecured creditors may take place.

The ranking for the treatment of claims against the company in a winding up and administration, and the distribution of assets in those procedures, is discussed next. Briefly, the holders of proprietary claims come first, except that there are some statutory exceptions to the priority of a floating chargee.[255] The unsecured creditors share in any remaining assets *pari passu*, and if there are any further assets available, these are shared *pari passu* by the shareholders.

3.3.1.1   The Holders of Proprietary Claims

On insolvency, a distribution can only be made by the liquidator or administrator out of the assets of the company. Thus, any assets which are owned outright by other persons do not fall within the insolvency process, and can be claimed outright. This applies both to legal ownership (for example, where property has already passed to a buyer under a contract of sale) and beneficial ownership (for example, where the company holds an asset on trust for a client). Certain financing structures involve either the reservation of an absolute interest in an asset (for example, hire purchase and finance lease transactions[256]) or the grant of an absolute interest (for example, receivables financing[257]).[258] In both cases, the creditor has a proprietary interest in the relevant assets and generally those assets do not fall within the insolvency process, although those with an interest based on retention of title will have to obtain the leave of an administrator or the court in order to enforce if the company is in administration.[259] Alternatively, such a creditor could wait until the assets are realised by the administrator and a distribution is made.

Similarly, if the company is being wound up, secured creditors[260] can remove the assets subject to their security interests from the pool and realise them to satisfy what is due to them, accounting to the liquidator for any surplus.[261] If the company is in administration, a secured creditor cannot enforce without the leave of the administrator or the court, but the administrator will realise the assets which are subject to the security interest and pay the secured creditor in priority to all other claims.[262] In certain circumstances prescribed

---

[250]   For a brief description of execution, see pages 220–21.
[251]   Insolvency Act 1986, Para 42 Sch B1.
[252]   Ibid, Para 65.
[253]   Insolvency Rules 1986, part 2 ch 10.
[254]   See Goode, n 8, 10–81.
[255]   Discussed in 3.3.1.2.
[256]   See 2.3.4.3.2.
[257]   See 2.3.4.1.
[258]   For discussion of the distinction between the two, see 6.2.2.
[259]   For discussion of the enforcement of such interests, see 6.5.2, discussing enforcement when the company is solvent, and 6.5.3, discussing the effect of administration.
[260]   For a detailed discussion of the different types of security see 6.3.
[261]   Insolvency Rules 1986, r 4.75(1)(g), r 4.88. For detailed discussion of enforcement see 6.5 below.
[262]   For full discussion, see 6.5.3 below.

by statute, assets subject to one type of security interest, the floating charge, are payable to unsecured creditors in priority to the holder of that floating charge, if the company does not have enough unencumbered assets to pay the unsecured creditors in full. The floating charge holder loses priority in three situations: first, to the costs of the liquidator or administrator, secondly, to preferential creditors and thirdly, to the prescribed part for unsecured creditors. These will be discussed in detail below.[263] The nature of the floating charge, and the reasons behind its loss of priority on insolvency are discussed in detail in chapter six.[264]

What follows will discuss the details of the legislation, and in particular the level of protection given to unsecured creditors on the insolvency of the corporate debtor. The priority of secured creditors (including those with an absolute interest) is not uncontroversial, and there is a detailed discussion of the policy arguments concerning this issue, particularly in relation to the protection of non-adjusting creditors, in chapter six.[265]

3.3.1.2   *The Order of Priority in Relation to Floating Charge Assets*

The order of priority of payments out of floating charge assets is first, the liquidator's or administrator's expenses,[266] second, the preferential creditors,[267] and third, the prescribed part for unsecured creditors.[268] What is left after these have been paid goes to the floating charge holder. If there is any surplus left of the floating charge assets after the floating chargee or chargees have been paid, this will go to the unsecured creditors *pari passu*. If the company has assets which are not subject to a floating charge, or any other security interest, the position changes. The liquidator's expenses are first paid out of such assets, then the preferential creditors,[269] then the claims of the general unsecured creditors. If the expenses and the preferential creditors are satisfied out of these non-floating charge assets, then they are not paid out of floating charge assets. However, even in this situation, the prescribed part will still be deducted from the floating charge assets.[270] It should be noted that some of the statutory provisions described in the following paragraphs are disapplied in relation to security and title transfer interests in financial collateral.[271]

---

[263]   See 3.3.1.2.

[264]   See 6.3.3.

[265]   See 6.6.

[266]   Insolvency Act 1986, s 176ZA in relation to the liquidator's expenses and Insolvency Act 1986, Para 99(3) Sch B1 in relation to the administrator's expenses. Para 99 does not expressly provide that the administrator's expenses have priority over the preferential creditors and the prescribed part, but s 176ZA does, and the reasoning behind the latter section was to put the liquidator in the same position as an administrator (Hansard, November 3, 2005).

[267]   Insolvency Act 1986, s 175.

[268]   Ibid, s 176A.

[269]   Ibid, s 176ZA and s 175.

[270]   Ibid, s 176ZA.

[271]   For further discussion of financial collateral see pages 224–25 and 6.4.1.1. Reg 10 of the Financial Collateral Arrangements (No 2) Regulations 2003 disapplies section 176A of the Insolvency Act (prescribed part) and section 754 of the Companies Act 2006 (priority of preferential debts when possession is taken by a debenture holder) but strangely not sections 40 and 175 Insolvency Act 1986 (dealing respectively with preferential debts when a receiver is appointed and when a liquidator is appointed) or para 65 Sch B1 of the Insolvency Act (applying the preferential debt regime to when an administrator makes a distribution). Further, none of the provisions concerning a liquidator's or an administrator's costs are disapplied.

3.3.1.2.1 Liquidator's or Administrator's Expenses

The expenses of a liquidation include all costs incurred by the liquidator in the course of the liquidation and claims by creditors in relation to contracts entered into by the liquidator after liquidation.[272] It had been thought for many years that such expenses were payable out of floating charge assets in priority to preferential creditors and floating charge holders: this stemmed from the interpretation of the relevant legislation by the Court of Appeal in *Re Barleycorn Enterprises Ltd*.[273] The House of Lords in *Buchler v Talbot*[274] held that this interpretation was wrong, and that liquidation expenses were not payable at all out of floating charge assets.[275] However, section 1282 of the Companies Act 2006 restored the former position, so that liquidation expenses are once again payable out of floating charge assets, this time in priority to both the preferential creditors and the prescribed part. There were a number of reasons for this statutory change. One very significant reason was to ensure that the same regime applied for liquidation expenses as had been set up for the expenses of an administration, which, by the reforms introduced by the Enterprise Act 2002, are payable out of floating charge assets.[276] Another significant reason was that, without being sure that the liquidation expenses would be paid out of floating charge assets, liquidators would refuse to act, or at least would only act if they had the agreement of the floating charge holder to fund the liquidation, which gave the banks control of the liquidation in a way considered undesirable since it might be to the detriment of the general body of unsecured creditors.[277]

However, section 1282 did not entirely reverse the position to that which applied after *Re Barleycorn Enterprises*. One of the main objections of floating charge holders, who were usually banks, to the 'top-slicing' of expenses from the floating charge assets was that a large part of the liquidation expenses was often the costs of actions brought by the liquidator to set aside transactions entered into by the company in the run-up to insolvency.[278] Not only were these actions costly (and often unsuccessful) but any recoveries were for the benefit of the unsecured creditors and not the floating charge holder. Further, such actions could be brought against the banks themselves, so that the floating charge holder could, at least in theory, be forced to foot the bill for a challenge to its own security.[279] Thus section 1282 was tempered by amendments to the Insolvency

---

[272] Insolvency Rules 1986, 4.218.

[273] [1970] Ch 465.

[274] [2004] UKHL 9; [2004] 2 AC 298.

[275] For discussion of the statutory background and the decision in *Buchler*, see L Gullifer, 'The Reforms of the Enterprise Act 2002 and the Floating Charge as a Security Device' in L Gullifer, W-G Ringe and P Théry (eds), *Current Issues in European Financial and Insolvency Law* (Oxford, Oxford University Press, 2009); R Mokal, 'Liquidation Expenses and Floating Charges – the Separate Funds Fallacy' [2004] *Lloyd's Maritime and Commercial Law Quarterly* 387; J Armour and A Walters, 'Funding Liquidation: a Functional View' [2006] *Law Quarterly Review* 295.

[276] Insolvency Act 1986, para 99 Sch B1. Parity between the two regimes was considered particularly important after the 2002 reforms since it was often envisaged that administration would lead into liquidation (Hansard, 3 November 2005).

[277] This was confirmed by the answers to a questionnaire sent out by the Insolvency Service in June 2005, which was answered by 428 Insolvency Practitioners.

[278] Discussed below in 3.3.2 and 3.3.3.

[279] This was attempted in *Re MC Bacon Ltd* [1991] Ch 127, although the Court of Appeal avoided this unattractive result by interpreting the (then) Insolvency Rules in such a way that the litigation expenses did not fall within the 'expenses of the liquidation'.

Rules 1986 to the effect that liquidators cannot incur litigation expenses in these kinds of proceedings without the consent of the floating charge holder.[280]

When the company is in administration, floating charge assets are even more vulnerable. The administrator, in the course of pursuing his statutory objectives, may well wish to keep the business of the company going. This can involve considerable expense, both in terms of meeting pre-existing obligations and in terms of incurring new obligations, and there are various provisions which mean that this expense is met out of floating charge assets in priority to the floating chargee. In addition to the 'top-slicing' of the administrator's expenses from the floating charge assets, the administrator is entitled to dispose of floating charge assets without the leave of the court.[281] Sometimes such a disposition will result in proceeds, for example where stock in trade is sold, in which case the floating chargee obtains the same priority in relation to such proceeds as it had in relation to the original asset.[282] However, more usually the asset will be used to meet expenses resulting from existing contracts (such as employment contracts), in which case there are no immediate proceeds and the assets subject to the floating charge diminish. Similarly, payments that the administrator makes under new contracts he enters into after his appointment fall within his expenses, which will be paid out of floating charge assets in priority to the claims of the floating chargee.[283] If the administrator does enable the company to trade out of its difficulties, of course, the floating chargee will be better off as there may be sufficient assets to pay all creditors, but if the rescue attempt does not succeed the floating chargee loses out considerably.[284]

3.3.1.2.2   Preferential Creditors

Prior to the Enterprise Act 2002, preferential debts comprised two main groups, namely various taxes collected by the debtor on behalf of the Crown, including some PAYE deductions, unpaid VAT, unpaid car tax, unpaid social security contributions and various other duties, and certain debts related to the insolvent's employees. The first of these categories (known as 'Crown preference') has now had its preferential status removed.[285] The other preferential class, namely the insolvent's employees, or those subrogated to them, has been retained.[286]

---

[280]   Insolvency Rules 1986, r 4.218A–E. The proceedings covered are those brought under Insolvency Act 1986, ss 212, 213, 214, 238, 239, 244 and 423. For discussion of these, see 3.3.2 and 3.3.3.

[281]   Insolvency Act 1986, Para 70 Sch B1.

[282]   Ibid, Para 70(2).

[283]   Ibid, Para 99.

[284]   For further discussion see pages 258–59.

[285]   Enterprise Act 2002, s 251. This followed an international trend, although Crown preference in some form is still retained in a number of countries. See B Morgan, 'Should the Sovereign be Paid First? A Comparative International Analysis of the Priority for Tax Claims in Bankruptcy' (2000) 74 *American Bankruptcy Law Journal* 461, 479–480. See pages 298–99

[286]   The policy reasoning behind these legislative moves can be questioned eg as regards preferential creditors see R Goode, 'The Death of Insolvency Law' (1980) 1 *Company Lawyer* 123, 129; R Mokal, 'Priority as Pathology: The *Pari Passu* Myth' [2001] *Cambridge Law Journal* 581; A Keay and P Walton, 'The Preferential Debts Regime in Liquidation Law: In the Public Interest?' [1999] *Company Financial and Insolvency Law Review* 84. See pages 298–99.

3.3.1.2.3 The Prescribed Part

The Enterprise Act 2002 recognised the need for further protection for unsecured creditors by providing that a proportion of the assets subject to the floating charge should be made available for the claims of unsecured creditors.[287] The prescribed part is calculated on the amount of floating charge assets after deduction of both the liquidation or administration expenses and the claims of the preferential creditors.[288] The prescribed part therefore means that the unsecured creditors will get something, even if the entire assets of the company fall within the floating charge. If the floating charge holder is not fully paid out of the remaining floating charge assets, it cannot prove for the balance with the other unsecured creditors out of the prescribed part.[289] This is because the prescribed part is to protect the unsecured creditors at the expense of the floating charge holder.[290]

3.3.1.2.4 General Unsecured Creditors

As mentioned above, if there are sufficient assets not subject to a security interest, the liquidator's or administrator's expenses are paid first out of these, then the preferential creditors, then the other unsecured creditors share in the rest *pari passu*. This means that if there are not sufficient assets left to pay all unsecured creditors in full, each creditor gets the same proportionate share of what is owed to it.[291] The effect of the statutory prescribed part provisions[292] is that unsecured creditors will always get something when a company is wound up (unless there are no or de minimis floating charge assets), but it is likely in most cases that they will still only recover a small proportion of what is owed to them.

3.3.1.2.5 The Shareholders

There are perhaps three different kinds of claims that could be brought by shareholders on insolvency which need to be distinguished. First, claims can be brought in relation to dividend payments or other payments arising out of the statutory contract, ie the articles of association of the company.[293] Second, there are claims arising outside the statutory

---

[287] Insolvency Act 1986, s 176A. For details of the prescribed proportion see Insolvency Act 1986 (Prescribed Part) order 2003 (SI 2003/2097), art 3. At present, the proportion is 50% where the floating charge assets are less then £10,000 (unless the costs of distribution are disproportionate to the benefits). If the assets exceed that amount, the proportion is 50% of the first £10,000 and 20% of the rest, with a ceiling of £600,000. The amount of the prescribed part was said to relate to the amount of floating charge assets which would have fallen within Crown preference, so that the net effect on floating charge holders was zero, see R Stevens, 'Security after the Enterprise Act' in J Getzler and J Payne (eds), *Company Charges: Spectrum and Beyond* (Oxford, Oxford University Press, 2006), 162. The Enterprise Act also abolishes administrative receivership which was regarded as unfair to the unsecured creditors: White Paper, para 2.2.

[288] Insolvency Act 1986, s 176A and s 176ZA.

[289] *Re Airbase (UK) Ltd: Thorniley v Revenue and Customs Commissioners* [2008] EWHC 124 (Ch); [2008] 1 BCLC 437.

[290] L Gullifer (ed), *Goode on Legal Problems of Credit and Security*, 4th edn, (London, Sweet & Maxwell, 2008) 5–67.

[291] Insolvency Act 1986, s 107 (winding up) and Insolvency Rules 1986, r 2.69. The meaning of *pari passu* is discussed at pages 103–104. See also 5.2.4.6.2.

[292] See 3.3.1.2.3.

[293] Companies Act 2006, s 33, discussed above at pages 66–67.

contract, such as a claim against the company brought by the shareholder for misrepresentations or breaches of corporate disclosure regulations, such as sections 90 and 90A FSMA, discussed in chapters nine and ten respectively.[294] Third, there are loans which are made to the company by shareholders.

As regards sums due to the shareholders in their capacity as shareholders, for example by way of declared but unpaid dividends, it is clear that these sums are not deemed to be a debt of the company, ie these claims do not rank alongside the claims of the unsecured creditors, but are only due to be paid after the unsecured creditors are paid in full, to the extent that any assets remain available for distribution at this time.[295] The consequence of this provision is that if the company is insolvent, these debts to the members will not be repaid because an insolvent company is, by definition, unable to satisfy all of its creditors' claims with its assets.

This is a clear example of the way in which Parliament is keen to ensure that on insolvency the shareholders claims qua shareholder will always rank behind the claims of the company's creditors.[296] The courts are also keen to ensure that the statutory order of payment out is not undermined.[297] There are numerous examples of this in insolvency cases. An interesting example of this principle at work in a company law case is the House of Lords' decision in *Johnson v Gore Wood & Co*.[298] In this case their Lordships considered whether a shareholder should be able to recover for reflective loss, ie loss which is merely a reflection of the loss suffered by the company and which will be fully compensated if the company sues successfully to recover that loss. If the shareholder is allowed to recover then either there will be double recovery at the expense of the defendant or the shareholder will recover at the expense of the company.

The problem can be solved either by disallowing the corporate claim and allowing the shareholders to sue individually or by disallowing the individual claims. The House of Lords preferred the latter approach. As Lord Millett explained, disallowing the corporate claim would prejudice the company's creditors if the company becomes insolvent as a result of the wrongdoing since on insolvency it is the creditors and not the shareholders who primarily benefit from the corporate action. To allow a corporate asset — the right to sue the wrongdoers — to be given to the shareholders individually at this point would subvert the normal positions of creditors and shareholders on insolvency.

As regards claims arising outside the statutory contract, the decision of the House of Lords in *Soden v British & Commonwealth Holdings plc*[299] is authority for the view that in relation to these claims the shareholders rank *pari passu* with the unsecured creditors. The House of Lords therefore determined that the relevant principle is not that 'members come last' but rather that the 'rights of members as members come last'. The rationale of section 74(2)(f) of the Insolvency Act was to ensure that the rights of members as such do

---

[294]   See 9.5.2 and 10.4.1.2. The fact that shareholders are entitled to bring these claims is made clear in Companies Act 2006, s 655.

[295]   Insolvency Act 1986, s 74(2)(f).

[296]   It is also relevant here that the shareholders are obliged to pay any unpaid subscription on insolvency, although most shares today are fully paid up so this issue rarely arises in practice.

[297]   This can also be seen in relation to creditors. It is one of the main justifications for the anti-deprivation principle (see page 100), and is demonstrated by the rule that parties cannot contract out of insolvency set-off (see 5.2.4.6.2) although limited 'contracting out' of the order of distribution is allowed by contractual subordination (see 5.3.4.1.3).

[298]   [2002] 2 AC 1.

[299]   [1998] AC 298.

not compete with the rights of the general body of creditors. However, a member having a cause of action independent of the statutory contract is claiming as a creditor and should be in no worse position than any other creditor.

The question of whether a shareholder bringing such a claim should rank *pari passu* with the unsecured creditors highlights a collision between securities law, and in particular the investor protection provided by statutory provisions such as sections 90 and 90A FSMA, and insolvency law.[300] Insolvency law is concerned predominantly with creditor protection. Subordinating the claims of shareholders creates greater certainty and, more importantly, increases the pool of capital available to creditors, particularly the unsecured creditors, if they do not have to share with the equity investors. However, subordinating these claims by equity investors fails to recognise that while they accept the ordinary business risk of insolvency, they do not assume the risk of corporate fraud or violations of securities legislation. Such subordination arguably punishes the innocent shareholder for the misconduct of corporate management, and undermines the goal of investor protection that provisions such as sections 90 and 90A FSMA are supposed to advance.[301] As a result these claims are not subordinated in the UK, but other jurisdictions, most notably the US, take a different approach to this issue.[302]

In relation to loans made by shareholders, while some legal systems provide for subordination of shareholder loans to the claims of other creditors in some circumstances, the UK provides no specific regulation of this issue.[303] Where a shareholder lends money (unsecured) to the company, he is prima facie entitled to recover that debt *pari passu* with the other unsecured creditors. Where the money is lent secured then the shareholder's claim qua creditor will rank ahead of the claims of the unsecured creditors. The decision in *Salomon v Salomon & Co Ltd*[304] is a good example of this principle in operation.

In terms of the payment out to the shareholders, should any money be available to distribute, for example on a voluntary winding up of a solvent company,[305] first the shareholders will be repaid their capital sums. There is a presumption that all shares rank equally with regard to the return of capital.[306] Any priority intended to be attached to preference shares regarding the return of capital must be expressly stated. The fact that preference shares have priority as to dividends does not mean that the shares are presumed to have priority as to a return of capital.[307] The sum repaid may be the par value of the shares, or the articles may provide for a higher sum.[308]

---

[300]   For discussion see 9.5.2 and 10.4.1.2.

[301]   See 9.5.1.

[302]   See §510(b) of the Bankruptcy Code; *Re Telegroup Inc* 281 F 3d 133 (3rd Cir, 2002). For discussion see J Sarra, 'From Subordination to Parity: An International Comparison of Equity Securities Claims in Insolvency Proceedings' (2007) 16 *International Insolvency Review* 181.

[303]   For example, in Germany, all shareholder loans are subordinated, subject to only limited exceptions: see the German Insolvency Statute, Insolvenzordnung (InsO) § 39(1) n5, as amended. For discussion see DA Verse, 'Shareholder Loans in Corporate Insolvency: A New Approach to an Old Problem' [2008] *German Law Journal* 1109.

[304]   [1897] AC 22.

[305]   Insolvency Act 1986, ss 89–90.

[306]   *Welton v Saffery* [1897] AC 299, 309 per Lord Watson.

[307]   *Birch v Cropper* (1889) LR 14 App Cas 525.

[308]   It is common to attach a Spens formula to preference shares which provides that on a repayment of capital the holders of the share capital are expressly entitled to a premium if, during a defined period prior to repayment, the shares have been standing in the market at a figure in excess of par. The premium is usually

Once the capital value of the shares has been repaid, the question then arises as to the distribution of any excess. In most insolvencies this issue is academic, as there is insufficient money available even to repay the unsecured creditors in full. However, where companies are successful this residual value of the company belongs to those entitled to the surplus. The default rule is that the surplus left after the paid up capital has been repaid is distributable equally amongst the ordinary shareholders in proportion to the nominal value of their shares.[309] As regards the right to share in the surplus capital of the company, where a share carries a preferential right to capital on insolvency, this displaces the principle of equality and it is presumed that the express preferential right to capital is the sum total of the entitlement.[310] It is for the preference shareholders to demonstrate that a provision in the company's constitution in the terms of issue of the shares confers an entitlement to share in any surplus assets. It is rare to see any provision providing preference shareholders with a right to share in the surplus.

3.3.2   Preservation of the Assets for Creditors on and during the Run-up to Insolvency.

It will be seen that it is usually the unsecured creditors who suffer on insolvency, as there will almost always be insufficient assets available to pay them in full, and, in fact, unsecured creditors are on average only paid a small fraction of what is owed to them.[311] As discussed earlier, while the company is solvent the creditors are usually expected to protect themselves against the prospective losses on insolvency and, subject to the priority given over floating charges to preferential creditors and the prescribed part, this largely holds good on insolvency as well.

However, there are various statutory provisions designed to prevent some kinds of reduction in the assets available to unsecured creditors both in the period running up to insolvency and after insolvency proceedings have commenced. There are also provisions to prevent some creditors getting paid before or on insolvency in a way considered unfair to other creditors, since if some creditors get paid in full, there is less to distribute *pari passu* to the other creditors. To some extent these two types of provisions overlap, although conceptually they are distinct. One type prevents reduction of the asset pool (the 'cake') while the other type prevents uneven distribution of the 'cake'. These statutory provisions are supplemented by the common law rule known as the anti-deprivation principle. This principle, which goes to the prevention of the reduction of the 'cake' at the time insolvency proceedings commence, is often linked with the *pari passu* principle, which goes to prevention of uneven distribution of the 'cake' by a liquidator or administrator.

---

ascertained by reference to the middle-market quotation in excess of par during the relevant period subject to adjustments to take account of any accrued arrears of dividend which is reflected in the market price of the shares.

[309]   *Birch v Cropper* (1889) LR 14 App Cas 525, 543 per Lord Macnaghten.

[310]   *Scottish Insurance Corporation Ltd v Wilsons & Clyde Coal Co Ltd* [1949] AC 462, criticising the earlier suggestion (*Birch v Cropper* (1889) LR 14 App Cas 525, 546 per Lord Macnaghten) that preference shares were entitled to share in the surplus assets unless their terms contained an express and specific renunciation of the right.

[311]   R Mokal, *Corporate Insolvency Law: Theory and Applications* (Oxford, Oxford University Press, 2005) 130; S Frisby, Interim report to the Insolvency Service on Returns to Creditors from Pre- and Post-Enterprise Act Insolvency Procedures (July 2007) 33–34.

In addition, there are a number of provisions designed to increase the money available to creditors on insolvency. Some of these are statutory, for example sections 213 and 214 of the Insolvency Act 1986 which allow the liquidator to pursue claims for wrongful trading or fraudulent trading against the directors and others, are discussed below at section 3.3.3.1.[312] Any successful recoveries under these sections flow to the unsecured creditors.[313] Other provisions have been developed by the common law, such as the general fiduciary duty owed by directors which becomes creditor-regarding once the company is insolvent, or close to insolvency.[314] Under this common law duty, in contrast to the statutory claims, the claim, and therefore any recoveries, are regarded as assets of the company.

3.3.2.1   Preventing Reduction of the Asset Pool

A reduction of the assets of the company in the period running up to insolvency is addressed by section 238 of the Insolvency Act 1986. Where a company has entered into a transaction at an undervalue within two years of the onset of insolvency this provision enables a liquidator or administrator to apply to the court for relief restoring the position to what it would have been had the company not entered into the transaction.[315] The company must have been section 123 insolvent,[316] or have become so as a result of the transaction.[317] A transaction at an undervalue could be a gift (or agreement to provide goods or services for no consideration), or a disposition for consideration worth less than the asset disposed. The effect of the transaction is to diminish the assets available for creditors generally, to the benefit of one particular person. The statutory provision has the effect of restoring the value of those assets, usually at the expense of the person benefitted. The scope of the order the court can make on an application under section 238 is very wide.[318] Any recovery pursuant to such an order is usually for the benefit of unsecured creditors;[319] however, it is possible to argue that if assets subject to a fixed charge have been disposed of, the recovery is for the benefit of the charge holder.[320]

Reduction in the assets in the period after the onset of insolvency[321] is dealt with by section 127 of the Insolvency Act 1986.[322] This section provides that any disposition of the company's property after that date is void unless the court otherwise orders. Not surprisingly, the section only applies to a winding up and not to anything done by an administrator (who has wide powers to carry on the company's business as mentioned earlier). If a liquidator, however, wishes to carry on the business (to a limited extent) by

---

[312]   In addition, the Company Directors Disqualification Act 1986, s 15 allows for the possibility that a disqualified director might be made liable for the debts of the company.

[313]   This is the general understanding of these provisions, see eg *Re Oasis Merchandising Services Ltd* [1997] BCC 282.

[314]   See eg *West Mercia Safetywear Ltd v Dodd* [1998] BCLC 250. Discussed further at pages 105–107.

[315]   For full discussion, see Goode, n 8, 11–12–11–68 and R Parry, *Transaction Avoidance in Insolvencies* (Oxford, Oxford University Press, 2001) ch 4.

[316]   See pages 88–89.

[317]   Insolvency Act 1986, s 240(2). There is a rebuttable presumption that this requirement is fulfilled if the transaction is entered into with a person connected with the company.

[318]   See Insolvency Act 1986, s 241.

[319]   *Re Yagerphone* [1935] Ch 392; *Re MC Bacon (No 2)* [1990] BCC 430.

[320]   See J Armour and A Walters, 'The Proceeds of Office-holder Actions under the Insolvency Act: Charged Assets or Free Estate?' [2006] *Lloyd's Maritime and Commercial Law Quarterly* 27, 44.

[321]   See page 88.

[322]   For full discussion see Goode, n 8, 11–124–11–133 and R Parry, *Transaction Avoidance in Insolvencies* (Oxford, Oxford University Press, 2001) ch 3.

making dispositions, he needs to obtain the leave of the court. The litmus test for giving leave will be whether the disposition is for the benefit of creditors generally: this can either be because carrying on business is considered to be for their benefit, or because a particular disposition does not diminish the asset pool, for example, if it is for full value.[323] Section 127 is disapplied in relation to dispositions of financial collateral.[324]

The common law principle known as the anti-deprivation principle deals with provisions in contracts entered into before the company becomes insolvent which have the effect of diminishing the asset pool on insolvency. The scope of this principle is not straightforward, as the courts have tried to maintain a balance between freedom of contract (usually between the company and its counterparty) and protecting the interests of the creditors. The latter is a policy task, and is normally done by legislation (as, for example, in relation to the provisions dealing with dispositions before and after insolvency described above) and so the courts have been loath to extend the common law principle in recent years.[325] The basic principle is that a provision in a contract which has the effect of diminishing the company's assets at the onset of insolvency is unenforceable. The trigger for the diminution of assets need not be the onset of insolvency but can be some other trigger (such as a specified date, or the insolvency of another person): the principle applies if the effect is that the diminution takes place on or after the onset of insolvency.[326]

However, there are various limitations on this principle. First, the assets must actually be diminished, so if the provision means that an asset is disposed of at full value,[327] or it actually has no value,[328] the provision is not unenforceable. Second, the principle does not relate to a diminution which takes place before the onset of insolvency.[329] As explained by Lord Neuberger in the recent decision of the Court of Appeal in *Perpetual Trustee Co Ltd v BNY Corporate Trustee Services Ltd*[330] this is because the basis of the anti-deprivation principle is to prevent companies contracting out of the insolvency scheme laid down by the Insolvency Act 1986. This provides that the assets of the company at the onset of insolvency are available for distribution by the liquidator (or administrator).[331] A diminution before that date, while it may have an adverse effect on creditors, does not conflict with that scheme, although it might fall within section 238. Another reason for this limitation is that it would lead to great uncertainty. If a company enters insolvency proceedings, this is a known fact and the date of commencement of insolvency is simple to determine. If a diminution before that time were included, issues might arise as to whether the company was insolvent at the time of the diminution, or whether the diminution should be set aside even if the company recovered.[332] In any event section 238 is designed to deal with such diminutions.

---

[323]   See guidelines for the exercise of the court's discretion in giving leave set out in *Denney v John Hudson & Co* [1992] BCLC 901, 904 per Fox LJ.

[324]   Financial Collateral Arrangements (No 2) Regulations 2003 (SI 2003/3226), reg 10.

[325]   *Perpetual Trustee Co Ltd v BNY Corporate Trustee Services Ltd* [2009] EWCA Civ 1160; *Money Markets International Stockbrokers Ltd v London Stock Exchange* [2002] 1 WLR 1150.

[326]   *British Eagle International Airlines Ltd v Cie Nationale Air France* [1975] 1 WLR 758.

[327]   *Borland's Trustee v Steel Bros & Co Ltd* [1901] 1 Ch 279.

[328]   *Money Markets International, Stockbrokers Ltd v London Stock Exchange* [2002] 1 WLR 1150, [110].

[329]   *Perpetual Trustee Co Ltd v BNY Corporate Trustee Services Ltd* [2009] EWCA Civ 1160, [71].

[330]   [2009] EWCA Civ 1160, [71].

[331]   The relevant provisions are Insolvency Act 1986, ss 107, 143 and 144.

[332]   *Perpetual Trustee Co Ltd v BNY Corporate Trustee Services Ltd* [2009] EWCA Civ 1160, [72] and [74] overruling, to this extent, the decision in *Fraser v Oystertec* [2004] BIPR 486.

A third limitation is that the principle does not apply if the asset consists of a limited interest (such as a lease or a license) which has been granted to the company on the basis that it terminates at the onset of insolvency.[333] Obviously, someone granting such an interest can grant as little or as much as he wishes, and if the interest inherently only lasts until insolvency the company grantee cannot be said to be deprived of anything at that time. However, the actual boundaries of this limitation do cause difficulties. First, it is uncertain how far the limitation goes. If the asset of which the company would be deprived is in any way created by the contract in question, it could be argued that this fact alone means that the asset is inherently limited. To give a crude example, a company could contract to provide services to X, with payment due from X on a certain date, the price being £50,000, unless the company was insolvent by that date in which case the price would be £20,000. In one sense this deprives the company of an asset (the right to £30,000) but in another sense, it never had that asset since the right to that £30,000 only arose if the company were not insolvent at the payment date, in other words, that the company's right was limited or flawed. The distinction between a deprivation and a flawed asset would then depend on niceties of drafting.

The uncertainty that this reasoning creates was addressed by Lord Neuberger in the *Perpetual* case,[334] who appeared to add an additional requirement to the limitation. This was that at least in the more difficult 'limited interest' cases, the principle would still apply unless the asset of which the company would be deprived was acquired (by the company) with finance provided by the person who benefits from the deprivation.[335] While this extra requirement made sense on the facts of the *Perpetual* case, it deals with a rather limited set of facts, namely where the relevant provision is really providing the beneficiary with some sort of purchase money security interest on insolvency. A purchase money security interest is a security interest which a financier has in the very asset which is acquired with the finance provided.[336] In many contexts it is seen as particularly deserving of protection as the company's assets are swelled by the addition of the asset so that the security interest has a neutral effect on the overall assets of the company.

However, the imposition of this additional requirement does not seem to go very far towards creating certainty in relation to the 'limited interest' exception. For example, it appears to have no bearing on facts such as in the case posited above, or the archetypal 'limited interest' cases such as where a lease terminates on insolvency. The line between a limited interest determining on insolvency (or another event) and an asset of which the company is deprived on insolvency is inherently difficult to draw, can be said to be artificial and enables parties to avoid the operation of the anti-deprivation principle by clever drafting.[337] However, it is difficult to think of a more satisfactory boundary to the anti-deprivation principle. Even if the principle were given a statutory basis, it would still be possible (and perhaps even easier) to draft around its application.

The diminution of the asset pool which all these provisions are designed to prevent nearly always benefits another person. Sometimes that other person is not a creditor of the

---

[333] *Perpetual Trustee Co Ltd v BNY Corporate Trustee Services Ltd* [2009] EWCA Civ 1160, [81].

[334] With whom Longmore LJ but not Patten LJ agreed.

[335] *Perpetual Trustee Co Ltd v BNY Corporate Trustee Services Ltd* [2009] EWCA Civ 1160, [64] and [67]. This is based on *Whitmore v Mason* (1861) 2 J & H 204.

[336] See pages 274–75 and page 309.

[337] See Goode, n 8, 7–14; *Money Markets International Stockbrokers Ltd v London Stock Exchange* [2002] 1 WLR 1150, [92]; *Perpetual Trustee Co Ltd v BNY Corporate Trustee Services Ltd* [2009] EWCA Civ 1160, [67].

company (for example, where assets are hived off to another company in the same group in the run-up to insolvency). However, in some cases the beneficiary will be a creditor of the company, and there is potential overlap between the provisions and principles already discussed and the next set of provisions and principles, which seek to preserve, at least to some extent, an even distribution of the assets. Of course, merely paying a creditor his pre-existing debt before the onset of insolvency will not diminish the asset pool, as the extinguishing of the debt cancels out the payment so that the net value of the assets is not affected. Sometimes, though, the same transaction falls under both sections 238 and 239, and it is up to the liquidator to decide which section to rely on.[338] Further, on or after the commencement of insolvency the payment of a creditor in full does diminish the asset pool in the sense that there is less to distribute *pari passu* to the other creditors. This means that courts and commentators have often used the term '*pari passu* principle' to apply both to the anti-deprivation principle and to the principle that the assets must be distributed to unsecured creditors in proportion to their claims.

One area of potential overlap between the policy of preventing reduction in the asset pool and the policy of preventing uneven distribution of assets is where a company grants a security interest during the run-up to insolvency to secure past indebtedness. The authorities here are to some extent contradictory. In *Re MC Bacon Ltd*[339] Millett J was of the view that where a charge was granted in these circumstances, there was no transaction at an undervalue within the meaning of section 238 since 'The mere creation of a security over a company's assets does not deplete them'. All that has happened is that the company has appropriated the charged assets to meet the secured liability, and therefore has adversely affected the rights of other creditors. On that view, the grant of a security interest can only be a preference, as discussed below. However, this view has recently been doubted by the Court of Appeal in *Hill v Spread Trustee Co Ltd*,[340] a case concerning section 423 of the Insolvency Act 1986 which covers transactions at an undervalue entered into by a company or an individual made with the intention of putting assets beyond the reach of, or otherwise prejudicing, a potential claimant. Arden LJ said, obiter, that the grant of a charge by way of legal mortgage could be a grant of a proprietary interest and so could be a transaction at an undervalue.[341] With respect, this must be right, since the effect of the grant of a mortgage[342] is to diminish the assets available for distribution under the insolvency regime.[343] It is an interesting question whether this reasoning can also apply to a mere charge, on the grounds that even here there is a grant of some sort of proprietary interest to the charge (though an interest less than ownership),[344] or whether, at least on

---

[338] As pointed out by Professor Goode (See Goode, n 8, 11–12) an office-holder is likely to decide to rely on s 238, which is wider in scope and reaches further back in time.

[339] [1990] BCLC 324.

[340] [2006] EWCA Civ 542.

[341] See J Levy and A Bowe, 'Transactions at an Undervalue – a New Departure?' (2006) 22 *Insolvency Law and Practice* 222 and R Stubbs, 'Section 423 of the Insolvency Act in Practice' [2008] *Insolvency Intelligence* 17.

[342] See 6.3.2.2.

[343] This, of course, largely affects the unsecured creditors, since if the assets are already subject to a security interest, the holder of that interest will usually have priority over the second mortgagee unless the first secured creditor gave permission for the grant of the second interest. See 6.4.3 below.

[344] See pages 241–42. See also H Beale, M Bridge, L Gullifer and E Lomnicka, *The Law of Personal Property Security* (Oxford, Oxford University Press, 2007) 4.16–4.33 and the discussion surrounding *Buchler v Talbot* [2004] 2 AC 298 HL: R Mokal, 'Liquidation Expenses and Floating Charges – The Separate Funds Fallacy' [2004] *Lloyd's Maritime and Commercial Law Quarterly* 387; J Armour and A Walters, 'Funding Liquidation: a Functional View' (2006) 122 *Law Quarterly Review* 295.

the present state of the authorities, the application of section 238 is another example of where the classification of a security interest as a mortgage or a charge makes a practical difference.[345]

This controversy also raises the question of whether section 245 of the Insolvency Act 1986 (which provides that floating charges created otherwise for new value[346] in the run-up to insolvency[347] are invalid), is a provision preserving the asset pool or preventing uneven distribution of assets. The answer is that it probably does both, but the question is significant in that it affects how section 245 falls within the statutory scheme of transaction avoidance on insolvency and also impacts on the question whether the scope of section 245 should be extended to cover other non-possessory security interests.[348] If section 245 is about preserving the asset pool, then arguably it should be subsumed into section 238 (where the time period requirements are more generous but the requirement of insolvency at the time of the transaction is stricter). Further, there would then be no need to extend section 245 to other secured transactions, since these would be covered within section 238. However, if section 245 is primarily about avoiding uneven distribution (in other words, if the *MC Bacon* reasoning is accepted), then it has a significant role: it is much wider than section 239 since the motivation of the company in granting the charge is irrelevant. However, this might be a reason not to extend section 245 to other secured transactions, but to continue to require the motivation requirement in those cases. It should also be noted that section 245 is disapplied in relation to charges created under a security financial collateral arrangement.[349]

3.3.2.2 Preventing Uneven Distribution of the Assets

A company is usually free to pay its creditors in whatever order it chooses. Further while a company is solvent, a creditor is not obliged to take account of the interests of the company's other creditors, and can therefore pursue its own interests in seeking to be paid in advance of other creditors.[350] This changes to some extent in the run-up to and after the onset of insolvency. One of the reasons for having a collective insolvency procedure is to avoid a race to be paid first. Such a procedure will result in the maximum benefit for all creditors, by avoiding duplication of costs, wasteful splitting up of assets and a disorderly process.[351] To gain these benefits it is necessary for all creditors without proprietary claims to be treated equally in terms of the distribution of assets so that each takes a proportionate reduction in his claim if the assets are not enough to pay everyone in full. In other words, the creditors must take *pari passu*.

Once insolvency proceedings have commenced, this *pari passu* principle is enforced reasonably strictly. It is itself prescribed by statute,[352] and there are, of course, exceptions

---

[345] See pages 241–42.

[346] For detailed discussion of this concept in this context see Goode, n 8, 11–111–11–115.

[347] Within 2 years if the recipient is connected with the company and one year if not: Insolvency Act 1986, s 245(3).

[348] This question is discussed in detail in chapter 6 at pages 259–60.

[349] Financial Collateral Arrangements (No 2) Regulations 2003, Reg 10.

[350] D Prentice, 'Some Observations on the Law Relating to Preferences' in R Cranson (ed), *Making Commercial Law* (Oxford, Clarendon Press, 1997) 439.

[351] R Mokal, *Corporate Insolvency Law*, n 311, ch 4, see also V Finch, 'Is *Pari Passu* Passé?' (2000) 5 *Insolvency Lawyer* 194, T Jackson, *The Logic and Limits of Bankruptcy Law* (Cambridge MA, Harvard University Press, 1986, reprinted in 2002) ch 2 and Goode, n 8, 2–03.

[352] Insolvency Act 1986, s 107 and Insolvency Rules 1986, r 2.69.

to it created by statute. Some of these are described above,[353] and another, insolvency set-off, is discussed in chapter five.[354] Contractual provisions which purport to create a different distribution from the statutory scheme are unenforceable. As with the anti-deprivation principle, the exact boundaries of this principle are hard to determine, since the same tension between freedom of contract (between two parties) and the policy of protection of the general body of creditors arises. Two areas of difficulty are set-off and subordination agreements, and these are discussed in chapter five below.[355]

In the period before the onset of insolvency, the policy of English law is to attempt to prevent a creditor obtaining an 'unfair' advantage over other creditors. Since, in insolvency proceedings, most unsecured creditors only obtain a small share of what is due to them, any creditor who is paid in full clearly obtains an advantage. However, not every creditor who is paid in full in that period is obliged to return the payment. Instead, only payments made to a creditor whom the company intends to prefer are covered. Section 239 of the Insolvency Act 1986[356] enables a liquidator or administrator to apply to a court for a remedial order[357] if a company has given a creditor a preference within a certain period of time before the onset of insolvency.[358] This only applies if the company is section 123 insolvent[359] at the time the preference is given, or becomes unable to do so as a result of the preference.[360] A preference is where a creditor is put into a better position than he would be in if the company went into liquidation,[361] and in order to trigger the section, the company, in giving the preference, must have been influenced by a desire to put that creditor in that better position.[362]

It is not always apparent why the motivation of the company in making the payment is the best test of whether the advantage obtained by the creditor is 'unfair':[363] one might have thought that the intention of the creditor would be more relevant, or that intention was not relevant at all, in that it is the mere receipt of payment which is unfair.[364] Further, if a creditor puts pressure on the company to pay, the resulting payment is not a preference under section 239: it might be thought that to reward the strongest creditor is not necessarily the best way to redress unfairness, nor does it further the aim of collective proceedings (to prevent a race to be paid). The shortcomings of the English law on preferences is the subject of much academic discussion.[365]

---

[353] 3.3.1.2.

[354] See 5.2.4 especially 5.2.4.6.

[355] See 5.2.4.6.2 and 5.3.4.1.3.

[356] For a full discussion of the scope of the section, see Goode, n 8, 11–69–11–104.

[357] The possible remedies are the same as for a transaction at an undervalue, see s 241.

[358] Two years if the preference is given to a person who is connected with the company and six months if the preference is given to someone else (Insolvency Act 1986, s 240(1)).

[359] See pages 88–89.

[360] Insolvency Act 1986, s 240(2).

[361] Ibid, s 239(4).

[362] Ibid, s 239(5).

[363] The basis for this limitation is probably that preferences were originally seen as a fraud on the insolvency laws, therefore the intention to commit fraud was relevant, see DD Prentice, 'Some Observations on the Law Relating to Preferences' in R Cranston (ed), *Making Commercial Law* (Oxford, Clarendon Press, 1997) 439, 441.

[364] There is no requirement of intention in US or Australian law, see Goode, n 8, 11–69.

[365] DD Prentice, 'Some Observations on the Law Relating to Preferences' in R Cranston (ed), *Making Commercial Law* (Oxford, Clarendon Press, 1997) 439; See Goode, n 8, 11–69; A Keay, 'Preferences in Liquidation Law: Time for a Change' [1998] *Company Financial and Insolvency Law Review* 198.

3.3.2.3   Protection of Creditors

It will be seen from the foregoing discussion that the law starts to offer some protection to unsecured creditors from a time before the actual commencement of insolvency proceedings. However, when that time begins is only known in retrospect, once proceedings do actually commence. This has the effect that companies (and creditors) have to have provisions such as sections 238 and 239 in mind when entering into any transaction or making any transfer of assets if at the time the company might be cash flow insolvent. It is, though, unclear whether the statutory provisions operate as a very effective deterrent to creditors or other beneficiaries against most transactions or transfers. Whether any transaction or transfer is actually reversed by the court depends, first, on whether the company actually goes into insolvency proceedings, secondly, on whether the liquidator or administrator actually brings proceedings and, thirdly, on what remedy the court orders. The remedy is not punitive or based on loss suffered but on the benefit gained by the beneficiary of the transaction or transfer, so the worst the beneficiary can suffer is having to pay back the benefit gained. For most creditors and beneficiaries, it is worth taking the benefit at the time, in return for the moderate risk of remedial redress later and few claims for such redress are actually made.[366]

3.3.3   The Balance between Creditors and Shareholders in an Insolvent Company

It is clear from the discussion in 3.3.1.2.5 that as between the shareholders and creditors of the company, the shareholders' claims qua shareholder rank behind those of the creditors and that both Parliament and the courts are keen to ensure that this ranking on insolvency is not undermined.

As discussed earlier in this chapter, the directors owe a general fiduciary duty to act in the best interests of the company.[367] When the company is solvent this duty is an obligation on a director to act in the long-term interests of the shareholders. While the directors have to take account of other stakeholder groups in determining how to fulfil this obligation, the company's creditors are not one of the relevant stakeholder groups. However, when the company is insolvent, or when it is nearing insolvency, the focus of the directors' attention when fulfilling their general fiduciary obligation switches from the shareholders to the creditors: they have to have regard to the creditors' interests.[368] However, this obligation is mediated through the company: the duty is owed to the company and not to the creditors directly.[369] Directors owe no general duty of care to

---

[366]   See Goode, n 8, 11–04.

[367]   See 3.2.1.3.1. The common law duty described here is owed by de jure and de facto directors. Whether it is also owed by shadow directors is an open question. There is little authority on this point. The better view is that shadow directors should also be subject to this duty, but a recent first instance decision (*Ultraframe (UK) Ltd v Fielding* [2005] EWHC 1638 (Ch)) came to the opposite conclusion. For discussion see pages 84–85.

[368]   *West Mercia Safetywear Ltd v Dodd* [1998] BCLC 250. The continued existence of this obligation is acknowledged by the Companies Act 2006, s 172(3).

[369]   *Yukong Line Ltd of Korea v Rendsburg Investments Corp of Liberia* [1998] 1 WLR 294. Early cases seemed to suggest that the duty was a direct duty to creditors (eg *Winkworth v Edward Baron Development Co Ltd* [1986] 1 WLR 1512, 1516 per Lord Templeman) although subsequent academic opinion regards this duty as an indirect one (eg D Prentice, 'Creditor's Interests and Director's Duties' (1990) 10 *Oxford Journal of Law Studies* 265, 275; S Worthington, 'Directors' Duties, Creditors' Rights and Shareholder Intervention' [1991] *Melbourne University*

creditors.[370] The directors are required to have regard to the creditors' interests generally and not to have regard to the interests of a particular creditor or section of creditors who have special rights once there is a winding up.[371] A breach of this duty can be litigated via section 212 of the Insolvency Act 1986. One consequence of this shift from a view of the company as shareholder-focused to creditor-focused is that shareholders lose their ability to ratify the wrongs that have been done to the company by the directors.[372]

This indicates that once the company is insolvent, or nearing insolvency, it is the creditors and not the shareholders that are in the driving seat. Once a company goes into liquidation, the shareholders cease to have any interest in the assets of the company,[373] and the interests of the company are equated with the interests of the creditors so that the directors must act so as to maximise creditor welfare. In a solvent company the proprietary interests of the shareholders entitle them as a general body to be regarded as the company but 'where a company is insolvent the interests of the creditors intrude'.[374] However this identification of the creditors with the company arises at a point before the company is insolvent, when the company is 'nearing insolvency'.

A number of cases make reference to this duty arising in the period prior to insolvency when the company is 'near insolvency' or of 'doubtful solvency' or if a contemplated payment or other course of action would jeopardise its solvency or would otherwise put the company in some form of dangerous financial position.[375] These terms are imprecise[376] and yet the trigger for the onset of this duty is significant for directors, and also in terms of defining the scope of protection available to creditors. It is likely that this shift in directors' duties from shareholders to creditors will occur very late however, in line with the time at which the courts have interpreted the section 214 duty as arising.[377] It would be surprising if the duty of loyalty required the directors to take account of creditors'

Law Review 121, 151; L Sealy, 'Personal Liability of Directors and Officers for Debts of Insolvent Corporations: A Jurisdictional Perspective (England)' in JS Ziegel, *Current Developments in International and Comparative Corporate Insolvency Law* (Oxford, Clarendon Press, 1994), 486; A Keay, 'Formulating a Framework for Directors' Duties to Creditors: An Entity Maximisation Approach' [2005] *Cambridge Law Journal* 614) and this is the approach followed by subsequent English cases, such as *Yukong Line Ltd of Korea v Rendsburg Investments Corp of Liberia* [1998] 1 WLR 294.

[370]   Although dictum in *Winkworth v Edward Baron Development Co Ltd* [1986] 1 WLR 1512 suggests that directors do owe a duty of care to creditors, this view has not been followed by subsequent English cases (eg *West Mercia Safetywear Ltd v Dodd* [1988] BCLC 250). Directors could owe specific duties to creditors eg in contract (though the contract is generally between the creditor and the company and directors are agents for the company not vice versa: *Salomon v Salomon & Co Ltd* [1897] AC 22) or tort. On this latter point the House of Lords in *Williams v Natural Life Health Foods Ltd* [1998] 1 WLR 830 made it clear that a director will only be personally liable for a negligent misrepresentation made in the course of acting qua director if he has assumed responsibility for the statement to the third party. However, where fraud is involved the courts will not allow a director to hide behind the company in this way and the director can be liable for deceit in addition to the company: *Standard Chartered Bank v Pakistan National Shipping Corpn* [2002] UKHL 43; [2003] 1 AC 959 (and see *Contex Drouzhba Ltd v Wiseman* [2006] EWHC 2708 (QB); [2007] 1 BCLC 758 on the particular application of this doctrine to creditors).

[371]   *Re Pantone 485 Ltd* [2002] 1 BCLC 266.

[372]   *Re Horsley & Weight Ltd* [1982] Ch 442; *Nicholson v Permakraft (NZ) Ltd* [1985] 1 NZLR 242 (New Zealand Court of Appeal); *Kinsela v Russell Kinsela Pty Ltd* (1986) 4 NSWLR 722 (Sup Ct NSW).

[373]   *Ayerst (Inspector of Taxes) v C & K (Construction) Ltd* [1976] AC 167.

[374]   *Kinsela v Russell Kinsela Pty Ltd* (in liq) (1986) 4 NSWLR 722, 730 per Street CJ (Sup Ct NSW) and see A Keay, 'Formulating a Framework for Directors Duties to Creditors: An Entity Maximisation Approach' (2005) 64 *Cambridge Law Journal* 614.

[375]   *Facia Footwear (in administration) v Hinchcliffe* [1998] 1 BCLC 218.

[376]   See page 88 et seq.

[377]   For discussion, see pages 110–11.

interests (under the directors' fiduciary duty to the company) at a time when they still owed their duty of care to the shareholders (because section 214 liability had not yet arisen). Although there is no strict link between the times that these two separate obligations will be judged to have arisen by the courts, it seems likely that the courts will apply similar tests for both.

This duty is significant in that it makes clear the focus of corporate law once the company is insolvent, however it is questionable whether this duty will provide any significant creditor protection. It only arises when the company is in, or near insolvency, despite some early cases which held that the duty could apply when the company was solvent,[378] and, as discussed, it is likely that the term 'near insolvency' will be interpreted to arise very late in the day. It remains a duty owed by the board to the company.[379] As a result enforcement of the duty is primarily on behalf of the company[380] and only indirectly on behalf of the creditors and the loss is measured according to the loss to the company.

Nevertheless, it is clear that creditors' interests dominate at this point in time. However, it will usually be the case that many creditors will not receive the full amount of the debt that they are owed in insolvency. In consequence, one issue which sometimes arises between the shareholders and creditors in an insolvent situation is whether the shareholders can be made liable for the debts of the company in some way. The unsecured creditors are on average paid only a small fraction of the debts due to them and therefore they may seek other avenues of recovery. The difficulty with any claim against the shareholders for the debts of the company is the concept of separate legal personality of the company and its corollary, limited liability, which prima facie protect the shareholders from such claims. However, in some circumstances it may be possible for the veil of incorporation to be lifted and liability for the debts of the company imposed on those standing 'behind' the company.

3.3.3.1 *Lifting the Veil between the Creditors and the Shareholders*

At common law the courts uphold the principle of limited liability almost in its entirety. The leading case is that of the Court of Appeal in *Adams v Cape Industries plc*.[381] This case makes it clear that the veil of incorporation will not be set aside by a court 'merely because it considers that justice so requires'[382] or simply because the company is a member of a group: 'the fundamental principle is that "each company in a group of companies ... is a

---

[378] Eg, *Ring v Sutton* (1980) 5 ACLR 546 (Sup Ct NSW).

[379] Cf Lord Templeman in *Winkworth v Edward Baron Development Co Ltd* [1987] 1 WLR 1512 who stated that the board, being the company's conscience, owed a duty to 'the company and the creditors of the company' to keep its property 'inviolate and available for the repayment of its debts' (at 1516). Subsequent decisions have made clear that the duty is owed to the company, but that in determining the company's interests regard shall be had to the creditors (*West Mercia Safetywear Ltd v Dodd* [1988] BCLC 250; *Re Produce Marketing Consortium Ltd* [1989] 1 WLR 745).

[380] A claim is brought by the liquidator under Insolvency Act 1986, s 212.

[381] [1990] Ch 433.

[382] Ibid, 536 per Slade LJ, although his Lordship did qualify this statement with the words 'save in cases which turn on the wording of particular statutes or contracts...' (at 536) cf *Re A Company* [1985] BCLC 333, 337–8 ('In our view the cases ... show that the court will use its power to pierce the corporate veil if it is necessary to achieve justice ...').

separate legal entity possessed of separate legal rights and liabilities'".[383] The courts may lift the veil where fraud is involved but only where the corporate entity is being used to evade a pre-existing liability.[384] The ability to use the corporate form to ensure that particular *future* liability does not fall on a particular company is a right which is 'inherent in our corporate law'.[385]

Similarly, the courts will attach liability to a shareholder or director if it is found that they are the principal and that the company is acting as a mere agent for that person. However, the Court of Appeal in *Adams v Cape* defined very narrowly the circumstances in which an agency relationship will be found to exist. Effectively an express agency agreement will be needed, and given that most companies are established in order for the business to be carried on by the company, and for the consequent liabilities to attach to the company, that kind of express agreement will be very rare.[386] To say that there is no presumption in favour of lifting the veil at common law 'may be regarded as an understatement'.[387]

It is sometimes suggested that even if the general principle is that the courts will not lift the corporate veil, they should be prepared to do so for certain sub-categories of unsecured creditor. The strongest arguments in favour of additional veil piercing are made in relation to non-adjusting creditors.[388] However, as is clear from the decision of the Court of Appeal in *Adams v Cape*, which did involve tort victims, no special rule is in place in the UK to deal with this category of unsecured creditor. In the UK compulsory insurance covers the majority of tort claims against companies, namely those arising from accidents at work and road traffic accidents.[389] As regards other forms of tort claim, the victims who claim against companies that subsequently become insolvent are in no worse position than those victims with claims against individuals who are unable to discharge the judgment debt. There is no good justification for altering the current veil-piecing rules in the UK for this reason.[390]

There are also some statutory mechanisms which can be used for veil-piercing albeit that they target those managing the company rather than shareholders per se.[391] The legislative response to the perceived need for creditor protection when the company is insolvent or on the verge of insolvency has been to impose liability on directors for

[383] Ibid, 532 per Slade LJ, quoting from *The Albazero* [1977] AC 774, 807 per Roskill LJ. This principle was reaffirmed by the Court of Appeal in *Ord v Belhaven Pubs Ltd* [1998] 2 BCLC 447.

[384] Eg, *Jones v Lipman* [1962] 1 WLR 832; *Gilford Motor Co Ltd v Horne* [1933] Ch 935; *Kensington International Ltd v Republic of the Congo* [2005] EWHC 2684 (Comm); [2006] 2 BCLC 296. See J Payne, 'Lifting the Veil: A Reassessment of the Fraud Exception' [1997] *Cambridge Law Journal* 284.

[385] *Adams v Cape Industries plc* [1990] Ch 433, 544 per Slade LJ.

[386] Although such an agreement does occasionally happen, see eg *Smith, Stone & Knight Ltd v Birmingham Corporation* [1939] 4 All ER 116.

[387] *Ord v Belhaven Pubs Ltd* [1998] 2 BCLC 447, 453 per Hobhouse LJ.

[388] H Hansmann and R Kraakman, 'Towards Unlimited Shareholder Liability for Corporate Torts' (1991) 100 *Yale Law Journal* 1879. For a discussion of the categories of non-adjusting creditors in UK law see 3.2.2.1 and 6.6.2.3.

[389] Employers' Liability (Compulsory Insurance) Act 1969; Road Traffic Act 1988. These two acts are coupled with the Third Parties (Rights Against Insurers) Act 2010 which transfers to the injured party an insolvent company's claim against the insurer. For further discussion see pages 297–98.

[390] This issue is discussed in chapter 6 at pages 297–98.

[391] However in small companies these will generally be the same individuals and in the group scenario there is the possibility that parent companies may become exposed to liability if they are in fact controlling the running of the subsidiary company.

fraudulent or wrongful trading via sections 213 and 214 of the Insolvency Act 1986 respectively. Significantly, recovery under these sections swell the assets available to the unsecured creditors.[392]

For over sixty years the UK has provided that directors who are responsible for fraudulent trading can be ordered without limit of liability to contribute to the asset pool[393] should the company go into insolvent liquidation.[394] The terms of this offence involve the business of the company being carried on[395] with an intent to defraud creditors of the company or creditors of any other person, or for any fraudulent purpose.[396] Liability will attach to those who are knowingly a party to the carrying on of the business in that manner. This can obviously include the directors of the company, and others involved in the management of the company[397] but it can also include outsiders,[398] providing they have actual knowledge[399] of the fraud at that time.[400] It is also possible for a company to be made liable for fraudulent trading[401] where the knowledge of one or more individuals can be attributed to a company,[402] and it can be appropriate to attribute knowledge of a fraud to a company even though the person with knowledge of the fraud

---

[392] Sections 213 and 214 are silent on this point. However, contribution orders under these sections are intended to benefit the creditors generally. By analogy with *Re Yagerphone Ltd* [1935] Ch 392 (a case dealing with preferences which held that the money recovered did not constitute an asset of the company and therefore did not fall into the charge because the recovery was intended to benefit the general body of creditors) the recoveries under these sections should not feed any charge but should form part of the assets available to unsecured creditors (and see *Re Oasis Merchandising Services Ltd* [1998] Ch 170). Compare the claims by the liquidator against the directors for breach of fiduciary duty where the company is insolvent or on the verge of insolvency where any recovery is the company's recovery and therefore available to satisfy the claims of the security holders (see pages 105–107).

[393] It used to be the case that the courts were prepared to countenance the inclusion of a punitive element in determining the quantum of recovery for fraudulent trading (eg *Re A Company No 001418 of 1988* [1990] BCC 526), cf wrongful trading actions (*Re Produce Marketing Consortium Ltd* [1989] 1 WLR 745). However, remarks of the Court of Appeal in *Morphitis v Bernasconi* [2003] EWCA Civ 289; [2003] Ch 552 make it clear that there is no power to include a punitive element in an award for fraudulent trading: the award is purely compensatory.

[394] There are two provisions relating to fraudulent trading: (i) a criminal provision, now found in Companies Act 2006, s 993 which allows an action to be brought against directors and others for fraudulent trading but does not depend upon the company being in winding up; and (ii) a civil provision, currently found in Insolvency Act 1986, s 213 which allows a liquidator to bring an action against directors and others where the company is in the process of being wound up.

[395] This is an odd phrase that does not appear elsewhere in statute. It has been interpreted to mean that a person can only be carrying on the business of the company if they take 'positive steps of some nature' (*Re Maidstone Buildings Provisions Ltd* [1971] 1 WLR 1085, 1092 per Pennycuick VC).

[396] Companies Act 2006, s 993(1); Insolvency Act 1986, s 213(1).

[397] An interesting question arises as to whether wealthy parent companies can be liable for fraudulent trading. In *Re Augustus Barnet & Son Ltd* [1986] BCLC 170 the parent company supplied letters of comfort to the auditors of the subsidiary and to the subsidiary's creditors to the extent that it would financially support the subsidiary. The subsidiary subsequently went into insolvent liquidation and the liquidator brought an action for fraudulent trading against the parent company. It was held that this level of involvement did not render the parent liable under the precursor to s 213.

[398] Eg *Re Gerald Cooper (Chemicals) Ltd* [1978] Ch 262.

[399] Actual knowledge of the fraud can include 'blind eye' knowledge: *Morris v Bank of India* [2005] EWCA Civ 93; [2005] 2 BCLC 328 ie ' . . .a suspicion that the relevant facts do exist and a deliberate decision to avoid confirming that they exist. But . . .the suspicion must be firmly grounded and targeted on specific facts. The deliberate decision must be a decision to avoid obtaining confirmation of facts in whose existence the individual has good reason to believe' (*Manifest Shipping Co Ltd v Uni-Polaris Insurance Co Ltd (The Star Sea)* [2001] UKHL 1; [2003] 1 AC 469, [116] per Lord Scott).

[400] The knowledge must exist at the time of the third party assistance of or involvement in the fraud.

[401] *Morris v Bank of India* [2005] EWCA Civ 693; [2005] 2 BCLC 328.

[402] See *Meridian Global Funds Management Asia Ltd v The Securities Commission* [1995] 2 AC 500 on the issue of attribution.

had acted dishonestly and in breach of his duty to his principal and employer.[403] One significant difficulty with this test in practice is the need to determine 'actual dishonesty …involving real moral blame'.[404] This is a subjectively assessed test,[405] and therefore it is generally going to be very difficult to satisfy this requirement. This difficulty was one of the predominant reasons for the introduction of the offence of wrongful trading in 1986 which has a lower mens rea requirement, being essentially a negligence test, as discussed below.

Section 214 of the Insolvency Act 1986, which deals with wrongful trading, applies where a company goes into insolvent liquidation,[406] and at some time before the commencement of the winding up the directors, including de facto directors[407] and shadow directors,[408] concluded or ought to have concluded that there was 'no reasonable prospect'[409] that the company could avoid going into insolvent liquidation. In determining whether or not the company's insolvent liquidation should have been foreseen by the directors, the directors will be treated as having the knowledge and skill of a 'reasonably diligent person' having both "(a) the general knowledge, skill and experience that may reasonably be expected of a person carrying out the same functions as are carried out by that director in relation to the company, *and* (b) the general knowledge, skill and experience that that director has'.[410] The directors are therefore judged by the higher of these two standards. When assessing this objective element the courts will take account both of the nature of the company[411] and the nature of that director's role within that company.[412]

Perhaps the most difficult aspect of section 214 is determining when there is 'no reasonable prospect' of the company avoiding insolvent liquidation. In practice the courts have adopted a test which means that insolvency must be almost inevitable before section

---

[403]   *Morris v Bank of India* [2005] 2 BCLC 328.

[404]   *Re Patrick & Lyon Ltd* [1933] Ch 786, 790 per Maugham J.

[405]   *Aktieselskabet Dansk Skibsfinansiering v Brothers* [2001] 2 BCLC 324.

[406]   Insolvency Act 1986, s 214(6) states that '[f]or the purposes of this section a company goes into insolvent liquidation if it goes into liquidation at a time when its assets are insufficient for the payment of its debts and other liabilities and the expenses of winding up' ie a balance sheet test.

[407]   *Re Hydrodan (Corby) Ltd* [1994] 2 BCLC 180. Section 214 is silent on this point but the definition of 'director' for the purposes of the Insolvency Act 1986 includes 'any person occupying the position of director, by whatever name called' (Insolvency Act 1986, s 251). It is also accepted that de facto directors are generally assumed to be subject to the same range of obligations and liabilities as de jure directors, see eg *Ultraframe (UK) Ltd v Fielding* [2005] UKHC 1638 (Ch).

[408]   Insolvency Act 1986, s 214(7). For a discussion of whether creditors can become shadow directors or de facto directors see pages 84–85.

[409]   Insolvency Act 1986, s 214(2)(a).

[410]   Ibid, s 214(4) emphasis added. This subsection has now been adopted to reflect the duty of care owed by directors while the company remains solvent: Companies Act 2006, s 174(2).

[411]   Eg *Re Produce Marketing Consortium Ltd* [1989] 5 BCC 569: 'the general knowledge skill and experience postulated will be much less extensive in a small company in a modes way of business, with simple accounting procedures and requirements than it will be in a large company with sophisticated procedures' (per Knox J at 594–95).

[412]   The fact that this duty contains a significant objective element is in contrast to the general duty, discussed above at pages 105–107, which is fundamentally a subjectively assessed obligation. The common law obligation on directors to act bona fide in the best interests of the company (ie the shareholders in a solvent company and the creditors in an insolvent company) was subjectively assessed (*Re Smith & Fawcett Ltd* [1942] Ch 304, 306 per Lord Greene MR. This principle is repeated in s 172(1) Companies Act 2006: it is for a director to act in what 'he considers in good faith' to be most likely to promote the success of the company, albeit that the obligation to take account of the interests of other stakeholders may have an objectively assessed element.

214 liability is potentially triggered.[413] On the face of the legislation a balance sheet test is adopted.[414] However, in practice, the courts seem to utilise a cash flow test when determining whether there is 'no reasonable prospect' of avoiding insolvent liquidation.[415] If there is merely a temporary cash flow problem then the directors will not be expected to put the company straight into liquidation providing their belief that the company can avoid insolvent liquidation is not unreasonable, for example where the company continues to have the support of its major lender. This means that section 214 is triggered at a later stage in practice that might appear to be the case on the face of the legislation. The consequential effect is to reduce the potential for section 214 to operate as a creditor protection device. However, there are also difficulties with trying to impose earlier obligations on directors to have regard to these types of issues,[416] whether as a result of the court applying existing obligations at an earlier point in time, or via the introduction of new obligations on directors.

The Company Law Review considered whether, in addition to the section 214 duty, directors should be required 'where they know or ought to recognise that there is a substantial probability of an insolvent liquidation, to take such steps as they believe, in their good judgment, appropriate to reduce the risk, without undue caution and thus continuing to have in mind the interests of members'.[417] This was not taken forward by the Government, and does not appear in the Companies Act 2006, as it was felt to be inconsistent with the policy of promoting a rescue culture for companies in financial difficulty.[418] Indeed it is easy to see how such a provision would be problematic, not only because of the difficult balancing decision that would be required, but also because of the potentially stultifying effect that such a provision may have on companies. Such an approach might well lead to the precipitate closure of otherwise viable concerns and directors failing to take risky decisions that would otherwise be in the interests of the company's creditors and shareholders. There would also be a social cost attached to the premature closure of otherwise viable concerns.

One of the significant benefits of section 214 is the fact that no specific course of action is mandated by the section. As discussed, it does not require the directors to put the company into insolvency when the company is in financial difficulties, or even necessarily where the company is balance sheet insolvent. The directors' actions will be judged by the court ex post by reference to the standard of the reasonable director. The directors will be able to escape liability if they behave reasonably and there is a defence if they take 'every step with a view to minimising the potential loss to the company's creditors as…[they] ought to have taken'.[419] If the directors put in place reasonable and sensible defence plans they will escape liability even if the plans subsequently fail and the company does go into insolvent liquidation.[420] Section 214 does not create a strict liability offence. The principal

---

[413]   *Rubin v Gunner* [2004] EWHC 316 (Ch); [2004] 2 BCLC 110.
[414]   Insolvency Act 1986, s 214(6).
[415]   See eg *Re Purpoint Ltd* [1991] BCLC 491 in which the company was balance sheet insolvent for some time but the court held the director liable under s 214 only later once it became clear that the company could not pay its debts as they fell due.
[416]   For discussion see Cheffins, *Company Law: Theory, Structure and Operation,* n 105, 540 et seq.
[417]   Company Law Review Steering Group, *Modernising Company Law for a Competitive Economy: Final Report* URN 01/942, July 2001 para 3.17.
[418]   DTI, *Modernising Company Law* (London, HMSO, July 2002, Cmnd 5553-I) para 3.11.
[419]   Insolvency Act 1986, s 214(3).
[420]   Eg *Re Continental Assurance Co of London plc* [2001] BPIR 733.

liability of a director who is found to have breached section 214 is to make such contribution as the court thinks proper to the assets of the insolvent company which are then available for distribution to creditors.[421]

One significant difficulty with a claim for either fraudulent or wrongful trading involves the funding of these claims. The action in both cases is brought by the liquidator[422] acting on behalf of the creditors as a general body. It is important to note that this section, and section 213, are therefore unavailable to an administrator, unlike some of the other provisions described earlier in this chapter.[423] Accordingly, if the company is dealt with by way of administration, these two sections do not operate.[424] Recovery cannot be ordered in favour of individual creditors[425] but any recovery under these sections swell the assets available to the unsecured creditors.[426] More significantly, perhaps, these actions have traditionally been funded from the pot of money available to pay the (unsecured) creditors and as a result liquidators would not commence an action unless there was a strong prospect that the money recovered would exceed the expenses of the litigation.[427] This had the effect of keeping the number of section 213 and section 214 actions very low.[428]

However, since 2002, amendments to the Insolvency Rules mean that office holder actions can be charged to liquidation expenses.[429] This change in the law had no immediate effect, perhaps because of the decision of the House of Lords in *Buchler v Talbot*[430] which provided that liquidation expenses, while taking priority over the claims of the preferential and unsecured creditors, did not enjoy the same priority over the claims of the floating charge holders. Although the decision in *Buchler v Talbot* has now been reversed by section 1282 of the Companies Act 2006, this was tempered by amendments to the Insolvency Rules 1986 to the effect that liquidators cannot incur litigation expenses in

---

[421]   Insolvency Act 1986, s 214(1) and *Re Produce Marketing Consortium Ltd* [1989] BCLC 520.

[422]   Ibid, s 213(2), s 214(1). This is in contrast to an action for breach of the directors' general fiduciary duty which on insolvency is a duty owed to the creditors as a whole (see eg *West Mercia Safetywear Ltd v Dodd* [1998] BCLC 250, discussed at pages 105–107). In relation to this latter action, the duty is owed to the company and therefore an action on behalf of the company may be brought by the liquidator, or an administrator or receiver.

[423]   Eg, actions under ss 238 or 239 of the Insolvency Act 1986.

[424]   Equally, if the company does not go into insolvency at all, even if it is later struck off the register of companies, these sections will not operate. For a discussion of these points see P Davies, 'Directors' Creditor-Regarding Duties in Respect of Trading Decisions Taken in the Vicinity of Insolvency' (2006) 7 *European Business Organization Law Review* 301, 321–324.

[425]   *London & Sugar Overseas (Sugar) Co Ltd v Punjab National Bank* [1997] 1 BCLC 705; *Re Purpoint Ltd* [1991] BCLC 491, 499. This is the same as the position regarding the general fiduciary duty owed by directors to creditors, discussed at pages 105–107.

[426]   *Re Oasis Merchandising Services Ltd* [1998] Ch 170 in the context of a s 214 action cf the position regarding the general fiduciary duty owed to creditors, at pages 105–107.

[427]   In addition, in *Oasis Merchandising* (ibid) the transfer of section 214 claims to a third party (willing to take up risky claims which the company is unwilling to pursue) by the liquidator was held to infringe the rule against champerty.

[428]   This can be compared to the number of actions brought against directors by the Secretary of State under the Company Directors Disqualification Act 1986. During 2009–10, for example, 1,388 disqualification orders or undertakings against directors of failed companies were secured (compared to 1,281 in 2008–09): Insolvency Service Annual Report and Accounts 2009–10, July 2010, 19. These actions are not confined to situations where the company is insolvent, though that is the usual scenario. In addition to a disqualification order (s 6) the Secretary of State can seek to impose personal liability for the company's debts in some circumstances (s 15). Disqualification actions are funded by the State.

[429]   Insolvency (Amendment) (No 2) Rules 2002, rule 23 which amended Insolvency Rules 1986, r 4.218.

[430]   [2004] UKHL 9; [2004] 2 AC 298.

proceedings such as sections 213 and 214 without the consent of the floating charge holder.[431] In addition, these changes do not alter the fact that directors of insolvent companies may have little or nothing by way of funds which it is worth the liquidator's while to pursue. As a result it is unlikely that the number of section 213 or section 214 actions will increase in the future.

As a result of these factors, lifting the veil, whether at common law or as a result of these two legislative provisions, is extremely rare in the UK. These are not mechanisms which lead to any significant increase in the funds available to creditors.[432]

3.4 Conclusion

As discussed in 3.1 above, the thesis of this chapter has been that shareholders are pre-eminent within a solvent company, because it is the shareholders (or at least the ordinary shareholders) that are the residuary claimants of the company, but that on insolvency there is a shift such that the creditors' interests dominate. It is suggested that this shift is entirely appropriate. In a solvent company, because the creditors' returns are fixed, they would tend to prefer excessively low risk projects as compared to the shareholders. Directors' duties are rightly shareholder-regarding at this point as broadly what is in the long-term interests of the shareholders will also be in the interests of the creditors at this point in time. If the creditors wish to have additional influence in this period then there are a number of different corporate governance rights for which they can bargain, and which can potentially provide them with a significant monitoring role.

On insolvency, however, there is a potential problem since at that point the shareholders 'come last' and yet, if the directors are too closely aligned with the shareholders then they might favour excessively risky projects that would potentially benefit the shareholders (who would take any upside of the decision but have nothing to lose if the risk does not pay off) at the expense of the creditors. The dominant interest on insolvency is therefore that of the creditors, as the discussion in 3.3 above demonstrates. At this point in time shareholders completely drop out of the picture and therefore it does seem entirely appropriate that when the company is in insolvency or in the vicinity of insolvency, the focus should shift from a shareholder-focused conception of the company, to a creditor-focused one.

This chapter has examined the means by which the general law seeks to regulate the conflict between creditors and shareholders when the company is insolvent, and to impose an orderly procedure within which creditors' claims can be met to the extent possible. The next chapter will discuss the mechanisms put in place by the law while the company remains solvent in order to regulate this conflict between creditors and shareholders.

---

[431] Companies Act 2006, s 1282, inserting new Insolvency Act 1986, s 176ZA; Insolvency Rules 1986, r 4.218A–E, For discussion see 3.3.1.2.1.

[432] There is one further possibility for recovery, which is aimed at directors rather than shareholders, but might be relevant if the shareholder becomes a de facto or shadow director, namely the Company Directors Disqualification Act 1986. This Act allows actions to be brought by the Secretary of State and the proceedings are publicly funded. The Act is primarily aimed at disqualifying unfit directors of insolvent companies but there is also provision for disqualified directors to be made liable for the debts of the company: Company Directors Disqualification Act 1986, s 15.

Creditors who are able to adjust, however, will seek to protect themselves against other creditors *ex ante*, by either or both of the contractual and proprietary means described in chapter two and in this chapter and discussed in more detail in chapters five and six which follow. The extent to which creditors can or should be prevented from putting in place this *ex ante* protection will also be discussed, but it will be seen that, except to the extent discussed in this chapter, English law largely adopts a view based on freedom of contract, so that adjusting creditors can avail themselves of very substantial protection against the competing claims of other creditors by having proprietary claims against what would otherwise be the company's assets.

4

Legal Capital

4.1 Introduction

The legal capital rules are a set of provisions that constrain corporate activity by reference to the shareholders' capital investment. Broadly, these rules fall into two categories: those that regulate how capital can be raised from shareholders, and in particular how much capital shareholders must invest into a company, and those that regulate whether and how capital can be returned to the shareholders. The primary purpose of these rules is to regulate the conflict that exists between creditors and shareholders regarding how to allocate a company's capital.[1] This conflict is obvious once the company is insolvent, at which point the company has insufficient money to meet all its financial obligations.[2] At that point, as discussed in chapter three, the interests of the creditors dominate and the shareholders 'come last'.[3] However, UK company law also regulates this conflict, in favour of creditors, by imposing legal capital rules when a company is solvent. The function and substance of the legal capital rules currently in place in the UK will be assessed in this chapter. These rules will then be analysed, to determine how well they operate to fulfil their purpose. The chapter will then examine alternatives to the legal capital rules, and will assess the desirability of a change in the law in this context.

4.2 The Function of the Legal Capital Rules

It is well understood that the interests of those who contribute to a company's cash flow will come into conflict. The most obvious conflict is that between the creditors and the shareholders of a company, although of course others can exist, not least between classes of shareholders, and between different creditors.[4] Some of the legal capital rules, such as

---

[1] Some of the legal capital rules can be seen as a device to protect shareholders. Other rules have been said to have a role in protecting market integrity. These are discussed in 4.2 below. However, the primary rationale behind the legal capital rules is creditor protection (see eg Company Law Review Steering Group, *Modern Company Law for a Competitive Economy: The Strategic Framework* (February 1999) URN 99/654, 81).

[2] For discussion see eg R Goode, *Principles of Corporate Insolvency Law*, 3rd edn (London, Sweet & Maxwell, 2005) ch 4.

[3] *Soden v British & Commonwealth Holdings plc* [1998] AC 298, 308. For discussion see 3.3, in particular 3.3.1.2.5.

[4] Disputes between creditors arise most acutely on insolvency, as a result of their respective priorities: see 3.3.1. As discussed above in chapters 2 and 3, adjusting creditors can protect themselves by contractual or proprietary means: see 3.2.2 above and chapters 5 and 6 below.

pre-emption rights,[5] can be seen as a device to protect shareholders.[6] Other rules have been said to have a role in protecting market integrity.[7] However, the primary rationale of the legal capital rules is the regulation of this conflict between shareholders and creditors, and the purpose of these rules has been to resolve the conflict in favour of the creditors.

As discussed at 3.2.2.2 the operations of a solvent company can create risk to a creditor. The particular risks that are relevant in this chapter are those that arise from the fact that whilst a company is solvent the shareholders generally control the operation of a company, directly through the general meeting, and indirectly through the directors. They are in a position to benefit themselves at the expense of the creditors in a number of ways.[8] They can withdraw assets from the pool available to the creditors for repayment (asset diversion). Common examples of this include distributions to themselves, such as dividend payments and share buy-backs. They can manipulate the investment profile of the company in a way which disadvantages creditors, for example by taking on riskier projects than the creditors contemplated when they extended credit to the company (risk shifting),[9] or by abandoning projects with a net positive value if the only benefit attaches to the creditors (underinvestment).[10] They may also disadvantage the existing creditors of a company by incurring additional debts to others which do not result in an equivalent increase in assets (claim dilution). This could result in a benefit to shareholders if the directors use the borrowed money to invest in risky projects that benefit shareholders at the expense of creditors.[11] Of course, creditors can also, potentially, engage in behaviour which advantages themselves at the expense of the shareholders, such as requiring the company to repay loans early or requiring it to decline to pay a dividend. Creditors could also encourage the company to invest in projects that are less risky than originally envisaged when the creditors invested, or not to invest in projects likely to accrue benefits only for the shareholders. The extent to which these matters might happen in practice is discussed in chapter three.[12]

The US and Europe have traditionally adopted quite different responses to the potential conflict between creditors and shareholders regarding the allocation of a company's legal capital. In the US, the legal capital rules have evolved to provide maximum flexibility to shareholders, and creditor protection devices are noticeable largely by their absence in

---

[5]   Companies Act 2006, ss 561–573.

[6]   This is discussed below at 4.3.1.

[7]   The rules restricting share repurchases have been said to have this role: *The Purchase by a Company of its Own Shares* (Cm 7944) (London, HMSO, 1980).

[8]   CW Smith and JB Warner 'On Financial Contracting: An Analysis of Bond Covenants' (1979) 7 *Journal of Financial Economics* 117, 118–9.

[9]   The evidence regarding the empirical significance of risk shifting is mixed: eg KH Daigle and MT Maloney, 'Residual Claims in Bankruptcy: An Agency Theory Explanation' (1994) 37 *Journal of Law and Economics* 157, G Andrade and S Kaplan, 'How Costly is Financial (not Economic) Distress? Evidence from Highly Leveraged Transactions that Became Distressed' (1998) 53 *Journal of Finance* 1443; A Eisendorfer, 'Empirical Evidence of Risk Shifting in Financially Distressed Firms' (2008) 63 *Journal of Finance* 609.

[10]   SC Myers, 'Determinants of Corporate Borrowing' [1977] *Journal of Financial Economics* 147.

[11]   MC Jensen and WH Meckling, 'Theory of the Firm: Managerial Behaviour, Agency Costs and Ownership Structure' (1976) 3 *Journal of Financial Economics* 305.

[12]   See chapter 3, particularly 3.2.

some State corporate laws.[13] Some creditor protection is provided by the Federal 'fraudu-lent transfer laws'[14] but the primary tool available to creditors who wish to protect themselves from opportunistic shareholders is contract.

By contrast, the European model has regarded the threat to creditors from shareholders as real and credible. This is the model on which the UK depends heavily because of the need to implement the Second Company law directive.[15] On this view the shareholders obtain the benefit of limited liability when they invest in a company, but this comes at a cost to the creditors. In the UK, common law exceptions to the principle of limited liability are rare and, where they do exist, very narrowly constrained.[16] The principal statutory exception, section 214 of the Insolvency Act 1986, is powerful in theory,[17] but difficulties with the funding of these actions in the past has meant that this section has rarely been invoked in practice.[18] So the principle of limited liability is very much intact in the UK.

Undoubtedly this principle constrains the amount available to creditors on insolvency. In Europe this has resulted in the view that creditors need to be compensated and that this compensation should be provided by law rather than being left to contract. The idea that creditors need protection is of significant longevity in the UK. The form of this protection has been rules that constrain corporate activity by reference to the shareholders' capital investment, principally by prescribing a minimum level of capital to be invested in a company by the shareholders, and a restriction on transfers to shareholders in some circumstances. The point is that creditors rank ahead of shareholders in a winding up,[19] and the purpose of the capital maintenance rules is to ensure that shareholders do not undermine that principle by improperly distributing assets to themselves, not only once the company is insolvent, but also while the company remains solvent.

It is interesting that of the various potential dangers which shareholders pose to creditors, namely asset diversion, altering the investment profile of the firm, or claim dilution by issuing additional debt, the focus of the Second Directive, and UK company law, has been on preventing the first. Both concentrate on creating and maintaining an equity cushion to protect the creditors in the event of insolvency, and one of the key factors in that approach has been the prevention of capital return to the shareholders. A rules-based approach[20] has been adopted to regulate this issue. These rules are examined at 4.3 below.

It may be that the focus on asset diversion of the Second Directive, and UK company law, is unsurprising. The idea of capital as a fund available to meet creditors' claims is

---

[13]   L Enriques and JR Macey 'Creditors Versus Capital Formation: The Case Against the European Legal Capital Rules' (2001) 86 *Cornell Law Review* 1165.

[14]   RC Clark, 'The Duties of the Corporate Debtor to its Creditors' (1977) 90 *Harvard Law Review* 505. In the UK the equivalent provisions are Insolvency Act 1986, s 238 and s 423.

[15]   Second Council Directive (EC) 77/91 [1977] OJ L26/1 as amended by Directive 2006/68/EC [2006] OJ L69/27.

[16]   To say that there is no presumption in favour of lifting the veil at common law 'may be regarded as an understatement': *Ord v Belhaven Pubs Ltd* [1998] 2 BCLC 447, 453 (Hobhouse LJ). For discussion see 3.3.3.1.

[17]   See eg P Davies, 'Directors' Creditor-Regarding Duties in Respect of Trading Decisions Taken in the Vicinity of Insolvency' (2006) 7 *European Business Organization Review* 301.

[18]   For discussion see 3.3.3.1.

[19]   See 3.3.1.

[20]   For discussion of this terminology see R Kraakman et al, *The Anatomy of Corporate Law: A Comparative and Functional Approach,* 2nd edn (Oxford, Oxford University Press, 2009), ch 2.

well-embedded.[21] When this view developed in the nineteenth century there was little in the way of publicly available information for creditors to assess the credit-worthiness of companies, other than statements about the company's capital, and it is perhaps understandable that the courts put emphasis on the retention of this fund. However, much more information is now available to creditors. There has been a significant expansion in the amount of information made available about a company via its annual report and accounts, and publicly listed companies are, in addition, under significant continuing disclosure obligations, as discussed in chapter ten.[22] In addition, it is generally recognised that many creditors can and will seek additional information from the company in order to determine whether, and on what terms, to lend.[23] Given these changes, a continuing commitment to capital rules as a creditor protection device needs to be examined closely. What is interesting to note is that of the three potential forms of abuse, asset diversion is one of the easier ones for the creditors, or at least the adjusting creditors, to monitor.[24] Creditors may also have contractual rights to prevent asset diversions, such as contractual restrictions on disposals[25] and the control rights which come from having fixed security.[26]

By contrast, in relation to the potential abuse of altering the investment profile of the company to the creditors' disadvantage, a standards-based approach has been adopted. This has been regarded as a matter for the directors, and regulated primarily through the duties imposed on directors. In particular, directors are under an obligation to make investment decisions bona fide in the best interests of the company, an obligation that has been subjectively assessed by the UK courts to date.[27] As discussed in chapter three, where the company is solvent this has traditionally meant acting in the interests of the shareholders as a whole.[28] Section 172 of the Companies Act 2006 potentially alters this, by adding a requirement that directors consider the interests of various other groups, such as employees and customers, when fulfilling this obligation. However, the position of the company's creditors does not form part of this analysis.[29] While the company is solvent, the interests of the creditors and the shareholders are broadly similar.[30] Only where the company is insolvent, or nearing insolvency, must the directors take account of the creditors' interests.[31] As regards the danger of claim dilution, it is largely left to creditors to protect themselves by contract where the company is solvent, by taking security[32] and

---

[21]   In the UK see eg *Ooregum Gold Mining Co of India v Roper* [1892] AC 125, 133 per Lord Halsbury ('[t]he capital is fixed and certain, and every creditor of the company is entitled to look to that capital as his security').

[22]   The continuing disclosure obligations regarding debt securities are discussed in chapter 11.

[23]   See 5.2.2 and 11.2.8.

[24]   This issue is discussed further at 5.2.2.

[25]   See pages 156–57.

[26]   See pages 242–43.

[27]   *Re Smith & Fawcett Ltd* [1942] Ch 304, 306 per Lord Greene MR, cf Companies Act 2006, s 172 which puts this obligation on a statutory footing. Section 172(1) provides that '[a] director of a company must act in the way he considers, in good faith…' (ie a subjective assessment) but goes on to provide 'and in doing so have regard (amongst other matters) to…' which introduces an objective element into the exercise of the directors' duties. For discussion see 3.2.1.3.1.

[28]   See 3.2.1.3.1.

[29]   Companies Act 2006, s 172, and in particular s 172(3).

[30]   For discussion see 3.2.2. However, this general statement will not work quite so well in some circumstances, for example where the company is highly leveraged.

[31]   *Winkworth v Edward Baron Development Co Ltd* [1986] 1 WLR 1512; *West Mercia Safetywear Ltd v Dodd* [1988] BCLC 250. See now Companies Act 2006, s 172(3). This is discussed in 3.3.3.

[32]   See chapter 6.

using negative pledge clauses which protect their priority,[33] and by using covenants restricting borrowing, and requiring certain gearing ratios.[34]

4.3   The Legal Capital Rules in the UK

The vast majority of the UK's legal capital rules are now in statutory form, and are primarily found in the Companies Act 2006. These statutory provisions have three origins. First, in the rules applicable to all companies, which originate in the nineteenth century, principally by way of case law. Second, in European legislation, principally the Second Company Law Directive,[35] which introduced legal capital rules for public companies.[36] When the UK initially implemented this directive it went beyond the strict requirements of that directive, extending many of the restrictions to private companies,[37] and gold-plating the regime in places.[38] Some of these extensions and some of this gold-plating have since been removed, by the Companies Act 2006. The third source, then, are the UK's statutory rules that pre-date the 2006 Act, and which introduced legal capital rules that were neither part of the common law, nor were they strictly required by European legislation.

The Companies Act 2006 was preceded by a substantial review of UK company law. The legal capital rules in place in the Companies Act 1985 and in the common law were carefully scrutinised by an independent Steering Group, the Company Law Review Steering Group, as part of this process. When this Company Law Review was established, it had been nearly 40 years since the last broad review of company law had been carried out, by the Jenkins Committee in 1962.[39] The Steering Group produced a large number of papers which considered the issue of legal capital, either specifically, or as part of the

---

[33]   See 5.2.1.

[34]   See page 156 and pages 168–69.

[35]   Second Council Directive (EC) 77/91 [1977] OJ L26/1. Reviews of the legal capital rules have also taken place in Europe: see Commission (EC), 'Simpler Legislation for the Single Market (SLIM): Extension to a Fourth Phase', SEC (1998) 1944 (Commission Staff Working Paper of 16 November 1998); High Level Group of Company Law Experts, 'Modern Regulatory Framework for Company Law in Europe' (Report) (Brussels, 4 November 2002) (the Winter Group Report). See also KPMG, 'Feasibility Study on an Alternative to the Capital Maintenance Regime established by the Second Company Law Directive', 2008. To date only modest amendments have been forthcoming, see eg Directive 2006/68/EC [2006] OJ L69/27.

[36]   It also creates other constraints for public companies, which arguably have little or no valid creditor protection role at all, such as the ban on financial assistance. According to Eilis Ferran, financial assistance rules are better regarded as an 'offshoot' of the legal capital rules: E Ferran, 'The Place for Creditor Protection on the Agenda for Modernisation of Company Law in the European Union' (2006) 3 *European Company and Financial Law Review* 178.

[37]   Often, although the Companies Act 1985 applied provisions from the Second Directive 77/91/EC to private companies, there were relaxations in the way in which the regime operated. For example, the financial assistance rules applied to private companies (Companies Act 1985, ss 151–153), but a whitewash procedure was put in place for private companies (ss 155–158). The ban on providing financial assistance for the purchase of a company's own shares is removed by Companies Act 2006 for private companies, but is left in place for public companies (see Companies Act 2006, ss 677–682).

[38]   For example, the definition of capital for the purposes of the Companies Act 2006 includes share premiums and any capital redemption reserve although this is not required by the Second Directive 77/91/EC: Companies Act 2006, s 610(4) and s 733(5)(6).

[39]   *Report of the Company Law Committee* (Cm 1749, 1962).

overall package of possible reforms[40] which were then considered and further amended by the Government in its response to these proposals.[41] Although the Company Law Review made a large number of recommendations for the reform of the legal capital rules of both private and public companies, many of these recommendations did not find their way into the final Act. This was in part as a result of the continuing obligation to implement the legal capital requirements of the Second Directive for public companies.

The rules relating to company capital can be divided into different parts. The first set of provisions deal with the raising of capital, and are generally creditor-neutral. There are then two sets of provisions that deal with the perceived dangers to the creditors more directly. These include provisions that are intended to ensure that a certain guaranteed cushion is created for creditors by ensuring that shareholders pay a certain amount into a company (the minimum capital rules) and those which attempt to ensure that this cushion isn't returned to the shareholders in certain circumstances (maintenance of capital).

4.3.1   The Raising of Capital

In order to issue new shares directors need to have authority to allot those shares. Prior to the Companies Act 2006 there was also a limit on the number of shares which directors were entitled to allot: the maximum authorised capital.[42] This concept has now been removed and is not found in the Companies Act 2006. The 2006 Act simply requires directors to obtain the power to allot shares from the shareholders. The rules regarding authorisation are different for different types of companies.[43] Directors of private companies with a single class of shares have authority to allot shares of that class unless the articles prohibit them from doing so.[44] For all other companies, directors can allot shares if they are authorised to do so by the company's articles or by ordinary resolution.[45] Instead, the 2006 Act permits an authorisation for a period of up to five years, stating the maximum amount of shares which can be allotted by the directors in that period.[46] For companies other than private companies with a single class of shares the need for the directors to go to the shareholders for their authority to allot shares is potentially important. Shareholders have the opportunity to exert control over share allotments, and they have flexibility as to how much control they wish to exercise, depending on the extent of the authorisation which they give to the directors. Where the authorisation given is extensive (eg five years and for a large number of shares) it has to be accepted that the level of control which shareholders then have is very limited.[47]

---

[40]   See Company Law Review Steering Group, *The Strategic Framework* n 1; *Company Formation and Capital Maintenance* (October 1999) URN 99/1145; *Developing the Framework* (March 2000) URN 00/656; *Completing the Structure* (November 2000) URN 00/1335; *Final Report* (July 2001) URN 01/942–3.

[41]   See White Papers DTI, *Modernising Company Law* (Cm 5553-I and Cm 5553-II, July 2002) and DTI, *Company Law Reform* (Cm 6456, March 2005).

[42]   Companies Act 1985, s 80.

[43]   Companies Act 2006, s 549.

[44]   Ibid, s 550.

[45]   Ibid, s 551.

[46]   Ibid, s 551(3).

[47]   However, additional constraints on the directors may be imposed by other means. For example, the Association of British Insurers (ABI) issues guidance on the authority which directors should be given to allot new shares. Until 2008 this was the lesser of (i) the company's unissued ordinary share capital and (ii) one-third

However, there is another, more significant, discipline which shareholders can impose on directors in the context of raising capital, via pre-emption rights. Under section 561 of the Companies Act 2006 any proposed allotment of equity securities[48] must first be offered to existing shareholders on a pre-emptive basis, ie the company must offer those securities first on the same or more favourable terms to existing shareholders in proportion to their existing holdings.[49] This is a form of option to acquire those shares before they are allotted to other people. The offer must be in writing and kept open for a minimum of 14 days.[50] Pre-emption offers can now be communicated to shareholders electronically.[51]

Pre-emption rights can be disapplied. Directors of a private company with only one class of shares can be given power by the articles or by a special resolution to allot shares without complying with the statutory pre-emption provisions.[52] For all other companies the pre-emption rights can be disapplied by special resolution.[53] Additional requirements are put in place for publicly listed companies. The Listing Rules, drawn up by the FSA to deal with companies with a listing on the Main London stock market, do not restrict disapplication of statutory pre-emption rights.[54] However, a set of guidelines drawn up by institutional investors does impose additional restrictions. A Statement of Principles drawn up by the Stock Exchange Pre-Emption Group[55] provides guidance on the circumstances in which certain institutional investors, namely ABI (Association of British Insurers) and NAPF (National Association of Pension Funds) members, should vote in

---

of the company's issued ordinary share capital. This was altered in 2008 to two-thirds of the company's issued ordinary share capital (although the additional one-third can only be used for rights issues): ABI, *Directors' Power to Allot Share Capital and Disapply Shareholders' Pre-Emption Rights*, December 2008. See also *A Report to the Chancellor of the Exchequer by the Rights Issue Review Group*, November 2008, available at www.hmtreasury.gov.uk/d/pbr08_rights issue 3050.pdf.

[48] The term 'equity securities' is defined in Companies Act 2006, s 560(1) as being ordinary shares in the company or rights to subscribe for, or convert securities into, ordinary shares in the company. The definition of an ordinary share is 'shares other than shares that as respects dividends and capital carry a right to participate only up to a specified amount in a distribution' (s 560(1)).

[49] There are a number of exceptions to pre-emption rights (Companies Act 2006, ss 564–566). Most notably the right of pre-emption does not apply where the shares are issues wholly or partly for non-cash consideration: s 565.

[50] Companies Act 2006, s 562(5). This period was initially 21 days, but the Myners' Report on Pre-Emption Rights (DTI, *Pre-emption Rights: Final: A Study by Paul Myners into the Impact of Shareholders' Pre-emption Rights on a Public Company's Ability to Raise New Capital*, February 2005, URN 05/679) recommended that the period for acceptances be reduced to 14 days on the basis that the existing procedure was too lengthy and cumbersome. The 2006 Act included a facility for the Secretary of State to reduce the period to less than 21 days (but not less than 14 days) by statutory instrument: s 562(6). The reduction of the period from 21 to 14 days was effected by the Companies (Share Capital and Acquisition by Company of its Own Shares) Regulations 2009 (SI 2009/2022) with effect from 1 October 2009.

[51] Ibid, s 562(2). Whatever form of communication is used, companies will have to communicate offers to all shareholders with a registered address in an EEA state, not merely those with a registered address in the UK (s 562(3)).

[52] Ibid, s 569. Directors of public companies and private companies with more than one class of shares can be given power by the articles or by a special resolution to allot shares pursuant to their general authorisation under s 551 without complying with the statutory pre-emption provisions (s 570 and see also s 571).

[53] Ibid, ss 570–571. In addition where the directors of the company are generally authorised to allot shares pursuant to Companies Act 2006, s 551 the directors may also be given power in the articles to allot shares without complying with the pre-emption provisions (s 570(1)).

[54] FSA, Listing, Prospectus and Disclosure Rules, available at www.fsa.gov.uk.

[55] The Pre-Emption Group comprises representatives of institutional investors, investment banks and listed companies.

favour of a resolution disapplying pre-emption rights.[56] Requests by a company to issue not more than five per cent of its issued share capital non pre-emptively in any given year are likely to be regarded as 'routine'.[57] However, a discount of more than five per cent is not likely to be regarded as routine.[58]

This Statement of Principles has a significant impact on the disapplication of pre-emption rights in practice because a company knows that if it wishes to have the support of the investor protection committees of the Association of British Insurers (ABI) and the National Association of Pension Funds (NAPF), whose members together own (on behalf of their clients) almost half of the share capital of UK companies,[59] it will need to adhere to the Statement of Principles, or make a very strong case for a waiver. Whilst the Statement of Principles does not have the force of law, this document represents the views of the majority of major UK institutional investors. In practice it is the Statement of Principles, rather than the statutory pre-emption provisions, that creates the significant restriction on companies, at least listed companies, raising capital.[60]

The perceived benefits of pre-emption rights for shareholders are various. They can help prevent dilution of shareholder voting control, and prevent value transfers from existing shareholders to new investors, given that new shares are typically offered at a discount to the prevailing market price.[61] Any discount in the price of a new issue relative to existing shares can be seen as representing a transfer of wealth from existing shareholders, whereas a new issue made to existing shareholders at less than the market price has no significant effect on an existing shareholder's financial position. However, pre-emption rights only protect shareholders to the extent that they wish to, and can afford to, take up the offer, and the protection may be less than it appears. In *Mutual Life Assurance Co of New York v Rank Organisation Ltd,*[62] a challenge was brought in relation to a rights issue which was in conformity with the legal requirements but which had a dilutive effect on shareholders resident in the US and Canada. The statutory pre-emption rights were disapplied by special resolution, to exclude US and Canadian shareholders, and to permit the company to pay the cash equivalent to those shareholders instead. The court rejected the challenge and held that no shareholder had the right to expect his or her fractional entitlement to remain constant forever.[63] The ability to prevent dilution of shareholder

---

[56]   See Pre-Emption Group, *Statement of Principles*, July 2008 available at www.pre-emptiongroup.org.uk/principles/index.htm. This Statement of Principles was formerly known as the Pre-Emption Guidelines. For discussion see DTI, *Pre-emption Rights (Myners Report)*, n 50 Chapter 3.

[57]   Ibid, Principle 8. The Principles also state that companies should not issue more than 7.5% of the company's ordinary share capital for cash other than to existing shareholders in any rolling three year period: Principle 10.

[58]   Ibid, Principle 11.

[59]   See eg National Statistics News Release, National Statistics, 10 June 2004 available at www.statistics.gov.uk/pdfdir/share0604.pdf.

[60]   See generally DTI, *Pre-emption Rights (Myners Report)*, n 50.

[61]   It is not a breach of directors' fiduciary duties to issue shares at a discount to market price with a view to ensuring the success of the issue: *Shearer v Bercain Ltd* [1980] 3 All ER 295. Additionally, an existing shareholder could fear the dilution of his/her income stream, since a new issue will introduce new claimants into the company.

[62]   [1985] BCLC 11.

[63]   Indeed, historically shareholders have not had a right to retain their proportionate holding in a company, after all, pre-emption rights were only introduced into UK law for the first time in 1980 (by way of Companies Act 1980, s 17) as a result of the need to implement the Second Directive.

voting control is not a right inherent in being a shareholder,[64] although of course it can be bargained for (and paid for) by shareholders if they wish to do so.

It is sometimes suggested that pre-emption rights are unduly short-term in focus and that the longer term financial interests of both the company and shareholders could be better served by allowing more flexible methods of raising capital. Of course, pre-emption rights do not prevent the company raising equity capital other than by issuing shares to existing shareholders. All that the statutory rules require is that any shares issued for cash consideration[65] are either issued *first* to the existing shareholders, or that the pre-emption rights have been disapplied. It is of course possible for offers to be more generous to shareholders than this, so that rights issues, for example, are generally made on a renounceable basis so that shareholders can trade the right to participate in the new issue of shares. As long as this process is complied with, companies then have significant flexibility as to their methods of raising new equity capital. It has been suggested in the past that the process itself is too slow and that this can act as an unnecessary constraint on companies,[66] but steps have been taken to deal with this point, with the period during which pre-emption offers remain open being reduced from 21 days to 14 days from 1 October 2009.[67]

The process required by these statutory provisions has important consequences. An influential report by Julian Franks and Colin Mayer has suggested that pre-emption rights have a significant disciplinary effect on underperforming management, by limiting their access to equity.[68] A significant advantage of the UK's opt-out system of pre-emption rights, as compared to the US system of opt-in rights, is the fact that the directors have to go to the shareholders to get pre-emption rights disapplied. This has two consequences. In the US directors may issue equity to a new shareholder at a discount in return for implicit or explicit agreements to leave the existing management in place.[69] Bypassing the existing shareholders in this way is not possible in the UK. Second, a potentially important tool is put in the hands of the institutional shareholders.

In the context of the public markets, institutional investors in the UK have a potentially significant role to play. Although, in general, each institutional investor holds a small percentage of each listed company, Franks and Mayer found that coalitions of five shareholders can on average control more than 30 per cent of the equity in a company. The fact that UK law requires the directors to go to the shareholders, and in particular the institutional investors, if they wish to disapply pre-emption rights, provides an opportunity for dialogue, certainly for non-routine disapplications, and an opportunity for the

---

[64]   See E Ferran, 'Legal Capital and the Pressure of the Securities Markets' in KJ Hopt and E Wymeersch (eds), *Capital Markets and Company Law* (Oxford, Oxford University Press, 2003) ch 5.

[65]   The pre-emption provisions do not apply where the shares are issued for non-cash consideration (Companies Act 2006, s 565) and therefore this is one way for companies to issue shares other than to existing shareholders. Companies are therefore able to make use of structures such as vendor placings which allow the company to sidestep the pre-emption rules.

[66]   DTI, *A Discussion Paper by Paul Myners into the Impact of Shareholders' Pre-emption Rights on a Public Company's Ability to Raise New Capital*, November 2004, 24.

[67]   Companies (Share Capital and Acquisition by Company of its Own Shares) Regulations 2009 (SI 2009/2022), amending Companies Act 2006, s 562(5). See also *A Report to the Chancellor of the Exchequer by the Rights Issue Review Group*, November 2008, available at www.hmtreasury.gov.uk/d/pbr08_rights issue-3050.pdf regarding other mechanisms for reforming the process.

[68]   J Franks and C Mayer, 'Governance as a Source of Managerial Discipline' available at www.nbb.be/doc/ts/publications/WP/WP31En.pdf.

[69]   Ibid, 20.

institutional investors to exercise a corporate governance role. The pre-emption principle is certainly strongly supported by investors such as insurance companies and pension funds who argue that pre-emption rights help to cement their long-term relationship with the companies in which they invest. Institutional investors argue that it is the investors who already have the greatest familiarity with the company and its prospects who can best judge the merits of the issue. Further, the need to obtain approval for a disapplication of pre-emption rights may help to deter companies from launching inappropriate capital issues, the proceeds of which may fail to generate value.

Pre-emption rights therefore do seem to have an important role to play. One question which may be asked, however, is whether it is necessary for pre-emption rights to be mandatory.[70] Despite the potentially valuable aspects of pre-emption rights as a form of shareholder protection, criticisms can be made regarding the unduly cumbersome nature of the procedure set out in the 2006 Act, and in particular the length of time which pre-emptive offers take.[71] The standard form transaction in place in the 2006 Act is a poor device because the prescribed requirements will often be less attractive to investors than the alternative requirements that could be developed by the market. If pre-emption rights are as highly regarded by shareholders (and in particular by institutional investors) as they appear to be, it is likely that they would remain a fixture in the UK system, if this issue were left to the market to regulate. The power and influence of institutional investors is such that it is likely that their pressure would result in publicly listed companies continuing to offer new shares to existing shareholders pre-emptively, either as a result of provisions included in the articles or in accordance with some market norm akin to the existing Statement of Principles.[72]

However, for private companies, where no market exists, pre-emption provisions would not develop in this way. In the smallest private companies, where the same individuals are both shareholders and directors, this may not be an issue. The shareholders may be in a position to control the board, and may choose to insert provisions into the articles providing them with protection akin to that currently provided by the statutory provisions. There is also the possibility that in some circumstances an interference with the percentage of their control rights, or a dilution in the value of their shares, could give rise to a petition on the grounds that the business of the company is being conducted in an unfairly prejudicial manner.[73] However, in other types of private companies, some form of compulsory pre-emption rights, imposed by the law, as at present, should remain in place as a valuable form of shareholder protection.[74]

---

[70]   See eg E Ferran, 'Legal Capital and the Pressure of the Securities Markets' in KJ Hopt and E Wymeersch (eds), *Capital Markets and Company Law* (Oxford, Oxford University Press, 2006) ch 5.

[71]   See DTI, *Pre-emption Rights (Myners Report)* n 50. One of the cumbersome aspects of the procedure identified by Paul Myners (namely the fact that the offer must be kept open for 21 days) has now been amended. In accordance with Myners's recommendation, this period has been reduced to 14 days: Companies Act 2006, s 562(5) as amended by the Companies (Share Capital and Acquisition by Company of its Own Shares) Regulations 2009 (SI 2009/2022) with effect from 1 October 2009.

[72]   For discussion of the role of institutional investors see 10.2.2.2.

[73]   Companies Act 2006, s 994. The shareholder would need to demonstrate that some kind of promise had been made to them, either formally or, more likely, informally, to the extent that their pro rata share of the company would not be reduced.

[74]   The Winter Group did not recommend any reform of pre-emption rights, but noted their importance, and in particular noted that should no par value shares be introduced (see 4.3.2.2) then pre-emption rights may become more important as they may be the only protection left at European level to prevent shareholder

4.3.2   The Minimum Capital Rules

These rules come in two parts: requirements as to the amount which must be invested by shareholders before business can be commenced, and rules governing the measurement of the consideration provided by the shareholders for those shares, to ensure that the proper value is received.[75]

4.3.2.1   *The Entry Price for Limited Liability*

The Companies Act 2006 imposes an obligation for public companies to have a minimum share capital of £50,000.[76] No minimum share capital is required for private companies.

4.3.2.2   *The Measurement of Consideration*

As for ensuring that appropriate consideration is received in return for shares issued to shareholders, the Companies Act 2006 requires that all shares have a fixed nominal value,[77] sometimes called the par value, and that companies may not issue shares at a discount to this nominal value.[78] Thus, if companies issue 50,000 shares at £1 each, the nominal value of those shares is £1, and the shares cannot be issued for less than £1 each. This nominal value is a somewhat arbitrary figure that is attached to the shares. It bears no relation to the market value of the shares, at the time of issue or later. Due to the existence of the 'no-discount' rule, companies often set the nominal value of their shares at a very low level. It is very common therefore for the issue price of shares to be well in excess of the nominal value.

Companies with share capital can have those shares denominated in any currency or in several currencies. However, to obtain a trading certificate as a public company, or to re-register as a public company, a company must have its authorised minimum capital denominated either in sterling or in euros[79] (but not in a mixture of the two).[80] The definition of cash for these purposes includes the release of a liability of the company for a liquidated sum.[81] As long as the shares are issued above the nominal value, the legislation is silent as to the actual price at which the shares are issued. Instead, this is a matter for directors' duties (the directors must act bona fide in the best interests of the company when setting the price), and a matter for negotiation with the new investor. The price can be below the market price as long as the directors do not breach their fiduciary duties in

---

dilution: High Level Group of Company Law Experts, 'Modern Regulatory Framework for Company Law in Europe' (Report) (Brussels, 4 November 2002) available at www.ec.europa.eu/internal_market/company/docs/modern/report_en.pdf (Winter Group Report).

[75]   Note that additional regulatory requirements regarding capital are imposed on certain kinds of financial institutions: see pages 25–26. These requirements are in addition to the legal capital requirements discussed in this chapter, and focus on investor protection and systemic risk issues, rather than creditor protection per se.

[76]   Companies Act 2006, ss 761, 763(1), as required by Second Directive, art 6. This is a repetition of the equivalent provisions in the Companies Act 1985 (ss 117–118), and gold plates the requirement of the Second Directive in this regard, which requires just €25,000. A quarter of this share capital needs to be paid up: s 586.

[77]   Ibid, s 542.

[78]   Ibid, s 580; *Ooregum Gold Mining Co of India v Roper* [1892] AC 125. This is a requirement of the Second Directive, art 8(1).

[79]   *Re Scandinavian Bank Group plc* [1988] Ch 87.

[80]   Companies Act 2006, s 765(1). One innovation in the 2006 Act was a new statutory procedure for all companies to redenominate the currency of share capital without an application to the court: ss 622–628.

[81]   Ibid, s 583(3)(c).

determining that price.[82] Any difference between the nominal price and the issue price is referred to as a premium and is treated in much the same way as capital. It is available to finance the company's activities, but is not generally available to distribute to shareholders as a dividend.[83]

In regard to shares issued for non-cash consideration, in private companies this is a matter for the directors' business judgement.[84] This would include the situation where shares are issued in return for an asset of some kind, such as the acquisition of property. In general the courts show a lack of interest in assessing the worth of non-cash consideration received by private companies as long as it is not 'colourable or illusory'.[85] However, for public companies the Second Directive requires a stricter rule.[86] As a result, the Companies Act 2006 requires a mandatory valuation of non-cash consideration received by public companies.[87] A detailed report[88] is required by an independent valuer during the six months preceding the allotment. The report must include a description of the asset, the method and date of valuation and it must support the conclusion that the consideration received by the company is not less than the nominal value of the shares plus any premium.[89] A copy of the report must be sent to the allottee before the allotment, and must be delivered to the registrar of companies when the company files the return of allotment of the shares.

Where the company allots shares in contravention of these requirements, the allottee can be liable to pay an amount equal to the aggregate of the nominal value of the shares and the whole of any premium, plus interest.[90] This is in addition to the original consideration provided for the shares and therefore the allottee may be required to pay twice.[91] Subsequent holders of shares allotted in contravention of these provisions may also be liable to pay for the shares in cash in some circumstances.[92] Directors who authorise the allotment may also be liable for breach of fiduciary duty.[93] In addition some forms of non-cash consideration, most notably an undertaking to do work or to perform services,[94] are prohibited altogether.

---

[82] *Mutual Life Insurance Co of New York v Rank Organisation Ltd* [1985] BCLC 11.

[83] Companies Act 2006, s 610.

[84] *Re Wragg Ltd* [1897] 1 Ch 796.

[85] Ibid, 835 per Smith LJ.

[86] Directive (EC) 2006/68 [2006] OJ L264/32 of 25 September 2006, amending Council Directive 77/91/EEC, as regards the formation of public limited liability companies and the maintenance and alteration of their capital. There are no plans to implement these changes into UK legislation at the present time.

[87] Companies Act 2006, s 593. There are exceptions (see ss 594–595). For the procedure regarding valuation of non-cash consideration for the shares of a public company see ss 596–597.

[88] Ibid, s 596. The requirements for this report, and the detailed requirements attached to it in the Companies Act 2006, are a repetition of the requirements of the Companies Act 1985 without any substantive changes.

[89] Ibid, s 596(3).

[90] Ibid, s 593(3).

[91] The harshness of this provision is mitigated by Companies Act 2006, s 606 which allows the court to grant relief from liability in some circumstances.

[92] Companies Act 2006, s 605, but see also s 606 in this regard.

[93] *Hirsche v Sims* [1894] AC 654; *Lowry (Inspector of Taxes) v Consolidated African Selection Trust Ltd* [1940] AC 648.

[94] Companies Act 2006, s 585, as required by Second Directive 77/91/EC, art 7.

Two explanations can be advanced to justify these rules in policy terms. The first suggests that these rules protect the existing shareholders of the company from dilution, the second suggests that these rules provide an important creditor protection function. These will be assessed in turn.

4.3.2.3   *The Efficacy of these Rules as a Form of Shareholder Protection*

It was discussed at 4.3.1 above that issues of new shares can impact on the existing shareholders in a company. In particular the issue of new shares can have a dilutive effect on the value of the existing shares of the company if inadequate consideration is received for those shares. Pre-emption rights can perform a valuable role in preventing this dilution, but the protection provided by pre-emption rights is limited in a number of ways. First, pre-emption rights do not apply where the issue is for non-cash consideration.[95] Second, pre-emption rights can be disapplied, and so do not necessarily protect minority shareholders. Third, they only protect existing shareholders to the extent that they can afford to take up the issue of shares offered to them.

It is sometimes suggested, therefore, that the rules regarding the adequacy of consideration received by the company in return for shares can have a role in protecting shareholders against dilution. However, the rules are not effective for this purpose. All they seek to ensure is that the directors receive at least par value for the shares. If the market value of the shares is below par value then the existing shareholders are not disadvantaged by an issue below par but at, or close to, market price. Similarly, the shareholders are not protected by this rule where the market price is significantly above the par value. What the existing shareholders need is a rule that ensures that the shares are issued at a fair price, which is likely to be market price, or just below. It is lawful for the directors to issue below market price and it may well be appropriate for them to do so in order to ensure that the issue is successful. However, there is already a rule in this regard. Directors are under a duty to act bona fide in the best interests of the shareholders as a whole,[96] which includes an obligation to achieve a fair price for the shares issued by the company. Of course the rules requiring expert valuations of non-cash consideration might provide the shareholders with some information to help them to determine whether the directors are in breach of their duties, but these rules are a cumbersome and expensive way to achieve that end.

4.3.2.4   *The Efficacy of these Rules as a Form of Creditor Protection*

If the idea behind these rules is to provide the creditors with the comfort of a guaranteed equity 'cushion', then they are ineffective. The rules adopt a 'one size fits all' approach which does not take account of the size of the debt which the company may incur or the riskiness of its activities. In addition, the minimum capital requirement for public companies is minuscule compared to the size of the debts of most public companies, and of course the 2006 Act imposes no minimum capital requirement for private companies, which are just as likely to have creditors potentially in need of protection.

There is also no ongoing obligation on the shareholders to retain this level of investment in the company. The 2006 Act does provide that if the net assets of a public

---

[95]   Companies Act 2006, s 565.
[96]   Ibid, s 172, this is subject to the obligation on directors to take account of other stakeholder interests in determining what the best interests of the shareholders actually comprise.

company fall to half, or less than half, of its called up share capital the directors must call a general meeting to consider whether any steps must be taken to deal with the situation.[97] However, this offers little or nothing by way of protection for the creditors. This rule is only likely to be invoked in extreme financial distress, when the shareholders' investment in the company has already been substantially depleted. Given that this calculation will generally depend on a complex accounting calculation, it may be difficult to discern when this point is reached. This provision imposes no obligation on the shareholders to inject any more capital,[98] nor does it require any particular form of action to occur at this point in time. Moreover, the damage to the company's reputation as a result of calling such a meeting may be significant, and it should be borne in mind that the meeting must be held even if the fall is only temporary.

Two points are worth noting in passing. The discussion here is intended to relate to the sorts of companies discussed in chapter one, ie manufacturing companies, retail companies, construction companies etc. There are other companies, not covered by this book, which have different rules as to capital adequacy, as discussed earlier.[99] A discussion of these issues falls outside the scope of this book. Second, as discussed in chapter five, an alternative method for ensuring capital adequacy is via the imposition of financial ratios by contractual means.[100]

As regards the consideration received for shares, the regime utilises the concept of par value by which to measure the adequacy of the consideration received, a concept that bears no relation to the market price of the shares. Indeed in this scheme it is entirely lawful for a company to issue shares below market price.[101] On one view this issue is of little relevance or interest to the creditors at all. In a case like *Ooregum Gold Mining Co of India v Roper*,[102] where the shares are allotted at 75 per cent of the par value, since the shares were then trading at a discount to the market price it is difficult to see why this impacts on creditors in any negative way: any money inputed to the company by the shareholders expands the potential pool of assets for creditors, even if issued at below the par value of the shares.[103] The no-discount rule provides no meaningful creditor protection.

It is particularly unfortunate that the anachronistic concept of par value was retained by the Companies Act 2006. The question of whether no par value shares should be

---

[97]   Ibid, s 656, implementing Second Directive 77/91/EC, art 17. This may be contrasted with some other European countries which have a rule of this kind in place. For instance, if the net assets of a Swedish company fall below half its share capital, then the shareholders must either inject fresh equity to restore the new asset level, or liquidate the company (see J Armour, 'Share Capital and Creditor Protection: Efficient Rules for a Modern Company Law' (2000) 63 *Modern Law Review* 355, 371).

[98]   Any obligation on the shareholders to inject further capital at this point would presumably undermine the principle of limited liability.

[99]   See pages 25–26.

[100]   See pages 168–70.

[101]   *Hilder v Dexter* [1902] AC 474, although this may be a breach of directors' duties (*Shearer v Bercain Ltd* [1980] 3 All ER 295).

[102]   [1892] AC 125.

[103]   This argument may have had less weight in earlier stages of company law development when mandatory accounting disclosures did not exist and creditors might have had little information other than par value to rely on. At that point future creditors of the company could potentially have been prejudiced if they relied on the par value as a measure of the capital actually subscribed. It is difficult to imagine that any creditors, present or future, would rely on par value in this way today.

introduced has been around for some time.[104] In the review that preceded the introduction of the 2006 Act the Company Law Review Steering Group stated that no par value shares should be introduced, arguing that there is no reason to impose any particular limit below which the issue price cannot fall as long as all of the proceeds of the issue are retained in an undistributable capital account.[105] However, the Second Directive prevents these reforms being introduced for public companies.[106] As a result, these proposals were dropped altogether for both public and private companies.[107] This is a great shame. Par value is a meaningless and valueless concept whose continued existence in the UK is difficult to justify, except insofar as the Second Directive continues to require it for public companies. By contrast, no par value shares are widely recognised elsewhere.[108]

As regards both cash and non-cash consideration, the legal capital rules provide little in the way of creditor protection. As regards cash consideration, the definition of cash for these purposes includes the release of a debt.[109] So, if the company owes A £120 and the company issues to A 100 shares of nominal value £1 this will be regarded as cash consideration and will not infringe the no-discount rule as long as the debt released is greater than the nominal value of the shares. This appears to be the case even if the company is insolvent at the time and the amount that the creditor is actually likely to receive is substantially below the nominal value of the shares issued.[110] So even if in the winding up the creditor will only receive 50 pence in the pound, ie just £60 in the above example, this does not infringe the no-discount rule. In the absence of deceit or fraud there is no authority for the court to inquire into the financial capacity of the issuing company to pay to the creditor-allottee the amount of the presently payable debt. This is subject to the proviso that the debt must have been genuinely created in the course of the company's business,[111] and must be immediately payable.

As regards non-cash consideration, the Second Directive specifies how this consideration should be valued when received by public companies.[112] Serious doubt can be cast on

---

[104] See eg Gedge Committee, *Report of the Committee on Shares of No Par Value*, Cmnd 9112 (1954); Jenkins Committee, *Report of the Company Law Committee*, Cmnd 1749 (1962) paras 32–34.

[105] See *The Strategic Framework*, February 1999 n 1, 88–91.

[106] Second Directive 77/91/EC, art 32 sets out safeguards for creditors on a capital reduction, including the right to apply to court, something which 'puts unjustified power in the hands of creditors': see *The Strategic Framework*, n 1, 84). See also Second Directive 77/91/EC, arts 19 and 22, 23. Although there is no formal requirement in the EU Company law directives for shares to have a nominal value, both the Second and Fourth directives require that shares have assigned to them, if not a nominal value then at least an 'accounting par' or 'accounting par value'. Second Directive 77/91/EC, art 8 requires that no par value shares of public companies should not be issued below their 'accountable par', thereby preventing a true no par value scheme being put in place.

[107] See CLR, *The Final Report*, n 40, para 10.7.

[108] Eg Australian Corporations Law, s 254C, inserted by Company Law Review Act 1998.

[109] Companies Act 2006, s 583(3)(c).

[110] *Pro-Image Studios v Commonwealth Bank of Australia* (1990–1991) 4 ACSR 586 (Sup Ct Victoria) cf *Re Jarass Pty Ltd* (1988) 13 ACSR 728 (Sup Ct NSW).

[111] In *Mosely v Koffyfontein Mines Ltd* [1904] 2 Ch 108 the Court of Appeal held that a proposal to issue convertible debentures at less than par where the debentures could immediately be converted into fully paid shares having a par value equal to the par value of the debentures was an infringement of the no-discount rule. The Court of Appeal deliberately left open the question of a debenture issued at a discount which was not *immediately* convertible into shares.

[112] As regards the assessment of non-cash consideration for private companies, this is not dealt with by statute, but by the common law: the courts will not investigate the adequacy of non-cash consideration received unless it is manifestly colourable or fraudulent: *Re Wragg Ltd* [1897] 1 Ch 796, 830; *Hong Kong & China Gas Co Ltd v Glen* [1914] 1 Ch 527.

the utility of these valuation rules. All that the rules aim to guarantee is that the value of the item on receipt is equal to the par value of the shares at that moment in time. For many items this will bear little relation to the value of the item at the (future) point in time when the creditors seek to realise their debts.[113] In fact, these valuation rules are costly for companies both in money, in that the independent reports need to be paid for, and in time, as they delay company formation and increases in capital through the issue of new shares. The prohibition on issuing shares in exchange for future services contained in the Second Directive is also problematic in the context of the financing of high tech start-up companies. Creditors deciding whether to lend to a company, and on what terms, will be interested in the net worth of the company, which will include the existing share capital of the company. In assessing this they will need to examine the current value of the firm's assets, rather than the value of the assets at the moment of purchase.[114]

One interesting question that arises is what remedy the company would have if it issued shares for non-cash consideration on the strength of an expert valuation which subsequently turned out to be negligent, so that the non-cash consideration is worth less than expected. This issue has arisen particularly in the context of share for share exchanges, where, in a takeover of a target company, the consideration paid to the target shareholders by the bidder is not cash but is rather shares in the bidder company. The shares in the target company clearly comprise non-cash consideration, paid by the bidder company. If the shares in the target turn out to be worth less than expected, the question arises whether the company has a claim for the difference between what it paid (the value of the shares it allotted to the target shareholders) and what it obtained.

It has been held, in the Australian case of *Pilmer v Duke Group Ltd*,[115] that a company does not have a proprietary interest in its own shares. A company, Kia Ora (the bidder), successfully made a share exchange offer with a cash component for another company, Western (the target). Kia Ora retained accountants, Nelson Wheeler, to prepare a report on Western. The acquisition of Western proved disastrous and Kia Ora went into liquidation. In an action by the liquidator against Nelson Wheeler one question for the High Court of Australia was the measure of damages payable by Nelson Wheeler in contract and tort arising from their incompetence in preparing the report on Western. Kia Ora argued that the loss it suffered was the difference in value between the shares it allotted to the Western shareholders (as consideration) and the shares of Western it acquired from Western's shareholders.

One approach to this issue is to regard the company as having no proprietary interest in its own shares. This is a view that has been advanced by Fidelis Oditah.[116] On this analysis, shares are not regarded as an asset of the company *prior* to the issue. When a company

---

[113]   Many assets devalue quickly (eg computers) and may have no value at a later date. In addition the 'independent' experts in this regard are repeat players in the market and will not wish to lose current or prospective clients by acting too independently in this regard. So long as the assets are not outrageously over-valued, it is likely that the non-cash consideration will be approved.

[114]   Clearly creditors are interested in just these issues in practice: see the discussion in 5.2.2 (regarding the initial information required by creditors) and chapter 11 (regarding the information required in relation to debt securities).

[115]   (2001) 75 ALJR 1067, (2001) 38 ACSR 121; [2001] 2 BCLC 773 (HC Aust).

[116]   See F Oditah, 'Takeovers, Share Exchanges and the Meaning of Loss' (1996) 112 *Law Quarterly Review* 424 (cf KR Handley, 'Takeovers, Share Exchanges and the Meaning of Loss' (1997) 113 *Law Quarterly Review* 51); DD Prentice and R Nolan, 'The Issue of Shares – Compensating the Company for Loss' (2002) 118 *Law Quarterly Review* 180.

issues shares it does create a proprietary interest, but that interest is a bundle of rights which are vested in the shareholder. Accordingly, once issued it is the shareholder and not the company that has a proprietary interest in the share; there is nothing that the company can turn to its own benefit. If correct, this approach has significant consequences. In a share for share exchange in a takeover situation, such as that in *Pilmer v Duke*, it would mean that a company such as Kia Ora should be regarded as having lost nothing, where the shares are worth less than expected:

> Prior to issuing the shares to the target shareholders, the bidder did *not* own or enjoy the contingent income and capital rights or the control rights transferred to the target's shareholders. In no true sense are the shares issued to the target's shareholders issued at the bidder's expense.[117]

This was the approach which the High Court of Australia adopted in *Pilmer v Duke*. Since Kia Ora had lost nothing, the court held that there was no basis for finding liability on the part of Nelson Wheeler in either contract or tort. If this is correct then it suggests that companies would also find it difficult to recover compensation from negligent expert valuers where they issue shares for non-cash consideration, since they have similarly lost 'nothing'. Of course, the shareholders in the bidder company (Kia Ora in the above example) can be said to have suffered a loss, or at least the existing shareholders in the bidder at the time of the new issue (for non-cash consideration) can be said to have suffered a loss as a result of the resultant dilution of their shareholdings. The 'new' shareholders coming in to the company (ie the shareholders in the target company— Western in the above example—who acquire shares in the bidder in the share exchange) have suffered no such loss.[118] If the shareholders of the bidder company are owed a duty by the expert valuer, then they may be able to claim for this loss.[119] Normally the reflective loss principle would prevent such a claim by the shareholders,[120] but this principle only applies where the company and the shareholder(s) both have claims arising out of the same set of facts, so that where the company has no claim, the principle does not apply.

However, it is to be hoped that the English courts would not follow this approach. There are at least two bases for regarding the company as having suffered loss in these circumstances. First, the primary purpose of a company issuing shares is as a capital raising exercise. It is clear that while shares are an asset of the shareholders, the capital raised by the issue of shares belongs to the company.[121] A company can receive consideration for the issue of its shares by a variety of means including the receipt of cash or non-cash assets, which can include the shares in another company. It was recognised in

---

[117]   F Oditah, 'Takeovers, Share Exchanges and the Meaning of Loss' (1996) 112 *Law Quarterly Review* 424, 434.

[118]   In this regard, the issue of shares for non-cash consideration is distinct from the share-for-share exchange in *Pilmer*, in which the shareholders could be regarded as a single, homogeneous body for these purposes.

[119]   It is not clear that the expert valuer (usually the company's auditor) would owe a duty to the shareholders in this regard. In general, courts have constrained the duty owed by auditors to shareholders (in relation to auditing the company's accounts) very narrowly: *Caparo Industries plc v Dickman* [1990] 2 AC 605. Although the situation is not identical, it seems likely that the shareholders would have to show that the expert knew that the advice would be communicated to the existing shareholders, and that the expert knew that the shareholders were likely to rely on that advice. The purpose of the expert's report will also be relevant. Was it merely for the purposes of giving the shareholders information that would allow them to sue the directors for breach of duty, should they have issued the shares in breach of the legal capital rules, or was the purpose to allow the shareholders to prevent dilution?

[120]   *Johnson v Gore Wood & Co* [2002] 2 AC 1.

[121]   *Bradbury v English Sewing Cotton Co Ltd* [1923] AC 744, 767 per Lord Wrenbury.

Pilmer that Kia Ora was entitled to recover the cash component of its offer. If Kia Ora had acquired all the target shares for cash, it could have obtained substantial damages. This distinction is difficult to justify. Once it is accepted that the company is employing its own capital in a share exchange takeover it follows that if the company does not receive full value it suffers exactly the same loss as would have occurred if only cash had been paid.[122] It should be noted also that where directors issue shares at a discount, the discount is recoverable.[123] This may be attributable to capital maintenance rules but it does indicate that when a company issues shares *it* can be considered to have suffered a loss.[124]

An alternative basis for the view that the company has suffered loss is to regard the company as having suffered an opportunity cost, ie it has lost the opportunity to enter into a different (better) bargain with the allottees, or to enter a different bargain altogether. The negligent advice prevents them from disposing of the shares in another manner and these foregone alternatives are its loss.[125] Rather than entering into *this* bargain, and exchanging its shares for an asset which turns out to be worth £100, the company could instead have exchanged these shares for an asset worth £100 plus x. Of course, quantifying the resultant loss will not be straightforward.[126]

In relation to an expert valuation, therefore, it would be preferable not to follow the *Pilmer* approach, and to allow the company to bring an action against the valuer where the report negligently undervalues the non-cash asset. This would mean, however, that the existing shareholders would be unlikely to be able to bring any claim, as a consequence of the reflective loss principle.

4.4   Maintenance of Capital

In the Companies Act 2006, the starting point for maintenance of capital issues is that any form of distribution of corporate assets to shareholders is prohibited except where the value of the distribution is less than that of the assets available for distribution. Distributions can be made to the shareholders in a number of ways, such as the payment of dividends, the redemption or purchase of the company's own shares, and a reduction of share capital. The central idea is that capital must not be returned to the shareholders.[127]

---

[122]   *Duke Group Ltd v Pilmer* (1998) 27 ACSR 1, 404 per Mullighan J (Sup Ct South Aust).

[123]   *Hirsche v Sims* [1894] AC 654.

[124]   DD Prentice and R Nolan, 'The Issue of Shares' (2002) 118 *Law Quarterly Review* 180, 181–82.

[125]   This argument is particularly powerful if the bidder is in the market to raise funds and it chooses the wrong option, although this argument may be difficult to run in relation to a bidder acquiring shares in another company since it may more appropriately be viewed as in the market to acquire assets (the shares in the target) rather than for fund raising purposes per se: F Oditah, 'Takeovers, Share Exchanges and the meaning of loss' (1996) 112 *Law Quarterly Review* 424, 441–42.

[126]   F Oditah, 'Takeovers, Share Exchanges and the meaning of loss' (1996) 112 *Law Quarterly Review* 424, 441–44.

[127]   The idea that capital must not be returned to the shareholders is central to the Second Company Law directive 77/91/EC, at least for public companies. This concept was gold-plated on implementation by the UK and was extended to include share premiums and the capital redemption reserve.

4.4.1 Dividend Payments

As regards dividend payments, there is a common law rule of long standing that a distribution of assets to a shareholder, except in accordance with specific statutory procedures, is a return of capital which is unlawful and ultra vires for the company.[128] These common law rules operate in tandem with the statutory rules, now contained in the Companies Act 2006, which lay down rules determining how companies may pay dividends.[129] The Act provides that dividends can only be made out of a company's distributable profits, which are the company's 'accumulated realised profits...less its accumulated realised losses'.[130] For public companies an additional hurdle is imposed: a dividend may not be paid if the result would be to reduce the value of its assets below that of liabilities and capital.[131] In the event of an unlawful dividend, the recipient is personally liable to repay the dividend, but only if they have knowledge of the unlawfulness of the payment.[132] In addition, the directors who authorise the unlawful dividend payment will be liable to the company for those sums,[133] unless they have acted under an honest and reasonable belief that the facts justified the payment, such as where the directors base their decision in good faith on accounts which are later found to be defective.[134]

4.4.2 Repurchases and Redemptions of Shares

There is a general rule that companies are not permitted to acquire their own shares.[135] However, the Companies Act 2006 contains a number of important exceptions to this rule. In particular, both redemptions and repurchases of shares are permitted in certain circumstances.[136] There are some significant similarities between these forms of distribution, which both involve a purchase of shares from a shareholder by the company. The procedures for financing the purchase of shares are broadly similar, as is the use of the capital redemption reserve as a mechanism for preserving the company's capital. The essential difference between the two is the fact that as regards repurchases of shares the agreement of both parties is required at the time of the purchase, and the terms of the purchase are set at that time, whereas for redeemable shares the terms are generally set in the articles and may not require the consent of both parties.

---

[128] Eg *Re Halt Garage (1964) Ltd* [1982] 3 All ER 1016. For a recent discussion of this principle see *Progress Property Co Ltd v Moorgarth Group Ltd* [2009] EWCA Civ 629. This rule prevents disguised distributions: *Aveling Barford Ltd v Perion Ltd* [1989] 1 WLR 360, although see, now, Companies Act 2006, ss 845–46.

[129] Note that there is often a contractual restriction on dividend payments in loans to private companies, see pages 157–58.

[130] Companies Act 2006, s 830.

[131] Ibid, s 831.

[132] Ibid, s 847(2) and see *Precision Dippings Ltd v Precision Dippings Marketing Ltd* [1986] 1 Ch 447 cf J Payne, 'Unjust Enrichment, Trusts and Recipient Liability for Unlawful Dividends' (2003) 119 *Law Quarterly Review* 583. The recipient must have knowledge of the facts giving rise to the contravention and does not need to know that the payment is a breach of the Act: *It's a Wrap (UK) Ltd v Gula* [2006] EWCA Civ 544; [2006] BCC 626.

[133] *Flitcroft's Case* (1882) LR 21 Ch D 519; *Precision Dippings*, ibid.

[134] Eg *Hilton International Ltd v Hilton* [1989] 1 NZLR 442, although in that case the directors failed to obtain a proper set of accounts and therefore were held liable to refund the amount of the dividend. See also *Re Paycheck Services 3 Ltd* [2009] EWCA Civ 625; [2009] 2 BCLC 309, [82]–[84], obiter.

[135] Companies Act 2006, s 658(1); *Trevor v Whitworth* (1887) LR 12 App Cas 409.

[136] Ibid, ss 684–689 as regards redemptions of shares and ss 690–708 as regards purchases of own shares.

Share buy-backs can be extremely beneficial, especially in small companies with little or no active market for the company's shares, as they provide an exit route for shareholders. Even in larger companies, they can be a useful tool where the company has surplus cash or wants to reorganise its capital by getting rid of a class of shares entirely. They also facilitate employee share schemes as they make it possible for the company to purchase the shares when the employee leaves the company. However, because share buy-backs potentially infringe the maintenance of capital principle, they have been curtailed by legislation.[137] For a share buy-back it is not necessary for a company proposing to purchase its own shares to have the authority to do so in its articles,[138] however a shareholder resolution is required to authorise the buy-back. This resolution[139] needs to be an ordinary resolution if the purchase is an 'on-market' purchase,[140] and a special resolution if it is an 'off-market' purchase.[141] Repurchases must be funded out of distributable profits or a fresh issue of shares in order not to reduce share capital.[142] Where the buy-back is funded wholly out of the company's profits the amount by which the capital of the company is reduced must be transferred to a capital redemption reserve[143] and this reserve is treated for most purposes as though it were share capital.[144] In addition to these company law requirements, the Listing Rules create some additional requirements for listed companies.[145]

However, a private company can buy back its own shares out of capital in certain circumstances.[146] In particular the directors must make a statement as to the solvency of

---

[137] Share buy-backs also give rise to other concerns, most notably the concern that they might be used by the company to bolster or stabilise the share price. These concerns are best dealt with via the specific provisions concerning market manipulation: Financial Services and Markets Act 2000, s 118, s 397 (discussed further in 10.5.2).

[138] However, the articles may restrict or prohibit the company's purchase of its own shares (s 690(1)).

[139] Shareholders cannot rely on the *Re Duomatic* principle of unanimous consent as an alternative to a resolution passed in a general meeting in this instance: *Re RW Peak (Kings Lynn) Ltd* [1998] BCC 596 (affirmed in *Wright v Atlas Wright (Europe) Ltd* [1999] 2 BCLC 301). The statutory protections are intended to protect the creditors as well as the shareholders and therefore it is not acceptable for the shareholders to waive that statutory protection.

[140] Companies Act 2006, s 701. The authority may be general and not linked to any particular purchase of shares (cf off market purchases). The maximum length of an authority is five years: s 701(5) (implemented by reg 4 of the Companies (Share Capital and Acquisition of its Own Shares) Regulations 2009 (SI 2009/2022)).

[141] Ibid, s 694. A general authorisation is not acceptable and the shareholders must approve the specific terms of the contract by which the shares are purchased: s 694(2). The special resolution may be of unlimited duration if a private company is involved (cf public companies: s 695(5)). A resolution approving an off market purchase of own shares will not be effective if any shareholder holding shares to which the resolution relates exercised the voting rights carried by those shares in voting on the resolution and the resolution would not have been passed if he had not done so: s 695(3).

[142] Ibid, s 692(2).

[143] Ibid, s 733(2). Where the buy-back is funded from a fresh issue of shares see s 733(3): normally the nominal value of the issued capital available to creditors will remain intact because the new shares will simply replace those being bought back.

[144] The exception to this situation is that the capital redemption reserve may be used to pay up fully paid bonus shares: s 733(5).

[145] See generally FSA Handbook, Listing Rules, LR 12.

[146] Initially the CLR recommended the repeal of these latter sections on the basis that the simplified reduction of capital procedure introduced for private companies would make them unnecessary. In practice the sections in the 1985 Act had been used by private companies as a simplified reduction procedure. However, these provisions were later reprieved on the basis that there would still be occasions when these sections would be useful to private companies, where the reduction procedure may not be available. The example given in the course of the parliamentary debate was where a company has no share premium or other capital reserves but wishes to purchase its shares at above the nominal value. The reduction procedure would not allow that, due to insufficient capital, but these sections might since they, unlike the reduction procedure, treat any revaluation

the company.[147] The directors must state that they have formed the opinion that if the payment is made the company will be able to pay its debts as they fall due for the coming 12 months, taking account of the company's liabilities, including its contingent and prospective liabilities.[148] Annexed to this statement is a report by the company's auditors stating that they are not aware of anything to indicate that the directors' opinion is unreasonable.[149] The directors commit a criminal offence with a maximum term of imprisonment of two years if they make their statement 'without having reasonable grounds for the opinion expressed in it'.[150] A special resolution approving the payment is also required.[151] When shares are repurchased they can either be treated as cancelled, or they can be held as treasury shares.[152]

As regards redemptions of shares, the Companies Act 2006 permits shares which are to be redeemed or are liable to be redeemed at the option of the company or of the shareholder.[153] The 2006 Act introduced some relaxations regarding the terms and manner of redemption. The 2006 Act allows the directors of both public and private companies to determine the terms and manner of the redemption if they are authorised to do so under the articles or by an ordinary resolution.[154] The terms of redemption no longer have to provide for payment on redemption.[155] The issue of redeemable shares by private companies no longer requires prior authorisation in the articles,[156] although this requirement remains in place for public companies.[157] The financing of redemptions broadly follows that of repurchases. Redemptions must be funded out of distributable profits or a fresh issue of shares in order not to reduce share capital,[158] but private companies are permitted to redeem shares out of capital if they follow the solvency statement procedure set out in the Act.[159]

4.4.3 Reductions of Capital

As regards reductions of capital, the Companies Act 2006 allows court-approved reductions of capital for both public and private companies. Section 641 of the Companies Act 2006 allows both public and private companies to reduce their capital by way of a special resolution, which is subsequently confirmed by the court. Creditors are entitled to object

---

reserves (unrealised profits) as being capital. This would allow companies to continue to distribute surplus cash in circumstances where they have no distributable profits (see Hansard, HL GC Day 10, cols 32–33).

[147] Companies Act 2006, s 714.

[148] Ibid, s 714(3)(4).

[149] Ibid, s 714(6).

[150] Ibid, s 715.

[151] Ibid, s 716. The votes of any member holding shares to which the resolution relates will be discounted for the purposes of determining whether the resolution has passed: s 717.

[152] Ibid, ss 724–732 and see G Morse, 'The Introduction of Treasury Shares into English Law and Practice' [2004] *Journal of Business Law* 303.

[153] Ibid, s 684.

[154] Ibid, s 685.

[155] Ibid, s 686. This allows for payment at a later date (s 686(2)) and for payment on more than one date (cf *BDG Roof Bond Ltd v Douglas* [2000] 1 BCLC 401). Somewhat strangely it is not open to a company to make payments on more than one date on a purchase of its own shares: s 691.

[156] It will still be possible to use the articles to exclude or restrict the use of redeemable shares: Companies Act 2006, s 684(2).

[157] Ibid, s 684(3).

[158] Ibid, s 687(2).

[159] Ibid, s 687(1).

to the reduction where their interests may be adversely affected, such as where the reduction involves a repayment to shareholders,[160] rather than merely cancelling share capital which is unrepresented by a company's available assets.[161] If creditors' interests are not properly dealt with in a reduction the court has discretion whether or not to confirm a reduction of capital.[162]

In addition, the Companies Act 2006 introduced a new method of reducing capital for private companies, by way of a special resolution coupled with a solvency statement from the directors. The Company Law Review initially recommended that this method should replace the court approval method for private companies, although this recommendation was later dropped.[163] The Company Law Review also recommended that public companies be allowed to reduce their capital on this basis, without having to seek court approval.[164] Compliance with the Second Directive requirement that creditors whose claims antedate the publication of the decision to reduce capital should be entitled to have a right to obtain security for their claims[165] would have been achieved by providing creditors with the opportunity, at their initiative, to challenge a reduction in court. However, the government decided against introducing this change for public companies.[166]

There are close similarities between this solvency statement and that required of directors in the procedure whereby private companies can repurchase their shares from capital,[167] although the statutory statement for a reduction of capital does not need to be accompanied by an auditors' report.[168] The statement must be made by all directors and the directors must take account of prospective and contingent liabilities of the company.[169] Making a statutory statement without having reasonable grounds for the opinions expressed in it is a criminal offence for which the maximum penalty is imprisonment for up to two years.[170] Although this procedure offers a measure of deregulation for private companies, there are many reasons, both presentational and practical, why private companies may still wish to follow the more cumbersome and expensive court approval route. These include the desire to draw as complete a line as possible under a particular change of share capital, and the desire to obtain the court's approval for an unusual reduction,[171] in circumstances where the directors are faced with a difficulty in forming

---

[160]   Ibid, ss 645(2), 645(4) and 646 (as amended by The Companies (Share Capital and Acquisition by Company of its Own Shares) Regulations 2009 (SI 2009/2022)).

[161]   Ibid, s 645(3).

[162]   Ibid, s 648, *Prudential Assurance Co Ltd v Chatterley-Whitfield Collieries Co Ltd* [1949] AC 512.

[163]   See *Company Formation and Capital Maintenance*, n 40, para 3.27; Company Law Review Steering Group, *Completing the Structure*, n 40, para 7.9.

[164]   Ibid, *Company Formation and Capital Maintenance*, paras 3.27–3.35.

[165]   Second Directive 77/91/EC, art 32.

[166]   Department for Trade and Industry, *Company Law Reform* (Cm 6456, 2005).

[167]   Companies Act 2006, ss 709–723 (discussed above at 4.4.2). The contents of the solvency statement required for a reduction of capital are almost identical to those of the statutory declaration or statement that used to be required of directors under the now repealed private company financial assistance 'whitewash' procedure (Companies Act 1985, s 155) although the statutory statement for a reduction of capital does not need to be accompanied by an auditors' report.

[168]   Ibid, s 643.

[169]   Ibid, ss 643(1) and (2).

[170]   Ibid, ss 643(4) and (5).

[171]   A private company cannot reduce its capital to zero except with court approval: s 641(2).

the opinion required for the solvency statement.[172] However, initial indications suggest that some private companies are beginning to make use of the solvency statement approach in preference to the court approval mechanism.

4.4.4   The Prohibition Against Financial Assistance

The rules prohibiting companies providing assistance for the purchase of their own shares have traditionally been regarded as part of the legal capital rules, but, as we will see in the next section, the root of these provisions has little in common with the rest of the capital maintenance provisions. In particular, creditor protection does not seem to be a strong driver behind these rules. The financial assistance rules are therefore best seen as an 'offshoot' of the legal capital rules as they have only a limited overlap with the idea that a company should maintain its capital.

Public companies are subject to a prohibition on the giving of financial assistance for the purchase of their own shares,[173] however this ban no longer applies to private companies.[174] These rules have been subject to substantial criticism as a result of both the complexity of the rules, and the costs associated with complying with them. As a result the Company Law Review suggested some significant reforms in relation to these provisions.[175] These proposals were not taken up and public companies continue to be faced with a prohibition on the giving of financial assistance for the purchase of their own shares in almost identical terms to that under the Companies Act 1985.[176]

The concept of 'financial assistance' is construed broadly to include not only assistance which directly or indirectly helps to pay the price of the shares but also other steps which merely smooth the path, for example the payment of concurrent benefits such as accountants' fees.[177] The assistance must fall within the forms of financial assistance specified in section 677 since only these forms of assistance are banned, but, importantly,

---

[172]   When the new solvency statement method for reducing capital was introduced, it was anticipated that reserves arising as a result of this procedure might be treated differently (and less favourably) than reserves arising from a court approved reduction of capital. However, the Secretary of State has made use of powers within the 2006 Act (specifically s 654) to introduce delegated legislation to clarify this issue. The Companies (Reduction of Capital) Order 2008 (SI 2008/1915) provides that when a company reduces its share capital (by any means) a reserve arising from that reduction is to be treated as a realised profit for the purposes of the rules about distributions of companies assets in Part 23 of the 2006 Act unless (in the case of a court approved reduction) the court orders otherwise.

[173]   Companies Act 2006, ss 677–683.

[174]   Since the rules on maintenance of capital continue to apply to private companies there is a danger that some corporate actions that would have infringed the ban on financial assistance will remain unlawful notwithstanding this repeal because they are contrary to the maintenance of capital regime. The Government agreed to make it clear in a saving provision under Companies Act 2006, s 1296 that the removal of the prohibition on private companies giving financial assistance for the purchase of own shares will not prevent private companies entering into transactions which they could lawfully have entered into under the whitewash procedure: Hansard HL vol 686 cols 443–44 (2 November 2006) (Lord Sainsbury). This has been achieved via the Companies Act 2006 (Commencement No 5, Transitional Provisions and Savings) Order 2007 (SI 2007/3495) para 52 (and see paras 7.2–7.9 of the accompanying Explanatory memorandum to the Order).

[175]   In 1996 and 1997 the DTI made proposals to improve the drafting of the sections on financial assistance: these proposals were endorsed in Company Law Review Steering Group, *Company Formation and Capital Maintenance*, (October 1999) URN 99/1145, paras 3.42–3.43.

[176]   Companies Act 2006, ss 677–680.

[177]   *Chaston v SWP Group plc* [2002] EWCA Civ 1999; [2003] 1 BCLC 675, cf *MT Realisations Ltd v Digital Equipment Co Ltd* [2002] EWHC 1628 (Ch); [2002] 2 BCLC 688. See generally E Ferran 'Corporate Transactions and Financial Assistance: Shifting Policy Perceptions but Static Law' (2004) 63 *Cambridge Law Journal* 225.

detriment to the company is not a necessary factor for section 677 purposes.[178] Finally it must be ascertained whether the assistance is given for the purpose of the acquisition and the assistance will not be caught by the provisions of the 2006 Act if the 'company's principal purpose in giving the assistance is not to give it for the purpose of any such acquisition' or is only an incidental part of some larger scheme.[179] However, the concept of a 'larger' or 'principal' purpose have been construed very narrowly by the courts.[180]

4.4.5   The Efficacy of these Rules as a Form of Creditor Protection

The capital maintenance rules appear to offer more protection to creditors than the minimum capital rules, since they aim to restrict distributions to shareholders and reductions of capital. However, in reality little, if any, protection is actually afforded by these rules. There are two reasons for this failure. First, distributions to shareholders are regulated by imposing a balance sheet test.[181] However, this balance-sheet information bears little relation to the company's true financial position.[182] It is calibrated by reference to historic contributions by shareholders, rather than by any calculation of a company's assets or financial needs on a going concern basis.[183] As a result, there is a disjunction between a company's real capacity to pay dividends, and the result under the distribution rules, which may produce either an unduly generous or unduly restrictive outcome.[184] It is likely that more effective controls on dividends can be put in place as a result of contract.[185]

Where a company has no positive net present value projects in which to invest, an inability to distribute its surplus as dividends can be regarded as a waste of resources. To the extent that the payment of dividends is a method by which companies can signal particular information to the market place,[186] an unduly restrictive policy on dividend payment constrains the company's ability to make use of this facility. An inability to do so can potentially have a negative impact on the efficiency of the equity market.[187]

Second, the distribution rules comprise only a narrow set of circumstances in which capital cannot be returned to the shareholders.[188] They do not prevent assets being

---

[178]   *Chaston v SWP Group plc* [2002] EWCA Civ 1999; [2003] 1 BCLC 675.

[179]   Companies Act 2006, s 678(2).

[180]   *Brady v Brady* [1989] AC 755; *Chaston v SWP Group plc* [2002] EWCA Civ 1999; [2003] 1 BCLC 675.

[181]   Second Directive 77/91/EC, art 15(1)(a) and see Companies Act 2006, Part 23.

[182]   L Enriques and JR Macey, 'Creditors Versus Capital Formation: The case against the European Legal Capital rules' (2001) 86 *Cornell Law Review* 1165, 1190; J Rickford, 'Reforming Capital: Report of the Interdisciplinary Group on Capital Maintenance' (2004) 15 *European Business Law Review* 919. This is discussed further at page 170.

[183]   Companies Act 2006, s 831 comes closer to an asset test, but this only applies to public companies. A similar point arises regarding the effectiveness of capital ratio tests, as opposed to cash flow tests: see pages 169–70.

[184]   J Rickford, 'Reforming Capital: Report of the Interdisciplinary Group on Capital Maintenance' (2004) 15 *European Business Law Review* 919, cf W Schön, 'Balance Sheet Tests or Solvency Tests – or Both' (2006) 7 *European Business Organization Law Review* 181.

[185]   See pages 161–62.

[186]   Eg A Brav, JR Graham, CR Harvey and R Michaely, 'Payout Policy in the 21st Century' (2005) 77 *Journal of Financial Economics* 483.

[187]   The use of dividend policy as a signalling device is discussed at 2.5.

[188]   It can be argued that this is a situation that particularly merits intervention (J Armour, 'Share Capital and Creditor Protection: Efficient Rules for a Modern Company Law' (2000) 63 *Modern Law Review* 355) since

distributed to shareholders in other ways, such as the payment of excessive compensation for shareholders who are also directors of the company. In the UK, directors of private companies can avoid the rules preventing the payment of dividends out of capital by returning capital to the shareholders by means of a share repurchase or a reduction of capital, providing the directors declare that the company will remain solvent for twelve months.[189] Neither do the capital maintenance rules prevent the assets being lost in other ways, for example through poor investments taken by directors, fraud by directors, or just unfortunate market conditions.

The ability of the company to recoup unlawfully paid distributions also needs to be considered. In order to provide protection for the creditors, the legal capital rules need to strive to achieve two goals. First they should aim to prevent unlawful distributions to the shareholders taking place. As discussed, the legal capital rules do not successfully achieve this goal. Second, however, the rules need to deal with the scenario in which unlawful distributions have occurred, in which event creditor protection will depend upon the ability of the company to recoup the unlawful payments and therefore regain the equity cushion. However, the present position regarding dividends is clear: recipients are only liable to repay if they know or have reasonable grounds for believing that the payment is made unlawfully.[190] Recipient liability for other forms of distribution to shareholders is dealt with by the common law, but the position is the same.[191] The requirement of knowledge means that few shareholders will be held liable to repay. Generally only shareholder-directors and parent companies are likely to have the requisite knowledge to render them potentially liable to repay. This has a significant impact on the ability of the company to recover these payments. Of course the directors who authorise the payments may be liable to compensate the company unless they acted under an honest and reasonable belief that the facts justified the payment,[192] but this relies on the company having an appetite to sue its directors, and on the directors having the capacity to compensate the company should the company be successful in its claim.[193]

As discussed above, the ban on financial assistance should be dealt with separately to the other forms of distributions to shareholders. This is because the link between capital maintenance and financial assistance is tenuous.[194] It is well understood that the mischief at which these sections are aimed is not abuse of creditors per se, but rather the prevention of the use of target company resources in a leveraged buyout to assist the acquisition of shares.[195] In many instances, for example where the form of assistance is a loan, no harm to the creditors will result from the assistance, and indeed it is clear from the case law that

---

dividends may be seen as harming only creditors whereas other kinds of losses (arising eg through poor investment decisions or unfortunate market conditions) harm shareholders too.

[189]   Companies Act 2006, Part 18 ch 5 (share repurchases), ss 642–644 (reductions of capital).

[190]   Ibid, s 847(2). This means knowledge of the facts giving rise to the contravention. It is not necessary for the recipients to appreciate that the payment involves a contravention of the Companies Acts: *It's A Wrap (UK) Ltd v Gula* [2006] EWCA Civ 544; [2006] BCC 626.

[191]   *Re Halt Garage (1964) Ltd* [1982] 3 All ER 1016.

[192]   *Flitcroft's Case* (1882) LR 21 Ch D 519; *Precision Dippings Ltd v Precision Dippings Marketing Ltd* [1986] 1 Ch 447.

[193]   This can be contrasted with the effect of breach of a contractual clause restricting excessive dividend payments, which allows the loan to be accelerated and terminated: see pages 157–58.

[194]   This was recognised by the Jenkins Committee in 1962: *Report of the Company Law Committee*, Cmnd 1749 (London, HMSO, 1962) paras 173–176.

[195]   J Armour, 'Share Capital and Creditor Protection: Efficient Rules for a Modern Company Law' (2000) 63 *Modern Law Review* 355, 378.

detriment to the company is not a prerequisite of the finding of financial assistance.[196] Indeed, the Company Law Review concluded that the prohibition 'can only endanger the interests of creditors in a situation of potential insolvency, when the directors' duties and the provisions on fraudulent and wrongful trading are likely to be relevant'.[197] It may also be noted that even though the ban on financial assistance is often said to be an impediment to leveraged buy-outs, it has not prevented the development of a significant European leveraged buy-out market.[198]

Not only do the legal capital rules not provide any significant levels of creditor protection, these rules also impose burdens on companies. One example, is the costs associated with the ban on financial assistance.[199] Another example relates to reductions of capital. If the company has to go to court to carry out the reduction,[200] this becomes a costly exercise. The amount of protection afforded to creditors via this procedure, where the company is undeniably solvent, is minimal. Although the court has to have regard to the creditors' interests when determining whether to allow the reduction, the evidence that the creditors' interests are protected is usually demonstrated by the company providing the court with evidence of a bank guarantee for all existing debts.

The legal capital rules also impose other costs on companies. For example, costs sometimes arise because transactions have to be ingeniously structured so as to avoid a particular legal capital rule. The legal capital rules rarely prevent transactions altogether. There are generally ways around the rules, although these often require expensive legal advice, and may require court orders,[201] and are therefore costly in terms of both time and money. Alternatively the costs may arise as a result of the lack of flexibility that the legal capital rules engender. For example, the rules excluding undertakings to perform services as an acceptable form of consideration for shares may hinder start-up companies, since they impose restrictions on the financing of those firms.[202]

---

[196] It has, alternatively, been suggested that the intention of the ban is to prevent discrimination between shareholders in takeover situations: *Chaston v SWP Group plc* [2002] EWCA Civ 1999; [2003] 1 BCLC 675, [31] per Arden LJ. However, this protection is already provided by directors' duties of good faith and the obligation to act for a proper purpose and the rules governing the equal treatment of shareholders in the City Code on Takeovers (see eg City Code, General Principle 1, and discussion in 12.3.4).

[197] See *Company Formation and Capital Maintenance,* n 40, 39.

[198] L Enriques, 'EC Company Law Directives and Regulations: How Trivial are They?' in J Armour and JA McCahery (eds), *After Enron: Improving Corporate Law and Modernising Securities Regulation in Europe and the US* (Oxford, Hart Publishing, 2006).

[199] The Company Law Review Steering Group estimated that the cost of legal advice regarding the financial assistance provisions amounted to £20 million per annum (See *The Strategic Framework,* n 1, para 5.4.21), a figure which is felt to be an underestimate by some practitioners.

[200] Only public companies are obliged to reduce their capital in this way (Companies Act 2006, s 641).

[201] Eg companies can sidestep the distribution rules by reducing the capital of the company, and returning the capital to the shareholders in this way. A public company will require a court order to reduce its capital. A private company may do so through the solvency statement procedure, although, as discussed, it is likely that many private companies will still opt for the court approval route.

[202] L Enriques and JR Macey 'Creditors versus capital formation: The case against the European Legal Capital rules' (2001) 86 *Cornell Law Review* 1165, 1195–96.

4.5   Alternatives to the Legal Capital Rules

In light of the apparent failure of the legal capital regime to provide meaningful creditor protection, a failure acknowledged by a wide range of academics and legislators and even accepted by the ECJ, at least as regards minimum capital requirements,[203] alternatives to the current regime need to be investigated. This section will assess creditor protection via contract, and creditor protection via insolvency law, before analysing the possibility of the introduction of a general solvency-statement approach to these issues.

4.5.1   Creditor Protection via Contract

One suggested alternative approach is that adopted by many US states, namely that the law need not and should not regulate this issue. Creditor protection, to the extent that it is required, can be provided via contract. On this view, there is no need for any protection to be provided to the creditors beyond what they might be able to bargain for themselves. To the extent that there is a danger of abuse by the shareholders,[204] the adjusting creditors have the opportunity to protect their own interests, by building in adequate interest rates to take account of the risk of lending, by taking some form of control rights over the company to monitor the directors' behaviour, and by taking security to protect themselves in the event of insolvency.[205] Chapters five and six analyse in detail the forms of protection that creditors can bargain for themselves.

One argument against this approach is that the legal rules mimic what can be achieved through contractual bargaining and that, because they provide a ready made solution, they reduce transaction costs. However, there seems little evidence for this in practice,[206] and even if there were, this does not present a compelling argument for retaining them as mandatory rather than optional rules.[207] As Eilis Ferran points out '[a] justification for legal capital rules that is based on their function as a transaction cost-reducing mechanism is only plausible where market participants are allowed the flexibility to choose between

---

[203]   Case C-212/97 *Centros Ltd v Erhvervs-og Selskabsstyrelsen* [1999] ECR I-1459.

[204]   It is questionable whether the dangers of shareholder abuse on which these rules are predicated are as acute as is supposed. Companies who engage in behaviour which systematically harms creditors are soon going to find that future creditors will refuse to extend credit to the company at competitive rates. This particularly applies to the danger of asset diversion since this form of shareholder abuse is the most easily detectable by creditors. Borrowing is a repeat game for companies. Although only a subset of creditors will be able to adjust their behaviour in this way, these adjusting creditors are likely to be the most crucial to a company's future financial success.

[205]   See 3.2.2.

[206]   Although see in this regard eg C Leuz et al, 'An International Comparison of Accounting-Based Payout restrictions in the United States, United Kingdom and Germany' (1998) 28 *Accounting & Business Research* 111, and more recently, M Bradley and MR Roberts, 'Are Bond Covenants Priced?' available at www.repec.org/esNASM04/up.21166.1069857472.pdf where the authors argue that dividend restrictions in State corporate law codes in the US are associated with better credit ratings for bonds issued by firms incorporated in those jurisdictions. However, these findings should be treated with care, not only because the results themselves may be questioned (in the Bradley and Roberts study many codes restricted dividends but not other forms of return of capital and so it is difficult to see how they could have any real effect) but also because even if there are some potential costs savings via this form of collective bargaining, it is not clear whether these are captured by the capital maintenance doctrine, and indeed the doctrine itself has a significant cost element.

[207]   E Ferran, 'The Place for Creditor Protection on the Agenda for Modernisation of Company Law in the European Union' (2006) 3 *European Company and Financial Law Review* 178.

the ready-made model provided by the law or a contractual model that may cost more to negotiate but which may be cheaper in the long run because of lower interest charges or otherwise more favourable financing terms'.[208] Contract-based systems have a flexibility and adaptability which is hard, if not impossible, to mimic in a statutory model. It is difficult to see why official lawmakers are in a better position to supply the terms for loams and debt securities than the users of such instruments in practice, and if standard terms are needed it seems sensible to leave it to the market participants themselves to generate them.

One further argument that is sometimes raised against the proposition that creditor protection can be left to contract is the fact that only some creditors are in a contractual relationship with the company and of those only a subset will have the incentive, bargaining power and resources necessary to improve their position by taking security or by other contractual means.[209] However, even non-adjusting creditors,[210] may be able to free ride on the covenants imposed by more sophisticated creditors.[211] This may not always work perfectly in practice and the benefits to weaker creditors will only arise where the contractual negotiation or creditor monitoring processes of the adjusting creditors works effectively. Nevertheless this system allows for the possibility of some protection for the non-adjusting creditors, and there are other mechanisms available to protect these creditors.[212]

As regards the involuntary creditors, compulsory insurance schemes cover the majority of tort claims against companies, namely those arising from accidents at work and road traffic accidents.[213] Employees are covered by a range of employment legislation to protect them, and are placed in the category of preferred creditors on a winding up as regards the payment of at least some of the money owed to them. This raises an important issue. Creditors are principally in need of protection from shareholders when the company is insolvent and the protections which adjusting creditors can bargain for themselves are of primary benefit in the event of insolvency. By the same token, non-adjusting creditors are most in need of protection when the company is insolvent. The availability of creditor protection once the company is insolvent is dealt with in the next section.

4.5.2   Creditor Protection via Insolvency Law

Protection of the creditors from the shareholders is of principal importance when the company is insolvent.[214] At that point there will generally be insufficient money to satisfy all the claims against the company and the conflict between the shareholders and the creditors will be clear. However, on insolvency the creditors are put in the driving seat and insolvency law protects the creditors from the shareholders' claims. As discussed in chapter

---

[208]   Ibid, 189.

[209]   See 3.2.2.1 and 6.6.2.3.

[210]   See 3.2.2.1 for a discussion of non-adjusting creditors.

[211]   Eg, L Enriques and JR Macey, 'Creditors versus capital formation: The case against the European Legal Capital rules' (2001) 86 *Cornell Law Review* 1165, 1172. For a specific example see pages 157–58.

[212]   See 3.2.2.1.

[213]   Employers' Liability (Compulsory Insurance) Act 1969; Road Traffic Act 1988. These claims are protected on insolvency: Third Parties (Rights Against Insurers) Act 2010. See pages 297–98 for further discussion.

[214]   This issue is discussed in 3.3, particularly 3.3.1.2.5.

three,[215] statutory provisions are in place to ensure that the shareholders do not under-mine the principle that creditors rank ahead of the shareholders at this point in time. In particular, section 74(2)(f) of the Insolvency Act 1986 provides that claims by a member in his character as a member by way of dividends, profits or otherwise are deemed not to be a debt of the company so that on a winding up these claims are subordinated to the claims of the unsecured creditors. The courts are also keen to ensure that the statutory order of payment out on a winding up is not undermined.[216] On insolvency, then, the rules regulating the order of payment out on a winding up or distribution by an administrator are effective at protecting creditors from the claims of shareholders, which is the principal concern of the legal capital rules. The protection of some types of creditors from the claims of other, more powerful, creditors is discussed in chapters three and six.[217]

The suggestion is, therefore, that while the company remains solvent creditors are in need of no special protection from the law. It is notable that at this point the law does not separate creditors' interests from those of the shareholders in determining the scope of directors' duties. Section 172 of the Companies Act 2006 does separate a number of other stakeholder groups which require consideration by directors when determining what is 'most likely to promote the success of the company for the benefit of its members as a whole'.[218] However, creditors are absent from this list, and rightly so.[219] The creditors' primary interest in the company is the return of their investment and while there is adequate money to pay them they have no need of additional protection from the law.[220] This changes only where the company is insolvent or on the threshold of insolvency. Where the company is insolvent, although the creditors do need protection from the shareholders, this protection is provided by insolvency law, as described above.

One argument that could be raised against this approach is that the definition of insolvency is notoriously difficult,[221] and therefore it should not be used as a hard boundary between creditor protection being provided by law, and no such creditor protection. There is obviously a period just prior to insolvency when the creditors do become in need of protection, although formal insolvency procedures have not begun. The law recognises this grey area already.[222] The directors' duty to have regard to the creditors' interests operates when the company is *nearing* insolvency[223] and many of the provisions in the Insolvency Act 1986 take account of behaviour in the period before insolvency. In particular section 214 of the Insolvency Act 1986 operates once the directors have concluded, or ought to have concluded, that there is 'no reasonable prospect' that the

---

[215] See 3.3.1.2.5.

[216] *Soden v British & Commonwealth Holdings plc* [1998] AC 298. For discussion see 3.3.1.2.5.

[217] 3.3.1, 3.3.2 and 6.6.2.3.

[218] Companies Act 2006, s 172(1), discussed at 3.2.1.3.1.

[219] See chapter 3, particularly 3.3.

[220] One gloss could be added to this: if the riskiness of the company's business increases dramatically this will increase the probability of default and may reduce the market value of debt claims, even if the company never does default. However, if the company remains solvent this does not impact on the creditors' likelihood to be repaid and so this does not seem to be an area in which the law needs to intervene.

[221] For discussion see eg Goode, *Principles of Corporate Insolvency Law*, n 2, ch 4. This is also discussed at pages 88–89.

[222] See 3.3.2 and 3.3.3.

[223] *West Mercia Safetywear Ltd v Dodd* [1988] BCLC 250, although the courts are not always consistent in their terminology (see eg *Facia Footwear Ltd (in administration) v Hinchliffe* [1998] 1 BCLC 218: the company must be in a dangerous financial position). See pages 105–107.

company can avoid going into insolvent liquidation.[224] This provision is important because it acts as a disincentive to directors to dispose of assets, or to trade wrongfully, and because it allows the creditors to obtain redress against those directors.[225] However, there are other provisions operating in the period prior to insolvency which enable the liquidator to get the assets back from the person to whom the assets were disposed,[226] although whether these sections deter dissipation of the assets in the first place is more difficult, since directors do not suffer any specific detriment as a result of an action under these provisions.[227]

If there is a concern that the boundary between solvency and insolvency means that creditors are potentially left unprotected in this twilight zone then it would be better to focus on providing more protection for creditors at this time, or clarifying the definition of insolvency, rather than legislating for the entire period when a company is solvent. However, there is a danger of over-regulation of this area.[228] The Company Law Review did consider increasing directors' obligations to creditors. One early suggestion was that the common law duty on directors to consider creditors' interests at or near insolvency should be moved further back into the solvent life of the company, so that this obligation should kick in when insolvency was merely in prospect. This was dropped due to fears that it would have a 'chilling effect' ie it would encourage directors to move too precipitously to put companies into liquidation, and not to risk trying to trade out of their difficulties with the attendant risk of being sued by the liquidator on the creditors' behalf if they failed and worsened the creditors' position in the meantime.[229] The Companies Act 2006 maintains the previous position regarding directors' duties to creditors.[230]

It is sometimes suggested that the rules relating to piercing the corporate veil need to be reconsidered in order to allow the creditors on insolvency to claim from the shareholders above and beyond the limit of their contributions to the company.[231] These arguments are not concerned with the need to ensure that the creditors rank ahead of the shareholders on a winding up but rather they question whether it is acceptable to undermine the concept of limited liability in some circumstances. The strongest arguments in favour of additional veil piercing are made in relation to involuntary creditors.[232] Yet, in the UK compulsory insurance covers the majority of tort claims against companies, namely those

---

[224] Insolvency Act 1986, s 214(2)(b) and see 3.3.3.1 for a discussion of when section 214 liability is triggered.

[225] See also the fraudulent trading provisions in Insolvency Act 1986, s 213, which allow personal liability to be attached to those carrying on the business of the company in certain circumstances, discussed at pages 109–10.

[226] See 3.3.2.1 and 3.3.2.2.

[227] See 3.3.2.3.

[228] See eg B Cheffins, *Company Law: Theory Structure and Operation* (Oxford, Oxford University Press, 1997) 540–48.

[229] Department for Trade and Industry, *Modernising Company Law* (Cm 5553-I, 2002), paras 3.8–3.14. For discussion see pages 110–11.

[230] Companies Act 2006, s 172(3) states that the duty imposed on directors by s 172 to promote the success of the company is subject to any enactment (eg Insolvency Act 1986, s 214) or rule of law (eg the common law duty to creditors: *West Mercia Safetywear Ltd v Dodd* [1988] BCLC 250).

[231] See 3.3.3.1.

[232] eg H Hansmann and R Kraakman, 'Towards Unlimited Shareholder Liability for Corporate Torts' (1991) 100 *Yale Law Journal* 1879. See page 108.

arising from accidents at work and road traffic accidents.[233] There is no good justification for altering the veil piercing rules in the UK.[234]

Another counter-argument is that even if the company does not become insolvent as a result of the distributions to shareholders, the creditors' interests can nevertheless be harmed because the distributions do reduce the company's net assets, and therefore make it more exposed to the risk of default.[235] Creditors, it could be argued, are still prejudiced if the risk of default increases above that at which they priced it, and if the value of their debt claim matters to them as an asset.[236] However, a restriction on the return of capital to shareholders per se is of little assistance to non-adjusting creditors.[237] Although some benefits may accrue to the adjusting creditors, because such restrictions may deter ex post actions by the shareholders,[238] this is a group which is in a position to protect itself by contract. It is accepted that this protection has its limits,[239] and there may be some inefficiencies, in the sense of failing to maximise the expected value of corporate assets, if such distributions are allowed. However, it may be questioned whether this justifies the imposition of the legal capital rules in a solvent situation when these inefficiencies are weighed against the costs of the legal capital rules themselves.

The suggestion therefore is that most creditors are able to protect themselves by contract, and that creditors only need additional protection on insolvency, at which point the insolvency rules are adequate to provide that protection. A natural follow-on from this proposition is the solvency statement approach, ie an approach which allows the directors considerable freedom to manipulate the company's capital while the company is solvent, subject of course to the agreement of the company's shareholders. Following this approach, no specific protection is provided by law to creditors while the company remains solvent. The UK has already adopted this approach in relation to certain aspects of the legal capital regime.[240] However, the solvency statement approach discussed in the next section would adopt this approach for all issues regarding a company's legal capital.

4.5.3   The Solvency Statement Approach

The solvency statement approach starts from the proposition that creditors only need protection when the company is insolvent. The law should provide protection for the creditors at that point, and it does so, via the insolvency provisions, but there is no need for the law to provide any protection while the company is solvent. Obviously there is a difficult period just prior to insolvency where the law may need to intervene, when the

---

[233] Employers' Liability (Compulsory Insurance) Act 1969; Road Traffic Act 1988. These claims are protected on insolvency: Third Parties (Rights Against Insurers) Act 2010. This issue is discussed further in chapter 6 (see 6.6.2.3).

[234] See page 108.

[235] See J Armour, 'Legal Capital: An Outdated Concept?' [2006] *European Business Organization Law Review* 5, 11–15.

[236] Eg where the creditor wishes to realise the value of the loan before maturity, as with bonds, factoring of book debts etc.

[237] This is because if creditors do not adjust, the optimal level of capitalisation by shareholders is zero: J Armour, 'Legal Capital: An Outdated Concept?' [2006] *European Business Organization Law Review* 5, 12.

[238] Ibid, 12–13.

[239] Eg there are limits to the interest rates which it is feasible to charge.

[240] Eg in relation to repurchases of shares out of capital by private companies (Companies Act 2006, ss 709–723) and in relation to reductions of capital by private companies, whereby private companies can bypass the need to go to court (Companies Act 2006, ss 642–644). For discussion see 4.4.2 and 4.4.3.

company is technically solvent, but creditors are in need of some protection against abuse from the shareholders, but the UK already has provisions in place to deal with this period.[241] The value of the UK's regulations in this regard has been recognised within Europe. When the Winter Group considered whether a general solvency statement should be adopted at EU level, it was suggested that *should* a solvency statement based system be put in place then a wrongful trading provision akin to section 214 of the Insolvency Act 1986 would be desirable throughout Europe.[242] In terms of regulating the relationship of the creditors and the shareholders, which, after all, is all that the legal capital rules aim to achieve, the existing provisions are pretty efficient. Even if some creditors are not protected against other creditors on insolvency, they are nevertheless protected against the possibility of shareholders ranking ahead of them, which is all that the legal capital rules aim to prevent.

The basis of the solvency statement approach is that solvent companies should be left unconstrained by the legal capital rules as regards the manipulation of their own capital. As long as a company is solvent, the directors should be able to make distributions of capital, including dividend payments, reductions of capital, repurchases and redemptions. Indeed the directors should be able to manipulate the company's capital as they see appropriate, without the need to have regard to creditors' interests, while the company remains solvent. That is not to say that constraints would not exist. Directors would be constrained by the need to gain shareholder approval for the measures they propose and by the need to comply with their directors' duties in proposing and carrying out those measures, ie a standards based approach. In relation to public companies the market would act as a constraint on the company's management. In particular the institutional shareholders within the UK have the potential to act as an important check and balance on management action. This has already been discussed in the context of pre-emption rights at 4.3.1 above and the corporate governance role of institutional shareholders is discussed further in chapter ten.[243] In addition, to the extent that the company has debt finance, the directors' behaviour will be considerably constrained by covenants.[244]

A general solvency test approach has been adopted elsewhere to deal with these issues.[245] It has already been adopted in the UK to deal with specific aspects of legal capital regulation, namely allowing private companies to repurchase shares out of capital and to reduce their capital without the need to go to court.[246] However, in order for this approach to be a successful tool in regulating company capital on the wholesale basis suggested above it will need careful application.

---

[241] For discussion of these issues see 3.3.2 and 3.3.3.

[242] The Report of the High Level Group of Company Law Experts, *A Modern Regulatory framework for Company Law in Europe* (The Winter Group Report), ch IV.

[243] See 10.2.2, particularly 10.2.2.2.

[244] See 3.2.2.4 and 5.1.

[245] See eg New Zealand Companies Act 1993, s 4; US Model Business Corporation Act, § 6.40, although in both cases an additional net assets test is added as a requirement. It is not suggested here that the UK would adopt an additional net assets test to supplement any general solvency based approach which it introduced. The disadvantages of basing a distribution policy on any accounts-based test have already been discussed and a net assets test does not appear to add anything advantageous to the general solvency test: for further discussion see J Rickford, 'Reforming Capital: Report of the Interdisciplinary Group on Capital Maintenance' (2004) 4 *European Business Law Review* 919, 978–82.

[246] As regards the procedure whereby private companies can repurchase their shares from capital: Companies Act 2006, ss 709–723. As regards the method by which private companies can reduce their capital without going to court: ss 642–644.

The solvency test itself needs to be carefully defined. What is needed is a test that requires directors to reach a view that for the reasonably foreseeable future, taking account of the company's expected prospects in the ordinary course of business, it could reasonably be expected to meet its liabilities.[247] The test of solvency currently adopted by the Companies Act 2006, in relation to repurchases of shares out of capital by a private company, is a good starting point. This test requires the directors to form an opinion about the company's ability to pay its debts at the time of making the solvency statement, and to look forward over the coming twelve months in order to determine whether the company will be able to pay its debts as they fall due over that period (or to pay its debts in full if it is wound up within that period).[248] This test rightly requires directors to take account of 'contingent or prospective' liabilities, in addition to existing liabilities, when making this assessment.[249] Rickford et al have suggested that 'contingent or prospective' liabilities should not be interpreted too narrowly in this context.[250] This phrase should not be confined to contingent liabilities that have already vested, or prospective liabilities that have already accrued. If this phrase is interpreted narrowly it could exclude, for example, salary costs for the coming year.[251] An overly technical interpretation of this kind would reduce the value of this solvency test as a creditor protection device. Instead, directors should take account of all the liabilities which the company will face in the following period, encompassing all of the normal trading prospects of the company.

A question arises as to whether the solvency test should adopt a cash flow test or an asset-based test or a combination of the two. For the purposes of assessing whether a company is insolvent a cash flow test (ie whether the company is unable to pay its debts as they fall due)[252] will often be the most useful test. After all, some companies will be balance sheet insolvent, ie the value of their assets is less than their liabilities,[253] from day one, but can nevertheless pay their debts as they fall due and can otherwise operate perfectly successfully. Insurance companies, for example, often operate on this basis. There is little doubt that a cash flow test should form the basis of the solvency statement approach. The question is whether an asset-based test should be added.

The test in place for dividend payments, and other forms of distribution, is an asset-based test. A distribution should be made only if, after it has been made, the company will retain assets whose value exceeds its liabilities by the amount of the company's legal capital. However, it is not enough that the company's assets should exceed its liabilities, ie that it should have positive net assets, at this point. The assets need to

---

[247] If a company is funded by debt it is likely that it will already have to report on its solvency as part of its contractual covenants: see discussion at page 169.

[248] Companies Act 2006, s 643(1), cf s 714(3) (regarding repurchases) which encompasses similar ideas, but is expressed in different terms.

[249] Ibid, s 643(2); s 714(4).

[250] J Rickford, 'Reforming Capital: Report of the Interdisciplinary Group on Capital Maintenance' [2004] *European Business Law Review* 919, 979–80. It is also suggested that prospective and contingent assets should be taken into consideration when assessing the solvency status of the company, although 'a measure of prudence is clearly required' (ibid, 980). The suggested test is that 'directors should be required to reach the view that *for the reasonably foreseeable future, taking account of the company's expected prospects in the ordinary course of business, it can reasonably be expected to meet its liabilities*' (ibid, 980, emphasis as original). This may be compared to the interpretation of the cash flow test under Insolvency Act 1986, s 123, discussed at pages 56–57 and pages 88–89.

[251] Ibid, 979.

[252] Insolvency Act 1986, s 123(1)(e).

[253] Ibid, s 123(2).

exceed the liabilities by a 'margin',[254] that margin being the amount of the company's legal capital. This chapter has argued that the legal capital rules do not provide any meaningful creditor protection, and as a result the addition of this 'margin' is unnecessary and indeed has costs attached to it, as discussed. However, the question arises as to whether a net assets test without this additional margin, sometimes called a 'bare net assets' test, is a meaningful form of creditor protection. Should a general solvency test, put in place following the dismantling of the legal capital regime, seek to combine a net asset test with the cash flow test? The general solvency based regime introduced in New Zealand, for example, requires certification of solvency by the directors based on both a cash flow test and a bare net assets test.[255] The solvency test currently adopted by the Companies Act 2006 also incorporates both a cash flow test and a balance sheet test.[256]

One argument in favour of the additional net assets test is that it can potentially provide more information to the directors when they are determining whether they can legitimately make a distribution. One problem with this argument is that the information provided by the net assets test, linked as it is to historical balance sheet information, does not per se provide useful information about whether a company should make a distribution. The fact that a company has a surplus on its balance sheet does not indicate that it would be prudent for the company to distribute that amount.[257] The net assets test fails to make proper allowance for the quality of the company's assets and liabilities. On the whole '[n]et assets tests are not well suited to covering these important forward looking indicators of the true financial position'[258] and it is of course this assessment of the company's true financial position which is of most interest, and relevance, to creditors. If the net assets test is too rigidly linked to the accounts therefore, it is likely to be of relatively little value.

One way to address these difficulties is to ensure that any net assets test is applied in a flexible way, which takes account of these issues and subjects the accounting figures to proper business appraisal.[259] For example, intangible assets, such as cash flows, need to be assessed realistically, taking account of issues such as the quality of the company's performance over time. However, if this approach is followed, there may be very little difference between an assessment of the net position of a company and an assessment of solvency using the cash flow test.[260] This is because the value of an asset is the discounted value of the cash which the asset is expected to realise and the value of a liability is the discounted value of the prospect of having to pay cash to satisfy it. If that is correct, then the additional net assets test may add little to a solvency statement approach based on a cash flow test.[261]

---

[254] J Rickford, 'Reforming Capital: Report of the Interdisciplinary Group on Capital Maintenance' [2004] *European Business Law Review* 919, 970.

[255] New Zealand Companies Act 1993, s 4.

[256] Companies Act 2006, s 643(1)(a) and s 714(3)(a) both refer to the ability of the company to pay its debts, a phrase which incorporates the insolvency provisions, which defines inability to pay tests as encompassing both the balance sheet test and the cash flow test: Insolvency Act 1986, s 123.

[257] J Rickford, 'Reforming Capital: Report of the Interdisciplinary Group on Capital Maintenance' [2004] *European Business Law Review* 919, 976.

[258] Ibid.

[259] See the discussion of the New Zealand test in this regard: ibid, 977–78.

[260] J Rickford, 'Reforming Capital: Report of the Interdisciplinary Group on Capital Maintenance' [2004] *European Business Law Review* 919, 978.

[261] It may be that if a narrow interpretation of 'contingent or prospective liabilities' is taken, ie taking account of only contingent liabilities that have already vested and prospective liabilities that have already accrued, then a

Once the decision is taken as to which solvency test to use, the next issue is how to apply that test in practice. It is generally accepted that directors do not need to consider extraordinary transactions. Drawing this line may not always be straightforward. In order to satisfy the requirement for the formation of an opinion on the ability of the company to pay its debts directors would have to make sufficient inquiries into the financial affairs of the company to satisfy themselves that the statement can be honestly made.[262] A further issue is whether this solvency statement by the directors should be audited. Of the two examples of the solvency statement method at work within the Companies Act 2006, one does require the statement to be audited,[263] and the other does not,[264] despite initial recommendations of the Company Law Review to this effect.[265] In practice this distinction may not be significant, since directors will often want to get the advice of the company's auditors before making a solvency statement, and therefore the auditors will be potentially liable both in contract and in tort if they act negligently. Therefore, although the auditors may not be liable on the face of the statute for negligent advice, in practice the auditors are likely to be joined in any action against the directors arising from an inaccurate solvency statement.

The second important component of an effective system based on a solvency statement method is to ensure that directors are made suitably accountable for their solvency statements. Again, the solvency statement test currently set out in the Companies Act 2006 provides a useful starting point. All directors are required to make the statement. Any directors unhappy about making the statement would have to resign or be removed from office before the procedure could be used.[266] If the directors make a solvency statement without having reasonable grounds for the opinions expressed in it, then every director in default commits a criminal offence.[267]

The difficulty with imposing a criminal sanction is that, although the aim of imposing criminal liability has the effect of focusing the directors' minds on the issue at hand, over-penalising this issue may not achieve the desired result. If the effect is to dissuade directors from manipulating the company's capital, by repurchasing the company's shares for example, this could be problematic. As discussed above, there may be good reasons for directors to make use of the company's capital, and if the capital is left unused and the company has no positive net value projects in which to invest, this could lead to a waste of the company's resources. By contrast, if any criminal provisions are rarely or never enforced it may be questioned how much of a deterrent effect they will have in practice. In relation to the criminal liability imposed for breach of the financial assistance provisions,

---

net assets test that is applied in a flexible way may add something of value to the cash flow test, as it would allow liabilities should as staff costs for the coming twelve months, to be taken into account.

[262] See *Re In A Flap Envelope Co Ltd* [2003] EWHC 3047(Ch); [2004] 1 BCLC 64 where this test was established in relation to the statutory declaration of solvency for the purposes of the whitewash test in Companies Act 1985, s 155 and see Companies Act 2006, s 714(3) which specifically requires directors to make inquiries.

[263] Companies Act 2006, s 714.

[264] Ibid, s 643.

[265] See Company Law Review Steering Group, *Company Formation and Capital Maintenance*, n 40, para 3.30. This recommendation was later dropped; See *Developing the Framework*, n 40, para 7.26; *Completing the Structure*, n 40, para 7.10.

[266] If such a resignation is made merely for the purposes of escaping liability for the solvency statement and the individual continues as a de facto director then this might call into question the validity of the solvency statement procedure: *Re In A Flap Envelope Co Ltd* [2003] EWHC 3047(Ch); [2004] 1 BCLC 64.

[267] Companies Act 2006, s 643(4)(5), s 715.

for example,[268] the view has tended to be that this is an over-penalisation of the issue and it is the civil consequences of breach on which directors will focus in practice.[269]

An alternative mechanism would be to adopt an approach similar to that in relation to section 214 of the Insolvency Act 1986 whereby the court … may declare that [the director] is to be liable to make such contribution (if any) to the company's assets as the court thinks proper'.[270] This could have distinct advantages over a section 214 claim since, for example, the company would not need to be in liquidation in order for liability to arise.[271] This liability is not without difficulty either. Often directors of insolvent companies will have few personal assets available to satisfy such claims, either because they have invested their personal wealth into the company or because they have been carefully advised to place their assets elsewhere to protect them. To the extent that Directors' and Officers' liability insurance (D & O insurance) is available to fill the gap the cost of such insurance falls on the company, and will presumably be passed on to the shareholders and creditors, ie those whom the protection is intended to benefit, and to the extent that payments are made out of insurance policies rather than the directors own pockets, the deterrent effect of such liability must be weakened. Of course, liability under the Company Directors Disqualification Act 1986 will potentially fall on the directors for their behaviour but it is unclear whether this will, of itself, provide the deterrent required.

It was suggested, above, that imposing criminal liability on directors might be problematic as it might act as a deterrent to directors manipulating the company's capital at all. Of course, directors are also likely to view civil liability as an unattractive potential consequence of the solvency statement approach. However, it should be recalled that directors face civil consequences for unlawful dividend payments at present.[272] It should also be borne in mind that if the company breaches any financial ratios laid down in its debt covenants, the creditors who have the benefit of those covenants will have the option of accelerating and terminating the loan, or could engage in dialogue with the company with the purpose of improving its position, for example by replacing the existing management.[273] These issues can also have an incentivising effect on the directors.

The third important component of such a system is to ensure that effective mechanisms for the recovery of wrongful payments are put in place. The current solvency tests within the Companies Act 2006 do not provide a good basis for the determination of this issue. The Companies Act 2006 is silent on the civil consequences of a distribution to shareholders paid consequent upon a false or inaccurate solvency statement. There is case law to the effect that an unlawful return of capital is void,[274] and this is so even where the failing is purely procedural, so it is likely that a flawed solvency statement would invalidate a distribution in a similar manner. In addition, the common law has established that the

---

[268]   Ibid, s 680. The Company Law Review considered decriminalising this offence but after receiving mixed views on this point it eventually recommended retention of the criminal sanctions: Company Law Review Steering Group, *Completing the Structure*, n 40, para 13.42.

[269]   In the event, criminal liability was retained in the Companies Act 2006: s 680(2).

[270]   Insolvency Act 1986, s 214(1); *Re Produce Marketing Consortium Ltd (No 2)* [1989] BCLC 520.

[271]   For a discussion of liability under Insolvency Act 1986, s 214 see pages 110–13.

[272]   Eg *Flitcroft's case* (1882) LR 21 Ch D 519; *Bairstow v Queens Moat Houses plc* [2001] EWCA Civ 712; [2001] 2 BCLC 531. However, it has been suggested that directors might consider a rule based system (such as the current rules) easier to comply with than one based on a standard (the proposed solvency statement test): P Davies, *Gower and Davies: Principles of Modern Company Law*, 8th edn (London, Sweet & Maxwell, 2008) 303.

[273]   See 3.2.2.4 especially pages 83–84.

[274]   *MacPherson v European Strategic Bureau Ltd* [2000] 2 BCLC 683.

responsible directors are in breach of their duties to the company.[275] However, in order for the solvency statement method to operate as an effective way of protecting the company's capital, a system of ensuring that the wrongful payments are returned to the company should be put in place.

The present position regarding dividends is clear: recipients are only liable to repay if they know or have reasonable grounds for believing that the payment is made unlawfully.[276] Recipient liability for other forms of distribution to shareholders is dealt with by the common law, but the position is the same. This seems to be an inappropriate way of dealing with this issue. There should be strict liability on those receiving wrongful payments, requiring those payments to be returned, with relief only if the recipients are in good faith, they have changed their position and if it would be unfair to insist upon recovery.

There are theoretical arguments in favour of such an approach rather than the present knowledge-based system which results in very few payments being recovered from the shareholders in practice.[277] There are also strong policy arguments available to support this approach, since the purpose of these rules is creditor protection and that is best served (if the rules are breached) by ensuring that the wrongfully paid sums are returned to the company for the benefit of the creditors. It is notable that in other jurisdictions that have adopted a solvency based approach, a much tougher statutory approach towards recipients of wrongful payments has been adopted than is present in the UK system.[278]

A solvency test has some significant attractions when compared to the present legal capital system, and would bring the EU in line with the trend in other industrialised economies.[279] In Europe, there has recently been a shift away from the view that creditors need statutory protection during the solvent life of the company and that detailed legal capital rules are the way to provide that protection. There has been strong academic support for a relaxation of the legal capital rules for some time, within the UK and beyond.[280] This support has now spread beyond the academic community.

There have been a number of strands to this development. First, the European Commission's Action Plan for Company Law marked a shift away from the role of company law at the European level being the protection of those who deal with companies in favour of an approach based on business efficiency and competitiveness.[281] Within this new approach creditor protection devices can still be retained if they are necessary on the

---

[275] *Aveling Barford Ltd v Perion Ltd* [1989] BCLC 626.
[276] Companies Act 2006, s 847(2). This means knowledge of the facts giving rise to the contravention. It is not necessary for the recipients to appreciate that the payment involves a contravention of the Companies Acts: *It's A Wrap (UK) Ltd v Gula* [2006] BCC 626.
[277] J Payne, 'Unjust Enrichment, Trusts and Recipient Liability for Unlawful Dividends' (2003) 119 *Law Quarterly Review* 583 cf CH Tham, 'Unjust Enrichment and Unlawful Dividends: A Step Too Far?' [2005] *Cambridge Law Journal* 177, 182.
[278] Eg Companies Act 1993, s 56(1) (New Zealand).
[279] See eg New Zealand Companies Act 1993, s 4; US Model Business Corporation Act, § 6.40, although in both cases an additional net assets test is added as a requirement.
[280] Eg J Armour, 'Share Capital and Creditor Protection: Efficient Rules for a Modern Company Law' (2000) 63 *Modern Law Review* 35, E Ferran, 'The Place for Creditor Protection on the Agenda for Modernisation of Company Law in the European Union' (2006) 3 *European Company and Financial Law Review* 178; J Rickford (ed) 'Reforming Capital' [2004] (No 4) *European Business Law Review*; J Payne, 'Legal Capital in the UK following the Companies Act 2006' in J Armour and J Payne (eds), *Rationality in Company Law: Essays in Honour of DD Prentice* (Oxford, Hart Publishing, 2008).
[281] Commission (EC), 'Modernising Company Law and Enhancing Corporate Governance in the European Union' (Communication) COM (2003) 284 final (21 May 2003).

grounds of efficiency and competitiveness, but, as we have seen, the current legal capital regime is hard to justify on this basis, and indeed can on one level be said to be hampering European competitiveness when compared to other jurisdictions, notably the US.[282] The European Court of Justice has stated that there is no unique value in the minimum capital rules as a creditor protection device.[283] In addition the *Centros* decision has led to a substantial numbers of entrepreneurs living and trading on the continent establishing private companies in the UK in order to take advantage of the comparatively more relaxed capital regime for private companies in the UK.[284] In turn this has led to a process of negative harmonisation and a relaxation of capital maintenance regimes in Europe.[285]

In the UK the Government has unequivocally stated its support for more flexibility than is permitted by the Second Directive.[286] There has also been a re-examination of the function and role of the Second Directive at European level,[287] although to date the amendments to the Second Directive have been minimal.[288] However, the Commission does seem to contemplate the possibility of more radical reform of the Second Directive than has occurred to date.[289] This is based in part on a consideration of the costs that the legal capital measures currently entail[290] and an appreciation that 'a rigid, harmonised European framework might sometimes appear to be more of an impediment to innovation than a benefit for the Internal Market'.[291]

[282]   Eg the fact that UK plcs cannot accept services as consideration for the payment of shares is said to be detrimental to high tech start-ups: L Enriques and JR Macey, 'Creditors versus capital formation: The case against the European Legal Capital rules' (2001) 86 *Cornell Law Review* 1165, 1195.

[283]   Case C-212/97 *Centros Ltd v Erhvervs-og Selskabsstyrelsen* [1999] ECR I-1459.

[284]   M Becht, C Mayer, HF Wagner, 'Where do Firms Incorporate? Deregulation and the Cost of Entry' (2008) 14 *Journal of Corporate Finance* 241.

[285]   J Simon, 'A Comparative Approach to Capital Maintenance: France' (2004) 15 *European Business Law Review* 1037.

[286]   DTI, *Company Law Reform* (White Paper) Cm 6456, 2005, 42–43.

[287]   The idea that the Second Directive should be amended was first raised as part of 'Simpler Legislation for the Single Market (SLIM): Extension to a Fourth Phase', SEC (1998) 1944 (Commission Staff Working Paper of 16 November 1998), and was later added to the agenda for the Commission's High Level Group of Company Law Experts: 'Modern Regulatory Framework for Company Law in Europe' (Report) (Brussels, 4 November 2002) (the Winter Group Report). More recently a study on an alternative to the capital maintenance system of the Second Directive was launched by the European Commission in September 2006, and has been published: KPMG, 'Feasibility Study on an Alternative to the Capital Maintenance Regime established by the Second Company Law Directive' available at http://ec.europa.eu/internal_market/company/capital/index_en.htm. The main conclusion of the study is that the minimum legal capital requirements and rules on capital maintenance do not constitute a major hurdle to dividend distribution.

[288]   Directive 2006/68/EC allowed a relaxation of the rules governing the need for an expert valuation when non-cash consideration is received by public companies in exchange for its shares (para 3), a relaxation of the rules governing financial assistance (para 5) and a relaxation as regards the rules regarding a public company's ability to purchase its own shares (para 4).

[289]   Commission (EC) a Simplified Business Environment for Companies in the Areas of Company Law, Accounting and Auditing (Communication), COM (2007) 394 final (10 July 2007). The Commission puts forward two different possible models for how to proceed with a number of company law directives, including the Second Directive, one of which would involve a dismantling of those directives so that the remit of EU regulation in those areas 'should be reduced to those legal acts specifically dealing with cross-border problems'.

[290]   The Commission has also started to measure the administrative burdens in company law throughout the EU: Commission (EC), 'First Progress Report on the Strategy for the Simplification of the Regulatory Environment', (Commission Working Document) COM (2006) 690 final (14 November 2006).

[291]   Ibid, 4.

4.6 Conclusion

Strong arguments can be made against most of the legal capital rules in place in the Companies Act 2006. It is difficult to justify the imposition of costly and burdensome legal capital rules constraining a company's actions while solvent, when the need for creditor protection arises predominantly on insolvency. These costly rules are also difficult to justify when many creditors are in a position to protect themselves by contract, and even those that are not able to do so are able to free ride to some extent. Even if the needs of non-adjusting creditors are not met via free riding, the legal capital rules do not provide them with any meaningful protection. In short, the legal capital rules in place under the Second Directive, and to date implemented into UK law by the Companies Act 2006, are expensive and largely ineffective as creditor protection devices. Even if small benefits are obtained, any benefit gained is outweighed by the costs of the system.

Most of the current legal capital regime should be dismantled, for both public and private companies. No par value shares should be introduced for all companies. The minimum capital rules should be abolished for public companies, as should the 'no issue at a discount rule' for all companies, since they fulfil no significant role as regards creditor protection at the present time. In relation to distributions of capital, provided the company is solvent (and not in the twilight period just before insolvency) the law should not intervene to protect the creditors. As this chapter has suggested, careful thought needs to be put into the operation of the solvency statement approach, and into the regulation of the pre-insolvency twilight period, but in principle this approach is superior to the majority of the legal capital rules currently in place at present. The one aspect of the legal capital rules which should be retained are not creditor-focused at all, and indeed are entirely creditor neutral in their effect, namely the pre-emption provisions. These provide potentially important protection for shareholders, and can have importance governance implications, especially in publicly listed companies.

5

Creditor Protection: Contractual

5.1 Introduction

In chapter two, the various ways in which a company might be financed through debt were considered, and the possibilities for mitigating the credit risk to the creditor were discussed.[1] The risks faced by creditors were further discussed in chapter three,[2] and it was pointed out that, although there is some very limited protection for creditors under the general law,[3] most creditors are expected to protect themselves by proprietary or contractual means, or both.[4] Not all creditors are in a position to obtain such protection: the extent to which creditors can adjust is discussed in chapter three,[5] and the policy issues surrounding the protection of non-adjusting creditors are discussed in chapter six below.[6] Adjusting creditors who are in a position to obtain proprietary protection are in a strong position. The advantages of such protection are discussed below,[7] but it should be noted at this point that all creditors who obtain proprietary protection also have contractual rights against the debtor company, quite often of a very extensive nature. Broadly speaking, such contractual rights give protection while the company is solvent,[8] while proprietary protection is most useful when the company is insolvent. This is an over-generalisation, however, and there can be significant advantages to proprietary protection even outside insolvency.[9] Contractual rights against the debtor company itself are of less use once the company is insolvent, but creditors can often also obtain contractual rights against third parties, which will be effective protection unless the third party is also insolvent.

In this chapter we discuss some of the main contractual provisions for reducing credit risk, both as against the debtor company and as against third parties. The discussion of debt covenants focuses on provisions which are included in agreements specifically for the provision of finance, typically loan agreements and (to a limited extent) issues of debt securities,[10] rather than all extensions of credit. Thus, except where otherwise indicated, the debtor is referred to throughout this chapter as the 'borrower' and the creditor as the

---

[1] 2.3.1.2 and 2.3.1.3.

[2] 3.2.2.2.

[3] The requirements for legal capital are discussed in chapter 4, and regulation is discussed in chapter 11.

[4] 3.2.2.2.

[5] 3.2.2.1.

[6] 6.6.2.3.

[7] 6.1.1.

[8] See 3.2.2.4.

[9] See page 221.

[10] Other agreements such as asset finance agreements (see 2.3.4.3.2) may also include similar clauses.

'lender'.[11] Not all of the covenants discussed will be included in all debt agreements: this will depend, inter alia, on the type of borrowing, on the credit-worthiness of the debtor and the respective bargaining powers of each party, as well as the state of the market.[12] In particular, the level of covenants in debt securities is generally lower than in loan agreements, with the possible exception of high yield bonds.[13] For ease of reference, the term 'loan agreement' will be used throughout. However, it should be noted that the provisions discussed are also used in debt securities, albeit to a lesser extent. Many of the provisions discussed (or variations of them) are contained in standard forms and precedents used by lenders and those extending credit, including standard contracts produced by organisations such as the Loan Market Association for use in syndicated loans.[14] It should also be noted that debt agreements will also include many other terms which are not discussed in this chapter, for example, provisions for interest, provisions concerning taxation and other administrative provisions. The purpose of the discussion in this chapter is to focus on the main means of contractual protection used by lenders, and to consider some important legal issues which impact on the effectiveness of that protection. It is not a comprehensive guide to drafting covenants in debt agreements: for this the reader is referred to more specialist literature.[15]

5.2   Contractual Rights Against the Borrower

The most basic contractual right that a lender has against the borrower is the right to be repaid, plus (usually) a right to some form of additional payment, often periodic, which represents payment for the making of the loan. Although this can come in many forms, we can loosely call this 'interest'.[16] As discussed in chapter three,[17] the contractual provisions considered in the current chapter are included in debt agreements in order to protect the lender from the risk of non-payment. This protection is achieved by restricting the borrower's activities, by requiring the borrower to meet certain financial ratios, and by requiring the borrower to provide information (usually financial) both at the time the loan is made and throughout the life of the loan. These covenants are discussed in 5.2.1 and 5.2.2 below. It should be noted that where a guarantee is taken,[18] similar covenants may be included against the guarantor in the guarantee agreement, and where the borrowing company is part of a group, the financial covenants and events of default are

---

[11]   The term 'lender' includes situations in which there are, in fact, multiple lenders, such as syndicated loans and bond issues. For ease of exposition other terminology is used when discussing specialised areas, such as guarantees: this is explained at page 192.

[12]   These issues are discussed in more detail in chapter 3 at 3.2.2.2.

[13]   See page 79, in which the reasons for this are discussed and it is pointed out that the purpose of covenants in debt securities is often to protect the value of the bond rather than directly against the risk of non-payment.

[14]   See page 358.

[15]   For example, see G Fuller, *Corporate Borrowing: Law and Practice*, 4th edn (Bristol, Jordan Publishing Ltd, 2009); P Cresswell, WJL Blair, GJS Hill, PR Wood (eds), *Encyclopaedia of Banking Law* (London, LexisNexis Butterworths, 2010); P Wood, *International Loans, Bonds, Guarantees, Legal Opinions*, 2nd edn (London, Sweet & Maxwell, 2007). For precedents, see the *Encyclopaedia of Forms and Precedents* (London, Butterworths Tolley) vol 4(1) (Banking).

[16]   See page 73.

[17]   See page 81.

[18]   See 5.3.1 below.

likely to apply to all group companies. Breach of any requirement, or any other specified event of default, will give the lender the right to accelerate the loan and terminate the agreement. These rights are discussed in 5.2.3 below. The way in which these contractual rights are used by lenders to influence the running of the borrower company is discussed in some detail in chapter three.[19]

At 5.2.4 we consider rights of set-off and netting which a lender may have in respect to the borrower's indebtedness. These rights can have a very considerable impact on the protection of a lender from credit risk, particularly since set-off is available on the insolvency of the borrower. Although some rights of set-off arise under the general law, these have limits, and financing agreements often include specific provisions relating to set-off. These may either extend its availability or restrict it. In addition, agreements may include provisions for netting which operate in conjunction with set-off to reduce risk. Set-off which operates on insolvency gives protection that is as powerful as proprietary protection, and in some cases more powerful, but it is reasonably clear that under English law set-off is not a proprietary interest, and so its discussion is included in this chapter and not in chapter six, which deals with proprietary protection.

5.2.1   Restrictions on the Borrower's Activities[20]

These covenants directly address the risks to creditors which arise because of the different interests of creditors and shareholders. These risks are identified and discussed in chapter three above:[21] in general terms they are that the borrower may incur further debts after borrowing from the lender, or may dispose of assets which otherwise would be available to pay the lender. Future borrowing can, broadly speaking, be controlled in two ways.[22] One way is by a general financial covenant, which requires the borrowing company (and often the entire group of companies) to comply with a specified gearing ratio. These seek to ensure that there is sufficient value in the company generally to repay the borrowing and are discussed below.[23] The second way is by a specific covenant restricting borrowing which conflicts with that of the lender, usually borrowing which ranks ahead of that from the lender. This will usually be secured borrowing, and so it is likely also to fall foul of a negative pledge clause. Broadly speaking, a negative pledge clause prevents the borrowing company from granting security over its assets. It comes in a number of forms, and gives significant protection to a lender. However, its use also raises a number of interesting legal issues, which are discussed below in considerable detail,[24] after a brief discussion of other forms of restrictive covenants which are used to protect lenders.

It is common for a lender to include a clause restricting the disposal of substantially all of the assets of the company: disposals in the ordinary course of trading, those for which full value is received and those with the consent of the lender are likely to be excluded.[25] It

---

[19]   3.2.2.4.

[20]   See 3.2.2.3.

[21]   3.2.2.2.

[22]   See the analysis by Fuller, who calls these the outer and the inner borrowing limits, see Fuller, *Corporate Borrowing: Law and Practice*, n 15, 168.

[23]   5.2.2.2.

[24]   5.2.1.1.

[25]   For further details, see Wood, *International Loans, Bonds, Guarantees, Legal Opinions*, n 15, 5–030–5–032; *Encyclopaedia of Forms and Precedents* (London, Butterworths Tolley) vol. 4(1) (Banking) [204] clause 19.10. This

is possible that a restriction on disposal would be interpreted as including restricting the grant of security to another lender (and could in particular include quasi-security structures which include the disposal of assets, such as the sale of receivables[26] or sale and lease-back devices[27]).[28] However, these transactions are much better dealt with by a negative pledge clause which covers them specifically,[29] and a clause restricting disposal will usually be coupled with a negative pledge clause. A restriction on disposal is particularly important if the lending is unsecured. If the lender is protected by a fixed charge or mortgage, there is no need to restrict disposal of those assets expressly, since it is in the nature of a fixed charge that the chargor cannot dispose of the charged assets without the consent of the chargee.[30] However, in relation to assets over which a lender has a floating charge,[31] there is some point in including the clause, since, without further restriction, the chargor is free to dispose of assets in the ordinary course of business, and this is given a very wide definition in the context of a floating charge.[32] The exact scope of the restrictions can then be a product of the negotiations between the borrower and the lender, and will represent a balance between protection of the lender and the freedom required to enable the borrower to carry on its business successfully.[33] Restrictions on disposal are particularly important where the borrower company is part of a group, since intra-group transfers are common, and yet, if made between the borrowing company and another company in the group, potentially damaging to the lender. If the borrower is the holding company, transfers between the subsidiary companies do not damage the lender, but a disposal of assets by a subsidiary company outside the group would be damaging and would be prohibited by covenant restricting disposals.[34]

The payment of dividends or other distributions to shareholders by the borrower company may also be restricted to a particular percentage of net profits.[35] Such a clause is less common when the borrower is a public company. This may be because public companies tend to present less credit risk, but also may be because dividend distributions by public companies are regulated further than those by private companies.[36] This is an example of where a 'default' level of protection is given to creditors by statute, rather than expecting creditors to bargain for their own protection. Whether statutory regulation is a

clause is known as a 'Tickler' clause after the case of *Commercial Union Assurance Co Ltd v TG Tickler Ltd* (unreported) 4 March 1959, in which it was held that the sale of a factory was not a sale of part of the company's 'undertaking': a specific contractual restriction was therefore required to prevent such actions, see Fuller, n 15, 181.

[26] 2.3.4.1.
[27] 2.3.4.3.1.
[28] See Wood, n 15, 5–030. Fuller, n 15, 181 points out that this would depend on the interpretation of the contract.
[29] Negative pledge clauses are discussed in detail below at 5.2.1.1.
[30] See pages 242–243.
[31] See 6.3.3 below for discussion of the floating charge.
[32] For the scope of 'ordinary course of business' in a floating charge see *Ashborder BV v Green Gas Power Ltd* [2004] EWHC 1517 (Ch), [2005] BCC 634 and page 243 below.
[33] A McKnight, 'Restrictions on Dealing with Assets in Financing Documents: Their Role, Meaning and Effect' (2002) 17 *Journal of International Banking Law* 193.
[34] E Ferran, *Principles of Corporate Finance Law* (Oxford, Oxford University Press, 2008) 333.
[35] See Wood, n 15, 5–045.
[36] In relation to all companies, dividends can only be paid out of distributable profits, see Companies Act 2006, s 830 and 4.4.1 above. Distributions to public companies are also subject to Companies Act 2006 s 831, see 4.4.1 above.

better means of protecting creditors than contractual protection is discussed above.[37] In addition to the points made in that discussion, it will appear from the current chapter that there is a complicated, and potentially varied, mix of covenants in loan agreements, which supplement the limited statutory protection available. It thus seems odd to provide such limited protection for creditors of public companies, when the major creditors are extremely likely to bargain for additional covenants anyway and so could easily include, for example, a covenant restricting dividend payments. Covenants can also be more closely tailored to the particular requirements of the lender, and the situation of the borrower. They can also overcome the shortcomings of the statutory tests, so that, for example, a clause restricting dividend payments can depend on cash flow tests rather than the historic balance sheet tests used by the Companies Act 2006.[38] Further, breach of a covenant leads to the right to accelerate the loan and terminate the contract, while breach of the statutory provisions only leads to a rather restricted ability to recover the payment.[39] Non-adjusting creditors (who, arguably, are the group that the statutory protection seeks to protect) would then be able to free ride on the benefits of the contractual protection.[40]

Sometimes covenants are also included which prohibit a substantial change of business of the borrower company, or prohibit mergers or change or control.[41] A change in the type of business carried out can greatly affect the credit risk faced by the lender: the new business may be much riskier, which may be good for the shareholders who will benefit from any increased gains, but bad for the creditors who will not benefit from gains, but who will suffer if the company becomes insolvent.[42] A merger or change of control will not necessarily affect the credit risk, but it may be perceived to do so, and so may affect the current value of the loan. This is especially important for bondholders, who may wish to sell their bonds, but also, maybe, for syndicated lenders, who may wish to transfer their interest.[43] For these reasons, the consequences are often not triggered unless the change of control is also accompanied by a downgrading in credit rating.[44]

Often the provisions referred to in the last paragraph are not drafted as restrictive covenants, but as events which give rise to certain consequences. In a loan agreement, this could be an event of default[45] or, in order not to trigger a cross-default, it could be a trigger for mandatory prepayment.[46] In bond issues, such events are not usually breaches as such, but trigger a 'put option', that is, gives the bondholders the right to require the issuer to redeem the bonds.[47] To the extent that such a provision acts as a disincentive to a

---

[37]   4.5.1.

[38]   For a critique of the balance sheet test imposed by the statute, see 4.4.5 above.

[39]   See page 139.

[40]   The free riding argument is discussed further in chapter 3 above, especially at page 85.

[41]   For a description of the ways changes of control can be effected, see page 19.

[42]   See page 76.

[43]   For a discussion of traded debt, see chapter 8.

[44]   M Hartley, 'Beyond Change of Control' (2006) 21 *Journal of International Banking and Financial Law* 475. See page 32 for a description of credit rating.

[45]   5.2.3.

[46]   See Cresswell et al, *Encyclopaedia of Banking Law,* n 15, F3238.

[47]   See Fuller, n 15, 8.52–53; M Hartley, 'Beyond Change of Control', (2006) 21 *Journal of International Banking and Financial Law* 475; M Hartley, 'Bondholder Protections Revisited' (2010) 25 *Journal of International Banking and Financial Law* 219.

takeover, it can be seen as a kind of poison pill,[48] and care would need to be taken by the directors of the borrowing company that, in agreeing to it, they were not in breach of their duties.[49]

Another area of debtor activity which may be restricted in a loan agreement is that of prepayment[50] or repurchase of the loan. Borrowers are usually permitted to prepay subject to certain restrictions, such as timing, and the giving of notice.[51] Repurchase by the borrower of the whole or part of a syndicated loan has become more common since the financial crisis, as loan often trade at below their face value and the borrower can thus, effectively, repay the loan at a discount, or, if the price of the loan goes up again, can sell at a profit.[52] Further, it can enable the borrower to have a say in any restructuring of the indebtedness. However, this causes problems with the democratic governance of the syndicate,[53] which lenders may wish to avoid. Thus the LMA documentation now contains an optional clause prohibiting or restricting debt buy-backs in the leveraged loan facilities agreement.[54]

5.2.1.1   The Negative Pledge Clause

A negative pledge clause provides important protection where a loan is unsecured. Where a lender takes fixed security, there is no need for a negative pledge clause, since the mortgagor or chargor is automatically prohibited from disposing of the secured assets (including creating security interests over them) without the consent of the mortgagee or chargee.[55] This is not the case where the lender takes a floating charge, and it is very common for a negative pledge clause to be included in such a charge. The effect of this is considered in chapter six below.[56] The following discussion is limited to the use of a negative pledge clause in unsecured lending. The primary purpose of such a clause is to protect the ability of the lender to enforce the loan against the assets of the borrower in the latter's insolvency: even though it may be an unsecured creditor and have to rank *pari passu* with all other unsecured creditors, at least all the assets of the company will be available for distribution if there are no secured creditors. Coupled with extensive rights to information about the company's financial position,[57] which enables a lender to take steps to accelerate and enforce a loan if the borrower gets into financial difficulties, a negative pledge clause gives good protection. Thus the lender may be able to complete enforcement[58] before the borrower becomes insolvent,[59] and even if this is not possible, may be able to prevent dissipation of assets before insolvency so that the lender is likely to be able

---

[48]   See Wood, n 15, 6–025.

[49]   For discussion see 12.3.2.1.1.

[50]   This is called repayment, in the case of loans, and redemption, in the case of debt securities.

[51]   For a detailed discussion, see Fuller, n 15, 5.5–5.16. Prepayment provisions in relation to a syndicated loan or bond issue usually include a system for sharing the prepayment pro rata among the multiple lenders, see page 357–58.

[52]   S Samuel, 'Debt Buybacks: Simply Not Cricket?' (2009) 24 *Journal of International Banking and Financial Law* 24.

[53]   See page 366 below.

[54]   At clause 30, inserted in September 2008. It seems that this clause has been little used, at least at first, see P Wood, 'Life after Lehmans: Survey of Changes in Market Practice' (2009) 24 *Journal of International Banking and Financial Law* 579.

[55]   See pages 242–43.

[56]   See pages 250, 276.

[57]   See 5.2.2.2 below.

[58]   See pages 220–21.

to recover all or most of the amount owed. Moreover, it is when the borrower is in financial difficulties that it will need to give security in order to raise new money.[60] If the grant of security is prohibited by a negative pledge clause, this enables the original lender to protect its interests either by refusing permission, or by giving consent on terms, such as limiting the amount of new borrowing.[61] This argument only works, of course, if the borrower asks for permission to breach the clause.[62] However, a breach of the clause would be an event of default, and so would enable the lender to take protective action at a point when its interests are threatened.[63] It should also be noted that a secured lender tends to have considerable power and influence on insolvency,[64] particularly in a restructuring: by preventing there being any secured creditors the lender increases its chances of being in a position to exercise influence itself.[65]

It might be asked why a lender would lend unsecured using the protection of a negative pledge clause, which, while valuable, is only a contractual right and not a proprietary right,[66] when it could take security which is a proprietary right. One answer may be that the balance of bargaining power is in favour of the borrower: this could be the case where the borrower is a very large credit-worthy company which can dictate the terms of the loan. Another might be that the cost of taking security can be very considerable, especially in complicated international transactions, and where the borrower appears very credit-worthy, that cost seems unnecessary.[67] Despite conferring merely a contractual right, a negative pledge can be very effective as a borrower will not wish to breach it and trigger an event of default. For many companies this is a very serious occurrence, as not only will it entitle the lender to accelerate or terminate the loan,[68] it may put the borrower in breach of cross-default clauses in other agreements, and have the effect of ruining the borrower's financial reputation.[69] Thus the clause regulates the borrower's behaviour by deterring breach: if, however, the borrower does breach the clause the remedies for the lender are rather limited. These will be discussed below.

In a eurobond issue, the purpose of a negative pledge clause is rather different. Rather than attempting to preserve priority over all the borrower's assets by preventing security being given for any borrowing, the object of the clause is to protect the trading value of

---

[59]   If there is sufficient pressure from the lender, it is unlikely that payment would count as a preference under Insolvency Act 1986, s 239, see 3.3.2.2 above.

[60]   See Wood, n 15, 5–009.

[61]   If the lender actually wants to control the amount of liabilities incurred by the borrower more generally, it is probably more effective to do this by a direct covenant restricting borrowing; see Wood, n 15, 5–009, and see above page 156.

[62]   The lender's options if the borrower breaches without permission are discussed below at 5.2.1.3.

[63]   J Arkins, '"OK – So You've Promised, Right?" The Negative Pledge Clause and the "Security" it Provides' (2000) 15 *Journal of International Banking Law* 198, 199. See 5.2.3 below.

[64]   This is particularly true of a holder of a floating charge, although the position has changed somewhat recently. See 6.3.3.4 and 6.5.1.4 below.

[65]   See Wood, n 15, 5–009.

[66]   See further discussion below pages 162–65.

[67]   J Arkins, '"OK – So You've Promised, Right?" The Negative Pledge Clause and the "Security" it Provides' (2000) 15 *Journal of International Banking Law* 198, 199.

[68]   5.2.3.

[69]   Benjamin calls it a 'financial death sentence': J Benjamin, *Financial Law* (Oxford, Oxford University Press, 2007) 8.25; A Hudson, *The Law of Finance* (London, Sweet & Maxwell, 2009) 8.44.

the issue, by preventing the issuer from issuing secured bonds into the same market, which would have the effect of making the unsecured issue less attractive and therefore less valuable.[70]

5.2.1.2 Forms of Negative Pledge Clause

There are three possible forms of negative pledge clause in unsecured lending (although the wording of each will, of course, vary). The first is a basic agreement not to grant security to any other person. Alternatively, the agreement could provide that the debtor can grant security to another person only if it grants matching security to the original lender. This can be drafted either so that the provision of matching security is a non-promissory condition of the granting of security to a third party, or that there is a positive promise to grant matching security.[71] Further, the agreement could provide that if security is given to a third party, a matching security in favour of the original lenders automatically attaches to the same asset. As negative pledge clauses are included in bond issues for a different purpose from when they are included in loan agreements, while all forms of the clause can be used in loan agreements, bonds tend to include the second type of clause,[72] and only cover the granting of security for issues of securities rather than for all kinds of debt.[73]

One challenge in drafting such a clause is to make sure that a wide enough class of transactions is prohibited to protect the lender, while not prohibiting transactions which the borrower needs to undertake in order to carry on its business.[74] This can be done by limiting the transactions to those creating security interests, but this will not catch 'quasi-security' transactions such as asset-based finance transactions,[75] so the clause is often extended to include these.[76] The balance can also be achieved by limiting the assets which are involved, so that the borrower is prohibited from alienating some, but not all, assets.[77]

5.2.1.3 Enforcement of Restrictive Covenants

The possible remedies of the lender for breach of the restrictive covenants discussed above fall into three classes: first, a personal (contractual) remedy against the borrower, second, a personal remedy (probably in tort) against the party to whom the disposition was made, or the security was granted, or who made the prohibited loan ('the third party') and, third, a proprietary remedy. A distinction needs to be made between those situations where the lender monitors the borrower's conduct extensively, and those, for example, in bond issues, where monitoring is very limited.[78] If there is extensive monitoring, then enforcement of a negative pledge clause by contractual remedies is not a problem. If the

---

[70]   See Fuller, n 15, 9.31 and fn 52; G Fuller, *The Law and Practice of International Capital Markets* (London, LexisNexis Butterworths, 2007) 8.24–25; see Wood, n 15, 12–012.

[71]   L Gullifer (ed), *Goode on Legal Problems of Credit and Security*, 4th edn (London, Sweet & Maxwell, 2008) 1–75.

[72]   See Fuller, n 15, 8.24.

[73]   For a discussion of when an 'all monies' negative pledge clause might be used in a bond issue, see M Hartley, 'Bondholder Protections Revisited', (2010) 25 *Journal of International Banking and Financial Law* 219.

[74]   A Hudson, *The Law of Finance*, n 69, 19–59.

[75]   2.3.4.2.

[76]   For an example of a negative pledge clause, see Fuller, n 15, 9.33. See also P Wood, n 15, 5–013.

[77]   See Hudson, n 69, 19–59.

[78]   For discussion of monitoring see pages 81–82 and 170.

lender knew or suspected in advance that a breach was going to occur, then in theory it could obtain injunctive relief to prevent it, or maybe even (at least in the case of an unauthorised disposition or security interest) appoint a receiver.[79] However, this is very unlikely unless there is very extensive monitoring. If the lender does not know about the breach for some time, the personal remedies will be of less use.[80] It has, of course, the right to rely on the event of default, to accelerate the loan and terminate the contract. If the borrower is solvent, then the threat of doing this might force the borrower to renegotiate the terms of the loan: this use of a breach of covenant is discussed above in chapter three as a method of corporate governance.[81] However, in a situation where the lender is seriously concerned about a disposal of assets or a grant of security, it is likely that exercising its rights to accelerate and terminate will force the borrower into insolvency. Faced with an insolvent borrower, the lender's personal rights are then of little use: in theory it has a right to damages for breach but this does not put it in a better position than its right to repayment of the loan under the loan agreement: both are unsecured claims.[82]

The lender might therefore wish to assert a remedy which will be effective against the third party. A possibility under all forms of the clause is that there is a tort action against the third party for inducing breach of contract or interference with contractual relations. This action is discussed in this paragraph in the context of a breach of a negative pledge clause, since that is the context in which it is most likely that a lender might wish to obtain such a remedy, but the same reasoning would apply to breaches of other restrictive covenants. The possibility of such an action in tort has been the subject of some debate,[83] but recent developments in the law of the economic torts have made it unlikely that it would succeed. It has been established that there is no independent tort of interference with contractual relations and that the two torts which remain are inducing breach of contract and causing economic loss by unlawful means.[84] There are clearly no unlawful means here: all the third party has done is to enter into a secured transaction with the borrower. Therefore the only possibility is the tort of inducing breach of contract. However, this requires an intention on the part of the defendant to induce breach, which means that the defendant has to know of the term breached (it is not enough that he ought to have known) and to have intended the breach either as an end or as a means to an end (not merely a foreseeable consequence of his actions).[85] Although it is not impossible that these criteria could be fulfilled where security is granted to a third party in breach of a negative pledge clause, it would be very rare.

A third possible remedy for breach of a negative pledge clause is a proprietary remedy against the borrower's assets (which, being proprietary, may bind the third party to whom security is granted). Such a remedy is a possibility where the clause is in the second or third forms discussed above which purport to give the lender a security interest if one is

---

[79]   D Allen, 'Negative Pledge Lending' [1990] *Journal of International Banking Law* 330.

[80]   This is likely to be the case in bond issues, because of the limited monitoring of the trustee, see page 344.

[81]   3.2.2.4.

[82]   It is possible that a disposal of assets at an undervalue in the run-up to insolvency could be avoided, see page 99 above.

[83]   J Stone, 'Negative Pledges and the Tort of Interference with Contractual Relations' (1991) 8 *Journal of International Banking Law* 310; TC Han, 'The Negative Pledge as a Security Device' [1996] *Singapore Journal of Legal Studies* 415; L Wo, 'Negative Pledges and Their Effect on a Third Party' (1999) 14 *Journal of International Banking Law* 360.

[84]   *OBG Ltd v Allan* [2007] UKHL 21; [2008] 1 AC 1, [189].

[85]   Ibid, [39]–[43].

granted to the third party: if successful this would make the lender a secured creditor with a proprietary right against the borrower's assets which ranked above or equally with that of the third party. Let us initially consider the case where the clause provides for automatic attachment of security. First, it is necessary to identify the asset over which security is given[86] so that if the clause only provides for 'matching security' this will not be enough and the clause will be ineffective.[87] If there is sufficient identification, all the lender has at the time of the contract is a contractual right and not an inchoate security,[88] since an agreement to grant security on a contingency is not in itself a security interest.[89]

Can the security interest in favour of the lender then attach automatically on the occurrence of the contingency, that is, the granting of the security to the third party? There is considerable debate about this, focusing on whether fresh consideration is required at that point. One view[90] is that consideration must be executed at the time when the security interest comes into existence, and since there is no new money extended at the time when the contingency occurs, the security interest in favour of the lender cannot arise or attach. The opposite view[91] is that the original loan by the lender is sufficient consideration. There are no direct English authorities.[92] Although there is dicta from the Singapore Court of Appeal supporting the view that no further consideration is required, this was not part of the ratio of the case, and arguably only refers to the obligation of the debtor to provide security rather than the automatic attachment of a security interest.[93]

Even if fresh consideration is required, it could be argued that since the breach of the negative pledge clause is an event of default, consideration is provided at that point by the lender by refraining from making demand.[94] The main problem with this argument is that the lender will normally be unaware that the breach has occurred: if it were aware, as

---

[86] See page 238.

[87] See Gullifer (ed), *Goode on Legal Problems of Credit and Security*, n 71, 1–75. However, it is not difficult to draft a clause which does sufficiently identify the assets; J Stone, 'The Affirmative Negative Pledge' (1991) 6 *Journal of International Banking Law* 364, 368.

[88] For further discussion of inchoate security, see pages 238–39.

[89] See Gullifer, n 71, 1–76; and see the decision of the Singapore Court of Appeal in *The Asiatic Enterprises (Pte) Ltd v United Overseas Bank Ltd* [2000] 1 SLR 300, [16]. For a view that, at least in relation to land, a negative pledge clause in this form does create an immediate security interest which is registrable as a floating charge, see G Hill, 'Negative Pledge with Provision for "Automatic Security" on Breach: a Form of Floating Charge?' (2008) 23 *Journal of International Banking and Financial Law* 528. This view has some support from an obiter dictum of Lord Scott in *Smith v Bridgend County Borough Council* [2002] UKHL 58 [2000] 1 AC 336, [61]–[63].

[90] See Gullifer, n 71, 1–76; J Maxton, 'Negative Pledges and Equitable Principles' [1993] *Journal of Business Law* 458; P Ali, *The Law of Secured Finance* (Oxford, Oxford University Press, 2002) 3.20–3.24; A McKnight, 'Restrictions on Dealing with Assets in Financing Documents: Their Role, Meaning and Effect', (2002) 17 *Journal of International Banking Law* 193, 203.

[91] P Gabriel, *Legal Aspects of Syndicated Loans* (London, Butterworths, 1986) 86–90; J Stone, 'The Affirmative Negative Pledge' (1991) 6 *Journal of International Banking Law* 364; H Beale, M Bridge, L Gullifer and E Lomnicka, *The Law of Personal Property Security* (Oxford, Oxford University Press, 2007) 6.77; TC Han, 'Charges, Contingency and Registration' (2002) 2 *Journal of Corporate Law Studies* 191.

[92] Two cases (*Re Jackson & Bassford Ltd* [1906] 2 Ch 467; *In re Gregory Love & Co* [1916] 1 Ch 203) which have been relied upon by both sides of the argument are not directly on the point since in both the security interest was expressly executed and did not arise automatically, and, further, was executed by deed so consideration was irrelevant; see Gullifer, n 71, 1–76.

[93] *The Asiatic Enterprises (Pte) Ltd v United Overseas Bank Ltd* [2000] 1 SLR 300, [18]: 'Where it is part of the agreement that the debtor will in certain event provide a certain security or further security, then upon the happening of that event, the debtor will be obliged to provide such security and no fresh consideration from the creditor is called for'.

[94] TC Han, 'Charges, Contingency and Registration' (2002) 2 *Journal of Corporate Law Studies* 191, 199.

would be the case had it been monitoring extensively, it will usually immediately exercise its right to terminate the loan agreement,[95] but if it is unaware how can the lender be said to have refrained from making a demand? It might also be possible to avoid the requirement for fresh consideration by making the original loan agreement by deed. However, it is difficult to see how the requirement for a further deed can be avoided if fresh consideration would, otherwise, be required. Further, the deed would only operate in relation to property owned by the borrower at the time of execution of the deed.[96]

If fresh consideration is not required, there are still further problems for the lender. First, the security interest created is likely to be registrable within 21 days.[97] Since the lender is unlikely to know that the interest has arisen, it will not know to register the charge,[98] and the prospect of the lender having to monitor the borrower's activities so as to know if it needs to register a charge is unattractive to some lenders. Second, the lender will only gain priority over the security interest granted to the third party if the lender's interest predates that of the third party. If the trigger for the lender's interest is the grant to the third party, the lender will lose priority. Therefore, if the lender wants priority, the clause would have to be drafted so that an earlier point (for example, the attempt to grant a security interest to a third party) was the trigger.[99] Third, there is still a possibility that the security interest in favour of the lender would be set aside as a preference under section 239 of the Insolvency Act 1986 if the borrower became insolvent within the relevant time.[100] The value given by the lender at the time of the original loan will not count as new value[101] even if it did count as sufficient consideration to support the grant of the security interest.

Given all these difficulties, it is unlikely that an 'automatic security' clause would be effective to create a security interest in favour of the lender. An unsecured lender who does not monitor, and who relies on a negative pledge clause to give quasi-proprietary protection is likely to fall into difficulty. However, if coupled with effective monitoring, the contractual remedies available for breach of negative pledge clauses and other restrictive covenants are likely to act as a deterrent against breach, and might provide adequate protection, particularly if an injunction could be obtained.

As well as the technical reasons discussed above, there are good policy reasons why it is not possible for a security interest to arise automatically on a particular contingency, when that contingency is not a public event. If the interest did arise, it would not be visible to the outside world, nor to the third party grantee of the security interest which triggered the clause, whose security would be severely cut down by the lender's interest. Since a third

[95]   See Gullifer, n 71, 1–76; A McKnight, 'Restrictions on dealing with assets in financing documents: their role, meaning and effect' (2002) 17 *Journal of International Banking Law* 193 at 203.

[96]   See Ali, *The Law of Secured Finance,* n 90, 3.57.

[97]   Companies Act 2006, s 860: see 6.4.2 below.

[98]   Any leave for late registration would be given subject to the priority of other charges already created: 6.4.2 below.

[99]   Such drafting has succeeded in the context of automatic crystallisation: see *Re Manurewa Transport Limited* [1971] NZLR 909 (Sup Ct Auckland); *Fire Nymph Products Ltd v The Heating Centre Pty Ltd* (1992) 7 ACSR 365 (Sp Ct NSW CA). However, it has been doubted by some writers that this analogy would be accepted by the courts: see J Arkins, '"OK – So You've Promised, Right?" The Negative Pledge Clause and the "Security"it Provides' (2000) 15 *Journal of International Banking Law* 198.

[100]   This is two years where a preference is given to a connected person and six months for any other person, see page 104.

[101]   The presence of new value would prevent the security interest being a preference; R Goode, *Principles of Corporate Insolvency Law,* 3rd edn (London, Sweet & Maxwell, 2005) 11–81.

party security holder does not even have constructive notice of a negative pledge clause in a registered floating charge[102] (when it is relatively easy to discover it and when he is at least on notice of the existence of the charge), it seems very unsatisfactory for a third party to be bound by a security interest arising out of an unregistered loan agreement. If there is fresh consideration for the lender's interest at the time it arises, at least the assets of the borrower are swelled and the third party's position is not so adversely affected: thus there is a policy justification for the requirement of fresh consideration. In any event, there is also an argument for registration of the new interest at the time of its creation (so that other potential creditors are put on notice) and also, maybe, for registration at the time when the loan agreement is entered into, so that third parties know that an interest may arise. Of course, if such registration is required, some of the benefits of lending unsecured are lost and the lender might as well take a security interest in the first place.

Depending on the construction of the clause, even if there is no automatic security there is likely to be an obligation on the borrower to grant the lender security if security is granted to a third party. If the borrower does grant such security, it would have to be by deed,[103] or be over present but not future property, or there would have to be valid executed consideration.[104] It would also, probably, have to be registered. It would not have priority over the security granted to the third party as it would be created after that security interest. Given these drawbacks, it is only in certain circumstances that a right to security is of benefit to a lender in the context of a negative pledge clause.

5.2.2 Rights to Information and Financial Covenants

The credit-worthiness of a borrower, that is, its ability to pay interest payments and eventually to repay the loan, is of critical importance to a lender at all stages during the currency of the loan. The lender will want to be able to check the position throughout, and to be able to take action if the credit-worthiness of the borrower deteriorates. This section examines the lender's rights to information at various stages of the loan, which enables the lender to monitor both the borrower's credit-worthiness, and also whether the borrower's business is being conducted in a way which may jeopardise the interests of creditors.[105] The lender's ability to take protective action is also examined, as are the contractual provisions which trigger these rights. The method of protection is different before and after the loan is made, and the discussion is split up accordingly. After the loan is made, the protective rights are triggered by breaches of covenants and events of default, many of which involve the maintenance of certain financial standards. The covenants specifying such financial standards (financial covenants) are examined in section 5.2.2.2.

5.2.2.1   *Rights at the Time of Making the Loan*[106]

At this stage the lender wishes to be in a position to make an informed decision whether to lend, and also, if it does decide to lend, on the amount of risk it will take on. In theory, the

---

[102] See page 271.

[103] As in *Re Jackson & Bassford Ltd* [1906] 2 Ch 467 and *In re Gregory Love & Co* [1916] 1 Ch 203.

[104] See above.

[105] See 3.2.2.2 above for a discussion of the risks creditors face, particularly where the interests of shareholders and creditors diverge.

[106] See also discussion at 11.2.8 below.

greater the risk the more the lender can charge for lending, but in practice the interest rate is often not very negotiable, either because there are multiple lenders and the rate is already fixed, or because the weight of the bargaining power is tipped towards the borrower. The lender will then have to decide whether the risk is worth taking for the reward it will bring. On assessment of the risk the lender will also be able to decide what other protection it needs, for example, the level of proprietary protection and also the level of contractual protection, although the amount it can actually get is also a factor of the bargaining power between the parties.[107] The bottom line for many lenders is, therefore, that they will not lend if the information shows that the risk is too great for the combination of interest and protection they are able to obtain.

However, where loans are transferable, the ability to transfer the loan for a good price may be more important to the lender than the absolute credit risk, since the lender may have little intention of keeping the loan until it is due to be repaid. This may make a lender less concerned about the details of the borrower's financial position and more concerned about the marketability of that sort of loan. For example, in a securitisation structure where loans are bundled together and repackaged into securities which are then tranched,[108] the absolute credit risk of each loan becomes much less important than the likelihood of enough securities being sold to finance the purchase of the loans from the lender. Arguably, this decoupling of absolute credit risk from the lender can lead to less assiduous assessment of credit risk and loans being made to borrowers who cannot repay or on terms which do not accurately reflect the credit risk.[109]

The initial information on which a lender will make a decision will, in the case of a securities issue or a syndicated loan, be provided by a standard document produced for all potential bondholders or syndicated lenders. In the case of a public listed securities issue, this will be a prospectus or listing particulars which will have to comply with the appropriate regulations and which will be publicly available.[110] In relation to a non-listed offer of securities (which will be made to a limited number of potential investors) or a syndicated loan, information will be contained in an offering circular, an invitation letter or an information memorandum.[111] Further, those purchasing debt securities and entering into syndicated loans will have regard to the credit ratings of a borrower produced by the credit rating agencies.[112] A single bank lender, however, will have to obtain information from the borrower itself, although a considerable amount of historic information about a company's financial position is often publicly available.[113] In this form of relationship lending, which is usually undertaken by banks to small or medium sized companies, the lender will take steps to know the borrower's business well. The lending will usually be at least partly on the basis of an overdraft and so the bank's exposure at any

---

[107]   Borrowers may also prefer to agree to stricter covenants rather than let the whole risk be reflected in the interest rate, see page 78.

[108]   8.3.3.

[109]   See also the discussion at pages 86–87.

[110]   See page 325 and 11.2 where the regulation of initial issues of debt securities is discussed.

[111]   See pages 325 and 359. The question of redress for false statements in such documents is discussed in 7.4.4 (in relation to syndicated loans) and 11.2.7 (in relation to debt securities).

[112]   See pages 32–33 and 559–61.

[113]   This will vary according to the size of the company and whether it is public or private and whether it is listed or not, see 10.3.1.1 and 10.3.1.2. Any security interests granted by the company will be registered in the company charges register, see 6.4.

one time will not necessarily be great, and the bank will put great store by its own knowledge of the customer in deciding whether to loan and what the overdraft limit should be.

At this initial stage, the contractual protection a lender has is in the form of conditions precedent in the agreement. These relate to a number of matters which, from the lender's point of view, have to be in place before the loan will be made. For example, it will be a condition precedent that the borrower has capacity to enter into the loan and has delivered documents which prove this.[114] Another example of a condition precedent, if the loan is secured, will be that the security has been validly created and perfected, and again that supporting documentation has been delivered.[115] Another important condition precedent will be that the representations and warranties made by the borrower are true, that there has been no material adverse change in circumstances since the date of the information provided, for example, in the audited accounts, and that no event of default has occurred.[116] The term 'representations and warranties' relates to the information, provided by the borrower, on which the lender makes the lending decision. Usually, representations are statements of fact and warranties are promises that certain representations are true or that certain acts have been done.[117] The problem with all information provided is that the situation may change between the provision of the information and the time when the creditor actually acts on it. This time lag is dealt with by the condition precedent mechanism.

There is a distinction in contract law between a promissory condition and a contingent condition.[118] The former is a promise made by one party to a contract, and failure to do it entitles the other party to terminate the contract and sue the other party for breach.[119] A contingent condition, however, is a state of facts which has to be fulfilled, which may or may not be something within a party's control: if it is the former, the party is not obliged to bring that state of facts about, but (usually) must not prevent it coming about.[120] The exact consequences if the state of facts is not fulfilled is a matter of interpretation of the contract,[121] although the effect will always be that one party is not obliged to perform some or all of his obligations under the contract until the state of facts is fulfilled. In the present context, this means that the lender is not obliged to advance funds unless and until the condition precedents are fulfilled. However, there are various possibilities as to the state of the contract between the parties if the condition precedent is not fulfilled. One is that the contract never comes into existence at all,[122] or that if there is a contract, both parties are discharged, so that either party can withdraw from the contract. Another is that

---

[114] See Wood, n 15, 3–008; Fuller, n 15, 2.7.

[115] Wood, n 15, 3–009.

[116] Fuller, n 15, 2.7.

[117] Note that a distinction can be made between legal warranties, which are promises that legal prerequisites and formalities have been complied with in order for the loan agreement to be valid, and commercial warranties, which are promises about the financial position of the borrower at the relevant time: Wood, n 15, 4–003.

[118] H Beale (ed), *Chitty on Contracts*, 30th edn (London, Sweet & Maxwell, 2008) 12–027; *Trans-Trust SPRL v Danubian Trading Co Ltd* [1952] 2 QB 29, 304.

[119] Contractual promises may also be warranties, breach of which only entitles the innocent party to damages and not to termination, or intermediate terms, breach of which may entitle the innocent party to termination depending on the seriousness of the breach. See Beale, *Chitty on Contracts*, ibid, chapter 12 section 2.

[120] E Peel (ed), *Treitel on the Law of Contract*, 11th edn (London, Sweet & Maxwell, 2003) 2–114.

[121] *Total Gas Marketing Ltd v Arco British Ltd* [1998] 2 Lloyd's Rep 209, 215.

[122] Peel, *Treitel on the Law of Contract*, n 120, 2–112; *Pym v Campbell* (1856) 6 E & B 370.

one party can withdraw but the other cannot,[123] and another is that the contract is binding on both, but that the obligations of one or both are suspended pending the fulfilment of the condition.[124] The position in relation to conditions precedent in loan agreements appears to be the third of these: the lender is not obliged to lend if a condition precedent is not fulfilled, but the contract to lend (the underlying facility agreement) remains valid and binding unless there is an event of default.[125] Of course, non-fulfilment of a condition precedent may well be an event of default. It should also be remembered that in many loan facilities the advances are made in stages, so that each time the lender is called upon to make an advance it will be able to refuse if a condition precedent is not fulfilled, for example, if the financial state of the company has changed.

5.2.2.2 Ongoing Rights

After an advance has been made, a lender wants to protect itself against changes in circumstances which would make the borrower less likely to be able to repay the loan. Obviously, once the loan has been made, the technique of a condition precedent cannot be used, so the loan agreement will also contain covenants, breach of which is an event of default which will entitle the lender to accelerate the loan and terminate the loan agreement.[126] The agreement will also list events of default which are not breaches, but which again give the lender the right to accelerate and terminate.[127] One type of covenant seeks to enable the lender to take action if early warning signs of financial weakness appear: while the action taken might be drastic, such as acceleration, it is far more likely to involve a dialogue with the directors of the company which may culminate in the renegotiation of the loan.[128] Alternatively, a lender of tradable debt such as a debt security or a tradable loan may choose to 'exit' via sale. The actual content of these covenants will vary according to the circumstances,[129] particularly in relation to the credit-worthiness of the borrower.[130] However, they all require the company to meet particular financial targets, usually expressed as ratios.[131] The ratio requirements can often relate to the consolidated position of the corporate group rather than the individual borrowing company.

---

[123] Beale, *Chitty on Contracts,* n 118, 12–028.

[124] Ibid.

[125] Wood, n 15, 3–011.

[126] 5.2.3.1. For detailed empirical research about covenants see P Taylor and J Day, 'Evidence on the Practices of UK Bankers in Contracting for Medium-Term Debt' [1995] *Journal of International Banking Law* 394; P Taylor and J Day, 'Bankers' Perspectives on the Role of Covenants in Debt Contracts' [1996] *Journal of International Banking Law* 201; P Taylor and J Day, 'Loan Contracting by UK Corporate Borrowers' [1996] *Journal of International Banking Law* 318; P Taylor and J Day, 'Loan Documentation in the Market for UK Corporate Debt: Current Practice and Future Prospects' [1997] *Journal of International Banking Law* 7; P Taylor and J Day, 'Financial Distress in Small Firms: the Role Played by Debt Covenants and Other Monitoring Devices' (2001) 3 *Insolvency Lawyer* 97; J Day, P Ormrod and P Taylor, 'Implications for Lending Decisions and Debt Contracting of the Adoption of International Financial Reporting Standards' (2004) 19 *Journal of International Banking Law and Regulation* 475.

[127] 5.2.3.1.

[128] See pages 82–83 above.

[129] The Loan Market Association standard form does not even suggest a pro-forma but leaves this clause for individual negotiation, see M Campbell, 'The LMA Recommended Form of Primary Documents' (2000) 15 *Journal of International Banking and Financial Law* 53, and Clause 21 of the Loan Market Association loan documentation for Investment Grade Borrowers. The LMA form for leveraged finance does include some pro-forma covenants, but these also are expected to be tailored to the individual circumstances.

[130] Loans to highly rated borrowers may not include any financial covenants at all.

[131] P Taylor and J Day, 'Evidence on the Practices of UK Bankers in Contracting for Medium-Term Debt' [1995] *Journal of International Banking Law* 394, 397.

One type of ratio relates to the capital worth of the company. As explained earlier, a company will be balance sheet insolvent if its assets are insufficient to discharge its liabilities.[132] A financial covenant could use this measure and prescribe a minimum net worth of a certain amount.[133] Another assessment would focus on the balance sheet gearing of the company, and would provide that the company must meet a particular gearing ratio (borrowings expressed as a percentage of net worth). The balance of debt and equity in a company's financial structure was discussed earlier from the point of view of the company.[134] From the point of view of a lender, too high a level of debt can lead to insolvency risk,[135] although a certain level is desirable because of the discipline it exerts on the directors.[136] As mentioned above,[137] gearing covenants can act as a general restriction on borrowing, which mitigates the debt dilution risk which lenders face.[138] The main problem with reliance on capital ratios alone is that they are calculated historically and are susceptible to manipulation by the borrower[139] (although some control is exercised by the requirement of auditing).

Another type of ratio relates to the income of the company. A covenant may require that the ratio of the profit of the company to the interest payments that it has to make to service its debt is not less than a certain amount.[140] An alternative is to use a cash flow based ratio, such as the relationship between cash inflow and the costs of the business (including funding).[141] This has the advantage that it is not a historic measure, and cash flow information can be required from the borrower company at intervals more frequent than other financial information. However, it can be difficult to draft effective covenants based on cash flow.[142] All these financial covenants are very dependent on the accounting methods used to calculate these ratios,[143] and changes in accounting standards can lead to covenants operating in different ways from that originally intended.[144] As well as the financial covenants, the warranties relating to the pre-loan representations may also continue, so that the borrower warrants that there is no change in its financial position.[145]

---

[132] See pages 56–57.

[133] Minimum net worth is what would be left if all the assets were sold and all the liabilities paid: S Valdez, *An Introduction to Global Financial Markets*, 5th edn (Basingstoke, Palgrave Macmillan, 2007) 91. This would be of interest to a lender in asset-based lending.

[134] 2.6.

[135] Obviously, a higher level of debt.

[136] See Ferran, *Principles of Corporate Finance Law,* n 34, 65. See further discussion at page 683.

[137] See page 156.

[138] See page 77.

[139] See Hudson, n 69, 33–28; M Hughes, *Legal Principles in Banking and Structured Finance*, 2nd edn (Hayward's Heath, Tottel Publishing Ltd, 2006) 15.

[140] See Valdez, *An Introduction to Global Financial Markets*, n 133, 91; A Hudson, *The Law of Finance* (London, Sweet & Maxwell, 2009) 33–27. This covenant is particularly relevant to cash flow lending (overdraft and invoice discounting): P Taylor and J Day, 'Evidence on the Practices of UK Bankers' [1995] *Journal of International Banking Law* 394, 397. The way that the components of this ratio are calculated can be a matter of considerable negotiation (See Wood, *International Loans, Bonds, Guarantees, Legal Opinions*, n 15) 5–040 et seq). One common measure for 'profit' is EBITDA (earnings before interest, tax, depreciation and amortisation) or EBIT (earnings before interest and tax).

[141] See Hudson, n 69, 33–28.

[142] P Taylor and J Day, 'Evidence on the Practices of UK Bankers in Contracting for Medium-Term Debt' [1995] *Journal of International Banking Law* 394, 397.

[143] P Taylor and J Day, 'Loan Documentation in the Market for UK Corporate Debt: Current Practice and Future Prospects' [1997] *Journal of International Banking Law* 7, 10.

[144] See J Day, P Ormrod and P Taylor, 'Implications for Lending Decisions and Debt Contracting of the Adoption of International Financial Reporting Standards' (2004) 19 *Journal of International Banking Law and Regulation* 475 on the effects of the change from the GAAP standard to the IFRS standard.

[145] These are known as 'evergreen' covenants: see Wood, n 15, 4–007.

If a ratio is not met, this would enable the lender to decide what to do: it would not necessarily terminate the arrangement but could use its power to do so to put pressure on the borrower to improve the position, and, if necessary, to renegotiate the loan with more protection for the lender.[146] The clauses mentioned above all specify particular financial criteria, but often a more general clause covering any 'material adverse change' is also included: there is either a representation that no such change has occurred plus a continuing warranty, or such a change is an event of default.[147] The flexibility that such a clause gives can be useful, but, as with any clause requiring an assessment of materiality,[148] it can also lead to serious uncertainty.[149] Lenders will generally include such a clause as a general safety net to catch any events which they have not been able to foresee in the future, but will combine it with specific covenants and events of default dealing with foreseeable risks.[150]

Coupled with financial covenants are obligations to provide information, so that the lender can monitor the borrower's financial position. The effectiveness of these depends on the information being timely and reliable,[151] and also on the company being willing to provide the information.[152] The minimum information would be that which is publicly available, such as the information periodically made available by companies.[153] However, most of this information is historic and therefore do not give very timely and up-to-date information,[154] so further information, to be provided by the management, may be required.[155]

5.2.3   Termination and Acceleration Rights

As mentioned above, debt contracts usually stipulate a number of 'events of default', the occurrence of which entitles the lender to accelerate repayment of the loan and/or to terminate the loan contract (which has the same effect, but which also releases the lender

---

[146]   P Taylor and J Day, 'Evidence on the Practices of UK Bankers in Contracting for Medium-Term Debt' [1995] *Journal of International Banking Law* 394, 399. See pages 82–84 above.

[147]   J Day and E Kontor, 'Corporate Lending in an Intangibles Economy: Potential Solutions' [2002] *Journal of International Banking Law* 174, 177; Wood, n 15, 6–018–6–022.

[148]   Note the difficulties experienced by a bond trustee who has to certify that an event of default is 'materially prejudicial' to the bondholders, discussed at pages 346–48 below.

[149]   See, for example, the problems caused by a similar clause in the *Elektrim* litigation, discussed at pages 347–78 below.

[150]   R Youard, 'Default in International Loan Agreements: Part 2' [1986] *Journal of International Banking Law* 378, 390.

[151]   P Taylor and J Day, 'Financial Distress in Small Firms: the Role Played by Debt Covenants and Other Monitoring Devices' (2001) 3 *Insolvency Lawyer* 97, 111.

[152]   Thus very large companies may have the bargaining power to restrict the information provided to that which is publicly available: see P Taylor and J Day, 'Loan Contracting by UK Corporate Borrowers' [1996] *Journal of International Banking Law* 318, 323.

[153]   See Chapter 10.3. In relation to debt securities which are listed on the GEFIM or the PSM certain levels of ongoing disclosure are required, see 11.3.1.

[154]   Hughes, *Legal Principles in Banking and Structured Finance*, n 139, 2.10. Not all the information disclosed to the markets is historic, however, see pages 490–91.

[155]   Such a requirement is not always very effective: see P Taylor and J Day, 'Loan Documentation in the Market for UK Corporate Debt: Current Practice and Future Prospects' [1997] *Journal of International Banking Law* 7, 13.

from the obligation to make further advances).[156] For a lender this is a very significant right: it should however be noted that it is only a right, which the lender can decide not to rely on, and that acceleration or termination does not happen automatically.[157] A lender has a discretion whether to waive a breach or to enforce it. Although the best way of exercising this discretion is by making a positive communication to the borrower, there is often a concern that inaction may be seen as a waiver, and so an agreement will often contain a 'no-waiver' clause. Such a clause, though useful, does not completely block a successful argument of waiver by estoppel when the facts support this.[158]

At its strongest, when it includes a 'cross-default' clause so that any default on any borrowing by the borrower is an event of default, it enables a lender to drive a borrower into insolvency very quickly.[159] The ability to accelerate a loan means that a lender can, if it wishes, seek to get paid (or to enforce its liability against the assets of the company) at the first sign of financial trouble. It might be thought to be a way to 'steal a march' on other creditors, although if all the borrower's credit agreements include cross-default clauses this will not be successful as all other creditors will also be able to accelerate their claims, thus driving the borrower into insolvency. Conversely, the cross-default clause can lead to inertia as there is no incentive on any particular lender to take action.[160]

The acceleration clause also, however, enables a lender to force a renegotiation of the loan as a price for not activating the clause: most lenders would prefer to do this as they are more likely to get paid if the borrower overcomes its financial troubles. The right is obviously of most use in term loans where the amount outstanding is considerable. The right to terminate its own further obligations to lend is also important to the lender, especially where the facility is revolving rather than for a term. A lender will have no desire to advance further funds when the likelihood of being repaid the funds already advanced is reduced. Further, the ability to refuse to advance further funds is an important way of forcing a renegotiation. The forced renegotiation may be on terms which include changes in the way that the company is managed, thus giving a lender an important corporate governance role when the company is in difficulties.[161]

---

[156]   Wood, n 15, 6–001. Where a loan is secured, events of default are usually also triggers for crystallisation of a floating charge, see P Mather, 'The Determinants of Financial Covenants in Bank-Loan Contracts' (2004) 19 *Journal of International Banking Law and Regulation* 33, 35. For further discussion of crystallisation, see 6.3.3.2 below.

[157]   R Youard, 'Default in International Loan Agreements' [1986] *Journal of International Banking Law* 276, 278. Note that the decision whether or not to accelerate a loan can be complicated where there are multiple lenders. In a bond issue, a trustee usually has the discretion whether to waive a breach, and also has the power to accelerate a loan if it decides that an event of default is materially prejudicial to the bondholders, and is obliged to do so if instructed by the bondholders and is satisfactorily indemnified. The difficulties this can cause are discussed below at pages 345–48. In a syndicated loan, the decision whether to waive the breach or to accelerate can be taken by a majority of lenders, except in relation to breaches of certain provisions, such as conditions precedent. See page 365 below.

[158]   *Tele2 International Card Company SA and others v Post Office Limited* [2009] EWCA Civ 9 and see E Nalbantian, M Brown, H Territt and N Davies, 'Drowning about Waiving?' (2010) 25 *Journal of International Banking and Finance Law* 195.

[159]   See Benjamin, *Financial Law*, n 69, 8.25; Hudson, n 69, 8.44; K Clark and A Taylor, 'Events of Default in Eurocurrency Loan Agreements' (1982) 1 *International Financial Law Review* 12, 13, who point out that the effectiveness of cross-default clauses can be limited by banks' standards of secrecy, so that one lender will not necessarily know of a default on another loan.

[160]   Wood, n 15, 6–013.

[161]   See 3.2.2.4 above.

5.2.3.1   Events of Default

The loan contract will stipulate such events of default as, from the lenders' view, are thought to be suitable indications of the borrower's inability to repay the loan, and, from the borrower's view, are not so easily triggered as to make it impossible to carry on its business. This balancing exercise is difficult, and is often the product of considerable negotiation. Some events of default will be breaches of the agreement, but others will be events outside the control of the borrower and will not amount to breach (so that they will not, for example, give rise to a right of damages). The most obvious breach is failure to pay the lender amounts due, whether of principal or interest.[162] Since a failure to pay can arise from a minor administrative error, there is usually a short grace period.[163] Any breach of warranty (including the warranty that all representations remain accurate) or breach of covenant will also be an event of default. These events, and a failure to pay, amount to breaches. Non-breach events may include insolvency proceedings, or actual insolvency, default on other loan or other types of contracts (these are cross-default clauses)[164] and any change in circumstances which might have a materially adverse effect on the financial condition of the borrower.[165]

5.2.3.2   Effect of Wrongful Acceleration

In some circumstances, especially where the event of default in question requires the lender to interpret a widely drafted clause, such as to decide whether an adverse change of circumstances is 'material', a borrower may allege that the lender has sought to exercise its right to accelerate wrongfully. It appears from the House of Lords decision in *Concord Trust v Law Debenture Trust Corporation plc*[166] that a wrongful exercise of the right to accelerate is of no legal effect. This means that it is ineffective to achieve anacceleration,[167] and that, in the absence of an implied term to the effect that the lender agreed not to give an invalid notice of acceleration, the lender is not contractually liable for doing so. Such a term would only be implied if it were necessary to give business efficacy to the contract[168] and this is unlikely to be the case in most circumstances.[169] It would, of course, be a breach of contract if the lender refused, on the basis of the wrongful acceleration, to make further advances which it was contractually obliged to do, or if it wrongfully enforced security.[170]

---

[162]   It should be noted that loans payable on demand do not require an acceleration clause, see R Youard, 'Default in International Loan Agreements' [1986] *Journal of International Banking Law* 276, 276.

[163]   S Lear and M Lower, 'Events of Default' [1993] *Law Society Gazette*, 21 Apr, 90 at (31); Wood, n 15, 6–009; K Clark and A Taylor, 'Events of Default in Eurocurrency Loan Agreements', (1982) 1 *International Financial Law Review* 12.

[164]   Such clauses can be justified on the basis that a default in meeting the obligations to one creditor is a good advance warning of financial difficulty: R Youard, 'Default in International Loan Agreements' [1986] *Journal of Business Law* 378, 384.

[165]   Wood, n 15, 6–018. See above page 170.

[166]   *Concord Trust v Law Debenture Trust Corporation plc* [2005] UKHL 27.

[167]   See the decision of the Court of Appeal in the same case at [2004] EWCA Civ 1001, [71] (Jonathan Parker LJ), approved by Lord Scott at [2005] UKHL 27, [37].

[168]   *The Moorcock* (1889) LR 14 PD 64, 68.

[169]   This is clear both from the House of Lords decision in the *Concord* case and in the decision of *BNP Paribas SA v Yukos Oil Company* [2005] EWHC 1321 (Ch) in which the approach of the House of Lords was followed.

[170]   [2005] UKHL 27 at [41]; E Peel, 'No Liability for Service of an Invalid Notice of "event of default"' (2006) 122 *Law Quarterly Review* 179, 182–83.

There are other possible causes of action for which a lender might be liable for wrongful acceleration. A discussion of these and of the policy implications of the *Concord* decision can be found in chapter seven in the context of the obligations of bond trustees.[171]

5.2.3.3 Validity of Acceleration Clauses

When the trigger for the acceleration of the payment obligation is a breach of contract,[172] the question arises as to whether the clause can be challenged under the jurisdiction of the courts to set aside penalties. It is clear that the mere fact that the loan becomes repayable early does not make it a penalty, as long as no extra interest is payable other than that which has already accrued and continues to accrue.[173] This seems to be the case despite the fact that early payment is usually more expensive for the payer and more valuable to the payee, at least where there is a positive rate of inflation.[174] If, however, the obligation accelerated includes unaccrued interest, this may be set aside as a penalty:[175] the test to be applied will be that discussed in the next paragraph.

If the provision also provides for an additional rate of interest after default, this also might potentially be struck down as a penalty. The penalty jurisdiction is an exception to the general rule that the courts should uphold the terms of the contract as agreed between the parties.[176] A clause will be struck down as a penalty if its primary contractual function is deterrence of breach, and not compensation of the innocent party for the breach:[177] the primary test for this (though maybe not the only one) is whether the amount payable under the clause is a genuine pre-estimate of the loss flowing from the breach.[178] However, it appears from the judgment of Colman J in *Lordsvale Finance v Bank of Zambia*[179] that being a genuine pre-estimate of loss is not the only reason why a clause providing for payment on breach might not be a penalty: it can also be if there is another good commercial reason why the dominant contractual purpose of the clause is not to deter breach.[180] In that case, which concerned an increase in the rate of interest on default of a loan, the increase was of one per cent. Colman J explained that this was explicable since the credit risk of the borrower had increased after the default, and that interest rates were

---

[171]   See pages 345–48.
[172]   The rules against penalties only applies to sums payable on breach of contract, and not to sums specified as payable on other non-breach events, *Export Credits Guarantee Department v Universal Oil Products Co* [1983] 1 WLR 399.
[173]   *Oresundsvarvet AB v Lemos (The Angelic Star)* [1988] 1 Lloyds Rep 122; *Wadham Stringer Finance Ltd v Meaney* [1981] 1 WLR 39; *O'Dea v Allstates Leasing Systems (WA) Pty Ltd* (1983) 152 CLR 359 (HC Aust); GA Muir 'Stipulations for the Payment of Agreed Sums' (1985) 10 *Sydney Law Review* 503; *AMEV-UDC Finance Ltd v Austin* (1986) 162 CLR 170 (HC Aust); *BNP Paribas v Wockhardt EU Operations (Swiss) AG* [2009] EWHC 3116 (Comm); cf *Esanda Finance Corp Ltd v Plessing* (1989) 166 CLR 131 (HC Aust); (1989) ALJ 238.
[174]   M Furmston (ed), *The Law of Contract*, 2nd edn (London, Butterworths, 2003) para 8.118.
[175]   *Oresundsvarvet AB v Lemos (The Angelic Star)* [1988] 1 Lloyds Rep 122, 125.
[176]   *Robophone Facilities v Blank* [1966] 1 WLR 1428, 1446–47; *Murray v Leisureplay plc* [2005] EWCA Civ 963, [29].
[177]   *Lordsvale Finance plc v Bank of Zambia* [1996] QB 752, 762.
[178]   *Dunlop Pneumatic Tyre Co Ltd v New Garage & Motor Co Ltd* [1915] AC 79, 86.
[179]   [1996] QB 752. See also Hughes, n 139, 2.4–2.5.
[180]   Ibid at 763, cited with approval by Mance LJ in *Cine Bes Filmcilik ve Yapimcilik AS v United International Pictures* [2003] EWCA Civ 1669, [15]. Cf *Jeancharm Ltd v Barnet Football Club Ltd* [2003] EWCA Civ 58, where the Court of Appeal explained the decision in *Lordsvale* on the grounds that the provision was a genuine pre-estimate of loss, and *Murray v Leisureplay plc* [2005] EWCA Civ 963, [111], where Buxton LJ appears to the limit the test to whether there is a genuine pre-estimate of loss.

generally higher where credit risk was higher. Thus an increase was to be expected and could not be said to be for the dominant purpose of deterring default.

It is, however, a question of degree. In *Jeancharm Ltd v Barnet Football Club Ltd*[181] default interest was charged at an uplift of five per cent: this was held to be a penalty on the grounds that it could not be justified on the basis that the credit risk of the borrower had increased, and that it was not a genuine pre-estimate of loss.[182] This does not undermine the approach of the court in *Lordsvale*, where the judge took account of the commercial reasons for the provision, the prevalence of such clauses in international loan agreements and the attitude of the courts of other countries to them. In particular, he took regard of the fact that the law of New York upheld such clauses, and commented that

> It would be highly regrettable if the English courts were to refuse to give effect to such prevalent provisions while the courts of New York are prepared to enforce them. In the absence of compelling reasons of principle or binding authority to the contrary there can be no doubt that the courts of this country should adopt in international trade law that approach to the problem which is consistent with that which operates in that nation which is the other major participant in the trade in question. For there to be disparity between the law applicable in London and New York on this point would be of great disservice to international banking.[183]

This pragmatic attitude to terms in commercial contracts has been much approved by those in practice.[184]

It should also be mentioned that the penalty jurisdiction has also been applied to acceleration clauses in hire purchase and conditional sale agreements.[185] The relevant principles are now well-established and tend to be followed in the drafting of all such clauses. The question of relief against forfeiture of the subject matter of a finance lease has also been considered, and this will be discussed in chapter six.[186]

The penalty clause jurisdiction does not apply when the trigger for acceleration is not a breach of contract. However, where the event of default is that formal insolvency proceedings have been commenced against the borrower company, the question arises whether the acceleration clause falls foul of the anti-deprivation principle.[187] The first question to ask is whether the effect of the clause is to deprive the insolvent company of an asset it would otherwise have. It could be said that, by accelerating the loan, the company becomes liable for a sum for which it would not otherwise be liable, and that increasing a company's liabilities has the same effect as diminishing its assets.[188] However, on insolvency all future and contingent debts become immediately provable anyway,[189] which means that they are, in effect, accelerated. Thus unless the acceleration clause contained some element of penalty for acceleration (that is, an extra payment which was only to be

---

[181]   [2003] EWCA Civ 58.

[182]   Ibid, [16], [22] and [29].

[183]   [1996] QB 752, 767.

[184]   Hughes, n 139, 2.5; See also *BNP Paribas v Wockhardt EU Operations (Swiss) AG* [2009] EWHC 3116 (Comm) [23]–[25].

[185]   *Bridge v Campbell Discount Co Ltd* [1962] AC 600. For the possible application of the principle to finance leases, see R Goode, 'Penalties in Finance Leases' (1988) 104 *Law Quarterly Review* 25.

[186]   6.5.2.1 below.

[187]   See pages 100–101.

[188]   That an increase in liabilities can be seen as a deprivation was accepted in *Ex p Mackay* (1873) LR 8 Ch App 643 (an early case in which the principle was applied), where James LJ commented that a clause where the price of an article sold would be doubled if the buyer became insolvent would fall foul of the principle (at 647).

[189]   Insolvency Rules 1986, r 11.13, r 12.3(1), r 13.12.

made if the loan were accelerated) there cannot be said to be a deprivation. It should be noted that an acceleration clause is often combined with a right of set-off on insolvency, but even here the principle will not be contravened providing that the right of set-off falls within insolvency set-off.[190]

If the acceleration clause is coupled with the termination of the right to call for future advances, this, in theory, could amount to a divesting of an asset of the company on insolvency. However, since the insolvency is bound to be an anticipatory breach by the borrower (since it will be unable to repay the loan),[191] this brings the obligation of the lender to make the loan to an end, and a clause stating that this is the case (or terminating the contract before the actual onset of insolvency) cannot be said to divest the company of any asset which would otherwise be available to creditors.[192]

5.2.4 Set-off [193]

Set-off can arise in a number of forms, but the basic idea is the same. If A owes money to B and B owes money to A the two debts can be set off against each other so that only the balance is payable. Set-off operates both outside and within insolvency, although in the latter situation it is restricted by statutory criteria. Set-off can operate to the advantage or disadvantage[194] of a creditor in a number of ways. Outside insolvency, its prime function is to avoid circuity of action, so that instead of a creditor having to sue a debtor for the debt, it can (in certain circumstances) merely cancel its own debt to the debtor. This not only saves litigation and enforcement costs, but can also reduce the creditor's exposure to the debtor's credit risk (both actually and in its books, which can have an effect on capital adequacy) and also the creditor's own debts. When combined with netting,[195] set-off is extensively used by those who trade on the financial markets to reduce exposure and risk, and also to reduce the volume of settlements.[196] Although set-off operates by operation of law, its limits (outside insolvency) can be extended or reduced by agreement between the parties. Thus, with agreement, a lender can set off the debt owed by a borrower against a debt the lender owes to a third party, such as a parent company of the borrower.[197] Conversely, the parties can exclude the right of set-off, so that, for example, loans[198] and

---

[190]   See below 5.2.4.6. For a decision that an acceleration provision, coupled with a provision that the payment of the loan must be by way of set-off, did not contravene the anti-deprivation principle, see *Re Mistral Finance Ltd (In Liquidation)* [2001] BCC 27, [56]–[61].

[191]   *Sale Continuation Ltd v Austin Taylor & Co Ltd* [1968] 2 QB 849.

[192]   F Oditah, 'Assets and the Treatment of Claims in Insolvency' (1992) 108 *Law Quarterly Review* 459, 494–499. See also Goode, *Principles of Corporate Insolvency Law*, n 101, 7–09.

[193]   See, generally, R Derham, *The Law of Set-Off* (Oxford, Oxford University Press, 2003); Gullifer, n 71, ch 7; P Wood, *Set-off and Netting, Derivatives and Clearing Systems* (London, Sweet & Maxwell, 2007) ch 1.

[194]   Where it is to the disadvantage of the creditor, it is possible to exclude all but insolvency set-off: see below page 182.

[195]   See pages 180–81.

[196]   Benjamin, n 69, 8.25; Hudson, n 69, 12.03–12.07.

[197]   Such an agreement would normally be coupled with a guarantee from the parent company.

[198]   Wood, n 15, 3–058.

bonds may provide that payment must be made without set-off.[199] While such a clause is valid outside insolvency, it does not apply within insolvency as insolvency set-off is mandatory.[200]

5.2.4.1   Use of Set-off and Flawed Asset Structures in Lending

If the borrower becomes insolvent, set-off has an important protective function for the lender. Under English law, mutual debts are set off on insolvency so that only the balance due to the solvent party is provable. Thus if a borrower owes £1m to the lender, and the lender owes £750,000 to the borrower, the lender's liability to the borrower is discharged and the lender need only prove for the £250,000 balance. A lender is very unlikely to receive the full amount owed in relation to the amount proved for, but the effect of insolvency set-off is that it does 'receive' the full £750,000 which is set off, as the lender no longer has to pay this to the borrower. Insolvency set-off therefore puts the lender in the same economic position as if the debt were secured, in that it gets the full amount in priority to the unsecured creditors. In fact, it is in a better position than, for example, the holder of a floating charge, since the liquidator's costs, preferential creditors and the prescribed part for the unsecured creditors are paid out of floating charge assets in priority to the floating chargee.[201]

Lenders, especially bank lenders, may structure transactions to enable themselves to be 'paid' by set-off if the borrower becomes insolvent. Thus, to give a very simple example, if a borrower has a deposit account with a bank, the bank will rely on being able to set off its debt to the borrower against the amount due on the loan if the borrower becomes insolvent. The bank may seek to protect itself further by a provision in the deposit agreement that the deposited funds cannot be withdrawn while the loan remains extant. This changes the nature of the bank's obligation to pay the borrower into a contingent debt, often known as a 'flawed asset'. The 'flaw' in the asset (that the debt is not payable to the borrower until the lender has been paid) is inherent, and as such survives the insolvency of the borrower.[202] A provision which has the effect that a debt owed to a company is not repayable in certain circumstances might be thought to fall foul of the anti-deprivation principle, if the company became insolvent. There is, as yet, no English authority on this point.[203] However, the principle does not apply to an inherently limited

[199]   This is a requirement for any debt securities traded through CREST, see below page 396 and is also invariably included in issues of stock, see page 391. This was not necessarily the case for bearer bonds which were negotiable instruments, since they were transferred free from equities including set-off (see below 8.2.3 and Fuller, n 15, 323.

[200]   *National Westminster Bank Ltd v Halesowen Presswork and Assemblies Ltd* [1972] AC 785.

[201]   3.3.1.2.

[202]   *In re Bank of Credit and Commerce International S.A. (No 8)* [1996] Ch 245, 262–63 (*BCCI (No 8)*); Ali, n 90, 18; *Enron Australia v TXU Electricity Ltd* (2003) 204 ALR 658 (Sup Ct NSW) and *Marine Trade SA v Pioneer Freight Futures Co Ltd BVI* [2009] EWHC 2656 (Comm), cf Beale et al, n 91, 6.89 where it is doubted whether the actual clause in the *BCCI (No 8)* case created a true flawed asset rather than a charge. The distinction between the two can be problematic, see *Fraser v Oystertec plc* [2004] EWHC 1582 (Ch).

[203]   Note, though, that a case raising this point is due to be heard in the High Court in November 2010 (*In Re Lehman Brothers International (Europe); In the matter of the Insolvency Act 1986*, No 7942 of 2008).

asset,[204] and there is a strong argument that either a contingent debt falls within this category, or that the reasoning is sufficiently analogous for the principle not to apply.[205]

Where the depositor and the borrower are the same person, the flawed asset device merely preserves the value of the deposit so that the lender can benefit from the application of insolvency set-off if the borrower becomes insolvent. If the deposit is by another party, such as a parent company, insolvency set-off will not apply, and so the flawed asset has independent value. As explained by Rose LJ, in the Court of Appeal decision in *BCCI (No 8)*,[206]

> It will almost invariably be in the interests of the general body of creditors for [the depositor's liquidator] to permit the bank to recoup itself out of the deposit, take delivery of any other securities which the bank holds for the principal debt, and seek to recover from the principal debtor.

However, if the depositor has guaranteed the borrowing, insolvency set-off will apply in any case since the obligation under the guarantee will be set off against the deposit.[207]

It has frequently been the practice of bank lenders to take a 'triple cocktail' of protection: a flawed asset, a contractual set-off and a charge-back (a charge taken by the lender over the deposit).[208] This represented a 'belt and braces' approach, which was perhaps appropriate when there was doubt about the validity of charge-backs[209] and the scope of insolvency set-off was more limited.[210] Triple cocktails, and, indeed, flawed assets, are now much less common.[211]

Whether the advantage insolvency set-off gives to a creditor is justified in policy terms will be discussed below, when the requirements for insolvency set-off are considered.[212] First, the various types of set-off outside insolvency will be discussed briefly. The labels for these types sometimes vary: the titles used here are those coined by Philip Wood, which are now widely used.[213]

5.2.4.2 Independent Set-off

This originated from the Statutes of Set-Off, and is sometimes called statutory set-off. Now it also includes that form of set-off which was applied by analogy where one of the claims was equitable which, confusingly, was called legal set-off. It is really a procedural defence: where a claim for a liquidated sum is brought, a cross-claim for a liquidated sum can be asserted to extinguish or reduce the judgment which the claimant can obtain.[214]

---

[204]   See page 101 above.

[205]   This view obtains support from the reasoning of the Court of Appeal in *Perpetual Trustee Co Ltd v BNY Corporate Trustee Services Ltd* [2009] EWCA Civ 1160, see Butterworths Corporate Law Service, I[9.510]–[9.519]; (2009) All England Annual Review (Company Law) 4.50.

[206]   [1996] Ch 245, 263.

[207]   This is now so even if there has been no demand under the guarantee, see Gullifer, n 71, 7–96.

[208]   Charge-backs are discussed below at 6.3.2.4.

[209]   Now resolved, see 6.3.2.4.

[210]   In particular, contingent debts owed to the insolvent party could not be the subject of set-off. This is now changed, see Insolvency Rules 1986, r 2.85(4) and r 4.90(4) as amended by the Insolvency (Amendment) Rules SI 2005/527.

[211]   R. Calnan, *Taking Security, Law and Practice* (London, Jordan Publishing Ltd, 2006) 432–33; Ali, n 90, 280.

[212]   5.2.4.6.3.

[213]   P Wood, *English and International Set-Off* (London, Sweet & Maxwell, 1989). See also Gullifer, n 71, 7–03.

[214]   Independent set-off is not a defence, although usually pleaded as such (CPR r 16.6), and thus does not actually reduce the defendant's liability but only takes effect on and from the date of judgment: see Gullifer, n 71,

The significance of this is that it only applies where an action has actually been brought: where the claimant seeks to exercise a self-help remedy, independent set-off does not apply. Thus, for example, a borrower cannot rely on independent set-off to reduce the amount payable on an instalment of a loan, or an instalment under a hire purchase agreement. In these circumstances the lender could invoke an acceleration clause,[215] or could terminate the agreement and repossess the goods, on the grounds that an instalment had not been fully paid.[216]

Independent set-off has significant other limitations, in that it can only apply to debts (liquidated claims for money) and not to claims for damages, and only to debts due at the start of the action. For these reasons, it is rarely relied on, since transaction set-off[217] is more liberal. However, there is one situation where independent set-off can be used when transaction set-off cannot be. Independent set-off applies even where the claim and the cross-claim are unconnected, whereas transaction set-off, which is based on the principle that it is inequitable for the claimant to succeed on the claim without giving credit for the cross-claim, requires an inseparable connection.

5.2.4.3   Transaction Set-off

Where there is sufficient connection between the claim and the cross-claim, this form of set-off operates as a substantive defence. This means that, unlike the situation in relation independent set-off discussed above, where a payment is made taking account of transaction set-off, a self-help remedy for underpayment is not triggered.[218] This proposition is not uncontroversial. In two fairly recent cases[219] Buxton LJ has doubted whether transaction set-off can be used as a substantive defence and appeared to say that it could only be used at the time of litigation;[220] however, there is considerable authority against this view.[221] The availability of a self-help remedy by the assertion of transaction set-off creates considerable uncertainty in practice as to the operation of an acceleration or termination clause. This is a strong reason for providing that payments under a loan agreement or in an issue of securities should be made without set-off.[222] It is also unclear at what point transaction set-off should be asserted in order for it to be effective to prevent self-help remedies. Again, the position is not certain, but the better view is that where the claimant

---

7–36; *Stein v Blake (No 1)* [1996] AC 243, 251 (Lord Hoffmann); *Glencore Grain Ltd v Agros Trading* [1999] 2 Lloyd's Rep 410, [28]; *Henriksens Rederi A/S v Centrala Handlu Zagranicznego (CHZ) Rolimpex (The Brede)* [1974] QB 233 at 245–46 (Lord Denning M.R.); *Fuller v Happy Shopper Markets Ltd* [2001] 1 WLR 1681, [21].

[215] See above 5.2.3.
[216] See Gullifer, n 71, 7–38–39. The question whether the same is true for transaction set-off is discussed below. If the borrower had sufficient bargaining power, it could, of course, include contractual set-off with a wider scope in the agreement.
[217] 5.2.4.3.
[218] Gullifer, n 71, 7–55.
[219] *Mellham Ltd v Burton (Inspector of Taxes)* [2003] EWCA Civ 173; *Smith v Muscat* [2003] EWCA Civ 962.
[220] [2003] EWCA Civ 173, [11]; [2003] EWCA Civ 962, [44].
[221] *Federal Commerce & Navigation Co Ltd v Molena Alpha Inc (The Nanfri)* [1978] QB 927 at 974 (Lord Denning) and 982 (Lord Goff); *Aectra Refining and Manufacturing Inc v Exmar NV (The New Vanguard and The Pacifica)* [1994] 1 WLR 1634, 1650; *Eller v Grovecrest Investments Ltd.* [1995] 1 QB 272; *Pacific Rim Investments Pte Ltd. v Lam Seng Tiong* [1995] 3 SLR 1 (Sing CA); *Fuller v Happy Shopper Markets Ltd* [2001] 1 WLR 1681, [22]. See also R Derham, 'Equitable Set-Off: A Critique of Muscat v Smith' (2006) 122 *Law Quarterly Review* 469.
[222] The advantages of an acceleration clause are dependent on speed and certainty, and if a paying borrower could claim to pay less than the due amount on the grounds of set-off, this would prevent the timely operation of the clause, even if the cross-claim turned out later to be without merit.

is relying on a self-help remedy the set-off must have been asserted before the reduced payment is made:[223] there is no need for the claimant to wait after payment to see whether any set-off is asserted.[224] The substantive operation of transaction set-off means that (once asserted) it can operate as payment. This is supported by the House of Lords decision in *Mellham v Burton*,[225] where, after considering the views of Buxton LJ discussed above, the House held that 'payment' under section 87 of the Taxes Management Act 1970 could be made by transaction set-off.

One way of expressing the test for the necessary link between the claim and the cross-claimis that there must be an 'inseparable connection'. However, this test is less suitable where the claim and cross-claim derive from different contracts, and the Court of Appeal has recently endorsed as more appropriate a slightly redrafted version of the statement of Lord Denning in *The Nanfri*:

> cross-claims . . . so closely connected with [the Plaintiff's] demands that it would be manifestly unjust to allow him to enforce payment without taking into account the cross-claim.[226]

The test relates to the substance rather than the form of the claims, so even if the claims arise out of the same transaction this does not necessarily mean that they are sufficiently connected, while claims arising out of separate contracts may qualify if they are sufficiently connected. Providing there is sufficient connection, it does not matter that one claim is liquidated and the other unliquidated (for example, a claim for damages).[227] Further, the claims must be mutual, although in determining mutuality account is taken of equitable interests as well as legal interests. Thus if a beneficiary is sued, it can set off a claim held on trust for him by a trustee.[228]

5.2.4.4 Banker's Right to Combine Accounts

For bank lenders, a significant part of the law of set-off is the right to combine current accounts. This is probably best analysed as an implied contractual right to set off the credit balance on one account (a debt due by the bank to the customer) against a debit balance on another account.[229] This is because there is no obligation on the banker to combine accounts,[230] and the right to do so can be excluded by express or implied agreement. Where a customer has a loan account and a current account, it will be presumed that there

---

[223] Although there is no reported case where a self-help remedy was used where set-off had not been asserted beforehand, there are cases supporting the obverse position, that where set-off is asserted, the creditor cannot use a self-help remedy: *Santiren Shipping Ltd v Unimarine SA* [1981] 1 Lloyd's Rep 159; *Pacific Rim Investments Pte Ltd v Lam Seng Tiong* [1995] 3 SLR 1; *Eller v Grovecrest Investments Ltd* [1995] 1 QB 272 and *Fuller v Happy Shopper Markets Ltd.* [2001] 1 WLR 1681.

[224] Gullifer, n 71, 7–55. *Cf* R Derham, 'Equitable Set-Off: A Critique of Muscat v Smith' (2006) 122 *Law Quarterly Review* 469, 477.

[225] [2006] UKHL 6.

[226] *Federal Commerce & Navigation Co Ltd v Molena Alpha Inc.*, (*The "Nanfri"*) [1978] QB 927, 974–5, as approved by Rix LJ in *Geldof Metallconstructie NV v Simon Carves Ltd* [2010] EWCA Civ 667 [43]. For a discussion of the position before this Court of Appeal decision, with examples of the necessary connection, see R Derham, *The Law of Set-Off* (Oxford, Oxford University Press, 2003) 4.02–4.20; Gullifer, n 71, 7–50–7–51.

[227] *Hanak v Green* [1958] 2 QB 9.

[228] *Cochrane v Green* (1860) 9 CB (NS) 448.

[229] Gullifer, n 71, 7–32. *Cf* Derham, *The Law of Set-Off*, n 226, 15.03 et seq.

[230] *Halesowen Presswork and Assemblies Ltd v National Westminster Bank Ltd* [1971] 1 QB 1, 34; *Re EJ Morel Ltd* [1962] Ch 21, 31.

is no right to combine without express agreement.[231] This makes obvious sense, since the customer will normally want to carry on its business by writing cheques on its current account, even though it has borrowed from the bank. However, the bank will want, and will have, a right of set-off on insolvency (since insolvency set-off cannot be excluded) and will often provide for a contractual right of set-off under certain circumstances.

5.2.4.5   *Contractual Set-off and Exclusion of Set-off*

Although in many circumstances a lender might be sufficiently protected by relying on set-off which arises under the general law, it is likely to wish to provide in the agreement for the precise application of set-off to the transaction. This is as much in the interests of certainty as because it is wished to extend or reduce the application of set-off, although this may also be desired. However, as can be seen even from the brief discussion above, the scope of independent and transaction set-off or the application of set-off to a particular transaction is not always absolutely clear, and providing for the precise operation of set-off in the agreement prevents any possible dispute as to whether set-off is available.

Contractual set-off can also be used to provide for set-off to occur where otherwise it would not. For example, an agreement can provide that unconnected debts between the same parties can be set off in a way that the amount payable is reduced, either immediately or at a later date at the option of one party.[232] This is significantly beyond the application of independent set-off, where such debts can only be set off once litigation has commenced. Independent set-off does not constitute payment, and transaction set-off only does when asserted, but contractual set-off can do so immediately (depending on the terms of the contract). Thus, when combined with netting, contractual set-off is a useful tool to reduce the number of settlements and exposure risk.

Netting comes in various forms, which are closely related to but distinct from set-off.[233] The title netting covers various contractual provisions which change the nature of the parties' obligations to each other either to have the effect of set-off or so that set-off (contractually provided for) can take place. Novation netting is an agreement whereby all contracts between the parties are consolidated into one single contract, with one payment obligation. Usually, as each new contract is entered into, it is consolidated with the single contract so that there is only ever one balance payable. The actual time of payment is provided for separately by the contract. One use of this technique is where there is a clearing house in a market. The clearing house rules usually provide that each time two members of the market trade with each other, each transaction is novated to the clearing house (so that the clearing house then has two contracts, one with each party) and consolidated with each party's other obligations to and rights against the clearing house so that only one balance is payable either to or from the clearing house.[234] Settlement netting

---

[231]   *Bradford Old Bank Ltd v Sutcliffe* [1918] 2 KB 833.

[232]   Derham, *The Law of Set-Off*, n 226, 713.

[233]   Gullifer, n 71, 7–17–7–20. The threefold analysis discussed there has been adopted widely: see *Enron Europe Ltd (In Administration) v Revenue and Customs Commissioners* [2006] EWHC 824 (Ch), [20]–[22] and B Muscat, 'Developments in Netting Legislation: The Silent Revolution in the Financial Markets' (2008) 23 *Journal of International Banking and Financial Law* 470.

[234]   See description of rules of the London Clearing House (LCH Clearnet Ltd) in Gullifer, *Goode on Legal Problems of Credit and Security*, n 71, 7–18. This means that LCH Clearnet Ltd assumes the risk that a member might default on payment and become insolvent, and therefore requires members to post margin with it as security.

relates purely to payment, so that when amounts become due from and to two or more parties, they are netted out so that only one sum is payable. Thus it is distinct from novation netting, which applies to executory contracts. Settlement netting is to deal with the rather specific risk that A will pay the gross amount to B but B will not be able to pay the gross amount due back to A: the operation of settlement netting means that A's risk of B's non-payment is limited to the net amount.[235] It is often used in the settlement of payment through a clearing house, although, as will be seen, novation netting is a safer method in the event of the insolvency of one of the members.

It is a requirement of both these methods of netting, and any consequential set-off, that the claim and cross-claim be monetary. However, many contracts involve at least one obligation which is to do something other than pay money, for example, to transfer assets such as securities. Until that obligation is performed, the corresponding money obligation is not due. Thus there can be no possibility of netting or set-off while the contract remains executory, and on insolvency a liquidator can elect not to perform the insolvent's side of the bargain, leaving the other party as an unsecured creditor. To avoid this problem, many contracts contain a provision for close-out netting, so that on a specified event (either insolvency or default or some other such event) the contracts between the parties are terminated or accelerated so that money claims become due either way (the calculation of the amount due on non-monetary obligations is normally carried out using the usual-principle of contractual damages: the difference between the contract price and the market price) and these are then set off so that only a net sum is payable.[236] Close-out netting provisions are extensively used in the financial markets and are found in many master agreements governing such transactions.[237]

Another way in which contractual set-off can extend the scope of set-off which arises by operation of law, is to provide that set-off will occur even where there is no mutuality of parties. Thus, a lender could have the right to set off a claim owed to party B against the obligation of borrower A.

There is no problem with the effectiveness of any of these provisions outside of insolvency, since parties have freedom of contract.[238] However, if a party becomes insolvent, as a general rule any contractual terms providing for set-off which operates more widely than insolvency set-off are unenforceable. Further, any attempt to rely on them may be set aside as a preference or a transaction at an undervalue.[239] Insolvency set-off is mandatory and parties cannot contract out of it.[240] Mutuality of parties is required for insolvency set-off. Where this exists, however, insolvency set-off is very wide in scope, and includes unrelated, future and contingent claims. Therefore, the main

---

[235]   *Enron Europe Ltd (In Administration) v Revenue and Customs Commissioners* [2006] EWHC 824 (Ch) [22].

[236]   See definitions of close-out netting in EU Collateral Directive (2002/47/EC of the European Parliament and of the Council (02/47/EC) art 2(1)(n); Financial Collateral Arrangements (No. 2) Regulations 2003 reg 3.

[237]   For example, the ISDA master agreement, which relates to the trading of derivatives, and the London repo and securities lending agreements. See J Benjamin, *Financial Law* (Oxford, Oxford University Press, 2007), 12.10–12.22, 8.25; Hudson, n 69, 12.13 and 13.43.

[238]   There are some limits, however, on the effectiveness of set-off against third parties: see Gullifer, n 71, 7–26– 8. For example, no new set-off (contractual or otherwise) can arise between debtor and creditor once the debtor has had notice that the debt has been assigned, see page 375.

[239]   Provisions which do fall within insolvency set-off cannot have this result: see *Re Washington Diamond Mining Co* [1893] 3 Ch 95, 104. See Derham, *The Law of Set-Off*, n 226, 16.04.

[240]   *National Westminster Bank Ltd. v Halesowen Presswork & Assemblies Ltd* [1972] AC 785.

situation where contractual set-off is likely to be unenforceable is where it is sought to set off debts where there is no mutuality. The mandatory nature of insolvency set-off is discussed further in the next section.

Set-off can also work to the disadvantage of a lender in that the borrower may seek to rely on it to avoid making repayments in full or at all. Obviously, if a cross-claim exists the lender will eventually have to pay the borrower, but it may not wish to have to do so immediately. For example, the lender may have itself to make back-to-back payments on its own arrangementsfor financing the loan, such as a securitisation, or it may wish to have the ability to challenge the cross-claim as a defendant rather than as a claimant,[241] or it may wish to take away from the borrower any incentive to make spurious cross-claims. Alternatively, the debt obligation may be transferable, and there is a doubt as to whether it can be transferred free from equities, including set-off.[242] Thus the lender may wish to exclude the operation of set-off by contractual terms, so that payment will take place in full.

Outside insolvency, there now seems little doubt that such a clause is effective.[243] Although the width of application of the exclusion will depend in each case on the exact wording of the term, independent set-off can be excluded as well as transaction set-off, and it seems there is no policy objection to this.[244] This is also the case where the exclusion is by reason of the CREST rules (incorporated into the contract):[245] this is particularly critical as the operation of the CREST system depends upon the immediate completion of bargains without regard to any other transactions between the parties.[246] There is, however, a presumption that parties to an agreement do not intend to abandon remedies for breach which arise by operation of law, and clear words must be used to rebut this.[247] Generally, therefore, set-off cannot be excluded without clear words, although in deciding whether a more general clause (which does not use the word 'set-off') excludes it, the whole contractual context will be considered.[248] Despite this, it is clear that where a debt security is sought to be transferred through the CREST system an exclusion of set-off will be incorporated even without express words.[249]

---

[241] There are great advantages in being a defendant: most notably that the defendant has, at least temporarily, the money that is being claimed. Further, if a cross-claim cannot be set up as a defence, the lender can obtain summary judgment under Civil Procedure Rules r 24 which is quicker and much less expensive than a defended claim. A similar advantage is obtained by the payee of a negotiable instrument, in that only cross-claims which amount to a total or partial failure of consideration can be defences to a claim on such an instrument by an immediate, see E McKendrick (ed), *Goode on Commercial Law*, 4th edn, (London, Penguin/LexisNexis, 2010) 561–62.

[242] This is unlikely to be the case where the debt obligation is a bearer security which is a negotiable instrument, but will be where the transfer is by way of assignment, and may be when there is a novation. Therefore issues of stock usually include a clause excluding set-off: see *Hilger Analytical Ltd v Rank Precision Industries Ltd* [1984] BCLC 301, and the CREST rules provide that a security traded through the system must be 'transferable free from any equity, set-off or counterclaim between the issuer and the original or any intermediate holder of the security' (rule 7 3.2). These issues are discussed in more detail in chapter 8.

[243] *Hong Kong and Shanghai Banking Corporation v Kloeckner & Co AG* [1990] 2 QB 514 at 521; *Coca-Cola Financial Corp v Finsat International Ltd (The Ira)* [1998] QB 43.

[244] *Coca-Cola Financial Corp v Finsat International Ltd (The Ira)* [1998] QB 43, 52.

[245] *Re Kaupthing Singer and Friedlander Ltd (In Administration)* [2009] EWHC 740 (Ch); *Newcastle Building Society v Mill* [2009] EWHC 740 (Ch).

[246] Ibid, [19]. See page 396 below.

[247] *Gilbert-Ash (Northern) Ltd v Modern Engineering (Bristol) Ltd* [1974] AC 689, 717.

[248] *BOC Group plc v Centeon LLC* [1999] CLC 497, 503. For a full discussion, see Derham, n 226, 5.78–5.99.

[249] See page 396.

5.2.4.6   *Insolvency Set-off*

5.2.4.6.1   The Limits and Operation of Insolvency Set-off [250]

Insolvency set-off applies both on liquidation and in administration where the administrator chooses to make a distribution.[251] In this section reference will only be made to the rules on liquidation in the interests of simplicity. The idea is that an account is taken of mutual dealings between the insolvency company and a creditor to produce a net balance: if a debit balance, the creditor may only prove for that balance in the liquidation.

Insolvency set-off is mandatory and as such operates automatically.[252] This means that there needs to be a specific cut-off date early on in the insolvency process when it operates. However, the actual accounting process and the actual amounts to be taken into calculation will not be known until later when the liquidator has been appointed and is able to do the necessary work. Two principles[253] deal with this problem: the retroactivity principle and the hindsight principle. The former deems the account to be taken at the 'date of the account' even though it does not actually happen till later. The latter means that the liquidator can take into account events happening after the date of the account when calculating the balance due.[254]

Two specific issues are of particular interest in the context of this chapter. The first is the inclusion of contingent debts in insolvency set-off. A creditor may prove for a contingent debt in the liquidation,[255] and so consistency requires that such debts can be set off. In any event, it makes sense to include them in both proof and set-off, and for there to be a procedure for estimating their value, since otherwise the liquidation process would be unduly protracted while the liquidator waits for contingencies to eventuate. Recent developments to the Insolvency Rules[256] have clarified that contingent claims against the insolvent company are included,[257] as are contingent claims by the company (against the creditor), although if the account results in a balance payable to the company by the creditor, this does not need to be paid until it becomes due.[258] The liquidator estimates the value of a contingent claim, taking into account both the possible amount of the debt and the probability of it arising.[259]

The second issue is whether the mutuality required for insolvency set-off is destroyed by the presence of a charge-back. A charge-back, it will be recalled, is a charge taken by a lender over a debt owed by it, usually a credit balance in an account held with it. It might be thought that such a charge is not required, since the lender is in any event protected by

---

[250]   For detailed discussion, see Gullifer, n 71, 7–76–7–101.

[251]   The relevant rule in liquidation is Rule 4.90 of the Insolvency Rules 1986, and, in administration, Rule 2.85. Amendments in 2005 brought the two regimes in line as far as possible, although there are significant, though inescapable, differences, see Gullifer, n 71, 7–85.

[252]   *Stein v Blake* [1996] 1 AC 243, 254–55 and *Gye v McIntyre* (1991) 171 CLR 609, 622 (HC Aust). The mandatory nature of insolvency set-off is discussed below at 5.2.4.6.2.

[253]   Articulated by Hoffmann LJ (as he then was) in *MS Fashions Ltd. v Bank of Credit and Commerce International SA (No. 2)* [1993] Ch 425, 432–33.

[254]   Gullifer, n 71, 7–80 and 7–81.

[255]   Insolvency Rules 1986 r 12(3)(1).

[256]   By the Insolvency (Amendment) Rules 2005 SI 2005/527.

[257]   The House of Lords had already made this clear in *Re West End Networks Ltd, Secretary of State for Trade and Industry v Frid* [2004] UKHL 24.

[258]   Insolvency Rules 1986 r 2.85(4) and (8) and r 4.90 (4) and (8).

[259]   See Goode, n 101, 4–41.

set-off, but despite this many lenders do take such a charge. One reason for this is that the lender wishes to have a choice whether and when to enforce the security, rather than having it operate automatically by insolvency set-off. A lender might wish to have this choice, for example, where the debt and the credit balance are in different currencies and it is sought to exploit the varying exchange rates to the lender's advantage.[260] However, this choice will not be available unless mutuality is destroyed by the charge. Usually, where the solvent party has security for a debt, it has a choice either to enforce its security, in which case insolvency set-off will not apply,[261] or to prove in the liquidation. The problem is that at the date of the account it is not known whether the creditor will enforce the security or prove in the liquidation. However, if the creditor does enforce the security by the time of the actual taking of the account then the liquidator, by application of the hindsight principle, must conclude that the mutuality is broken and automatic insolvency set-off does not apply. One could go further and say that the mere potential for being able to enforce the security means that the mutuality is broken at the date of the account, but that this lack of mutuality can be reversed if the creditor makes it clear by the time that the account is actually taken that it intends to prove and not to rely on its security. The position has been left open by authority. Hoffmann LJ and the Court of Appeal in *MS Fashions Ltd v Bank of Credit and Commerce International SA (No 2)*[262] appeared to take the view (in a slightly different context) that a charge did not break the mutuality or prevent set-off. However, Lord Hoffmann in *BCCI (No 8)*[263] left the point open, and did not appear to have a firm view in support of the views expressed in *MS Fashions*. There is strong academic and practitioner opinion to support the view that mutuality is destroyed, and this view seems preferable.[264]

5.2.4.6.2   The Mandatory and Exclusive Nature of Insolvency Set-off

It will be recalled that it is a basic principle of insolvency law that the insolvent company's assets are to be distributed *pari passu* to its unsecured creditors.[265] This principle, however, applies to such a limited extent in practice that many commentators have suggested that it does not exist,[266] or that it should be reformulated.[267] Any creditor with a proprietary claim falls outside the principle (an alternative formulation of this is that since the asset is no longer owned by the company, the principle does not apply to it), and there are

---

[260]   M Evans, 'Triple Cocktail Becomes a Single Malt' (1998) 13 *Journal of International Banking Law* 115, 116; R Calnan, 'The Insolvent Bank and Security Over Deposits' (1996) 4 *Journal of International Banking and Financial Law* 174, 177.

[261]   *Re Norman Holding Co Ltd* [1991] 1 WLR 10; *Stewart v Scottish Widows and Life Assurance Society plc* [2005] EWHC 1831 (QB), [185] (appealed [2006] EWCA Civ 999, but not on this point). See also *Re Bank of Credit and Commerce International SA (In Liquidation) (No 8)* [1996] Ch 245, 256: 'Set-off ought not to prejudice the right of a secured creditor to enforce his security in any order he chooses and at a time of his choice'.

[262]   [1993] Ch 425, 438, 446.

[263]   [1998] AC 214, 225.

[264]   Derham, n 226, 16.68–16.73; M Evans, 'Triple Cocktail Becomes a Single Malt', [1998] *Journal of International Banking Law* 115; C Farner, 'Charges over Bank Accounts' (1998) 13 *Journal of International Banking and Financial Law* 85; R Calnan, 'The Insolvent Bank and Security Over Deposits' (1996) 11 *Journal of International Banking and Financial Law* 185.

[265]   See page 95 and 103.

[266]   R Mokal, 'Priority as Pathology: The Pari Passu Myth' (2000) 60 *Cambridge Law Journal* 581 (esp 616–21).

[267]   L Ho, 'The Principle Against Divestiture in Insolvency Revisited: *Fraser v Oystertec*' (2004) 19 *Journal of International Banking and Financial Law* 54. 'Unfair' unequal distribution before insolvency is dealt with by Insolvency Act 1986, s 239 which is discussed at 3.3.2.2.

significant statutory exceptions.[268] Insolvency set-off can be seen as another exception to the principle, in that it enables some unsecured creditors to recover the whole or part of their claim in full.[269] Whether it is justifiable to have such an exception is discussed in detail below.[270] However, because it is an exception to the principle, its limits are clearly defined by statute, as discussed above.

The common law anti-deprivation principle, which is aimed at preventing the diminution of an insolvency company's assets, will also be recalled.[271] It can be seen that set-off could offend against the anti-deprivation principle since if the claim of the debtor against the creditor is seen as an asset of the debtor, then requiring that asset to be used to fulfil the creditor's claim against the debtor is divesting the debtor of that asset.

If set-off (or netting) offends both these principles, then it could be said that neither should be permitted in insolvency except to the extent that the situation falls within statutory insolvency set-off. Set-off arising by operation of law does so, but where set-off or netting is provided for contractually, it may fall outside the bounds of insolvency set-off, for example, by providing for set-off where there is no mutuality. Even so, it could be said that the contractual provisions agreed by the parties should survive the insolvency of one party unless they fall foul of either of the insolvency principles discussed above. The boundaries of these two insolvency principles are, however, not absolute or straightforward. For example, a company is free to dispose of its property if it wishes at any time up to insolvency, subject to the provisions against transactions at an undervalue and preference.[272] Further, a person is free to transfer to a company as much or as little of the interest in an asset as it wishes, so that if an interest in an asset is transferred to a company on the basis that the interest is determined on insolvency, the agreement is unimpeachable.[273]

Bearing these matters in mind we should consider the case of *British Eagle International Air Lines Ltd v Compagnie Nationale Air France*.[274] In that case, airlines were members of a clearing house (IATA) and amounts due to and from member airlines were netted out by the clearing house each month, at which point the clearing house would pay or receive the net balances to or from the airlines (a form of settlement netting). British Eagle became insolvent and was owed a sum by Air France. The question was whether the liquidator could claim this amount in full, or whether it could only claim the net balance from IATA taking into account the sums that British Eagle owed other airlines.

The House of Lords (by a majority) held that the effect of the clearing house netting arrangements contravened the *pari passu* principle in that the creditor airlines were put in a better position than other creditors as they were 'paid' in full. It made no difference that the arrangements were not intended to put those creditors in a better position in the insolvency of a member, but were merely to improve payment mechanisms, although the two dissenting judges did think that the lack of intention to avoid the rules of insolvency

---

[268] These are discussed above at 3.3.1.2.

[269] See above page 176.

[270] 5.2.4.6.3.

[271] This principle is discussed at pages 100–101. The same principle applies to non-corporate debtors, but these will not be considered here.

[272] See 3.3.2.1 and 3.3.2.2 above.

[273] *Money Markets International Stockbrokers Ltd (In Liquidation) v London Stock Exchange Ltd* [2002] 1 WLR 1150 at [37]. This is one of the limits of the anti-deprivation principle, see page 101.

[274] [1975] 1 WLR 758.

law was significant. Although the House of Lords relied on the *pari passu* principle, it can be argued that what was really at stake was the anti-deprivation principle, in that the effect of the agreement was to take the asset (the claim against Air France) out of the general pool of assets of British Eagle and distribute it to the member airlines. If that asset was not an asset of British Eagle at the time of the insolvency, then the principle did not come into play, so that if the rules of the clearing house provide that all inter-member claims are immediately novated to the clearing house (novation netting) the arrangement could not be challenged.[275]

Further where a clearing house arrangement provided that no claims ever arose between members but only between members and the clearing house, this did not infringe the principle either (as there was nothing to divest or of which to deprive the other creditors).[276] Concerns about the invalidity of settlement netting in clearing house arrangements in insolvency (bilateral settlement netting would fall within insolvency set-off and would therefore be valid) have led to statutory intervention, so that settlement netting arrangements in financial markets are statutorily protected on insolvency.[277]

It is reasonably clear that a bare provision for non-mutual set-off, however, would still be invalid on insolvency.[278] Such a provision would clearly fall foul of the anti-deprivation principle, since the claim due to the insolvent company is being disposed of to a third party, rather than enuring to the benefit of all unsecured creditors. It should be noted, however, that if the real basis of the invalidity is the anti-deprivation principle, there should be no reason why a liability of the insolvent company to a creditor should not be able to be set off, pursuant to an agreement, against the liability of that creditor to third party.[279] If, however, there is a free-standing principle that all unsecured creditors should be paid *pari passu*, to which insolvency set-off is the only exception, then such a provision should not be valid, since that creditor is, effectively, being paid the full amount due to it by not having to pay the third party.[280]

To the extent that close-out netting provisions might be seen as violating either principle (which is unlikely if there is mutuality since future and contingent claims are now included in insolvency set-off in either direction)[281] such provisions in financial

---

[275]   Gullifer, n 71, 7–30. Such an arrangement would be unlikely to appeal to a body such as the IATA as it would then bear the risk of a member's insolvency itself. Such a body would be unlikely to be able to call for margin as security, unlike the London Clearing House (see n 234 above).

[276]   *Ansett Australia Holdings Ltd v International Air Transport Association* [2008] HCA 3 (HC Aust).

[277]   Financial Markets and Insolvency (Settlement Finality) Regulations 1999 reg 14 enacting the 1998 Settlement Finality Directive (EC 98/26 art 3(2)).

[278]   *Re Bank of Credit and Commerce International SA (In Liquidation) (No 8)* [1996] Ch 245, 272–73.

[279]   Derham, n 226, 16.20.

[280]   This can be illustrated by a rather basic example: A (the insolvent company) owes £50 to B. B owes £50 to C. If the two debts can be 'set off' then the effect is that B does not have to pay C. B therefore obtains the benefit of £50, rather than merely receiving the proportion it would have received if it had proved in A's liquidation. In effect, C is paying A's debt for it, but, when A is insolvent, this could be seen as contrary to *pari passu*, since if C wished to make a gift of £50 to A, it should become part of A's assets and be available for all of A's creditors.

[281]   In some situations, a close-out netting provision may benefit the insolvent company, as, although contingent claims by the company can now be set-off under the Insolvency Rules 1986 (see the Insolvency (Amendment) Rules SI 2005/527 amending rules 2.85(4) and 4.90(4)), if the taking of the account results in a balance due to the company, this only has to be paid when it is due and payable (Rules 2.85(8) and 4.90(8)) whereas under a close-out netting provision the balance is immediately due. However, even if contractual provisions do benefit the insolvent company, it appears that parties cannot contract out of the application of the rules of insolvency set-off: *National Westminster Bank Ltd. v Halesowen Presswork and Assemblies Ltd* [1972] AC 785.

collateral arrangements are rendered valid in insolvency by Regulation 12 of the Financial Collateral Arrangements (No 2) Regulations 2003.[282]

As mentioned above, set-off can also be excluded contractually for various reasons.[283] However, when the borrower becomes insolvent, the exclusion is ineffective.[284] This is strange, in that, where the borrower is insolvent, set-off almost invariably operates to the advantage of the creditor, so by excluding it the creditor is swelling the assets available for the unsecured creditors and taking its chance by proving for the full amount in the insolvency.[285] The justification for the rule appears to be that the insolvency set-off legislation is beneficial for the orderly administration of insolvent estates[286] and that, if the creditor did not pay, the liquidation proceedings might be held up by lengthy and costly litigation against it.[287] This justification, weak even on its face,[288] does not counterbalance the freedom of contract argument allowing a creditor to exclude set-off if it wishes.[289] Further, in one specific situation there is a strong argument for allowing such exclusion. This is where an insolvent company, in the course of restructuring under an agreed moratorium with creditors, opens a current account with a bank who has lent to it in order to pay in its earnings. If the bank did not agree to exclude insolvency set-off, all credits to that account would go to reduce the company's indebtedness to the bank, and would not be available for creditors generally.[290] For this reason the Cork Committee on Insolvency Law and Policy[291] recommended that the prohibition on contracting out of insolvency set-off be reversed. However, no legislation has resulted from this.

5.2.4.6.3   Policy Justifications for Insolvency Set-off

As has been mentioned earlier, insolvency set-off is a significant exception to the related principles of insolvency law that a company cannot agree to divest itself of assets on insolvency in a way that deprives unsecured creditors of those assets, and the *pari passu* principle that all creditors within a particular class should be treated alike.[292]

The policy justifications for this are varied. It can be argued that, since the parties have given credit to each other outside of insolvency on the basis that they would be able to rely

---

[282] SI 2003/3226. Carve-outs such as this provision and the settlement finality provision mentioned earlier are justified by the benefits of set-off and netting in the financial markets: see below 5.2.4.6.3.

[283] See page 182.

[284] *National Westminster Bank Ltd v Halesowen Presswork and Assemblies Ltd* [1972] AC 785; *John Dee Group Ltd v WMH (21) Ltd* [1998] BCC 972, 976.

[285] Take the following examples: (1) Lender (L) owes borrower (B) £100, B owes L £200. If B is insolvent and insolvency set-off operates, L can prove for £100 and is released from its debt (so gets 'paid' £100 and pays nothing). If insolvency set-off does not operate, L must pay B £100 and can prove for £200. (2) L owes B £200, B owes L £100. If insolvency set-off operates, L must pay £100 and is released from £100 of its debt (so gets 'paid' £100). If insolvency set-off does not operate, L must pay £200 and can prove for £100.

[286] *National Westminster Bank Ltd v Halesowen Presswork and Assemblies Ltd* [1972] AC 785, 808–09.

[287] *Re Maxwell Communications Corp plc (No 2)* [1993] 1 WLR 1402, 1411.

[288] See the critique in Derham, n 226, 6.72. The quantification of claims in insolvency is complicated whether or not there is set-off, especially now that contingent claims (which must be quantified) can be set off in both directions.

[289] A term which excludes set-off outside insolvency would, in any case, only operate within insolvency if it was clear that it was intended to do so: *National Westminster Bank Ltd v Halesowen Presswork and Assemblies Ltd* [1972] AC 785.

[290] This problem can be avoided by opening the current account with a bank other than the original financier, but such a bank has less incentive to take on an insolvent client.

[291] Report of the Review Committee of Insolvency Law and Practice ('Cork Report') Cmnd 8558 (1982).

[292] See page 185.

on set-off to ensure payment, it would be unfair to deprive the creditor of this benefit on the insolvency of the other party.[293] One problem with this argument is that, to the extent that the set-off relied on is contractual (rather than independent or transaction set-off), reliance on it is no different from reliance on any other contractual term which seeks to give a creditor an advantage in insolvency. A right to set-off is not a proprietary right like a security interest:[294] secured creditors are clearly in a different class, and the line between proprietary and personal rights is (relatively) easily drawn and justified. A line between contractual rights which survive insolvency and those which do not is both less easy to draw and to justify. Further, many contractual provisions (such as close-out netting) are designed merely to protect the creditor in the event of the debtor's insolvency, and so an argument based on reliance on the use of set-off outside insolvency does not apply. If the reliance argument applies to a creditor who has, by the use of contractual terms, attempted to put himself in a better position than other creditors on the insolvency of the debtor, then this argument should result in all such bargains being effective in insolvency, when, in fact, the reverse is true in that a desire to improve a creditor's position on insolvency is a reason for contractual provisions being ineffective[295] and transfers being set aside.[296]

The argument is stronger, in a way, in relation to set-off which would have arisen outside insolvency by operation of law: reliance on this surviving insolvency is, perhaps, more justifiable, although if the law did not allow set-off on insolvency (as is the case in many jurisdictions[297]) parties would be expected to know this and not to rely on pre-insolvency law. Further, in many cases the possibility of set-off, or even of there being a cross-claim, is not in the parties' minds at the time of entering into the transaction, so that the reliance argument does not apply.[298] Thus we should look for other justifications for insolvency set-off to bolster the reliance argument.

A related justification is that if an insolvent company can receive the full amount of a claim due from another person, it is only fair that that person should be able to receive its claim against the company in full.[299] This justification was noted by Lord Hoffmann in his

---

[293]   Goode, n 101, 8–01.

[294]   This is clearly explained in a Singaporean case: *Electro-Magnetic (S) Ltd (Under Judicial Management) v Development Bank of Singapore Ltd* [1994] 1 SLR 734, 738 (Sing CA) where LP Thean JA said: 'A security over a property consists of some real or proprietary interest, legal or equitable, in the property as distinguished from a personal right or claim thereon. A right of set-off is a personal right; it is a right given by contract or by law to set one claim against the other and arrive at a balance'. See also Gullifer, *Goode on Legal Problems of Credit and Security*, n 71, 1–19, the 2nd edition of which was cited with approval in that case. Where Lord Hoffmann in *Stein v Blake* [1996] AC 243, 251 described insolvency set-off as 'a form of security', he was clearly describing its functional use rather than classifying it as a security interest. However, see now the Canadian Supreme Court decision of *Caisse Populaire Desjardins de l'Est de Drummond v Canada* [2009] SCC 29 where a majority of the court held that a right to set off an amount deposited with the lender bank against the loan was held to be a 'security interest' within the meaning of the Income Taxes Act. This decision turned on the particular wording of the contractual provisions, and also (arguably) on the functional view of 'security interest' which applies in the Canadian Personal Property Securities Acts.

[295]   *Money Markets International Stockbrokers Ltd (In Liquidation) v London Stock Exchange Ltd* [2002] 1 WLR 1150, [103].

[296]   As transactions at an undervalue under Insolvency Act 1986, s 238 and as preferences under s 239 Insolvency Act 1986, see 3.3.2 above.

[297]   See P Wood, *Set-off and Netting, Derivatives, Clearing Systems*, n 193, 1–015 for a summary of insolvency set-off and netting worldwide.

[298]   Derham, n 226, 6.12.

[299]   *National Westminster Bank Ltd. v Halesowen Presswork and Assemblies Ltd* [1972] AC 785 at 813 (Lord Cross).

masterly analysis of insolvency set-off in *Stein v Blake*,[300] where he pointed out that, for example, in *Forster v Wilson*[301] Parke B said that the purpose of insolvency set-off was 'to do substantial justice between the parties'. It is difficult to see how, in the absence of reliance (which is discussed above), it is any more fair to pay a person with a cross-claim in full than any other creditor. The amount which that creditor receives over and above the proportion which all unsecured creditors receive is an amount that those unsecured creditors do not receive, so the 'fairness' in favour of the cross-claimant is balanced out by the unfairness to the other creditors.[302] Lord Hoffmann also pointed out, perhaps by way of justification, that the rule was of extreme longevity in that it had been part of the law of England since the time of Queen Elizabeth I.[303]

Another justification, which is articulated by the House of Lords in *National Westminster Bank Ltd v Halesowen Presswork and Assemblies Ltd*, is that insolvency set-off simplifies the liquidation process so that the estate of an insolvent company can be administered in a 'proper and orderly way'.[304] Unfortunately, the decision gives no further explanation of what is meant by this, but it can be surmised that the reduction of claims to net claims would relieve the liquidator's burden of having to deal with the gross payments. However, even to administer the net claims requires the liquidator to value each claim before set-off, and it is difficult to see that a great deal of time and costs is saved, especially now that contingent claims can be set off. It should be remembered that the effect of insolvency set-off is that other creditors who do not have the benefit of set-off lose out as the proportion of their own claims which are recoverable is reduced. Thus the justification for insolvency set-off needs to be strong, and it is hard to see that the saving in costs and time for a liquidator outweighs the disadvantages to the other creditors.

A further justification is that set-off on insolvency is critical to the management of risk in the financial markets, as well as more generally in the commercial world. Philip Wood points out that the effect in reducing exposure is huge[305] and without it the risk of systemic collapse, with the concomitant cost to the public purse, is greatly increased.[306] Effects of this reduction in risk are that less collateral has to be held against exposure, both in relation to individual transactions, which frees up capital and improves the liquidity and capacity of the markets, and also in relation to the general exposure of banks as capital adequacy requirements are reduced.[307] He thus argues that 'the economic advantages of

---

[300]   [1996] 1 AC 243, 251.

[301]   (1843) 12 M & W 191, 204.

[302]   See Derham, n 226, 6.11 who points out that the existence of a cross-claim may be wholly fortuitous and not be the result of forethought of the benefited party at all.

[303]   [1996] 1 AC 243, 251.

[304]   [1972] AC 785, 809 (Lord Simon).

[305]   95% in the foreign exchange markets.

[306]   P Wood, n 193, 1–012. It might be said that the financial markets have recently collapsed at great expense to the taxpayer even with the benefit of insolvency set-off: however, it can be argued that without insolvency set-off it would have been much worse. For example, when Lehman Brothers collapsed, it owed £400 billion to counterparties of credit default swaps, but, after netting, the total amount actually payable was $5.2billion, see 'The Future Regulation of Derivatives Markets: is the EU on the Right Track? (House of Lords 10th report 2009–10 (HMSO 31 March 2010) 20 citing evidence from the Association for Financial Markets in Europe (AFME), British Banking Association (BBA) and International Swaps and Derivatives Association (ISDA) para 4.4. (annexed to report at annex 1)).

[307]   See pages 25–26. It is now thought, however, that larger capital adequacy requirements would assist in preventing a financial collapse such as that which happened in 2007–09, and the Basel II requirements are being reviewed, see chapter 2, n 102.

insolvency set-off seem overwhelming'.[308] The question is whether the undoubted advantages in the financial markets outweigh the disadvantages to unsecured creditors elsewhere in the commercial world.

If the justifications for insolvency set-off do not obviously outweigh the disadvantages, should it be permitted? The answer is probably that it should be allowed in certain circumstances, but the difficulty is drawing the lines around those circumstances. One way is to provide by statute that certain contractual provisions which limit market risk are valid, within the context of that particular market, which has been done in the cases of settlement of market transactions and financial collateral arrangements.[309] Apart from such provisions, the limits on set-off in insolvency under English law are in theory the *pari passu* and anti-deprivation principles. In practice, this broadly means that any contractual provisions for set-off which are wider in scope than the statutory limits of insolvency set-off are unenforceable on insolvency. These statutory limits are now quite extensive, having been widened by legislation over the years,[310] but it is hard to rationalise these limits on the basis of any of the justifications of insolvency set-off discussed above.

5.3 Contractual Rights Against Third Parties

As will be clear from the above discussion, contractual rights against the borrower have one major drawback: on the insolvency of the borrower the lender will only be able to prove in the insolvency for a fraction of the amount due (set-off, as explained above, is an exception to this). One way of overcoming this problem is for the lender to have a contractual right against a third party who is more likely to remain solvent.[311] The lender can also take security over the assets of the third party, or take other steps to protect itself against the third party's credit risk.[312] There are two main categories of third parties: those who are connected to the borrower and who give the protection without payment, such as a parent company, or a director, and those whose do so for a fee, such as a financial company or bank whose business is providing credit protection.

There are other related benefits which accrue, some to the borrower and some to the lender. First, in a bond issue or securitisation, the fact that such protection exists will make the securities more marketable and also more valuable.[313] Second, the existence of such protection may mean that the borrower can borrow on more advantageous terms. Third, where the person giving the credit protection has some control over the behaviour of the borrower, for example a parent company or a director, the existence of the credit protection aligns the interests of that person with that of the lender and helps to ensure

---

[308] Wood, n 193, 1–012.

[309] 5.2.4.6.2.

[310] The most recent widening being the extension of set-off of contingent claims to those made by the insolvent company, see page 183 above.

[311] This is neatly put by Professor Wood, who says 'Guarantees are usually taken to provide a second pocket to pay if the first should be empty': Wood, *International Loans, Bonds, Guarantees, Legal Opinions*, n 15, 18–002.

[312] For a description of techniques for doing this where the third party is a bank, see C Kerrigan and J Wyatt, 'The Strength of a Bank Guarantee: A Credit Risk?' (2009) 24 *Journal of International Banking and Financial Law* 488.

[313] Fuller, n 15. 9.01.

that the borrower does not conduct itself in a way which makes it less likely that the loan will be repaid.[314] This is most graphically illustrated in the case of small private companies, where the directors are a small number of natural persons. If a director gives a guarantee of a loan or overdraft, backed up with a charge over his or her home, he or she has a large incentive to take steps to make sure that the lending bank is repaid. Fourth, a protection right against a third party is useful if the lender wishes to exercise rights of set-off against that third party in any circumstances, for example in order to net all the accounts of a group company or in the event of the insolvency of both the borrower and the third party.[315] Fifth, for tax reasons the borrower may be a particular member of a group of companies; that member then on-lends the money to a trading company who really needs it: that latter company would then guarantee the original loan.[316] Sixth, in certain transactions the creditor or lender would like to know it is getting paid irrespective of any underlying dispute over whether payment is due: this gives that party a procedural advantage so that it becomes the defendant in any subsequent litigation rather than the claimant,[317] and also so that payment is made on the due date (when the creditor or lender may need the money to pay another party) rather than being postponed while the dispute is resolved. Third parties who give credit protection for a fee sometimes prefer this sort of structure, since they know that they will have to pay under any circumstances, rather than having the uncertainty of waiting until a dispute is resolved. Since the third party will normally have a right of indemnity against the debtor, upon which it can call immediately on payment, the third party will only be out of its money for a short time. Examples of this structure are performance bonds (also called demand guarantees) and standby credits.

Rights against a third party take a number of forms, some of which are very similar to each other. They can be called, variously, guarantees, indemnities, performance bonds, standby credits and insurance. Further, there are less formal arrangements such as comfort letters. These are considered below at 5.3.1 and 5.3.2. A structure that is in some ways similar to a guarantee is a credit default swap, which is a form of credit derivative. It has the effect of shifting the risk, or part of the risk, of default onto a third party for a fee. It is considered below at 5.3.3.

Another technique used by a creditor to improve its chances of being paid out of the insolvent borrower's limited assets is to agree with another creditor, such as a parent company or a member of the same group, that the latter's claim will be subordinated to that of the creditor. This technique, known as subordination, is also used extensively to enable lenders to take a specific amount of credit risk in, for example, a bond issue, where lower ranking lenders will receive a higher rate of return as they are taking on more risk than those to whom they are subordinated.[318] Subordination is considered below at 5.3.4.

---

[314] Wood, n 15, 18–003.
[315] Ibid, 18–006. Note that set-off will only be effective in insolvency if there is mutuality, see above 5.2.4.6.2.
[316] See 2.3.5.2.
[317] See n 241.
[318] This is called 'tranching': for a fuller description see pages 403–404.

5.3.1   Guarantees, Indemnities and Performance Bonds[319]

5.3.1.1   *Introduction*

There are numerous different kinds of contract which can come under the loose term of 'guarantees', in that they a give a creditor a contractual right against a third party which is referable to the borrower's obligation.[320] This section will consider suretyship guarantees, indemnities, performance bonds and standby credits, which can all be used for similar purposes but which have different legal characteristics. The differences between the various legal forms have significant consequences, so that although the legal effect of any such contract will depend on its terms, it is sometimes necessary for the court to characterise the agreement as being that of a particular form. Despite this, this is an area where lawyers draft the agreements in order to obtain the best of all worlds, which often means contracting out of some of the consequences of, for example, an agreement being a guarantee, but trying to avoid the agreement being recharacterised as, for example, an indemnity or a contract of insurance.

In this chapter, to aid comparison between the various legal forms, the following terminology will be used. The lender, who might be investors in a bond issue,[321] or a syndicate of lenders, or a single bank, or a company extending credit to another company, will be called the 'creditor'. The borrower, who is the recipient of the loan or credit in such transactions, will be called the 'principal debtor'. The third party, who is the provider of the credit protection, will be called the 'third party', rather than variously described as the guarantor, the indemnifier and so on.

5.3.1.2   *Important Distinctions*

One major distinction is between contracts where the liability of the third party is triggered by a default on the part of the principal debtor, and those where the trigger is a demand by the creditor, often coupled with other requirements, such as the presentation of documents.[322] The former can be subdivided into suretyship guarantees, where the third party agrees to pay the principal debtor's outstanding liability, if the principal debtor does not pay, and indemnities, where the third party agrees to make good any loss suffered by the creditor,[323] so that liability is triggered by the loss caused by the failure of the principal debtor to pay the creditor.

The third party's obligation under a suretyship guarantee is a secondary liability, while liability under the other types of transaction referred to above is primary. This means that

---

[319]   What follows is of necessity a very brief discussion of the voluminous law surrounding guarantees. For a full discussion, see G Andrews and R Millett, *Law of Guarantees*, 5th edn (London, Sweet & Maxwell, 2007); G Moss, *Rowlatt on Principal and Surety*, 5th edn (London, Sweet & Maxwell, 1998); J Phillips and J O'Donovan, *The Modern Contract of Guarantee*, English edn (London, Sweet & Maxwell, 2004); and KP McGuinness, *The Law of Guarantee*, 2nd edn (Toronto, Carswell, 1996).

[320]   For a list of such contracts, see Wood, n 15, 18–007.

[321]   When a guarantee is given for a bond issue where there is a trustee, the guarantor is a party to the trust deed and the trustee holds the benefit of the guarantee on trust for the holders of the securities: Fuller, n 15, 9.03. Bond issues are discussed in chapter 7.

[322]   Examples of the latter type of contracts are performance bonds (also known as demand guarantees) and standby letters of credit.

[323]   *Yeoman Credit Ltd v Latter* [1961] 1 WLR 828. This means that the liability on an indemnity is unliquidated, Gullifer, n 71, 345.

under a suretyship guarantee the third party's liability only arises when the principal debtor defaults,[324] and is co-extensive with that of the principal debtor. Thus it is for the same amount[325] and cannot be enforced if the obligation of the principal debtor cannot, for example if it is illegal or void or released by the creditor. Further, if the third party pays, it is entitled to be subrogated to the rights that the creditor had against the principal debtor.[326] Thus, to protect the third party, if those rights are changed, either by agreement between the creditor and the principal debtor, or because of the conduct of the creditor, the surety is discharged.[327] Where the third party's obligation is primary, this means that it is independent of that of the principal debtor and arises whether or not there is default, although, in the case of an indemnity, it is the loss caused by default against which the creditor is indemnified, so if there is no default there will be no loss. In the case of a performance bond or a standby credit, the obligation to pay arises on demand irrespective of whether a default has occurred. Where the obligation is primary, the third party's liability is not affected by matters affecting the contract between the creditor and the principal debtor. It is this point which is the principal consequence of the distinction between guarantees and indemnities, and on which many of the cases turn. Another consequence is that contracts of guarantee must be in writing and signed by the guarantor to be enforceable.[328] Since most modern credit protection contracts with third parties will be in writing and signed, this is rarely of much importance.[329]

Another distinction, which can be important in practice, is whether the liability of a third party is in debt or damages. If the claim is for damages, the creditor has to prove its loss, and will have to take reasonable steps to mitigate its damage, whereas a claim in debt is for a liquidated sum. Further, claims for contribution under section 1 of the Civil Liability (Contribution) Act 1978 (between co-sureties) can be made in respect of damages claims but not claims in debt, and therefore a different limitation period applies to such claims.[330] Again, the position depends on the true construction of the agreement. Two possible constructions were identified by Lord Reid in *Moschi v Lep Air Services Ltd*.[331] The first is that there is an undertaking that if the principal debtor fails to pay the debt the third party will pay it. The third party's obligation, which would be in debt, would arise on the principal debtor's failure to pay. The second is that the third party promises that the principal debtor would fulfil its obligation: if it failed to do so, the third

---

[324] *Ex p Gardom* (1808) 15 Ves. 286; G Andrews and R Millett, *Law of Guarantees*, 5th edn (London, Sweet & Maxwell, 2007) 7–001.

[325] The actual amount for which the third party is liable may be modified by the terms of the contract of guarantee.

[326] *Davies v Humphreys* (1840) 6 M & W 153.

[327] See below, 5.3.1.3.2.

[328] Statute of Frauds 1677, s 4.

[329] For an example where s 4 of the Statute of Frauds was not complied with, see *Actionstrength Ltd v International Glass Engineering In.GL.en SpA* [2003] UKHL 17, [2003] 2 AC 541.

[330] Limitation Act 1980, s 10; *Hampton v Minns* [2002] 1 WLR 1.

[331] [1973] 1 AC 331, 344–45. Later cases have considered and followed this distinction, see *General Produce Co v United Bank Ltd* [1979] 2 Lloyds Rep 255, 258; *Hampton v Minns* [2002] 1 WLR 1 (where the guarantee was said to be of the first construction); *Carlton Communications plc v The Football League* [2002] EWHC 1650 (Comm), [84] (where the second construction was preferred). See also *Barnicoat v Knight* [2004] EWHC 330 (Ch) and *Nearfield Ltd v Lincoln Nominees Ltd* [2006] EWHC 2421 (Ch). See also Gullifer, n 71, 8–09; G Andrews and R Millett, *Law of Guarantees*, 5th edn, (London, Sweet & Maxwell, 2007) 16.0126–002; Fuller, n 15, 9.08.

party would be in breach of contract and liable for damages.[332] The first construction causes difficulties if, for example, payments are to be made by instalments and the principal debtor fails to pay one instalment. This is often a repudiatory breach or triggers a termination clause so that the contract is terminated, and the principal debtor is no longer liable to pay the rest of the instalments, but is liable in damages for the creditor's loss caused by the termination. On the first construction, the debt in relation to the rest of the instalments never falls due, so the third party is not liable to pay it, whereas on the second construction the third party is also in breach and therefore liable for damages. It should be remembered, though, that in relation to the instalments which had already accrued, the third party is liable in debt.[333]

5.3.1.3　*Guarantees*

5.3.1.3.1　Protection of the Third Party: Construction of the Guarantee

Each of the different legal forms has disadvantages for one or more parties. It is proposed now to outline some of these before considering ways that parties attempt to obtain the maximum advantage from the agreement without the concomitant disadvantages. The main disadvantage of a guarantee is to a creditor, in that the law protects a third party guarantor in several ways. The first of these is that the guarantee agreement is construed strictly against the creditor.[334] This is, at least in part, because the balance of bargaining power usually favours the creditor, who would normally draft the contract,[335] and also because a third party guarantor often receives no direct benefit for his guarantee.[336]

Recent cases have shown a retreat from the strict principle, at least where an objective approach taking into account the factual matrix would render a different result,[337] but there are certain areas in which it is particularly important for a creditor that clear words are used. One is where the creditor is seeking to exclude the protection that a third party guarantor would have by operation of the general law.[338] Another relates to the definition of the actual liability of the third party guarantor, as defined in the agreement. For example, if a guarantee of an overdraft does not state that it is a continuing guarantee, the guarantor's liability is reduced by payments into the account, under the rule in *Clayton's case*,[339] and later drawings are not covered.[340] To take another example, a guarantee which, by its terms, covered 'every sum of money [the principal debtor is] obligated to pay' including 'monetary damages arising out of any failure by [the principal debtor] to

---

[332]　Note that many standard guarantees include both types of obligation in two separate clauses, see X Lok, 'Guarantees and Indemnities: the Issues' (2007) 22 *Journal of International Banking and Financial Law* 491.

[333]　*Chatterton v Maclean* [1951] 1 All ER 761; *Moschi v Lep Air Services Ltd* [1973] 1 AC 331, 354–55; *Hyundai Heavy Industries Co Ltd v Papadopoulous* [1980] 1 WLR 1129, 1136–37.

[334]　Beale, *Chitty on Contracts,* n 118, 44–056. A guarantor is sometimes referred to as a 'favoured debtor', *Halsbury's Laws of England* Volume 49 para 1093.

[335]　*Eastern Counties Building Society v Russell* [1947] 1 All ER 500; Andrews and Millett, *Law of Guarantees*, n 331, 4–002.

[336]　*Blest v Brown* (1862) 4 De GF & J 367. It should be borne in mind, however, that there are often considerable indirect benefits, especially when the third party is part of the same corporate group.

[337]　Fuller, n 15, 9.75; *Static Control Components (Europe) Ltd v Egan* [2004] EWCA Civ 392 [12]; *Vodafone Ltd v GNT Holdings Ltd* [2004] EWHC 1526 (QB) [71].

[338]　*Trafalgar House Construction (Regions) Ltd v General Surety & Guarantee Co Ltd* [1996] AC 199, 208. For discussion of such protection, see below 5.3.1.3.2.

[339]　(1816) 1 Mer 572.

[340]　Wood, n 15, 19–006; Gullifer, n 71, 8–06.

perform its obligations', was held not to cover the obligations of the principal debtor arising out of an arbitration award, since the third party guarantor would then be bound by the outcome of proceedings in which it had had no chance to participate.[341]

For a creditor, the best way to avoid strictness of construction is to try and define the liability of the third party guarantor as clearly as possible, without any ambiguity. In the event of any ambiguity, it might be possible for a creditor to argue that the strict approach is inapplicable, since the reasons for the fiercely protective attitude the law has towards third party guarantors is not necessary where the third party is, for example, a well-advised parent company.[342] However, this argument is unlikely to work where the third party is an individual director, or a member of his or her family. A creditor cannot avoid the strict construction approach by drafting the agreement as an indemnity, since the principle of strict construction applies, if anything, even more strongly to indemnities than to guarantees.[343]

5.3.1.3.2   Protection of the Third Party: Discharge of the Third Party

Another principle protecting a third party guarantor is that his liability is discharged if the liability of the principal debtor is void or voidable[344] (and avoided) or unenforceable[345] or discharged[346] or released by the creditor.[347] This partly comes from the co-extensiveness principle,[348] so that if the principal debtor is not liable, the third party cannot be either, and partly (at least in relation to release) that the third party loses its right of indemnity and subrogation against the principal debtor if the latter is released.[349]

A further related principle, sometimes called the rule in *Holme v Brunskill*,[350] is that a third party guarantor is discharged if the creditor varies the terms of its contract with the principal debtor without the third party's consent, including giving the principal debtor extra time to pay.[351] The rationale of this principle is the protection of the third party, who is taken to have agreed only to guarantee the precise liabilities that were in the original agreement and no other.[352] Further, the third party's rights of indemnity and subrogation could be damaged by an agreement between the creditor and the principal debtor, which the third party may not know about and has no ability to affect. The rule, however, takes little account of whether the variation of the contract causes any actual damage to the third party. Unless the creditor can show that the variation is 'unsubstantial or that it

---

[341]   *Sabah Shipyard (Pakistan) Limited v The Islamic Republic of Pakistan* [2007] EWHC 2602 (Comm); B Cain, 'Devil in the Detail: Messages from Recent Guarantee Cases' (2008) 23 *Journal of International Banking and Financial Law* 128.

[342]   Beale, n 118, 44–056.

[343]   Andrews and Millett, n 331, 4–003.

[344]   Ibid, 6–024.

[345]   For example, time-barred, see Andrews and Millett, n 331, 6–027.

[346]   By the acceptance by the principal debtor of a repudiatory breach by the creditor, *Watts v Shuttleworth* (1861) 7 H & N 353. The position where the principal debtor affirms the contract after a repudiatory breach is less clear, but the position is probably that the third party guarantor's liability remains, see Andrews and Millett, n 331, 9–017.

[347]   *Mahant Singh v U Ba Yi* [1939] AC 601.

[348]   See above pages 192–193.

[349]   For the third party's right of indemnity see below 5.3.1.3.3.

[350]   (1878) 3 QBD 495.

[351]   *Swire v Redman* (1876) 1 QBD 536, 541.

[352]   A Choy, 'Discharge of Guarantees: the Rule in Holme v Brunskill Revisited' (2007) 22 *Journal of International Banking and Financial Law* 450.

cannot be otherwise than beneficial to the [third party]',[353] the third party is discharged: there is no requirement for it to show detriment or for a court to inquire into whether there is such detriment. However, the variation must affect the risk of non-fulfillment of the guaranteed obligation:[354] if it merely affects the amount for which the third party is liable, the third party will only be discharged in relation to the amount by which the liability is increased.[355]

It can be seen that the application of the rule in *Holme v Brunskill* can be very detrimental to creditors in corporate finance transactions. It effectively means that any restructuring of financing arrangements will potentially discharge the third party unless the latter's consent is obtained. However, this introduces a moral hazard problem, as the third party has an incentive to withhold consent to a variation if it would like to be discharged from the guarantee, or to extract concessions as a price for giving consent.[356] Even if an attempt is made to obtain consent, disputes may arise as to whether this had been done successfully.[357] The rule in *Holme v Brunskill* has been criticised for its width, and it has been suggested that it would be sufficient to protect a third party for it to be discharged pro tanto for any detriment it suffers from the variation of the principal contract.[358] Creditors, however, tend to seek to avoid the rule by employing various drafting techniques, used also to avoid the principle, discussed earlier, that a third party is discharged if the principal debtor's liability is void or discharged.

One such technique is for the guarantee to provide directly that the liability of the third party is not to be prejudiced or diminished if certain listed events occur (including defects in the principal contract, discharge or release of the principal debtor and variations to the principal contract).[359] Alternatively, the agreement could provide for consent by the third party in advance to any variation of the principal contract, or that the creditor has authority to agree to a variation without reference to the third party. Yet another possibility is to provide that the third party is deemed to be liable as a principal debtor.[360] In theory, parties to a contract can agree whatever rights and obligations they like, and if a third party agrees that the usual protection of a guarantee contract is not available to it, that agreement will be upheld by the courts, providing clear and unambiguous language is

---

[353]   *Holme v Brunskill* (1878) 3 QBD 495, 505; *Ankhar Pty Ltd v National Westminster Finance (Australia) Ltd* (1987) 162 CLR 549, 559 (HC Aust).

[354]   Andrews and Millett, n 331, 9–024.

[355]   So that, for example, where security held for the debt by the creditor was sold at an undervalue, the third party was *pro tanto* released, *Skipton Building Society v Stott* [2001] QB 261, [21]. If the creditor's actions were repudiatory, however, the third party might be fully discharged [22]. See also *Barclays Bank plc v Kingston* [2006] EWHC 533 (QB).

[356]   A Choy, 'Discharge of Guarantees: the Rule in Holme v Brunskill Revisited' (2007) 22 *Journal of International Banking and Financial Law* 450.

[357]   *Moat Financial Services v Wilkinson* [2005] EWCA Civ 1253, discussed by S Bradshaw, 'Keeping your Guarantee Alive' [2006] *International Company and Commercial Law Review* 300.

[358]   A Choy, 'Discharge of guarantees: the rule in *Holme v Brunskill* revisited' (2007) 22 *Journal of International Banking and Financial Law* 450, relying on the Court of Appeal's decision in *Mercers Co v New Hampshire Insurance Co* [1992] 2 Lloyd's Rep 365, 377.

[359]   For examples of such clauses, which are often drafted so as to be very comprehensive, see Wood, n 15, 19–018; Fuller, n 15, 9.77. The effectiveness of such a clause is not without doubt, see Andrews and Millett, n 331, 9–034.

[360]   Such 'principal debtor' clauses have other purposes as well, in that they create enough mutuality for insolvency set-off to apply, even though no demand has been made under the guarantee (*MS Fashions Ltd v Bank of Credit and Commerce International SA (No 2)* [1993] Ch 425; Gullifer, n 71, 7–95). This is now less important after the change in the scope of insolvency set-off to include contingent debts owed by and to the insolvent party.

used to displace the normal incidents of such a contract.[361] However, the effect of such clauses is dependent on issues of construction which are sometimes problematic.[362] It can be uncertain whether the events that occur actually fall within the words of the clause (bearing in mind the strict construction applied to guarantees). For example, if there is authority to agree to a variation, but a restructuring can be characterised as a new contract rather than a variation of the old one, then the third party will not be liable in respect of this.[363] Further, a clause may be interpreted to cover situations where the principal debtor's liability is discharged or released, but not where the principal agreement is void because it was prohibited by statute.[364] The insertion of these protective clauses, especially a principal debtor clause, might also have the effect that the agreement is recharacterised as an indemnity.[365]

It is also possible, even if there is no such clause in a contact of guarantee, for a creditor to protect its position against a surety on release of the principal debtor or variation of the principal contract, by reserving its rights against the third party at the time of the release or variation. This might seem odd, in that the third party is not a party to this transaction and cannot be said to have agreed in advance to the preservation of its liability. However, there is longstanding authority supporting the effectiveness of such a reservation, and it can be justified on the basis that, in agreeing to the release or variation on these terms, the principal debtor is agreeing that the third party's rights against it are preserved[366] (it will be recalled that one of the main reasons for the third party's discharge is that it could lose its rights of indemnity and subrogation against the principal debtor[367]).

5.3.1.3.3 Protection of the Third Party: Third Party's Rights against the Principal Debtor

A third party guarantor is protected by having an indemnity against the principal debtor, which arises either by express or implied agreement between the third party and the principal debtor or in restitution.[368] However, there cannot be any such agreement, or such a right to restitution, where the guarantee is not given at the request of the principal debtor but is arranged solely between the creditor and the third party.[369] In addition to

---

[361] *Trafalgar House Construction (Regions) Ltd v General Surety & Guarantee Co Ltd* [1996] AC 199, 208; *Liberty Mutual Insurance Company (UK) Ltd v HSBC Bank plc* [2002] EWCA Civ 691, [49].

[362] The courts have generally construed such provisions restrictively. Often, but not always, construction will involve application of the contra proferentum rule as the wording will have been put forward by the creditor. However, this has not always led to clarity. See *Coutts & Co v Stock* [2000] 1 WLR 906, where Lightman J commented (at [17]): 'Provisions such as clause 10 have grown like Topsy. As each possible ground for a challenge by a guarantor to the validity or enforceability of his guarantee has seen the light of day, further protective provisions for the bank have been devised designed to head off that challenge and tagged onto the clause. The present compilation of words is in dire need of revision. If a guarantor is intended to be made primarily liable when there is no primary liability for any reason on the part of the debtor, this could and should be spelt out explicitly'.

[363] *Triodos Bank NV v Dobbs* [2005] EWCA Civ 630. For a similar debate about the meaning of 'release' see *General Produce Co v United Bank Ltd* [1979] 2 Lloyd's Rep 255, 258.

[364] *Heald v O'Connor* [1971] 1 WLR 497. Cf *General Produce Co v United Bank Ltd* [1979] 2 Lloyd's Rep 255, where the third party's liability was held to remain despite the release of the principal debtor by operation of law.

[365] See below.

[366] *Cole and Another v Lynn* [1942] 1 KB 142, 146; *Greene King plc v Stanley* [2001] EWCA Civ 1966 [80].

[367] See page 201.

[368] Andrews and Millett, n 331, 10–002.

[369] *Owen v Tate* [1976] QB 402. This rule is subject to some exceptions, for example, where the guarantee is given in cases of necessity.

any indemnity, when a third party has paid the principal debtor's liability, it is subrogated to the rights of the creditor against the principal debtor, which includes the right to any security which the creditor holds.[370] Although this is an equitable right, the right to security is also contained in section 5 of the Mercantile Law Amendment Act 1856. This is important since the equitable right of subrogation may well not be available to a third party where the principal debtor does not request the guarantee, but it would seem that the statutory right is not so limited.[371]

5.3.1.4   Indemnity and Performance Bond

5.3.1.4.1   Nature of Third Party's Liability

Although the methods discussed above can be effective, from a creditor's point of view, to preserve a third party's liability under a guarantee when that of the principal debtor is discharged or varied, uncertainty remains. Creditors often, therefore, seek to take an indemnity either instead of, or as well as,[372] a guarantee. It is also possible that attempts to exclude the protection given by the general law to third party guarantors have the effect of turning a guarantee into an indemnity. It should be remembered that is no hard and fast line between guarantees and indemnities. Neither are they completely distinct concepts. As mentioned above, there are two main reasons why a court might need to distinguish one from the other. The first is to decide whether the third party is liable even though the principal debtor is not, and the second is to decide whether the requirement of writing under the Statute of Frauds applies. It is only in the latter context that a bright line has to be drawn: the contract either falls within the statute or it does not.[373] A considerable jurisprudence has therefore grown up surrounding the distinction.[374] The distinction was described in one Statute of Frauds case in the following terms: 'An indemnity is a contract by one party to keep the other harmless against loss, but a contract of guarantee is a contract to answer for the debt, default or miscarriage of another who is to be primarily liable to the promisee.[375] It will be seen that the chief differentiating feature, therefore, is whether the third party's liability is primary or secondary; there are, however, other touchstones that have been used to answer this question in this context, such as whether the third party is separate from or 'interested in' the transaction.[376]

---

[370]   *Craythorne v Swinburne* (1807) 14 Ves 160.

[371]   Andrews and Millett, n 331, 11–019.

[372]   A common combination is that of a pure guarantee (the second 'Moschi' category giving rise to a liability in damages), a conditional payment guarantee (the first 'Moschi' category giving rise to a liability in debt) and an indemnity: this is included in the LMA standard syndicated loan agreements, see Fuller, n 15, 9.13 (for further discussion of the 'Moschi' categories see pages 193–94 above). Of these three elements, the first two create secondary liability on the third party, A Berg, 'Rethinking Indemnities' (2002) 17 *Journal of International Banking and Financial Law* 360, 403. Whether contracts including both a guarantee and an indemnity are treated as giving rise to two separate obligations (one secondary and one primary) or just one secondary obligation is a matter of construction: Andrews and Millett, n 331, 1–014; *Western Credit Ltd v Albery* [1964] 2 All ER 938; *Stadium Finance Co Ltd v Helm* (1965) 109 Sol Jo 471; *Citicorp Australia Ltd v Hendry* [1985] 4 NSWLR 1 (Sup Ct NSW CA).

[373]   The Statute does not actually refer to the word 'guarantee' but the requirement of writing applies to 'any special *promise* to answer for the debt default or miscarriages of another person': not all guarantees fall within the statute (Andrews and Millett, n 331, 3–005).

[374]   Andrews and Millett, ibid, 3–006–3–016.

[375]   *Yeoman Credit Ltd v Latter* [1961] 1 WLR 828, 831.

[376]   *Sutton & Co v Grey* [1894] 1 QB 285; *Pitts v Jones* [2007] EWCA Civ 1301.

Where the issue to be determined is whether the third party's liability is discharged by the discharge of the principal debtor or under the rule in *Holme v Brunskill*, the question could be said to have become circular: the third party is discharged if its liability is secondary, it is secondary if the contract is one of guarantee, the contract is one of guarantee if the liability of the third party is secondary. The knot can be untied by treating the issue as one of construction of the particular agreement in these cases, without the court having to make a decision as to whether the contract is one of guarantee or of indemnity. Thus the labels used by the parties are not conclusive,[377] and the courts will look at the rights and obligations created by the word used.[378] This approach means that clauses such as those referred to earlier can be successful in preventing a third party being discharged from liability without that party's liability necessarily being characterised as primary, and the agreement being characterised as one of indemnity.[379]

An indemnity, being a contract to keep another harmless against loss, will normally result in the indemnifier being liable in damages rather than in debt.[380] Difficult questions of quantification can arise, particularly where the creditor is said to be contributorily negligent, or has failed to mitigate its loss.[381] In practice these are usually overcome by the inclusion of a liquidated damages clause.[382] In corporate finance transactions, the usual position is that the principal debtor is itself liable in debt, and so the indemnity analysis is not attractive. There is, however, another possible analysis. This is that a third party can undertake liability in debt (on the basis of a similar construction to the first category suggested by Lord Diplock in the *Moschi* case)[383] but in such a way that it is not discharged if the principal debtor is.[384] The difficulty with this construction is that it is not clear how the third party's obligation can be a principal and not a secondary liability if it is dependent upon failure to pay by the principal debtor. If it is not so dependent, then it becomes akin to a performance bond. This in itself would not be a problem, were it not for the 'presumption' that is said to exist against a contract being a performance bond if the third party is anything other than a bank. This comes from the case of *Marubeni Hong Kong and South China Ltd v Government of Mongolia*,[385] where the Court of Appeal made it clear that specific language would be required in the agreement to displace this presumption.[386] This presumption has been much criticised,[387] and rightly so, as although

---

[377]   *Seaton v Heath* [1899] 1 QB 782, 792; *Gold Coast Ltd v Caja De Ahorros del Mediterraneo* [2001] EWCA Civ 1806 [21].

[378]   For a recent example, see *Associated British Ports v Ferryways NV* [2009] EWCA Civ 189.

[379]   *General Produce Co v United Bank Ltd* [1979] 2 Lloyd's Rep 255; A Berg, 'Rethinking Indemnities' (2002) 17 *Journal of International Banking and Financial Law* 403.

[380]   *Firma C-Trade SA v Newcastle Protection and Indemnity Association (The Fanti)* [1991] 2 AC 1.

[381]   A Berg, 'Rethinking Indemnities' (2002) 17 *Journal of International Banking and Financial Law* 360.

[382]   Ibid.

[383]   [1973] 1 AC 331, 344–45.

[384]   Fuller, n 15, 9.09.

[385]   [2005] EWCA Civ 395.

[386]   Ibid, [30]. In that case, the use of words such as 'unconditionally pledges' and 'simple demand', were not enough to displace the presumption, as the agreement also said that the third party's liability only arose if 'the amounts payable under the agreement (are) not paid when the same becomes due'. For another case where a contract called a 'bond' was characterised as a guarantee, see *Trafalgar House Construction (Regions) Ltd v General Surety & Guarantee Co Ltd* [1996] AC 199. Where the third party is a bank, however, the courts seem happy to go the other way and characterise an agreement labelled as a guarantee as a performance bond (*Gold Coast Limited v Caja de Ahorros del Mediterraneo* [2001] EWCA Civ 1806).

[387]   Hughes, n 139, 15.12; P McGrath, 'The Nature of Modern Guarantees: *IIG v Van Der Merwes*' (2009) 2 *Corporate Rescue and Insolvency* 10.

performance bonds are chiefly given by banks as a 'guarantee' (in a loose sense) of performance of non-monetary obligations such as those under a construction contract[388] or in a contract for international sale of goods,[389] there is no reason why they cannot be used in the context of corporate finance as a 'guarantee' of performance of a loan contract. They offer more protection to the creditor than a true guarantee as the creditor is assured of payment and does not need to prove loss even for non-accrued liabilities.[390] There are indications, however, that the courts are prepared to displace the *Marubeni* presumption in some circumstances, for example where the agreement included a clause providing that the third party was liable as principal debtor coupled with provision for a certificate of the amount payable by the third party to be conclusive in the absence of manifest error.[391] Thus the analysis mentioned above, which results in the third party remaining liable even if the principal debtor is discharged, could apply.

The above discussion is predicated on the basis that, if the third party's liability is primary, there is no danger that it will be discharged under the rule in *Holme v Brunskill*. This, however, was doubted (obiter) by Cresswell J in the *Marubeni* case,[392] and it has even been argued that the rule should apply to a performance bond as well.[393] To the extent that the rule in *Holme v Brunskill* (and the related rules about discharge of the third party when the contract with the principal debtor is void, or discharged) depends on the secondary nature of the third party's liability, then this argument is clearly fallacious. But to the extent that the rule is to protect the ability of the third party to have recourse against the principal debtor, it might be said that the third party needs as much protection where its liability is primary as where it is secondary.[394] One counter-argument is that where the third party is being paid (by the principal debtor) to take on primary liability, it can make whatever arrangements it likes about reimbursement, and these need not depend upon the liability of the principal debtor to the creditor. It is only really where the third party and the surety do not involve the principal debtor in the transaction that the third party is obliged to rely on its rights under the general law for reimbursement[395] and therefore needs the protection of the general law, such as the rule in *Holme v Brunskill*.

Under a contract of indemnity it seems (although there is no direct authority) that the third party has a right of indemnity against the principal debtor, in a similar way to that of a third party guarantor.[396] With a performance bond, an indemnity will usually be given expressly by the principal debtor as a condition of the third party giving the performance bond,[397] and in the absence of an express indemnity, it seems that one will be implied.[398]

---

[388]   Ibid, 16–004.

[389]   Ibid, 16–005.

[390]   Hughes, n 139, 15.12, postscript to chapter 5.

[391]   *IIG Capital LLC v Van Der Merwe* [2008] EWCA Civ 542. The presumption, however, was not rebutted in the case of *Carey Value Added SL v. Grupo Urvasco SA* [2010] EWHC 1905 (Comm).

[392]   *Marubeni Hong Kong and South China Ltd v Government of Mongolia* [2004] EWHC 472 (Comm) [142]. This point was not considered by the Court of Appeal in that case.

[393]   G Bhattacharyya, V Reynolds and A White, 'Differentiating and Identifying Primary and Secondary Liability Instruments in the Law of Guarantees' (2005) 20 *Journal of International Banking Law and Regulation* 488, who support this conclusion.

[394]   For the ability of a third party under an indemnity and a performance bond to recover against the principal debtor, see below.

[395]   Whether by indemnity or by subrogation.

[396]   Andrews and Millett, n 331, 10–002.

[397]   Ibid, 16–012.

[398]   *IIG Capital LLC v Van Der Merwe* [2008] EWCA Civ 542, [26]–[27].

The principal drawback of a performance bond, from the point of view of the principal debtor (and maybe the third party) is that the third party is still obliged to pay even if the creditor makes a demand when nothing is due from the debtor. If, for example, the third party's liability is fixed by a conclusive certificate, it is possible that the amount paid may eventually be seen to be too much. This loss will usually fall on the principal debtor, who would be obliged to indemnify the third party: the principal debtor would also have a right of restitution against the creditor as regards the overpayment, to which the third party would be subrogated.[399] In the first place, though, the absolute nature of the third party's obligation means that it is obliged to pay. This is the case even if nothing is due and the demand is made fraudulently. In this situation, it is very unlikely that the debtor will be able to obtain an injunction stopping the third party from paying,[400] although in a case of fraud there does appear to be a possibility of obtaining an injunction to prevent the creditor from making the demand in the first place.[401] Although the contract between the creditor and debtor could include an express term prohibiting the creditor from making an unjustified demand, such a term is unlikely to be implied,[402] so that the demand will not constitute a breach. However, there will be a duty on the creditor to account for any sums received to which it is not entitled under the debt contract:[403] this could be on the basis of an implied term,[404] or on restitutionary grounds.[405]

5.3.2   Credit Insurance

Where a company extends credit to customers, who are usually other companies, there is always a risk that the customers will not pay their debts. If the creditor is supplying goods, it may be able to protect itself by using retention of title terms,[406] but this may not always be possible, for example because the goods are to be immediately used in manufacture or sold on. Alternatively the creditor may not be supplying goods but services. In these circumstances, a creditor will usually take out credit insurance, whereby an insurance company agrees to pay the creditor the insured sum if the debtor becomes insolvent. To avoid the moral hazard of creditors not making proper credit checks on their customers if they could claim the full amount of the loss, the amount covered is usually only about 80 per cent to 95 per cent of the debts.[407] The insurance can cover some or all of the creditor's debtors: whether an insurance company will be prepared to cover any particular debtor will depend on that debtor's credit rating.[408] The fact that a company has credit insurance also makes it easier for that company to obtain receivables financing, as it makes it more likely that the receivables will be paid. Credit insurance can also be used to protect other

---

[399]   *IIG Capital LLC v Van Der Merwe* [2008] EWCA Civ 542, [27].
[400]   Andrews and Millett, n 331, 16–021.
[401]   *Themehelp Ltd v West* [1996] QB 84; Andrews and Millett, n 331, 16–025.
[402]   *The State Trading Corporation of India Ltd v ED & F Man (Sugar) Limited and The State Bank of India* [1981] Com LR 235 per Shaw LJ; *Costain International Ltd v Davy McKee (London) Ltd* (unreported 26 November 1990 per Russell LJ; Andrews and Millett, n 331, 16–026.
[403]   *Cargill International SA v Bangladesh Sugar and Food Industries Corp* [1998] 1 WLR 461.
[404]   *Tradigrain SA v State Trading Corporation of India* [2005] EWHC 2206 (Comm), [26].
[405]   Andrews and Millett, n 331, 16–033.
[406]   2.3.4.3.4.
[407]   J Wright, 'Insuring against Insolvency' (2009) 20 *Construction Law* 26.
[408]   *Close Invoice Finance Ltd v Watts* [2009] All ER (D) 09 (Sep) (Unreported).

lenders, such as those investing in securities issued in a securitisation.[409] In the context of exporting goods, the Export Credit Guarantee Department provides insurance against non-payment by foreign counterparties.

Credit insurance performs a similar function to a guarantee, and in certain cases it may be difficult to tell whether the contract in question is one or the other. It is important to distinguish the two, however, since the protection that the law gives to the insurer is different to that given to the guarantor.[410] As discussed above, the secondary nature of the guarantor's liability means that release of the principal debtor or variations to the principal's contract discharges the guarantor. By contrast, the insurer's protection consists of the law providing every possibility of assessing the risk it is taking correctly. Thus an insured party is under an obligation to make full disclosure of all material facts.[411] The difference in protection is justified by the usual background to the two types of contract: an insurer is usually at arm's length to the insured party, and is paid a premium for taking the risk, which it must therefore assess accurately, while the guarantor is usually not paid for giving the guarantee, and usually knows the debtor well, so that it is in a good position to assess the risk it is taking on.[412] It is clear that the label given to the transaction by the parties is not determinative of the characterisation issue,[413] but that the distinction depends on the 'substantial character' of the transaction.[414] Unfortunately, this does not mean that there are any definitive touchstones for characterisation, but it appears[415] that the courts will look at whether the guarantor/insurer is paid,[416] whether the guarantor/insurer deals with the creditor (which would make it a contract of insurance) or the debtor (which would make it a contract of guarantee),[417] and whether the guarantor/insurer has easy means of discovering the credit-worthiness of the debtor.[418]

5.3.3   Credit Default Swaps

Although structurally different, credit default swaps can perform a similar function to guarantees. They are a mechanism for transferring risk of default from one party to another. They are part of a broader category of transactions known as financial derivatives, which are parasitic transactions which derive value from an underlying product.[419] All derivatives have two possible functions, and this is particularly true for credit derivatives. Those entering into such a transaction may want to protect themselves against risk resulting from a particular transaction. This process is known as 'hedging'. This risk

---

[409]   Fuller, n 15, 4.81. For an example of credit insurance being used to cover the exposure of a bank under derivative transactions, see *Merrill Lynch International Bank Ltd (formerly Merrill Lynch Capital Markets Bank Ltd) v Winterthur Swiss Insurance Co* [2007] EWHC 893 (Comm).

[410]   Hughes, n 139, 5.25.

[411]   This means that contract is one of the utmost good faith (*uberrimae fidae*) which is different from most contracts, where there is no duty of disclosure but only liability for misrepresentation.

[412]   *Seaton v Heath* [1899] 1 QB 782, 793 per Romer LJ. This distinction breaks down when considering some of the examples of guarantees discussed earlier.

[413]   Ibid, 292.

[414]   Ibid.

[415]   J Benjamin, *Financial Law* (Oxford, Oxford University Press, 2007) 5.129.

[416]   Although guarantors do sometimes get fees, Hughes, n 139, 5.25.

[417]   This is not always conclusive, see *In re Denton's Estate* [1904] 2 Ch 178, 189.

[418]   This is not always the case with guarantors, see Hughes, n 139, 5.25.

[419]   Hudson, n 69, 1087. For an argument that credit default swaps are not derivatives, see M Smith, 'The Legal Nature of Credit Default Swaps' [2010] *Lloyds Maritime and Commercial Law Quarterly* 386, 408.

could be the risk of market movement (for example, a futures contract[420]), or the risk of interest rate movement (for example, an interest rate swap[421]) or the risk of non-payment (a credit derivative). An alternative use for derivatives is for making money through speculation and trading.[422] Credit derivatives can themselves be divided into end-user instruments, which relate to a specific asset, and trading instruments, which relate to general credit-worthiness of the reference entity.[423] Here we are merely concerned with end-user instruments, which are used by lenders to protect themselves in a corporate finance transaction against risk of default by the borrower.

In a typical credit default swap, the buyer of protection (in our case, the lender) enters into a contract with the seller of protection whereby the latter agrees to bear the credit risk of a particular entity ('the reference entity') and pay on certain events of default (but is under no obligation to pay unless such an event occurs).[424] These events could be a failure to make an instalment payment on a loan, or a bond, or could be any material breach of covenant, including financial covenants.[425] The seller of protection is paid a fee by the buyer of protection for taking on the risk. It can be seen that the protection given to the lender is similar in many ways to that under a guarantee or indemnity: the lender is protected against the credit risk of the borrower but is exposed to the credit risk of the seller of protection, as it is to the credit risk of the third party in a guarantee.[426] It can, however, be argued that the risk of using credit derivatives is greater, in that the law on guarantees has been developed over many years, and the documentation reflects this,

[420]   A company could hedge against the risk of increase in the price of a commodity by entering into a futures contract to buy that commodity in the future at a price fixed at the time of the contract (or entering into an option to buy that commodity at a fixed price) or by entering into a futures contract or option to sell that commodity at a fixed price: if the market price then rises the profit on the futures sale will cancel out the loss on the actual purchase price paid. See further D Abbey, 'The Use of Derivatives in the Airline Industry' (2007) 5 *Journal of Business and Economics Research* 7. Abbey notes a large discrepancy in the amount of hedging used by different airline companies against a rise in the price of fuel, ranging from 0% to 85% of liabilities.

[421]   Here a company who has to make payments on a loan at a floating rate of interest will enter into a transaction whereby it pays a counterparty a sum based on a fixed rate of interest and the counterparty pays it a sum based on a floating rate of interest (in fact, the payments are netted off so that only the difference is paid): the company's interest costs are thereby pegged at the fixed rate. See ISDA, 'An Introduction to the Documentation of OTC Derivatives' at www.isda.org/educat/pdf/documentation_of_derivatives.pdf and Benjamin, *Financial Law*, n 69, 4.37 for further explanations of interest rate swaps.

[422]   Hudson, n 69, 43–10 et seq. The use of credit derivatives for speculation can lead to systemic risk, as exemplified by the global financial crisis of 2008: investors would purchase derivatives which related purely to the risk of entities rather than specific transactions, so that the amount counterparties (such as Lehmann Brothers) had to pay out on the failure of such entities was huge.

[423]   S Henderson, 'Credit Derivatives – At a Crossroads?' (2001) 16 *Journal of International Banking and Financial Law* 211. It should be realised that those who provide protection under a credit default swap also may protect themselves by entering into a credit default swap with another entity, S Henderson, 'Regulation of Credit Derivatives: to What Effect and for Whose Benefit?' Part 5 (2009) 24 *Journal of International Banking and Financial Law* 413. This passing on of risk can take place several or even many times, so that hedge funds, banks, investment funds and even individuals had some involvement in the credit risk of the original loan: M Todd Henderson, 'Credit Derivatives are Not "Insurance"' University of Chicago Law and Economics, Olin Working Paper No. 476 at 8, available at www.ssrn.com/abstract=1440945.

[424]   Benjamin, n 69, 4.59.

[425]   Hudson, n 69, 43–44–43–46. As noted above, a credit event can also refer to the credit-worthiness of a particular entity, so that the trigger for payment is the insolvency of that entity or a downgrade in its credit rating, Hudson, n 69, 43–47. However, this is usually a feature of trading instruments which are not considered here.

[426]   For discussion of more complex uses of credit derivatives, see Benjamin, n 69, 4.4.6, S Henderson, 'Regulation of Credit Derivatives: to what effect and for whose benefit?' Part 5 (2009) 24 *Journal of International Banking and Financial Law* 413.

while that of derivatives is relatively untested.[427] Some of the legal uncertainties concerning credit default swaps are discussed below. Unlike a guarantee, which is usually seen as a means of credit enhancement to be used in conjunction with the taking of security and other methods of reducing credit risk,[428] a credit default swap can be seen as an alternative to transferring the debt,[429] so that the lender is no longer economically involved in the debt, even though it still keeps its relationship with the borrower.[430] The disadvantage, from the lender's point of view, compared to a transfer of the debt is that it still retains the credit risk of the counterparty to the credit default swap.[431]

Credit default swaps are merely contracts, and many legal issues will largely be a matter of construction of the contract.[432] In the past it was an important issue whether a credit derivative was a gaming contract, as such contracts were unenforceable.[433] This is no longer a live issue, since gaming contracts are no longer unenforceable.[434] Another important issue, however, is whether a credit derivative contract is one of insurance. There are two reasons why this is of significance. If a credit default swap were an insurance contract, those who sold protection, would be required to be authorised by the FSA to carry out insurance business.[435] Banks, and other financial institutions, who act as sellers of protection, are, of course, authorised by the FSA to carry out various functions. However, the regulation of insurance companies is different from that of banks,[436] so that a bank authorised to carry out banking business will not be authorised to carry out insurance business. Further, if a bank were to seek such authorisation, it would be prohibited from carrying out any business other than insurance.[437] For this reason, banks would not wish to be authorised to carry out insurance business.[438] Secondly, as mentioned above,[439] an insured party[440] is required to make full disclosure of all material facts:

---

[427] FSA Handbook, The Interim Prudential Sourcebook for Investment Businesses, Appendix 63 [10App63.5].

[428] Such as due diligence in assessing the credit risk of the borrower, and monitoring of the borrower.

[429] M Todd Henderson, 'Credit Derivatives are not "Insurance"', n 423; A Morrison 'Credit Derivatives, Disintermediation and Investment Decisions' Oxford Financial Research Centre Working Paper 2001-FE-01, available at www.ssrn.com/abstract=270269. See 8.3.2 below.

[430] When done on a large scale, this process is a synthetic securitisation: the economic effects of a securitisation are replicated, but the former legal relationships remain in place. This will reduce the capital adequacy requirements of the lender, but only to the extent that the credit of the counterparty to the swap is better than that of the borrower, or to the extent that the swap is collateralised. See Benjamin, n 69, 18.33; FSA Prudential Sourcebook for Banks, Building Societies and Investment Firms, BIPRU 9.5.

[431] Benjamin, n 69, 18.32; Fuller, n 15, 4.77. This risk is usually covered by the provision of collateral by the counterparty.

[432] For an example, see *Nomura International Plc v Credit Suisse First Boston International* [2002] EWHC 160 (Comm). For a general discussion of the construction of contracts in the context of credit default swaps, see M Smith, 'The Legal Nature of Credit Default Swaps' [2010] *Lloyds Maritime and Commercial Law Quarterly* 386.

[433] See Benjamin, n 69, 5.135–143. See further M Smith, 'The legal nature of credit default swaps' [2010] *Lloyd's Maritime and Commercial Law Quarterly* 386, 400, 406.

[434] Gambling Act 2005 s 335.

[435] Financial Services and Markets Act 2000 (Regulated Activities) Order 2001 (SI 2001/544) ('Regulated Activities Order') art 10. See page 533 for a brief account of the regulatory process.

[436] The insurance regime is set out in the Prudential Sourcebook for Insurers (INSPRU), whereas banks are regulated under the General Prudential Sourcebook (GENPRU) and the Prudential Sourcebook for Banks, Building Societies and Investment Firms (BIPRU).

[437] 1.5.13 INSPRU.

[438] M Smith, 'The legal nature of credit default swaps' [2010] *Lloyd's Maritime and Commercial Law Quarterly* 386, 387.

[439] See page 202.

[440] Here this would be the buyer of protection, ie the lender.

this would not be the case if the swap were not an insurance contract. The basic structure of a credit default swap does seem very similar to an insurance contract: the buyer pays the seller to pay it if an event occurs. In considering whether it is an insurance contract, it is first important to consider precisely what such a contract involves.

There is no statutory definition of an insurance contract, nor any very satisfactory common law one.[441] One description is found in *Prudential Insurance Company v Commissioners of Inland Revenue.*[442] This stresses three aspects: first, it is a contract whereby one secures for oneself a sum of money upon the happening of an uncertain event. Secondly, the insured must have an insurable interest and thirdly, the sum of money is to meet a loss or detriment which will occur because of the event. While the first is certainly the case in credit default swaps, the second two are not necessarily the case. It is quite possible to have a credit default swap where the buyer of protection has no interest in the underlying loan, and even when it does in fact have such an interest, its rights depend on the contract between the parties and not on the existence of that interest. Further, the obligation on the seller of protection to pay is not dependent on any loss on the part of the buyer of protection: it is an absolute obligation which arises on the event of default (rather like the obligation to pay on a performance bond), and the amount may be fixed without reference to the amount of future loss.[443]

These two technical differences between a credit default swap and a contract of insurance were relied upon in an opinion given to International Swaps and Derivatives Association in 1997 by the late Robin Potts QC, which has been relied upon by whole industry ever since as conclusive, at least as to English law.[444] However, the presence of an insurable interest, and the fact that the payment meets a loss are not strictly speaking necessary for a contract to be a contract of insurance. Some further explanation is required. Many types of insurance are 'indemnity insurance' where the insurer pays out a sum of money representing the loss suffered by the insured on the occurrence of the insured event. However, there are also many types of 'non-indemnity' insurance, such as life insurance, where the amount paid out is fixed in advance and does not depend on loss.[445] The fact, then, that a credit default swap does not provide for an indemnity does not prevent it being a contract of insurance.[446]

Whether an insurable interest is a requirement for a contract to be a contract of insurance is more complicated. If a contract is an indemnity insurance contract, then payment is only made if the insured suffers loss: the insured, then, must have an interest in

---

[441] FSA Consultation Paper No 150, *Draft Guidance on the identification of contracts of insurance* (2002) 5.

[442] [1904] 2 KB 658.

[443] JJ de Vries Robbe, *Securitisation Law and Practice in the Face of the Credit Crunch* (Alphen aan den Rijn, Netherlands, Kluwer Law International, 2008) 3.42.1.

[444] J Benjamin, *Financial Law* (Oxford, Oxford University Press, 2007) 5.140–142. However, doubts about the effectiveness of the opinion in all circumstances were raised by the FSA in their Discussion Paper 11, Cross-section risk transfers, Annex B, on the basis that the wording of the contract might not make it clear that the parties did not intend to enter into a contract of insurance and that in any particular contract, the true intention of the parties was to insure against loss. It should also be pointed out that even if the parties include a 'no intention to insure' clause in the contract, this would not be definitive if the court held that the terms of the contract otherwise created an insurance contract, see discussion of the courts' approach to characterisation at 6.2.2.

[445] For a full analysis, see Law Commission, *Insurable Interest Issues Paper 4* (January 2008) 1.14–18 and chapter 3.

[446] M Smith, 'The legal nature of credit default swaps' [2010] *Lloyd's Maritime and Commercial Law Quarterly* 386, 405.

the subject matter of the insurance for there to be any loss.[447] However, in non-indemnity insurance contracts this is not the case. In order to distinguish such contracts from wagers, which used to be (as a matter of policy) unenforceable,[448] and in order to prevent moral hazard[449] statute requires an insurable interest for such contracts to be enforceable.[450] An insurable interest, however, is not a requirement at common law for a contract to be a contract of insurance.[451] In fact, if it had been there would have been no point in statutorily providing that an insurance interest was necessary for a contract of insurance to be enforceable.[452] Thus the two differences identified by Robin Potts QC do not appear to prevent a credit default swap being a contract of insurance.[453] Of course, the kind of credit default swap we are concerned with in this book does include an insurable interest, in that the buyer of protection will be protecting its credit risk under a loan to a company. Thus it would not fall foul of the statutory requirement in the Life Assurance Act 1774. However, there is no insurable interest in the 'naked' credit default swaps entered into for speculative purposes, and so potentially, these could be void under English law.[454] If a credit default swap is a contract of insurance at common law, then the requirement of full disclosure[455] would apply. Even more significantly, it is possible that the insurance regulatory regime of the FSA would apply.

The lack of clarity as to the definition of a contract of insurance prompted the FSA to issue guidance as to what they consider relevant when deciding whether a contract is a contract of insurance, for the purposes of deciding whether authorisation is required under the Financial Services and Markets Act 2000.[456] The FSA's guidance lists a number of general principles as to characterisation, such as the dominance of substance over form,[457] which apply in most contexts,[458] as well as more specific factors which are said to be indicative of a contract of insurance. Three that seem relevant to the question of credit

---

[447] See Law Commission, *Insurable Interest Issues Paper 4*, n 445, 1.16.

[448] This is not the case now, see page 204 above.

[449] Such as the risk that A, who insured the life of B, might murder B to claim on the insurance policy.

[450] The statutory provisions are complicated, and the law is not entirely clear, see Law Commission, *Insurable Interest Issues Paper 4*, n 445, part 2 for an account of the history of the statutory requirements and the resulting lack of clarity. It is, however, clear that the Life Assurance Act 1774 requires an insurable interest for non-indemnity insurance that does not cover goods, merchandises and ships.

[451] FSA Policy statement 04/19, 2004.

[452] M Smith, 'The legal nature of credit default swaps' [2010] *Lloyd's Maritime and Commercial Law Quarterly* 386, 397.

[453] This is the conclusion also reached by Marcus Smith QC, see M Smith, 'The legal nature of credit default swaps' [2010] *Lloyd's Maritime and Commercial Law Quarterly* 38, 409.

[454] This depends on the scope of Life Assurance Act 1774 s 3. This section has been held not to apply to contracts not in the form of a 'policy' of insurance (see N Legh-Jones, J Birds, D Owen (eds), *MacGillivray on Insurance Law*, 11th edn (London, Sweet & Maxwell, 2008), [1.030] and M Smith, 'The legal nature of credit default swaps' [2010] *Lloyd's Maritime and Commercial Law Quarterly* 386, 398) and so may well not apply to naked credit default swaps.

[455] See page 202 above.

[456] FSA Perimeter Guidance Manual (PERG 6) 'Guidance on the Identification of Contracts of Insurance', available at www.fsa.gov.uk. Prior to this the FSA issued a consultation paper No 150 on Draft Guidance on the Identification of Contracts of Insurance (2002) and Policy statement 04/19 2004 dealing with the responses. Further, the lack of clarity as regards the statutory requirement of an insurable interest led the Law Commission to issue an Issues Paper on the subject (Law Commission, *Insurable Interest Issues Paper 4*, n 445).

[457] PERG 6.5.4. Despite this, a relevant factor is whether the contract is described as one of insurance, see PERG 6.6.8.(3).

[458] See, for example, the characterisation of an interest as an absolute or a security interest, discussed at 6.2 below, and the characterisation of fixed and floating charges, discussed at 6.3.3.3.2 below.

derivatives are whether the provider 'assumes risk',[459] whether the amount paid by the 'recipient' is related to the likelihood of the event occurring or the seriousness of the event[460] and whether the provider may either make a profit or bear a loss (a 'speculative risk') or only bear a loss (a 'pure' risk).[461] It will be seen that the lack or presence of an insurable interest is not part of the test, although the emphasis on 'assuming risk' might lead to the inference that the provider is 'assuming' a risk the 'recipient' has, and there would only be such risk if the 'recipient' had some form of interest which could be damaged in some way.[462] The FSA also lists as relevant whether the contract is described as an insurance contract, and whether it includes terms (such as obligations of the utmost good faith) which are usually found in insurance contracts.[463] However, the absence of usual terms is not conclusive, since the test is one of substance rather than form.[464] The exact interpretation of this substance test could be crucial in deciding whether credit default swaps are insurance contracts. If a similar approach is followed to that of the courts when deciding whether an interest is an absolute or a security interest,[465] namely whether the rights and obligations created are consistent with the label put on the transaction by the parties,[466] then it is likely that they will not be held to be insurance contracts. If the approach is similar to that followed when deciding whether a charge is fixed or floating, namely that the rights and obligations created by the contract are decided using the usual rules of interpretation, and then the contract is characterised in law ignoring the labels used by the parties,[467] then it seems much more strongly arguable that credit default swaps are insurance contracts. However, this could have very far reaching consequences. For example, if an agreement to pay a specific sum on a contingency were an insurance contract, then this would surely include some types of performance bond, as well as other contingent debts.[468]

It could be argued that this is an overly technical approach to the question, and that the real question is whether credit default swaps should be treated as insurance contracts from a regulatory point of view. Here there are two questions: the first is whether credit default swaps should be regulated in the same way as insurance contracts, and the second is whether they should be regulated at all. This latter point is complex, and will be dealt with briefly below. In relation to the former point, it is necessary to consider why insurance contracts are regulated in the way that they are. Reasons include the fact that insurance companies have particular corporate governance problems in that they take in premiums up front, and deliver the 'product' (paying out on claims) later, so that there is a particular need to make sure that they are in a position to pay out.[469] Further, many insurance contracts are entered into by consumers who need protection against entering into

---

[459]   PERG 6.6.2.
[460]   PERG 6.6.8(1).
[461]   PERG 6.6.8(2).
[462]   Law Commission, n 445, 7.17.
[463]   PERG 6.6.8 (3).
[464]   PERG 6.6.8(4).
[465]   See 6.2 below.
[466]   See pages 228–29.
[467]   *Agnew v Commissioner of Inland Revenue* [2001] UKPC 28, [2001] AC 710, [32] and see 6.3.3.3.3 below.
[468]   See below at 5.3.4.1.2 for discussion about the use of contingent debts in debt subordination.
[469]   M Todd Henderson, 'Credit Derivatives are not "Insurance"' University of Chicago Law & Economics, Olin Working Paper No 476, available at www.ssrn.com/abstract=1440945.

contracts which they do not understand.[470] The second of these arguments does not apply to credit default swaps, since buyers of protection are either lenders or sophisticated investors. The risk for the buyer of protection is counterparty risk, that is that the seller of protection will not pay. This is a very significant risk, and in one sense is analogous to the risk by an insured party that an insurance company will not pay on an insurance contract.[471] The seller faces the risk of moral hazard, in that the lender who has divested itself of risk using a credit default swap will have little incentive to monitor the borrower, which may affect the likelihood of payment out by the seller of protection.

It can be argued that these risks apply to many transactions, not just to those credit default swaps. To the extent that all a credit default swap is doing is transferring risk, this is done by many types of transactions, both debt and equity,[472] which are not regulated or are regulated in a different way to insurance contracts. If it were sought to regulate credit default swaps that looked like insurance, there would be great difficulty drawing lines to decide which did and which did not. Further, parties would then contract around those lines and enter into synthetic transactions which had the same economic effect but a different legal structure.[473] It is more satisfactory to make a decision about regulating the whole credit derivatives market. This issue is considered briefly in the next paragraph, but first it should be pointed out that, from a regulatory perspective, the credit default swaps which protect a lender against credit risk are seen as the 'safest' kind, since they are limited in scope to protection against actual risks in relation to actual transactions.[474]

The question of whether the whole market should be regulated is one which has been much debated in the wake of the financial crisis.[475] This has resulted in an agreement by

---

[470] Ibid. Both these reasons are similar to those applying to the regulation of public issues of securities, which is discussed in 9.3.

[471] P Vasudev, 'Credit Derivatives and Risk Management: Corporate Governance in the Sarbanes-Oxley World' [2009] *Journal of Business Law* 331, 337. This counterparty risk is ameliorated by the posting of collateral by the seller of the swap. This may be adequate in the case of the simple credit support discussed in this section. In relation to credit default swaps relating to complicated portfolios, the requirement to post collateral was marked to market, and increased as the value of the portfolio diminished. In the financial crisis this requirement became excessively onerous for some swap counterparties, such as AIG, which, ironically, was an insurance company. See S Henderson, 'Regulation of Credit Derivatives: To What Effect, and For Whose Benefit?' (Part 6) (2009) 24 *Journal of International Banking and Financial Law* 480.

[472] Todd Henderson, 'Credit Derivatives are not "Insurance"' University of Chicago Law & Economics, Olin Working Paper No 476, available at www.ssrn.com/abstract=1440945 argues that for a company to issue shares is just another way of transferring risk, except that the sequence of payments is reversed, in that the shareholders pay the amount relating to the risk up front (but will lose it if the company becomes insolvent) while the 'price' is paid periodically in dividends.

[473] M Todd Henderson, 'Credit Derivatives are not "Insurance"' University of Chicago Law & Economics, Olin Working Paper No 476, available at www.ssrn.com/abstract=1440945.

[474] S Henderson, 'Regulation of Credit Derivatives: To What Effect, and For Whose Benefit?' (Part 6) [2009] 24 *Journal of International Banking and Financial Law* 480.

[475] The matter was considered in the Turner Review: Lord Turner, *The Turner Review, A Regulatory Response to the Global Banking Crisis*, March 2009 at 3.1. Further discussion in the UK included Financial Services Authority and HM Treasury 'Reforming OTC Derivatives Markets: A UK Perspective' (December 2009); 'The Future Regulation of Derivatives Markets: is the EU on the Right Track?' (House of Lords 10th report 2009–10 (HMSO 31 March 2010); S Henderson, 'Regulation of Credit Derivatives: To What Effect, and For Whose Benefit?' (2009) 24 *Journal of International Banking and Financial Law* 3–8, 11; T Strong and I Wilkinson, 'Derailing Derivatives' (2009) 24 *Journal of International Banking and Financial Law* 666; R Ayadi and P Behr, 'On the Necessity to Regulate the Credit Derivatives Markets' (2009) 10 *Journal of Banking Regulation* 179. There was also an extensive debate in Europe and the US.

the G20 nations in relation to how the derivatives market should be regulated.[476] The main problems identified are lack of transparency and counterparty risk. Both problems stem largely from the fact that most credit derivative contracts are not traded on a market with a central counterparty but 'over the counter' (OTC). Lack of transparency can lead to systemic risk, since it is not clear to parties what their counterparties' total exposure is, nor can such exposure be monitored by regulatory agencies, so dangerous levels of risk can pass unnoticed.[477] More transparency would also increase the utility of credit default swap pricing in signalling credit risk to the market and to other creditors of the reference entity.[478] Counterparty risk, as mentioned above, is a significant danger both to individual contracting parties and more generally, since if one counterparty fails to pay, there is a danger of a domino effect. The G20 agreement states that these problems should be dealt with by greater standardisation of contracts, by (where possible) requiring derivatives to be traded on exchanges and cleared through central counterparties, for contracts to be reported to trade repositories and for there to be higher capital requirements for non-exchange derivative contracts. Nations are now considering how to translate this into regulatory law: the US has already enacted the Dodd-Franks Act[479] which includes many of these provisions, and the EU has issued several consultations on the issue.[480] Opinion seems divided at present about the utility of these regulatory changes: there seems little doubt that it will raise the cost of credit derivatives. This may be necessary in order to prevent further systemic collapse, but it is unfortunate for those who use credit derivatives merely as a way of hedging risk.

5.3.4   Subordination

A lender can protect itself against the credit risk of the borrower by making sure that it gets paid before other creditors. One way of doing this is to take security over the borrower's assets;[481] another is to achieve a higher ranking by means of subordination, so that subordinated creditors are not paid until the lender has been paid in full. While this is particularly important on the insolvency of the borrower, it may also have cash flow implications while the borrower is still solvent. Subordination is used to allocate risk among different lenders in a particular funding structure. One example is in a leveraged buyout,[482] where the subordination is usually achieved by using a chain structure of several companies.[483] The legal effects of this structural subordination are discussed at

---

[476]   This was part of the agreement at the Pittsburg summit held on 25 September 2009, see www.g20.org/Documents/pittsburgh_summit_leaders_statement_250909.pdf at para 13. The commitment to achieve these goals by the end of 2012 was reaffirmed at the Toronto summit on 27 June 2010, see www.g20.org/Documents/g20_declaration_en.pdf at para 25.

[477]   'The Future Regulation of Derivatives Markets: Is the EU on the Right Track?' (House of Lords 10th report 2009–10 (HMSO 31 March 2010) 18.

[478]   See page 86, where the role of credit default swap pricing in corporate governance is briefly discussed.

[479]   Enacted on 21 July 2010.

[480]   'Ensuring Efficient, Safe and Sound Derivatives Markets' (July 2009) see http://ec.europa.eu/internal_market/financial-markets/docs/derivatives/report_en.pdf; 'Ensuring Efficient, Safe and Sound Derivatives Markets: Future Policy Actions' (October 2009) see http://ec.europa.eu/internal_market/financial-markets/docs/derivatives/20091020_563_en.pdf; 'Public Consultation on Derivatives and Market Infrastructures' (June 2010) see http://ec.europa.eu/internal_market/consultations/docs/2010/derivatives/100614_derivatives.pdf.

[481]   Discussed in chapter 6.

[482]   Discussed in chapter 14.

[483]   See 14.4.

5.3.4.1.4 below. Another common example is in a securitised bond issue,[484] where the different tranches of securities rank in order: this can be achieved by a turnover trust or by contractual subordination, or by providing that the senior ranked tranches are secured, but the lowest rank is not. It is also common for a parent company to agree to be subordinated to other lenders to a subsidiary company, or, where a company is in difficulties, for lenders to agree to be subordinated to a party who is willing to lend in an attempt to enable the company to trade out of its difficulties.

It is possible for a subordination agreement to be made between secured or unsecured lenders. Where the lenders are secured, the agreement determines their priority, which would otherwise be determined by the general law.[485] Such agreements are very common. A lender taking a charge over the borrower's assets will normally know of any earlier charges, either because the borrower has informed it or because it has searched the register: the lender can then come to a subordination agreement with the previous secured creditor, if the latter will agree. There is no need to obtain the borrower's consent or to make it party to the subordination agreement.[486] It would normally be advisable for the lenders to agree to subordinate the debt as well as the security interest, so that the senior lender is protected even if the security is ineffective or insufficient.[487]

Where a subordination agreement is made between unsecured lenders, the main question is whether it will be effective on the insolvency of the borrower. Unless the borrower is insolvent the order of payment of lenders is not critical, since all will be paid eventually, although timing of payments can make a difference to cash flow.[488] In insolvency, though, the order of payments is likely to make the difference, for some lenders, between being paid and not being paid. It will be recalled that the default rule for distribution of assets in insolvency to unsecured creditors is *pari passu*[489] and that it not possible to contract out of its operation by agreeing that insolvency set-off should not apply to particular debts.[490] There has been concern that contractual subordination would be likewise ineffective as an attempt to contract out of *pari passu* distribution, both on the basis of the *Halesowen case*[491] and the *British Eagle* case.[492]

5.3.4.1 *Types of Subordination*

In order to assess this concern, it is necessary to consider the various types of subordination which have been developed. In this analysis, the subordinated lender is known as the junior creditor, and the lender who benefits from the subordination is known as the senior

---

[484] See 8.3.3.

[485] See 6.4.4.

[486] *Cheah Theam Swee v Equiticorp Finance Group Ltd* [1992] 1 AC 472.

[487] P Wood, *Project Finance, Securitisations, Subordinated Debt*, 2nd edn (London, Sweet & Maxwell, 2007) 10–031.

[488] It should be noted that in a tranched securitisation, the order of payment outside insolvency is controlled by a 'waterfall' clause. This may provide for sequential payments (top tranches first) or pro rata payments (each tranche gets paid something), see Fuller, n 15, 4.67. These clauses can be very complex and their interpretation has been the subject of much recent litigation, see, for example, *Re Sigma Finance Corp (in administrative receivership)*; [2009] UKSC 2.

[489] See pages 184–85 above. The principle is given statutory force in Insolvency Act 1986, s 107.

[490] See page 187.

[491] *National Westminster Bank Ltd v Halesowen Presswork & Assemblies Ltd* [1972] AC 785; above page 187.

[492] *British Eagle International Air Lines Ltd v Compagnie Nationale Air France* [1975] 1 WLR 758; see page 185.

creditor. In reality, the senior or junior creditor could be one or many creditors, or could be all other debt owed by the borrower (so that one or more junior creditor can be subordinated to all other creditors, for example). The subordination may also be 'springing', in that it only takes effect if a particular event happens, such as the insolvency of the borrower,[493] or it can apply at all times (a 'complete' subordination).[494]

5.3.4.1.1 Turnover Trust

One type of subordination is known as a turnover subordination. Here, either the junior creditor agrees to hold the proceeds of the debt it is owed on trust for the senior creditor (including dividends paid in the borrower's insolvency) until the senior creditor is paid in full, or the junior creditor merely agrees to pay over such proceeds or dividends which it receives to the senior creditor until the latter is paid in full. It will be seen that this second method is less attractive to the senior creditor as it takes the risk of the junior creditor's insolvency, and so this method is rarely used.[495] In both methods, the junior creditor proves as normal in the borrower's insolvency, and thus the *pari passu* principle cannot be said to be infringed.[496] The senior creditor, in fact, is greatly benefitted by this method, since it gets a 'double dividend' in the borrower's insolvency.[497] To illustrate this, suppose that the borrower's assets were £1 million and its liabilities £10 million, of which £1 million was owed to the senior creditor, £1 million to the junior creditor and the rest to other unsecured creditors. Each creditor would therefore obtain a dividend of one tenth. The senior creditor would, under the turnover method, obtain £200,000: £100,000 from each of its own dividend and that of the junior creditor. Under other methods of contractual subordination, the junior creditor would not prove, or its proof would be assessed as nil, and so there would be £1 million to be distributed among nine creditors, so that each would get a dividend of one ninth: under this method the senior creditor would therefore get £111,111.[498]

There is no problem with an agreement by a creditor to hold the proceeds of a debt on trust for another party, however, an issue does arise whether the trust is absolute or by way of security. It is important to know this since if it is a security interest,[499] it could be registrable, either as a charge over book debts[500] or as a floating charge.[501] Further, entering into the agreement might be a breach of a negative pledge clause in another agreement to which the junior creditor was a party.[502] As discussed below,[503] when characterising a transfer of an asset as absolute or by way of security, the court will look at

---

[493] This is the common form in relation to subordinated securities issues, see Fuller, n 15, 10.38.

[494] This is more likely to be the situation where the subordinated creditor is a parent company or otherwise connected with the borrower, Fuller, n 15, 10.38.

[495] Wood, *Project Finance, Securitisations, Subordinated Debt*, n 487 10–022.

[496] *Re NIAA Corp Ltd* (1993) 12 ACSR 141 (Sup Ct NSW); H Beale, M Bridge, L Gullifer and E Lomnicka, *The Law of Personal Property Security*, n 91, 6.103.

[497] Gullifer, n 71, 8–24, *Re SSSL Realisations* [2004] EWHC 1760 (Ch), [27], affirmed on appeal sub nom *Squires v AIG Europe Ltd* [2006] EWCA Civ 7.

[498] See Wood, n 487, 10–027 for a similar worked example.

[499] Such a security interest could be an equitable mortgage, created by an equitable assignment of the proceeds, or a charge. The term 'charge' in the Companies Act includes both a mortgage and a charge, so either would potentially be registrable.

[500] Registrable under Companies Act 2006, s 860(7)(f).

[501] Registrable under s 860(7)(g), ibid.

[502] Wood, n 487, 11–017.

[503] 6.2.

whether the indicia of security are present, namely, the right of the transferee to any surplus value over and above the underlying obligation, the obligation of the transferor to pay the balance if the transfer does not fulfil the underlying obligation and the right of the transferor to redeem the security if the underlying obligation is fulfilled in another way. Here one could say that the underlying obligation was for the junior creditor to pay to the senior creditor such amount of the proceeds or dividend as will result in the senior creditor being fully paid. That amount might be all, or only some of the proceeds received by the junior creditor. It cannot be more, so the second indicia of security cannot be present. The question, therefore, is whether, if the amount due is only some of the proceeds, this amounts to a right to the surplus or an equity of redemption (the first and third indicia of security). This will not be the case if the trust is only over that portion of the proceeds that is equal to the amount required to enable the senior creditor to be paid in full. To some extent, therefore, the question of whether a turnover trust is a charge will depend on the wording of the declaration of trust. In *Re SSSL Realisations*[504] Lloyd J held that, on construction of the relevant clause, the trust obligation was limited to the sums due to the senior creditor, and therefore was not a charge.[505]

While this seems an eminently sensible solution, it does entail an analysis that there can be a trust of part of a fund, that is, the proceeds or dividend received by the junior creditor.[506] One could argue that this falls foul of the requirement of certainty of trusts,[507] particularly since the sums held on trust are not segregated from the assets of the trustee (the balance of the fund). The argument is that a person cannot declare a trust of an amount of money which it owns (whether in cash or in a bank account) without separating out that sum of money from any other money by, for example, transferring it to a separate bank account.[508] The main authority cited in support of this is *MacJordan Construction Ltd v Brookmount Erostin Ltd*[509] where, pursuant to a contract between a developer and a builder, the developer was to make interim payments to the builders on production of an architect's certificate, but was entitled to retain three per cent of each amount, which sum it was to hold on trust for the builder. The Court of Appeal held that the developer was under a contractual obligation to separate and set aside the three per cent as a trust fund. This was never done, and any money retained was kept by the developer among its own assets. The Court of Appeal held that the builder could have no proprietary remedy against the insolvent developer, since no trust had been validly created, and there was no equity which bound the bank (which had a floating charge over the developer's assets) to set aside the amount that should have been separated. This decision was followed in *Re Global Trader Europe Ltd*[510] where client money which should have been segregated by a broker was not, and was mixed with the brokers' own funds: it was held that the clients had no proprietary claim on the insolvency of the broker.

---

[504]   [2004] EWHC 1760 (Ch), [49], [51].

[505]   This was upheld by the Court of Appeal, *Re SSSL Realisations, sub nom Squires v AIG Europe (UK) Ltd* [2006] EWCA Civ 7; [2006] Ch 610, [122].

[506]   This could be a debt due to the junior creditor, if it were paid into its bank account, or it will be a debt to the junior creditor from the liquidator who is usually mandated to distribute the amount due directly to the senior creditor. Fuller, n 15, 10.59.

[507]   Discussed in chapter 7 at page 318 et seq.

[508]   D Hayton, 'Uncertainty of Subject-matter of Trusts' (1994) 110 *Law Quarterly Review* 335, 337; Hudson, n 69, 21–04.

[509]   [1994] CLC 581.

[510]   [2009] EWHC 602 (Ch); [2009] 2 BCLC 18.

However, it could be said that the situations in both these cases fell foul of the certainty requirement in two ways: not only was the trust money not segregated from the trustee's money, but it was also unidentifiable by any means, since it formed part of the trustee's general assets. It was not an unsegregated part of a particular fund.[511]

The difference between being part of a fund and being part of the trustee's general assets can be explained by reference to the argument made by Professor Goode. He starts from the premise that money is not fungible, in that although a debt is enumerated in units of currency, say, £100, those units cannot be split off from the debt in the way that bottles of wine can be taken out of a bulk.[512] Each debt, he says, is capable of separate ownership, but when part of a debt is assigned this results in co-ownership of the debt. It is clear that part of a debt can be assigned in equity, though not by statutory assignment,[513] and Professor Goode explains that because of the lack of fungibility of the subject matter, such an assignment can only result in (equitable) co-ownership of the debt. If this is correct, there is no problem of certainty or identification with a declaration of trust over part of a debt, for example, a bank account, by the person to whom the debt is owed as this will have the effect that the trustee then holds the debt on trust for himself and the beneficiary. In certain circumstances, the trustee may be under an express or implied obligation to segregate money held on trust for others from money held for himself. An example is where this is required by the Financial Services Authority Rules if the money belongs to a client of the trustee,[514] by paying that money into a separate bank account. Where this is not the case, segregation is not necessary to constitute a trust providing that the intention to create a trust is clear. This view is supported by considerable authority to the effect that the main relevance of segregation is as evidence of intention, so that an obligation to segregate money, and/or actual segregation shows that it was intended to declare a trust, while if there is no obligation to segregate then this is evidence that a trust was not intended.[515] Where, however, there is a very clear intention to create a trust, actual segregation is not essential to create a trust providing that the trust assets can be identified.[516] This identification can take place where the trust relates to part of a specified debt, as the obligations of the trustee are clearly defined in relation to that debt.[517]

[511] Thus, for example, the situation can be distinguished from that in *Hunter v Moss* [1994] 1 WLR 452, which is discussed in detail below at page 320. This view also obtains some support from the judgment of Arden LJ in *Lehman Brothers International (Europe) (in admin)* [2010] EWCA Civ 917, [171].

[512] R Goode, 'Are Intangible Assets Fungible?' [2003] *Lloyds Maritime and Commercial Law Quarterly* 379.

[513] *Re Steel Wing Co Ltd* [1921] 1 Ch 349.

[514] CASS 5.5; CASS 7.4.

[515] *Henry v Hammond* [1913] 2 KB 515, 521; also *Re Nanwa Gold Mines Ltd* [1955] 1 WLR 1080; *R v Clowes* [1994] 2 All ER 316, 325.

[516] In *Re Kayford Ltd* [1975] 1 WLR 279, 282; *R v Clowes* [1994] 2 All ER 316; *Re ILG Travel Ltd (in administration)* [1995] 2 BCLC 128; *Re Lewis's of Leicester Ltd* [1995] BCC 514; *Stephens Travel Service International Pty Ltd (Receivers & Managers Appointed) v Qantas Airways Ltd* (1988), 13 NSWLR 331 (CA) (at 348 Hope JA specifically distinguished *Henry v Hammond* as dealing merely with the case where intention is unclear); *Air Canada v. M & C Travel Ltd* (1991) 77 DLR (4th) 536 (Sup Ct Canada). See also *In The Matter Of Lehman Brothers International (Europe) (In Administration)* [2009] EWHC 2545 (Ch), [54].

[517] This view has been supported by a number of commentators, see P Parkinson, (2002) 61 *Cambridge Law Journal* 657, 668; J Martin, 'Certainty of Subject Matter: a Defence of Hunter v Moss' [1996] *Conveyancer* 223; S Worthington, 'Sorting Out Ownership Interests in a Bulk: Gifts, Sales and Trusts' [1999] *Journal of Business Law* 1.

There are, however, two particular questions in the turnover trust situation. One is whether it is intended to create a trust over part of the proceeds,[518] as opposed to the creation of a charge over the whole of the proceeds, and the other question is whether such a trust is possible. The two questions are intertwined in that if a trust is not possible, the intention of the parties to create a proprietary interest would mean that the court is likely to hold that a charge has been created. If the arguments made above, however, are correct so that a trust of part of the proceeds is possible, the question is reduced to ascertainment of the intention of the parties. For example, in *Re ILG Travel Ltd*, Jonathan Parker J held that in fact what was intended to be created was a charge,[519] although he accepted that it was possible for parties to intend to create a 'bare trust' where beneficiaries' money was mixed with that of the trustee.[520] In other cases where a separate bank account was set up into which money held on trust was paid, the fact that some of the money paid in belonged to trustee did not prevent the trust being valid.[521] If the intention to create a trust over part of the proceeds is made clear enough in a turnover trust, it should therefore be upheld by the court.[522] This was the view of the High Court of Australia in the case of *Associated Alloys Pty Ltd v ACN 001 452 106 Pty Limited*.[523] Here a contract for the sale of goods on retention of title provided that such part of the proceeds of such goods as equaled the amount due from the buyer to the seller were to be held on trust by the buyer for the seller. The High Court held that the trust took effect when the proceeds were received by the buyer, so that the constitution of the trust over the relevant part of the cash or bank account amounted to fulfillment of the buyer's obligation to pay the seller under the contract of sale.[524]

Even if the turnover trust does create a charge and not a trust, it is not necessarily registrable, at least as a charge over book debts. This was the conclusion of Lloyd J in *Re SSSL Realisations*,[525] on the grounds that a charge over the proceeds of a debt is not a charge over the debt itself. If the proceeds were in the junior creditor's bank account, the charge would, of course, have been over the debt represented by that account but it is generally thought that a bank account is not a book debt.[526] If the junior creditor were

---

[518]   The arguments made here only really work if the proceeds are in the form of a debt owed to the junior creditor. It is submitted that this is inevitably the case: either the debt is owed by the liquidator (although note that a dividend paid by a liquidator is not a debt it the sense that it can be recovered by action), or the money is paid into the junior creditor's bank account, in which case the debt is owed by the bank. The analysis would be more difficult were the proceeds to be paid in cash (that is, legal tender) but this possibility is so unlikely that it can be dismissed.

[519]   [1995] 2 BCLC 128, 156–157.

[520]   An example given was the Australian case of *Stephens Travel Service International Pty Ltd (Receivers & Managers Appointed) v Qantas Airways Ltd* (1988) 13 NSWLR 331 (CA).

[521]   *Re Kayford Ltd* [1975] 1 WLR 279; *Re Lewis's of Leicester* [1995] BCC 514.

[522]   See also in support of this view, L Ho, 'A Matter of Contractual and Trust Subordination' (2004) 19 *Journal of International Banking Law and Regulation* 494.

[523]   [2000] 202 CLR 588, [34].

[524]   It is true that it is unlikely that the actual decision would be followed in this country, but this is because it is unlikely that the courts would interpret a contract of sale to have the effect that the buyer could pay the seller only out of the proceeds of sale (as opposed to any other source of payment), rather than because of the reasoning in relation to the effectiveness of the trust. See page 235.

[525]   [2004] EWHC 1760 (Ch), [54], upheld by the Court of Appeal at *Re SSSL Realisations, sub nom Squires v AIG Europe (UK) Ltd* [2006] EWCA Civ 7; [2006] Ch 610, [122].

[526]   *Re Brightlife* [1987] Ch 200. *Northern Bank v Ross* [1991] BCLC 504.

able to withdraw from the bank account without the consent of the senior creditor, however, the charge could be a floating charge which would be registrable.[527]

5.3.4.1.2 Contingent Debt

Another way of structuring a subordination so that it does not infringe the *pari passu* principle, is as a contingent debt. There are various drafting techniques, but the basic idea is that the junior creditor and the borrower agree that if the borrower is insolvent[528] the junior creditor will not recover (or will be treated as a holder of preference shares) unless the senior creditor has been paid in full.[529] In order to create a contingent debt, it is important that the borrower is a party to the agreement, but this is likely to be the case in, for example, a securities issue. Contingent claims are, of course, provable in a liquidation,[530] but they are valued by the liquidator, and if the junior creditor is not going to receive anything under the arrangement, the conditional debt will be valued at nil (and if it is valued at more than this, it is because it is entitled to recover on a *pari passu* basis with the other creditors).[531]

5.3.4.1.3 Contractual Subordination

Another formulation is for the junior creditor to agree with the senior creditor that it will not claim until the senior debt has been paid in full,[532] or to agree with the debtor that the senior creditors are entitled to be paid in full before any payments are made to the junior creditor.[533] Potentially, this could infringe the *pari passu* principle, although it has now been held in two cases that it does not.[534] Various arguments persuaded the judge in *re Maxwell Communications Corporation plc*, where the parties to the agreement included the debtor.[535] First, if a creditor can waive its right to prove in the liquidation after it has commenced, there is no reason why it cannot do so in advance, and partially (in case any assets remain once the senior creditor has been paid in full). Secondly, to disallow contractual subordination would have widespread repercussions.[536] Thirdly, since a subordination is possible by the use of the trust formulation, to disallow contractual subordination would 'represent a triumph of form over substance'.[537] Fourthly, since other jurisdictions give effect to such a form of subordination, it would be 'a matter of grave concern' if English law did not.[538]

---

[527] This point was not considered in *SSSL Realisations*. See Beale et al, n 91, 6.113.

[528] The test for insolvency may be defined so as to exclude the liabilities owed to the junior creditor, Fuller, n 15, 10.49.

[529] Wood, n 487, 10–024; Fuller, n 15, 10.49; Beale et al, n 91, 6.95. For examples of clauses, see Fuller, n 15; Wood, n 15, 10–024–025.

[530] Insolvency Rules 1986, r 12.3(1).

[531] Fuller, n 15, 10.49; Beale et al, n 91, 6.109.

[532] This was the position in *SSSL Realisations*.

[533] This was the formulation in *Re Maxwell Communications Corp plc (No 2)* [1993] 1 WLR 1402, 1411–12.

[534] *Re Maxwell Communications* [1993] 1 WLR 1402; *Re SSSL Realisations Ltd* [2004] EWHC 1760 (Ch). The latter decision was confirmed by the Court of Appeal at [2006] EWCA Civ 7.

[535] [1993] 1 WLR 1402, 1406.

[536] Ibid, 1416. This argument may have been too strong, in that subordinations were, and still usually are, drafted as turnover trusts or contingent debt subordinations because of the uncertainty about the validity of contractual subordinations, so the use of the latter was not widespread.

[537] Ibid, 1417.

[538] Ibid, 1420.

Other arguments could also be marshalled. One is that the *pari passu* principle is designed to prevent one unsecured creditor obtaining an advantage over another in the distribution on insolvency, and there is no objection to one creditor agreeing to be paid after all the other creditors, as this merely gives that creditor a disadvantage.[539] It could be said that although this argument makes some sense where the agreement is only between the creditors, it is less successful where the borrower is also a party.[540] However, Lloyd J in *Re SSSL Realisations* thought that it made no difference to the validity of the agreement that the borrower was a party,[541] and it is difficult to see why this should be the case where it is the *pari passu* principle itself which is in issue. The anti-deprivation principle,[542] though, only applies to contracts made by the debtor: the debtor is not permitted to agree that part of its assets shall pass to another on its insolvency so that those assets are not available for the general body of creditors. It could be said that a subordination agreement whereby all the creditors agree with the debtor that one senior creditor should be paid in full before any other creditors obtained anything infringes this principle. It is, however, hard to see why the principle should render such agreement void if all creditors have consented to it, unless the true meaning of *National Westminster Bank v Halesowen*[543] is that consent is irrelevant in relation to any attempt to contract out of insolvency distribution.

One could argue that the anti-deprivation principle applies where both the borrower and the junior creditor are insolvent, as in the *Re SSSL Realisations* case. In this situation, the effect of the subordination agreement is that the creditors of the junior creditor are deprived of an asset (the debt owed by the borrower to the junior creditor) as a result of the subordination agreement. This argument was (strongly) made in the *Re SSSL Realisations* case in relation to the debtor's insolvency, and rejected on the sensible grounds that the insolvency of each company had to be looked at separately.[544] Thus, on that view the principle clearly did not apply in the insolvency of the debtor.

In relation to the insolvency of the junior creditor, the judge in *SSSL Realisations* at first instance held that the subordination agreement did not contravene the anti-deprivation principle.[545] The point was not raised on appeal. However, the matter did not appear to be analysed in detail. The subordination considered was a contractual agreement, and such a provision could be seen as a deprivation, in that the junior creditor had an asset (the debt) and agreed with the other creditors not to enforce it. However, one of the limitations of the principle may still apply. There might be full value for the deprivation.[546] Further, the timing might be such that the diminution takes place before the junior creditor's

---

[539]   Wood, n 15, 11–025.

[540]   Beale et al, n 91, 6.109.

[541]   [2004] EWHC 1760 (Ch) [45].

[542]   See discussion at pages 100–102.

[543]   [1972] AC 785.

[544]   [2004] EWHC 1760 (Ch) [45]. See L Ho, 'A Matter of Contractual and Trust Subordination' (2004) 19 *Journal of International Banking Law and Regulation* 496.

[545]   [2004] EWHC 1760 (Ch) [45]. This appears to be what was meant, although the judge referred to the principle as the *pari passu* principle. Both the judge and the Court of Appeal (at [2006] EWCA Civ 7) held that the subordination agreement could not be disclaimed as an onerous contract.

[546]   See page 100 above. This appears to have been the case in *SSSL Realisations*, see [88] where the judge pointed out, in the context of whether the subordination was an onerous contract, that the disability was part of the price paid for the financing of the group of companies. It could also be the case if, for example, the subordinated creditor obtains a higher interest rate, which would be the case where there are various tranches of debt.

insolvency.[547] Thirdly, the subordination could be seen as an inherent limitation of the debt,[548] if the whole arrangement was entered into under one contract.

If a subordination agreement is structured as a turnover trust, the analysis is likely to be that the junior creditor has disposed of an asset (the proceeds of its claim against the debtor), but the disposition has happened before the insolvency of the junior creditor. Thus the issue is not governed by the anti-deprivation principle, but by section 238 of the Insolvency Act 1986 covering transactions at an undervalue.[549] If the subordination is structured as a contingent debt, then this will probably be seen as a flawed asset. The reasoning above in relation to flawed assets will therefore apply.[550]

5.3.4.1.4 Structural Subordination

As mentioned above,[551] debt can be subordinated structurally: this is particularly common in private equity transactions,[552] but also in other lending to and within group companies. This utilises a tiered company structure whereby the senior debt is lent to company A, which will actually make use of the money, and the junior debt is lent to a company B. Company B owns 100 per cent of company A. As a result the senior creditor has a direct debt claim against company A whereas the junior creditor only has a debt claim against company B. Company B's claim against company A is a qua shareholder claim and is thus subordinated to all of the creditor claims of company A (including of course that of the senior creditor).[553] This has the effect that the junior creditors will only receive some value (maybe not to the full amount) if the senior creditor has been paid in full.

5.5 Conclusion

This chapter has examined various ways in which creditors can be protected by contractual means. It is clear that, at least for all creditors who are able to adjust by using contractual protection, the protection against the risks posed by the actions of directors which favour shareholders is superior to that provided by the general law under the legal capital rules discussed in chapter four. In relation to such risks, non-adjusting creditors may well be able to free ride and obtain some protection. Much of the protection discussed in this chapter, then, deals with the risks posed to a particular creditor from other creditors in the event of the borrower's insolvency. Insolvency set-off, for example, enables a creditor to recover its debt or part of it pound-for-pound in a situation when most unsecured creditors would receive a mere proportion of what is owed to them. By

---

[547] See page 100.
[548] See page 101.
[549] F Oditah, 'Assets and the Treatment of Claims in Insolvency' (1992) 108 *Law Quarterly Review* 478; L Ho, 'A Matter of Contractual and Trust Subordination' (2004) 19 *Journal of International Banking Law and Regulation* 498. Whether the transaction was at an undervalue would depend on a number of circumstances which will not be reviewed here.
[550] See page 177.
[551] See page 209.
[552] See 14.4.
[553] 3.3.1.2.5.

obtaining contractual rights against solvent third parties, a creditor is able to safeguard its position when the borrower is insolvent. A creditor can also neutralise the competition other creditors pose when the borrower is insolvent, by using covenants against further borrowing, restrictive debt/equity ratios and negative pledge clauses, as well as by obtaining agreement from other creditors that they will subordinate their claims. It is, of course, the case that any of this protection is only available to a creditor if it is able to adjust.[554] Non-adjusting creditors may need some protection under the general law, but this is better dealt with on insolvency and is discussed below at 6.6.2.3.

Despite all these devices, a creditor is still better off obtaining proprietary protection if it can. The benefits of proprietary protection, as compared to contractual protection, are discussed in the next chapter.[555] It is important to realise, however, that the two are not mutually exclusive. In fact, virtually all secured creditors will also take extensive contractual protection, both in the form of covenants, and in the form of rights against third parties, such as guarantees, and usually would seek to take security interests over the assets of the guarantor as well. Most lenders want as much protection as they can get, and the only restraining factors are the bargaining power of the borrower,[556] and the availability of assets over which to take security or third parties who can give contractual protection.

---

[554] See 3.2.2.1 above for a discussion of which creditors can and cannot adjust, and of ways of adjusting which are not covered in this chapter, such as adjusting the price, diversification, refusing to contract and requiring payment in advance.

[555] 6.1.1.

[556] This can be considerable, so that large public companies rarely borrow on a secured basis.

6

Creditor Protection: Proprietary

6.1 Introduction

This chapter considers the proprietary protection that a creditor might have. The advantages of proprietary protection are very considerable, and are discussed in the first section below. However, the very advantages that having a proprietary interest gives to a lender are potential disadvantages to other, less protected, lenders and other creditors. For this reason, there are some limits on the freedom of lenders to demand proprietary protection. These limits take two main forms. The first is the statutory alteration of priorities on insolvency: this device is used to protect non-adjusting creditors. The details of this have already been set out in chapter three,[1] while the policy considerations are dealt with below in 6.6.[2] The second is the statutory disclosure of certain types of proprietary interests, in order to enable subsequent lenders and creditors to make adjustments so as to protect themselves.[3] The current system of registration of security interests, and the priority scheme which relates to it, is discussed throughout this chapter, but particularly in 6.4.

It is very important that a legal system enables creditors to protect themselves by taking proprietary interests: this is vital for the availability of credit. There are certain basic attributes which a law should have in this regard. One such attribute is that the law is clear, certain and easily accessible. Another is that it should be possible to obtain a proprietary right over any asset of a borrower, and that the process of doing so should be as easy and cheap as possible. Further, it must be possible to acquire proprietary rights over both the present and future assets of the borrower, without any additional formalities in the future, and to acquire a non-possessory proprietary interest which does not prevent the borrower from disposing of the asset subject to that interest in the ordinary course of business. It should be possible for any creditor (with or without proprietary protection) to find out sufficient information to enable it to adjust adequately to the risks it takes in advancing credit.[4] There should also be a simple and straightforward way for a creditor taking a proprietary interest to protect itself from losing priority to a future creditor taking a proprietary interest in the same asset. Further, it should be possible to enforce a proprietary claim effectively whether or not the borrower is insolvent.

It is important to bear these ideal attributes in mind when considering the English law discussed in this chapter. In 6.7 we will reintroduce the theme of an ideal law, will consider how English law shapes up to that ideal and will discuss a possible alternative system.

---

[1] 3.3.1.2.
[2] Especially at 6.6.2.3.
[3] For discussion of possible adjustments, see 3.2.2.1.
[4] Non-adjusting creditors are discussed at 3.2.2.1 and 6.6.2.3.

As this is a lengthy chapter, a more systematic description of the sections is in order. 6.1 looks at the advantages to a creditor of obtaining a proprietary interest and various distinctions relating to that interest. 6.2 considers the important distinction between absolute and security interests. 6.3 discusses non-possessory true security interests, that is, mortgages and fixed and floating charges. 6.4 discusses the registration requirements, and the extent to which registration constitutes notice, and then also priority between two or more security interests, and between a security interest and an absolute interest. 6.5 discusses briefly the enforcement of security and quasi-security interests. 6.6 discusses the various economic justifications for secured credit, both from the US and the UK standpoint. 6.7 considers the arguments for and against reform of the law of personal property security in England and Wales.

6.1.1   Purpose of Obtaining Proprietary Rights

In the previous chapter we considered the various ways in which a creditor[5] could protect itself by obtaining contractual rights. In many of the situations considered, an important question was whether those contractual rights gave the creditor sufficient protection if the debtor became insolvent. In some cases, such as set-off, the protection given is indeed extensive. However, as a general rule, one of the main drawbacks of contractual protection is that contractual rights merely entitle a creditor to prove in the liquidation of the insolvent debtor, which generally results in recovery of little or none of the outstanding debt. In contrast, a creditor who has proprietary rights[6] is in a position to enforce them either outside of the liquidation altogether, or, at least, in priority to the claims of most of the general body of creditors. The acquisition of proprietary rights is, then, a very significant part of the protection of creditors in corporate finance. However, it should be noted that only adjusting creditors are able to protect themselves in this way.[7]

The ease of enforcement of a proprietary interest is also a significant advantage, whether or not the debtor is insolvent. If a creditor merely has a contractual right to payment, and the debtor will not pay, the creditor has to sue it for the debt. If the creditor obtains a judgment against the debtor, and the debtor still will not pay, the creditor has to execute that judgment, either by obtaining seizure and sale of goods by a sheriff or other enforcement officer,[8] or by obtaining an attachment of debts in third party proceedings,[9]

---

[5]   In this chapter the terms 'creditor' and 'lender' will be used when appropriate in the context. When specific situations of corporate finance are discussed the term 'lender' will be used, even where the transaction involves the retention or grant of an absolute interest. This is because the position of the financier in these cases is analogous, and is often compared to, that of a financier making a secured loan.

[6]   There is considerable academic discussion about the nature of property and proprietary rights. For a brief discussion, see M Bridge, *Personal Property Law*, 3rd edn (Oxford, Oxford University Press, 2002) 12–13. For more detailed discussion, see AW Scott 'The Nature of the Rights of the Cestui Que Trust' (1917) 17 *Columbia Law Review* 269; JW Harris, 'Trust, Power and Duty' (1971) 87 *Law Quarterly Review* 31; A Honoré, 'Trusts: The Inessentials' in J Getzler (ed), *Rationalising Property, Equity and Trusts* (Oxford, Oxford University Press, 2003) 1; P Birks, 'Personal Property: Proprietary Rights and Remedies' (2000) 11 *King's College Law Journal* 1; R Nolan, 'Equitable Property' (2006) 122 *Law Quarterly Review* 232; R Nolan, 'Understanding the Limits of Equitable Property' (2006) 1 *Journal of Equity* 18; B McFarlane, *The Structure of Property Law* (Oxford, Hart Publishing, 2008).

[7]   See 3.2.2.1.

[8]   County Courts Act 1984, Part V, and the Courts Act 2003, Sch 7, paras 6–11.

[9]   Civil Procedure Rules Part 72.

or by obtaining a charging order.[10] The creditor then becomes an execution creditor, and obtains proprietary rights against the company's assets, which will have priority over unsecured creditors on insolvency. A creditor who already has a proprietary interest is in a position (subject to contractual restriction) to enforce its interest on default even if the debtor is not insolvent, without going through this process. The threat of this is often enough to persuade a recalcitrant debtor to pay. Further, if the debtor is insolvent, the procedure for enforcing a proprietary interest is often quicker and easier than proving in a liquidation, although it should be noted that if the debtor goes into administration, there will be a moratorium on the enforcement of nearly all proprietary interests, whether absolute interests or security interests.[11]

There are other significant advantages in having proprietary rights, even outside insolvency. Such rights will usually enable the creditor to monitor what the company does with the assets over which it has such rights and, if the rights extend broadly enough, to monitor the entire operation of the company.[12] These monitoring rights are coupled with the right to control what the company does with the assets. The ability to control does depend, to some extent, on the nature of the proprietary rights. The holder of a fixed charge, for example, has to give consent each time a charged asset is disposed of by the company, while assets subject to a floating charge can be disposed of without the charge holder's consent. The 'ultimate weapon' of the floating charge holder, the ability to appoint an administrative receiver to manage the company if the charge holder's interests were threatened, has now been removed by statute[13] and so, arguably, the control power of the floating charge holder has been significantly diminished.[14] It can be said that the control power of a creditor with proprietary rights is analogous to that of an unsecured creditor with detailed financial covenants in its loan agreement, coupled with strict events of default and an effective termination and acceleration clause.[15] Security, though, gives a creditor an additional advantage, since the secured creditor is in a position to enforce against the secured assets on default without having to go through an execution process, and is also in a position to influence insolvency proceedings.[16] The extent to which a floating charge holder can still influence insolvency proceedings is discussed below.[17]

6.1.2 Absolute Interests

So far we have talked generically about proprietary rights. However, as will be recalled from the discussion in chapter three,[18] a distinction should be made between absolute

---

[10] Charging Orders Act 1979 and Civil Procedure Rules part 73.

[11] Insolvency Act 1986, Sch B1 para 43. See 6.5.3.

[12] It is, of course, possible for a creditor to have extensive contractual monitoring rights without a security interest, see pages 81–82 and 5.2.2.2.

[13] Insolvency Act 1986, s 72A, as inserted by the Enterprise Act 2002, s 250.

[14] This will be discussed in more detail later in the chapter, see pages 248–49, 260–61 and 285.

[15] Secured loan agreements often include such provisions as well: the control power of proprietary rights comes from the general law, but lenders prefer to have the details spelt out in the agreement in the interests of clarity and certainty.

[16] J Armour, 'The Law and Economics Debate About Secured Lending: Lessons for European Lawmaking?' (2008) 5 *European Company and Financial Law Review* 3, 8–9. Other advantages of security are discussed at 6.6.2.

[17] See pages 260–61.

[18] 3.3.1.1.

interests and security interests. Under English law, the difference between the two is not the purpose for which the interest is obtained, but the legal form of it. Many absolute interests are obtained by creditors, either by grant or by reservation,[19] for exactly the same purpose for which a creditor would obtain a security interest. Such interests are often called 'quasi-security' interests, and there is a strong argument that they should be treated, at least in some respects, such as the requirement of registration, in the same way as security interests. This argument will be considered later.[20] Other absolute interests are obtained by grant or reservation for other reasons, for example, an absolute interest in goods is granted to a buyer of those goods, and the absolute interest in goods which are hired to a company is retained by the hire company. Although the purpose of these transactions is not security for an advance (in the first example the grantee of the interest is a debtor of the company, though in the second the party reserving the interest is a creditor) the effect on the insolvency of the company is the same: the party who has the absolute interest can claim the asset irrespective of the insolvency.[21]

6.1.3   Distinctions in Relation to a Company's Assets

There are a number of important distinctions to bear in mind in relation to the types of assets which a company may have and over which a creditor can obtain a proprietary interest. The first distinction is between tangible and intangible property. Tangible property[22] has a corporeal existence, put briefly, they are things that can be touched. In the context of corporate assets, tangible assets will usually include equipment, raw materials (if the company is a manufacturing company) and stock in trade[23] (manufactured goods or goods bought by the company for resale or to hire to others). It also includes land, but, as will be explained below, land falls into a slightly different category. The most significant point about tangible assets is that they can be possessed, and that there is no necessary link between who has possession and who has another proprietary interest in those assets.[24] Although, in the absence of other evidence, possession is evidence of title, if there is contrary agreement, there is no problem in English law with the creation of non-possessory proprietary interests, whether absolute or security interests. This is critically important in relation to corporate financing, since, in relation to tangible assets, it is usually important for the company to have possession of the assets in which the creditor has a proprietary interest.[25] This is because those assets are used by the company in its business, either as equipment or plant, or as raw materials, or as stock which the company will sell.

---

[19]   3.3.1.1.

[20]   6.7.4.1.

[21]   The examples that are given are of absolute legal interests, but the same point applies to absolute equitable interests, in other words, to the interest of a beneficiary under a trust.

[22]   This can also be called choses in possession, see Bridge, *Personal Property Law*, n 6, 3, although this term does not include land.

[23]   This may also be called inventory.

[24]   Possession can be seen as a proprietary interest, see E McKendrick (ed), *Goode on Commercial Law*, 4th edn (London, LexisNexis UK, 2009) 45-49, W Swadling, 'The Proprietary Effect of a Hire of Goods' in N Palmer and E McKendrick (eds), *Interests in Goods*, 2nd edn (London, Lloyd's of London Press, 1998).

[25]   Recent empirical research shows that there is a strong correlation between the introduction of non-possessory security and an increase in bank lending in the transition economies of Eastern Europe: J Armour, 'The Law and Economics Debate About Secured Lending: Lessons for European Lawmaking?' (2008) 5 *European*

For many companies, most of their wealth will be found in their intangible assets. These are assets which cannot be possessed, and which form a residual category of assets once the category of tangible assets have been taken out.[26] Intangible assets are usually rights against other people, either a specific person (such as a right to sue that person for a sum of money, in other words, a debt, including cash in a bank account) or people in general (such as the various forms of intellectual property, namely trade marks, patents and copyright). In relation to this type of property there is clearly no problem about a split between who has possession and who has proprietary rights, but the question of how these rights are transferred does have to be addressed.[27] Sometimes it is difficult to categorise assets as tangible or intangible (for example, when software was stored on disks, the disk was said to be tangible, but the software intangible).[28] There is one case where there is a distinct overlap: where intangible rights are contained in a document so that they can be transferred by transfer of that document, much of the law governing tangible property applies to that document. In the context of corporate finance, negotiable instruments, such as bills of exchange and bearer bonds,[29] come into this category.

The next important distinction is between real and personal property. Real property is land, or rights to land, and personal property is everything else. This distinction is largely historical, and this is reflected in different rules for, for example, the creation of security interests in land and the transfer of rights to land. However, much of the difference is technical, and will not be addressed in this book except to the extent that it impinges on the actual use of proprietary rights in land as protection for creditors. Largely, creditors are very happy to obtain proprietary rights in land owned by a company. Land is seen as a safe asset, the value of which is reasonably stable (although the recent experience of sub-prime mortgages in the US and in the UK has shown that this is not always the case).

Another distinction, which has to be approached with considerable care, is between fixed and circulating assets. Fixed assets are assets which a company does not dispose of in the ordinary course of business, while circulating assets are acquired by the company with the aim of disposing of them in its course of business. The characteristics of circulating assets are that they are usually only in the ownership (and/or the possession) of the company for a relatively short time, they are disposed of for a greater price than the price at which they were acquired and more assets are acquired on a regular basis. Examples of circulating assets that fit this description are raw materials and stock in trade. However, receivables can also be seen as circulating assets. They fit a different part of the cycle, in that they include the profit obtained by disposal of tangible circulating assets (if this is the business of the company) but the company has them for a relatively short time, until they are paid. The company obtains new receivables on a regular basis. Many companies, of

---

Company and Financial Law Review 3, 15 citing R Haselmann, K Pistor and V Vig, 'How Law Affects Lending' (2006) *Columbia Law and Economics Working Paper* No 285 and M Afavuab and S Sharma, 'When Do Creditors Rights Work?', *World Bank Policy Research Working Paper* No 4296 (2007), 36 (Table 8).

[26] Bridge, n 6, 4. It should be pointed out that not all writers accept that intangible property is actually property, see A Pretto, *Boundaries of Personal Property: Shares and Sub-Shares* (Oxford, Hart Publishing, 2005).

[27] This question is addressed in Chapter 8.

[28] *St Albans City and District Council v International Computers Ltd* [1997] FSR 251. Sir Ian Glidewell considered that computer disks, as tangible media, qualified as 'goods' within the definition of Sale of Goods Act 1979, s 18 and Supply of Goods and Services Act 1982, s 61. A computer program, as intangible software, was not considered to be 'goods' (265–66).

[29] Discussed in 8.2.3.

course, have no circulating tangible assets: the business of the company may be providing services, or making loans, or creating intellectual property, but most have circulating receivables in some form or other.[30]

The distinction between fixed and circulating assets is not a hard and fast one, and can cause considerable confusion. First, most companies will dispose of their fixed assets from time to time, either to replace them or to raise money, or, because their operation has changed, so that the assets are no longer needed. Assets which are replaced regularly, such as information technology (IT) equipment, may be owned by the company for not much longer than circulating assets, as defined above (although if this is the case, most companies would use some form of hire to obtain such equipment rather than obtaining full ownership). Second, a particular type of asset, such as a car, may be a circulating asset for one company (a car sale or hire company) but a fixed asset for another company (a taxi company). Third, the structure of a transaction may affect whether a company owns one asset or many circulating assets. For example, a company may hire equipment to other companies either on a number of separate consecutive contracts, or under one long-term contract. The receivables stemming from this transaction, which is an asset of the leasing company, could in the first instance be seen as a long-term fixed asset and in the second instance be seen as circulating assets.[31] The points made in this paragraph need to be borne in mind when considering the distinction between fixed and floating charges, which is discussed below.[32] They show that there is a danger in characterising a charge merely by looking at the type of assets it covers.

A further, though related, distinction is between present and future assets. If a lender lends money generally to a company,[33] it will usually want proprietary rights not only in the assets presently owned by the company, but also in the assets to be owned by the company in the future. This is particularly true of circulating assets (they are constantly being disposed of, so eventually there will be nothing left of those assets which were 'present assets' at the time of the loan) but also of 'fixed' assets, since these will be replaced over time or new ones will be acquired. The ability for creditors to take proprietary rights over future assets is therefore critical to an effective corporate finance law, and the way in which it has been achieved in English law will be discussed in detail later on in this chapter.[34]

It should also be noted that security interests over financial collateral are treated somewhat differently from security interests over other kinds of assets. This stems from the Financial Collateral Directive,[35] enacted in the United Kingdom as the Financial Collateral Arrangements (No 2) Regulations 2003,[36] although some of the provisions largely reflect the preceding law. The Regulations disapply certain formality requirements (including registration)[37] and some insolvency provisions.[38] They also provide that certain provisions often found in such arrangements, such as a provision for close-out netting,[39] a

---

[30]   This is not necessarily true of investment companies.
[31]   See page 252.
[32]   6.3.3.3.2.
[33]   As opposed to lending merely for the acquisition of a particular asset.
[34]   6.3.2.1.
[35]   Directive 2002/47/EC.
[36]   SI 2003/3226.
[37]   Ibid, reg 4.
[38]   Ibid, reg 8 and 10.
[39]   See page 181.

right of use and a right of appropriation,[40] are effective.[41] The provisions of the Regulations apply both to absolute interests (called title transfer financial collateral arrangements) and security interests (called security financial collateral arrangements) over financial collateral. This covers both cash (money credited to an account) and financial instruments (both debt and equity securities). The Directive has recently been amended to include within financial collateral credit claims by credit institutions who grant credit in the form of a loan.[42]

A security financial collateral arrangement is one where the collateral holder has possession or control of the collateral.[43] The precise meaning of this is a matter of much debate[44] and the position in English law is uncertain. The issue is discussed in detail below.[45] The policy behind the special treatment of interests in financial collateral is to improve the efficiency and stability of the financial markets, by reducing administrative burdens, promoting certainty and harmonising the position in relation to financial collateral across the European Union.[46]

6.2   Absolute and Security Interests

6.2.1   What is a Security Interest?[47]

A security interest is a proprietary interest that A obtains in relation to property owned by B to secure an obligation owed to A by B or, more rarely, by C. In relation to corporate finance, this obligation is nearly always an obligation to pay money, and it is on this that this book will concentrate. Therefore, A can be called the creditor,[48] and B the debtor. There are various forms of security interest (pledge, lien, mortgage and charge[49]): the first

---

[40]   6.5.1.2.

[41]   Financial Collateral Arrangements (No 2) Regulations 2003 (SI 2003/3226), regs 12 and 16–18.

[42]   Directive 2009/44/EC. 'Credit institutions' bears the meaning it has in Article 4(1) of Directive 2006/48/EC, that is, deposit taking institutions such as banks. The Financial Collateral Arrangements (No 2) Regulations 2003 have not yet been amended as a result of this amendment to the Directive, but HM Treasury has recently published a consultation paper on implementation: 'A consultation on the implementation of EU Directive 2009/44/EC on settlement finality and financial collateral arrangements' (August 2010).

[43]   Financial Collateral Arrangements (No 2) Regulations 2003 (SI 2003/3226) reg 3.

[44]   Law Commission No 296, *Company Security Interests: Final Report*, Cm 6654 (2005) Ch 5; L Gullifer (ed), *Goode on Legal Problems of Credit and Security*, 4th edn (London, Sweet & Maxwell, 2008) 6–38; H Beale, M Bridge, L Gullifer and E Lomnicka, *The Law of Personal Property Security* (Oxford, Oxford University Press, 2007) 10.24–10.40; M Hughes, 'The Financial Collateral Regulations' (2006) 21 *Journal of International Banking and Financial Law* 64; D Turing, 'New Growth in the Financial Collateral Garden' (2005) 20 *Journal of International Banking and Financial Law* 4; A Zacaroli, 'Taking Security over Intermediated Securities: Chapter V of the UNIDROIT (Geneva) Convention on Intermediated Securities' in L Gullifer and J Payne (eds), *Intermediated Securities: Legal Problems and Practical Issues* (Oxford, Hart Publishing, 2010) 167.

[45]   6.4.1.1.

[46]   See the Recitals in the Financial Collateral Directive, especially recitals 3, 5, 9 and 10.

[47]   See Gullifer, *Goode on Legal Problems of Credit and Security*, n 44, 1–16–1–38.

[48]   The term 'creditor' will be used throughout this chapter rather than the term 'lender' which is used in other chapters.

[49]   *Re Cosslett (Contractors) Ltd* [1998] Ch 495, 508 (Millett LJ).

two are possessory and the second two non-possessory. They will be discussed in more detail below: the discussion of a security interest in this section is generalised and largely applies to all types of security interest.

In English law it is the location of ownership which determines whether an interest is absolute or by way of security (as mentioned above, the actual purpose of the transaction is largely irrelevant). Ownership is an illusive concept. There are a number of rights which a person may have in relation to a thing, including the right to use it, to possess it, to dispose of it and so on. An owner of a thing may have all these rights in relation to that thing, but it can also give away most of these rights, and still remain the owner.[50] For example, a seller of goods may retain title (ownership) in those goods when the buyer has possession and use of those goods and is permitted (by contract) to dispose of them as it wishes.[51] Ownership can therefore be seen as the residual right; what remains when other rights in respect of the thing have been given away. On this view, the location of ownership could be seen as a matter merely of the intentions of the parties and to have no relation to the rights that each party to the transaction actually has. However, as we shall see, the courts do not allow parties complete freedom of contract to decide on the location of ownership if it is felt that the 'reality' is truly otherwise.

If a creditor has a proprietary interest in assets which are still owned by the debtor, then that interest is a security interest if it is for the purpose of securing an obligation. There are various features, known as the indicia, or incidents, of security,[52] which, if present, indicate that an interest is a security interest and which, if an interest is a security interest, it is likely to have. The first is that if the asset in question is realised in order to meet the secured debt, and the amount realised is more than the debt, the debtor has a right to that surplus. The second is that if the amount realised is less than the secured debt, the debtor remains liable for the balance. The third is that the debtor is always able to rid the asset of the creditor's proprietary interest by paying the debt by means other than by the realisation of the asset: this is known as the 'right to redeem'. Another main feature of a security interest is that it can only be created by grant and not by reservation.[53] If a debtor grants an interest to a creditor, therefore, this can either be an absolute interest or a security interest: which it is will depend on whether the incidents of security are present. If a creditor reserves an interest, however, this can only be an absolute interest, even if the debtor is granted many of the rights which usually go with ownership such as the right to possess, the right to use and the right to dispose of the asset.

The importance of this discussion, which might be thought rather theoretical, is at least twofold. First, since there are a number of statutory and other consequences if an interest is a security interest, most notably that most security interests are required to be registered, creditors may attempt to avoid creating a security interest. This conclusion may be challenged by other creditors if the debtor is insolvent, and the courts on a number of occasions have had to decide whether a particular interest is absolute or by way of security.

---

[50]　Bridge, n 6, 30. A Honoré, 'Ownership' in A Guest, *Oxford Essays in Jurisprudence* (Oxford, Clarendon Press, 1961) 107, 126–28.

[51]　For further discussion and more examples, see Beale et al, *The Law of Personal Property Security* n 44, 2.08–2.11.

[52]　*Re George Inglefield* [1933] Ch 1, 27–28.

[53]　*McEntire v Crossley Brothers Ltd* [1895] AC 457, 462; *Clough Mill v Martin* [1985] 1 WLR 111, 116, 119, 120–21 (CA); *Armour v Thyssen Edelstahlwerke AG* [1991] 2 AC 339, 351–52 per Lord Keith, 354 per Lord Jauncey. See Beale et al, n 44, 2.22 for further discussion of this proposition.

This process of characterisation will be examined shortly. The second is that in many countries the technical differences between some absolute interests and security interests have been statutorily abolished, and all transactions which have the purpose of security are treated in the same way. Such systems will be examined later in this chapter in the course of a discussion as to whether the same route should be followed in England and Wales.[54]

6.2.2   The Characterisation of Interests as Absolute or Security Interests

Courts have to characterise in many contexts, usually where a concept appears in a statute. Particular consequences may flow from the characterisation of a contract (for example, as a contract of service or for services[55]), of a person (for example, whether a company is an enemy alien[56]), of a tangible asset (for example, whether it is a motor vehicle[57]) and so on. We are concerned here with the characterisation of a proprietary interest. This means that, possibly unlike other types of characterisation, the result of the court's decision is likely to affect not only the parties to the transaction by which the interest was created, but other parties as well.[58] In the context of security interests, this is usually because the debtor is insolvent, and the general creditors are competing for the scarce resources. Thus, if an interest is a security interest but is unenforceable against the liquidator as it has not been registered,[59] this increases the assets available for distribution to the general creditors. It should be noted that the courts have also had to characterise a charge as fixed or floating since, as will be recalled, preferential creditors, and now the prescribed part, are paid out of floating charge assets in priority to the floating chargee, but not out of fixed charge assets.[60] This characterisation process will be discussed later in the chapter.[61] It is important, however, to appreciate that where third parties are affected by the characterisation of an interest, there is an argument that the parties creating that interest cannot have total freedom of contract to label that interest what they will, so that they cannot have the benefits of a certain type of interest without suffering the detriment which follows from having that type of interest. This argument has been much more strongly endorsed by the courts in the context of the fixed/floating charge characterisation than in the context of absolute/security interest characterisation.

In relation to the absolute/security interest characterisation, the courts have identified two approaches, called the 'external' and the 'internal' approach by Staughton LJ in *Welsh Development Agency v Export Finance Co Ltd.*[62] In both approaches, the court has to

---

[54]   6.7.

[55]   This is of significance in considering whether a person employed under such a contract is an employee (contract of service) or an independent contractor (contract for services). This has a number of effects, including whether an employer is vicariously liable for that person's acts, see A Dugdale and M Jones (eds), *Clerk and Lindsell on Torts*, 19th edn (London, Sweet and Maxwell, 2006) 6.02.

[56]   *Daimler Company, Ltd v Continental Tyre and Rubber Company (Great Britain) Ltd* [1916] 2 AC 307.

[57]   Hire Purchase Act 1964, s 29(1).

[58]   This is not necessarily the case, for example, in theory characterisation may be necessary in order to determine whether a party is in breach of a negative pledge clause by creating a security interest. This would only affect the position between the parties to the negative pledge clause (see 5.2.1.1).

[59]   Companies Act 2006, s 860.

[60]   3.3.1.2.

[61]   6.3.3.3.2.

[62]   *Welsh Development Agency v Export Finance Co Ltd* [1992] BCLC 148, 186.

determine what rights and obligations are created by the contract: the labels put on the rights and obligations by the parties, and the label put on the interest created, are not determinative at this stage, although they can be take into account. The 'external approach' is where it is contended that the parties did not intend to create the rights and obligations which the contract purports to create.[63] If this is made out, the document is said to be a 'sham' and will be recharacterised or declared a nullity. In order to determine this question, the court can look at evidence external to the agreement itself, including evidence of what the parties have done after the date of the contract.[64] The 'internal approach' is where the court accepts that the parties did intend to create the rights and obligations created by the contract: the court then looks at those rights and obligations to decide what interest is, in law, actually created.[65] Since a finding of a sham involves a finding of at least some dishonesty, the courts are slow to come to this conclusion,[66] and, in the context of corporate finance, the internal approach is more likely to be followed. This should not mean, however, that the courts will never consider whether a commercial agreement is a sham: this point will be considered further in the context of the characterisation of charges as fixed or floating.[67] It should also be pointed out that doubt has been cast on the analysis of Staughton LJ by Lord Walker in *Re Spectrum Plus*[68] and by later commentators, particularly as to whether it covers all possible cases.[69] It is certainly true that parties can change the nature of an agreement after it has been made, by variation, waiver or estoppel, and such an analysis may be a half-way house between a court finding a sham and not recharacterising at all, where conduct after the contract was made is inconsistent with the nature of the agreement if the internal route is followed.[70]

There is a strong argument that the courts' approach to characterisation of security interests differs between the absolute/security interest cases and the fixed/floating charge cases. One reason is that there is a reasonably clear touchstone as to whether a charge is fixed or floating: this is whether the chargee has control over the charged assets,[71] whereas the position is much less clear in relation to the absolute/security interest cases. Another is

---

[63]   *Snook v London and West Riding Investments Ltd* [1967] 2 QB 786, 802C–E. The law on shams has developed in a number of different contexts, such as whether a tenancy agreement is a license. Leading cases include *Snook v London and West Riding Investments Ltd* [1967] 2 QB 786; *A-G Securities v Vaughan* [1990] 1 AC 417; *National Westminster Bank v Jones* [2001] 1 BCLC 98. There is considerable academic discussion of the concept of sham, see, for example, N Briggs, 'Sham Transactions' [2003] *Insolvency Lawyer* 7; A Berg, 'Recharacterization' (2001) 16 *Journal of International Banking and Financial Law* 346, J Vella, 'Sham Transactions' [2008] *Lloyd's Maritime and Commercial Law Quarterly* 488.

[64]   When construing a contract, the normal rule is that the court cannot look at evidence of post-contractual conduct, *James Miller & Partners Ltd v Whitworth Street Estates (Manchester) Ltd* [1970] AC 583, 603, 611, 614. This issue is discussed in more detail below at page 255 in the context of the characterisation of a charge as fixed or floating.

[65]   This is the approach advocated in relation to the fixed/floating charge characterisation by Lord Millett in *Re Brumark Investments* Ltd [2001] 2 AC 710, [32], and approved by the House of Lords in *Re Spectrum Plus Ltd (In Liquidation)* [2005] 2 AC 68 (see Lord Walker at [141]).

[66]   *National Westminster Bank v Jones* [2001] 1 BCLC 98, [46] per Neuberger J.

[67]   See page 255.

[68]   [2005] 2 AC 680, [160].

[69]   S Atherton and R Mokal, 'Charges over Chattels: Issues in the Fixed/floating Jurisprudence' (2005) 26 *Company Lawyer* 10; A Berg, 'The Cuckoo in the Nest of Corporate Insolvency: some Aspects of the Spectrum Case' [2006] *Journal of Banking Law* 47.

[70]   This approach is problematic in the context of fixed and floating charges, however, because of Insolvency Act 1986, s 251 which provides that the Insolvency Act consequences of a charge being floating apply to the charge 'as created', see page 255.

[71]   6.3.3.3.2. This touchstone may, of course, be difficult to apply in practice.

that even if a charge which is labelled fixed is recharacterised as floating, the consequences for the chargee (that priority is ceded to the liquidator's costs, the preferential creditors and the prescribed part) are not as drastic as where an unregistered 'absolute' interest is recharacterised as a security interest (the creditor becomes unsecured). The result appears to be that in the latter cases, the courts tend to ask the question whether the rights and obligations created are consistent with the label put on the transaction by the parties,[72] rather than the more open question 'what is the correct legal label to put on the rights and obligations created in this agreement?' This is despite the fact that the rhetoric of the courts in the absolute/security interest cases is that they are looking at the substance and not the form of the agreement.[73] This, of course, does not mean the economic substance: it is quite clear that under English law the parties can choose whatever legal form they wish to achieve an economic result.[74]

6.2.3   Reasons for Choosing a Structure based on an Absolute or a Security Interest

Before discussing the policy considerations that apply to the absolute/security interest characterisation process, we should consider why companies, and their lenders, choose a structure involving retention or grant of an absolute interest rather than a security interest. One reason which applies to all such structures is that there is no registration requirement under section 860 of the Companies Act 2006 in relation to absolute interests. Other reasons are more transaction specific. In relation to devices based on retention of title, these usually give the lender priority over secured creditors.[75] Certain structures, such as hire purchase arrangements,[76] also give the lender priority over bona fide purchasers of the asset. The lender may be interested in having the surplus value in the asset, for example this is the case in an operating lease.[77] A lender may perceive that an absolute interest is a 'stronger' interest than a security interest.[78] Where the company has already borrowed on terms which include a negative pledge clause, a transaction involving an absolute interest may not be in breach of this clause.[79] A lender may prefer to finance receivables by factoring or invoice discounting as it is now much more difficult to create a fixed charge over receivables because of the House of Lords decision in *Re Spectrum Plus*,[80] and to take a floating charge is less attractive for the reasons discussed in chapter three and

---

[72]   *Orion Finance Ltd v Crown Financial Management Ltd (No 1)* [1996] BCC 621, 625–26.

[73]   *McEntire v Crossley* [1895] AC 457, 462; *Helby v Matthews* [1895] AC 471, 475; *In re George Inglefield Ltd* [1933] Ch 1, 27. For an attack on that rhetoric, see A Berg, 'Recharacterisation after Enron' [2003] *Journal of Business Law* 205, 237.

[74]   *Re Polly Peck International* plc [1996] BCC 486, 495; *Chow Yoong Hong v Choong Fah Rubber Manufactory* [1962] AC 209, 216–17; *Beconwood Securities Pty Ltd v Australia and New Zealand Banking Group Limited* [2008] FCA 594, [53].

[75]   See page 274; *Welsh Development Agency v Export Finance Co Ltd* [1992] BCC 270, 300G.

[76]   Except in relation to motor vehicles, see Hire Purchase Act 1964, Part III.

[77]   Some finance lessors also take part of their return in the form of a share in the sale proceeds of the asset at the end of the lease, see Inland Revenue, Finance Leasing Manual 6.44.

[78]   See, for example, 5.05 ibid, 'Lessors are therefore more prepared to lend to less solid businesses and, perhaps, to lend cheaper than ordinary lenders (even leaving aside tax considerations)'.

[79]   See *Welsh Development Agency v Exfinco* [1992] BCLC 148, 154. Clauses, however, are usually now drafted widely enough to catch absolute interests, see page 161.

[80]   J Armour, 'Should we Redistribute in Insolvency?' in J Getzler and J Payne (eds), *Company Charges: Spectrum and Beyond* (Oxford, Oxford University Press, 2006).

below.[81] Security interests cannot be enforced by a lender if the borrower is in adminis-tration without the permission of the administrator or the leave of the court.[82] The same applies to certain absolute interests, such as those created by retention of title.[83] However, the 'enforcement' of other absolute interests is free of these restrictions, which may make them more attractive to certain lenders.

For both parties there may be tax advantages, although these have been steadily whittled away by the Inland Revenue.[84] These depend on whether the criteria in the relevant legislation are fulfilled. Whether the interest created is absolute or by way of security either is irrelevant or only partially relevant.

From the borrower's point of view, certain structures, such as securitisation, are attractive in that assets are removed from the borrower's balance sheet, since an absolute interest is granted to the lender. This may improve the borrower's debt to equity ratio,[85] or, in the case of a bank or financial institution, affect how much capital has to be retained to comply with capital adequacy requirements.[86] However, like tax, accounting and capital adequacy are governed by particular and strict rules and are not specifically dependent upon the nature of the transaction. For example, the International Accounting Standard 39 'de-recognises' assets if the originator has 'no continuing involvement' in them, and this can be the case either if there is a true sale or if there is a 'pass-through' arrangement, which need not be a true sale.[87] Of course, it may be that a structure involving an absolute interest may be the only way a lender is prepared to lend, or the terms, such as the rate of interest, may be more attractive than borrowing on security. Such a structure may be riskier for a borrower than a straight loan on security. Depending on the terms of the transaction, the borrower may lose any surplus value in the asset if it defaults. Further, even if there is a contractual obligation on the lender to repay any surplus to the borrower, the borrower takes the credit risk of the lender in relation to this, and if the lender becomes insolvent, the borrower will only have an unsecured claim.[88] In contrast, where a secured creditor enforces security it holds any surplus value on trust for the borrower.

6.2.4   Policy Considerations

The process of recharacterisation is not a merely technical one: there are significant policy issues to be considered. On one hand there is the policy of freedom of contract: this has to

---

[81]   See page 257.

[82]   Insolvency Act 1986, Sch B1 para 43(2).

[83]   Insolvency Act 1986, Sch B1 para 43(3) is in similar terms to para 43(2) and applies to hire purchaser agreements. A hire purchase agreement is defined in Sch B1 para 111(1) as including 'a conditional sale agreement, a chattel leasing agreement and a retention of title agreement'.

[84]   For example, a finance lease is much less advantageous from a tax point of view than it used to be, see page 41 above.

[85]   P Wood, *Project Finance, Securitisations, Subordinated Debt,* 2nd edn (London, Sweet & Maxwell, 2007) 6.010.

[86]   See pages 25–26.

[87]   Implemented in the UK by FRS 26 (Financial Reporting Standard). Note also that the economic effects of other receivables financing transactions such as invoice discounting must be reflected in accounts, see FRS 5.

[88]   This risk was graphically experienced by those who had provided collateral to Lehman Brothers for financial transactions under 'title transfer collateral arrangements' whereby an absolute interest in collateral was transferred to Lehman as prime broker, with only a contractual right to its return, or who gave Lehman a 'right of use' of collateral provided as security. See, for example, M Yates, 'Custody, Prime Brokerage and Right of Use: a Problematic Coalition?' (2010) 25 *Journal of International Banking and Financial Law* 397.

be the default position in a commercial contract unless there is any reason to qualify it. Of course, freedom of contract cannot permit parties to create contracts which are internally inconsistent, or to put a label on an interest which is completely inappropriate. Having said this, where only the parties to the contract are affected, they are (sometimes) allowed to agree that black is white,[89] but the position is different when third parties are affected. Against the policy of freedom of contract has to be weighed a policy in favour of publicity of interests where those interests are not readily apparent by external examination. Those dealing with companies should have a simple means of discovering their true financial state, and this includes knowing whether the assets they appear to have are encumbered by security interests or actually belong to other parties. At present, however, only security interests are registrable, and the fact that assets which appear to belong to the company actually belong to a financier is not. This distinction will be discussed in detail below,[90] but it is important to note at present that where an English court characterises an interest as absolute this means that it is not registrable, and is therefore 'hidden'.[91] It should be remembered, however, that there are other ways of discovering the state of a company's finances than consulting the Company Charges Register: the company produces annual accounts which are public,[92] and if a company has sold an asset, such as its receivables, in theory the balance sheet will show that the company's assets are reduced. However, the assets will be increased by the purchase price obtained for the receivables. Often this cash will be used to pay other liabilities, so that these will reduce (and the assets will also reduce). Thus, although the balance sheet will reflect the transaction, it may not be obvious to those looking at it that the receivables have been sold.[93] If publicity of interests is considered important, it can be argued that companies should not be able to 'hide' interests by entering into transactions which create absolute interests rather than security interests, when the purposes are virtually identical.

One argument that is made in relation to characterisation of fixed and floating charges is that the very benefit parties want when they take a floating charge, namely the ability to take a wide-ranging charge over circulating assets of the company, is the reason for the statutory consequences which chargees seek to avoid by attempting to create a fixed charge.[94] Thus, a policy justification for recharacterisation is that lenders cannot have the benefit without having the statutory detriment which Parliament has decided goes with it. However, it is not so clear that this argument can be applied to the sale/charge characterisation. It can be argued that the legislature has decided what interests are registrable, and provided that the parties have actually created an absolute interest, the policy of publicity

---

[89] One example of this is a non-reliance clause in a contract, where both parties know that there actually was reliance. That the clause is effective can be explained on the basis of estoppel by convention, see J Cartright, 'Excluding Liability for Misrepresentation' in A Burrows and E Peel (eds), *Contract Terms* (Oxford, Oxford University Press, 2007) 224–25; A Trukhtanov, 'Misrepresentation: Acknowledgement of Non-reliance as Defence' [2009] *Law Quarterly Review* 648; *Peekay Intermark Ltd v Australia and New Zealand Banking Group Ltd* [2006] EWCA Civ 386; [2006] 2 Lloyd's Rep 511; *JP Morgan Chase v Springwell Navigation Corp* [2008] EWHC (Comm) 1186; *Trident Turboprop (Dublin) Ltd v First Flight Couriers Ltd* [2008] EWHC 1686 (Comm); affirmed on appeal without discussion of the point, [2009] EWCA Civ 290; [2009] 1 Lloyd's Rep 702. See also page 364.

[90] 6.4.1 and 6.7.

[91] *Associated Alloys Pty Ltd v ACN 001 452 106 Pty Ltd* (2000) 202 CLR 588, [95] (HC Aust).

[92] See 10.3.1. Note that listed companies are required to produce more frequent reports (see 10.3.1.2).

[93] Also balance sheets are historic so do not necessarily give an up to date picture.

[94] See *Re Spectrum Plus* [2005] 2 AC 680, [111], [141].

should not affect characterisation: it is up to the legislature to further this policy by widening the category of registrable interests, not the courts by recharacterising interests.[95]

One other policy consideration is that many of the financing transactions which operate on the basis of a grant or reservation of an absolute interest are in forms that are used extensively on a daily basis in the financial world, and which account for many billions of pounds worth of lending every year. Thus the recharacterisation of a 'true sale' securitisation[96] or an invoice discounting transaction as a registrable security interest would have very widespread consequences. However, the strength of this argument should be doubted. The courts should not determine the boundaries of concepts on the basis of the damage done or not done to the financing industry by their decisions. Therefore, if there is serious concern, the better course may be express legislation to deal with the problem, for example, a 'safe harbour' for securitisations,[97] or a reform of the registration requirements.[98]

6.2.5   The Detailed Process of Characterisation[99]

6.2.5.1   Grant and Grant-back

The structure of sale and lease-back[100] constitutes a grant by the company of an absolute interest in an asset to the lender, and a grant-back by the lender of a possessory interest to the company. The economic purpose of the transaction is (virtually) always for the lender to provide finance to the borrower. However, as we have seen the economic purpose is irrelevant to the legal process of characterisation. In relation to this structure, the court will look at the transaction as a whole;[101] this is important since if the constituent parts were examined separately it could not be a secured transaction, since the grant-back involves the retention of an absolute interest and cannot be a security interest.[102] In fact, the courts have only recharacterised such agreements as secured loans in what appear to be sham cases,[103] and where the borrower genuinely intends to enter into a sale and

[95]   *McEntire v Crossley Brothers* [1895] AC 457, 466; *Helby v Matthews* [1895] AC 471, 477; *Associated Alloys Pty Ltd v ACN 001 452 106 Pty Ltd* (2000) 202 CLR 588, [49]–[51].

[96]   See 8.3.3.

[97]   V Seldam, 'Recharacterisation in "True Sale" Securitisations: The "Substance Over Form" Delusion' [2006] *Journal of Business Law* 637, 643.

[98]   See 6.7 below.

[99]   In this section the party providing the finance is called the 'lender' and the company receiving the finance is called the 'borrower' despite the form of the transaction. This is to aid comparison with structures involving 'true' security interests. Of course, if the transaction is not recharacterised as a secured loan, the parties are not lenders and borrowers in law.

[100]   Described above at 2.3.4.3.1.

[101]   *Re Curtain Dream Ltd* [1990] BCLC 925, 934; See also the approach of the Court of Appeal in *Welsh Development Agency v Export Finance Co Ltd* [1992] BCLC 148, 187–88 per Staughton LJ; *In re Bond Worth* [1980] Ch 228, 248; *Orion Finance Ltd v Crown Financial Management Ltd* [1996] 2 BCLC 78, 85; *Ex p Odell* (1878) 10 Ch D 76, 85; *Beckett v Tower Assets* [1891] 1 QB 638, 646.

[102]   See page 226.

[103]   *Cochrane v Matthews* (1878) 10 Ch D 80; *Re Watson* (1890) 25 QBD 27; *Madell v Thomas* [1891] 1 QB 230; *British Railway Traffic & Electric Co v Jones* (1931) 40 Lloyd's Rep 281; *Polsky v S and A Services* [1951] 1 All ER 185; *North Western Central Wagon Finance Co Ltd v Brailsford* [1962] 1 WLR 1288.

lease-back the courts have upheld the structure.[104] Where, however, a transaction was completely circular (a sale and sale-back) the court did recharacterise it as a secured loan.[105] This is generally seen as a one-off case depending on some (rather unclear) terms in the agreement. The fact that there was an obligation to repurchase the same assets as were sold to the financier meant that there was exact mutuality.[106] It can be argued that in other sale and sale-back transactions, such as repos and securities lending transactions, the obligation is to transfer equivalent securities and so the exact mutuality is not present.[107]

6.2.5.2   Grant

There are at least two structures which fall into the category of grant. One is the very common receivables financing transaction.[108] The other is the sale of goods to a financier who then sells as an undisclosed agent.[109] Since the relevant interest is granted to the lender, it can potentially be either absolute or by way of security.[110] One might, then, have thought that the courts would approach characterisation by looking at the rights and obligations created and deciding whether they created an absolute or a security interest. In fact, in the case of both structures, the courts have looked at the legal form of the transaction (as creating an absolute interest) and then looked to see if the exact terms of the agreement are consistent with that form. The difference is, perhaps, subtle but has had the effect that no agreement in this category has actually been recharacterised by the courts, despite the fact that in both structures there are provisions which, looked at from a different perspective, could be seen as indicia of security.[111]

In a receivables financing transaction, for example, the sale of the receivables is often with recourse, so that the credit risk of non-payment by the debtors is on the borrower and not the lender.[112] This might be seen as indicative of the second of the indicia of security discussed above: that the borrower is always liable for the balance if the 'security' does not realise enough to repay the 'loan'. However, the courts have taken the view that this does not convert a contract expressed to be a sale into a charge.[113] Further, a

---

[104]   *Yorkshire Railway Wagon Co v Maclure* (1882) 21 Ch D 309. The company was legally advised and it was clear 'that the advisers of the railway company perfectly well knew what they were doing' (per Jessel MR 313). See also *Staffs Motor Guarantee v British Wagon Co Ltd* [1934] 2 KB 305.

[105]   *Re Curtain Dream Ltd* [1990] BCLC 925.

[106]   Ibid, 939.

[107]   This was one of the reasons given by Finkelstein J for not recharacterising a securities lending transaction as a mortgage in *Beconwood Securities Pty Ltd v Australia and New Zealand Banking Group Limited* [2008] FCA 594, [50]. However, if it is right that shares and bonds are fractional interests (see page 321 and Gullifer, n 44, 6.09) this may need some qualification, G Tolhurst, 'Securities Lending in Australia' (2009) 1 *Corporate Rescue and Insolvency* 22. Another way of looking at the issue, however, is that although shares and bonds are fractional interests so that there is no identification problem in relation to a declaration of trust, different 'parcels' of shares or bonds acquire a different history so that they can be seen as different 'things' so that they can be seen as 'equivalent' rather than the 'same'. See Gullifer, n 44, 6.09.

[108]   2.3.4.1.

[109]   *Welsh Development Agency v Export Finance Co Ltd* [1992] BCLC 148; [1992] BCC 270.

[110]   See page 226 above.

[111]   See page 226 above.

[112]   This is done by the borrower guaranteeing the debts, or agreeing to repurchase debts which are not paid within a certain period.

[113]   *Lloyds & Scottish Finance Ltd v Cyril Lord Carpets Sales Ltd* [1992] BCLC 609, 616. Lord Wilberforce explained the provision by saying that a purchaser can provide for 'security' to make sure he gets what he bargained for without altering the 'nature of the contract' or converting it into a charge. The recourse provisions are often bolstered by provision for periodic payments from the seller to the purchaser, paid by direct debit or similar arrangements, instead of the seller accounting to the purchaser as and when the receivables are paid. The

receivables financing agreement often provides for the borrower to keep any surplus generated by the debtors over and above the original purchase price and the discount charge, which resembles the first indicia of security.[114] Despite this, the courts have held that this provision is consistent with a sale rather than a charge.[115] Receivables financing has also increased hugely in popularity since the *Spectrum* decision[116] in order to avoid the danger of any security interest being characterised as a floating charge. If the transaction creates an absolute interest there is no danger of such characterisation, and so financiers would clearly wish to rely on the approach of the courts in a sale/charge characterisation as discussed above, and have the interest characterised as absolute, rather than be involved in a fixed/floating charge characterisation dispute.

The other structure, where goods are sold to a financier and then sold by the company as undisclosed agent, was considered in the important case of *Welsh Development Agency v Export Finance Co Ltd*[117] The Court of Appeal again took the view that freedom of contract was to be upheld, and features which might have been thought to indicate security, such as a 'right of redemption', were said not to be inconsistent with the structure of the transaction by the parties as a sale.[118]

6.2.5.3   *Retention of Title*

Structures such as credit sales on retention of title terms,[119] hire purchase[120] and conditional sale agreements[121] and finance leases[122] all depend on the device of retaining title. Since a security interest cannot be created by the retention (as opposed to the grant) of title, such transactions will not be recharacterised as creating a security interest even if they include terms which otherwise would appear to be indications of security, such as a right to the surplus.[123] However, many contracts of sale on retention of title terms also provide that the seller shall 'retain' title in any products made with the goods sold, or in any proceeds of resale. Whether such a provision creates an absolute or a security interest

---

courts have also said that this method of payment is not inconsistent with a charge, even though it closely resembles repayment of a loan (and interest) by instalments; *Olds Discount Co Ltd v John Playfair Ltd* [1938] 3 All ER 275, 280.

[114]   See page 226.

[115]   *In re George Inglefield Ltd* [1933] Ch 1, 20; *Olds Discount Co Ltd, v John Playfair Ltd* [1938] 3 All ER 275, 276–77.

[116]   J Armour, 'Should we Redistribute in Insolvency?' n 80. S Frisby, 'In re Spectrum Plus – Less a Bang than a Whimper' in P Omar (ed), *International Insolvency Law – Themes and Perspectives* (Aldershot, Ashgate Publishing Ltd, 2008). For discussion of the *Spectrum* decision see 6.3.3.3.2 below.

[117]   [1992] BCLC 148. See also *In re Lovegrove* [1935] Ch 464; *Palette Shoes Pty Ltd v Krohn* (1937) 58 CLR 1 (HC Aust).

[118]   [1992] BCLC 148, 168–69, 189. Indeed, Dillon LJ says that the parties were 'entitled to choose' how to raise finance, and Ralph Gibson LJ says that 'If any mischief arising from off balance sheet financing is judged to be serious it could be prohibited by legislation'.

[119]   2.3.4.3.4.

[120]   See page 40.

[121]   See page 41.

[122]   See pages 40–41.

[123]   See *Clough Mill v Martin* [1985] 1 WLR 111, 117 where there was held to be an obligation to account and *McEntire v Crossley* [1895] AC 457, 465 per Lord Herschell. In that case the same effect was specifically provided for in the contract. See also the agreement in *Kinloch Damph Ltd v Nordvik Salmon Farms Ltd* (1999) Outer House Case, June 30, 1999, where the seller's right to repossess was limited to the amount outstanding under the contract. Similar reasoning applies where the contract provides that title will not pass until all monies due from the buyer to the seller have been paid.

in the products or proceeds depends on the precise terms of the contract in question, but certain general propositions can be stated. Let us first consider products. If the product is a new thing,[124] then it is initially owned by the producer (the buyer). The actual effect of the 'retention' provision is that the buyer grants an interest in the product to the seller. Being by grant, that interest can be either an absolute or a security interest. However, it is likely that the parties intended the buyer to have the right to any surplus value over and above the purchase price, and to be able to pay the purchase price from any source of finance, after which it will own the product outright. These are the first and third indicia of security mentioned above,[125] and therefore the transaction will be characterised as a security interest.[126]

Next we will consider a provision that the seller 'retains' an interest in the proceeds of a sub-sale. It is even clearer here that the seller's interest is by grant from the buyer, since the sub-buyer clearly intends to transfer the legal interest in the proceeds to the buyer. Therefore, the test is once again whether the indicia of security are present. Since the sub-sale is likely to be at a profit, the buyer will be entitled to any surplus, and will be able to pay the seller's purchase price from other funds, thus 'redeeming' the sub-sale proceeds: thus the two indicia of security are present. The seller's interest in the proceeds will be recharacterised as a charge.[127] One case in which the opposite result was reached is the Australian case of *Associated Alloys Pty Ltd v ACN 001 452 106 Pty Limited*.[128] In that case, the purchase price was expressed to be payable by a trust which arose over the proceeds of the sub-sale as soon as they were received, but the trust only extended to the amount of the purchase price due. It is unlikely that this result would be achieved in other cases, since the courts would probably not interpret a contract of sale to have the effect that the buyer could pay the seller only out of the proceeds of sale (as opposed to any other source of payment).

6.2.5.4 *Quistclose Trusts*

A device which has sometimes been said to be a security interest is that under a 'Quistclose' trust.[129] This device is sometimes used to protect a lender against the insolvency of a borrower where money is lent for a specific purpose. The security-like purpose of the device was noted by Lord Millett in *Twinsectra Ltd v Yardley*, where he commented on its similarity to a retention of title clause, in that the lender 'enables the borrower to have recourse to the lender's money for a particular purpose without entrenching on the lender's property rights more than necessary to enable the purpose to be achieved'.[130] Where a lender makes it clear that money is lent for a specific purpose, the courts are likely to hold that the borrower holds the money on resulting trust for the

---

[124]   That is, the goods sold cannot be removed from the product: where this is the case then title continues to be retained, see *Hendy Lennox (Industrial Engines) Ltd v Grahame Puttick Ltd* [1984] 1 WLR 485.

[125]   Page 226.

[126]   See, for example, *Clough Mill v Martin* [1985] 1 WLR 111; *Ian Chisholm Textiles v Griffiths* [1994] 2 BCLC 291; *Modelboard Ltd v Outer Box Ltd* [1993] BCLC 623.

[127]   *E Pfeiffer Weinkellerei-Weineinkauf GmbH & Co v Arbuthnot Factors Ltd* [1988] 1 WLR 150; *Tatung (UK) Ltd v Galex Telesure Ltd* (1988) 5 BCC 325; *Compaq Computers Ltd v Abercorn Group Ltd* [1993] BCLC 602.

[128]   [2000] 202 CLR 588, [34] discussed above at page 214.

[129]   So called because this form of trust was first recognised in *Barclays Bank Ltd v Quistclose Investments Ltd* [1970] AC 567. See also M Bridge, 'The Quistclose Trust in a World of Secured Transactions' [1992] *Oxford Journal of Legal Studies* 383.

[130]   [2002] 2 AC 164, [81].

lender, in circumstances that the lender's beneficial interest is qualified by a power of the borrower to use the money for the specified purpose. If the purpose fails, the power disappears and the money is held on the original unqualified resulting trust.[131] It will be seen that on this analysis, the trust cannot be said to be a security interest, as there is no separate obligation to be secured: the borrower's obligation to pay the money to the lender comes from the trust itself.[132] A different analysis may apply where the trust is not created by the payment from the lender to the borrower, but is declared by the borrower after the payment has been made (in order to protect the lender). This is more analogous to the extended reservation of title cases discussed above, since the lender's interest is granted by the borrower, and also appears to secure a separate and pre-existing obligation to repay.[133]

6.3 Types of Security Interests

6.3.1 Introduction

This section is concerned solely with 'true' security interests, that is, those interests characterised in English law as security interests. There are four types of consensual security interests, which can be said to form a *numerus clausus* so that no new forms of security interest will be recognised. These are the pledge, the contractual lien, the mortgage and the charge.[134] There are also other variants of security interest which arise by operation of law, for example, the possessory lien and the equitable lien, but these will not be considered further here.[135] The pledge and the contractual lien are both possessory interests. The latter arises where possession is given for a purpose other than security (such as storage), and is really a contractual extension of the possessory lien, giving security for sums due from the owner to the party in possession. The pledge is created when possession of goods is given to the pledgee for the purpose of securing an obligation owed by the pledgor to the pledge. Pledges and liens are relatively little used in corporate finance,[136] although the pledge of documents of title to goods is important in the financing of international trade,[137] and the pledge of negotiable instruments is of

---

[131]   Ibid, [100]. However, this analysis has been doubted by some academics see eg R Chambers, *Resulting Trusts* (Oxford, Oxford University Press, 1997) ch 3; see generally W Swadling (ed), *The Quistclose Trust: Critical Essays* (Oxford, Hart Publishing, 2004).

[132]   Beale et al, n 44, 6.143. See J Glister, 'Trusts as Quasi-Securities? The Law Commission's Proposals for the Registration of Security Interests' [2004] *Lloyd's Maritime and Commercial Law Quarterly* 460; Law Commission Consultative Paper No 164, *Registration of Security Interests: Company Charges and Property other than Land* (July 2002), Part VII.

[133]   Beale et al, n 44, 6.145.

[134]   *Re Cosslett (Contractors) Ltd* [1998] Ch 495, 508.

[135]   For further discussion of these interests see Beale et al, n 44, 3.57–3.76 and 4.105–4.128.

[136]   The amount secured by a lien is rarely significant, but a lien can arise over goods of a very high value, such as aircraft, see *Bristol Airport plc v Powdrill* [1990] Ch 744.

[137]   See Beale et al, n 44, 3.26–3.32; for a detailed discussion, see R Jack, A Malek and D Quest, *Documentary Credits*, 3rd edn (London, Butterworths, 2001) ch 11 and R King, *Gutteridge and Megrah's Law of Bankers' Commercial Credits*, 8th edn (London, Europa, 2001) ch 8.

considerable importance where debt instruments are in negotiable form.[138] Since in English law pledges are only created by the transfer of possession, there cannot be a pledge of an intangible that is not a documentary intangible, such as a registered share.[139] The term 'pledge' is often used in practice in relation to financial collateral: this is a non-technical use meaning 'security interest'.

The other two types of security interest, mortgage and charge, are non-possessory. This makes them far more suitable for most kinds of secured lending. First, since many corporate assets are intangibles, this is the only type of security interest that can be taken over them.[140] Second, even over tangible assets, a non-possessory security interest allows the borrower to have the use of the assets and yet use them as security. For most tangible assets, including land, this is vital.[141]

6.3.2   Non-possessory Security Interests

6.3.2.1   *Security over Future Property*

The ability to take security over future property of a company is critical for a lender. If this were not possible, the lender's security would be limited to the assets the borrower had at the time of the loan, and each new asset acquired would necessitate a new security agreement.[142] Of course, there are some situations where a security interest will be limited to assets owned by the borrower at the time of the loan, for example, a security interest over a particular item to secure money advanced to finance that particular purchase. However, the bulk of security interests are more general than this, and even fixed security interests (where the consent of the security holder is required for disposal of any assets) would normally cover future assets since even 'fixed' assets such as land or equipment are usually replaced from time to time.[143] Where a security interest is floating, so that the secured assets can be disposed of without the consent of the security holder, the need for the security interest to cover future property is self evident.

It has for many years been straightforward to create a security interest over future assets under English law.[144] However, this is not possible under common law. At law it is only possible to transfer assets which exist at the time of transfer. An agreement can be made at law to transfer future assets, but there will only be an actual transfer when there is a new act of transfer, such as the taking of possession.[145] However, in equity an agreement to transfer future assets will have the effect that the assets are transferred automatically

---

[138]   For a discussion of the form in which debt securities are now usually held, see pages 327–28. Negotiable instruments are discussed below at 8.2.3.

[139]   Beale et al, n 44, 10.12–10.13; Gullifer, n 44, 1–47.

[140]   See above page 223.

[141]   See above page 222.

[142]   This is one of the reasons why pledges are of such limited use in corporate finance.

[143]   See above page 224.

[144]   This has not been the case in the past in other jurisdictions. For example, in France, assets subject to security interests had to be specifically described, which limited the ability of the borrower to pledge its future receivables. The position in France in relation to receivables has now been amended by the new book IV of the Code Civil (2006), especially art 2355. Denmark recently amended its law (January 2006) so that security over some future assets, especially receivables, could be created. In Slovakia, reform of the law in 2002 allowed future assets to be used as security.

[145]   *Robinson v Macdonnell* (1816) 5 M & S 228; *Holroyd v Marshall* (1861–62) 10 HL Cas 191, 210–11 per Lord Westbury; WJ Gough, *Company Charges*, 2nd edn (London, Butterworths, 1996) 65–68.

without a future act. This was confirmed in the nineteenth century case of *Holroyd v Marshall*.[146] The basis for this is the doctrine that 'equity considers as done that which ought to be done',[147] coupled with the fact that equity would specifically enforce the agreement to transfer.[148] This does not mean, however, that all the criteria for specific performance must be fulfilled: that would be overly restrictive and technical.[149] It is necessary, however, for the consideration for the transfer to be executed, which will usually mean that at least some of the loan must have been advanced, and that the assets in question be identifiable. The latter criterion can be fulfilled by a general description such as 'all the book debts due and owing or which may during the continuance of this security become due and owing to the said mortgagor'.[150]

Another remarkable feature of the *Holroyd v Marshall* doctrine is that it has the effect that the security interest arises at the time that it is created, rather than at the time at which each asset is acquired. Of course, this does not tell the whole story, since obviously a secured lender cannot have a proprietary interest in an asset until it is acquired by the borrower: it is therefore often said that the security interest does not 'attach' to the asset until it is acquired. However, for priority purposes at least, once the asset is acquired the security interest is treated as having arisen at the time it was created.[151] This is very important, since if the priority point in relation to each asset was the date on which it was acquired, this would lead to considerable complexity.[152]

On this reasoning, where a security interest covers present and future assets, it is clearly a valid security interest at the time of creation, which attaches to the future assets as they are acquired by the borrower. However, if the security interest only covers future assets, or when the borrower owns no assets falling within the description at the time of creation, the question arises as to whether the lender has any sort of security interest at that time. There seems little doubt that the effect of *Holroyd v Marshall* in this situation is that as soon as an asset falling within the description is acquired by the borrower the security interest immediately attaches to that asset in the same way as if a security interest over present and future assets had been created. Before that moment, though, the lender can have no interest in that particular asset.[153] But does the secured lender have some sort of inchoate security interest dating from the time when the security agreement is executed?

The question could be said to be hypothetical, in that until an asset is acquired, no secured lender would wish or be able to enforce the security interest, and so the nature of it, or whether it exists at all, is irrelevant. It is not irrelevant, however, once assets are acquired. The date of the creation of the security interest is relevant for a number of reasons. First, it may affect priority. Second, if it falls within section 860 of the Companies Act it is necessary to register it within 21 days of creation. Third, some event may occur between the date of the execution of the document creating the security interest and when the borrower first acquires any assets, which would affect certain types of rights and not

---

[146]   (1862) 10 HL Cas 191.

[147]   *Tailby v Official Receiver* (1888) 13 App Cas 523, 546.

[148]   *Holroyd v Marshall* (1862) 10 HL Cas 191, 210–11.

[149]   *Tailby v Official Receiver* (1888) 13 App Cas 523, 547.

[150]   Ibid.

[151]   Ibid, 533 per Lord Watson; Beale et al, n 44, 4.14; Gullifer, n 44, 2–13.

[152]   This, of course, is on the basis that the priority point is the date of creation of the security interest, see page 273 below. As to reform of the law on this point, see below 6.7.

[153]   This has led some commentators to say that a charge cannot be created over a future asset, see Beale et al, n 44, 6.91.

others. For example, if the borrower were not a company, the discharge from bankruptcy of the borrower would terminate any contractual rights, or the expropriation of property rights situated in a certain jurisdiction.

In relation to priority, it is clear from *Re Lind*[154] that the 'priority point' in this situation is the date of the agreement creating the security interest and not the date when the assets are acquired. In that case, L mortgaged property he expected to receive under his mother's will to N in 1905 and to A in 1908. Ignoring his intervening bankruptcy (for the purposes of the discussion in this paragraph), he then assigned the property to P in 1911. His mother died in February 1914, L obtained the property and he assigned it (again) to P in May 1914. The mortgages to N and A were held to have priority over the assignment to P. On its own this could be said to have a number of explanations: one is that once the asset is acquired, the date of priority 'relates back' to the date of execution, another is that although each person's interest attaches automatically at the time that the asset is acquired, they attach in the order of the purported assignments. A third would be that the secured lender has an inchoate interest from the moment of execution over a fund of assets, which just happens to be empty at that time.[155] This last analysis is the most attractive.

The other context in which this issue has arisen is where the assignor's bankruptcy has intervened between the execution of the security agreement and the acquisition of the asset. Once a bankrupt has been discharged, all merely contractual rights anyone had against him will be terminated. Therefore, if all the assignee had was a contract to assign the asset, this would not survive the discharge of the bankruptcy.[156] In *Re Lind*, L became bankrupt in 1908 and was discharged in 1910. It was held by the Court of Appeal that N's and A's mortgages survived the bankruptcy so that when the asset was finally acquired, it was automatically subject to their mortgage.[157] The alternative, that they had a contractual right only, was rejected, and a case in which this had been held, *Collyer v Isaacs*,[158] was distinguished[159] (and, to the extent that it could be said to be inconsistent with the ruling in *Re Lind*, overruled).[160] The nature of the assignee's right, then, is that is a right, 'higher' than a contractual right,[161] 'something in the nature of an estate or interest'.[162] This is not a very exact description, but maybe no more precision is possible.[163]

---

[154] *Re Lind* [1915] 2 Ch 345.

[155] Gullifer, n 44.

[156] *Re Lind* [1915] 2 Ch 345, 364 per Phillimore LJ.

[157] The actual debt was, of course, discharged by the bankruptcy, but the right of the mortgagee in relation to the future property was not merely ancillary to this debt; ibid, 370 per Bankes LJ.

[158] (1881) 19 Ch D 342.

[159] Ibid, 363 per Swinfen Eady LJ.

[160] Per Bankes LJ, 375. RP Meagher, JD Heydon and MJ Leeming (eds), *Meagher, Gummow and Lehane's 'Equity, Doctrine and Remedies'*, 4th edn (Sydney, Butterworths LexisNexis, 2002) suggests that it is more satisfactory to see *Collyer v Isaacs* as overruled, a view which has some support from the judgment of Neuberger J in *Peer International Corporation and others v Termidor Music Publishers Ltd* [2002] EWHC 2675, [79].

[161] Ibid, 365 per Phillimore LJ.

[162] Ibid, 364 per Phillimore LJ. It should be borne in mind that Phillimore LJ was not particularly happy with the conclusion as he thought it would be better as a matter of policy that all assignments of bare futurities should be made impossible.

[163] See Meagher et al, *Meagher, Gummow and Lehane's 'Equity, Doctrine and Remedies'*, n 160, 256 where it is called a sui generis right. For a persuasive analysis concluding that the interest of the assignee is 'an equity', see G Tolhurst, *The Assignment of Contractual Rights* (Oxford, Hart Publishing, 2006) 4.33.

6.3.2.2 Mortgage

In a mortgage, title in the mortgaged assets passes from the mortgagor to the mortgagee with an obligation to retransfer on payment of the secured obligation.[164] Where legal title is transferred to the mortgagee, the mortgage is a legal mortgage. The right to retransfer will be enforced by equity, and is seen as an equitable interest in its own right: the equity of redemption.[165] This is a proprietary interest in the assets, which the mortgagor can encumber and even alienate, for example, to a second mortgagee.[166] The value of the equity of redemption will, of course, depend on the amount outstanding on the secured obligation at any time. Arguably, if the mortgagee is undersecured, so that the amount of the loan is more than the value of the mortgaged assets, the mortgagor has no interest in the assets. However, this misstates the position as the mortgagor always has the ability to redeem the mortgage by paying off the loan, and the better view is that, in equity, the mortgagor owns the assets subject to the mortgage.[167]

A legal mortgage is, in one sense, the 'best' security which can be taken: its priority position is advantageous in that no subsequent interest can gain priority over it without the agreement of the mortgagee, and the legal mortgagee can in theory enforce by foreclosure and obtain full legal ownership of the assets.[168] These advantages are somewhat illusory, however, in that the legal mortgagee will still take subject to any prior legal interest and some prior equitable interests[169] and foreclosure is only obtained by applying to court, which has various powers to enable the mortgagee to take steps to protect its equity of redemption.[170] Obtaining a legal mortgage can involve formal steps, depending on the nature of the asset mortgaged, so that, for example, a legal mortgage of shares requires a transfer to the mortgagee in the issuer's register[171] and a legal mortgage of debts requires transfer by statutory assignment[172] or novation.[173] If the formal steps are not followed, the mortgage usually will take effect as an equitable mortgage.

An equitable mortgage involves the transfer of equitable title to the mortgagee, subject, again, to the mortgagor's right to retransfer, which is the mortgagor's equity of redemption. The equitable interest in the mortgaged assets is thus split between the mortgagor and the mortgagee. Again, the position could be rationalised, so that, in equity, the mortgagor owns the assets subject to the mortgage. However, the mortgagor is likely also to be the legal owner, unless either the mortgage is a second mortgage and the first mortgage is legal, or the mortgagor only ever had a beneficial interest in the assets, in that

---

[164]   *Santley v Wilde* [1899] 2 Ch 474.

[165]   *Paulett v AG* (1667) Hard 465, 469; *In re Sir Thomas Spencer Wells* [1933] Ch 29, 44, 46.

[166]   Although that mortgage will of necessity be equitable, *King v Hussain* 2411/05, 2005 NSWSC 1076 (Supreme Ct NSW).

[167]   *In re Sir Thomas Spencer Wells* [1933] Ch 29, 52; *Cunliffe Engineering Ltd v English Industrial Estates Corp* [1994] BCC 972, 976; cf *Railton v Wood* (1890) LR 15 App Cas 363.

[168]   See 6.5.1.1 for a brief account of foreclosure.

[169]   Any prior legal interest would have priority under the *nemo dat* rule, and the legal mortgagee would have constructive notice of any prior equitable security interest which is registered, and therefore would take subject to it, see page 273.

[170]   See 6.5.1.1.

[171]   See 8.2.7.

[172]   See 8.2.2.1.

[173]   8.2.1. Other legal mortgages also require entries in the relevant register, such as mortgages of ships (s16 and Schedule 1 of the Merchant Shipping Act 1995), aircraft (Mortgaging of Aircraft Order 1972, SI 1972/1268) and intellectual property (Patents Act 1977, ss 30–33), (Trade Marks Act 1994, s 25), (Registered Designs Act 1949, s 19).

they were held on trust for him. If the mortgagor only has an equitable interest in the asset, for example, where it is the holder of securities held with an intermediary, only an equitable mortgage can be granted.

One significant advantage of an equitable mortgage over a legal mortgage is that the former can be taken over future assets.[174] The lack of formal requirements can also be seen as an advantage, so that, for example, an equitable mortgage can be taken over intellectual property without registering it,[175] and it is possible to create an equitable mortgage over debts without giving notice to the debtor.[176] However, the concomitant disadvantage is that the equitable mortgagee is more likely to lose priority to later interests than a legal mortgagee.[177]

6.3.2.3 *Charge*

Unlike a mortgage, a charge is a security interest which entails no transfer of title to the chargee. Despite this, it is a proprietary interest and fully enforceable on insolvency. It is a 'mere encumbrance', whereby the charged property is appropriated to the discharge of an obligation.[178] A charge is always equitable, and is clearly different from a legal mortgage, which entails a transfer of legal ownership. The difference between a charge and an equitable mortgage is sometimes illusory and difficult to draw, in that the law treats both in the same way for certain purposes. For example, the priority position of a fixed charge is virtually identical to that of an equitable mortgage, and the registration requirements are the same, so that the word 'charge' in part 25 of the Companies Act 2006 includes a mortgage.[179] The chief practical (as opposed to conceptual) difference arises on enforcement. Even in the absence of specific words in the agreement creating the security agreement, a mortgagee, by virtue of its ownership, can enforce the mortgage by foreclosure[180] or by taking possession of, and selling, the asset. A chargee may not foreclose or take possession, and will only have a right of sale or to appoint a receiver[181] if the charge is made by deed[182] or if it applies to the court for an order for sale or the appointment of a receiver. However, power to take possession, to sell the assets and to appoint a receiver are routinely included in the document creating a charge, and in these circumstances it is hard to know whether the document creates a charge or an equitable

---

[174] See discussion at 6.3.2.1.

[175] Beale et al, n 44, etc. 13.90–91, 13.97, 13.101–102. However, registration is a priority point, and an unregistered equitable mortgage will lose priority to a later registered mortgage or charge, whether legal or equitable.

[176] This is by equitable assignment; see discussion at 8.2.2.1.

[177] See 6.4.3.

[178] *Carreras Rothmans Ltd v Freeman Mathews Treasure Ltd* [1985] Ch 207, 227.

[179] Companies Act 2006, s 861(5). In section 205(1)(xvi) of the Law of Property Act 1925, the word 'mortgage' includes a charge. In many judgments, the court uses the two terms interchangeably, see *In re Richardson* (1885) LR 30 Ch D 396; *In re Regent's Canal Ironworks Company ex p Grissell* (1876) LR 3 Ch D 411; *In re Yorkshire Woolcombers Association Ltd* [1903] 2 Ch 284, 293 and 298; *In re Crompton & Co Ltd* [1914] 1 Ch 954, 967; *London County and Westminster Bank, Limited v Tompkins* [1918] 1 KB 515, 528–29.

[180] Foreclosure is where the mortgagee's ownership interest is made absolute, and the mortgagor's equity of redemption is extinguished. See 6.5.1.1.

[181] A receiver is a person appointed to take control of the asset(s) which are the subject matter of the security interest, in order to realise their value or to receive the income from them. See 6.5.1.4.

[182] By virtue of Law of Property Act 1925, s 101 which also applies to a mortgage. The right of sale given by this section is limited to certain situations by s 103.

mortgage. Since the situations in which it is necessary to distinguish between the two are very limited,[183] the courts have given little attention to this particular characterisation.[184]

6.3.2.4   Security Interest over Lender's own Indebtedness

Where a company who borrows from a bank has an account at that bank, the bank often wishes to take a security interest over that account as security for the loan. The account is, in fact, only a debt owed by the bank to the account holder,[185] and so the security interest is taken over the lender's own indebtedness. There has been much debate over whether such a security interest was valid, which was put to rest by the decision of the House of Lords in *BCCI (No 8)*.[186] There a bank's charge over its own indebtedness was held to be a valid proprietary interest, a decision which was greatly welcomed by the banking industry, who had been taking such charges for some time. One objection had been that if the debt owed by the bank was assigned to the bank, the debt would be released:[187] this objection would still apply to a mortgage-back, but not if the security interest were a mere charge.[188] Another objection was that if the secured obligation was owed by the account holder, the charge was indistinguishable from a set-off,[189] and if it was owed by a third party, this undermined insolvency set-off.[190] Although the position is not clear, the better view is that a charge-back breaks the mutuality required by insolvency set-off.[191]

6.3.3   The Floating Charge

6.3.3.1   Introduction

A charge can be fixed or floating. A fixed charge is a security interest which attaches to specific assets either on creation of the charge or, in the case of future property, when the relevant asset is acquired by the chargor. This means that the charge can be enforced on default without any further action by the chargee and that the chargor cannot dispose of the charged assets without the consent of the chargee. These characteristics of a fixed charge mean that anyone who takes the asset under an unauthorised disposition takes subject to the charge, unless that person is a good faith purchaser of the legal interest without notice of the fixed charge.[192] They also mean that the fixed charge operates like a negative pledge clause, so that any unauthorised disposition is a breach of contract, which

---

[183]   See Beale et al, n 44, 4.16–4.41. A local authority may distrain for rates over assets which are the subject of a 'mere charge' but not those which are the subject of a 'charge by way of mortgage' (*Re ELS Ltd* [1995] Ch 11). It is not possible to take a mortgage (as opposed to a charge) over one's own indebtedness (*Re BCCI (No 8)* [1998] AC 214, 227). A valid power of appropriation in relation to financial collateral can be included in a mortgage but (it appears) not a charge (such a power is valid under Regulation 17 of the Financial Collateral Arrangements (No 2) Regulations 2003), see below 6.5.1.2.

[184]   The matter is discussed by Ferris J in *Re ELS Ltd* [1995] Ch 11, 24.

[185]   *Foley v Hill* (1848) 2 HL Cas 28.

[186]   *Re Bank of Credit and Commerce International SA (No. 8)* [1998] AC 214, 227.

[187]   *Re Charge Card Services Ltd* [1987] 1 Ch 150, 175.

[188]   This was made clear by Lord Hoffmann in the *BCCI* case, [1998] AC 214, 226: 'A charge is a security interest created without any transfer of title or possession to the beneficiary'.

[189]   R Goode, *Legal Problems of Credit and Security*, 2nd edn (London, Sweet & Maxwell, 1988) 128.

[190]   R Goode, *Commercial Law*, 2nd edn (London, Butterworths, 1995) 660.

[191]   For a full discussion see pages 183–84.

[192]   See page 273.

may give the lender the right to accelerate and terminate the loan.[193] Thus, taking fixed security enables a creditor to prevent asset diversion, one of the main dangers faced by creditors.[194] It will be seen that, as mentioned above, there is very little difference between a fixed charge and an equitable mortgage.

However, the inability of the chargor to dispose of the charged assets in the ordinary course of business means that there are severe practical restrictions on what assets can be the subject of a fixed charge. It will be recalled that earlier there was discussion of a distinction between fixed and circulating assets.[195] Although this distinction is by no means hard and fast, it will be seen that it is vital for a company to be able to dispose of circulating assets such as raw materials and stock in trade quickly and easily, and also to be able to use the proceeds of receivables (themselves the proceeds of the disposition of the other circulating assets) to meet current expenses, such as the wage bill. Thus in order to be able to give security over the entire undertaking of the company, the floating charge developed in the nineteenth century out of the mortgage over the company's undertaking sanctioned by the Companies Clauses Consolidation Act 1845.[196] Thus the chargor had a power to dispose of the charged assets either absolutely or by way of security in the ordinary course of business: this power could be express but was usually implied as a necessary incident of a charge over the whole undertaking of the company.[197] Although the power only authorises dispositions in the ordinary course of business, this concept has been interpreted very widely in this particular context to include exceptional and unusual transactions, particularly if they are necessary for the survival of the business[198] (but not transactions which are intended to bring the business to an end or which have this effect).

6.3.3.2   *Crystallisation*

An important feature of the early floating charge was that it could not be enforced until the company had ceased to be a going concern,[199] whereas a fixed charge or mortgage could be enforced against any charged or mortgaged assets immediately on default. Thus, before enforcement, the floating charge had to crystallise, that is, attach to specific assets. Until fairly recently, crystallisation could only occur on events which signalled the end of the ordinary course of business of the company, that is, winding up[200] or cessation of business,[201] or the active intervention by the chargee, for example, by taking

---

[193]   5.2.1.1.

[194]   See page 77. Asset diversion is the main danger against which the legal capital rules seek to protect a company, see pages 117–18.

[195]   See pages 223–24.

[196]   For accounts of the history of the floating charge, see R Pennington, 'The Genesis of the Floating Charge' (1960) 23 *Modern Law Review* 63; R Gregory and P Walton, 'Fixed and Floating Charges – a Revelation' [2000] *Lloyd's Maritime and Commercial Law Quarterly* 123.

[197]   *In re Panama, New Zealand and Australian Royal Mail Company* (1870) 5 Ch App 318, 322; *In re Florence Land and Public Works Company* (1878) 10 Ch D 530, 546.

[198]   *Ashborder BV v Green Gas Power Ltd* [2004] EWHC 1517(Ch), [2005] BCC 634; *Re Borax Ltd* [1901] 1 Ch 326.

[199]   This was also a feature of the mortgage over the company's undertaking mentioned in the text.

[200]   *In re Panama, New Zealand and Australian Royal Mail Company* (1870) 5 Ch App 318, 322; *Hodson v Tea Company* (1880) 14 Ch D 459.

[201]   *Davey & Co v Williamson and Sons Ltd* [1898] 2 QB 194, 200–01; *In Re Woodroffes Ltd* [1986] Ch 366; *Re Sperrin Textiles* [1992] NI 323, 329; *Bank of Credit and Commerce International SA v BRS Kumar Brothers Ltd* [1994] 1 BCLC 211, 221; *William Gaskell Group Ltd v Highley* [1994] 1 BCLC 197; *Mallett v The Real Meat Producers Ltd* [1996] BCC 254.

possession[202] or by appointing a receiver.[203] The appointment of an administrator by the chargee under the power in paragraph 14 of Insolvency Act Sch B1 might be thought also to have the effect of crystallising a floating charge, since this amounts to intervention by the chargee,[204] see, however, the argument against this made below.[205] It is now possible for the charge agreement to provide that a floating charge will crystallise by the giving of notice by the chargee to the chargor[206] or on the occurrence of an event which does not involve the intervention of the chargee. Such events are often similar to the events of default which enable the lender to accelerate the loan,[207] for example, the giving of security to another creditor, the levying of execution by another creditor,[208] a cross-default[209] or the breach of a prescribed financial ratio.[210] Such clauses are known as automatic crystallisation clauses, and, although contentious, are likely to be held to be valid on the grounds that the parties are free to agree any trigger for crystallisation.[211] The policy ramifications of this are considered below.

The effect of crystallisation is that the floating charge becomes a fixed charge.[212] Practically, this means that the chargor no longer has the power to dispose of the charged assets (including the creation of a security interest over them) without the consent of the chargee. If the chargor does make such a disposition, this is a breach of contract, and may trigger a right to accelerate or terminate the loan, and will also give the chargee the right to restrain such a breach by injunction.[213] In theory, the disponee will take subject to the charge, but this may not actually be the case because of one or both of two reasons. First, the disponee may acquire the legal interest for value without notice of the charge, and so would take free of the prior equitable interest.[214] This is likely to be the case if the disposition is a sale of stock in trade in the ordinary course of business, or the payment of a trade bill in cash. Thus although in theory crystallisation prevents the chargor from carrying on business, in practice it is possible to do so, at least if the chargee waives the breaches of contract.[215] Second, if the disponee only acquires an equitable interest (for

---

[202]   *Mercantile Bank of India Ltd v Chartered Bank of India, Australia and China, and Strauss & Co Ltd* [1937] 1 All ER 231, 241; *Dresdner Bank Aktiengesellschaft v Ho Mun-Tuke Don* [1993] 1 SLR 114 (Singapore CA).

[203]   *Evans v Rival Granite Quarries Ltd* [1910] 2 KB 979, 986–87, 1000; *George Barker (Transport) Ltd v Eynon* [1974] 1 WLR 462.

[204]   Gullifer, n 44, 4–42. The same cannot be said for an administrator appointed by the directors or by the court.

[205]   Page 245.

[206]   *Re Brightlife Ltd* [1987] Ch 200.

[207]   See page 172.

[208]   See pages 220–21.

[209]   See page 171.

[210]   See pages 169–70.

[211]   See *Re Brightlife Ltd* [1987] Ch 200; *Fire Nymph Products Ltd v The Heating Centre Property Ltd* (1992) 7 ACSR 365 (Sup Ct NSW CA); *Re Manurewa Transport Limited* [1971] NZLR 909 (Sup Ct Auckland); *DFC Financial Services Ltd v Coffey* [1991] 2 NZLR 513 (PC); *Covacich v Riordan* [1994] 2 NZLR 502 (HC Auckland). This line of New Zealand authority is probably now inapplicable since the enactment of the New Zealand Personal Property Securities Act 1999 (see M Gedye, R Cuming and R Wood, *Personal Property Securities in New Zealand* (Wellington, Brookers, 2002) 159).

[212]   *Evans v Rival Granite Quarries Ltd* [1910] 2 K.B. 979, 999 per Buckley LJ; *NW Robbie & Co Ltd v Witney Warehouse Co Ltd* [1963] 1 WLR 1324; *Cretanor Maritime Co. Ltd v Irish Marine Management Ltd* [1978] 1 WLR 966, 978; *Covacich v Riordan* [1994] 2 NZLR 502, 514.

[213]   This would only have practical effect if the chargee were able to obtain an injunction before the disposition was made.

[214]   See below page 273.

[215]   This may result in refloatation of the charge, see below pages 247–48.

example, a charge or equitable mortgage) or acquires a legal interest but with notice of the (floating) charge (for example, a legal mortgage),[216] there is a strong argument that it will not take subject to the charge unless it has notice that the authority of the chargor to dispose of the assets free of the charge has been terminated, that is, that the charge has crystallised.[217] It is very unlikely that the disponee will have such notice if the crystallisation is automatic.

The conceptual effect of crystallisation is a matter of some debate, as this depends on how the nature of the floating charge before crystallisation is seen.[218] One view is that, until crystallisation the chargee does not have any form of proprietary interest.[219] On crystallisation, therefore, the chargee obtains such an interest. Although this view has met with some support in Australia,[220] it does not appear to represent English law. Another is that, prior to crystallisation, the floating chargee has an interest in a fund rather than in specific assets.[221] The composition of the fund can change, but the interest remains the same. On this view, it does not matter whether the fund is closed so that no further assets can be added, or open so as to include future assets. On crystallisation the charge attaches to the assets which are presently in the fund.[222] Another view is that the nature of the charge before and after crystallisation remains the same, so that the chargee has a proprietary interest in each of the charged assets at all times. However, on this view the chargee's interest before crystallisation is qualified in that (on one view[223]) it is defeasible and disappears on permitted dealings or that (on another view[224]) it is overreachable so that on disposition the disponee obtains good title. Both these views are hard to reconcile with the reasoning in many of the cases, which is based on the idea that the charge attaches to specific assets on crystallisation, and which specifically denies that a floating charge is a fixed charge with a license to deal.[225] Therefore the 'interest in a fund' theory is the most attractive explanation of the present law.[226] However, in terms of conceptual purity there is a great deal to be said for the idea of a single type of charge under whose terms the chargor has a limited or full power to dispose of the charged assets. If the law

---

[216]   The mortgagee would either have actual notice through checking the register or constructive notice, see below 6.4.3.2.

[217]   Gullifer, n 44, 5–50; Gough, *Company Charges*, n 145, 255–56.

[218]   For a full discussion see Beale et al, n 44, 4.45–4.51.

[219]   Gough, n 145, 97–101, 341–48.

[220]   *Tricontinental Corporation Ltd v Federal Commissioner of Taxation* (1987) 73 ALR 433, 444 per Williams LJ (Queensland CA); *Lyford v Commonwealth Bank of Australia* (1995) 17 ACSR 211, 218 per Nicholson J (Federal Court of Australia).

[221]   Gullifer, n 44, 4–03–4–04.

[222]   Of course, if the charge is expressed to cover future assets, assets acquired by the chargor will continue to fall within the charge after crystallisation, in the same way as if the charge had been a fixed charge from the start, *NW Robbie & Co Ltd*, n 212. The one Australian case which appears to throw doubt on this proposition, *Re Rex Development Pty Ltd* (1994) 13 ACSR 485 (Sup Ct Aust Cap Terr), was based on the construction of the particular charge document. See Beale et al, n 44, 4.53.

[223]   S Worthington, *Proprietary Interests in Commercial Transactions* (Oxford, Clarendon Press, 1996) 81.

[224]   R Nolan, 'Property in a Fund' (2004) 120 *Law Quarterly Review* 108.

[225]   *Evans v Rival Granite Quarries Limited* [1910] 2 KB 979, 999; *In re Colonial Trusts Corporation ex p. Bradshaw* (1879) 15 Ch D 465, 472. See also other cases on priority of execution creditors, such as *In re Standard Manufacturing Company* [1891] 1 Ch 627, 639–41; *In Re Opera Ltd* [1891] 3 Ch 260; *Taunton v Sheriff of Warwickshire* [1895] 2 Ch 319, 323, and on distress for rates *Re ELS Ltd* [1995] Ch 11.

[226]   There is some support for this view from Lord Walker in *Re Spectrum Plus* [2005] 2 AC 680 [139], but he immediately afterwards cites with apparent approval the analysis by Professor Worthington in *Proprietary Interests in Commercial Transactions* n 223, 74–77, which suggests the theory of the defeasible fixed charge.

were to be reformed on the lines discussed below[227] the usefulness of the floating charge could be retained on this basis, without the complicated conceptual structure of crystallisation, or the difficulties of categorising a charge as fixed or floating.[228]

Does the conceptual debate discussed above have any practical significance? Generally it does not, but there are three areas on which it has some bearing. First is the effect of decrystallisation.[229] Second, if the nature of the charge when floating is different from a fixed charge, it makes more sense for there to be a bright line between a fixed and a floating charge which can be determined by the courts rather than the intentions of the parties, while if the nature of the charge is the same, then it makes more sense for the incidents of that charge to be solely a matter for the parties. Third, in the rare case where a disponee takes subject to an uncrystallised floating charge, the priority position will depend on the nature of that charge.[230] However, this is rarely significant as usually the charge will have crystallised by the time that the chargee wishes to enforce the charge.[231]

Another controversial area is the use of automatic crystallisation clauses. The arguments against them centre on the fact that after the clause has triggered crystallisation the chargor still appears to have authority to dispose of the charged assets, when in fact such authority has been terminated: it has been said that 'The debenture-holder would have all the advantages of allowing the company to continue in business and all of the advantages of intervening at one and the same time, to the prejudice of all other creditors'.[232] As we have seen, there is unlikely to be actual prejudice to subsequent disponees, but an unsecured creditor who does not complete execution until after crystallisation will lose priority to the crystallised charge.[233] This priority rule applies whether or not the execution creditor has notice of the charge, or of the fact that it has crystallised;[234] so it is hard to see that the execution creditor is prejudiced by the secret nature of the crystallisation. But it is prejudiced by the fact that it appears possible to crystallise a charge and yet for the charger to continue trading. Obtaining priority over execution creditors is now one of the main purposes that automatic crystallisation clauses are now included in charge documents.[235] Automatic crystallisation would only be effective to achieve priority over disponees other than execution creditors if, first, it was possible to publicise the crystallisation and second, it was possible for the charge to operate before any subsequent interest in the assets was granted. There have been various unsuccessful attempts to reform the law

---

[227] 6.7.

[228] Discussed below at 6.3.3.3.2 and 6.3.3.3.3.

[229] Discussed below at pages 247–48.

[230] See Beale et al, n 44, 13.28.

[231] See the Australian cases of *Hamilton v Hunter* (1982) 7 ACLR 295 (Sup Ct NSW); *Torzillu Pty Ltd v Brynac Pty Ltd* (1983) 8 ACLR 52 (Sup Ct NSW) and *Re Bartlett Estates Pty Ltd* (1988) 14 ACLR 512 (Sup Ct Qnd), although the matter was not discussed in any detail in any of these cases. For further discussion see Gullifer, n 44, 5–39 and 5–41.

[232] *R v Consolidated Churchill Copper Corp* (1978) 90 DLR (3d) 357 [22] (Sup Ct BC) per Berger J; See also A Boyle, 'The Validity of Automatic Crystallization Clauses' (1979) *Journal of Business Law* 231.

[233] *Evans v Rival Granite Quarries Ltd* [1901] 2 KB 979. Berger J considered that the effect of a valid automatic crystallisation clause was that 'the debenture-holder would be able to arrange the affairs of the company in such a way as to render it immune from executions' *R. v Consolidated Churchill Copper Corp* (1978) 90 DL (3d) 357, [22].

[234] Gough, n 145, 319–20.

[235] Gullifer, n 44, 4–53. One other reason, which is no longer valid, is that a charge which crystallised before winding up did not count as a floating charge in the statutory provisions applicable on insolvency (listed on page 249), such as those giving priority to preferential creditors (see 3.3.1.2.2). This was changed in 1986 so that the statutory provisions apply to a charge which 'as created' was a floating charge (Insolvency Act 1986, s 251).

to achieve the former by statutory means,[236] but requiring crystallisation to be registered is unlikely to be helpful since in most cases the chargee will not be aware that automatic crystallisation has taken place. The latter can be achieved by careful drafting so that the trigger for the crystallisation was an event before the subsequent interest was created, for example, the attempt to create that interest.[237]

Automatic crystallisation clauses can be drafted so that the charge crystallises on an event which is not so serious that the company stops trading. Matters may then improve so that the continuance of trading is the preferred option by all parties. Once automatic crystallisation takes place, if the company continues to trade, the chargee either has to consent actively to all dispositions (which is impractical) or, if it just stands by and does nothing, may well be taken to have waived the crystallisation.[238] The effect of such a waiver is unclear: it may mean that the charge never crystallises or that it decrystallises. Decrystallisation, by notice or on certain events, may also be provided for expressly in the charge agreement, so that if the situation which caused the crystallisation (such as the breach of a financial ratio) improves, the company can continue trading.[239]

The actual effect of decrystallisation is untested in the courts, and is unclear. One possibility is that the charge can move from floating to fixed to floating at the will of the parties: it is purely a matter of freedom of contract.[240] Another is that, on decrystallisation, the assets are released from the fixed charge and a new floating charge is created.[241] This is based on the view that when a floating charge crystallises, its nature changes so that it becomes a charge over specific assets as opposed to an interest in a fund (or in no assets at all), so that once it has attached to specific assets its nature cannot be reversed.[242] If the charge is of the same nature before and after crystallisation, then there seems to be no objection to the 'license to deal' being imposed or removed at the will of the parties, so that a new charge is not created.

The debate also raises the wider question, which also arises in the context of the characterisation of fixed and floating charges, as to how far the parties can be free to determine the incidents of the charge without regard to specific legal concepts or the interests of third parties. If the effects of crystallisation applied only to the parties themselves, then there would be no objection to an approach based solely on freedom of contact, but to the extent that third parties are affected such freedom should be controlled. The effect of decrystallisation on third parties, on one level, is minimal, since if the powers

---

[236]   Companies Act 1989, s 100 introducing a new s 410 into the Insolvency Act 1986 (the Companies Act 1989 was never brought into force); see also Company Law Review Steering Group, *Modern Company Law for a Competitive Economy: Final Report* URN 01/942 (July 2001) para 12.28, Law Commission, *Registration of Security Interests: Company Charges and Property other than Land*, Consultation Paper No 164 (2002) para 4.143, BIS, *Registration of Charges Created by Companies and Limited Liability Partnerships, Proposals to Amend the Current Scheme and relating to Specialist Registers*, 12 March 2010, paras 25–27.

[237]   Attempts at such drafting have succeeded in Australia (*Fire Nymph Products Ltd v The Heating Centre Pty Ltd* (1992) 7 ACSR 365 (Sup Ct NSW CA) and New Zealand (*Re Manurewa Transport Limited* [1971] NZLR 909 (Sup Ct Auckland). A similar problem occurs with a negative pledge clause in an unsecured loan agreement, see page 164.

[238]   For a detailed discussion, see Beale et al, n 44, 4.61.

[239]   See Encyclopaedia of Forms and Precedents, Vol 4(1) Banking 576.

[240]   See Gough, n 145, 404–06 and R Pennington, 'Recent Developments in the Law and Practice relating to the Creation of Security for Companies' Indebtedness' (2009) 30 *Company Lawyer* 163.

[241]   R Grantham, 'Refloating a Floating Charge' [1997] *Company Financial and Insolvency Law Review* 53; C Tan, 'Automatic Crystallization, De-crystallization and Convertability of Charges' [1998] *Company Financial and Insolvency Law Review* 41.

[242]   See the discussion of the nature of the uncrystallised charge at page 245.

of the chargor to dispose of the charged assets are restored, disponees taking after that date will take free of the charge anyway, and it does not matter to them whether the charge is new or the original charge. Previous disponees might benefit if the charge is new, in that date of creation affects priorities.[243] However, if it were possible to decrystallise a charge with no adverse consequences, then this would act as an incentive to chargees to include 'hair trigger' automatic crystallisation clauses in their charges, which might have an adverse effect on other creditors. If the effect of decrystallisation were to create a new charge, however, this acts as a disincentive on its use, since the new charge might require a new registration[244] and could be set aside under section 245 of the Insolvency Act 1986 if created within one year of the chargor's insolvency.[245]

A further problem arises if it is possible to decrystallise a fixed charge, for example, by the fixed chargee standing by and permitting disposal of assets by the chargor. If this creates a new floating charge, then the issues of registration and priorities mentioned above arise. If, however, the same charge remains, then arguably it is a charge which is, as created, a fixed charge and so does not fall within the statutory definition of a floating charge in section 251 of the Insolvency Act, despite the ability of the chargor to dispose of the assets without the permission of the chargee. Such a result would be very unfortunate, as the statutory provisions on insolvency which apply to floating charges[246] would not apply here. Thus there is a strong policy argument at least for the effect of the decrystallisation of a fixed charge to be to create a new floating charge.[247]

As mentioned above, crystallisation will occur if the chargor company ceases trading, or if the chargee intervenes to take control of the assets. The problems associated with automatic crystallisation will not apply here, since the event is a public one. Until recently a chargee would normally enforce a floating charge by the appointment of an administrative receiver, that is, a receiver who took control of all the assets of the company,[248] and this would amount to sufficient intervention to crystallise the charge. With some exceptions, the ability of a floating chargee to appoint an administrative receiver has been abolished[249] but a floating chargee may now appoint an administrator out of court.[250] It is not at all clear whether such an appointment would crystallise the charge, since the effects of crystallisation do not seem to apply, and although the chargee is initially intervening it is not taking control of the assets.[251] The first in the hierarchy of objectives of an

---

[243] See page 273.

[244] B Collier, 'Conversion of a Fixed Charge to a Floating Charge by Operation of Contract: Is it Possible?' (1995) 4 *American Journal of Comparative Law* 488; C Tan, 'Automatic Crystallization, De-crystallization and Convertability of Charges', [1998] *Company Financial and Insolvency Law Review* 41, 45. It has been argued that, even if a new charge is created, it would not fall within s 860 Companies Act 2006 as it was not 'created by the company', see A Berg, 'The Cuckoo in the Nest of Corporate Insolvency: Some Aspects of the Spectrum Case' [2006] *Journal of Banking Law* 42.

[245] Another effect, which could still apply, is that the new charge would attract the provisions of the Enterprise Act 2002, such as the abolition of the right to appoint an administrative receiver and the application of the prescribed part, while the old one might have been created before the commencement date of 15 September 2003.

[246] Discussed in 3.3.1.2 above, and see also page 249.

[247] See Beale et al, n 44, 4.65.

[248] An administrative receiver is defined in Insolvency Act 1986, s 29.

[249] Insolvency Act 1986, s 72A. This applies to floating charges created after 15 September 2003. See pages 279–80 below.

[250] Insolvency Act 1986, Sch B1 para 14.

[251] This is contrary to the view expressed in Gullifer, n 44, 4–42 but on further reflection appears to be correct.

administrator is to rescue the company as a going concern, and in order to do this the administrator may wish to dispose of floating charge assets in the ordinary course of business. Paragraph 70 of Schedule B1 of the Insolvency Act 1986 provides that the administrator 'may dispose of or take action relating to property which is subject to a floating charge as if it were not subject to the charge'. The consent of the chargee is therefore not required for a disposition made pursuant to this power, and so it would appear that any disponee would not take subject to the charge. Further, while making such a disposition, the administrator acts as agent of the chargor (not the chargee or even all the creditors).[252] One could even argue that if the charge had crystallised by other means before the appointment of the administrator, the effect of the appointment is a statutory 'decrystallisation'.

6.3.3.3   The Distinction between Fixed and Floating Charges

6.3.3.3.1   Introduction

As discussed in chapter three,[253] statute provides that certain creditors of the company have priority over the floating (but not fixed) chargee in relation to floating charge assets, namely, the liquidator or administrator in relation to costs, the preferential creditors and the unsecured creditors to the extent of the 'prescribed part'. There are also other statutory provisions which apply only to floating charges and not to fixed charges. These include section 245 of the Insolvency Act 1986, which provides that floating charges created in the run-up to the insolvency of the chargor are set aside on insolvency, the requirement that floating charges be registered[254] and the ability of an administrator to dispose of floating charge assets without the leave of the court.[255] Thus it may become necessary for the court to decide whether a charge is fixed or floating in order to know whether these provisions apply.[256] This process has spawned a great deal of litigation. It should be remembered, though, that the cases are primarily about statutory interpretation, that is, what is meant by 'floating charge' in the statute in question (and, presumably, in other statutes dealing with related issues).[257] Because of this, the court has to take a black or white view on the substance of the interest created by the parties: the charge must be either fixed or floating. However, if there were a different trigger (or triggers) for the statutory consequences, it would be possible to permit the parties to decide the incidents of a charge for themselves, so that it had some features of a fixed charge and some of a floating charge.

6.3.3.3.2   The Defining Features of a Fixed Charge and a Floating Charge

The statutory consequences of a charge being floating have acted as a strong incentive to chargees to draft charge documents which create fixed charges over as many of the chargor's assets as possible. Thus charges, labelled as fixed charges, would be created over

---

[252]   Insolvency Act 1986, Sch B1 para 69.
[253]   3.3.1.2.
[254]   Companies Act 2006, s 860.
[255]   Insolvency Act 1986, Sch B1 para 70.
[256]   Note that in relation to financial collateral most, though not all, of these provisions are disapplied, see pages 92 and 262.
[257]   L Gullifer and J Payne, 'The Characterization of Fixed and Floating Charges' in J Getzler and J Payne (eds), *Company Charges: Spectrum and Beyond* (Oxford, Oxford University Press, 2006) 63; P Turner, 'Floating Charges, a 'No-theory' Theory' [2004] *Lloyd's Maritime and Commercial Law Quarterly* 319.

not only fixed assets but circulating assets as well. As we have seen from the discussion earlier,[258] there is no problem with there being a fixed charge over future assets as well as present assets; however, practically, the chargor will also need to dispose of circulating assets and a power to do so without the chargee's consent will lead to the charge being characterised as floating. This is established by the decision of the Privy Council in *Agnew v Commissioner of Inland Revenue*[259] and of the House of Lords in *Re Spectrum Plus*.[260] These confirmed that the defining characteristic of a floating charge is the third of the characteristics identified by Romer LJ in *Re Yorkshire Woolcombers Association Ltd*,[261] namely the ability of the company to 'carry on business in the ordinary way' in relation to those assets.

What amounts to 'carrying on business in the ordinary way' has been further refined by these cases to mean disposal of the relevant assets free from the charge.[262] The other two characteristics identified by Romer LJ,[263] while often present in a floating charge, appear not to be definitive: thus, a charge can be floating even if it is over a present and unchanging asset, provided that the chargor has the power to dispose of it without the consent of the chargee. Lord Scott in the *Spectrum* case illustrated this by giving the example of a floating charge over a specific debt.[264] This point is also illustrated by the decision of the House of Lords in *Smith v Bridgend County Borough Council*,[265] where a charge over two huge coal washing plants (which took years to install) was held to be floating because the chargor had, in theory, the ability to replace them.[266]

Thus a charge will be floating if the chargor has the power to dispose of the charged assets without the consent of the chargee, and will be fixed if it does not have this power, or, in other words, if the chargee has control of the charged assets. Of course, the terms of a charge are often not this clear cut. For example, most floating charges will contain a negative pledge provision, prohibiting the creation of charges over the charged assets which rank in priority to that of the chargee,[267] but will permit the chargor to dispose of the charged assets by sale, and many other charges will include more complex mixtures of prohibitions and permissions. The application of the *Spectrum* test thus can be uncertain: two uncertainties remain in particular. It is not always clear what amounts to the 'charged assets' over which the chargee must have control, nor it is clear what amounts to control.

First, let us consider what is meant by the 'charged assets'. If the charge is over a debt, it appears that the chargee must exercise control over both the debt and its proceeds, on the

---

[258]   6.3.2.1.

[259]   [2001] AC 710.

[260]   [2005] 2 AC 680.

[261]   [1903] 2 Ch D 284, 295.

[262]   *Agnew v Commissioner of Inland Revenue* [2001] UKPC 28, [2001] AC 710, [32].

[263]   'If it is a charge on a class of assets of a company present and future' and 'if that class is one which, in the ordinary course of the business of the company, would be changing from time to time', *Re Yorkshire Woolcombers Association Ltd* [1903] 2 Ch D 284, 295.

[264]   *Re Spectrum Plus* [2005] 2 AC 680, [107]. He also confirmed (at [111]) that the essential characteristic of the floating charge was that until crystallisation 'the chargor is left free to use the charged asset and to remove it from the security'.

[265]   [2001] UKHL 58, [2002] 1 AC 336.

[266]   Ibid, [44] per Lord Hoffmann. The plants were also included in a description which included assets more likely to be replaced.

[267]   Such a provision is only effective to give the first chargee priority over the subsequent chargee if the latter has notice of the provision, see page 276 below.

basis that the proceeds are the traceable assets of the debt and represents its entire value.[268] In both the *Agnew* and the *Spectrum* cases the chargor collected the proceeds from the debtors and was free to dispose of those proceeds, though not the debts themselves, and therefore the charges were held to be floating. There are really only two effective ways for a chargee to take control of the proceeds: either the chargee itself must collect in the debts for its own benefit, or the chargor must pay the proceeds into a blocked bank account (either with the chargee or with another bank).[269] It can be seen that these options are usually unattractive to a company granting security to a lender over its receivables, since the proceeds from receivables will be used by the company to pay its ongoing expenses, such as rent, wages and utilities bills.

The structure of the lending, however, must be considered. If the loan is a term loan, or represents capital start-up funding which cannot easily be repaid, then it would seem impossible for fixed security over receivables to be given, for the reasons set out above.[270] However, if the lending is purely to provide cash flow, so that the amount that is lent is roughly equivalent to the receivables owed to the company, the lending can be repaid by the incoming receivables (either collected by the lender or by the borrower on behalf of the lender) and ongoing expenses can be funded by further borrowing. This, of course, is the structure of receivables financing[271] and can be achieved either by outright assignment of receivables or by lending secured by a fixed charge over those receivables using one of the methods outlined above. One effect of the *Agnew* and *Spectrum* decisions has been that many lenders to small and medium sized enterprises have opted to lend against receivables on the basis of invoice discounting (often as part of asset-based financing[272]) rather than by an overdraft secured by charges.[273]

Most charged assets generate income (or proceeds) or have the potential to do so. Whether it is necessary for the chargee to control the income as well as the asset for a charge over that asset to be fixed depends on a number of factors.[274] One is how directly the asset generates income; for example, machinery enables the company to make things to generate income but there would be no need for the chargee to control the products made by the machinery to have a fixed charge over the machinery itself. Another is how close the generation of proceeds or income comes to being the sole value of the asset.[275] Another is whether the asset is destroyed in the generation of the proceeds or income; for

---

[268] *Agnew v Commissioner of Inland Revenue* [2001] UKPC 28, [2001] AC 710, [46]. This view is not universally accepted, see D Henderson, 'Problems in the Law of Property after Spectrum Plus' [2006] *International Company and Commercial Law Review* 30; R Pennington, 'Recent Developments in the Law and Practice Relating to the Creation of Security for Companies' Indebtedness' (2009) 30 *Company Lawyer* 163.

[269] This is a summary of the account given by Lord Hope in *Re Spectrum Plus*, n 65, [54]. See also S Worthington and I Mitchkovska, 'Floating Charges: the Current State of Play' (2008) 23 *Journal of International Banking and Financial Law* 467.

[270] See G Yeowart, 'Why Spectrum Plus is Bad News for Banks' (2005) 24 *International Financial Law Review* 19.

[271] See 2.3.4.1.

[272] See pages 38–39.

[273] See page 38. Armour, 'Should we Redistribute in Insolvency?' n 80. S Frisby, 'In re Spectrum Plus – Less a Bang than a Whimper' in P Omar (ed), *International Insolvency Law – Themes and Perspectives* (Aldershot, Ashgate Publishing Ltd, 2008).

[274] See Beale et al, n 44, 4.99.

[275] For example, Lord Millett pointed out that the whole value of a receivable was its proceeds, see *Agnew v Commissioner of Inland Revenue* [2001] UKPC 28, [2001] AC 710, [46].

example, this is true of a receivable.[276] One analogy that is often used in relation to the destruction of a receivable is that of a caterpillar becoming a butterfly: this is distinguished from a tree which bears fruit.[277] The tree remains (and thus is a separate asset from the fruit) while the chrysalis becomes the butterfly. Examples of 'tree and fruit' cases include land and the rent from it,[278] and shares and the dividends from them.[279] It is possible therefore to grant a fixed charge over the land, or shares, and a floating charge over the income stream derived from them.

However, these analogies are only useful to illustrate the distinction between two extremes: they do not help with intermediate cases which resemble neither the tree nor the chrysalis. One example of this is a long-term income producing contract, such as a chattel lease charged by the lessor or a contract to operate an infrastructure project for a limited period charged by the operator in a project finance transaction. Both these contracts generate the proceeds directly, and only exist economically as income-producing assets, so that the payments due represent the whole of their value. However, the asset survives separately from the payments made, until the end of its term: on this basis it could be said to have a separate existence. Despite this, it is strongly arguable that such contracts are to be treated as receivables payable over a long period of time, so that for a charge over such a contract to be fixed the chargee must control the proceeds as well as the contract itself.[280] This is an unpalatable view for those who provide finance for special purpose vehicles and other companies whose sole assets are income-producing long-term contracts.[281] While the proceeds from such contracts are not usually all used to pay running expenses, there is often some form of payment waterfall whereby the destinations of the incoming payments is agreed in advance and not all the destinations will be under the control of the lender.[282] Whether this amounts to sufficient control for a charge to be fixed will be discussed below.

The control required on the part of the chargee for the charge to be fixed is that the chargee's actual consent must be required for every disposition of the charged assets: it is not enough for consent to be given in advance or for the chargee to be obliged to give

---

[276] For an argument that this is the sole criterion for whether control over proceeds is required for a fixed charge over the asset see N Frome and K Gibbons, 'Spectrum – an End to the Conflict or the Signal for a New Campaign?' in J Getzler and J Payne (eds), *Company Charges: Spectrum and Beyond* (Oxford, Oxford University Press, 2006).

[277] See R Stevens, 'Security after the Enterprise Act' in J Getzler and J Payne (eds), *Company Charges: Spectrum and Beyond* (Oxford, Oxford University Press, 2006) 165–66.

[278] *Rhodes v Allied Dunbar Pension Services Ltd* [1989] 1 WLR 800, 807. The case is also referred to as *Re Offshore Ventilation Ltd* [1989] 5 BCC 160.

[279] *Arthur D Little Ltd (in administration) v Ableco Finance LLC* [2003] Ch 217.

[280] S Worthington and I Mitchkovska, 'Floating Charges: The Current State of Play', (2008) 23 *Journal of International Banking and Financial Law* 467. In *Re Atlantic Computer Systems Ltd* [1992] Ch 505, the Court of Appeal held that a charge over sub-leases of computers was fixed despite the right of the chargor to use the income in the ordinary course of business. This case was followed in *Re Atlantic Medical Ltd* [1993] BCLC 386, but it is now widely accepted that both cases must be seen as wrong in the light of the *Agnew* and *Spectrum* decisions, see, for example, F Oditah, 'Fixed Charges and Recycling of Proceeds of Receivables' (2004) 120 *Law Quarterly Review* 533; A Berg, 'The Cuckoo in the Nest of Corporate Insolvency: Some Aspects of the Spectrum Case' [2006] *Journal of Banking Law* 22, 30; C Addy, 'Re Spectrum Plus, a Year (and a Bit) On – What Conclusions Can Now be Drawn?' (2007) 22 *Journal of International Banking and Financial Law* 67.

[281] It should, however, be pointed out it is still possible for such lenders to take floating charges over such contracts. Note also that Insolvency Act 1986, s 176A does not apply to many project finance arrangements.

[282] Payment waterfalls are common in project finance transactions and also in securitisations, see pages 43 and 403.

consent.[283] This is made very clear by the reasoning in *Agnew*[284] and *Spectrum;*[285] this seems to overrule the reasoning in *Queen's Moat Houses plc v Capita*[286] where the right of a chargor to require the chargee to release the charged property from the charge was considered consistent with the charge being fixed.[287] Thus, where the proceeds of charged receivables are paid to the chargor, they must be paid into a blocked account, that is, an account from which the chargor cannot withdraw without the consent of the chargee.[288]

A number of practical issues arise from this. First, there is the question whether the restrictions on the use of proceeds contained in a payment waterfall is enough to give a chargee (if a party to the waterfall agreement) sufficient control for a charge to be fixed. While it is true that the waterfall clause does control the application of the proceeds so that the chargor does not have an unfettered right to their disposition, there are two reasons why the control is not sufficient.[289] First, the clause amounts to consent to disposal in advance, and secondly, it is often the case that at least the residual amount of the proceeds is paid to the chargor, who then has control over its disposition.[290]

Another issue is whether a fixed charge can be created over receivables by a 'two account' structure, such as that considered in *Re Keenan Brothers Ltd*[291] This structure consists of a blocked account, into which the proceeds of the charged receivables must be paid (by the terms of the charge), and another current account. The chargee may then permit the chargor to transfer funds from the blocked account (so long as a certain level of funds remain to the credit of the account) to the current account, at which point the chargor obtains free use of the funds, thus enabling it to meet cash flow expenses. The requirement that the proceeds be paid into a blocked account is clearly consistent with the chargee having sufficient control, but it would also be necessary that the consent to the transfer to the current account was, for every transfer, an independent act of will by the

---

[283] Beale et al, n 44, 4.82–4.84.

[284] [2001] AC 710, [27] and [22]: in the latter paragraph Lord Millett cited with approval Henchy J in *Re Keenan Bros Ltd* [1986] BCLC 242, 246, where he said that where assets were 'made undisposable save at the absolute discretion of the debenture holder' this had the distinguishing features of a fixed charge.

[285] [2005] 2 AC 680, [138], where Lord Walker says that under a fixed charge 'the assets can be released from the charge only with the active concurrence of the chargee', and [140]. Lord Walker also made it very clear (at [158]) that agreements other than the charge agreement can be taken into account when characterising a charge, so it will not make any difference if consent in advance is given in another agreement.

[286] [2004] EWHC 868 (Ch).

[287] A Zacaroli, 'Taking Security Over Intermediated Securities', n 44, 167. A Berg, 'The Cuckoo in the Nest of Corporate Insolvency: Some Aspects of the Spectrum Case' [2006] *Journal of Banking Law*, 32. Vos J in *Gray v G-T-P Group Ltd* [2010] EWHC 1772(Ch) held that a charge was floating where the chargor was entitled to require the chargee to transfer some or all of the charged assets to it on request. Although he distinguished *Queen's Moat* as relating to a different context, he said that if it did have a bearing on the case before him 'the very clear dicta of their Lordships in *Spectrum* came after [*Queen's Moat*] and must take precedence over it'. See further page 264.

[288] *Agnew v Commissioner of Inland Revenue* [2001] UKPC 28, [2001] AC 710 [48]; *Re Spectrum Plus* [2005] 2 AC 680, [54].

[289] See A Berg, 'The cuckoo in the Nest of Corporate Insolvency: Some Aspects of the Spectrum Case' [2006] *Journal of Banking Law* 33. For a contrary argument, see Frome and Gibbons, 'Spectrum – an End to the Conflict or the Signal for a New Campaign?' n 276.

[290] Arguably this would be the case in a project finance waterfall clause where the residual sum left after all obligations have been paid is earmarked under the waterfall clause for dividends to the sponsor shareholders, since there is no obligation on the special purpose vehicle to pay dividends.

[291] *Re Keenan Brothers Ltd* [1986] BCLC 242.

chargee, so that the chargee was not under any obligation to permit transfers.[292] There are, however, practical problems with this. First, it is expensive and time-consuming for the chargee[293] and secondly it has the effect that the chargor cannot be assured of having cash available to meet the expenses it incurs in the ordinary course of business. This is not only inconvenient; it could mean that the continuation of business under these circumstances was a breach of duty by the directors of the chargor company.[294]

It might be argued that, so long as the amount of the funds which had to remain in the blocked account was more than the secured indebtedness, this amounts to sufficient control for a fixed charge. However, this argument is fallacious. What is being characterised (usually) is the charge over the book debts, and the question is whether there is sufficient control of 'the charged assets': this includes the debts and the proceeds. To obtain a fixed charge over all the book debts, it is necessary to control all the proceeds. It makes no logical sense to say that there is a fixed charge over all the book debts but control only over part of the proceeds. In addition, there is the simple point that in characterising a charge, the court looks at control over the charged assets, which may at any time be worth more (or less) than the secured indebtedness. Whether it is possible to have a fixed charge over part of a fund of debts or money and a floating charge over the rest is an interesting question. In theory it must be possible, but only if the part is sufficiently identified. This raises the issues of identification which are discussed in different contexts throughout this book.[295] Identification issues do not usually arise in relation to a security interest, since a security interest can be taken over a body of assets worth more than the secured debt, and so such assets can be generically defined.[296]

In past cases where the characterisation of fixed and floating charges has been considered, there has usually not been a credit balance in the bank account into which receivables proceeds are paid, since the chargor has had the ability to dispose of the funds, and has used them to pay bills. The asset which was in issue in these cases was the receivables themselves. However, if an attempt is made to block or partially block an account, there may be a credit balance. It should be noted that it is likely that that the charge in relation to the credit balance at the bank (though not in relation to the receivables) is a financial collateral security arrangement and therefore many of the insolvency provisions are disapplied, thus removing one of the main reasons why a chargee would want a fixed charge.[297]

---

[292]   In *Re Keenan*, an attempt was made to do this by providing in the charge document that the chargee was under no obligation to permit transfers, and the fact that it might do so on any number of occasions should not be taken or construed as giving rise to any express or implied right to the company to do so: see first instance decision at [1985] BCLC 302, 305.

[293]   G Yeowart, 'Why Spectrum Plus is Bad News for Banks', (2005) 24 *International Financial Law Review* 19.

[294]   A Berg, 'The Cuckoo in the Nest of Corporate Insolvency: Some Aspects of the Spectrum Case' [2006] *Journal of Banking Law* 45.

[295]   Pages 212–13 and 318–22.

[296]   For example, 'all existing and future book debts' as in *Tailby v Official Receiver* (1888) 13 App Cas 523.

[297]   Reg 8 of the Financial Collateral Arrangements (No 2) Regulations 2003 disapplies para 70 Sch B1 Insolvency Act 1986 (ability of administrator to use the floating charge assets without leave of the court, see pages 248–49 above) and Regulation 10 disapplies s 176A (prescribed part) and s 245 (invalidity of floating charge not for new value in the run-up to insolvency) Insolvency Act 1986 and s 754 Companies Act 2006 (preferential creditors priority when a secured creditor takes possession), although (strangely) not s 176ZA (liquidator's expenses) or para 99 Sch B1 (administrator's expenses) Insolvency Act 1986, nor s 40 or s 175 Insolvency Act 1986 (preferential creditors' priority on appointment of receiver or on winding up).

A third issue arising from *Agnew* and *Spectrum* is that Lord Millett said that the question of whether the chargee had sufficient control is not determined merely by the wording of the charge document, but by the post-contractual conduct of the parties. Thus, it is not enough to provide contractually for a blocked account if it is not operated as one in fact.[298] The difficulties stemming from this proposition are largely caused by the fact that, because of section 251 of the Insolvency Act 1986, it is the nature of the charge *as created* which is relevant to whether the statutory consequences on insolvency apply. Thus, *prima facie*, what the courts are characterising is whether the transaction entered into by the parties created a fixed or floating charge. This depends on the construction of the agreement between the parties. However, usually the conduct of parties after a contract is made cannot be taken into account in construing that contract.[299] One exception to this is where the court is considering whether the original agreement is a sham,[300] so that if an account is never treated as blocked this is good evidence that the blocking provision was not intended by the parties to represent the rights and obligations between them. In this situation, the court would have no difficulty in characterising the charge as floating. However, such a clear case will be rare, and since a finding of a sham involves a finding of dishonesty, it is unlikely that the court will reach this conclusion if there is evidence that the parties did, at least initially, intend to create a blocked account, or other structure which gave the chargee sufficient control.

If the court does not find a sham, the failure of the chargee to exercise the potential control given to it by the charge document could give rise to a variation of the original agreement,[301] or a waiver of the chargee's rights,[302] either of which could have the effect of decrystallising the fixed charge created by the original agreement.[303] As pointed out earlier, whether decrystallisation creates a new floating charge or merely changes the incidents of the existing fixed one is not entirely clear. However, in the present context, if a new charge is not created the result is surprising, since it means that a charge which is operated as a floating charge is still a fixed charge 'as created' and the statutory consequences on insolvency do not apply to it. This is highly undesirable from a policy point of view, if it is considered that those who take the 'benefit' of a floating charge

[298] *Agnew v Commissioner of Inland Revenue* [2001] UKPC 28, [2001] AC 710, [48].

[299] *James Miller & Partners Ltd v Whitworth Street Estates (Manchester) Ltd* [1970] AC 583, 603, 611, 614; *L Schuler AG v Wickman Machine Tool Sales Ltd* [1974] AC 235, 252, 260–61, 265–68, 272–73; *Dunlop Tyres Ltd v Blows* [2001] EWCA Civ 1032, [21]–[22].

[300] *AG Securities v Vaughan* [1990] 1 AC 417, 466 and see above pages 227–28.

[301] For example, by an agreement that the chargee will give consent to withdrawals or dispositions in the future.

[302] For example, by the chargee's failure to prevent a withdrawal or a disposition. While one waiver would not result in decrystallisation, repeated waivers could create a representation leading to an estoppel which would prevent the chargee from relying on its control in the future. Cf A Berg, 'The Cuckoo in the Nest of Corporate Insolvency: Some Aspects of the Spectrum Case' [2006] *Journal of Banking Law* 43 who sees the operation of an estoppel as likely to be only temporary.

[303] S Atherton and R Mokal, 'Charges over Chattels' : Issues in the Fixed/floating Jurisprudence' (2005) 26 *Company Lawyer* 10, 17. It should be pointed out that in the reverse situation, where proceeds subject to a floating charge were paid into a blocked account from four months after the charge was created, this conduct was ignored and the charge was held to be 'floating as created', see *Fanshaw v Amav Industries Ltd* [2006] EWHC 486 (Ch). The question of whether payment into the blocked account had the effect of crystallising the charge was not considered. Where a charge was created as fixed, the charge document gave the chargee the option of requiring payment into a blocked account and this was actually done, the charge was characterised as fixed, see *In the matter of Harmony Care Homes Ltd* [2009] EWHC 1961 (Ch).

should also take the burden of the statutory consequences.[304] However, if a new charge is created, it will require registration, and, if not, will be void against the liquidator and secured creditors.[305] This could lead to a paradox, where if the court finds a sham, the charge will be floating not fixed, but will be valid in insolvency while if the court finds that there has been a waiver of rights, leading to a new floating charge, this charge could be void for non-registration.

Yet another issue arising from the *Spectrum* decision on control is whether a charge can be fixed when the chargor cannot dispose of the charged assets generally but has the right to substitute other assets for the charged assets without the consent of the chargee. This is of significance in relation to financial collateral, where a right to substitute is very common indeed,[306] but can also be relevant in relation to machinery, for example, which the chargor may wish to update. It is, of course, not the right to acquire new assets which is the problem, but the concomitant right to dispose of the old assets without the chargee's consent which could be inconsistent with the necessary level of chargee control. The authorities are inconclusive.[307] The right to substitute would normally require that the value of the charged assets remains constant, or at least above the level of the secured borrowing, so, to that extent, the chargee is retaining control over its security. However, there seems to be no suggestion in *Agnew* and *Spectrum* that the necessary control is limited to charged assets to the value of the borrowing: it appears to have to extend to all the charged assets, and in normal circumstances it would be very difficult to limit control to a certain part of the charged assets.[308] For this reason, it would seem that a general power to substitute assets is not consistent with a fixed charge, and to achieve the necessary control the chargee would have to give consent to every substitution. However, a power to substitute, for example, machinery for the purposes of updating with very specific criteria for substitution might be sufficient.[309]

6.3.3.3.3   The Methodology of Characterising a Charge as Fixed or Floating

It is now necessary to address the actual process of characterisation carried out by the courts in this context. It will be noted that the approach is somewhat different from that in relation to characterising a transaction as a sale or charge, and the differences and possible

---

[304]   See also discussion above at page 248.

[305]   6.4.3.1.

[306]   The Financial Collateral Directive (2002/47/EC) (Art 2(2)) and the Financial Collateral Arrangements (No 2) Regulations 2003 (reg 3) both provide that any right of the collateral-provider to substitute equivalent financial collateral or withdraw excess financial collateral does not prevent the collateral being in the possession or control of the collateral taker so that the arrangement does fall within the definition of a security financial collateral arrangement. The limit of the right to substitute to equivalent collateral makes this exception very narrow, see page 266 below.

[307]   Weak support for the proposition that a limited right to substitute is consistent with a fixed charge can be found from *Holroyd v Marshall* (1861–62) 10 HLC 191, which was decided before the floating charge was developed, *Re Cimex Tissues* [1995] 1 BCLC 409, (a first instance decision which is unlikely to have survived the *Spectrum* decision) and *Re TXU Europe Group plc* (in administration) [2004] 1 BCLC 519, where a statement by Blackburne J that a right to substitute was not inconsistent with a fixed charge was clearly obiter. Support for the contrary proposition can be found in three Singaporean cases on financial collateral: *Re Lin Securities* [1988] 1 SLR 340 (HC Singapore); *Dresdner Bank Aktiengesellschaft v Ho Mun-Tuke Don* [1993] 1 SLR 114 (Singapore CA) and *Re EG Tan & Co (Pte)* [1990] 1 SLR 1030 (HC Singapore). For full discussion see Beale et al, n 44, 4.90–4.96; Zacaroli, n 44, 167.

[308]   See page 254.

[309]   Beale et al, n 44, 4.96.

reasons for them are discussed above.[310] Lord Millett laid down some very specific methodology for this process in *Agnew*.[311] In the first stage the court construes the agreement between the parties to ascertain what rights and obligations are intended to be created by the parties. The court then characterises the charge as fixed or floating, based on the criteria discussed above, but without reference to the label put on the transaction by the parties. To what extent, then, is the intention of one or both parties to create a particular type of transaction relevant to the process? It can be relevant during the first stage, in conjunction with other factors such as the nature of the assets charged, in order to assist in ascertaining the parties' intentions as to the rights and obligations created, if these are not fully spelled out in the charge document.[312] Otherwise, and particularly during the second stage of the characterisation process, it is not relevant, and it is clear that the characteristics of fixed and floating charges are matters of law and cannot be changed by the agreement of the parties. Thus, in this particular characterisation process, policy considerations trump those of freedom of contract. In characterising a charge as floating, the courts are deciding that certain statutory consequences apply, and so the line drawn by the courts should reflect the policy reasons for those statutory consequences. It is to these that we now turn.

6.3.3.3.4   Should Floating Charges be Treated Differently?

As mentioned in chapter three, floating charges are treated differently from other security interests, especially when the chargor is insolvent. One aspect of this is that certain groups of unsecured creditors have priority over the floating chargee in relation to floating charge assets.[313] Whether unsecured creditors should have any kind of statutory priority is discussed below,[314] but it should also be asked whether, if such priority is given, it should be over all security interests rather than just floating charges.[315] The features of a floating charge which can be said to justify the different treatment are that, unlike a fixed charge, a floating charge can be given over all the assets of the company, so that there is nothing left for the unsecured creditors, and also that the existence of the floating charge does not prevent the company from trading and thus incurring further debts to unsecured creditors.[316] On the face of it, these are not insignificant differences. However, different treatment means that creditors are given an incentive to try and avoid having floating, as opposed to fixed, charges. This involves unproductive and wasteful costs, and so, arguably, it would be more cost-effective for priority to be given over all chargees. It is also necessary to consider whether the benefits of priority outweigh these costs.[317]

A possible solution to the problem of these costs would be to redefine the statutory trigger for priority so that it would be easier to administer and less easy to avoid, while

---

[310]   See pages 228–29.
[311]   *Agnew v Commissioner of Inland Revenue* [2001] UKPC 28, [2001] AC 710, [32].
[312]   S Atherton and R Mokal, 'Charges over Chattels: Issues in the Fixed/floating Jurisprudence' (2005) 26 *Company Lawyer* 10, 15.
[313]   The details of these are discussed at 3.3.1.2.
[314]   6.6.
[315]   See R Calnan, 'Floating Charges: A Proposal for Reform' (2004) 19 *Journal of International Banking and Financial Law* 341; Armour, n 80.
[316]   L Gullifer and J Payne, 'The Characterization of Fixed and Floating Charges' in J Getzler and J Payne (eds), *Company Charges: Spectrum and Beyond* (Oxford, Oxford University Press, 2006) 80.
[317]   See Armour, n 80, who concludes that, with the possible exception of employees, the benefits achieved by preferential status are small or non-existent and do not justify the costs of any redistribution scheme.

keeping roughly the same result, that is, mostly the same charges would be subject to the statutory priority consequences as at the moment. A contender is the criterion used in New Zealand, which is that priority is given over charges over accounts receivable and inventory of the company.[318] Although there will always be arguments at the edges of the definition of 'accounts receivable' and 'inventory' there is a clear core area which will always be included. Further, by concentrating on the type of assets over which the charge is given, it is much more difficult for creditors to avoid the trigger by clever drafting.

If there is to be any statutory trigger which differentiates between charges for the purpose of priority for certain unsecured creditors, it should reflect the reasons for this differentiation, namely, those referred to above.[319] The *Spectrum* criterion, that is the ability of the chargor to dispose of any of the charged assets without the consent of the chargee, could be said to be over-inclusive as it does not just include charges which cover all the assets of the company or those which permit the company to trade. Is a differentiation that depends on the type of assets charged more appropriate? It can certainly be said that a company needs the ability to dispose of assets such as inventory or receivables (or at least the proceeds of receivables) and so these assets would not be charged were the charge not floating. However, modern financing techniques raise a problem. Both these types of assets can be the subject of an absolute disposition which does not stop the company trading. Most obviously, receivables can be sold to a financier, and, less commonly, inventory also can be sold to a financier and then sold to customers by the company as an undisclosed agent.[320] Even were the statutory trigger to be changed, such dispositions would not be included. Nor, arguably, should they be. These sales bring new money into the company, and the financier's interest relates only to that money, while assets subject to a floating charge are security for all past and future borrowing.[321]

Another aspect of the different treatment of fixed and floating charges on insolvency is that floating charge assets can be used by an administrator to fund the attempted rescue of the company (both by the top-slicing of the administrator's expenses and by the power of the administrator to use floating charge assets without the leave of the court[322]) and by a liquidator to fund the liquidation, subject to the floating chargee's veto on certain litigation expenses.[323] It is this aspect of the insolvency consequences that most concerns chargees whose charges are, or might be characterised as, floating. While the priority of employees and the ring-fenced is reasonably finite, can be roughly calculated in advance

---

[318]   New Zealand Personal Property Securities Amendment Act 2001 Sch 1, amending cl 9 of Sch 7 to the Companies Act 1993. This criterion was also proposed by the Law Commission, see Report No 296, *Company Security Interests: Final Report*, Cm 6654, paras 3.165–170. The position in Australia under the new Personal Property Securities Act 2009 is rather more complicated. Statutory triggers which referred to a floating charge will now operate in relation to a charge over circulating assets. The definition of circulating asset is complex, but includes two alternative elements. These are either that the chargor has general power to dispose of assets in the ordinary course of business (as opposed to a limited power, such as to substitute assets) or that the asset is a current asset, which includes accounts receivable, inventory, currency and bank current accounts.

[319]   See page 257.

[320]   As in *Welsh Development Agency v Exfinco* [1992] BCLC 148. See above 6.2.5.2.

[321]   This last point refers to a distinction between a charge over future property, where new assets can secure payment in relation to old lending, and a purchase, where new money comes into the company for each receivable sold. A financier's interest which is acquired for new money is excluded from the New Zealand definition of security interests over which preferential creditors have priority (but in New Zealand 'security interests' include some outright transfers).

[322]   Insolvency Act 1986, Sch B1, paras 70 and 99 and see page 94 above.

[323]   Insolvency Act 1986, s 176ZA and see 3.3.1.2.1 above.

and can be allowed for by taking extra security, the use of floating charge assets in insolvency proceedings is open-ended and can result in a very considerable reduction in floating charge assets.[324]

Despite the fact that the argument for parity between an administrator's costs and a liquidator's costs was one of the main reasons for the statutory reversal of *Buchler v Talbot*,[325] different justifications apply for the use of floating charge assets in funding each process. The administrator, to the extent that he is seeking to rescue the company, should be able to operate in the ordinary course of business, in the same way as the company operated before administration. This will include disposing of circulating assets such as stock-in-trade, making payments to creditors, employees and utilities and entering into new contracts. Arguably, he should be able to do this using assets which the company was able to use before administration.[326] Further, the floating charge holder is most likely to gain from a rescue of the company, since its lending is given on the basis that it will be paid out of income rather than out of specific assets,[327] so arguably it makes more sense that it should fund the rescue attempt.[328]

Yet another difference in treatment is that a floating charge created in the run-up to insolvency can be set aside if not given for new value, while this is not the case in relation to fixed charges.[329] It is difficult to discern a coherent rationale for this position.[330] The argument for the setting aside of a floating charge is that a lender who takes a charge when the borrower is in financial difficulties improves its position significantly vis-à-vis all the other creditors. This improvement in position can only be justified if, and to the extent that, the lender provides the borrower with new value. First, new value may enable the borrower to keep trading so that its financial position improves and all creditors benefit. Second, although the lender taking the charge is then in a better position than other creditors, the borrower itself is no worse off.[331] However, both these arguments apply equally to fixed and floating charges. Further, even if no new value is given, a lender who

---

[324] R Calnan, 'Floating Charges: A Proposal for Reform' (2004) 19 *Butterworth's Journal of International Banking and Financial Law* 341.

[325] Hansard, 3 November 2005. For a discussion of the statutory overruling of this case, see 3.3.1.2.1.

[326] This was the view of the Law Commission, see Report No 296, *Company Security Interests: Final Report*, Cm 6654 at 3.166 fn 205, in relation to the power of the administrator to use floating charge assets without the leave of the court (Insolvency Act 1986, Sch B1 para 70).

[327] See the discussion of the distinction between relationship lending and asset-based lending at pages 38–39.

[328] It should be noted that the floating charge assets would not necessarily fund the rescue attempt directly, but would be used to pay the costs of additional finance raised by the administrator. Of course, if the rescue attempt failed, the repayment costs would form part of the administration expenses. A proposal to rank finance costs above all other administration expenses, in an attempt to assist corporate rescue, was made, inter alia, by the Insolvency Service in *Encouraging Corporate Rescue – a Consultation* (June 2009) Proposal C. The responses to the proposals on rescue funding were mixed, and the Government has decided not to take them forward at the moment, although it should be noted that the negative comments were mainly aimed at proposals to allow administrators to grant new security interests.

[329] Insolvency Act 1986, s 245.

[330] For a full discussion see Gullifer and Payne, 'The Characterization of Fixed and Floating Charges', n 316, 85–87. See further page 103 above.

[331] This argument, however, ignores the fact that the creditor is better off than other creditors. The transaction could thus be seen as a 'preference' even if not a 'transaction at an undervalue' (see 3.3.2). These terms are used here loosely rather than referring to the exact statutory definitions in the Insolvency Act. It is very unlikely that a charge will ever fall within the current test of preference, since the borrower will usually grant the charge in order to obtain new value, or to avoid enforcement of an existing debt, and not to put the lender in a better position, although this will be a consequence of the grant of the charge.

refrains from enforcing the debt due because a charge is granted to it is enabling the borrower to keep trading. This is true for both fixed and floating charges.

The Cork Committee supported the present position by arguing that the grant of a floating charge (as opposed to a fixed) was more damaging to unsecured creditors because of the width of the charge, and because it encompassed future assets which could be acquired on credit by the borrower, thus prioritising the floating chargee over the unpaid vendors.[332] This latter argument is open to several objections. First, both fixed and floating charges can cover future assets, although it is true that future circulating assets are more likely only to be the subject of a floating charge. Second, unpaid vendors are in a position to protect themselves,[333] and if they fail to do so when a borrower has granted a (registered) floating charge it is hard to see why insolvency law should protect them. In fact, it is the unsecured creditors existing at the time that the charge is granted who are worse off, since they did not know of the existence of the charge when they extended credit. However, this argument applies to both fixed and floating charges. The only justification for the existing width of section 245 is that floating charges are wider in scope than fixed charges, and this does not seem a good enough reason to limit section 245 to floating charges.

6.3.3.4   *The Future of the Floating Charge*[334]

The floating charge has suffered many blows over the years, and yet retains its popularity amongst lenders. To some extent, this is hard to fathom. As a priority device, it is severely limited.[335] The assets within its scope can be disposed of by the chargor, and by an administrator, so that unless the administration is successful in rescuing the business, there will be nothing left for the floating chargee. Further, any assets that are left will go first to meet the administrator's, and subsequent liquidator's, costs, then the claims of the preferential creditors, and then the prescribed part. Admittedly, the *Spectrum* decision has meant that there are now assets over which it is very hard to take a fixed charge, and so there may be more assets within the scope of floating charges than there used to be. However, as discussed above, lenders are developing new ways of obtaining proprietary protection in relation to such assets, by using receivables financing and other asset-based techniques, involving the transfer of an absolute and not a security interest.

The main benefit of taking a floating charge used to be the ability to take control of enforcement, by the appointment of an administrative receiver, and floating charges were taken for control rather than for priority. Except in certain circumstances, this is now not possible.[336] Instead the floating chargee can appoint an administrator out of court. This right is still valuable to a lender, although in fact many administrators are now appointed by the directors or the company.[337] Despite the rhetoric of the administrator's duties being owed to all creditors which now appears in the legislation, the appointing lender still has

---

[332]   *Report of the Review Committee on Insolvency Law and Practice* (Cmnd 8558, June 1982) para 1553.

[333]   See page 75 above.

[334]   See R Goode, 'The Case for the Abolition of the Floating Charge' in J Getzler and J Payne (eds), Company Charges: Spectrum and Beyond (Oxford, Oxford University Press, 2006).

[335]   R Mokal, *Corporate Insolvency Law: Theory and Application* (Oxford, Oxford University Press, 2005).

[336]   It should not be forgotten, though, that in those exceptional cases, for example, project finance, the ability to appoint an administrative receiver is still very important.

[337]   S Frisby, 'Not quite Warp Factor 2 yet? The Enterprise Act and Corporate Insolvency (Pt 1)' (2007) 22 *Journal of International Banking and Financial Law* 327. This seems to be for public relations purposes, to prevent

considerable influence over the conduct of the administrator. First, the lender is in a position to choose the identity of the administrator. This means that it can choose an insolvency practitioner sympathetic to the interests of banks, and also that the chosen person has an incentive to comply with the lender's wishes to ensure future business. Second, the administration is funded by the principal lender, through the top-slicing of expenses and the unrestricted use of floating charge assets. Thus the lender has a strong incentive to monitor the actions of the administrator closely. The presence of a monitoring lead creditor is valuable to other creditors both within and outside insolvency.[338] In English law, the way of identifying a lead creditor is to see who has fixed and floating charges over all the assets of the company. The growth in asset-based lending in recent years could threaten this structure, if different financiers lent against different assets.[339] However, to the extent that one financier can lend against all the assets of the company, as in 'true' asset-based lending,[340] this replicates the lead creditor. Since an asset-based lender takes a mixture of absolute interests and charges, it may end up qualifying to appoint an administrator, since it will have charges over all the assets of the company (any other assets are already owned by the asset-based financier).

Where, then, does this leave the floating charge? Probably still with a residual role: largely to enable the appointment of an administrator, but also for priority where nothing else is possible. A lender is likely to prefer to have a floating charge rather than being unsecured, despite the disadvantages of this form of security. It should be remembered, that when it comes to taking security, lenders will usually try and have security over every asset possible (the 'crown jewels') and if a floating charge is the only way to achieve this, then this is the route that they will take.

6.4   Registration and Priorities[341]

6.4.1   The Requirement of Registration

Under English law, many, but not all, security interests created by companies[342] are required to be registered in the register of company charges. The purpose of this requirement is to give publicity to security interests the existence of which would not otherwise be obvious to third parties, including any person taking an interest in the assets and others extending credit to the company. For this reason, only non-possessory security interests are registrable, since possession is seen as sufficient publicity in itself.[343] The registration requirements are set out in section 860 of the Companies Act 2006, and apply

---

the banks looking too predatory. Of course, the directors are under great pressure from the lender to make the appointment, and if they did not the lender would do so.

[338] See pages 294–95.

[339] S Frisby, *Report in Insolvency Outcomes, prepared for the Insolvency Service*, June 2006, 9, 39–43.

[340] See pages 38–39.

[341] For a detailed discussion of the registration of company charges, see G McCormack, *Registration of Company Charges*, 3rd edn (Bristol, Jordan Publishing, 2009).

[342] Security interests which arise by operation of law, such as an equitable lien, are not required to be registered.

[343] Law Commission, *Registration of Security Interests*, Consultation Paper No 164, n 236, para 1.6.

only to charges listed in the section.[344] Thus, while all floating charges are required to be registered, only some fixed charges are. While it is unsatisfactory that the statutory position is drafted as 'not registrable unless listed' rather than 'registrable unless excepted',[345] in fact the exceptions are few and to some extent are justified by policy considerations. The following sections consider certain exceptions in detail.

6.4.1.1   Charges over Securities[346]

First, and most important, fixed charges over shares in a company are not registrable.[347] Similarly, fixed charges over debts which are not book debts are not registrable. Thus fixed charges over securities, whether debt or equity, are not registrable. However, registration requirements are disapplied anyway in relation to security financial collateral arrangements,[348] in the interests of reducing administrative burdens in relation to dealings on the financial markets.[349] It will be remembered that to qualify as a security financial collateral arrangement, the collateral taker needs to have 'possession or control' of the securities.[350] Thus it could be argued that where this is the case there is no need for registration, since 'possession or control' in itself acts as sufficient publicity.

This, of course, depends on what is meant by 'possession or control' in the definition of a security financial collateral arrangement in the Financial Collateral Directive ('FCD')[351] and the Financial Collateral Arrangements (No 2) Regulations 2003 ('FCAR').[352] The concept of possession is straightforward when securities are in tangible form. Thus, if securities are bearer securities and the security holder takes possession of them, or where registered shares are certificated and possession is taken of the certificates, this falls within the definition. This is understandable as there is clearly sufficient publicity of the security interest.

Control could be seen as the equivalent of possession where security is taken over intangibles, but is less easy to define. There are two helpful distinctions that can be made

---

[344]   The term 'charge' in this section includes a mortgage, s 861(5) and is used in this sense throughout this section.

[345]   There have been proposals to amend the list in this way, see Company Law Steering Group 12.54, Law Commission No 296, *Final Report*, n 44, paras 1.6, 3.14–3.16; BIS, *Registration of Charges created by Companies and Limited Liability Partnerships*, n 236, paras 16–21.

[346]   For further discussion, see Gullifer, n 44, 6–38; Law Commission No 296, Final Report, n 44, chapter 5; Tolley Company Law Service 'Charges over Shares'.

[347]   A charge over (declared) dividends could be seen as a charge over a book debt, which would be registrable under Companies Act 2006, s 860(7) and for this reason in the past many charges over shares have been registered as a cautionary measure, see Gullifer, n 44, 3–26.

[348]   See above pages 224–25.

[349]   The term 'markets' is used widely here, in that the scope of the financial collateral regime is not limited to transactions on recognised financial markets, or, indeed, to any sort of market transaction, but includes transactions whereby securities are used as security for any kind of loan. It also appears to be the case that shares in private companies are financial collateral: this point was agreed between the experts who gave evidence to the British Virgin Islands Court of Appeal in *Alfa Telecom Turkey Ltd v Cukurova Finance International Ltd* HCVAAP2007/027.

[350]   See pages 224–25. Financial Collateral Arrangements (No 2) Regulations 2003 (SI 2003/3226), reg 3 (definition of 'security financial collateral arrangement'). See also Financial Collateral Directive 2002/47/EC Article 2(2).

[351]   Directive 2002/47/EC.

[352]   SI 2003/3226. This point has attracted a great deal of debate, see Law Commission No 296, *Final Report*, n 44, Ch 5; Gullifer, n 44, 6–38; Beale et al, n 44, 10.24–10.40; M Hughes, 'The Financial Collateral Regulations' (2006) 21 *Journal of International Banking and Financial Law* 64; D Turing, 'New Growth in the Financial Collateral Garden' (2005) 20 *Journal of International Banking and Financial Law*; Zacaroli, n 44, 167.

in this area:[353] that between positive and negative control,[354] and that between legal and operational control. Positive control is where the chargee has the right to dispose of the securities without any further reference to the chargor, and negative control is where the chargor is prohibited from disposing of the securities without the consent of the chargee.[355] Legal control refers to control established by the rights and prohibitions in the agreement, while operational control refers to the practical ability of the chargee to dispose of the collateral, or to prevent the chargor disposing of it, as the case may be.

Negative operational control would give publicity of the security interest to others seeking to take an interest in those securities, since the company cannot in fact dispose of them without the consent of the chargee. An example of negative operational control would be where money was held in a blocked bank account, as discussed earlier in relation to floating charges.[356] In fact, negative operational control is often coupled with positive operational control, for example, where the chargee is registered as the owner of shares in the books of the company, or in the CREST register.[357] Another example is, where securities are held through an intermediary,[358] where the intermediary is the chargee, or is notified of the charge by the chargee, or the securities are transferred to the chargee's account.[359] Given that in these situations there is sufficient publicity of the security interest, registration might, therefore, be seen as unnecessary. It would, however, still provide information for unsecured creditors who would otherwise be unaware of the security interests, unless they made extensive investigations. Further, unsecured creditors would also not usually be aware, without making investigations, that the company owned the securities in the first place.

If 'control' also includes legal control without operational control, however, it is less clear that publicity is achieved. Negative legal control could merely mean that the chargor is prohibited by the charge document from disposing of the assets, and unless some mechanism is put in place to prevent the chargor actually making such a disposal (which would amount to negative operational control), the control would not be apparent to the outside world.

There are arguments, however, which suggest that legal control without operational control is not the meaning of 'control' in the FCD and the FCAR, even if such control were enough to render a charge fixed. The phrase used in the Directive ('possession or control') and the context indicates that control refers to the functional equivalent of possession, that is, operational control.[360]

The UNIDROIT Geneva Securities Convention 2009, which sets out a harmonised framework for the holding of intermediated securities, largely mirrors the FCD in relation to security interests over intermediated securities. In the Convention, the situations in which a charge is to be exempt from registration requirements are spelt out specifically.[361]

---

[353] J Benjamin, *Financial Law* (Oxford, Oxford University Press, 2007) 478, fn 192.
[354] This distinction is also made by the Law Commission in Report No 296, *Final Report*, n 44, para 5.46.
[355] Beale et al, n 44, 10.27–10.30.
[356] 6.3.3.3.2.
[357] For an account of CREST see page 238. There are other methods of taking security in relation to securities held through CREST which have a similar effect, see Beale, et al, n 44, 10.29.
[358] See page 238.
[359] These methods are those listed by the Law Commission as amounting to control under the scheme it proposed, see Law Commission No 296, *Final Report*, n 44, para 5.20.
[360] See Zacaroli, n 44, 167.
[361] Ibid, Zacaroli, 172–73.

All are instances of operational as well as legal control. The first situation is where the securities are transferred into the name of the chargee.[362] The second is where the intermediary is itself the chargee.[363] The third is where the intermediary is not permitted to deal with the securities without the permission of the chargee,[364] (this would be negative operation control). The fourth is where the intermediary is obliged to comply with the instructions of the chargee without requiring the consent of the chargor,[365] (positive operational control).

It could also be argued that merely legal control without at least some operational control is not even enough for a charge to be fixed rather than floating where the subject matter of the charge is intangible: this certainly seems to be the case in relation to, for example, cash in a bank account, where the account itself must be blocked and operated as such, but is not necessarily true in every case, so that, for example, there can be a fixed charge or equitable mortgage over certificated securities merely by assignment.[366] The same is true in relation to receivables, although there would have to be operational control over the proceeds.

It can be also asked whether operational control is sufficient without any legal control. This issue arose recently in the case of *Gray v G-T-P Group Ltd*[367] In this case, which concerned money in a bank account rather than securities,[368] there was an agreement between the chargee and the chargor whereby money, paid by third parties to the chargee, would be held by the chargee in its bank account on trust for the chargor.[369] The chargee provided certain services to the chargor for which fees were payable. The charge was created since, on the occurrence of certain events such as the insolvency of the chargor or where fees payable by the chargor to the chargee were more than 14 days overdue, the chargee was entitled to withdraw any sums due to it from the bank account.[370] However, until the occurrence of a specified event, the chargee was obliged to transfer all of the balance of the funds in the account to the chargor if the chargor requested it to do so. Thus the chargee had operational control over the charged funds, since it was the account holder and only it could withdraw the money from the bank, but not legal control, since it

---

[362]   UNIDROIT Geneva Securities Convention 2009, article 11.

[363]   Ibid, article 12(3)(a).

[364]   Ibid, article 12(3)(b) and (c). This is by means of a 'designating entry', which is an entry in the securities account, (article 1(l)) or a 'control agreement', which is an agreement between the intermediary, the chargor and the chargee (article 1(k)).

[365]   Ibid, articles 12(3)(b) and (c). Again, this would be by a designating entry or a control agreement.

[366]   Beale et al, *The Law of Personal Property Security* (Oxford, Oxford University Press, 2007) 4.10. In practice, however, the chargee will take possession of the certificate, (and often also take a signed transfer form) for the very reason that otherwise the chargor can, practically, dispose of the securities even though legally prohibited from doing so. Even this is not necessarily safe since duplicate certificates may be obtained, see Law Commission, *Company Security Interests: A Consultative Report*, Consultation Paper No 176 (2004), 4.44 and fn 55.

[367]   *Gray v G-T-P Group Ltd (Re F2G Realisations Ltd)* [2010] EWHC 1772 (Ch).

[368]   It will be recalled that money in a bank account is 'cash', as defined in the Financial Collateral Arrangements (No 2) Regulations 2003, and security interests over cash fall within their scope, see reg. 3 and pages 224–25 above.

[369]   The chargor was a retailer of laminated floors, and the chargee provided debit card services to the chargor's customers.

[370]   It was conceded that the agreement created some form of charge, see *Gray v G-T-P Group Ltd (Re F2G Realisations Ltd)* [2010] EWHC 1772 (Ch), [18]. It would appear that the subject matter of the charge was the beneficial interest of the chargor in the debt owed to the chargee by the bank, which the chargee held on trust for the chargor (although this was not spelt out in these terms in the judgment).

was obliged to transfer those funds to the chargor on request. If it had not made a requested transfer, the chargee would have been in breach of trust as well as in breach of the agreement.

The judge held that the charge was floating, on the grounds that the chargee's consent was not required for the chargor to withdraw the funds.[371] This seems correct. The situation was wholly analogous to where the chargor pays funds into a bank account over which the bank has a charge. Unless the account is blocked, the chargor can withdraw from the account without the consent of the bank, even though, in actual fact, the bank has to 'do' something to effect the withdrawal.[372] This was exactly the situation in the *Spectrum* case[373] (where the charge was held to be floating) and also in the *Siebe Gorman* case[374] (where the decision that the charge was fixed was overruled by the House of Lords in *Spectrum*).

However, the judge then held that there was no 'possession or control' to bring the charge within the scope of the FCAR. This was disastrous for the chargee as the charge was not registered, and so was void against the liquidators of the chargor. The grounds for the decision were that operational control alone is not enough to constitute control: legal control is also required.[375] If we consider this decision from the point of view of whether registration should be required in such circumstances, it seems a little odd. To the extent that control gives publicity, it is operational and not legal control that does so,[376] in the same way that actual possession gives publicity even if there is a (private) agreement that the possessor is holding for someone else. Of course, when considering other issues, such as whether the insolvency provisions relating to a floating charge should apply, different considerations apply.

In relation to charges over intermediated securities, the *Gray* decision appears potentially inconsistent with the UNIDROIT Geneva Securities Convention 2009, since one of the situations set out there as being a situation in which the registration requirements do not apply is where an intermediary is the chargee.[377] As will be seen from the discussion in chapter seven,[378] an intermediary holds the securities in its account on trust for the investor, and if those securities are charged to the intermediary the situation seems analogous to that in *Gray*. Of course, the agreement between the intermediary and the investor may provide that the investor cannot give instructions freely to the intermediary in relation to the charged securities, but that does not appear to be a requirement under the Convention for the disapplication of registration provisions, and it may not be the case where the securities are held under a prime brokerage agreement, where it is envisaged that the securities will be used to execute trades as instructed by the client.[379]

---

[371] See pages 252–53.

[372] Of course, given that withdrawals can now been made electronically without the intervention of a human being, the idea of the bank 'doing' anything is rather illusory.

[373] *Re Spectrum Plus* [2005] UKHL 41; [2005] 2 AC 680.

[374] *Siebe Gorman & Co Ltd v Barclays Bank Ltd* [1979] 2 Lloyd's Rep 142.

[375] *Gray v G-T-P Group Ltd, (Re F2G Realisations Ltd)* [2010] EWHC 1772 (Ch), [62].

[376] An argument on these lines was made by the chargee in the *Gray* case (see n 287, [56]) but this did not appear to persuade the judge.

[377] In the *Explanatory Report* (2008 UNIDROIT Document 4, February 2008, available at http://www. unidroit.org/english/conventions/2009intermediatedsecurities/conference/conferencedocuments2008/conf11–004-e. pdf) on a previous draft of the Convention the rationale of this provision was described as follows: 'The rationale for such self-perfection is that the relevant intermediary has control over the account'.

[378] See page 337.

[379] Zacaroli, n 44, 184–85.

It can be seen from the foregoing discussion that the relationship between the boundaries of where there is 'possession or control' within the FCAR and the boundary between a fixed and a floating charge is problematic, at least in the context of charges over securities.[380] However, it is clearly envisaged in the FCAR that at least some floating charges will come within the definition of 'security financial collateral arrangement'. Some of the provisions disapplied to such arrangements only apply to floating charges.[381] 'A charge created as a floating charge' is expressly included in the definition of security interest,[382] where the collateral is within the possession or control of the collateral taker. This seems to indicate that if the charge is crystallised by the chargee acquiring control (probably both positive and negative) the FCAR apply at that stage. This may have an effect on the application of insolvency provisions, but it cannot affect registration, since that must take place on creation. On first blush, then, it might seem that all floating charges over financial collateral need to be registered.

However, the definition of a floating charge in the FCAR also provides that a right of the collateral provider to substitute equivalent collateral or to withdraw excessive collateral does not prevent the collateral being within the possession or control of the collateral taker.[383] It is arguable that if a chargor had such a right, the charge would be characterised as a floating charge under English law.[384] Therefore, it may only be where a charge is floating merely because of such a right that it falls within the FCAR. Both limbs of this exception are potentially problematic.

The right of substitution as defined in the FCAR is particularly narrow as it only applies to 'equivalent securities' which are defined as securities of the same issuer or debtor, and forming part of the same issue or class.[385] The definition in the FCD is wider, merely referring to a right of substitution of financial collateral. It is difficult to see why a chargor would want, or use, a right to substitute securities of the same issue: in this context substitution would have to take place immediately and there seems little purpose in substituting shares or bonds with those of the same issue.[386]

---

[380] It is to be hoped that this problem will be tackled when the Financial Collateral Arrangements (No 2) Regulations 2003 are amended, as they have to be, to include the latest amendments to the Financial Collateral Directive (see EU Directive 2009/44/EC). However, the current consultation by HM Treasury 'A consultation on the implementation of EU Directive 2009/44/EC on settlement finality and financial collateral arrangements' (August 2010) only raises one particular aspect of the problem, namely, whether 'collateral security charges' under the Financial Markets and Insolvency (Settlement Finality) Regulations 1999, SI 1999/2979 should be included within the definition of 'financial collateral' (see paras 3.1–3.7).

[381] Regulation 8 disapplies Insolvency Act 1986, Sch B1 para 70 (right of administrator to dispose of floating charge assets without leave of the court) and Regulation 10 disapplies Insolvency Act 1986, s 176A (prescribed part out of floating charge assets), Insolvency Act 1986, s 245 (avoidance of floating charge not for new value created in the run-up to insolvency) and Companies Act 1985, s 196 (now Companies Act 2006, s 754, establishing priority of preferential creditors over a floating charge where debenture holders take possession). Further, the disapplication in Regulation 4 of the registration requirements in Companies Act 2006, s 860 will potentially only apply to floating charges, since fixed charges over securities and bank accounts are not registrable (see 6.4.1.1 and 6.4.1.2).

[382] Reg 3.

[383] Ibid.

[384] See page 256.

[385] This appears to be a drafting error in the Regulations, for the reasons given in the text. 'Equivalent collateral' is defined in the Financial Collateral Directive (Article 2(1)) but this is for the purpose of the article concerning the right of use, where, since there is a time lag between withdrawing the collateral and replacing it, there is some purpose to requiring equivalent collateral.

[386] If the view discussed below at page 321 is taken, that is, that shares or bonds of the same issue are merely fractional interests, then substitution of one for the other is entirely pointless.

In contrast, the right of withdrawal is potentially very wide, especially in the context of cash in a bank account.[387] If a borrower charges its credit balance at a bank on terms that it can withdraw funds so long as the balance of the account does not fall below a certain amount, which equals or exceeds the secured debt, this could be seen as a right to withdraw excessive collateral. However, such a charge is probably floating.[388] Here, then, is a potentially wide category of floating charges to which the registration and insolvency provisions are disapplied.

6.4.1.2   Other Fixed Charges which are Not Registrable

Apart from charges over debt securities, fixed charges over debts which are not book debts are the other main exception to the requirement of registration. The exact scope of the term 'book debts' is unclear, but it is established that it does not include charges over insurance policies[389] or over a credit balance in a bank account,[390] although the latter probably falls within the financial collateral exception anyway. It is hard to see why fixed charges over debts in general are not registrable, and there have been many suggestions that the law should be reformed to effect this.[391] Other fixed charges that are not required to be registered are those over goods (other than ships and aircraft) which are created orally,[392] and charges on imported goods which, if executed by an individual, would be exempt from registration as a bill of sale.[393] As can be seen, apart from the exception of charges over securities and other financial collateral, the statutory provisions are unclear and arcane[394] and are hard to justify on any principled grounds.[395]

6.4.1.3   Other Registers

There are also other registers in which charges created by companies over certain assets, such as registered land,[396] unregistered land,[397] ships,[398] aircraft,[399] patents,[400] trade marks,[401] and registered designs,[402] are either required to be registered, or can be

---

[387]   Financial collateral includes 'cash' and 'cash' includes a credit balance in a bank account (Regulation 3).

[388]   See pages 253–54. It does not appear to have been argued in the *Gray* case discussed above that the right of the chargor to withdraw the funds in the account was a right to withdraw 'excess collateral'. This could depend on what obligation it was thought the charge was securing: was it any obligation owed by the chargor to the chargee, or only the obligation to pay which existed once a specified event had arisen?

[389]   *Paul and Frank Ltd v Discount Bank (Overseas) Ltd and Board of Trade* [1967] Ch 348.

[390]   *Re Brightlife Ltd* [1987] Ch 200 cf *Re Permanent Houses (Holdings) Ltd* [1988] BCLC 563.

[391]   Company Law Steering Group 12.60; Law Commission, *Registration of Security Interests*, n 236, para 5.47.

[392]   If created in writing such charges fall within Companies Act 2006, s 860(7)(b) as charges evidenced by an instrument which, if executed by an individual, would be a bill of sale.

[393]   Bills of Sale Act 1890, s 1.

[394]   In particular, they include references to out-of-date concepts such as book debts, and complex and obscure legislation such as the Bills of Sale Acts.

[395]   Reform is being considered by the Government, see BIS, *Registration of Charges created by Companies and Limited Liability Partnerships*, n 236, paras 16–18.

[396]   That is land registered under the Land Registration Act 2002.

[397]   Maintained in the Land Charges Registry under the Land Charges Act 1972.

[398]   Merchant Shipping Act 1995, Sch 1

[399]   Maintained under the Mortgaging of Aircraft Order 1972, SI 1972/1268.

[400]   Patents Act 1977, s 33.

[401]   Trade Marks Act 1994, s 25.

[402]   Registered Designs Act 1949, s 19.

registered (usually to obtain priority over subsequent charges). The position is complex and varies according to the type of asset in question.[403]

6.4.2   The Registration Process

Charges can only be registered once created, and must be registered within 21 days of creation.[404] Registration involves sending the original charge document, together with the relevant form,[405] to Companies House where the application is checked, the charge is registered and a 'certificate of registration' is issued.[406] Once such a certificate is issued, it is definitive as to registration even if the registered particulars are wrong,[407] and might mislead a later person searching the register.[408] Late registration is only permitted on application to the court,[409] although leave will usually be granted on terms that no one taking a security interest between the date of creation of the charge and the date of the late registration will be prejudiced.[410] However, unsecured creditors who have relied on the absence of registration are not generally protected, although they are if the company is in liquidation (when late registration will not be ordered). Further, the imminence of insolvency is a matter for the court to take into account when making the order for late registration.[411]

6.4.3   The Effect of Registration

6.4.3.1   *Consequences of Failure to Register*

In relation to the effect of registration, there are two issues requiring discussion. The first is the consequence of failure to register a charge, and the second is the extent to which registration amounts to notice to third parties. The Companies Act 2006 provides for the consequences of failure to register.[412] It should first be pointed out that the obligation to register is on the company, and not the secured creditor, although either the company or the secured creditor can register. A company failing to register commits a criminal offence.[413] Despite this, it is usually the secured creditor who registers, since the sanction of invalidity, discussed below, which affects the secured creditor, is the most powerful disincentive against non-registration. The seems little point in putting the obligation to register on the company (who has no real interest in registering) and when the Law

---

[403]   For detailed discussion see Beale et al, n 44, 13.59–13.105.
[404]   Companies Act 2006, ss 860(1) and 870(1).
[405]   MG01 available for download from http://www.companieshouse.gov.uk/forms/generalForms/MG01_particulars_of_a_mortgage_or_charge.pdf. The details on the form include the details of the chargor and chargee, the date of creation of the charge, details of the charging instrument, amount secured and short particulars of the property charged.
[406]   Companies Act 2006, s 869.
[407]   *National Provincial and Union Bank of England v Charnley* [1924] 1 KB 431.
[408]   See discussion in McCormack, *Registration of Company Charges,* n 341, 6.42–6.55.
[409]   Companies Act 2006, s 873.
[410]   Beale et al, n 44, 8.35.
[411]   *Re Ashpurton Estates Ltd* [1983] Ch 110.
[412]   Companies Act 2006, s 874.
[413]   Ibid, s 860(4).

Commission suggested abolishing the criminal sanction, only one consultee disagreed.[414] The company is also penalised in another way for failing to register: on the expiration of 21 days after the creation of the charge the money secured by the charge becomes immediately payable.[415] This provision is supposed to protect the secured creditor, who no longer has security for its loan, although the company or the secured creditor can, of course, apply to register out of time.

The most powerful sanction for non-registration is the provision that an unregistered charge is void against 'a liquidator [or] an administrator..[or] a creditor of the company'.[416] This provision requires some explanation. The word 'creditor' appears to mean a creditor taking a proprietary interest in the company's assets, that is, either a secured creditor[417] or a creditor who has completed execution.[418] Thus, before the onset of insolvency proceedings, if such a creditor enforces its proprietary interest it does not have to pay the proceeds to a prior unregistered chargee. However, an unregistered charge is not void against the company (or unsecured creditors) before the onset of insolvency, so that an unsecured creditor could not prevent an unregistered chargee enforcing its security.[419] Once insolvency proceedings have commenced[420] the unregistered charge is void against the company in liquidation or in administration.[421] This effectively means that it is void against the unsecured creditors, so that the unregistered chargee itself becomes an unsecured creditor. It is not clear what the position is regarding a purchaser of assets which are subject to an unregistered charge. Usually such a person will take free of the charge as they are obtaining the legal interest for value without notice of the charge.[422] However, where, for example, a receivables financier takes an absolute assignment, yet an unregistered chargee is the first to give notice to the obligors and so obtains priority under the rule in *Dearle v Hall*,[423] the question would arise whether the unregistered charge was void against the purchaser.[424] The section is silent on this matter, and the position should

[414] Law Commission No 296, *Final Report*, n 44, 3.72. The abolition of the criminal sanction had also been proposed by the Diamond report, the Crowther report and the Final Report of the Steering Group of the Company Law Review. Despite this, the latest Government consultation paper proposes retention of the criminal sanction (BIS *Registration of Charges*. n 236, 2010, para 42). This is because it is thought that requiring the chargor (and only the chargor) to register would eliminate the risk of malicious registration which would arise if the original charge document were not required to be presented on registration (Proposal J and para 78). However, an easier way to deal with this risk is to require the chargor to confirm registration, a process which could be achieved using electronic means.

[415] Companies Act 2006, s 874(3). This seems to mean that the loan is automatically accelerated, although the meaning is not entirely clear. Automatic, rather than optional, acceleration is not necessarily helpful to the secured creditor (see McCormack, *Registration of Company Charges*, n 341, 6.05 and G Gretton, 'Registration of Company Charges' (2002) 6 *Edinburgh Law Review* 146, 164). In theory this would mean that if the chargee applied to register the charge late, this would be to secure the accelerated obligation rather than the loan on the original terms.

[416] Companies Act 206, s 874(1).

[417] *Re Monolithic Building Co* [1915] 1 Ch 643, 662.

[418] *Re Ashpurton Estates Ltd* [1983] Ch 110, 123.

[419] *Re Ehrmann Bros Ltd* [1906] 2 Ch 697, 708.

[420] That is, when a winding up petition has been presented (Insolvency Act 1986, s 129) or when an administrator is appointed (Insolvency Act 1986 Sch B1 paras 10, 19, 31).

[421] *Smith (Administrator of Cosslett (Contractors) Ltd) v Bridgend County Borough Council* [2001] UKHL 58, [2002] 1 AC 336, [21], [31].

[422] See page 273. If the absolute transfer is first in time, the chargor would not have notice of it since it is not registrable.

[423] (1828) 3 Russ 1. See below, pages 273–74, for a discussion of the rule in *Dearle v Hall*.

[424] In theory the question arose in *E Pfeiffer Weinkellerei-Weineinkauf GmbH & Co v Arbuthnot Factors Ltd* [1988] 1 WLR 150, where an extended retention of title clause over proceeds of sale (receivables) was held to be

be clarified.[425] One suggestion is that the word 'creditor' could be interpreted to include 'purchaser' but this seems to do violence to the language. It is also inconsistent with the Court of Appeal's interpretation of 'creditor' in section 895 of the Companies Act 2006 in *Re Lehman Brothers International (Europe)(in administration)* where the word was held not to include a person with an absolute interest, namely a beneficiary under a trust of which the company was trustee, albeit in a different context.[426]

6.4.3.2 Registration as Notice

The whole point of registration is to enable other parties who may be affected by a security interest to find out about it easily, quickly and cheaply without having to rely on the honesty of the company who has granted the interest, or on expensive due diligence exercises. The Company Charges register can now be searched electronically, by inputting the name or number of the relevant company.[427] Those lending to companies[428] will usually search the register, which entitles them to see the relevant form. At least where the chargee is a bank or other financial institution, it will have registered the charge itself and will have included as much information as possible by 'cutting and pasting' sections from the charge agreement onto the form. The searcher will usually be able to see, and will therefore have notice of, whether the charges are described as fixed or floating, and any negative pledge clauses as well as the details of the property charged. The party searching can then make adjustments as a result of that information. This could include refusing to lend at all, entering into agreements with other chargees, taking security interests over different assets from the ones originally contemplated, charging more for the loan or limiting the amount lent. If it does lend, the fact that it has notice may affect its priority position.[429] However, since a chargee has 21 days in which to register, it is possible that a second chargee may search the register before a previous charge is registered, yet the previous charge, registered later yet within 21 days of creation, has priority. To avoid this, chargees usually do not advance any funds until 21 days after the creation of a charge, and check the register before making such an advance. Further, it will be an event of default[430] for a borrower to have created a charge ranking in priority to the charge in question.

Since notice may be relevant to priorities, it is necessary also to consider the position where a person taking a proprietary interest does not search the register. It should be stressed that in the case of commercial lenders, this is very unlikely to occur: most lenders will search before advancing any funds. This is fortunate, since the law as to whether such

a registrable charge, and competed with an absolute assignment of receivables to a financier. The argument that the unregistered charge was valid against the purchaser appears not to have been taken and the case appears to have been dealt with on the basis that the purchaser was a 'creditor of the company' (at 155).

[425] Companies Act 1989, s 399 would have clarified the matter, but this never came into force and has now been repealed. This point is raised in the Government's consultation paper BIS, *Registration of Charges*, n 236, para 46).

[426] [2009] EWCA Civ 1161, [169]–[177]. This related to Companies Act 2006, s 899 which defines who is bound by a scheme of arrangement. For further discussion, see pages 630–31.

[427] Although the resulting search lists all entries that have been made for the company, and not just registered charges, which makes the search more complicated. The cost of searching is low (£1 per charge).

[428] This includes those extending credit to companies, although it is less clear that trade creditors will actually search the register. However, if they do not, they will rely on credit rating agencies who do.

[429] See 6.4.3.

[430] Enabling the lender to accelerate the loan and terminate the charge agreement, see 5.2.3.

a person has constructive notice of a registered interest is unclear.[431] The best attempt at rationalising the law is that registration is constructive notice to those who would reasonably be expected to search the register. Unfortunately, there is no direct authority on the point, nor any provision in the Companies Act 2006.[432] The view taken, is, however, consistent with section 199 of the Law of Property Act 1925 which provides that a purchaser shall not be prejudicially affected by notice of' a thing unless 'it is within his own knowledge, or would have come to his knowledge if such inquiries and inspections had been made as ought reasonably to have been made by him'. The contrary view, that registration is notice to all the world, would appear to lead to unreasonable and undesirable results.[433] This still leaves open, however, the question of who would reasonably be expected to search the register.

While it seems clear that those taking registrable charges are in this category, and that trade purchasers in the ordinary course of business are not, the position is far less clear in relation to those taking non-registrable security interests (such as pledges) and those taking absolute transfers made in the financing context (such as absolute assignments of receivables). It is strongly arguable, however, that those in the latter category must be expected to search the register and so would have constructive notice, since they are financiers operating in a similar way to those making secured loans.

Of what is registration constructive notice? The position established by the cases is that a party has constructive notice of particulars which are required to be included on the register.[434] This does not include a negative pledge clause in a floating charge (although these are commonly included in the registered particulars). This has the result that a party who takes a subsequent charge without searching the register will obtain priority over the floating charge.[435] Since negative pledge clauses are ubiquitous in floating charges, it has been argued that persons taking charges have inferred knowledge of the negative pledge clause, even though they do not have constructive notice. Although this argument has not been directly considered by an English court, there are two Irish decisions which affirm the current state of the law (albeit without detailed consideration of an argument based on inferred knowledge as opposed to constructive notice)[436] and a decision of the Hong Kong Court of First Instance where an argument based on inferred knowledge was rejected for lack of evidence that negative pledge clauses were regularly included in registered particulars.[437]

If a charge is registered as fixed, since that is the label put on it by the parties, but is (on a true characterisation) floating it is unclear whether a party who did not search would have notice of restrictions. Actual knowledge that there was a fixed charge over an asset must now be taken as constructive notice of (very extensive if not total) restrictions on

---

[431]   For a detailed discussion see Beale et al, n 44, chapter 11.

[432]   The Companies Act 1989 s 103 would have inserted a new s 416 into the Companies Act 1985 providing that registration was constructive notice to anyone taking a charge on the company's property and no one else. The current consultation by BIS includes this issue, see n 439.

[433]   Gough, n 145, 842.

[434]   *English and Scottish Mercantile Investment Co v Brunton* [1892] 2 QB 700; *Standard Rotary Machine Co Ltd* (1906) 95 LT 829; *Wilson v Kelland* [1910] 2 Ch 306; *G & T Earle Ltd v Hemsworth* (1928) 44 TLR 605; *Siebe Gorman & Co Ltd v Barclays Bank Ltd* [1979] 2 Lloyd's Rep 142, 160; *Welch v Bowmaker (Ireland) Ltd* [1980] IR 251 (Sup Ct Ireland); *Re Salthill Properties Limited* (2004) IEHC 145 (HC Ireland).

[435]   See page 276.

[436]   *Welch v Bowmaker (Ireland) Ltd* [1980] IR 251; *Re Salthill Properties Limited* (2004) IEHC 145.

[437]   *ABN Amro Bank NV v Chiyu Banking Corp Ltd* [2001] 2 HKLRD 175, 196–97.

disposal in that charge.[438] However, where the party has no knowledge that there is a charge at all, the question arises whether it should be fixed with constructive notice in relation to how the charge ought to have been registered (as a floating charge) or how it was registered (as a fixed charge).

The law relating to constructive notice is disgracefully unclear and is scarcely fit for purpose. There should not be such uncertainty as to who is affected by constructive notice of registration, and it seems very odd that a common clause designed to achieve priority is ineffective in the very situation in which it would be most useful. Large scale reform is discussed below, but it should be noted that the Government has proposed reform, both to clarify the parties who are affected with constructive notice[439] and to make negative pledge clauses registrable.[440] Having said all this, actual problems caused by the weaknesses in the present law are likely to be relatively rare. This is firstly because most lenders will search the register, so the question of constructive notice does not arise, and secondly because priority contests will only occur when a corporate borrower either deliberately or mistakenly creates competing interests over the same asset without disclosing the true position. It should also be pointed out that since the basic priority rule is first in time, notice is not usually relevant to priority contests between two legal interests or two equitable interests,[441] but only where there is a contest between a prior equitable interest and a later legal interest.

6.4.4 Priorities

In this section we will consider the position where more than one person has a competing proprietary interest in assets which have some sort of connection with a company. This language is very loose, but it is hard to be more precise, since proprietary claimants may be purchasers from the company, sellers to the company who have reserved title, those for whom the company holds an asset on trust, those who have a security interest (possessory or non-possessory) granted to them by the company or creditors who have executed judgment against the company's assets. It is thus not possible to say with precision whose assets the subject of the competing claims are, as this would prejudge the issue.

Even if we leave aside the priority consequences of non-registration, the English law rules on priority are highly technical and complex. It is not proposed to do more than give an outline of them here.[442] The complexity of these rules is one of the key arguments for reform, which will be addressed below.[443] However, it should be pointed out that these are only default rules, and are rarely relied upon in their raw state by commercial parties. Instead, most of the sophisticated lenders we are considering in this book will make sure that the priority of their interests is determined contractually, by using the register and

---

[438] Cf *Siebe Gorman & Co Ltd v Barclays Bank Ltd* [1979] 2 Lloyd's Rep 142, 160 which must now be seen as turning on a very different view of what restrictions were required for a charge to be fixed.

[439] BIS, *Registration of Charges*, n 236, paras 47–50. The proposal is that those taking registrable charges should be affected with constructive notice and no one else. If the list of registrable charges is not expanded to include those taking an outright assignment of receivables, this seems an odd result.

[440] Ibid, para 64 proposal G.

[441] Unless the rule in *Dearle v Hall* applies, see pages 273–74.

[442] For detailed discussion see Beale et al, n 44, chapters 11–15; Gullifer, n 44, chapter 5; R Calnan, *Taking Security: Law and Practice* (Bristol, Jordans, 2006) chapter 7.

[443] 6.7.

performing due diligence to discover what other proprietary interests there may be and, if necessary, by making agreements with those with competing interests.[444] In fact, for this very reason there are few cases about the default rules, which in turn is a major reason why the law in this area is so uncertain. It should be pointed out, though, that agreement is not always possible, particularly where discovering the existence of those with a prior claim would be expensive or time-consuming. This might be, for example, where their consensual interests are not registered, where interests arise by operation of law or where the register does not give an up to date position (for example, where a floating charge has crystallised automatically). For a secured lender, there is also the danger of further security interests being created in the future over the same assets, and an understanding of the priority rules is necessary so that a lender can protect itself against this danger. Such protection may take the form of a negative pledge clause,[445] or of attempting to take the 'strongest' security interest possible.

The basic priority point in English law is the date of creation. This is articulated in relation to legal interests by the maxim: *nemo dat quod non habet* (you cannot give what you have not got) and in relation to equitable interests by the proposition that the first in time has priority. There are a number of exceptions to this basic rule. First, if A acquires an equitable interest in an asset, and then B acquires a legal interest, B will take free of A's interest if B acquired its interest in good faith, for value and without notice of A's interest. An example of this rule in the corporate finance context is that a purchaser of goods or other assets in the ordinary course of business will nearly always take free from a prior equitable charge, since the purchaser will not search the register nor be expected to search and so will not have constructive notice of the charge. Trade buyers of stock in trade would fall into the category of 'purchaser of goods in the ordinary course of business', but it is less clear that buyers of equipment or other movable corporate infrastructure would do so.[446] A lender taking a legal mortgage would be expected to search the register and so would take subject to a prior equitable security interest.

However, if B is a statutory assignee of a debt, then the reasoning is different. Since section 136 of the Law of Property Act 1925 provides that a statutory assignment is 'subject to equities', the legal interest exception does not apply and the governing rule is, instead, the rule in *Dearle v Hall*.[447] This rule is the second exception to the basic first in time doctrine. It provides that, where there are successive assignments of a debt or chose in action, the first assignee to give notice to the obligor gains priority, providing that that assignee did not take its assignment with notice of the other assignment.[448] If B takes a statutory assignment, it will have given notice to the obligor, whereas if A (the prior

---

[444] See R Calnan, 'Taking Security in England' in M Bridge and R Stevens (eds), *Cross-Border Security and Insolvency* (Oxford, Oxford University Press, 2001) 33. Secured lenders can agree among themselves to reverse the default priorities without obtaining the borrower's consent or, indeed, even informing it, *Cheah Theam Swee v Equiticorp Finance Group Ltd* [1992] 1 AC 472.

[445] See 5.2.1.1 and page 271.

[446] Law Commission, *Registration of Security Interests*, n 236, para 2.61.

[447] (1828) 3 Russ 1; *Harding Corp. Ltd v Royal Bank of Canada* [1980] WWR 149; *E Pfeiffer Weinkellerei-Weineinkauf GmbH & Co v Arbuthnot Factors Ltd* [1988] 1 WLR 150; *Compaq Computers Ltd v Abercorn Group Ltd* [1991] BCC 484. This view is not uncontroversial, see F Oditah, *Legal Aspects of Receivables Financing* (London, Sweet & Maxwell, 1991) 6.15, and G Tolhurst, *The Assignment of Contractual Rights* (Oxford, Hart Publishing, 2006) chapter 5.

[448] This proviso is known as the 'second limb' of the rule and was added by cases decided after *Dearle v Hall* (1828) 3 Russ 1.

assignee) has an equitable assignment this is probably because it has not given notice.[449] However, B will not necessarily win, since if B had notice of A's assignment when B took its assignment, A will have priority.[450] If B is a financial institution, it is likely to have searched the register and so will have notice of A's assignment. B will thus lose priority, unless it has entered into an agreement with A. If B has not searched the register, it may have constructive notice of A's interest, if B would reasonably be expected to search the register.[451] The position is even less straightforward where A's interest is not registered, for example, where it has taken an absolute assignment which is not registrable. Here B will only be able to find out about A's interest by obtaining information from the borrower, C, or by asking the debtor. Enquiry of the debtor is impractical where the assignment is of a large number of debts.[452] If C does not disclose A's interest, and B has not discovered it by a due diligence exercise, then B will lose priority to A (since A is first in time) unless B has given notice to the debtor first. B can, of course, protect itself to some extent by taking a warranty from C that there have been no previous assignments of the debts, and making breach of warranty an event of default. Breach would then enable B to accelerate any obligations C has and to terminate the agreement. However, this will not fully protect B if C is insolvent.

Another situation which creates a potential exception to the first in time rule is where a lender has taken a security interest over (present and) future property of the borrower, and the borrower then acquires an asset solely with finance provided by another lender, who wishes to take a security interest over that asset. There are a number of reasons why that second secured party should have priority over the first. The asset is a 'windfall' to the first chargee: it merely increases its security when it has done nothing to assist its acquisition. Further, if the first chargee could just keep increasing its security in this way, there would be no incentive for subsequent lenders to lend on security at all. A subsequent lender who lent in relation to a particular asset might be a specialist in the field, and therefore able to lend at a more advantageous rate than the original lender.[453] In many cases of corporate finance, of course, the second lender will be an asset financier, who will supply the asset on retention of title terms.[454] Since the second lender's interest is a legal interest by retention, the borrower never acquires any interest at all, and so the asset cannot fall within the after-acquired property clause in the original charge. Therefore the second lender has priority in relation to that asset. However, if the second lender does take a charge, it will lose priority to the first charge, since on acquisition there is a *scintilla temporis* (a tiny amount of time) when the asset belonged to the borrower before the grant

---

[449]   If A has given notice, its assignment is likely to have become statutory, at least in relation to present debts.

[450]   This is an application of the 'second limb' of the rule.

[451]   See 6.4.3.2.

[452]   Also, the debtor is under no obligation to provide any information (*Ward v Duncombe* [1893] AC 396, 387, 393–94 per Lord McNaghten) and is not liable for negligence for any inaccurate information given (*Low v Bouverie* [1891] 3 Ch 82).

[453]   For further discussion, see C Walsh, 'The floating charge is dead; long live the floating charge', in A Mugasha (ed), *Perspectives in Commercial Law* (Sydney, Prospect, 2000) 129 at 134. See also below page 308 where purchase money security interest (PMSI) superpriority in a notice filing scheme is discussed.

[454]   This includes a conditional sale, hire purchase or finance lease, see 2.3.4.3 above.

of the charge to the second lender, within which time the asset fell within the after-acquired property clause in the first charge. There have been a few cases in which a *scintilla temporis* has been held not to exist,[455] but the law in this area is still unclear.[456]

Another category of exceptions to the first in time doctrine is the series of exceptions to the *nemo dat* rule contained in sections 21 to 25 of the Sale of Goods Act 1979. These exceptions only relate to priority between legal interests in goods[457] and apply to situations where a person who is not the owner of goods appears to be in a position to dispose of them, usually because that person is in possession of the goods. There is not a general principle that a good faith disponee obtains good title in these circumstances, but the Act contains a series of specific situations where this is the result. Only some are relevant to the proprietary protection taken by lenders discussed in this book. One situation is where the goods are disposed of with the authority or consent of the owner.[458] This is commonly the case where goods are sold on retention of title terms, but the contract provides that the buyer has the power to sell the goods in the ordinary course of business. The sub-buyer thus obtains good title, free from any interest of the original seller. Another situation is where a retention of title device is used but there is no power to sell the goods, for example, in asset financing.[459] If the device is a conditional sale, section 25 of the Sale of Goods Act 1979 provides that a good faith disponee taking delivery of the goods similarly obtains good title. Asset financing by means of a hire purchase agreement[460] or a finance lease, however, are not included. If a legal mortgagor of goods sells them to a good faith buyer, the *nemo dat* rule applies so that the buyer takes subject to the mortgage. Section 24 of the Sale of Goods Act 1979, which provides that a good faith buyer from a seller in possession takes free of the first buyer's interest, does not apply here.[461]

In a way similar to the situation in which goods are disposed of with the authority or consent of the owner, a third party taking an interest in assets subject to a security interest will take free from that security interest if the grant of the interest to the third party is with the authority or consent of the secured lender. The extent of authority or consent may be made clear *ex ante* in the security agreement (as in the case of a floating charge) or may be given at the time of the grant (as where assets are subject to a fixed charge but consent to a particular disposition is made. In that situation, the third party takes in priority to the prior security interest. In other words, the first in time rule does not apply. For example, let us take the situation where an asset subject to a fixed charge is sold by the chargor to a third party who had actual or constructive notice of the charge. On the priority rules set out above (*nemo dat* and first in time), the third party would take subject to the charge. However, if the chargee had consented to the disposition and given the chargor power to dispose of the asset, then the third party will take free of the charge.

---

[455] For example, *Abbey National v Cann* [1991] 1 AC 56; *Wilson v Kelland* [1910] 2 Ch 306; *Security Trustee Co v Royal Bank of Canada* [1976] AC 503.

[456] See Gullifer, n 44, 5–62–5–64.

[457] Priority between a prior equitable interest and a subsequent legal interest has already been dealt with.

[458] Sale of Goods Act 1979, s 21.

[459] 2.3.4.3.2.

[460] *Helby v Matthews* [1895] AC 471. The position is different (and more complicated) where the goods are a motor vehicle: this is governed by Hire Purchase Act 1964, s 27.

[461] Sale of Goods Act 1979, s 62(4), which provides that provisions in the Act about contracts of sale do not apply to mortgages or charges.

This reasoning can also explain the position of a party taking an interest in an asset falling within a floating charge. The chargor has power to dispose of the asset in the ordinary course of business so the third party would take free of the charge. Thus where a floating chargor creates a subsequent fixed charge over the assets subject to the floating charge, the fixed charge has priority, since a floating chargee is taken to have power to create fixed charges ranking in priority to the floating charge.[462] This is also true of an absolute assignment of receivables: the rule in *Dearle v Hall* does not apply.[463] However, if the disposition were outside the ordinary course of business, the third party would take subject to the charge.[464] A common situation is where the chargor's powers to dispose are limited in the charge agreement.[465] In this situation, the disponee will take subject to the charge, but only if it has notice (actual or constructive) of the limitation of power. Otherwise the disponee is entitled to assume that the floating chargor has the power to dispose of the asset free of the charge, and will therefore take free of the charge. A floating charge will commonly contain a negative pledge clause, prohibiting the creation of any charge ranking in priority to the floating charge. A party taking a subsequent fixed charge with notice of the negative pledge clause will cede priority to the floating charge, but if the fixed chargee does not have notice it will take free of, and in priority to, the floating charge.[466] In practice, most parties taking a charge search the register, and will know of the restriction, so that they can either adjust to the loss of priority or overcome it with a subordination agreement.

Where a fixed charge takes subject to a floating charge, either because of a subordination agreement or because the fixed charge has notice of a negative pledge clause in a prior floating charge, there is a potentially problematic circularity problem which arises because of the statutory priority of the preferential creditors.[467] Normally, the fixed charge has priority over the preferential creditors who have priority over the floating charge, but here the floating charge has priority over the fixed charge. In *Re Portbase Ltd*,[468] Chadwick J held that, on the interpretation of the relevant statute, the preferential creditors had priority over both the fixed and the floating chargees. This, however, improves the position of the preferential creditors because of factors which have nothing to do with them,[469] and the preferable approach is to treat the floating chargee as subrogated to the fixed chargee's claim.[470]

---

[462] *Wheatley v Silkstone and Haigh Moor Coal Company* (1884) 29 Ch D 715; *Cox Moore v Peruvian Corporation Ltd* [1908] 1 Ch 604. This power is usually restricted in the charge agreement, see discussion later in the paragraph.

[463] *Ward v Royal Exchange Shipping Co Ltd* (1887) 58 LT 174; *Re Ind Coope & Co Ltd* [1911] 2 Ch 223.

[464] For a discussion of what effect this actually has, see Gullifer, n 44, 5–40. This situation would, though, be very rare since 'the ordinary course of business' is very widely defined, see *Ashborder BV v Green Gas Power Ltd* [2004] EWHC 1517 (Ch), [2005] BCC 634; *Re Borax Ltd* [1901] 1 Ch 326 and page 243 above.

[465] It should be borne in mind that a charge where nearly all, but not all, dispositions without the consent of the chargee are prohibited will now be characterised as floating as a result of the *Spectrum* decision.

[466] *English and Scottish Mercantile Investment Co v Brunton* [1892] 2 QB 700; *Welch v Bowmaker (Ireland) Ltd* [1980] IR 251(Sup Ct Ireland).

[467] Here 'preferential creditors' includes all creditors having statutory priority over the floating charge, namely, the expenses of the liquidator or administrator, the preferential creditors and the prescribed part, see 3.3.1.2.

[468] [1993] Ch 388.

[469] Namely, the subordination agreement or the notice of the negative pledge clause.

[470] For a detailed discussion, see Gullifer, n 44, 5–60. This reasoning was conceded as correct in *Re Woodroffe's (Musical Instruments) Ltd* [1986] Ch 366.

In the same way, where a floating charge has crystallised automatically or by notice (as opposed to by a more public trigger, such as cessation of business) a third party acquiring an interest who does not know of the crystallisation is entitled to assume that the floating chargor has the power to dispose of the charged assets free of the charge, and will therefore take free of the charge.[471] If the third party has searched the register, it may know that the charge includes an automatic crystallisation clause, but it will not know of a 'private' crystallisation. If the third party has not searched, there will be no constructive notice even of the clause, as it is not required to be registered. The Government are proposing to address the problem by making automatic crystallisation clauses registrable.[472] However, even if a third party has notice of the clause, this will not give it notice (actual or constructive) that the charge has crystallised: to safeguard its position it would have to make enquiries of the prior chargee and maybe enter into an agreement as to priorities.

The rules as to priority between two floating charges are also rather obscure. The two English cases on the subject both involve detailed consideration of the terms of the charge agreements, rather than laying down any general rules. However, it seems reasonably clear from the decision in *Re Benjamin Cope & Sons Ltd*[473] that even where a floating charge provides that the chargor has a general power to deal with the charged property in the ordinary course of business, this is to be interpreted as not including a power to create a second floating charge over the same assets ranking *pari passu* or in priority to the first charge. The basis of the decision appears to be that the first chargee 'could not have intended to authorise a competing charge upon the entirety of the property comprised in the earlier charge'.[474] Whether the decision would have been the same were the second floating charge to only cover part of the assets charged by the first charge is unclear.[475] In *Re Automatic Bottle Makers Ltd*, where the *Benjamin Cope* decision was extensively considered, a great deal of stress was placed on the fact that in the latter case the charged assets were the same.[476] In that case, the second charge was over only part of the assets, but there was express authorisation of such a charge. The presumption underlying the two cases appears to be that a second charge over part of the assets is authorised by a general power[477] but the position is very unclear. It does, however, seem reasonably clear that the priority between floating charges depends on authority reasoning as set out above and not on the date of crystallisation.[478] Given the lack of clarity in the law, it is no surprise that priority issues in this area are usually dealt with by agreement, and there have been no decided cases for a very considerable time.

Having discussed priority issues involving floating charges which depend on authority reasoning, we now turn to other priority issues where such reasoning is wholly or partially absent. An execution creditor will not obtain priority over a floating charge unless it has

---

[471]   See pages 244–45 above.

[472]   BIS *Registration of Charges created by Companies and Limited Liability Partnerships*, n 236, para 64 proposal G. Views are also elicited on whether automatic crystallisation itself should be registrable. However, since even the chargee does not usually know that the charge has crystallised, this appears impractical.

[473]   [1914] Ch 800 per Sargant J.

[474]   *Re Automatic Bottle Makers Ltd* [1926] Ch 412, 427, where Sargant LJ explains his previous decision.

[475]   Ibid, 417, where Sargant LJ intervened in the argument to say that this point was not decided in *Re Benjamin Cope & Sons Ltd* [1914] 1 Ch 800.

[476]   *Re Automatic Bottle Makers Ltd* [1926] Ch 412, 420 per Lord Hanworth MR, 423 per Warrington LJ, 427 per Sargant LJ.

[477]   Ibid, 423 per Warrington LJ.

[478]   *Re Household Products Co Ltd* (1981) 124 DLR (3d) 325 (Sup Ct Ontario).

completed execution by the time the charge crystallises.[479] Similarly, a local authority cannot distrain for rates once a floating charge has crystallised, unless the charge is a 'mere charge' and not by way of equitable mortgage.[480] A landlord, however, can levy distress for rent on the goods of a company whether or not a floating charge over those goods has crystallised.[481] Obtaining priority over execution creditors is one of the main reasons why automatic crystallisation clauses are included in a floating charge. Even if an execution creditor has no notice that the charge has crystallised, it still takes subject to the floating charge.[482] Creditors obtaining rights of set-off before a floating charge over the debt set-off has crystallised take free of the charge,[483] and also if the right of set-off arises after crystallisation but before notice of the charge to the debtor (the person asserting the set-off).[484]

So far in discussing priorities between charges we have assumed that the loan secured is made at the time of the creation of the charge, or at least before the competing charge is granted. However, if the first chargee makes a further loan or advances credit after the second charge is created, this potentially prejudices the position of the second chargee, who cannot adjust specifically in relation to such an advance, but can only adjust generally *ex ante*.[485] English law gives limited protection to the second chargee, in that the first chargee cannot 'tack' further advances onto its original security interest once it has notice of the second charge, unless it is obliged to make the further advance in its charge agreement.[486] The boundaries of the 'rule against tacking' are very complex, and riddled with uncertainties.[487] Therefore, as in so many contexts in relation to the law of priorities, the answer is for the default position to be circumvented by agreement.

As can be seen from this discussion of the principal priority rules, the English law in this area is complex and, to a large extent, uncertain. The ability of parties to overcome this uncertainty by agreement is not a sufficient justification for the law to remain in its present state. Agreements are not costless, and the law should reflect an easily ascertained default position, that is, the priority position most usually adopted by parties, so that the costs of negotiating around that position are minimised. Reform of the law in this area, and in relation to registration, are discussed below.[488]

---

[479]   *Re Opera Ltd* [1891] 3 Ch 260; *Robson v Smith* [1895] 2 Ch 118; *Evans v Rival Granite Quarries Ltd* [1910] 2 KB 979.

[480]   *Re ELS Ltd* [1995] Ch 11.

[481]   *Re Coal Consumers Association* (1876) LR 4 Ch D 625; *Cunliffe Engineering Ltd v English Industrial Estates Corporation* [1994] BCC 972.

[482]   *Robson v Smith* [1895] 2 Ch 118.

[483]   *Biggerstaff v Rowatt's Wharf Ltd* [1896] 2 Ch 93.

[484]   *Business Computers Ltd v Anglo-African Leasing Ltd* [1977] 2 All ER 741.

[485]   This could be either by charging a higher interest rate (which is unlikely to be a fine tuned adjustment) or by including a covenant prohibiting future borrowing. However, such a covenant (at least in a bald state) may be difficult to include in a loan agreement. See page 156.

[486]   Law of Property Act 1925, s 94.

[487]   For discussion, see Beale et al, n 44, 13.106–13.130 and Gullifer, n 44, 5–17–5–21.

[488]   See 6.7.

6.5 Enforcement

One of the advantages of security is that the secured lender can usually enforce its proprietary rights without using a court process. This can be contrasted with the position of an unsecured creditor, who has to obtain a judgment on its claim and then execute it.[489] If winding up of the company commences before execution is complete, however, the unsecured creditor loses the benefit of the execution and is merely entitled to prove *pari passu* with all the other unsecured creditors.[490] The benefits of security as a means of protecting against credit risk are only as good as the ability of the secured lender to enforce its security.[491] This means that a creditor must have remedies which enable it to assert its proprietary rights effectively and to turn non-cash assets into money out of which it can pay itself. Although the best protection for the secured creditor is if it can enforce without needing to go to court (and this, largely, is the position under UK law, although not in many other countries[492]), there needs to be effective court procedures as a longstop.

The freedom of a secured creditor to enforce its proprietary rights needs to be balanced against the interests of all those who have an actual or potential interest in the relevant assets. This can be said to be a policy of protection of the debtor company, but in fact, since the company is likely to be insolvent at the time of enforcement, the interests that are protected are those of its creditors. More specifically, those most closely interested in the particular asset against which enforcement is being made are creditors who also have a security interest in that asset (either senior or junior to the enforcing creditor) and any surety of the secured debt, since it will have a right to the security if it pays the debt.[493] It is only if there is surplus value in the asset once these parties have been paid that the unsecured creditors (for whom the term 'debtor' is often used as a shorthand) are interested. The danger for these parties is that the asset will decline in value, through mismanagement, or will be sold or otherwise realised at an undervalue. It will be seen that UK law gives a certain level of protection against this danger, but it is by no means comprehensive.

Another danger for all the company's creditors is that enforcement of security results in individual assets being sold at a lower value than if all the assets of the company, or indeed the whole business of the company, were sold together. The former type of sale is often referred to as a 'fire sale'. One way of preventing this is if there is one lead secured creditor, who runs the enforcement process.[494] However, another response is for there to be a

---

[489] For the forms of execution, see pages 220–21.

[490] Insolvency Act 1986, s 183.

[491] Whether enforcement procedures were effective was an important issue, for example, for the European Bank for Research and Development when setting up new systems for secured lending in the Eastern block countries in Europe. F Dahan, E Kutenicova and J Simpson 'Enforcing Secured Transactions in Central and Eastern Europe: An Empirical Study, Part 1' (2004) 19 *Journal of International Banking and Financial Law* 253.

[492] In civil law jurisdictions the original position was that security could only be enforced by a judicially monitored public auction, in order to protect the debtor. Although this position has been substantially changed in recent years, so that private sales are permitted under certain circumstances, the court still plays an important part in enforcement in many countries. For an overview, see P Wood, *Comparative Law of Security Interests and Title Finance*, 2nd edn (London, Sweet & Maxwell, 2007) 20–026–20–037.

[493] See pages 197–98.

[494] This benefit of a lead creditor is discussed below at page 295 and also above at pages 260–61 in the context of the benefits of the floating charge.

collective insolvency procedure, which involves a stay on enforcement of security interests, while attempts are made either to rescue the company or to sell the business as a whole.[495] In the UK, there has been a recent move from the first situation to the second. Before 2003, the floating chargee, who would typically have fixed and floating charges over all the company's assets, would enforce by appointing an administrative receiver, who would enforce outside any insolvency proceedings. The company would go into liquidation, and any assets which were not included within the charge, or which were left over once the chargee had enforced, would be got in and distributed by the liquidator. The Enterprise Act 2002 abolished the power of the floating chargee to appoint an administrative receiver,[496] and instead provided a power for the floating chargee to appoint an administrator out of court.[497]

Administration is a collective insolvency procedure, as referred to above, and a moratorium on the enforcement of security and quasi-security is imposed on the appointment of an administrator.[498] A similar moratorium applies in relation to small companies while a Company Voluntary Arrangement is being discussed,[499] and there are Government proposals to extend to this to larger companies.[500] The moratorium enables the administrator to attempt to rescue the company, but if this is not possible (and it rarely is) the administrator will realise the assets, often by selling the business as a going concern, and distribute the proceeds to the secured creditors who are entitled.[501] If there is any surplus for unsecured creditors, the administrator can distribute this to them,[502] or can put the company into liquidation.

Although certain rights to enforce security interests come from the general law, most secured loan documentation will include provisions about enforcement which extend the general law. The right to enforce security will normally arise on default in payment, and also on acceleration as a result of an event of default.[503] The loan documentation will usually provide for a wide variety of enforcement powers which will enable the creditor to do anything permissible to obtain the value of the secured assets, including taking possession, selling the assets, collecting receivables and other debts, notifying the debtor (in order to turn an equitable assignment into a statutory one) and appointing a receiver.[504]

A secured creditor is not obliged to enforce its security. It can choose to enforce as an unsecured creditor or pursue contractual rights it has against third parties, such as claiming under a guarantee or a credit default swap.[505] Unless it is restricted by contract, it has a totally free choice as to its actions: it does not owe a duty to the debtor or to any

---

[495]   For a global overview of such procedures, see Wood, *Comparative Law of Security Interests and Title Finance*, n 492, 21–011–21–022.

[496]   Insolvency Act 1986, s 72A inserted by Enterprise Act 2002, s 250.

[497]   Insolvency Act 1986, Sch B1 para 14.

[498]   Ibid, para 43.

[499]   Insolvency Act 1986, Sch A1.

[500]   The Insolvency Service: 'Encouraging Corporate Rescue – a consultation' June 2009. For criticism, see R Calnan, 'Encouraging Company Rescue' (2009) 24 *Journal of International Business and Financial Law* 443.

[501]   The administrator has power to distribute to the secured and preferential creditors under Insolvency Act 1986, Sch B1 para 65.

[502]   Leave of the court is required: Insolvency Act 1986, Sch B1 para 65(3).

[503]   Such an event may not be a breach, but will give the creditor the right to accelerate the loan, see above 5.2.3.

[504]   For an example of a clause providing for very wide powers of enforcement, see Wood, n 492, 32–086.

[505]   See above 5.3.

counterparty to act in a particular way.[506] To the extent that one form of enforcement does not fully satisfy the debt, usually the creditor can pursue another form, unless there is a contractual restriction on this.[507] However, if a creditor has security over several assets (A, B and C) and another creditor has security over only one of those assets (A), the doctrine of marshalling operates to prevent the first creditor enforcing over asset A, and leaving the second creditor unsecured.[508]

As discussed earlier in this chapter, a creditor can have proprietary protection in the form of a security interest or an absolute interest. While all of the foregoing two paragraphs applies to both kinds of proprietary protection, the details as to enforcement vary. One of the chief differences, which will be apparent from the discussion above in relation to characterisation of interests, is that on enforcement of a security interest there is an obligation to account for any surplus, that is, the amount of any proceeds over and above the sum required to pay off the secured debt.[509] This is expressly provided for in section 105 of the Law of Property Act 1925 in relation to a sale by a mortgagee or chargee under the power of sale provided for in that Act.[510] This section rarely applies, since enforcement is usually under the terms of the mortgage or charge rather than under the Act, but the same principles apply, and is usually provided for expressly in the terms of the loan agreement.[511] The right of the debtor to the surplus is a proprietary right, that is, it is a right to be paid out of the proceeds of the enforcement themselves and is not just a personal right to be paid the equivalent of the surplus.[512] This is of considerable importance if the enforcing creditor is itself insolvent.

If another creditor also has a security interest in the asset, which ranks below that of the enforcing creditor, then the enforcing creditor is obliged to pay the surplus to the subordinate creditor.[513] Although it will normally be the most senior secured creditor who enforces, in theory a subordinate (or junior) creditor can do so. It can either do so with the consent of the senior secured creditor, in which case it is liable to account to the senior creditor before meeting the costs of enforcement and its own claim,[514] or without consent, in which case the sale is subject to the interest of the senior creditor who can enforce its interests against that of the buyer.[515]

---

[506] *China & South Sea Bank Ltd v Tan* [1990] 1 AC 536, 545; *Cheah Theam Swee v Equiticorp Finance Group Ltd* [1992] 1 AC 472, 476.

[507] This statement may need some qualification in relation to title finance agreements, see below 6.5.2.1.

[508] For details see Beale et al, n 44, 17.05–17.09 and, generally, P Ali, *Marshalling of Securities* (Oxford, Clarendon Press, 1999).

[509] This does not apply on foreclosure, see below 6.5.1.1.

[510] Law of Property Act 1925, s 101 provides that a mortgage (or charge) made by deed includes such a power of sale. It also provides that the costs of enforcement are payable out of the proceeds before the enforcing creditor is paid.

[511] Wood, n 492, 32–089.

[512] Law of Property Act 1925, s 105 expressly provides that the proceeds are held on trust. Earlier cases had already provided that the mortgagee held the proceeds on constructive trust (*Banner v Berridge* (1880) LR 18 Ch D 254, 269), and this therefore would be the case if s.105 did not apply. The loan agreement may provide that the proceeds are held on trust.

[513] This is provided for in section 105, by the words 'the residue of the money so received shall be paid to the person entitled to the mortgaged property': this includes subordinate secured creditors. Beale et al, n 44, 17.54. An obligation to account to subordinate secured creditors is often also included in the loan agreement, see Wood, n 492, 32–089.

[514] Law of Property Act 1925, s 105. This is usually also provided for in the loan agreement.

[515] *Manser v Dix* (1857) 8 De G M & G 703. Such a sale would not be in the ordinary course of business, and so it is very unlikely indeed that a buyer would be a bona fide purchaser without notice of the prior security interest.

Apart from these general points, the legal position in relation to enforcement varies according to the kind of interest that is being enforced. The discussion that follows will concentrate on non-possessory interests, both security interests and absolute interests.[516] The various means of enforcement outside insolvency proceedings are discussed first. These are available to a secured creditor if the company is being wound up, but if an administrator has been appointed, there is a statutory moratorium which prevents the enforcement of any security interest (and some quasi-security interests) without the leave of the court. The circumstances in which such leave will be given are briefly discussed below.[517]

6.5.1   Methods of Enforcement: Security Interests

6.5.1.1   *Foreclosure*

Foreclosure is a remedy only available to a mortgagee, and not to a chargee. It will be recalled that legal or equitable title is transferred to the mortgagee, subject to the mortgagor's right to redeem and equity of redemption. On foreclosure, the mortgagor loses its rights, so that the mortgagee becomes the absolute legal or equitable owner of the assets. It will be seen that, if the assets are worth more than the secured indebtedness, this remedy is greatly to the disadvantage of the mortgagor, who loses the surplus. For this reason, foreclosure is only available by order of the court. On application by the mortgagee, the court can make an order for sale (which would release the surplus value which would be paid to the mortgagor) or can make a foreclosure order nisi, usually for six months, to allow the mortgagor to redeem, for example, by refinancing. If the debt is not paid within that time, the court will make a final order for foreclosure. It will be seen that foreclosure is a remedy with many difficulties and few advantages, and in fact is very rarely used.[518]

6.5.1.2   *Appropriation of Financial Collateral*

This is another remedy which appears to be limited to a mortgage and not a charge.[519] If the terms of the mortgage include a power for the secured party to appropriate the collateral, this power can be exercised by the secured party without any order of the court. The secured party appropriates the collateral by becoming absolute owner. On doing this, it is obliged to value the collateral in a commercially reasonable manner, and account to

---

[516] As noted above, possessory interests are little used in corporate finance outside certain specialist situations.

[517] 6.5.3.

[518] It has recently been described by the Privy Council as 'obsolescent' (*Cukurova Finance International Ltd v Alfa Telecom Turkey Ltd* [2009] UKPC 19, [13]).

[519] This follows from the wording of Regulation 17 of the FCAR. It is not very clear why there is this limitation: the FCD does not, of course, refer to the distinction between a charge and a mortgage: it merely refers to a security financial collateral arrangement, which is defined in Regulation 3 of the FCAR as including both a mortgage and a charge. It is possible that the right to appropriate was seen as analogous to foreclosure, although, of course, there are considerable differences as discussed below. The Privy Council in the *Cukurova* case mentioned this point, but expressed no view on it (at [14]). It is likely, however, that if a security interest expressed as a charge were to include the remedy of appropriation, it would be characterised as an equitable mortgage, see Tolley's Company Law Service C4210.

the collateral giver for any surplus value.[520] If the value of the collateral is insufficient to meet the secured obligation, the debtor remains obliged to pay the outstanding amount.[521] These features make the remedy crucially different from foreclosure, so that it is a novel remedy, previously unknown to English law.[522] It is closer to a sale by the secured party to itself,[523] previously prohibited under English law:[524] sale, as will be seen below, is subject to an equitable duty to take reasonable care to obtain true market value.[525] Furthermore, the appropriation can be of the absolute legal title (which would usually be case if the mortgage was legal) or the absolute equitable title (if the mortgage was equitable).[526] The nature of appropriation as a sale to the mortgagee, however, means that the obligation to account for the surplus is not proprietary but is merely a personal obligation to pay the surplus to the collateral giver. This puts the collateral giver at risk of the secured party's insolvency, and is in contrast to enforcement by sale to a third party or other means. It should be remembered, though, that appropriation is only available if the mortgagor has agreed to it in the security agreement.

6.5.1.3 *Possession and Sale*

A mortgagee or chargee may enforce its interest itself by taking possession of the assets and, if necessary to realise their value, to sell them. There is no doubt that a legal mortgagee has a right to take possession:[527] it is less clear that an equitable mortgagee has such a right, and clear that a chargee does not have it, but the agreement will nearly always make express provision for both a right to take possession and also for a right to sue to enforce choses in action (such as receivables) which are the subject of the mortgage or charge.

The right of sale of a mortgagee or chargee may arise in several ways. First, there is a right of sale on default implied by the general law in relation to mortgages.[528] Second, where a mortgage or charge is made by deed, there is a power of sale implied by section 101 of the Law of Property Act 1925. However, this is limited by certain restrictions set out in section 103, and although these are customarily excluded in a security agreement, the statutory power of sale is usually superceded anyway by an express power of sale.

Although the mortgagee[529] is under no duty to enforce in a particular way, or to enforce at all, once it undertakes enforcement it comes under duties which are owed not only to

---

[520] FCAR reg 18(2).

[521] FCAR reg 18(3).

[522] *Cukurova Finance International Ltd v Alfa Telecom Turkey Ltd* [2009] 1 CLC 701 [14] (CA British Virgin Islands).

[523] Ibid, [27].

[524] *Martinson v Clowes* (1882) 21 Ch D 857.

[525] *Cuckmere Brick Co v Mutual Finance Ltd* [1971] Ch 949, 965, 972, 977.

[526] *Cukurova Finance International Ltd v Alfa Telecom Turkey Ltd* [2009] 1 CLC 701, [34]–[36]. It is, however, necessary that there is a positive act evincing the intention to appropriate, which is communicated to the collateral giver.

[527] *Four-Maids Ltd v Dudley Marshall (Properties) Ltd* [1957] Ch 317, 320. The agreement normally provides that this right only arises on default, *Johnson v Diprose* [1893] 1 QB 512; *Birmingham Citizens Permanent Building Society v Caunt* [1962] Ch 883.

[528] *Re Morritt* (1886) 18 QBD 222, 233 per Cotton LJ; *Deverges v Sandeman, Clark & Co* [1902] 1 Ch 579, 588–89 per Vaughan-Williams LJ, 592–93 per Stirling LJ; *Stubbs v Slater* [1910] 1 Ch 632, 639 per Cozens-Hardy MR.

[529] The analysis in this and the following paragraphs applies equally to a mortgagee and a chargee, and therefore only the term 'mortgagee' will be used for clarity.

the mortgagor, but also to other secured creditors,[530] and to sureties,[531] as they are affected by diminution in the value of the assets. There is a basic duty to act in good faith;[532] apart from this, the secured party is free to act in its own interests, subject to certain equitable duties. These duties are imposed only when the secured party actually takes steps to enforce. Thus, for example, there is no duty on a mortgagee to sell the assets[533] or to sell at any particular time,[534] even if those decisions result in detriment to the mortgagor. Generally, the duties of a mortgagee only arise where their imposition would not result in a conflict of interest between it and the mortgagor. Where there is such a conflict, the mortgagee is entitled to protect its own interests.[535]

When a mortgagee does take possession of the mortgaged assets, it is under a duty to take reasonable care to manage[536] and preserve them, the standard of care being a flexible one of reasonable competence.[537] If a mortgagee decides to sell the mortgaged assets, it comes under a duty to take reasonable care to obtain the true market value at the time of sale.[538] The mortgagee will not be liable just because a higher price could be obtained: it is enough if it obtained a 'proper price',[539] and it is under no duty to improve the assets to obtain a higher price.[540]

6.5.1.4 Appointment of a Receiver

The (albeit light) duties imposed on a mortgagee in possession has meant that in the past most mortgagees have preferred to appoint a receiver over the mortgaged or charged assets, rather than take possession and sell themselves. This has the effect of protecting the mortgagee from liability, since usually the receiver is the agent of the mortgagor.[541] The mortgagee can act totally in its own interests in deciding whether or not to appoint a receiver[542] (providing that it acts in good faith) although if it does decide to appoint it is probably under some sort of minimal duty to appoint a competent person.[543] Where a mortgage or charge is made by deed, the mortgagee or chargee has a right to appoint a receiver under section 101 of the Law of Property Act 1925. Such a receiver has very limited powers[544] and there is usually a much wider power included in the mortgage or

---

[530]   *Tomlin v Luce* (1889) 43 ChD 191; *Downsview Nominees Ltd v First City Corporation Ltd* [1993] AC 295, 311.
[531]   *American Express International Banking Corporation v Hurley* [1986] BCLC 52, 61.
[532]   *Downsview Nominees Ltd v First City Corporation Ltd* [1993] AC 295, 317.
[533]   *Raja v Austin-Gray* [2002] EWCA Civ 1965, para 55; *Silven Properties Ltd v Royal Bank of Scotland plc* [2003] EWCA Civ 1409 [14]; [2004] 1 WLR 997, 1004.
[534]   *Cuckmere Brick Co v Mutual Finance Ltd* [1971] Ch 949, 965; *Tse Kwong Lam v Wong Chit Sen* [1983] 1 WLR 1349, 1355.
[535]   *Cuckmere Brick Co v Mutual Finance Ltd* [1971] Ch 949, 965; *Shamji v Johnson Matthey Bankers Ltd* [1991] BCLC 36, 42. Beale et al, n 44, 17.38.
[536]   *Palk v Mortgage Services Funding plc* [1993] Ch 330, 338 per Sir Donald Nicholls VC; *McHugh v Union Bank of Canada* [1913] AC 299.
[537]   *Medforth v Blake* [1999] EWCA Civ 1482; [2000] Ch 86, 93.
[538]   *Cuckmere Brick Co v Mutual Finance Ltd* [1971] Ch 949, 965, 972, 977.
[539]   *Parker-Tweedale v Dunbar Bank plc* [1991] Ch 12.
[540]   *Silven Properties Ltd v Royal Bank of Scotland plc* [2003] EWCA Civ 1409; [2004] 1 WLR 997.
[541]   See page 286.
[542]   *In re Potters Oils Ltd* [1986] 1 WLR 201, 206; *Shamji v Johnson Matthey Bankers* [1991] BCLC 36, 42.
[543]   *Shamji v Johnson Matthey Bankers* [1991] BCLC 36, 42.
[544]   There is no power of sale, and the statutory power is limited by the restrictions in s 103.

charge agreement.[545] In the past, a floating chargee would routinely appoint a receiver over all the assets of the company: this would be an administrative receiver and, latterly, had extensive powers set out in Insolvency Act 1986. However, except in limited cases, the power to appoint an administrative receiver has been abolished and a floating chargee can, instead, appoint an administrator out of court.[546] A mortgagee or chargee, however, can still appoint a receiver over part of the company's assets under section 101 Law of Property Act 1925 or under a power in the security agreement.

Chargees under charges created before 15 September 2003 are still able to appoint an administrative receiver. Interestingly, however, the official statistics showed a rapid drop-off in receiverships after 2003, coupled with a rapid rise in administrations, indicating that chargees were preferring to appoint an administrator rather than an administrative receiver, even where they had the right to do so.[547] However, in 2008 and 2009 the numbers of receiverships increased considerably.[548] There was also a marked increase in administrations and liquidations,[549] which indicates (unsurprisingly) that the number of companies in financial difficulties rose generally during those years as a result of the economic crisis. Further, the statistics do not distinguish between administrative receiverships and receivers appointed under section 101 of the Law of Property Act 1925 or under a power in the security agreement. One possible explanation, therefore, is that more secured creditors are appointing receivers over part of the assets as an alternative to putting the company into administration.[550] The advantage of doing this is that enforcement can take place straight away, unless another creditor[551] or the company's directors[552] appoint an administrator, in which case the moratorium would apply.

It should be pointed out that the cases in which a floating chargee can still appoint an administrative receiver are significant in terms of the sums involved. These cases are set out in sections 72B to 72GA of the Insolvency Act 1986, and broadly cover two areas: charges in relation to the capital and financial markets, and in relation to project finance, including projects in the public sector. The carve-outs were as a result of considerable lobbying from interested parties, and as such are connected more by policy considerations than by matters of principle.

---

[545] There is also a residual power to apply to the court for the appointment of a receiver, but again this will be superceded by the express power in the agreement.

[546] Insolvency Act 1986, Sch B1 para 14.

[547] Insolvency Service statistics, Receiverships, Administrations and Company Voluntary Arrangements. This is confirmed by a Report Prepared for the Insolvency Service by John Armour, Audrey Hsu and Adrian Walters in December 2006 (page 16).

[548] From 337 in 2007 to 1,468 in 2009: figures from the Insolvency Service statistics.

[549] Insolvency Service statistics, n 547.

[550] See V Finch, 'Reinvigorating Corporate Rescue' [2003] *Journal of Business Law* 526, 537 and R Stevens, 'Security after the Enterprise Act' in J Getzler and J Payne (eds), *Company Charges: Spectrum and Beyond* (Oxford, Oxford University Press, 2006) 166–67.

[551] A creditor can only appoint an administrator by application to the court under Insolvency Act 1986, Sch B1 para 12.

[552] The company's directors can appoint an administrator out of court under Insolvency Act 1986, Sch B1 para 22. The company can also make such an appointment, where there is a resolution of shareholders to that effect (Insolvency Rules 1986, Rule 2.22).

A receiver is usually the agent of the mortgagor and not the mortgagee.[553] The agency is not a usual one, however.[554] The relationship is tripartite, including the receiver, the mortgagee and the mortgagor.[555] The receiver owes duties (which are equitable, and not common law duties) both to the mortgagee and to all those interested in the equity of redemption, which includes the mortgagor and other creditors. The receiver owes a duty of good faith, and then other duties, which will vary depending on the circumstances. If the receiver chooses to manage the mortgaged assets, he owes an equitable duty of care, the primary duty of which is to bring about a situation in which the secured debt is repaid.[556] In relation to sale of the mortgaged assets, the receiver owes the same duty as the mortgagee does:[557] thus there is no positive duty to sell, nor to sell at any particular time, nor to do more than obtain a proper price (for example, there is no duty to improve the property to obtain a higher price[558]). Since the receiver is the agent of the mortgagor, the mortgagee will not be liable for his acts, unless the mortgagee treats him as an agent,[559] or specifically directs him to do particular acts.[560]

It will be seen that, apart from a general duty of good faith and some limited duties if he actually manages or sells the property, a receiver is free to act in the interests of the mortgagee, and, to some extent, to protect his own interests by not taking on tasks which might leave him open to liability.[561] In relation to an administrative receiver, it was this focus on furthering the interests of the floating chargee, rather than on operating for the benefit of all the creditors, which persuaded the Government that this gave too little protection to unsecured creditors.[562] This was especially so where the floating chargee was oversecured, as there was no incentive for the administrative receiver to do anything other than realise from the charged assets the amount due to the floating chargee.[563] The Government responded by abolishing administrative receivership and replacing the floating chargee's remedy with a fast-track into administration. The administrator, unlike a receiver, owes a duty to act in the interests of all the company's creditors,[564] unless he has decided that he cannot either rescue the company or achieve a better result for the company's creditors as a whole than if it were wound up.[565] If he does so decide, he can pursue the tertiary objective of realising property in order to distribute to secured and preferential creditors, but even so he is under a duty not to unnecessarily harm the interests of the creditors of the company as a whole.[566] Thus, in theory, the administrator's

---

[553] Law of Property Act 1925, s 109(2), where the receiver is appointed under section 101; Insolvency Act 1986, s 44 in relation to administrative receivers. The security agreement will also usually provide that the receiver is the agent of the mortgagor.

[554] Although it is a real agency, *Rhodes v Allied Dunbar Pension Services Ltd* [1989] 1 WLR 800, 807.

[555] The relationship and the duties arising from it are considered in *Silven Properties Ltd v Royal Bank of Scotland plc* [2003] EWCA Civ 1409 [27]; [2004] 1 WLR 997, 1007–08.

[556] *Medforth v Blake* [2000] Ch 86, 102.

[557] *Medforth v Blake* [2000] Ch 86, 99; *Silven Properties Ltd v Royal Bank of Scotland plc* [2003] EWCA Civ 1409, [27]; [2004] 1 WLR 997, 1007–08.

[558] *Silven Properties Ltd v Royal Bank of Scotland plc* [2003] EWCA Civ 1409 [28]; [2004] 1 WLR 997, 1008.

[559] *American Express International Banking Corporation v Hurley* [1986] BCLC 52, 57.

[560] *Standard Chartered Bank v Walker* [1982] 1 WLR 1410, 1418; *Medforth v Blake* [2000] Ch 86, 95.

[561] Stevens, 'Security after the Enterprise Act' n 550, 159.

[562] Insolvency Service, *Insolvency – A Second Chance* (Cm 5234, 2001), para 2.2, 2.3.

[563] Mokal, *Corporate Insolvency Law*, n 335, 212.

[564] Insolvency Act 1986, Sch B1 para 3(2).

[565] Ibid, para 3.

[566] Ibid, para 3(4).

duties when realising security are more onerous than those of an administrative receiver, but this is unlikely to make much difference in the application of those duties in practice.[567]

6.5.2 Methods of Enforcement: Absolute Interests

6.5.2.1 Devices Based on Retention of Title[568]

Where the lender[569] has retained title to goods, enforcement consists of the retaking of possession. The borrower will have the right to possession under the agreement, and so, for the lender to retake possession, that right has to have reverted. This could be because the borrower is in repudiatory breach of the agreement, which has been accepted by the lender, or because the agreement provides that the lender has the right to terminate the right to possession on a particular breach (such as non-payment of an instalment) or event (such as insolvency of the lessee,[570] or indication of financial distress). The effect of retaking on the borrower will vary depending on two linked matters: the current value of the goods (whether they are worth more or less than the amount agreed to be paid) and the amount already paid by the borrower to the lender pursuant to the agreement. If the value of the goods has risen, or (perhaps more likely to be the case) a substantial amount has already been paid pursuant to the agreement, the borrower will be left 'out of pocket' by the retaking. However the lender, as the owner, prima facie has no obligation to account to the borrower for any surplus value of the goods over and above the outstanding debt. There are various ways that the issue is dealt with in the current law, which will be examined in the next paragraphs.

One technique is for the parties to provide in the agreement for the surplus, or part of it, to be returned to the borrower. Since the transaction involves a reservation of title rather than a grant of an interest, this will not result in the interest being recharacterised as a security interest.[571] Such a provision may well be found in a transaction where title is reserved until all monies due from the buyer to the seller are paid (an 'all monies' clause),[572] or the court may imply a right to the surplus.[573] In conditional sale, hire purchase and finance lease transactions, which have a fixed amount of payments due over a particular term, there are usually provisions which have the effect that the seller is to be put into a position as if the buyer had committed a repudiatory breach of contract. Thus

---

[567] Calnan, n 442, 319.

[568] There are sales on retention of title terms, conditional sales, hire purchase agreements and finance leases. For discussion of these devices see 2.3.4.3 above. For detailed discussion of enforcement in relation to such devices, see Beale et al, n 44, chapter 18.

[569] The word 'lender' will be used throughout this section to refer to the financier who extends credit, either for the acquisition of assets on the basis of retention of title (see 2.3.4.3.2) or who buys assets from the borrower company who then buys or leases them back (see 2.3.4.3.1). The word 'borrower' will be used for the borrower company.

[570] Such a provision, or a provision that the agreement terminated automatically on the insolvency of the lessee could be said to fall foul of the anti-deprivation principle discussed in *Perpetual Trustee*, see above 3.3.2.1, but in the case of leases and licenses, this is not the case, since it can be said that a limited interest has been granted in the first place. *Perpetual Trustee Co Ltd v BNY Corporate Trustee Services Ltd* [2009] EWCA Civ 1160, [81].

[571] See pages 226 and 234–35.

[572] See above n 123.

[573] *Clough Mill Ltd v Martin* [1985] 1 WLR 111, 117–18.

the lender is compensated for the loss of bargain, either by keeping the payments made or suing for payments due or both, but has to give credit for the amount realised by the sale of the repossessed goods, and for early repayment of the outstanding debt. The borrower is, to some extent, protected by the rule against penalties,[574] and also, in some situations, by the ability to obtain relief against forfeiture of sums already paid.[575]

A further possible technique, which applies only to some kinds of transactions, is the use of the restitutionary right of the borrower to recover payments made on the grounds of total failure of consideration.[576] This only applies where the transaction is structured as a sale, and then only where it can be shown that goods repossessed have actually been paid for or if the goods are sold on conditional sale and a number of instalments have already been paid. In relation to hire purchase agreements and finance leases, no such recovery is possible as the contract is seen as partially performed by the period of hire that has elapsed.[577] Even in conditional sale agreements, this method of recovery is usually expressly excluded. Thus in relation to all three types of transaction, recovery of sums paid would only be possible if the court were prepared to grant relief against forfeiture of sums paid. In relation to corporate, non-consumer borrowers, the courts have so far been very unwilling to do this.[578]

However, the courts have been more willing to grant relief against forfeiture of goods, when a lender seeks repossession. The jurisdiction to grant relief exists where there is a transfer of possessory or proprietary rights[579] (in the situations discussed in this section the rights transferred are possessory) and where the object of the transaction and the insertion of the right to forfeit is essentially to secure the payment of money.[580] These criteria are fulfilled in the cases of conditional sale, hire purchase and finance lease transactions, and the jurisdiction has been held to exist in all three situations,[581] although

---

[574]   Although it should be noted that the scope of this rule is limited to sums paid on breach, and so does not extend to sums payable on a non-breach event which entitles the lender to terminate the contract, *Associated Distributors Ltd v Hall* [1938] 2 KB 83; *Bridge v Campbell Discount Co Ltd* [1962] AC 600; *In Re Apex Supply Co Ltd* [1942] Ch 108; *Transag Haulage Ltd v Leyland DAF Finance plc and another* [1994] 2 BCLC 88.

[575]   The law on this is technical and complicated, and still, to a certain extent, unclear. See H Beale (ed), *Chitty on Contracts,* 30th edn (London, Sweet & Maxwell, 2008) chapter 26 section 7, Beale et al, n 44, 18.12–18.16; 18.26–18.28; 18.33–18.36 and L Gullifer, 'Agreed Remedies' in A Burrows and E Peel (eds), *Commercial Remedies* (Oxford, Oxford University Press, 2007) 200–12.

[576]   This would be subject to a claim for damages for loss of bargain. *Clough Mill Ltd v Martin* [1985] 1 WLR 111, 117.

[577]   *Brooks v Beirnstein* [1909] 1 KB 98; *Chatterton v Maclean* [1951] 1 All ER 761.

[578]   This is despite the fact that a majority of the Court of Appeal in *Stockloser v Johnson* [1954] 1 QB 476 said (at 485 and 490) that there was jurisdiction to grant such relief where it was unconscionable for the lender to retain such sums. Unconscionability would depend on a number of factors, including how much had been paid, compared to the benefit that the borrower already had had out of the contract, which would indicate whether the lender was unjustly enriched (see Denning LJ in Stockloser above at 492). However, the minority view (that there was no such jurisdiction) has been followed at first instance in *Galbraith v Mitchenall Estates Ltd* [1965] 2 QB 473 and *Windsor Securities v Loreldal* (The Times) 1 January 1975. For further discussion, see Beale, *Chitty on Contracts,* n 575, 26–146–150; Beale et al, n 44, 18.16, 18.28, 18.36, and Gullifer, 'Agreed Remedies', n 575, 208–11.

[579]   *The Scaptrade* [1983] 2 AC 694.

[580]   *Shiloh Spinners Ltd v Harding* [1973] AC 691, 722.

[581]   Hire purchase: see *Goker v NWS Bank plc,* 1 August 1990 (Lexis); *Transag Haulage Ltd v Leyland DAF Finance plc and others* [1994] 2 BCLC 88; *More OG Romsdal Fylkesbatar AS v The Demise Charterers of the Ship 'Jotunheim'* [2004] EWHC 671 (Comm); Finance lease: see *On Demand Information plc v Michael Gerson (Finance) plc* [2003] 1 AC 368. There are no direct cases on conditional sale, but Romer LJ accepted obiter that it would be available in *Stockloser v Johnson* [1954] 1 QB 476. It could be argued that in some cases of conditional sale the more appropriate response is relief against forfeiture of payments, see L Smith, 'Relief Against Forfeiture: A Restatement' (2001) 60 *Cambridge Law Journal* 178, 183.

not in the case of an operating lease.[582] The relief is discretionary, and will only be granted if the lender can be protected financially, either by the continuation of periodic payments,[583] or by the payment of all outstanding debts.[584] The conduct of the borrower is also relevant (repeated default is a reason not to grant relief)[585] as is the size of any windfall the lender will obtain were relief not to be given.[586]

At least in situations where relief is granted on payment of the outstanding amount, this jurisdiction can be seen as treating a device based on retention of absolute title like a security interest, since the borrower is effectively given a right to redeem.[587] This is particularly striking in a case like *On Demand Information plc v Michael Gerson (Finance) plc*[588] where relief was given despite the fact that the goods themselves had been sold, so that all that was being protected was the borrower's financial position, that is, the surplus value in the goods over and above the outstanding debt. The result is analogous to that where a security interest is enforced. In a case where the borrower is entitled to retain the goods themselves, this can be seen as enabling the borrower to use the goods in its business.[589] Protection of this non-financial interest was the original reason for granting relief against forfeiture, in the context of interests in land, and to the extent that this is the reason for giving relief in the retention of title cases, it is less easy to see the grant of such relief as treating the lender's interest as a security interest. After all, if a secured party has the right to take possession and sell the collateral on default,[590] the borrower cannot ask the court for relief against the loss of the use of the asset.

Outside of the situation where the borrower is insolvent,[591] and therefore use of the goods may be temporarily critical to enable the business to be sold quickly, it is hard to see why relief should be given for non-financial reasons where the subject matter of the contract is goods, which are not unique, as opposed to land, which is unique. It should always be possible for the borrower to refinance and acquire replacement goods, and if it is not, this indicates that the lender will be disadvantaged by being forced to continue in a relationship with the borrower. This type of reasoning underlay the decision in *Celestial Aviation Trading 71 Ltd v Paramount Airways Private Ltd*[592] where the court decided that there was no jurisdiction to give relief against forfeiture in relation to an operating lease,

---

[582] *Celestial Aviation Trading 71 Ltd v Paramount Airways Private Ltd* [2010] EWHC 185 (Comm) cf *Barton Thompson & Co Ltd v Stapling Machines Co* [1966] Ch 499 where the point was left open.

[583] This was offered in *More OG Romsdal Fylkesbatar AS v The Demise Charterers of the Ship 'Jotunheim'* [2004] EWHC 671 (Comm) although the court decided not to award relief on other grounds.

[584] *Transag Haulage Ltd v Leyland DAF Finance plc* [1994] 2 BCLC 88. This was also effectively the position in *On Demand Information plc v Michael Gerson (Finance) plc* [2003] 1 AC 368.

[585] *Goker v NWS Bank plc*, 1 August 1990; *More OG Romsdal Fylkesbatar AS v The Demise Charterers of the Ship 'Jotunheim'* [2004] EWHC 671 (Comm).

[586] *Transag Haulage Ltd v Leyland DAF Finance plc* [1994] 2 BCLC 88, 101.

[587] L Smith, 'Relief Against Forfeiture: A Restatement' (2001) 60 *Cambridge Law Journal* 178. See also *Celestial Aviation Trading 71 Ltd v Paramount Airways Private Ltd* [2010] EWHC 185 (Comm) [53] where Hamblen J described the interest of a lessor under a finance lease as 'more of a security interest than an ownership interest'.

[588] [2003] 1 AC 368.

[589] This was the reason for seeking relief in *Transag Haulage Ltd v Leyland DAF Finance plc* [1994] 2 BCLC 88 since the borrower's business could not be carried on and sold as a going concern without the use of the fleet of lorries which were the subject of the application.

[590] See page 283.

[591] A similar effect to relief against forfeiture is achieved within insolvency by the moratorium imposed on the appointment of an administrator, see below 6.5.3, since the borrower is enabled to retain the goods providing that the administrator pays the rent or other periodic payments.

[592] [2010] EWHC 185 (Comm).

since the point of the termination provisions was not just to secure the payment of rent. In that case, a stark distinction was drawn between the retention of title devices discussed above, which were treated as security interests, and an operating lease, where the interest of the lessor was in more than merely getting paid: it was also in receiving back the aircraft which was the subject of the lease.[593]

6.5.2.2   *Devices based on the Grant of an Absolute Interest*[594]

As discussed in 2.3.4.1 above, there are two possible types of receivables financing structure which involve the transfer of an absolute interest to the lender. A factor, who takes a statutory assignment of the debts and who provides a debt collection service to the borrower, is in a position to sue any non-paying debtor in its own name.[595] In an invoice discounting arrangement, the lender normally takes only an equitable assignment and the debtors are not notified.[596] The borrower thus collects in the debts itself, but will hold the proceeds on trust for the lender. As trustee, the borrower will be obliged to account to the lender for the proceeds, and, in relation to those proceeds, the lender will have priority over all other claimants to the borrower's assets if the borrower is insolvent. In most invoice discounting agreements, the lender will have the right to give notice to the debtors and convert its equitable assignment into a statutory assignment, so that it can sue the non-paying debtors itself. As mentioned above, many receivables financing transactions contain terms giving the lender a right effectively to recover any shortfall and an obligation effectively to account for a surplus to the borrower, but this has not led the courts to recharacterise the arrangement as a charge.[597]

6.5.3   The Effect of Administration

If an administrator is appointed, the effect on enforcement by secured creditors is immediate and dramatic: there is a moratorium on the enforcement of security and the repossession of goods under hire purchase agreements, as well as other legal process against the property of the company.[598] The imposition of the moratorium means that no steps may be taken to enforce security or repossess goods without the consent of the administrator or the leave of the court while the company is in administration. The effect of the moratorium is merely procedural: the secured creditor retains its proprietary rights.[599] The reason for the moratorium is to permit the administrator during the temporary period of the administration to use the company's property to carry on the

---

[593]   Ibid, [64].

[594]   The term 'lender' is used in this section to mean the receivables financier (the purchaser of the receivables) and the term 'borrower' for the seller of the receivables.

[595]   See pages 374–75.

[596]   See page 375.

[597]   See pages 233–34.

[598]   Insolvency Act 1986, Sch B1 para 43. An interim moratorium, which has the same effect, takes effect while certain procedural steps prior to the appointment of an administrator are being taken (Insolvency Act 1986, Sch B1 para 44).

[599]   *Barclays Mercantile Business Finance Ltd v Sibec Ltd* [1992] 1 WLR 1253; [1993] BCLC 1077, 1081; *Centre Reinsurance International Co v Freakley* [2006] UKHL 45, [7], [16].

business with a view to rescue, or to carrying out one of his other purposes.[600] It will be recalled that the administrator, in order to further the purposes of the administration, also has the power to dispose of floating charge assets without leave of the court,[601] and to dispose of assets subject to fixed charges and hire purchase property with the leave of the court,[602] in which case the secured party is protected by obtaining an interest in the proceeds.[603] There is thus a balance between the rights of secured creditors to enforce against the secured assets, and the benefits which come to all the creditors from keeping the assets together, and from allowing the administrator freedom to act.[604]

Two further points need to be made about the moratorium. First, it does not just extend to the enforcement of true security interests,[605] but to title retention devices as well. 'Hire purchase agreements' are defined in paragraph 111(1) of Schedule B1 of the Insolvency Act 1986 as including a conditional sale agreement, a chattel leasing agreement and a retention of title agreement'.[606] Second, a secured creditor (used in the wide sense) can ask the administrator for permission to enforce, and, if this is not forthcoming, apply to the court for leave.

The principles on which permission and leave should be granted were set out in *Re Atlantic Computer Systems plc.*[607] In that case, the Court of Appeal gave guidance on what is generally the approach of the court in leave applications in order to assist administrators and parties. The court stressed that usually the decision whether to agree to enforcement should be that of the administrator, and that applications to court should be the exception rather than the rule, and this has proved to be the case. The general principles set out related to the previous legislation,[608] but the wording of the current legislation is the same,[609] and recent cases have applied the *Re Atlantic Computers* guidance to applications under the current legislation.[610]

The guidelines make it clear that it is for the secured creditor to make out a case for permission to enforce, but that the moratorium is imposed so as to enable the administrator to carry out the purpose of the administration,[611] so if enforcement will not interfere with that purpose, then it will normally be permitted. If it would interfere with the purpose, then the administrator, or the court, has to carry out a balancing exercise between the interests of the secured creditor and of the other creditors of the company,

---

[600] See page 90. His purpose may be, or may become, the realisation of assets for distribution to the secured creditors, see pages 286–87 above.

[601] Insolvency Act 1986, Sch B1 para 70.

[602] Ibid, para 71(1).

[603] The nature of this interest varies according to the type of security or quasi-security: ibid, paras 70(2), 71(3) and 72 (3).

[604] Mokal, n 335, 254.

[605] 'Security' is defined in s 248(b) Insolvency Act 1986 as 'any mortgage, charge, lien or other security', and clearly includes pledges, as well as non-consensual security interests (R Goode, *Principles of Corporate Insolvency Law,* 3rd edn (London, Thomson, 2005) 10–53).

[606] For further discussion see R Goode, *Principles of Corporate Insolvency Law,* 3rd edn, (London, Thomson, 2005) 10–59.

[607] [1992] Ch 505, 541 et seq.

[608] Insolvency Act 1986, s 11(3)(c).

[609] Ibid, Sch B1 para 43(2) and (3).

[610] *Fashoff (UK) Ltd v Linton* [2008] EWHC 537 (Ch).

[611] The possible purposes are now set out in Insolvency Act 1986 Sch B1 para 3. See page 90 above and pages 286–87 above. The administrator has to, as soon as practicable after the company enters administration, identify which purpose is achievable and explain how he envisages that it is to be achieved (Insolvency Act 1986, Sch B1 para 49 and Insolvency Rules 1986, r 2.33(2)).

including an assessment of what likely loss will be caused to each party by the giving of permission. Although the exercise is one of balance, there appears to be a considerable amount of extra weight given to the interests of those creditors with proprietary protection (the guidelines in *Re Atlantic Computers* were given in relation to the whole moratorium, which also covers enforcement by unsecured creditors).[612] However, the administrator or court should also take into account the extent of the creditor's proprietary protection: if the creditor is under-secured delay in enforcement is more likely to be prejudicial than if it is fully secured.[613] Permission, or leave, can be given on terms, and terms can also be imposed by the court if no leave is given, in that the court can give directions to the administrator. Thus a secured or quasi-secured creditor can be protected even though it cannot enforce immediately, by terms which oblige the administrator to continue to pay rent (in the case of, for example, a finance lease or hire purchase) or interest payments.

In common with many other insolvency provisions, the moratorium provisions are disapplied in relation to financial collateral arrangements.[614] The purpose of the disapplication of these provisions is said to be to prevent systemic risk and to promote the certainty of such arrangements, by taking away the various insolvency provisions in different Member States which inhibit effective realisation of financial collateral.[615] Thus, even if the borrower company is in administration, secured or quasi-secured creditors can freely enforce their interests over securities, and also over cash in bank accounts provided that their security interest meets the criterion of 'control' in the Regulations.[616] In relation to a bank account, an ability of the chargor to withdraw cash if the credit is over the amount of the secured debt seems not to prevent the chargee having control within the meaning of the regulations.[617]

6.6 Economic Arguments about Secured Credit

So far we have assumed that companies should generally be free to grant proprietary interests in their assets (both absolute and by way of security), although we have noted that English law places some restrictions on this, both in terms of registration requirements and (in relation to the floating charge) in terms of loss of priority and other effects on the insolvency of the chargor. We now turn to the question of whether the institution of secured credit is desirable at all from an economic point of view and, if it is, what system achieves the best economic outcome, in the sense of eliminating inefficiencies and maximising added value.

---

[612] Insolvency Act 1986, Sch B1 para 43(4) covers the right of forfeiture by peaceful re-entry by a landlord, and para 43(6) covers all legal proceedings as well as execution.
[613] *Re Atlantic Computer Systems plc* [1992] Ch 505, 544.
[614] Financial Collateral Arrangements Regulations 2003, reg 8.
[615] Financial Collateral Directive preamble para 5 and Article 4.
[616] Discussed above pages 262–67.
[617] See above page 267.

6.6.1   Means of Assessing a System of Secured Credit

There is extensive literature on this subject, mainly generated by scholars from the United States.[618] It is necessary to appreciate that there are different viewpoints as to what is a 'good' system. One view is to judge a system by the criterion of economic efficiency. This can be judged by one of two standards: the Kaldor-Hicks test, which sees an activity as efficient if it maximises value overall even if some participants are worse off, and the Pareto test, which only sees it as efficient if it maximises overall value without any participants being worse off.[619] At first sight, a system of secured credit clearly does make some participants worse off, as the priority of secured creditors in insolvency automatically means that the unsecured creditors do not recover in full. However, if it can be argued that the unsecured creditors are either made better off by the general institution of security, or that they are not made worse off by the grant of a security interest in a specific situation, then the system is potentially efficient even on the Pareto test.

Another possible viewpoint is to assess a system in terms of fairness,[620] which would usually focus on the question of fairness to the unsecured creditors of the borrower in insolvency. This can be seen as an extended application of the Pareto test: it can be unfair for some creditors to suffer for a system which brings overall benefit. However, it can also include other kinds of arguments, such as the argument that the employees of a company have contributed towards the assets and so should share in them. A third possible viewpoint is to prioritise freedom of contract:[621] this view would see the borrower's right to alienate its own property as critical, and the system would be judged on how well it facilitated the granting of security (and other) interests by borrowers.[622] Another possible line of enquiry is to consider whether there are benefits in the institution of secured credit which are not available (or are available only at greater cost) if creditors only protected themselves by means of contractual protection such as covenants.[623] In considering the literature, it needs to be remembered that the US system is very different from that of the UK, both in terms of the law of secured transactions,[624] and in terms of the general law.[625] It is useful, however, to consider some of the arguments made and to apply them to current English law as well as to any proposals for reform.

---

[618]   For an interesting overview of much of the literature, see G McCormack, *Secured Credit under English and American Law* (Cambridge, Cambridge University Press, 2004) chapter 1.

[619]   McCormack, *Secured Credit under English and American Law,* ibid, 23.

[620]   See, for example, E Warren, 'Making Policy with Imperfect Information: the Article 9 Full Priority Debates' (1997) 82 *Cornell Law Review* 1373; V Finch, 'Security, Insolvency and Risk: Who Pays the Price?' (1999) 62 *Modern Law Review* 633.

[621]   See, for example, S Harris and C Mooney, 'A Property-based Theory of Security Interests' (1994) 80 *Virginia Law Review* 2021.

[622]   This is not necessarily the best criterion, however. One could produce an effective and efficient system for the buying and selling of slaves: this does not make it desirable, see P Shupack, 'Solving the Puzzle of Secured Transactions' (1988) 41 *Rutgers Law Review* 1067, 1072 fn 15.

[623]   For contractual protection by covenants see chapters 3 and 5.

[624]   Which is governed in the US by Uniform Commercial Code Article 9.

[625]   For example, the position in relation to tort claims.

6.6.2   The Puzzle of Secured Credit

6.6.2.1   *Monitoring*

The 'puzzle' first addressed by the law and economics scholars is why debtors grant security interests. They have argued that because of the advantages of security to a creditor, a secured loan attracts a lower rate of interest than an unsecured one, but this is offset exactly by a raising of interest rates by unsecured creditors.[626] They then look for other possible benefits of secured credit. One possible benefit was that of monitoring. All creditors need to protect themselves against two dangers: the first is that the borrower will deplete its assets either by diminishing their value or by substituting its safe assets for more risky ones[627] and the second is that it will dilute the value of the creditor's debt by adding more liabilities without correspondingly increasing the asset pool.[628] To achieve this protection, unsecured creditors need to have extensive covenants which give them the ability to monitor the entire business of the borrower and, in conjunction with that monitoring, to stop the borrower depleting the asset pool or increasing liabilities.[629] The same benefits can be achieved by taking a security interest, but this has the added benefit that the creditor's monitoring can be focused solely on the asset which is given as security, and therefore monitoring costs are reduced.[630] Asset withdrawal and substitution can be prevented more effectively by a security interest than by covenants, since the secured creditor not only has the right to prevent disposition (if it knows about it in advance) but also the right to 'follow' the asset so that the person who takes the asset may take subject to the security interest.[631] Furthermore, certain creditors can reduce monitoring costs further by taking security over assets in respect of which they have a specialised knowledge. The reduction in costs lowers the cost of credit, and therefore, it is argued, the taking of security is efficient.

Against this argument it could be said that the savings in monitoring costs from the taking of security are equalled by the increase in monitoring required by unsecured creditors in relation to the assets which are not subject to security.[632] However, this is not necessarily the case. It could be argued that, if the assets monitored by the secured creditor were representative of the health of the business, unsecured creditors could 'free ride' on that monitoring and could save the costs of monitoring themselves.[633] Shareholders could also benefit from this free riding.[634] Taking this argument to its logical conclusion, the most effective monitoring can be done by a creditor with a security interest over all the

---

[626] TH Jackson and AT Kronman, 'Secured Financing and Priority among Creditors' (1989) 88 *Yale Law Journal* 1143; A Schwartz, 'Security Interests and Bankruptcy Priorities' (1981) 10 *Journal of Legal Studies* 1.

[627] This is a concern as creditors do not benefit from any increase in value which may come from risky projects, while shareholders do, while creditors are more likely to suffer first from any loss. Shareholders thus have an incentive to indulge in risky projects, and creditors wish to prevent them.

[628] For a helpful analysis of these dangers, see R Squires, 'The Case for Symmetry in Creditors' Rights' (2009) 118 *Yale Law Journal* 806, 819–20. For further discussion of the points made in the text, see 3.2.2.2 above.

[629] The benefits of monitoring and the use of covenants in this regard is discussed in more detail in 3.2.2.3 above.

[630] TH Jackson and AT Kronman, 'Secured Financing and Priority among Creditors' (1989) 88 *Yale Law Journal* 1143, 1153. Security also results in reduced enforcement costs, see above page 221.

[631] This depends on the rules of priority, which are discussed above at 6.4.4.

[632] A Schwartz, 'Security Interests and Bankruptcy Priorities' (1981) 10 *Journal of Legal Studies* 1.

[633] S Levmore, 'Monitors and Freeriders in Commercial and Corporate Settings (1982) 92 *Yale Law Journal* 49.

[634] Ibid, 50, 68–71.

assets of the company, since its interests are most closely aligned with both the shareholders and the unsecured creditors (who are the residual claimants unless there is a surplus).[635] However, it is unclear that the taking of security is an essential element in this argument. Wouldn't the benefits of having a 'lead' creditor to monitor be just as great if that lead creditor were unsecured?[636]

To reach a negative answer to this question it is necessary to focus on the issue of enforcement, either in the run-up to insolvency, or on insolvency itself. While the company is solvent a secured lead creditor would only be more efficient if it could be shown that the secured creditor charged a lower interest rate because of the security, and this was not offset by higher rates charged by the unsecured creditors. This could be the case if some of the unsecured creditors did not fully adjust.[637] However, on enforcement the existence of the 'lead' secured creditor can be shown to have a beneficial impact on all creditors. There is a danger for unsecured creditors as a whole that, on insolvency, the total assets of the company will be depleted by a 'race to be first' by specific creditors who are in a position to enforce before others. Obviously, this has distributive effects (in that there is less for the other creditors) but it also may have an effect on the overall size of the pot, in that the value of the assets is less when broken up than when held together as a whole.

The presence of a lead secured creditor can help in several ways. First, by being able to make an effective threat to remove assets from the business (as well as to accelerate the loan) the secured lead creditor is more likely to be able to force the company to make the necessary restructuring to keep it going. This will be to the benefit of all creditors. Second, other creditors know that they cannot enforce against assets subject to security and so the 'race to be first' is deterred.[638] Third, if security gives 'control' rights (such as the right to appoint an administrative receiver under English law, now abolished for all but certain categories of floating chargee) this enables the lead creditor to take control of the whole enterprise, to keep the business going and realise maximum value by selling it as a going concern, or, at least, not disposing of assets in a piecemeal fashion.[639] The extent to which this is still an advantage of a floating charge is discussed above.[640] Fourth, if the lead creditor is secured, its incentive to intervene in the running of the company and, eventually, to enforce, is increased as the company's financial position deteriorates, since until that stage the secured creditor may have sufficient 'cushion' of assets not to need to take action.[641] Since it is at this stage when lead creditor intervention is most useful to other creditors, this can be seen as a factor in favour of the lead creditor being secured.

---

[635] R Scott, 'A Relational Theory of Secured Financing' (1986) 876 *Columbia Law Review* 901. The single creditor can also be more efficient as it can negotiate with the borrower as a proxy for the other creditors, thus saving duplication of costs, see J Armour and S Frisby, 'Rethinking Receivership' (2001) 21 *Oxford Journal of Legal Studies* 73, 84.

[636] P Shupack, 'Solving the Puzzle of Secured Transactions' (1988) 41 *Rutgers Law Review* 1067.

[637] This argument will be examined at 6.6.2.3.

[638] J Armour and S Frisby, 'Rethinking Receivership' (2001) 21 *Oxford Journal of Legal Studies* 73, 87. This argument is of limited value in relation to assets over which the lead creditor has a floating charge, as execution creditors who complete execution before crystallisation obtain priority over the floating chargee, see above pages 277–78.

[639] R Mokal, 'Administrative Receivership and the Floating Charge' in *Corporate Insolvency Law: Theory and Applications* (Oxford, Oxford University Press, 2005); J Armour and S Frisby, 'Rethinking Receivership' (2001) 21 *Oxford Journal of Legal Studies* 73.

[640] 6.3.3.4.

[641] J Armour, 'The Law and Economics Debate about Secured Credit: Lessons for European Law-making' (2008) 5 *European Company and Financial Law Review* 3.

6.6.2.2   Signalling

Another possible benefit from security is said to be that it acts as a signal to other creditors. One view is that the grant of security signals that the borrower is of good quality. This is because security is costly to grant, and so a company will only be prepared to incur those costs if it has faith in its projects and wishes to signal to the market that its projects are worthwhile, that is, more worthwhile than the market is likely to think on other information that is available.[642] The main problem with this argument is that it does not reflect the real world. In fact, security is demanded by creditors rather than offered by borrowers, and is demanded in those situations where it is of most use, that is, where the borrower's credit-worthiness is weak.[643] Thus to the extent that it is a signal, it is a signal that the borrower is of poor quality. It is difficult to see the value of this signal as significant enough to explain why security is efficient.

6.6.2.3   Non-adjusting Creditors

A third explanation of why the lower cost of secured lending is not completely outweighed by the higher cost to the borrower of unsecured credit, is that some unsecured creditors cannot adjust, therefore the full cost of the security interest is not reflected in the increased costs of unsecured credit. This argument has been used by some commentators to conclude that secured lenders and borrowers are deliberately exploiting non-adjusting creditors to obtain more advantageous rates on secured lending than would be the case were these creditors to adjust fully.[644] Empirical studies appear to show no support for the deliberate exploitation thesis.[645] It is, however, said to be the case that the presence of security does damage the position of unsecured creditors, and that some unsecured creditors are not in a position to adjust fully.[646]

This bald statement of fact deserves examination. Let us consider the categories of creditors discussed in chapter three.[647] The first category is those who choose to extend credit to the company. Of these, some may be secured creditors (in the wide sense of having proprietary protection) and others may adjust by using the contractual means outlined in chapter five.[648] If a creditor chooses to contract with a company, it has the means of discovering what security interests that company has granted over its assets (either by checking the register or by using a credit rating agency, who use the information in the company charges register to compile their ratings).[649] If the company has assets over

---

[642]   A Schwartz, 'Security Interests and Bankruptcy Priorities' (1981) 10 *Journal of Legal Studies* 1.

[643]   For this and other arguments against the signalling theory, see V Finch, 'Security, Insolvency and Risk': Who Pays the Price?' (1999) 62 *Modern Law Review* 633, 649.

[644]   L LoPucki, 'The Unsecured Creditors' Bargain' (1994) 80 *Virginia Law Review* 1887; V Finch, 'Security, Insolvency and Risk: Who Pays the Price?' (1999) 62 *Modern Law Review* 633, 645.

[645]   R Mokal, 'The Priority of Secured Credit' in *Corporate Insolvency: Theory and Applications* (Oxford, Oxford University Press, 2005); Y Listokin, 'Is Secured Debt Used to Redistribute Value from Tort Claimants in Bankruptcy? An Empirical Analysis' (2008) 57 *Duke Law Journal* 1037.

[646]   V Finch, 'Security, Insolvency and Risk: Who Pays the Price?' (1999) 62 *Modern Law Review* 633.

[647]   3.2.2.1.

[648]   These include set-off, insurance and guarantees, as well as contractual terms.

[649]   The use of information on the Company Charges Register by credit rating agencies (on whose information unsecured creditors rely) was made clear to the Law Commission during its consultation on the reform of the registration of company charges, see Law Commission, *Company Security Interests: A Consultative*

which it could grant security in the future, the creditor can adjust either by taking security itself, or by attempting to prevent security being granted to any other creditor by use of a negative pledge clause,[650] or by charging more for its loan to reflect the increased risk of security being given in the future. A creditor also has the capacity to adjust by the various means discussed in 3.2.2.1 above: by adjusting price (either for this particular company or for all its customers), by not extending credit, by diversification, or by refusing to contract with companies who appear to be in financial difficulties.

One could argue that if a creditor (such as a trade creditor) is not able to adjust to the presence of security using one of these means, then it clearly cannot adjust to the other risks that are in the market, and the fact that such a creditor may itself become insolvent as a result of non-payment by the company is not a cause for great concern.[651] It should also be mentioned that many loans by directors and group companies are unsecured. This may well be because of agreements with other creditors (such loans may also be subordinated) and are a product, therefore, of conscious choice. These loans are often made when the company is in difficulties, and these lenders have a strong incentive to benefit the company, and therefore will knowingly take on the risk of being unsecured.

It is possible to have more sympathy for the second category of creditors, namely those who, while they chose to have dealings with the company, did not choose to extend credit but have become creditors because the company has become liable to them, usually for breach of contract or in tort.[652] Although it is possible for such creditors to protect themselves (for example, by refusing to pay for goods until they have been examined thoroughly to make sure that they conform to the contract, or by keeping running accounts with the company so that they can assert set-off), this is not always possible. They are therefore in a similar position to the third category of claimants, those who have no prior contact with the company before becoming creditors (such as tort claimants).

In relation to tort claimants,[653] there is a distinction between the US and the UK position.[654] Much of the US literature focuses on the weak position of tort claimants. Many tort claimants are the victims of accidents at work or road accidents. In the UK there is compulsory liability insurance in respect of both these types of claims.[655] Further, the victims will have the right to claim direct against the insurance company if the insured company is insolvent by a statutory transfer of the insured company's rights to the victim on the insolvency of the insured company.[656] This right to claim direct may also benefit other tort and contract claimants, since the company may well be insured for liability other than for employment and road accidents, such as liability for defective products, and damage caused to third parties through polluting or other dangerous activities. These

---

Report, n 366, 3.152 and fn 200. The ease with which this information can be procured by a creditor depends on the efficiency of the registration system: this argument has more weight where there is an effective, low cost system of registration.

[650] 5.2.1.1. Note that a negative pledge clause can also be included in a floating charge see page 276.

[651] Mokal, 'The Priority of Secured Credit', n 645, 152 et seq.

[652] Utility companies could also be included here, as well as the tax authorities. See below for discussion of these.

[653] See also the discussion at pages 108 and 144–45.

[654] Mokal, n 645, 151–52.

[655] Employers' Liability (Compulsory Insurance) Act 1969, s 1 and Road Traffic Act 1988, s 143.

[656] Third Party (Rights against Insurers) Act 2010. This is also provided by statute in some US states, such as Louisiana, Wisconsin and New York.

kinds of claims figure significantly in the US literature.[657] It should be pointed out, though, that (in the UK) in relation to non-compulsory third party insurance, the insured is free to charge or assign the proceeds of the policy to a lender. If this security or absolute interest is not a floating charge, the lender will have priority over the victim in respect of the proceeds of the insurance policy.[658]

Despite this, it appears to be the case that tort claimants are not a substantial category of unsecured creditor in most insolvencies. There are a number of differences between the UK and the US which may explain this.[659] One is the structure and funding of class actions, which means that these are more common in the US. Coupled to this is the quantum of damages, which is much larger in the US as damages include a punitive element which is usually assessed by a jury. The quantum of damages for personal injury is also affected by the difference in provision of health care and social security between the two countries.[660] Thus the arguments made about tort claimants in the US context must be treated with care in the UK.

There are two types of non-adjusting creditors which deserve special mention. First, employees of the company are not in a position to take security nor, usually, to adjust in any meaningful way. Most employees cannot negotiate their level of wages, especially once they have commenced employment, and it may be difficult for them to leave the company and obtain another job. Second, the tax authorities and utility companies cannot adjust (for example, by charging higher interest rates), except by being more aggressive in enforcing debts. However, this course of action may send the company into insolvency, and so the authorities have to balance the negative effects of this against their own protection.

Those who consider that there is a transfer of wealth from secured lenders to non-adjusting creditors suggest various ways to protect the latter. One possibility is for certain classes of non-adjusting creditors to be given priority over secured lenders (or a class of secured lenders).[661] This course suffers from the objection that it does not assist all non-adjusting creditors, but could be worth considering for particular disadvantaged groups. However, in the UK there are arguments against this course for the three main groups in contention. First, tort claimants are protected to some extent by a direct claim against an insurance company, as discussed above. Second, although the priority course is in fact followed to some extent for employees, who have preferential status above floating charge holders, employees actually have a much better route for recovery. They are entitled to claim a sum direct from the Secretary of State, who is then subrogated to their

---

[657]   L LoPucki, 'The Unsecured Creditors' Bargain', (1994) 80 *Virginia Law Review* 1887, 1897.

[658]   Law Commission report 272, 'Third Parties – Rights Against Insurers' (2001), paras 7.13–7.14.

[659]   Although it is not necessarily the case that tort claimants figure extensively in most US insolvencies either, see Mokal, *The Priority of Secured Credit in Corporate Insolvency*, n 645, 138–152; C Hill, 'Is Secured Debt Efficient?' (2002) 80 *Texas Law Review* 1117, fn 241.

[660]   Most health care in the UK is provided by the National Health Service, and although there is a certain degree of 'claw-back' from tortfeasors in relation to liability for road traffic accidents, (Road Traffic Act 1988 ss 157–158) this is limited. The Law Commission recommended a much wider claw-back (see Law Commission Report No 262 *Damages for Personal Injury: Medical, Nursing and Other Expenses* (1999), paras 3.19–3.43) but this recommendation has not been enacted. However, the State does have the right to claw back certain Social Security payments made to an injured person from a tortfeasor (Social Security (Recovery of Benefits) Act 1997).

[661]   L LoPucki, 'The Unsecured Creditors' Bargain' (1994) 80 *Virginia Law Review* 1887, 1908 et seq discusses this possibility in relation to tort claimants.

preferential claim against the company.[662] This directly claimed sum is greater than the amount of the employees' preferential claim.[663] Third, the tax authorities did have preferential status above floating charge holders until 2002 (Crown preference), when this was abolished in order to fund the 'prescribed part', which is discussed below.[664] Many countries have totally or partially abolished tax preference, largely because the tax authorities can protect themselves to a considerable extent by more efficient enforcement mechanisms.[665] The strongest argument in favour of tax preference relates to tax collected or withheld by the company from others (for example, employees' income tax and value added tax paid by customers). This tax, in one sense, has already been collected and 'belongs' to the tax authorities, and it is hard to see why it should be available for the unsecured creditors.[666] However, it was the preferential status in relation to this tax which was given up by the UK Government in 2002,[667] as it was considered more important for this asset to be available for the unsecured creditors generally.

Another possible mechanism for protecting non-adjusting creditors would be to set aside for those creditors a certain percentage of assets subject to a security interest. Various such schemes have been suggested. One is for secured creditors to cede some priority to unsecured creditors who were non-adjusting in respect of the particular secured claim asserted by the secured creditors.[668] The problem with this idea is that it is very difficult (and costly) to identify who the non-adjusting, as opposed to adjusting, unsecured creditors are.[669] Another scheme considered by US writers is the 'fixed-fraction' scheme, whereby secured creditors are only secured for a specific fraction of their secured claim, and the balance of the assets forming security are available for unsecured creditors.[670] This can be contrasted with the actual position in the UK, where the prescribed part (available to all unsecured creditors) is a fixed fraction of the assets subject to the floating charge, whatever the amount of the debt owed to the floating chargee.[671] Both schemes can be criticised on the basis that they will increase the cost of credit, either because lenders will charge more for credit (as their recovery is diminished) or that they will lend less. The latter danger is more likely in the UK, where a floating charge lender can protect itself by oversecuring, that is, attempting to ensure that there is a 'cushion' of floating charge assets which exceed the value of the debt, and which are available for the preferential creditors and the prescribed part. In fact, a floating chargee is better off under the present scheme

---

[662]   The claim against the Secretary of State is for a maximum of eight weeks at £350 per week: Employment Rights Act 1996, ss 182–186. The weekly limit is raised regularly: the current limit is imposed by SI2008/3055 art 3 Schedule para 7.

[663]   An employee's preferential claim relates to wages for four months before the date of administration or winding up, with a maximum of £800, plus any accrued holiday pay within certain limits (Schedule 6, Insolvency Act 1986, Insolvency Proceedings (Monetary Limits) Order 1986 (SI 1986/1996) para 4).

[664]   See also pages 94–95.

[665]   B Morgan, 'Should the Sovereign be Paid First? A Comparative International Analysis of the Priority for Tax Claims in Bankruptcy' (2000) 74 *American Bankruptcy Law Journal* 461, 505–06. (Although this needs to be balanced against the risk of sending the company into insolvency, see above page 298).

[666]   Report of The Review Committee, Insolvency Law and Practice, 1982, Cmnd 8558 (The Cork Report), on which the Insolvency Act 1986 is based, para 1418.

[667]   Preferential status for taxes paid directly by the company was abolished in 1986.

[668]   L Bebchuk and J Fried, 'The Uneasy Case for the Priority of Secured Claims in Bankruptcy' (1996) 105 *Yale Law Journal* 857, 905.

[669]   Ibid, 908.

[670]   L Bebchuck and J Fried, 'The Uneasy Case for the Priority of Secured Claims in Bankruptcy: Further Thoughts and a Reply To Critics' (1997) 82 *Cornell Law Review* 1279, 1323.

[671]   Insolvency Act 1986, s 176A and s 176ZA and see 3.3.1.2.3.

than when there was Crown preference, since the amount of the prescribed part is easily calculated in advance, as is the amount payable to preferential creditors, which depends largely on the number of employees the borrower company has. The amount due to the Crown, of course, was more difficult to predict, since it depended on how effective the Crown was in enforcing the sums due to it.

Another problem with a partial priority scheme is that the costs of redistribution may not outweigh the benefits to the non-adjusting unsecured creditors. First, as all unsecured creditors benefit equally, those who do adjust will obtain a double benefit. Those who could have adjusted but chose not to (for whatever reason) will also benefit. This could act as a disincentive to adjustment.[672] The amount left for genuine involuntary creditors is therefore small.[673] If there is real concern about such creditors, and a desire to ensure that costs of torts are internalised within the borrower company, a better route is likely to be compulsory insurance against such liability.[674] The premiums which the company has to pay thus internalise the cost, and provide a disincentive against risky behaviour.[675] Second, a rule of partial priority provides an incentive for secured creditors to structure their transactions so that the rule does not apply to them. This is particularly marked in the UK, where lenders have developed structures which do not include taking a floating charge,[676] but is also a danger in the US.[677]

Other methods for improving the position of unsecured creditors should also be mentioned. Transactions in the run-up to insolvency likely to damage unsecured creditors, including the grant of security for existing debt, attract remedies which are usually purely for the benefit of unsecured creditors.[678] Such transactions potentially damage all unsecured creditors, as it is difficult to adjust accurately in relation to such transactions.[679] Strengthening these provisions (such as by extending section 245 of the Insolvency Act 1986 to cover fixed charges[680]) would protect unsecured creditors in a way that is targeted at the most objectionable types of security or other interests.[681] Another possibility is to make it easier for unsecured creditors to adjust accurately, by improving transparency, and reducing the costs of obtaining information about the credit of the borrowing company. Arguably the reforms discussed in the next section would do this.

---

[672] However, at least on the UK figures, the benefits from the prescribed part to individual creditors are unlikely to be significant enough to preclude adjustment.

[673] It is likely that the actual benefit to unsecured creditors generally of the prescribed part will be, on average, tiny. See Mokal, n 645, 129–30.

[674] This would need to be coupled with a right of the tort claimant to sue the insurance company direct, as currently exists under the Third Party (Rights against Insurers) Act 2010, although at present there is the danger of loss of priority to secured lenders for non-compulsory insurance, see above pages 297–98.

[675] S Block-Lieb, 'The Unsecured Creditors' Bargain: a Reply' (1994) 80 *Virginia Law Review* 1989, 2002; Mokal, n 645, 151.

[676] See page 257.

[677] C Hill, 'Is Secured Debt Efficient?' (2002) 80 *Texas Law Review* 1176.

[678] See 3.3.2. Note that the remedies do not always only benefit unsecured creditors as they can involve the setting aside of the transaction: if a security interest is set aside, this may benefit another creditor who holds a security interest over the same asset.

[679] This is because adjustment usually has to be done before the transaction takes place, and therefore can only reflect the chance of it happening. If such a transaction were prohibited, then unsecured creditors would not need to make such a speculative adjustment.

[680] See pages 259–60.

[681] Mokal, n 645, 186.

6.7   Reform

Over the last forty years, there has been much discussion about the need to reform the law governing personal property security in England and Wales.[682] There have been various suggestions for reform dating back to the report of the Crowther Committee in 1971,[683] whose proposals were endorsed by the Insolvency Law Review Committee.[684] The Diamond Report also suggested reform of the law in 1989,[685] making similar recommendations. Reform was also suggested in the Final Report of the Company Law Review Steering Group, which recommended that further work be undertaken by the Law Commission.[686] The Law Commission published a Consultation Paper in 2002,[687] followed by a Consultative Report in 2004[688] and a Final Report in 2005.[689] The proposals contained in that report, with some very limited exceptions,[690] have not been enacted. There is still ongoing consideration of reform, both at Governmental level,[691] and in the practitioner and academic fields.[692] In the following section, we set out the arguments for and against reform, and give a brief description of what a reformed system might look like. It is not possible to include a detailed discussion in a book of this size, and the reader is referred to the Law Commission papers and more specialist literature.[693]

6.7.1   Attributes of an Ideal Law

It is important, first, to consider what are the most desirable attributes of a law governing the proprietary protection of creditors. One such attribute is that the law is clear, certain and easily accessible. As discussed in this chapter, proprietary protection lowers the cost of credit, and, in order to price such reduction accurately, lenders need to be able to predict their position in law if the borrower defaults. There should be certainty whether a proprietary interest is effective against third parties, both when the borrower is solvent and on its insolvency, and whether that interest is subject to any other interest in the same asset. In other words, the priority rules must be clear. Another attribute is that it should be possible to obtain a proprietary right over any asset of a borrower, and that the process of doing so should be as easy and cheap as possible. A further attribute is that it must be possible to acquire proprietary rights over both the present and future assets of the

---

[682]   The discussion in this section relates solely to the law of England and Wales. The Scottish law of security is different and the considerations in relation to reform are not the same.

[683]   *Report of the Committee on Consumer Credit*, Pts IV and V, Cmnd 4596 (1971).

[684]   See The Cork Report, n 666, paras 1620–23.

[685]   A Diamond, *A Review of Security Interests in Property* (London, HMSO, 1989).

[686]   *Modern Company Law for a Competitive Economy: Final Report* (2001 URN 01/942).

[687]   Law Commission, *Registration of Security Interests: Company Charges and Property other than Land*, Consultation Paper No 164 (2002).

[688]   Law Commission, *Company Security Interests: A Consultative Report*, n 366.

[689]   Law Commission No 296, *Company Security Interests: Final Report*, Cm 6654 (2005).

[690]   These relate to registration of charges created by overseas companies over property in the UK (Overseas Companies Regulations 2009).

[691]   BIS, *Registration of Charges created by Companies and Limited Liability Partnerships*, 2010.

[692]   Secured Transactions Law Reform Project (project director: Sir Roy Goode).

[693]   Beale et al, n 44, chapter 21; J de Lacy (ed), *The Reform of UK Personal Property Security Law* (Abingdon, Routledge-Cavendish, 2010).

borrower, without any additional formalities in the future, and to acquire a non-possessory proprietary interest which does not prevent the borrower from disposing of the asset subject to that interest in the ordinary course of business.

Further, it should be possible for any creditor (with or without proprietary protection) to find out sufficient information to enable it to adjust adequately to the risks it takes in advancing credit.[694] This means both that it should have accurate information about the extent of the borrower's assets at the time it advances credit, and that it should be able to monitor what happens to those assets during the time it is exposed to the credit risk of the borrower, that is, after it has advanced credit but before it is paid. There should also be a simple and straightforward way for a creditor taking a proprietary interest to protect itself from losing priority to a future creditor taking a proprietary interest in the same asset. Further, it should be possible to enforce a proprietary claim effectively whether or not the borrower is insolvent. Lastly, although it should be possible for creditors to contract out of most default rules in relation to priority and enforcement, that default position should be the one most likely to be required in general, so as to minimise transaction costs. It will be noticed that these attributes refer to a 'proprietary interest' rather than to 'security'. That is because if a lender relies on such an interest to protect it in the event of a borrower's default, the desirable attributes of the relevant law are the same whether or not the interest is a 'true' security interest or an absolute one.

6.7.2   Unsatisfactory Aspects of English Law

With these desirable attributes in mind, it can be said that the English law of personal property security is unsatisfactory from a practical point of view for several reasons. First, it is difficult to access. Most of English personal property security law is found not in statute, but in case law dating from the middle of the nineteenth century. One example of this is the rule in *Dearle v Hall* governing the priority of successive assignments.[695] The fact that so much of the law consists of case law, not legislation, means that substantial amounts of time and money are spent in research. In addition, the absence of a modern statute means that the UK has no exportable product – this limits its ability to influence the future shape of the law in continental Europe.[696]

Secondly, once located, the law in this regard is confusing and over-complicated. English law has a range of devices which fulfil a security function, such as legal and equitable mortgages, legal and equitable charges, title transfer and title retention devices, and hire purchase agreements. For each there exist separate creation, perfection and priority rules. The complexity of the priority rules is apparent from the discussion earlier in this chapter.[697] The law is also unclear in many respects. For example, the relation between registration and priority is complex, the scope of constructive notice arising from registration is uncertain[698] and so is the effect of non-registration.[699] The difficult distinction between the fixed and the floating charge has considerable priority and

---

[694]   See pages 296–97.
[695]   See pages 273–74.
[696]   For example, the Draft Common Frame of Reference book IX relates to personal property security, but draws little on English law.
[697]   6.4.
[698]   6.4.3.2.
[699]   6.4.3.1.

insolvency consequences. Priority of competing assignments of receivables is governed by the *Dearle v Hall* rule, criticised above, and a lender taking an absolute assignment of receivables cannot protect its priority position by registration.[700] Where a debtor wrongly disposes of property, the priority rules are different according to whether the creditor is a legal or equitable mortgagee or chargee, a seller under a conditional sale agreement, or the owner under a hire purchase agreement. The lack of clarity has been exacerbated by the introduction of the FCAR which are uncertain in their scope and application.[701]

Thirdly, the system of registration is flawed in a number of ways. The process itself is cumbersome and expensive, and, although searching can now be done electronically, depends upon the submission of the original charge document in paper form. The risk of mistakes (if not spotted by Companies House during the checking process) is on those who subsequently search the register, rather than the person registering.[702] The register itself can be misleading, and does not include all non-possessory interests which could affect secured or unsecured creditors.[703] Further, the requirement of registration within a 21 day period leads to the invisibility period of 21 days[704] and, if parties fail to register in time, they face unnecessary costs in order to obtain a court order to register out of time.[705] The fact that there are specialist registers for particular types of assets also makes the system more complex.

6.7.3   Options for Reform

There are several options for reform. The first, and more conservative, is to reform the law governing company charges registration. This could include such changes as making all charges registrable unless excepted, clarifying the scope of constructive notice, clarifying against whom an unregistered charge is invalid and including negative pledge clauses within the prescribed particulars. Such reforms were included within the ill-fated 1989 Companies Act, and have again recently been suggested by the Department of Business, Innovation and Skills ('BIS').[706] These reforms would be a start: they deal with some rather obvious defects of the registration system, and would be reasonable interim measures pending more widespread reform. Professor Diamond suggested a similarly two stage process in his report in 1989, although his 'interim' measures, which were enacted in the 1989 Companies Act, were wider than those suggested by BIS.

Another possible option is to make amendments to English law in a wider area than just registration of company charges. This could include the law relating to priority, not just between security interests but including absolute interests as well. It could also include the law of insolvency, so that, for example, the trigger for various statutory consequences

---

[700]   See pages 273–74.
[701]   6.4.1.1.
[702]   See page 268.
[703]   This comes both from the limits of the *numerus clausus* list (see pages 261–62) and from the omission of interests created by retention of title and absolute transfer.
[704]   See page 270.
[705]   See page 268.
[706]   BIS, *Registration of Charges created by Companies and Limited Liability Partnerships*, n 691.

could be something other than the distinction between fixed and floating charges.[707] While, obviously, there could be considerable discussion about the content of such amendments, and they could be quite far-reaching, the resulting system would still fall foul of the first and second criticisms of English law set out above. Unless the whole system were codified, it would still be difficult to know what the law was (and we would still lack an exportable product), and even if it were codified (if that were possible) the distinctions between the different types of interests would remain.

A third option is wholesale reform of the English system, similar to that adopted recently in some other common law jurisdictions, namely a notice filing system, which utilises a functional approach when determining when its rules apply, where priority is usually determined by date of filing, and where there are common rules for enforcement for all interests falling within the scheme. Such a scheme was first introduced in the United States in Article 9 of the Uniform Commercial Code ('UCC'),[708] and has been broadly followed in the Personal Property Security Acts ('PPSAs') of Canada,[709] New Zealand[710] and, now, Australia.[711] The Law Commission, in their Consultative report of 2005,[712] set out a version of such a scheme for England and Wales. The following discussion sets out the main features of such a scheme, and seeks to point out where there would be significant change were such a scheme to be introduced in England and Wales.

6.7.4   Outline of Notice Filing Scheme[713]

6.7.4.1   *Functional Approach*

All interests created with the function of security are included within the scheme, and are, largely, treated the same way. Differences of form are, therefore, disregarded. Thus the rules apply equally to pledges, liens, mortgages and charges,[714] and also to title retention devices such as sales on retention of title terms, conditional sales, hire purchase agreements and finance leases. Transactions where title is transferred with the function of security are also included. Title retention and title transfer devices for the purposes of security can be referred to as 'quasi-security' interests. Furthermore, two forms of

---

[707]   See, for example, R Calnan, 'What is Wrong with the Law of Security' in J de Lacy (ed), *The Reform of UK Personal Property Security Law* (Abingdon, Routledge-Cavendish, 2010). For general discussion, see also Beale et al, n 44, 21.25–21.70.

[708]   Now Article 9 (revised).

[709]   The first such Act was the Ontario PPSA in 1967. There are PPSAs in nine out of the ten provinces, and the three territories. The Ontario Act differs in some significant respects from the other Acts. For detailed commentary, see R Cuming and R Wood, *Saskatchewan and Manitoba Personal Property Security Acts Handbook* (Ontario, Carswell, 1994); J Ziegel and D Denomme, *The Ontario Personal Property Security Act Commentary and Analysis*, 2nd edn (Toronto, Butterworths, 2000).

[710]   New Zealand Personal Property Securities Act 1999, which introduces a wholly electronic registration system. For detailed commentaries, see M Gedye, R Cuming and R Wood, *Personal Property Securities in New Zealand* (New Zealand, Brookers, 2002); L Widdup and L Mayne, *Personal Property Securities Act: A Conceptual Approach* (Wellington, LexisNexis Butterworths, 2002).

[711]   Personal Property Securities Act 2009, which is expected to come into force in May 2011. For detailed discussion, see V Barns-Graham and L Gullifer, 'The Australian PPS Reforms: What Will the New System Look Like?' (2010) 4 *Law and Financial Markets Review* 394.

[712]   Law Commission, *Company Security Interests: A Consultative Report*, n 366.

[713]   The references that are given are to Article 9 (revised) UCC, Ontario PPSA (OPPSA), Saskatchewan PPSA (SPPSA), which was used as a model for the New Zealand Act, New Zealand PPSA (NZPPSA) and Australian PPSA (APPSA).

[714]   Although possessory interests do not require registration.

transactions which do not perform the function of security are included in the rules governing registration and priorities,[715] because of their similarity to transactions which do have a security function: these transactions are known as 'deemed security interests'. They are absolute assignment of receivables[716] and (operating) leases for over a year.[717]

The functional approach is often justified on the basis that these transactions all have a common function and so should be treated alike.[718] The approach brings simplicity and clarity to a system where otherwise there would a number of different ways of doing the same thing, each with slightly different legal consequences, which can be exploited by those aware of them, and which confuse those who are not. However, it also could be argued that the different forms of transactions do involve genuine (though, in some cases minor) differences and so the decision to treat them alike in law is a policy choice, which requires further justification. Such justification has to be made in relation to each area of law (registration, priorities and enforcement) and, in some cases, exceptions to uniform treatment are themselves justified. Thus, for example, in the PPSA scheme registration is not required for possessory interests, and the priority position of purchase money security interests is different from that of other security interests.[719] It should be noted, however, that in relation to generalised arguments about secured credit (such as those discussed in 6.6. above) all creditors with a proprietary interest are treated alike, and treated as different from unsecured creditors.

In relation to registration, parity of treatment for non-possessory interests with the function of security can be justified on the basis of false wealth. In other words, the borrower appears to own more assets than he actually does. Against this, it can be argued that lenders know that borrowers usually encumber their assets (either with true security interests or quasi-security interests), and so can discover this by due diligence exercises, coupled with warranties in lending agreements, so that a register is not necessary. Even if it is accepted that there is little danger of an interest being so hidden that it is impossible to discover it, registration which is cheap to do and easy to access can cut the costs of taking security (including quasi-security) since an accurate register can form the basis of enquiries and prevent unnecessary investigation. Thus, for example, if a lender is lending against equipment which may be the subject of quasi-security interests, it is cheaper to make the necessary investigations (for example, as to how much is left to pay under the agreement) if there is a definitive list available which does not depend on the veracity of the borrower.

---

[715] But not the rules relating to enforcement, UCC (revised) 9–601(g), SPPSA s 55(2)(a), NZPPSA s 105, APPSA s 109(1).

[716] UCC (revised) 1–201(37), OPPSA s 1(1), SPPSA s 2(1)(qq), NZPPSA s 17(1)(b), APPSA s 12(3). Certain types of assignments of receivables are excluded, such as those taking place on the sale of a business, and those that take place only to facilitate collection: UCC (revised) 9–109(d), OPPSA s.4, SPPSA s 4(g) and (h), NZPPSA s 23 (e)(viii)–(x), APPSA s 8(f)(vi)–(x).

[717] OPPSA s 2(c) (added by amendment in 2006); SPPSA s 2(1)(qq), NZPPSA s.17(b), APPSA s 12(3) and 13. Operating leases are not deemed security interests under UCC Article 9, although they are very often registered anyway (Law Commission, *Company Security Interests: A Consultative Report*, n 366, para 3–37).

[718] See, for example, JS Ziegel, 'The New Provincial Chattel Security Law Regimes' (1990) 70 *Canada Bar Review* 681 at 685–86.

[719] See page 308.

6.7.4.2   *Registration*

All interests within the scheme require 'perfection' if they are to be enforceable against third parties. 'Enforceable' in this context means to have priority over unperfected interests and later registered interests, and to be enforceable against a liquidator or administrator in the insolvency of the debtor. Possessory interests are perfected by the taking of possession (in English law pledges and liens are not created until possession is taken, so perfection and creation would be simultaneous).[720] Some schemes provide that interests over financial collateral may be perfected by control.[721]

Most other security interests are perfected by registration, which means the filing of a financing statement giving certain minimum details about the identity of the debtor and of the secured party and a description of the collateral.[722] In most schemes this information can be (or must be) submitted electronically by filling in an online form.[723] There is no need to submit (in any form) the agreement creating the interest, or to include details of its terms. The information is submitted directly to the register, and the risk of any errors is on the person submitting it, usually the secured party, since registration is conclusive evidence of the scope of the security interest.[724] Although the information is relatively sparse, it is sufficient to enable any interested party to make enquiries of the registered secured party, who is obliged to provide fairly extensive further information.[725] The financing statement can be filed at any time before or after the creation of the security interest. This is so that a secured party can protect itself from the time that it is envisaged that it will obtain a security interest, and removes the problem of the invisibility period.[726] The secured party is not obliged to file at any particular time, but if it files after creation it risks losing priority to another secured party who files earlier. To avoid the risk of a filing being entered or remaining on the register if no security interest is actually granted, most systems require the debtor to be notified of the filing,[727] and give the debtor power to remove an incorrect filing, or to require the filing of a statement correcting the position.[728] Only one financing statement is required to be filed in relation to all security interests taken by the secured party over the assets specified. This means that where there are likely to be multiple interests (such as when goods are sold on retention of title terms) only one registration is required.

One of the main advantages of a modern notice filing system, such as that established in New Zealand, and soon to be established in Australia, is that it is fully electronic. This means that both a security interest can be registered and the register can be searched

---

[720] NZPPSA, s 41; UCC (revised), 9–313; OPPSA, s 22; SPPSA, s 24; APPSA, s 21(2).

[721] UCC (revised) 9–312, 314; APPSA s 21(2)(c). What amounts to control is defined in APSSA, ss 25–29.

[722] The information varies from system to system, but see UCC (revised), 9–502(a), NZPPSA, s 142; APPSA, s 153.

[723] The New Zealand system is wholly electronic and the Australian system will be.

[724] Thus, if certain collateral is omitted, the security interest is valid in relation to the collateral mentioned, but not in relation to the omitted collateral. NZPPSA, s 152; SPPSA, s 43(9); APPSA, s 164(3). This is in contrast to the current English system, where the conclusive certificate system (see page 268) means that the risk of error is on subsequent persons searching the register.

[725] NZPPSA, s 177; SPPSA, s 18; OPPSA, s 18; UCC (revised) 9–210; APPSA, s 275.

[726] See above page 270.

[727] NZPPSA, s 148; SPPSA, s 43(12); OPPSA, s 46(6); APPSA, s 157; UCC (revised), 9–509 (requires the debtor's authorisation for filing, but this is usually by being bound by the security agreement).

[728] NZPPSA, s 162; UCC (revised), 9–518; SPPSA, s 50; OPPSA, s 56; APPSA, s 178.

online. The New Zealand computer system is cheap and easy to use,[729] and requires very little maintenance. Further, such a system can be linked up to other registers, such as, in England, those relating to land, ships and aircraft, so that information registered on one register could be forwarded to another.[730] A notice filing system would also address the other problems with the current system identified above.[731] There would be no need for an application for registration to be checked, those relying on the register would be protected from mistaken registration, and there would not be any period during which a subsequent interest could lose priority to a prior invisible interest. There would also be no need for a secured creditor to apply for permission to register late, since registration can take place at any time. There would still be a significant incentive to register, since unregistered interests would be void against unsecured creditors in insolvency,[732] and would lose priority to all registered security interests in the same assets.

6.7.4.3 Priorities

The basic priority rule is very simple: where interests in relation to any particular asset are perfected, priority is determined by the date of perfection. In most cases, this will mean that priority is by date of registration. The date of creation of the interest is irrelevant. A perfected interest has priority over an unperfected one, and unperfected ones rank in order of attachment.[733] These rules determine the priority of security interests in relation to all advances made by the secured party, at whatever time, so that the rules on tacking do not apply.

Although these are the basic rules, there are some exceptions. Where one interest in an asset is perfected by registration and another by control, the interest perfected by control has priority, regardless of the dates of perfection.[734] The parties can agree a different order of priority from that laid down by the basic rules. This can either be done by a subordination agreement, or by the debtor being given specific permission by a secured party to create security interests ranking in priority to that of the secured party. However, unlike a floating charge, a security agreement which merely gives the debtor permission to dispose of the assets in the ordinary course of business will only relate to dispositions which are not for the purpose of security, and will not (without more) cover the creation of subsequent security interests. Since the default position is that priority is by date of registration, there is no need for negative pledge clauses or automatic crystallisation to protect the position of a 'floating chargee'.[735] The troublesome question of whether registration is constructive notice also disappears.[736]

---

[729] Registration costs $3 and searching the register $1.

[730] There is power in the Companies Act 2006 to introduce such a system to the current register, see s 893.

[731] See 6.7.2.

[732] This is not the position in New Zealand.

[733] Attachment is the moment when the security interest is effective as against the debtor and any creditors against whom an unperfected interest is not void, for example, unsecured creditors before insolvency. It is defined in the PPSAs, as are the conditions that are necessary for an interest to attach, which are usually that value is given and that the debtor has rights in the collateral. NZPPSA, s 40; SPPSA, s 12; OPPSA, s 11; UCC (revised), 9–203; APPSA, s17.

[734] APPSA, s 57(1).

[735] In most schemes perfected security interests have priority over execution creditors who execute later than the date of perfection thus removing another reason for automatic crystallisation, see above pages 277–78.

[736] UCC (revised), 9–331(c), OPPSA, s 46(5), SPPSA, s 47, NZPPSA, s 20, APPSA, s 300.

An interest in an asset to secure an advance made to acquire that asset (a purchase money security interest or 'PMSI') has priority over a previously perfected interest which would attach to that asset under an after-acquired property clause. Most interests created by retention of title, such as conditional sale agreements and finance leases, fall into the category of PMSI, since title is retained to secure the purchase price. Leases which are deemed security interests are also treated as PMSIs.[737] Some schemes also permit cross-collateralisation, so that an interest retains PMSI status not only to the extent that it secures the obligation to pay or repay the purchase price of that asset, but to the extent it secures all obligations owing from the debtor to the creditor;[738] this is, in effect, an 'all monies' clause.[739] Other schemes limit the PMSI status to the obligation securing the purchase price of that asset.[740] To obtain PMSI status, the interest must usually be registered within a certain (short) period of its attachment[741] or of the debtor taking possession of the relevant asset, and some schemes require notice to be given to holders of prior registered interests, when the PMSI is in inventory.[742] Many schemes also provide that the perfected interest (together with its PMSI status) automatically continues to the proceeds of sale of the asset or to products made from it. In relation to proceeds in the form of receivables, this causes a conflict with a receivables financier, over whom the PMSI holder would, without more, have priority. Many jurisdictions have recognised this tension and, as a matter of policy, have provided that, in this particular case, the PMSI super priority should not apply and that priority should be by date of registration. Even this does not fully solve the conflict, since if the debtor refinances with a new receivables financier, who registers after the PMSI is registered (and it must be remembered that a supplier of raw materials only needs to register once to cover all its future ROT supply contracts), the ROT supplier will still have priority over the receivables financier. Arguably, this could raise the cost of receivables financing, since the financier will, in order for its financing to be effective, have to make subordination agreements with all the debtor's suppliers.

There are many policy reasons for the PMSI super priority.[743] These include preventing the first registered financier having a monopoly on lending to a debtor (since one registration covers all future advances, any subsequent non-PMSI lenders would have to obtain a subordination agreement from the first lender in order to get priority) and considerations of fairness, as the PMSI lender swells the debtor's assets by the amount lent, and if the asset falls within the first financier's security interest, that financier obtains a 'windfall'. PMSI lending is also seen as efficient, since those who lend on this basis are specialists in the field, and not only price the credit more accurately than a general financier, but also are in a better position to realise the asset if there is a default, and therefore can reflect this in the price of credit.

---

[737] APPSA, s14(1)(c).
[738] UCC, 9–103(b)(2).
[739] See page 287.
[740] APPSA, s 14(3).
[741] UCC (revised), 9–324, SPPSA, s 34, OPPSA, s 33, NZPPSA, s 74, APPSA, s 62. In all these schemes, in the case inventory, the registration must be before attachment or possession.
[742] UCC (revised), 9–324(b) and (c); OPPSA, s 33(1); SPPSA, s 34(3).
[743] For a full discussion, see L Gullifer, 'Retention of Title Clauses: a Question of Balance' in A Burrows and E Peel (eds), *Contract Terms* (Oxford, Oxford University Press, 2007) 287–289. See also pages 274–75.

The circumstances in which a buyer[744] would take free of security interests are specified separately from the rules governing priority between security interests. Basically, a buyer takes assets subject to any prior security interests unless the sale is permitted in the security agreement (a type of floating charge) or either the security interest is unperfected, or the disposition is of goods sold in the ordinary course of business of the debtor. The schemes vary as to whether the buyer's knowledge of the security interest, or that the disposition is in breach of the security agreement, prevents the buyer taking free.

6.7.4.4 *Enforcement*

The schemes also normally provide a default code for enforcement outside insolvency.[745] This will provide for various methods of enforcement, which will vary according to the type of asset, but which broadly speaking involve the secured party taking control of the asset, and then realising its value. A form of foreclosure, called retention, is also usually included. The debtor and other secured creditors (who may have an interest in the asset) are safeguarded by notice requirements. The default code will also include general obligations, such as the obligation to obtain a market value when realising collateral, and an obligation to act with commercial reasonableness.[746] Further, the order of distribution on realisation will be prescribed, including an obligation to account to the debtor for any surplus after the enforcing secured creditor, and all other secured parties with an interest in the collateral, have been paid. To some extent, the parties can contract out of these enforcement provisions, but not if third parties are affected. Further, there are certain provisions, such as the debtor's right to the surplus and the right to redeem, which are mandatory.[747]

6.7.5 Assessment of Reform

The attributes of an ideal system, and an assessment of how English law fails to match up to this, are set out above. There is therefore a strong case for reform, and for a wholesale reform which not only produces a modern, wholly electronic registration system, but involves a rational and integrated system of registration and priorities, together with a codification of the law on enforcement. What arguments, then, can be made against this? The most general argument (which can be expressed in a variety of ways) is that the current system is not broken enough to warrant the costs of wholesale reform. It is said that the problems identified above can, largely, be overcome by drafting and devices which are now very familiar to the legal profession, and that the uncertainties, which are unsatisfactory in theory, rarely cause important or expensive problems in practice. The costs, though, of a wholly new system would be considerable; not so much in terms of

---

[744] Similar rules also apply to lessors.

[745] See UCC part 6; OPPSA, Part V; SPPSA, Part V; NZPPSA, Part 9; APPSA, chapter 4.

[746] UCC (revised), 9–610(b); OPPSA, s 63(1); SPPSA, s 65(3); NZPPSA, s 110; APPSA, ss 111 and 131.

[747] It will be recalled that these two rights are indicia of security under English law (see page 226). The precise position varies between the jurisdictions. Some legislation lists the provisions that may be contracted out of (eg NZPPSA, s 107; APPSA, s 115), some lists the provisions which may not be contracted out of (UCC (revised) 9–602) and some do both (SPPSA, s 56(3), which provides that there can be no waiver or variation by agreement of the enforcement provisions, with some limited exceptions, such as that in s 59(4) that the payment for collateral disposed may be deferred if agreed in the security agreement. The order of distribution can also be changed, but only by agreement of all interested parties after default, not by the security agreement (s 60(2)).

setting up the central system but in terms of re-educating the users of that system (both lenders and borrowers and their lawyers) and the inevitable uncertainty which comes from a new system, even if the final result is law that is more certain. To some extent, an assessment of this argument is an empirical matter, since the actual level of problems caused by the present law across the entire spectrum of borrowers and lenders is largely unknown, and the actual costs of reform can only be estimated. One way of assessing the situation is to look at other countries, where the need for reform has been accepted and reform has been introduced relatively recently. The New Zealand experience has been largely favourable.[748] It is still too early to see how the reforms in Australia fare, although the introduction of reform itself (as opposed to some of the details of the drafting of the Act) has generally been well received.[749] It should also be borne in mind that the transitional costs of any reform are immediate but transitory, while reform (if it is worthwhile) lasts for generations.

There are other arguments that are also made against wholesale reform. One is that the current English law has the benefits of flexibility and upholds freedom of contract. Thus the 'hierarchy' of interests between a legal and an equitable interest means that the parties can choose a more formal approach to creation and either have the priority protection of a legal interest, or can choose the more informal and flexible approach of equity, and still have an interest which is effective in insolvency and has relative priority against other interests.[750] Further, new security devices can be created to deal with specific problems, in the way that the floating charge was developed over time to deal with circulating assets.[751]

However, these concerns can be met within a reformed system. The functional approach means that all interests with the purpose of security are treated alike in relation to registration and priorities, but within that approach there is freedom for the parties to agree whatever terms they like in the security agreement. The floating charge, in function if not in name, can remain and, in fact, aspects of it are built into the system.[752] As mentioned above, the priority rules are largely default rules which can be varied by the parties, but the advantage is that the default position is that which most parties would wish to adopt.[753] There is no predetermined extent to which the parties can contract out of the enforcement scheme: this varies within the established schemes, and so could be

---

[748]   See S Flynn 'Personal Property Securities Reform' (INSOL World – Second Quarter 2008); G Brodie, 'Personal Property Securities: A New Zealand Maritime Perspective' (2008) 22 *Australia & New Zealand Maritime Law Journal*; P Wells, 'Personal Property Securities: Possibilities, Problems and Peculiarities' [2008] *Journal of the Australasian Law Teachers Association* 335; M Gedye, R Cuming and R Wood, *Personal Property Securities in New Zealand* (Wellington, Brookers, 2002).

[749]   See P Quirk, 'Whether Australian Secured Transactions Law will Transition from the English System to the Personal Property Securities Act?' (2009) 31 *Thomas Jefferson Law Review* 219; Access Economics Party Ltd Report, 'The Costs and Benefits of Personal Property Securities (PPS) Reform' (6 July 2006); C Wappett 'Personal Property Securities Reform: An Overview of the Proposed PPSA and Implementation' in 2010 *Personal Property Securities Conference, Tuesday 18 May 2010* Law Society of South Australia, [Adelaide]; J Boncales and S Henderson-Kelly, 'Personal Property Securities Reform – the Australian Experience' (Personal Property Securities Branch, AG's Department, 2 March 2009); J Popple, 'Personal Property Securities Reform' (Credit Law Conference – LexisNexis Professional Development).

[750]   City of London Law Society Financial Law Panel commentary on the Law Commission, *Company Security Interests: A Consultative Report*, Consultation Paper No 176 (2004) para 1.19.

[751]   Ibid, para 1.16.

[752]   Such as the priority of a purchaser in the ordinary course of business over a secured party, see pages 307 and 309 above.

[753]   Unlike, for example, the present position in relation to floating charges, where, to obtain priority over a fixed charge, an effective negative pledge clause is necessary.

very extensive in an English scheme. The present system, where only specified interests are registrable, is in some ways restrictive of the development of new interests, in that there is uncertainty whether such interests are registrable or not. For example, over the years many attempts have been made to draft clauses in relation to the proceeds of sale of goods sold on retention of title terms which do not require registration, since they are, at present, hard or impossible to register, and any interests created are void if they are not registered as they are likely to be characterised as charges.[754] If the position in relation to registration were clear, then such interests could have been developed more readily.

A further argument made against reform is that, although superficially simple, a notice filing system is actually too complex. It is true that there have to be some exceptions to the simple general rules to cover particular situations, for example, the PMSI exception, and this does add complexity. The experience of other jurisdictions is relevant here. Some, at least, of the complexity comes from the way that legislation is drafted rather than from the rules themselves. UCC Article 9 seems, to English eyes, to be rather impenetrable, and the Australian Act, which tries to cover every possible situation, is long and detailed. However, the Canadian PPSAs and the New Zealand Act are relatively short and are drafted in a straightforward manner, as was the draft suggested by the Law Commission. To some extent there is a trade off between having enough rules so that the law is certain and clear in most situations, and simplicity. Since the principles behind a notice filing scheme are clear and straightforward, it can be argued that adding further detail does not detract from the basic clarity of the scheme.

One other objection is that the information on the register is reduced in a notice filing scheme. This is undoubtedly true, in that at present virtually all the terms of the original charge are copied and pasted into the form that forms the basis of registration. However, the point of the notice filing is that it gives the searcher notice of the interests registered, so that further enquiries can be made. As was pointed out earlier, it provides a definitive list of interests which need to be investigated, and therefore cuts the cost and risk of investigations, rather than precluding the need for them altogether.

The weighing up of the advantages and disadvantages of wholesale reform depends, to some extent, on the perspective from which one comes. From a theoretical point of view, there is a strong case for adopting a codified system based on rational and coherent principles. From a practical point of view, too, an electronic notice filing scheme is attractive and has proved successful in a number of jurisdictions similar to our own. There would be some costs and disruption while the system was changed, and so, from the perspective of those familiar with the existing system, change can be seen as undesirable. In assessing the impact of change, the experience of Australia in introducing their reforms will be instructive and is worth monitoring closely.

Are the arguments for wholesale reform stronger than those for a more piecemeal approach to reform of the registration system, or the wider law as discussed above?[755] If one is replacing the current system with an electronic one, reforming the list of registrable charges and changing the priority structure to make registration a priority point, for example, it could be said that it is much more conceptually coherent to take on the whole jurisprudence of notice filing, rather than trying to 'bolt on' some of its ideas onto our current law. It could be said that a whole new system would also involve working out how

---

[754]   See page 235.
[755]   See pages 303–304.

it fitted with the rest of the English law of personal property, and so achieving total conceptual coherence is never possible. However, other jurisdictions with similar common law jurisprudence to our own have incorporated notice filing schemes, and the experience of Canada and New Zealand is that they, after some transition, fit well into the rest of the existing law. Changing the law to deal with a few particular problems would only be a temporary solution, in that new problems would emerge and new changes would then need to be made: this would mean that the law would be forever in a state of flux, which in the end is inimical to certainty.

7

Multiple Lenders

7.1 Introduction

Where a company borrows money from one lender, such as a bank, the organisation of the loan is relatively straightforward. The loan agreement is a contract between the borrower and the lender, and the terms of it govern their relationship. As we have seen, this relationship may include contractual protection for the lender, which can be enforced by the lender taking whatever action the provisions allow. This could involve refusing to lend because a condition precedent has not been fulfilled, acceleration of the loan, relying on a right of set-off (outside or within insolvency), or obtaining an injunction to prevent the borrower from breaching a covenant. Alternatively, it may entail the lender suing the borrower for the debt owed, or for breach of contract. Again, if the lender has rights against a third party, it can enforce these directly against that third party. Similarly, if the lender has proprietary protection, such as a security interest, that means that the lender itself has a proprietary right in a particular asset or assets, and can assert this under the circumstances envisaged in the loan agreement either outside or within the insolvency of the borrower. A single bank lender is likely to have monitoring rights in relation to the borrower's business and assets, and this means that the transaction is often seen as a relationship between lender and borrower (and is often referred to as 'relationship lending').[1]

Where a company wishes to access funds from more than one lender, it could take out a series of loans or other borrowing. An example of this is where each loan or borrowing is secured on a different asset. This sequential lending can cause problems of priority, which can be dealt with by subordination agreements (where the borrowing is unsecured)[2] and the general law of priority, usually modified by priority agreements, where the borrowing is secured.[3] If a company is large, and requires considerable funds, however, it will want to access a number of lenders simultaneously, either by taking out a syndicated loan or by issuing debt securities.

Having multiple lenders raises a number of issues which do not arise where there is a single lender. First, there needs to be an organisational structure so that one (legal) person sets up the transaction, collects in and distributes payments and is able to set in train the enforcement procedure, maybe even enforcing the debt obligation on behalf of all the

---

[1] It is not always the case that finance from a single lender will be in the form of 'relationship lending'. Asset-based finance, which is discussed at 2.3.4.2 above, depends less on the relationship between lender and borrower since it is not based on cash flow. However, the lender will monitor the assets of the company closely to make sure that it retains its proprietary protection.
[2] 5.3.4.
[3] 6.4.4.

lenders. There are considerable advantages to the borrower in having only one person to deal with, especially where the lenders are numerous and diverse, as in a bond issue. It is usually necessary to have some sort of decision-making procedure included in the structure of the transaction, and often having one person who can make relatively minor decisions on behalf of the lenders is advantageous to all.[4] A decision-making procedure also has to deal with the potential problem of one lender holding out against the rest, since if one person can exercise termination provisions against the wishes of the others, this may well affect everyone due to the operation of cross-default clauses.[5] Further, if each lender can enforce on its own, there is a danger that those who get in early will recover all that the issuer has, leaving the other bondholders to prove against an insolvent issuer.[6] As will be seen below, these problems are overcome in whole or in part by the use of agents or trustees.

Secondly, in order to attract lenders there needs to be a mechanism for conveying information to potential lenders. In relation to both syndicated loans and issues of debt securities fairly standard mechanisms have developed, which involve the use of specialist advisers, usually investment banks. There is considerable regulation of this process in relation to debt securities, but not in relation to syndicated loans. The content of this regulation, and the reasons for the difference in approach, are discussed below in chapter eleven, while the operation of the mechanisms themselves is discussed in this chapter.

Thirdly, although not essential, it is desirable to have a system of transferring the company's obligation to pay from one lender to another, both so that the potential pool of lenders can be increased and also to attract more lenders in the first place. The ways in which transfer of debt can be effected are discussed in the following chapter.

Issues similar to those discussed above arise in relation to shares as well as debt. Shareholders, especially in public companies, can be numerous, and can have diverse interests and therefore the issue of who makes decisions on behalf of the shareholders as a whole, and the question of potential minority abuse arise in that context just as they do with debt securities. Subject to that, issues of collective enforcement do not arise in quite the same way as they do in relation to debt. Shareholders are purchasing the 'hope' that the company will make profit rather the promise of a specific payment in the future (they are the residual claimants in the company). As a result there is no ultimate payment obligation to enforce. Shareholders can be involved, however, in the enforcement of obligations owed by the directors to the company.[7] These issues are discussed in relation to shareholders in chapter three above.[8] Further, mechanisms similar to those used to attract investors in a bond issue are used in an initial public offering of shares. These mechanisms and the regulation governing them are discussed in chapter nine below. Transfers of shares raise similar issues to the transfer of debt securities and will be discussed in chapter eight below.

---

[4]   Decision-making procedures are discussed at 7.3.3 in relation to bonds and 7.4.6 in relation to syndicated loans.

[5]   See page 171.

[6]   This issue is dealt with by the 'no-action' clause found in debt securities, discussed at pages 332–33 below and the 'pro rata' clause found in syndicated loan agreements, discussed at pages 357–58 below.

[7]   For example, by way of a derivative action: Companies Act 2006 ss 260–264 (England, Wales and Northern Ireland) and ss 265–269 (Scotland). See generally P Davies, *Gower and Davies Principles of Modern Company Law,*8th edn (London, Sweet & Maxwell, 2008) ch 17.

[8]   See 3.2.

The transferability of debt or shares gives rise to one point that will be discussed in this chapter. If the company's obligation to the lender is transferable, then it has a value in the hands of the transferor, and falls within its assets. As regards third parties (both transferees and an insolvency officer of the transferor[9]) it is seen as property, and the transferor is seen as having a proprietary interest in the debt due to it or the shares. Thus the transferor is seen as the owner of the debt or shares, and can sell or create a security interest over it or them. This is true in relation to loans (even loans made by one lender). However, the idea of ownership seems even more obvious when the debt is in some way reified by being divided up into securities, so that a person can say 'I own a bond',[10] in a similar way to saying 'I own a share'.

The ownership of debt securities by the holders is largely taken for granted. However, the nature of this ownership right is not always clear cut, particularly where the debt obligation is not owed directly to the actual investor, for example, in an issue of stock, or where securities are held through an intermediary. These issues are discussed below.

Before dealing with the specific application of the law to syndicated loans and bond issues, it is worth considering two important legal concepts that have been used to deal with the issues relating to multiple lenders set out above. These are trust and agency.

7.2   Basic Concepts

7.2.1   Trust

The concept of a trust is largely peculiar to common law jurisdictions,[11] and arose from the division of the law in England and Wales into that administered by the courts of common law and that administered by the Court of Chancery, which was known as equity.[12] The trust has been called 'the outstanding creation of equity'.[13] It was developed originally from the medieval device of the use, whereby land was conveyed to a 'feoffee' by a common law conveyance, with directions to hold it for other persons, known as the 'cestui que use'.[14] Although the use was largely abolished by the Statute of Uses in 1535, the concept remained and was developed in the seventeenth century into the trust: a concept whereby one person owned property at law, but was obliged in equity to deal with it in accordance with the terms of the trust for the beneficiary (or beneficiaries) of the

---

[9]   The definition of property in Insolvency Act 1986, s 436 includes things in action.

[10]   It is also more obvious where the securities are bearer securities, so that each debt is represented by a piece of paper.

[11]   As opposed to civil law or other types of jurisdictions.

[12]   For the historical background leading to the development of the trust, see P Pettit, *Equity and the Law of Trusts*, 11th edn (Oxford, Oxford University Press, 2009) Ch 1; DJ Hayton and C Marshall, *Hayton and Marshall: Commentary and Cases on The Law of Trusts and Equitable Remedies*, 12th edn (London, Sweet & Maxwell, 2005) 1–23–1–24; J Martin (ed), *Hanbury and Martin: Modern Equity*, 18th edn (London, Thomson Reuters, 2009) 1–003–1–017.

[13]   Pettit, *Equity and the Law of Trusts*, n 12, 12.

[14]   Ibid.

trust. A relatively recent statement of the basic principles of trust law was that of Lord Browne-Wilkinson in *Westdeutsche Landesbank Girozentrale v Islington LBC:*[15]

(i) Equity operates on the conscience of the owner of the legal interest. In the case of a trust, the conscience of the legal owner requires him to carry out the purposes for which the property was vested in him (express or implied trust) or which the law imposes on him by reason of his unconscionable conduct (constructive trust).

(ii) Since the equitable jurisdiction to enforce trusts depends upon the conscience of the holder of the legal interest being affected, he cannot be a trustee of the property if and so long as he is ignorant of the facts alleged to affect his conscience, i.e. until he is aware that he is intended to hold the property for the benefit of others in the case of an express or implied trust, or, in the case of a constructive trust, of the factors which are alleged to affect his conscience.

(iii) In order to establish a trust there must be identifiable trust property. The only apparent exception to this rule is a constructive trust imposed on a person who dishonestly assists in a breach of trust who may come under fiduciary duties even if he does not receive identifiable trust property.

(iv) Once a trust is established, as from the date of its establishment the beneficiary has, in equity, a proprietary interest in the trust property, which proprietary interest will be enforceable in equity against any subsequent holder of the property (whether the original property or substituted property into which it can be traced) other than a purchaser for value of the legal interest without notice.

Although this statement has not proved uncontroversial[16] it is a good starting point to considering the basic features of a trust. In the eighteenth and nineteenth centuries, and for a portion of the twentieth century, the main use of a trust was in relation to the protection of family assets, but over the years, and particularly recently, it has been developed widely for use in commercial transactions,[17] including those involving multiple lenders. Its use in this field has been based upon the two main distinctive features of a trust.[18] First, there is the separation of title between the legal owner and the beneficiaries. The beneficiaries have an equitable proprietary interest in the trust property, which persists against the trustee, and also against any subsequent owner of the property, except a bona fide purchaser of the legal interest without notice, although enforcement against such an owner has to be by the trustee rather than the beneficiaries.[19] This persistence is effective even in the insolvency of the trustee or the third party, so that the beneficiaries have priority over all the other creditors of that party in relation to that asset. This persistence in insolvency is one of the main reasons why the trust structure is the best

---

[15]   [1996] 1 AC 669, 705.

[16]   This is especially true of the second proposition as to the role of conscience in the law of property (see W Swadling, 'Property and Conscience' (1988) 12 *Trusts Law International* 228), and as to whether a trust can arise without the trustee being aware of it (see, in relation to a resulting trust, the discussion in Pettit, n 12, 14).

[17]   For discussion of this phenomenon, see P O'Hagan, 'The Use of Trusts in Finance Structures' [2000] *Journal of International Trust and Corporate Planning* 85; D Hayton, H Pigott and J Benjamin, 'The Use of Trusts in International Financial Transactions' (2002) 17 *Journal of International Banking and Financial Law* 23; D Hayton, P Matthews and C Mitchell (eds), *Hayton and Underhill: Law of Trusts and Trustees*, 17th edn (London, Sweet & Maxwell, 2007) 1.97–1.138.

[18]   P O'Hagan, 'The Use of Trusts in Finance Structures' [2000] *Journal of International Trust and Corporate Planning* 85. These two aspects follow the third and fourth, and then the first and second propositions of Lord Browne-Wilkinson set out above.

[19]   Martin, *Hanbury and Martin Modern Equity*, n 12, 1–019; Hayton and Marshall, *Hayton and Marshall: Commentary and Cases on The Law of Trusts and Equitable Remedies*, n 12, 1–54–1–59.

explanation of the rights of owners of securities who hold them through an intermediary. As we shall see, such owners include many bondholders, where the bond is issued as a global note.[20] Moreover, the trust property can be held for any number of beneficiaries, which makes the structure particularly useful in the situation of multiple lenders. Thus, where security is given for the loan, the security can be granted to the trustee to hold on behalf of the lenders.[21]

Secondly, the fiduciary obligation owed by the trustee to the beneficiaries imposes a number of duties on the trustee. The precise nature of the trustee's duties in any situation is governed by the terms of the trust deed, and the primary duty of the trustee is to comply with those terms. However, there are some basic duties common to all trustees, such as the duty to exercise their powers in the best interests of the beneficiaries,[22] to preserve the trust fund[23] and not to put themselves in a position of conflict of interest with the beneficiaries of the trust, including obtaining unauthorised benefits from the use of the trust property.[24] Trustees also owe a duty of care to the beneficiaries of the trust, although the precise boundaries of that duty will depend upon the provisions in the trust deed, and on the status of the trustee. A professional corporate trustee owes a duty of special care and skill, because of the expertise it professes to have,[25] although the extent of this, too, will depend on the terms of the trust deed. The extent to which the trust deed can define the trustee's obligations and exclude liability is a matter of considerable debate and is discussed below in the context of bond trustees.[26]

It is the ability of the trustee to act on behalf of the beneficiaries with respect to the trust property that is of particular use in relation to issues of stock and bonds. Although a bond trustee's powers and duties are usually limited to some extent by the trust deed,[27] it performs many functions which would be difficult or expensive for the bondholders to perform collectively, such as dealing with modifications to the terms of the bonds, receiving information from the issuer and taking action on possible events of default.[28] The ability to enforce the security on behalf of bondholders or syndicated lenders is one of the main benefits of having a security trustee.

Although trusts can be created by operation of law, it is with the creation of express trusts that we are concerned here. The trust is created by a trust deed, which is one of the several documents drawn up when the bond or stock issue takes place or a secured syndicated loan is set up. In order to create an express trust, three certainties must be present: certainty of intention to create a trust, certainty of object (that is, who is to

---

[20] 7.3.2.3.2.

[21] See page 333.

[22] *Armitage v Nurse* [1998] Ch 241. Millett LJ said at 253 that 'there is an irreducible core of obligations owed by the trustees to the beneficiaries and enforceable by them which is fundamental to the concept of a trust'. However, he considered that these did not include 'the duties of skill and care, prudence and diligence', but rather that 'The duty of the trustees to perform the trusts honestly and in good faith for the benefit of the beneficiaries is the minimum necessary to give substance to the trust'. For further discussion see pages 353–54.

[23] *Re Brogden* (1888) 38 Ch D 546 (deals with duty to safeguard trust assets); *Buttle v Saunders* [1950] 2 All ER 193 (could not accept lower offer even if felt honour bound to); *Jobson v Palmer* [1893] 1 Ch 71 (duty in relation to land).

[24] *Bray v Ford* [1896] AC 44; *Boardman v Phipps* [1967] 2 AC 46.

[25] *Bartlett v Barclays Bank Trust Co Ltd (No. 2)* [1980] 1 Ch 515, 534.

[26] 7.3.4.

[27] So that, for example, there is usually only a very limited duty to monitor the financial position of the borrower, see page 344.

[28] See 7.3.3 below.

benefit from the trust) and certainty of subject matter of the trust.[29] These will now be considered in turn. The intention to create a trust must be apparent from the words of the documentation (and any surrounding circumstances) but there is no need for any particular form of words to be used.[30] This is not usually an issue where there is a trustee of a stock or bond issue, or where the security for a syndicated loan is held by a trustee, since the trust deed will expressly use the word 'trust'. However, the question might conceivably arise where it is sought to use a trust structure to explain the holding of securities by an intermediary, if the agreement is not so explicit. The need for certainty of objects means not only that it must be certain for what purpose the trust was created, but that there needs to be one or more beneficiaries who are either legal or natural persons.[31] There is no need for these beneficiaries to be identified when the trust is created[32] so long as they form an ascertainable class.[33] Thus it can be seen how beneficial the trust structure is when there is a class of multiple lenders, the membership of which can change frequently, without the knowledge of the issuer, by transfer of the stock, bonds or loans. The issuer or borrower only has to deal with one trustee without worrying about the identity or the whereabouts of the lenders.

The third requirement of certainty, that of subject matter, is potentially more problematic, especially when applying a trusts analysis to securities held through an intermediary. The principle will be discussed at this point, and its application discussed later on in the chapter.[34] The rule is that there cannot be a valid trust unless the subject matter of the trust can be identified. The identification can be very wide, such as 'all my property', but any further act of appropriation cannot be left to be done by the trustee or a third party. The main difficulty arises where there is a defined pool of assets of which a part is declared to be held on trust. The argument is that there cannot be a valid trust, since it is not known which of the assets form the trust property. Thus if A owns ten bottle of wine, he cannot declare himself trustee of five bottles of this wine for B, as it is not known which five bottles are held on trust for B.

Three cases are said to establish this proposition in relation to tangible assets. In the first, *Re London Wine Co (Shippers) Ltd*,[35] a company which sold wine to customers buying for investment had granted a floating charge to a bank. The receiver appointed under that charge claimed that all the stocks of wine held by the company belonged to it and not to the buyers, and so were subject to the charge. No wine was ever appropriated to each customer and it was held that no property could therefore pass under a contract of sale because of section 16 of the Sale of Goods Act 1893.[36] The buyers also argued that the sellers held 'the wine that they had bought' on trust for them. This entailed arguing that the contract of sale manifested an intention to create a trust (which in itself was dubious) and that there was sufficient certainty of subject matter, on the basis that there was an

---

[29]   *Knight v Knight* (1840) 3 Beav 148, 173.

[30]   Pettit, n 12, 47–50; *Re Kayford* [1975] WLR 279, 282.

[31]   This is known as 'The Beneficiary Principle' and is discussed at Pettit, *Equity and the Law of Trusts*, n 12, 58; Martin, n 12, 3–024; G Moffat, G Bean and R Probert, *Trusts Law*, 5th edn (Cambridge, Cambridge University Press, 2009) 216.

[32]   Martin, n 12, 3–024; Pettit, n 12, 55–56.

[33]   *Inland Revenue Commissioners v Broadway Cottages Trust* [1955] Ch 20.

[34]   See page 338.

[35]   [1986] PCC 121.

[36]   Now Sale of Goods Act 1979, s 16. This says that where there is a contract of sale of unascertained goods, no property in goods is transferred until the goods are ascertained.

identifiable mass and a declaration of trust of a quantitative interest within that mass. This argument was rejected on two grounds. First, there was no ascertainable mass, since the company remained free to fulfil its contracts to the purchasers from any source.[37] Second, even if there had been an identifiable mass, the declaration of trust could only have taken effect as a trust of the whole, giving effect to the proportionate interest of the beneficiary, so that, in the example above, A would hold all ten bottles of wine on trust for itself and B in equal shares.

Similar reasoning applied in *Re Goldcorp Exchange Ltd.*[38] Here, customers bought gold from a company, and were led to believe that the company was storing gold in its vaults on their behalf. In fact it only stored enough gold to meet its commitments to deliver on a daily basis. Despite the customer's belief, it was clear from the contracts that the sale was not out of an identified bulk, and the subject matter of the contract was therefore totally unascertained. Therefore no property could pass when the contract was made,[39] nor was there any trust created when the company acquired gold from which it was going to fulfil its obligations (since there was no obligation to fulfil any obligation out of the gold acquired: the company could have bought in more gold).[40]

In the third case, *Re Wait*,[41] the sale actually was out of an ascertained bulk, but since it was clear that property could not pass at law because of section 16 of the Sale of Goods Act, the claimants claimed an order for specific performance under section 52 of the Sale of Goods Act, and, in the alternative, that there had been an equitable assignment of part of the bulk. The first argument failed since specific performance under the section was only available where the goods were 'specific or ascertained', and clearly the goods in this case did not fit that description.[42] The second argument failed largely on the grounds that where there was a contract for the sale of goods, the parties would not be taken to have intended to create equitable rights or interests in the absence of express words, especially where the creation of a legal interest failed.[43] However, it is true that Lord Hanworth also said that the argument that there was an equitable assignment failed as the subject matter was not specific. As can be seen, neither of the first two cases is direct authority for the proposition that there cannot be a declaration of trust of a certain number of goods out of a mass, since in neither case was there a mass. In fact, in both cases it was envisaged that such a trust could be declared,[44] although at least in *Re London Wine* it was envisaged that this would be a trust of the whole, held in proportionate shares. In *Re Wait*, there was no declaration of trust, nor could such a declaration be implied from the contract made. However, from these three cases, none of which is directly on the point, the doctrine has been developed that it is not possible to declare a trust of a certain number of tangible objects out of a mass of such objects. It is, though, possible for a trustee to hold a mass on trust for himself and/or others in undivided shares, that is, fractional interests in the mass.

---

[37] *Re London Wine Co (Shippers) Ltd* [1986] PCC 121, 156. This was the ratio of the case.
[38] [1995] 1 AC 74.
[39] Ibid, 91.
[40] Ibid, 96–97.
[41] [1927] 1 Ch 606.
[42] Ibid, 621 (Lord Hanworth), 630 (Atkin LJ).
[43] Ibid, 636 (Atkin LJ).
[44] *In Re Goldcorp Exchange Ltd* [1995] 1 AC 74. Lord Mustill said at 91: 'Their Lordships do not doubt that the vendor of goods sold ex-bulk can effectively declare himself trustee of the bulk in favour of the buyer, so as to confer pro tanto an equitable title'. See also *In Re London Wine Co* [1986] PCC 121, 136–37.

The next series of cases involve intangible property. In *Hunter v Moss*,[45] A declared himself trustee for B of five per cent of the issued share capital of a company whose share capital consisted of 1000 shares. A was the registered owner of 950 shares, so the declaration of trust was said to apply to 50 shares out of 950. Colin Rimer QC held at first instance that the trust did not fail for uncertainty of subject matter, and his judgment was upheld in the Court of Appeal. The first instance judgment is more detailed than that of the Court of Appeal, and the reasoning is easier to follow. It is based on there being a difference between a trust of tangible objects, which can be separated and which each have a different existence, and intangible assets, which cannot physically be separated or allocated, and so the requirement of certainty can be satisfied in a different way from that required in relation to tangibles. The requirement of certainty, the judge said, was not based on some immutable principle about allocation but on 'whether, immediately after the purported declaration of trust, the court could, if asked, make an order for the execution of the purported trust'.[46] This was entirely possible: if the court had made such an order 50 shares out of the 950 registered in A's name could have been transferred to B and registered in his name, and this would have executed the trust. B could not have complained that he had received the 'wrong' shares because the shares were completely indistinguishable from each other, not just contractually (as with bottles of wine, where delivery of any out of a mass might satisfy a contract of sale, but there might be real differences between them, in that one might be corked or stored badly and so deteriorated)[47] but absolutely, so that it is not possible to separate one from another.

The decision in *Hunter v Moss* has been extensively criticised.[48] However, it has been (rather unenthusiastically) followed in England in the subsequent case of *Re Harvard Securities Ltd*[49] and (more enthusiastically) in Hong Kong.[50] In the Australian case of *White v Shortall*, the question was considered at some length at first instance.[51] The judge supports the result in *Hunter v Moss*, though not the reasoning of the Court of Appeal. His process of reasoning is particularly interesting as he focuses on the nature of the property (shares). He points out that the choses in action which a shareholder has (and which therefore represent the value of his shareholding) are not necessarily divided up on a share by share basis. For example, in relation to the right to be paid a dividend he says: 'In that way, the chose in action — the thing that the law regards as a piece of property because it can be sued for — is the single right to be paid the dividend, the measure of which is the number of shares held'.[52] He then goes on to say 'Given the types of rights that are involved in holding shares in a company, the way that rights of a shareholder need not be identified only in terms of owning particular identified shares, how identification of

[45]   *Hunter v Moss* [1994] 1 WLR 452, upholding decision at first instance [1993] 1 WLR 934.
[46]   (1993) 1 WLR 934, 945.
[47]   Ibid, 940.
[48]   Pettit, n 12, 51; A Hudson, *The Law of Finance*, (London, Sweet & Maxwell, 2009) 526–30; D Hayton, P Matthews, C Mitchell (eds), *Hayton and Underhill: Law of Trusts and Trustees*, n 17, 8.18–8.21. However, Martin in *Hanbury and Martin: Modern Equity*, n 12 takes a different view at 3–022–3–023, arguing that the *Hunter v Moss* solution is 'fair, sensible and workable'.
[49]   *Re Harvard Securities Ltd* [1997] 2 BCLC 369.
[50]   *In Re CA Pacific Finance Ltd* [2000] 1 BCLC 494.
[51]   *White v Shortall* [2006] NSWSC 1379. As the discussion in the first instance judgment was strictly obiter the point was not considered by the Court of Appeal of NSW who dismissed the appeal at [2007] NSWCA 372.
[52]   Ibid, [199].

individual shares can be unimportant for a transfer of some of the shares in a shareholding, and how these particular shares in [the relevant company] were in any event not numbered and were held as an undifferentiated balance in a share register, there is nothing in the nature of the trust property that is inconsistent with recognising the validity of the trust'.[53]

This argument reflects that which has been put forward for many years by Professor Goode;[54] namely that shares (and other intangible property) are not separate pieces of property but that the number of shares is merely a way of determining the size of each shareholding. Thus, even the legal owner of shares does not own a number of separate pieces of property but owns an undivided share in the share capital of the company. When a person is registered as the legal owner of 250 shares out of a share capital of 1000, what he really owns is 25 per cent of the share capital.[55] If he declares himself trustee of 50 shares out of his 250 for B, the question 'of which shares is he the trustee?' does not arise. The position must be that he is holding 20 per cent of his 25 per cent for B, and therefore holds his 25 per cent as tenants in common for himself and B in the proportions 80 per cent to 20 per cent.

There are thus a number of different ways of approaching the question of certainty of subject matter in relation to a declaration of trust which relates to part of the intangible property of a certain description owned by a certain person. One approach is to say that the only way there can be sufficient certainty of subject matter is if the trustee declares that he is holding the property for the beneficiaries (which could include himself) in undivided shares as tenants in common.[56] There is no real doubt that this would be effective: the main problem is where the declaration of tenancy in common is not express, and so the question is whether this would be implied to give effect to the trust. It clearly will not be in relation to tangible property[57] but in commercial situations where such express declarations are common, and where the trust would otherwise fail, it could be argued that such terms of the trust would be more readily implied.[58] Another approach is to say that dividing intangible property, such as share capital or debts, into units is merely for convenience, and what is really owned is an undivided share of the whole: this is the approach discussed in the last paragraph. A third approach is to say that the purpose of the rule that the subject matter must be certain is to enable the trust to be administered and executed, and so long as this is possible, then the requirement is fulfilled.[59] This view is consistent with a view of a trust as primarily concerning obligations in relation to property, rather than conferring equitable ownership on the beneficiaries. Obviously, it is important to know in respect of which property the obligations are owed (otherwise the

---

[53]   Ibid, [211].

[54]   L Gullifer (ed), *Goode on Legal Problems of Credit and Security*, 4th edn (London, Sweet & Maxwell, 2008) 6–09. See also E Micheler, *Properties in Securities* (Cambridge, Cambridge University Press, 2007) 30 and M Ooi, *Shares and Other Securities in the Conflict of Laws* (Oxford, Oxford University Press, 2003) 3–14.

[55]   Note that in *Hunter v Moss* [1994] 1 WLR 452 and [1993] 1 WLR 934 '5% of the issued share capital' is used synonymously with '50 shares'.

[56]   See the approach suggested by Oliver J in *Re London Wine Co* [1986] PCC 121, 137.

[57]   *Re London Wine Co* [1986] PCC 121.

[58]   G Morton, 'Commentary on The Dematerialisation of Money Market Instruments' in S Worthington (ed), *Commercial Law and Commercial Practice,* (Oxford, Hart Publishing, 2003).

[59]   This approach was taken by Campbell J in *White v Shortall* [2006] NSWSC 1379, and has a number of adherents, including S Worthington, 'Sorting Out Ownership Interests in a Bulk: Gifts, Sales and Trusts' (1999) *Journal of Business Law* 1, 18–20; P Parkinson, 'Reconceptualising the Express Trust' (2002) 61 *Cambridge Law Journal* 657.

trust is no more than a contract); however, it is possible for the obligations to be owed in relation to part of a larger mass of property if the declaration of trust is sufficiently clear for the trustee to know what to do in any given circumstance,[60] for example, if he disposes of any of the mass, if profits accrue to the mass, or if a disposal is taxed.[61]

So far we have considered the situation where a person who owns a certain amount of intangible property declares himself trustee of part of that property for another. This situation needs to be distinguished from that in which there is no express declaration of trust, but a person mixes property which it is claimed he holds on trust with his own. The mere fact of mixing cannot prevent there being a trust, if there is the intention to declare one, but such an intention will not be implied where the property is mixed with that of the trustee.[62] Moreover, many trust deeds oblige a trustee to hold his own property separately from that he holds on behalf of the beneficiaries. Having said this, if he does mix trust property with his own, it remains trust property and can be traced.[63] In that situation, the trustee holds the property (for example, a credit balance at a bank) partly for himself and partly for the beneficiaries rateably according to their contributions.

Another situation to be considered is where the trustee has no beneficial interest at all in the mass of property, for example, where A transfers the property to B to hold on trust for C and D. In this situation, it is, perhaps, even easier to imply that B is holding for C and D as tenants in common, either in equal shares or in some other proportions if this is made clear, even if the instructions as to proportions are given in absolute figures rather than as shares (ie 10 out of 100 rather than one tenth).[64] Yet another possibility is that C and D transfer their property to B to hold on trust for them. There would have to be an agreement from C and D that the property could be mixed, as otherwise the mixing would be a breach of trust (although in that situation, each would be able to trace into the fund). Given that agreement, it is also easier to imply an agreement that B is holding for C and D as tenants in common.

An interest of a beneficiary under a trust is an equitable interest, and thus attracts certain rules which do not apply to ownership or other interests at law. One difference relates to formalities: transfer of an equitable interest must be in writing.[65] However, certain formalities which are necessary for a legal interest to be transferred (such as the registration of a transfer of shares at law) are not necessary in relation to the transfer of equitable interests. Another difference relates to priorities, namely that where an equitable interest is transferred to another who is unaware of an inconsistent equitable right or interest, the transferee does not take free of that right or interest, while the transferee of a legal interest in property (absolute ownership or a security interest) will take free if in good faith and without notice of the inconsistent equitable right or interest.

---

[60]   P Parkinson, 'Reconceptualising the Express Trust' (2002) 61 *Cambridge Law Journal* 674, 676.

[61]   S Worthington, 'Sorting Out Ownership Interests in a Bulk: Gifts, Sales and Trusts' (1991) *Journal of Business Law* 18; *White v Shortall* [2006] NSWSC 1379, [251]–[263].

[62]   *Henry v Hammond* [1913] 2 KB 515; *R v Clowes (No 2)* [1994] 2 All ER 316; *Commissioners of Customs and Excise v Richmond Theatre Management Ltd* [1995] STC 257.

[63]   *Foskett v McKeown* [2001] 1 AC 103, 110.

[64]   D Hayton, 'Uncertainty of Subject Matter of a Trust' (1994) 110 *Law Quarterly Review* 338, 339. C and D can call for the entire mass of property, under the doctrine in *Saunders v Vautier* (1841) 4 Beav 115 and distribute it among them. See *In The Matter Of Lehman Brothers International (Europe) (In Administration)* [2009] EWHC 2545, [54].

[65]   Law of Property Act 1925, s 53(1)(c).

7.2.2 Agency

The concept of an agent is a very simple: it is a person who acts on behalf of another person. Unlike a trustee, the agent is not appointed in relation to any particular property, but the scope of his duties and powers is usually defined by an agency agreement, although it can also be wholly or partially implied from his situation, for example, the nature of his employment. This scope is known as the agent's authority, and is important in two ways. First, we should consider the position as between the agent and his principal. If the agent acts outside his authority, he is in breach of contract, and the principal can, in extreme cases, terminate the agency agreement. Second, we should consider the position between the agent and a third party. An agent is only any use to the principal if he can make binding contracts between the principal and third parties. Although any attempt to bind the principal to a contract in a way which is outside the agent's actual (express or implied) authority is, as between the agent and the principal, a breach of contract, it may nevertheless be successful in binding the principal to the third party. This would be the case if the principal had held the agent out as having authority (ostensible or apparent authority), and the third party had relied on that holding out, or if the principal had later ratified the unauthorised transaction. It is also possible for an agent to act on behalf of a principal without disclosing the fact that he is an agent: the principal will be bound where the agent acts within his authority and also, exceptionally, where the agent is in a position which would have given rise to apparent authority had the agent been disclosed.[66]

The position between the principal and the agent is of significance where an agent represents multiple lenders. Although the agent's authority and specific duties are defined by the agency agreement, there are certain duties which are inherent to agency, at least unless excluded by the agency agreement. Not only does an agent owe a duty of care and skill in performing his duties, but he is usually treated as a fiduciary, so that he owes a duty to act in good faith, to avoid conflicts of interest between his principal and any other principals he has, and between himself and his principal.

7.3 Issue of Debt Securities

It will be recalled from the discussion in chapter two,[67] that debt securities are tradable instruments issued by a company to multiple lenders. They are tradable by nature, and are usually listed for trading on a public secondary market, although there is no requirement for them to be so. Debt securities can vary enormously, in terms of the amount repayable, the term of repayment, whether and how interest is charged and so on.[68] There are also more complicated types of debt securities: those which are convertible into, or exchangeable for, equity securities,[69] those which are backed by assets,[70] and those which have

---

[66] *Watteau v Fenwick* [1893] 1 QB 346, although this decision has been much criticised.
[67] 2.3.3.
[68] The varieties of debt securities are discussed in 2.3.3 and especially at 2.3.3.5.
[69] See page 45.
[70] See page 35.

equity-like features and are known as 'hybrids'.[71] The discussion in this chapter seeks to make general legal points about debt securities, although not every point will apply to every type. There is one crucial distinction made, however: that between bonds (or notes) and stock.[72] These two types of securities are structured differently and so are subject to a different legal analysis in what follows.

7.3.1   Attracting Lenders

The first question in a securities issue is attracting lenders who are prepared to invest. Where the securities are listed on a regulated exchange, and sometimes in other circumstances, the process of eliciting lenders will attract regulatory supervision. Regulation of debt is dealt with in chapter eleven and what follows is merely a short description of the varieties of process by which buyers of debt securities are found.

There are two main ways in which bond issues are sold: either by a single stand-alone issue, or under a 'programme'. Short-term securities such as commercial paper and medium-term notes are very often issued under a programme,[73] where the documentation for a series of issues is drafted and agreed in advance, so that each issue only requires very limited documentation.[74] Stand-alone issues require full documentation for each issue, and are therefore more expensive and time-consuming. They are rarely used for plain 'vanilla' issues, but are for more complicated issues, such as convertible or high-yield bonds requiring more negotiation.[75] Domestic stock is issued in a different way again, the most common method being a 'placing', which is a one-off process, and which can also be used for bonds.[76]

The basic ideas behind all issues of debt securities are the same. One or more investment banks organise the issue for the issuer: these are called 'arrangers'[77] or 'managers'[78] or 'dealers'.[79] These banks will advise the issuer on the best market for the securities: both in terms of the primary market, that is whether they should be offered only to a small number of selected institutions or more widely, and in terms of the secondary market, whether they should be listed and admitted to trading on one of the financial markets.[80] There is often one lead bank, who does most of the administration, but several other banks who join with the lead bank in underwriting the issue,[81] that is, agreeing to buy the bonds if no one else will, usually with a view to selling them on to investors quickly, or, alternatively, to buying all the bonds which they then sell on to

---

[71]   2.4.

[72]   7.3.2.1.

[73]   Known as ECP and EMTN programmes respectively: see G Fuller, *The Law and Practice of International Capital Markets* (London, LexisNexis Butterworths, 2007) 1.102 and 1.169 et seq.

[74]   This has many similarities with a revolving loan facility: see above and M Hughes, *Legal Principles in Banking and Structured Finance*, 2nd edn (Hayward's Heath, Tottel Publishing Ltd, 2006) 4.8.

[75]   M Doran, D Howe and R Pogrel, 'Debt Capital Markets: an Introduction' (2005) 16 *Practical Law Company* 21, 23–24. For a description of high-yield bonds, see pages 32–33.

[76]   See 9.2.2 below for a discussion of placing in relation to shares.

[77]   Usually in relation to stock: G Fuller, *Corporate Borrowing: Law and Practice*, 4th edn (Bristol, Jordan Publishing Ltd, 2009) 13.3.

[78]   Generally in relation to stand-alone issues: see Fuller, *The Law and Practice of International Capital Markets*, n 73, 6.02.

[79]   Generally in relation to programmes: see ibid.

[80]   See pages 326–27 below.

[81]   For a discussion of underwriting in relation to equity securities see page 411 below.

investors.[82] This is an incentive on the banks to try and find investors, and to advise accurately on the price and terms that the market will bear.[83] By this means the issuer knows that it will obtain the financing represented by the bond issue. This, however, comes at a price, and the investment banks are well paid for taking on the underwriting risk.

The most important documents are also common to all procedures. First, a mandate letter appoints the lead manager(s) or arranger. This may follow a period of bidding, where potential managers compete for the position by setting out their credentials and their suggested terms for the issue. The lead manager(s) will then prepare for the launch, by discussing with the issuer the details of the terms of the securities, and by deciding whom to appoint as trustee. At the launch, the issue is announced to potential co-managers, who will buy or underwrite the issue, and potential investors. Next comes the subscription agreement, which is an agreement between the issuer and the managers[84] including representations and warranties from the issuer and an agreement from the managers to subscribe to, or to procure others to subscribe to, the issue. The liability of the managers under this agreement is usually joint and several, so that any one of them might be liable to buy the whole issue if the other managers all fail and there are no investors.[85] There will also be an agreement between the managers, setting out the obligations of each.

The issue will be marketed to investors by the managers by means of an offering circular or prospectus. This is the document which must comply with the regulatory requirements, which are set out in chapter eleven.[86] It will contain information, often prescribed by regulation, about the issuing company and the issue itself. Other documentation which must be prepared includes the trust deed (if there is a trustee), agreements with paying and/or fiscal agents[87] and the bond itself.

The details of the process vary according to the type of issue. With stock, a placing takes place on one day (the 'impact' day) with one arranger sending provisional invitation letters and preliminary offering circulars to potential buyers in the morning. The stock is priced later in the day on the basis of the response, and formal documents are sent out the following morning.[88]

In a stand-alone issue of Eurobonds,[89] a lead manager will be appointed and the issue is launched. At this point, the preliminary offering circular is sent to potential investors and

[82] This is termed a 'bought deal', see P Wood, *Law and Practice of International Finance,* (London, Sweet & Maxwell, 2008) 11–33; Fuller, n 73, 6.17. If the on-sale is to a small group of selected investors, this would be a 'private placing'.
[83] Hudson, *The Law of Finance*, n 48, 35–07. Note that the price in most ordinary bond issues is now likely to be determined before the manager is appointed, rather than the more traditional 'open-priced' structure where the price was determined after receiving feedback from potential investors, see Fuller, n 73, 6.16–6.19.
[84] In relation to stock this is called a placing agreement. In relation to a programme, the equivalent document is the programme agreement, but under this agreement the dealers only agree to subscribe on an uncommitted basis, so that there will be a subscription agreement for each issue as well; Fuller, n 73, 6.06–6.08; M Doran, D Howe and R Pogrel, 'Debt Capital Markets: an Introduction' (2005) 16 *Practical Law Company* 21, 24.
[85] Hudson, n 48, 35–17.
[86] 11.2.
[87] See pages 331 and 339–40.
[88] Fuller, *Corporate Borrowing: Law and Practice,* n 77, 13.3.
[89] For detailed description, see Fuller, n 77, 13.5–13.8; P Wood, *International Loans, Bonds, Guarantees, Legal Opinions,* 2nd edn (London, Sweet & Maxwell, 2007) 10–035; Fuller, n 73, ch 6; Tolley's Company Law Service B5049–5052; M Doran, D Howe and R Pogrel, 'Debt Capital Markets: an Introduction' (2005) 16 *Practical Law Company* 21, 24.

also other potential managers (who will underwrite the issue). The price may either be specified by the issuer when appointing the lead manager, or may be determined after feedback from potential investors and managers. The next stage is the signing of the subscription agreement, after which the sales to investors are confirmed, as is the listing and the rating (if the issue is listed and/or rated). The issue is then closed, at which time the final documents are produced, the global note is delivered to the depositary[90] and the price is paid by the buyers, via the paying agent,[91] to the issuer. In a programme issue, the general process is the same, but the offering circular and other major documentation are agreed and signed when the programme is set up, so for each issue only the price and other key terms need to be agreed and documented.

There is a danger, when a new issue of securities is launched on the market, that the price will be very volatile in the period after the launch. This is often because those who initially bought the securities (such as the managers or initial investors) may offload securities onto the market to make a quick profit, or because they have initially asked for more securities than they actually want. In order to combat such volatility, the lead manager may buy a large number of securities in the market, thus artificially pushing up the price. This process is called 'stabilisation'. It will enable itself to do this by over-allotting the securities in the first place to the managers, that is, by allotting more securities than are actually being issued. The managers will not be aware of this, or at least, not of the extent of over-allotment. The lead manager will then be able to 'buy-back' the over-allotted securities before the issue is closed. This creates an artificial demand and drives up the price which otherwise would be depressed by the large amount of sales by the managers.[92] The main problem with stabilisation is that it would be likely to fall foul of the statutory provisions against market abuse.[93] Since stabilisation is seen as a beneficial activity, safe harbours have been created from the market abuse offences. These are discussed in chapter eleven.[94]

Part of the process will usually involve the rating of the issue by a rating agency,[95] and often an application for listing on a stock exchange, so that the bonds can be traded on a public market.[96] Not all bonds are listed,[97] but listing has certain advantages for the issuer. It gives a wider market for the bonds, including, in theory, the public. However, in order to escape certain regulatory requirements,[98] very few bonds are actually offered to members of the public, but are limited to sophisticated investors such as pension funds and investment funds. Much of the trading of bonds is actually done off the market (or 'over the counter') but many institutional investors are not permitted, either by law or by their own prudential guidelines, to invest in non-listed securities.[99] Therefore, many issues are

---

[90]   See below page 335 et seq.

[91]   See below page 331.

[92]   For a full description of stabilisation, see Fuller, n 77, 13.71–13.73 and Fuller, n 73, 6.144–6–150.

[93]   See 10.5.

[94]   11.4.1.

[95]   See above pages 32–33 and 11.7 below.

[96]   The two debt securities markets on the London Stock Exchange are the Gilt Edged and Fixed Interest Market, which is a regulated market and the Professional Securities Market, which is an unregulated market. See chapter eleven below, in particular page 540.

[97]   For example, commercial paper is rarely listed: M Doran, D Howe and R Pogrel, 'Debt Capital Markets: an Introduction' (2005) 16 *Practical Law Company* 21, 25.

[98]   See chapter 11.

[99]   Wood, *International Loans, Bonds, Guarantees, Legal Opinions*, n 89, 10–039; Hudson, n 48, 35–38.

listed although traded over the counter. In addition, listing gives a benchmark price for over the counter trades, which can be helpful to investors.[100] Further, a 'quoted Eurobond', which is one which is listed on a recognised stock exchange, is exempt from the requirement to withhold tax at source when interest is paid: this is very important for investors, who would otherwise receive a very reduced interest payment.[101] The disadvantages of listing are the regulatory requirements, which apply both at the listing stage and throughout the life of the bond.[102] These not only add to the expense, but are time-consuming and may delay an issue, which makes it difficult to take advantage of favourable market conditions.[103]

7.3.2 Structure of Securities Issue

7.3.2.1 *Difference Between Bonds and Stock*

One of the fundamental distinctions in relation to debt securities is that between bonds[104] and stock.[105] Loan stock is issued by a company to the domestic market, and comprises just one debt obligation, held either by a trustee or created by deed poll. As it is a single obligation, it can be split up into as many parts as there are people who want to hold it (though not in units of less than £1). Bonds (or notes), however, are individual debt obligations owed by the company to each holder. Bonds of this structure were originally only issued for the international market (as Eurobonds) but the bond structure is now used for many domestic issues as well.[106]

Another important difference between the two is that stock is usually in registered form, while bonds are usually bearer instruments.[107] This is because, in the past, this enabled the identity of the bond investor to be kept secret from the issuer.[108] This distinction is best understood by looking at the position before dematerialisation of securities.[109] The title to registered securities was derived from the register kept by the issuer, which was evidenced by a certificate issued to the holder. In order to transfer registered securities, it was necessary to execute a stock transfer form, and deliver this to the issuer together with the certificate. The issuer would then amend the register. The

---

[100] Wood, n 89, 10–039.

[101] Income Tax Act 2007, s 882; Inland Revenue Manual Company Taxation Manual 35218.

[102] These are discussed in chapter 11 below.

[103] Wood, n 89, 10–040.

[104] The term 'bonds' is used here to cover bonds of all types of maturity, including commercial paper and -medium term notes: see above, pages 30–31 for discussion of the different terms.

[105] See Fuller, n 77, 3.3–3.5. For further discussion of the differences, see Fuller, n 73, 1.168 et seq.

[106] Ibid, 3.2.

[107] Now, bonds are usually issued as global bearer notes. However, they are also sometimes issued in registered global note form, see below page 336. This is more likely where they are intended to be bought by US buyers, in order to comply with US tax regulations (see Fuller, n 73, 12.10 and Wood, n 89, 11–008).

[108] M Doran, D Howe and R Pogrel, 'Debt Capital Markets: an Introduction' (2005) 16 *Practical Law Company* 21.

[109] Dematerialsation was brought about by the Uncertificated Securities Regulations 2001 (SI 2001/3755) as amended by Uncertificated Securities (Eligible Debt Securities) Regulations 2003 (SI 2003/1633) and the Uncertificated Securities (Amendment) Regulations 2007 (SI 2007/124).

actual piece of paper (the certificate), however, did not give the holder any particular rights, unlike a bearer security, which is owned by the holder and transferable by delivery.[110]

Although it is in theory possible to have this situation today, it is unlikely. Registered securities are now able to be held in dematerialised form through the CREST system. The CREST system, which is operated by Euroclear UK and Ireland Ltd (EUI), was established in 2001 to enable certificated securities to be converted to uncertificated form, and for uncertificated new issues to be made. EUI maintains the CREST register, on which the securities are registered and which is the root of title for a CREST member.[111] The registration has to be in the name of a CREST member, which can be either a direct member[112] or a sponsored member.[113] The securities are transferred between members[114] by an entry in the CREST system. EUI has no proprietary interest in the securities: the registered member is the legal owner. Thus stock is usually now held through CREST, although it is still possible to hold it in certificated form. Bonds can still be held as bearer bonds, but the cost of producing individual definitive notes[115] and the requirements of the US securities laws have led to them largely being issued as global notes.[116] This means that, at least initially, only one note is issued representing the whole of the bond issue. It is held in a depositary, usually by or on behalf of Euroclear (in Belgium) or Clearstream (in Luxembourg).[117] The holders of the bonds are account holders with Euroclear or Clearstream (or hold through account holders who act as intermediaries), and the securities are transferred through the clearing systems operated by those companies. Bearer securities can also be held through CREST,[118] and this is common for money market instruments such as commercial paper.

It is now common for securities of any type to be held through an intermediary rather than directly by the owner. One reason for indirect holding is, as indicated above, because a bond is issued in global form and so is held by the legal owner for account holders. Another reason is that intermediation itself brings benefits. These include ease of settlement and transfer,[119] the use of local intermediaries in cross-border investment,[120]

---

[110]   A bearer instrument is likely to be a negotiable instrument, where the bona fide transferee gets a better title than the transferor, see 8.2.3. below.

[111]   Uncertificated Securities Regulations 2001 (SI 2001/3755) reg 24(2) and (3).

[112]   An institution which has an electronic connection directly with the settlement system.

[113]   This can be anyone (including individuals) who has a sponsorship arrangement with a direct member.

[114]   It is only possible to transfer between members, but any buyer who is not a member can become a sponsored member, or have a member hold for him as an intermediary.

[115]   Which have complicated and expensive security features, since, as bearer securities, possession of the note confers ownership and all the rights of a holder.

[116]   M Doran, D Howe and R Pogrel, 'Debt Capital Markets: an Introduction' (2005) 16 *Practical Law Company* 21; Tolley's Company Law Service B5034; Fuller, n 77, 1.222. For further discussion of global notes see page 335 et seq.

[117]   It is also possible for registered securities to be held through Euroclear or Clearstream: see Fuller, n 73, 1.119. See 7.3.2.3.2 for more detailed discussion of the rights of holders of bonds under a global note.

[118]   Tolley's Company Law Service, C4009, 4015. The ambit of the CREST system was widened to include debt securities by the Uncertificated Securities (Amendment) (Eligible Debt Securities) Regulations 2003 (SI 2003/1633). In order for a bearer security to become dematerialised, it in effect becomes a registered security, since the root of title becomes the CREST register: Uncertificated Securities Regulations 2001 (SI 2001/3755) reg 24(2) and (3).

[119]   This is discussed at 8.2.5.

[120]   J Benjamin, *Financial Law*, (Oxford, Oxford University Press, 2007) 8.68.

and services provided by the intermediaries, such as management services or financial services.[121] The legal analysis of indirect holding of securities is discussed in the context of bond issues below.[122]

7.3.2.2 Stock

There are two possible structures for the holding of stock, both of which are consonant with it being just one single debt owed by the issuing company. The first is that the debt is owed to a trustee, and the second is that the debt is contained in a deed poll.

7.3.2.2.1 Debt Owed to a Trustee

Where there is a trustee of the stock, it[123] holds the benefit of the covenant to pay on behalf of the stockholders. No direct covenant to pay principal or interest is made with the stockholders, which means that a stockholder is not a creditor of the company.[124] The stockholders, even collectively, can have no legal title to the debt, but it is held for them as beneficiaries under a trust, so they become equitable co-owners of the debt, which they hold as tenants in common, in proportion to the amount of stock they own.[125] However, it is the stockholders who are entered on the register of holders kept by the company[126] and issued with certificates (if the stock is certificated) which evidence the holder's equitable interest, and the trust deed normally provides that the company recognises the holder as absolute owner of the stock.[127] If the stock is dematerialised, and is admitted to CREST then a similar register is kept in the CREST system.[128]

The fact that the stockholders' interest is an equitable interest has various consequences, some of which are mentioned above. One is that any transfer of an equitable interest has to be in writing.[129] This requirement is disapplied when securities are transferred through the CREST system.[130] Another is that a stockholder can only grant an equitable and not a legal mortgage of his stock.[131] Normally, having an equitable mortgage could present a problem to the mortgagee, since it would lose priority to a subsequent legal mortgagee.

---

[121] The provision of finance by an intermediary for the investor to buy the securities is one of the chief reasons for the prime brokerage agreement, whereby the intermediary makes an advance to the investor to buy the securities, which it (the prime broker) then holds on the investor's behalf subject to a security interest to secure the advance. See S Worthington and I Mitchkovska, 'Pitfalls with Property Claims: Lehman Bros Again' (2009) 24 *Journal of International Banking and Financial Law* 321.

[122] See page 337, and for discussion of the transfer of intermediated securities see 8.2.5 below.

[123] As in most of the situations described in this chapter, the trustee (or agent) is likely to be a department of a bank, or other financial institution; thus the pronoun 'it' will be used.

[124] And therefore cannot petition for its winding up for non-payment of interest: *Re Dunderland Iron Ore Company* [1909] 1 Ch 446, 452.

[125] Gullifer, *Goode on Legal Problems of Credit and Security*, n 54. This satisfies any requirement as to certainty of subject matter of the trust. It is also inevitable, since there is only one obligation, so no question of ascertainment of separate units can arise, see above pages 318–22.

[126] Note that this is different from the position in relation to shares, since no notice of a trust can be entered on the register of members of a company, Companies Act 2006, s 126. See 8.2.7.

[127] Tolley's Company Law Service C4002.

[128] Uncertificated Securities Regulations SI 2001/3755 (as amended by Uncertificated Securities (Amendment) (Eligible Debt Securities) Regulations 2003 SI 2003/1633), reg 22 and Sch 4 para 14.

[129] Law of Property Act 1925, s 53(1)(c).

[130] Uncertificated Securities Regulations SI 2001/3755, reg 38.

[131] Tolley's Company Law Service C4006, which explains that if the stock is transferred into the name of the mortgagee in the stock register, this has an effect very like a legal mortgage, because of the provision in the trust deed that the company recognises the registered holder as owner.

However, since it is not possible to grant a legal mortgage, any subsequent mortgage would also be equitable, and so the first equitable mortgagee would always have priority on the grounds of being first in time.[132] Also, a transferee of stock, even if without notice, in theory takes subject to any equitable rights or interests affecting that stock.[133]

Stock can be structured in this way whether or not the company's covenant to pay is secured, but where there is security, it will be granted to the trustee to hold on behalf of the stockholders. Secured loan stock is usually called debenture stock (although this term can also be used for unsecured stock).[134] In either case, it is the trustee which has the power to enforce the covenant to pay, and the security, if any. The stockholders cannot enforce directly, but they have the power to force the trustee to enforce on their behalf, and, if he will not do so, to bring an action themselves under the *Vandepitte*[135] principle so long as they join the trustee as co-defendant.[136] The advantages of having a trust structure as opposed to a deed poll are in many ways similar to those in relation to a Eurobond issue, which are discussed below.[137]

7.3.2.2.2   Debt Contained in a Deed Poll

An alternative way to structure stock is by means of a deed poll. A deed poll is an instrument executed by one party, which contains a promise that can be enforced by anyone who is benefitted by the promise.[138] Thus, the company executes a deed making a promise to pay those registered as holders of the stock, which is enforceable by whoever are the holders from time to time. Although enforceable rights can now be conferred on third parties to a contract under the Contracts (Rights Against Third Parties) Act 1999, a deed poll is still significant in that it is unilateral, whereas the Act only applies to contracts made between two or more people.[139] Although it is possible to transfer stock issued by deed poll, this structure tends to be used for larger denominations of stock, where there will not be many holders and where there is not an active market. For smaller denominations, where there are many holders and an active market, the trustee structure is usually used.[140]

7.3.2.3   Eurobonds

Although this section is headed 'Eurobonds', the structure discussed is that of bonds and notes of all maturities, including short-term notes such as commercial paper. The term 'bonds' will be used throughout, unless the context demands otherwise. As mentioned above, bonds are bearer instruments, and, for the purpose of analysis, it is worth

---

[132]   See page 273 where the relevant priority rules are discussed. The proposition in the text is potentially qualified by the application of the rule in *Dearle v Hall* (see pages 273–74), but this is unlikely to affect the result, see discussion in Tolley's Company Law Service C4029/2 and pages 390–91 below.

[133]   This will rarely cause problems in practice, see the discussion at 8.2.4.

[134]   Butterworths Corporate Law Service CAF 16.17.

[135]   [1933] AC 70. For discussion of the *Vandepitte* principle, see below page 383.

[136]   Tolley's Company Law Service C4002.

[137]   7.3.2.3.1.

[138]   *Moody v Condor Insurance Ltd* [2006] 1 WLR 1847, [16].

[139]   Fuller, n 77, 3.8. However, if the person making the obligations intends a deed to operate as a deed poll, it will be held to do so, despite the fact that there are in fact two or more parties to the deed: *Moody v Condor Insurance Company Ltd* [2006] 1 WLR 1847, following *Chelsea and Walham Green Building Society v Armstrong* [1951] 1 Ch 853.

[140]   Butterworths Corporate Law Services CAF 16.231–16.232.

considering the position if individual bearer securities were issued.[141] Each bearer security constitutes an independent debt and promise to pay the bearer.[142] This obligation is 'locked up' in the document (and passes by delivery of the document): the bond is a documentary intangible.[143] Therefore, each holder is the legal owner of the bond and the obligation locked up in it. A bearer bond is transferable by delivery and there seems little doubt that a bearer bond is a negotiable instrument.[144] The problem of there being multiple lenders in a bond issue can be dealt with in two ways: either a fiscal agent is appointed, or there is a trustee.

7.3.2.3.1   Advantages and Disadvantages of the Trustee Structure

There are a number of advantages in using the trustee structure, both from the perspective of the bondholders and the issuer. However, a fiscal agent structure is cheaper, and is used extensively in issues of short-term securities (such as commercial paper) and plain 'vanilla' issues.[145] The main difference between a fiscal agent and a trustee is that the fiscal agent acts on behalf of the issuer, while the trustee acts on behalf of the bondholders, to whom he owes fiduciary duties. The primary function of the agent is to make payments on the bonds to the bondholders, and thus it is common for there to be a paying agent even where there is a trustee.[146] A trustee has a much more extensive role, as it is acting as the representative of all the bondholders and therefore its role includes all the steps one would expect a single lender to take to protect its interests. The trustee has a monitoring role,[147] is expected to consider the seriousness of events of default and, if the default is serious enough, can accelerate and enforce payment of the bonds. The trustee is also able to negotiate restructuring on behalf of the bondholders, and is able to agree minor modifications to the terms of the issue during the life of the bonds.[148]

There are advantages in having a trustee for both the bondholders and the issuer.[149] For the bondholders, the main advantage is to have an expert person to deal with the issuer. A bond trustee will be a specialist corporate trustee[150] and will be in a position to evaluate financial information produced by the issuer. Moreover, the presence of a trustee means that the issuer is more likely to agree to disclose confidential information, when it will only be seen by the trustee. It will also be more likely to agree to include in the

---

[141]   Although this is unlikely in practice because of the factors of cost and difficulty of settlement.

[142]   In a typical issue, this covenant is qualified by the bearer's promise not to enforce the issuer's debt unless the trustee refuses to sue. The question of whether the bearer can actually enforce this covenant will be discussed later (pages 348–49).

[143]   For a discussion of documentary intangibles generally, see E McKendrick, *Goode on Commercial Law*, 4th edn (London, LexisNexis UK, 2009) Ch 18, and, in relation to bearer bonds, see 611–15.

[144]   See 8.2.3.

[145]   M Doran, D Howe and R Pogrel, 'Debt Capital Markets: An Introduction' (2005) 16 *Practical Law Company* 21, 24.

[146]   Fuller, n 77, 3.02–3.04.

[147]   Though note the limitations of this, see below page 344.

[148]   For further discussion see 7.3.3 below.

[149]   See generally Fuller, n 77, 213–14 and Fuller, n 73, 3.73–3.76; Wood, n 89, 16–002–16–005; R Tennekoon, *The Law and Regulation of International Finance* (London, Butterworths, 1991) 247; C Duffett, 'Using Trusts in International Finance and Commercial Transactions' (1992) 1 *Journal of International Trust and Corporate Planning* 23; P Rawlings, 'The Changing Role of the Trustee in International Bond Issue' [2007] *Journal of Business Law* 43; Financial Markets Law Committee, Issue 62 'Trustee Exemption Clauses' 16–17.

[150]   As opposed to an agent, which will usually be a bank. Fuller, n 73, 3.06.

documentation covenants which require expert evaluation, such as financial ratio covenants, or which require a decision to be made, such as whether a breach is 'material'.[151] As we shall see, the obligations on a trustee to monitor are limited, but even so the trustee is more likely to be aware of financial difficulties or a default at an earlier stage than individual bondholders would: this enables action to be taken which can either aid restructuring of the debt or facilitate orderly enforcement. In the case of restructuring, the trustee will be in a stronger position to negotiate than any individual bondholder, as it represents a large amount of debt. It will, however, need authority from the bondholders to agree any major changes. This will necessitate arrangements for obtaining the consent of a majority of the bondholders, which can either be contained in the original documentation or set up after the event.[152] Furthermore, since it is the trustee who decides when to accelerate payment on default,[153] a trustee will be in a position to waive or take no action on a minor breach. This prevents one or two 'mad bondholders' from enforcing their rights which could cause detriment of all the others and also to the issuer,[154] since acceleration is likely to trigger cross-default clauses in other agreements, which is likely to push the issuer into insolvency. Having a trustee also makes enforcement easier, since it is the trustee who has the right to bring enforcement proceedings: this is cheaper and more convenient where there are numerous and dispersed bondholders, and preserves the anonymity of bondholders.

Bolstering up the trustee's position in relation to acceleration and enforcement is the 'no-action' clause, which provides that no bondholder can enforce its rights against the issuer unless the trustee has been directed to do so and has taken no action.[155] The other advantage brought by the no-action clause is that the proceeds recovered on enforcement are distributed rateably, as no bondholder can gain more by being the first to sue.[156] Interestingly, the development of this clause, and the analogous clause in syndicated loans, the 'pro rata' clause, is evidence that there is substance behind the theoretical argument justifying the *pari passu* rule in insolvency: in collective situations, parties really will bargain for a pro rata distribution to avoid the race to the courtroom door, as each rationally, when behind a veil of ignorance, will perceive it to be the best outcome for it in all possible worlds.[157] Where the issuer is not in difficulties, but a change in circumstances make it desirable for a change to be made to the terms of the issue, a trustee can agree to minor changes without troubling (or having to find) the bondholders,[158] who generally do

---

[151] Wood, n 89,16–002.

[152] R Karia and K Hargreaves, 'Negotiating with Bondholders' (2009) 24 *Journal of International Banking and Financial Law* 259.

[153] Subject to the power of the bondholders, if acting by a large majority, to direct acceleration if the trustee refuses to do so: see 7.3.3 below.

[154] It should be pointed out that such bondholders are not necessarily mad; it may be quite rational in terms of its own interests to accelerate although harmful to the collective interests of the bondholders and to the issuer. For examples of such situations, see P Rawlings, 'The Changing Role of the Trustee in International Bond Issue' [2007] *Journal of Business Law* 43, 47. For further discussion of the 'no-action' clause and its use in dealing with the 'mad bondholder' problem, see below page 348 et seq.

[155] There is no need to use the *Vandepitte* procedure here, as there is in the case of stock (see page 330 above), as the bondholder will have an independent obligation owed to it, albeit qualified by the no-action clause: see below.

[156] Wood, n 89, 16–002.

[157] T Jackson, The *Logic and Limits of Bankruptcy Law* (Cambridge, Mass, Harvard University Press, 1986) ch 1.

[158] See pages 343–44 below.

not pay much interest in the administration of the bond issue, provided that the payments are made on time and the issuer is not in financial difficulties.[159]

Having a trustee poses some disadvantages for the bondholders. There is some rather minor expense. More significantly, there is a general loss of control, since the advantages listed above can only be given effect to by giving the trustee discretion to act without consulting the bondholders at every turn. Further, negotiation and restructuring on default, which is facilitated by the presence of a trustee, is not necessarily always beneficial to the bondholders, who may consider that they are better off being paid (although they will only get paid in full if the issuer is solvent).[160] Obviously, the advantages of a trustee for bondholders are greatest where the bondholders are numerous and diverse, as the problems of co-ordinated action are very great, and also where there is no desire on the holders to expend their own resources on the protection of their economic interest in relation to the bond (although, of course, the trustee has to be paid). While it used to be compulsory for an issue of domestic bonds which was listed on the London Stock Exchange to have a trustee,[161] this is no longer the case.

The present of a trustee can also have advantages for the issuer. The advantages largely stem from the convenience of dealing with one person rather than a large number. Examples of this are the ability to agree minor modifications with the trustee alone, the ability to negotiate with just the trustee in the event of rescheduling and only having to deal with one person enforcing the bonds. Further, the no-action clause gives the issuer considerable protection against the 'mad bondholder' problem: an acceleration by a single bondholder on the basis of default may harm the interests of the other bondholders, but it will be even more disastrous for the issuer, as it is likely to lead to its insolvency. Many Eurobond issues also permit the trustee to agree that another entity be substituted as the debtor in place of the issuer:[162] this may be desirable, for example, for tax reasons.[163]

There is one situation in which the advantages of having a trustee are overwhelming: where security is given for the obligation to pay. While this is not common in Eurobonds, it is fundamental to other structures, such as securitisation and project finance. If security had to be given to each bondholder, not only would this be expensive and complicated at the start, but each time a bond was transferred to another holder, the security interest would have to be re-registered.[164] Further, the trustee can enforce on behalf of all the bondholders. These benefits stem from the fact that it is possible to have a trust with a changing group of beneficiaries,[165] so that the trustee holds the trust property for those who are bondholders for the time being. The free tradability of the bonds is thereby preserved. Other advantages include common terms for all secured creditors, and more efficient administration of subordination, for example, turnover trusts.[166]

---

[159]   R Karia and K Hargreaves, 'Negotiating with Bondholders' (2009) 24 *Journal of International Banking and Financial Law* 259.

[160]   Wood, n 89, 16–002, who points out that this disadvantage, if it is such, is often overcome by the creation of a committee of bondholders.

[161]   Hudson, n 48, 35–22.

[162]   Fuller, n 77, 12.8.

[163]   Wood, n 89, 16–003.

[164]   P Ali, 'Security Trustees' in P Ali (ed), *Secured Finance Transactions: Key Assets and Emerging Market* (London, Globe Business Publishing Ltd, 2007) 33.

[165]   See pages 317–18 above.

[166]   Hughes, *Legal Principles in Banking and Structured Finance*, n 74, 13.10–13.12.

7.3.2.3.2   Subject Matter of the Trust[167]

It will be recalled from the discussion of the concept of trust earlier in the chapter that its most distinctive feature was that the obligations of the trustee are owed in relation to property. This is true of even the most 'obligation-centred' view of trust,[168] otherwise a trust is indistinguishable from a contract. Whether a trust deed is also a contract is a matter which we will consider later,[169] but the argument that it is in no way detracts from the need for there to be some property as the subject matter of a trust. In a secured bond issue, there is no problem: the subject matter of the trust is the security interest granted to secure the issuer's obligations. However, in an unsecured bond issue there is no such obvious answer. One view is that the trustee does not hold assets like an ordinary trustee, but instead has a collected delegation of authority from the bondholders[170] or is a fiduciary representative of the bondholders.[171] This view contradicts the orthodox notion of a trust, and would appear to make the 'trustee' merely a fiduciary agent of the bondholders, whose authority could be revoked by any bondholder at any time, and who therefore could not be relied upon to bind all the bondholders when waiving the right to accelerate on breach.[172] It is also not necessary to take such a radical view since, as will be discussed in the next paragraph, there is something which can be the subject matter of the trust.

Let us again start with the position where bearer bonds are issued. Here the issuer makes separate promises to pay to all the bondholders, but also a parallel covenant to the trustee, which is satisfied by payment made to the bondholders.[173] It is not the case that the trustee holds the promises to the bondholders on trust for them: this would reduce their interests to equitable interests, which would prevent the bonds being negotiable instruments.[174] However, the trustee can hold the parallel covenant made to it on trust for the bondholders.[175] This makes sense: the trustee's obligations all relate to the protection of that covenant for the benefit of the bondholders, since the 'no-action' clause means that it is enforcement by the trustee which is the bondholders' route to protecting their economic interest in the bond. The structure might be seen as a little artificial or even circular, in that the covenant is given to the trustee merely so that it can hold it on trust for the bondholders, and the trustee's covenant is valuable to the bondholders purely because they agree not to enforce their own covenants unless the trustee unreasonably refuses to

---

[167]   For an interesting discussion of this and the other difficulties in seeing the bond trusteeship as an orthodox trust, see A Hudson, *The Law on Investment Entities* (London, Sweet & Maxwell, 2000) ch 6.

[168]   See P Parkinson, 'Reconceptualising the Express Trust' (2002) 61 *Cambridge Law Journal* 657 and pages 321–22 above.

[169]   See pages 352–53.

[170]   McKendrick, *Goode on Commercial Law*, n 143, 166; P Rawlings, 'The Changing Role of the Trustee in International Bond Issue' [2007] *Journal of Business Law* 48.

[171]   Wood, n 82, 9.12(3)(b). However, Professor Wood's views have changed: see Wood, n 89, 16–013. See also S Schwartz, 'Commercial Trusts as Business Organisations: Unravelling the Mystery' (2003) 58 *Business Lawyer* 559, 569, in relation to the US position.

[172]   Tennekoon, *The Law and Regulation of International Finance*, n 149, 227, who also takes the view that a no-action clause would be ineffective on termination of authority.

[173]   Or payment to the paying agent who will then pay the bondholders: Wood, n 89, 16–13; Fuller, n 73, 3.44.

[174]   McKendrick, n 143, 614; Tennekoon, *The Law and Regulation of International Finance*, n 149, 226; Fuller, n 77, 3.10.

[175]   Wood, n 89, 16–013; Fuller, n 77, 3–10; Tennekoon, n 149, 226; Hudson, n 48, 35–25. This trust is usually expressly declared in the trust deed: see Tolley's Company Law Service B5050.

enforce its own covenant (which it holds on trust for the bondholders).[176] However, it is no more artificial than many other structures, and at least it is consistent with the usual understanding of trust law. One might ask why it is necessary for the bondholders to have their own covenants: why is the transaction not structured like stock, where there is only one covenant which is made to the trustee? The answer is that, when bonds were issued as bearer bonds, it was seen as very important that bondholders had legal title to the bond. This was partly because legal title was necessary for the bond to be a negotiable instrument, partly because disposal of an equitable interest would require writing,[177] and partly because, as it was to be traded on the international markets, the bondholders' title would need to be recognised in countries which did not recognise or understand equitable interests.[178]

There are, however, two potential problems with this analysis. One, pointed out by Tennekoon,[179] is that the promise made by the issuer to the trustee is an asset of which only the trustee can declare a trust, since the issuer is the debtor. If the trust deed (executed by the issuer) declares that the trustee holds this covenant on trust for the bondholders, is this sufficient to create a valid trust? Tennekoon's view is that such a trust should be valid,[180] but that it would be safer for the trustee itself to declare the trust. This is achieved in practice by including an express declaration of the trust in the trust deed, to which the trustee is a party.[181]

The other complication is that bonds are usually no longer bearer bonds, but are constituted by a global note,[182] which is held by a depositary (usually a bank) for a clearing system (one or both of Clearstream and Euroclear[183]). The bondholder's rights either derive from entries on the books of the clearing system, if the bondholder has an account with that system, or from entries on the books of an intermediary who does have an account and who holds the securities for the bondholder. Trading takes place through the clearing system, by book entry. The global note itself is in the form of a bearer bond,[184] with provision for the issue of definitive securities in certain situations, such as an event of

---

[176]   It would be possible to see the no-action clause as a contractual version of the '*Vandepitte* procedure' (based on *Vandepitte v Preferred Accident Insurance Corporation of New York* [1933] AC 70, 79) whereby the beneficiaries of a trust have the right to bring an action, joining the trustee as defendant, if the trustee unreasonably refuses to enforce the trust (see Fuller, n 73, 1.145 and 3.45). However, this seems to assume that the trustee holds the bondholders' rights on trust as well as its own, which, for the reasons given in the text, it is argued is not the case.

[177]   Hudson, n 48, 35–25. This is a not a problem with stock as registration provides the necessary writing, and the section is disapplied to CREST transfers, see page 329 above.

[178]   Tennekoon, n 149, 226.

[179]   Ibid, 226–27.

[180]   There is authority for such a declaration of trust in *Fletcher v Fletcher* (1844) 4 Hare 67, although whether there was actually intention to create a trust of the promise in that case is open to doubt, see Martin, n 12, 136–37. The view expressed by Hanbury and Martin is that, where there is consideration for the promise, the relevant intention to create a trust is that of the promisee, while if the promise is voluntary, the intention of the promisor will suffice.

[181]   Tolley's Company Law Service B5050.

[182]   While what is described here is a global bearer note, it is also possible to have global registered notes which are held by a depositary: this is largely where there are potential US buyers, see footnote 107 above.

[183]   These are International Central Securities Depositaries and will be referred to in this chapter as ICSDs.

[184]   See page 392 for discussion of whether it is a negotiable instrument.

default by the issuer or the closure of the clearing system.[185] It is clear, then, that the bondholders do not have legal title to the bond in the way described above in relation to bearer bonds.

There are two possible ways of analysing the relationship between the depositary and the ICSDs.[186] One is that the depositary holds the obligation contained in the global note on trust for the ICSD. This would be on the basis that the depositary is treated by the issuer as the person entitled to receive payment (this is usually stated on the face of the security itself),[187] and since the security is a bearer security it makes sense for the holder to be the legal owner. The other possibility, which is more attractive, is that the depositary holds the global note as bailee for the ICSD, who then hold it on trust for the investors.[188] The entitlement of the depositary to receive payment can be explained by its position (usually) as both the issuer's paying agent,[189] and the agent of the ICSD to whom it immediately will transfer the payment,[190] rather than as holder. The drawback with this analysis is that the documentation usually provides that only the 'holder' is entitled to payment, and the depositary can be seen as 'holder'.[191]

The above description is based on the Classic Global Note ('CGN') structure[192] which, although still in use, has been largely supplanted by the New Global Note ('NGN') structure.[193] In this structure, there is no depositary as such, but the global note is held by a 'common safekeeper' and the payment and other function previously carried out by the depositary will be carried out by a 'common service provider': the ICSD will usually be both the common safekeeper and the common service provider.[194] There will be a direct contractual relationship between the issuer and the ICSD, and the legally relevant record of the indebtedness of the issuer is maintained by the ICSD.[195] Under this structure, it seems even more appropriate that the ICSD is the legal owner, since it will usually hold the global note as common safekeeper. Even if it does not, it makes sense for the common safekeeper to be merely a bailee.

---

[185]   Fuller, n 73, 1.124; M Doran, D Howe and R Pogrel, 'Debt Capital Markets: an Introduction' (2005) 16 *Practical Law Company* 21. The problems caused by the absence of definitive securities are discussed below page 342.

[186]   This analysis is on the basis that English law applies. However, it may not, since the ICSDs are both situated in Luxembourg and Belgium).

[187]   Fuller, n 73, 1.129.

[188]   Benjamin, *Financial Law,* n 120, 8.71.

[189]   Fuller, n 73, 1.129.

[190]   Fuller, n 73, 3.20.

[191]   C Maunder, 'Bondholders' Schemes of Arrangement: Playing the Numbers Game' [2003] *Insolvency Intelligence* 73, 74. The question of who is the holder of Eurobonds is discussed by Tennekoon, n 149, 171–76, who reaches no firm conclusion. However, it should be noted that the bulk of his discussion concerns bearer bonds which are held by the depositary and not a permanent global note.

[192]   This is the technical term for the structure described, used throughout Europe.

[193]   The NGN structure was introduced for global bearer notes from 1 January 2007 and for global registered notes from 30 June 2010. See J Machin, 'Registered Notes: ECB Eligible Collateral and the Proposed New Safekeeping Structure' (2010) 25 *Journal of International Banking and Financial Law* 53. The new structure is compulsory if the securities are to constitute eligible collateral for Eurosystem operations: see press release of European Central Bank 13 June 2006, at http://www.ecb.int/press/pr/date/2006/html/pr060613.en.html.

[194]   In order to constitute eligible collateral as above, both the common safekeeper and the common service provider must be one of the ICSDs.

[195]   See ECB press release, above.

In order to simplify the analysis in the next few paragraphs, it will be assumed that the ICSD is the legal owner of the obligation contained in the global note.[196] The ICSD would then hold the obligation on trust for all those with accounts with it in relation to securities from that particular issue. If an account holder is an intermediary, it will then hold its beneficial interest on trust for its own account holders, who may be the ultimate bondholders or may be intermediaries themselves. This structure of sub-trusts is the best way under English law to explain the relationships in the holding of intermediated securities,[197] since an important feature of a sub-trust is that the sub-beneficiary only has rights against its immediate sub-trustee and not against the trustees higher up the chain.[198] This is important given that trading systems operate by trading taking place at the lowest level, so that higher level intermediaries have no knowledge of those holding accounts with lower tier intermediaries. The other important feature of the trust structure is the persistence of the beneficiary's interest against all others, except a *bona fide* purchaser of a legal interest without notice, including the insolvency officer of the trustee: in this context this means that those ultimately beneficially entitled to the bonds (that is, investors) are protected against the other creditors of anyone higher up in the chain who was to become insolvent. It can therefore be seen that the features of the trust discussed above[199] make it an important and useful structure in this modern way of holding securities, designed to speed up the process of issuance and of trading.

So far we have considered the position in relation to the obligation of the issuer contained in the global security, so that what is being held on trust is the ICSD's right to sue the issuer. However, this right is likely to be very limited, because of the 'no-action' clause, discussed above.[200] The important right to enforce is that of the trustee, who has its own separate covenant.[201] If, as we concluded earlier, it is this right which is the subject matter of the trust of which the bond trustee is trustee, who is the beneficiary where there is a deposited global note? Again, the best analysis appears to be that the legal owner of the global note is the beneficiary, and holds this interest on trust for the account holders, in addition to holding its own right to sue on trust.[202]

In practice, the clearing systems (and maybe the depositary) will be in jurisdictions which are not governed by English law, and under whose law there is no concept of trust.[203] The problems caused by cross-border holdings of intermediated securities are

---

[196]   This will almost certainly be the case in a NGN structure. Under the CGN structure, it is possible that the depositary will be the legal owner, as discussed above.

[197]   For detailed discussion of the position in English law in relation to intermediated securities, see J Benjamin, *Interests in Securities*, (Oxford, Oxford University Press, 2000); R Goode, 'The Nature and Transfer of Right in Dematerialised and Immobilised Securities' [1996] *Journal of International Banking and Financial Law* 167; Law Commission, 'The UNIDROIT Convention on Substantive Rules regarding Intermediated Securities: Further Updated Advice to the Treasury' (May 2008); Gullifer, *Goode on Legal Problems of Credit and Security*, n 54, ch 6; L Gullifer, 'Protection of Investors in Intermediated Securities' in J Armour and J Payne (eds), *Rationality in Company Law* (Oxford, Hart Publishing, 2009); L Gullifer and J Payne (eds) *Intermediated Securities: Legal Problems and Practical Issues* (Oxford, Hart Publishing, 2010) chapters 1, 2 and 3.

[198]   *Hayim v Citibank NA* [1987] AC 730.

[199]   See pages 316–18.

[200]   See pages 332–33.

[201]   See pages 334–35.

[202]   Hudson, n 48, 35–26.

[203]   This is another reason why it is probably best to see the relationship between the depositary and the ICSD as a bailment, as it is clear that English law does not apply.

outside the scope of this book, but have been much discussed.[204] The latest attempt to deal with such issues is the UNIDROIT Convention on Substantive Rules regarding Intermediated Securities 2009 ('the Geneva Securities Convention'),[205] which, if adopted by the relevant countries, would provide some uniformity of rules in relation to such securities. The specific issue of the obligations of bond trustees, however, is not addressed directly by this Convention. Generally, the exact analysis and classification of the obligations owed by participants in the intermediation process might be seen as less important than having a system which works efficiently and well. However, it is critical that the rights and obligations of all parties are clear and certain in the global markets, where huge amounts of securities are bought and traded. The Convention addresses this issue of certainty at an international level. However, until it is adopted, and even if it is, a robust domestic analysis is also necessary to provide that certainty.

If the trust analysis[206] is accepted, the certainty requirements of a trust need to be considered. First, is there sufficient intention to create a trust? This will be no problem where there is an express declaration of trust, but where there is not, such an intention will have to be implied from the circumstances. This is likely given that that under current English law this is the only feasible way to give the investor a proprietary interest in the securities. Secondly, the question of certainty of subject matter needs to be considered. Although the whole issue is now represented by a global security, the entitlement of individual investors is still described in money denominations. Thus, an investor can buy any number of bonds from one issue at, say, £100,000 par value from an issue of 1000. However, where the issue is represented by one global bond, the ICSD holds the single obligation represented by the bond on trust for all the account holders as co-owners, despite the convenience of the issue being split up in denominations. This overcomes the problem of identification of subject matter when the securities are held in a pooled account, although in fact it would be the case even if the ICSD (or other intermediary) held each account holder's securities in a separate account, since the interest of the account holder is of its nature a co-ownership interest, that is, a one thousandth share of the entire issue. In practice, such securities are always held in pooled accounts as this facilitates dealing.[207] The trust analysis, of course, is specific to English law,[208] but the problem of identification is universal. If Belgian or Luxembourg law applies, as is likely if the ICSD is Euroclear or Clearstream, account holders are in a similar position, but without using the concept of trust: they have a proprietary co-ownership right which is proportionate to the credit of securities in their account.[209]

Therefore, what is it that the investor in a Eurobond actually has, where the issue is represented by a global note? On the above analysis, he has a beneficial co-ownership interest in the obligation represented by the global note, which is held by the ICSD as

---

[204]   See the Hague Convention on the Law Applicable to Certain Rights in Respect of Securities held with an Intermediary 2006 ('Hague Securities Convention'); and also Gullifer and Payne, *Intermediated Securities*, n 197, especially chapters 1, 2 and 9; H Kronke, 'The Draft Unidroit Convention on Intermediated Securities: Transactional Certainty and Market Stability' in *International Monetary Fund: Current Developments in Monetary and Financial Law* Volume 5 (Washington D.C., International Monetary Fund, 2009), 619.

[205]   For discussion, see Gullifer and Payne, n 197.

[206]   Set out at page 337.

[207]   Benjamin, n 120, 19–06.

[208]   Which would probably apply, for example, if an English account holder with Euroclear held as an intermediary for English investors.

[209]   Tolley's Company Law Service C401.

trustee pooled with other co-ownership interests. The interest is beneficial, and therefore proprietary, vis a vis the ICSD (and therefore survives its insolvency) but is a proprietary interest in a contractual right against the issuer.[210] The investor may hold through another intermediary (who itself has an account with the ICSD) and in this case the investor has a beneficial interest, via a sub-trust, in the beneficial interest that its intermediary has.[211] The investor has no direct relationship with the issuer, although he may have a right (through the layers of intermediaries) to call for a definitive bond in certain circumstances.[212]

Furthermore, the bond trustee holds the covenant made to it on trust for the ICSD,[213] who holds that beneficial interest also on trust for the account holders. The investor's interest in the bond trustee's covenant is thus held under a sub-trust. If this is correct, then, technically, it is the ICSD who should give instructions to the trustee in relation to all matters where the trustee requires consent, and to whom the trustee's duties are owed. This, of course, makes no sense in that it is the ultimate investors who have the economic interest in the proper performance of the trustee's duties, so provision has to be made in the trust deed to deal with this issue. First, the deed is likely to provide that, if a bond is held through an ICSD, a trustee must consider the interests of the account holders rather than the depositary or the clearing system.[214] Secondly, the bond itself or the trust deed may provide that account holders shown in the records of an ICSD will be treated as holders for the purposes of giving instructions to the trustee.[215] Alternatively, the depositary or ICSD is treated as the holder, and itself sets up a system for ascertaining the instructions of the account holders, which it passes on to the trustee.[216] The powers and duties of the trustee and the way in which the balance between discretion and direction from the bondholders is struck are considered below.[217]

7.3.2.3.3 Bond Issue Without Trustee

Despite the advantages of having a trustee, discussed above, some debt securities are issued without a trustee. Various administrative tasks will still be undertaken by agents[218] (as they often are even if there is a trustee). At the very least there is likely to be a fiscal agent, who is responsible for making payments to bondholders.[219] Since any agents

---

[210] The bondholder is thus exposed to the credit risk of the issuer, but not the credit risk of the ICSD.

[211] See Hughes, n 74, 4.3–4.4 who makes the point that this is a long way from the bearer bond and the basic concept of a negotiable instrument. How this affects trading of securities is discussed below at 8.2.5.

[212] See above pages 335–36, R Goode, 'The Nature And Transfer Of Rights In Dematerialised And Immobilised Securities' (1996) 11 *Journal of International Banking and Financial Law* 17.

[213] Or the depositary if it is the holder and holds on trust for the ICSD.

[214] Financial Markets Law Committee Issue 62 *Trustee Exemption Clauses* (2004) 27, sample clause at 1.1.12. However, this does not deal with the situation where the account holder is itself an intermediary and holds for the ultimate investor.

[215] E Cavett and J Walker, 'New Issues for Trustees in the Credit Crunch' (2009) 24 *Journal of International Banking and Financial Law* 215. Such a provision is called a 'look through' provision: Fuller, n 73, 14.19.

[216] Fuller, n 73, 14.19. The way in which the instructions of the bondholders are ascertained is discussed below at 7.3.3. A further alternative, mainly used in the US, is for the registered holder to issue an omnibus proxy to the trustee or paying agent, who then issues sub-proxies to account holders, who can issue them to their account holders and so on: C Maunder, 'Bondholders' Schemes of Arrangement: Playing the Numbers Game' [2003] *Insolvency Intelligence* 73, 74; Fuller, n 73, 14.21.

[217] 7.3.3.

[218] For a full account of the tasks agents often undertake, see Fuller, n 73, 3.01–3.39.

[219] Where the bond issue is represented by a global note, the depositary or ICSD is very often appointed as a fiscal or paying agent: Fuller, n 73, 3.20.

appointed are agents of the issuer and not of the bondholders, it is clear that where the bonds are bearer bonds, there is a direct relationship between each bondholder and the issuer, which is enforceable by each bondholder. Where a global note is immobilised, however, the same structure applies as discussed above, so that the interest of each bondholder is a beneficial co-ownership interest under a trust. Enforcement therefore presents a problem, since the depositary or ICSD would be the only party entitled to enforce, on the instructions of all the bondholders. Without more, an individual bond-holder would not be able to enforce on its own. The way of overcoming this is for the issuer to execute a deed poll at the time of issue, assuming a direct obligation to pay the bondholders if a default occurs. As was pointed out earlier in the context of stock,[220] a deed poll enables the issuer to undertake unilateral obligations which can be enforced by persons not a party to the deed. The problem with this structure in this context, however, is that the obligation to the bondholder arises at the moment of default, rather than at the time of issue, which may well be at a point when the issuer is insolvent and may even be once insolvency proceedings have started.[221] An alternative analysis, put forward by Martin Hughes, is that the Contract (Rights of Third Parties) Act 1999 can be used, so that the bond could provide that the benefit of the obligation owed to the holder (the depositary or ICSD) is enforceable by the bondholders as a class.[222] So long as the class is sufficiently specified, this should be effective. Another possibility would be for the bondholder to call for the issue of a definitive security, which is a right usually exercisable in the event of a continuing default.[223]

It is also necessary to have a system to deal with any modifications the issuer wishes to make to the terms of the securities. Such modifications potentially affect all bondholders, and so each should have the opportunity of expressing a view as to whether they should be allowed. As will be seen later, where there is a trustee, it will be given powers to agree to minor modifications.[224] Where there is no trustee it is common for a fiscal agent to have similar but more limited powers.[225] However, with regard to more far-reaching modifica-tions, the bond will provide that the bondholders' views are expressed through the requirement for majority approval at a bondholders' meeting, which will now be dis-cussed. The following discussion applies both to issues where there is a trustee and where there is not: in the former case any resulting decision will constitute instructions to the trustee to act, rather than approval direct to the issuer.

7.3.3 Ascertaining the Views of Holders[226]

Where there are multiple lenders there is always the danger that a course of action which is in the interests of some will not be in the interests of others. Although there has to be a

---

[220] 7.3.2.2.2.

[221] Hughes, n 74, 4.11; Tolley's Company Law Service B5038.

[222] Hughes, n 74, 4.14.

[223] Fuller, n 73, 1.124. It is one of the functions of a fiscal agent to receive the definitive security from the issuer and to pass it on to the bondholder: Fuller, n 77, 3.19.

[224] See pages 343–44 below.

[225] Fuller, n 77, 14.04, 14.09.

[226] This discussion also applies to stock. For a detailed discussion of the meeting of holders, see Fuller, n 73, 14.10–14.38.

decision-making process, it includes some protection for those who would be disadvantaged by the proposed course of action. This is the case whether the proposed action relates to modification of the terms of the issue, or acceleration or enforcement, or restructuring within or outside insolvency. In relation to decisions outside insolvency proceedings, the bond or the trust deed will specify that decisions shall be taken at a bondholders' meeting. All bondholders are entitled to attend, and there will be a procedure for giving notice,[227] thus protecting the opportunity of all to take part in the decision-making process. Where bonds are held through a clearing system, notice is given through that system. Bondholders can attend the meeting or appoint a proxy. However, bearer bonds, or bonds held through a clearing system, are easily traded without the knowledge of the issuer and notice might be given to the wrong party. To ensure that those voting are entitled to vote, where the bonds are held through a clearing system, the holder has to 'block' its account. In the case of bearer bonds, the holder must either produce them at the meeting or, if appearing by proxy, deposit the bonds with the paying agent until the meeting is completed.[228] This system ensures that those voting are those entitled to vote, although in the case of bonds held indirectly, it only works in relation to the account holders at the ICSDs, who may themselves be intermediaries for investors or for other intermediaries. Unless the blocking system works all the way down the chain, there is no guarantee that the ultimate beneficial owners of the bonds are actually those giving voting instructions: this will depend on the position between each intermediary and its clients.[229]

The interests of bondholders are also protected by both quorum and majority requirements. A meeting is only valid if the quorum requirements are met: these vary according to the type of business, but most require a quorum of a majority, with changes to fundamental terms (known as entrenched terms) requiring a higher number, which can be as much as 75 per cent.[230] In each case, the numbers are calculated on the nominal amount of bonds held by those present, in person or by proxy.[231] A resolution will then be binding if 75 per cent of those present vote in favour.[232] It is very important, in order that decisions can be made and a course of action taken, that the majority of voting bondholders can bind the minority. However, this has to be tempered by protecting the minority against oppressive conduct by the majority. Thus, it is well-established in case law that the majority must act in good faith[233] and for the purpose of benefitting the class of bondholders as a whole.[234] This is similar to the obligation owed by shareholders to one

---

[227] G Fuller, *The Law and Practice of International Capital Markets* (London, LexisNexis Butterworths, 2007) 14.24. Where the securities are listed on the London Stock Exchange the Listing Rules para 17.3.10 and 17.3.12. prescribe certain matters which must be included in the notice.

[228] E Cavett and J Walker, 'New Issues for Trustees in the Credit Crunch' (2009) 24 *Journal of International Banking and Financial Law* 215; G Fuller, n 73, 14.28, 14.30

[229] For discussion of similar issues in relation to shares, see 10.2.2.1 below.

[230] See Fuller, n 77, 14.34; Wood, n 89, 16–043.

[231] There may in fact only be one person present, since where the bonds are held through a clearing system and the depositary or ICSD is treated as holder, its representative will be the only person voting, although in accordance with the account holders' wishes.

[232] Lower percentages to quorum and majority apply to meetings adjourned for lack of quorum. In practice, the combination of quorum and majority percentages mean that quite a low percentage of holders can bind a majority: see R Wedderburn-Day and P Phelps, 'The Enfranchisement of Bondholders in the Marconi Schemes of Arrangement' (2003) 18 *Journal of International Banking and Financial Law* 421.

[233] *Goodfellow v Nelson Line (Liverpool) Ltd* [1912] 2 Ch 324, 333.

[234] *British America Nickel Corporation Ltd v MJ O'Brien* [1927] AC 369, 371; *Greenhalgh v Arderne Cinemas Ltd* [1951] Ch 286, 291, which, although this case related to shareholders, was applied to syndicated loans in

another when voting to change the articles of association.[235] This obligation is not as onerous as it might sound, since it is recognised that not all bondholders will have identical interests, and each is entitled to vote according to his own interests.[236] The position is very similar to that relating to syndicated lenders[237] and the principle established in *Redwood Master Fund Ltd v TD Bank Europe*,[238] that where the documentation specifies different classes of lenders there is no need for each to vote in the interests of the lenders as a whole so long as they act in good faith, applies here.

Ascertaining the views of holders, and making decisions about how to proceed, are issues that are particularly troublesome in the context of restructuring bond issues. Although major decisions require the calling of a meeting and formal resolutions, in complicated transactions trustees like to consult bondholders on a more informal basis, and there is increasing use of bondholder committees to sound out views more informally.[239]

It may be desirable to have the sanction of the court for a restructuring, either (outside insolvency) in a scheme of arrangement under section 895 of the Companies Act 2006[240] or (where the company is insolvent) by a company voluntary arrangement.[241] In these situations, statute provides that a majority of the creditors (if over 75 per cent in value) can bind the minority. However, the requirement for 'a majority of the creditors', which appears to require a majority in number in addition to 75 per cent in value, may cause problems where the bond issue is represented by a global bond as it is not entirely clear who the 'creditors' are. As discussed earlier, the holder is either the depositary, or the ISCD, but is not those beneficially entitled to the bonds. The trustee, if there is one, is also a creditor, but in many cases it is the same entity as the depositary. If there is a trustee, there is even a doubt as to whether the depositary (or ICSD) is a creditor, since the 'no-action' clause means that it cannot enforce the obligation owed to it unless the trustee refuses to act.[242] A 'no-action' provision did not prevent bondholders taking part in safeguard proceedings in France, which are similar to a scheme of arrangement in the UK.[243] However, who counts as a creditor is ultimately a matter of interpretation of the relevant UK statutory provisions.

This means that, where there is a global bond, there is likely to be only one creditor or maybe two, in which case a majority in number seems impossible, even though the depositary and/or trustee can represent the wishes of the beneficial holders who have

---

Redwood Master Fund Ltd v TD Bank Europe Ltd [2002] EWHC 2703, [2006] 1 BCLC 149, [84]. See also *Law Debenture Trust Corporation plc v Concord Trust* [2007] EWHC 1380, [123].

[235]   *Allen v Gold Reefs of West Africa Ltd* [1900] 1 Ch 656. See generally 3.2.
[236]   *Goodfellow v. Nelson Line (Liverpool) Ltd* [1912] 2 Ch 324, 333.
[237]   7.4.4 below.
[238]   [2002] EWHC 2703, [2006] 1 BCLC 149.
[239]   E Cavett and J Walker, 'New Issues for Trustees in the Credit Crunch' (2009) 24 *Journal of International Banking and Financial Law* 215; R Karia and K Hargreaves, 'Negotiating with Bondholders across Multiple European Jurisdictions: What are the Key Issues?' (2009) 24 *Journal of International Banking and Financial Law* 259, 261.
[240]   See the discussion of schemes of arrangement in chapter 13 below.
[241]   R Goode, *Principles of Corporate Insolvency Law*, 3rd edn (London, Sweet & Maxwell, 2005) 10–134 (schemes of arrangement) 10–106–10–133 (company voluntary arrangements).
[242]   Fuller, n 77, 3.10. Where there is only one obligation owed to the trustee, as in the case of stock, the trustee is the only creditor who can petition for winding up: *Re Dunderland Ore* [1909] 1 Ch 446.
[243]   *Elliott International LP v Law Debenture Trustees Ltd* [2006] EWHC 3063.

instructed it, and can exercise its vote split as to value.[244] One possible way of avoiding this problem is for the issuer to issue definitive bonds to all the beneficial bondholders. However, whether this is possible will depend on the terms of the global note, and in any event it is slow and expensive as the definitive instruments have to be security printed.[245] Other possible ways round the problem are to amend the trust deed to allow beneficial owners to sue, or to treat the holder as the only creditor, and to procure contractual release from all the beneficial owners.[246] None of these are particularly satisfactory, and it might have been better had section 425 of the Companies Act 1985 been amended (when re-enacted as section 899 of the Companies Act 2006) to take out the requirement for a majority of creditors, leaving in just the value requirement, especially since any minority is protected by the power of the court to refuse the scheme.[247]

7.3.4 Trustees' Obligations[248]

The large number and dispersed nature of bondholders means that the trustee plays a pivotal role in the way the bond issue is administered. Although its obligations are owed to the bondholders, the trust structure is of most use if the trustee is given enough discretion to deal with most matters without having to consult the bondholders. However, the benefits of having a trustee are that it acts as a fiduciary and therefore is accountable to the bondholders for its actions. The tension between these two objectives and the way in which they are balanced, has led to a considerable amount of discussion about the role of the trustee in recent years. The problem is exacerbated by the fact that the trustee's powers and obligations (or lack of them) are laid down in the trust deed, which is a document executed by the issuer and negotiated with the trustee, but not necessarily with the original bondholders, and certainly not with any bondholders who acquire securities in the secondary market.

The three main functions of a trustee are to deal with modifications to the terms of the securities or the trust deed, to receive information from the issuer which indicates whether it is able to comply with its obligations, and to take action on possible events of default.[249] The first two can be dealt with swiftly, but the third requires more discussion.

It is likely that, if the issue of securities is for a reasonable duration, the issuer will want minor modifications to the terms of the securities to be made at some point. If all or a majority of the bondholders were required to agree to every modification, this would be very cumbersome. While bondholders are often prepared to play an active part in making

---

[244] C Maunder, 'Bondholders' Schemes of Arrangement: Playing the Numbers Game' [2003] *Insolvency Intelligence* 73, 75.

[245] This is true at least where the issue is listed on a recognised Stock Exchange. For details of the way this problem was overcome in the Marconi scheme of arrangement, see R Wedderburn-Day and P Phelps, 'The Enfranchisement Of Bondholders In The Marconi Schemes Of Arrangement' (2003) 18 *Journal of International Banking and Financial Law* 421.

[246] R Karia and K Hargreaves, 'Negotiating with Bondholders' (2009) 24 *Journal of International Banking and Financial Law* 259, 263.

[247] This amendment had been suggested in the DTI report: *Modern Company Law for a Competitive Economy: Final Report* (2001) but did not form part of the new Act. For a detailed argument in favour of this reform, see C Maunder, 'Bondholders' Schemes of Arrangement: Playing the Numbers Game' [2003] *Insolvency Intelligence* 73 and for further discussion see page 647 below.

[248] This discussion applies to both stock and bond issues, except where the context makes clear.

[249] Financial Markets Law Committee Issue 62 *Trustee Exemption Clauses* (2004) 17.

decisions if the issuer gets into financial difficulties, until then they usually wish to remain passive, and often anonymous. This is accentuated where the securities are held through intermediaries, since the issuer does not know who the ultimate bondholders are, and it is difficult and time consuming to discover this information. The trustee is therefore given power to agree modifications when, in its opinion, they are not materially prejudicial to the interests of bondholders or they are to correct a manifest error or they are of a formal, minor or technical nature.[250] Any other sort of modification will require the consent of the bondholders.[251]

One might have thought that a useful role which a bond trustee could play would be to monitor whether the issuer had complied with its obligations, and whether it looked as though it could comply with them in the future. In one sense, the trustee is in a position to do this, as it is usually the recipient of considerable financial information which the issuer is obliged to provide under the bond covenants. However, the monitoring role of the trustee is greatly limited by provisions in the trust deed. These usually provide that the trustee is under no duty to take any steps to find out whether an event of default has happened and is entitled to assume that no event of default or potential event of default has occurred unless it has actual notice of this occurrence.[252] In practice, this means that the trustee relies on certificates issued by the directors of the issuer that no default has occurred.[253] While this will be satisfactory for the holders so long as the directors are diligent and honest, it does mean that there will be no advance warning of a deliberate breach. Some such breaches are difficult to remedy if the issuer becomes insolvent, such as a breach of a negative pledge clause.[254]

This limited monitoring role can be justified by arguing that trustees are not accountants or financial analysts, that market practice does not demand such monitoring and that the fees charged reflect the limited level of service provided.[255] It must be remembered, however, that trustees (in this context) are professionals who provide a service: the real question is as to who should decide what service is provided. If those benefitting from a service are happy with low fees and minimal obligations, and are given a genuine choice as to the level of service provided and the level of fees, then there can be no complaint. It is true that the terms of the trust deed are negotiated between the issuer and the trustee, and the bondholders have no say in the matter, but the participants in the bond markets are sophisticated investors who will investigate the terms of the trust deed before buying the

---

[250] Fuller, n 77, 12.8.

[251] For the procedures for this, see above 7.3.3.

[252] Fuller, n 77, 12.28; P Rawlings, 'The Changing Role of the Trustee in International Bond Issue' [2007] *Journal of Business Law* 43, 54; P Ali, 'Security Trustees', n 164, 33–34. For alternative formulations of these provisions, see the Financial Markets Law Committee Issue 62 *Trustee Exemption Clauses* (2004) ch 4, sample clauses 1.1.2, 1.1.8 and 1.1.11.

[253] The trustee does have to exercise reasonable care and skill in examining the certificate: see Fuller, n 77, 12.19.

[254] P Rawlings, 'The Changing Role of the Trustee in International Bond Issue' [2007] *Journal of Business Law* 43, 55, and see above 5.2.1.3 for the effectiveness of certain types of negative pledge clauses in providing security for the lender. If the grantee of the security has no notice of the breach, it is likely to have priority over the holders. In this case there may be little left if the issuer becomes insolvent. This may well happen as a result of acceleration of the bond, this being the only remedy left to the holders, except to sue the directors for fraud (which may be a possibility if the certificate is deliberately untrue).

[255] Financial Markets Law Committee Issue 62 *Trustee Exemption Clauses* (2004) ch 4, comment to 1.1.8 and p18.

bonds.[256] Further, it is possible to make a distinction between contractual terms which limit the obligations undertaken by a party and contractual terms which exclude or limit liability for breach of obligations which a party does undertake.[257] The arguments in favour of controlling the latter are stronger, since the former allow flexibility in the actual subject matter of the contract. The same arguments apply in relation to trusts,[258] as can be seen by the operation of section 750 of the Companies Act 2006, which is discussed below.[259]

The trustee plays a particularly important role if there is a breach of the terms of the securities, and/or an event of default has occurred.[260] While provisions of trust deeds and securities will, of course, vary, it is usual to provide that most events of default do not entitle the trustee to accelerate payment of the securities unless it has certified that the event of default is materially prejudicial to the interests of the holders.[261] As pointed out above, the trustee is not obliged to monitor to check if a breach or event of default has occurred. However, if it does have actual notice of a breach, it usually has two (linked) areas of discretion, which it is obliged at least to consider whether to exercise,[262] although not unless it is satisfied that it will be indemnified by the holders.[263] First, it has the discretion whether to waive the breach, and, second, it has the discretion whether or not to certify that the event of default is materially prejudicial to the holders. If the trustee does not so certify, and the event of default is not a breach, this means that no further action can be taken; if it is a breach, then in theory at least the decision has to be taken whether or not to waive it, since otherwise the issuer is potentially liable for damages even though no acceleration will take place.

If the trustee does certify material prejudice, it will then usually have the power to accelerate payment. It has the obligation to do this if it is directed to do so by the holders[264] and indemnified to its satisfaction.[265] Once accelerated, it is for the trustee to enforce the issuer's obligations, although, again, it is only obliged to do so if directed by the holders and indemnified. The 'no-action' clause mentioned above,[266] will normally

---

[256] Law Commission, *Trustee Exemption Clauses* Report No 301 (2006) Appendix C, C36.

[257] For example, only the latter are controlled by the Unfair Contract Terms Act 1977, although both are controlled in relation to consumers under the Unfair Terms in Consumer Contract Regulations 1999. See the reasoning of Gloster J in *JP Morgan Chase Bank (formerly Chase Manhattan Bank) v Springwell Navigation Corp* [2008] EWHC 1186, [602], discussed at footnote 405 below.

[258] Which in any event (in this context) can be seen as contracts; Hughes, n 74, 13.3. For an application of such arguments to clauses limiting obligations in trust deeds, see Law Commission Report No 301, n 256, 5.46–5.91. It has, of course, to be remembered that the same clause may include both limitations of obligations and limitation or exclusion of liability.

[259] Page 350 et seq.

[260] Not all events of default are breaches: see discussion at page 168 above, and see 5.2.3 for a discussion of acceleration and termination rights generally.

[261] Certain events of default are exempt from this provision, such as failure to pay or the winding up of the issuer: see P Rawlings, 'The Changing Role of the Trustee in International Bond Issue' [2007] *Journal of Business Law* 43, 49. For a sample clause, see Fuller, n 77, 5.19.

[262] Trustees who are given discretionary powers must give consideration to the exercise of those powers, see Martin, n 12, 6–006; *Re Manisty's Settlement* [1974] Ch 17, 25.

[263] See Financial Markets Law Committee Issue 62 *Trustee Exemption Clauses* (2004) pages 20–23 and chapter 4 1.3.2; *Concord Trust v Law Debenture Trust Corporation plc* [2004] EWHC 1216, [33].

[264] The way in which decisions such as whether to accelerate can be taken by holders is discussed above at 7.3.3.

[265] Fuller, n 77, 216.

[266] See pages 332–33.

mean that only the trustee can enforce the issuer's obligations and the holders are not permitted to do so, unless the trustee fails to enforce within a reasonable time of being instructed.[267]

It can be seen that this scheme draws a balance between the convenience of allowing the trustee to deal with less serious matters on its own, while it has the power to consult the holders on critical matters such as acceleration and enforcement. The operation of this balance depends largely on the extent to which the trustee is prepared to act on its own, without the instructions of the holders. There are two particular concerns for trustees. The first is that, given the complex financial matters which have to be considered in exercising its discretion, it may have to incur considerable expenditure in obtaining expert advice. As pointed out above, trustees' fees are often set at a reasonably low level,[268] and so a trustee would look to be indemnified for any additional expenditure. While a trustee has a statutory right to be indemnified out of a trust fund,[269] in this case there is no trust fund as such,[270] only the issuer's obligation to pay. If the trustee eventually recovers the amount due from the issuer, it will normally have a right to deduct its expenses before paying the balance to the holders.[271] However, the discretions we are talking about arise in the context of a possible default, and it may not be at all clear when or if payment will be made by the issuer. A trustee is not required to make a personal loss out of acting in accordance with the trust[272] and trust deeds invariably make provision for the trustee to be indemnified to its satisfaction before exercising these discretions.[273]

What amounts to satisfactory indemnification can be open to question. In *Concord Trust v Law Debenture Corporation Ltd*,[274] which was part of the *Elektrim* litigation discussed below,[275] the trustee refused to accelerate the bond as it said that the indemnity offered was not satisfactory. There were two main reasons. The first, argued only at first instance, was that the conditions of the indemnity were not satisfactory, in that it was not joint and several (between the holders and the guarantor) and that the creditworthiness of one of the major bondholders was in doubt. The second related to the amount of the indemnity: the trustee contended that it could be liable to the issuer for very considerable damages if it was held not to be entitled to accelerate the bond.[276] It is clear from the decisions of all the courts in the *Concord* case[277] that a trustee is entitled to refuse to act on the grounds that the indemnity offered is unsatisfactory, provided that the decision to refuse is not unreasonable according to the *Wednesbury* principle (that is, that no

---

[267] For a sample clause, see Fuller, n 77, 216.

[268] For example, in the *Concord* case discussed below, the trustees' fees were an initial acceptance fee of £2,000 and an annual management fee of £2,500 ([2004] EWCA Civ 1001, [38]) in relation to a bond issue of €510M par value.

[269] Trustee Act 2000, s 31(1).

[270] This is true even for a security trustee, since the security is only available on enforcement of the issuer's obligations.

[271] This is known as 'top-slicing': see Fuller, n 77, 217 for a sample clause.

[272] *Re Grimthorpe* [1958] Ch 615, 623, cited by Sir Andrew Morritt V-C in *Concord Trust v Law Debenture Trust Corporation plc* [2004] EWHC 1216, [33].

[273] Financial Markets Law Committee Issue 62 *Trustee Exemption Clauses* (2004) 4 1.2.3 and 1.3.2.

[274] [2004] EWHC 1216, [2004] EWCA Civ 1001, [2005] UKHL 27.

[275] Page 347 et seq.

[276] This issue is discussed below.

[277] That is, the High Court, the Court of Appeal and the House of Lords.

reasonable trustee could have come to it).[278] Although the actual decision (especially in the Court of Appeal and the House of Lords) related to the amount of the indemnity, it seems reasonably clear that this principle applies to any aspect of the indemnity to which a trustee could reasonably object.[279]

As well as concern about being indemnified against expenditure, a trustee will also worry that its actions may expose it to considerable liability, and that the indemnity offered may not be enough to cover this. Unlike an indemnity against expenditure, here there is real uncertainty as to whether the liability will ever eventuate, and, if so, how much it would be.[280] It is clear from the *Concord Trust* litigation that, although the amount of possible liability will be looked at on a 'worst-case scenario', a trustee cannot insist on an indemnity against a risk unless it is 'more than fanciful'.[281] Concern about possible liability may also act as a disincentive to a trustee to exercise its discretionary power to accelerate rather than to ask the holders for instructions.[282]

It is worth considering in more detail what a trustee's rights and obligations are when deciding some of the matters mentioned above. First, the trustee is likely to have to decide whether an event of default is 'materially prejudicial to the interests of bondholders'.[283] In the first case in the *Elektrim* litigation ('the *Acciona* case')[284] the relevant event of default was the suspension of the bondholders' nominated director (of the issuer), which was a clear breach of the terms of the trust deed. The bondholders contended that it was materially prejudicial. The issuer suggested to the trustee that, in financial terms, it was not. The trustee, presumably in an attempt to protect itself, asked the court for directions as to the meaning of the phrase 'materially prejudicial to the interests of the bondholders'. The steps which Peter Smith J held to be necessary seem fairly self-evident: the trustee must ascertain whether there is a breach, and if there is, it must ascertain the consequences of that breach. It must then decide whether the interests of the bondholders (defined as the interests in being paid under the bond, and any ancillary interests which protect that right, such as security) have been materially prejudiced.[285] Sometimes this will involve extensive factual investigation and sometimes this will be self-evident (as it was held to be in this case).

It will be noted that the only parties to the *Acciona* case were the trustee and the bondholders. The issuer, therefore, was not bound by the decision, and was free to challenge it. This meant that even though the trustee then issued a certificate of material prejudice and was duly instructed by the bondholders to accelerate liability, the trustee refused to accelerate as it was not satisfied with the indemnity offered, as discussed above. The trustee was concerned that if it did so, the issuer would sue it for substantial damages

---

[278]   The burden of proof is on the party or parties challenging the decision, which in that case were the bondholders.

[279]   For example, the failure to provide security if the creditworthiness of the bondholders was very suspect, or a provision that the bondholders' liability was several rather than joint and several.

[280]   It is reasonably clear from the *Concord* litigation that an indemnity would have to cover possible costs if there was a chance of the issuer or a third party commencing proceedings: see [2005] UKHL 27, [34].

[281]   Ibid.

[282]   P Rawlings, 'The Changing Role of the Trustee in International Bond Issue' [2007] *Journal of Business Law* 43, 50.

[283]   It may also have, at times, to consider whether a proposed modification is materially prejudicial.

[284]   *Law Debenture Trust Corporation plc v Acciona SA* [2004] EWHC 270. The subsequent case was the *Concord Trust* case discussed above.

[285]   [2004] EWHC 270, [42] and [48]. The judge found that there was material prejudice.

on the basis that it was not entitled to accelerate. However, the House of Lords held that it was very unlikely that this would give the issuer a valid cause of action. A wrongful acceleration had no contractual effect, and therefore did not actually have the effect of accelerating the liability:[286] there was therefore no need to imply a term prohibiting the service of such a notice.[287] Nor was there an action in tort, since there was no duty of care owed, and no intention to found a conspiracy or other economic tort claim.[288]

It might be thought that this is an unfortunate state of the law. If a trustee, and therefore the bondholders, were liable for wrongful acceleration, this acts as a deterrent against opportunist interpretations of events of default clauses in order to trigger renegotiations, and preserves some sort of balance between issuer and bondholders.[289] In a difficult economic climate there is a greater incentive for bondholders to seek to renegotiate, and therefore to become more activist, which is likely to result in more trustees being instructed to serve acceleration notices. Even if, technically, it has no legal effect, a wrongful acceleration can have deleterious effects on an issuer, especially if it became public knowledge either through an obligation to disclose,[290] or in any other way. Such information might discourage other lenders or other companies from doing business with the issuer. Furthermore, the mere service of a notice might constitute default in other agreements the issuer may have, although this would depend on the wording of the particular agreements. There are two possible lines of argument left open by the House of Lords' decision. The first is that the service of the notice gives rise to a cause of action in defamation.[291] The second, which would be far more likely to apply where the lending was by way of syndicated or other loan, is that by serving the notice the lenders are evincing an intent not to make further advances to the borrower. If they are contractually obliged to do so, this in itself would be a breach, maybe even a repudiatory breach.[292]

On the other side of the coin, the issuer has some protection against bondholder activism through the 'no-action' clause. The point of such a clause is to prevent what is called the 'hold-out' problem: where one or a small number of bondholders wish to take action which is damaging to the interests of the bondholders as a whole, or which is unmeritorious and potentially damaging to the issuer who has to defend the action (and therefore is also damaging to the interests of the bondholders as a whole).[293] The clause also stops multiplicity of actions, as enforcement can only take place by the trustee.[294] An example of where it could be effective was given in *Re Colt Telecom Group plc*[295] where one

---

[286] This follows the position already established in *Bournemouth and Boscombe Athletic Football Club v Lloyds TSB Bank plc* [2003] EWCA Civ 1755 (see A McKnight, 'A Review of Developments in English Case Law During 2004: Part 1' [2005] *Journal of International Banking Law and Regulation* 105).

[287] [2005] UKHL 27, [37]. This has been followed in two more recent cases: *Jafari-Fini v Skillglass Ltd* [2007] EWCA Civ 261 and *BNP Paribas v Yukos Oil Company* [2005] EWHC 1321.

[288] [2005] UKHL 27, [38]–[43].

[289] S Wright, 'Making Lenders Liable for Damage Caused by "Wrongful Acceleration" of Loans' (2006) 27 *Company Lawyer* 123.

[290] See 11.3.1.

[291] E Peel, 'No Liability for Service of an Invalid Notice of "Event of Default"' (2006) 122 *Law Quarterly Review* 179, 183; Hughes, n 74, 11.20.

[292] A McKnight, 'A Review of Developments in English Case Law During 2004: Part 1' [2005] *Journal of International Banking Law and Regulation* 117, 117–118.

[293] *Feldbaum v McCrory Corporation* 18 Del J Corp L 630, 642; *Elektrim SA v Vivendi Holdings 1 Corp* [2008] EWCA Civ 1178, [1]–[4]. See pages 332–33 for discussion of the mad bondholder problem.

[294] *Elektrim SA v Vivendi Holdings 1 Corp* [2008] EWCA Civ 1178, [91], [101].

[295] *Re Colt Telecom Group plc* [2002] EWHC 2815.

hedge fund acquired seven per cent of the bonds at a discount and sought to put the company into administration, with a view to making a profit if the value of the bonds rose as a result of restructuring. None of the other bondholders supported the petition. The court held that the no-action clause prevented all enforcement, including 'non-contractual claims', that is, those not based on a breach of contract, and also enforcement where there had not been an event of default.[296] It was argued that if the no-action clauses were interpreted in this way, this could lead to situations where no one could enforce, not even the trustee.[297] Whether this would be the case, of course, would depend not only on the construction of the no-action clause but on the construction of the powers of the trustee as set out in the trust deed. In the situation in *Colt Telecom*, however, the trustee, as a creditor, would have been able to petition for administration, both under the Insolvency Act and so would have been able to enforce.

In subsequent cases it has also been held that a no-action clause covers 'any claim designed to vindicate the rights of a bondholder in his capacity as such' including claims in both contract and tort,[298] although not the bringing of opposition proceedings to safeguard proceedings[299] in the French Commercial Court.[300] The court also held in the *Colt Telecom* litigation that there was no rule of English public policy prohibiting the use of such clauses.[301] It is difficult to see how the argument that there was such a rule could stand any chance of success. It was based on an argument that any creditor should be free to wind up a company, and that this freedom could not be bargained away. However, there are other instances of such bargains, and no absolute right exists, statutory of otherwise, to be able to bring insolvency proceedings. Further, the advantages of the no-action clause are clear and well-established. The fact that the courts are prepared to interpret the scope of such clauses expansively means that a no-action clause gives wide and strong protection, and when combined with a bond trustee (who will hold any payments made by the issuer on trust for the bondholders) has been described as a 'robust fortress against holdout litigation'.[302]

---

[296] The bonds were governed by New York law, and so this was actually a decision on what the law of New York was, but the cogent reasoning supporting this decision, namely that the limitations argued for gave rise to distinctions which were illogical, would surely also apply to English law.

[297] This argument was based on M Kahan, 'Rethinking Corporate Bonds: The Trade-off between Individual and Collective Rights' (2002) 77 *New York University Law Review* 1040. Professor Kahan was called as an expert in the case. See also P Rawlings, 'Reinforcing Collectivity: The Liability of Trustees and the Power of Investors in Finance Transactions' (2009) 23 *Trust Law International* 14, 24.

[298] *Elektrim SA v Vivendi Holdings 1 Corp* [2008] EWCA Civ 1178, [92]–[93]. It should be remembered, however, that a no-action clause does not prevent the bondholders bringing actions which are not related to enforcing the obligations in the bonds, such as a misrepresentation action against the issuer in relation to statements made in the prospectus (either at common law or for a breach of the regulatory regime under FSMA s.90: see 11.2.7 below) or against other parties, such as a negligent intermediary, or an action for breach of trust against the trustee: see P Rawlings, 'Reinforcing Collectivity: The Liability of Trustees and the Power of Investors in Finance Transactions' (2009) 23 *Trust Law International* 14, 22.

[299] Safeguard proceedings are corporate rescue proceedings in French law, which are somewhat similar to administration proceedings in the UK.

[300] *Elliott International LP v Law Debenture Trustees Ltd* [2006] EWHC 3063.

[301] *Re Colt Telecom Group plc* [2002] EWHC 2815, [62]–[77].

[302] N Ishikawa, 'Towards the Holy Grail of Orderly Sovereign Debt Restructuring. Part 2: Optimum Architecture of Collective Action Clauses' (2007) 22 *Journal of International Banking and Financial Law* 404. See also P Rawlings, 'Reinforcing Collectivity: the Liability of Trustees and the Power of Investors in Finance Transactions' (2009) 23 *Trust Law International* 14, 32, who argues that this gives the issuer too much protection to the detriment of minority bondholders.

These cases demonstrate that there appears to be an increase in the appetite of bondholders and issuers to become involved in the acceleration and enforcement of bonds, either by seeking to take action themselves, or by mobilising themselves to give directions to the trustee, and for issuers to oppose this, either through the courts or by putting pressure on the trustee in other ways. It may well be that one reason is the large number of junk or high yield bonds in circulation:[303] the return is higher, which attracts more aggressive investors, but default is more likely,[304] so the stakes are higher and the perceived benefits of interference are greater. The trustee is left in the middle of this surge of activism and, not unexpectedly, tries to protect itself against liability and challenge as much as possible. It is to this that we now turn.

7.3.5   Excluding Trustees' Duties

As mentioned above trustees are under various duties to the beneficiaries of the trust in relation to the trust property. A trustee owes a duty to carry out its administration of the trust with care and skill, the standard being higher in relation to professional trustees, depending on the level of expertise they hold themselves out as having.[305] Bond trustees are invariably professional trustees, and will have of necessity held themselves out to have certain types of expertise in order to be used in the first place. Since the duty will have prima facie arisen, any protection from liability has to be achieved by means of an exclusion or limitation clause.[306] However, in relation to bond issues, section 750(1) of the Companies Act 2006[307] provides that:

> Any provision contained in (a) a trust deed for securing an issue of debentures, or (b) any contract with the holders of debentures secured by a trust deed, is void in so far as it would have the effect of exempting a trustee of the deed from, or indemnifying him against, liability for breach of trust where he fails to show the degree of care and diligence required of him as trustee, having regard to the provisions of the trust deed conferring on him any powers, authorities or discretions.

For the purposes of the Companies Act, 'debenture' is defined as including debenture stock, bonds and any other securities of a company, whether or not constituting a charge on the assets of the company.[308] This is a wide definition and will cover most bond and stock issues, but, because of the jurisdiction of the Act, only those issued by UK

---

[303]   P Rawlings, 'The Changing Role of the Trustee in International Bond Issue' [2007] *Journal of Business Law* 43, 65.

[304]   Both because of the nature of the issuer and also because the covenants are likely to be stricter: see pages 32–33 and page 79.

[305]   *Bartlett v Barclays Bank Trust Co Ltd (No 2)* [1980] 1 Ch 515, 534. There is also a limited duty of care and skill imposed by s.1 of the Trustee Act 2000, which is wider than the *Bartlett* duty in that the test of knowledge and expertise does not just depend on what the trustee has held itself out as having, but includes a more objective test of what it is reasonable to expect of a person acting in the course of that kind of business. This only applies to certain activities, which are set out in Schedule 1 of the Act, and which do not include many of the main activities of a bond trustee, as discussed in the previous paragraphs.

[306]   The statutory duty in Trustee Act 2000 s 1 does not apply where excluded by the trust deed: Sch 1 para 7.

[307]   Re-enacting Companies Act 1985, s 192, which itself re-enacted Companies Act 1948, s 88, the provision having been first introduced in the Companies Act of 1947.

[308]   Companies Act 2006, s 738. See also pages 546–47.

companies.[309] The effect of this section is that any clause which expressly excludes liability for breach of the equitable duty of care and skill[310] will be void, and as a result such clauses are not included in bond issue trust deeds. However, the last part of section 750(1), 'having regard to the provisions of the trust deed conferring on him any powers, authorities or discretions', indicates that the section is limited to actual exclusion clauses and does not cover clauses which contain powers to do things which would otherwise be in breach of trust, such as taking advice from specialists or which confer discretion on the trustee or which limit the duties of the trustee.[311] Such clauses were described by the Law Commission in their consultation paper on trustee exemption clauses as extended powers or authorisation clauses, and duty exclusion clauses,[312] but despite their difference in structure, the actual effect of them is to protect trustees from liability.[313] Bond issue trust deeds, therefore, include such clauses in order to give trustees a comprehensive package of protection and it is to these clauses that the following discussion is addressed.

There seems to be no doubt that, since the trust is created by the trust deed, the terms of the deed define the trustee's obligations. The deed can therefore impose obligations on the trustee or not, and can exclude liability for breach of obligations imposed. However, such terms only have effect within the limits of their true construction, so that the debate is partly at least about the relevant principles of construction. A second possible limit is based on public policy, so that, at least in certain situations, a trustee should not be able to restrict its obligations or liability beyond a certain point. The construction question will be considered first.

One well known approach to construction of terms is that applied to construing the terms of a contract. The starting point is that the parties are free to agree whatever rights and obligations they like, providing that there are no statutory or common law controls against unfairness.[314] Most of these controls are based on protection of parties with weaker bargaining power or who do not have enough information to make an informed decision. Apart from the requirement of consideration (which usually means that there have to be reciprocal promises) there is no pre-conceived idea of the content of contractual obligations, or that one party rather than the other should owe any particular duties to anyone.[315] However, terms which exclude or restrict liability for breaches of those

---

[309]   In practice, similar wording is included in many trust deeds for issues of international securities: Financial Markets Law Committee Issue 62 *Trustee Exemption Clauses* (2004) 4; Fuller, n 77, 12.15.

[310]   The duty referred to in *Bartlett v Barclays Bank Trust Co Ltd* [1980] 1 Ch 515, 534. The section does not prevent the exclusion of the statutory duty under the Trustee Act 2000; Fuller, n 77, 12.12. This is because it is the duty that is excluded and not the liability: see Law Commission '*Trustee Exemption Clauses*' (2002) Consultation Paper No 171, 82 (sample clause A3).

[311]   Fuller, n 77, 12.14; Tennekoon, n 149, 238. Examples of such clauses can be found in Fuller, n 77, 12.28; Financial Markets Law Committee Issue 62 *Trustee Exemption Clauses* (2004) ch 4; Law Commission '*Trustee Exemption Clauses*' (2002) Consultation Paper No 171 appendix A, A3 and A4.

[312]   Law Commission, *Trustee Exemption Clauses* (2002) Consultation Paper No 171, chapter 2.5–2.6.

[313]   It should be noted that the possibility of these sorts of clauses was acknowledged when the Unfair Contract Terms Act 1977, which seeks to control clauses excluding contractual and other common law liability, was drafted so that some duty defining clauses also trigger the controls, see s 3(2)(b) and s 13.

[314]   For example, the Unfair Contract Terms Act 1977 or the rule against penalties.

[315]   This is, of course, subject to the qualification that in certain types of contracts there are specified duties, so that, for example, in a sale of goods contract the seller owes certain duties to the buyer and in an employment contract the employer owes certain duties to the employee. However, if the configuration of rights and obligations does not bring the contract into a particular category (for example, in a contract of barter there is no seller and no buyer) there is still an enforceable contract.

obligations will be construed strictly against the person relying on them (*contra proferentum*). Further, the more deliberate and serious the breach, the more unlikely it is that it will be covered by an exclusion clause[316] if the result would be against 'business common sense', even if that would be the literal meaning of the word used.[317] This approach is largely to preserve internal consistency. If the parties have agreed that one party should be under a particular obligation, it makes no sense if he is not liable even for a deliberate and serious breach: it means that the obligation has no contractual content.

There has been considerable discussion as to whether these principles apply to the construction of exclusion clauses in trust deeds. It can be said that a trust deed, especially in a commercial context, is like a contract. It sets out the rights and obligations as between the trustee and the settlor (here the issuer) so that, for example, the House of Lords in *Concord Trust v Law Debenture Trust Corporation plc*[318] construed the trust deed as if it were a contract, applying the usual contractual principles relating to the implication of terms and referring to breach of a possible implied term as 'breach of contract'.[319] It is, of course, possible that the same document has two functions: one as a declaration of trust and the other as (evidence of) a contract between the issuer and the trustee. However, even on this analysis, it could be said that the contract can qualify and refine the terms of the trust.[320] An alternative view is that the exclusion of liability is not a matter of contract, but can only be by means of equitable provisions.[321]

It is certainly true that a trust is different from a contract, and that the differences between them should qualify the application of contractual principles of construction to some extent. One rather obvious difference is that the people for whose benefit many of the duties are undertaken, and who have the capacity to enforce them, are not parties to the trust deed at all, and in theory play no part in the bargaining process.[322] As pointed out earlier, though, in the case of a bond issue, the bondholders will usually be in a position to see the terms of the trust deed before they invest[323] and although they have no bargaining power as such, they have the opportunity not to buy, or, at least in relation to bonds traded on a market, to exit from the transaction if they do not like the terms. In any event, many of the terms used are very standard, and so are familiar to everyone involved in the transaction (although, of course, this could also be said to reduce the ability of the potential bondholder to 'shop around' for better terms).

Another difference is said to be that a trust is based on a grant of property rather than an agreement.[324] This has various ramifications. One is that the terms of the trust deed bind subsequent beneficiaries as well as the original beneficiaries. This, of course, is true in relation to a bond issue, but the same arguments apply as made above, and, in addition, similar considerations apply to any traded debt, even when only purely contractual rights

---

[316]   *Photo Production Ltd v Securicor Transport Ltd* [1980] AC 827, 850–51.
[317]   *Internet Broadcasting Corporation v MAR LLC* [2009] EWHC 844, [27], [32].
[318]   [2005] UKHL 27, discussed above page 346 et seq.
[319]   Ibid, [37] and see Hughes, n 74, 11.4–11.5.
[320]   Financial Markets Law Committee Issue 62 *Trustee Exemption Clauses* (2004) 1–2.
[321]   A Hudson, *Equity and Trusts*, 5th edn (Abingdon, Routledge-Cavendish, 2008) 360 relying on *Re Duke of Norfolk Settlement Trusts* [1982] Ch 61, 77.
[322]   M Bryan, 'Contractual Modification of the Duties of a Trustee' in S Worthington (ed), *Commercial Law and Commercial Practice* (Oxford, Hart Publishing, 2003) 513, 518.
[323]   The terms of the trust deed will usually be described in the offering circular, see page 325 above and Law Commission, *Trustee Exemption Clauses* Report No 301 (2006), Appendix C, C36.
[324]   Law Commission, *Trustee Exemption Clauses* (2002) Consultation Paper No 171, 2.60–2.61.

apply. The proprietary basis of the trust also means that the beneficiaries may have remedies other than damages, such as orders for restitution of trust property and for disgorgement of profits. In relation to trusts in general this is a very telling point, and, in fact, a clause excluding liability for breach is unlikely to be held to cover either remedy.[325] However, in the context of a bond issue it is not the misappropriation of property which is likely to be at issue, or covered by the exculpation provisions, but the duty to act with care and skill, or maybe the duty to avoid a conflict of interest, so this distinction from contract is not particularly relevant.

If a trust deed were seen as a contract, section 2(2) of the Unfair Contract Terms Act 1977, which subjects a contract term or notice excluding liability for negligently caused economic loss to a test of reasonableness, might apply. However, it seems reasonably clear that this does not apply to trustee exemption clauses in bond issues, for several reasons. First, it can be argued that a trust deed is not a contract, and so the exclusion clause is not a contract term. The Law Commission thought that this was the case[326] and it was conceded in the only case to consider the matter, *Baker v Clark*.[327] It is, of course, arguable that the reverse is true,[328] but this argument is context dependent, and there are other good reasons why section 2(2) does not apply to bond issues. One is that the duty of care and skill to which the clause relates is not a 'common law duty' as required by section 1(1) of the Unfair Contract Terms Act, but an equitable duty imposed because of the trustee's status as trustee. Where there is no explicit additional duty stated in the trust deed, this would appear to be correct.[329] Further, section 2 of the Unfair Contract Terms Act does not apply to 'any contract so far as it relates to the creation or transfer of securities or of any right or interest in securities'.[330] This reflects the freedom of contract policy in relation to the capital markets that has so far resulted in very little regulation of the actual terms of contracts[331] as well as the concerns that were expressed to the Law Commission in relation to commercial trusts.[332]

The basis in recent case law for the courts' approach to construction of trustees' exclusion clauses is the case of *Armitage v Nurse*.[333] In this case the Court of Appeal had to consider whether liability for the trustee's (maybe gross) negligence was covered by a wide exclusion clause. In holding that it was, Millett LJ considered both the construction of the clause, and whether there was any public policy against the validity of a wide exemption

---

[325] This will generally be the case on a straightforward construction of the clause; Bryan, 'Contractual Modification of the Duties of a Trustee', n 322, 518–19; *Armitage v Nurse* [1998] 1 Ch 241, 253. See also Bryan, n 322, 513, 519, where the author points out that this is especially so if unauthorised profits are seen as trust property: *Foskett v McKeown* [2001] 1 AC 102.

[326] Law Commission, *Trustee Exemption Clauses* (2002) Consultation Paper, No 171, 2.60–2.61.

[327] [2006] EWCA 464, [19].

[328] Hughes, n 74, 11.5–11.6. Hughes then, however, points out that if the trust deed were to be seen as a contract *simpliciter*, the beneficiaries' enforcement of the duty of care and skill would be either in tort, or in reliance on the Contracts (Rights of Third Parties) Act 1999. Section 7(2) of that Act provides that section 2(2) of the Unfair Contract Terms Act does not apply where a third party is relying on the 1999 Act to enforce a breach of a contractual duty of care and skill.

[329] Law Commission, *Trustee Exemption Clauses* (2002) Consultation Paper No 171, 2.63. Although the judge assumed that there was a common law duty in *Baker v Clark* [2006] EWCA Civ 464, [20] this appears to have been because of the way the case was pleaded and argued, rather than an actual decision on this point.

[330] Unfair Contract Terms Act 1977, Sch 1 para 1(e). Fuller, n 77, 12.16.

[331] For a discussion of the regulation of debt more generally, see chapter 11.

[332] For example by the Financial Markets Law Committee, in Issue 62 *Trustee Exemption Clauses* (2004); Hughes, n 74, 11.7.

[333] [1998] 1 Ch 241.

clause, such as one covering any liability except for actual fraud. In relation to construction, he appeared to be applying contractual principles. The clause excluded liability for all loss and damage unless it was caused by 'actual fraud'. Millett LJ rejected an argument that fraud was to be given an extended meaning, and limited it to dishonesty, thus construing the clause literally and strictly. This approach has been followed in some subsequent cases.[334] In relation to public policy, Millett LJ took the view that any large-scale control of trustee exclusion clauses was a matter for Parliament.[335] However, he did say that there was an irreducible core of trustee's obligations which could not be excluded for there still to be a trust. These were the duty of the trustee to perform the trust honestly and in good faith for the benefit of the beneficiaries.[336] This is not so much a matter of public policy, as one of definition, and herein lies an important difference between trust and contract.

As with many transactions that confer particular benefits on the parties, there are certain definitional criteria which need to be fulfilled for those benefits to be obtained. In relation to contract, the criteria are limited (agreement, consideration, some degree of certainty). However, to obtain proprietary benefits such as accrue under a trust, the criteria are stricter. The three certainties have already been discussed, but it is also the case that, for a trust to exist, the trustee must be under these minimum duties, otherwise the link between it, the property and the beneficiaries is not sufficiently strong. Without that link, the beneficiaries should not be entitled to priority in insolvency over the trustee's creditors, and the other benefits of there being a trust. It could, of course, be said that this reasoning is undermined as it is the trustee who has to suffer the detriment of the fiduciary duties but the beneficiaries who obtain the benefit. However, the whole transaction is interlinked: the higher the duties on the trustee, the more fees the beneficiaries (at least in a bond issue) have to pay.[337]

Even on the reasoning in *Armitage v Nurse*, it is not clear how far this idea of an irreducible core extends. It is clear that it does not cover the duty of care and skill, so that any form of negligence can be excluded. However, there must be some fiduciary duties which are fundamental to the trust structure which cannot be excluded or modified. It can be argued, for example, that, at least where the trustee holds security, it must have some management function in relation to that property, which includes monitoring its value.[338] There are, however, indications that in commercial transactions the court is prepared to interpret the 'core' very narrowly and to strive to give effect to the trust. In *Citibank NA v MBIA Assurance SA*,[339] the trust deed provided that the trustee was obliged to follow the instructions of the guarantor of a bond issue without having regard to the interests of the noteholders, and excluded the trustee from liability to the noteholders when so doing. It

---

[334] *Bogg v Raper* (Times, 22 April 1998); *Alexander v Perpetual Trustees WA Ltd* [2001] NSWCA 240.

[335] [1998] 1 Ch 241, 256. Since that case, the Law Commission has considered the issue, see Law Commission, *Trustee Exemption Clauses* (2002) Consultation Paper No 171 and Law Commission, *Trustee Exemption Clauses* Report No 301 (2006).

[336] [1998] 1 Ch 241, 253–54. For a similar approach in Australia, see *Australian Securities and Investments Commission v Citigroup Global Markets Australia Limited* [2007] FCA 963.

[337] One could make a similar argument in relation to the fixed charge: in order to have a fixed charge it is the chargor and not the chargee who suffers the detriment of lack of ability to deal with the assets. However, the chargor will benefit from a lower rate of interest.

[338] J Getzler, 'Equitable Compensation and the Regulation of Fiduciary Relationships' in P Birks and F Rose (eds), *Resulting Trusts and Equitable Compensation* (London, Mansfield Press, 2000) 256 and Ali, 'Security Trustees', n 164, 38.

[339] [2006] EWHC 3215, [2007] EWCA Civ 11.

was argued by the noteholders that this clause reduced the obligations of the trustee below the irreducible core. However, the Court of Appeal held, having interpreted the clause, that this was not the case. The trustee continued to have an obligation of good faith, and also had discretion to act in other areas. The approach of the Court of Appeal was to lean against an interpretation that the trustee was not a trustee at all, although it did not rule out the possibility of this if it were justified on the documentation.[340] On this approach, there seems to be little 'downside' to suffer in order to get the benefit of a proprietary interest.[341] That can be seen as a commercial approach to the development of the law, but it must be realised that the corollary of giving the benefit of a trust lightly is that other creditors may lose out in the event of insolvency of the trustee.

When the Law Commission considered the question of whether there should be statutory control of trustee exclusion clauses, it initially proposed that professional trustees should not be able to exclude liability for negligence.[342] There was considerable adverse reaction to this from those who used trusts in a commercial context, who argued that restricting the ability of trustees to have extensive protection from liability would mean that trust corporations would refuse to act as trustees, so that the use of the trust structure would die out in favour of fiscal agency, and the benefits of using the trust would therefore be lost. Furthermore, where there was a trust, the trustees would be reluctant to exercise their discretion without consulting the beneficiaries, which would make the operation of the trust much more inefficient.[343] These arguments persuaded the Law Commission that statutory control was not desirable, and in their final report they recommended merely a rule of practice that paid trustees should take reasonable steps to ensure that settlers are aware of exemption clauses included in trust deeds.[344] Such a rule is likely to have little impact in relation to bond issues, where the terms of the trust deed are already made known both to the settlor and the beneficiaries.[345] In any event, the Law Commission proposed that the rule would not apply where the trustee was already subject to statutory regulation of exemption clauses,[346] although the statutory regulation of debenture trust deeds, of course, only extends to a limited type of clause.[347]

The current position, then, in relation to bond issue trust deeds, is a balance. It is not possible for a trustee expressly to exclude liability for breach of the duty of care and skill, but a similar effect can be achieved by indirect means, which are not subject to regulation but which are, as a matter of practice, known both to the settlor (the issuer) and to the beneficiaries (the bondholders). Such clauses are likely to be interpreted strictly, but will be enforceable unless they reduce the irreducible core of the trustee's obligations, which is very unlikely in relation to the standard type of clause. However, unusual arrangements, such as in the *Citibank* case, are potentially more open to challenge, although where the alternative to holding a clause enforceable is deciding that there is no trust, the courts are likely to be very loathe to go down that route, and are likely to give force to the parties' intentions.

---

[340] Ibid, [82].

[341] A Trukhtanov, 'The Irreducible Core of Trust Obligations' (2007) 123 *Law Quarterly Review* 342.

[342] Law Commission '*Trustee Exemption Clauses*' (2002) Consultation Paper No 171.

[343] Financial Markets Law Committee Issue 62, Trustee Exemption Clauses (2004) 1–3.

[344] Law Commission,'*Trustee Exemption Clauses*' Report No 301 (2006).

[345] Ibid, 6.81.

[346] The predecessor to Companies Act 2006 s 750, Companies Act 1985 s 192, was given as an example.

[347] See pages 350–51 above.

7.4 Syndicated loans

7.4.1 Comparison between Agency in Syndicated Loans and Trustee in Bond Issues

Like an issue of debt securities, a syndicated loan is a way of enabling the borrower to borrow from more than one lender. The usual impetus is that the borrower wishes to borrow more money than one lender is prepared to lend. The arranging bank thus organises a syndicate of banks all of whom participate in making the loan, thus spreading the risk of non-payment amongst them. Unlike bonds, syndicated loans are not of their nature tradable, although they can be transferred and there is now a well-developed secondary market in such loans. However, the fact that the transferability of loans is an 'add-on' to their intrinsic nature[348] means that their structure is more geared to lenders who intend to remain locked into the deal, and take a longer term view, rather than bondholders who can offload their investment in the market whenever they wish.[349] This is reflected, for example, in the more extensive covenants which normally appear in a loan, whereas bonds often just include little more than a negative pledge.[350]

Another difference is that a bond issue is a one-off event: there is no obligation on the bondholders to lend more money, while a syndicated loan, even if it is a term loan, can be drawn down in tranches, so that the lenders have an obligation to lend in the future. This means, for example, that the method of transfer of loans is more complicated than the transfer of bonds, in that obligations are transferred as well as rights, and that borrowers may want to protect themselves against a loan being transferred to a person who would be unable to fulfil the lending obligations.[351] Having said this, even this difference between the two methods of borrowing has been eroded, in that many bonds are now issued under a programme, with common documentation for a series of issues and which enables the issuer to obtain more credit when it needs to, which in some ways is similar to a revolving loan facility.[352] However, there are still differences, since the dealers in a bond programme are not obliged to subscribe for any further issues: the programme agreement is on an uncommitted basis, whereas the participants in a syndicated loan are obliged to lend within the terms of the loan.[353]

Another difference which stems largely from their tradability, and from the identity of the investors, is that bonds are rated and that, apart from high-yield issues, are only issued by investment grade companies.[354] Loans can, and are, lent to any company, although the terms on which they will be made depend on the creditworthiness of the borrower. Obviously, the size of the company to whom a syndicated loan is made will be large, but that does not always ensure creditworthiness. This is another reason for the more extensive covenants in loans, and also may be a reason for the loan to be secured.

---

[348] Hughes, n 74, 4.2, Fuller, n 77, 1.4.
[349] This, of course, depends on a level of liquidity in the market.
[350] Fuller, n 73, 1.57; Wood, n 89, 10–018. See above page 79.
[351] Hughes, n 74, 4.8. See below 8.2.1.
[352] See page 324.
[353] Fuller, n 73.
[354] See pages 32–33 above.

Other points of distinction between bonds and syndicated loans will emerge in the ensuing discussion. However, there is an important similarity as well. Both structures involve multiple lenders, and one of the most important elements of the structure is the balance between the individual interests of each lender and the collective interests of the whole group.[355] One might have thought that, since syndicated lenders are less able to 'exit' and are therefore more likely to be part of the group for longer, there would be more protection of the group as a whole. This is true to some extent, but against this it must be remembered that lenders have obligations as well as rights. It is the disinclination of syndicated lenders to be liable for the failure to lend of the other participants that has led to the rights (and therefore) obligations of lenders being several rather than joint.[356] Further, since the lenders are banks, and may have other relationships with the borrower, such as a deposit account, a lender may want to be able to set off the debt due to it under the loan against what it owes the borrower on the deposit account, and this would not be possible if the debt was jointly owned with the other participants.[357] The several nature of the lenders' rights means that each lender can enforce the debt owed to it individually. As we have seen, owners of debt securities are not able to do this if there is a trustee (in relation to either stock or bonds). The position of holders of stock issued under a deed poll, and of bonds issued without a trustee, is more similar to that of syndicated lenders.[358] The right of each lender to enforce is, however, qualified in practice by a provision that enforcement can only occur after an event of default has been declared by the agent, on the directions of a majority of the lenders.[359] Where a syndicated loan is secured, however, security cannot conveniently be held separately by each lender, and it is necessary for there to be a security trustee to hold the security for the benefit of all the banks. In this situation there will be a parallel covenant to pay the security trustee who will be responsible for enforcing this and the security on the direction of a majority of the lenders,[360] thus giving rise to a more collective procedure.

Although each lender can enforce separately, collectivism is to some extent restored with the inclusion of a 'pro rata' clause. Since bonds are collectively enforced, if an issuer is insolvent, each bondholder will get a pro rata share of whatever is recovered. However, in the case of syndicated loans, separate enforcement could lead to a 'race to the bottom', so that a lender which enforced early can obtain full payment while all others recover proportionately less. The 'pro rata' clause therefore provides that if a bank recovers more than it would have done on collective enforcement, it must pay the excess to the agent who distributes it pro rata.[361] However, this clause can also operate to give the syndicated lenders a collective advantage over other creditors. As mentioned earlier, the several nature of the lenders' rights means that deposits can be set off against the borrower's obligations

---

[355] The balance in any individual transaction will, of course, depend on the terms of that particular transaction: Hudson, n 48, 34–12. The discussion following is based on some of the more usual provisions in loan agreements, but the situation will vary according to the context of the loan and the negotiating powers of the borrowers.

[356] Fuller, n 77, 2.17; Hughes, n 74, 9.2. There is also no question of the syndicate being a partnership, for similar reasons: see Benjamin, n 120, 8.25; Hudson, n 48, 34–11–34–13.

[357] Fuller, n 77, 2.17.

[358] For details, see above 7.3.2.2.1 and 7.3.2.3.3.

[359] A Mugasha, *The Law of Multi-bank Financing*, (New York, Oxford University Press, 2007) 5.11.

[360] See below 7.4.6.

[361] For examples of such a clause, see Fuller, n 77, 2.20 and Wood, n 89, 7–029. See earlier pages 332–33 for discussion of the similarity between this and the compulsory pari passu rule on actual insolvency.

under the loan. If one lender has such a right of set-off, the pro rata clause means that it enures to the benefit of all the lenders, and, providing that the lenders collectively have counterclaims against the borrower equal to the amount of the loan, the entire loan can be paid through set-off.[362] This may give the same effect as if the loan had been secured, although without the actual grant of security, which could infringe negative pledge clauses in other agreements with the borrower.[363] It is not entirely clear (and would in any event depend on the actual wording) whether the pro rata clause applies to a buy-back of the debt by the borrower, which has the effect of extinguishing the debt.[364] While still advantageous to the borrower, if the lender has to share the proceeds of a buy-back with the other lenders, it is no more advantageous to the lender than selling on the loan. On the other hand, if it does not, it is not consistent with the collective spirit of a syndicated loan.

A further feature of the collectivism is that, although the rights and obligations of the lenders are several, there is only one agreement to which all are parties, so that the terms and conditions are identical.[365] In order to simplify the drafting process for each agreement, and to save on lawyers' time and costs, the Loan Market Association has put together standardised loan agreements, which are periodically revised to reflect market practice.[366] Some provisions in these agreements are reasonably standard, others are still very dependent on the position of the parties, so that the LMA form is just the starting point for negotiations.[367] A market standard agreement is also a significant advantage where there is a thriving secondary loan market, since traders are not keen to examine the terms of the loans traded, nor are they in a position to negotiate such terms.[368] This can also lead to disadvantages, for example, what was drafted as a standard form for loans to investment grade companies has become standard for all types of borrowers[369] as well, which could be detrimental to lenders who are not prepared to negotiate every point (or who intend to sell the loan on).[370]

7.4.2   Finding Lenders

As with bonds, it is necessary for there to be an institution which puts together the group of lenders. In relation to a syndicated loan, this is done by an arranger, which is a bank (or

---

[362]   This is by the process of double dipping. If lender A owes the borrower more than the amount of A's share of the loan, A can set off its entire share, the excess is then shared between the other lenders, and A is subrogated to the rights of the other lenders for the amount distributed. A can then set off the balance of the debt it owes the borrower against these subrogated loans. For a full explanation, see Wood, n 89, 7–030 or P. Cresswell, general editor; W Blair, G Hill, P Wood (editors) Encyclopedia of Banking Law (London, Butterworths) 3503.

[363]   Wood, n 89, 7–030. Whether the double-dipping would be effective in insolvency would depend on the timing of the 'dips': it is unlikely that any 'dipping' would be permitted after the onset of insolvency.

[364]   S Samuel, 'Debt Buybacks: Simply Not Cricket?' (2009) 24 *Journal of International Banking and Financial Law* 24. See also page 159 above.

[365]   Loan Market Association, 'Guide to Syndicated Loans' 1.

[366]   Most of the changes are negotiated between the Loan Market Association and the Association of Corporate Treasurers.

[367]   M Campbell, 'The LMA Recommended Form of Primary Documents' (2000) 15 *Journal of International Banking and Financial Law* 53; K Clowry, 'LMA Credit Documentation: Recent Key Negotiation Issues' (2008) 23 *Journal of International Banking and Financial Law* 6. Such terms include the events of default, the financial covenants and terms as to transferability.

[368]   Hughes, n 74, 9.8.

[369]   For examples of such terms, see the Association of Corporate Treasurers, 'Guide to the Loan Market Association Documentation for Investment Grade Borrowers' (2007) 6.

[370]   Ibid.

more than one bank) which will also itself be a participant lender. The arranger is granted a 'mandate' to solicit other banks to join the syndicate: this is often expressed not to be legally binding on the arranger, who is therefore not committed to lend, but gives a 'best efforts' undertaking to put together the syndicate which would lend. It is also possible for the arranger to underwrite the loan, thereby promising to lend if no other banks can be found. In this case the underwriting obligation is likely to be subject to changes in the market, which can entitle the arranger to change the terms of the loan or even to pull out altogether.[371] The arranger advises the borrower on putting together the information memorandum, which gives information about the borrower in a similar way to a preliminary offering circular in a bond issue.[372] On the basis of this document, the arranger finds other banks to participate and the loan documentation is negotiated.[373]

7.4.3   The Role of the Arranger

One issue that arises in relation to this process is the legal position of the arranger, and, in particular, to what extent the arranger acts as agent for the borrower, or the participant banks. This issue includes the question whether the arranger is liable for false statements in the information memorandum. If the borrower is insolvent, the lenders will seek to sue a 'deep-pocketed' defendant such as the arranging bank for such false statements. If the arranger owes a fiduciary duty to the lenders, this would include a duty to make full disclosure. However, there are also alternative causes of action relating to false statements; these are considered below.[374] The question of whether an arranging bank is a fiduciary, however, goes further than just this type of liability. If the arranger were a fiduciary, it would be under a duty of the utmost good faith and honesty and to act in the best interests of the person to whom the duty is owed: this would include a duty to avoid conflict of interest (which could be difficult),[375] a duty of due diligence and, maybe, a duty to account to the participants for fees received from the borrower.[376]

The arranging bank's factual position changes in the course of the transaction. In the first place, it is instructed by the borrower, with regard to drawing up the information memorandum and maybe advising the borrower on the type of transaction that is suitable for its requirements.[377] Its next task is to solicit other potential participants, but when it has done that, it negotiates the loan documentation with the borrower and appears to be acting for the participant banks as much or more than for the borrower.

---

[371]   Fuller, n 77, 13.2; Wood, n 89, 1–005–1–007; 'Guide to Syndicated Loans', n 365, 4.1.

[372]   Note, however, that there are no regulations governing this document, unlike a bond prospectus, see 11.2.8.

[373]   Wood, n 89, 1–008; 'Guide to Syndicated Loans', n 365, 2–4.

[374]   7.4.4. A comparison can also be made with the liability of a manager or underwriter for misstatements in a bond prospectus, see 11.2.7 below.

[375]   Wood, n 89, 1–009.

[376]   G Skene, 'Syndicated Loans: Arranger and Participant Bank Fiduciary Theory' (2005) 20 *Journal of International Banking Law and Regulation* 269. It can be argued, however, that in this context a fiduciary duty is not more than an aspect of a duty of care, which is often owed to the participant banks in relation to certain functions: see *Henderson v Merrett Syndicates Ltd (No.1)* [1995] 2 AC 145, 205, and D Halliday and R Davies, 'Risks and Responsibilities of the Agent Bank and the Arranging Bank in Syndicated Credit Facilities' (1997) 12 *Journal of International Banking Law* 182, 183. However, while it is possible to owe duties of care in relation to specific tasks to two people at once, it is surely more difficult to owe fiduciary duties to two people, especially if their interests are, to some extent, opposed.

[377]   'Guide to Syndicated Loans', n 365, 2.

The question of whether an arranger is a fiduciary has, then, two aspects. First, does it owe fiduciary duties to anyone and second, if so, to whom and when. The second question may throw some light on the answer to the first. Since it is impossible to owe fiduciary duties to each of two parties negotiating with each other, and it is very difficult to pinpoint a time when the duties of the arranger shift from the borrower to the lenders, the best solution is that the arranger does not owe fiduciary duties to anyone.[378] There is, however, Court of Appeal authority for the proposition that the arranger owes a fiduciary duty to the participant banks. In *UBAF Ltd v European American Banking Corporation*[379] Lords Justice Ackner and Oliver said

> The transaction into which the plaintiffs were invited to enter, and did enter, was that of contributing to a syndicate loan where, as it seems to us, quite clearly the defendants were acting in a fiduciary capacity for all the other participants. It was the defendants who received the plaintiffs' money and it was the defendants who arranged for and held, on behalf of all the participants, the collateral security for the loan. If, therefore, it was within the defendants' knowledge at any time whilst they were carrying out their fiduciary duties that the security was, as the plaintiffs allege, inadequate, it must, we think, clearly have been their duty to inform the participants of that fact and their continued failure to do so would constitute a continuing breach of their fiduciary duty.

This statement is often said to be obiter,[380] since the purpose of the application was to set aside leave to serve out of the jurisdiction. The two grounds for this were that the claims in deceit and under section 2(1) of the Misrepresentation Act 1967 were precluded by section 6 of the Statute of Frauds Amendment Act 1928 and that the claim in negligence was statute barred. No independent claim based on breach of fiduciary duty was in fact pleaded: the relevance of the existence of a fiduciary duty was that it would give rise to a duty of disclosure which might enable the claimant to rely on section 32(1)(b) of the Limitation Act 1980 (based on deliberate concealment) which would have the effect of making the limitation period run from the time when the facts were first known by the claimant. The statement quoted above does, therefore, appear to be relevant to the decision in the case (that leave should not be set aside) but despite that, it is not necessarily of general import. The claimant's case was based on false statements about the value of the collateral. The defendant was not only the arranging bank, but was also security trustee for the transaction and the agent bank. It would appear that the statement that the defendant owed fiduciary duties could be because of its role as security trustee rather than its role as arranger. Furthermore, the defendant had previously acquired knowledge which put it in a different position from most arrangers.[381]

The case has never been expressly followed in the UK, and, it is submitted, should be treated with great care as an authority, since every case will depend on its own facts. First

---

[378] Wood, n 89, 1–009.

[379] *UBAF Ltd v European American Banking Corporation* [1984] QB 713.

[380] G Bhattacharyya, 'The Duties and Liabilities of Lead Managers in Syndicated Loans' (1995) 10 *Journal of International Banking and Financial Law* 172; D Halliday and R Davies, 'Risks and Responsibilities of the Agent Bank and the Arranging Bank in Syndicated Credit Facilities' (1997) 12 *Journal of International Banking Law* 182, 183; G Skene, 'Syndicated Loans: Arranger and Participant Bank Fiduciary Theory' (2005) 20 *Journal of International Banking Law and Regulation* 269, 273.

[381] G Bhattacharyya, 'The Duties and Liabilities of Lead Managers in Syndicated Loans' (1995) 10 *Journal of International Banking and Financial Law* 172; G Skene, 'Syndicated Loans: Arranger and Participant Bank Fiduciary Theory' (2005) 20 *Journal of International Banking Law and Regulation* 269, 273.

and foremost, the existence and extent of a fiduciary relationship between parties will depend on the contractual position between them.[382] The arranger will therefore seek to exclude any fiduciary duties, whether owed to the borrower or to the lending banks (and will probably also seek to exclude liability in negligence and for misrepresentation[383]): to the extent that it sought to exclude equitable duties this would not seem to fall within the Unfair Contract Terms Act[384] and would seem to be effective to prevent a fiduciary relationship arising.[385] This is desirable given the difficulties of analysis discussed above, and also given that the participants (both borrower and lenders) are sophisticated and experienced financial institutions which are in a good position to protect themselves.

7.4.4   Liability of the Agent Bank in Relation to False Statements in the Information Memorandum

The information memorandum used in syndicated loans, which is usually drawn up by or on the advice of the arranging bank, provides important information to potential lenders. The loan documentation will include a warranty by the borrower of the correctness of the information in the memorandum, so that if information is found to be inaccurate, this would be an event of default.[386] There would also be a claim against the borrower for misrepresentation and deceit.[387] However, an action against the borrower is unlikely, in the absence of special circumstances, to add anything to the claim for the amount due on the loan[388] and, in any event, if the borrower is unable to pay back the loan and is insolvent, there is no point in suing for damages. The lenders would then look to sue other persons with deeper pockets; this might, of course, include guarantors or insurers,[389] but is likely also to include the bank who acted as arranger.[390] It should be pointed out that there is no equivalent action to that under section 90 of the Financial Services and Markets Act. This action arises where there is a misstatement in disclosure required by regulatory rules, and therefore only arises where those rules apply, namely in relation to offers of shares and debt securities.[391]

The question of whether the arranger owes a fiduciary duty to the lenders has just been discussed. There are also potential claims in tort and under the Misrepresentation Act 1967. One possible tortious cause of action is deceit, but this will depend on dishonesty on the part of the arranger. Another possibility is that the arranger owes a duty of care to the

---

[382]   *Henderson v Merrett Syndicates Ltd (No 1)* [1995] 2 AC 145, 206 (Lord Browne-Wilkinson).

[383]   See 7.4.4. below.

[384]   See page 353 above.

[385]   G Skene, 'Syndicated Loans: Arranger and Participant Bank Fiduciary Theory' (2005) 20 *Journal of International Banking Law and Regulation* 269, 279, takes the view that this would be the position under Australian law. It also appears to be the position under US law: see *Banque Arabe et Internationale D'Investissement v Maryland National Bank* 810 F Supp 1282, 1296 (SDNY, 1993), aff'd 57 F 3d 146 (2d Cir. 1995); *Banco Español de Crédito v Security Pacific National Bank,* 763 F Supp 36, 45 (SDNY, 1991), aff'd 973 F.2d 51 (2d Cir. 1992), cited by Skene, n 376, 277.

[386]   For example clauses, see Clause 24 and Clause 19 of the LMA Investment Grade Loan Agreement (2008). See also 5.2.3 above.

[387]   As there is against the issuer of debt securities, see 11.2.7 below.

[388]   Wood, n 89, 1–019.

[389]   See 5.3 above.

[390]   G Bhattacharyya, 'The Duties And Liabilities Of Lead Managers In Syndicated Loans' (1995) 10 *Journal of International Banking and Financial Law* 172.

[391]   See 9.5.2 and 11.2.7 below.

lenders under the doctrine in *Hedley Byrne & Co Ltd v Heller & Partners Ltd.*[392] There are two cases in which an arranger was held to owe a duty of care to lenders participating in a syndicated loan, although in neither was the issue merely one of negligent misstatement, and both, arguably depend on their own facts.

In *Natwest Australia Bank Ltd v Tricontinental Corp Ltd*[393] the arranger, who was also one of the lending banks, drew up the information memorandum but failed to disclose that the borrower had a contingent liability to it, the arranger. The claimant, another of the lending banks, had actually made enquiries of this very matter from the arranger and had been told that the contingent liabilities were only nominal. In these circumstances, the Supreme Court of Victoria held that the arranger owed a duty to disclose the contingent liabilities to the lending banks, of which it was in breach, and that the lending bank was not contributorily negligent in failing to pursue the matter or to make its own enquiries. The reasoning of the court depended heavily on the facts: there was said to be an assumption of responsibility based on the facts that the arranger was acting in the course of business and had been paid a substantial fee and that a prudent bank would realise that the existence of the contingent liability would be an important factor in the decision of the lending bank whether to participate in the syndicate.[394] The duty of care was not affected by the inclusion of a disclaimer in the information memorandum which read: 'The information herein has been obtained from the borrower and other sources considered reliable. No Representation or Warranty expressed or implied is made with respect to this information'. This was interpreted as only relating to information provided, rather than information which was omitted, and also did not relate to the express question asked by the lending bank.[395] However, as with many such negligence cases, this finding of an assumption of responsibility is fact-specific. For example, the arranger actually knew about the contingent liabilities, so the duty was one of disclosure rather than a duty of care. Also, the lending bank made a specific enquiry, which meant that the arranger knew of the importance to it of the existence of contingent liabilities.[396] Moreover, the disclaimer was narrow and a wider disclaimer in the mandate agreement might have been more effective, as discussed below.

In the case of *Sumitomo v Banque Bruxelles Lambert SA*[397] the arranger had failed to make disclosure to an insurance company which rendered mortgage indemnity guarantees, taken out to protect the security for the loan, invalid. Here, the limited contractual duties owed by the arranger to the lending banks did not prevent a duty of care arising in relation to the arrangement of the insurance policy: there was sufficient assumption of responsibility in relation to that particular task.[398] The exclusion clause in the loan agreement was interpreted only to apply to the arranger's liabilities qua agent bank and

---

[392]   [1964] AC 465.
[393]   1993 VIC LEXIS 743.
[394]   Ibid, 164.
[395]   Ibid, 167.
[396]   G Bhattacharyya, 'The Duties And Liabilities Of Lead Managers In Syndicated Loans' (1995) 10 *Journal of International Banking and Financial Law* 172.
[397]   [1997] 1 Lloyd's Rep 487. See S Sequiera, 'Syndicated Loans – Let The Arranger Beware!' (1997) 12 *Journal of International Banking and Financial Law* 117.
[398]   [1997] 1 Lloyd's Rep 487, 514.

not as arranger[399] (and in fact, was not wide enough even to exclude liability for negligent execution of the bank's tasks qua agent: the clause, as all exclusion clauses, was interpreted strictly).

The position, therefore, appears to be that, although each case will depend on its own facts, the court will be prepared to find a duty of care in relation to specific tasks if they are foreseeably important to the lenders. Whether a more widely drawn duty of care in relation to the information memorandum exists is a matter for considerable doubt. In *IFE Fund SA v Goldman Sachs International*,[400] where it was made clear in the information memorandum that the arranging bank was accepting no responsibility for the accuracy of the information, the Court of Appeal held that there was no duty of care owed,[401] and that the court would be very slow to 'superimpose' a duty of care where obligations between the various parties had been carefully agreed.[402]

In any event, such a duty can be satisfactorily excluded both by a notice given to the participants in relation to the information memorandum[403] and/or by a term in the loan agreement excluding liability of the arranger for representations made.[404] Such a disclaimer would be subject to the requirement of reasonableness in section 2(2) of the Unfair Contract Terms Act 1977,[405] but it is submitted that, given the relatively equal bargaining power of the parties and the fact that the lending banks are sophisticated commercial institutions, such an exclusion is likely to be held to be reasonable.[406] The counter-argument to this is that the arranger is in a better position to assess the credit-worthiness of the borrower,[407] and so it should bear some responsibility (apart from its own liability as lender) if disclosure is inaccurate. One could argue that this concern is covered, however. First, it is covered by the fact that the arranger would still be liable for fraud, (including recklessness) since this liability cannot be excluded. In addition, it is covered by the fact that the banks, unlike bondholders, do negotiate the agreement which includes the exclusion clauses and can put pressure on the arranger to take them out.

There is also potential liability under section 2(1) of the Misrepresentation Act 1967, which applies where a person has entered a contract after a misrepresentation has been made to him by another party thereto. If the arranger is also a party to the loan agreement

---

[399] Ibid, 493.

[400] [2007] EWCA Civ 811.

[401] Ibid, [28].

[402] Waller LJ in the Court of Appeal at [28] agreed with the reasoning of the judge to this effect, set out at [17].

[403] Wood, n 89, 1–021.

[404] For examples, Encyclopedia of Banking Law 2125 cl 19(5), n 362.

[405] Note, though, that Gloster J in *JP Morgan Chase Bank (formerly Chase Manhattan Bank) v Springwell Navigation Corp* [2008] EWHC 1186, [602] said that contractual provisions which merely confirm the basis upon which the parties are transacting business are not subject to section 2(2) of the Unfair Contract Terms Act 1977, since 'Otherwise, every contract which contains contractual terms defining the extent of each party's obligations would have to satisfy the requirement of reasonableness'. While this makes a great deal of sense, it might still be possible to argue that such duty-defining clauses are 'excluding . . . the relevant obligation or duty' under section 13 of that Act, and thus are brought within section 2. This argument does not appear to be available in relation to section 3 of the Misrepresentation Act 1967, to which section 13 does not apply.

[406] G Bhattacharyya, 'The Duties And Liabilities Of Lead Managers In Syndicated Loans' (1995) 10 *Journal of International Banking and Financial Law* 172. In *Raiffeisen Zentralbank Osterreich AG v Royal Bank of Scotland plc* [2010] EWHC 1392 the judge held that if the relevant clause did exclude liability for misrepresentation it satisfied the requirement of reasonableness in section 11 of the Unfair Contract Terms Act (at [319]–[327]).

[407] Hughes, n 74, 9.5.

(usually this would be the case as the arranger is likely to be another lender, and also the agent bank) then the Act applies. Liability by this route is easier for the lending bank, in the sense that no duty of care needs to be established, and the burden of proof of breach of duty is reversed. However, clauses in the information memorandum can also affect whether such liability arises. If it is made clear that the arranging bank is making no representations in relation to the information provided in the memorandum, then this is binding on the parties as a matter of contractual estoppel[408] and there can be no liability for misrepresentation.[409] Such a clause is not subject to the requirement of reasonableness imposed by section 3 of the Misrepresentation Act 1967 as it does not exclude or restrict liability for misrepresentation.[410] If the clause provides that there is no reliance on any representations made, then this too can take effect as a contractual estoppel, but section 3 will apply.[411] Of course, if the clause expressly excludes or restricts liability, section 3 will also apply. In any event, where the lenders are experienced financial institutions, or where the wording used is common in the context of syndicated loan agreements, the clause is likely to be held to be reasonable.[412]

7.4.5   The Position of the Agent Bank

The actual structure of the loan transaction reflects the need to have efficient day-to-day administration, and to have effective decision-making at critical moments. Again the balance is between collectivity and enabling individual banks to protect their own interests. One of the lending banks is usually appointed as the agent bank: this is largely an administrative position and does not attract such high fees as the position of arranger.[413] The position of the agent bank can be compared with that of a trustee in a bond issue, in that it is a person who carries out functions on behalf of the lenders. In fact there is a considerable difference, in that the agent is seen as mainly a functionary which deals with specific administrative tasks.[414] This is supported by the documentation, which provides for certain specific powers, but which has heavy exclusionary provisions. A loan agreement will usually state expressly that the agent bank is not a fiduciary,[415] unlike a bond trustee, and the agreement may provide for the agent to do things which would otherwise be a breach of fiduciary duty, such as receiving sums from the borrower on its own account.[416] If an agent bank is also a security trustee then it will, of course, owe fiduciary duties, but

---

[408]   *Peekay Intermark v Australia and New Zealand Banking Group* [2006] EWCA Civ 386; *JP Morgan Chase Bank (formerly Chase Manhattan Bank) v Springwell Navigation Corp* [2008] EWHC 1186, [558]–[568] and *Raiffeisen Zentralbank Osterreich AG v Royal Bank of Scotland plc* [2010] EWHC 1392, [250]–[255].

[409]   *Raiffeisen Zentralbank Osterreich AG v Royal Bank of Scotland plc* [2010] EWHC 1392, [267].

[410]   Ibid, [316]. However, even this depends on the particular circumstances of the case: where a clear statement of fact is made which is (objectively) intended to be a representation and to be relied upon, but the terms of the contract state that no representation has been made, section 3 may apply, ibid, [307]–[308].

[411]   Ibid, [286]. See also *E A Grimstead & Son Ltd v McGarrigan* [1999] EWCA Civ 3029 and *Government of Zanzibar v British Aerospace (Lancaster House) Ltd* [2000] 1 WLR 2333 though cf *Watford Electronics Ltd v Sanderson CFL Ltd* [2001] EWCA Civ 317.

[412]   *Raiffeisen Zentralbank Osterreich AG v Royal Bank of Scotland plc* [2010] EWHC 1392, [319] to [327].

[413]   Encyclopedia of Banking Law 3405, n 362.

[414]   Hughes, n 74, 9.14. For a list of the agent bank's functions, see Encyclopedia of Banking Law 3406 and Fuller, n 77, 22–23.

[415]   Encyclopedia of Banking Law 2122, cl 19(3), n 362; Hughes, n 74, 9.18.

[416]   Hughes, n 74, 9.18. Such an authorisation of conflict may also be included in a trust deed: see Fuller, n 77, 12.28(3), but since the agent bank is usually one of the lenders, an actual conflict is much more likely to arise.

many of these are usually excluded. Further, a bond trustee is responsible for enforcement, and individual enforcement is prevented by a no-action clause, whereas syndicated lenders can enforce the liability due to them individually. The agent is largely expected to act on the instructions of the lenders, and it is to the democratic structure of the syndicate that we now turn.

7.4.6 Majority Lenders[417]

Most important matters concerning the loan will require the consent of 'the majority lenders'. This term will be defined in the loan agreement: usually consisting of holders of a majority (50 per cent or 66 per cent) of the loan outstanding.[418] These matters include modification of the loan agreement, waiver of breaches, determining whether an event or breach is material so as to amount to an event of default, directing the agent bank to accelerate the loan if there is an event of default and giving consent to the provision of security by the borrower.[419] In relation to modification, certain entrenched provisions, such as the pro rata clause, definition of 'majority lenders' and subordination provisions cannot be modified without the consent of all the lenders.[420] Certain breaches, for example, of a condition precedent, cannot usually be waived by a majority.[421] Thus, despite the general idea of democratic decision-making which is discussed in the next paragraph, there is some protection for the individual lender which wishes, rationally or irrationally, to hold out against the collective view.

It is necessary for the agreement to provide expressly that the decision of the majority binds all the lenders: this is not inherent in the agreement.[422] Obviously, the effect of such a provision is potentially to damage the interests of the minority lenders, and the question arises whether, and in what circumstances, they should be given some protection. It now seems reasonably clear that the majority are under some restraints in the way in which they exercise their power, and, indeed, their vote, but that these restraints are to prevent a dishonest abuse of power and nothing more. Thus, the majority must not exercise their power in a manner motivated by a desire to damage or oppress the minority,[423] nor to

---

[417] For discussion of the ascertainment of the views of bondholders, see above 7.3.3.

[418] Hughes, n 74, 9.7; Wood, n 89, 7–014; Mugasha, *The Law of Multi-bank Financing*, n 359, 5.118. The LMA agreement cl 1 provides for a majority of 66⅔%. Compare the position with bonds, where a numerosity requirement is more common than in syndicated loans, 7.3.3. Again, unlike in a bond issue, voting procedures are rarely formalised in the loan agreement, so that when it becomes necessary to ascertain the views of the majority, some sort of '*de facto* mechanism' has to be set up by the lenders: *Redwood Master Fund Ltd v TD Bank Europe Ltd* [2002] EWHC 2703, [97].

[419] Hughes, n 74, 9.7; Wood, n 89, 7–014; Mugasha, n 359, 5.118.

[420] Tolley's Company Law Service 5027; Mugasha, n 359, 5.116; Wood, n 89, 7–015.

[421] Wood, n 89, 7–015. This enables an individual lender to refuse to advance further funds if such a breach occurs.

[422] This is implicit in the judgment of Lindley LJ in *Sneath v Valley Gold Ltd* [1893] 1 Ch 477, 489, where he says: 'Powers given to majorities to bind minorities are always liable to abuse; and, whilst full effect ought to be given to them in cases clearly falling within them, ambiguities of language ought not to be taken advantage of to strengthen them and make them applicable to cases not included in those which they were apparently intended to meet'. It would not have been necessary to provide either that full effect should be given to such powers, or that they should be strictly construed, unless only the express power enabled the majority to bind the minority.

[423] *Redwood Master Fund Ltd v TD Bank Europe Ltd* [2002] EWHC 2703, [105]. See above pages 340–41. It is, of course, not easy to prove bad faith, but it may be inferred from the effect that the exercise of the power has on the minority, if the result is extreme enough. However, there is no reason why, absent bad faith, a lender should not vote according to its own interest: ibid, [105].

confer special collateral benefits on the majority. The principles in relation to syndicated loans are very similar to those applicable to bonds, which are discussed above.[424]

There is therefore a balance between the advantages of majority rule, which is necessary to get things done and to avoid the 'holdout' problem, where one lender can prevent a beneficial course of action by refusing to consent, and the possible oppression of the minority. It is still possible, and indeed likely, that the majority vote will damage a minority lender, who is only protected by the 'good faith' requirement discussed above, and it may be that where there are several tranches of subordinated lenders, there is more likely to be a true divergence of interests than where there is only one tier of lenders,[425] where interests are more likely to be aligned and where the dissenting lender is more likely to be irrational, or, at least, trying to obtain an individual advantage which could well damage the interests of the whole.

The effect of a debt buy-back on syndicate democracy should also be noted. If the borrower buys back the loan itself, this may have the effect of extinguishing the loan, but if it does not, or if the buy-back is made by a sponsor, this gives the borrower a voice in the syndicate democracy, and can give rise to conflicts of interest.[426] Of course, where the decision requires a majority vote, it is unlikely that the borrower will have bought back enough debt for its vote to make a difference,[427] but where a unanimous decision is required, the borrower could hold out against a decision.[428]

7.5 Conclusion

The presence of more than one lender gives rise to a number of additional issues which do not need to be considered when there is only one lender. There is a need for the transaction to be structured in such a way that there can be efficient administration, without undue cost and duplication, which necessitates the use of either a trust or agency structure. This in itself necessitates the protection of individual rights, and the balance between this and collectivity is critical. One particular feature of both syndicated loans and bonds is their transferability. There is no reason why loans by single lenders, or, indeed, any extension of credit, cannot be transferred[429] and so the transfer of loans will be discussed separately in the next chapter.

---

[424] 7.3.3.
[425] This is noted in *Redwood Master Fund Ltd v TD Bank Europe Ltd* [2002] EWHC 2703, [95].
[426] S Samuel, 'Debt Buybacks: Simply Not Cricket?' (2009) 24 *Journal of International Banking and Financial Law* 24; P Clark and A Barker, 'The Evolution of Debt Buybacks' (2009) 24 *Journal of International Banking and Financial Law* 359.
[427] A decision to accelerate the loan would normally fall into this category.
[428] This might, for example, be to improve its position in restructuring negotiations.
[429] Subject to some legal restraints discussed at pages 373–74.

8

Transferred Debt

This chapter is an attempt to draw together all the situations in which debt is transferred,[1] but also includes a section on the transfer of shares by way of comparison. In most cases, we will be looking at transfers by and from people who are lending to companies, but the same techniques are also used by companies in order to raise finance by transferring debts which are owed to them. Indeed, one technique, securitisation, is used both by companies and by lenders, which after all are companies whose business is finance; to raise money. One reason why a lender, or indeed a company, might want to transfer debt (among others) is to offload the credit risk of the debtor. In order to do this, there is no need actually to transfer the debt: the credit risk can be partially or wholly transferred to another party by other means, such as sub-participation or by using derivatives such as credit default swaps, or by the use of synthetic securitisation. These are therefore also considered in this chapter. Debts may also be transferred as security for a loan or other credit: this can be by way of mortgage or by way of charge.[2] This aspect of the transfer of debt is discussed in chapter six except insofar as it overlaps with the subject matter of the current chapter.

8.1 Why is Debt Transferred?

The first distinction that needs to be made is between debt which is created to be traded, and other debt. Of course, as other debt, for example, syndicated loans, comes to be transferred more frequently so that a market grows up, the distinction between the two somewhat collapses. However, historically bonds and other debt securities, as well as other money market instruments such as bills of exchange, were designed to be traded, and were therefore negotiable.[3] This meant that the borrower knew that the debt was going to be transferred, and that it would have to pay the holder, whoever that might be. The relationship between the borrower and the original lender was, therefore, only temporary. This had a number of ramifications for the original lenders. First, it knew that, provided that the market was functioning normally, it could sell the securities at any time, and so it could afford to take a greater risk than with 'relationship' lending. Such risk included not

---

[1] The term 'transfer' is here used in a rather loose and non-legal sense. As will be seen, in some cases there is an actual transfer of the debt, in others a new debt arises in the place of the old debt, and in other cases still, only the credit risk is transferred and the debt remains owing to the same creditor.

[2] With a charge there is, again, technically not an actual transfer, but many of the legal features of an assignment also apply to a charge, for example, the rules on set-off, see H Beale, M Bridge, L Gullifer and E Lomnicka, *The Law of Personal Property Security* (Oxford, Oxford University Press, 2007) 4.26.

[3] The concept of negotiability is discussed below at 8.2.3.

only the credit risk of the borrower, but the liquidity risk of the lender (the risk that it might need the cash tied up in the loan for other ventures or to pay back its own debt) and, to some extent, market risk (although if the market became too adverse it might not be possible for the lender to sell the securities at all). Second, it could use the securities for other purposes, such as collateral for its own borrowing, in a very straightforward way as they could be mortgaged, charged or (in the case of negotiable instruments) pledged. Third, since the securities were designed to be traded on a market, there was generally a transparent pricing structure which could be used to value them at any time. Fourth, the presence of a market meant not only that there were generally willing buyers to whom to transfer the securities, but that there was a structure whereby these transfers could take place quickly, cheaply and easily.[4]

These factors translated into certain benefits for the issuer of the securities. The interest rate payable might well be lower than that charged by a 'relationship' lender.[5] Further, as the lenders can offload the credit risk, there is less incentive for extensive credit checks at the time of issue, or for extensive monitoring during the life of the security. Similarly, although there are covenants which the issuer has to observe, they are usually less stringent than those in relationship lending.[6] The presence of a market meant not only that there was a larger pool of potential investors initially than with 'relationship' lending, but also that there was an even larger pool of investors who were potentially willing to buy the securities and therefore ensure continuing finance for the issuer. Further, the presence of a market meant that even if it were only possible to issue relatively short-term debt, since long-term debt would be too expensive, there was usually a liquid enough market for replacement debt to be reissued, thus achieving a rolling over of the finance, while with a 'relationship' loan this would entail complicated and expensive refinancing negotiations.

The lack of incentive and capacity to investigate and monitor the financial state of the borrower in the case of traded debt is one of the main reasons for the regulation of the issue of debt listed on the Stock Exchange, and for the continuing disclosure obligations which also apply. Regulation of debt is discussed below in chapter eleven.

Other debt, which was not created in order to be traded, can also be transferred. As mentioned in the last chapter, it is common for a lender in a syndicated loan to transfer its interest. This could be for a number of reasons. It might be a way of transferring the credit risk as mentioned above. For example, if the borrower looks unlikely to be able to repay in full, the lenders might wish to 'crystallise' their loss and sell to less risk-averse institutions which specialise in distressed debt.[7] Or a lender might just decide that it wanted a different

---

[4]   This is not just referring to the ease of transfer by delivery, which is a feature of negotiability, but to the presence of (originally) a physical market so that not only the physical transfers could take place easily but that settlement of payment was facilitated, and now the presence of an electronic market which enables transfer and settlement to take place virtually instantaneously.

[5]   A Morrison, 'Credit Derivatives, Disintermediation and Investment Decisions' (2003) 78 *Journal of Business* 621–47.

[6]   See discussion at page 79 above.

[7]   LMA Guide to Syndicated Loans 6.1.4.; P Wood, *International Loans, Bonds, Guarantees, Legal Opinions*, 2nd edn (London, Sweet & Maxwell, 2007) 7–019; A Mugasha, *The Law of Multi-Bank Financing*, (New York, Oxford University Press, 2007) 2–57, 2–61. Buyers of distressed debt may hope to make an eventual profit on the debt, and can spread the risk of loss by holding a wide portfolio bought at heavily discounted prices. In some circumstances, a buyer of distressed debt may buy the debt in order to pursue remedies against the arranger of the syndicated loan, rather than sue the borrower, although if this is achieved by way of assignment it may be

risk profile for its assets, and transfer its interest in a certain type of risk, or a certain type of borrower, in order to use the capital to lend elsewhere.[8] The lender, of course, might need capital for other reasons, or might decide that it does not want to retain any loans for their term, but wishes to sell on all its loans and use the proceeds to make more loans. This phenomenon becomes more likely as transfer of loans becomes easier and more common, and if there are other advantages to transfer as well, and is likely to lead to a situation where lenders 'originate to distribute' as happened in the period after 2000.[9] In this situation, the differences between debt issued to be traded, which is discussed above, and debt which on its face is not created to be traded begins to collapse, and the features of the former, such as the lack of incentive to monitor, become apparent in the latter. Despite this, there is little regulation of the issue or transfer of syndicated or other loans, and any protection for lenders or buyers has to come from private law rights and remedies.[10]

Other reasons for transfer relate largely to the regulation of lenders, and, in particular, banks. As described in chapter two,[11] banks are required to keep a certain amount of capital against risky assets, of which loans are a category. If the loans can be removed from the banks' balance sheet by transfer, then the amount of capital that has to be held decreases.[12] Of course, the bank no longer has the source of income from the loan, but the future income will be taken into account in the pricing of the sale, discounted, of course, for the risk of default in both income and capital repayments. A bank also might wish to transfer a loan to an associate or to another jurisdiction,[13] and a buyer might wish to purchase a loan to build up a set-off.[14]

Similar reasons apply to the transfer of single lender loans, and other types of smaller scale financing, such as credit card debts and asset-based lending. These debts tend to be transferred as part of a securitisation, where the purchase price for them is funded by an issue of securities, thus spreading the risk very widely and taking advantage of the lower cost of borrowing money by issuing securities. Of course, both bond issues and syndicated loans can also be securitised. A company can also securitise its receivables, but, at least in relation to smaller companies, financing of receivables is more easily achieved by transfer to a factor or an invoice discounter.[15] The prime motivation for a company is liquidity: receivables financing is a way of turning illiquid assets into ready cash[16] which can then be used to improve the company's cash flow or generally to finance the company's operations.

---

void as against public policy: A Chakrabarti and D Pygott, 'Trading Claims' (2007) 22 *Journal of International Banking and Financial Law* 645. In certain circumstances, it might also be possible for the lender to sell at a profit, thus locking in the gain.

[8] LMA Guide to Syndicated Loans, ibid, 6.1.2.; Wood, *International Loans, Bonds, Guarantees, Legal Opinions*, ibid, 7–019; Mugasha, *The Law of Multi-Bank Financing*, ibid, 2.58.

[9] D Llewellyn, 'The Global Financial Crisis: The Role of Financial Innovation' in P Booth (ed), *Verdict on the Crash: Causes and Policy Implications* (London, Institute of Economic Affairs, 2009).

[10] See 11.2.8 and 11.4.2. below.

[11] See pages 25–26.

[12] LMA Guide to Syndicated Loans, n 7, 6.1.3; Wood, n 7, 7–019; Mugasha, n 7, 2–534.

[13] Wood, n 7, 7–019.

[14] Wood, n 7, 7–109. This is not permitted after the 'cut-off' date for insolvency set-off: see Insolvency Rules 1986, r 2.85(2)(e) and r 4.90(2)(d) (as amended) and L Gullifer (ed), *Goode on Legal Problems of Credit and Security*, 4th edn (London, Sweet & Maxwell 2008) 7.90.

[15] 2.3.4.1.

[16] This is often said to be the major point of all securitisations, but where financial institutions are involved, the other reasons discussed, especially capital adequacy, are also important.

8.2 Methods of Transfer

The most suitable method of transfer of a debt will depend upon the nature of the debt, but also on the circumstances of the transfer. Detailed comparison between methods will take place as part of the discussion of each method, but there are a few general points to be made. First, the position of the borrower needs to be considered. Some methods require the borrower to consent to the transfer (either at the time or in advance). Even if active consent is not required, a borrower can, to some extent, prevent transfer of the benefit of any contract to which it is a party. In these circumstances, a method which transfers risks and rewards but which does not involve a transfer is preferable. Further, the parties to the transfer may not wish the borrower to know that the debt has been transferred. This may be because they wish to retain a particular relationship with the borrower, or because they think that the publicity would harm it, the lender, in its future dealings with the borrower or more generally, or merely because it is simpler for the borrower to pay the original lender than to direct it to pay someone else, when it might make a mistake.[17]

Another relevant point is whether merely rights are being transferred or whether there are obligations to transfer as well. Where a loan is a revolving facility, or has not been fully drawn down, the lender will owe the borrower an obligation to advance funds. Obligations cannot be assigned, but can be transferred by novation.[18] This is not a problem with an issue of debt securities, where there is never any outstanding obligation to advance funds.

A third question is whether there is any restriction on transfer in the original loan agreement. This will not apply in the case of securities or other negotiable instruments, where transfer is inherent in their nature, but could apply in the case of any other debt, including a loan. It may be that there is a restriction imposed by the borrower, or, though unusual, a restriction imposed by law.

A fourth potential problem is where security is given for the original loan. Transferring merely the benefit of the loan is likely to be construed as transferring the entitlement to the security as well,[19] but if there is a new obligation of the borrower to pay the transferee, then the entitlement to security will not automatically follow.[20]

8.2.1 Novation

The concept of novation is very simple: the original contract between A and B is terminated and a new one arises between B and C. Where there are mutual obligations still outstanding, the mutual agreement by A and B to release each other from these is consideration for the termination, and the agreement by B and C to take on new obligations provides sufficient consideration for the new agreement. C's obligations to B can be on exactly the same terms as A's obligations to B, but they are new obligations: A's

---

[17]   This would be true, for example, with some consumer debts.

[18]   It will be seen that this principle is not absolute, as an obligor can be prejudiced by events after assignment, for example, once notice is given to the obligor further set-off or other equities cannot arise between the assignor and the obligor, and the obligor must pay the assignee and not the assignor.

[19]   This would usually be done expressly as well, see Wood, n 7, 9–033. There is no requirement to register the transfer of security, Beale et al, *The Law of Personal Property Security*, n 2, 8.58.

[20]   Wood, n 7, 10–32.

obligations are not transferred to C. Nor are A's rights against B transferred to C (as in an assignment): B takes on new obligations which are owed to C. It can be seen that the idea of novation can solve the problem of outstanding debt in relation to the 'transfer' of syndicated loans.

It will be recalled that although the rights of the creditor can be assigned the obligations of the assignor cannot.[21] The problem is solved, however, at the 'cost' of the agreement of the borrower being necessary for the novation to take place. Furthermore, since all parties to a contract must consent to a novation, in a syndicated loan every party to the loan agreement (that is, the whole syndicate of lenders) would have to consent every time a novation takes place. This problem is overcome by including a unilateral offer in the original loan agreement made by all the parties, to accept a novation within the limits laid down in the agreement.[22] Strictly speaking, there are two offers: one to agree to the termination of the original contract and another to agree to the formation of a new contract, on exactly the same terms as the old, with whoever is the purchaser of the loan.[23]

Transferability is made easy by a provision in the loan agreement that the novation can be effected by the delivery, by the selling bank, of a 'transfer certificate' to the agent bank.[24] The legal effect of this was analysed by Aikens J in *The Argo Fund Ltd v Essar Ltd*[25]

> The offer to terminate the old contract is made to each original participant. The offer to conclude a new contract is made to all those who are eligible, ie are within the definition of 'bank or other financial institution'. In the case of the old contract, the offer of [the borrower] is accepted by the original participant by the delivery of the Transfer Certificate. In that case there is mutual consideration, because each side agrees to give up all its rights and obligations as against the other. In the case of the new contract, [the borrower]'s standing offer to all those eligible has to be accepted by a Transferee. The act of acceptance by the Transferee is not spelt out in Clause 27. It must be the fact that the Transferee agrees to the transfer with the Transferor on the terms of the Agreement (as set out in the Transfer Certificate) and agrees to the Transferor sending the Transfer Certificate to the Agent, thus permitting the Transferor to send it to the Agent on behalf of both Transferor and Transferee.

Since novation results in the borrower being in a new relationship with a different party, including, in some cases, that party being obliged to advance further funds to the borrower, it is understandable that the borrower will wish to have some control over who that party might be. A primary motivation is to ensure that any future party to the loan is sufficiently credit-worthy,[26] but there are other reasons as well: the borrower might wish to ensure that the new lender complies with regulatory requirements,[27] or might wish to retain rights of set-off against particular lenders, or might wish to ensure that lenders

---

[21] See above and M Hughes, *Legal Principles in Banking and Structured Finance*, 2nd edn (Hayward's Heath, Tottel Publishing Ltd, 2006) 9.21–9.22, 10.4–10.5.

[22] Hughes, *Legal Principles in Banking and Structured Finance*, ibid, 9.23–9.24. The concept of a unilateral contract was originally spelt out in *Carlill v Carbolic Smoke Ball Company* [1893] 1 QB 256. A unilateral offer requires no overt acceptance, but can be accepted by the performance of an act, at which point the offeror is bound. The concept has been used to analyse situations when otherwise it would be difficult to explain why a party was bound, for example, in *New Zealand Shipping Co Ltd v AM Satterthwaite & Co Ltd (The Eurymedon)* [1975] AC 154.

[23] Mugasha, n 7, 8.12.

[24] See *Habibson's Bank Ltd v Standard Chartered Bank (Hong Kong) Ltd* [2010] EWHC 702 (Comm), [28] and [29] for a recent statement in support of the efficacy of this arrangement.

[25] [2005] EWHC 600 (Comm), [51]–[52], aff'd [2006] EWCA Civ 241.

[26] *The Argo Fund Ltd v Essar Ltd* [2005] EWHC 600 (Comm), [28]; Hughes, n 21, 9.25.

[27] Ibid, [29].

would be benign in their decisions as to when and how to enforce the loan.[28] As a result, loan agreements usually restrict 'transfer' of the loan to a bank or financial institution; although, since 2001, this has been extended in the LMA documentation to include: 'a trust, fund or other entity which is regularly engaged in or established for the purpose of making, purchasing or investing in loans, securities or other financial assets'. It is sometimes possible for the borrower to negotiate specific exclusions from this very broad list, for example, by negotiating a list of unacceptable institutions.[29]

The restriction 'bank or other financial institution' (without the 2001 additions) was considered by the Court of Appeal in *The Argo Fund Ltd v Essar Ltd*,[30] where the relevant loan had been transferred to a hedge fund. The Court of Appeal rejected the first instance judge's approach that the 'other financial institution' should be a lender of money which had the ability to advance the agreed loan during the draw-down period,[31] and held that 'other financial institution' meant '"a legally recognised form or being, which carries on its business in accordance with the laws of its place of creation and whose business concerns commercial finance" … whether or not its business included the lending of money on the primary or secondary lending market'.[32]

This decision, affirming that of the first instance judge, was on the grounds that the inclusion of 'other financial institution' made it clear that a transfer to a non-bank was permitted, that the agreement permitted assignment (as opposed to novation) to anyone[33] and that there was a well-developed secondary market in loans.[34] It is hard to see why the ability to assign to anyone was relevant. An assignment would only transfer rights and the assignee would not be obliged to make further loans. The Court of Appeal considered that the ability of the transferee to be able to advance any loan not drawn down at the time of the transfer was immaterial, as that would make the interpretation of the words 'other financial institution' depend on whether the loan had been fully drawn down or not at the time of the transfer.[35] This particular argument may have depended on the short draw-down period of the loan in question (45 days), but otherwise it seems strange. Given that a transfer could take place at any time, why should a borrower not wish to protect itself against transfer to an institution which could not advance funds due, thus necessitating expensive restructuring of the borrower's financing, even if such a restriction limited possible transferees throughout the whole period of the loan? The extent of the protection a borrower may be able to obtain at the time of negotiation of the syndicated loan agreement will depend on the strength of the bargaining powers of the parties at the time of the agreement itself. The actual decision in Argo appears to have been motivated

---

[28]   These reasons also apply to a restriction on assignment.

[29]   See The Association of Corporate Treasurers, *Guide to the Loan Market Association Documentation for Investment Grade Borrowers* (2007) 60.

[30]   [2006] EWCA Civ 241.

[31]   Ibid, [32], [43]–[44].

[32]   Ibid, [51]. The hedge fund was held to fall within the definition.

[33]   Assignment of a syndicate member's rights was permitted by clause 27.1 of the agreement without restriction: see ibid, [42].

[34]   Ibid, [43].

[35]   *The Argo Fund Ltd v Essar Ltd* [2006] EWCA Civ 241, [44].

in part by a desire not to allow the defaulting borrower to escape from its obligations on what amounted, in the circumstances, to a technicality.[36]

One further problem with novating a syndicated loan is that, if a new contract is entered into, this does not automatically transfer the rights to any security given to the transferor for the original repayment obligation. One way of overcoming this is for the security to be given to a trustee who holds it on behalf of all the lenders.[37] The obligation that is secured is a parallel covenant made to the trustee[38] (again held on trust for the lenders from time to time) and the transferor's rights in respect of this can easily be assigned to the transferee (there being no obligations to the borrower to worry about in this transaction).

8.2.2   Assignment[39]

Assignment is a technique which is used in a number of different contexts. It can be used when a company transfers an absolute or security interest in receivables to a bank or other financier in order to obtain finance. The generic term for this is receivables financing, and various types of it are discussed in chapter two above.[40] It can also be used when a lender wishes to transfer the benefit of a loan it has made.

There are a number of significant differences between assignment and novation. First, an assignment is the transfer of rights: no new contract is created and none is terminated. The amount of involvement the assignor still has following the assignment depends on whether the assignment takes place at law or in equity,[41] and also on whether the assignment is permitted under the terms of the original agreement.[42] Second, as mentioned above, obligations cannot be assigned, only rights. Third, the consent of the obligor[43] is not required for a valid assignment to take place. As explained above, the requirement that the borrower must consent to a novation has led to specific provisions in a syndicated loan transaction. Nor, if the contractual rights to be assigned are owed to more than one person, do all the obligees have to consent, unless the obligation is joint and not several. All obligees, in contrast, must consent to a novation, hence specific provisions are required in a syndicated loan agreement.[44] Fourth, the obligor need not be given notice of the assignment for it to be valid in equity.[45] Fifth, an assignment takes place subject to equities (including rights of set-off), whereas if a loan contract is novated the new contract will not be affected by any prior dealings between the transferor and the borrower, although there can, of course, be a set-off between the borrower and the

---

[36]   Ibid, [52]. It was not clear why Argo did not take an assignment of the rights of the transferring banks and sue on that, but, as it had not done so, the Court of Appeal held that it could not now argue that the transfer to it should be construed as an assignment, since assignment and novation were entirely different concepts under English law: see [62].

[37]   Mugasha, n 7, 8.15; Hughes, n 21, 9.28. See page 357 above.

[38]   See page 357.

[39]   See generally G Tolhurst, *The Assignment of Contractual Rights* (Oxford, Hart Publishing, 2006) and M Smith, *The Law of Assignment* (Oxford, Oxford University Press, 2007).

[40]   2.3.4.1.

[41]   See below 8.2.2.1.

[42]   See below 8.2.2.2.

[43]   The word 'obligor' is used here as any non-personal obligation can be assigned, including but not limited to, debts. A borrower, or any other debtor, would be an obligor.

[44]   For example, clause 29 of the LMA Leveraged Loan Agreement.

[45]   See below 8.2.2.1.

transferee. Sixth, an agreement to assign future rights is given effect in equity,[46] so that there can be a valid equitable assignment of both present debts and those to arise in the future, which is critical in receivables financing. Seventh, there are limitations on the kind of rights which can be assigned: rights which are personal to the assignor cannot be assigned, so that the identity of the obligee is material to the obligor,[47] nor can rights which have been made non-assignable (or personal[48]) in the original contract,[49] nor can an assignment of a bare right of action take place.[50]

Assignment is the transfer of a chose in action, that is, a personal right to property which can only be enforced by bringing an action, as opposed to taking possession.[51] A chose in action can be either legal, that is, originally only enforceable in a court of law, or equitable, that is, enforceable in equity. Most of the rights we are considering here will be legal choses in action, as they are legal debts. However, an interest under a trust is an equitable chose in action, which would include, for example, an interest in securities held by an intermediary or the interest of a holder of stock.

8.2.2.1   Statutory and Equitable Assignments

Originally, assignment of a chose in action was not possible either at law or in equity.[52] However, by the beginning of the eighteenth century the courts of equity recognised the rights of an assignee as against an assignor, although the latter had to bring any necessary action on the chose against the obligor.[53] Eventually, the Judicature Act 1873 provided that the assignee of a chose in action could sue on it in its own name, if certain conditions are fulfilled.[54] The present form of this provision is section 136(1) of the Law of Property Act 1925, and the conditions are that the assignment is in writing, is absolute (not by way of charge only), and that written notice of the assignment has been given to the obligor. There also cannot be a statutory assignment of a future chose in action,[55] nor of part of a debt as opposed to the whole debt.[56] An assignment under section 136(1) is often called a 'legal' assignment, but this can be misleading as the section's only effect is to enable the

---

[46]   *Holroyd v Marshall* (1861–62) 10 HLC 191.
[47]   *Tolhurst v Associated Portland Cement Manufacturers* (1900) Ltd [1902] 2 KB 660, 668 per Collins MR 'neither at law nor in equity could the burden of a contract be shifted off the shoulders of a contractor on to those of another without the consent of the contractee'.
[48]   Gullifer, *Goode on Legal Problems of Credit and Security*, n 14, 3–39.
[49]   See below 8.2.2.2.
[50]   This amounts to champerty and is against public policy. However, if the assignee can show that he has an interest in enforcing the claim, such assignment would be permitted: *Trendtex Trading Corp v Credit Suisse* [1982] AC 679, 703. Lord Roskill required a 'genuine commercial interest' and this would certainly be the case where a debt is assigned as a matter of property, even though the assignee has to sue on it to recover it: see *Camdex International v Bank of Zambia (No 1)* [1998] QB 22.
[51]   *Torkington v Magee* [1902] 2 KB 427, 439; Smith, *The Law of Assignment*, n 39, 2.22.
[52]   This was, at least in part, because a transfer of claims was seen as champertous: see V Waye and V Morabito, 'The Dawning of the Age of the Litigation Entrepreneur' (2009) 26 *Civil Justice Quarterly* 389, 391. Tolhurst, *The Assignment of Contractual Rights*, n 39, ch 2; Smith, n 39, ch 5.
[53]   Tolhurst, n 39, 26.
[54]   Judicature Act 1873, s 25(6). This Act had the effect of enabling actions at law and in equity to be brought in the same courts.
[55]   Gullifer, n 14, 3.11. See discussion in Smith, n 39, 2.38–2.49.
[56]   *Re Steel Wing Co Ltd* [1921] 1 Ch 349; Smith, n 39, 10.22. The reason for this rule is that if only part of the debt is assigned, and the 'assignee' could sue on part of the debt by reason of section 136, the debtor would be exposed to a multiplicity of suits, which could result in conflicting decisions (*Re Steel Wing Co Ltd* [1921] 1 Ch 349, 357).

assignee to sue on the chose at law: it does not attract the priority rules which usually apply to a legal interest (the rule that a bona fide purchaser of the legal interest takes free of prior equitable interests[57]) in that the assignee takes 'subject to equities', including a prior equitable assignment.[58] Priority is instead determined by the rule in *Dearle v Hall*,[59] which is that the first assignee to give notice to the obligor has priority.[60] It is therefore better to refer to an assignment under section 136 of the Law of Property Act 1925 as a 'statutory assignment'. Whether the effect of the section is indeed procedural, as suggested above, or substantive is a matter of some debate.[61] Even the procedural significance has been undermined to some extent by the courts.[62]

In many cases of transferred debt, the conditions for a statutory assignment will not be fulfilled, at least at first. In many situations the lender or creditor will not want the debtor to know that the debt has been assigned. This might be so that the lender can continue its relationship with the debtor, or for reputational reasons, particularly if the creditor is obtaining financing by assigning the debt. If no notice is given to the debtor, the assignment cannot be a statutory one. However, if all other conditions are fulfilled, it can become a statutory assignment later when notice is given, for example prior to enforcement. Failure to give notice to the debtor has a number of consequences apart from (possibly) preventing the assignee from suing on the debt in its own name. First, until the debtor is given notice set-offs can continue to arise between the assignor and the debtor.[63] Second, until the debtor has received notice of assignment, it does not know to pay anyone other than the assignor, and can obtain a good discharge by so doing. Once the debtor has notice of assignment it can be made to pay again if it pays the assignor.[64] Third, until notice is given to the debtor, the debtor and assignor can agree to modify the contract and the assignee is bound by this[65] (although it might be a breach of the contract between the assignee and the assignor). Fourth, as mentioned above, until notice of an assignment is given to the debtor, the assignee may lose priority to a subsequent assignee who does give notice to the debtor under the rule in *Dearle v Hall*.[66]

Once notice has been given to the debtor, many assignments in the context of transferred debt will be statutory, as they are likely to have been made in writing and to be absolute, that is, not by way of charge.[67] However, an assignment will not be statutory if only part of a debt is assigned, or if the debt is a future debt. Of particular importance, therefore, is the ability of a creditor to assign a future debt in equity. This means that,

---

[57] See page 273.

[58] E Peel (ed), *Treitel on the Law of Contract*, 12th ed (London, Sweet & Maxwell, 2007) 15–037.

[59] (1828) 3 Russ 1.

[60] *Pfeiffer Weinkellerei-Weineinkauf GmbH & Co v Arbuthnot Factors Ltd* [1988] 1 WLR 150; *Compaq Computers Ltd v Abercorn Group Ltd (t/a Osiris)* [1991] BCC 484.

[61] Tolhurst, n 39.

[62] See below pages 376–77.

[63] *Roxburghe v Cox* (1881) 17 Ch D 520. Although set-off is specifically mentioned this rule applies to all equities. It only applies to defences arising after notice to the debtor, and not, for example, to defences arising out of the original contract. Nor does it apply to set-off closely or inseparably connected with the original claim: Gullifer, n 14, 7–66.

[64] *Brice v Bannister* (1878) 3 QBD 569, 578.

[65] *Brice v Bannister* (1878) 3 QBD 569.

[66] (1828) 3 Russ 1. This is subject to the so-called 'second limb' of the rule, that if the second assignee has notice of the first assignment at the time of its assignment it will not gain priority over the first assignment.

[67] Even an assignment by way of a mortgage, which is a transfer of the absolute interest subject to an obligation to reassign, is absolute within the terms of s 136: *Tancred v Delagoa Bay & East Africa Railway Co* (1889) 23 QBD 239.

providing there is executed consideration, an agreement to assign debts which may arise in the future is binding on the assignor, and will have the effect that the debts will be automatically assigned (in equity) to the assignee when they do arise, provided they have been sufficiently identified.[68] It is often the case, particularly in receivables financing, that all the present and future debts of a company are assigned to the financier, for example, in a 'whole turnover' agreement.[69]

It is important to consider what happens when a debt is assigned in equity.[70] One view could be that all that happens is that the assignee acquires a right to force the assignor to enforce the debt, in other words, the assignment only affects the relations between the assignor and the assignee.[71] If this right is seen as merely personal (a contractual right against the assignor) then this is surely wrong.[72] The assignee must have some sort of proprietary right, as there seems no doubt that if the debtor pays the debt to the assignor, the assignor holds the proceeds on trust for the assignee, and thus the assignee would have priority over the creditors of an insolvent assignor.[73] Further, if the assignor becomes insolvent before the debt is paid, the assignee again has priority over the assignor's creditors:[74] this also leads to the conclusion that the assignee's right in relation to the unpaid debt must be proprietary. It might be possible still to see the assignee's proprietary right as only relating to the relationship between the assignee and the assignor: this could be an interpretation of the statement that the assignor holds the right to sue the debtor on trust for the assignee.[75] On this view, the assignee has no relationship with the debtor, and cannot sue it.

However, there are good reasons to argue that an equitable assignment does more than this: it does give the assignee a relationship with the debtor, although one founded in equity rather than at law.[76] If notice is given to the debtor, yet the assignment remains equitable only, the debtor is obliged to pay the assignee and cannot get a good discharge by paying the assignor.[77] Further, case law establishes that an equitable assignment gives the assignee substantive rights, and the requirement to join the assignor when the assignee sues is merely procedural, so that it can be waived if there is no reason for the assignor to be joined.[78] Such reasons might include the possibility that the assignor will contest the

---

[68]   *Tailby v Official* Receiver (1888) 13 App Cas 523. See 6.3.2.1 above.

[69]   Beale et al, n 2, 5.112; E McKendrick (ed), *Goode on Commercial Law*, 4th edn (London, LexisNexis UK, 2009) 843–76 (draft whole turnover agreement).

[70]   For detailed consideration of this point, see Tolhurst, n 39, 4.05–4.09 and Smith, n 39, ch 6.

[71]   Tolhurst, n 39, 4.05–4.06.

[72]   Smith, n 39, 6.07.

[73]   Gullifer, n 14, 3–35.

[74]   This means that the assignee can either force the assignor's liquidator to enforce the debt for its (the assignee's) benefit, or can sue the debtor itself, joining the assignor (or its liquidator) if necessary.

[75]   See the analysis by B McFarlane in *The Structure of Property Law* (Oxford, Hart Publishing, 2008) 1.2.2. where he describes an equitable assignment as the acquisition by the assignee of a 'persistent right' against the assignor, which is a right against the assignor's right against the debtor (a persistent right, in McFarlane's terminology, is a right against a right which imposes a duty on the holder of the second right in favour of the holder of the persistent right, and which gives the latter a power to impose a duty on anyone acquiring a right which depends on the former's right).

[76]   See Tolhurst, n 39, 4.07–4.09.

[77]   *Jones v Farrell* (1857) 1 De G & J 208; *Brice v Bannister* (1878) 3 QBD 569; *William Brandt's Sons & Co v Dunlop Rubber Co Ltd* [1905] 2 AC 454.

[78]   *William Brandt's Sons & Co v Dunlop Rubber Co* Ltd [1905] 2 AC 454; *Sim Swee Joo Shipping Sdn Bhd v Shirlstar Container Transport Ltd* (unreported) 17 February 1994; *Raiffeisen Zentralbank Österreich AG v Five Star General Trading LLC* [2001] EWCA Civ 68, [60]. *Cf* M Smith, 'Equitable Owners Enforcing Legal Rights?' (2008)

assignment, or that the assignment is only of part of a debt, so that the debtor might otherwise face multiple actions.[79] There is also other evidence of the substantive nature of the rights of an equitable assignee. First, where an equitable assignee brings an action in its own name without joining the assignor, this counts as commencing proceedings for the purposes of limitation.[80] Second, an action commenced by an equitable assignee is not a nullity, even though in a proper case it will be stayed for the assignor to be joined.[81] Third, the rights of an equitable assignee have been considered (as a matter of substantive law) not sufficiently different from those of a statutory assignee for the former not to be entitled to the protection of an Act protecting bank depositors.[82]

If this is correct, what is the basis of the equitable assignee's right of action against the debtor? One view is that it is an equitable cause of action and can only attract equitable relief, but that in order to obtain a legal remedy, the assignor has to be joined.[83] Another view is that the courts of law will enforce the equitable rights of the assignee, providing that the position of the debtor and the legal rights of the assignor are protected (by joinder if necessary).[84] This is a practical view, which seems to accord with what most commercial parties would want and expect. However, it is conceptually rather difficult to explain, in that it appears that an equitable right is being treated exactly like a legal right, when the common law has consistently refused to enforce an assignment except when made in accordance with section 136. Thus, another view of the assignee's right to sue is that the assignee is 'enforcing the claim of the assignor but in its own name'.[85] This is justified by characterising the assignee's interest as that of a beneficiary under a trust and invoking the *Vandepitte* principle.[86] This view, then, sees the right of an equitable assignee as only a right against the assignor (or, against the assignor's right[87]) so that the equitable assignee is not brought into a direct relationship with the debtor.

It should be noted that this debate in itself is not of great practical consequence in relation to transferred debt, since if the only reason that the assignment is equitable is that no notice is given to the debtor, this is usually remedied before any action is taken on the debt, at which point the assignment becomes statutory. The same is true if the reason that the assignment is equitable is that the debt is a future debt, as ex hypothesi it will have

---

124 *Law Quarterly Review* 517, 523, who argues that the explanation for the requirement to join the assignor being procedural only lies in 'a regrettably silent, but otherwise wholly beneficial, expansion of the *Vandepitte* procedure'.

[79]   *William Brandt's Sons & Co v Dunlop Rubber Co Ltd* [1905] 2 AC 454, 462; *Performing Right Society Ltd v London Theatre of Varieties* [1924] AC 1, 14 (Viscount Cave); *Weddell v JA Pearce & Major* [1988] Ch 26, 40; *Central Insurance Co Ltd v Seacalf Shipping Corporation (The Aiolos)* [1983] 2 Lloyd's Rep 25, 33; *Deposit Protection Board v Barclays Bank plc* [1994] 2 AC 367, 381 (Simon Brown LJ); *Three Rivers DC v Bank of England (No 1)* [1996] QB 292, 309 (Peter Gibson LJ).

[80]   *Central Insurance Co Ltd v Seacalf Shipping Corporation (The Aiolos)* [1983] 2 Lloyd's Rep 25.

[81]   *Weddell v JA Pearce & Major* [1988] Ch 26.

[82]   See the decision of the Court of Appeal in *Deposit Protection Board v Barclays Bank plc* [1994] 2 AC 367. The decision was overruled by the House of Lords, but not on this point but on the basis that on its true construction the relevant statute did not include any assignees in its protection.

[83]   Tolhurst, n 39, 88–90. This is consistent with the view of Staughton LJ in *Three Rivers DC v Bank of England (No 1)* [1996] QB 292, 303. However, this view does not necessarily seem to be shared by the other two members of the Court of Appeal in that case.

[84]   This appears to be the view put forward in most of the cases, see those cited in footnote 78 above.

[85]   Smith, n 39, 6.30.

[86]   Smith, n 39, 6.31. Under this principle, a beneficiary can sue a third party in its own name if the trustee refuses to sue, but the right that is being enforced is that of the trustee and not of the beneficiary.

[87]   McFarlane, *The Structure of Property Law*, n 75, 1.2.2.

arisen, and thus be a present debt, before it can be sued on. The only two situations where an assignment might realistically remain equitable even when notice has been given and when the debt has arisen are where the assignment is of part of the debt, in which case there are very strong reasons for joining the assignor,[88] and where the assignment is 'by way of charge'. In the latter case, however, the charge document will usually provide for the chargee to take a statutory assignment of the debt if it wishes to enforce it, thus turning the charge into a mortgage.[89] However, the conceptual basis of an equitable assignment may be important for other reasons, such as when determining the effect of an anti-assignment clause.[90]

Given that some of the transfers we are considering in this chapter are of equitable interests, for example interests in securities held by an intermediary and the interest of a stockholder,[91] it is necessary also to consider the means of transfer of an equitable chose in action. Such a chose may be transferred in equity,[92] the result of this being that the assignee replaces the assignor as beneficiary under the trust, and can enforce the equitable chose (against the trustee) in its own name.[93] There appears to be authority in favour of the view that an equitable chose can also be assigned under section 136,[94] but this seems inconsistent with the wording of the section, and unnecessary since an equitable assignee of an equitable chose can in any event sue in its own name.[95]

8.2.2.2   Clauses Prohibiting Assignment

As mentioned above, it is possible for the original contract to provide that the rights created cannot be assigned, or can only be assigned under certain circumstances, such as if the obligor consents.[96] There are various reasons why a debtor might want to protect itself in this way.[97] One is that a debtor might not wish to risk paying the wrong party by inadvertently ignoring a notice of assignment. Another is that it wishes to continue to rely

---

[88]   *Walter & Sullivan Ltd v J Murphy & Sons Ltd* [1955] 2 QB 584; *Re Steel Wing Co Ltd* [1921] 1 Ch 349.

[89]   See Encyclopaedia of Forms and Precedents Vol 10(2) F28 clause 4.7.2.

[90]   See below 8.2.2.2.

[91]   Although in fact, the most attractive analysis in relation to intermediated securities is that these are transferred by novation: see below page 392.

[92]   This would require writing, however, under Law of Property Act 1925, s 53(1)(c).

[93]   *Cator v Croydon Canal Co* (1841) 4 Y & C Ex 405, 593; Peel, *Treitel on The Law of Contract*, n 58, 15–008; Tolhurst, n 39, 4.30; Smith, n 39, 6.04. There might, of course, be a good procedural reason for the assignor to be before the court, for example, if only part of the equitable chose were to be transferred. However, in the cases discussed here, the assignor will be an equitable owner in common and the effect of the assignment will be that the assignee also becomes an equitable owner in common. Any rights of enforcement on the debt itself will be exercised by the trustee of the issue.

[94]   See the cases discussed by Smith, n 39, 10.08–10.12.

[95]   Tolhurst, n 39, 5.07–5.15.

[96]   See, for example, the restriction on assignment in the agreement at issue in the case of *Barbados Trust Co Ltd v Bank of Zambia* [2007] EWCA Civ 148 at [5]. Consent of the debtor was required for assignment, but the consent was not to be unreasonably withheld, and was deemed to have been given if the debtor did not reply within 15 days of a request for consent.

[97]   These are similar to the reasons for limiting consent to a novation (see *Barbados Trust Co Ltd v Bank of Zambia*, ibid, at [6] where reference is made to the reasons given for limitation in the *Argo* case) although they do not relate to the ability of the assignee to fulfil future obligations since these cannot be assigned. However, the effect of a 'non-assignment' clause is different in that there is no need for the debtor to consent to an assignment, so, unlike a novation, there is no question of a consent being given subject to conditions. Instead, the nature of the debtor's obligation is changed.

on set-offs between it and the original creditor.[98] Yet another is that it may have a relationship with the original creditor, or it may trust the original creditor not to behave unreasonably, whereas it cannot be so sure that an assignee would behave in this way.[99] A borrower might, for example, wish to avoid the sale of distressed debt to a vulture fund.[100]

There has been much discussion over the effect of such a clause.[101] These discussions reveal an inherent policy tension between a freedom of the debtor to contract in such a way as to protect himself from having to deal with persons other than the original creditor, and a freedom of the creditor to alienate his right to performance, which can be seen as his own property.[102] The importance of the free flow of the funding of credit has been seen as so important in many jurisdictions that, at least in the context of receivables financing, and sometimes in a wider context, anti-assignment clauses have been deprived of virtually all effect. This has been done by legislation, and such an approach will be discussed later.[103]

First, we shall consider the effect of such a clause under current English law and in accordance with existing principles. Even this is not at all clear cut, but there are certain effects upon which all judges and writers are agreed. The first is that any given clause has to be construed in order to determine its legal effect. There are many permutations, four of which were identified by Professor Goode in an early article[104] commenting on the case of *Helstan Securities Ltd v Hertfordshire County Council*:[105]

(1) that the term does not invalidate a purported assignment by the 'assignor' to the 'assignee' but gives rise only to a claim by the debtor against the 'assignor' for damages for breach of the prohibition; (2) that the term precludes or invalidates any assignment by the 'assignor' to 'the assignee' (so as to entitle the debtor to pay the debt to the 'assignor') but not so as to preclude the 'assignor' from agreeing, as between himself and the 'assignee', that he will account to the 'assignee' for what the 'assignor' receives from the 'debtor': *In re Turcan* (1888) 40 Ch.D. 5; (3) that the 'assignor' is precluded not only from effectively assigning the contractual rights to the 'assignee', but also from agreeing to account to the 'assignee' for the fruits of the contract when received by the 'assignor' from the debtor; (4) that a purported assignment by the 'assignor' to the

---

[98] It will be recalled that where a debt is assigned, the debtor cannot rely on set-offs arising between him and the assignor once he has received notice of the assignment, see above page 375. However, the assignee does take subject to set-offs arising between the debtor and the assignor up to that time.

[99] R Goode, 'Contractual Prohibitions against Assignment' in J Armour and J Payne (eds), *Rationality in Company Law* (Oxford, Hart Publishing, 2009).

[100] This appears to have been what happened in *Barbados Trust Co Ltd v Bank of Zambia* [2007] EWCA Civ 148.

[101] R Goode, 'Inalienable Rights?' (1979) 42 *Modern Law Review* 553; Tolhurst, n 39, 6.82–6.90; G McMeel, 'The Modern Law of Assignment: Public Policy and Contractual Restrictions on Transferability' [2004] *Lloyd's Maritime and Commercial Law Quarterly* 483; A Tettenborn, 'Prohibitions on Assignment – Again' [2001] *Lloyd's Maritime and Commercial Law Quarterly* 472; B Allcock, 'Restrictions on the Assignment of Contractual Rights' (1983) 42 *Cambridge Law Journal* 328; *Helstan Securities Ltd v Hertfordshire CC* [1978] 3 All ER 262; *R v Chester and North Wales Legal Aid Area Office, ex p Floods of Queensferry Ltd* [1998] 1 WLR 1496; *Linden Gardens Trust Ltd v Lenesta Sludge Disposal Ltd* [1994] 1 AC 85; *Don King Productions Inc v Warren (No 1)* [2000] Ch 291; *Barbados Trust v Bank of Zambia* [2007] EWCA Civ 148.

[102] Rix LJ in *Barbados Trust v Bank of Zambia* [2007] EWCA Civ 148, [112].

[103] See pages 388–89.

[104] Goode, 'Inalienable Rights?' (1979) 42 *Modern Law Review* 553.

[105] [1978] 3 All ER 262. In this and what follows the words 'assignor' and 'assignee' are in inverted commas to reflect the uncertainty about the status of the assignment. It is still preferable to use these words rather than others, since it is easier then to compare the position where there is an anti-assignment clause to one where there is not.

'assignee' constitutes a repudiatory breach of condition entitling the debtor not merely to refuse to pay the 'assignee' but also to refuse to pay the 'assignor'.

This analysis was approved by Lord Browne-Wilkinson in *Linden Gardens Trust Ltd v Lenesta Sludge Disposals Ltd*,[106] who pointed out that constructions (1) and (4) were very unlikely to occur. In practice, construction (2) is the construction usually intended and preferred by the courts,[107] but even then there are still further construction issues which will arise, for example, whether the clause covers an equitable as well as a legal assignment, and whether it covers a declaration of trust.[108]

There now appears to be little doubt that such a clause is effective as far as the debtor is concerned, in other words, if there is such a clause in the agreement the debtor need not trouble itself over whom to pay. It will obtain a good discharge by paying the original creditor whether or not any attempt has been made to assign the debt. The debt cannot be the subject of a successful statutory assignment.[109] Further, the debtor retains the ability to assert rights of set-off arising even after notice of the purported assignment has been given to it.[110] The attempted assignment is also a breach of the contract between the original creditor and the debtor, although there is unlikely to be any substantive loss flowing to the debtor from this breach. It follows from this that the 'assignee' is not able to sue the debtor in order to enforce the debt: only the assignor can do this.[111] Thus the debtor is able to achieve its purpose of maintaining a relationship with the original creditor, which it knows and trusts, and the policy of allowing him to do this is achieved. However, there is the possibility that this policy will conflict with a policy against alienation, when we come to consider the position between the 'assignor' and the 'assignee'.[112]

There is one significant distinction to be borne in mind, between the position after the debt has been paid to the 'assignor' and the position before that time. After payment, the debtor can have no interest in preventing the 'assignee' from having proprietary rights to the proceeds. The debtor does not need to be sued: it has already paid. Thus the question of who can sue on the debt is irrelevant: the debt has been extinguished by payment. However, before payment the value of the debt (because it is a chose in action) is the right to sue on it and receive the proceeds: there is no value in merely having the right to sue but not the right to the proceeds, but equally there is no value in having a right to the proceeds but no means of enforcing the debt, as the debtor might then never pay. This means that in order for an 'assignee' to have some value in the debt before it is paid, it must have some means either of suing in its own name, or of forcing the 'assignor' to sue. An anti-assignment clause can prevent the first (we have just seen that) but the question is whether it can prevent the second.

---

[106]   [1994] 1 AC 85, 106–09.
[107]   G McMeel, 'The Modern Law of Assignment: Public Policy and Contractual Restrictions on Transferability' [2004] *Lloyds Maritime and Commercial Law Quarterly* 483, 500.
[108]   See pages 383–84.
[109]   Gullifer, n 14, 3–40. *Linden Gardens Trust Ltd v Lenesta Sludge Disposals Ltd* [1994] 1 AC 85, 106–09. Of course, the true effect of a clause will always depend on its exact wording, and the case of Linden Gardens, though laying down certain principles, was considering a particular form of words.
[110]   Gullifer, n 14, 3–39; Peel, n 58, 6.88–6.89; R Goode, 'Inalienable Rights?' (1979) 42 *Modern Law Review* 553, 553; *Christie v Taunton, Delmard Lane & Co* [1893] 2 Ch 175.
[111]   Though note that the 'assignee' might be able to force the assignor to sue the debtor, see discussion below.
[112]   These terms are in inverted commas as, ex hypothesi, an assignment has not actually taken place.

With this in mind, let us first consider the position if the 'assignor' has been paid by the debtor. It is clear that as the 'assignor' has agreed, for valuable consideration, to assign the debt to the 'assignee' it cannot retain that money as against the 'assignee'. Thus even an ineffective assignment (vis-a-vis the debtor) will have the effect of causing the 'assignor' to hold any proceeds of the debt on trust for the 'assignee'.[113] Further, if a clause in the original agreement purported to prevent this occurring, it might well be void as against public policy,[114] since the debtor has no interest in preventing such a trust arising[115] and cannot, by contract, prevent the creditor from alienating what has become its own property (presumably it could make it a breach of contract for it to do so, but cannot stop such an alienation being effective vis-a-vis the beneficiary of the trust). If the assignment was expressed to cover both the debt and any proceeds, the assignment would be valid as regards any proceeds actually received.[116]

It also needs to be considered how the interest of the 'assignee' in the proceeds is created. One way is to see it as an assignment of future property, which is valid in equity without more when the property is acquired under the principle in *Holroyd v Marshall*[117] and *Re Tailby*.[118] On this view, what has actually been assigned is reinterpreted in the light of the anti-assignment clause: since the contractual right itself cannot be assigned, the assignment takes effect only in relation to the proceeds. Allcock suggests that this takes effect by means of a constructive trust, but it is not clear that this concept is required. If the intention to assign the proceeds is clear, as it must be from the agreement between the 'assignor' and the 'assignee': the 'assignee's' interest in the proceeds will be express and will be an equitable interest by way of assignment.[119] Another view is that the 'assignee's' interest in the proceeds flows from the interest it had in the debt itself.[120]

We should now consider the position before the debtor pays the assignor. Given that an anti-assignment clause can, uncontroversially, prevent a statutory assignment from taking place, we will consider its effect on an equitable assignment. It will be apparent from the discussion above[121] that the exact nature of the equitable assignee's rights is open to debate. If the assignment merely gives the assignee rights against the assignor and does not affect the relationship between the assignee and the debtor, then it must be questioned whether an anti-assignment clause can have any effect. On this view, the position between

---

[113] Gullifer, n 14, 3–41; *Re Turcan* (1888) 40 Ch D 5, 10–11, supported by Lord Browne-Wilkinson in *Linden Gardens Trust Ltd v Lenesta Sludge Disposal Ltd* [1994] 1 AC 85, 106 and Rix LJ in *Barbados Trust Co Ltd v Bank of Zambia* [2007] EWCA Civ 148, [77]. See also B Allcock, 'Restrictions on the Assignment of Contractual Rights' [1983] *Cambridge Law Journal* 328, 335–36; G Tolhurst, 'Prohibitions on Assignment and Declaration of Trust' [2007] *Lloyd's Maritime and Commercial Law Quarterly* 278; G McMeel, 'The Modern Law of Assignment: Public Policy and Contractual Restrictions on Transferability' [2004] *Lloyd's Maritime and Commercial Law Quarterly* 483, 507–08; Smith, n 39, 347. P Zonneveld, 'The Effectiveness of Contractual Restrictions on the Assignment of Contractual Debts' (2007) 22 *Journal of International Business and Financial Law* 313 (relies on *Hodder & Tolley Ltd v Cornes* [1923] NZLR 876 and *Atwood & Reid Ltd v Stephens* [1932] NZLR 1332).

[114] R Goode, 'Inalienable Rights?' (1979) 42 *Modern Law Review* 553.

[115] As by the time the trust arises, the debtor will already have paid the original creditor and will be discharged.

[116] *Re Turner Corporation Ltd (In Liq)* (1995) 17 ACSR 761, 767.

[117] (1862) 10 HL Cas 191.

[118] (1888) 13 App Cas 523. Also B Allcock, 'Restrictions on the Assignment of Contractual Rights' [1983] *Cambridge Law Journal* 328, 335.

[119] Smith suggests that the effect of an equitable assignment in any event is that the assignee's interest arises by means of a constructive trust: Smith, n 39, 6.12.

[120] Goode, 'Contractual Prohibitions Against Assignment', n 99, 362.

[121] 8.2.2.1.

the assignor and the debtor has not changed, and so one might think that the debtor has no interest in preventing such an assignment. However, this analysis is wrong for a number of reasons, which arise from the earlier discussion. First, it seems reasonably clear from the authorities that the relationship between the assignee and the debtor is affected by an equitable assignment, so that a debtor with notice has to pay an equitable assignee,[122] and an equitable assignee can sue a debtor without the consent of the assignor (either without joining the assignor or, if there is reason to do so, by joining the assignor as defendant).[123] Second, even on the view that the relationship is not affected, the assignor holds the debt as trustee for the assignee, and therefore must enforce the debt if instructed to do so by the assignee (and can be forced to do so if it refuses),[124] and, further, in certain circumstances, the assignee may be able to sue in its own name, in the right of the assignor.[125] Third, on either view, once notice is given to the debtor, equities such as set-off arising between the assignor and the debtor will no longer arise.[126] Therefore, it would seem that the debtor does have an interest in preventing an equitable assignment, and, indeed, a clause prohibiting the assignment of the whole or any part of a contract was held to prohibit both a legal and an equitable assignment.[127]

This interest of the debtor would be protected only if, first, the debtor could always get a good discharge by paying the assignor, second, it could be sure that the assignor always had control over enforcement of the debt and, third, it could be sure that set-off and other equities would always continue to arise between the assignor and the debtor, even after notice to the debtor. An anti-assignment clause can achieve the first and the third, by making any notice of assignment ineffective, in that a debtor cannot be bound by a notice of something which the assignor is contractually forbidden to do.[128] Thus the debtor could rely on a set-off arising between him and the assignor even after receiving notice of the purported 'assignment'. However, it is less clear that such a clause can prevent the second. The 'assignee' will be unable to sue in its own right, as it could if the clause was not there,[129] as the effect of the clause is to prevent the assignee obtaining any rights against the debtor. However, it cannot prevent the 'assignee' obtaining rights against the 'assignor' which the 'assignee' can enforce, and this includes the right to force the assignor to enforce the debt against the debtor, which would come from an express or implied term of the contract of assignment.[130] Thus the 'assignee's' position is made procedurally more difficult, as it can only obtain the proceeds of the debt by the convoluted procedure of suing the assignor, but it will get the money in the end (and is protected if the assignor becomes insolvent), as its right against the assignor is not merely contractual but is an equitable proprietary right which survives the assignor's insolvency.[131]

---

[122] See pages 376–77.
[123] See page 377.
[124] See above page 377. See eg *Barbados Trust v Bank of Zambia* [2007] EWCA Civ 148, where this reasoning was used to support allowing the assignee to sue the debtor directly using the *Vandepitte* procedure, although in that case there was an express declaration of trust.
[125] Ibid.
[126] *Roxburghe v Cox* (1881) 17 Ch D 520.
[127] *R v Chester and North Wales Legal Aid Area Office, ex p Floods of Queensferry Ltd* [1998] 1 WLR 1496.
[128] Goode, n 99, 360; Gullifer, n 14, 3–39.
[129] By obtaining a statutory assignment.
[130] *MH Smith (Plant Hire) Ltd v DL Mainwaring (t/a Inshore)* [1986] 2 Lloyd's Rep 243, 246.
[131] In McFarlane's terminology, a persistent right; McFarlane, n 75, 1.2.2.

Attempts have been made to circumvent an anti-assignment clause by, instead of assigning the debt, the 'assignor' declaring a trust of it in favour of the 'assignee'.[132] We will initially consider the position where such a trust is expressly declared. Arguably, the 'assignor's' rights against the debtor are its own property, and it can declare a trust of its own property. One practical effect of such a trust is unobjectionable: it means that the 'assignor' will hold the proceeds of the debt, once paid, on trust for the 'assignee' (as discussed above), and the debtor cannot prevent this, and has no interest in doing so.

However, before the debt is paid, what is the effect of such a declaration of trust? First, there is no question of the 'assignee'[133] giving notice to pay to the debtor: the debtor continues to be able to pay the 'assignor' and obtain a good discharge. Second, since no notice can be given, one might have thought that set-offs could continue to arise between the 'assignor' and the debtor. This is likely to continue to be the case as long as the 'assignor' is solvent, since both independent set-off and transaction set-off arise where there is mutuality at law. However, there could be a problem where the 'assignor' is insolvent, as insolvency set-off[134] requires strict mutuality, so that a claim against the 'assignor' in its own right cannot be set off against a claim which the 'assignor' holds on trust for the 'assignee'.[135] In terms of enforcement of the debt, the 'assignee' cannot sue in its own right, as it is merely a beneficiary under a trust and it does not obtain the substantive interest an equitable assignee obtains against the debtor.[136] Nor can it, unlike many equitable assignees, give notice to the debtor and obtain a statutory assignment which would give it an unquestionable right to sue in its own name.[137] However, as beneficiary, it can force the trustee to sue.[138] Further, if the trustee refuses to sue, a beneficiary can bring an action against the debtor, under the procedure established in *Vandepitte v Preferred Accident Insurance Corp of New York*.[139] Under this procedure, a beneficiary can bring what is effectively the trustee's action, but in its own name, joining the trustee as defendant. Obviously, where there is no anti-assignment clause, there is no objection to this procedure being used. If, however, there is an anti-assignment clause, can this prevent an effective declaration of trust, or, if not, can it prevent the *Vandepitte* procedure being used?

It has been held that a clause which expressly prohibits only assignment will not be held to prevent a declaration of trust, since a declaration of trust is different in character from an assignment.[140] There are a number of judicial statements that an equitable assignment

---

[132] *Don King Productions Ltd v Warren* [2000] Ch 291.
[133] This person is no longer even a failed assignee, but a beneficiary under a trust, but the term 'assignee' is used to show that it is in the same position as a failed assignee.
[134] Under rule 4.90 or rule 2.85 Insolvency Rules 1986.
[135] Gullifer, n 14, 7–84. R Derham, *The Law of Set-Off* (Oxford, Oxford University Press, 2003) 11–04; J Marshall, 'Declaring a Trust over Rights to an "Unassignable" Contract' (1999) 12 *Insolvency Intelligence* 1. However, this reasoning may not apply where the 'assignor' only declares a trust of the proceeds and not of the debt itself: see M Feely, 'Can Set-off Prejudice a Debt Subordination Agreement?' (2009) 24 *Journal of International Banking and Financial Law* 64, which discusses this question in the context of a turnover trust (see 5.3.4.1.1.) where there seems little doubt that the junior creditor holds only the proceeds on trust for the senior creditor.
[136] See below.
[137] This difference between a declaration of trust and an equitable assignment was noted by Waller LJ in *Barbados Trust Co Ltd v Bank of Zambia* [2007] EWCA Civ 148, [43].
[138] See page 382 above.
[139] [1933] AC 70. See also *Harmer v Armstrong* [1934] Ch 65, 82–83.
[140] *Don King Productions Inc v Warren* [2000] Ch 291, 321; *Barbados Trust Co Ltd v Bank of Zambia* [2007] EWCA Civ 148, [43] (Waller LJ), [80]–[89] (Rix LJ).

is different from a declaration of trust,[141] and there are certainly some differences, such as the inability of a beneficiary to convert its position into that of a legal assignee by giving notice, to require the debtor to pay it direct and (probably) to prevent set-off arising, at least outside insolvency. Further, if there is an equitable assignment, the assignor cannot sue without joining the assignee, whereas if there is a trust, the trustee can sue without joining the beneficiary,[142] and, as we have seen, an equitable assignee can, in some circumstances, sue the debtor without joining the assignor, while even if a beneficiary can sue under the *Vandepitte* procedure the trustee has to be joined. There is also another rather technical distinction, in that an assignment is a transfer of rights, and a declaration creates a new right, that of the beneficiary against the trustee.[143] For these reasons, it seems correct that a clause which does not in its terms prohibit a declaration of trust should not be interpreted to do so. Against this it has been argued that the effect of an equitable assignment is that the assignor holds the debt on trust for the assignee, and therefore the effect of an equitable assignment and a declaration of trust is exactly the same. On this view, a clause prohibiting the former should also be held to prohibit the latter.[144] These arguments fail to take account of the differences discussed above, which, although in some cases rather technical, demonstrate that an equitable assignment affects the position of a debtor to a greater extent than does a declaration of trust, and so a debtor might justifiably wish to prohibit the former and not the latter.

Of course, a debtor might wish to prohibit both. If the clause is drafted so as to prohibit a declaration of trust expressly, can this prohibition prevent a trust arising? One possible view is that it cannot, in that an agreement between A and B cannot stop B declaring a valid trust over what is B's own property.[145] Applying the same analysis as that applied to an anti-assignment clause, the result would be that the clause could only prevent any consequences from the declaration of trust which actually affected the debtor.[146] As has been pointed out, these would be few; the only one of possible substance is that the requisite mutuality for insolvency set-off might be broken.[147] Arguably, however, if there is a clause prohibiting the declaration of trust, it might not be broken if the clause were taken into account in assessing mutuality.[148] This would be on the basis that, although the 'assignor' held the claim on trust for the 'assignee', the debtor was not bound by that trust as, vis-a-vis the debtor, the declaration of trust was contractually prohibited, and further, that any notice given to the debtor of the trust was ineffective, for the same reason. Further, a clause prohibiting both an assignment and a declaration of trust would have rendered a declaration of trust a breach of the contract between the 'assignor' and the

---

[141]　*Barbados Trust Co Ltd v Bank of Zambia*, ibid, [43] (Waller LJ); *Don King Productions Inc v Warren*, ibid, 319 (Lightman J); *Re Turcan* (1888) 40 Ch D 5, 10–11; *Devefi Pty Ltd v Mateffy Perl Nagy Pty Ltd* (1993) 113 ALR 225, 236.

[142]　*Three Rivers DC v Bank of England* [1996] QB 292, 311.

[143]　Goode, n 99, 366. But note that Professor Goode points out that the distinction appears to have no legal significance except in relation to imperfect gifts. Also, this distinction collapses on the view of an equitable assignment that it merely creates rights against the assignor, such as that of McFarlane, n 75, 1.2.2.

[144]　A McKnight, 'Contractual Restrictions on a Creditor's Right to Alienate Debts' [2003] *Journal of International Banking Law and Regulation* 1 and 43; G McMeel, 'The Modern Law of Assignment: Public Policy and Contractual Restrictions on Transferability' [2004] *Lloyd's Maritime and Commercial Law Quarterly* 48.

[145]　As opposed to creating a trust by transferring the property to someone else, which could be prevented. See M Smith, 'Equitable Owners Enforcing Legal Rights?' (2008) 124 *Law Quarterly Review* 517, 519.

[146]　Goode, n 99, 362.

[147]　See above page 383.

[148]　Marshall, 'Declaring a Trust over Rights to an "Unassignable" Contract' (1999) 12 *Insolvency Intelligence* 1.

debtor, although whether the debtor would have suffered any loss is not clear. It is also unlikely that the debtor could obtain an injunction to prevent a declaration of trust, if it knows about it in advance.[149] The possible adverse consequences to the debtor of the beneficiary ('assignee') being able to force the trustee ('assignor') to sue would be no greater than the adverse consequences of an equitable assignment and are not in the power of the debtor to prevent.

A different view is that the clause can stop both an equitable assignment and a declaration of trust, since both have the same effect and both affect the interest of the debtor.[150] This view is on the basis that an anti-assignment clause does more than merely prevent the assignee having any relationship with the debtor, it actually changes the nature of the debt so that it becomes inalienable (in the same way as personal rights are inalienable).[151] The argument is that there is no policy reason against this, and, although the proceeds cannot be rendered inalienable, the rights against the debtor can. This is justified on the grounds of the freedom of contract of the debtor to protect itself. However, if this means that the 'assignee' has no proprietary (or 'persistent') rights against an insolvent 'assignor', this is very undesirable and thus there is a good policy argument against this state of affairs.[152] If the 'assignee' can obtain proprietary rights which give priority in insolvency, then it is difficult to see how the debt has become inalienable. This divergence of view points up the policy dilemma identified earlier between the freedom of the debtor to protect himself and the freedom of the 'assignor' to alienate its property. In the context of transferred debt, one might also consider the wider policy issue of developing a market in such debt, and, in particular, in distressed debt, which, if not transferred by lenders, could cause systemic collapse.

The next question is whether the debtor can prevent the *Vandepitte* procedure being used. In *Don King Productions Ltd*[153] Lightman J envisaged a limit on the powers of the beneficiary to control the trustee, so that the trust would not 'abrogate the fullest protection that the parties to the contract have secured for themselves under the terms of the contact'.[154] Thus he envisaged that, where there was an anti-assignment clause (let alone a clause prohibiting a declaration of trust) the court would disallow the *Vandepitte* procedure and that the rule in *Saunders v Vautier*,[155] which enables a beneficiary to give directions to the trustee and to call for the trust to be wound up, would not apply.[156] However, it is unclear how far the parties to the debt contract can change the normal

---

[149]   Goode, n 99, 363.

[150]   A McKnight, 'Contractual Restrictions on a Creditor's Right to Alienate Debts' [2003] *Journal of International Banking Law and Regulation* 43; G McMeel, 'The Modern Law of Assignment: Public Policy and Contractual Restrictions on Transferability' [2004] *Lloyd's Maritime and Commercial Law Quarterly* 483. See also the views of Rix LJ and Hooper LJ in the *Barbados Trust* case, both of which appear to think that a properly drafted clause could prevent a valid declaration of trust: [2007] EWCA Civ 148, [88] and [139]. See also *Don King Productions Inc v Warren* [2000] Ch 291, 321.

[151]   *Tolhust v Associated Portland Cement Manufacturers (1900) Ltd* [1902] 2 KB 660, 668; R Goode, 'Inalienable Rights?' (1979) 42 *Modern Law Review* 553, 556–57; *Helstan Securities Ltd v Hertfordshire County Council* [1978] 3 All ER 262, 266.

[152]   Goode, n 99, 361.

[153]   [2000] Ch 291.

[154]   Ibid, 321.

[155]   (1841) 4 Beav 115.

[156]   This latter point was justified on the basis that the trust was an 'active' trust, in that the trustees had duties to perform and not a 'bare' trust to which *Saunders v Vautier* would apply.

incidents of a trust, before the trust ceases to be such.[157] The question arose in the case of *Barbados Trust Co Ltd v Bank of Zambia*.[158] There, again, an anti-assignment clause was held not to prohibit a declaration of trust,[159] but it was argued that the clause prevented the use of the *Vandepitte* procedure as it laid the debtor open to an action by the 'assignee' which was the very thing that the clause was designed to prevent. Waller LJ took the view that if there was a valid declaration of trust, this conferred on the beneficiary a right to force the trustee to sue, and the *Vandepitte* procedure was merely a procedural means of achieving this:

> It is important to bear in mind when considering the above questions that what has for shorthand been referred to as the *Vandepitte* short cut is a matter of *procedure* to enable a beneficiary under a trust to obtain what he is beneficially entitled to in a situation in which the trustee will not sue — will not sue for what the trustee is legally entitled to but which if he succeeds he must hold for the beneficiary. It would be understandable if the court would not allow the procedure to be misused to obtain rights that the beneficiary is not otherwise entitled to, but otherwise if the beneficiary has an unanswerable right under a trust and the trustee has an unanswerable claim, why should the court's procedure not be available to enable the rights to be established or brought to fruition?[160]

Rix LJ agonised more over whether the *Vandepitte* procedure could be used:

> What is a court to do in such circumstances? It seems to me that there is a tension between (a) the interests of those whose contracts, either because they are of an inherently personal nature or because of agreed restrictions on alienability, should not readily be intruded upon by strangers to them, (b) the interests of those who seek to arrange their affairs on the basis of holding property in trust for others, and (c) the public interest, which is concerned to see that contracts are performed, that the beneficiaries of trusts are protected, and that financial assets are not too readily made inalienable especially where markets regularly provide liquidity for the trading of them. If a prohibition on assignment carried all before it, destroying all alienability whatever the circumstances, even to the extent of making it impossible for beneficial interests to be protected in any circumstances in the absence of the legal owner as a formal claimant, it seems to me that the public interest in freedom of contract and the freedom of markets could be severely prejudiced.[161]

However, having reviewed a number of situations where an anti-assignment clause which prevented the *Vandepitte* procedure would be commercially undesirable, on balance he decided that the procedure should be used.[162] Hooper LJ took the opposite view: that the spirit of the anti-assignment clause would be contravened if the procedure were allowed.[163]

---

[157] P Turner, 'Charges of Unassignable Rights' (2004) 20 *Journal of Contract Law* 97. There is an irreducible core of trustee's obligations that cannot be contracted out of: see *Armitage v Nurse* 1998] Ch 241, 253–54. See in a different context, the discussion on trustees' exemption clauses at 7.3.4.

[158] [2007] EWCA Civ 148.

[159] Waller LJ did appear to say that if the clause had expressly prohibited a declaration of trust, this could place an embargo on the declaration of such a trust: ibid at [43]. Rix LJ also took this view at [88].

[160] [2007] EWCA Civ 148, [29].

[161] *Barbados Trust Co Ltd v Bank of Zambia* [2007] EWCA Civ 148, [112].

[162] Ibid, [119].

[163] Ibid, [139].

The views of the Court of Appeal in this case do not give any definitive guidance on whether the *Vandepitte* procedure should be available where a clause prohibits a declaration of trust. The clause in the case itself did not do this: it merely prohibited assignment. Also, all the reasoning on the *Vandepitte* procedure was actually obiter, since a majority of the Court of Appeal held that the debt had not been properly assigned to the 'assignor' in the first place. The question is therefore an open one. As the effect of an anti-assignment clause is to prevent the 'assignee' suing the debtor in its own name (which would otherwise be possible)[164] then logically a clause which prohibited a declaration of trust should prevent the use of the *Vandepitte* procedure. If the right of an equitable assignee to sue the debtor in its own name (albeit joining the assignor if necessary) is seen as affecting the debtor, so that it has a justifiable interest in preventing it, then the same must be true of the *Vandepitte* procedure, which is analogous to (and on one view identical to[165]) the right of the equitable assignee to sue.

Against this, it can be argued that the *Vandepitte* procedure is merely a procedural mechanism to enable the 'assignee' to enforce the 'assignor's' rights.[166] It can be seen as a 'shortcut', to avoid the circuity of action whereby the 'assignee' sues the 'assignor', compelling the 'assignor' to sue the debtor. If this is the case, it is said, the debtor is no worse off by the use of the *Vandepitte* procedure than by the normal operation of the rights of a beneficiary to force the trustee to enforce the trust. In one sense this is true, but there seems to be little to distinguish this argument from an analogous argument that the right of an equitable assignee to sue in its own name is based on exactly the same principle (avoiding circuity of action). The question of whose right is being enforced (the 'assignee's' or the 'assignor's') is at best unclear in the case of an equitable assignment, and in any event is irrelevant to the debtor, who only knows that he is being sued by the assignee, who can bring proceedings without the consent of the assignor. In any event, there should be consistency between the position where there is an equitable assignment and where there is a declaration of trust. A prohibition clause should not prevent the 'assignee' suing in either case, or it should prevent it in both cases.

There are two further points to make. From a practical point of view, if the 'assignor' is able to cede control over the bringing of an action to the 'assignee', so that the 'assignee' can force the 'assignor to sue, then it could be said to make little difference to a debtor whether the ensuing action is technically brought by the 'assignee' or the 'assignor': the point is that the debtor's fate is being determined by someone other than the 'assignor'. Here the policy point is clear. Either a debtor should be able to prevent an 'assignor' ceding that control (which would give the debtor all the protection which it seeks and would swing the pendulum completely in the direction of the debtor's freedom of contract) or the policy of allowing people to alienate rights to their own property should prevail. This would mean that the debtor would not be able to prevent the ceding of control by the 'assignor', but could only protect itself to the extent of always being able to get a good discharge by paying the 'assignor' and always being able to maintain a right of set-off against the 'assignor'. Professor Goode favours this latter view, and points out that there

[164] As a statutory assignee, see above page 380.
[165] Smith, n 39.
[166] Goode, n 99, 373. This has some support from the judgment of Waller LJ at [45].

are a number of other reasons why an 'assignor' could cede control over enforcement which cannot be prevented, for example, by a takeover of the 'assignor' by another company.[167]

In the context of transferred debt, there are important policy reasons to facilitate the ability of a creditor to transfer to another not only the economic interest in the debt, but some rights of control over its enforcement, since no transferee would want to buy a debt which might or might not be enforced by the transferor.[168] This is particularly true where loans are assigned in the distressed debt market, since a major point of the transaction is that the transferee is the specialist in recovering such loans, and the transferor is keen not to have to spend time and money concerning itself with this. It could be said, of course, that this is the very situation against which the debtor wishes to protect itself.

The second point stems from the actual nature of a trust. If the beneficiary under a declaration of trust cannot call for the trust property under *Saunders v Vautier*, nor enforce the trustee's claim against the debtor under the *Vandepitte* procedure, arguably there is no trust and therefore no proprietary interest, so that the 'assignee' merely has a contractual right against the 'assignor' and will not obtain priority in the 'assignor's' insolvency. Again, this is of no use to transferees of debts in the contexts we are considering. In receivables financing, the whole point of taking an assignment is to ensure that the financier recovers money equivalent to the finance provided (plus interest), even in the insolvency of the company financed. In securitisation, the whole point is that the entire beneficial interest is transferred to the special purpose vehicle so that, in the event of the originator's insolvency, its other creditors have no claim on the receivables. Where assignment is used in the transfer of loans made by financial institutions (as in the *Barbados* case itself) this point might be less critical, since usually it is the debtor which is in financial difficulties, but, however, the transferor wishes to divest itself of any interest in the (now unprofitable) loan.

8.2.2.3   Reform

These policy considerations could be taken one stage further, to support an argument for anti-assignment clauses to be ineffective. Legislation to this effect has been passed in a number of jurisdictions, although the precise scope of the override varies.[169] Is there a need for such legislation in UK law? The arguments in favour are that, at least in the context of receivables financing, the uncertainty surrounding the legal effect of such clauses, and the disproportionate cost of examining every receivable to discover whether it includes such a clause where the receivables are of low value, means that it would be cost effective to have such a prohibition. This, it is argued, would lower the cost of credit and

---

[167]   Goode, n 99, 372. Another possibility is that other parties have become sub-participants in the loan (see below 8.3.1) or have an interest as a result of a credit default swap (see below 8.3.2.) and so are in a position to influence enforcement. Neither of these 'transfers' of risk would be prohibited by an anti-assignment clause.

[168]   Ibid.

[169]   US Uniform Commercial Code Article 9–406; The Canadian Personal Property Security Acts (see page 304 above); German Commercial Code HGB, s 354(a); Korean Civil Code, s 449(2); Japanese Civil Code, s 466(2); Italian Civil Code, s 1260(2); Greek Civil Code, s 466(2); Portuguese Civil Code, s 577(2); Spanish Civil Code, s 1112. See also the UN Convention on the Assignment of Receivables in International Trade (2002) Art 9(1) and the UNIDROIT Convention on International Factoring (1988) Art 6(1). I am indebted to Mr Woo-Jung Jon for his analysis in his MSt thesis which led to this list.

make receivables financing a more streamlined operation.[170] The arguments against such a reform are that it interferes with freedom of contract, and that if it were to be limited to only certain types of obligations (for example, receivables) there would be problems of categorisation. Despite these objections, the Law Commission has proposed such a change in the law,[171] which, it said, was strongly supported by those in the receivables financing industry. However, as with most of the other proposals by the Law Commission in their report on Company Security Interests, this proposal has not been enacted.[172]

8.2.3 Negotiable Instruments

Probably the simplest way in which the benefit of a loan contract can be transferred is if the obligation is embodied in an instrument. An instrument is a piece of paper which does not just evidence the obligation, but which entitles the holder (if it is a bearer instrument) or the indorsee (if an instrument payable to order) to payment. This means that the obligation represented by a bearer instrument can be transferred merely by delivery to another person. If the instrument is payable 'to order' it can only be transferred by delivery and indorsement (signing by the original payee). The payee can either sign and name the indorsee, in which case a signature continues to be required for transfer, or it can just sign ('indorse in blank') in which case the instrument becomes a bearer instrument.[173]

A negotiable instrument has an additional advantage. If it is effectively transferred to a bona fide purchaser, the transferee obtains two benefits. It obtains good title to the obligation even if the title of the transferor is defective, and it takes the obligation free of any equities which affected it in the hands of the transferor. An instrument is negotiable if it is recognised by mercantile usage as such:[174] so long as the volume of usage is established the courts will recognise a document as negotiable even if it is of recent origin.[175]

These two attributes (a convenient and easy manner of transfer, and negotiability) have meant that such instruments have played a significant part in corporate finance in the past, since they could be easily traded on open markets. A buyer would not have to investigate the provenance of the instrument, and could decide whether to buy purely on the basis of the credit risk of the promisor. For example, where companies received payment by bills of exchange or other similar instruments, these could be sold to banks or other financiers, who would easily be able to sell on the instrument in the money

---

[170]   Goode, n 99, 374–76.

[171]   Law Commission Report No 296, 'Company Security Interests', 4.35–4.40.

[172]   See page 301.

[173]   McKendrick, n 69, 513, 528. Note that in the case of instruments governed by the Bills of Exchange Act 1882, where an order bill is transferred by delivery only, without indorsement, the transferee obtains the title which the transferor had, and also the right to obtain an indorsement from the transferor (BEA s.31(4)).

[174]   *Edelstein v Schuler & Co* [1902] 2 KB 144, 154. Bills of exchange, promissory notes and cheques (which are now rarely negotiable) are specifically covered by the Bills of Exchange Act 1882 which provides that a bona fide purchaser is a 'holder in due course' and takes free of any defect of title of prior parties (ss 29 and 38(2)).

[175]   *Edelstein v Schuler & Co* [1902] 2 KB 144, 154. A modern example is the certificate of deposit, which is a certificate that money has been deposited with a bank. Certificates of deposit are actively traded on the money markets: see S Valdez, *An Introduction to Global Financial Markets*, 5th edn (Basingstoke, Palgrave Macmillan, 2007) 124.

markets.[176] As mentioned earlier[177] bonds issued by companies were usually in the form of bearer bonds, which enabled them to be traded easily.[178]

It will be seen that the benefits of negotiability are not available when the technique of assignment (discussed above) is used. An assignee (statutory or equitable) takes 'subject to equities'.[179] There appear to be at least two reasons for this. One is the basic principle of nemo dat quod non habet: the assignor cannot transfer more than it has.[180] This principle applies to all transfers of property (including tangible property) unless there is an exception. Negotiability is such an exception, and is justified by mercantile usage and the smooth operation of markets. Another reason is a (weaker) principle that assignment should not prejudice the position of the obligor, so that the obligor is in the same position vis-a-vis the assignee as it would have been vis-a-vis the assignor. An obligor under a negotiable instrument accepts, when undertaking the obligation, that it will be liable to any holder, and that equities and defences which exist between it and the original obligee will no longer apply.

8.2.4 Transfer of Stock

Stock is either transferred through CREST[181] or, if certificated, is transferred by the delivery up of the certificate to the issuer's registrar together with a transfer form.[182] The legal analysis of the transfer is not entirely clear. One view is that it takes place by novation, since, by accepting the registration, the company is agreeing that the transferee should take the place of the transferor.[183] Thus the transfer of registered debt securities is seen as the same as the transfer of shares. However, this analysis requires modification in relation to stock, where there is only one obligation which cannot be novated in the ordinary sense. Where the stock is created by deed poll, the process could be seen as analogous to novation, since although the company's obligation to the original stock-holder is not contractual, as it is effectuated by the deed poll, it is replaced by a new obligation to the new stockholder, and the company, by registering the transfer, agrees with this transfer.[184]

In relation to stock issued under a trust deed, the interest of the stockholder is merely equitable, since the legal interest to the debt is held by the trustee.[185] This may mean that there cannot be a novation, and the means of transfer is by assignment.[186] In either case,

---

[176] For detailed discussion of the law relating to bills of exchange, see N Elliot, J Odgers and J Phillips, *Byles on Bills of Exchange* (London, Sweet & Maxwell, 2007), AG Guest, *Chalmers and Guest on Bills of Exchange, Cheques and Promissory Notes* (London, Sweet & Maxwell, 2009); McKendrick, n 69, ch 19.

[177] 7.3.2.1.

[178] Hughes, n 21, 4.3.

[179] *Mangles v Dixon* (1852) 3 HLC 702, 731–32.

[180] See, for example, Smith, n 39, 13.47–13.51, citing *Phillips v Phillips* (1861) 4 De GF & J 208, 215–16.

[181] For analysis of CREST transfers, see below 8.2.6.

[182] G Fuller, *Corporate Borrowing: Law and Practice*, 4th edn (Bristol, Jordan Publishing Ltd, 2009) 3.3; Tolley Company Law Service C4002. If the instrument does not provide for the procedure for transfer, this is governed by the Stock Transfer Act 1963.

[183] J Benjamin, *Interests in Securities* (Oxford, Oxford University Press, 2000) 3.07; Tolley Company Law Service C4029.

[184] This analysis is not without problems, as it means that a new debt arises each time the stock is transferred which could have repercussions, for example, on insolvency, see Hughes, n 21, 4.3.

[185] 7.3.2.2.1.

[186] Although see below in relation to transfers of interests in intermediated securities: 8.2.5.

potentially the transferee takes subject to defects in title and equities. If the transfer takes place by assignment, the rule of priority would be that in *Dearle v Hall*.[187] Even this is not straightforward, since it is not clear whether notice of an assignment can be received by an issuer.[188] Such a notice cannot be received by an issuer of shares,[189] but this prohibition is based on the fact that no notice of trust shall be entered in the company's register.[190] However, in relation to stock held on trust the registrar does enter a notice of trust, and it does appear that this entry is effective in some way. Thus the reasoning applicable to shares may not apply here, although the position is likely to depend on the exact words of the trust deed. Further, it is not clear whether giving notice to the issuer is sufficient to gain priority under *Dearle v Hall* if the trustee is not also given notice, since what is actually being assigned is the right against the trustee and not a direct right against the issuer.[191] Even if no qualifying notice under *Dearle v Hall* is given, the transferee who registers may well succeed against someone who acquires an earlier unregistered interest, since the first transferee has failed to take any steps to prevent the original stockholder from transferring the stock to someone else, such as dispossessing him of the certificates or stock transfer form.[192]

In any event, in most cases a priority battle is unlikely to arise, since the trust deed will invariably provide that, as between the company and stockholder, a registered holder is treated as the absolute owner whose claim against the issuer is free from any equities or set-offs between the company and any holder, including the current holder.[193] Such a provision will have the effect of excluding the usual rule that an assignee takes subject to equities,[194] although it is clear from recent cases concerning the exclusion of the right of set-off that clear words must be used.[195] The effect of such a provision is that, despite the fact that the transfer is on the register rather than by delivery, and the interest of the transferor is equitable, the transaction is similar to the transfer of a negotiable instrument, in that a kind of contractual negotiability is conferred.[196]

---

[187] (1828) 3 Russ 1. As explained at pages 273–74 above, this rule is that priority is in the order that the debtor is notified of the assignments.

[188] Tolley Company Law Service C4029(2).

[189] *Société Générale de Paris v Walker* (1885) 11 App Cas 20. See 8.2.7 below.

[190] Companies Act 2006, s 126.

[191] Law of Property Act 1925, s 137(2) which requires notice to a trustee in respect of an equitable interest in securities, and *Re Dallas* [1904] 2 Ch 385. Fuller, *Corporate Borrowing: Law and Practice*, n 182, 15.18 notes that the trustee will usually have the right to inspect the register, and this may count as sufficient notice.

[192] Tolley Company Law Service C4029(2).

[193] Fuller, n 182, 3.7(d). This provision is also required if the security if traded through CREST, see Rule 7 paras 3.2 and 5.

[194] *Re Blakely Ordnance Co* (1867) 3 Ch App 154; *Re Agra and Masterman's Bank* (1866–7) 2 Ch App 391; *Hilger Analytical Ltd v Rank Precision Industries Ltd* [1984] BCLC 301.

[195] *Gilbert-Ash (Northern) Ltd v Modern Engineering (Bristol) Ltd* [1974] AC 689, 717; *BOC Group plc v Cention LLC* [1999] CLC 497. If the provisions in the trust deed comply with the CREST requirements then they will be effective: *Re Kaupthing Singer and Friedlander Ltd; Newcastle Building Society v Mill* [2009] EWHC 740 (Ch). Insolvency set-off cannot be excluded: *Halesowen Presswork and Assemblies Ltd v Westminster Bank Ltd* [1971] 1 QB 1.

[196] M Hughes, *Legal Principles in Banking and Structured Finance*, 2nd edn (Hayward's Heath, Tottel Publishing Ltd, 2006) 4.3. This does not mean, however, that all aspects of the law applicable to negotiable instruments also apply: *Re Kaupthing Singer and Friedlander Ltd; Newcastle Building Society v Mill* [2009] EWHC 740(Ch), [22].

8.2.5   Transfer of Intermediated Securities

As discussed above in chapter seven[197] most bonds are now issued in the form of a global immobilised note rather than as bearer bonds. The global note is in the form of a bearer bond, but it is not clear that it is a negotiable instrument, since it is never intended to be transferred.[198] In any event, what is traded is not the global note but the bondholders' entitlements, and these are co-ownership interests under a trust or sub-trust.[199] Such an interest cannot, of course, be a negotiable instrument: it is not transferred by delivery (there is nothing to deliver).[200] So how are bondholders' interests (held through an intermediary) transferred? And is such transfer in any way analogous to the transfer of a negotiable instrument? To take the simplest case, where the transferor and the transferee have accounts with the same intermediary, a debit entry is made in the account of the transferor and a credit entry in the account of the transferee. The effect of these entries is that the transferee has replaced the transferor (as regards the securities transferred) as a co-beneficiary under the trust whereby the intermediary holds its own co-ownership interest on trust for those of its account holders who own those particular securities. The book entries become more complicated when the parties have accounts with different intermediaries, since debit and credit entries must be made up the chain until two intermediaries have accounts with the same intermediary,[201] but the effect is the same: the transferor ceases to be a beneficiary in relation to that co-ownership interest and the transferee becomes a beneficiary. What is the best legal analysis of this event?

Clearly the transfer has not taken place by negotiation. Assignment also seems inappropriate, since it is hard to describe the transferee's interest as the same as the transferor's, although the two are connected. The most appropriate analysis would seem to be some sort of novation, in that the transferor's beneficial interest no longer exists and has been replaced by the new beneficial interest of the transferee. This is the conclusion reached by Joanna Benjamin.[202] It is further supported by the use of netting in the settlement of securities, so that there is rarely a straight 'transfer' from A to B.[203] Of course, to achieve novation the consent of the obligor is required.[204] However, since what is being 'transferred' is the interest of a beneficiary against a trustee, it is surely the trustee's consent which is required. Since the trustee/intermediary makes the book entries, this requirement is satisfied.[205] The ultimate obligor, the issuing company, has no knowledge or involvement in the transfer.

There are two potential problems which arise on this analysis. First, section 53(1)(c) of the Law of Property Act 1925 provides that a disposition of an equitable interest must be

---

[197]   7.3.2.3.2. Intermediated holdings of shares are discussed in 10.2.2.1 in the context of corporate governance.

[198]   Hughes, n 21, 4.4; McKendrick, n 69, 615.

[199]   See pages 338–39.

[200]   J Benjamin, 'Ease of Transfer and Security of Transfer in the Securities Markets' (2001) 16 *Journal of International Banking and Financial Law* 219, 221; Law Commission Updated Advice (May 2008) 5.39.

[201]   For a worked example, see L Gullifer, 'Protection of Investors in Intermediated Securities' in J Armour and J Payne (eds), *Rationality in Company Law* (Oxford, Hart Publishing, 2009), 232–33. This is in the context of shares held with an intermediary, but the principle is the same for debt securities.

[202]   Benjamin, *Interests in Securities*, n 183, 3.27–3.33. See also Tolley Company Law Service C4029(3).

[203]   See Gullifer, 'Protection of Investors in Intermediated Securities', n 201, 232–33.

[204]   See pages 370–71.

[205]   Law Commission 'Issues Affecting Transferees of Intermediated Securities' (Third Seminar) at http://www.lawcom.gov.uk/docs/investment_securities_seminar_paper_3.pdf (accessed 13 November 2009) 1.33.

in writing and signed by the person disposing of the interest. It should first be noted that this provision does not apply where the transaction is a financial collateral arrangement.[206] It is not at all clear whether the transfer of an interest in intermediated securities as described above is a 'disposition' within the section. On one view, it could be argued that what is happening is that a new interest is created[207] (or that the transferee joins the 'group' of equitable co-owners of the pool of securities held by the intermediary by way of succession rather than disposition) and on either analysis this is not a disposition.[208] These arguments are perhaps bolstered by the fact that a straight 'transfer' rarely happens so that unless the transferor and transferee both have accounts with the same intermediary, the operation of the tiered system, and in particular the occurrence of netting, means that the intermediary of the transferee will make a credit entry without knowing where the 'securities' it is crediting come from. However, there is very considerable uncertainty about the issue, as the word 'disposition' is not defined in the Act.[209]

One rationale of the rule in section 53(1)(c) is that, where an equitable interest is transferred, the trustee ceases to owe duties to the transferor and owes them to the transferee,[210] and so any requirement which enables the trustee to discover this change in duties is helpful (although it would be more consistent with the rationale if written notice to the trustee were required, as section 136 of the Law of Property Act 1925 requires in relation to assignments).[211] This rationale does not apply in relation to transfers of intermediated securities, in that the intermediary who is the trustee in relation to the transferee is well aware of the transfer, since it makes the credit entry in the transferee's account (similarly, the transferor's intermediary is aware that it is no longer a trustee by making the debit entry). This argument could lead to the conclusion that the records of the intermediaries are sufficient 'writing' for the purposes of section 53(1)(c).[212] However, for the avoidance of doubt it is generally recognised that legislative reform would be desirable.[213]

The second problem is more complex.[214] It will be recalled that the advantages of negotiability are, first, that the transferee obtains good title even if the transferor's title is

---

[206]   Financial Collateral Arrangements (No 2) Regulations 2003, SI 2003/3226, reg 4(2) and *Mills v Sportsdirect.com Retail Ltd* [2010] EWHC 1072 (Ch).

[207]   The declaration of a new trust is not a 'disposition' under s.53(1)(c): A Hudson, *Equity and Trusts*, 5th edn (Abingdon, Routledge-Cavendish, 2008) 255–56.

[208]   Benjamin, n 183, 72 at fns 48 and 51. While setting out these arguments, Benjamin herself thinks that the position is uncertain.

[209]   The section was considered in *Grey v Inland Revenue Commissioners* [1960] AC 1, where the House of Lords expressed the view that 'disposition' was to be given its 'natural' meaning (at 13).

[210]   Another rationale may be to protect those entitled to property from hidden transactions: see Hudson, *Equity and Trusts*, n 207, 245.

[211]   McFarlane, n 75, 120.

[212]   A Austin-Peters, *Custody of Investments: Law and Practice* (Oxford, Oxford University Press, 2000) 69.

[213]   Benjamin, n 183, 3.41; Financial Markets Law Committee paper 'Property Interests in Investment Securities' issue 3 (July 2004) at www.fmlc.org/papers.html 6.9; B McFarlane and R Stevens, 'Interests in Securities: Practical Problems and Conceptual Solutions' in L Gullifer and J Payne (eds), *Intermediated Securities: Legal Problems and Practical Issues*, (Oxford, Hart Publishing, 2010) 54–55; Law Commission Further Updated Advice 4.53. See article 11(2) Geneva Securities Convention 2009 which disapplies all formalities required for a credit to a securities account to be effective. Note also that s 53(1)(c) is disapplied in relation to transfers through the CREST system (considered below 8.2.6.): Uncertificated Securities Regulations 2001 Reg 38(5).

[214]   For detailed analysis of this issue, see Law Commission 'Issues Affecting Transferees of Intermediated Securities' (Third Seminar) at http://www.lawcom.gov.uk/docs/investment_securities_seminar_paper_3.pdf (accessed 13 November 2009) 1.117–164; Law Commission, 'The UNIDROIT Convention in Intermediated Securities Further Updated Advice to HM Treasury' (May 2008), part 5; McFarlane and Stevens, 'Interests in Securities, n 213, 52–54.

defective and, second, the transferee takes free from equities. In the absence of the negotiability exception to the *nemo dat* rule, a transferee can only obtain as good a title as that of the transferor.[215] If, for example, a transfer of intermediated securities is not authorised by the transferor, the transferor will have a personal claim against its intermediary who made the unauthorised transfer (which amounts to a breach of trust by the intermediary), but it may also seek to assert an equitable tracing claim against the equitable interest of the transferee.[216] One possible defence to such a claim is that the recipient transferee is a bona fide purchaser of the legal interest without notice of the breach (the 'equity's darling' defence). However, since the transferee only has an equitable interest, this defence is not available.[217] It has been suggested that this result, which means that those holding securities with an intermediary are in a different position from those holding bearer securities,[218] or those holding through the CREST system,[219] or those registered as the holder of securities,[220] is unsatisfactory and that statutory reform is required.[221] It should, however, be pointed out that in practice such a tracing claim would be rare. First, the transferor has a good personal claim against its intermediary, which it is probably more convenient to bring if the intermediary is solvent.[222] Second, because of the use of netting in the settlement system, it is often difficult or impossible to track the exact recipient of 'transferred' securities. However, even a small amount of legal risk can cause systemic problems in certain circumstances and so legislative reform is desirable.[223]

To the extent that the transferee takes subject to defects in the title of the transferor, it is also arguable that it takes subject to equities (such as vitiating factors or set-off[224]).[225] If, as suggested above, the transfer takes place by novation, then this may not be the case.[226] In any event, most bonds provide contractually that the holder takes free from all equities

---

[215]   This is not necessarily the case where there is a novation, since the new obligation undertaken by the new intermediary is not necessarily the same as that given up by the old intermediary, but the position is not clear.

[216]   Benjamin, n 183, 3.59 and 2.53–2.55. Since equity will trace into substitute assets as well as the original assets, the fact that the transfer takes place by novation will not prevent such a claim arising.

[217]   Benjamin, n 183, 3.64; Law Commission Further Updated Advice 5.40–5.43. *cf* McFarlane and Stevens, n 213, 54.

[218]   Which are negotiable instruments.

[219]   See 8.2.6.

[220]   These are the legal owners, so that the defence does apply. For further protection of transferees of registered shares, see Law Commission Further Updated Advice, n 214, 5.24 and E Micheler, 'Farewell Quasi-Negotiability? Legal Title and Transfer of Shares in a Paperless World' [2002] *Journal of Business Law* 358 and 'The Legal Nature of Securities: Inspirations from Comparative Law' in L Gullifer and J Payne (eds), *Intermediated Securities: Legal Problems and Practical Issues* (Oxford, Hart Publishing, 2010) ch. 5

[221]   Law Commission: Further Updated Advice, n 214, 5.67; Financial Markets Law Commission, 'Property Interests in Investment Securities' (July 2004) Issue 3 at www.fmlc.org/papers.html, 6.8.

[222]   Intermediaries are regulated under the Financial Services Authority and so in theory should not become insolvent (see Law Commission: Further Updated Advice, n 214, 5.5) although the recent experience of Lehman Brothers belies this point.

[223]   The UNDROIT Convention addresses this point in detail: see Articles 18 and 19; L Gullifer, 'Ownership of Securities' in L Gullifer and J Payne (eds), *Intermediated Securities: Legal Problems and Practical Issues*, (Oxford, Hart Publishing, 2010) 26–30 and C Mooney and H Kanda 'Core Issues under the UNDROIT (Geneva) Convention on Intermediated Securities: Views from the United States and Japan' in L Gullifer and J Payne (eds), *Intermediated Securities: Legal Problems and Practical Issues* (Oxford, Hart Publishing, 2010) 94–119.

[224]   For a definition of equities to which assignees take subject, see Smith, n 39, 13.33–13.37.

[225]   Law Commission: Further Advice, n 214, 5.47, where it is argued that the rule in *Phillips v Phillips* [2007] All ER (D) 178 (that a bona fide transferee of an equitable interest does not take subject to equities) does not apply to choses in action including intermediated securities.

[226]   See also E Micheler, 'Farewell Quasi-Negotiability? Legal Title and Transfer of Shares in a Paperless World?' [2002] *Journal of Business Law* 358, 360.

between the company and any existing holder. This is a similar provision to that included in registered stock.[227] Where the bonds are held through intermediaries, the provision would have to make it clear that 'holder' included 'account holder'.[228] It is clear that a provision excluding set-off can be effective,[229] since the party who would otherwise assert the set-off would be the issuer, who is a party to the agreement. However, it would be more difficult to provide contractually for each transferee to take free from defects in title, as this would have to bind successive bondholders so that each was prevented from pursuing any proprietary claim against transferees. Thus, as discussed above, the protection can only be given by legislation.

8.2.6 Transfers via CREST

If debt securities are dematerialised and held through the CREST system (but not through an intermediary)[230] they in effect become registered securities, since the CREST register is the root of title.[231] Until fairly recently money market instruments, which were bearer securities, were settled through the Central Moneymarkets Office.[232] Such securities have now become 'eligible debt securities' and can be held in a dematerialised form and traded through the CREST system.[233] The transfer of such securities through CREST takes place, as with all transfers through CREST, by an entry in the CREST register, which has the effect of transferring legal title. Although it is not entirely clear, it would seem that this transfer takes place by novation. When certificated registered shares were transferred by entries in the company's register, the conventional analysis was that they were transferred by novation.[234] On the basis that all that has changed in relation to the transfer of shares with the introduction of the CREST system is the location of the register (the definitive register is now that of CREST), it would seem to be arguable that the explanation for the transfer of shares through CREST is also that of novation. If that is the case, then since debt securities, including eligible debt securities, are traded through CREST in exactly the same way as shares, the novation analysis would also apply to them.

It should be pointed out that the novation analysis in relation to shares is not universally accepted. It has been argued, in fact, that it can no longer apply as the company cannot be said to agree to a novation, since it is not involved in the transfer process.[235] The argument is then made that this means that the transferee cannot take free from equities,

---

[227] See page 391.

[228] As with the sample clause at 1.1.12 of Financial Markets Law Committee, Issue 62 'Trustee Exemption Clauses'.

[229] For a discussion of the effectiveness of such provisions, see page 182.

[230] This is common for some short-term bonds traded on the money market: see Tolley Company Law Service C4009. For a brief description of the CREST system see page 328, and for a more detailed discussion see Tolley Company Law Service, CREST ([C8001] et seq).

[231] Uncertificated Securities Regulations 2001 (SI 2001/3755) reg 24(2) and (3).

[232] Benjamin, n 183, 9.72; M Evans, 'Moving to a Dematerialised Capital Market' (2003) 18 *Journal of International Banking Law and Regulation* 121.

[233] This is the effect of the amendments to the Uncertificated Securities Regulations 2001 made by the Uncertificated Securities (Amendment) (Eligible Debt Securities) Regulations 2003 (SI 2003/1633).

[234] E Micheler, *Property in Securities: A Comparative Study* (Cambridge, Cambridge University Press, 2007) chapter 2.1; RR Pennington, *Company Law*, 8th edn (Oxford University Press, 2001) 398–99; Benjamin, n 183, 3.05.

[235] E Micheler, 'Farewell Quasi-Negotiability? Legal Title and Transfer of Shares in a Paperless World' [2002] *Journal of Business Law* 358 at 363; Micheler, *Property in Securities*, n 234, 5.2.3.

as the company has not agreed to waive its rights to assert equities against that transferee.[236] This then forms the basis of a new theory that shares are quasi-negotiable because of the importance that shares are freely transferable.[237]

It is submitted that the novation analysis is acceptable at least when applied to debt securities which are traded through CREST. First, a security can only be an eligible debt security if the terms of issue provide that its units may only be issued in uncertificated form.[238] Although in theory securities originally issued as bearer securities can be converted to uncertificated form, this is very rare, and in any event requires the participation of the issuer.[239] Thus, the issuer must be taken to have agreed in advance to the transfer of securities through the CREST system, and, thus, to novation (if that is the legal method by which such transfer is effected). Secondly, for a security other than a share to comply with the CREST rules for entry into the system, it must be 'transferable free from any equity, set-off or counterclaim between the issuer and the original or any intermediate holder of the security'.[240]

This provision in the CREST rules means that one of the advantages of negotiability is maintained when a debt security is transferred through CREST. When it was proposed to include transfers of money market instruments in the CREST system, those consulted made it very clear that it was important to keep all the benefits of negotiability.[241] The other aspect of negotiability, that the transferee takes free from any defect of title of the transferor, has not been dealt with expressly in the legislation or the CREST Rules as it was thought to be sufficiently covered by the existing provisions.[242] The dangers were considered to be those of a forged or otherwise defective transfer instruction (so that an unauthorised transfer was made), and adverse claims by third parties. The former is covered under Regulation 35[243] in that where there is a 'properly authenticated dematerialised instruction' the purported transferor cannot deny that it was authorised, and an addressee without actual notice of a defect can accept that an instruction was sent with

---

[236]   Ibid.

[237]   E Micheler, 'Farewell Quasi-Negotiability? Legal Title and Transfer of Shares in a Paperless World' [2002] *Journal of Business Law* 358; Micheler, n 234, chs 5 and 6.

[238]   Uncertificated Securities Regulations 2001 (SI 2001/3755) reg 3 (as amended by the Uncertificated Securities (Amendment) (Eligible Debt Securities) Regulations 2003 (SI 2003/1633).

[239]   Ibid, reg 33.

[240]   CREST Rule 7 3.2. Normally this would be contractually incorporated into the terms of the security and is included in the pro forma terms for an eligible debt security published by the Bank of England (see http://www.bankofengland.co.uk/markets/money/edsterms.pdf at 6.4): if not, it would clearly be implied. Both statutory and equitable set-off are included: see *Re Kaupthing Singer and Friedlander Ltd; Newcastle Building Society v Mill* [2009] EWHC 740 (Ch).

[241]   Bank of England consultation paper 'The Future of Money Market Instruments' (November 1999), appendix II; Bank of England consultation paper 'The Future of Money Market Instruments: Next Steps' (March 2000), 11; Bank of England interim report 'The Future of Money Market Instruments' (January 2001) 6 (proposal (v).

[242]   'The Future of Money Market Instruments' (November 1999), n 241, appendix II, including notes of an advice by Richard Sykes QC on this very point. *Cf* the view of Benjamin, who argues that, as the original regulations were not designed to replicate negotiability, they only achieve integrity of the system itself but do not prevent reversal of a transfer under the operation of the general law, for example, the law of tracing: Benjamin, n 183, 213 at fn 131.

[243]   Uncertificated Securities Regulations 2001 (SI 2001/3755) reg 3 (as amended by the Uncertificated Securities (Amendment) (Eligible Debt Securities) Regulations 2003 (SI 2003/1633).

authority.[244] As regards the latter, competing claims could (in theory) be either legal or equitable. Since the CREST register is the definitive record of legal title,[245] a competing legal claim cannot arise: only the registered legal owner can issue the relevant transfer instruction. There could, however, be competing equitable claims, since these cannot be registered on the CREST register.[246] The transferee, however, will have the protection of the equity's darling defence unless it has notice of the competing claim: this is a position similar to where there is a negotiable instrument.[247]

8.2.7   Transfers of Shares[248]

As discussed in chapter two,[249] once a shareholder has purchased shares in a company, it will generally only be able to exit if the company buys back the shares or if the shareholder finds a purchaser to buy the shares. In practical terms, companies will only infrequently repurchase shares, and will only do so if the shares were issued as redeemable shares or if the rules regarding the purchase of shares by a company[250] are observed. In either event the capital maintenance rules discussed in chapter four must be observed.[251] If a shareholder wishes to realise its investment, the ability to transfer the shares will therefore be important.

Broadly, share transfers involve two stages. First the buyer and seller conclude a sales contract in which they agree the price of the shares and the other terms of the agreement. The second stage is then the transfer of the shares to the buyer, and the buyer becomes the owner of the shares. However, when considering transfers of shares it is helpful to separate the discussion of transfers in relation to different sizes of company, with small private companies at one end of the spectrum, and large publicly listed companies at the other.

In a small private company, as discussed in chapter two, the importance of shares is not predominantly as a source of financing for the company, but rather as a device for allocating control within the company. As a result the transfer of shares in such companies will often be subject to restrictions.[252] Common restrictions include a requirement that the permission of the board is obtained before the shares can be transferred, or that the shares are offered first to the existing shareholders of the company.[253] Shares that are not publicly traded have no market as such and therefore agreeing the price of shares in a private company is not generally straightforward.

---

[244]   Ibid, reg 35 (2)(4) and (5). The requirement of actual notice may even put the transferee in a better position than where there is a negotiable instrument, since this may be narrower than the notice required to prevent a transferee being a holder in due course.

[245]   Ibid, reg 24.

[246]   Ibid, reg 23(3).

[247]   Ibid, reg 35(4). See further, 'The Future of Money Market Instruments' (November 1999), n 241, appendix II, advice of Richard Sykes QC.

[248]   See generally P Davies, *Gower and Davies Principles of Modern Company Law*, 8th edn, (London, Sweet & Maxwell, 2008) ch 27.

[249]   See page 12.

[250]   See 4.4.2.

[251]   See 4.4.

[252]   Davies, *Gower and Davies Principles of Modern Company Law*, n 248, 942–45.

[253]   This is a form of pre-emption, but these pre-emption rights arise only on transfer and only bind the selling shareholder as a matter of agreement between the parties (albeit that the agreement may be contained in the articles of association). This may be compared to the pre-emption rights discussed in 4.3.1 which arise when the company issues new shares, and bind the company as a result of statute.

Companies issuing registered shares must keep a register containing the names of the members.[254] In relation to non-listed shares (ie shares in private companies and public companies whose shares are not listed on the London Stock Exchange) the shares are generally in certificated form and every shareholder will, in addition to having their name in the share register of the company, have a paper certificate evidencing their shareholding.[255] To transfer the shares the seller completes and signs a transfer form and delivers this together with the share certificate to the buyer. The buyer then lodges the certificate with the company to have his name entered on to the share register.[256] Only once the buyer has his name entered onto the register of members does he become a member of the company. The general view is that there is then a novation rather than an assignment of the transferor's rights to the transferee.[257] However, it should be noted that the beneficial interest in the shares may well already have passed before this point.[258]

However, this raises an important issue, namely the difference between legal and equitable title to the shares. The process described above, the end result of which is that the buyer's name is entered on the company's register of members, deals with a transfer of legal title. However, it is perfectly possible for shares to be the subject of a trust, either arising from an express declaration of trust or arising by operation of law, as described above. Section 126 of the Companies Act 2006 makes it clear, however, that the company is unaffected by any trust that exists in relation to its shares. The company's relationship is with the person who is registered as a member of the company, who is the legal owner of the shares. The purpose of this provision is to preserve security of title (broadly, it is clear that someone owns a share because they are entered on the register of members) and security of transfer. This latter point is important. The fact that companies can remain unaffected by trusts of their shares is important for the efficient transfer of company shares, otherwise any transfer of shares which a company has to register might result in the company being sued over some breach of duty relating to the transfer. A transfer of beneficial interest in the shares will, therefore require an agreement to sell and a transfer, but will not involve the company's register. The beneficial owner has a relationship with its trustee and not with the company. The trustee will have to account to the beneficiary for any dividends it receives, and it is a well-established principle that the beneficial owner of shares, if absolutely entitled as against the registered owner, can instruct the registered owner how to deal with the shares, and how votes should be cast.[259]

By contrast, in publicly listed companies, the holding of shares is predominantly for the purpose of investment (on the part of the shareholder) and finance-raising (on the part of the company. One of the requirements of the London Stock Exchange means that to be listed shares must be freely transferable,[260] and of course this secondary market makes

---

[254]   Companies Act 2006, s 113.

[255]   It is possible for non-listed shares to be held in uncertificated form but this is rare. If uncertificated the shares have to be freely transferable: Uncertificated Securities Regulations 2001 (as amended), regs 14–16.

[256]   Even entry onto the register is only prima facie evidence of title (Companies Act 2006, s 127) and rectification of the register is possible: Davies, n 248, 957–58.

[257]   For discussion see page 395.

[258]   The delivery of the signed transfer form and certificate to the seller and payment by the buyer is generally accepted to effect a transfer of the beneficial interest, and the beneficial interest may even pass before that point, on the agreement to sell, if that agreement is held to be specifically enforceable: *Michaels v Harley House (Marylebone) Ltd* [1997] 2 BCLC 166; *Kilnoore Ltd (in liq) Unidare plc v Cohen* [2006] 1 Ch 489.

[259]   *Kirby v Wilkins* [1929] 2 Ch 444, 454 per Romer J.

[260]   FSA Handbook, Listing Rules, LR 2.2.4(1).

investment in shares in a listed company attractive and this is one of the reasons why companies choose to list in the first place.[261] The transfer is still a two stage process. However, to sell listed shares an investor will generally enlist the services of a broker who will sell the shares through the electronic trading system operated by the London Stock Exchange or by making contact with another financial services provider.

In contrast to the paper-based system described above, listed shares are now generally dematerialised (ie uncertificated) and as a result although the buyer's name will again be entered on the shareholder register, this settlement process is carried out electronically through CREST, which maintains the register for uncertificated shares.[262] The CREST register is the record of legal title. Only the registered legal owner can issue the relevant transfer instruction.[263] As regards transfers of shares via CREST, much of the discussion in 8.2.6 will be relevant.

Of course, shares in listed companies are frequently beneficially owned. There are a number of reasons why this might be the case. First, as with private companies, the shares could be made the subject of a traditional trust, although this is not the most common reason for the shares in listed companies to be held beneficially. Second, as with bonds,[264] shares are often held indirectly through intermediaries, although it should be noted that there is no immobilised global share akin to the global immobilised note described in chapter seven. The third reason arises from the shift from certificated to uncertificated issues and transfers described above. Dematerialisation does not itself affect the direct relationship between investor and issuer. Investors generally have the option of holding an account directly or through an intermediary. However, in some instances there will be no choice, for instance shares held in ISAs or PEPs must be held via an intermediary. Even where there is choice, small investors may feel that it is simpler to vest the legal title to their shares in a nominee who is a member of the system and then hold their shares indirectly. Where the transfer occurs via an intermediary much of the discussion in 8.2.5 dealing with transfers of intermediated securities will be relevant.

Additionally, many financial products, such as pensions and unit trusts, will involve individuals investing in the stock market via a financial institution which holds the legal title to the shares in question. In the case of pension funds, for example, the pension scheme will usually be constituted as a trust, separate from the sponsoring entity. The beneficiaries of the scheme are, collectively, the ultimate beneficial owners of the scheme's equity investors.[265] In these circumstances the private investor will hold indirectly via an intermediary, and indeed it is likely that the intermediary is holding for very many private investors in this way.

Section 126 of the Companies Act 2006 applies equally to listed companies and the beneficial owner prima facie has a relationship with its trustee rather than with the

---

[261] See 9.2.1.

[262] For discussion see 8.2.6.

[263] See page 397.

[264] For a general account of intermediated holdings, see pages 328 and 337, and for discussion of the transfer of intermediated securities see 8.2.5.

[265] Generally the trustees will contract out the investment of the pension contributions to specialist fund managers. The contract with the fund manager is likely to give the manager the right to vote the shares it purchases on behalf of the fund (although the trustees may reserve to themselves the right to take voting decisions). In general the fund manager will not hold the shares it purchases on behalf of the fund but, rather, they will be held by a separate custodian company. However, in some circumstances the intermediary will engage a custodian to buy the shares, and to hold legal title to those shares.

company. The increase in the number of listed shares held via an intermediary, and the consequences of this for the investor are explored further in chapter ten.[266]

8.3 Structures which have a Similar Effect to Transfer

8.3.1 Sub-participation[267]

Another method of 'transfer' that is often used in the context of an interest in a syndicated loan, is sub-participation. This is not, strictly speaking, a transfer, since the original lender retains exactly the same legal position vis-a-vis the borrower. Instead, new contractual rights between the original lender ('lender') and the new participant ('participant') are created. Since no interest is transferred, the contract between the lender and the participant can be on any terms they wish. There are, however, two main forms. Either the participant pays the lender a sum of money (equivalent to the 'price' of the debt), and the lender agrees to account to the participant for any money it receives from the borrower (this is called a 'funded sub-participation') or no money is paid by the participant, but it agrees to accept the risk of non-payment by the borrower, by giving a guarantee or indemnity of the borrower's obligations to the lender (this is called a 'risk participation').[268] This latter structure has now, in practice, largely been replaced by the use of credit derivatives.[269]

The precise legal nature of each agreement is, of course, a function of the exact words used[270] but the usual structure is that there are two back-to-back contracts: the original loan contract between the lender and the borrower, and the contract between the lender and participant. The participant is therefore merely an unsecured creditor of the lender and has no proprietary interest in the loan or the proceeds.[271] The result of this is that the participant takes on the credit risk of both the borrower and the lender. If the borrower does not pay, the participant does not get paid, and will only receive whatever the lender receives in the borrower's insolvency. If the lender is insolvent, as the participant has no proprietary right to proceeds of the loan already or subsequently received by the lender, all it has is an unsecured claim to the amount of those proceeds, and has no right to sue the borrower direct.[272]

---

[266] See 10.2.2, especially 10.2.2.2.

[267] This method of transferring the risk and benefit of a loan without changing the contractual relationship between the lender and borrower is that used where English law applies. In the US a different legal method is used, called 'loan participation', which has very similar practical effects. For a discussion of the legal position in the US see Mugasha, n 7, ch 6.

[268] Mugasha, n 7, 7.04–7.05.

[269] Fuller, n 182, 15.41; Mugasha, n 7, 7.02. See 8.3.2 below, and, for discussion of credit default swaps, see 5.3.3.

[270] *Lloyds TSB Bank plc v Clarke* [2002] UKPC 27, [14]. If the parties make it clear that a sub-participation structure is intended, the court will not recharacterise the transaction as an assignment.

[271] *Lloyds TSB Bank plc v Clarke* [2002] UKPC 27, especially [16] approving the description of a sub-participation agreement by Professor Wood, of which the most up to date version is Wood, *International Loans, Bonds, Guarantees, Legal Opinions*, n 7, 9–039.

[272] Wood, n 7, 9–039. Note, though, that in a risk participation where the participant guarantees the loan, the participant might, on payment under the guarantee, obtain rights against the borrower by way of subrogation.

In most circumstances, the additional credit risk of the lender adds little extra risk to the transaction, since the lender is likely to be a bank or a stable financial institution. However, in times of financial uncertainty, when banks can become insolvent, this can become a concern.[273] Several possible ways for a participant to protect itself have been discussed. One possibility is for the participant to take a charge over the loan or the proceeds of the loan.[274] A charge over the loan itself would, without more, normally give the participant a charge over the proceeds as well, which would mean that it would have priority over unsecured creditors of the lender in relation to proceeds which had been paid or which continued to be paid during insolvency.[275] There are, however, a number of potential problems with this structure. First, the obligation secured by the charge is the lender's obligation to pay the participant under the sub-participation agreement. This obligation only arises when the borrower pays the lender, at which point the subject matter of the charge (the loan) ceases to exist. There is, therefore, no equity of redemption.[276] Arguably, if the proceeds are also charged, this objection is less strong, as once the proceeds are received the obligation to account has arisen, and can be fulfilled by the payment of any money the lender has. There is, therefore, an equity of redemption in the proceeds. There is thus more sense in taking a charge over the proceeds alone, although until the borrower makes the first payment there is no secured obligation (and therefore no executed consideration so the charge cannot be enforceable in equity) nor is there any subject matter of the charge.[277] Further, the ability of the lender to use the proceeds for its own purposes and to pay the participant the money due from any source means that if there is a charge, it is a floating one.[278] If the arrangement is not held to be a charge, it is likely either to be completely ineffective or to be characterised as an absolute transfer of

This issue is not without difficulty. The guarantee is (usually) given without the consent of the borrower and in these circumstances a surety has no right of indemnity as such (*Owen v Tate* [1976] QB 402; M Hughes, 'A Commentary on the Recent Report by the Financial Law Panel on the Secondary Debt Market' (1997) 12 *Journal of International Banking and Financial Law* 75. However, a surety might have a right of subrogation under the Mercantile Law Amendment Act 1856 s 5, although if this does not apply it is not clear that subrogation would apply under equitable principles, see Gullifer, n 14, 8–08.

[273]   For example, in 2008 the Loan Market Association produced a discussion paper 'LMA Sub-Participation Agreements and Grantor Insolvency' (C Winkworth and L Watt, Richards Kibbe & Orbe LLP available at http://www.lma.eu.com/uploads/files/RK_O%20paper.pdf) which has since been the subject of discussion in legal journals: see M Daley, 'Funded Participations – Mitigation of Grantor Credit Risk' (2009) 24 *Journal of International Banking Law and Regulation* 288.

[274]   Wood, n 7, 9–039; Loan Market Association discussion paper 'LMA Sub-Participation Agreements and Grantor Insolvency' (C Winkworth and L Watt, Richards Kibbe & Orbe LLP available at http://www.lma.eu.com/uploads/files/RK_O%20paper.pdf) 2, where it is suggested that the charge would be in favour of a security trustee. See also Fuller, n 182, 301, fn 107.

[275]   The insolvency of the lender will not stop the borrower making payments to the lender, which, in the absence of a charge, would be part of the lender's assets for distribution to all its creditors.

[276]   M Daley, 'Funded Participations – Mitigation of Grantor Credit Risk', (2009) 24 *Journal of International Banking Law and Regulation* 288, 289.

[277]   For a discussion of whether there can be a charge over purely future property, see 6.3.2.1.

[278]   This seems reasonably clear in the light of *Re Spectrum Plus* [2005] UKHL 41: the question is raised by Daley at the end of his paper (at 289–90). The participant would therefore lose priority to preferential creditors and the ring-fenced fund: see 3.3.1.2 and would require registration. Some of these provisions would be disapplied if the charge was seen as a security financial collateral arrangement (see pages 224–25 above). While this would not be the case at the moment, it might well be the case (depending on who the lender was) once the Financial Collateral Arrangements (No 2) Regulations 2003 are amended to take into account the recent amendments to the Financial Collateral Directive (see page 225).

the loan. This is usually not what the parties to the transaction intended, since the reason for using the sub-participation structure is usually that an assignment has adverse consequences.[279]

If the lender has other borrowings, then, if these are secured, the chargee is likely to lose priority to earlier security holders, or, if unsecured, the grant of the charge is likely to be in breach of a negative pledge clause.[280] Such a charge is likely to be registrable, especially if it is floating, unless it is a security financial collateral arrangement. It has also been suggested that if the charge is given when the lender is in financial difficulties, it could be vulnerable to being set aside as a preference.[281] However, the giving of security for a contemporaneous or subsequent advance is not usually seen as a preference,[282] so that, at least to the extent that the charge secures the lender's obligation to pay in relation to payments not yet received from the borrower, it would not be a preference. Nor, if the charge were floating, would it be vulnerable to being set aside under section 245 of the Insolvency Act 1986.[283] These problems in taking a charge appear to have led to it being a very rare occurrence in practice.[284]

Another way for a participant to protect itself against the credit risk of the lender is to include a provision in the sub-participation agreement giving it the right to request a transfer of the loan, either to itself or to a third party,[285] such a transfer taking place by way of an assignment or a novation. The problem with this course of action is that if there is a reason not to assign or novate the loan in the first place, for example, because the borrower's consent is required, then this reason may still prevent this course of action even if the lender is in financial difficulties.

As has been seen, the position of a sub-participant is considerably weaker than that of an assignee or a party to whom a loan has been novated.[286] One might, then, wonder why a participant would enter into such a structure. One reason may be that the loan contains restrictions on assignment or novation. The difficulties that such restrictions cause have been discussed earlier, and one way of bypassing them is to transfer the credit risk without transferring the loan, by means of a sub-participation or credit derivative.[287] Other reasons for using sub-participation include tax or regulatory disadvantages to the sub-participant if it became the 'lender of record'[288] or practical reasons, for example, where the loan is the subject of arbitration proceedings which require the lender of record to be registered.[289]

---

[279]   See discussion below.

[280]   Wood, n 7, 9–039. This may also be the case if the earlier borrowing is secured by a floating charge. Note that the sub-participation agreement itself is likely to contain a promise by the lender not to create any security interest in the loan.

[281]   Wood, n 7, 9–039. For a brief discussion of preferences, see page 104.

[282]   R Goode, *Principles of Corporate Insolvency Law*, 3rd edn (London, Sweet & Maxwell, 2005) 11–82.

[283]   See page 103.

[284]   Wood, n 7, 9–039. Fuller, n 182, 301 at fn 107.

[285]   Loan Market Association discussion paper, 'LMA Sub-Participation Agreements and Grantor Insolvency' (C Winkworth and L Watt, Richards Kibbe & Orbe LLP available at http://www.lma.eu.com/uploads/files/RK_O%20paper.pdf) 3.

[286]   For other weaknesses, see Wood, n 7, 9–040–9–047.

[287]   Goode, n 99, 374; Hughes, n 21.

[288]   Loan Market Association discussion paper,See 'LMA Sub-Participation Agreements and Grantor Insolvency' (C Winkworth and L Watt, Richards Kibbe & Orbe LLP) available at http://www.lma.eu.com/uploads/files/RK_O%20paper.pdf) 3.

[289]   M Hughes, 'Legal Liability In The Secondary Debt Market' (1997) 12 *Journal of International Banking and Financial Law* 469, who gives such an example where the registration process was complicated and expensive.

If the loan is syndicated, obviously the sub-participant does not acquire any rights against the agent bank or direct rights against the borrower. However, whether the loan is syndicated or not, the participant could acquire contractual rights against the lender to direct the conduct of enforcement or other administration of the loan. Thus, where an anti-assignment clause is inserted to protect the borrower against someone other than the lender having control over the enforcement of the debt,[290] sub-participation, while not being a breach of the clause, can still have adverse effects on the borrower.[291]

8.3.2 Credit Derivatives

A similar effect to a risk sub-participation can be achieved by the use of a credit default swap. Like sub-participation, this cannot be seen as a transfer of the loan obligation itself, but involves the transfer of credit risk, so that risk is divorced from legal ownership. As with a sub-participation, this can have an effect on the way that the lender behaves vis-a-vis the borrower. Credit default swaps are discussed in detail in chapter five.[292]

8.3.3 Securitisation[293]

Securitisation is a technique which can be used either by a company or a lender to transfer the credit risk of receivables (either trade receivables in the case of a company, or loan receivables, or even bonds, in the case of a lender), and/or to receive immediate finance for rights to payment in the future. 'Traditional' or 'true sale' securitisation is where the receivables are transferred to a special purpose vehicle ('SPV') in exchange for a price, and the SPV issues securities to the market to fund the acquisition.[294] The payments on the securities are funded by the income from the receivables, now owned by the SPV, and the securities are secured by a charge over the receivables for the benefit of a security trustee, who is usually also trustee of the issue.[295] The SPV (and therefore the holders of the securities) takes the risk that the receivables will not be paid, but is otherwise 'insolvency remote' so that it incurs no other risks which might render it insolvent. Therefore, as it has no employees the actual administration of the receivables is usually carried out by the company which originated the transaction.[296] An important feature of securitisation is that the securities are usually 'tranched'. This means that there is a pre-set order of payment to different groups of investors in the securities. The senior ranking tranches are paid first, followed by lower ranking tranches, which are often called 'mezzanine notes' followed by 'junior' notes (sometimes called 'equity' as the risk is analogous to an equity

---

[290] See pages 378–79.
[291] M Hughes, 'Legal Liability In The Secondary Debt Market' (1997) 12 *Journal of International Banking and Financial Law* 469.
[292] 5.3.3.
[293] See pages 35–36. For a detailed discussion, see Fuller, n 182, ch 7; G Fuller, *The Law and Practice of International Capital Markets*, (London, LexisNexis Butterworths, 2007) ch 4, A Hudson, *The Law of Finance*, (London, Sweet & Maxwell, 2009) ch 47; P Wood, *Project Finance, Securitisations, Subordinated Debt*, 2nd edn (London, Sweet & Maxwell, 2007) part 2.
[294] For discussion of the basic features of such a securitisation, see *MBNA Europe Bank Ltd v Revenue and Customs Commissioners* [2006] EWHC 2326 (Ch), [45]–[49].
[295] See chapter 7 for a discussion of the position of trustees.
[296] Fuller, n 182, 7.25.

risk, since the holders are the first to take a loss and yet are entitled to any surplus). The greater risk in holding lower-tranched notes is offset by a higher rate of interest payment. This tranching is achieved by subordination[297] and actual payment is often in accordance with a 'waterfall' clause which pre-determines the order of payment, and will include other payments such as tax and an administration payment to the originator.[298]

The technique usually used to transfer the receivables to the SPV in such a structure is that of assignment. This is because the originator does not usually want the obligors to know that the receivables have been securitised,[299] so novation is unsuitable. Indeed, since the obligors are not notified, even an assignment can only be equitable.[300] This creates a number of different risks and effects.[301]

First, the enforcement of the receivables has to be by the originator (the assignor). This is hardly a problem, since the originator is usually administering the collection of the receivables. Second, there is in theory a risk of loss of priority if the originator assigns the receivables to someone else and gives notice. However, this would normally be in breach of, and an event of default of, the originator's sale contract with the SPV and so could cause the whole structure to terminate. Third, set-offs can continue to arise between the originator and the obligor.[302] Further, the fact that the receivables are assigned (whether by statute or in equity) means that the SPV takes subject to equities between the originator and the obligor. It also means that if a receivable is not assignable, then in theory the assignment is ineffective, although, as we have seen, if the SPV can force the originator to recover from the obligor, the originator will hold the proceeds on trust for the SPV. The SPV and the holders of the securities cannot be protected from these risks, or the general credit risk of the obligors, by having recourse against the originator, as would be common in a straightforward receivables financing, as this might prejudice the 'true sale' nature of the assignment, which is discussed below.[303] These risks are therefore reflected in the price paid for the receivables, which is discounted from their face value, and/or in the amount of lower rate notes issued, which bear the very high risk of being paid last. Credit enhancement, by third party guarantees or insurance, can also cover the risk.[304]

The most important aspect of the transfer to the SPV in this form of securitisation is that it is a 'true sale'. This is critical for a number of reasons. First, if the transfer were to be recharacterised as merely granting the SPV a security interest, it would be void if not registered, and enforcement would be rendered difficult or impossible if the originator became insolvent.[305] Second, usually one reason for securitisation is to move the receivables off the balance sheet of the originator for regulatory capital adequacy purposes, and

---

[297] For the various techniques, see 5.3.4.

[298] Wood, *Project Finance, Securitisations, Subordinated Debt,* n 293, 7–010.

[299] This is particularly true where there is an ongoing relationship between the originator and the debtor, for example, in the context of credit card receivables: see *MBNA Europe Bank Ltd v Revenue and Customs Commissioners* [2006] EWHC 2326(Ch), [59].

[300] Of course, it is sometimes the case that the obligors do know that their obligations are being securitised, such as where a bank acts as an intermediary to obtain finance more cheaply from the securities market than a company can do so, by making a loan to the company, which is then securitised. In this case the transfer can be by novation or statutory assignment.

[301] See 8.2.2.1 for a discussion of statutory and equitable assignments.

[302] J Benjamin, *Financial Law* (Oxford, Oxford University Press, 2007) 406 at fn 28.

[303] Wood, n 293, 7–026; *MBNA Europe Bank Ltd v Revenue and Customs Commissioners* [2006] EWHC 2326 (Ch), [48].

[304] See 5.3.1 and 5.3.2. Benjamin, *Financial Law,* n 302, 18.23.

[305] Wood, n 293, 8–002.

this would not be achieved if there were no true sale.[306] Third, there must be no question that the originator is collecting the receivables on its own behalf, as on its insolvency any payments made to the SPV might be set aside.

The approach of the courts in characterising transactions as an outright sale or the creation of security for a loan has been discussed above.[307] In the present context, it is absolutely clear that the form of the transaction is that of a sale. Further, the rights and obligations of the parties set out in the (usually very complicated) documentation are intended to bind the parties: there is no question of a sham. Therefore, the approach to be taken is that of the internal route,[308] that is, whether the rights and obligations created are consistent with the label that is given to the transaction by the parties.[309] The approach of the court acknowledges that parties may structure a transaction as a sale even though the economic purpose of it is security for a loan.[310] It is only if the legal structure of the transaction (taken as a whole) amounts to the creation of a secured loan that the courts will recharacterise it.[311]

The possible features of securisation which could cause problems in relation to characterisation are if the originator still bore some of the credit risk of the receivables (for example, if the sale was to some extent with recourse) or if the originator was entitled to any surplus value generated by the receivables once the amounts due on the securities had been paid.[312] The originator often does want that benefit, and various techniques are used to achieve this: the originator may make a subordinated loan to the SPV, or may buy the 'equity' tranche of the securities, or may charge high servicing fees for the administration of the receivables.[313] Neither recourse to the seller nor the ability of the seller to receive a surplus have prevented the courts upholding the characterisation of invoice discounting agreements as sales of the receivables.[314] This line of cases is relied upon in the 'true sale' opinions produced by lawyers in each securitisation transaction. There are, as yet, however, no English cases dealing with the characterisation of a securitisation true sale. The nearest the English courts have come to considering the matter is the case of *MBNA Europe Bank Ltd v Revenue and Customs Commissioners*[315] where the issue was whether the assignment in the course of a securitisation was a 'supply' within the VAT regime. Briggs J held that the transfer was not by way of security[316] but by way of sale, although he said that it was not a 'simple' sale[317] and did not constitute a supply under the VAT regime. The case is therefore far from conclusive, and even less so as it did not involve a securitisation as described above but a 'master trust' structure whereby the receivables

---

[306]   The criteria for a true sale which is effective under Basel II are found in the FSA Handbook BIPRU 9.4. See pages 25–26.

[307]   6.2.2.

[308]   See pages 227–28 and *Welsh Development Agency v Export Finance Co Ltd* [1992] BCLC 148, 186.

[309]   That, at least, seems to be the approach of the courts in the cases involving characterisation as a sale or loan, see above pages 228–29. The approach in relation to characterisation of a charge as fixed or floating appears to be different, at least in emphasis.

[310]   See, for example, the cases discussed in 6.2.5.1.

[311]   *Re Curtain Dream* [1990] BCC 341; V Seldam, 'Recharacterisation in "True Sale" Securitisations: The "Substance Over Form" Delusion' [2006] *Journal of Business Law* 637, 641.

[312]   Hudson, *The Law of Finance*, n 293, 47–15 fn 14.

[313]   These and other techniques, together with the risks they pose, are discussed by Wood, n 293, 7–031.

[314]   See pages 233–34.

[315]   [2006] EWHC 2326 (Ch).

[316]   Ibid, [95].

[317]   Ibid, [98].

are assigned to another SPV which holds them on trust for the originator and the first SPV jointly.[318] It is, however, an indication that the courts will uphold the structure of a securitisation as the parties have set it up rather than be quick to recharacterise it.[319]

If the originator does not wish to transfer receivables, it can transfer risk either by making a 'whole business' securitisation,[320] where the SPV makes a loan to the company secured on the company's assets, funded by the issue of securities or a synthetic securitisation. The latter achieves the same economic effect as a true sale securitisation by the use of credit derivatives.[321]

In each of these structures, the original obligors play no part in the securitisation and, indeed, are usually unaware of it. This is, then, another example of where debt is transferred in such a way that the 'control' of it passes to a third party, who may have an adverse effect on the obligor and about which the obligor can do very little. Further, the risk of the debt moves away from the original lender, which, if it happens on a large scale, may render the lender less cautious about the loans it makes in the first place.

8.4 Conclusion

This chapter has sought to differentiate the different ways in which a lender's entitlement under a debt contract can be transferred, and also ways in which the credit risk can be transferred without actually transferring the debt. There are only three transfer techniques: novation, assignment and negotiation, and the advantages and disadvantages of each have been discussed. The technique of negotiation has proved valuable for market transfers in the past, and it is not surprising that it has been sought to incorporate the advantages of negotiation in current methods of market transfers, which do not involve tangible representations of the debt obligation. Where debt is not designed to be traded, that is, when it is not incorporated in a security, a question of balance arises between the right of the borrower to prevent or limit the transfer of the debt, and the right of lender to alienate its own property, namely the debt or the proceeds. This is a difficult issue: so far the development of English law in this area has been exclusively by the courts, although many other jurisdictions have legislation on the subject. The transfer of risk by other methods, such as sub-participation and securitisation (which can involve actual transfer of debts) raise the question of protection of the 'transferee' against the credit risk of the 'transferor' as well as of the borrower.

The transfer of debt, or the risk of debt, potentially can lead to lower standards of risk assessment or protection on the part of the original lenders. This issue arises in different contexts throughout this book,[322] and can be seen as one of the contributing causes of the recent global financial crisis.

---

[318]   Fuller, *The Law and Practice of International Capital Markets*, n 293, 4.71.
[319]   *MBNA Europe Bank Ltd v Revenue and Customs Commissioners* [2006] EWHC 2326 (Ch), [90]–[91].
[320]   See pages 35–36.
[321]   See page 36.
[322]   See pages 80, 86–88.

9

Public Offers of Shares

9.1 Introduction

In this chapter we consider the issue of how companies can raise money by offering their shares to the public. This is an important issue. Although fewer than one per cent of the overall companies registered are public companies,[1] the economic power of these companies belies this low figure. This chapter will concentrate primarily on the issues related to the initial public offer of shares (IPO). The following chapter will deal with the issue of the ongoing regulation of the market, once securities have successfully been offered to the public.

Most companies will raise external equity finance only once — at the time of their IPO. Thereafter they tend to rely upon retained earnings and debt, either from banks or through the issue of bonds in order to finance their operations, although rights issues and seasoned equity offerings do occur once a company's shares are traded on the public markets. However, it is also possible for a company to arrange to have its debt securities traded on a public market. If the company wishes to offer debt securities to the public it must satisfy most of the same requirements as when offering shares to the public. This is discussed in more detail in chapter eleven.

As we will see in the next section, the ability to offer shares to the public confers significant advantages on companies. However, these advantages come at the cost of additional regulation, both of the companies themselves and of the capital markets within which those companies operate. All jurisdictions regulate the institutions of the capital markets to some extent and the UK is no exception. This chapter will consider why that additional regulation is thought necessary at the IPO stage, and will then assess the extent to which the regulation in place in the UK fulfils these goals.

9.2 Why would a Company Consider an IPO?

9.2.1 The Advantages of an Offer of Shares to the Public

The advantages of an offer of shares to the public, especially when combined with a listing of those shares,[2] are clear. If, as is usual, the IPO involves the issue of new shares, the funds

[1] See eg Statistical Tables on Companies Registration Activities 2008–09 compiled by Companies House available at www.companieshouse.gov.uk/about/pdf/companiesRegActivities2008_2009.pdf.
[2] It is not necessary to list the shares that are offered to the public, but it is very common as this provides a liquid secondary market for the shares, increasing their marketability and therefore their value.

raised are received by the company. The company may want to increase its equity base in order to fund business expansion plans, to introduce new products or to reduce borrowings. The capital required may exceed the amounts that the original shareholders can, or wish to, contribute. This will place limits on the company's development if further sources of funding are not tapped. An IPO allows the company to have access to outside investors who can participate substantially in the company. This access to significantly increased levels of equity capital is one of the major advantages of offering shares to the public especially when combined with a listing.[3] In addition to providing additional equity capital, an IPO may also improve the rate at which the company can borrow from banks.[4]

In addition, the original shareholders are able to arrange their exit by selling their shares in the IPO.[5] In a private company there are limited exit options for shareholders. Shareholders are normally unable to exit the company unless they hold redeemable shares, or the company repurchases its shares, or the shareholder manages to find a private purchaser for the shares, or the company is wound up. It is quite common for the shares sold at the IPO to be both newly created shares and existing shares, in order to allow the exit of existing shareholders, although it is possible for IPOs to consist of shares in just one of these categories. Going public therefore can potentially constitute an opportunity for the original investors to realise their profits from the company. Shareholders are then faced with the choice of exiting entirely or selling part of their investment while retaining a stake in the company.

The shares in a publicly listed company are generally more flexible investments than shares in private companies. Not only is there a ready market for the shares, but the requirements of the London Stock Exchange mean that to be listed shares must be freely transferable.[6] As a result any restrictions on the transfer and registration of shares must be removed before the shares can be offered to the public.[7] The marketability of the shares tends of itself to increase the value of the investment. Investors tend to look on the increased liquidity of shares favourably, and shares in public companies are therefore valued more highly. Shareholders may also find that banks will accept listed shares as security for loans. From the company's perspective, listed shares can be used as a form of payment, for example as consideration in share-for-share acquisitions, thereby widening the company's financing options compared to unlisted companies which can effectively only make cash offers. The

---

[3] These issues are discussed in chapter 2, especially 2.2.2. However, most companies will also want to retain a significant debt element to their financing portfolio: see 2.6 for a discussion of 'optimal' debt-equity ratios.

[4] M Pagano and A Röell, 'The Choice of Stock Ownership Structure: Agency Cost, Monitoring, and the Decision to Go Public' (1998) 113 *Quarterly Journal of Economics* 187.

[5] Studies have suggested that companies underprice their shares when going public eg JR Ritter, 'The Costs of Going Public' (1987) 19 *Journal of Financial Economics* 269; T Jenkinson and C Mayer, 'The Privatisation Process in France and the UK' (1988) 32 *European Economic Review* 482. This would suggest that the original shareholders are not always best advised to sell their shares in the IPO as they can potentially receive higher prices by retaining their shares and selling them in the after-market. However, the validity of this proposition will depend on a number of factors including the size of the shareholding which the shareholder wishes to sell.

[6] FSA Handbook, Listing Rules, LR 2.2.4(1). For a discussion of the transfer of shares see 8.2.7.

[7] It is also common market practice for IPOs to have capital structures comprising a single class of ordinary shares adhering to the 'one-share-one-vote' principle, not because of any regulatory requirement but because that is the structure which institutional investors in the UK markets expect: MJ Brennan and J Franks, 'Underpricing, Ownership and Control in Initial Public Offerings of Equity Securities in the UK' (1997) 45 *Journal of Financial Economics* 391.

liquidity associated with listed shares also provides greater scope for the company to offer remuneration packages to its employees that include shares and options.

Other perceived advantages in going public include the additional prestige that is felt to attach to a company with 'plc' in its title[8] and a flotation is often an opportunity for publicity for the company.[9] In addition, the change from a private company to a publicly listed company entails a number of corporate governance changes,[10] and is often a catalyst for developments in the professional management systems of a company. Key managers are often recruited and non-executive directors may be introduced. The fact of going public may also allow some additional pressure to be exerted on managers to act in the shareholders' interests. The existence of a share price may allow managers' performance to be assessed externally since share prices in large and liquid markets continuously aggregate information about a company's performance.

The liquidity of the shares also makes them valuable as a tool for incentivising managers and it is common for managers in the US and UK in particular to use pay-for-performance strategies to encourage managers to pursue shareholders' interests. The issuing of share options and other similar strategies as a form of performance-based compensation may be a potentially valuable tool, especially where shareholders are widely dispersed and may not be able to monitor the manager's actions effectively.[11] However, equity-based compensation schemes for directors and managers can introduce their own difficulties. In particular such schemes increase the windfalls resulting to these individuals if they manipulate the share price of the company and therefore increase the possibility of market abuse,[12] or if the strike price/conditions are set too low, making it too easy to profit from the scheme. In addition, if the strike conditions focus on short-term performance objectives, such schemes may encourage managers to take excessive short-term risks at the expense of sustainable long-term profits. Alternative tools are available to discipline poorly performing managers. In relation to UK public companies, for example, a positive relation between UK rights issues and managerial change has been found to exist.[13] In the US, takeover bids are also thought to play an important role in disciplining poorly performing managers,[14] although empirical studies have concluded that in the UK takeovers do not appear to operate as a disciplinary device of this kind.[15] This is discussed further in chapter twelve.

---

[8] 'Plc' stands for public limited company not public listed company and therefore is the suffix for all public companies, whether listed or not.

[9] See Eversheds (Sponsor), 'Going Public 2: A survey of recently floated companies', London Stock Exchange plc, 2003 in which one in ten respondents to a survey conducted on behalf of the London Stock Exchange said that the extra credibility and profile was a major motivation in going public.

[10] See Financial Reporting Council, *The UK Corporate Governance Code* (formerly the Combined Code on Corporate Governance), June 2010, discussed further at 10.3.1.1.

[11] This depends on shareholders having enough control over the process of setting the strike price of the options.

[12] For discussion see chapter 10 and in particular 10.5.

[13] J Franks, C Mayer and L Renneboog, 'Who Disciplines Management in Poorly Performing Companies?' (2001) 10 *Journal of Financial Intermediaries* 209; D Hillier, SC Linn and P McColgan, 'Equity Issuance, CEO Turnover and Corporate Governance' (2005) 11 *European Financial Management* 515. Discussed further at 4.3.1.

[14] Eg HG Manne, 'Mergers and the Market for Corporate Control' (1965) 73 *Journal of Political Economy* 110. For discussion of this issues see J Coffee, 'Regulating the Market for Corporate Control: A Critical Assessment of the Tender Offer's Role in Corporate Governance' (1984) 84 *Columbia Law Review* 1145.

[15] J Franks and C Mayer, 'Hostile Takeovers and the Correction of Managerial Failure' (1996) 40 *Journal of Financial Economics* 163, 180. See also B Clarke, 'Articles 9 and 11 of the Takeover Directive (2004/25) and the Market for Corporate Control' [2006] *Journal of Business Law* 355.

9.2.2   The Disadvantages of a Public Offer

The disadvantages of an IPO are also clear. The process can be time consuming, complex and costly, as the UK position demonstrates. In order to offer securities to the public in the UK, companies need to be public companies.[16] A public company does not need to offer its shares to the public. A public company is simply one that has fulfilled the requirements of the Companies Acts in order to be registered as a public company and whose certificate of incorporation states that it is such.[17] However if a company does want to offer its shares to the public, being a public company is a necessary first step. A company will therefore need to follow the requirements of the Companies Act 2006 in order to set itself up as a public company.[18] This includes complying with the minimum share capital requirements that apply to public companies,[19] but not to private companies.[20] The Companies Act 2006 imposes a more onerous regime on public companies as regards its legal capital, as we saw in chapter four. However the Companies Act 2006 also includes many other instances of additional regulation, including increased obligations regarding AGMs,[21] a continuing obligation to have a company secretary[22] and a minimum of two directors rather than one,[23] a requirement to lay its accounts and reports before the general meeting[24] and an inability to make use of the written resolution procedure which is available to private companies.[25] Some of these issues may seem small matters, but cumulatively the effect is that it is administratively more complicated, and more expensive, to run a public company than a private company.

However, being a public company is a necessary but not a sufficient step. In addition the company will need to make an offer to the public, and this is usually accompanied by an admission of the company's securities to trading on a public market. This latter step is not vital: a company may offer its shares to the public without securing their admission to a public market. While the number of UK public companies is approximately 10,000,[26] the number of listed companies is much smaller. The advantage of an admission to listing is to provide a market for the investors in its shares, on which they can trade the shares that they obtain from the company. Companies are generally able to raise money more easily and obtain a better price if, after the initial issue of shares to the public, there is a healthy secondary market available to investors on which they can sell their shares and realise their investment, if they so choose. The lack of liquidity in the shares in a private company is one of the significant disadvantages of this form of capital and it is therefore unsurprising that many public offers are accompanied by an admission to listing. However, it is possible

---

[16]   Private companies are prohibited from offering their shares to the public: Companies Act 2006, s 755.

[17]   Companies Act 2006, s 4(2).

[18]   Alternatively a private company can be converted into a public company: Companies Act 2006, ss 90–96.

[19]   Companies Act 2006, s 763 (£50,000).

[20]   See 4.3.2.

[21]   Companies Act 2006, s 336 cf private companies which need no longer have an AGM.

[22]   Ibid, s 271 cf private companies which no longer need to have a secretary: s 270.

[23]   Ibid, s 154. There are also additional requirements regarding the appointment of directors of public companies: s 160.

[24]   Ibid, s 437–438 cf private companies which are under no statutory obligation to hold an AGM or to lay accounts and reports in general meetings.

[25]   Ibid, s 288.

[26]   As at 31 March 2009 there were 9,800 public companies on the register for Great Britain: Statistical Tables on Companies Registration Activities 2008–09, n 1 (these statistical tables do not incorporate the figures for Northern Ireland).

that where the company does not expect or want the shares to be traded very widely it may not seek a listing, and will rely on the investors to trade their shares privately.[27]

There are two primary ways in which the company can offer its securities to the public for the first time.[28] For large issues the most appropriate method is generally an offer for sale or subscription coupled with a listing on a stock exchange. The offer[29] is made via a prospectus which is a lengthy and heavily regulated document, designed to provide potential investors with the information they need to decide whether or not to invest.[30] In order to ensure that the issue is fully subscribed the offer will usually be underwritten.[31] Underwriting is a form of insurance for the company and its shareholders if the issue does not prove popular with the market in general.[32] This can either be via a sponsoring investment bank agreeing for a fee to subscribe for the whole issue and for it, rather than the company, to make the offer to the public (an offer for sale) or for the underwriting bank to agree to take up any securities for which the public have not subscribed (an offer for subscription).[33] The offer price is usually stated as a fixed and pre-determined amount per share.[34] This amount will be fixed as late as possible. Obviously, since the offer involves, by definition, shares of a company which are new to the public, there is no existing market price to act as a yardstick for the issue price. The aim is to set the price at a level which will ensure a modest over-subscription, and that trading will open at a small premium.

The second method, which may be used where smaller amounts of capital are being raised, is a placing.[35] A public offer is both expensive and time consuming, involving a team of people at the company, at the company's advising bank and at the company's solicitors' firm working for months. Additionally, an IPO will involve paying for the services of the sponsoring investment bank, and paying commissions for the underwriters and sub-underwriters and probably paying a specialist share registrar. These costs are likely to be prohibitive unless a large amount of capital is being raised. A placing is a less expensive endeavour. A placing usually involves the investment bank obtaining firm commitments to take up the shares in the company. Usually these commitments will be from the bank's institutional investor clients. There is therefore no general offer to the public. These commitments can then be coupled with a listing on a stock exchange. A

---

[27] For a discussion of the advantages and disadvantages of listing debt see pages 326–27.

[28] The offer may include the shares that were owned by existing shareholders of the company who want to realise some or all of their investment.

[29] This is not an offer in a contractual sense and any acceptance is not binding on the offeror. Rather it is an invitation to make an offer which the company may or may not accept. This allows the offeror company (or sponsoring bank) to deal with the situation where the offer is over-subscribed, usually by accepting in full offers for small numbers of shares and scaling down large applications (the details of which would need to be set out in the prospectus).

[30] For further details on the content of the prospectus see 9.4.2.

[31] The offer will not always be underwritten, eg if the lead banks only take the shares on a 'best efforts' basis, which they may wish to do in difficult market conditions.

[32] For a discussion of underwriting in the context of debt securities see pages 324–25.

[33] Generally the sponsoring bank will attempt to arrange for the offer to be sub-underwritten by other institutions in order to spread the risk.

[34] Alternatives are available however. For example, a minimum price can be stated and applicants invited to tender at or above that price, the issue price then being fixed at the highest price that will enable the issue to be subscribed in full, all successful applicants paying that same price and those tendering below the issue price being eliminated. This pricing structure is rare today.

[35] For a discussion of placing in the context of debt securities see page 324.

variation on this method is an intermediaries offer where financial intermediaries take up the offer for the purpose of allocating their securities to their own clients.[36]

Next, the company will have to apply for listing on a stock exchange. A number of options are available for this listing.[37] In the UK there is the Main Market, for well-established companies, and the Alternative Investment Market (AIM) for less well-established companies. These markets are run by the London Stock Exchange (LSE). Even within these markets, choices exist. It was announced in October 2009 that companies listing on the Main Market (whether UK companies or overseas companies) can now choose whether to obtain a 'premium' or a 'standard' listing.[38] A 'standard' listing requires the issuer to comply with the minimum standards required by EU legislation,[39] whereas a number of obligations have been 'super-added' for those wishing to acquire a premium listing, such as additional obligations regarding substantial and related party transactions[40] and an obligation to 'comply or explain' with the requirements of the UK Corporate Governance Code.[41] Prior to this date, UK companies had to apply for listing under the 'primary' listing and overseas companies applied for a 'secondary' listing. These changes to the listing rules are intended to create a level playing field for all companies listing on the Main Market.[42] As a result UK companies now have the choice to have a 'premium' listing, a 'standard' listing, or a listing on AIM.

However, the LSE has no monopoly on the operation of public markets for securities within the UK and a number of alternative markets exist, mostly for companies wishing to raise relatively small sums of money,[43] although the PLUS Markets Group launched a new market in July 2007 intended to compete with the Main Market.[44]

There is no obligation on UK companies to list their shares on a UK market. A UK company has complete freedom to decide where to list its shares, either as a primary or, more commonly, as a secondary cross listing. Equally, non-UK companies can choose to list their shares in London. There has been an erosion of the concept of 'national'

---

[36] Of course, once an initial public offer has taken place the company can subsequently raise new equity capital by way of a rights issue, and indeed if it is issuing new shares for cash it will be obliged to do so unless the shareholders have agreed to set aside pre-emption rights (see 4.3.1). A variation on a rights issue is an open offer, where, as in a rights issue, the offer is made to the company's existing shareholders pro rata to their existing holding, but unlike a rights issue the shareholders are not able to renounce their rights. It is technically possible for an initial public offering to be via a rights issue, but this would require the shares to be sufficiently widely held to make it possible to raise the necessary capital from existing shareholders. It is really in relation to subsequent offers that rights issues and open offers come into their own.

[37] For a discussion of the position regarding debt securities see chapter 11.

[38] See the Listing Rules Sourcebook (Amendment No 3) Instrument 2009 available at www.fsahandbook.info/FSA/handbook/LI/2009/2009_54.pdf and FSA, *Listing Regime Review*, CP09/24, October 2009. For further discussion see FSA, *Consultation on amendments to the Listing Rules and feedback on DP08/1 (A Review of the Structure of the Listing Regime)* CP 08/21, December 2008. The effective date for most of these rules is 6 April 2010, but standard listing was made available to UK companies from 6 October 2009.

[39] See the Consolidated Admissions Requirements Directive (CARD) 2001/34/EC, discussed further below.

[40] See FSA Handbook, Listing Rules, LR 10 and LR 11, discussed further at 10.3.2.4.

[41] See *The UK Corporate Governance Code*, n 10, discussed further at 10.3.1.1.

[42] FSA, *Consultation on amendments to the Listing Rules and feedback on DP08/1 (A Review of the Structure of the Listing Regime)* CP 08/21, December 2008. The changes also allow companies to migrate between the premium and standard segments of the market, without cancelling their listings, subject to certain procedural requirements eg companies migrating from premium to standard listing are required to obtain shareholder approval via a special resolution; companies migrating from standard to premium listing will need to appoint a sponsor.

[43] Eg PLUS-quoted market, a stock market for small and mid-cap companies in London: www.plusmarketsgroup.com, which is intended to compete with AIM.

[44] See the PLUS-listed market, ibid.

exchanges in recent years. Companies may be attracted by lower trading costs in one regime compared to another for a number of reasons. A regime may be able to offer the presence of skilled analysts and institutional investors, more advanced technology, greater liquidity, or higher accounting standards and better shareholder rights protection than exist in the issuer's home jurisdiction.[45] Alternatively it has been suggested that issuers might want to 'bond' themselves to a regime with higher disclosure standards and a stricter enforcement regime in order to attract investors who would otherwise be reluctant to invest.[46] Securities markets can then respond, and compete, by adopting techniques designed to persuade companies to list with them.[47] In Europe there is evidence that the traditional emphasis on home listing is diminishing,[48] and a level of regulatory competition is developing.[49] This phenomenon is also observable globally.[50] At one point, for example, the US was regarded as a particularly popular destination for cross listing.[51] However, recent studies suggest that the impact of the US Sarbanes-Oxley Act has led many foreign firms cross listed on US exchanges to delist, or to consider delisting.[52]

---

[45] M Pagano, AA Röell and J Zechner, 'The Geography of Equity Listing: Why Do Companies List Abroad?' (2002) 57 *Journal of Finance* 2651.

[46] For a discussion of the bonding hypothesis, see eg JC Coffee, 'The Future as History: The Prospects of Global Corporate Convergence in Corporate Governance and its Implications' (1999) 93 *Northwestern University Law Review* 641; JC Coffee, 'Racing Towards the Top?: The Impact of Cross Listings and Stock Market Competition on International Corporate Governance' (2002) 102 *Columbia Law Review* 1757; RM Stulz, 'Globalization, Corporate Finance and the Cost of Capital' (1999) 12 *Journal of Applied Corporate Finance* 8.

[47] According to the theory of regulatory competition, offering market participants a choice of legal regimes results in optimal regulation. For a discussion of the advantages of a regulatory competition approach see eg R Romano, 'Empowering Investors: A Market Approach to Securities Regulation' (1998) 107 *Yale Law Journal* 2359; SJ Choi and AT Guzman, 'Portable Reciprocity: Rethinking the International Reach of Securities Regulation' (1998) 71 *Southern California Law Review* 903, further developed in AT Guzman, 'Capital Market Regulation in Developing Countries: A Proposal' (1999) 39 *Virginia Journal of International Law* 607 cf MB Fox, 'Retaining Mandatory Securities Disclosure: Why Issuer Choice is Not Investor Empowerment' (1999) 85 *Virginia Law Review* 1335.

[48] L Baele, A Ferrando, P Hördhal, E Krylova and C Monnet, 'Measuring Financial Integration in the Euro Area' *European Central Bank Occasional Paper Series* No 14 (April 2004) ch 8.

[49] L Enriques and TH Tröger, 'Issuer Choice in Europe' (2008) *Cambridge Law Journal* 521; J Payne, 'The Way Forward in European Securities Regulation: Regulatory Competition or Mandatory Regulation?' in S Weatherill (ed), *Better Regulation* (Oxford, Hart Publishing, 2007). Note that in Europe it is possible for issuers to make use of a prospectus passport: once a prospectus is approved in a home state it is valid for public offers or the admission of securities to trading on a regulated market in any number of states within the EU: Prospectus Directive 2003/71/EC, art 17.

[50] The number of foreign listings in the UK has increased in recent years, though that is predominantly due to an increasing number of small foreign firms listing on AIM: C Doidge, GA Karolyi and RM Stultz, 'Has New York Become Less Competitive than London in Global Markets? Evaluating Foreign Listing Choices Over Time' (2009) 91 *Journal of Financial Economics* 253.

[51] A premium has been observed in relation to cross listings in the US, though it is suggested by some academics that changes to the US regulatory regime, and in particular the introduction of the Sarbanes-Oxley Act in 2002, has had a dampening effect on cross listings to the US. For discussion see C Doidge, GA Karolyi and RM Stulz, 'Has New York Become Less Competitive than London in Global Markets? Evaluating Foreign Listing Choices over time' (2009) 91 *Journal of Financial Economics* 253 who find that although cross listings have fallen in both New York and the Main Market in London, the premium for US listings has not been eroded cf K Litvak, 'Sarbanes-Oxley and the Cross-Listing Premium' (2007) 105 *Michigan Law Review* 1857.

[52] See Committee on Capital Market Regulation, The Competitive Position of the US Public Equity Market (2007) available at www.capmktsreg.org. Of course firms may decide to delist for many reasons other than because of the impact of Sarbanes-Oxley: GA Karolyi, 'The World of Cross-Listings and Cross-Listings of the World: Challenging Conventional Wisdom' (2006) 10 *Review of Finance* 99.

414   *Public Offers of Shares*

For companies which decide to list their securities in London, there may also be further requirements imposed by European regulation. The Consolidated Admissions Requirements Directive (CARD)[53] requires that securities may not be admitted to official listing on a stock exchange unless certain merit requirements have been satisfied.[54] The FSA, acting as the United Kingdom Listing Authority (UKLA), maintains the official list in the UK, and sets out the requirements for inclusion to the official list in the Listing Rules.[55] Since only companies whose securities are in the official list will be admitted by the London Stock Exchange to its Main Market, an admission to trading on that market in practice requires companies to satisfy both requirements, ie to seek inclusion in the official list and to apply for admission of the securities to trading on the market, a matter governed by the London Stock Exchange.[56] This chapter will focus on the admission of securities to the Main Market.[57] No equivalent requirement exists for an application for securities to be traded on AIM[58] or the Plus-quoted market.[59]

It should be clear from this discussion that the process involved for a company to put itself in a position where it can offer its securities to the public is a substantial one, with significant costs attached to it,[60] which will not be entered into lightly by companies. The additional costs and regulation do not end once the IPO is complete. Additional obligations follow as a result of obtaining a listing on the Main London Market, not least the need to comply with the Financial Services Authority (FSA)'s Prospectus Rules, Listing Rules, Disclosure Rules and Transparency Rules. The company faces increased obligations in relation to its accounts.[61] The level of disclosure of information also increases. This disclosure occurs not only on the IPO itself, but also on an ongoing basis.[62] The information to be published includes important financial data such as announcements of results and dividends, events which affect the management of the company, such as changes of directors, and alterations in capital structure. Publicly traded companies must disclose any price sensitive information to the market as soon as possible.[63] In addition

---

[53]   Directive 2001/34/EC.

[54]   Ibid, art 5.

[55]   The Listing Rules are included in the FSA Handbook, available at www.fsahandbook.info/FSA/html/handbook. The Listing Rules also fulfil a number of other important functions including containing the rules relating to related party transactions and additional corporate governance requirements that apply to listed companies. For a discussion of the future role of the FSA in regulating the capital markets see 9.4.1.

[56]   See LSE, *Admission and Disclosure Standards*, April 2010 (regarding admission to the Main Market) cf LSE, *AIM Rules for Companies*, February 2010 (regarding admission to AIM).

[57]   In order to trade on the Plus-listed market an issuer will need to make an application to have the securities admitted to the Official List, and the content of this chapter will therefore apply to these applications.

[58]   Eligibility requirements for admission to trading on AIM are a matter for the exchange itself (ie it is an exchange-regulated market) and the London Stock Exchange lays down no general eligibility requirements, relying mainly on certification from the 'nominated adviser' that the issuer is appropriate for that market: LSE, *AIM Rules for Companies*, February 2010, Rule 1.

[59]   See Plus, *Rules for Issuers*, March 2010, available at www.plusmarketsgroup.com.

[60]   Research conducted for the London Stock Exchange found that flotation costs were typically 10 per cent of the capital raised: Eversheds (Sponsor), 'Going Public 2: A survey of recently floated companies' London Stock Exchange plc, 2003.

[61]   See Companies Act 2006, Part 15 generally which distinguishes between different types of company according to their size and whether or not they are quoted, reserving the most onerous obligations for quoted companies (as an example see ss 444–447).

[62]   Ongoing disclosure requirements are discussed in detail in chapter 10.

[63]   FSA Handbook, Disclosure Rules and Transparency Rules, DTR 2.2, discussed further at 10.3.2.1.

shareholders holding more than three per cent of the company will have to disclose the size of their holdings and any material changes in them.[64]

Directors' duties also become more onerous in a public company. Companies listed with a 'premium' listing on the Main Market become subject to the requirements of the UK Corporate Governance Code.[65] These are a set of corporate governance principles that include the requirement that at least one half of the board should be independent non-executive directors;[66] the board should have nomination, remuneration and audit committees on which the non-executive directors are the only or dominant representatives;[67] and the CEO and the chair of the board should not be the same person.[68] The Listing Rules require all companies with a premium listing of equity shares in the UK to disclose in their annual report the extent to which they have complied with the UK Corporate Governance Code in the previous twelve months and to give reasons for any non-compliance.[69] Constraints on directors' actions may also arise from the need to consider and deal with arms length investors, and in particular institutional investors.[70] It is usual in the UK for controlling shareholders in a private company to lose their control when the company is floated. There is also more external scrutiny of the company and the share price often becomes a barometer for the company's fortunes.

9.2.3 Summary

These advantages and disadvantages need to be weighed up. Clearly becoming a public company, obtaining a listing and offering its securities to the public will not suit all companies. Another possibility, which will operate as a good alternative for some companies, is to seek an injection of capital from a private equity fund. This alternative is discussed in detail in chapter fourteen.[71] For many companies, however, once they reach a particular size or stage in their development, the need to access the additional funds which can be tapped in the equity capital markets by offering shares to the public, and to benefit from the reduced cost of capital which flows from the enhanced liquidity of the shares, becomes too compelling to ignore, and outweighs the attendant disadvantages.[72]

---

[64] Ibid, DTR 5.1, discussed at 10.3.2.3.

[65] *The UK Corporate Governance Code,* n 10.

[66] Ibid, B.1.2 although in companies below the FTSE 350 the requirement is only for two independent non-executive directors.

[67] Ibid, B.2.1, C.3.1, D.2.1.

[68] Ibid, A.2.1.

[69] FSA Handbook, Listing Rules, LR 9.8.6(5) and (6), 9.8.7. Companies whose securities are traded on a public market but are not admitted to the Official List (eg companies trading on AIM) are not required to comply with the UK Corporate Governance Code.

[70] The role of institutional investors is discussed at 10.2.2.2.

[71] For a discussion of the comparisons between a private equity structure and a public company see 14.6.

[72] This analysis may well be different for debt and equity securities. There may be more marginal benefits to be gained from an offer of debt securities to the public, when weighed against the very considerable disadvantages that follow from a public listing. This issue is discussed further at chapter 11.

9.3   The Theory of Regulation of Public Offers

As will be clear from the previous section, potentially significant advantages flow to the company from an offer of its securities to the public, but these are accompanied by considerable levels of additional regulation. This section will consider the aims of this additional regulation. The following sections will then assess the regulation of public offers of shares with a premium listing on the Main Market in the UK in the light of these goals. This chapter concentrates on the investor protection that arises from the regulation of the markets. It should be noted that the UK regulatory regime also regulates the providers of financial products, so that no-one may carry on regulated activities without authorisation from the FSA.[73] Those who act as intermediaries in relation to issues of equity securities carry on regulated activities, for example, by advising on investments,[74] arranging deals in investments,[75] or managing investments,[76] and usually are required to be authorised. Regulating these intermediaries is another way in which a regime can seek to ensure investor protection. However, a full discussion of this form of regulation falls outside the confines of this book.[77]

9.3.1   Objectives of Regulation

The overarching aim behind capital market regulation at the IPO stage is undoubtedly investor protection, but the goal is not to insulate investors from sustaining losses.[78] Instead the aim is to enable investors to make informed choices and efficient resource allocation decisions, and for them to be protected from fraudulent issuers. The primary problem for investors in a public offering is valuing the offered securities. Issuers and their insiders enjoy an informational advantage over outside investors. The risk for outside investors is that issuers will use this advantage to sell overvalued shares. However, there are risks for issuers too. More sophisticated investors can compensate by demanding a lower price to purchase the shares, with the result that issuers would be forced to accept less for their securities than they would if investors had full information on which to value the securities. This would raise the cost of capital for issuers.

As we will see in chapter ten, the position is more complex once the securities have been admitted to trading. It is generally accepted that at that stage there are two objectives being pursued in capital markets regulation: first to ensure that the prices of publicly traded securities are reasonably well informed, ie to promote the efficiency of the market through the promotion of an efficient market price,[79] and, second, to ensure that shareholders are protected by effective corporate governance institutions once they invest in publicly traded shares. The latter objective is only of significance after the IPO and will be dealt

---

[73]   FSMA, s 19.

[74]   Financial Services and Markets Act 2000 (Regulated Activities) Order 2001 (SI 2001/544) art 53. The same issue arises in the context of debt securities, see page 533.

[75]   Ibid, art 25. But note the issue by a company of its own securities is not included (ibid, arts 18 and 34).

[76]   Ibid, art 37.

[77]   For further reading see eg A Hudson, *The Law of Finance* (London, Sweet & Maxwell, 2009).

[78]   Eg the FSA operates on 'the general principle that consumers should take responsibility for their decisions': FSMA, s 5(2)(d).

[79]   Another, closely allied, goal, may be said to be to safeguard the quality of publicly traded investments.

with in the next chapter. The former objective also operates differently at the IPO stage as compared to the position once the securities are being publicly traded. In the IPO there is only a market for shares once the shares have been issued and are actually available to be traded. Those who subscribe to the offer cannot therefore rely on the market to ensure that the price is efficient, though those that buy in the after-market may be able to do so. In order to protect those who subscribe to the offer a slightly different set of investor protection devices need to be put in place. These are based on disclosure, as we shall see, but rather than relying on the market to provide the requisite level of investor protection, there are a number of structures and processes put in place that result in a partial reversal of the usual 'caveat emptor' principle. These are discussed further below.

9.3.2   The Need for Regulation

We should consider why investors in publicly traded securities are in need of this protection. It stems in part from the nature of the assets in question. Securities are intangible goods which cannot be inspected in the same way as other consumer products. Indeed many investors do not even want to inspect: they aim to be passive recipients of an income stream rather than active investigators in the product.[80] Buying a security is not like buying a car. There is no opportunity to walk around the asset, to inspect its material condition or to take it for a test drive. In addition, unlike other consumer products where the value of the asset depends on what has happened to it to date (to continue the car analogy, how many miles it has driven, the quality of the service history, whether it has been in any serious accidents), the value of securities is largely contingent on the expected future performance of the issuing company.

Securities are claims to the future income of companies. The quality of these securities cannot be fully assessed in advance. The problem with selling securities is that this future income is subject to many unknowns. No entrepreneur can make binding promises about the future income that will be generated by the company. Nevertheless the directors and managers in a company are in a better position than prospective investors to judge the likely nature of the risks that the company will face, and how it is likely to fare under them. However, this creates a risk that they will misrepresent the company's prospects in order to encourage investors to invest. It is this risk, caused by the asymmetry of information between companies and market participants, that capital market regulation seeks to address.[81]

However, these same points could be made in relation to the investments in private companies, which are not regulated in the same way. As we saw in chapter four, the law

---

[80] Public company shareholders have traditionally been regarded as passive (for a discussion of the 'rational apathy of such shareholders' see AA Berle and GC Means, *The Modern Corporation and Private Property* (London, Transaction Publishing, 1991)). Of course, investors come in all shapes and sizes. Retail investors are classically passive investors, but institutional investors can be either passive investors (eg tracker funds) or more active (eg hedge funds). This is discussed further in 10.2.2.

[81] These arguments are starker in relation to shares than debt securities. The future income of a debt security will generally be certain (in terms of the amount owed and the dates of payment) albeit that whether the lender will be repaid will depend on the financial state of the company at the time. However, with shares, the amount that the shareholder will receive is uncertain in all respects. As discussed in 3.2.1 there is no entitlement to dividend payments. Although the shareholders, or at least the ordinary shareholders, are the residual claimants on the company, taking the lion's share of the risks and rewards in the company, this makes the income stream entirely dependent on the future fortunes of the company.

does put in place protections for shareholders in private companies: some of the legal capital measures, such as pre-emption rights, are there in order to provide shareholder protection.[82] However, these measures are in place to protect existing members of the company, not incoming shareholders, whose position is left primarily to contract law. What is it about publicly traded securities that requires this additional protection?

Both of the above objectives of regulating the capital markets, namely an efficient market and investor protection, require the law to constrain opportunistic managers and controlling shareholders, in other words to regulate the conflict between corporate insiders and corporate outsiders. There is a general assumption that investors in private companies tend to have some link or connection with the company and so not to be corporate outsiders in quite the same way as public company shareholders. However, this distinction is not an exact one: not all private company investors will be insiders, particularly in large private companies, and some public company investors, for example the founder shareholders, can still be regarded as 'insiders' to some extent. In private companies with small numbers of shareholders, the shareholders are more likely to be involved in the management of the firms and therefore to have direct knowledge of the corporate affairs. However, this argument weakens as the private company increases the number of its shareholders.

There may be other reasons to distinguish between public and private companies. The level of sophistication amongst public company investors is sometimes said to be lower so that such investors may lack the capacity to evaluate shares based on the information provided to them. However, this is not going to be true of all public company investors. Some public company shareholders, such as institutional investors, will have the sophistication necessary to evaluate this information, should they choose to do so. A stronger argument for differentiating between public and private companies is the idea that a fraud in a publicly traded company may impact on the prices of independent but similar companies in the market place, whereas a fraud at a private company is unlikely to have a similar spillover effect.[83]

Perhaps one significant difference between public companies and private companies is the fact that private company share purchases are generally a matter of negotiation. Investors purchasing a significant stake in a private company are able to contract their own protection, including their own disclosure regime. The foundational documents in venture capital financing arrangements attest to the possibility that shareholders can contract the necessary protective structures in some circumstances.[84] 'Outside' investors in private companies still need information, but will need to bargain for this disclosure themselves on a company by company basis, but this obviously comes with costs attached to it which make it unsuitable for use in the public company context. In public companies it is unreasonable to expect most retail investors to conduct, and pay for, their own disclosure regime. There can be a transaction cost benefit in public companies, therefore, to imposing a mandatory regime of disclosure. Although a regime of this kind could be of

---

[82] In addition there are general company law devices in place to protect minority shareholders in private companies eg Companies Act 2006, ss 994–996.

[83] R Kraakman et al, *The Anatomy of Corporate Law*, 2nd edn (Oxford, Oxford University Press, 2009), 9.1.

[84] Eg SN Kaplan and P Strömberg, 'Financial Contracting Theory Meets the Real World: An Empirical Analysis of Venture Capital Contracts' (2003) 70 *Review of Economic Studies* 281. The position of private equity investors is discussed further in chapter 14.

benefit to some private companies, this type of regulatory mechanism will be too costly for most private firms to support, and therefore disclosure in private companies remains a matter for individual investors to negotiate.

9.3.3   Regulatory Strategies

It is suggested that there are three principal strategies for regulating this conflict between corporate insiders and corporate outsiders: the mandatory disclosure strategy, governance strategies or trusteeship, and affiliation strategies.[85] The second and third of these can be dealt with relatively quickly here as it is mandatory disclosure which forms the central plank of the UK's regulatory strategy.[86]

9.3.3.1   Trusteeship

Governance strategies can arise in a number of forms. One form of trusteeship involves a disinterested third party screening companies that wish to enter the public securities market. In the UK a prospectus must be vetted by the FSA[87] (acting in its capacity as the UK Listing Authority)[88] and section 75(5) of FSMA entitles the FSA to refuse an application for listing if that listing would be detrimental to investors.[89] However, time constraints mean that this review is by no means full and comprehensive. The primary aim of this review is to ensure that the prospectuses' contents comply with the Prospectus Directive, and not to ensure that the information provided is correct. The FSA can be expected to spot glaring omissions or inaccuracies in the information provided, but it cannot guarantee the completeness or accuracy of all of the information in the prospectus.[90] In general the costs of a trusteeship system are deemed to be too great to be justified in a mature market.

In the UK, therefore, the FSA has taken on the role of a general watchdog,[91] rather than a more formal role at entry level which would lead to a complete ban of companies at that stage. The concept of trusteeship can also be regarded more widely, as comprising any strategy designed to provide oversight of the directors in a public company context. On this analysis rules relating to the structure of boards, such as the need for independent directors, or rules providing shareholders with corporate governance rights in the public company context could be regarded as part of the trusteeship strategy. In the UK the

---

[85]   Kraakman et al, *The Anatomy of Corporate Law,* n 83, ch 9.

[86]   It is also worth noting that although issuers are not required to be authorised by the FSA, those acting as financial intermediaries are so required, thereby protecting the investors who make use of them: FSMA Part II and for discussion see J Benjamin, *Financial Law* (Oxford, Oxford University Press, 2007) 10.2.

[87]   For a discussion of the future of the FSA as regulator see 9.4.1.

[88]   FSMA, s 87A, implementing Prospectus Directive 2003/71/EC, art 13. The draft prospectus, and other relevant documents, must be submitted to the FSA at least 10 days prior to the intended publication date in order to allow this process to occur.

[89]   In fact it is more likely that the FSA will simply require the issuer to remedy the inaccuracy, and to refuse approval only if that does not occur: FSMA, s 87J.

[90]   It is worth noting that the FSA and its officers are protected from liability in damages for acts and omissions in the discharge of their functions, unless bad faith is shown or there is a breach of the Human Rights Act 1998, s 6, so it will usually not be worth suing the FSA if the prospectus is incomplete or inaccurate: FSMA, s 102.

[91]   For a discussion of the future of the FSA as regulator see 9.4.1.

Corporate Governance Code[92] is an example of the first strategy, whereas the advisory vote taken by shareholders in public companies each year is an example of the latter.[93]

9.3.3.2   Affiliation Strategies

The affiliation strategy involves rules being introduced to govern the characteristics and behaviour of public firms. For example, it is possible to impose rules relating to the minimum size of corporate issuers, a minimum float for listed securities and a minimum history for published accounts. The UK adopts this strategy to some extent, so that, for example, the expected market value of the equity securities to be admitted must be at least £700,000.[94] In addition, where shares, rather than debt securities, are being issued, the company must produce audited accounts for a period of three years, ending not earlier than six months before the application for admission.[95]

To help investors understand these figures the company must show that 'at least 75% of the applicant's business is supported by a historic revenue earning record' for the three years in question, that it controls the majority of its assets and that it will be carrying on an independent business as its main activity.[96] Finally the applicant must show that it will have sufficient working capital to meet its requirements for the twelve months after listing.[97] These requirements aim to ensure that issuers have a certain quality that is demonstrated by the company's trading history and size. However, it is clear that rules of this kind can only go so far towards protecting investors from possible abuse, and very few company law rules protect issues such as the price and voting rights of public company shares.[98] It is also notable that this is a very limited list of issues compared to the very significant amount of information which a company must disclose in its prospectus as a result of the imposition of mandatory disclosure, discussed next. The value of these requirements must therefore be questioned. In a regime that is so heavily geared towards mandatory disclosure, an alternative approach would be not to mandate these issues but to allow companies to determine these issues for themselves, so that they could include less than three years of accounting records, for example, but then disclose that fact to the public.

Liability regimes for ongoing disclosure obligations, such as section 90A of FSMA, can also be regarded in this category since they aim to ensure the reliability of ongoing

---

[92]   *UK Corporate Governance Code,* n 10.

[93]   Companies Act 2006, ss 420–421, 439. For further discussion of the corporate governance rights of shareholders in public companies see 10.2.2.

[94]   FSA Handbook, Listing Rules LR 2.2.7(1)(a). The value is £200,000 for debt securities: LR 2.2.7(1)(b) (discussed further at 11.2.1.3). This is a requirement of the Consolidated Admissions Requirements Directive 2001/34/EC (CARD): CARD, arts 43 and 58. Other UK requirements, which all flow from CARD, are that the securities on offer must be admitted to listing (LR 2.2.9), the securities must be freely transferable (LR 2.2.4(1)) and, in the case of shares, a 'sufficient number' of the class of shares in question must be distributed to the public (LR 6.1.19(1)).

[95]   Ibid, LR 6.1.3, implementing CARD, art 44. For a discussion of the position regarding debt securities see chapter 11.

[96]   Ibid, LR 6.1.4. This requirement does not flow from CARD.

[97]   Ibid, LR 6.1.16. This requirement is subject to exceptions: LR 6.1.17, 6.1.18. Again these requirements do not flow from CARD and are super-added by the UK.

[98]   One of the exceptions is the company law rule that, once listed in the UK, shares cannot generally be issued at a 10% discount to the market price (LR 9.5.10), unless as part of a rights issue or if the discount is specifically approved by shareholders.

corporate disclosures. These are discussed further in chapter ten. Liability regimes for disclosures made in prospectuses are more usually regarded as part of the disclosure strategy, discussed below.

9.3.3.3   *Mandatory Disclosure*

Although the UK does make use of both of the above strategies to a small extent, the primary mechanism for regulating its capital markets is via the use of mandatory disclosure. As discussed above, equity securities are intangible goods, which are claims to the future income of companies, and insiders are in a better position than investors to evaluate the risks faced by the company and its potential to overcome those risks. It is clear that to be effective a securities system needs to regulate the agency relationship between directors, as insiders, and investors, as outsiders, by preventing fraud by the insider. Most of the major jurisdictions have developed anti-fraud rules to counteract this possibility. The UK was in fact one of the first to do so, with its Directors' Liability Act of 1890. However, if a system has an anti-fraud rule in place, to prevent insiders abusing their position and defrauding investors by lying to them about the company and its prospects, but the system has no disclosure obligations, then companies could potentially stay silent and avoid liability.[99] It is therefore extremely common to see anti-fraud rules being coupled with mandatory disclosure rules in order to ensure that prices are as undistorted as possible.

Mandatory disclosure is the strategy adopted in the UK to deal both with the need to regulate IPOs, discussed in this chapter, and also to regulate the ongoing market, once shares have been listed, discussed in chapter ten. However, the rationale for mandatory disclosure is not identical in these two scenarios. The primary rationale to explain the need for disclosure in relation to the ongoing market is to ensure market efficiency, although disclosure can also perform other useful functions, such as allowing shareholders to exercise a corporate governance role and allowing lenders to reduce monitoring costs. This is discussed at 10.2.1. The efficient capital market hypothesis suggests that investors (including unsophisticated investors) are protected providing all relevant information is disclosed as this is then reflected in the price of the securities. However, at the IPO stage no market yet exists for the securities and therefore no market price has yet been established. The rationale for disclosure at this stage is linked to that at the ongoing market regulation stage, but is nevertheless distinct. Its basis is the informational asymmetry which exists between corporate insiders and outsiders, but the disclosure rules at the IPO stage operate to modify the caveat emptor principle, in order to provide investors in the public offering with the information they need to assess whether to purchase the offered shares.

It is generally accepted that in order to allow investors to make efficient choices about the securities in which to invest, a system of *mandatory* disclosure is required.[100] Due to the

---

[99]   In principle there is no liability for silence unless it makes something already said misleading see eg *Derry v Peek* (1889) 14 App Cas 337.

[100]   For discussion of the utility of mandatory disclosure see generally, JC Coffee, 'Market Failure and the Economic Case for a Mandatory Disclosure System' (1984) 70 *Virginia Law Review* 717; FH Easterbrook and DR Fischel, 'Mandatory Disclosure and the Protection of Investors' (1984) 70 *Virginia Law Review* 669; MB Fox. 'Retaining Mandatory Disclosure: Why Issuer Choice is not Investor Empowerment' (1999) 85 *Virginia Law Review* 1335; R Romano, 'Empowering Investors: A Market Approach to Securities Regulation' (1998) 107 *Yale Law Journal* 2359; A Ferrell, 'The Case for Mandatory Disclosure in Securities Regulation Around the World' (2007) 2 *Brooklyn Journal of Corporate Financial and Commercial Law* 81. For a good summary of the empirical evidence on this issue see Kraakman et al, n 83, 9.2.1.2.

agency problem between investors and corporate insiders it is believed that managers would not disclose bad news to the market without some incentive to do so. A system of voluntary disclosure would therefore lead to the under-production of information. Investors operating within such a system would then make assumptions about the information they were not being told and discount the value of the information they did receive. To avoid this scenario, confident managers would have to reveal all of the information relating to their company, good or bad, but there would be no guarantee that the benefit of doing so would outweigh the costs involved. There is a financial cost involved in disclosure that cannot be ignored. Revealing information may also harm the company, for example by providing commercially valuable secrets to the company's competitors, and therefore managers would be unlikely to reveal some information even if it would be relevant to investors.

However, arguments can be made in favour of voluntary disclosure. One suggestion is that differentiation between the good and bad securities can take place as a result of the efforts of financial intermediaries. Analysts will actively search for information before they invest in a company, follow up tips and look at global information such as the price of raw materials before they invest, and other investors can piggy back on their efforts. The imposition of the burden of mandatory disclosure on companies, which carries a cost element with it, can be regarded as an implicit subsidy by companies to analysts working in the securities markets. It can be justified as a more efficient way of making available to the market information regarding specific companies as compared to the situation where analysts are left with the whole burden of information acquisition. If analysts were left to carry the burden it is likely that fewer companies would be followed by analysts and the result is therefore likely to be a less efficient price formation process, especially outside the area of the largest companies.[101]

Alternatively, companies can attempt to differentiate their securities as a high quality product through other means, although these all come with significant costs attached to them. For example the company can use reputational means, such as employing a respected merchant bank or stockbroker to bring them to the market, or employing well respected outsiders, such as accountancy firms, to certify the accuracy of the company's representations. Investors ought to be able to trust reputable intermediaries to report truthfully, even if they do not trust the issuing companies themselves to do so because, in theory, these intermediaries are repeat players who face serious sanctions but make no significant gains from misreporting. This mechanism is in use in the UK. A company applying for a premium listing of its equity securities on the Main Market must appoint a sponsor, normally an investment bank, whose role is to provide assurance to the FSA that the responsibilities of the applicant under the listing rules have been met, and to guide the applicant in understanding and meeting its responsibilities under the listing rules.[102] The sponsor therefore owes duties to its client and to the FSA.[103]

---

[101]   JC Coffee, 'Market Failure and the Economic Case for a Mandatory Disclosure System' (1984) 70 *Virginia Law Review* 717.

[102]   FSA Handbook, Listing Rules, LR 8.3.1. It is the sponsor who submits the application for listing to the FSA and accompanies it with a sponsor's declaration that it has fulfilled its two duties (LR 8.4.3). Where a prospectus is required, the sponsor must not submit the application unless it has come to the reasonable opinion that the applicant has also met all of the requirements set out in the prospectus rules: LR 8.4.2 and LR 8.4.8. These obligations are super-added, and don't fall on an issuer seeking a standard listing. There is no requirement for an issue of debt securities to have a sponsor: see 11.2.1.3.

[103]   In relation to an admission to AIM the 'nominated adviser' plays a similar role in relation to the admission document required for admission to AIM, see *AIM Rules for Nominated Advisers*, February 2007. For a discussion of the future of the FSA as regulator see 9.4.1.

Companies could also attempt to differentiate themselves by requiring directors to hold substantial quantities of shares: the higher the quality of the securities the more directors are likely to be prepared to hold. However, directors are likely to want to be compensated if they have to hold undiversified portfolios. Alternatively the company could make promises regarding dividend payments, or may even use leverage in order to demonstrate their confidence in the company's prospects.

Perhaps the most significant problem in a voluntary system, and therefore the most compelling argument in favour of mandatory disclosure, is the fact that the information provided under a voluntary system would be idiosyncratic. Without standardisation of the information involved it would be difficult if not impossible for most investors to make use of it. Standardisation improves comprehensibility and comparability and thereby increases the value of the information to investors. In addition, standardisation solves the problem of under-production of information. If every company must disclose the same things, there are reciprocal benefits to each company's investors even though the company will be compelled to disclose things of advantage to its rivals. While it is technically possible for standardisation of this kind to arise through private ordering, a mandatory system ought to be cheaper and quicker to establish.

Therefore, although arguments in favour of voluntary disclosure can be made, and there are those who question the benefits of mandatory disclosure, most academics and regulators now accept that mandatory disclosure is an essential feature of company law and capital markets regulation. This is certainly the accepted position in the EU,[104] and it is from the EU that the UK's mandatory disclosure rules now originate, in the form of the maximum harmonisation Prospectus Directive and its implementing Regulation. This is discussed in the next section. However this ex ante protection is not sufficient in and of itself and a legal system must also ensure that the information disclosed by companies under its mandatory disclosure system is reliable. In order to achieve this, the UK has in place an elaborate system of ex post protection in the form of liability rules for misstatements. This is discussed at 9.5 below.

9.4 The Regulation of Public Offers in the UK: Ex Ante Protection via Mandatory Disclosure

9.4.1 Regulatory Structure

The regulatory structure in this area is complex, being a mixture of EU legislation, UK domestic legislation, rules generated by the UK regulator, currently the Financial Services Authority (FSA), and rules generated by the stock exchanges themselves. There has been a slew of EU directives aimed at promoting the concept of a single market for financial services.[105] In order to facilitate this process, the Lamfalussy process was introduced, to

---

[104] See eg Report of the High Level Group of Company Law Experts on a Modern Regulatory Framework for Company Law in Europe, Ch II.3 (4 November 2002).
[105] The genesis of many of these directives was the Financial Services Action Plan: European Commission, 'Financial Services: Implementing the Framework for Financial Markets: Action Plan' COM (1999) 232.

make the law-making process in this area more streamlined, more flexible and faster.[106] The Prospectus Directive, a maximum harmonisation directive, was introduced as part of this process, in order to regulate the disclosure of information required in securities prospectuses within the EU.[107] The implementation of the Prospectus Directive into UK law was achieved in large part via amendments to the Financial Markets and Securities Act 2000 (FSMA).[108] In addition, a directly applicable Regulation was adopted at Community level, which provides over a hundred pages of detailed information regarding the information to be disclosed in public offers.[109]

In the UK, a single financial regulator, the FSA, was established by FSMA.[110] In fact the UK's statutory regime for financial services has a relatively short history. A series of financial scandals and failures of financial institutions during the 1970s and early 1980s, which showed that the traditional self-regulation of the UK's financial services industry presented serious systemic weaknesses. This led to a review of the existing position[111] and to the subsequent enactment of the Financial Services Act 1986, designed to create a new and more efficient regulatory regime governing financial services in the UK. Reforms of the London Stock Exchange were also implemented.[112] However, the regulatory regime established by the 1986 Act proved ineffective in many respects, including inadequate enforcement because of regulatory fragmentation. This led to a new series of initiatives in the late 1990s for the radical restructuring of the supervisory edifice of the UK financial services and banking sector. These included the transfer of regulatory and supervisory responsibility for banking, securities and insurance sectors from the Bank of England, the Securities and Investment Board (SIB) and several other bodies involved in the supervision of the financial services industry in the post-1986 era, including the Securities and Futures Authority, to a new body, the FSA.[113]

It is important to realise that with the implementation of FSMA in 2000 the FSA became a single regulator, with responsibility for a wide range of disciplines, including the capital markets and the banking sector.[114] The FSA has a wide remit in the area of financial services, with substantial rule-making and enforcement powers. For these purposes its rule-making powers are particularly important. The FSA is responsible for the

[106] For a detailed account of the implementation and effect of the Lamfalussy proposals see N Moloney, *EC Securities Regulation,* 2nd edn (Oxford, Oxford University Press, 2008) ch 3.

[107] Directive 2003/71/EC. This Prospectus have been under review and amendments have been proposed (see European Parliament, Draft Report, 2009/0132 (COD) September 2009). For the text of the amendments see Council of the European Union, 10254/2010, May 2010.

[108] At EU level an important distinction is drawn between regulated and non-regulated markets. Within the UK, the Main Market of the London Stock Exchange is a regulated market for the purposes of the Prospectus Directive but the decision was taken by the London Stock Exchange not to seek regulated status for AIM, which is, instead, an exchange-regulated market (ie self-regulated).

[109] Commission Regulation (EC) No 809/2004. No implementing legislation was required to give effect to this Regulation in UK law, but the relevant disclosures are reproduced for ease of reference in the FSA Handbook.

[110] FSMA, Part I.

[111] See LCB Gower, *Review of Investor Protection: A Discussion Document* (HMSO, 1982); LCB Gower, *Review of Investor Protection, Part I,* (Cm 9125, 1984) and *Part 2* (HMSO, 1985) and the Government's White Paper: DTI, *Financial Services in the UK- A New Framework for Investor Protection,* (Cm 9432, 1985).

[112] See eg BAK Rider et al, *Guide to Financial Services Regulation,* 3rd edn (Bicester, CCH Editions Ltd, 1997) 22–26.

[113] See I MacNeil, 'The Future of Financial Regulation: The Financial Services and Markets Bill' (1999) 62 *Modern Law Review* 725.

[114] For discussion see E Ferran 'Examining the UK's Experience in Adopting the Single Financial Regulator Model' (2002–3) 28 *Brooklyn Journal of International Law* 257.

FSA Handbook which contains the Prospectus Rules, the Listing Rules and the Disclosure and Transparency Rules. It is the Prospectus rules which are of particular importance for the purpose of IPOs.[115]

However, this position is not static, and the role of the FSA has been under review again as a result of the financial crisis. In a speech given in June 2010 the Chancellor, George Osborne, announced an end to the FSA in its current form.[116] He stated that from 2012 banking regulation will be transferred from the FSA to a new prudential regulatory authority, a legally separate but subsidiary part of the Bank of England. As regards the regulatory activity of the FSA that is described in this chapter, one possibility is that it will be carried out by a new Consumer Protection and Markets Authority, possibly with a new Economic Crime Agency to take over the role of criminal enforcement, although other possibilities have also been suggested, including that the Financial Reporting Council take over this role. The exact remit of any such Authority remains unclear at the time of writing. However, there is no suggestion that the substantive rules governing IPOs described in this chapter are going to change significantly. It is possible that these new authorities may have more energy and enthusiasm for enforcement, discussed in 9.5.3 below, but that remains to be seen.

The final level of regulation exists at the level of the stock exchanges themselves, which also have an important rule-making function. As discussed, in the UK admission of securities to trading on the Main Market requires companies to seek inclusion in the official list (currently governed by the FSA in its capacity as the UK Listing Authority) *and* to apply for admission of the securities to trading on the market (a matter governed by the London Stock Exchange). The LSE's rules governing this process are therefore of considerable importance.[117]

9.4.2 Mandatory Disclosure in the UK

The key mechanism by which UK law achieves its disclosure objectives is the prospectus. A prospectus is required whenever admission of securities to trading on a regulated market, such as the LSE's Main Market is sought,[118] or indeed whenever a company offers its securities to the public.[119] There are a number of exceptions to the concept of 'an offer of securities to the public', including where the offer is addressed to 'qualified investors'

---

[115]   However, note that the Listing Rules are also relevant because of the threshold requirements for a listing of securities stipulated by the Consolidated Admissions Requirements Directive (CARD) Directive 2001/34/EC.

[116]   George Osborne, Mansion House speech, 16 June 2010 and see HM Treasury, *A New Approach to Financial Regulation: Judgment, Focus and Stability* (Cm 7874, 2010).

[117]   See London Stock Exchange, Admission and Disclosure Standards, April 2010 (regarding admission to the Main List). Debt securities admitted to the Professional Securities Market are still part of the official list and the admission process is therefore under the remit of both the FSA (as the UK Listing Authority) and the London Stock Exchange. This is in contrast to the position of AIM. Eligibility for admission to trading on AIM is entirely a matter for the LSE to regulate: LSE, *AIM Rules for Companies*, February 2010. The role of the exchange in relation to securities such as those admitted to AIM, is, therefore, potentially even more significant than for securities admitted to the official list.

[118]   FSMA, s 85(2). AIM is not a regulated market and therefore an admission to AIM per se will not trigger the need for a prospectus, although if the admission is accompanied by an offer to the public then a prospectus will be required: FSMA s 85(1). However, even if no prospectus is required, the LSE rules require an applicant for admission to AIM to produce a publicly available admission document which includes disclosure requirements and is in effect a slimmed down version of a prospectus.

[119]   Ibid, s 85(1).

only,[120] or where the total amount to be raised in the offer is no more than 2,500,000 euros over a period of 12 months,[121] or the offer is to fewer than 100 persons per EEA state.[122] The idea behind these exceptions is to exclude the need to provide a prospectus (and thereby the information provided in that prospectus) where the costs of providing it would be unlikely to outweigh the benefits of having it provided. However, there are other exemptions which are based on other rationales,[123] such as the exemption for the target shareholders in a share exchange takeover bid,[124] or where the offerees receive the offer other than as part of a fundraising exercise by the company eg those receiving bonus shares, shares issued under employee or directors' share schemes.[125]

However, even if an offer falls within one of these exceptions, the need for a prospectus can still be triggered by a request for admission of securities to a regulated market such as the Main Market in London. Although there are exceptions to this requirement too,[126] the exceptions are narrower in scope so that, for example, there is no 'qualified investor' exception, which is unsurprising given that there is no mechanism for controlling the ownership of the shares once they have been admitted to the market.[127]

The overriding purpose of the prospectus is to provide the information which is 'necessary to enable investors to make an informed assessment of (a) the assets and liabilities, financial position, profits and losses, and prospects of the issuer . . .and (b) the rights attaching to the transferable securities',[128] ie to provide disclosure to investors.[129] This document is intended to provide useful information to investors and therefore the information in a prospectus 'must be presented in a form which is comprehensible and easy to analyse',[130] and issuers need to provide a summary[131] as part of the prospectus in order to further this aim. As discussed, the source for the rules regarding the need for a prospectus, and the contents of the prospectus, is the Prospectus Directive and its supporting Regulation. However, the EU legislation did not introduce an entirely novel

---

[120]   Ibid, s 86(1)(a), implementing Prospectus Directive 2003/71/EC, art 3(2)(a).

[121]   Ibid, s 85(5)(a), Sch 11A, para 9, implementing Prospectus Directive, art 1(2)(h).

[122]   Ibid, s 86(1)(b), implementing Prospectus Directive, art 3(2)(b) (note that the draft text Amending Directive, Council of the European Union, 10254/2010, May 2010, envisages this figure rising to 150). Qualified investors do not count against this figure (Prospectus Directive, art 2, although the draft text of the Amending Directive suggests changes to this definition). For a discussion of the exemptions available in the context of debt securities see 11.2.1.

[123]   For discussion see P Davies, *Gower and Davies: Principles of Modern Company Law,* 8th edn (London, Sweet & Maxwell, 2008) 873–75.

[124]   Ibid, s 85(5)(b) implementing Prospectus Directive, art 4(1)(b)(c).

[125]   Ibid, s 85(5)(b) implementing Prospectus Directive, art 4(1)(a)(d)(e).

[126]   FSA Handbook, Prospectus Rules, PR 1.2, implementing Prospectus Directive, art 4(2).

[127]   However, there is one exception here that does not exist for offers to the public, namely that no prospectus is required to admit shares representing less than 10% of the number of shares of the same class already admitted to trading on that regulated market, measured over a twelve month period: FSA Handbook, Prospectus Rules, PR 1.2.3, implementing Prospectus directive, art 4(2).

[128]   FSMA, s 87A(2), implementing Prospectus Directive, art 5(1).

[129]   There is also an obligation to provide a supplementary prospectus if information arises after the prospectus has been published that requires the published information to be qualified: FSMA, s 87G, implementing Prospectus Directive, art 16.

[130]   FSMA, s 87A(3) implementing Prospectus Directive, art 5(1).

[131]   FSMA, s 87A(5). The summary should convey the essential characteristics and risks associated with the issuer and the securities: FSMA, s 87A (6), implementing Prospectus Directive, art 5(2). Changes are suggested to the provisions relating to summaries by the draft text of the Amending Directive: Council of the European Union, 10254/2010, May 2010.

disclosure regime: many of the disclosure rules required by the EU legislation replaced the entirely domestic disclosure rules which were previously in place.

A good idea of the nature of the disclosure requirements created by this Regulation can be gained by examining the minimum disclosure requirements[132] for a share registration document.[133] Full details of the issuer itself must be given, including its legal and commercial name, its place of registration, date of incorporation and its registered office[134] as well as the details of the existing share capital of the company[135] including a description of the rights, preferences and restrictions attaching to each class of the existing shares.[136] The information which issuers must provide includes details of the members of the administrative, management or supervisory bodies of the company and any senior manager who is relevant to establishing that the issuer has the appropriate expertise and experience for the management of the issuer's business,[137] including their remuneration,[138] details of the company's employees,[139] and details of major shareholders within the company.[140] Unsurprisingly, the issuer must disclose risks which are specific to the issuer or its industry.

Issuers are, unsurprisingly, required to disclose audited historical financial information covering the latest three financial years (or such shorter period that the issuer has been in operation), and the audit report in respect of each year).[141] The names and addresses of the issuer's auditors for the period covered by the historical financial information must also be disclosed.[142] Issuers must also provide, inter alia, a description (including the amount) of the issuer's principal investments for each financial year for the period covered by the historical financial information up to the date of the registration document;[143] a description of, and key factors relating to, the nature of the issuer's operations and its principal activities;[144] a description of the principal markets in which the issuer competes;[145] details of the risks which are specific to the issuer or to its industry;[146] information regarding any existing or planned material tangible fixed assets, including leased properties, and any major encumbrances thereon;[147] the most significant recent trends in production, sales and inventory, and costs and selling prices since the end of the

---

[132] Note that although the Prospectus directive is a maximum harmonisation directive, the Commission Regulation creates minimum disclosure requirements. Issuers may need to provide more information than is contained in the annexes, in order to comply with the overarching requirement to provide investors with all of the necessary information in accordance with FSMA, s 87A(2).

[133] Commission Regulation, Annex 1. This annex is reproduced at FSA Handbook, Prospectus Rules, PR App 3.1. This may be contrasted with the requirements for non-equity issues, set out in the other annexes to the regulation.

[134] Ibid, para 5.1.

[135] Ibid, para 21.

[136] Ibid, para 21.2.3.

[137] Ibid, para 14.1.

[138] Ibid, para15.1.

[139] Ibid, para 17.

[140] Ibid, para 18.1.

[141] Ibid, para 20.1.

[142] Ibid, para 2.1.

[143] Ibid, para 5.2.1.

[144] Ibid, para 6.1.1.

[145] Ibid, para 6.2.

[146] Ibid, para 4.

[147] Ibid, para 8.1.

last financial year to the date of the registration document;[148] and a summary of each material contract for the two years immediately preceding publication of the registration document.[149]

It can be seen that the information required is predominantly historical in nature. It describes the issuer, its managers, its shareholders, its financial situation etc up to the date of application for admission. For the most part the information required of issuers does not look forward at all, although it can be seen that some of the information required of issuers can be regarded as forward-looking to a minor extent. So, for example, issuers are required to provide information concerning the issuer's capital resources (both short and long-term)[150] and 'information regarding any governmental, economic, fiscal, monetary or political policies or factors that have materially affected, *or could materially affect*, directly or indirectly, the issuer's operations'.[151]

It might seem surprising that the mandatory disclosure requirements focus so strongly on the provision of historical information given that the value of the securities to the investor is in their *future* potential and it is information about the company's future performance and profits which is likely to be of most interest to a potential investor. However, a recitation of specified objective facts is the lowest cost method of disclosure. If the costs of mandatory disclosure become excessively high then alternative methods whereby high quality businesses can distinguish themselves (eg employing high reputation outsiders, or promising significant dividends in the future) all start to look like more attractive options. Historical facts are also the easiest to compare across companies. Verification is cheapest and the enforcement of an anti-fraud system works best where it is relatively simple, and cheap, to verify the accuracy, or inaccuracy, of a statement made by the company. There are costs attached to both over-enforcement and inaccurate enforcement.[152]

There are also dangers associated with the inclusion of forward-looking information in prospectuses, which does not attach to the provision of historical information, because it provides the issuer's directors with an opportunity to present the company's future in an over-optimistic manner. This danger is clearly recognised by the EU's regulatory regime. In only one respect does EU legislation allow issuers to include genuinely forward-looking information in their prospectuses: issuers can choose to include profit forecasts in their prospectuses, though they are not obliged to do so.[153] These profit forecasts have the potential to be particularly influential for unsophisticated investors. As a result the assumptions underlying profit forecasts have to be stated and a distinction made between assumptions which directors can influence and those which are outside their control. The assumptions must also be specific and precise and readily understandable by investors. In addition the company's auditors or accountants must confirm that the forecast has been

---

[148]   Ibid, para 12.1.
[149]   Ibid, para 22.
[150]   Ibid, para 10.1.
[151]   Ibid, para 9.2.3 (emphasis added).
[152]   FH Easterbrook and DR Fischel, 'Mandatory Disclosure and the Protection of Investors' (1984) 70 *Virginia Law Review* 669, 678.
[153]   Commission Regulation, Annex 1 (reproduced at FSA Handbook, Prospectus Rules, PR App 3), para 13.

properly compiled, that the basis of the forecast is compatible with the issuer's general accounting policies and the forecast is compatible with the company's historical accounts.[154]

However, whatever the reasons behind the provision of largely backward-looking information, the effect is that this information disclosure will be of relatively little benefit to investors in determining what the future value of the securities is likely to be, which after all is what investors are most concerned to determine. This is in contrast to the position regarding the ongoing regulation of the markets, discussed in chapter ten, where some 'forward-looking' information is included in annual reports as a result of section 417 of the Companies Act 2006.[155]

9.5 The Regulation of Public Offers in the UK: Enforcement of the Mandatory Disclosure Regime

As discussed, investor protection requires two matters to be put in place: first, that information is disclosed to the investor to allow him to make a decision whether or not to invest, and, second, that information needs to be accurate. There are relatively few ex ante mechanisms put in place in the UK to ensure that the information disclosed in the prospectus is accurate. As we have seen, the FSA (acting as the UK Listing Authority) has a very low level vetting role in relation to prospectuses[156] which should prevent glaring inaccuracies or omissions getting through, but this process does not guarantee the accuracy and completeness of the document, although it is sometimes suggested that the obligation to submit the prospectus to the FSA for vetting may act as a valuable discipline upon issuers and their advisers.

Another form of ex ante protection arises from the need for the issuer to appoint a sponsor who has to assure the FSA when required that the responsibilities of the applicant company under the Listing Rules have been met.[157] Finally, certain items of information within the prospectus will need to be verified by third parties, so that the accounts provided by the issuer need to have been audited, and the auditors, or reporting accountants, will also have to confirm that any profit forecast within the prospectus has been properly compiled.[158] However, these forms of ex ante review are fairly light touch and the main remedies for omissions or inaccuracies in a prospectus are provided ex post. This section will consider the range of ex post protections on offer.

In the context of ex post remedies it has been suggested that it is not just 'law on the books' but also the level of enforcement of those laws in practice that is important in

---

[154] Ibid, 13.2–13.3.
[155] See 10.2.1.1. The US makes even greater use of forward-looking disclosure by providing an extensive Discussion and Analysis of Financial Condition and Results of Operations (MD & A report) (Regulation S–K, Item 303) which supplements historical accounting data with narrative information on the accounts and a forward-looking review of the business.
[156] FSMA, s 87A. For a discussion of the FSA as regulator in the future see 9.4.1.
[157] FSA Handbook, Listing Rules, LR 8.4.3.
[158] Ibid, Prospectus Rules, PR App 3.1, Annex I, para 13.

determining the quality of a jurisdiction's regulatory regime.[159] On this analysis, the level of enforcement practised within a regime will depend both on the existence of rights to enforce, for example the rights of private citizens to bring an action or the extent of the public authority's powers to enforce, and on the intensity or frequency with which enforcement occurs in practice. This section will therefore discuss each of these issues in turn.

9.5.1   The Aims of Enforcement

The liability regime for inaccurate information provided in securities prospectuses is a matter of choice for each jurisdiction. Even within the EU, although the Prospectus Directive requires Member States to apply 'their laws, regulation and administrative provisions on civil liability' to those responsible for the information contained in prospectuses,[160] it does not go on to stipulate the nature of the regime that should be imposed. This is therefore a matter of choice for individual Member States. In order to judge the effectiveness of the UK's enforcement regime it is first necessary to consider what are the aims of a liability regime. The UK's enforcement regime can then be judged according to these aims.

A liability regime is one of the blocks in the capital markets regulation regime of a jurisdiction and as such the aims of a liability regime are the same as the aims of the capital markets regulation regime set out above, namely to protect investors and, more generally, to promote the efficient allocation of financial resources in the economy as between competing projects. There are two ways in which a liability regime might contribute to these goals. First, a liability regime can encourage the accurate and timely disclosure of information by issuers by deterring misstatements, and second a liability regime can contribute to the goal of promoting investor confidence by providing compensation to those who suffer loss as a result of a misstatement in a prospectus.

9.5.1.1   *Encouraging the Accurate and Timely Disclosure of Information*

A liability regime can contribute to the goal of encouraging the disclosure of accurate and timely information by deterring misstatements. However, in order for a liability regime for misstatements in prospectuses to have a deterrent effect, that liability needs to fall on the directors and others who actually make the statement, rather than on the company. If the liability falls only on the company, that liability will then be borne by the shareholders rather than the makers of the misstatements, such as the directors. The shareholders may put pressure on the directors as a consequence of the liability imposed on the company, but such deterrence would operate only indirectly.

In reality, where liability falls on the company the result is that one set of shareholders recover at the expense of another set of shareholders.[161] Company liability for misstatements in those circumstances can be seen as little more than a redistribution of value

---

[159] JC Coffee, 'Law and the Market: The Impact of Enforcement' (2007–8) 156 *University of Pennsylvania Law Review* 229.

[160] Prospectus Directive 2003/71/EC, art 6(2).

[161] Of course the position will be different where the claim is from the purchaser of debt securities.

among shareholders.[162] The consequences of this are discussed further below. This is not to suggest that situations where liability is imposed only on the issuer can have no deterrent effect. It is possible that reputational and other losses will fall on the makers of the misstatements as a result of the company being involved in litigation, but the deterrent effect is likely to be less pronounced in this situation than where liability falls on the statement makers directly.

In addition, even if the liability regime does not make the directors liable to the investors, the directors might nevertheless be liable to the company, for breach of their directors' duties. Thus, the director might have to reimburse the company for the loss suffered by the company in compensating the investor, but the decision to seek recovery from the director would be a decision to be taken by or on behalf of the company.[163] The decision to bring such an action could be brought by the board, or by the shareholders. Shareholders in the UK have the ability to bring a minority shareholders' action against misbehaving directors either by way of a derivative action,[164] or by way of a statutory petition for relief from unfair prejudice.[165] However, the level of enforcement of directors' duties by shareholder litigation is close to nil for listed companies.[166]

Of course, even if liability falls only on the company, the actions of the directors and advisers of the company will remain of primary importance since the company, while a separate legal person, can nevertheless only act via its human agents. Liability can generally only be imposed on the company if its agents have acted in a way which allows liability to be attributed to the company. Usually it is only the acts and state of mind of those who are the 'directing mind and will' of the company, ie its directors, that can be attributed to the company.[167] It might be thought that imposing liability on the company could induce senior managers and directors to screen more carefully against misleading statements. However, this possibility is significantly undermined by the fact that the company is only likely to be made liable for misstatements committed by these same individuals, and it is these individuals who have the greatest stake in keeping the company's share price high.

In order to have a deterrent effect, liability needs to fall directly on those that make the misstatements. This will normally be the directors, but might also be the company's advisers, such as its auditors. However, even imposing liability on the directors might not secure any deterrent purpose in practice if the effect of Directors and Officers Liability

---

[162]   Where the company is insolvent, it appears that the defrauded investors are allowed to compete with the other unsecured creditors of the company for a share of the assets (see *Soden v British & Commonwealth Holdings plc* [1998] AC 298), in contrast to the usual position that shareholders claims (eg to declared but unpaid dividends) are subordinated to the claims of the unsecured creditors on insolvency (Insolvency Act 1986, s 74(2)(f)).

[163]   Companies Act 2006, s 463 provides that a director is liable to compensate a company for any loss it incurs as a result of an untrue or misleading statement or omission from the directors' report or the directors' remuneration report that accompany the annual accounts (or from summary financial statement derived from them). However, a director will only be liable if the untrue or misleading statement is made deliberately or recklessly or the omission amounts to dishonest concealment of a material fact (s 463(3)).

[164]   Companies Act 2006, Part 11.

[165]   Ibid, ss 994–996. For discussion of the ability of shareholders to make use of this remedy to provide a remedy for the company (ie the overlap between the unfair prejudice remedy and the derivative action) see J Payne, 'Shareholders' Remedies Reassessed' (2004) 67 *Modern Law Review* 500.

[166]   J Armour, 'Enforcement Strategies in UK Corporate Governance' in J Armour and J Payne (eds), *Rationality in Company Law: Essays in Honour of DD Prentice* (Oxford, Hart Publishing, 2009) 79–85.

[167]   *Meridian Global Funds Management Asia Ltd v Securities Commission* [1995] 2 AC 500.

insurance (D&O insurance) is to transfer the costs of the liability back to the company. In the US even where liability can potentially fall on directors, in practice the system of D&O insurance operates so that little liability remains with the directors.[168] In the UK, D&O insurance is generally unavailable to cover fraudulent behaviour, however this difficulty may be bypassed if D&O insurance cover is extended to include directors' liabilities under settlements of claims brought by investors in which the directors do not admit liability. If this is the case, imposing liability on directors might simply add to the incentives for defendants to settle investors' claims out of court.[169] In relation to the company's auditors, new provisions in the Companies Act 2006 make it possible for auditors to limit their liability by agreement with the company, as long as that agreement is fair and reasonable.[170] However, liability limitation agreements are confined to liability owed by the auditor to the company, and does not seem to extend to auditors' liability to third parties.[171]

So, one aim of a liability regime might be to encourage the accurate disclosure of information through the use of deterrence. However, it is not necessarily the case that the most appropriate way to achieve this is by imposing the maximum level of liability possible, say a strict liability regime with onerous penalties for issuers, directors and others held responsible for the misstatement, and easy access to the regime for a wide range of potential applicants. Three different issues need to be weighed in the balance. First, the costs of any liability regime need to be borne in mind. It is accepted that the standard of accuracy in prospectuses is high and that this can be attributed in part to the imposition of the significant liability regime which currently exists in the UK regarding misstatements in prospectuses.[172] However, it is also accepted that the verification process to which prospectuses are subject is both time consuming and costly. It seems clear that the costs could be reduced if the standard of the liability regime were reduced.[173] The benefits of imposing a particular standard for liability must therefore be weighed against the costs.

Second, it may be that a more stringent liability regime might actually reduce the incentives for issuers to make timely and full disclosure of information, even if the level of accuracy of the information disclosed increased. Concerns about liability might lead issuers to check and double check the accuracy of information before release. This might make the information actually released more accurate but would be likely to slow down the release of that information. This is not likely to be a concern regarding the publication of a prospectus for an IPO, since that document is the first information received by the public from the company and therefore any delay cannot be said to be prejudicial to the public, but it might be of concern regarding ongoing obligations to disclose. Where the

---

[168] JC Coffee, 'Reforming the Securities Class Action: An Essay on Deterrence and its Implementation' (2006) 106 *Columbia Law Review* 1534.

[169] It is also the case that the cost of the misstatements will be transferred back to the company if the company undertakes to provide to the directors an indemnity against liability to third parties, as is now permitted by Companies Act 2006, s 234.

[170] Companies Act 2006, Part 16, Ch 6.

[171] Ibid, s 534(1).

[172] See eg HM Treasury, *Davies Review of Issuer Liability, Liability for Misstatements to the Market: A Discussion Paper* (March 2007) para 71.

[173] In the context of liability for misstatements for ongoing disclosures, the accountancy firm PriceWaterhouseCoopers estimates that if the current fraud-based regime (see FSMA, s 90A) were to be changed to a more onerous negligence based regime (akin to the regime for misstatements in prospectuses) then this would be likely to increase the audit costs for annual statements by a fifth and that a similar further increase would be generated by additional legal work which would be involved: HM Treasury, *Davies Review of Issuer Liability*, ibid.

disclosure relates to some kind of inside information, any slowing down of the release of this information could be deleterious to the market.

Of more concern in the context of IPOs is the fact that issuers have some control not only over the amount of checking which occurs before a statement is made but also over the content of the statement itself. In relation to many disclosure obligations the law requires that a statement be made but does not determine how detailed that disclosure should be. The danger is, therefore, that if liability regimes are too onerous the level of detail in disclosures, and therefore the potential benefit of disclosures to investors, might actually reduce. There might therefore be less information in the market place if the liability regime is too stringent. Alternatively, the quality or utility of the information might decrease because it could conceivably be subject to all sorts of qualifications, assumptions and disclaimers.

Finally, the ultimate purpose of these measures needs to be borne in mind, namely the promotion of investor confidence in the market, and of an efficient market for securities. It is generally accepted that permitting fraudulent statements to be made would have a corrosive effect on market confidence. However, by contrast, investors do not expect to see a strict liability regime in place, and therefore it is difficult to argue that a strict liability regime is needed to secure that confidence. The clearly stated general principle under which the FSA operates, after all, is that consumers need to take responsibility for their own decisions.[174] The issue is rather the extent to which misstatements involving some wrongdoing short of fraud should be brought within the liability regime.

9.5.1.2   Providing Compensation to Those Who Suffer Loss

The second way in which a liability regime might contribute to the goal of promoting investor confidence in the market is by providing compensation to those who suffer loss as a result of a misstatement in a prospectus. There are two elements that need to be considered. The first is what investors should be protected against. The point has already been made that regulation of the capital markets in the UK does not aim to insulate investors from sustaining losses. It is expected that investors should take responsibility for their own decisions. However, it is well accepted that investors should be protected against some misstatements made in company prospectuses. These are selling documents, intended to persuade investors to buy securities in the company and it is not surprising that the law has protected investors from fraudulent misstatements made in those prospectuses for over a hundred years. More interesting is the question whether the law should protect investors against other forms of misstatement, namely those made negligently or even innocently. The same points can be made here as are discussed above, namely that a balance needs to be struck between the benefits of accurate information versus the costs involved if the level of liability is set too high. As regards prospectus liability, as we will see, the position in the UK is generally that liability can be imposed for negligent misstatements in some circumstances, though generally not for innocent misstatements.

Attention also needs to be given to the amount of compensation to which investors should be entitled. If an investor, A, buys a share for £2 which subsequently turns out to have been worth just £1.50 at the date of purchase should A be able to recover just 50p?

---

[174]   FSMA, s 5(2)(d).

Should A be able to recover any diminution in the future income stream of those shares, ie the reduced dividends which may also flow from the misstatement? What if the share is actually only worth £1.20 at the date when A sells it, can the additional 30p be recovered by A in any circumstances? Should A in fact be able to return the shares to the issuer, and recover the entire £2 investment? The level of compensation available to the investor will have an impact on the value of compensation as a tool for investor protection. The definition of investor for these purposes will also be relevant. Should it include only those initial subscribers who purchase from the company or the underwriting bank, or should investors in the after-market also be included in this protection?

As discussed previously, it is well understood that private enforcement is a poor remedy in the situation where shareholders are suing the company because this essentially involves shareholders suing other shareholders. Inevitably the cost of the damages imposed on the defendant company falls principally on the shareholders. The claimant shareholder recovers from the other shareholders with the result that this form of litigation involves pocket-shifting wealth transfers. For institutional investors such as pension funds holding a portfolio of companies they are just as likely to be among the shareholders in the issuer which has made the misleading statement as among the investors who were misled. The benefits they might gain in their latter capacity are likely to be balanced out by the losses they suffer in the former. However these payments will not entirely balance out in practice because of the fact that the litigation has transaction costs, such as the lawyers' fees involved in bringing and defending the litigation. These transaction costs mean that from a compensatory perspective shareholders are likely to be made systematically worse off by private litigation.[175] As a result long-term shareholders should not — rationally — engage in private litigation.

9.5.2   Private Enforcement: Civil Liability for Defective Prospectuses

Civil remedies for misrepresentations which have caused loss to those who have relied on them have existed in the UK for well over a hundred years. The first remedy was provided by the common law: liability for fraudulent misrepresentations was introduced via the tort of deceit.[176] A statutory liability regime for prospectuses followed shortly afterwards.[177] The current version of this statutory regime is to be found in section 90 of FSMA.[178]

---

[175]   JC Coffee, 'Reforming the Securities Class Action: An Essay on Deterrence and its Implementation' (2006) 106 *Columbia Law Review* 1534; MB Fox, 'Civil Liability and Mandatory Disclosure' (2009) 109 *Columbia Law Review* 237. This argument works better in the context of securities litigation arising once a company is trading its shares on the public market than it does at the IPO stage since investors are only buyers and not sellers at the IPO stage.

[176]   *Derry v Peek* (1889) 14 App Cas 337. It is notable that this common law liability for misstatements in prospectuses is in sharp contrast to the position regarding misstatements in disclosures made by the company once it has floated on the public market, discussed in detail in chapter 10. Perhaps the reason for this distinction is the origin of the liability regime in the tort of deceit, which as we shall see, requires that the maker of the statement should have intended that the recipients of the statement rely on it. This reliance is easier to establish in relation to prospectuses, which are selling documents, intended to persuade those that read them to buy shares in the company, than in relation to annual reports and accounts that are aimed at the shareholders of the company and are not primarily intended to induce the reader to engage in securities trading in the same way. The liability regime in relation to continuing disclosures is discussed in detail in 10.4.1 and 10.4.2.

[177]   Directors' Liability Act 1890.

[178]   In contrast the statutory liability regime for issuers in relation to continuing obligations to disclose was only introduced in 2006: FSMA, s 90A, introduced by Companies Act 2006, s 1270 (discussed at 10.4.1). See also

In addition to the claim under section 90 FSMA and liability in deceit, there are a number of other civil remedies which have developed in relation to misstatements in prospectuses. Two different claims for negligent misstatement have arisen: a claim under section 2(1) of the Misrepresentation Act 1967 and a claim for negligent misstatement based on the decision of the House of Lords in *Hedley Byrne & Co Ltd v Heller & Partners Ltd*.[179] The substance of this latter claim is that the defendant owes the claimant a duty of care not to cause the claimant economic loss by negligent misstatement. It may, in addition, be possible for the courts to treat the misrepresentation as having been incorporated into the subsequent contract concluded between the parties, giving rise to the possibility of a breach of contract claim by the investor against the company as the other party to the contract.[180] The nature of these claims will be discussed in the next section. As will become clear, the claim under section 90 is likely to produce the most favourable result for investors on most occasions and therefore this section will focus on an analysis of this claim, and then compare and contrast the other forms of civil liability where relevant.

9.5.2.1 The Nature of the Claim under Section 90 FSMA

In principle, section 90 FSMA makes those responsible for the prospectus (or supplementary prospectus) liable to pay compensation to any person who has acquired any of the debt[181] or equity securities to which the prospectus relates and has suffered loss as a result of any untrue or misleading statement in it or of the omission of any matter required to be included under FSMA. Under section 90 FSMA, anyone who has acquired the securities whether for cash or otherwise and can show that he has suffered loss as a result of the misstatement will have a prima facie case for compensation.

Under section 90 FSMA an investor can claim compensation for the distortion of the operation of the market through the provision of false information, arising either from positive statements included in the prospectus or from the omission of information required to be disclosed in the prospectus.[182] There is no requirement for the claimant to demonstrate that he or she relied on the misstatement, or even that they had read the prospectus, in order to establish a cause of action.[183] It is enough that the error affected the market price. This is sometimes described as 'fraud on the market', whereby a misstatement which has an effect on the market price can be said to cause an investor loss, even though that particular investor was not aware of the misstatement.

---

in this regard, HM Treasury, *Davies Review of Issuer Liability: Final Report* (June 2007), www.hm-treasury.gov.uk/media/4/7/davies_review_finalreport_040607.pdf; HM Treasury, *Extension of the Statutory Regime for Issuer Liability* (July 2008) www.hm-treasury.gov.uk/media/2/5/issuerliability_170708.pdf. As we shall see in 10.4.1 the scope of this liability regime is more limited than that which relates to prospectuses.

[179] [1964] AC 465.

[180] See eg *Jacobs v Batavia and General Plantations Trust Ltd* [1924] 2 Ch 329. Shareholders have faced difficulties bringing damages claims against companies in the past. Companies Act 2006, s 655 makes it clear that it is possible for a shareholder to bring such an action while continuing to hold shares in the company, ie it is not necessary for a shareholder to rescind the allotment before bringing the damages claim.

[181] For a discussion of the regulation of debt securities see chapter 11.

[182] FSMA, s 90(1)(b).

[183] Presumably, however, some causal connection will need to be shown between the misstatement or omission in the prospectus and the loss, so that if the claimant who buys the shares after a significant lapse of time will find it hard to demonstrate that the prospectus continues to have any significant impact on the price of the securities.

There are defences available for those responsible for the prospectus. The defendant will be 'exempted' from liability if he reasonably believed (having made such enquiries, if any, as were reasonable) that the statement was true and not misleading or that the matter whose omission caused the loss was properly omitted.[184] If the statement is made by an expert then the non-expert will escape liability if he or she acted on the reasonable belief that the expert was competent and had consented to the inclusion of the statement in the prospectus.[185] As a result, the standard for liability is negligence liability, but a particularly strong form of negligence liability since it is for the defendant to prove that he was not negligent rather than the claimant to prove that he was.[186] Alternatively he will not incur liability under section 90 FSMA if he can demonstrate that the claimant acquired the securities with knowledge that the statement was false or misleading or with knowledge of the matter omitted.[187] The breadth of this claim can be contrasted with the far narrower claims available in relation to the other civil law actions.

The tort of deceit consists of the act of making a wilfully false statement with intent that the claimant will act in reliance on it, and with the result that he does so act and suffers harm as a consequence.[188] In contrast with section 90 FSMA, in order to succeed the investor must demonstrate that he or she was induced to act by the false statement.[189] The investor must also demonstrate that the maker of the statement knew that it was false, did not have an honest belief in its truth, or was reckless as to its accuracy.[190] Under section 90 FSMA the investor need not demonstrate that the maker of the statement knew that the statement was wrong.[191] These elements are significant and make it difficult to establish deceit claims in practice. In addition, again in contrast to the section 90 FSMA claim, claims in deceit do not cover omissions per se, although omissions which cause the document as a whole to be misleading will be actionable.[192]

As regards a claim in negligence under *Hedley Byrne*, the scope of this duty was narrowly defined by the House of Lords in *Caparo Industries plc v Dickman*.[193] A claim in negligence arising from misstatements in a prospectus is a claim for pure economic loss, ie financial or pecuniary loss unrelated to physical injury or damage to property. The House of Lords in *Caparo* rejected the view that foreseeability is the touchstone of liability in

---

[184]   FSMA, Sch 10 para 1(2).

[185]   Ibid, para 2(2).

[186]   This is similar to the position under the Misrepresentation Act 1967, s 2(1) but very different to the position regarding common law negligence where the burden of proof is on the claimant.

[187]   FSMA, Sch 10 para 6. In this respect, the position of an investor under a s 90 claim is identical to that under the other forms of civil liability. A claim brought by an investor who knows that the information contained in the prospectus is false is likely to fail irrespective of the remedy he pursues. An investor who knows that the information is false cannot claim to have been induced to act on it and a claim for deceit or misrepresentation under the Misrepresentation Act 1967 will fail for that reason. Similarly, in a case based on breach of the duty of care, an investor could not credibly claim that the mistaken advice caused loss where he or she was actually aware of the mistake and proceeded anyway.

[188]   *Bradford Building Society v Borders* [1941] 2 All ER 205.

[189]   *Smith v Chadwick* (1884) 9 App Cas 187. The statutory liability for misstatements in continuing disclosures, under FSMA s 90A follows the deceit rule and requires reliance by the claimant (for discussion, see 10.4.1.2.2).

[190]   *Derry v Peek* (1889) 14 App Cas 337.

[191]   Lack of knowledge on the part of the responsible person is relevant only to the extent that it may provide a basis for the defence that they believed on reasonable grounds that the information was true: FSMA, Sch 10 para 1.

[192]   *R v Kylsant* [1932] 1 KB 442.

[193]   [1990] 2 AC 605.

such cases. In *Caparo* the claimant had acquired shares in a target company as part of a takeover. The claimant contended it had relied on the company's accounts for the accounting year 1983–4 which had been audited by the company's accountants, Touche Ross. Caparo asserted that these accounts, although gloomy, in fact overvalued the company and that the auditors had been negligent in not detecting the irregularities or fraud which had led to the overstatements in the accounts and in certifying the accounts as representing a true and fair view of the company's financial position. The House of Lords held that the auditors owed Caparo no duty of care in negligence. Their Lordships seemed particularly keen to avoid the imposition of 'a liability in an indeterminate amount for an indeterminate time to an indeterminate class'.[194] Instead, the House of Lords established three criteria for the imposition of a duty of care in a particular situation: foreseeability of damage, proximity of relationship and reasonableness.

Proximity, ie the closeness and directness of the relationship between the parties, is particularly important in this context. The court will have particular regard to the purpose for which the statement is made and communicated, the knowledge of the maker of the statement and the reliance on the statement by the recipient, in determining whether the necessary proximity is established. For those claiming, under *Hedley Byrne*, that they have suffered loss as a result of the negligent misstatement of another it will be crucial to demonstrate that the defendant 'knew' that the advice or statement would be communicated to the claimant either directly or indirectly and that the defendant 'knew' that that claimant was very likely to rely on that advice or statement.[195]

The way in which the courts have interpreted the concept of duty of care in this context has necessarily limited the occasions on which the investor may be able to bring a claim. A further limitation in negligence claims, when compared to section 90 FSMA, is that claims in negligence will not generally cover omissions. Where the negligent misstatement claim is instead brought under the Misrepresentation Act 1967, there is again no claim for misrepresentation in relation to omissions unless silence has the effect of making what is said untrue. Another important disadvantage of a claim under the Misrepresentation Act 1967 when compared to section 90 FSMA, is that, as with deceit claims, the investor must demonstrate reliance. If the evidence shows that the investor was unaware of the statement or took no notice of it, the claim will not succeed.[196]

The nature of the breach of contract claim is that the misrepresentation which appears in the prospectus has been incorporated into the subsequent contract between the parties. However, these claims face two significant difficulties. First, it is rare for prospectuses to make the kind of explicit promises about future value or performance which might give rise to a breach of contract claim for those future earnings. The prospectus will include representations of course, but these are generally statements of fact rather than promises and therefore can only protect the claimant's negative interest, not his expectation interest

---

[194]   *Ultramares v Touche* (1931) 255 NY 170, 179 per Cardozo CJ.

[195]   In the context of the statutory accounts provisions, which were the subject matter of the decision in *Caparo*, the House of Lords determined that the purpose of these accounts, as far as the shareholders were concerned, was to put them in a position where they could effectively exercise their governance rights over the board (for example, by replacing ineffective management), not to enable them to take investment decisions. Accordingly, a duty of care did not exist in relation to purchases of shares in the company, whether by existing shareholders or non-shareholders. On the other hand, the court also made it clear that liability could arise for auditors (and presumably others) where the financial statements were given to a known recipient for a specific purpose of which the auditors were aware and upon which the recipient had relied and acted to his detriment.

[196]   *Smith v Chadwick* (1884) 9 App Cas 187.

in future earnings. Second, in effect there are two separate contracts: the first is the contract of purchase of the shares, which may be with the company but may alternatively be with the underwriter, depending on the method chosen by the company to offer its shares to the public;[197] and the second is the contract between the shareholder and the company (and between the shareholders inter se) comprising the company's constitution (predominantly now the company's articles of association) with which the shareholder becomes bound once entered into the company's register.[198] The two are quite separate and even if the prospectus did contain explicit promises of the kind referred to above, the process of allotment of shares and the entry in the register are regarded as a complete novation, so that any such representations made in the prospectus will not automatically be carried through to the new contract.

It should be clear that the nature of the claim under section 90 FSMA is likely to be far more useful to an investor than the other civil law claims. In particular the fact that section 90 FSMA includes omissions, that the investor need not show reliance and the fact that the investor does not need to demonstrate knowledge on the part of the statement-maker, are all significant advantages of this claim. However, it is worth pointing out one limitation in the substance of a section 90 FSMA claim as compared to the other civil claims: the statutory claim only extends to situations where the allegedly false information is contained in the prospectus. This definition will include supplementary prospectuses and the summary[199] but will not include false information included in other documents, such as broker's circulars. There is some doubt as to whether this section applies if the misstatement appears in the Admission document required for an AIM admission.[200] In these instances the investor would have to pursue remedies other than section 90 FSMA.

9.5.2.2   Who Can Claim?

Section 90 FSMA provides that those responsible for the prospectus are liable to pay compensation to any person who has acquired any of the securities to which it relates and suffered loss as a result of any untrue or misleading statement in it or of the omission of something required to be included under the Act. The category of claimants includes both those who subscribe for securities and those who buy in the market when dealings commence, since the Act relates to all those who have 'acquired securities to which the particulars apply'.[201] Anyone who has acquired the securities whether for cash or otherwise, whether from the company or by purchase in the after-market, will have a case for compensation if they can demonstrate loss as a result of the misstatement or omission. The requirement of a causal link between the inaccurate prospectus and the loss operates to exclude purchasers whose acquisition occurs after the distorting effect of the wrong information has been exhausted. Presumably this will usually occur once it has become public knowledge that the information in the prospectus was wrong, so that the share price will have adjusted accordingly.

---

[197]   See pages 411–12.

[198]   Companies Act 2006, s 33.

[199]   However, liability in relation to the summary is restricted to situations where the summary is misleading when read together with the rest of the prospectus: FSMA, s 90(12).

[200]   The word 'prospectus' is not defined for the purposes of FSMA, s 90. It could be argued that s 90 should also apply to the AIM admission document, which is in effect a cut-down version of the prospectus required by the Prospectus Directive.

[201]   FSMA, s 90(1)(a). For the definition of 'acquisition' see FSMA, s 90(7).

This is in contrast to the position in the other claims available to the investor. One of the significant limitations which exist in bringing a claim in deceit is that in general only initial subscribers are able to bring a claim. The tort of deceit consists of making a wilfully false statement with intent that the claimant will act in reliance on it, and with the result that he does so act and suffers harm as a consequence.[202] A decision of the House of Lords has held that subsequent purchasers in the marketplace have no cause of action even though they may have relied on the prospectus because the purpose for which a prospectus is issued is to induce subscriptions of shares.[203] The purpose of the prospectus is therefore, for these purposes, exhausted once the initial allotment is complete.[204] This is an important point. Drawing a distinction between subscribers and market purchasers in the immediate period after dealings begin is highly artificial, at least in commercial terms, especially where the offer is fully underwritten and the lead managers are the initial subscribers for the shares and then on-sell or place them with investors in the market. The better view is that this form of action should extend to the purchasers in the after-market.[205] Companies have an interest not only in the issue being fully subscribed but also in the development of a healthy secondary market for the shares so that the initial subscribers can sell their shares in the market should they wish to do so.

As regards negligence claims, it is clear from the decision in *Caparo* that establishing proximity between the claimant and defendant is particularly important in the context of misstatements in prospectuses. The requisite proximity is likely to be established only as between the maker of the relevant statement and persons to whom the document is specifically directed. However, defining the category of those to whom a prospectus is directed is not straightforward. Those responsible for prospectuses will try to restrict this category, either by contractual exclusion clauses or on the basis that their statements were only intended for a limited audience, namely the initial subscribers. Support for this latter approach can be found in *Al-Nakib Investments (Jersey) Ltd v Longcroft*,[206] in which the court held that misleading statements in a prospectus issued in connection with a rights issue could form the basis of a claim by a shareholder who took up his rights in reliance upon the prospectus, but not when the same shareholder purchased further shares in the market.

However, it might be argued that the public at large could be expected to have sight of the prospectus. Indeed one of the purposes of a prospectus could be said to be the creation of a healthy after-market for the securities. On that analysis, investors in that after-market ought to be able to hold the authors of the prospectus to account in some circumstances. Support for this view can be found in *Possfund Custodian Trustee Ltd v Diamond*[207] in which Lightman J refused to strike out a claim that an additional and intended purpose of a prospectus issued in connection with a placing of securities was to inform and

---

[202]   *Bradford Building Society v Borders* [1941] 2 All ER 205.

[203]   *Peek v Gurney* (1873) LR 6 HL 377.

[204]   However, where the investor can demonstrate that the prospectus was only one of a series of false statements made by the defendants whose purpose was to encourage purchases in the secondary market as well as to induce initial subscribers, then subsequent purchasers may be able to maintain their claims: *Andrews v Mockford* [1896] 1 QB 372.

[205]   See eg J Cartwright, *Misrepresentation, Mistake and Non-Disclosure* (London, Sweet & Maxwell, 2007) para 7.52 who argues that liability should properly be regarded as extending to purchasers in the after-market as well as initial subscribers.

[206]   [1990] 1 WLR 1390.

[207]   [1996] 1 WLR 1351.

encourage purchasers in the after-market. This is a compelling argument. Unlike a set of company accounts, a prospectus is not a private document being prepared for the benefit of a limited class of people, but rather a public document required by statute to be prepared for the benefit of the public at large and for the proper regulation of the securities markets. Prospectuses are known to fulfil this function by the persons responsible for preparing them and therefore it can quite properly be said that the entire investing public is within the contemplation of the persons responsible for the contents of the prospectus. Of course if the offer of securities is actually to a more restricted class of investor, such as in a placing, then it would follow that the investing public at large would not be within the contemplation of those responsible for the prospectus.

The preferable view is that where offers of securities are made to the public, then those responsible for the prospectus should be liable to account to any investor for any loss suffered as a result of some misstatement in that prospectus. However, the present view in relation to claims in deceit or under *Hedley Byrne* appears to be narrower than this, restricting claims to the initial subscribers, unless the investor in the after-market can establish that the purpose of the prospectus was also to encourage purchases in the after-market. Where the investor's claim is based on the contractual relationship between themselves and the statement-maker, either a claim under the Misrepresentation Act 1967 or a claim for breach of contract, the claim can only be brought by the counter party to the contract, ie there is no possibility of claims by those in the secondary market. On this analysis, then, the claim under section 90 FSMA is significantly more powerful than the other possible civil liability claims because it clearly extends to purchasers in the after-market, subject to the limitation regarding causation, discussed above.

9.5.2.3   Who Can Be Sued?

The range of potential defendants under section 90 FSMA is much more wide-ranging than under the other potential forms of liability. The availability of a claim against persons other than the company will be particularly valuable as the company may be insolvent by the time that the claim is made. The claim under the Misrepresentation Act 1967 and the claim for breach of contract are limited in scope in that there must be a contractual nexus between the claimant and the defendant.[208] This significantly reduces the deterrent effect of this form of liability. In deceit claims the action can be against anyone who can be shown to be responsible for the statement, including the directors, accountants or other experts, but only if they have knowledge of the falsity of the statement or were reckless as to the truth.[209] The mens rea requirement is significant. An honest, even if wholly unreasonable, belief in the truth of the statement will not amount to deceit.[210] This will be difficult to establish in practice. In a claim of negligence, the claim can be brought not only against the company but also against directors and others but only if they can be

---

[208]   Eg, in a rights issue there will be a nexus between the company and the shareholders who take up the offer, such that the company can be sued, but not its directors or other experts and advisors who are involved in the offer. Statements made by an agent, such as a director, to the party to the subsequent contract (the investor) can form the basis of a claim but only to the extent of making the principal (the company) liable to the third party: *The Skopas* [1983] 1 WLR 857. Presumably the agent's behaviour could have consequences for the agent, eg they could constitute a breach of directors' duties.

[209]   Recklessness here must be understood to indicate the absence of any genuine belief in the truth of the matter rather than recklessness in the sense of gross negligence: *Derry v Peek* (1889) 14 App Cas 337, 375.

[210]   *Derry v Peek*, ibid.

shown to have owed a duty of care to the claimant not to cause loss or damage caused by breach of that duty. As discussed above, the courts have adopted a restrictive test as to when this duty will arise. These are significant constraints in practice.

Under section 90 FSMA liability falls on all those who are responsible for the prospectus.[211] For equity shares these include the issuer,[212] usually the company,[213] the directors of the issuer,[214] each person who accepts, or is stated to accept, responsibility for any part of the prospectus (but the liability only relates to that part)[215] and any other person who has authorised the contents of the prospectus or any part of it (again, in relation to the part authorised).[216] Experts, such as the reporting accountant, are therefore potentially included in this list,[217] and in relation to these experts, there is no need to demonstrate that the maker of the statement assumed responsibility towards the claimant. This is obviously in sharp contrast to liability under a common law negligence claim.

As discussed, a significant deterrent effect is only likely to occur where the liability falls directly on the makers of the statement, as it does in claims under section 90 FSMA, deceit claims and the negligence claim under *Hedley Byrne*. However, the legal and practical hurdles involved in the latter two claims mean that such claims are extremely unlikely to succeed in practice. This is likely to reduce their potential deterrent effect. The deterrent effect of a section 90 FSMA claim will be undermined if D&O insurance and other devices mean that the costs of any potential liability are transferred back to the company in practice and will this ultimately be borne by the shareholders of the company themselves.

9.5.2.4 *Remedy*

Under section 90 FSMA the only available remedy is financial compensation. The section is silent as to the basis on which compensation is to be assessed. In relation to the statutory compensation regime for inaccurate prospectuses which predated FSMA, the courts applied the deceit rules.[218] On this basis the measure of damages is tortious, ie to restore the claimant to his or her former position. A tort action involves an action for a wrong done whereby the claimant was tricked out of money in his pocket. As a result the highest limit of his damages is the whole extent of his loss, and that loss is measured by the money which was in his pocket and is now in the pocket of the company. However, in so far as he

---

[211]   FSMA, s 90 and Sch 10 covers misstatements in prospectuses and listing particulars. The only distinction is that the list of those responsible for prospectuses is found in the FSA Handbook (Prospectus Rules, PR 5.5) and those responsible for listing particulars is found in FSMA 2000 (Official Listing of Securities) Regulations 2001 (SI 2001/2956) reg 6. All those responsible for the prospectus must be identified in the prospectus itself as a result of the Prospectus Directive, art 6.

[212]   FSA Handbook, Prospectus Rules, PR 5.5.3(2)(a).

[213]   The issuer will be the company where the company is making the offer (in an offer for subscription or a rights offer or open offer) or seeks admission or has authorised these steps.

[214]   FSA Handbook, Prospectus Rules, PR 5.5.3(2)(b)(i) unless the prospectus was published without the director's knowledge or consent: PR 5.5.6. Liability also falls on those who authorise themselves to be named in the prospectus as a director, or having agreed to become a director, immediately or in the future: PR 5.5.3 (2)(b)(ii).

[215]   Ibid, PR 5.5.3(2)(c).

[216]   Ibid, PR 5.5.3 (2)(f).

[217]   Ibid, PR 5.5.9 provides that nothing in the rules shall be construed as making a person responsible by reason only of his giving advice in a personal capacity. This is generally assumed to exclude certain professionals (eg lawyers) although not the reporting accountants, or the sponsor required by the Listing Rules.

[218]   *Clark v Urquhart* [1930] AC 28.

has got an equivalent for that money, that loss is diminished.[219] So, in the example set out above where the investor pays £2 per share for shares which were worth £1.50 each at the time of the sale, the investor can recover 50 pence per share. This measure of damages includes no forward-looking element, ie there is no possibility of recovery in respect of any prospective gains which the investor may have been expecting. This tortious measure of damages also applies to claims for deceit, claims under the Misrepresentation Act 1967,[220] and claims for a breach of duty in negligence under *Hedley Byrne*.

By contrast damages for breach of contract protect the investor's expectation/positive interest, which does take account of the prospective gains which the investor, under the contract, was entitled to expect. So, for example, the investor may recover for loss of the expected profits on the shares, in the shape of future dividends and capital growth, although assessing these, necessarily speculative, claims, will be very difficult.[221] This difference makes a possible claim for breach of contract potentially very attractive. However, as discussed, significant difficulties attach to this claim which mean that breach of contract claims in this area are extremely rare in practice.

In terms of the rules of remoteness, there are two different tests that could be applied. In negligence the recoverable loss is defined by reference to the scope of the duty broken. In relation to claims relating to misstatements in prospectuses, it is likely that recovery will be limited to the loss caused by having a security worth less than the investor expected. So, the investor can only recover 50 pence per share in the above example, even if something else has occurred which caused the shares to be worth only, say, £1.20 at the date of claim. By contrast, the deceit test allows a person to claim all of the losses flowing from the misstatement. This can have important consequences. In *Smith New Court Securities Ltd v Scrimgeour Vickers (Asset Management) Ltd*[222] Smith New Court were induced to buy shares in a company by the fraudulent misrepresentations of one of Scrimgeour's executive directors. The purchase price was just over 82 pence per share, but the market price of the shares on the acquisition date was 78 pence per share. Usually the measure of damages would be the difference between these two sums. However, the company in question was subject to a substantial but entirely unrelated fraud, unknown to either the claimant or defendant, which occurred before Smith New Court's purchase. When this fraud became known the company's share price dropped considerably so that Smith New Court was only able to sell its shares in the company for between 30 and 40 pence over a period of time. Could Smith New Court recover the whole of these losses from Scrimgeour? The House of Lords held that in these circumstances Scrimgoeur was liable for *all* damage directly caused by the deceit.

Although the normal measure of damages is the difference between the purchase price and the market price at the date of purchase, this rule should not be rigidly applied if it would do an injustice. Here it was more accurate to assess the true value as comprising only the proceeds received for the shares. It is not surprising that distortions in the market

---

[219] *McConnel v Wright* [1903] 1 Ch 546, 554–55 per Romer LJ. So, for example, if the fraudulent misrepresentation in the prospectus stated that the company had already acquired valuable property, but that property was only acquired afterwards, credit for the value of this subsequently acquired property will be given in assessing the damages.

[220] *Royscot Trust Ltd v Rogerson* [1991] 2 QB 297.

[221] This may lead the court to assess damages on the reliance basis eg *Anglia Television Ltd v Reed* [1972] 1 QB 60, and *McRae v Commonwealth Disposals Commission* (1951) 84 CLR 377.

[222] [1997] AC 254.

price caused by the defendant should be taken into account by the court, as fraudulent defendants should not profit from their own wrongdoing. In some situations distortions caused by unrelated third party frauds will be regarded as a risk that is borne by the fraudulent defendant.

Of the civil law claims, not surprisingly the deceit test of remoteness applies to deceit claims and the negligence test of remoteness to claims under *Hedley Byrne*. As regards claims under the Misrepresentation Act 1967, there is some disagreement as to whether the remoteness test should be that applied to the tort of deceit or that applied to negligence. The difference between these measures may be significant. In *South Australian Asset Management Corpn v York Montague Ltd,*[223] for example, the same court as in the *Smith New Court* applied a different test where a surveyor had negligently valued properties for a lender proposing to take security over the properties. In this case, the surveyor's liability was limited to the loss caused to the lender from having a security worth less than it had expected but the surveyor was not liable for the loss caused by the subsequent drop of values in the property market generally. The Court of Appeal in *Royscot Trust Ltd v Rogerson*[224] felt that the appropriate measure was the deceit test, but this has been doubted by the House of Lords.[225]

As regards section 90 FSMA, the statute is silent as to the correct remoteness test to be applied. However, the fact that the deceit rules have been applied to the statutory liability regime in the past to determine the measure of damages suggests that the remoteness rules for deceit might also apply, ie that the claimant can recover all actual losses flowing directly from the transaction, potentially including losses caused by the independent fraud of a third party.

However, in one important respect the common law rules are potentially more powerful than the section 90 FSMA claim, because the investor may be able to rescind the contract for misrepresentation. This possibility does not exist in relation to section 90 FSMA which is purely a claim for financial compensation.

Rescission involves a reversal of the contract, so that the claimant hands back the shares and the company hands back the purchase price.[226] This right is exercisable against the contracting party,[227] ie the company, if the contract for the purchase is with the company (as it will be for example in an offer for subscription or rights issue of some kind), or against the investment bank acting on behalf of the company (where it is an offer for sale), or the transferor if the acquisition is from the previous holder of the shares. It will be necessary to demonstrate that the misrepresentation was made by the transferor. Where the transferor was the company, statements included in the prospectus, even if made by experts rather than the company directors, will generally be held to have been made by the company for these purposes.[228]

However, two barriers stand in the way to a successful rescission claim. First, the court has discretion to substitute damages for the remedy of rescission in appropriate cases.[229]

---

[223] [1997] AC 191.
[224] [1991] 2 QB 297.
[225] *Smith New Court Securities Ltd v Scrimgeour Vickers (Asset Management) Ltd* [1997] AC 254.
[226] *Re Scottish Petroleum Co* (1883) 23 Ch D 413. The investor may also recover interest: *Karberg's Case* [1892] 3 Ch D 1.
[227] *Collins v Associated Greyhound Racecourse Ltd* [1930] 1 Ch 1.
[228] *Mair v Rio Grande Rubber Estates Ltd* [1913] AC 853.
[229] Misrepresentation Act 1967, s 2(2).

The court may well decide that damages are more appropriate where it believes that the rescission is motivated by subsequent adverse movements in the stock market rather than by the misrepresentation made by the defendant.

Second, there are a number of significant limitations on the right to rescind. If the investor accepts dividends,[230] or attends meetings[231] (in the case of shares) or, presumably, accepts interest payments (in the case of debt securities), or if the investor sells or attempts to sell the securities[232] after the truth has been discovered, or even if the investor delays too long, then the contract will be taken to have been affirmed, and the right to rescind lost. The case law suggests that the investor must act promptly after the discovery of the misrepresentation or risk losing the right to rescind.[233] As you might expect, the liquidation of the company will also defeat a rescission claim, since at that point the interests of the company's creditors intervene. Likewise, the fact that the company is insolvent will bar rescission, even if winding up has not yet commenced.[234] In addition, rescission will be barred where restitution in integrum is not possible, such as where the shareholder has disposed of the securities before discovering the misrepresentation,[235] or if the investor has used the securities as security for its own borrowings or a third party has otherwise acquired an interest in them, at least until that third party interest has been unwound.

Although rescission appears to be a powerful remedy for investors, these difficulties mean that it has limited practical significance, and there is little evidence that this remedy is used much in practice.

9.5.2.5   Summary

On the whole, then, the statutory liability regime is more powerful than the other potential civil law claims. It also seems to be more likely to fulfil the aims of a liability regime. Section 90 FSMA targets the makers of the statements and therefore has the potential to have a significant deterrent effect. It also provides a generous level of compensation if the deceit rules regarding the measure of damages are applied. In addition, section 90 FSMA adopts a generous definition of 'investor' by allowing all acquirers the potential to bring an action, whether they are initial subscribers or purchasers in the after-market, although this is subject to a causation test, as described above.

9.5.3   Public Enforcement

There are two forms of sanction available under this heading: criminal and administrative. There is no element of compensation for investors in these sanctions, but the possibility of deterrence can still exist. The FSA's role in this context is significant, particularly in

---

[230]   *Scholey v Central Railway of Venezuela* (1868) LR 9 Eq 266n.

[231]   *Sharpley v Louth and East Central Coast Railway Co* (1876) 2 Ch D 663.

[232]   *Ex p Briggs* (1866) LR 1 Eq 483.

[233]   Eg *Sharpley v Louth and East Coast Railway Co* (1876) 2 Ch D 663.

[234]   *Tennent v The City of Glasgow Bank* (1879) 4 App Cas 615. The investor must therefore have issued a writ or had their name removed from the register before the company's insolvency or liquidation: *Oakes v Turquand* (1867) LR 2 HL 325.

[235]   If the shareholder has disposed of only part of the shares it seems reasonable in principle that rescission should still be possible since the investor can go back into the market to buy substitute shares: see *Re Mount Morgan (West) Gold Mines Ltd* (1887) 3 TLR 556 and *Smith New Court Securities Ltd v Scrimgeour Vickers (Asset Management) Ltd* [1997] AC 254, 262 per Lord Browne-Wilkinson for support of this view but cf *Re Metropolitan Coal Consumers' Association Ltd* (1890) 6 TLR 416.

relation to administrative sanctions. It was noted in 9.4.1 above that the FSA's role in this regard may be taken over by a new organisation, the Consumer Protection and Markets Authority, in the future. There is no suggestion at the time of writing that this change will entail any significant change to the substantive powers described in this section, but it is possible that it may have an effect on the intensity of enforcement, discussed at 9.5.4.

9.5.3.1   Criminal Sanctions

Under section 85 FSMA it is unlawful to make a public offer for securities or to request admission of securities to a regulated market unless an approved prospectus has been made publicly available.[236] On indictment the maximum penalty is a prison term of not more than two years or a fine or both.[237] The FSA has the power to invoke this provision.[238]

9.5.3.2   Administrative Sanctions

The primary sanctions in this area are the administrative sanctions operated by the FSA. The FSA has a number of sanctions that it can use prior to the allotment of the securities.[239] It has the power to refuse to approve a prospectus, thereby preventing the public offer or the admission to a regulated market from proceeding.[240] Alternatively, if approval has been given and the offer launched or the admission process begun, the FSA has power to suspend further action for up to ten days if it suspects that a provision of Part VI of FSMA, or a provision in the Prospectus Rules, or any other provision required by the Prospectus Directive, has been infringed. If it finds that such a provision has been infringed, it may require the offer to be withdrawn or the market operator to be prohibited from trading in the securities.[241] The FSA must give reasons for any suspension or prohibition decision in writing and the applicant has the right to appeal to the Tribunal.[242]

Alternatively the FSA can publicly censure the issuer or other person offering the securities or seeking admission for failure to comply with these requirements.[243] These are potentially very powerful weapons in the FSA's armoury for ensuring compliance with the relevant rules. However, the value of this sanction is limited to breaches of the rules which the FSA picks up in advance of the offer to the public (or admission to trading). As regards misstatements in the prospectus, the review carried out by the FSA in advance of publication[244] is very light touch and is not likely to reveal any but the most glaring inaccuracies. It is also notable that these sanctions fall predominantly on the company

---

[236]   FSMA, s 85. See the exemptions from liability listed in s 86.

[237]   Ibid, s 85(3).

[238]   Ibid, s 401.

[239]   It is possible for the FSA to make use of these sanctions once an admission to trading has been secured, but it is unlikely that the FSA will wish to exercise its power to prohibit trading at this point.

[240]   FSMA, s 87D. This section sets out the procedure the FSA must follow if it proposes to refuse to approve a prospectus. More likely the FSA will require the inaccurate information to be corrected and will refuse permission only if that is not forthcoming (s 87J).

[241]   Ibid, s 87K and 87L.

[242]   Ibid, s 87Q.

[243]   Ibid, s 87M. This is subject to the right to appeal to the Tribunal: s 87N.

[244]   Ibid, s 87A.

rather than the officers of the company who are likely to be the ones responsible for the misstatement or non-compliance. For these reasons the potential deterrent effect of these measures is diminished.

However, the FSA also has the power to impose monetary penalties on the issuer or on any other person offering shares to the public, seeking approval for a prospectus or requesting their admission to trading on a regulated market.[245] This power extends to any person who was a director of a company where the director was 'knowingly concerned' in the contravention.[246] The amount of the penalty will be such amount as the FSA considers appropriate. This power to impose a monetary penalty is a general power of the FSA, not confined to the Prospectus Rules or the Prospectus Directive. The FSA has the power to publicly censure the issuer or any other person offering securities or seeking admission in lieu of imposing a penalty.[247] A proposal to impose a penalty must be communicated to the person by way of a warning notice and a decision to impose a penalty may be appealed to the Tribunal.[248]

9.5.3.3   Summary

It is clear from this analysis that some significant ex post measures are available in the UK. These target misstatements in prospectuses and provide for both public and private enforcement of those misstatements, at least in terms of the law on the books. As regards private enforcement, the liability regime in place under section 90 FSMA is particularly valuable as a potential tool for providing both compensation and deterrence. The public enforcement measures available to the FSA also have a potentially important deterrent role. The next section will consider how these provisions operate in practice.

9.5.4   Intensity of Enforcement

It is not just the law on the books that is important. The enforcement of those laws is also an important consideration. There is some international and comparative research which associates the presence of deep and liquid securities markets with the presence in those jurisdictions of a vigorous system of private enforcement of obligations under securities law.[249] Other research has suggested that measures of *public* enforcement are more strongly associated with robust financial markets.[250] When Coffee carried out an analysis of the levels of both public and private enforcement in practice he concluded that enforcement intensity matters.[251]

There are two ways in which the intensity of enforcement can be measured, which can be termed inputs and outputs. 'Inputs' are essentially the resources (budget and staff) given to the securities enforcer, and 'outputs' are what they do with those resources, ie

---

[245]   Ibid, s 91(1A).
[246]   Ibid, s 91(2).
[247]   Ibid, s 91(3).
[248]   Ibid, s 92.
[249]   R La Porta, F Lopez-de-Silanes and A Shleifer, 'What Works in Securities Laws?' (2006) 61 *Journal of Finance* 1.
[250]   HE Jackson and MJ Roe, 'Public and Private Enforcement of Securities Laws: Resource-based Evidence' (March 16, 2009) *Harvard Public Law Working Paper* No. 08–28; *Harvard Law and Economics Discussion Paper* No. 638, available at www.ssrn.com/abstract=1000086.
[251]   JC Coffee, 'Law and the Market: The Impact of Enforcement' (2007)156 *University of Pennsylvania Law Review*, 229.

actions brought and sanctions imposed.[252] When inputs are considered the UK does well. When the overall regulatory costs for ten major jurisdictions are considered (Australia, Canada, France, Germany, Hong Kong, Singapore, Sweden, the UK and the US) and that data is adjusted for the relative size of those securities markets, the UK was found to rank third in the table behind Australia and Canada, but well ahead of the US.[253] However, when outputs are considered the position is quite different.

The number of public enforcement actions brought by the FSA is a fraction of those brought by the US regulator, and even when those numbers are adjusted to reflect relative market size the UK brings only 60 per cent of the actions brought by the SEC.[254] The picture is even starker when the aggregate monetary sanctions are compared. Over a two year period public securities enforcement monetary sanctions imposed by the US exceeded those imposed in the UK, even after adjusting for relative market size, by more than a ten to one margin.[255]

This differentiation between levels of enforcement in the US and the UK continues when private enforcement is considered. Private enforcement of securities law violations is frequent in the US,[256] and it is estimated that private enforcement in the US imposes even greater financial penalties than public enforcement.[257] By contrast, in the UK a recent study found only two instances of private rights of action brought in relation to misleading statements or omissions in disclosures since 1990[258] and there is no reported case of an investor succeeding in bringing a claim under section 90 FSMA or its predecessor, the Financial Services Act 1986. There are a number of important differences between the two civil litigation systems that might help to explain this disparity. These include the absence of class actions in the UK,[259] the absence of contingent fees for this type of claim[260] and the fact that the UK operates a 'loser pays' rule.[261]

Studies have found that there is a significant difference between the percentage of the FSA's and SEC's budget that goes to enforcement activity. The SEC devoted a percentage of

---

[252] Ibid.

[253] HE Jackson, 'Variation in the Intensity of Financial Regulation: Preliminary Evidence and Potential Implications' (2007) 24 *Yale Journal on Regulation* 253, 272 (Figure 3). Australia spent $279,587 per billion dollars of stock market capitalisation to the UK's $138,159 and the US's $83,943.

[254] Ibid, 284 (Figure 10).

[255] Ibid, (Figure 11) and JC Coffee, 'Law and the Market: The Impact of Enforcement' (2007) 156 *University of Pennsylvania Law Review* 229, 262. The two year period was 2000–2002.

[256] J Armour, B Black, BR Cheffins and R Nolan, 'Private Enforcement of Corporate Law: An Empirical Comparison of the US and UK' (2009) 6 *Journal of Empirical Legal Studies* 687.

[257] HE Jackson, 'Variation in the Intensity of Financial Regulation: Preliminary Evidence and Potential Implications' (2007) 24 *Yale Journal on Regulation* 253, 280 (Table 3).

[258] J Armour, 'Enforcement Strategies in UK Company Law: A Roadmap and Empirical Assessment' in J Armour and J Payne (eds), *Rationality in Company Law: Essays in Honour of DD Prentice* (Oxford, Hart Publishing, 2009) 85.

[259] Indeed class actions are basically unknown in Europe: C Hodges, 'Europeanisation of Civil Justice: Trends and Issues' (2007) 26 *Civil Justice Quarterly* 96.

[260] In the UK the Courts and Legal Services Act 1990, s 58 permits conditional fee arrangements by which lawyers can agree to no payment if the case is unsuccessful and an increase in their normal fee (but, crucially, not a share of the recoveries) if the case is successful. Fees can be doubled (but no more) through these agreements: The Conditional Fee Agreements Order SI 2000/823.

[261] It has also been suggested that the fact that in the UK it is relatively easy for a defendant to have the claim against it struck out at an early stage of the litigation has helped to impair the development of speculative litigation that is observed in the US eg HM Treasury, *Davies Review of Issuer Liability, Liability for Misstatements to the Market: A Discussion Paper* (March 2007) para 113.

its budget to enforcement that was roughly three times that devoted by the FSA.[262] The US also has a track record of imposing criminal penalties (fines and imprisonment)[263] far in excess of that of the FSA.

In general, then, the US invests more in both public and private enforcement than the UK. By contrast, European jurisdictions (eg Germany, France, Italy) invest in enforcement less than the UK. Explaining this difference is not straightforward and a number of different explanations have been put forward. One recent study, for example, suggests that the legal regimes of investor protection seem roughly to match the size and maturity of national capital markets.[264] Another suggestion is that differences in ownership regimes go some way towards explaining these differences.[265]

It has been suggested that the fact that the US is far ahead of the UK (and indeed all other securities regimes) in the number of public and private securities enforcement actions helps to explain the valuation premium which has been measured in relation to foreign firms which cross list in the US,[266] but which is not observed as occurring in any other jurisdiction, including the second most common cross listing destination, namely the London Stock Exchange.[267] The bonding explanation for cross listing suggests that managers 'bond' themselves not to divert excessive private benefits to themselves by deliberately subjecting themselves to a stricter regulatory standards under which the company is exposed to high levels of mandatory disclosure and faces significant private and public enforcement to ensure that those disclosures are full and accurate.[268] The bonding hypothesis has its critics, and at least part of the difference between the US and the UK regarding cross listing premiums in the past may have been due to the fact that cross listed firms in the US are subject to the same disclosure and enforcement standards[269] as domestic firms. Until 2010, overseas companies were subject to lower disclosure obligations than UK incorporated companies, under the UK disclosure regime. Following the introduction of the two tier listing regime in the UK, overseas companies will have a choice whether to apply for a standard listing or a premium listing. A standard listing will involve them complying with the same requirements with which all overseas companies have had to comply in the past, and with which all UK companies opting for a standard

---

[262]   JC Coffee, 'Law and the Market: The Impact of Enforcement' (2007) 156 *University of Pennsylvania Law Review* 229, 278–79.

[263]   Ibid, 274–76. Criminal enforcement is carried out by the Department of Justice, or the State criminal law enforcement authority.

[264]   R La Porta, F Lopez-de-Silanes and A Shleifer, 'The Economic Consequences of Legal Origins' (2008) 46 *Journal of Economic Literature* 285.

[265]   For discussion see Kraakman et al, n 83, 9.4.

[266]   C Doidge, GA Karolyi, and RM Stulz, 'Why Are Foreign Firms Listed in the US Worth More?' (2004) 71 *Journal of Financial Economics* 205.

[267]   According to Coffee, it might also help explain why firms appear to be increasingly choosing not to cross list in the US, despite the existence of this cross listing premium: JC Coffee, 'Law and the Market: The Impact of Enforcement' (2007) 156 *University of Pennsylvania Law Review* 229.

[268]   See JC Coffee, 'The Future as History: The Prospects for Global Convergence in Corporate Governance and its implications' (1999) 93 *Northwestern University Law Review* 641.

[269]   It has been suggested that US enforcement, both public and private, rarely focuses on foreign issuers in practice: J Siegel, 'Can Foreign Firms Bond Themselves Effectively by Renting US Securities Laws' (2005) 75 *Journal of Financial Economics* 319, 321.

listing now have to comply. A premium listing includes certain super-added requirements, previously reserved for UK companies, which will now be required of all companies (UK or overseas) who take up this option.[270]

Nevertheless, this historical difference cannot explain all of the differences observable between the valuation premium available in the US and UK. There does appear to be some value attached to the high enforcement standards that are observed in the US. If this is the case, should we be concerned about the relative lack of enforcement observable in the UK? Not necessarily. The explanation for this distinction may arise in part from the different shareholder protection regimes in place in the two jurisdictions. The suggestion is that the US expends more on enforcement than the UK because its corporate law gives shareholders less control rights than exist in the UK, so that enforcement in the US might to some extent be a substitute for weaker corporate governance.[271]

Of course, differences between the US and the UK in the levels of shareholder protection on offer are observable. Shareholders in the UK have the power to remove directors by an ordinary resolution at any time[272] whereas the staggered board provisions commonly used by US managers allow them to entrench themselves against the possibility of removal.[273] Unlike their US counterparts, UK shareholders vote on executive pay at the AGM.[274] The UK's Takeover Code imposes a 'no frustrating action' principle upon the managers of a target company which prohibits them from taking, once a bid is launched or anticipated, any actions that might have the consequence of frustrating its success, without first obtaining the consent of the shareholders.[275] This is in sharp contrast to the US 'board choice' model.[276] In contrast with the US, in the UK shareholder approval is necessary for certain types of corporate transaction, namely those involving either a risk of a conflict of interest or those which are of significant magnitude in relation to the size of the company.[277]

---

[270] See the Listing Rules Sourcebook (Amendment No 3) Instrument 2009 available at www.fsahandbook.info/FSA/handbook/LI/2009/2009_54.pdf and FSA, *Listing Regime Review*, CP09/24, October 2009. For further discussion see FSA, *Consultation on Amendments to the Listing Rules and Feedback on DP08/1 (A Review of the Structure of the Listing Regime)* CP 08/21, December 2008. The effective date for most of these rules is 6 April 2010, but standard listing was made available to UK companies from 6 October 2009.

[271] However, the fact that shareholders of UK companies have greater powers than their US counterparts to control managers means that there is a risk that shareholders may use their power opportunistically and this gives rise to a need for greater intra-shareholder protections in the UK than the US: J Armour and J Gordon, 'The Berle-Means Corporation in the 21st century' (work-in-progress on file with authors).

[272] Companies Act 2006, s 168(1). The default rule for appointment in UK public companies is for retirement by rotation (Model Articles for Public companies, Art 21: The Companies (Model Articles) Regulations 2008 (SI 3229/2008), Sch 3, but this is subject to the exercise of the mandatory removal power.

[273] LA Bebchuk, JC Coates and G Subramanian, 'The Powerful Antitakeover Force of Staggered Boards: Further Findings and a Reply to Symposium Participants' (2002) 55 *Stanford Law Review* 885.

[274] Since 2002 publicly traded UK companies have been required to send shareholders each year a directors' remuneration report on which an advisory shareholder vote must be taken at the AGM: Companies Act 2006, ss 420–421; 439. Studies suggest that this has had a restraining impact on executive pay: S Balachandran, F Ferri and D Maber, 'Solving the Executive Compensation Problem through Shareholder Votes? Evidence from the UK' *Working paper Columbia Business School/Harvard Business School* (2007).

[275] City Code, GP 3 and Rule 21. This is discussed in detail in chapter 12.3.2.2.1.

[276] For discussion see 12.3.2.2.1.

[277] FSA Handbook, Listing Rules, LR 10, LR 11. In addition company law requires that for certain transactions to which the counterparty is either a director or a related party shareholder approval must be sought eg Companies Act 2006, ss 190–196 (substantial property transactions) and ss 197–214 (corporate loans or similar transactions with directors).

Pre-emption rights are also treated differently: they are opt-out in the UK as opposed to the opt-in structure in place in the US.[278] In addition the waiver of pre-emption rights is governed by a well-established set of voting guidelines adhered to by institutional investors in the UK.[279] In addition to the protection from dilution provided by pre-emption rights, they also appear to have an important governance role in the UK by providing a focal point around which shareholders can centre monitoring and engagement with the company.[280] Pre-emption rights in the UK are strongly correlated with managerial turnover.[281] From this follows another distinction: institutional investors in the UK generally both own a higher percentage of shares and exercise closer oversight of managers than in the US.[282] For all these reasons UK shareholders have greater powers than their US counterparts to control managers using governance mechanisms and therefore it could be argued that the need for ex post enforcement in general is reduced.

The different levels of enforcement as between the US and UK may also be explained by different regulatory styles adopted by the SEC and FSA, at least historically. In contrast to the approach of the SEC which seems to focus on ex post enforcement to a significant extent, the FSA's approach appears has been more ex ante, ie it appears to have opted for a more advisory and consultative relationship with issuers. This type of discursive consultative approach is one that has been utilised by the Takeover Panel for many years with considerable success. It is also notable that one of the sanctions developed by the Takeover Panel, namely the threat of censure, is also one which exists in the FSA's armoury, and it is exercised periodically. In practice this is a powerful substitute for ex post formal enforcement. Public censure is cheap to impose compared to formal ex post enforcement since no legal proceedings are required, merely a public announcement.[283]

However, these issues of regulatory style are obviously not static. In the wake of the financial crisis the FSA has suggested that it plans to change its regulatory style, to be less light touch in future.[284] In addition, as discussed in 9.4.1, it is suggested that from 2012 the FSA's role in this regard will be taken over by a new organisation, the Consumer Protection and Markets Authority, with a new Economic Crime Agency with control of criminal enforcement. At the time of writing it is not suggested that this change will make any difference to the substantive enforcement powers discussed in 9.5.3, but it is possible that these new authorities will have more energy and enthusiasm for enforcement than that displayed by the FSA at present. There are also changes afoot at the European level with a new European Securities and Markets Authority in development which will have an enhanced enforcement role as compared to existing EU regulatory authorities, but again the detail of these proposals is still in development at the time of writing.[285]

---

[278]   For discussion see 4.3.1.

[279]   Pre-Emption Group, *Disapplying Pre-Emption rights: A Statement of Principles*, July 2008, available at www.pre-emptiongroup.org.uk.

[280]   DTI, *Pre-emption Rights: Final: A Study by Paul Myners into the Impact of Shareholders' Pre-emption Rights on a Public Company's Ability to Raise New Capital*, February 2005, URN 05/679.

[281]   J Franks, C Mayer and L Renneboog, 'Who Disciplines Management in Poorly Performing Companies?' (2001) 10 *Journal of Financial Intermediation* 209, 234.

[282]   BS Black and JC Coffee, 'Hail Britannia?: Institutional Investor Behaviour under Limited Regulation' (1994) 92 *Michigan Law Review* 1997.

[283]   See Armour, 'Enforcement Strategies in UK Corporate Governance', n 166.

[284]   H Sants, Annual Lubbock Lecture in Management Studies, Said Business School, Oxford, 12 March 2010.

[285]   European Commission, Proposal for a Regulation Establishing a European Securities and Markets Authority, COM (2009) 503 final, September 2009.

It could be that in part the difference between the US and the UK is due to the fact that higher levels of ex ante regulation of managers' behaviour exist in the UK in terms both of regulation by the shareholders through governance mechanisms and of regulation by the FSA, through consultation and advice. If this is the case then these ex ante mechanisms may reduce the need for ex post enforcement to some extent, so that the comparatively low levels of ex post enforcement observable in the UK would not be a particular cause for concern. These arguments are compelling but it is not clear that they can provide a full answer to the specific issues regarding misstatements in prospectuses, at least at the IPO stage. Most of the ex ante mechanisms available to shareholders to control managers that are outlined above will only take effect once the company has floated[286] and, prior to the IPO, there will be little opportunity for consultation with the FSA. As we have seen, the FSA's vetting role at this stage is fairly rudimentary.

However, there are other differences between the US and UK which could help to explain this difference in the levels of private enforcement. In addition to the differences between litigation systems described above, namely the lack of class actions and contingency fees in the UK, and the existence of the 'loser pays' rule, which undoubtedly have a significant impact, the different levels of institutional investor presence in the market could be a factor. It is well understood that private enforcement is a poor shareholder remedy in the situation where shareholders are suing the company because this essentially involves shareholders suing shareholders. Inevitably the cost of the damages imposed on the defendant company falls principally on the shareholders. The plaintiff shareholder recovers from the other shareholders with the result that this form of litigation involves pocket-shifting wealth transfers. For institutional investors such as pension funds holding a portfolio of companies they are just as likely to be among the shareholders in the issuer which has made the misleading statement as among the investors who were misled. The benefits they might gain in the latter capacity are likely to be balanced out by the losses they suffer in the former. However these payments will not entirely balance out because of the fact, discussed above, that the litigation has transaction costs which mean that from a compensatory perspective shareholders are likely to be made systematically worse off by private litigation.[287]

Indeed these problems have led to a number of recent studies in the US which suggest dissatisfaction with the system of private litigation in the US,[288] one of the major criticisms being that levels of private enforcement in this context are too high.[289] A drive towards higher levels of private enforcement might not necessarily be a good thing. Unless an investor thinks that there is some reason why it will systematically be on one side rather than the other of the litigation, then it will be rational for a widely dispersed long-term investor to support a system of letting the losses lie where they fall, and not bringing private litigation, thereby saving the transaction costs required to shift the loss. Securities

[286] For example, pre-emption rights do exist for private companies, although they are more lightly regulated than in public companies. In practice the most significant constraints exist as a result of the Statement of Principles drawn up by the Pre-Emption Group (www.pre-emptiongroup.org.uk/principles/index.htm) which only apply to public companies. For discussion see 4.3.1.

[287] JC Coffee, 'Reforming the Securities Class Action: An Essay on Deterrence and its Implementation' (2006) 106 *Columbia Law Review* 1534.

[288] Interim Report of the Committee on Capital Markets Regulation (November 2006).

[289] JC Coffee, 'Reforming the Securities Class Action: An Essay on Deterrence and its Implementation' (2006) 106 *Columbia Law Review* 1534.

litigation is therefore likely to be less attractive to long-term investors than to short-term ones, and if the UK market has higher levels of long-term investors then it would not be surprising to find lower levels of private litigation being initiated.

There are a number of differences between the US and the UK, both legal and practical which help to explain the differences in the levels of public and private enforcement observable in the two jurisdictions, and which suggest that the very low levels of private and public enforcement in the UK are not necessarily a problem. It is interesting that, given the very low levels of formal enforcement activity, the standard of accuracy of information included in prospectuses is still perceived to be high, and indeed that this is linked in part to civil liability standards. This would suggest that the low levels of formal enforcement observable in practice have not compromised the theoretical deterrent effect of the liability regime.

9.6 Conclusion

UK capital markets regulation rests on two dominating principles. The first is that members of the public who are offered company securities are entitled to full disclosure to them of the nature of what is on offer before they make a financial commitment. The second is that effective remedies should be available to redress any loss incurred as a result of failure on the part of the company to make complete or accurate disclosure.

The principle of mandatory disclosure is central to the regulatory regime in the UK described in this chapter. Companies listing on the London Main Market will have to comply with significant levels of information disclosure, the content of which mainly flows from EU legislation. However, as discussed, the vast majority of this information is backward-looking, namely historical data relating to the company, its directors, its shareholders, its advisers and its business to date. There is very little of the forward-looking data which investors might find helpful in assessing the future prospects of the company. Forward-looking data carries with it the risk that directors might be over optimistic about the company's prospects. The provision of historical data is cheaper to produce, easier to compare across companies, and easier to verify. However, the fact that the information provided to investors is backward-looking necessarily limits the value of information disclosure as a device for assessing the future value of the securities on offer in an IPO.

The use of mandatory disclosure is also coupled with provisions to allow enforcement actions to be brought in the event that the information disclosed is inaccurate or incomplete. These are an important adjunct to the mandatory disclosure rules since the value of the mandatory disclosure regime is significantly diminished if there is no reasonable prospect that the information actually provided is full and accurate. In the context of IPOs the UK provides relatively minimal ex ante verification processes but there is a range of ex post measures available which allows for both private and public enforcement of misstatements in prospectuses. In terms of the law on the books, the ex post enforcement measures on offer are substantive and potentially provide both compensation to the investors who have suffered loss as a result of the misstatement, and a deterrent effect on directors and others who may make misstatements in prospectuses in the future. Although the levels of both public and private enforcement in practice are low in the UK this is not an issue that need necessarily be of concern. In large part the fact that these levels are lower than the US, for example, can be explained by systemic differences between the two jurisdictions. Perhaps most reassuring is the fact that despite the low levels of enforcement it is generally felt that the level of accuracy in UK securities prospectuses remains high.

In the next chapter the continuing obligations of issuers, once their shares have been listed, will be discussed. In chapter eleven we will then discuss these issues in the context of debt securities. Although there are many similarities in the way in which the issue of debt and equity securities are regulated, particularly where debt securities are offered to the public, there are also a number of significant and important differences which require separate analysis.

10

Ongoing Regulation of the Capital Markets

10.1 Introduction

In chapter nine we analysed the regulation of initial public offers, when companies offer their shares to the public for the first time. This chapter will consider the distinct, but allied, topic of the ongoing regulation of the capital markets. In order to understand and evaluate the regulation that has been put in place to deal with this issue, the aims of regulating the ongoing market must first be understood. Section 10.2 considers these aims. Broadly, two mechanisms are put in place to regulate the market at this stage: mandatory disclosure rules (the predominant technique utilised at the IPO stage) and rules designed to prevent market abuse, although there is some overlap between these concepts in practice. This chapter will consider each of these techniques, both in terms of the content of the rules (the law on the books) and the enforcement regime in place. This chapter deals with the ongoing regulation of equity securities. Some of the issues raised here are also relevant to debt securities but the extent of this overlap, and the regulation of debt securities more generally, are discussed in the next chapter.

10.2 The Objectives of Ongoing Capital Market Regulation

The primary goal of ongoing capital market regulation is to ensure that the prices of publicly traded securities are reasonably well informed, which is similar to the goal in regulating IPOs, discussed in chapter nine. However, a second goal is to ensure that public company shareholders are protected by effective corporate governance institutions once they invest in publicly traded shares. This latter goal only really comes to the fore once the IPO has taken place. Mandatory disclosure is the main regulatory technique utilised at the IPO stage, and this technique is again used in relation to ongoing market regulation, although the purpose of mandatory disclosure is somewhat different, and it is not the only regulatory technique employed. This section will discuss the objectives of ongoing market regulation in detail, and highlight the differences between the techniques employed here and those employed at the IPO stage.

10.2.1   Promoting an Efficient Market Price

As discussed in chapter nine, mandatory disclosure is used at the IPO stage in order to provide investors with the information they need to decide whether to purchase the offered securities. Mandatory disclosure at this point operates to modify the principle of caveat emptor (buyer beware). However, once the securities have been listed, a market for those securities develops. As a result, the rationale for the regulation of the market changes. The primary rationale to explain the need for disclosure in securities markets after the IPO stage is the promotion of market efficiency. This section will first assess the theory behind market efficiency, and will then consider the form that ongoing capital market regulation takes in practice.

10.2.1.1   *Efficient Capital Markets Theory*

Efficient capital markets theory is based on the idea that prices within the market at any given time 'fully reflect' available information.[1] Three different forms of efficiency have been identified: weak form efficiency, semi-strong form efficiency and strong form efficiency.[2] In a weak form market the current prices of securities reflect all relevant historical information. In a semi-strong form efficient capital market the prices adjust rapidly to information as it becomes available. In a strong form efficient capital market the prices reflect all relevant information, including information not yet made public. There is significant support for the view that securities markets in major jurisdictions, including the US and UK, are efficient in both the weak form and semi-strong form, with the semi-strong version being most favoured.[3] The major problem with the strong form hypothesis is the fact that it seems that profits can still be made by insider trading. Clearly the fact that insiders can make profits from information which is known to them but which is not yet public suggests that the market price does not reflect that non-public information, and the market is thus not strong form efficient.

Once the semi-strong form of market efficiency is accepted then this suggests that the more information that can be made available to the public, the better. A deficiency of information is seen as reducing allocative efficiency.[4] Accurate information is necessary to ensure that money moves to those who can use it most effectively and that investors make optimal choices about their investment decisions. Without adequate information investors will not be able to distinguish the 'good' investments from the 'bad' investments and since those offering the 'better' securities will not be able to distinguish themselves, investors will view all securities as average. Therefore higher quality securities will sell at lower prices than they would if the information were available,[5] there will be too little

---

[1]   EF Fama, 'Efficient Capital Markets: A Review of Theory and Empirical Work' (1970) 25 *Journal of Finance* 383.

[2]   Ibid.

[3]   EF Fama, 'Efficient Capital Markets: II' (1991) 46(5) *Journal of Finance* 1575. However, some empirical studies also identify market phenomena that are inconsistent with the efficient capital market hypothesis (for a summary see JW Brudney and WW Bratton, *Corporate Finance: Cases and Materials*, 4th edn (New York, Westbury, 1993) 133–36).

[4]   RJ Gilson and RH Kraakman, 'The Mechanisms of Market Efficiency' (1984) 70 *Virginia Law Review* 549.

[5]   This analysis assumes that the information can be made available costlessly. However, there are those who draw a distinction between informational efficiency of the kind proposed by the efficient capital market hypothesis and fundamental efficiency, by which they mean that prices should reflect the best current estimate of the present value of future cash flows from the security. If prices are informationally efficient but not

investment in the good businesses and the low quality businesses, the 'lemons', will attract too much money.[6] Investors lose because they invest in the wrong securities, and society loses because the high quality shares are undervalued, and there is the possibility that investors may, in the long run, not invest at all in such a market. The disclosure of information about the companies concerned is a way of dealing with these issues.[7] An informed securities market enhances not only the value of high quality companies, but also the value of the marketable securities of public companies in aggregate.[8]

It is widely accepted that the efficiency of the price formation process in a securities market depends in large part upon the mechanisms whereby information is produced, verified and analysed.[9] Analysis is a process which is largely left to market participants, but most jurisdictions put measures in place to regulate the production and verification of the information. It is these measures that will be discussed in this chapter, however, given that much of the analysis on which individual investors actually rely is performed by intermediaries on their behalfs, an alternative form of investor protection would be to regulate the intermediaries who channel the information to the investors.[10]

However, the efficient capital market hypothesis on which this theory of regulation is based has come under attack.[11] In particular, this hypothesis has been under threat from the advent of behavioural analysis.[12] The work of behavioural analysts causes difficulties for the efficient capital market hypothesis because this hypothesis does not capture socio-psychological factors, such as herding, which may lead investors to engage in irrational trading activities that affect the prices of securities. Behavioural finance shifts attention from the analysis of the relationship between prices and information, to investor behaviour, using the findings of behavioural psychologists about individuals' departures from rational decision-making. In particular very large market changes and excessive volatility (booms and busts) are attributed to 'irrational' investors who over-react to a

---

fundamentally efficient then this may result in an allocative efficiency problem as scarce resources may not be allocated to their most productive use: LA Stout, 'The Mechanisms of Market Inefficiency: An Introduction to the New Finance' (2003) 28 *Journal of Corporate Law* 635. Gilson and Kraakman have expressed doubt about the existence of these two separate concepts of market efficiency: RJ Gilson and RH Kraakman, 'The Mechanisms of Market Efficiency: Twenty Years Later: The Hindsight Bias' (2003) 28 *Journal of Corporate Law* 715.

[6]   G Ackerlof, 'The Market for "Lemons": Qualitative Uncertainty and the Market Mechanism' (1970) 84 *Quarterly Journal of Economics* 488.

[7]   The primary value associated with disclosure is therefore that of ensuring accurate share values. However, some academics also associate disclosure with other important corporate benefits: R Kraakman, 'Disclosure and Corporate Governance: An Overview Essay' in G Ferrarini et al (eds), *Reforming Company and Takeover Law in Europe* (Oxford, Oxford University Press, 2004). In particular disclosure can provide an enforcement function (eg it allows shareholders to decide whether to vote to ratify a self-dealing transaction by directors), an educative function (eg when public shareholders need to ratify an important corporate decision) and a regulatory function (eg companies must disclose the extent to which they comply with corporate governance regimes such as the UK Corporate Governance Code).

[8]   See RJ Gilson and RH Kraakman, 'The Mechanisms of Market Efficiency' (1984) 70 *Virginia Law Review* 549 on the role of mandatory disclosure in economising on investor information costs.

[9]   RJ Gilson and RH Kraakman, 'The Mechanisms of Market Efficiency: Twenty Years Later: the Hindsight Bias' (2003) 28 *Journal of Corporation Law* 715. This proposition remains robust despite developments in behavioural science: for discussion see E Avgouleas, *The Mechanics and Regulation of Market Abuse: A Legal and Economic Analysis* (Oxford, Oxford University Press, 2005) ch 2.

[10]   To some extent this happens already. The FSA has a system in place for regulating the providers of financial products, for example, see eg A Hudson, *The Law of Finance* (London, Sweet & Maxwell, 2009) chs 8–11. Reference is also made to this issue in the context of debt securities in chapter 11. However, detailed discussion of these issues fall outside the scope of this book.

[11]   For an overview of the literature see Avgouleas, *The Mechanics and Regulation of Market Abuse*, n 9, 44–74.

[12]   Eg, A Shleifer, *Inefficient Markets: An Introduction to Behavioural Finance* (Oxford, Clarendon Press, 2000).

given flow of information.[13] Proponents of the efficient capital market hypothesis find these bubbles particularly difficult to explain. Where irrational behaviour in the market is inconsistent, then it can be expected that some investors' biases or irrational behaviour will cancel out that of others. However, a bubble results from investors all operating according to a single or common bias.[14]

It seems that investors do not always behave rationally and that markets can sometimes diverge from estimated economic values as a result of self-reinforcing herd and momentum effects. The fact that the market can behave irrationally is important. It has implications for regulators. For example, the basis of the current system of financial regulation is premised on the idea that liquidity is good and therefore that more liquidity is better. However, there may be occasions, when the market is behaving irrationally, in the middle of a bubble effect, when the regulator needs to reconsider this position, and constraints on liquidity may be justified in order to preserve the smooth functioning of the market. The decision of the FSA to ban short selling for a period in autumn 2008 when some banking shares were in free fall, was an example of this.[15]

However, the view that investors can be irrational does not mean that liquid and efficient markets have no benefits. The proposition that new information influences price behaviour still holds true, as does the fact that investors rely on market prices to make investment decisions. Markets still appear to be 'informationally' efficient even if we may doubt the market's fundamental efficiency (ie whether the prices reflect the underlying value of companies). New information regarding a security is quickly incorporated into the market via the price of that security. Even in the midst of a bubble, liquid markets can provide useful and accurate price signals as to the relative attractiveness of different securities even if the overall level of prices is affected by the irrationality. Market prices may be regarded as the best indicator of value, even if they are not the most effective and accurate carriers of market information in all circumstances.[16] A financial market system based on disclosure which aims to provide investors with accurate share prices is still a valuable and appropriate regulatory goal.[17]

10.2.1.2　Regulation of the Ongoing Market: The Role of Mandatory Disclosure

As a consequence of the efficient capital market hypothesis, one of the foundation stones in the regulation of the ongoing market is mandatory disclosure. We saw in chapter nine

---

[13] A Tversky and D Kahneman, 'Judgment Under Uncertainty: Heuristics and Biases' (1974) 185 *Science* 1124.

[14] Even in a 'mispriced' market it may be that some large arbitrage traders, such as hedge funds, will enter the market and help to correct the pricing inefficiencies. However, fund managers acting for 'arbitrageurs' depend for their jobs and bonuses on performing equal to or better than the market and will make decisions in order to make money and keep their jobs rather than to correct prices. As a result they, too, are likely to herd: A Shleifer and LH Summers, 'The Noise Trader Approach to Finance' (1990) 4 *Journal of Economic Perspectives* 19; RJ Gilson and RH Kraakman, 'The Mechanisms of Market Efficiency: Twenty Years Later: The Hindsight Bias' (2003) 28 *Journal of Corporate Law* 715.

[15] For discussion see Lord Turner, *The Turner Review, A Regulatory Response to the Global Banking Crisis*, March 2009, 112.

[16] The adoption of a number of institutional investors of passive investment strategies (ie index tracking) on the assumption that this will ensure them the best returns, seems to support this view.

[17] It is notable that in the Turner Review, which reviewed the causes and implications of the financial crisis, although investor irrationality was accepted to exist in certain circumstances, there was no suggestion that the FSA's policy of regulation based on disclosure needed to be reconsidered: See *The Turner Review*, n 15.

that mandatory disclosure is the core form of regulation in place at the IPO stage too. However, mandatory disclosure operates in a different way post-IPO, as this section will discuss.

It was explained in chapter nine that at the IPO stage the aim of investor protection is pursued primarily by providing investors with the information they need to make efficient resource allocation decisions and for them to be protected from fraudulent (and negligent) issuers. In the UK this is primarily achieved via a combination of mandatory disclosure and anti-fraud rules. However, both the mandatory disclosure and the fraud rules discussed in chapter nine focus on the prospectus. The information disclosed presents a picture of the company at the moment in time that the shares are offered to the public. As discussed the prospectus contains a significant amount of historical information about the company, but very little by way of future projections.[18] The focus is on a particular, and narrow, window of time.

The aim of the enforcement regime associated with disclosure at the IPO stage is primarily to protect those who are the initial subscribers to the company's prospectus. There is some protection of those who trade in the market once dealings commence, but even here the protection is tied to the prospectus. Under section 90 FSMA the claim for compensation depends on the investor demonstrating that the loss results from a misstatement or omission in the prospectus.[19] The requirement of a causal link between the inaccurate prospectus and the loss operates to exclude purchasers whose acquisition occurs after the distorting effect of the wrong information has been exhausted.[20] Similarly, in order to succeed in a negligent misstatement claim arising out of the prospectus, a purchaser in the after-market would need to demonstrate that he was in the contemplation of the statement makers, and that the purpose of the prospectus was to encourage purchases in the after-market.[21]

There are significant differences between the initial disclosures made to the public in the prospectus and the ongoing disclosures made once the company has been listed. The prospectus is first and foremost a selling document. The aim is to convince investors to purchase shares in the company, on the basis that this is a liquid investment which investors could sell for a profit in the future. The fact that the purpose of the prospectus is to promote securities to investors justifies the tough legal regime, described in chapter nine, which is in place to regulate the accuracy of statements placed in the prospectus.

By contrast periodic and ad hoc disclosures made once the company has been listed are generally expressions of routine reporting requirements, as discussed below, and do not typically coincide with a selling effort on the part of the company. That is not to say that disclosure rules are not needed at this stage. Bad news will hurt directors by reducing their compensation and diminishing their job security. The increasing incidence of equity-based compensation schemes such as share options, also means that directors suffer personally if the share price of the company drops. The worse the news, the less likely directors are to disclose it voluntarily and the more likely they are to be tempted to

---

[18]   See 9.4.2.

[19]   FSMA, s 90(1)(b).

[20]   For further discussion see 9.5.2.2.

[21]   *Caparo Industries plc v Dickman* [1990] 2 AC 605. There is some debate as to whether the purchasers in the after-market can be said to be within the contemplation of those responsible for a prospectus (see *Al-Nakib Investments Ltd v Longcroft* [1990] 1 WLR 1390 cf *Possfund Custodian Trustee Ltd v Diamond* [1996] 1 WLR 1351). For discussion see 9.5.2.2.

misrepresent the company's finances. As discussed in chapter nine, mandating the disclosure of information can minimise the agency cost for public investors, and this is as true for ongoing disclosures as for those made on the initial public offering of shares. Rules are also needed once the company has successfully offered its securities to the public, in order to reduce informational asymmetries in financial markets and to increase the quality and quantity of information to which outside investors have access at that point in time.

So, one purpose of regulating the market on an ongoing basis is to provide information to investors in order to enable them to make investment decisions about whether to buy, or sell, securities in a particular company. This is similar to the arguments made in favour of regulation at the IPO stage. However, regulation of the ongoing market is more complex than at the IPO stage. First, ongoing disclosures are sometimes regarded not as investor-focused (ie providing information to all those who may make investment decisions about the company, both those who have already invested and those yet to do so) but as specifically shareholder-focused, and are seen as providing information to share-holders in order to enable them to perform their corporate governance function. This is discussed in the next section, 10.2.2. It is also worth noting that disclosures can benefit groups outside the specific focus of the disclosure. Lenders and other financial intermediaries may employ corporate disclosure to reduce monitoring costs, for example.[22]

Second, the need to protect investors goes further than requiring the disclosure of adequate and accurate information to investors. Disclosure alone will not be enough to protect investors and the integrity of the marketplace more generally. The disclosure will only be beneficial if it is both timely and accurate and therefore rules are needed to ensure the timeliness and quality of that information. However, the need to reduce informational asymmetries in the ongoing market, once companies have succeeded in offering their securities to the public, requires more than just placing disclosure obligations on the issuer. It also requires rules to be put in place to prevent insiders[23] using their position to make gains at the expense of outsiders. It is possible for insiders to release misleading information into the marketplace, or to withhold significant information about the company from the marketplace, and thereby distort the market. However, other forms of market abuse move away from the principle of disclosure and tackle different kinds of manipulation or improper behaviour, such as 'wash sales', where a trader simultaneously buys and sells the same securities (ie trades with himself) to give the appearance of a legitimate transfer of title or risk, or both, at a price outside the normal trading range for that investment in order to artificially move the price of those securities. Capital market regulation of the ongoing market therefore tackles informational asymmetries both by the use of mandatory disclosure obligations and by regulating market abuse.

10.2.1.3 Regulation of the Ongoing Market: The Role of Market Abuse

There are two forms of recognised market abuse: insider dealing and market manipulation. In the UK and EU the term 'market abuse' covers both of these terms.[24] Both are said to impair market integrity and the current regulatory approach is to treat both forms of conduct under one umbrella.

---

[22] See 5.2.2.
[23] For discussion of the definition of insider see 10.5.2.
[24] FSMA, s 118 and see Market Abuse Directive 2003/6/EC, article 1.

Insider dealing is the situation in which those with inside information about securities use that information to make a profit or avoid a loss. An obvious example is where a director of a company knows, as a result of his position, that a takeover offer is about to be made for the company and that the price offered will be at a substantial premium to the current market price of the shares, and before that information is made public he buys more shares in the company at the current market price in order to participate in the windfall. Alternatively the director may know that the company is about to announce substantial losses and so may sell his shares in advance of the disclosure of that information in order to avoid the inevitable drop in share price that will result from the announcement. It is not the holding of information which is relevant. There is no offence of receiving or holding inside information. The offence involves the use, or misuse, of that information.[25] The original justification for regulating insider dealing was because it was seen as an abuse of the fiduciary relationship which exists between the fiduciary (generally the director) and his or her principal (the company). As a result company law rules were used to regulate it.[26] Consequently the initial concept of insider trading was a narrow one. This concept can be widened, to treat outsiders in possession of inside information as temporary insiders, where they have been entrusted with information, or to construct the necessary fiduciary relationship between the parties. This would involve the expansion of the concept of the fiduciary relationship beyond its traditional understanding in company law. However, the result is likely to be unsatisfactory: the links created would be somewhat artificial and the reach of insider dealing as a concept would still be limited.

The approach adopted by the EU has been somewhat different. The rationale for regulating insider dealing at EU level is to facilitate the 'smooth functioning of securities markets',[27] rather than a reliance on the fiduciary relationship. Instead, as we shall see, the modern approach to insider dealing defines inside information as material non-public information, irrespective of its source and insiders are defined principally by reference to their possession of that information, not by their relationship to the issuer.[28] Consequently insider dealing has become a securities law matter, with a focus on protecting investors and the market generally, rather than a company law matter.

However, the idea that insider dealing needs to be regulated at all has proved controversial. A number of arguments are advanced against regulating insider dealing.[29] There are those who argue that inside information is a property right of the company, allocation of which is better left to purely contractual negotiations rather than formal law. An adjunct of this argument is that the use of inside information is an appropriate way to compensate corporate personnel, particularly directors, as a mechanism for encouraging innovation.[30]

---

[25]   *AG's Ref (No 1 of 1988)* [1989] 1 AC 971. There is no offence committed if the insider makes use of the information in order to decide not to sell. A failure to sell is not illegal because there has been no securities transaction.

[26]   P Davies, 'The European Community's Directive on Insider Dealing: From Company Law to Securities Markets Regulation' [1991] *Oxford Journal of Legal Studies* 92.

[27]   Market Abuse Directive, 2003/6/EC, 2nd Considerandum.

[28]   For discussion see 10.5.2.

[29]   One of the arguments against regulating insider dealing is based on the perceived inability of regulators to monitor and enforce insider dealing. This will be discussed below at 10.5 when enforcement is discussed more generally.

[30]   HG Manne, 'In Defence of Insider Trading' (1966) 44 *Harvard Business Review* 113; JR Macey, *Insider Trading: Economics, Politics and Policy* (New York, Free Press, 1966).

This argument is rooted in a time when insider dealing was regarded as an aspect of company law, since it focuses predominantly on insiders who are directors,[31] a view which is no longer current in the UK. It also suffers from a number of other defects. There is no evidence that directors are undercompensated, and, to the extent that they are, there are many other mechanisms for compensating them. The growth of equity-based compensation schemes in particular might be said to be better targeted at achieving this goal. More problematically, insider dealing is a poor tool for incentivising managers. In particular, it is unpredictable since the opportunity to exploit inside information comes along infrequently. In addition, managers can make just as much money from trading on bad news about the company as good news. This moral hazard where managers become 'indifferent between working to make the firm prosperous and working to make it bankrupt'[32] is particularly unacceptable.

Another argument put forward is that insider dealing is a victimless crime. Investors who trade with, or at the same time as, insiders are willing buyers/sellers. They do not know the identity of the counterparty to the transaction and would have bought or sold to someone else in any case, even if the insider had not been in the market. Since there is no inducement by the insider to trade there is no loss in the investor's hands which can be said to have been *caused by* the insider. An argument is even mounted that investors benefit because if an insider goes into the market to buy shares it increases the demand for shares and the third party seller of shares will therefore benefit from any consequential increase in price.

The points about causation and inducement may be relevant to determining the rationale of insider trading in a system which allows individual investors to bring civil claims against the insider in relation to the insider trading, but the UK has no such system. Insider dealing is dealt with by way of a mixture of criminal and administrative sanctions in the UK, not civil law remedies.[33] More importantly, insider dealing is a zero sum game, ie the net benefits of insider dealing must equal the net losses.[34] Although individual investors may benefit from insider dealing on occasion, the fact remains that the net result to investors generally is negative. The victims are therefore all those who constitute the market, other than the insiders. The losses are real, albeit thinly spread, and the concern is that insider dealing can impact investor confidence in the accuracy of market prices and reduce investment in the market in the first place.

This issue is an important one. Arguments in favour of regulating insider dealing often commence from the notion that insider dealing is 'unfair'. These arguments run the risk of being vague and based predominantly on a sense of moral outrage.[35] However, the approach of the EU to insider dealing does put flesh on the bones of this concept. Insider dealing laws are regarded as necessary to promote fair and orderly markets. According to the Market Abuse Directive, the objective of legislation against insider dealing is 'to ensure the integrity of Community financial markets and to enhance investor confidence in those

---

[31]   Manne initially referred only to entrepreneurs but subsequently expanded his ambit to include managers: HG Manne, 'Insider Trading and the Law Professors' (1970) 23 *Vanderbilt Law Review* 547.

[32]   WD Carlton and DR Fischel, 'The Regulation of Insider Trading' (1983) 35 *Stanford Law Review* 857, 873.

[33]   This is discussed further at 10.5 below.

[34]   M Klock, 'Mainstream Economics and the Case for Prohibiting Inside Trading' (1994) 10 *Georgia State University Law Review* 297; MP Dooley, 'Enforcement of Insider Trading Restrictions' (1980) 66 *Virginia Law Review* 1, 33.

[35]   HG Manne, 'In Defence of Insider Trading' (1966) 44 *Harvard Business Review* 114.

markets'.[36] Investor confidence is a key component in creating efficient markets. It is not the fact of trading with an insider per se which causes the problem, or the fact that insiders induce investors to trade at the 'wrong price'. The insider dealing itself does not harm investors. What is damaging is the nondisclosure of material information, ie the information asymmetry between insiders and public investors.[37]

Investors who buy and sell in the market know that they run the risk that they may deal in securities just before the issuer discloses information about the company to the market. This may have favourable or unfavourable results for the investor depending on the nature of the disclosure, and whether the investor is buying or selling. Over the long run, and in the absence of insider dealing, any gains or losses should even out. However, the presence of insider dealing undermines investor confidence by undermining investors' beliefs that the market is fair and that they have an equal chance of profiting from securities trades. The effect of insider dealing is that market prices do not reflect the true worth of securities, in a way which is unfavourable to outsiders.

Investors who believe that the system is rigged are likely either to withhold their investment or alternatively to build this risk into their investment decisions, by lowering the price they are prepared to pay for companies' shares. Either of these outcomes will increase companies' cost of capital.[38] Importantly, in the first successful criminal conviction for insider dealing brought by the FSA the judge stated in the course of his judgment that this should not be regarded as a victimless crime, but was instead a crime which undermined confidence in the integrity of the market.[39] This was a sentiment reiterated by the Court of Appeal: 'The principles of confidentiality and trust, which are essential to the operations of the commercial world, are betrayed by insider dealing and public confidence in the integrity of the system which is essential to its proper function is undermined by market abuse'.[40]

Following the shift from regarding insider dealing as company law-based to securities law-based, these market-focused arguments have become the dominant rationale for regulating insider dealing in the UK. In opposition to this view, arguments have been put forward to suggest that the allocative efficiency of the market can be increased by *allowing* insider dealing to occur. It has been suggested that insider dealing provides a good method of channelling information to the market, including information that companies would not disclose publicly because it would be too expensive, or would not be believable, or because disclosing it publicly would destroy the value of the information.[41] Insider dealing, it is suggested, allows all information, not just that which is publicly available, and which has a bearing on the prospects of the company, to be factored into the price of the company's shares. This increases allocative efficiency, since the price at which the company's shares trade more accurately reflects the company's prospects.

---

[36]   Market Abuse Directive 2003/6/EC, 12th Considerandum.
[37]   See eg SM Bainbridge, *Corporation Law and Economics* (New York, Foundation Press, 2002) 72.
[38]   H Schmidt, 'Insider Dealing and Economic Theory' in KJ Hopt and E Wymeersch (eds), *European Insider Dealing* (London, Butterworths, 1991).
[39]   *R v McQuoid*, Southwark Crown Court, 27 March 2009 (unreported).
[40]   *R v McQuoid* [2009] EWCA Crim 1301; [2009] 4 All ER 388, [8] per Lord Judge CJ.
[41]   Eg DW Carlton and DR Fischel, 'The Regulation of Insider Trading' (1983) 35 *Stanford Law Review* 857.

However, dealing alone is an inefficient way to impart information to the marketplace,[42] so this system would only work efficiently if the insider's identity, and presumably their status as an insider, is known to the market. On this analysis the extent to which insiders make a profit on this information is the price that is paid by society for the greater efficiency that is generated.[43] However, the stock market is already perceived to be efficient and any gains from insider trading would at best be marginal.[44] Any gains would also have to be weighed against the cost to the system arising from loss of investor confidence and the consequential increase in the cost of capital. There is some evidence that although merely adopting insider laws does not affect the cost of equity in a country, enforcement of those insider dealing laws does affect the cost of equity, with the cost decreasing significantly after the first prosecution.[45]

By contrast, little doubt is generally expressed about the economic need for the prohibition of market manipulation. Once one of the goals of capital market regulation is the smooth functioning of the market, the rationale for regulating market manipulation is clear.[46] Market manipulation involves the unwarranted interference in the operation of the ordinary market forces of supply and demand. It is an interference with the market's normal price-forming mechanism and it thereby undermines the integrity and efficiency of the market.

Common examples of market manipulation involve the dissemination of misleading information, such as the publication of false accounts, or the retention or concealment of material market information. False rumours, of a possible take-over bid, for example, may be circulated in the market purely in order to drive up the share price. Alternatively artificial transactions may be made in order to create the appearance of active trading and to convey false information regarding the supply and demand for investments. This may be carried out by company insiders, and the increase in equity-based compensation packages for corporate executives has been linked with some of the recent market manipulation schemes, such as Enron.[47] Share options provide a pay-off only where the price of the company's shares has moved above the strike price at which the options were granted, and the pay-off may increase exponentially based on the increase in reported earnings. Pay packages based on share options do not penalise executives when the company's shares underperform. This creates a recognised moral hazard problem and can

---

[42]   It is the release of new information rather than the supply of a particular security which is the primary driver of share price movements: RJ Gilson and RH Kraakman, 'The Mechanisms of Market Efficiency' (1984) 70 *Virginia Law Review* 549, 629–34.

[43]   It can be doubted whether insider dealing will always be of value to society. In advance of a takeover for example the inside information will be of significant value to insiders (and therefore be of high private value) but is of dubious societal value since its effect will simply be to drive up the share price. For discussion see H McVea, 'What's Wrong with Insider Dealing?' (1995) *Legal Studies* 390, 395.

[44]   It is generally accepted that the stock market is one of the most efficient markets in existence: RJ Gilson and RH Kraakman, 'The Mechanisms of Market Efficiency' (1984) 70 *Virginia Law Review* 549.

[45]   U Battacharya and H Daouk, 'The World Price of Insider Trading' (2002) 57 *Journal of Finance* 75.

[46]   The common law has dealt with cases of market manipulation for some time, see eg *R v De Berenger* (1814) 3 M&S 67 (KB), 105 Eng Reports 536; *R v Aspinall* (1875–76) 1 LR 730, although the courts regarded these manipulative schemes as amounting to straightforward fraud, albeit that the misrepresentations were addressed to the public at large and had no specific recipients. The creation of the modern securities law-based offence of market manipulation only arose in 1986 with the Financial Services Act 1986, s 47.

[47]   LA Bebchuk and O Bar-Gill, 'Misreporting Corporate Performance' Discussion Paper 400, Harvard Law School, Dec 2002.

increase incentives for market manipulation by corporate executives.[48] However it is not limited to this group, as others within the market, such as traders in investment banks or other professional advisers, could carry out this form of market abuse. The core of market manipulation is the improper use of market power which interferes with the market's normal price-forming mechanism.

Any doubts expressed about the regulation of market manipulation tend to relate to the form and content of the prohibition.[49] The difficulty with forming a workable definition of market abuse in practice is to define what is an inappropriate interference with 'normal' market forces, since some interference is allowed.[50] The price stabilisation rules are an example of accepted interference with normal market forces.[51] These issues are discussed further at 10.5.2 below. However, the difficulties with drawing the boundaries of market manipulation in practice do not detract from the clear rationale for regulating market manipulation in principle.

10.2.2   Promoting Corporate Governance

In the previous section we discussed the need for the law to provide protection for investors. The focus of this section is somewhat different and considers the need to provide assistance to those who are shareholders in a public company. Although one well accepted role for mandatory disclosure is to prevent the undersupply of information necessary for the efficient pricing of securities, mandatory disclosure has also been said to perform an important function regarding the governance of public companies.[52] It is even suggested by some commentators that the governance functions of mandatory disclosure are its most important functions.[53] While this is debatable, it is certainly true that '[i]nformation and disclosure is an area where company law and securities regulation come together'.[54] Of course some disclosures might perform both functions simultaneously, as where a director has committed a major fraud on the company. This information would be material to pricing the securities accurately, and the disclosure of this information would also be necessary in order to allow the shareholders to perform their role of monitoring the board. Other disclosure rules may be geared primarily to investors, such as the insider dealing rules, while others may have a predominantly governance-based function. For example, the rules governing self-dealing transactions between the company and its directors,[55] may be triggered by transactions that are trivial in comparison to the

---

[48]   JN Gordon, 'What Enron Means for the Management and Control of the Modern Business Corporation: Some Initial Reflections' (2002) 69 *University of Chicago Law Review* 1233.

[49]   Eg DR Fischel and DJ Ross 'Should the Law Prohibit "Manipulation" in Financial markets?' (1991) 105 *Harvard Law Review* 503.

[50]   E Lomnicka, 'Preventing and Controlling the Manipulation of Financial Markets: Towards a Definition of Market Manipulation' (2001) 8 *Journal of Financial Crime* 297.

[51]   The safe harbour for price stabilisation rules is created by Market Abuse Directive 2003/6/EC, art 8 and its implementing regulation, which is directly effective: Commission Regulation (EC) 2273/2003 implementing the Market Abuse Directive. This safe harbour has been extended by domestic legislation (Criminal Justice Act 1993, Sch 1, para 5; FSMA, s 397(4)(a)(c) and (5)(b)(d) and FSMA, s 118(5)(b), 144) so that it extends to the whole range of market abuse provisions in place in the UK.

[52]   RH Kraakman, 'Disclosure and Corporate Governance: An Overview Essay', n 7.

[53]   Ibid, 96.

[54]   *Report of the High Level Group of Company Law Experts: A Modern Regulatory Framework for Company Law in Europe* (Brussels, Nov 4, 2002) ch II.3, 34.

[55]   Companies Act 2006, ss 177–187.

company's asset value or market capitalisation, so will be relevant for governance reasons, but are unlikely to have any material impact on share price.

Shares in publicly quoted UK companies are typically dispersed amongst many holders.[56] The central problem of corporate governance for UK publicly quoted companies is therefore holding managers accountable to the shareholders.[57] It is well understood that shareholders have two main mechanisms for exercising their corporate governance function: 'voice' and 'exit'.[58] They can use their status to attend meetings and vote, to remove the directors of the company for example, or they can express their displeasure by selling their shares in the company, which could affect the company's share price if a large enough percentage of the shareholders adopt this tactic. Given the small size of shareholdings of most public company shareholders in the UK, where even institutional shareholders hold relatively small holdings of less than five per cent, exit as a mechanism for corporate governance is not well developed. It is undoubtedly true that the disclosure of information to shareholders in a company allows them to make investment decisions about their shareholding, but English law has regarded this as being a private investment issue rather than a corporate governance matter.[59] 'Corporate governance' in the UK public company context has therefore tended to focus on issues of 'voice' rather than 'exit', but this is not to deny that exit can have a role in some circumstances.[60]

The UK has traditionally adopted a shareholder-centred approach to company law. In a solvent company directors have owed their duties to the shareholders as a whole.[61] Section 172 of the Companies Act 2006 continues this approach. The Act specifically rejects the 'pluralist approach' to directors' duties and adopts the 'enlightened shareholder value' recommendations of the Company Law Review Steering Group.[62] Section 172 provides that a director must 'act in the way he considers, in good faith, would be most likely to promote the success of the company for the benefit of its members as a whole'. Although section 172 goes on to provide that in doing so the director must have regard to a number

[56] R La Porta, F Lopez-de-Silanes and A Shleifer, 'Corporate Ownership Around the World' (1999) 54 *Journal of Finance* 471; M Becht and C Mayer, 'Introduction' in F Barca and M Becht (eds), *The Control of Corporate Europe* (Oxford, Oxford University Press, 2001). For an excellent discussion of the development of dispersed ownership in the UK see BR Cheffins, *Corporate Ownership and Control: British Business Transformed* (Oxford, Oxford University Press, 2008).

[57] See R Kraakman et al, *The Anatomy of Corporate Law*, 2nd edn (Oxford, Oxford University Press, 2009) 35–36. This is in contrast to the governance concerns in UK private companies which tend to revolve around inter-shareholder disputes and conflicts between the shareholders and the creditors (P Davies, *Introduction to Company Law* (Oxford, Oxford University Press, 2002) 215–17.

[58] AO Hirschman, *Exit, Voice, and Loyalty: Responses to Decline in Firms, Organizations and States* (Cambridge MA, Harvard University Press, 1970).

[59] *Caparo Industries plc v Dickman* [1990] 2 AC 605 and see the discussion below at 10.3.

[60] For example, if a large number of investors sell their shares in a company in which they are dissatisfied with the company's performance, the share price will be depressed, making the company potentially vulnerable to a takeover, which is likely to result in the managers being displaced. This issue is discussed further in 12.3.2.2.2. Empirical evidence suggests that, in the UK at least, the market for corporate control does not in fact operate as a disciplinary device for poorly performing companies: J Franks and C Mayer, 'Hostile Takeovers in the UK and the Correction of Managerial Failure' (1996) 40 *Journal of Financial Economics* 163, 180.

[61] Eg *Smith and Fawcett Ltd* [1942] Ch 304, 306 per Lord Greene MR. As a rule directors do not owe duties to individual shareholders although they may do so in specific factual circumstances: *Peskin v Anderson* [2001] 1 BCLC 372.

[62] DTI, *Company Law Reform*, (Cm 6456, 2005), para 3.3.

of other stakeholder interests, such as the company's employees, suppliers, customers etc.[63] The preferable analysis of section 172 is that it requires directors to have regard to the long-term interests of the shareholders and that in doing so the directors may have to take account of other stakeholder groups in order to determine what best ensures the long-term growth of the company. Following the introduction of the Companies Act 2006, it is clear that UK company law remains predominantly shareholder-focused while the company remains solvent.[64]

Shareholders in UK companies have a number of governance entitlements.[65] As regards the company's board, shareholders have the right to remove directors at any time by an ordinary resolution.[66] Further, the UK Corporate Governance Code now provides that directors of FTSE 350 companies should be re-elected annually.[67] This is in contrast to the 'staggered board' provisions, commonly used in the US, which allow US directors to entrench themselves against the possibility of shareholder removal.[68] Shareholders in UK public companies also have a significant role in relation to directors' remuneration. Since 2002 publicly traded companies are required to send shareholders a directors' remuneration report each year on which an advisory vote must be taken at the AGM.[69]

In relation to takeovers, in the UK it is the shareholders who determine the outcome of the bid. The Takeover Code imposes a 'no frustrating action' principle upon directors of the target company. Once a bid is launched or anticipated the directors are prohibited from taking any actions that might frustrate the bid without first obtaining the consent of the shareholders.[70] This is in contrast to the position in the US, discussed further at 12.3.2.2.

The shareholders also have substantial control rights in relation to a number of corporate transactions. They have a significant role in approving certain categories of corporate transaction, particularly those involving a risk of conflict of interest or which are of a significant size in relation to the company. General company law requires transactions to which the counterparty is a director or connected party[71] to be approved

---

[63]   Companies Act 2006, s 172(1). While the company remains solvent directors do not owe any duties to the creditors. Of course, once the company is insolvent, the position changes and directors do fall under an obligation to take account of creditors' interests, as Companies Act 2006, s 172(3) recognises.

[64]   For further discussion of the role of both shareholders and creditors when the company is solvent see 3.2.

[65]   These entitlements are generally recognised as being greater than their counterparts in the US: J Armour and JN Gordon, 'The Berle-Means Corporation in the 21st Century' (work-in-progress on file with authors); CM Bruner, 'Power and Purpose in the "Anglo-American" Corporation' (2010) 50 *Virginia Journal of International Law* 579.

[66]   Companies Act 2006, s 168(1). Shareholders holding more than 5% of the company's voting rights may require the holding of a general meeting for the purpose of removing directors, and may require the proposed resolutions to be circulated to shareholders at the company's expense: Companies Act 2006, ss 303–305 (this 5% minimum stake was introduced by the Companies (Shareholders' Rights) Regulations 2009 (SI 2009/1632), reg 4 implementing Shareholders Rights Directive 2007/36, art 6). Shareholders holding more than 5% of the voting rights in public companies may require resolutions to be put on the agenda for the AGM, and circulated in advance, at the company's expense: Companies Act 2006, ss 338–339.

[67]   FRC, *UK Corporate Governance Code*, June 2010, B.7.1.

[68]   See eg LA Bebchuk, JC Coats and G Subramanian, 'The Powerful Antitakeover Force of Staggered Boards: Theory, Evidence and Policy' (2002) 54 *Stanford Law Review* 887.

[69]   Companies Act 2006, ss 420–421, 439.

[70]   The City Code on Takeovers and Mergers, General Principle 3 and Rule 21. For discussion see chapter 12.3.2.2.

[71]   Companies Act 2006, ss 252, 254.

by the shareholders.[72] These include substantial property transactions[73] and corporate loans.[74] There is also a long standing tradition of the shareholders ratifying breaches of directors' duties.[75] The UK Listing Rules add to these provisions. All transactions of a value between five per cent and 25 per cent of the company's business must be disclosed to shareholders,[76] and for transactions in excess of a 25 per cent threshold the disclosure must be supplemented by a shareholder vote on the transaction.[77] In relation to 'related party transactions'[78] there must be disclosure plus a shareholder vote.[79]

Finally, UK shareholders have control over the issue of new shares as a result of pre-emption rights. These rights are applied as default rules to all companies[80] and supplemented by the Listing Rules for firms with a premium listing in the UK Official List.[81] The application of these rules can be waived by shareholder authorisation.[82] However, in relation to listed companies, the grant of such a waiver is subject to a well-established set of voting guidelines adhered to by institutional investors in the UK.[83] In short, consent will be granted uncontroversially for issues amounting to less than five per cent of the ordinary share capital in any given year, but where the issue amounts to more than 7.5 per cent of the ordinary capital a business case for waiver must be made.[84]

It may therefore be seen that UK law creates a potentially significant governance role for shareholders in public companies. Although recent studies have demonstrated that the level of enforcement of directors' duties by way of listed company shareholders bringing shareholder litigation is close to nil,[85] it has been suggested that the shareholders in listed companies can have a significant role in corporate governance via more structural and/or informal measures, such as the control which shareholders exercise over pre-emption rights. There will typically be a dialogue between the company and its major institutional shareholders in the period prior to a rights issue.[86] This provides a focal point for

---

[72] Ibid, s 180, although the directors can avoid the need to do so in some circumstances, eg by declaring the interest in the proposed transaction to the other directors (s 177).

[73] Ibid, ss 190–196.

[74] Ibid, ss 197–214.

[75] See eg *North West Transportation Co Ltd v Beatty* (1887) LR 12 App Cas 589; *Atwool v Merryweather* (1867) LR 5 Eq 464, although it is now clear, contrary to some of the earlier case law, that the resolution will only be effective if it is passed without votes in favour of the resolution by the director (if a member of the company) and any shareholder connected with him: Companies Act 2006, s 239.

[76] FSA Handbook, Listing Rules LR 10.4.1. LR 10.2.2 sets out a series of different ratio tests to be used when applying this test See 10.3.2.4.

[77] Ibid, LR 10.5.1.

[78] The concept of 'related party' is defined in LR 11.1.4. See 10.3.2.4.

[79] The votes of the related party and their associates are excluded from the vote: LR 11.1.7(4).

[80] Companies Act 2006, ss 560–577. See 4.3.1.

[81] See Listing Rules, LR 9.3.11–9.3.12.

[82] Companies Act 2006, ss 570–571; ibid, LR 9.3.12(1).

[83] Pre Emption Group, *Disapplying Pre-Emption Rights: A Statement of Principles* July 2008 available at www.pre-emptiongroup.org.uk/principles/index.htm. See 4.3.1.

[84] Ibid.

[85] J Armour, B Black, BR Cheffins and RC Nolan, 'Private Enforcement of Corporate Law: An Empirical Comparison of the US and UK' (2009) 6 *Journal of Empirical Legal Studies* 687; J Armour, 'Enforcement Strategies in UK Corporate Governance: A Roadmap and Empirical Assessment' in J Armour and J Payne (eds), *Rationality in Company Law: Essays in Honour of DD Prentice* (Oxford, Hart Publishing, 2009).

[86] GP Stapledon, *Institutional Shareholders and Corporate Governance* (Oxford, Clarendon Press, 1996) 129–130; Myners' Report on Pre-Emption Rights (DTI, *Pre-emption Rights: Final: A Study by Paul Myners into the Impact of Shareholders' Pre-emption Rights on a Public Company's Ability to Raise New Capital*, February 2005, URN 05/679. See 4.3.1.

shareholders to engage with the company and potentially provide a monitoring role. Indeed a positive relation between UK rights issues and managerial change has been found to exist.[87]

It seems unarguable that if public shareholders are to make use of these various governance rights they will need accurate and complete information from the directors in order to perform this role. In order for shareholders to exercise their function of making or ratifying fundamental corporate decisions, they will need to have information about the proposed transactions. Shareholders who are asked to propose a merger transaction need information which, in the absence of a legal requirement to do so, neither the directors nor the outside party might be prepared to disclose voluntarily.

In order to assess the corporate governance role of public company shareholders in practice, however, a distinction needs to be drawn between private, or retail, investors and institutional shareholders.

10.2.2.1   Private Investors

The percentage of listed company shares in the hands of private investors has declined over the last fifty years or so, from well over 60 per cent in the late 1950s to less than 20 per cent in 2006.[88] As discussed, the traditional model of a UK public company is one with widely dispersed share ownership. Within this model, the concept of 'rational apathy' amongst public company shareholders is well known.[89] Gains resulting from shareholder activism are expensive to produce and other shareholders cannot be excluded from taking a pro rata share in the benefits created.[90] Accordingly it is rational for small retail investors to utilise their 'exit' rights rather than 'voice' rights if they are unhappy with the direction the company is taking. Accordingly such investors traditionally don't have a significant governance role, despite being provided with a range of governance rights by the law.

Recent developments have potentially exacerbated this effect. In the UK, a large number of shareholders in public companies now hold their shares in an intermediated way, ie they do not hold the shares directly, but through an intermediary. The intermediary is on the share register of the company and is the legal owner of the shares and the underlying indirect holder's relationship is with the intermediary and not with the company.[91]

---

[87]   J Franks, C Mayer and L Renneboog, 'Who Disciplines Management in Poorly Performing Companies?' (2001) 10 *Journal of Financial Intermediaries* 209; D Hillier, SC Linn and P McColgan, 'Equity Issuance, CEO Turnover and Corporate Governance' (2005) 11 *European Financial Management* 515. This effect is similar to the argument, discussed in chapter 3 regarding the corporate governance role of creditors which involves a dialogue between the company and the creditor following a trigger of acceleration: 3.2.2.4.

[88]   J Moyle, 'The Pattern of Ordinary Share Ownership: 1957–70' University of Cambridge Department of Applied Economics Occasional Paper no 31 (1971) 6–7; Office for National Statistics, *Share Ownership: A Report on Ownership of Shares as at 31st December 2006* (London, ONS, 2007).

[89]   AA Berle and GC Means, *The Modern Corporation and Private Property* (New York, Macmillan, 1932) although it was Robert Clark who actually coined the phrase 'rational apathy': RC Clark, 'Vote Buying and Corporate Law' (1979) 29 *Case Western Reserve Law Review* 776, 779.

[90]   FH Easterbrook and D Fischel, *The Economic Structure of Corporate Law* (Cambridge MA, Harvard University Press, 1991).

[91]   The company remains 'blind' to the underlying indirect holder of the shares: Companies Act 2006, s 126 supplemented by the Model Articles for Private Companies limited by Shares, reg 23, and the Model Articles for Public Companies, reg 45, for Companies incorporated after 1 October 2009: The Companies (Model Articles) Regulation 2008 SI 2008/3229. This is a repetition of the law as it existed before the introduction of the 2006 Act (see Companies Act 1985, s 360 and reg 5 of 1985 Table A), despite proposals from the Company Law Review Steering Group that Companies Act 1985 s 360 be amended to enable companies to recognise the rights of

In the UK there are a number of reasons why shares may be held indirectly. The first reason has existed for as long as shares have existed. Shares, just like any other asset, may be the subject of a trust of the traditional variety, ie a settlor, the legal owner of shares, transfers that legal title to a trustee, or declares himself a trustee, of those shares for the benefit of another. In these circumstances the trustee will be the registered owner and will have the right to vote, although it is a well-established principle that the beneficial owner of shares, if absolutely entitled as against the registered owner, can instruct the registered owner how to deal with the shares, and how votes should be cast.[92] However, the use of trusts of this kind is not a particularly common occurrence in relation to shares in public companies.

The second reason, which does have a potential impact on retail investors, is the shift, in recent years, from certificated to uncertificated issues and transfers.[93] In the UK most of these are effected through the CREST computer system, operated by Euroclear UK and Ireland.[94] A company which joins CREST can issue paperless shares and register transfers of those shares electronically, thereby saving money.[95] Dematerialisation does not itself affect the direct relationship between investor and issuer. Investors generally have the option of holding an account directly or through an intermediary, the exception being that for certain kinds of investments, such as PEPs, investors are required to hold their investment via an intermediary. Even where investors have a choice, many small investors find that it is simpler to vest the legal title to their shares in a nominee who is a member of the system and then hold their shares indirectly. In practical terms a decision of a company to join CREST will involve many private investors holding their shares indirectly and companies that have joined CREST are likely to have a large number of indirect investors. Approximately 85 per cent of listed share capital in the UK is held through CREST in book entry form,[96] and a recent consultation recommended the compulsory dematerialisation of listed UK shares.[97]

The effect of intermediation in the UK is that the indirect investor is regarded as the beneficial owner of the shares.[98] However, the governance rights attached to the share per se belong to the intermediary who is on the share register and is the legal owner of the shares. This poses a potential corporate governance problem since these intermediaries gain no economic benefit from any activism. It has been recognised that these beneficial owners are in danger of being effectively disenfranchised.

---

persons other than the registered holder: Company Law Review Steering Group, *Modern Company Law for a Competitive Economy – Final Report* (URN 01/942 and 01/943), 2002, vol 1, para 7.4.

[92] *Kirby v Wilkins* [1929] 2 Ch 444, 454 per Romer J.

[93] The system of dematerialisation in existence in the UK is in contrast to the systems in place elsewhere, most notably the US which involve immobilisation of a global note which is kept by a depositary. The depositary then holds for one or more intermediaries who hold for investors. For discussion see L Gullifer, 'The Proprietary Protection of Investors in Intermediated Securities' in J Armour and J Payne (eds), *Rationality in Company Law: Essays in Honour of DD Prentice* (Oxford, Hart Publishing, 2009). Transfers of shares are discussed further at 8.2.7.

[94] See the Uncertificated Securities Regulations 2001 SI 2001/1633 (as amended) and as supplemented by CREST rules and conditions (see Euroclear UK & Ireland Ltd, CREST Reference Manual, September 2009).

[95] For a discussion of transfers via CREST see 8.2.6.

[96] *The Dematerialisation of Shares and Share Transfers – A Proposal to Remove the Requirement for Paper Share Certificates and Stock Transfer Forms*, ICSA, April 2006, 4.

[97] Ibid. Other EU states, such as Denmark, France and Italy, have already adopted a system of compulsory dematerialisation.

[98] For a discussion of transfers of intermediated securities see 8.2.5.

It seems right that these indirect investors should not be disadvantaged by their method of holding shares. They may want to engage in the governance of the company, and if they do their wishes should be facilitated. There are two basic mechanisms that can be used to enfranchise indirect investors: the intermediary can act in accordance with the wishes of the indirect investor or the intermediary can delegate rights, such as the right to vote, to the indirect investor. Reforms put in place by the Companies Act 2006 aim to facilitate both of these mechanisms. In order to facilitate intermediaries exercising their vote in accordance with the instructions of the indirect investor, the 2006 Act provides that where a registered holder holds shares for more than one person, then the rights attached to the shares (including the right to vote) need not all be exercised in the same way.[99] An intermediary who holds for a number of indirect investors can therefore vote in a way that accommodates the wishes of all of those underlying investors.

In terms of delegating rights to the indirect investor, the 2006 Act does two things. First, it strengthens the right of registered shareholders to appoint another as a proxy[100] and these rights can be used by intermediaries to appoint an indirect investor as a proxy and thereby give that indirect investor the right to vote in relation to its own shares. Second, the Act creates new rights for intermediaries to delegate information rights[101] or a broader range of rights (including the right to requisition a meeting or require circulation of a resolution) to indirect investors in some circumstances.[102]

One downside of these rights, however, is that to a large extent they depend on the relationship between the indirect investor and the intermediary. They do not create any rights for the indirect investor against the company, instead they allow the intermediary to take account of the indirect investor's wishes, or to delegate rights to that individual, without compelling the intermediary to do so. Whether the indirect investor can compel the intermediary will depend on the terms of the contract between them.[103] It is common for this contract to exclude the obligation to vote. Another issue is that they may facilitate the engagement of an indirect investor with the company *if* the indirect investor wishes to be engaged. However, they clearly do not tackle the more fundamental problem of rational apathy underlying the engagement between retail investors and public companies.[104]

10.2.2.2   Institutional investors

While there has been a decline in the numbers of private investors holding listed company shares over the past fifty years, there has been a corresponding increase in the number of institutional investors. The proportion of UK shares owned by pension funds, insurance

---

[99]   Companies Act 2006, s 152(1).

[100]   Ibid, s 324. The 2006 Act makes the ability to appoint a proxy mandatory for the first time. The 2006 Act also makes mandatory for the first time the right of proxies to attend, speak and vote at meetings of the company on a show of hands as well as on a poll. This is an important extension of the previous regime in which, typically, public companies' articles would not allow a proxy to speak at a meeting *or* to vote on a show of hands. The 2006 Act allows proxies to vote on a show of hands as well as on a poll: ss 284–285 (the text of these sections was amended by the Companies (Shareholders' Rights) Regulations 2009 (SI 2009/1632) regs 2–3, in order to clarify the rights of proxies voting on a show of hands).

[101]   Ibid, s 146 (traded companies only).

[102]   Ibid, s 145 which allows any company, public or private, to amend its articles to allow any shareholder on the register to nominate someone else to exercise his rights as a shareholder in his place.

[103]   For discussion see J Payne, 'Intermediated Securities and the Right to Vote in the UK' in L Gullifer and J Payne (eds), *Intermediated Securities: Legal Problems and Practical Issues* (Oxford, Hart Publishing, 2010).

[104]   For a discussion of the problems caused to bondholder democracy by immobilisation see 7.3.3.

companies and unit trusts has risen dramatically in this period.[105] The effect of institutional shareholders on corporate governance needs to be carefully assessed.

There is no doubt that one significant impact which institutional investors have had in this context is the development of the shareholder-friendly corporate governance regime for public companies which currently exists in the UK. A number of examples of this influence can be given. First is the influence which institutional shareholders have had on the development of the UK Corporate Governance Code. This was first appended to the Listing Rules on a 'comply or explain' basis in 1992.[106] The basis for this Code, drawn up by Sir Adrian Cadbury, was the pre-existing guidelines of the Institutional Shareholders' Committee's Statement of Directors.[107] Second, the introduction of pre-emption rights into the Listing Rules pre-dated their introduction in general company law, and apparently followed pressure from institutional investors.[108] The institutional investors have taken a further role in regularising the position regarding pre-emption rights in public companies by drafting and publishing the Pre-Emption Guidelines,[109] which now have a significant impact on the operation of shareholder control over rights issues in public companies.[110] Third, institutional shareholders had a significant role in preparing the predecessor to the Takeover Code,[111] entrenching a pro-shareholder stance which was carried over into the setting up and operation of the Panel on Takeover and Mergers in 1968.[112] Finally, institutions were responsible for the introduction of the provisions in the Listing Rules requiring shareholder approval for significant corporate transactions.[113] It is undoubtedly the case, then, that institutional investors have had a significant role in establishing the framework of corporate governance in the UK. However, it is also important to determine how much use institutional investors make of these corporate governance tools.

One mechanism for institutional shareholders to exercise a corporate governance role is to exercise their right to vote.[114] Concerns have been raised about the level of voting by institutional investors. When Paul Myners conducted his Review of the Impediments to Voting UK shares for the Shareholder Voting Working Group in 2004, voting levels at company meetings were around 50 per cent. Improvements have been made in the interim

---

[105]   For a discussion of the impact of tax law on this developments see BR Cheffins and SA Bank, 'Corporate Ownership and Control in the UK: The Tax Dimension' (2007) 70 *Modern Law Review* 778.

[106]   It was called the 'Cadbury Code' at that time. See Committee on Corporate Governance, Report of the Committee on the Financial Aspects of Corporate Governance (the Cadbury Report) (London, Gee, 1992).

[107]   For discussion see GP Stapledon, *Institutional Shareholders and Corporate Governance* (Oxford, Clarendon Press, 1996) 67–69; J Holland, 'Self-Regulation and the Financial Aspects of Corporate Governance' [1996] *Journal of Business Law* 127.

[108]   Stapledon, *Institutional Shareholders and Corporate Governance,* ibid, 56; LCB Gower, *Gower's Principles of Modern Company Law,* 4th edn (London, Stevens & Sons, 1979) 223, 343.

[109]   Pre-Emption Group, *Disapplying Pre-Emption Rights: A Statement of Principles* July 2008 available at www.pre-emptiongroup.org.uk/principles/index.htm. See 4.3.1.

[110]   Myners' Report on Pre-Emption Rights, n 86.

[111]   See Issuing Houses Association, *Notes on Amalgamation of British Businesses* (1959). For discussion see A Johnston, *The City Takeover Code* (Oxford, Oxford University Press, 1980) ch 3. For discussion see 12.2.1.

[112]   J Armour and DA Skeel Jr, 'Who Writes the Rules for Hostile Takeovers, and Why? The Peculiar Divergence of US and UK Takeover Regulation' (2007) 95 *Georgetown Law Journal* 1727.

[113]   Stapledon, n 107, 60.

[114]   Given the relatively small size of the stakes of most institutional investors (2% is common) these are not particularly illiquid and therefore institutions are not locked into their investments. Exit is therefore still an option, although some institutional investors (eg index tracking funds) have effectively abandoned exit as an option.

and by the time of his fourth progress report in 2007 the level had risen to 63 per cent for FTSE 100 companies.[115] However, there are still a lot of voting rights not being cast, and the focus of attention for this deficit has fallen in large part on institutional investors holding shares in UK public companies. Given that such a high percentage of the UK market is held by institutional investors a lack of voting by institutional investors must be at least part of the problem. Indeed a number of reports have concluded that the level of institutional intervention in the affairs of the companies in which the institutions have invested is less than optimal.[116]

There has been a debate for a number of years about the best way to encourage institutional investors to be more active in the corporate governance of companies.[117] The Myners Report on Institutional Investment in the UK in 2001 recommended an obligation on fund managers to monitor and to engage in corporate governance where there was a reasonable expectation that such an activity would increase the value of the portfolio investments.[118] The possibility of mandatory voting by institutional investors has also been discussed in the past. In 1998, the then Secretary of State for Trade and Industry, Margaret Beckett, demanded that institutional investors should vote all their shares and should annually disclose their voting policies and records so that they could be held accountable.[119] There has now been a legislative response to this issue. Unsurprisingly, this response does not amount to a requirement that institutions must vote their shares. There are difficulties attached to mandating shareholders to vote. There is a long standing tradition in English law of shares being regarded as the property of the shareholders to do with as they wish,[120] and this includes voting as they like, without being subject to fiduciary duties,[121] or not voting at all. It is also appreciated that the introduction of mandatory voting would need to be accompanied by an obligation that the vote be informed. However, placing a legal obligation on institutions to vote in a sensible and informed manner is likely to be a practical impossibility. In particular it is unclear how such a provision would be policed. The courts have not had an easy time assessing the validity of shareholder voting in other contexts and there is no reason to believe it would

---

[115]   P Myners, '*Review of the Impediments to Voting UK Shares: Fourth Report to the Shareholder Voting Working Group*' (July 2007) 1.

[116]   Eg, P Myners, *Institutional Investment in the UK: A Review* (HM Treasury, London, 2001); Company Law Review Steering Group, *Modern Company Law For a Competitive Economy: Final Report*, (URN 01/942, July 2001) para 3.54.

[117]   There is a debate as to whether the corporate governance role of institutional investors can be increased through legal change (see eg BS Black, 'Agents Watching Agents: The Promise of Institutional Investor Voice' (1992) 39 *UCLA Law Review* 811) or whether there are strong non-legal reasons for shareholder passivity (JC Coffee, 'Liquidity versus Control: The Institutional Investor as Corporate Monitor' [1991] *Columbia Law Review* 1277). For some of the dangers that might arise from giving institutional investors a dominant role in corporate governance see JC Coffee, ibid; P Davies, 'Institutional Investors in the UK' in DD Prentice and PRJ Holland (eds), *Contemporary Issues in Corporate Governance* (Oxford, Clarendon Press, 1993) 78–81.

[118]   Myners, *Institutional Investment in the UK: A Review*, n 116, para 5.89. This suggestion did not amount to a mandatory obligation to vote the shares. This Report did not propose that this requirement would be legislative, but rather envisaged a voluntary code being put in place to govern these issues.

[119]   Margaret Beckett, speech held at the PIRC Annual Conference, London, 4 March 1998, available at: www.dti.gov.uk/ministers/archived/beckett040398.html.

[120]   *Pender v Lushington* (1877) LR 6 Ch D 70.

[121]   However, at times, shareholders have been constrained as to how they exercise their votes, eg the requirement to vote their shares bona fide in the best interests of the company on an alteration of articles: *Allen v Gold Reefs of West Africa Ltd* [1900] 1 Ch 656).

be easier here.[122] It is likely that the voting policy statements produced by institutions would be broad and general and unlikely to commit institutions to specific actions. Such a provision would also not prevent institutions choosing to exercise their 'exit' rather than 'voice' and indeed it may even reinforce a preference for that action.

Instead, the Companies Act 2006 introduces a power for the Secretary of State to make regulations requiring certain institutions to provide information, either to the public or to specified persons only, regarding the exercise of voting rights attached to shares.[123] The relevant institutions include unit trusts, investment trusts, pension schemes, entities carrying out long-term insurance business and collective investment schemes.[124] Information may be required by the regulations regarding the manner in which voting rights are exercised, any exercise of voting rights by the institution's agent (eg a fund manager), any instructions given by an institution to its agents as to the exercise of voting rights, and any delegation of voting rights by an institution.[125] However, there has been a considerable amount of opposition to these sections in the 2006 Act,[126] and there seems little likelihood that these regulations will be introduced soon.[127] Instead, a new code, the UK Stewardship Code, published by the Financial Reporting Council, sets out seven principles of good practice for institutional investors, intended to 'enhance the quality of engagement' between institutional investors and the companies in which they invest.[128] Whereas the UK Corporate Governance Code deals with corporate governance issues for companies, this Code deals with corporate governance issues for institutional investors. The matters included in the Stewardship Code include that: institutional investors should have a policy on how it will discharge its stewardship responsibilities (including its policy on voting), which must be publicly disclosed, it should have a robust policy on managing conflicts of interest in relation to stewardship matters, and it should periodically report on its stewardship and voting activities. The Code also suggests that institutional investors should consider obtaining an independent audit opinion on its engagement and voting processes which should be publicly disclosed. The Code follows the 'comply or explain' principle established by the UK Corporate Governance Code, requiring institutional investors to provide a statement on their website that details how the principles of the Code are applied by that investor, discloses any information required by the Code, and explains if and to what extent any elements of the Code have not been complied with.

---

[122] See the difficulties the courts have faced when applying the test in *Allen v Gold Reefs of West Africa Ltd* [1900] 1 Ch 656 regarding the validity of votes to alter the articles of a company: *Constable v Executive Connections Ltd* [2005] EWHC 3 (Ch); [2005] 2 BCLC 638. See also M Kahan and EB Rock, 'On Improving Shareholder Voting' in J Armour and J Payne (eds), *Rationality in Company Law: Essays in Honour of DD Prentice* (Oxford, Hart Publishing, 2009) 267–70, where the authors explain the problems with applying such a standard in the US context.

[123] Companies Act 2006, s 1277.

[124] Ibid, s 1278. The regulations may extend this provision to other forms of institution or alternatively limit the application of this provision: s 1278(2).

[125] Ibid, s 1280(1).

[126] For example, the Association of Investment Trust Companies (AITC) has expressed doubts about a real demand from retail investors and raised concerns as to the practical feasibility of a disclosure requirement, since the vast majority of trusts outsource their day-to-day fund management activities, including voting, to external fund managers: AITC Comments on Company Law Reform Bill: Draft Clauses, available at www.aitc.co.uk.

[127] The Government has said that it is willing to see how market practice evolves before deciding whether and how to exercise the power: HL Debs, vol 682, col 787, May 23 2006 (Lord Sainsbury).

[128] FRC, *UK Stewardship Code*, July 2010 available at www.frc.org.uk. This code is based on the code on the responsibilities of institutional investors issued by the Institutional Shareholders Committee. The FRC will be responsible for the oversight and development of the Stewardship Code.

Whether this Code will be a catalyst for institutional investors to engage more actively in the stewardship of those companies in which they invest remains to be seen.

This is not to suggest that institutional investors do not exercise their votes. Clearly they do. Some are more activist than others,[129] although in general institutional investors tend to vote on issues which are of general relevance to all companies, such as the introduction of non-voting shares,[130] the disapplication of pre-emption rights, issues of executive pay or board structure.[131] It is also possible for institutional investors to requisition a meeting to remove directors.[132] These forms of activism within the UK do occur, although they are relatively rare.[133] This allows institutions to economise on their decision-making costs by adopting a standardised policy.[134] Only in cases of severe under-performance does it seem that institutions will provoke a change of management.[135]

However, an analysis of the role that institutional investors play in UK corporate governance would not be complete without an assessment of their more informal forms of influence. It is common for listed companies to meet regularly with major institutional investors to discuss governance practices, strategy and financial issues.[136] In addition, a rights issue by the company, and the need for shareholder approval to disapply pre-emption rights, provides a specific occasion for a dialogue between the shareholders, particularly the institutional investors, and the management of a company. This provides a focal point for shareholders to engage with the company and potentially provide a monitoring role. As discussed, a positive relation between UK rights issues and managerial change has been found to exist.[137]

10.2.2.3   Summary

In chapter nine the purpose of capital market regulation at the IPO stage was discussed. At that point in time there is only one purpose for the regulation: to protect investors by ensuring that they have the information they need to help them make efficient resource

---

[129]   Stapledon, n 107, 92–98.

[130]   Non-voting and dual class shares are not expressly prohibited by the Listing Rules but they are strongly discouraged by institutional investors: ibid, 58–59.

[131]   See Davies, 'Institutional Investors in the UK', n 117.

[132]   Shareholders holding more than 5% of the company's voting rights may require the holding of a general meeting for the purpose of removing directors, and may require the proposed resolutions to be circulated to shareholders at the company's expense: Companies Act 2006, ss 303–305. Shareholders holding more than 5% of the voting rights in public companies may require resolutions to be put on the agenda for the AGM, and circulated in advance, at the company's expense: ss 338–339.

[133]   M Becht, J Franks, C Mayer and S Rossi, 'Returns to Shareholder Activism: Evidence from a Clinical Study of the Hermes UK Focus Fund' (2009) 22 *The Review of Financial Studies* 3093. Shareholder activism seems more developed in the US (see LA Bebchuk, 'The Case for Increasing Shareholder Power' [2005] *Harvard Law Review* 1735; M Harris and A Raviv, 'Control of Shareholder Decisions: Shareholders vs Management' (2009) CRSP working paper 620; for a recent review of the literature see L Renneboog and PG Szilagi, 'Shareholder Activism Through the Proxy Process' (2010) available at www.ssrn.com/abstract=1460578).

[134]   BS Black and JC Coffee, 'Hail Britannia?: Institutional Investor Behaviour under Limited Regulation' (1994) 92 *Michigan Law Review* 1997, 2034–55.

[135]   R Crespi-Cladera and L Renneboog, 'Corporate Monitoring by Shareholder Coalitions in the UK' ECGI Finance Working Paper 12/2003 (2003); J Franks, C Mayer and L Renneboog, 'Who Disciplines Management in Poorly Performing Companies?' (2001) 10 *Journal of Financial intermediation* 209.

[136]   Stapledon, n 107, 101–06.

[137]   J Franks, C Mayer and L Renneboog, 'Who Disciplines Management in Poorly Performing Companies?' (2001) 10 *Journal of Financial Intermediation* 209; D Hillier, SC Linn and P McColgan, 'Equity Issuance, CEO turnover and Corporate Governance' (2005) 11 *European Financial Management* 515. See 4.3.1.

allocation decisions. This is achieved via mandatory disclosure obligations, so that at the IPO stage potential investors are made aware of the nature of what is on offer before they make a financial commitment, coupled with remedies to redress any loss in some circumstances should the information supplied prove incomplete or inaccurate. By contrast, after the company has succeeded in offering its securities to the public, the regulatory rationale becomes more complicated. At this stage there are two broad aims in place: to allow shareholders of public companies to exercise their governance role, and to promote the smooth operation of the market. This latter aim comprises two aspects: to provide information to shareholders, and to investors more generally, in order to enable them to make investment decisions, and to prevent market abuse.

The aims of regulation discussed in this section need to be borne in mind when considering the tools which the UK has adopted to achieve the regulation of the ongoing markets. Two strategies have been adopted: disclosure and rules aimed at preventing market abuse. These are dealt with in the next sections.

10.3 The Use of Mandatory Disclosure

As we saw in chapter nine, when a company seeks to offer its securities to the public it becomes subject to mandatory disclosure obligations. The mandatory disclosure obligations facing companies once the securities have been successfully listed will be discussed in this section. The reasons why this disclosure needs to be mandatory and not voluntary were dealt with in chapter nine and will not be repeated here.[138]

A number of important distinctions arise between mandatory disclosure at the IPO stage and continuing disclosure obligations. First, as noted in the previous section, the purpose of disclosures once the company has succeeded in offering its shares to the public is both to inform investors and to provide information to the existing shareholders of the company, whereas at the IPO stage only the first of these functions is performed. Second, and following from that, the aim of a prospectus is solely to persuade investors to buy the company's securities, whereas the purposes of continuing disclosures are more varied. Sometimes the information is being provided to shareholders in their capacity as shareholders, sometimes to shareholders in their capacity as investors. Sometimes the information is to enable recipients to carry out a governance role within the company. Some disclosures are intended to inform investment decisions, and others are intended to prevent insider dealing. However, selling the company's securities is rarely the predominant reason for these disclosures being made. Third, at the IPO stage the disclosures are all made by the company, via its directors and advisers, to investors. By contrast, continuing disclosures comprise both disclosures by the company to its shareholders and investors, and disclosures to the company by corporate insiders or major shareholders, often with a further disclosure obligation on the company. These differences alter the nature of the continuing mandatory disclosures facing companies.

For a long time, ongoing disclosures were regarded as being fundamentally shareholder-focused, and the purpose of providing the shareholders with information was to enable them to exercise a corporate governance role within the company, rather than to inform

---

[138] See 9.3.3.3.

their investment decisions. In *Caparo Industries plc v Dickman*[139] the claimant, Caparo, had acquired shares in a target company as part of a takeover. Caparo contended that it had relied on the company's accounts for the accounting year 1983–1984 which had been audited by the company's accountants, Touche Ross. At the time the annual report and accounts were the primary form of ongoing disclosure obligation imposed on a company. Caparo asserted that these accounts overvalued the company and that the auditors had been negligent in not detecting the irregularities or fraud which had led to the overstatements in the accounts and in certifying the accounts as representing a true and fair view of the company's financial position. The House of Lords held that the auditors owed Caparo no duty of care. They held that the purpose of the statutory accounts provisions was not to supply information to investors, but to provide information to the shareholders and that the purpose of this information provision was to enable them to exercise their governance rights over the board effectively.

There have been important changes in the context of ongoing disclosures since *Caparo*, both in terms of the disclosures themselves and the liability regime attaching to those disclosures. Since *Caparo* new investor-focused disclosure obligations have been added and even some of the obligations which have traditionally been regarded as shareholder-focused are now understood as having, additionally, an investor protection element. Since *Caparo* there has also been the introduction of a new statutory remedy for investors regarding misstatements in ongoing disclosures and there has been the introduction of new administrative remedies for market abuse. These are discussed in the following sections. Nevertheless, the purpose for which ongoing disclosures are being made remains a relevant consideration, and one which informs the potential liability for inaccurate statements to a certain extent. As a result, it is important to consider not only the nature of the disclosure requirements in place, but also the purpose of those requirements.

10.3.1   Periodic Disclosures

10.3.1.1   Annual Reports

Obligations have been placed on all UK companies to provide annual reports and accounts since the nineteenth century. A number of directives at EU level relating to annual reports have had an impact on the disclosure requirements now facing all UK companies.[140] In relation to *quoted* companies, these general disclosure requirements have been supplemented by the rules of the public securities markets. Again, European law has had an important part to play in setting these disclosure rules.

The basic periodic reporting requirements for companies whose securities are traded on *regulated markets* originate in EC law, via the Transparency Directive.[141] The Transparency

---

[139]   [1990] 2 AC 605.

[140]   See especially the Fourth Council Directive on the Annual Accounts of Certain Types of Companies, Directive 78/660/EEC ([1978] OJ L222/110 as amended); the Seventh Council Directive on Consolidated Accounts, Directive 83/349/EEC ([1983] OJ L193/1 as amended).

[141]   Directive 2004/109/EC on transparency requirements in relation to issuers. For implementation see Companies Act 2006, Part 43, which adds new ss 89A-89O, 90A and 100A to Part 6 of FSMA 2000. This is a minimum harmonisation directive. Implementation of the directive has also taken place via amendments to the FSA Handbook, specifically the new Disclosure and Transparency Rules (DTR).

Directive applies to companies whose securities are listed on the Official List,[142] but not to issuers whose securities are traded on AIM, or the Plus-quoted market, for example.[143] Article 4 of the Transparency Directive requires the publication of audited annual accounts and reports for companies with securities listed on a regulated market. To a large extent the requirements of this article are met by the rules contained in the Companies Act 2006.[144]

In general the Companies Act 2006 imposes an obligation on the directors of companies to produce annual reports and accounts, to have financial statements and parts of the reports audited, to circulate the reports and accounts to shareholders and lay them before the shareholders in a general meeting and to file them at Companies House.[145] Different obligations are placed on different kinds of companies, so that, for example, a different and reduced regime is in place for small (private) companies.[146] The reporting obligations placed on companies outside the small company regime (which will include all public companies and some private companies) are more extensive, particularly for quoted companies.[147]

The general principle governing the content of annual accounts is that the accounts must give 'a true and fair view of the assets, liabilities, financial position and profit or loss'[148] of the individual company or companies included in the consolidation of the group accounts.[149] Detailed guidance is provided for companies as to the specific information that needs to be included. A company which is under an obligation to produce individual accounts may choose[150] to produce accounts by reference to the rules set out in the Companies Act 2006 and the regulations made thereunder,[151] or by reference

---

[142] This includes companies listed on the Main Market and also companies on the Plus-listed market (see www.plusmarketsgroup.com). These obligations relate both to companies with a premium listing and to those with a standard listing, following the segmentation of the UK Official list: See the Listing Rules Sourcebook (Amendment No 3) Instrument 2009 available at www.fsahandbook.info/FSA/handbook/LI/2009/2009_54.pdf and FSA, *Listing Regime Review*, CP09/24, October 2009.

[143] However, issuers on these exchanges still face periodic disclosure obligations in excess of those found in the Companies Acts eg, LSE, AIM Rules for Companies, February 2010, para 18 (half yearly reports).

[144] To the extent that the Directive required more onerous reporting obligations than are found in the 2006 Act, these additional obligations have been implemented via the FSA's Disclosure and Transparency Rules, eg, FSA Handbook, Disclosure and Transparency Rules, DTR 4.1.3. In addition, because the Transparency Directive is a minimum harmonisation directive there are some 'super-equivalent requirements' ie requirements not required by the Directive but imposed on listed companies by the FSA, which appear in the Listing Rules, eg LR 9.8.4.

[145] See generally Companies Act 2006, Parts 15 and 16.

[146] Companies Act 2006, Part 15, in particular s 381. A public company cannot be a 'small company' for these purposes: s 384(1)(a).

[147] A 'quoted company' is a company officially listed in any EEA state or admitted to trading on the New York Stock Exchange or Nasdaq: Companies Act 2006, s 385(2). The power to review the accounts and reports of companies for compliance with the relevant requirements is one which has been delegated by the Government to the Financial Reporting Review Panel. That Panel's powers extend to all of the periodic reports required to be produced by listed companies, whether annual or otherwise (see www.frc.org.uk).

[148] Companies Act 2006, s 393(1).

[149] For many years this was almost all that companies legislation said about the content of accounts. That is not the case today (see Parts 15 and 16 Companies Act 2006) but the true and fair view remains an overriding principle in this area (see eg s 393(1); s 396(4)(5); s 404(4)(5)).

[150] Companies Act 2006, s 395.

[151] Even the content of the 2006 Act and the regulations made thereunder are not sufficient to provide fully the detailed information needed to produce a set of accounts for any particular company and these provisions are supplemented by accounting standards drawn up by the Accounting Standards Board (ASB), an operating

to International Financial Reporting Standards (IFRS).[152] The same choice is available to companies producing group accounts although companies with securities traded on a regulated market must use IFRS for their group accounts.[153] The annual accounts must be audited[154] and detailed guidance is laid down in this regard.[155] The auditors' report is addressed to the shareholders and must state whether in their opinion the annual accounts have been prepared in accordance with the Companies Act or the IFRS and in particular whether they give a true and fair view.[156]

A directors' report must accompany both individual and group accounts. This has been a requirement of domestic legislation for some time[157] and is also a requirement of EC legislation.[158] This report must include a variety of information, both general[159] and specific.[160] European regulations require that a company whose securities are admitted to trading on a regulated market must also include a corporate governance statement in its annual report.[161] In the UK, from April 2010, under the FSA's revised Listing Regime, all companies with a premium listing are required to report on how they have applied the UK Corporate Governance Code (previously known as the Combined Code) regardless of their country of incorporation.[162] New rules require that overseas issuers with a standard listing of certain securities, including shares, need to make a corporate governance statement in their directors' report covering the governance code to which the issuer is subject, and providing certain details of its share capital.[163]

The UK Corporate Governance Code is a set of corporate governance principles drawn from the work of a number of reports published from 1992 onwards, most notably the Cadbury Committee.[164] The Code sets out standards of good practice in relation to issues

body of the Financial Reporting Council. The ASB is the body prescribed by the Secretary of State to issue accounting standards which have statutory recognition: Companies Act 2006, s 464 and Accounting Standards (Prescribed Body) Regulations 2008/651.

[152]   Regulation (EC) No 1606/2002 on the Application of International Accounting Standards ([2002] OJ L243/1). International Accounting Standards (IAS) have now become International Financial Reporting Standards (IFRS).

[153]   Ibid, art 4 (which is directly applicable).

[154]   Companies Act 2006, s 475. Certain companies, such as small companies and dormant companies, are exempt from this requirement: s 475(1).

[155]   Companies Act 2006, Part 16. The detailed requirements of the audit report are established by an International Standard on Auditing (United Kingdom and Ireland), ISA 700.

[156]   Companies Act 2006, s 495(3).

[157]   Most recently Companies Act 2006, s 415.

[158]   Fourth Directive 78/660/EEC, art 46ff, Seventh directive 83/349/EEC, art 36ff.

[159]   Eg details of the company's principal activities: Companies Act 2006, s 416(1)(b).

[160]   Eg details about the employment, training and promotion of disabled persons: The Large and Medium Sized Companies and Groups (Accounts and Reports) Regulations 2008 (SI 2008/410), Sch 7, Part 3.

[161]   Fourth directive 78/660/EEC, art 46A, inserted by Directive 2006/46/EC. This corporate governance statement must deal, inter alia, with the company's control structures, compliance with the relevant corporate governance code, and must contain a description of the company's internal control and risk management systems in relation to financial reporting.

[162]   FSA Handbook, Listing Rules, LR 9.8.6–9.8.7. For discussion of the changes introduced in April 2010 see the Listing Rules Sourcebook (Amendment No 3) n 142 and FSA, *Listing Regime Review*, n 142. Prior to this date, whilst all UK companies were required to report on how they have applied this Code, overseas companies listed on the Main Market were merely required to explain whether they complied with the corporate governance code of their country of incorporation and how that code differed from the UK Corporate Governance Code.

[163]   As a result overseas companies with a standard listing must now comply with DTR 7.2.

[164]   Report of the Committee on the Financial Aspects of Corporate Governance (Gee, London, 1992) (Cadbury Report). See also Directors' Remuneration, Report of a Study Group (Gee, London, 1997) (Greenbury

such as board composition and development, remuneration, accountability and audit and relations with shareholders. The Code sets out a number of principles, with which companies must comply.[165] There are then a number of lower-level, more specific provisions.[166] It is not obligatory for companies to follow these but companies must state whether they have complied, and explain any areas of non-compliance. Although the FSA can impose sanctions for non-compliance with the Listing Rules,[167] if a company fulfils the requirements of the Listing Rules by disclosing its non-compliance with the Corporate Governance Code, this is a matter for the shareholders, as the recipients of this information, rather than the FSA.

Two developments deserve particular comment in relation to the directors' report. First, the directors of quoted companies are required to produce a directors' remuneration report.[168] The Financial Services Act 2010 gives the Treasury power to expand the disclosure regime beyond quoted companies, and to employees who are not directors.[169] Information is required about the company's remuneration policy, including the composition of the remuneration committee, and disclosure must be made of the payments actually made to directors in the financial year in question, including salary, bonuses, non-cash benefits, share option schemes and pension benefits.[170] This latter disclosure is audited. The fact that details of the directors' remuneration should be disclosed is not new[171] but the requirement of an advisory vote is an innovation.[172] The directors must give notice to the shareholders of their intention to move an ordinary resolution approving the remuneration report at the meeting at which the accounts are laid before the shareholders, and they must ensure that the resolution is put to the vote at the meeting.[173] However, '[n]o entitlement of a person to remuneration is made conditional on the resolution being passed' by reason only of these provisions.[174]

The second development which requires comment is the use of the directors' report to include forward-looking 'narrative' reporting to accompany the backward-looking financial information contained in the accounts. Section 417 of the Companies Act 2006 requires all companies, other than those benefitting from the small companies regime, to

---

Report); Final Report of the Committee on Corporate Governance (Gee, London, 1998) (Hampel Report); Review of the Role and Effectiveness of Non-Executive Directors (London, The Stationery Office, 2003) (Higgs Report).

[165] For example, Main Principle B.1 states: 'The board and its committees should have the appropriate balance of skills, experience, independence and knowledge of the company to enable them to discharge their respective duties and responsibilities effectively' (UK Corporate Governance Code, June 2010).

[166] For example, Principle B.1.2 states that at least one half of the board as a whole should be non-executive directors, all of whom should be independent (UK Corporate Governance Code, June 2010). In companies below the FTSE 350 the requirement is only for two independent non-executive directors.

[167] See 10.4.2.1.

[168] See Companies Act 2006, s 420. This report was first introduced in the Directors' Remuneration Report Regulations 2002 (SI 2002/1986). Although the directors' remuneration report is usually presented with the directors' report it is not technically part of the directors' report.

[169] Financial Services Act 2010, s 4.

[170] Large and Medium-Sized Companies and Groups (Accounts and Reports) Regulations 2008/410 Sch 8.

[171] The Listing Rules required disclosure of much the same information even before the introduction of the Directors' Remuneration Report Regulations 2002 (SI 2002/1986). For the current Listing Rules requirements see LR 9.8.8.

[172] See Companies Act 2006, s 439.

[173] Ibid.

[174] Companies Act 2006, s 439(5). Presumably the director and the company could agree to the remuneration being conditional in this way.

contain a business review, although the intensity of this review is weaker for companies that are not quoted. Companies are required to produce a fair review of the company's business and a description of the principal risks and uncertainties facing it,[175] the purpose of the review being to 'inform members of the company'.[176]

For quoted companies the business review must deal with a number of additional matters including the 'main trends and factors' likely to affect the future of the company's business, the impact of the company's business on the environment, the employees, social and community issues and contractual arrangements essential to the company's business (such as supply chains and out-sourcing arrangements),[177] unless, in the opinion of the directors, such disclosure would be seriously prejudicial to those persons or to the public interest.[178] Indeed directors can decline to disclose any of these matters if in their opinion disclosure would be seriously prejudicial to the interests of the company.[179] Concerns have been raised that the information required by the business review is general rather than specific,[180] leading to doubts as to whether the information produced will be of value to shareholders.[181] It is also notable that, in contrast to the annual accounts, the business review is not audited,[182] and although the Accounting Standards Board has produced a reporting standard for the business review[183] this is merely a statement of best practice and compliance with it is purely voluntary.

The inclusion of forward-looking information in the directors' report contrasts sharply with the information disclosure obligations regarding the prospectus. The information included in the prospectus is predominantly backward-looking, even though this is of relatively little benefit in helping investors to determine what the future value of securities is likely to be, which, after all, is their primary concern when deciding whether to invest.[184]

Other jurisdictions, notably the US, do require more forward-looking information from issuers. In the US, the management of issuers are required to provide an extensive Management Discussion and Analysis of Financial Condition and Results of Operations (MD&A report)[185] which supplements historical accounting data with narrative information on the accounts and a forward-looking review of the business. When the US introduced provisions to allow forward-looking data to be included, concerns were

---

[175]   Companies Act 2006, s 417(3). This review applies equally to the companies in a group where group accounts are required: s 417(9).

[176]   Ibid, s 417(2).

[177]   Ibid, s 417(5).

[178]   Ibid, s 417(11).

[179]   Ibid, s 417(10).

[180]   There is a requirement for directors to make use of 'key performance indicators', both financial and non-financial, to the extent necessary for an understanding of the material, in an attempt to inject some quantitative analysis in to the review: s 417(6), although this is not the case for medium-sized companies in some circumstances (s 417(7)).

[181]   The forerunner to the business review, the Operating and Financial Review, which was recommended by the Company Law Review Steering Group (see Company Law Review Steering Group, *Modern Company Law For a Competitive Economy: Final Report*, URN 01/942, July 2001, Vol I, paras 3.33–3.45) required more specificity and detail regarding the information supplied by directors than the equivalent provisions in the Business Review.

[182]   The audit requirement for the directors' report is simply that the auditors' certify that the directors' report is consistent with the accounts: Companies Act 2006, s 496.

[183]   ASB, *Reporting Statement: Operating and Financial Review*, January 2006.

[184]   See chapter 9.4.2.

[185]   The SEC (Securities and Exchange Commission) requires extensive annual disclosure via Form 10-K. The financial date required to be disclosed is specified in Regulation S-K. The financial disclosures are supplemented by Regulation S-K Item 303: the MD&A section.

expressed by directors regarding liability should their estimates prove wrong and as a result a safe harbour rule was designed to protect directors from law suits[186] and thereby to encourage them to provide this forward-looking material, although many managers are still reluctant to do so because of liability concerns should the estimates prove wrong. Section 463 of the Companies Act 2006 provides a similar safe harbour for directors regarding statements in the directors' report and directors' remuneration report.[187] Directors' liability in negligence to their company for statements in these reports is excluded entirely, although liability for fraud is maintained.[188] However, the directors' liability to other persons is excluded entirely, even in the case of fraud.[189]

10.3.1.2 Half Yearly and Quarterly Reporting

Although article 4 of the Transparency Directive did not introduce significant changes when implemented in the UK, other articles of the Directive have had an important impact. In particular articles 5 and 6 introduce a requirement for more regular reporting than the annual reporting required by the Companies Act 2006. Article 5 of the Directive requires half yearly reports to be published within two months of the end of the half year.[190] These reports are less detailed than the annual ones and are not required to be audited.[191] The half year report contains a condensed set of financial statements and an interim management report, which indicates the important events that have occurred during the first six months of the financial year and their impact on the financial statements, plus an assessment of the principal risks and uncertainties for the remaining six months.[192]

Article 6 goes further and requires reporting on a more frequent basis than half yearly. Quarterly accounting is contentious. The potential benefit of more frequent reporting is that it might add to the efficiency of the securities markets. However, there is a danger that it might promote an overly short-term approach amongst management. Article 6 of the Directive requires the publication of quarterly interim management statements by issuers but does not go as far as requiring quarterly accounts. This interim statement must give an explanation of material events and transactions which have taken place and their impact on the issuer and a general description of the company's financial position and performance.[193]

---

[186] Securities Act 1933, Rule 175.

[187] As such section 463 therefore goes beyond protecting directors from liability in relation to forward-looking statements since it covers all statements contained in these reports.

[188] The director is liable for untrue or misleading statements in the reports or omissions if the director has been fraudulent: s 463(2)(3). Fraud for these purposes is defined in the same way as common law deceit: the maker of the statement must know it is untrue or misleading or be reckless as to whether this is the case: *Derry v Peek* (1889) LR 14 App Cas 337.

[189] Companies Act 2006, s 463(4)(5). Third parties may still have a claim for fraud against the company: FSMA s 90A, discussed at 10.4.1.2. In fact s 463 excludes the third party liability of any person (s 463(4)), not just directors, although in most cases it will only be the directors and the company who will be responsible for statements in the reports, and therefore only they will potentially be liable for any errors.

[190] FSA Handbook, Disclosure and Transparency Rules, DTR 4.2.

[191] However, if they are audited or reviewed, the audit report or review must be published: Transparency Directive 2004/109/EC Art 5(4); DTR 4.2.9.

[192] See Transparency Directive 2004/109/EC, art 5 and DTR 4.2.

[193] DTR 4.3.

The issuer is required to disseminate this information throughout the EC 'in a manner ensuring fast access to such information on a non-discriminatory basis'.[194] Where the UK is the home state of the issuer this means that periodic reports are to be distributed through a Regulated Information Service (RIS)[195] and are made available on the issuer's website.[196]

10.3.1.3   The Function of Periodic Disclosures

Periodic disclosures seem to be both investor-focused and shareholder-focused. Some of these disclosures are targeted specifically at shareholders, and address corporate governance issues. The fact that the annual accounts of a public company must be circulated to the shareholders,[197] and laid before the shareholders in general meeting,[198] suggests that the shareholders are regarded as a significant focus for these documents. Although there is no specific requirement for shareholders to consider a resolution to approve the accounts and report, shareholders in public companies must be afforded the opportunity to discuss them. It can also be seen that the auditors' report on the annual accounts and reports is addressed to the shareholders,[199] which lends further weight to the view that the primary focus, of the annual reports and accounts at least, is the shareholders. Of course the annual accounts are a public document and where there is a public market for the company's securities, the annual accounts will be widely read not only by existing shareholders but also by creditors and the wider, investing public. Nevertheless, as discussed, it is the corporate governance function of the annual report and accounts that was recognised and emphasised by the House of Lords in *Caparo Industries plc v Dickman*.[200]

Innovations since the decision in *Caparo* suggest that the shareholders remain the significant focus of disclosures in the annual report and accounts. For example, the requirement for the directors' remuneration report to be disclosed to shareholders, and, more particularly, the need for an advisory vote of the shareholders on this report, is a strong indication as to the focus of this information. Even though a rejection of the remuneration report by the shareholders has no effect on the directors' receipt of remuneration,[201] nevertheless this vote gives shareholders a guaranteed opportunity to express their views on directors' remuneration, and in practice those companies who have experienced a negative vote on their remuneration report have moved to amend their remuneration arrangements.[202] The business review also seems to be focused on providing

---

[194]   Transparency Directive 2004/109/EC, art 21.

[195]   An RIS is an information service approved by the FSA which carries news about all companies to the market.

[196]   DTR 6.

[197]   Companies Act 2006, s 423(1). The obligation to circulate the company's annual report and accounts extends beyond the shareholders and includes debenture-holders and others who are entitled to receive notice of general meetings.

[198]   Companies Act 2006, ss 437–38 cf private companies where there is an obligation to circulate the accounts and reports but any further action is a matter for the shareholders or the company's articles.

[199]   Companies Act 2006, s 495(1).

[200]   [1990] 2 AC 605.

[201]   Companies Act 2006, s 439(5).

[202]   Since the introduction in 2002 of the requirement to put the remuneration report a number of companies have faced shareholder revolts over their remunerations reports, eg GlaxoSmithKline in 2003, RBS and Shell in 2009.

information to the shareholders, indeed the 2006 Act specifically provides that the purpose of the review is to 'inform members of the company'[203] rather than investors more generally.[204]

By contrast the half yearly and quarterly yearly disclosures are not tied to a shareholder meeting at all. Further, the dominant objective of the Transparency Directive appears to be investor protection, rather than shareholder protection, although shareholders do benefit from these disclosures as well. It is also noticeable that although the measures regarding the annual report and accounts are largely to be found in companies legislation, the implementation of articles 5 and 6 of the Transparency Directive, introducing the half yearly and quarter yearly disclosures, has been effected via securities legislation. This underlines the function of these latter disclosure requirements being primarily the disclosure of information to the market rather than to shareholders.

10.3.2   Ad hoc Disclosures

In addition to the periodic reports that publicly quoted companies must make every three months, these companies also have to make disclosure of certain information as and when it arises. Four kinds of ad hoc disclosures will be considered in this section: inside information, directors' shareholdings, major shareholdings and disclosures required by the Listing Rules.

10.3.2.1   Inside Information

An obligation is placed on companies to disclose inside information to the market 'as soon as possible'. The origin of the current requirement is found in the Market Abuse Directive[205] which is implemented into UK law via the FSA's Disclosure and Transparency Rules.[206] In general, inside information is information which is not known to the market but if it were known would have a significant effect on the price of the company's securities because it is precise information relating either to the company or to its securities.[207] Common examples are the discovery of a fraud committed within the company or its subsidiaries, or that the company is in discussions about a takeover bid.

The obligation on the company is to display the information on the company's website,[208] and to release the information via a Regulated Information Service (RIS).[209] The information should be disseminated to the public simultaneously, as nearly as

---

[203]   Companies Act 2006, s 417(2).

[204]   This is contrary to the recommendations of the Company Law Review Steering Group which proposed that the Operating and Financial Review (the precursor to the business review) should be more widely-targeted, to include investors more generally (Company Law Review Steering Group, *Modern Company Law in a Competitive Economy: The Final Report*, URN 01/942, July 2001, para 3.33).

[205]   Directive 2003/6/EC on insider trading and market abuse (the 'Market Abuse Directive'), art 6.

[206]   FSA, Disclosure and Transparency Rules, DTR 2. Although these rules only apply to companies whose securities are admitted to a regulated market, ad hoc disclosure rules are imposed on AIM companies under the AIM rules: LSE, *AIM Rules for Companies*, Feb 2010, Rule 11.

[207]   Market Abuse Directive, n 205, art 1.

[208]   Market Abuse Directive, n 205, art 6(1); DTR 2.3.5.

[209]   DTR 2.2.1. These provisions apply to all companies whose securities are traded on the Official List (ie both premium and standard listings following the segmentation of the Official list into a two tier system: see the Listing Rules Sourcebook (Amendment No 3) n 142 and FSA, *Listing Regime Review*, n 142) and also to companies on the Plus-listed market.

possible, in all EEA Member States[210] and it must be communicated to the FSA.[211] The Market Abuse Directive permits an issuer 'under its own responsibility' to delay disclosure to protect its 'legitimate interests' but subject to the rider that the non-disclosure must not be likely to mislead the public and provided the company can ensure confidentiality on the part of those to whom the information will have to be disclosed.[212]

It could be said that one aim of this disclosure requirement is to make shareholders and investors aware of this information as it may impact on their decision to deal in the shares. However, the predominant purpose of the disclosure seems to be to deprive the information of its 'inside' character so as to remove the potential for gain from the insider with the information. It is notable that the primary obligation here is on the company to disclose this information, unlike the second and third types of ad hoc disclosure, discussed below, in which the primary obligation is on the holder of shares to disclose certain information to the company, and the company's obligation to disclose to the market is secondary. In those circumstances the role of information provision *to* the company (and thereby its shareholders) is clear, whereas here the disclosure obligation is purely on the company to disclose to the market. Again it is significant that these disclosure obligations are part of securities legislation rather than companies legislation. The predominant purpose of these disclosure obligations is to provide information to the market rather than to shareholders.

Insider dealing is both a criminal offence under the Criminal Justice Act 1993 and a breach of FSMA 2000 provisions and is dealt with in detail in section 10.5 below.

10.3.2.2   Disclosure of Directors' Shareholdings

There has been a long-standing requirement in UK law for directors of companies to disclose their interests in securities of the companies of which they are directors, and over time this has also been extended to the interests of spouses, civil partners and children. The current rules, which originate in the Market Abuse Directive,[213] relate only to companies incorporated in the UK whose securities are admitted to trading on a regulated market. Those discharging managerial responsibilities for these companies, and those connected with them,[214] are required to disclose their dealings in the shares, derivatives, or other financial instruments of the issuer.[215]

---

[210] DTR 6.3.4.

[211] DTR 6.2.2.

[212] DTR 2.5.1, implementing Market Abuse Directive, n 205, art 6(2).

[213] Directive 2003/6/EC.

[214] FSMA, s 96B(2). Note that the core of the definition of 'connected person' for these purposes is found in Companies Act 1985, s 346, a section which is for other purposes revoked and replaced by Companies Act 2006 ss 252–254, but which is preserved for this purpose by the Companies Act (Commencement No 3, Consequential Amendments, Transitional Provisions and Savings) Order 2007/2194, Sch 3 para 50.

[215] Market Abuse Directive, art 6(4), implemented into UK law via DTR 3. These provisions apply to all companies on the Main list (ie both premium listed and standard listed companies) and to Plus-listed companies. Interestingly, following the implementation of the Market Abuse Directive and the introduction of the Companies Act 2006, the scope of the obligation on directors to disclose their shareholdings has actually reduced. For example, prior to these measures, directors' shareholding disclosure obligations applied to all companies (see eg Companies Act 1985, ss 324–326 and s 328) and not just to companies whose securities are admitted to trading on a regulated market. The AIM rules require companies to disclose transactions by directors and require the company to have in place rules and procedures under which the director is to provide the necessary information to the company but they do not directly impose obligations on the directors: *LSE, AIM Rules for Companies*, February 2010, rules 17 and 31 and Sch 5.

Those discharging managerial responsibilities include not only directors but also senior managers who have regular access to inside information relating to the issuer and have the power to make managerial decisions affecting the issuer's development and business prospects.[216] Those discharging managerial responsibilities need to disclose transactions relating to the shares (but not the debt securities) of the issuer, including where the director has a purely economic interest in the shares, but no ownership interest, for example where the transaction involves a contract for differences, in which the contracting party becomes entitled to the difference between the price of the share at two different times without actually acquiring a property interest in the share. A range of transactions are covered, including the use of shares as collateral for a financing transaction (eg as security for a loan from a bank). The transaction needs to be disclosed to the issuer within four business days of the transaction occurring and the issuer must then give the information to the market[217] and to the FSA.[218] Both the price and volume of the transaction need to be disclosed.[219]

One purpose of these disclosure rules is corporate governance-focused. The rules provide information to shareholders about a director's interests in the company, and therefore the existence of any particular financial incentives the director has to improve the performance of the company, as part of the process of shareholder monitoring of the directors' stewardship of the company.[220] However, the predominant purpose is to curb insider trading, with the focus being on the market rather than shareholders. Again, it is relevant that these provisions are now found in securities legislation, whereas at one time they were regarded as part of company law.[221]

10.3.2.3 Disclosure of Major Shareholdings

The idea that an interest in shares should be declared once certain size thresholds have been reached is a well-established principle of UK law.[222] Although the names of the legal owners of shares is a matter of public record, appearing on the share register and reported to Companies House in the annual return, it is common for shares to be held beneficially, via a nominee. The dematerialisation of shares in recent years, has made this even more common. Although dematerialised shares can be held directly, it is also very common for them to be held indirectly.[223] Therefore merely examining the share register will not provide a full picture of those with an interest in the shares of the company.

The origins of the current regime are, again, European law, in this instance the Transparency Directive.[224] This directive applies only to companies whose securities are

---

[216] FSMA, s 96B(1). This definition does not appear to include shadow directors, a category which was specifically included in the Companies Act 1985 disclosure obligations (see Companies Act 1985, s 324(1)).

[217] DTR 3.1.2, 3.1.4.

[218] DTR 6.2.2.

[219] DTR 3.1.3(7).

[220] See eg Law Commission and the Scottish Law Commission, *Company Directors: Regulating Conflicts of Interest and Formulating a Statement of Duties: A Joint Consultation Paper* (Law Com Consultation Paper No 153, Scot Law Com Discussion Paper No 105,1998) para 5.2.

[221] See Companies Act 1985, ss 324–329, repealed by the Companies Act 2006 (Commencement No 1, Transitional Provisions and Savings) Order 2006 (SI 2006/3428) Sch 4.

[222] See eg the recommendations of the Cohen Committee, *Report of the Committee on Company Law Amendment* (Cm 6659, 1945) 39–45.

[223] Discussed at 10.2.2.1.

[224] Directive 2004/109/EC on transparency requirements in relation to issuers.

admitted to trading on a regulated market.[225] However, in implementing the directive into domestic law in this context the scope of the regime was broadened to include all companies with securities traded on a prescribed market.[226] This includes the Main Market of the London Stock Exchange (both premium and standard listings), AIM and the Plus Markets, and these disclosure obligations are therefore more wide ranging than those relating to directors' disclosures, discussed above.[227] The disclosure obligation arises when the shareholder holds three per cent of the total voting rights in the company and at every one per cent increase thereafter.[228] Decreases must also be notified.[229] The shareholder must notify the percentage of shares now held and the date upon which the threshold was crossed.[230] Disclosure must take place as soon as possible but in any event by the end of the second trading day following the day on which the obligation to disclose arose.[231] When issuers on a regulated market receive this information they are under an obligation to make public the information received as soon as possible and in any event by the end of the following trading day.[232]

In order to capture the disclosure of *beneficial* interests, the rules require disclosure of voting rights arising out of a person's 'direct or indirect holding of financial instruments'.[233] So, for example, voting rights attached to shares held by a nominee on behalf of another will constitute an indirect holding of voting rights by that other person. The crucial issue is the control of the exercise of the voting rights. If the nominee has the control of the exercise of these rights then it will be regarded as the direct holder for these purposes, whereas if the nominee may only act on the instructions of the beneficial holder then it is the beneficial holder who will be regarded as having a disclosable interest, if the threshold test is met.

Similarly, it is common for institutional investors such as pension funds to vest the legal title of the shares in a custodian but outsource the management of their investment portfolio to a fund manager. The question of who has a potentially disclosable interest in the shares will depend upon who has control of the voting rights. If, as is usual, the custodian can only vote upon instruction then it will not have to disclose. As between the fund manager and the institutional investor, it will depend upon whether the instructions to the custodian come from the fund manager alone, or whether the fund manager is operating under a mandate from the institutional investor. Where the shares are held

---

[225]   Ibid, art 9(1).

[226]   FSMA, s 89A(1), 3(a); DTR 5.1.1(3).

[227]   However, the current regime is still narrower than that in place prior to the implementation of the Transparency Directive. Under Companies Act 1985, s 198 the regime applied to all public companies.

[228]   DTR 5.1.2. These disclosure triggers are more demanding than the Transparency Directive requires, which sets the thresholds at 5, 10, 15, 20, 25, 30, 50 and 75%: Transparency Directive, art 9(1). Exemptions are in place to cover certain categories, eg market makers who hold shares on their own account in order to be able to offer continuous trading opportunities for those who want to buy and sell shares, thereby increasing market liquidity (DTR 5.1.3(3) and 5.1.4) although often these exemptions are limited, eg the market maker exemption does not apply when the market maker's holding in a particular company reaches 10%.

[229]   DTR 5.1.2.

[230]   DTR 5.8.1.

[231]   DTR 5.8.3. The obligation to disclose arises when the person 'learns of the acquisition or disposal or of the possibility of exercising voting rights' or 'having regard to the circumstances, should have learned of it' rather than the date on which the acquisition or disposal actually occurred: DTR 5.8.3(1).

[232]   DTR 5.8.12. For issuers whose securities are traded on a prescribed (but not regulated) market the period is slightly longer and they have until the end of the third trading day to disclose to the public.

[233]   DTR 5.1.2. Relevant financial instruments in this context will be instruments giving the holder an unconditional right to acquire a share carrying voting rights, eg an option to purchase (see DTR 5.3).

indirectly, in addition to disclosing the percentage of shares now held and the date that the threshold was crossed, details of the indirect nature of the holding are required. For example, where the shares are held by a nominee who can vote only under instructions, the name of the nominee must be disclosed by the beneficiary when making his disclosure, even though that nominee has no disclosable interest.[234] Once the issuer receives this information, it must again make disclosure of this information to the public.[235]

One of the reasons to require the holders of large shareholdings to disclose their interests publicly is to deter insider dealing. As with those discharging managerial responsibilities, large shareholders may be in a position to discover inside information about the company. However, this is only one aspect, and a rather minor aspect, of the role that these rules play. More important is the dissemination of information regarding those who have positions of influence or control over the company as a result of large shareholdings. Support for this view can be found in the fact that holdings of non-voting shares do not have to be disclosed.[236] Similarly, where shares are held via a nominee the person with the disclosable interest is the person in control of the voting rights, irrespective of whether they have the legal or beneficial title to the shares. It is the issue of control and influence rather than the economic stake in the company per se which seems to be an important driver in these rules.[237] Indeed it is notable that the origin of the current rules in this regard is the Transparency Directive and not the Market Abuse Directive.

However, there is still the question of at whom this information dissemination is aimed. This information is certainly useful to those inside the company, particularly as an early warning signal about potential takeover bids.[238] In addition, this information can be useful to investors more generally in order to give them as full a picture of the company as possible when deciding whether to invest. The fact that the obligation on shareholders to disclose was moved from company law to become part of securities law when the Transparency Directive was implemented into domestic law is no doubt significant.[239] The preamble to the Transparency Directive suggests that improving the functioning of the securities market is the dominant concern of the disclosure requirements contained in the Transparency Directive.

---

[234] DTR 5.8.1.

[235] DTR 5.8.12.

[236] Similarly holdings of shares that are only allowed to vote in certain circumstances (such as preference shares that can only vote if the preferential dividend has not been paid) do not have to be disclosed: DTR 5.1.1(3).

[237] By contrast, those exercising managerial responsibilities do have to disclose holdings in non-voting shares under the provisions requiring directors' disclosure because opportunities to engage in insider dealing can still arise in these shares since the economic incentives to deal still arise in relation to these shares.

[238] As another device to try to elicit this information, the company can ask any person to reveal the extent of their interest in the company's voting shares: Companies Act 2006, ss 793–796.

[239] Companies Act 2006, s 1266, introducing FSMA, ss 89A–G. Previously these disclosure rules were to be found in the Companies Act 1985 (repealed by Companies Act 2006 (Commencement No 1, Transitional Provisions and Savings) Order 2006/3428, Sch 3). By contrast the company's ability to request disclosure of someone's interest in the company's voting shares remains part of company legislation (CA 2006, ss 793–796).

10.3.2.4   *Disclosures Required by the Listing Rules*

The Listing Rules impose a number of ad hoc disclosure requirements on companies with a premium listing on the Main Market.[240] Two are worth noting. First is the requirement for companies whose shares are listed on the Main Market to disclose related party transactions to the shareholders and to seek shareholder approval for these transactions.[241] Related party transactions include transactions between a listed company and any of its subsidiaries, on the one side, and, on the other, a director or shadow director of the listed company or another company within the corporate group or a person who has been such a director within the previous twelve months or an associate of such a director.[242] However, the requirement for shareholder approval also applies to transactions between the listed company and any person where the purpose and effect is to benefit a related party.[243] On the approval resolution the related party may not vote and the related party must take all reasonable steps to ensure that any associates do not vote either.[244] Although the Listing Rules require this information to be disclosed to shareholders in a circular,[245] companies are also under an obligation to disclose this information to the market, via the RIS system.[246]

Second, the Listing Rules require disclosure by companies listed on the Main Market to their shareholders of certain 'significant' transactions, whether or not there is an element of self-dealing involved, and approval of some of those transactions.[247] Classification is by reference to the size of the transaction relative to the size of the issuer.[248] The general principle is that the more substantial the transaction is for the issuer, the greater the protection afforded to its investors either through disclosure or ultimately through consent at a general meeting. Four 'class tests' (gross assets; profits; consideration; and gross capital) are used to determine the 'ratio' of the size of the transaction relative to the issuer,[249] and consequently the regulatory requirements that apply to the transaction. A Class 3 transaction is one where each percentage ratio is less than five per cent. A limited announcement is required in these circumstances if the consideration includes the issue of securities for which a listing will be sought[250] or if the issuer releases any details of the transaction to the public.[251] A Class 2 transaction is one where any percentage ratio is five per cent or more, but each is less than 25 per cent. A more detailed announcement than a

---

[240]   Following the segmentation of the UK Official List into a two tier regime, these obligations apply to those companies with a premium listing but not to those with a standard listing: See the Listing Rules Sourcebook (Amendment No 3) n 142 and FSA, *Listing Regime Review*, n 142. Similar, though in general less demanding, rules may be imposed on companies listed on other UK public markets as a matter of contract between the company and the body organising the relevant exchange. For example AIM companies are subject to similar ad hoc requirements by virtue of the AIM rules, which apply as a matter of contract between the company and the London Stock Exchange: eg, LSE, *AIM Rules for Companies*, February 2010, rules 12–13.

[241]   FSA Handbook, Listing Rules, LR 11.1. There are some exemptions eg for small transactions: LR 11.1.6 and LR 11 Annex 1R.

[242]   Ibid, LR 11.1.4.

[243]   Ibid, LR 11.1.5.

[244]   Ibid, LR 11.1.7(4).

[245]   Ibid, LR 11.1.7(2).

[246]   Ibid, LR 11.1.7(1).

[247]   Ibid, LR 10.

[248]   Ibid, LR 10.2.1.

[249]   Ibid, LR 10 Annex 1.

[250]   Ibid, LR 10.3.1.

[251]   Ibid, LR 10.3.2.

Class 3 announcement is required, the content requirements for which are set out in the Listing Rules.[252] A Class 1 transaction is one where any percentage ratio is 25 per cent or more. The issuer must comply with the Class 2 requirements and, in addition, send an explanatory circular to its shareholders,[253] and obtain the prior approval of the transaction by its shareholders in a general meeting.[254] The content requirements for a Class 1 circular are again set out in the Listing Rules.[255] Following the circular to shareholders the company is also under an obligation to make disclosure to the market by way of a RIS circular.[256]

Despite the fact that the company is under an obligation to disclose the details of both significant transactions and related party transactions to the market via a RIS circular, there is little doubt that the predominant concern of these disclosure requirements is to provide information to the shareholders in order to allow them to perform their corporate governance functions. The fact that shareholder approval is required for related party transactions and the larger significant transactions makes this point clear. It is a well-established principle of company law to further good corporate governance by requiring shareholder approval for particular transactions, especially where the transaction is particularly sensitive or important. For example, shareholder approval is needed for the transaction if it is being entered into by directors or their associates with the company,[257] and shareholder approval is required for the appointment of the company's auditors.[258] The Listing Rules take this principle further, extending the requirement for shareholder approval in the context of directors and their associates contracting with the company, and adding a new category of transaction where approval is necessary, based on the size of the transaction. The corporate governance focus of these rules in the Listing Rules seems clear.

10.3.2.5 The Function of Ad Hoc Disclosures

As discussed, regulation of the capital markets has a number of aims. It variously seeks to inform shareholders for corporate governance purposes, to inform shareholders and investors regarding their investment decisions, and to protect the market (and thus investors) more generally by preventing market abuse. All of these aims are now visible in the mandatory disclosure obligations which exist for publicly traded companies.

Traditionally the emphasis was on the provision of information to the shareholders of the company with the purpose of that information being corporate governance-focused. Many of the disclosure obligations were found in the Companies Acts rather than in securities legislation, and the House of Lords in *Caparo* made it clear that the annual report and accounts, until relatively recently the only mandatory periodic disclosure requirement, was governance-focused rather than providing the shareholders with information with which to make investment decisions. The force of this argument is strong in relation to the annual report and accounts which are required to be circulated to shareholders and laid before them in a general meeting. It is also strong in relation to

---

[252] Ibid, LR 10.4.
[253] Ibid, LR 10.5.1(2).
[254] Ibid, LR 10.5.1(3).
[255] Ibid, LR 13.4 and 13.5.
[256] Ibid, LR 10.3.1; 10.4.1; 10.5.1.
[257] Companies Act 2006, Part 10, Ch 4.
[258] Ibid, Part 16, Ch 2.

those ad hoc disclosure requirements where there is a significant internal corporate rationale, such as the disclosures of significant transactions and related party transactions by companies to their shareholders. However other ad hoc disclosures appear to have little or no internal corporate rationale.

There has undoubtedly been a shift in emphasis regarding the purpose of ongoing disclosure rules in recent years, allowing for the development of disclosure requirements which have little to do with corporate governance aims. Recent European legislation, in particular the Market Abuse Directive and the Transparency Directive, has had a significant impact in this area. The implementation of these directives has resulted in a shift from ongoing disclosures being located in companies legislation to them being placed in securities legislation. There has been an important shift in emphasis from a shareholder focus to an investor protection focus. Recital 1 of the Transparency Directive for example, states that '[t]he disclosure of accurate, comprehensive and timely information about security issuers builds sustained investor confidence and allows an informed assessment of their business performance and assets. This enhances both investor protection and market efficiency'.[259] An obvious example of this approach is the disclosure of inside information. It cannot be ruled out that shareholders might obtain some information from these disclosures that might be relevant to them in making investment or governance decisions. However, the predominant purpose of these disclosures is one based on a market protection approach.

The current position is therefore that ad hoc disclosures perform a number of functions. Some are aimed at providing shareholders with information to allow them to perform their governance functions, some provide shareholders and investors more generally with information on the basis of which to make their investment decisions, and some are intended to protect investors by preventing market abuse. Of course some disclosures are intended to perform more than one of these functions. This may be compared with the disclosures associated with initial public offers where the information is only provided for one function: to enable investors to decide whether to purchase securities in the issuer. When assessed against this objective it was stated that the large amounts of information that companies are actually required to produce at the IPO stage are relatively unhelpful. Whereas shareholders want to assess the future potential of a company, and therefore might be expected to find information relating to an issuer's future plans and likely performance to be most helpful, the information actually provided is predominantly historical.[260] There are compelling practical reasons for this, not least that the recitation of specified objective facts is the lowest cost method of disclosure and is open to least abuse by corporate insiders, nevertheless the effect is that the information provided will be of relatively little value to investors in helping them to determine what the future value of the securities is likely to be.

By contrast, there is no single unitary purpose behind periodic disclosures against which those disclosures can be judged. The nature of the information provided is also different. Some is of a largely factual historical nature, such as the annual accounts of the company, but some is more forward-looking, such as the business review which must now accompany most company accounts and which must include a fair review of the

---

[259]   2004/109/EC.
[260]   See 9.4.2.

company's business and a description of the principal risks and uncertainties facing it.[261] Even in relation to the information (which is factual) the predominant purpose is not generally to provide investment information to investors. For example, in relation to the remuneration report provided to shareholders, the predominant purpose is to enable the shareholders to perform their governance role more effectively. These disclosures are therefore likely to be more valuable than the mandatory disclosures made at the IPO stage.

This makes it important to ensure that the information is accurate and reliable. Again, as with the IPO stage, the protections in place to try to ensure that the information is accurate are predominantly applied ex post. There are a range of mechanisms which allow for public and private actions in the event of misstatements in ongoing disclosures. These are discussed next, in section 10.4. However the regulation of the ongoing market is concerned with more than just ensuring that ongoing disclosures are accurate and timely. The protection of the market also requires that abuse more generally is prevented and for this reason protection mechanisms have also been developed which aim to prevent fraud by creating liability in the event of market abuse. These measures are discussed at 10.5 below.

10.4   Enforcement of the Mandatory Disclosure Obligations

10.4.1   Private Enforcement

Options exist for private enforcement by shareholders and investors in the context of ongoing disclosures. Until relatively recently the only possible claim arose from a duty of care that was recognised to exist between shareholders and those responsible for producing ongoing disclosures (specifically the annual report and accounts) but only in the context of information that was governance-focused. The options have recently been expanded to allow claims by investors for fraudulent misstatements in ongoing disclosures in some circumstances. There was even a clause included in the Financial Services Bill which would have allowed a court to authorise collective proceedings to be brought on behalf of a group of financial services claims that share the same, similar or related issues of fact or law, although this was dropped from the final Act (the Financial Services Act 2010).[262] These latter claims are not intended to cover disclosures that are shareholder-focused (the purpose being to enable the shareholders to fulfil their governance functions) but investor-focused. In order to determine the nature and extent of any private remedy for misstatements made in ongoing disclosures, the purpose of the disclosure is a relevant consideration.

---

[261]   Companies Act 2006, s 417, discussed above at 10.3.1.1.
[262]   The Financial Services Act 2010 does however give the FSA rule making powers to provide (effectively) civil compensation for customers: s 14.

10.4.1.1   Enforcement by Shareholders of Misstatements in Governance-based Disclosures

Shareholders have rights to bring civil litigation claims regarding misstatements in ongoing disclosures made to them in some circumstances. The decision of the House of Lords in *Caparo Industires plc v Dickman*[263] determines the limits of this liability. As discussed, in *Caparo* the House of Lords decided that the purpose of the statutory accounts provisions was not to supply information to investors, but to inform shareholders. In addition, their Lordships held that, to the extent that the report and accounts provide information to shareholders, the purpose of this information-provision is to enable them to exercise their governance rights over the board effectively, rather than to enable them to take investment decisions. A duty of care does not arise from the annual accounts and reports for auditors in relation to purchases of shares in the company, whether by existing shareholders or investors more generally.[264] By extension the annual report and accounts do not give rise to a duty of care owed by directors and other advisers to any shareholder or investor in relation to a decision to buy the shares.[265]

Since *Caparo* the number of ongoing disclosure obligations made has grown considerably. Many of these are predominantly investor-focused, with little, if any, element of governance, such as the disclosures regarding inside information. The law could have developed to allow common law *Caparo*-style claims by investors in relation to these disclosures. Indeed the fear that this might happen goes some way towards explaining the development of the new statutory liability regime, discussed in 10.4.1.2. However in practice the law has not developed in this way and these investor-focused disclosures have not been regarded as giving rise to a claim by investor/shareholders in the event of misstatement. Even as regards those disclosures where the aims could be said to be mixed, and to include some governance aspects and some investor protection aspects, such as the disclosures regarding directors' shareholdings and major shareholdings, the application of *Caparo* in practice suggests that no common law duty of care will be found to exist between the statement makers (the directors and other advisers) and either the shareholders or other investors in relation to the investment decisions which they make in reliance on those statements.

However, the decision in *Caparo* makes it clear that shareholders can bring a claim for negligent misstatement against the makers of the statement where the statement is located in an ongoing disclosure *if* the purpose of the statement is to provide information to the shareholders to enable them to carry out their governance rights. The House of Lords in *Caparo* accepted that the annual report and accounts can provide information of this kind to the shareholders. The other obvious disclosures that perform this function are the disclosures which provide the shareholders with information about significant transactions or related party transactions, as required by the Listing Rules.[266] The purpose of these disclosures is predominantly governance-focused. However, as discussed, there can

---

[263]   [1990] 2 AC 605.

[264]   Their Lordships left open the question of whether sales of shares might be within the scope of this duty.

[265]   Of course, a duty of care could arise if there is an assumption of responsibility by the maker of the statement to the claimant on the facts, ie if it can be shown that the statement-maker knew that the claimant was likely to use the statement for a particular purpose (such as a purchase of shares in the company) of which the defendant was, or ought to have been, aware eg *Galoo Ltd v Bright Grahame Murray* [1994] 1 WLR 1360.

[266]   FSA Handbook, Listing Rules, LR 10, LR 11 (see 10.3.2.4).

also be a governance benefit to shareholders from other disclosures made to the market, even those that are primarily focused on investors. Where a shareholder can demonstrate that the purpose of a disclosure is to provide information to the shareholders to enable them to perform their governance function then any negligent misstatement in that disclosure will potentially give rise to a claim against the maker of the statement, most likely the directors of the company. This (negligence-based) liability to shareholders in respect of governance-based disclosures should not be impacted by the introduction of the statutory (fraud-based) liability to investors for misstatements in ongoing disclosure documents, discussed in the next section.[267]

This is not an area in which there has been much litigation and the exact parameters of shareholders' rights in this area are not well-defined. One of the reasons for this lack of litigation may be the fact that the recovery will generally flow to the company rather than the shareholder, due to the principle of reflective loss. This principle dictates that shareholders are not able to recover loss which is merely reflective of the company's loss. Where the defendant owes a duty to the company, and not to the shareholder, the claim belongs to the company to the exclusion of the shareholder,[268] who is restricted to a derivative action or a claim under section 994 of the Companies Act 2006 to pursue a remedy for the company. Likewise where the defendant breaches a duty to a shareholder and has never owed a duty to the company then it is easy to see that the claim belongs to the shareholder to the exclusion of the company, even if the only loss suffered by the shareholder is a diminution in the value of his or her shares in the company.[269] However, the difficulty arises in circumstances where the defendant breaches separate duties to the company and to the shareholder. This will be the case where the director makes a misstatement in an ongoing disclosure since the director will owe a duty to the company, as part of his directors' duties, as well as (potentially) the duty of care to the shareholders recognised by the House of Lords in *Caparo*.

In these circumstances the House of Lords in *Johnson v Gore Wood & Co*[270] determined that the shareholder is debarred from claiming this personal loss, not because he has suffered no loss[271] but for policy reasons. In order to avoid the spectre of double recovery, justice to the defendant requires that the claim in relation to a wrong which causes loss to both the company and the shareholder be given to one victim at the expense of the other. Their Lordships chose to give the claim to the company in order to deal with the collective action problem and to protect the interests of the company's creditors.[272] As a result, if the misstatement occurs in a circular to the shareholders regarding a significant transaction, which, say, causes the company to enter into a contract it would not otherwise have entered into, both the company and the shareholder are likely to suffer loss (the latter

---

[267] HM Treasury, *Davies Review of Issuer Liability: Final Report* (June 2007), http://www.hm-treasury.gov.uk/media/4/7/davies_review_finalreport_040607.pdf, paras 42–45; HM Treasury, *Extension of the Statutory Regime for Issuer Liability* (July 2008) www.hm-treasury.gov.uk/media/2/5/issuerliability_170708.pdf paras 5.12–5.15. The introduction of FSMA, Sch 10A, para 7(3)(a)(v) by the Financial Services and Markets Act 2000 (Liability of Issuers) Regulations 2010 (SI 2010/1192) seems to make this point clear.

[268] Eg, *Stein* v *Blake* [1998] 1 All ER 724.

[269] See *George Fischer (Great Britain) Ltd* v *Multi Construction Ltd* [1995] 1 BCLC 260.

[270] [2000] UKHL 65; [2002] 2 AC 1.

[271] Cf *Prudential Assurance Co Ltd* v *Newman Industries Ltd (No 2)* [1982] Ch 204, 223.

[272] Shareholders can recover if they can show that the company has never had a cause of action against the defendant or if they can show that they suffer loss which is 'separate and distinct from that suffered by the company' ([2002] 2 AC 1, 35 per Lord Bingham) as a result of the wrongdoer's action.

through the reduction in share price). However, it is the company and not the shareholder which is regarded as having a claim for damages, so that the shareholder will not be able to recover damages for him/herself, even if the company chooses not to bring a claim.[273]

In practice, the incidence of such claims being brought is 'close to nil'.[274] Indeed the incidence of actions by shareholders in public companies generally is almost non-existent.[275] However the lack of formal enforcement of these issues by shareholders does not mean that these disclosures are unimportant or that enforcement of these issues by shareholders does not occur at all. Shareholders, particularly institutional investors, have a number of important informal mechanisms whereby they can exercise control within a company, including ultimately requisitioning a shareholders' meeting and removing the directors. These informal mechanisms are likely to be more effective in ensuring compliance with these disclosure requirements than a formal court hearing.

10.4.1.2   Enforcement by Shareholders and Other Investors of Investor-focused Disclosures

10.4.1.2.1   Background

As we saw in chapter nine, liability to investors for misstatements in prospectuses has had a long history in the UK, with a statutory liability regime in place since 1890, and common law liability existing even earlier.[276] By contrast, liability to investors for misstatements in relation to ongoing disclosures has been slow to develop.[277]

There are a number of reasons for this. As we have seen, by contrast with disclosures in prospectuses, many ongoing disclosures were, until relatively recently, regarded as company law matters, with obligations to produce annual accounts, for directors to disclose their interests in the company's shares and for major shareholders to disclose their shareholdings, all being located in the Companies Acts (notably the obligation to produce annual accounts). Investor protection was not, therefore, regarded as a relevant consideration. By contrast, the need to disclose any price sensitive information was not part of company law, but was regarded as a matter for the Stock Exchange rather than for the legislator to regulate. The Stock Exchange was not in a position to develop a wide ranging compensation system. It is no coincidence that the introduction of a statutory remedy for investors facing misstatements in ongoing disclosures[278] has followed two important developments: (i) the transfer of disclosure obligations from companies legislation to securities legislation and (ii) the transfer of rule-making power in this context from the London Stock Exchange to the FSA.[279]

---

[273]   For discussion see C Mitchell, 'Shareholders' Claims for Reflective Loss' (2004) 120 *Law Quarterly Review* 457.

[274]   See Armour, 'Enforcement Strategies in UK Corporate Governance', n 85, 86.

[275]   Ibid, 79–86.

[276]   Directors' Liability Act 1890. The common law developed a liability regime even earlier, via the tort of deceit (see 9.5.2).

[277]   For these purposes, shareholders who make use of statements in ongoing disclosures to make investment decisions, rather than for governance purposes, can be regarded as investors.

[278]   FSMA, s 90A, introduced by the Companies Act 2006, s 1270, and which came into effect on 8 November 2006, as amended by the Financial Services and Markets Act 2000 (Liability of Issuers) Regulations 2010 (SI 1192/2010).

[279]   For a discussion of the possible future of the FSA in this regard see 10.4.2.

It is easy to understand why the common law has not developed in such a way to produce a remedy for investors in this context, in contrast to the position regarding prospectuses. The tort of deceit, which provided the first common law remedy for inaccurate prospectuses, requires the recipient to demonstrate that the maker of the statement intended the recipient to rely on it. This makes sense in the context of the prospectus which is a selling document, but is not easily adapted for use in relation to ongoing disclosures. The primary ongoing obligation which existed in the late nineteenth century, when the tort of deceit was being adapted for use in prospectuses, was the obligation to produce annual reports and accounts. Yet, as developed, this obligation was intended primarily as a report to shareholders on the directors' stewardship and was not intended to induce reliance by way of securities trading. Although the annual reports and accounts have undergone some significant changes in the intervening period, this statement still remains a fair reflection of these documents today. It is not surprising that the tort of deceit was not adapted to provide a remedy for misstatements in annual reports and accounts.[280]

The tort of negligence could have provided an alternative common law avenue for a remedy in this context. It is accepted that this tort can give rise to a remedy where misstatements made by one person fall below the standard set by the law and thereby cause purely economic loss to another. This principle could easily have been used to provide a remedy to investors where directors or their advisers were negligent in the misstatements made in a company's continuing disclosure documents and an investor relied on these statements and suffered loss as a consequence. However, as discussed, in *Caparo Industries plc v Dickman*[281] the House of Lords decided that the purpose of the statutory accounts provisions was not to supply information to investors, and to the extent that it provided information to shareholders the purpose of this information provision was to enable them to exercise their governance rights over the board effectively, rather than to enable them to take investment decisions.[282] As a result of the way that the tort of negligence has developed it has not been available as a general remedy to investors.

Until 2006, then, there was no statutory regime for inaccurate statements other than those contained in prospectuses, and the common law offered no protection to investors unless the defendant knew that a particular person was likely to use the statement for a particular purpose (such as a purchase of shares in the company) of which the defendant was, or ought to have been, aware.

This was made clear in a recent decision, *Hall v Cable & Wireless plc.*[283] When Cable & Wireless sold One2One to Deutsche Telekom in August 1999, it agreed to indemnify Deutsche in respect of One2One's tax liabilities. Cable & Wireless also agreed that, if its debt rating fell below a particular level, it would either provide Deutsche with a bank guarantee in the sum of £1.5 billion or pay £1.5 billion into escrow to back up its

---

[280] For a discussion of the tort of deceit in the context of misstatements in prospectuses see 9.5.2.

[281] [1990] 2 AC 605.

[282] Only if the maker of the statement makes the statement knowing that it will be made available to a particular person who will rely on it for a particular type of transaction which is known or ought to be known to the maker of a statement, will a duty of care be found by the court. So, for example, where the auditors of a company's accounts send the accounts to a person who is contemplating a purchase of shares in that company, and that purpose is known to the auditors, the auditors will owe that person a duty of care: See eg *Galoo Ltd v Bright Grahame Murray* [1994] 1 WLR 1360.

[283] [2009] EWHC 1793 (Comm).

indemnity. This obligation was not included in Cable & Wireless's announcement of the sale or in its subsequent annual accounts. In December 2002, since Cable & Wireless's debt rating had fallen below the relevant level, it issued a press release to the effect that it was obliged to procure a bank guarantee for £1.5 billion or pay that sum into escrow. Not surprisingly, its share price then fell. Four shareholders, who had bought shares between August 1999 and December 2002, sued the company for losses suffered on their shares alleging, inter alia, breach of statutory duty, as Cable & Wireless had failed to announce under the Listing Rules its potential obligation to obtain the guarantee.[284] The judge rejected these claims. The appropriate body to take action in these cases is the FSA, which has powers to impose penalties under FSMA, as discussed below in 10.4.2. The judge held that shareholders do not have rights to bring such a claim directly against the company.

However, in 2006 a new statutory provision, section 90A FSMA, was introduced to provide a remedy for investors regarding misstatements in continuing disclosure documents in some circumstances.[285] The background to the introduction of this section is interesting. With the implementation of the Transparency Directive into UK law, a concern was expressed that some kind of liability between issuers and investors arising from continuing disclosure obligations could come into existence where none had existed before. This was not due to any specific provision in the Transparency Directive.[286] Rather, this concern arose from the directive's emphasis on investor protection rather than corporate governance as being the dominant purpose of the disclosures. It was feared that this shift in emphasis might lead a future court to reconsider the *Caparo* decision and to create issuer (and director) liability to investors based on ongoing disclosures.[287]

The Government's response to these concerns was to introduce section 90A FSMA, which is intended to replace any common law liability for behaviour falling within the scope of the section.[288] A review of this section was conducted by Professor Paul Davies, at the request of the Government, in 2007,[289] with a Final Report in June 2007.[290] As a result, the provisions regarding issuer liability for ongoing disclosures have been substantially amended by the Financial Services and Markets Act 2000 (Liability of Issuers) Regulations 2010.[291] Section 90A remains on the statute book but the detail of the provisions is now contained in a new schedule to FSMA, schedule 10A. These will be referred to here as the 'section 90A provisions'.

---

[284]   These continuing obligations are now in the Disclosure Rules and Transparency Rules.

[285]   This provision was introduced via Companies Act 2006, s 1270.

[286]   Transparency Directive 2004/109/EC, art 7 merely requires Member States to apply their existing liability regimes to misstatements in the disclosures required by the directive, rather than create any new ones.

[287]   See eg House of Lords, European Union Committee, 15th Report of Session 2003–04, Directors' and Auditors' Liability, HL Paper 89, May 2004.

[288]   For a discussion of the comparison of the UK liability regime under this section with comparable regimes in the US, Australia and Canada see E Ferran, 'Are US–style investor suits coming to the UK?' [2009] *Journal of Corporate Law Studies* 315.

[289]   HM Treasury, *Davies Review of Issuer Liability: Liability for Misstatements to the Market: A Discussion Paper* (March 2007).

[290]   HM Treasury, *Davies Review of Issuer Liability: Final Report* (June 2007).

[291]   See Financial Services and Markets Act 2000 (Liability of Issuers) Regulations 2010 (SI 1192/2010) which substitute s 90A and insert a new Schedule 10A, into FSMA 2000. These amendments take effect from 1 October 2010. For discussion see HM Treasury, *Extension of the Regime for Issuer Liability: A Response to Consultation* (March 2010).

10.4.1.2.2   Scope of the Section 90A FSMA Provisions

The section 90A provisions confirm the prior common law position of no liability in *negligence* for the company, its directors or advisers for misstatements made in relation to continuing disclosure obligations,[292] although the liability of advisers *to* the company for negligent misstatements remains intact.[293] However, in a departure from the pre-existing common law principles, the section 90A provisions provide for the liability of issuers to investors for *fraudulent* behaviour regarding ongoing disclosures in certain circumstances.

The section 90A provisions provide three different types of potential liability for an issuer of securities.[294] First, an issuer can be liable if it makes a statement in the documents to which these provisions apply, and which a person discharging managerial responsibilities within the issuer[295] knows to be untrue or misleading or is reckless as to whether it is untrue or misleading.[296] Second, an issuer can be liable where there is an omission of a required fact, if a person discharging managerial responsibilities within the issuer knew that the omission was a dishonest concealment of a material fact.[297] Third, the issuer can be liable if an investor suffers loss as a result of a delay by the issuer in publishing information to which these provisions apply, if a person discharging managerial responsibilities within the issuer acted dishonestly in delaying the publication of the information.[298] This last form of liability was introduced by the 2010 Regulations.[299]

The scope of liability is relatively tightly constrained. Recklessness involves deliberately disregarding an obvious risk and is not to be equated with negligence or even gross negligence.[300] This is in contrast to other jurisdictions, such as the US, which have adopted liability regimes that render the issuer liable for gross negligence for misstatements in ongoing disclosures.[301] For the purpose of both omissions and dishonest delay, the statute sets out the test of dishonesty to be applied: the person's conduct must be 'regarded as

---

[292]   FSMA, Sch 10A para 7(1). Prof Davies's view was that s 90A does not remove negligence liability where statements accepting responsibility for the accuracy of a document are made outside the company's reporting processes: *Liability for Misstatements to the Market: A Discussion Paper*, n 289, para 49. This was accepted by the Government: HM Treasury, *Extension of the Regime for Issuer Liability*, ibid, 7.

[293]   Ibid, Sch 10A, para 7(2). Companies Act 2006, s 463 excludes directors' liability to the company for negligent misstatements in the directors' report or directors' remuneration report but other advisers, in particular auditors, continue to be liable in contract and tort to the company, subject to the terms of their contract: see Companies Act 2006, Part 16, Ch 6.

[294]   'Securities' means 'transferable securities' as defined in FSMA, s 102A(3): FSMA Sch 10A para 8(1). In the case of depositary receipts and other secondary securities giving a right to acquire or sell other transferable securities, the issuer liable to pay compensation is the issuer of the underlying securities, provided that the secondary securities concerned have been admitted to trading by or with its consent. For depositary receipts and other secondary securities admitted to trading without the consent of the issuer of the underlying securities, and for all other derivative instruments, the issuer of the depositary receipts, other secondary securities or derivative instruments will be liable to pay compensation under the regime (see FSMA, Sch 10A, para 8(2)).

[295]   A person 'discharging managerial responsibilities' within an issuer is defined by FSMA, Sch 10A para 8(5). For most issuers these will be the directors of the company.

[296]   FSMA, s 90A(a) and Sch 10A para 3(1)(2).

[297]   Ibid, s 90A(a) and Sch 10A para 3(1)(3).

[298]   Ibid, s 90A(b) and Sch 10A para 5. The extension of s 90A liability to cover dishonest delay was one of the recommendations of the Davies Review: n 290, paras 47–50.

[299]   *Extension of the Regime for Issuer Liability*, n 291, 23–24.

[300]   *Derry v Peek* (1889) 14 App Cas 337, 361; *OBG Ltd v Allan* [2007] UKHL 21, [2008] 1 AC 1 [40]–[41] per Lord Hoffmann.

[301]   The Davies Review did consider whether the fraud-based regime under section 90A FSMA should be extended to include gross negligence, even if it was not extended to simple negligence, but concluded that it should not (*Davies Review of Issuer Liability: Final Report*, n 290, paras 24–30). There were two principal reasons

dishonest by persons who regularly trade on the securities market in question' and the person must be aware (or can be taken to have been aware) that it was so regarded.[302] The introduction of this test in the 2010 Regulations clarifies the fact that it is a criminal, and not a civil, test for dishonesty which applies.

The issuer will be liable to any investor, whether already a shareholder or not, who acquires securities and suffers loss as a result of the misstatement or omission,[303] where that person relied on the information and it was reasonable for him to do so,[304] or where that person suffers loss as a result of dishonest delay.[305] Following the 2010 Regulations, the issuer will also be potentially liable to investors who dispose of securities and even to those who continue to hold securities.[306] The extension to holders of securities was controversial, and was not recommended by the Davies Review.[307] However, the statutory provisions are not unconstrained in this regard, in particular the provisions are clear that there must be reliance by the holders of securities before they will be able to bring a claim under section 90A: there is 'a clear difference between an active holder and a passive holder — the latter will not be entitled to bring an action as they would not be able to show reliance upon the statement in making their investment decision'.[308] So, for example, it is expected that a claimant would have to demonstrate that he had instructed his broker to cancel a sell order. A holder of securities who continued to hold without giving the matter any thought would be considered to have held those securities passively and therefore would be unable to demonstrate the necessary reliance to bring a claim.

Section 90A was initially enacted to provide a statutory regime for liability in respect of only some ongoing disclosures. Specifically it was intended to provide a remedy for misstatements in annual reports and accounts, half yearly reports and quarterly interim management statements.[309] The section was therefore intended to relate to periodic disclosures and not to ad hoc disclosures. However, the Davies Review of section 90A recommended that the section be extended to cover ad hoc disclosures as well.[310] The line between periodic disclosures and ad hoc disclosures is not always clear, since some ad hoc disclosures have to be repeated in periodic statements,[311] and therefore distinguishing between the two for section 90A purposes is hard to justify. There are also strong policy arguments for attempting to ensure that ad hoc disclosures are as accurate as possible. The avoidance of fraud, accepted for periodic disclosures, seems no less important for ad hoc

---

for this conclusion: that gross negligence is an untested standard in English law and therefore would create legal uncertainties; and that the same problems of defensive reporting and speculative litigation would arise here as in relation to simple negligence.

[302]   FSMA, Sch 10A para 6.

[303]   At common law, the tort of deceit only applies to omissions that render what has been said misleading, it does not apply to 'pure' omissions: *R v Kylsant* [1932] 1 KB 442. Section 90A does cover omissions but it is not enough that the omission be intentional or reckless, it must also amount to a dishonest concealment of a material fact: FSMA, Sch 10A para 3(3).

[304]   Ibid, Sch 10A para 3(1). There is no requirement that the issuer intended the claimant to rely on the statement cf common law liability for deceit: *Smith v Chadwick* (1884) 9 App Cas 187.

[305]   Ibid, Sch 10A para 5.

[306]   Ibid, Sch 10A para 3(1)(a), para 5(1)(a). The extension to sellers was recommended by the Davies Review: *Davies Review of Issuer Liability: Final Report*, n 290, paras 51–53.

[307]   For discussion see *Extension of the Regime for Issuer Liability*, n 291, 15–16.

[308]   Ibid, 15.

[309]   Ie those disclosures required by articles 4, 5 and 6 of the Transparency Directive, discussed above at 10.3.1.

[310]   *Davies Review of Issuer Liability: Final Report*, n 290, paras 31–35.

[311]   See eg FSA Handbook, Prospectus Rules, PR 5.2.

disclosures. The Government accepted this recommendation,[312] and section 90A was amended accordingly by the 2010 Regulations.[313] Now, the regime extends to cover all information disclosed by a 'recognised means'[314] which includes a RIS or other means of disclosure used to communicate information to the relevant market.[315] It also includes other methods used when a RIS is unavailable.[316]

A further recommendation of the Davies Review was the extension of the regime beyond the Official list, to UK exchange-regulated markets, such as AIM and the Plus-quoted market and to UK multilateral trading facilities.[317] This change was also accepted by the Government. Indeed, the Government has gone further in its amendments to section 90A, extending the statutory regime to issuers of securities admitted to trading on an EEA regulated market or multilateral trading facility, where the UK is the home state for the issuer under the Transparency Directive or the issuer has its registered office in the UK.[318] Accordingly, for example, AIM issuers and UK incorporated issuers with securities admitted to trading on a US market will fall within the scope of the new regime.

Neither section 90A nor its accompanying schedule deal with the issue of the measure of damages to be awarded if an investor's claim is successful, or the correct test of remoteness to apply. However, it seems likely that the courts will apply the same approach as is followed in the case of common law claims for deceit since the section is so closely modelled on the common law tort. The overriding aim in the assessment of damages is to put the claimant into the position it would have been in if no false representation had been made. In general the claimant is entitled to recover by way of damages the full price paid but must give credit for any benefits received. These benefits will usually be the value of the property (the securities) at the date of the transaction, but in some circumstances the court will adopt a different method for calculating this benefit.

In *Smith New Court v Scrimgeour Vickers (Asset Management) Ltd*[319] Smith New Court were induced to buy shares in a company by the fraudulent misrepresentations of one of Scrimgoeur's executive directors. The purchase price was just over 82 pence per share, but the market price of the shares on the acquisition date was 78 pence per share. Usually the measure of damages would be the difference between these two sums. However, the company in question was subject to a substantial but entirely unrelated fraud, unknown to either the claimant or defendant, which occurred before Smith New Court's purchase. When this fraud became known the company's share price dropped considerably so that Smith New Court was only able to sell its shares in the company for between 30 and 40 pence over a period of time. The House of Lords held that in these circumstances Scrimgoeur was liable for *all* damage directly caused by the deceit, rather than the usual

---

[312]   *Extension of the Statutory Regime for Issuer Liability,* n 291, ch 6.

[313]   FSMA, Sch 10A para 2, inserted by Financial Services and Markets Act 2000 (Liability of Issuers) Regulations 2010 (SI 1192/2010).

[314]   Ibid, para 2(1). It is irrelevant whether the information was required to be published (by recognised means or otherwise): para 2(2).

[315]   Ibid, para 2(3).

[316]   Ibid, para 2(4).

[317]   *Davies Review of Issuer Liability: Final Report,* n 290, paras 36–39. See *Extension of the Statutory Regime for Issuer Liability,* n 291, ch 3.

[318]   FSMA, Sch 10A para 1, inserted by Financial Services and Markets Act 2000 (Liability of Issuers) Regulations 2010 (SI 1192/2010).

[319]   [1997] AC 254. For a more recent case applying this approach see *Dadourian Group International Inc v Simms* [2009] EWCA Civ 169; [2009] 1 Lloyd's Rep 601.

measure of damages in negligence which would limit the recovery to the loss caused by having a security worth less than the investor expected. This distinction is discussed further at 9.5.2.4.

Finally, issuers should not be subject to any liability other than under section 90A in respect of any loss suffered by an investor in relation to an untrue or misleading statement, or omission in published information or dishonest delay in publishing information covered by the section. There were exceptions to this safe harbour set out in section 90A before the 2010 amendments, and these were added to by the 2010 Regulations.[320] The exceptions include civil liability under section 90 FSMA (compensation for statements in prospectuses or listing particulars), liability for breach of contract, and civil liability arising from someone 'having assumed responsibility, to a particular person for a particular purpose, for the accuracy or completeness of the information concerned'.[321] This last exception aims to maintain an issuer's liability for negligent misstatement on a *Caparo Industries plc v Dickman*[322] basis, ie where a person has provided advice to another person for a particular purpose, the adviser is aware that the recipient is relying on that advice for that purpose and the recipient suffers loss as a result of relying on the negligent advice.

10.4.1.2.3   A Comparison of Section 90A FSMA (Liability in Relation to Ongoing Disclosures) and section 90 FSMA (Liability for Misstatements in Prospectuses)

In a number of important respects this statutory liability regime is narrower than that in place regarding statements in prospectuses in section 90 FSMA.[323] First, of course, section 90 covers liability for negligent as well as fraudulent behaviour.[324] Professor Davies considered whether section 90A should also be extended to cover liability for negligence.[325] Two particular factors weighed against such an extension. Concerns were raised about the additional costs, in terms of time and money, which would arise from ensuring that periodic and ad hoc statements met this standard. It was also said that the imposition of such a standard could lead to delays in disclosures, as a result of increased verification, and the possibility of less useful disclosures being made by issuers in an attempt to avoid liability. In fact negligence-based liability does exist for issuers in relation to continuing disclosures. Under the rules set out in the FSA Handbook, the issuer 'must take all reasonable care to ensure that any information it notifies to a RIS is not misleading, false or deceptive and does not omit anything likely to affect the import of the information'.[326]

The remedy for breach of this provision is a penalty imposed by the FSA, generally a fine or censure, rather than compensation for the investor ordered by the court.[327] The

---

[320] FSMA, Sch 10A para 7(3).

[321] Ibid, Sch 10A para 7(3)(a)(v).

[322] [1990] 2 AC 605.

[323] FSMA, s 90, and see chapter 9.5.2 for detailed discussion.

[324] FSMA, Sch 10 para 6. This is a particularly strong form of negligence liability since it is for the defendant to prove that he or she was not negligent rather than the claimant to prove that he or she was.

[325] *Liability for Misstatements to the Market: A Discussion Paper*, n 289, paras 70–77. For further discussion see P Davies, 'Liability for Misstatements to the Market: Some Reflections' [2009] *Journal of Corporate Law Studies* 295, 301–04. These arguments have been accepted by the Government: *Extension of the Regime for Issuer Liability*, n 291, 7.

[326] FSA Handbook, Disclosure and Transparency Rules, DTR 1.3.4 and 1A.3.2.

[327] In fact one of the options open to the FSA is to make a restitution order to obtain recompense for investors in appropriate cases (see FSMA, ss 382–383) but these are rarely used in practice (see for discussion of

view of the Davies Review was that public enforcement of a negligence-based liability for ongoing disclosures, via administrative sanctions, was more appropriate than private enforcement. Liability in civil litigation is measured by the loss suffered to the claimants, which in the case of heavily-traded stock could be very substantial. In principle the loss is caused to those who acquire securities, or, now, sell or hold securities, during the period between the statement being made and the truth becoming known, providing securities are still held at the end of the period and the 'prospect of a very large liability for only a very minor deviation from the standard of conduct of the reasonable person is likely to induce potential defendants to stay well on the non-liability side of the line, and, as part of that, to engage in "defensive" and unhelpful disclosure'.[328] By contrast, the FSA can take account of these issues when fixing the size of the penalty it will impose.[329] As a result of these concerns, the Davies Review did not recommend the extension of section 90A to cover liability for negligent misstatements.[330]

Second, a section 90 claim can be brought against all those responsible for the prospectus, including the company, its directors and each person who accepts or is stated to accept responsibility for any part of the prospectus (although liability will relate only to that part).[331] By contrast only the issuer can be liable to investors under section 90A, not its directors or advisers.[332] Of course the behaviour of these individuals will still be relevant, since it is the state of mind of 'a person discharging managerial responsibilities'[333] (whether knowledge or recklessness of the misleading statement, or dishonesty in concealing a material fact or dishonesty in delaying publication of information) that renders the issuer liable under this section. However those individuals are not made personally liable to investors under this section, although directors will remain liable to their company for this behaviour,[334] and may be subject to FSA sanctions.[335]

Third, in section 90 there is no requirement for the claimant to demonstrate that he or she has relied on the statement or even that they have read the prospectus in order to establish a cause of action.[336] This is sometimes described as 'fraud on the market' since

---

this issue FSA, Consultation Paper 07/02 *Review of the Enforcement and Decision-making Manuals*, esp para 5.31). A new provision, introduced by the Financial Services and Markets Act 2000 (Liability of Issuers) Regulations 2010 (SI 2010/1192) makes it clear that the FSA's power in this regard remains intact despite the introduction of s 90A: FSMA, Sch 10A para 7(4).

[328] *Davies Review of Issuer Liability: Final Report*, n 290, para 11.

[329] FSMA 2000, s 93(2)(a).

[330] *Davies Review of Issuer Liability: Final Report*, n 290, para 23. This recommendation has been accepted by the Government: HM Treasury, *Extension of the Statutory Scheme for Issuer Liability* (July 2008) para 2.9, and see HM Treasury, *Extension of the Regime for Issuer Liability*, n 291, 7.

[331] FSA Handbook, Prospectus Rules, PR 5.5.3(2).

[332] For a discussion of this point see E Ferran, 'Are US-style Investor Suits Coming to the UK?' [2009] *Journal of Corporate Law Studies* 315, 342–45.

[333] FSMA, Sch 10A para 3(2)(3), para 5(2), for definition of 'a person discharging managerial responsibilities' see para 8(5).

[334] Companies Act 2006, s 463 will not protect a director in these circumstances.

[335] Eg, directors of companies on regulated markets can be subject to FSA sanctions (public censure and penalties) where the company is in breach of its disclosure obligations under the Disclosure Rules and Transparency Rules and the director is 'knowingly concerned' in the contravention on the part of the issuer: FSMA, s 91(2).

[336] FSMA, s 90(1)(b). No requirement of reliance is included but causation must still be established for s 90 (FSMA, Sch 10 para 6) and presumably some causal connection will need to be shown between the misstatement or omission in the prospectus and the loss, so that if he claimant buys the shares after a significant lapse of time they will find it hard to demonstrate that the prospectus has any significant impact on the price of the securities.

the misstatement can be said to have caused the investor loss even though that particular investor was unaware of the misstatement. No such fraud on the market concept has been adopted for section 90A and for these purposes the claimant can only succeed if he or she can demonstrate that they relied on the publication,[337] although it is possible for an inference of reliance to be drawn from the facts.[338]

10.4.1.2.4   Assessment of section 90A

As discussed in chapter nine, a liability regime is one of the blocks in the capital market regulation regime of a jurisdiction and as such the aims of a liability regime are the same as the aims of the capital market regulation regime set out above, namely to protect investors and, more generally, to promote the efficient allocation of financial resources in the economy as between competing projects. There are two ways in which a liability regime might contribute to these goals. First, a liability regime can encourage the accurate and timely disclosure of information by issuers, and, second, a liability regime can contribute to the goal of promoting investor confidence by providing compensation to those who suffer loss as a result of a misstatement in a prospectus.

One way in which the goal of encouraging the disclosure of accurate and timely information may be achieved is through deterrence. However, in order for a liability regime for misstatements in periodic and ad hoc disclosures to have a deterrent effect, that liability needs to fall on the directors and others who actually make the statement, rather than on the company.[339] If the liability falls only on the company, that liability will then be borne by the shareholders rather than the makers of the misstatements (eg the directors). The shareholders may put pressure on the directors as a consequence of the liability imposed on the company, but such deterrence would operate only indirectly. In reality where liability falls on the company the result is that one set of shareholders recover at the expense of another set of shareholders. Company liability for misstatements can therefore be seen as little more than a redistribution of value among shareholders.[340] This is not to suggest that situations where liability is imposed only on the issuer can have no deterrent effect. It is possible that reputational and other losses will fall on the makers of the misstatements as a result of the company being involved in litigation, but the deterrent effect is likely to be less pronounced in this situation than where liability falls on the statement makers directly. In addition, even if the liability regime does not make the directors liable to the investors, the directors might nevertheless be liable to the company, for breach of their directors' duties. Thus, the director might have to reimburse the

---

[337]   FSMA, Sch 10A para 3(4), para 5(1)(b). Cf the position in the US where the fraud on the market theory has been adopted for misleading continuing disclosures as well as for misstatements in prospectuses: *Basic v Levinson* 485 US 224 (1988).

[338]   *Smith v Chadwick* (1884) 9 App Cas 187.

[339]   Recent studies suggest that even in regimes which prima facie allow claims by investors against directors for misstatements in ongoing disclosures, those directors are rarely held accountable for their misconduct (see eg M Klausner, 'Personal Liability of Officers in US Securities Class Actions' [2009] *Journal of Corporate Law Studies* 349).

[340]   Interestingly where the company is insolvent, it appears that the defrauded investors are allowed to compete with the other unsecured creditors of the company for a share of the assets (see *Soden v British & Commonwealth Holdings Ltd* [1998] AC 298), in contrast to the usual position that shareholders claims (eg to declared but unpaid dividends) are subordinated to the claims of the unsecured creditors on insolvency (Insolvency Act 1986, s 74(2)(f)). *Soden* was followed in Australia in *Sons of Gwalia v Margaretic* (2007) HCA 1 but this is being overturned by statute: see Corporations Amendment (Sons of Gwalia) Bill 2010 (Australia).

company for the loss suffered by the company in compensating the investor, but the decision to seek recovery from the director would be a decision to be taken by or on behalf of the company.[341]

The second way in which a liability regime might contribute to the goal of promoting investor confidence in the market is by providing compensation to those who suffer loss as a result of a misstatement in a prospectus.[342] There are two elements that need to be considered. The first is what investors should be protected against. The point has already been made that regulation of the capital markets in the UK does not aim to insulate investors from sustaining losses. It is expected that investors should take responsibility for their own decisions.[343] However, it is now accepted that investors should be protected against some misstatements found in periodic and ad hoc disclosures. The changes introduced to section 90A as a result of the 2010 Regulations significantly extend the reach of the regime in relation to ongoing disclosures, extending it to dishonest delays, to the sellers of securities, as well as those who continue to hold securities in some circumstances, extending the securities to which these provisions apply, and extending it to all ongoing disclosures published by 'recognised means'. These changes are to be welcomed. Attention also needs to be given to the amount of compensation to which investors should be entitled. If, as expected, the courts adopt the measure of remoteness established in *Scrimgoeur Vickers* to this issue, the level of compensation to which shareholders might be entitled is potentially substantial.

However, as discussed, the cost of the damages imposed on the defendant company falls principally on the shareholders. The claimant shareholder recovers from the other shareholders with the result that this form of litigation involves pocket-shifting wealth transfers.[344] Long-term investors in the market are just as likely to be among the shareholders in the issuer which has made the misleading statement as among the investors who were misled. The benefits they might gain in the latter capacity are likely to be balanced out by the losses they suffer in the former. However these payments will not entirely balance out in practice because of the fact that the litigation has transaction costs, such as the lawyers' fees involved in bringing and defending the litigation. For these investors the benefits of any compensation received will be minimal.[345]

10.4.1.3   Summary of Private Enforcement Mechanisms

Two points are worth noting. First, as with the mandatory disclosure rules themselves, understanding the different aims involved in regulating the ongoing market helps to explain the private remedies available to shareholders and to investors. In relation to mandatory disclosure we saw that the evolution of capital market regulations from a wholly shareholder-focused regime, to one which is also market-focused has led to the

---

[341]   Companies Act 2006, s 463 does not protect the director from this liability where the director knows of the untruth of the statement or is reckless with regard to its truth or acts dishonestly in relation to an omission.

[342]   See MB Fox, 'Civil Liability and Mandatory Disclosure' (2009) 109 *Columbia Law Review* 237, who suggests that, although buyers in relation to a particular transaction can be regarded as having suffered a loss, looking at the operation of disclosure requirements across all transactions, no loss is suffered by investors.

[343]   FSMA, s 5(2)(d).

[344]   Following the amendments to FSMA, s 90A, to include sellers as well as buyers, this argument will clearly not work where the claimant is a seller.

[345]   See RA Booth, 'The Future of Securities Litigation' (2009) 4 *Journal of Business and Technology Law* 129.

addition of a number of mandatory disclosure requirements. In the context of this section on private remedies, the effect of this evolution has been the addition of a statutory remedy, under section 90A FSMA and its accompanying schedule, for fraudulent behaviour in relation to ongoing disclosures.

Second, it is notable that the incidence of claims in this context is low. The incidence of formal claims by shareholders is close to nil. As discussed, as regards the governance-focused disclosures this is not particularly surprising, given the operation of the reflective loss principle. Nor is it necessarily a cause for concern since to some extent the shareholders, particularly the institutional investors, may be able to make use of informal mechanisms to ensure compliance with the disclosure requirements. As regards investor-focused disclosures, it is still too early to tell whether much use will be made of the new section 90A regime. However, section 90 has not been used a great deal, and section 90A is narrower in scope than that regime.[346] It would not be surprising if section 90A were not much used.[347]

10.4.2   Public Enforcement

Given the low levels of private enforcement of investor protection laws, the potential for public enforcement of these laws is important.[348] At the time of writing the role of enforcement is mainly with the FSA, although the Financial Reporting Review Panel has a role. However, this position is not static, and the role of the FSA has been under review recently as a result of the financial crisis. In a speech given in June 2010 the Chancellor, George Osborne, announced an end to the FSA in its current form.[349] He stated that from 2012 banking regulation will be transferred from the FSA to a new prudential regulatory authority, a legally separate but subsidiary part of the Bank of England. As regards the regulatory activity of the FSA that is described in this chapter, it is suggested that it may be carried out by a new Consumer Protection and Markets Authority, with a new Economic Crime Agency potentially to take over the role of criminal enforcement, although other options are also being considered. This issue, together with the exact remit of these authorities, remains unclear at the time of writing.

10.4.2.1   The FSA

The FSA has power, under Part VI of FSMA, to make the rules that appear in the FSA Handbook. In the context of ongoing disclosures, the FSA has the power to make the

---

[346]   However, two points which might suggest the alternative view are that (i) secondary market trading is much larger than primary market issuance so that the number of disappointed investors in the secondary market is likely to be much greater than in the primary market; and (ii) while prospectuses are issued only sporadically, periodic and episodic disclosures occur frequently in an issuer's life. For discussion see E Ferran, 'Are US style investor suits coming to the UK?' [2009] *Journal of Corporate Law Studies* 315.

[347]   Eilis Ferran has conducted a comparison of the new UK regime with the regimes in the US, Australia and Canada. She concludes that s 90A does not look likely to trigger an explosion of investor claims: E Ferran, 'Are US-style investor suits coming to the UK?' [2009] *Journal of Corporate Law Studies* 315.

[348]   For a discussion of private vs public enforcement see eg R La Porta, F Lopez-de-Silanes and A Shleifer, 'What Works in Securities Laws?' (2006) 61 *Journal of Finance* 1; HE Jackson and MJ Roe, 'Public and Private Enforcement of Securities Laws: Resource-based Evidence' (2009) 76 *Journal of Financial Economics* 207.

[349]   George Osborne, Mansion House speech, 16 June 2010 and see HM Treasury, *A New Approach to Financial Regulation: Judgment, Focus and Stability* (Cm 7874, July 2010).

Disclosure and Transparency rules (which implement the Market Abuse Directive and the Transparency Directive) and the Listing Rules (which include obligations relating to related party transactions and significant transactions).[350] The FSA Handbook places an obligation on an issuer to 'take all reasonable care to ensure that any information it notifies to a RIS is not misleading, false or deceptive and does not omit anything likely to affect the import of the information'.[351] The FSA's rules thus impose liability for negligent misstatements. An issuer which fails to comply with its obligations under the Listing Rules, Disclosure Rules or Transparency Rules is liable to a penalty to be imposed by the FSA.[352] In addition a director of the issuer who was 'knowingly concerned' in the contravention of the rules will be liable to pay a penalty as well.[353] A recent paper from the FSA states that it is committed to increasing the levels of penalty it imposes on both issuers and individuals, in order to 'achieve credible deterrence'.[354] As an alternative to imposing a penalty the FSA may issue a statement of censure.[355]

As an alternative to imposing a penalty or issuing a statement of censure, the FSA has the power to apply to the court for a restitution order.[356] Where someone has infringed Part VI FSMA and made a profit as a result (or caused loss to another as a result) the court can require an amount it considers just (having regard to the profit made or loss suffered) to be paid by that person to the FSA, for distribution to the persons who appear to the court to have suffered loss. The FSA also has power to bring criminal prosecutions in some circumstances. An offence is committed by a person who makes a statement which he knows to be misleading, false or deceptive in a material particular or is reckless as to whether it is so, and does so for the purpose of inducing another to take an investment decision or is reckless whether it has that effect.[357] This offence can also be committed where there is dishonest concealment of the material facts.

There is little formal enforcement by the FSA of these provisions. Professor Davies looked at the incidence of formal enforcement of issuer liability as part of his review for the Treasury in 2007.[358] He found no case in which the FSA had used its restitution powers.[359]

---

[350] FSMA, Part VI. These obligations relate only to issuers whose shares are admitted to trading on a regulated market ie not to AIM companies (cf the FSA's powers in relation to market abuse more generally, described at 10.5 below, which relate to securities trading on a prescribed market (see s 118(1)), thus including AIM). The main responsibility for supervision of disclosures made to the market by AIM companies lies with the London Stock Exchange, which has delegated that responsibility on a day to day basis to the 'Nominated Advisor' which all AIM companies are required to have: London Stock Exchange, *AIM Rules for Companies*, February 2010. For the quoted market segment of PLUS, its rules are similar to those of the LSE and AIM: see PLUS, *Rules for Issuers*, March 2009. For discussion see P Davies, 'Liability for Misstatements to the Market: Some Reflections' [2009] *Journal of Corporate Law Studies* 295, 309–11.

[351] DTR 1.3.4; DTR 1A.3.2.

[352] FSMA, s 91(1) for the listing rules, s 91(1ZA) for the disclosure rules and s 91(1B) for the transparency rules.

[353] FSMA, s 91(2). Accordingly if a director knows that the issuer has failed to take due care to establish the accuracy of the statement, he or she will be liable to a penalty.

[354] FSA, *Enforcement Financial Penalties*, CP 09/19, July 2009. In 2010 the FSA imposed its largest ever fine, of £33.32 million on JP Morgan Securities Ltd, for failing to protect client money by segregating it appropriately (see FSA/PN/089/2010, 3 June 2010).

[355] FSMA, s 91(3).

[356] FSMA, s 382.

[357] FSMA, s 387(1)(2).

[358] These figures were updated by Eilis Ferran in 2009, to show 12 enforcement actions by the FSA in relation to continuing disclosure obligations since 2002, of which only two involved the imposition of fines on directors: E Ferran, 'Are US-style Investor Suits Coming to the UK' [2009] *Journal of Corporate Law Studies* 315, 326–29.

[359] *Davies Review of Issuer Liability: A Discussion Paper*, n 289, para 63.

Looking at the four year period 2003–2007 Professor Davies found that little use was made of the FSA's criminal enforcement powers and he only found seven sets of penalties or censures imposed over that period for misstatements or delays in disclosing information (as opposed to market abuse).[360] This is not a high level of enforcement.

However, the FSA's stated policy is to avoid formal disciplinary action where possible: 'Where a firm or other person has failed to comply with the requirements of the Act, the rules, or other relevant legislation, it may be appropriate to deal with this without the need for formal disciplinary or other enforcement action. The proactive supervision and monitoring of firms, and an open and cooperative relationship between firms and their supervisors, will, in some cases where a contravention has taken place, lead the FSA to decide against taking formal disciplinary action'.[361] In these circumstances it has been argued that we should be wary of drawing inferences about the UK system based solely on the low formal enforcement rates.[362] However, this may be in the process of changing. As a result of the recent financial crisis, the FSA has abandoned its previous proclaimed approach to regulation,[363] which was regarded as 'light touch'. The FSA's new regulatory efforts are not focused directly on enforcement of continuing disclosures, but rather on financial regulation more generally, plus insider dealing and market abuse, but the new approach may also have an effect in this area.[364]

10.4.2.2   The Financial Reporting Review Panel

The Financial Reporting Review Panel (FRRP) is one of several bodies operating under the Financial Reporting Council. The FRRP was established in 1991[365] in order to investigate material departures from accounting standards by large companies (both public companies and large private companies)[366] and to persuade companies to rectify those errors where appropriate. The FRRP has the power to apply to court for an order mandating the revision of those errors.[367] Initially the FRRP carried out its functions reactively, responding to investors' complaints about particular financial statements. More recently, the FRRP has been given a more pro-active role in relation to listed firms.[368] The FRRP now scrutinises more than 300 sets of financial statements a year, which are selected on the basis of a risk-assessment based on sectoral, firm-specific and statement-specific risk factors.[369] Most of the accounts reviewed are of listed companies. The bulk of the FRRP's enforcement activity is informal.[370] Since 1991 in no case has the FRRP sought a

---

[360]   Ibid, Appendix, Table 1.

[361]   FSA Handbook, Enforcement Guide, eg 2.4.

[362]   Armour, 'Enforcement Strategies in UK Corporate Governance', n 85.

[363]   Eg, *The Turner Review,* n 15, 86–89; Hector Sants, Annual Lubbock Lecture in Management Studies, Said Business School, Oxford, 12 March 2010.

[364]   P Davies, 'Liability for Misstatements to the Market: Some reflections' (2009) *Journal of Corporate Law Studies* 295, 308.

[365]   See Financial Reporting Council, *The State of Financial Reporting: A Review* (London, FRC, 1991).

[366]   Oversight of small private companies is carried out by BERR: *Memorandum of Understanding between the FRRP and the FSA* (6 April 2005) para 3.

[367]   Companies Act 2006, ss 456–457. The FRRP was authorised to exercise those powers by the Companies (Defective Accounts)(Authorised Person) Order 1991 (SI 1991/13).

[368]   Supervision of Accounts and Reports (Prescribed Body) Order 2005 (SI 2005/715).

[369]   See eg Financial Reporting Review Panel, Activity Report 2008–09 (London, FRRP, 2009) 4–6.

[370]   Armour, n 85, 91; K Cearns and E Ferran, 'Non-enforcement Led Oversight of Financial and Corporate Governance Disclosures and Auditors' [2008] *Journal of Corporate Law Studies* 191.

court order and although action is taken relatively often[371] in the vast majority of these cases the companies in question remedied the defective accounting practice without the need for a public notice.[372]

10.5 The Regulation of Market Abuse

The regulation of market abuse is an important element of the ongoing regulation of the capital markets. It is closely related to the regulation of accurate, complete and timely ongoing disclosures by issuers. One of the aims of mandating ongoing disclosures is to provide investor protection, indeed, as discussed, the 'smooth operation of the market' is now arguably the predominant aim of ongoing disclosures. Similarly, both insider dealing and market manipulation are aimed primarily at protecting investors.[373] The division between protecting investors via disclosure and via a prevention of market abuse is not always clear cut. The rules governing disclosure of directors' shareholdings, for example, allow shareholders and other investors to make investment decisions by providing information about the level of directors' holdings in their own companies[374] (buying shares in their own companies can be read as a sign of confidence in the company and the future investment potential of its shares). However, it is clear that these rules are also aimed at preventing insider dealing by the directors. In addition, the disclosure of misleading information or non-disclosure of information may constitute market abuse in some circumstances.[375]

The aim of both mechanisms for investor protection is ultimately the same, namely an attempt to deal with asymmetrical information. The theory of capital markets regulation requires investors to have accurate and timely information about the company in order to decide whether to buy or sell shares in the company. Relevant information about the company is held primarily by insiders who would not necessarily disclose that information voluntarily. Indeed, as discussed in 10.2.1, the increasing incidence of equity-based compensation schemes such as share options have given directors further reason to want to retain bad information about the company, given the choice, since they will suffer personally if the share price drops. The mechanism used to ensure that the outsiders obtain that information is mandatory disclosure.

Similarly, with insider dealing, the need to regulate this behaviour arises from the information asymmetry between insiders and public investors. It is not the fact of trading with an insider which causes the problem, or the fact that insiders induce investors to trade at the 'wrong price'. The insider dealing itself does not harm investors. What is

---

[371] Eg, there were 112 cases of action being taken in 2008–09: Financial Reporting Review Panel, *Activity Report 2008–09* (London, FRRP, 2009) 4.

[372] Armour, n 85, 91.

[373] As discussed in 10.3 above, some ongoing disclosures, such as the disclosure of significant transactions and related party transactions, are predominantly aimed at shareholders rather than investors.

[374] See 10.3.2.2.

[375] For example, the disclosure of misleading information or the non-disclosure of information may constitute market abuse under FSMA, s 118 in the shape of behaviour 'likely to be regarded by a regular user of the market as a failure on the part of the person concerned to observe the standard of behaviour reasonably expected of a person in his position in relation to the market': s 118(4)(8).

damaging is the nondisclosure of material information.[376] Market manipulation, as we shall see, comes in two forms, namely misinformation (either disclosing wrong information or a failure to disclosure required information) or some other form of market distortion, such as misuse of a dominant position. In the first case the asymmetry of information is clear as this is similar to the general argument, above, regarding the need for mandatory disclosure. In the second, insiders are again using their position to manipulate the market to benefit themselves and this can again undermine investor confidence.

It may not be possible to tackle these information asymmetries via mandatory disclosure rules. These rules generally detail what a company must disclose, but do not detail what a company must not disclose, ie they do not cover the use of incorrect information. They are also limited in their scope in the sense that they place obligations on only limited parties to make disclosure, eg the obligation to disclose inside information is placed only on the company.[377] Others who are inside the company may have inside information and be in a position to make use of it for their own advantage, but have no obligation to disclose, or are not in a position to disclose. Disclosure rules alone will not be enough therefore. To ensure investor protection the regime needs to combine disclosure rules with rules designed to prevent fraud. In this context this involves rules designed to prevent market abuse. This section will deal with the possibility of both private and public claims for market abuse.

10.5.1 Private Enforcement of Market Abuse

The UK does not have any civil remedies for market manipulation or insider dealing.[378] At the present time these are dealt with entirely by way of public enforcement measures, as discussed in section 10.5.2.[379] This is in contrast to other jurisdictions, most notably the US. Explicit civil remedies for market manipulation and insider dealing exist in the Securities and Exchange Act 1934[380] and in addition the US courts have been willing to imply rights of action from criminal law prohibitions such as SEC Rule 10(b)-5.[381]

Any civil claim for market abuse faces some significant obstacles. The most obvious route for a civil claim for market abuse is some kind of fraudulent misrepresentation claim. In the UK, at common law a claim for fraudulent misrepresentation requires proof that a false statement of fact (or omission of material information) was made with an intention to induce the innocent party to rely on it and enter into the injurious course of conduct. It is, in addition, necessary to demonstrate that the claimant was induced to enter into the agreement by specifically relying on the misrepresentor's statement, omission or

---

[376] See eg SM Bainbridge, *Corporation Law and Economics* (New York, Foundation Press, 2002) 72.

[377] See 10.3.2.1.

[378] The Companies Bill 1973 purported to give a right to seek compensation from insiders to contractual parties who had dealt with them and who were not in possession of insider information (clause 15(3)) ie this clause required privity. The Companies Bill 1978, clause 61(1) gave a right of rescission and clause 61(2) a right to sue in damages to those directly affected by insider dealing. However by the time of implementation of the Companies Act 1980 any attempt to introduce civil remedies for insider dealing had been abandoned.

[379] See *Hall v Cable & Wireless plc* [2009] EWHC 1793 (Comm) esp [23]-[24].

[380] 9(e), 15 USC 78i and 16(b), 15 USC 78p(b).

[381] See eg *Kardon v National Gypsum Co*, 69 F Supp 512 (ED Pa, 1946); *Superintendent of Insurance v Bankers Life & Casualty Co*, 404 US 6 (1971).

conduct.[382] This is usually going to be difficult to demonstrate where individuals have engaged in insider dealing or manipulated the market since these forms of wrongdoing generally arise in the context of arm's length open market transactions. In the anonymous modern financial marketplace it is extremely unlikely that the maker of the misrepresentation or the initiator of the abusive practice and those injured by that behaviour will ever have any kind of contact. The issue of reliance is therefore likely to be very difficult to establish in most circumstances.

This problem has been solved in the US by adopting the fraud on the market theory. US courts have accepted that in a class securities fraud action involving open market transactions, the reliance element is practically impossible to prove. However, they have established that proving reliance is theoretically unimportant to the claim.[383] As originally conceived the fraud on the market theory held that 'causation is adequately established in the context of impersonal stock markets through proof of purchase and proof of the materiality of the representations'.[384] In the court's view the proof of the materiality of the representations circumstantially established the reliance of market traders. Subsequent cases endorsed the view that purchasers do not need to rely on the misstatements, but moved away from the need to demonstrate materiality. Instead, the view has been taken that where there is a market in securities 'the market is performing a substantial part of the valuation process performed by the investor in a face-to-face transaction'.[385]

The efficient capital markets hypothesis[386] has been used to argue that since most publicly available information is reflected in market price, an investor's reliance on any public material misrepresentations can be presumed for the purposes of a Rule 10b-5 action brought by an investor.[387] Instead of having to demonstrate materiality, ie that the price of the security was adversely affected, under this later theory of fraud on the market it is sufficient to show that the security is traded on an efficient market.[388] This presumption relieves plaintiffs from having to prove either loss causation or reliance affirmatively. Instead the defendant has the burden of disproving both. This later approach has been criticised.[389] Some commentators prefer to regard the fraud on the market presumption as a procedural device, that dispenses with the requirement to prove specific reliance, and not as a new theory of liability that replaces separate inquiries into materiality, causation and damages in securities fraud cases.[390]

The UK has now adopted the fraud on the market theory to enable investors to bring a compensation claim in relation to misstatements in the prospectus in section 90 FSMA.[391]

---

[382] *Smith v Chadwick* (1884) 9 App Cas 187.

[383] *Blackie v Barrack* 524 F 2d 891, 902 (9th Cir 1975), 429 US 816, for comment see 'Note, The Reliance Requirement in Private Actions under SEC Rule 10b-5' (1975) 88 *Harvard Law Review* 584.

[384] Ibid, 906–07.

[385] *Basic v Levinson*, 485 US 224, 244 (1988).

[386] EF Fama, 'Efficient Capital Markets: A Review of Theory and Empirical Work' (1970) 25 *Journal of Finance* 383, discussed in 10.2.1.1.

[387] *Basic v Levinson*, 485 US 224, 244, 247 (1988).

[388] This presumption can be rebutted eg by the plaintiff's knowledge of the abuse, or the public dissemination of the information that guided the defendants' abusive actions, or statements that correct and dissipate the influence on the market of the relevant misrepresentation (eg *Basic v Levinson*, 485 US 224, 249 (1988)).

[389] JR Macey and GP Miller, 'Good Finance, Bad Economics: An Analysis of the Fraud-on-the-Market Theory' (1990) 42 *Stanford Law Review* 1059; For discussion see Avgouleas, n 9, 481–85.

[390] DR Fischel, 'Use of Modern Finance Theory in Securities Fraud Cases Involving Actively Traded Securities' (1982) 38 *Business Lawyer* 1.

[391] See 9.5.2.

Under section 90 there is no requirement for the claimant to demonstrate that he or she has relied on the misstatement or even that they read the prospectus in order to establish a cause of action.[392] The use of the concept of fraud on the market dispenses with the need to demonstrate reliance. However, it is still necessary to demonstrate a causal link. The person claiming compensation must have suffered a loss as a result of the untrue or misleading statement in the prospectus, or the omission of information which should have been included.[393] Likewise if the claimant is fully aware of the defect and acquired the securities anyway, there will be no causation and the claim will not be made out.[394] This is a narrower version of fraud on the market than is in use in the US.

However, the UK has not adopted this fraud on the market theory in the context of insider dealing and there is no civil remedy for insider dealing at present.[395] This is not surprising. There are difficulties with giving a civil remedy to the person with whom the insider dealt. Not only is there the difficulty of identifying that particular individual, but it is difficult to justify the preferential treatment of that individual over and above all the others dealing in the market on the same day. It is just random chance that puts an investor in one category rather than another. Of course the fraud on the market theory deals with this difficulty by providing a remedy to all of those who dealt in the market on that day. However, to give a remedy to all of those individuals might be regarded as disproportionate and oppressive to the insider, and it appears to provide a windfall to those who dealt with the company's securities on the day in question. In the absence of causation it seems preferable to regard the wrong as being done to the market, but to give the cause of action to the regulatory authorities (such as the FSA)[396] to bring an action on behalf of all investors. The FSA has a broad range of remedies at its disposal, including restitution orders if it feels that compensation needs to be made to particular individuals on the facts of a particular case.[397] As a result any claim at common law for misrepresentation based on insider dealing will fail unless both reliance and loss causation can be established. In the modern anonymous marketplace this will rarely occur.

Another circumstance in which a civil claim for insider dealing might arise however is where the basis of the claim is not misrepresentation but breach of fiduciary duty. The advantage of such a claim is that there is no need to show loss on the part of the investor, just that the fiduciary has made an undisclosed profit. However, generally directors do not owe fiduciary duties to those with whom they deal. Even where directors are buying from the existing shareholders in their own company they do not per se owe a duty to those shareholders. Their fiduciary duties are to the company, ie the shareholders as a whole in a solvent company, not to individual shareholders.[398] As a general rule, then, they do not

---

[392]   FSMA, s 90(1).
[393]   Ibid, s 90(1)(b).
[394]   Ibid, Sch 10 para 6.
[395]   Early case law held that a sale of shares in breach of insider dealing regulations was unenforceable (*Chase Manhattan Equities Ltd v Goodman* [1991] BCLC 897) but subsequent changes in legislation have rendered this argument unworkable: see Criminal Justice Act 1993, s 63(2), although this provision relates only to consequences 'by reason only of' the Criminal Justice Act being contravened, and therefore if the contract is voidable at common law for misrepresentation then such a consequence, not being based on the Act, is not affected by the Criminal Justice Act 1993. However any claim based on common law would still have to surmount the difficulties of demonstrating reliance and causation.
[396]   As discussed at 9.4.1, the role of the FSA is planned to change in this regard from 2012.
[397]   FSMA, s 382.
[398]   *Percival v Wright* [1902] 2 Ch 421; *Peskin v Anderson* [2001] 1 BCLC 372.

have to reveal to the shareholders that negotiations are in progress for the sale of the company's undertaking at a favourable price — information which will have a favourable impact on the share price when made public. However, in certain circumstances, directors can owe a duty to one or more shareholders, for example where the directors of a small company act as the agents of the individual shareholders on a takeover.[399] However, it would be unusual for this kind of relationship to arise in the listed company context.[400]

10.5.2   Public Enforcement of Market Abuse

As discussed, there is no civil remedy for market abuse and the enforcement of insider dealing and market manipulation has been left to the public authorities. There are three different offences of market abuse that need to be considered in this context: the criminal offence of insider dealing under the Criminal Justice Act 1993; the criminal offence of market manipulation under section 397 FSMA; and the offence of market abuse under section 118 FSMA.[401] These will be examined in turn. As discussed, the Chancellor, George Osborne, announced an end to the FSA in its current form in a speech given in June 2010.[402] He stated that from 2012 the regulatory activity of the FSA that is described in this chapter will be transferred away from the FSA, possibly to a new Consumer Protection and Markets Authority, with a new Economic Crime Agency to potentially take over the role of criminal enforcement. These issues, and the exact remit of these organisations remains unclear at the time of writing, but it is not suggested that the substantive rules described in this section will change significantly.

10.5.2.1   The Criminal Offence of Insider Dealing under the Criminal Justice Act 1993

The offence of insider dealing was initially based on a breach of fiduciary duty by directors. The root of the offence was in company law and as such the primary focus was on shareholder protection. As discussed, the rationale for regulating insider dealing has undergone a shift, and is now regarded as market-focused, ie as an aspect of securities law. The Criminal Justice Act 1993 primarily adopts this later, investor-focused, approach to insider dealing.

---

[399]   Eg *Allen v Hyatt* (1914) 30 TLR 444.

[400]   A final possibility is a claim for breach of confidence against someone who receives information in confidence: *Schering Chemicals Ltd v Falkman Ltd* [1982] QB 1. The potential reach of this claim is broader than that based on a fiduciary duty but to date this civil claim has not been developed in the context of insider dealing.

[401]   One further provision which can be said to be aimed at preventing insider dealing is the Model Code, developed by the FSA and appended to Chapter 9 of the Listing Rules. In addition to stating that in no circumstances should directors deal when they are forbidden to do so under insider dealing legislation, it prescribes that in general directors should not deal within a period of two months preceding the announcement of the company's annual results, and similar limitations are imposed in relation to half yearly and quarterly reports. Breach of these Code provisions by a director involves a breach of his duty to the company, not to the FSA or to the investor in the market (see eg *Chase Manhattan Equities Ltd v Goodman* [1991] BCLC 897).

[402]   George Osborne, Mansion House speech, 16 June 2010 and see *A New Approach to Financial Regulation*, n 349, (Cm 7874, 2010).

10.5.2.1.1   Definition of an Insider

The Act creates two categories of insiders. 'Primary insiders'[403] are those who have their information through being a director, employee, or shareholder of an issuer of securities[404] or have access to the information by virtue of their 'employment, office or profession',[405] such as professional advisers to the company. 'Secondary insiders' by contrast are those who obtain their information from a primary insider.[406] Due to the criminal nature of this offence it is not enough for the individual to have information as an insider, that individual must also know that it is inside information and that he has it, and know that he has it, from an inside source.[407]

This definition of an insider is not status-based. The definition of primary insiders is not limited to the director of *the* issuer, but the director, employee or shareholder of *an* issuer,[408] and indeed anyone who has their information by reason of their employment, office or profession, but without that employment having to be with the issuer in question. This offence of insider dealing is therefore not based on the nature of the insiders' relationship with the company. A person is not defined as an insider because of their status, but by reference to the information they hold. The definition of inside information within the Criminal Justice Act is therefore key.

10.5.2.1.2   Definition of Inside Information

Inside information must relate either to particular securities or to a particular issuer of securities,[409] ie it must not be general in nature. An example might be that a takeover bid of a particular company is imminent. This information can include information which may affect the company's business prospects,[410] and can therefore include information coming from an outside source, such as a competitor company announcing a new and superior competing product. Presumably, however, information about the market sector to which a company belongs will not be inside information. So a report from the Government intending to remove the monopoly position of a particular company would be inside information, but plans to regulate a particular market sector, or information of general application, such as the state of the economy, are unlikely to be particular enough to count as inside information. However, the distinction will not always be easy to draw, as the information may impact differentially on companies, and some information which appears generic will be of key significance to some securities. For example, information about planned interest rate changes will have specific relevance to the price of gilts. Further, the information must be specific *or* precise.[411] Although these terms have

---

[403]   The terms 'primary' and 'secondary' insiders are not used in the legislation but were endorsed by the House of Lords in *AG's Ref (No 1 of 1988)* [1989] 1 AC 971.

[404]   Criminal Justice Act 1993, s 57(2)(a)(i). It has been suggested that the 'through being' test is a 'but for' test ie that there must be a causal link between the employment and the acquisition of the information, but not in the sense that the information must be acquired in the course of the employment: P Davies, *Gower and Davies Principles of Modern Company Law,* 8th edn (London, Sweet & Maxwell, 2008) 1102.

[405]   Ibid, s 57(2)(a)(ii).

[406]   Ibid, s 57(2)(b).

[407]   Ibid, s 57(1). As long as the secondary insider knows that the source of the inside information is a primary insider, he need not know the identity of that individual: *AG's Ref (No 1 of 1988)* [1989] 1 AC 971.

[408]   Ibid, s 57(2)(a)(i).

[409]   Ibid, s 56(1)(a).

[410]   Ibid, s 60(4).

[411]   Ibid, s 56(1)(b).

sometimes been regarded as synonymous, the two concepts do seem distinct. Information that a company's profits are in excess of expectations would be specific (as to the company and its prospects) but not precise, if the amount of the excess is not stated.

The information must not have been made public.[412] A non-exhaustive definition of this concept is provided in the Act,[413] so, for example, information has been made public if it is published in accordance with the rules of a regulated market for the purpose of informing investors and their professional advisers.[414] The definition of 'made public' is intended to provide a generous test for analysts. Analysts are in a potentially difficult position. Their role is to look at the information disclosed by companies and to look for further information of their own, and to use any information they acquire to their own advantage. The Criminal Justice Act 1993 does not aim to prevent the use of informational advantages of this kind. Indeed, on one view, analysts are crucial for the efficient functioning of the market. As discussed in chapter nine, much of the information actually disclosed by companies is technical and detailed and is not likely per se to provide very useful guidance to investors. The particular value of disclosure is that it impacts on the market price of the securities and therefore investors trading at the market price are protected even if they never read the particular disclosures made by the company.

Analysts are one of the bridging mechanisms for turning company disclosures into a market price which reflects the true value of the securities.[415] The acquisition of informational advantages through skill and diligence, rather than because that individual holds a particular position, is not improper and indeed is to be encouraged. As a result the Criminal Justice Act 1993 provides that 'information is made public if . . . it is derived from information which has been made public'.[416] Further, information is public if that information can be 'readily acquired'[417] by those likely to deal in the securities, whether the information has in fact been acquired or not. It can be public even though it can only be acquired by payment of a fee, it is only published outside the UK, or can only be acquired by those exercising 'diligence or expertise'.[418] Finally, the information, if made public, must be likely to have a significant effect on the price of any securities.[419]

---

[412]   Ibid, s 56(1)(c).

[413]   Ibid, s 58.

[414]   Ibid, s 58(2)(a).

[415]   See eg Z Goshen and G Parchomovsky, 'The Essential Role of Securities Regulation' (2006) 55 *Duke Law Journal* 711.

[416]   Criminal Justice Act 1993, s 58(2)(d).

[417]   Ibid, s 58(2)(c).

[418]   Ibid, s 58(3).

[419]   Ibid, s 56(1)(d). No advice is provided as to the meaning of 'significant' in this context, although in the context of takeovers the Panel regards a 10% movement in one day as sufficiently significant to require the announcement of a pending bid. In New Zealand the word 'likely' has been interpreted to mean that there must be a 'substantial risk' of this occurring: *Colonial Mutual Life Assurance Society v Wilson Neill Ltd* [1994] 2 NZLR 152 (Sup Ct NZ).

Under the Criminal Justice Act 1993 an "individual who has information as an insider"[420] is guilty of the offence of insider dealing in three different circumstances: actual dealing in securities,[421] encouraging another person to deal[422] and disclosing inside information to another person.[423]

10.5.2.1.3   The Offence of Actual Dealing in Securities

For the offence of actual dealing the individual must have inside information as an insider and must deal[424] on a regulated market[425] or rely on a professional intermediary to do so, or themselves be acting as a professional intermediary.[426] Dealing is defined to include both acquiring and disposing of securities, so inaction is not caught by the Act. Dealing which occurs off a regulated market is not caught by these provisions, once again reinforcing the rationale of this offence as being directed towards maintaining the integrity of the markets. The individual must deal in securities that are price-affected securities in relation to that information.

The fact that this is a criminal offence means that there is a significant mens rea element to the offence. The insider must know that the information is inside information and that that he has it, and knows he has it, from an inside source. This is subjectively assessed and accordingly will be difficult to establish. A number of defences are available. The main defence for the defendant is if he can show he would have done what he did even if he had not had the information, for example he would have traded anyway to meet a pressing financial need or legal obligation.[427] There is also a defence if the defendant can show that he did not expect the dealing to result in a profit attributable to the fact that the information was price sensitive information in relation to the securities.[428] This is likely to be narrowly construed and is unlikely to be very beneficial to defendants. Alternatively the defendant has a defence if he can show that he believed on reasonable grounds that the information had been disclosed widely enough to ensure that none of those taking part in the dealing would be prejudiced by not having the information.[429] There is also a general defence, which applies to all of the offences, for market makers. If the defendant can show

---

[420]   Ibid, s 52(1). Notice that this offence can only be committed by an individual, not a company (although the offence can be committed by an individual if he causes a company to deal or discloses information to it). This contrasts with the position under FSMA, s 397 and under FSMA, s 118, both of which can be committed by companies (see s 397(1) and s 118(1) respectively).

[421]   Ibid, s 52(1)(3). For the definition of securities see Criminal Justice Act 1993, s 54, Sch 2 and the Insider Dealing (Securities and Regulated Markets) Order 1994 (SI 1994/187). In general the definition covers shares, debt securities, options, futures, but not units in unit trusts.

[422]   Ibid, ss 52(2)(a), 52(3).

[423]   Ibid, s 52(2)(b).

[424]   For the definition of dealing in securities see Criminal Justice Act 1993, s 55.

[425]   For the definition of regulated markets see the Insider Dealing (Securities and Regulated Markets) Order 1994 (SI 1994/187). This Order extends the application of the Criminal Justice Act 1993 to securities which are officially listed in or are admitted to dealing under the rules of any investment exchange established within any of the States of the EEA, but see Criminal Justice Act 1993, s 62(1) on the need for a territorial connection with the UK.

[426]   Ibid, s 52(3). For the definition of professional intermediary for these purposes see Criminal Justice Act 1993, s 59.

[427]   Ibid, s 53(1)(c).

[428]   Ibid, s 53(1)(a).

[429]   Ibid, s 53(1)(b). This defence is mainly aimed at underwriting arrangements where those involved in the underwriting trade amongst themselves on the basis of shared knowledge about the underwriting proposal but the information is not known to the market generally.

that he acted in good faith in the course of his business as a market maker then he will have a defence to any of the insider dealing offences under this Act.[430]

10.5.2.1.4 The Offence of Encouraging another Person to Deal

For the second offence, the individual will be liable if he has the information as an insider and if he encourages another person to deal in price-affected securities in relation to the information.[431] It is not necessary for dealing to actually take place. The dealing need not be on a regulated market or in reliance on a professional intermediary, although the defendant must have reasonable cause to believe that the dealing would be prohibited. The other person need not know that the securities are price-affected securities nor need he actually receive the inside information. The mens rea element for this offence is that the individual must know or have reasonable cause to believe[432] that the dealing will take place on a regulated market or by or in reliance on a professional intermediary. The defences for this offence are the same as those for the actual dealing offence, set out above.[433]

10.5.2.1.5 The Offence of Disclosing Inside Information to Another Person

The final offence is the disclosing offence. The defendant must have information as an insider and must disclose that information 'otherwise than in the proper performance of the functions of his employment, office or profession'[434] to another person. Again the individual must know that the information was inside information and that he has it, and knows he has it, from an inside source. There is a defence if the defendant did not expect any person, because of the disclosure, to deal on a regulated market as, or in reliance on, a professional intermediary,[435] such as where the information is disclosed to a journalist to use as part of a story. There is also a defence if the defendant did not expect the dealing to result in a profit attributable to the fact that the information was price sensitive information in relation to the securities.[436]

10.5.2.1.6 Penalties and Enforcement

The penalties for insider dealing under this Act are up to seven years imprisonment or an unlimited fine.[437] A person found guilty can also be disqualified by court order from being a company director.[438] There are no civil law consequences of a breach of these provisions: no contract is rendered void or unenforceable as a result of a breach of section 52 of the Criminal Justice Act 1993.[439] A court by whom a person is convicted can make a compensation order requiring the insider to pay compensation to any person who has

---

[430] Ibid, s 53(4) and Sch 1.
[431] Ibid, s 52(2)(a).
[432] Ibid. Since it is enough for the defendant to have 'reasonable cause to believe' an objective element is introduced to this offence (cf the purely subjective approach adopted under the actual dealing and disclosing offences).
[433] Ibid, s 53(2). See pages 514–15.
[434] Ibid, s 52(2)(b).
[435] Ibid, s 53(3)(a).
[436] Ibid, s 53(3)(b).
[437] Ibid, s 61.
[438] Company Directors Disqualification Act 1986, ss 2, 8 and see *R v Goodman* [1993] 2 All ER 789.
[439] Criminal Justice Act 1993, s 63(2).

suffered loss from the offence,[440] although it will be difficult to identify an individual who has suffered loss in the faceless transactions that occur in the modern marketplace. In addition the FSA can make use of its range of remedies for market abuse, such as injunctions and restitution orders.[441]

The fact that this is a criminal offence raises a number of difficult enforcement issues.[442] An element of culpability is required as part of the offence. As we have seen with the offences of insider dealing under the Criminal Justice Act, for the offence to be established a mens rea element must be proved. In general it must be established that the individual knows that it is inside information and that he has it, and knows he has it, from an inside source.[443] This is subjectively assessed and accordingly it will be difficult to establish in court. Coupled with this is the fact that the burden of proof in criminal cases is higher than in civil cases: beyond reasonable doubt rather than merely on the balance of probabilities.

These offences have in the past needed to compete for police and prosecutor attention with other crimes which are generally regarded as more serious and worthy of attention, such as assaults and murders. However, it is now possible for the FSA to prosecute an offence under the Criminal Justice Act 1993,[444] which deals with this difficulty to some extent, and adds a specialist element into the prosecution of the offence, even if the judge and jury in such trials remain non-specialists.[445] The FSA secured its first criminal conviction for insider dealing in March 2009, and a number of other prosecutions have followed.[446] A lawyer, McQuoid, employed by a company, TTP communications plc (TTP), tipped off his father in law that TTP was about to be taken over. The father in law bought shares in TTP before the takeover was announced. Following the announcement TTP's share price soared, resulting in a profit of almost £49,000 on the shares. Both McQuoid and his father in law were given jail sentences of eight months, although the father in law's sentence was suspended for 12 months.[447] Dismissing McQuoid's appeal, the Court of Appeal stated that deliberate insider dealing was a species of fraud for which prosecution, rather than regulatory proceedings, would often be more appropriate.[448] This is intended to be part of a new, tougher stance on financial crime on the part of the FSA. Margaret Cole, director of enforcement at the FSA, said: 'By pursuing a criminal prosecution in this case, the FSA has shown that we will take tough action to achieve our

---

[440]   Powers of Criminal Courts Act 1973, s 35.
[441]   FSMA, ss 380, 382.
[442]   For a discussion see B Rider, 'Civilising the Law – The Use of Civil and Administrative Proceedings to Enforce Financial Services Law' [1995] *Journal of Financial Crime* 11.
[443]   Criminal Justice Act 1993, s 57(1).
[444]   FSMA, s 402. There is no need for the FSA to obtain the consent of the Secretary of State or the Director of Public Prosecutions before bringing a prosecution under section 402: *R (on the application of Matthew Francis Uberoi, Neel Akash Uberoi) v City of Westminster Magistrates' Court* [2008] EWHC 3191 (Admin).
[445]   For a discussion of the role of juries in particular see Home Office, *Juries in Serious Fraud Trials: A Consultation Document* (February 1998) chs 1–2.
[446]   Details of these prosecutions can be found on the FSA's website (www.fsa.gov.uk) see eg Press release FSA/PN/042/2009, 27 March 2009.
[447]   *R v McQuoid*, Southwark Crown Court, 27 March 2009 (unreported), upheld on appeal: *R v McQuoid* [2009] EWCA Crim 1301; [2009] 4 All ER 388.
[448]   *R v McQuoid* [2009] EWCA Crim 1301; [2009] 4 All ER 388.

aim of credible deterrence in the financial markets ... Anyone engaging in similar acts should see this as a clear warning that the FSA intends to bring all its powers to bear to protect the integrity of our markets'.[449]

Levels of enforcement of the criminal offence of insider dealing have been low. Between 1997 and 2006, for example, proceedings were brought against 15 individuals, of which eight were successful.[450] Although these levels are likely to rise given the new role for the FSA in this regard, the overall numbers are likely to remain small since it does not solve the two primary difficulties with these criminal prosecutions, namely the need to establish a mens rea element and the need to satisfy the high criminal law burden of proof.

10.5.2.2   *The Criminal Offence of Market Manipulation under Section 397 FSMA*

The movement away from regarding market abuse as based on fiduciary duties has allowed the concept of market manipulation to develop, based as it is on attempts to protect the 'smooth operation of the market' rather than any fiduciary relationship. The basic concept of market manipulation is easy to understand. It involves an unwarranted interference in the operation of the market's normal price-forming mechanisms. It is therefore an activity which is seen as undermining the integrity, and hence the efficiency, of markets. Obvious examples include the dissemination of misleading statements which move the price of the shares up or down, such as false rumours of a takeover bid made purely to drive the share price up. Another form of market manipulation is artificial transactions which create the appearance of active trading and convey false information about the supply and demand for investments.

However, creating a definition of market manipulation is not straightforward.[451] If an overly rigid definition is adopted then new and ingenious schemes that result in a manipulation of the market may be excluded, and yet overly flexible or open-ended definitions will cause difficulties where market manipulation may result in criminal penalties. Article 7 of the European Convention on Human Rights requires the contours of criminal behaviour to be delineated with clarity. Any ambiguity needs to be resolved in favour of the accused. This does not suggest that a high level of definitional complexity will be possible for any criminal offence of market manipulation. Only Parliament can create and define criminal offences and so amending these offences will be a slow process.[452] In addition, some interference with normal market forces is accepted within the UK capital markets. It is a defence to an action under section 397 if the defendant acts in conformity with the FSA's price stabilisation rules[453] or with its 'control of information

---

[449]   FSA Press release FSA/PN/042/2009, 27 March 2009.

[450]   Hansard HC vol 442 col 1635W (13 February 2006) (Parliamentary Question No 2005/3120 from Austin Mitchell).

[451]   For discussion see E Lomnicka, 'Preventing and Controlling the Manipulation of Financial Markets: Towards a Definition of Market Manipulation' (2001) 8 *Journal of Financial Crime* 297.

[452]   Another restrictive element that exists in relation to the criminal offence of market manipulation is the fact that international law imposes territorial limits on the enforceability of criminal law, whereas global financial markets mean that market abuse may often be conducted in a number of jurisdictions. For the territorial reach of these provisions see FSMA, s 397(6)(7).

[453]   FSMA, s 397(4)(a); s 397(5)(b). The FSA's price stabilisation rules are set out in the Code of Market Conduct in the FSA Handbook, MAR 2.

rules'[454] such as its rules regarding Chinese walls, which restrict the flow of information around large conglomerates and can result in the firm giving a misleading impression.[455]

The criminal offence of market manipulation can be committed by any person, including a company.[456] There are two forms of the offence: misleading statements and dishonest concealment;[457] and misleading conduct.[458] The two are not mutually exclusive.[459] The first of these is a natural corollary of the requirement to disclose information. The second can also encompass behaviour stemming from the disclosure obligations. A failure to disclose information required by the Listing Rules, for example, could conceivably fall within either form of the offence. However, the second form of the offence also ranges more broadly, to cover behaviour which does not per se involve misinformation but can nevertheless be seen as an interference with market mechanisms.

10.5.2.2.1   Misleading Statements and Dishonest Concealment

A defendant will be liable under section 397 for making a misleading statement if he makes a statement, profit or forecast which he knows to be misleading, false or deceptive in a material particular,[460] or is reckless in that regard. The requirement of knowledge here includes actual knowledge and wilful blindness, ie closing one's eyes to the obvious. The definition of recklessness should be given its ordinary meaning in English, ie a rash statement or promise made heedless of whether the person making it had any real facts on which to base it.[461]

A common example of this form of market manipulation is where brokers or other investment advisors provide misleading advice, in order to promote the sale of shares in which they make a market, or to offload securities which are marketed or have been underwritten by their firm, by 'talking up' the securities to unsuspecting investors. Another example is market rigging. An early form of this offence, which pre-dated statutory forms of market manipulation, involved a syndicate conspiring with a man (De Berenger) in order for the latter to appear at Dover as a French officer to bring the false news of Napoleon's death. This led to City stockbrokers and the public buying government debt which pushed the prices considerably higher, while the members of the syndicate offloaded their holdings, as planned, at a considerable profit.[462] Modern variants on this practice make use of the internet to perpetrate practices resembling market rigging.[463]

For the offence of making a misleading statement either recklessly or with knowledge that it was misleading, there is no requirement that the statement be made dishonestly. However, in order to establish liability based on an *omission*, dishonesty is required. The defendant will be liable if he dishonestly conceals material facts whether in connection

---

[454]   Ibid, s 397(4)(b); s 397(5)(c).
[455]   See FSA Handbook, Senior Management Arrangements, Systems and Controls, SYSC 10.2.
[456]   FSMA, s 397(1) which refers to a 'person' rather than an individual cf Criminal Justice Act 1993, s 52(1).
[457]   Ibid, s 397(1). This replicates the prohibition previously in place in Financial Services Act 1986, s 47(1).
[458]   Ibid, s 397(3). This replicates the prohibition previously in place in Financial Services Act 1986, s 47(2).
[459]   Various kinds of behaviour, such as false rumours and artificial transactions, could conceivably fall within both forms of the offence.
[460]   FSMA, s 397(1)(a),(c).
[461]   *R v Grunwald* [1963] 1 QB 935 per Paull J, upheld by the Court of Appeal in *R v Page* [1996] Crim LR 821, in the context of the Financial Services Act 1986, s 47.
[462]   *R v De Berenger* (1814) 3 M & S 67; 105 Eng Rep 536.
[463]   See IOSCO, *Report on Securities Activity on the Internet III*, October 2003.

with a statement, promise or forecast made by the person concealing the facts or otherwise.[464] Section 397 does not create any independent obligation to disclose and therefore the concealment must be of facts which the defendant is required by other provisions of the law to disclose,[465] such as those created in the Disclosure Rules and Transparency Rules. The test of dishonesty is objective and is defined by reference to the ordinary standards of reasonable and honest people.[466] Even in the commercial context it is the standards of ordinary people, not just those operating in a commercial context, which are relevant,[467] therefore the fact that it is an accepted market practice does not preclude a finding of dishonesty if the accused is subjectively aware that the relevant practices fall short of the standards regarded as honest by the general public.

In addition, the purpose of the statement or concealment must be either to induce someone (or be reckless whether it may induce someone) to enter into or refrain from entering into an investment agreement, or to exercise or refrain from exercising a right conferred by an investment.[468] The misleading statement or concealment must therefore be for the required purpose. The mere fact that a recipient of the statement makes an investment decision on the basis of a statement which the maker knows to be false is not enough. By contrast, if the defendant intends the consequences, the inducement need not be successful, and the consequences need not actually occur.[469]

A good example of this offence in practice is *R v Bailey and Rigby*.[470] The chief executive and chief financial officers of a company were found liable under this section. They were convicted of issuing a misleading trading statement which caused the share price to rise and investors to purchase its shares. The officers were found to have been reckless both as to the truth of this statement and as to whether investors would rely on it. They received custodial sentences of eighteen months and nine months respectively.

10.5.2.2.2 Misleading Practices and Conduct

In terms of the offence of misleading practices and conduct, it is an offence to carry out an act or course of conduct which creates a false or misleading impression as to the market in, or price or value of, any investment, if done for the purpose of creating that impression and thereby inducing a person to acquire or dispose of investments, or to refrain from doing so, or to exercise or not to exercise rights attached to investments.[471] The use of the phrase 'any course of conduct' leaves open the issue of whether both activity and inactivity by the defendant could potentially fall within this offence.[472] A false impression can be created by inaction on the part of the defendant, particularly where the defendant is under an obligation to act (eg to disclose certain information) and fails to do so. Unlike the

---

[464] FSMA, s 397(1)(b).
[465] *Aldrich v Norwich Union Life Insurance Co Ltd* [1998] CLC 1621 (Ch D); The Times, 13 August 1999 (CA).
[466] *R v Ghosh* [1982] QB 1053, per Lord Lane CJ. This test was laid down for dishonesty offences under the Theft Act 1968, as amended, but has been applied in the context of FSMA, s 397(1)(b): see *R v Lockwood* (1987) 3 BCC 333.
[467] *R v Lockwood* (1987) 3 BCC 333.
[468] FSMA, s 397(2). For the broad range of investments caught by this prohibition see FSMA, s 397(9)–(14) and FSMA, 2000 (misleading statements and practices) Order 2001 (SI 2001/3645) as amended.
[469] See *R v Finnegan*, The Independent, 27 November 1995 (CA), in relation to a similarly worded provision in the Banking Act 1987, s 35(1).
[470] [2006] 2 Cr App R (S) 36.
[471] FSMA, s 397(3).
[472] Cf FSMA, s 118(8) which clearly includes inaction.

offence of misleading statements or concealments, there is no need to demonstrate that the defendant had knowledge that the impression was misleading, or was reckless as to that fact, as long as it can be demonstrated that he acted for the purpose of creating an impression which was in fact misleading. It must be demonstrated that the purpose of creating the impression was to induce the other to act in a certain way. The defendant must intend the consequences, it is not enough if he is reckless as to the consequences. However, as with the misleading statements offence, the inducement need not be successful. It is enough if the defendant intends to create the impression, he need not intend the impression to be false and misleading.

However, the defendant has a defence if he can demonstrate that he reasonably believed that the impression was not misleading.[473] This defence includes objective ('reasonably') as well as subjective elements, and therefore does not wholly exonerate honest defendants. This is an attenuated form of mens rea when compared to the criminal offence of insider dealing, and the offence of misleading statements under section 397. Nevertheless even this reduced form of mens rea is problematic for two reasons. First, if the aim is to protect investors by preventing a market being manipulated then on one view the state of mind of the perpetrator should be irrelevant. The dissemination of false information, for example, will create a false market whether or not it was done with knowledge that the information was untrue, so that the market will be manipulated even if the wrongdoers did not intend to do so, or were not reckless or even negligent as to the result. Second, a mens rea element creates difficulties of proof for prosecutors, and makes successful prosecution of these offences significantly more problematic.

Trading designed to influence (or lead) market prices, or even to mislead other market players, is a common phenomenon in competitive markets. It is only if the conduct is capable of misleading the market and affecting the price formation mechanism that such conduct should be outlawed. This limb of the offence is rarely prosecuted so concrete examples are thin on the ground.[474] However, a good example of such a distortion would be where directors persuade the company's brokers to buy shares in the market at four times the previous market price in order to move the market price closer to that which the directors believe to be the 'true' value of the shares.[475]

10.5.2.2.3   Penalties and Enforcement

A person guilty of an offence under this section is liable, on conviction on indictment, to seven years imprisonment, or a fine, or both.[476] As with the insider dealing offence discussed above, a breach of section 397 does not render any contract void or unenforceable.[477]

---

[473]   FSMA, s 397(5)(a).
[474]   The FSA provides guidance however: see FSA Handbook, Code of Market Conduct, MAR 1.9.4 and see FSA Consultation Paper 10, *Consultation on a Draft Code of Market Conduct, Part 1* June 1998, para 37
[475]   *North v Marra Developments* [1982] 56 ALJR 106.
[476]   FSMA, s 397(8).
[477]   Unlike the offence of insider dealing under the Criminal Justice Act 1993, there is no express provision to this effect (cf CJA 1993, s 63(2), and in the context of the market abuse offence see FSMA, s 131). However, this has been assumed to be the case: *Aldrich v Norwich Union Life Insurance Co Ltd* [1998] CLC 1621 (Ch D) per Rimer J. In addition there is assumed to be no possibility of a breach of statutory duty claim arising under s 397. Again the statute is silent on this point, but this was the case under the common law, and again in *Aldrich* was assumed to be the position under s 397.

In addition the FSA can make use of its range of remedies for market abuse, such as injunctions and restitution orders.[478]

The criminal nature of these provisions creates difficulties. Chiefly, of course, the fact that this is a criminal offence means that there is a higher evidential burden than exists for a civil offence (the offence must be proved beyond reasonable doubt rather than merely on the balance of probabilities). The prosecution also needs to establish a mens rea element. For the offence of making a misleading statement the defendant must be demonstrated to know that the statement is misleading, false or deceptive or be reckless in that regard. If the offence involves an omission then dishonesty on the part of the defendant must be established. For the offence of misleading practices, it need not be shown that the defendant had knowledge, or was reckless, as to the fact that the impression was misleading, but it must be demonstrated that the defendant acted for the purpose of creating an impression that was misleading, and intended to do so. The defendant must be shown to have intended the consequences.[479] These requirements, particularly those in relation to misleading statements and dishonest omissions, create significant barriers for any prosecution. The FSA's metamorphosis into a regulator keen to bring criminal prosecutions in relation to financial crime may also impact on the number of section 397 prosecutions, but these cases are likely to remain rarer than insider dealing cases because of their complexity.

10.5.2.3   The Regulatory Offence of Market Abuse under Section 118 FSMA

The criminal offences of insider dealing and market manipulation, discussed above, have proved very difficult to enforce, principally due to the need to demonstrate mens rea on the part of the defendant and to satisfy the higher evidential burden imposed by the criminal law. As a result in 2000 a new offence of market abuse was introduced in section 118 FSMA with administrative rather than criminal sanctions. It was amended in 2005 to give effect to the Market Abuse Directive.[480] These amendments involved some re-casting of the existing provisions, rather than wholesale change. Section 118 covers activity on the Main Market and Plus-listed market and also on the AIM and Plus-quoted markets.[481]

Section 118 FSMA deals with both insider dealing and market manipulation in one section, although it is still useful to treat these two forms of market abuse separately. Section 118 divides market abuse into seven types of behaviour, which relate to qualifying investments[482] on a prescribed market. The first three relate broadly to the use of inside information[483] and the last four to market manipulation.[484] These offences can be

---

[478]   FSMA, ss 380, 382.

[479]   The defendant has a defence if he can demonstrate that he reasonably believed the impression was not misleading: FSMA, s 397(5)(a).

[480]   Directive 2003/6/EC, OJ L96/16. The necessary changes to FSMA were effected by the Financial Services and Markets Act 2000 (Market Abuse) Regulations 2005 (SI 2005/381).

[481]   Prior to the implementation of the Market Abuse Directive, s 118 FSMA applied to 'prescribed markets'. The Market Abuse Directive only required the provisions to apply to regulated markets but in implementing the directive it was decided to retain the previous, broader, coverage: Financial Services and Markets Act 2000 (Prescribed Markets and Qualifying Investments) Order 2001 (SI 2001/996), art 4.

[482]   The definition of qualifying investments is found in Financial Services and Markets Act 2000 (Prescribed Markets and Qualifying Investments) Order 2001 (SI 2001/996) art 5. They include transferable securities and any other instrument admitted to trading on a regulated market.

[483]   FSMA, s 118(2)(3)(4).

[484]   Ibid, s 118(5)–(8).

committed by any person, ie companies fall within the ambit of these provisions.[485] Further guidance is provided by the FSA in its Code of Market Conduct.[486] The Code does not attempt to describe exhaustively the types of conduct which may or may not constitute market abuse, but it does identify some conduct that will not amount to market abuse, ie it creates some safe harbours.[487]

10.5.2.3.1   Insider Dealing

The first and second types of behaviour prohibited under section 118 are very similar to the actual dealing and disclosing offences under the Criminal Justice Act 1993.[488] An offence is committed 'where an insider deals, or attempts to deal, in a qualifying investment . . .on the basis of inside information . . .'.[489] One issue that has arisen for discussion is whether it needs to be established that the person with inside information has an intention to use that inside information as the basis of the trades. In *Spector Photo Group NV*[490] the ECJ had to determine the definition of insider dealing for the purposes of article 2 of the Market Abuse Directive, and held that the mere fact that a person with inside information acquires or disposes of financial instruments to which that information relates is enough. The ECJ thereby created a presumption of intention to use the inside information where a person satisfies the constituent elements of article 2, providing the use made of the inside information is against the purpose of the Directive.[491] This should make it easier for regulators to establish breach of article 2. In the UK context, section 118(2) specifically requires that the insider deals 'on the basis of' the information before insider dealing is committed. The FSA's Code of Market Conduct clarifies the meaning of 'on the basis of'[492] and provides guidance as to when the FSA will consider trading to be on the basis of inside information.[493] Under current UK law, therefore, the FSA is required to establish that the trading has been informed by the inside information. It is too soon to say whether the effect of the *Spector* decision will be to prompt an amendment of the provisions of section 118(2), to follow the ECJ's approach on this issue. Following the ECJ's line on this issue would certainly make it easier for the FSA to prove that insider dealing has taken place. It is not likely that the decision in *Spector* will have any effect on the criminal law offence of insider dealing in the Criminal Justice Act 1993 (which does clearly require a mens rea element, as described at 10.5.2.1), since that Act does not implement the Market Abuse Directive.

---

[485]   Ibid, s 118(1), the same approach that is taken under FSMA, s 397(1) but cf Criminal Justice Act 1993, s 52(1).
[486]   FSA Handbook, Code of Market Conduct.
[487]   For a discussion of the role of the Code of Market Conduct see *Winterflood v FSA* [2010] EWCA Civ 423.
[488]   See Criminal Justice Act 1993, ss 52(1) and 52(2)(b). There is no equivalent of Criminal Justice Act 1993, s 52(2)(a) within s 118 but encouraging another to deal is caught by FSMA, s 123(1)(b).
[489]   FSMA, s 118(2).
[490]   [2009] EUECJ C-45/08 (23 December 2009).
[491]   The ECJ identified the purpose of the Directive as being: to protect the integrity of the financial markets; to enhance investor confidence; and to provide investors with the assurance that they are on an equal footing to all other investors.
[492]   Code of Market Conduct, MAR 1.3.3.
[493]   Ibid, MAR 1.3.4.

Alternatively the insider will be liable if he discloses insider information otherwise than in the proper course of the exercise of his employment, profession or duties.[494] An insider is defined to include those who have inside information as a result of being part of the management of the issuer, or who hold capital in the issuer, or as a result of their employment profession or duties, or as a result of criminal activities.[495] This is similar to the definition of an insider found in the Criminal Justice Act 1993,[496] and therefore raises the same issue about whether analysts, for example, should be regarded as insiders. For the reasons discussed above, there are good policy reasons why they should not necessarily be treated as insiders and the FSA seems to recognise this, stating that market makers will not be liable for insider dealing in some circumstances even when they do possess inside information.[497]

The definition of insiders for the purposes of section 118 extends beyond the Criminal Justice Act 1993 definition in one important respect: under section 118 an insider is also someone who obtains inside information 'by other means and which he knows, or could reasonably be expected to know, is inside information'.[498] Thus an insider is someone with inside information, however obtained, but with the qualification that the holder ought to know this fact. An example of the sort of behaviour that falls within these provisions can be found in the Final Notice issued by the FSA to Brian Taylor in 2008.[499] In May 2007, Mr Taylor was a private retail investor. One of the stocks that he regularly dealt in was Amerisur Resources plc. Amerisur is an oil and gas exploration company with projects in South America. The company's shares were admitted to trading on AIM. Blue Oar Securities Plc (Blue Oar) acted as broker for Amerisur in a share placing which took place on 24 May 2007. On 23 May 2007, Blue Oar contacted a number of existing Amerisur shareholders, including Mr Taylor, to invite them to participate in the placing. Blue Oar spoke to Mr Taylor at 9.35am and made Mr Taylor an insider in relation to the placing of Amerisur shares to be announced to the market on 24 May 2007. In the course of this conversation, Blue Oar advised Mr Taylor that the placing price was six pence, that the placing would be announced the next day and that Mr Taylor was not permitted to speak to anyone about the placing until it was announced to the market on 24 May 2007.

Following the receipt of this inside information, Mr Taylor sold 150,000 Amerisur shares at 9.095 pence at 9.46am on 23 May 2007. Mr Taylor then purchased 500,000 shares in the placing at six pence. Following the announcement of the placing on 24 May 2007 the price of Amerisur's shares fell to 7.5 pence. By his actions, Mr Taylor realised a profit of £4,642.50. The FSA found that Mr Taylor held this information 'by other means', because he had been telephoned by Blue Boar and asked whether he wanted to take part in the placing, and as a result of that conversation he could be expected to know that the information he received was inside information. He was therefore an insider for these

---

[494] FSMA, s 118(3). This is akin to Crimninal Justice Act 1993, s 52(2)(b).
[495] Ibid, s 118B(a)–(d).
[496] Criminal Justice Act 1993, s 57, although the reference to criminal activities is new.
[497] Code of Market Conduct, MAR 1.3.7–1.3.8. See pages 513–14
[498] FSMA, s 118B(e).
[499] FSA, Final Notice to Brian Valentine Taylor, 16 October 2008.

purposes. The FSA found Mr Taylor liable for market abuse under section 118(2) and imposed a penalty on him designed to strip away the whole of his profit.[500]

Again it may be said that in a regime that has moved away from a view of insider dealing as rooted in the fiduciary relationship, towards one based on a market approach, the definition of inside information is key. An insider is defined (almost) as anyone in possession of inside information. If the definition is too lax then the market will be impaired, but if it is too strict then this will impede legitimate information gathering and this will also have a potentially negative impact on market efficiency. The definition of 'inside information' is again similar to the definition under the Criminal Justice Act 1993,[501] ie it is information of a precise nature[502] which is not generally available,[503] which relates, directly or indirectly, to one or more issuers or qualifying investments,[504] and would, if generally available, be likely to have a significant effect on the price of the qualifying investments.[505] Information is likely to have a significant effect on price if and only if it is information of a kind that a reasonable investor would be likely to use as part of the basis for his investment decisions.[506] This is an ex ante test, made at the point when the information becomes available to the public. Whether the prices are in fact affected ex post seems irrelevant. It is worth noting that the inside information does not have to be 'inside' in any meaningful sense: it can also cover information which affects the market as such.

The main difference between section 118 and the offence under the Criminal Justice Act 1993 is the lack of a mens rea element. In principle a person can be liable under section 118 if they deal with inside information, even if they are unaware that the information is inside information or that they are an insider. A number of important qualifications exist however. First, if the insider obtains the information 'by any other means' then they must know or be reasonably expected to know, that it is inside information. There are also protections created at the imposition of penalty stage. The FSA may decide not to impose a penalty if it is satisfied that the person believed on reasonable grounds that he was not acting in breach of the insider dealing provisions, or that they had taken all reasonable precautions and exercised all due diligence to avoid the prohibition.[507] The FSA can also take account of these factors when deciding on the amount of penalty to be imposed.[508] Mens rea is not wholly irrelevant for these offences, therefore, although its role is significantly diminished as compared to the position under the Criminal Justice Act 1993.

The next offence under section 118 is somewhat different. It is not found in the Criminal Justice Act 1993 and it in fact adds a potentially significant extension to the first two forms of insider dealing. Section 118(4) was introduced in 2000 and is super-equivalent to the provisions in the Market Abuse Directive. This provision survived the

---

[500]   The FSA found that Mr Taylor's behaviour merited the imposition of a total penalty of £24,462.50 (being a penalty of £20,000 plus disgorgement of Mr Taylor's profit) but because of his financial circumstances this was reduced to £4,642.50.

[501]   See Criminal Justice Act 1993, s 56 discussed above at 10.5.2.1.

[502]   FSMA, s 118C(2) and see s 118C(5) for a definition of 'precise' in this context.

[503]   FSMA, s 118C(2)(a). See for further guidance Code of Market Conduct, MAR 1.2.12 which provides guidance on when information will be generally available to the public, and is akin to Criminal Justice Act 1993, s 58(3).

[504]   Ibid, s 118C(2)(b).

[505]   Ibid, s 118C(2)(c).

[506]   Ibid, s 118C(6).

[507]   Ibid, s 123(2)

[508]   Ibid, s 124(2).

amendments to section 118 introduced to give effect to the directive, because the FSA was loath to reduce the existing scope of its jurisdiction. However, it was agreed that over time the UK regime would be reduced to bring it into line with the more restricted EU regime introduced by the Market Abuse Directive. As a result it was agreed that section 118(4) would be subject to a sunset clause. This sunset clause has subsequently been extended. At the time of writing this clause is due to expire on 31 December 2011.[509] This extension is intended to allow the EU time to complete its planned review of the Market Abuse Directive.[510]

This provision is supplementary to the first two kinds of insider dealing. An offence is committed where there is behaviour which is based on information that 'is not generally available to those using the market'[511] and the behaviour is likely to be regarded by a regular user of the market as a failure on the part of the person concerned to observe the standard of behaviour reasonably expected of a person in his position in relation to the shares.[512] This extends the reach of these provisions beyond 'inside information' to include 'information which is not generally available'. However, there is a qualification: the information 'if available to a regular user of the market, would be, or would be likely to be, regarded by him as relevant when deciding the terms on which transactions in qualifying investments should be effected'.[513] It might include information which is not specific enough to be defined as inside information but which a 'regular user of the market' would regard as relevant. A regular user is defined as a reasonable person who regularly deals on that market in investments of the kind in question.[514] This definition also extends the notion of insider dealing beyond 'dealing' to include behaviour generally, including, potentially, a decision not to deal (subject to significant evidentiary problems being overcome). This offence is not limited to 'insiders' but includes any person whose behaviour falls within the subsection.

10.5.2.3.2   Market Manipulation

There are four different forms of market manipulation under section 118. The first of these involves effecting transactions or orders to trade which give, or are likely to give, a false or misleading impression about the supply of, or demand for, or the price of, qualifying investments, or which secure the price of such investments at an artificial level.[515] However this section will not apply where the transactions or orders to trade were for legitimate reasons and in conformity with accepted market practices.[516] The second

---

[509] Initially it was intended that this clause (and s 118(8)) would cease to have effect on 30 June 2008, but this has been extended by the Treasury (for the most recent extension see the Financial Services and Markets Act 2000 (Market Abuse) Regulations 2009 (SI 3128/2009)).

[510] The European Commission launched a call of evidence for review of the Market Abuse Directive in April 2009, see www.ec.europa.eu/internal_market/consultations/2009/market_abuse_en.htm.

[511] FSMA, s 118(4)(a).

[512] Ibid, s 118(4)(b).

[513] Ibid, s 118(4)(a).

[514] Ibid, s 130A(3).

[515] Ibid, s 118(5).

[516] Ibid, s 130A(3). Accepted market practices are those reasonably expected in the financial markets in question and accepted by the FSA. This provides the FSA with a measure of control over the width of this offence.

form of market manipulation involves transactions or orders to trade which employ fictitious devices or any other form of deception or contrivance.[517]

These forms of market manipulation are similar to the behaviour caught by section 397(3) FSMA, ie conduct which creates a false or misleading impression as to the market in or price of any relevant investments.[518] However, section 397 requires a mens rea element. It must be demonstrated that the defendant acted for the purpose of creating that impression and of thereby inducing another person to deal in the investments in some way.[519] No such element attaches to these provisions in section 118, although, as discussed, the FSA can take account of the mental state of the relevant person when deciding whether to impose a penalty and, if so, what the size of penalty ought to be.[520] Section 118 therefore moves away from an intention-based conception of market manipulation towards one that is effects-based. One other point to note is that although section 397(3) is silent as to whether conduct for these purposes can include inactivity, section 118 is clear that 'behaviour' includes both action and inaction.[521]

Examples of this form of market manipulation include situations where a person simultaneously buys and sells the same qualifying investment, ie trades with himself, to give the appearance of a legitimate transfer of title or risk, or both, at a price outside the normal trading range for the qualifying investment. It may be that the price of the qualifying investment is relevant to the calculation of the settlement value of an option, and the trader holds a position in the option. The trader's purpose in trading with himself in this way is therefore to position the price of the qualifying investment at a false, misleading, abnormal or artificial level, making him a profit or avoiding a loss from the option.[522] Alternatively, a series of transactions might be publicly reported for the purpose of suggesting a level of activity or price movement which does not genuinely exist. Another common form of this type of market manipulation involves a trader taking a long position on an investment and then disseminating misleading positive information about the investment to increase the price, or taking a short position and disseminating misleading negative information in order to decrease the price.[523]

However, some forms of behaviour which would otherwise constitute market manipulation are specifically allowed by the Act. The most obvious example is the price stabilisation rules. These rules allow those issuing new securities, for an interim period, to set the price of the security at an artificial level in order to avoid short-term price fluctuations which are regarded as detrimental to both issuers and investors.[524] This safe harbour is created at European level, and applies across the range of market abuse provisions in place in the UK.[525]

---

[517]   Ibid, s 118(6).
[518]   Ibid, s 397(3).
[519]   Ibid.
[520]   Ibid, s 123(2), s 124(2) and see page 524.
[521]   Ibid, s 130A(3).
[522]   Code of Market Conduct, MAR 1.6.15.
[523]   Ibid, MAR 1.7.2.
[524]   For discussion see FSA, *The Price Stabilising Rules*, CP 40, January 2000.
[525]   The safe harbour is created by Market Abuse Directive 2003/6/EC, art 8 and its implementing regulation, which is directly effective: Commission Regulation implementing the Market Abuse Directive. This safe harbour has been extended by domestic legislation (Criminal Justice Act 1993, Sch 1, para 5; FSMA, ss 397(4)(a)(c) and (5)(b)(d) and FSMA, s 144) so that it extends to the whole range of market abuse provisions in place in the UK. For implementation see Code of Market Conduct, MAR 2. The other safe harbour created by the Market Abuse Directive, art 8, relates to share buy-backs in the period after a public offer of securities.

The next form of market manipulation is similar to that found in section 397(1) FSMA.[526] It involves disseminating information that is likely to give a false or misleading impression as to a qualifying investment by a person who knew or could reasonably be expected to have known that the information was false or misleading.[527] Under section 397(1), the person must know or be reckless as to the fact that the statement is misleading, or, in the context of concealment, that the concealment is dishonest.[528] By contrast, under section 118 liability can arise if the person knew or 'could reasonably be expected to have known' that the information was false or misleading. In other words, section 118 creates a negligence standard.[529] Also, in contrast to section 397, there is no need for the maker of the statement to have intended or induced someone else to rely on the statement.[530]

A good example of this form of market manipulation is provided by the FSA's prosecution of the Shell group of companies in 2004.[531] Shell was found to have made false or misleading statements in relation to its hydrocarbon reserves and reserves replacement ratios between 1998 and 2003, despite indications from 2000 to 2003 that its proved reserves as announced to the market were false or misleading. Shell did not correct its disclosures until 2004 when it announced the recategorisation of 4,470 million barrels of oil, approximately 25 per cent of Shell's proved reserves. On disclosure of this information Shell's share price fell from 401 pence to 371 pence, reducing its market capitalisation on that day by £2.9 billion. Shell was found liable for this form of market manipulation and fined £17 million.

These provisions are a way of supplementing the rules regarding the need for accurate and timely disclosures to the market, supporting the FSA's ability to bring an action against the issuer and its directors for negligently making a misleading disclosure required by the Disclosure Rules and Transparency Rules.[532] The FSA's decision to bring a market abuse action in relation to this situation, rather than just dealing with it as a misstatement issue, was due to the seriousness of the company's misconduct.

As with the insider dealing provisions under section 118, the market manipulation provisions also contain a provision which was not strictly required by the Market Abuse Directive and therefore continues to exist on borrowed time, subject to a sunset clause.[533] Section 118(8) only applies where behaviour does not fall within one of the other forms of market manipulation. It deals with behaviour which is likely to give a regular user of the market a false or misleading impression as to the supply or demand or price of qualifying investments and the behaviour is likely to be regarded by a regular user of the market as a failure to observe the standards of behaviour reasonably expected of a person in the defendant's position.[534] It is broader than the other forms of market manipulation in that

---

[526]   FSMA, s 397(1) (2).
[527]   FSMA, s 118(7).
[528]   FSMA, s 397(1)
[529]   The provisions in FSMA, s 123(2) and 124(2) are also relevant.
[530]   Cf FSMA, s 397(2).
[531]   FSA, Final Notice to The Shell Transport and Trading Company, Royal Dutch Petroleum Company NV, 13 August 2004.
[532]   FSMA, s 91.
[533]   Initially it was intended that sections 118(4) and 118(8) would cease to have effect on 30 June 2008, but this has been extended by the Treasury (for the most recent extension see the Financial Services and Markets Act 2000 (Market Abuse) Regulations 2009 (SI 3128/2009)).
[534]   Ibid, s 118(a).

it does not require the dissemination of information[535] and it is not limited to effecting transactions or orders.[536] However, as with section 118(4), this form of market abuse is subject to the regular user of the market test.[537] The sort of behaviour caught by this provision would be the movement of physical commodity stocks, which might create a misleading impression as to the supply of, or demand for, or price or value of, a commodity.[538]

10.5.2.3.3 Levels of Enforcement of Market Abuse under Section 118

The primary sanction for market abuse is the imposition of a penalty, such as the £17 million fine imposed on the Shell group of companies by the FSA in 2004.[539] However, the FSA can substitute a public censure for the penalty.[540]

The levels of enforcement of the market abuse provisions under section 118 FSMA are certainly higher than under the criminal provisions. Between 2001, when the new regulatory regime came into existence, and 2007 the FSA issued Final Notices against eight firms and 15 individuals for market conduct related offences[541] and the levels of enforcement appear to have continued at much the same level since 2007.[542] Some of the penalties imposed have been substantial, for example, the fine of Shell of £17 million. In 2006 the FSA imposed a penalty of £750,000 on each of Philippe Jabre and his firm (GLG).[543]

However, these levels of enforcement still appear comparatively low. In part this is because of the high standard of proof required by the Financial Services and Markets Tribunal in relation to offences of market abuse under section 118.[544] Although the civil standard of proof is applicable (balance of probabilities rather than beyond reasonable doubt) the Tribunal has stated that the standard is flexible and the more serious the allegation, or the consequences if the allegation is proved, the stronger the evidence must be before the Tribunal will find the allegation to have been proved on the balance of probabilities.[545] To some extent this may help to explain the FSA turning its attention back to the criminal offences of insider dealing and market manipulation. If a near-criminal standard is going to be applied in civil cases, then perhaps the FSA's energy is better directed at securing some high profile criminal convictions.

When compared to other jurisdictions, the UK does well in terms of the amount of resources which it commits to the public enforcement of its securities regime.[546] However, the UK does not fare so well once the numbers of public enforcement actions actually

---

[535] Cf FSMA, s 118(7).

[536] Cf FSMA, ss 118(5), 118(6).

[537] FSMA, s 118.

[538] Code of Market Conduct, MAR 1.9.2.

[539] FSMA, s 123.

[540] Ibid, s 123(3). In addition the FSA can apply to court for a restitution order, or impose one itself: FSMA s 383. The FSA can also apply to court for an injunction to restrain future market abuse: FSMA, s 381.

[541] Speech by Margaret Cole, Director of Enforcement, FSA Securities House Compliance Officers Group, 29 June 2007 available on www.fsa.gov.uk.

[542] See eg FSA, Annual Report 2009/10, Section 2.

[543] FSA, Final Notice issued to Philippe Jabre and GLG Partners LP, 1 August 2006.

[544] *Davidson v FSA*, Financial Services and Markets Tribunal, Case 031 (2006).

[545] Ibid.

[546] J Coffee, 'Law and the Market: The Impact of Enforcement' (2007) 156 *University of Pennsylvania Law Review* 229.

brought by national regulators are compared. In particular, the number of public enforcement actions brought by the FSA are a fraction of those brought by the US regulator, even when those numbers are adjusted to reflect the relative market size of the two jurisdictions. The picture is even starker when the overall level of monetary sanctions imposed by the US and UK regulators are compared.[547]

The relative lack of enforcement observable in the UK might not be a cause for concern. For instance, the lower levels of enforcement activity would not be problematic if they reflected lower levels of market abuse occurring in the UK market. Or, alternatively, it could be that although the same levels of market abuse occur in the UK as in the US, they are being dealt with by the regulators in a different way. It has been compellingly argued that the style of regulation employed by the FSA is more informal than that employed by other national regulators, most notably the US.[548] It may be that the FSA is therefore dealing with market abuse in an informal manner which is not immediately observable to the public, although this would be surprising given the need for publicity to fulfil the goals of deterrence of potential market abusers and building confidence in the market generally. Alternatively it might be that the market is not intrinsically cleaner, but that fewer public prosecutions are needed by the FSA in order to create the deterrent effect sought by them.

Unfortunately, for all of these possibilities, a recent study commissioned by the FSA into the cleanliness of the UK's market reported significant levels of unusual price movements prior to takeover announcements for UK listed firms.[549] Share price movements ahead of such announcements may reflect insider trading, although it is possible that other factors, such as good guesswork by sophisticated investors, are also relevant. Worse, for the FSA, this study reported that the levels of these price movements occurring prior to takeovers had not decreased since the introduction of FSMA and in particular the introduction of the regulatory offence of market abuse in section 118. This suggests that although the level of enforcement engaged in by the FSA in tackling market abuse is greater than that which occurs under the criminal law regime, this has not affected the level of abuse carried out in the market. It would seem that neither the criminal regime nor the regulatory regime has had a significant deterrent effect.

The effect of these regimes on market confidence is more difficult to measure. Empirical research seems to demonstrate that market abuse regulations do have an impact on the cost of capital, not when they are adopted but when they are enforced.[550] This suggests that enforcement is important. However, the research suggests that cost of capital gains can arise even following relatively low levels of enforcement. Indeed that research found that the cost of capital decreases significantly even after the first prosecution. A small number of high profile prosecutions may not be enough to ensure deterrence, but seems to be enough to have a beneficial effect on cost of capital.

---

[547] Ibid.

[548] Armour, n 85.

[549] N Moneiro, Q Zaman and S Leitterstorf, 'Updated Measures of Market Cleanliness' FSA Occasional Paper No 25, March 2007. See also FSA, Market Watch, April 2008 and FSA, Annual Report, 2009–10, Section 2 (both documents available on the FSA website).

[550] U Battacharya and H Daouk, 'The World Price of Insider Trading' (2002) 57 *Journal of Finance* 75.

10.6 Conclusion

In terms of what the future holds for this area of financial regulation, the effect of the recent financial crisis has been to cause policy makers and legislators to re-examine the financial regulation regime generally. Most of the focus has however been on the banking sector, an area which falls outside the remit of this book, rather than on capital market regulation. This form of corporate financing, particularly equity securities which are the focus of this chapter, has not been regarded as key to explaining the financial crisis.[551] Discussion of the regulation of debt securities, and the effect of the financial crisis on that issue, is considered in the next chapter. As a result, the regulatory changes envisaged generally do not concern equity financing, at least in terms of the substantive changes proposed. In a speech given in June 2010 the Chancellor, George Osborne, suggested an end to the FSA in its current form.[552] He announced that from 2012 banking regulation will be transferred from the FSA to a new prudential regulatory authority, a legally separate but subsidiary part of the Bank of England. As regards the regulatory activity of the FSA that is described in this chapter, it is suggested that it will be carried out by a new Consumer Protection and Markets Authority, possibly with a new Economic Crime Agency being in control of criminal enforcement. The exact remit of these organisations remains unclear at the time of writing, but there is no suggestion that the rules governing ongoing disclosure or market abuse described in this chapter are going to change significantly. It is possible that the new authorities may have more energy and enthusiasm for enforcement, but again that remains to be seen. There are also significant changes planned at European level, but again these are predominantly going to impact on prudential and systemic risk issues rather than the issues discussed in this chapter.[553]

We saw in relation to IPOs in chapter nine that in that context regulators make use of two primary tools to deal with the potential danger of inaccurate information being provided by companies and their advisers. First, ex ante protections in the form of mandatory disclosure rules are created to try to ensure that accurate information is disclosed in the first place. Second, enforcement mechanisms are put in place to provide remedies in the event that the information is incomplete or inaccurate. It is clear that a similar pattern is observable in relation to capital market regulation once the securities are being publicly traded. However, there is an important distinction between the two stages. At the IPO stage the reason for imposing disclosure rules is straightforward: it is to provide investors with the information they need to decide whether to buy the securities. However, the reasons for imposing disclosure once shares are being publicly traded are more varied. Some disclosures are aimed at the shareholders and intend to provide them with the information they need to carry out their corporate governance functions. Other disclosures are aimed at investors more generally, and aim to ensure the 'smooth

---

[551] *The Turner Review,* n 15.

[552] George Osborne, Mansion House speech, 16 June 2010 and see *A New Approach to Financial Regulation,* n 349.

[553] European Commission, Proposal for a Regulation Establishing a European Securities and Markets Authority, COM (2009) 503 final, September 2009.

functioning of the market', either by providing investors with the information they need to make their investment decisions, or by preventing market abuse. Some disclosures may fulfil more than one of these functions.

As a result of the variety of functions performed by ongoing disclosures when compared to initial disclosures by companies, the regulatory regime in the context of ongoing disclosures is also more complex, as this chapter has examined. There is greater variety in the mandatory disclosure obligations imposed on companies as compared to the IPO stage. The timing of these obligations varies (some being periodic and some ad hoc), as does their content and focus. An understanding of the purpose of the disclosure helps to explain these differences. Both public and private mechanisms for enforcement are put in place to provide remedies in the event that this information proves inaccurate. The purpose of the disclosure is also important at this stage since different remedies may be available according to the purpose of the disclosure in question. While investors have a general statutory remedy for fraudulent misstatements, corporate governance-focused disclosures give rise to an additional common law remedy for shareholders. Again differences are observable between the IPO stage and the ongoing market. Investors have greater protection at the IPO stage, under s 90 FSMA, than exists at the later stage under section 90A, reflecting the fact that the prospectus is solely a selling document and that there is value in timely non-defensive disclosure.

The greater complexity of the ongoing market is also apparent in the fact that disclosure alone is not enough to ensure the smooth functioning of the ongoing market. Market abuse rules are also needed to tackle the problem of asymmetrical information as between insiders and outsiders. The presence of market abuse undermines investor confidence by undermining investors' beliefs that the market is fair and that market prices reflect the true worth of securities. Investors who believe that the system is being abused by insiders are likely to either withhold their investment or to build this risk into their investment decisions, by lowering the price they are prepared to pay for companies' shares. Either outcome will increase companies' cost of capital. Although the levels of enforcement of market abuse in the UK are low, empirical research suggests that even very low levels of enforcement can have a beneficial impact on cost of capital. The market abuse regime is therefore an important aspect of the ongoing regulatory regime.

11

Regulation of Debt

11.1 Introduction

So far we have considered how those who lend to companies[1] can protect themselves against credit and other risks by private adjustment. This can involve obtaining contractual and proprietary rights against the borrower or against third parties, but also by pricing the debt to reflect the risks. It can also involve a decision not to lend (or not to increase a loan) because the risks are too great. Although there are some non-adjusting creditors,[2] most creditors are able to adjust in some way. Should, then, the general law provide any protection for creditors? This issue has already been considered in certain contexts. Insolvency law provides limited protection for non-adjusting creditors,[3] and also by seeking to preserve the assets for *pari passu* distribution.[4] The legal capital rules seek to protect creditors, particularly those who cannot adjust, although their efficacy can be questioned.[5] This chapter considers the extent to which those lending to companies are protected by regulation, and the rationale behind the various kinds of regulatory protection.

Regulation can take a number of forms and can be directed at protection against different types of risk. The risk of collapse of a financial institution is a significant risk both for other financial institutions (who will be counterparties to transactions) and for borrowers (who may be counterparties, but who will also suffer from the lack of availability of credit, particularly if there is a 'knock-on' effect on other financial institutions).[6] This risk is, at least in part, addressed by the capital adequacy requirements, which are briefly described in chapter two,[7] as well as by requiring such institutions to be authorised and supervised by the FSA, and other more specific means. The regulation of financial institutions is outside the scope of this book, and is not discussed here. What is addressed is the regulatory response to the specific risks that lenders run in relation to loans made to corporate borrowers,[8] the most important of which is credit risk, that is,

---

[1] As in earlier chapters, the term 'lenders' encompasses all those who consciously extend finance to a company, including holders of debt securities, and 'loans' encompasses all finance extended. Where loan finance in particular is considered, this is made clear by the context.

[2] See 3.2.2.1 for a discussion of who these are.

[3] See 6.6.2.3.

[4] See 3.3.2.

[5] See chapter 4.

[6] Note as well that the collapse of financial institutions may affect those who finance them, which, in the case of commercial banks, will include consumers who deposit money with the bank. Depositors can be protected by deposit insurance, such as the Financial Services Compensation Scheme established by FMSA 2000, ss 212–224A.

[7] See pages 25–26.

[8] These risks are discussed in 3.2.2.2.

risk of non-payment. Many of those 'loans' are made by investors who purchase debt securities, some of which are traded on markets. In addition to credit risk, the holders of these debt securities run another risk: that the market is inefficient so that the price that they pay for the securities in the secondary market is 'wrong'. This risk is also run by the holders of equity securities, as discussed in chapter ten. The regulatory response to this risk in relation to debt securities is very similar to that applying in the equity markets.[9]

There are a number of ways in which lenders can be protected against credit risk through regulation. One is by requiring authorisation by the FSA for those involved in the transaction and by requiring authorised persons to comply with the detailed principles set out in the FSA handbook.[10] Thus, for example, those lending to banks by depositing money are protected by requiring banks to be authorised before they can accept deposits, which is a regulated activity.[11] This technique is rarely used in the context of corporate finance. The very limited extent to which a corporate borrower might be required to be authorised as accepting deposits is discussed below.[12] However, as with equity securities,[13] those who act as intermediaries in relation to issues of debt securities carry on regulated activities, for example, by advising on investments,[14] arranging deals in investments,[15] or managing investments,[16] and usually are required to be authorised.[17] This provides some limited protection for those lenders, in that it gives reassurance that these intermediaries will act in a proper manner, but it does not in itself moderate the credit risk of lending. Further, merely authorising persons to act does not of itself mean that they are competent, honest or reliable. What it does do is to give the FSA power to call for information or to intervene in those persons' affairs, and also (in theory at least) certifies that such persons are 'fit and proper' and have adequate resources to carry on the regulated activity in question.[18]

Allied to authorisation is the concept of affiliation discussed in 9.3.3.2 in relation to equity securities. In the context of debt finance, this involves limiting which companies can borrow in particular ways. Thus private companies cannot offer debt securities to the public[19] and there are further restrictions on which companies can list on the public markets.[20] The details of this regulation are discussed below.[21] Further, as with equity securities, there is, at least, a theoretical vetting by the FSA of companies who list debt securities on a public market.[22]

---

[9] See chapter 10. This issue is discussed in the market abuse section below.

[10] The authorisation regime administered by the FSA is complex, as is the relevant legislation. For a good and concise account, see J Benjamin, *Financial Law*, (Oxford, Oxford University Press, 2007) 10.2.

[11] FSMA, s 19; Financial Services and Markets Act 2000 (Regulated Activities) Order 2001 (SI 2001/544) ('Regulated Activities Order'), art 5. There is further protection for small-scale investors and consumers under the Financial Services Compensation Scheme, mentioned earlier.

[12] 11.5.

[13] See page 416.

[14] Regulated Activities Order, art 53.

[15] Regulated Activities Order, art 25. But note that the issue by a company of its own securities is not included: (Regulated Activities Order, arts 18 and 34).

[16] Regulated Activities Order, art 37.

[17] Benjamin, *Financial Law*, n 10, 10.28.

[18] See, for example, Part XI FSMA for the investigatory powers of the FSA, s 45 FSMA for the power of the FSA to revoke authorisation, and Schedule 6 FSMA for the 'threshold conditions' for authorisation.

[19] Companies Act 2006, s 755, discussed below.

[20] 9.3.3.2.

[21] See pages 539–40.

[22] See 9.3.3.1 for a discussion of this, which is a rather limited example of trusteeship.

A further means of regulation is to regulate particular types of transactions, in order to reduce the risks involved in those transactions, usually by supplementing or varying the general law. An important example of this technique is the rules relating to financial collateral, some of which are discussed in chapter six.[23] Another example is the regulation of covered bonds. These are bonds which, although payable by the issuer, are backed by a pool of assets belonging to the issuer which is ringfenced, so that if the issuer became insolvent, the payments on the bonds would continue to be made from those assets in priority to other creditors.[24] A further example is the regulation of the credit derivative market.[25]

However, the main method of regulation of debt is by requiring disclosure. Mandatory disclosure of information enables lenders to adjust more effectively in the ways described above, without incurring the costs of making their own detailed enquiries. Further, if disclosure is mandatory it will be uniform in relation to all the transactions for which it is mandatory, so that a potential lender can make a meaningful comparison between the risks of different transactions. One example of mandatory disclosure, the registration of security interests, has already been discussed.[26] This requirement of disclosure enables lenders to adjust in the light of security interests granted by the borrower, for example by refusing to lend at all, or by adjusting the price of the loan, or by taking security over unencumbered assets, or by entering into a priority agreement with the prior secured creditor.[27]

Registration of security interests is almost always effected by the secured creditor (even though the borrowing company is primarily responsible). However, in this chapter we will consider disclosure by the borrowing company itself. This is important at two stages. The first is when the lender is considering whether to lend. The disclosed information will enable the lender to decide whether to lend, and also (if this is possible) to adjust the terms on which the loan is made. Disclosure at this stage is equivalent to disclosure at the IPO stage in relation to shares.[28] The other stage is once the loan has been made, when ongoing disclosure will enable the lender to decide whether to lend more, and what steps, if any, it needs to take to protect itself from credit risk, for example, whether to transfer the debt to another lender, or whether to activate its contractual right to accelerate the loan or take other enforcement measures, or whether to involve itself in some other way in the governance of the company.[29] This is similar to ongoing disclosure in relation to shares.[30]

In the last paragraph, the discussion was in general terms which could relate to any sort of lender. However, the actual position differs markedly depending on the type of financing. If the finance is by way of actual loan (whether a term loan or a revolving facility)[31] or a type of asset-based finance, such as receivables financing,[32] asset-based

---

[23] See pages 224–25.
[24] These are regulated by Art 22(6) of EC Directive 85/611 on Undertakings for Collective Investment in Transferable Securities, enacted in the UK as Regulated Covered Bonds Regulations SI 2008/346 as amended by Regulated Covered Bonds (Amendment) Regulations SI 2008/1714.
[25] See pages 208–209.
[26] 6.4.
[27] 6.4.3.2.
[28] Discussed in chapter 9.
[29] See the discussion of the corporate governance role of creditors in 3.2.2.4.
[30] Discussed in chapter 10.
[31] 2.3.2.
[32] 2.3.4.1.

lending[33] or asset finance,[34] disclosure is not required by regulation. Instead, most lenders will, and are expected to, protect themselves by 'due diligence' enquiries and investigations into the financial state of the borrower, by relying on information from rating agencies[35] and often by including provisions in the financing agreement. These provisions (representations and warranties) will be structured as conditions precedent, non-fulfilment of which will entitle the lender not to lend. Further, if the loan has already been advanced, breach of the representations and warranties will be an event of default entitling the lender to accelerate the debt or sue for damages. After the loan has been made, lenders usually require continuing disclosure by including provisions in the agreement. All these provisions are discussed in chapter five above.[36]

Where the financing takes the form of an issue of debt securities, however, disclosure is required by regulation in some circumstances. One reason for this is that where debt securities are offered to the public, or are intended to be traded among investors in an active secondary market, it is largely the issuer who sets their terms and conditions. This is in contrast to those making loans, who either impose or negotiate terms and conditions, depending on the relative bargaining power of the parties.[37] Because the issuer wants the offer to succeed, the terms and conditions of the securities will to a great extent be determined by market norms and the forces of supply and demand. As discussed in 7.3.1, the issuer will often engage and pay an investment bank to advise it in this regard, and perhaps also to underwrite the offer. Whilst there may be scope for negotiation between the issuer and the underwriters regarding the terms and conditions of the debt securities, the ultimate investor faces a 'take it or leave it' proposition, both when the securities are initially issued and when they are traded afterwards in the secondary market.[38] In this regard, an offer of debt securities is not all that different from an offer of shares, and it gives rise to analogous investor protection issues. It should be pointed out, however, that, if the issuer is properly advised, the terms and conditions will reflect what the market will bear for that particular issue. To this extent, the investment bank advising the issuer will represent the interests of the investors by negotiating terms and conditions which will make the issue succeed in the market. Where there is significant credit risk, more contractual protection is likely to be included to make the debt securities more attractive to buyers.[39]

The basic difference between debt and equity, however, is that the holder of a debt security has a different set of rights and remedies from those of a shareholder. This issue is discussed extensively in chapter three. Broadly, a debt security typically gives its holder an absolute right to payment of interest and repayment of capital when due in accordance with the terms and conditions of the security, whereas a shareholder can only hope for payment of a dividend, or that there will be surplus assets available for distribution to him in a winding up after all the creditors have been paid off. Creditors will generally have

---

[33]   2.3.4.2.
[34]   2.3.4.3.2.
[35]   See page 166.
[36]   5.2.2.
[37]   See 5.2 for a discussion of the possible contractual rights a lender may have against a borrower.
[38]   See page 79 for a discussion of other reasons why there may be less contractual protection for bondholders than for those making loans.
[39]   For a discussion of the process of issue of debt securities, see 7.3.1.

powerful mechanisms to enforce payment of these sums.[40] By contrast, a shareholder's rights are much more limited, although to compensate for the residual nature of the shareholder's economic 'entitlements', shareholders are given various governance rights which are exercisable at least until the company is insolvent.[41]

Debt market regulation does not significantly alter the balance of contractual entitlements that holders of securities have against the issuer, although it does give them remedies against other persons involved in the transaction in certain circumstances.[42] By contrast, regulatory requirements that apply to the equity markets give shareholders additional remedial rights[43] and, in some circumstances, additional substantive governance rights over and beyond their rights under generally applicable law, such as the right, acting by majority, to veto certain transactions with related parties and substantial acquisitions or disposals.[44] However, debt market regulation does reflect the different balance of entitlements discussed in the previous paragraph. For example, the initial disclosure requirements, where debt securities are offered to the public or admitted to trading (whether on a regulated or merely on an 'exchange-regulated' market[45]), are less onerous than those for shares. There are a number of probable reasons for this. One is that equity is inherently more risky in nature than debt, since the shareholder only has a hope of gain rather than a right to repayment, and ranks behind all creditors if the company becomes insolvent.[46] Another reason, which does not stem from the inherent nature of debt securities, but just from the way that the market has developed historically, at least in the UK, is that corporate debt securities (as opposed to shares or government debt securities) are usually bought and traded by sophisticated investors:[47] this means that there can be a hierarchy of protection depending on the perceived ability of investors in particular issues to protect themselves.[48] This will be discussed later. A third reason for the disclosure requirements for debt securities being less onerous than those for shares is that it is possible for debt securities to contain contractual protection for the holders. This will vary according to the type of security, but in situations where the credit risk is high, there can be considerable contractual protection for bondholders.[49]

For debt securities, as with shares, there are regulatory rules relating to initial issues, and to ongoing disclosure. These will be considered separately below. It will be seen that much of the detail of the regulatory structure and requirements is the same as for shares. A great deal of what is said in chapters nine and ten will therefore apply here, and there is therefore extensive cross-referencing. The discussion below seeks to point out the differences and similarities between the regimes for equity and debt securities, some of the

---

[40]   These mechanisms are discussed in chapters 5 and 6. The position of non-adjusting creditors is discussed at 3.2.2.1.

[41]   For discussion see chapter 3, in particular 3.2.2.

[42]   See 11.2.7 and 11.3.2.

[43]   In particular see FSMA 2000, ss 90 and 90A, discussed at 9.5.2 and 10.4.1.2 respectively.

[44]   10.3.2.4.

[45]   11.2.1.2.

[46]   3.3.1.2.5.

[47]   See pages 31–32 for discussion of who invests in debt securities.

[48]   Indeed, that there is a sensible hierarchy of disclosure requirements is recognised by Article 21(2) of the Prospectus Directive Regulation (Commission Regulation (EC) No 809/2004) ('PD Reg'), which essentially provides such a hierarchy, so that the disclosure requirements that apply to shares will also apply to debt securities, but not *vice versa*. The hierarchy is (1) shares (2) retail debt securities and (3) wholesale debt securities. For definitions of these terms, see 11.2.1.3 below.

[49]   See page 79.

reasons for which are outlined above, and also to discuss the differences between the regulatory regime for debt securities and the position in relation to loans. The discussion focuses on the regulatory regime in the UK, although much of this derives from the implementation of EU legislation. It should be noted, though, that in the context of the debt markets, UK law has been considerably shaped by the desire to attract foreign companies to list debt securities on the UK markets.

11.2   Regulation of Initial Issue of Debt Securities

11.2.1   Introduction

Regulation of initial issues of debt securities by mandatory disclosure is effected by a structure that is basically the same as that for shares, and the reader is referred to the discussion in chapter nine for a full description.[50] The general rule is that it is unlawful to offer transferrable securities to the public, or to request their admission to trading on a regulated market, unless an approved prospectus (meeting the requirements of the Prospectus Directive[51] and Prospectus Directive Regulation[52] as they have been implemented in the UK,[53] and referred to in this chapter as a 'PD prospectus'[54]) has been made available to the public before the offer or request is made.[55] If a PD prospectus is not required, disclosure pursuant to the Listing Rules stipulated by the UK Listing Authority (the 'Listing Rules') may nevertheless be required.[56] These two criteria, 'offering to the public' and 'admitted to trading on a regulated market' are discrete, and each has its own exceptions and qualifications. It is the ability of an issuer to take advantage of these exceptions and qualifications which is discussed in the paragraphs below.

However, there are considerable differences in the disclosure requirements applicable to an initial issue of debt securities, depending on a number of factors. Most of these factors are in the control of the issuer, who has to make various choices. The first choice is to whom the securities are to be offered, the second is whether the securities are to be traded on a market, and, if so, which one, and the third is the size of the denomination of the securities. Basically, the most onerous requirements apply where the securities are

---

[50]   9.4.1 and 9.4.2. The detailed requirements for debt securities are set out in Articles 7, 8, 12 and 16 of the Prospectus Directive Regulation, reproduced in PR 2.3 and Annexes IV, V, IX and XIII of the Prospectus Directive Regulation (reproduced in PR 2.3.1).

[51]   Directive 2003/71/EC. Note that amendments to the Directive have been agreed, and will come into force later in 2010, which will mean that the Prospectus Rules will have to be amended in due course. See Amending Directive, Council of the European Union, 10254/2010 (passed by a resolution of the European Parliament on 17 June 2010) ('the Amending Directive'). The only significant amendment in relation to debt securities is the denomination threshold for wholesale securities, see 11.2.1.3 below.

[52]   Commission Regulation (EC) No 809/2004.

[53]   FSA Handbook, Prospectus Rules ('PR').

[54]   Note that in chapter 9 reference is simply made to a prospectus rather than to a PD prospectus. This is because chapter 9 focuses on the listing of shares on the Main market, where a prospectus complying with the Prospectus Directive is required ie all references to prospectuses in chapter 9 are PD prospectuses. No other form of prospectus is discussed in chapter 9 and therefore there is no need to differentiate a PD prospectus from any other type.

[55]   FSMA 2000, s 85(2).

[56]   For a summary of when each requirement applies, see below page 541.

intended to be offered to, or traded among, retail investors, either as part of the initial offer or following admission to trading on a regulated market. The issuer can therefore choose to limit the issue to sophisticated investors, and/or list the securities on an exchange-regulated market, and thereby avoid the more onerous disclosure (although some disclosure still has to be made). Unlike offers of shares, where the issuer usually wishes to access the widest possible number of investors, and so little use is made of the exceptions to the rules,[57] many issuers of debt securities make a 'public offer' only to qualified investors, and list the securities on the Professional Securities Market,[58] so as to attract the less onerous regime.

Of course, where the issuer is a UK public company whose shares are admitted to the Main Market, it will have had to produce a PD prospectus when making the IPO[59] and it will have to comply with ongoing disclosure requirements anyway.[60] Thus it might be thought that, for these companies, even the most onerous debt regulation regime does not add to their burden, and so there would be no point in trying to fall within the less onerous regime. However, it must be borne in mind that putting together a PD prospectus, even if some or all of the information is already public, can be costly and time-consuming. Bond issues are often put together very quickly, and so there may be advantages in not having to produce a PD prospectus.[61] There is one advantage, though, which might lead a company (especially one who is a repeat issuer) to choose to publish a PD prospectus. This is that a PD prospectus approved by the relevant competent authority in one EEA member state can be 'passported' to another EEA member state, enabling the issuer to list the securities on a regulated market or make a public offer there without having to produce another prospectus or listing document, perhaps in a different language and complying with different local rules.[62]

11.2.1.1   To whom the securities are offered

It will be recalled that a company can issue shares which are not offered to the public. A private company cannot issue shares to the public, and so can only offer them to specified persons, who may well be, and usually are, connected to the company in some way. However, as is discussed in chapter nine, it is often advantageous for a company to offer shares to the public. The same distinction applies to issues of debt securities. Since one of the purposes of a bond issue is to reach a wider base of lenders[63] than can be achieved through a loan structure, it might be thought that most issues would be to the public. To some extent, this is true, in that totally 'private' issues to those connected to public companies are rare.[64] However, debt securities, particularly Eurobonds, are often offered only to a specific group of sophisticated investors by means of a placing, as is stock,[65] and

---

[57] Examples of exceptions relating to shares are discussed at pages 425–26.
[58] Discussed below at page 540.
[59] The disclosure requirements for such a prospectus are discussed at 9.4.2 above.
[60] See 10.3.1 above.
[61] P Wood, *International Loans, Bonds, Guarantees, Legal Opinions*, 2nd edn (London, Sweet & Maxwell, 2007) 10–047.
[62] Prospectus Directive 2003/71/EC art 17. See further pages 412–13.
[63] For the advantages of a bond issue as against a loan, see 2.3.3.2.
[64] Loan notes, however, are often issued to shareholders of private companies, particularly in private equity transactions. See 14.4.2.
[65] See page 324.

so there is no offer to the public. It should also be remembered that debt securities are typically purchased by institutional or other financial institutions rather than by individuals or other retail investors.[66] If this is the case, even if there is technically an offer to the public, the need for onerous disclosure is less apparent, and thus there are various exceptions to the application of the disclosure requirements where the investors are sophisticated.

For the purposes of the mandatory disclosure requirements, an offer of transferable securities to the public is defined in section 102B of FSMA 2000 as a communication to any person which presents sufficient information on the securities and the terms on which they are offered to enable an investor to decide to buy or subscribe for the securities. This definition is extremely wide, but there are certain exceptions which narrow down its application considerably. This is because the requirements of the Prospectus Rules do not apply to offers that fall within an exception (unless the securities are also admitted to trading on a regulated market,[67] in which case the Prospectus Rules do apply). Thus the issuer can avoid the application of the Prospectus Rules if the offer is made to 'qualified investors' only,[68] or to fewer than 100 persons per EEA state.[69] The other relevant exceptions relate to the size of the offer and the denomination of the securities and are discussed below.[70]

It should also be noted that the requirement to produce a prospectus may be triggered not only where securities are offered to the public by the issuer or someone on its behalf, but also by a third party to whom the securities have already been allotted (eg an underwriter).[71] Indeed, the means by which debt securities usually find their way into the hands of retail investors is via the so-called 'retail cascade', which is a process by which the debt securities are initially issued to the underwriters, who in turn sell them on to other distributors, who ultimately sell them to retail investors. Where the secondary offeror is not 'acting in association' with the issuer, the issuer is not obliged to prepare a PD Prospectus,[72] but the secondary offeror is so obliged, unless a valid prospectus is already available and the person responsible for that prospectus 'consents to its use as explicitly stated in the prospectus'.[73]

The criterion of whether an offer is 'an offer to the public' is also used to trigger a separate form of regulation which is not based on disclosure. Section 755 of the Companies Act 2006 prohibits public offers of securities (both debt and equity) by private companies. The term 'offer to the public' is defined in section 756 and includes all offers of securities made to any section of the public except where the offer is made just to persons receiving the offer,[74] and/or just to persons connected with the company.[75] In relation to

---

[66]   This, though, is changing, see pages 31–32.
[67]   Ie the GEFIM, see 11.2.1.2 below.
[68]   FSMA, s 86(1)(a).
[69]   Ibid, s 86(1)(b). See pages 425–26 for further discussion.
[70]   See page 541.
[71]   See pages 324–25.
[72]   See Question 54 of the CESR document, 'Prospectus Directive: FAQs' (July 2010), available on CESR's website: www.cesr-eu.org.
[73]   This is clarified by an amendment to the Prospectus Directive contained in the Amending Directive, art 1(3)(b).
[74]   Companies Act 2006, s 756(3). In theory this exception would include a situation where an offer was made personally to thousands of people, but it seems that it is intended only to apply where the offer is made personally to a small group of people.

debt securities, it can be seen that the prohibition in section 755 protects potential investors by requiring a particular level of corporate governance and administration, and a minimal level of legal capital,[76] from a company offering such securities.[77]

11.2.1.2   Trading on a Market

Whether or not debt securities have been offered to the public, the issuer may well wish them to be traded on a secondary market operated by the London Stock Exchange ('LSE'), which will involve them being listed.[78] The benefits of listing are discussed in chapter seven,[79] where it is pointed out that even listed bonds are usually traded over the counter, but that the listing is important since many institutional investors are not permitted to invest in non-listed securities.[80] The main reason for this is the protection provided by the regulatory requirements of listing, which are discussed below.

The issuer, then, must choose whether the debt securities should be admitted to trading on a 'regulated market', to trading only on an 'exchange-regulated market',[81] or not admitted to trading on any market at all. In the UK, the LSE's regulated market for debt securities is known as the Gilt-Edged and Fixed Interest Market, (referred to in this chapter as 'the GEFIM'[82]), and its exchange-regulated market for debt securities is the Professional Securities Market ('the PSM'). Both the GEFIM and the PSM are accessible to issuers incorporated in the UK or anywhere else in the world. Where debt securities are admitted to trading on the GEFIM, a PD prospectus is required, but it is not for those securities admitted to trading on the PSM (unless the securities are 'offered to the public' as discussed above). However, 'listing particulars' will be required where the securities are to be admitted to trading on the PSM.

The choice of market, however, is not totally free. To list on both markets, the securities must be admitted to the Official List of the UKLA. The process and requirements are very similar to those for equity securities, which are discussed in chapter nine.[83] One difference in the requirements is that debt securities may only be admitted if their aggregate expected value on admission will be at least £200,000,[84] while the equivalent amount for shares is £700,000.[85] Since the creation of the 'premium' and 'standard' listing categories, all listings of debt securities will be standard listings.[86] This means, among other things, that the issuer is not required to appoint a sponsor, which it would be required to do in many circumstances in relation to a premium listing of its shares.

---

[75]   Ibid, s 756(4). This includes shareholders and employees of the company and their immediate relatives or trustees, and existing debenture holders of the company (s 756(5)).

[76]   See page 410.

[77]   There is further discussion about the difference between private and public companies at pages 417–18.

[78]   This means that they will have to be admitted to the Official List of the UKLA, discussed at page 414. As pointed out at pages 412–13, issuers can list on any market anywhere in the world if they wish. This chapter will only consider listing on the two LSE markets.

[79]   See pages 326–27.

[80]   A further important reason is that listed Eurobonds are exempt from the requirement to withhold tax on interest at source, see page 327.

[81]   Sometimes described as a 'multilateral trading facility'.

[82]   This is also often called the 'Main Market' but since this term is potentially confusing with the use of 'Main Market' in chapters 9 and 10 to refer to the main equity securities market, this term will not be used here.

[83]   9.3.3.1 and 9.3.3.2.

[84]   FSA Handbook, Listing Rules, LR 2.2.7(1)(b).

[85]   FSA Handbook, Listing Rules, LR 2.2.7(1)(a).

[86]   LR 1.5.1. See the discussion at page 412.

11.2.1.3 Denomination of Securities

The Prospectus Directive recognises that some kinds of debt security are usually only bought and traded among sophisticated investors, and the view was taken that such investors were less deserving of the protection provided by mandatory initial disclosure requirements. The size of the denomination of the securities is used as a rather crude proxy for the sophistication of the investors. The critical difference is between securities with a denomination of at least €50,000 (so-called 'wholesale' debt securities) and those with a lower denomination (so-called 'retail' debt securities).[87] Where the Prospectus Rules apply,[88] a different disclosure regime applies to wholesale debt securities ('the wholesale regime') to that applying to retail debt securities ('the retail regime'). As discussed below, the disclosure requirements under the retail regime are more onerous then those under the wholesale regime. Denomination is also relevant to whether the securities are 'offered to the public' within the definition in section 102B of FSMA 2000.[89] Securities are not 'offered to the public' if they are wholesale securities[90] or if the total consideration for the securities offered cannot exceed €100,000.[91]

11.2.2 The Regulatory Regime in Outline

To summarise, then, if debt securities are admitted to trading on the GEFIM, a PD prospectus is required whether they are offered to the public or not.[92] The actual content of the requirements for a PD prospectus will vary depending on whether the wholesale or retail regime applies. If securities are admitted to trading on the PSM, a PD prospectus will be required only if the securities are offered to the public, and one of the exceptions to the 'public offer' requirement for a PD prospectus (discussed above) does not apply. This, though theoretically possible, is unlikely to happen since an issuer seeking to list its securities on the PSM will wish to make sure that the issue does fall within one of those exceptions. If a PD prospectus is not required, the issue is only required to publish 'listing particulars' pursuant to the Listing Rules. If the securities are not listed, then a PD prospectus will only be required if they are offered to the public and none of the exceptions apply. Otherwise, the only possible regulatory regime is that applying to financial promotion.[93] It would be very unlikely for debt securities to be 'offered to the public' but unlisted, since if it is sought to access a wide market on issue, it is likely that the issuer will wish to continue to access the widest possible number of potential investors in the secondary market.[94] Further, many institutional investors would not be able to buy unlisted securities: thus issues would normally be listed unless issued to a small group of

---

[87] This will be increased to €100,000 when the Amending Directive takes effect.
[88] Where the securities are admitted to trading on the GEFIM and/or where there is an offer to the public.
[89] See 11.2.1.1 above.
[90] FSMA 2000, s 86(1)(d)
[91] FSMA 2000, s 86(1)(e). The Amending Directive clarifies that the €100,000 'total consideration' condition refers to the total consideration for securities offered throughout the European Union, not in each member state.
[92] There are some limited exceptions to this, listed in FSMA 2000, Sch 11A, para 9 such as where the total consideration of the offer is less than €2,500,000 (FSMA 2000 s 85(5)(a)). The same is true for equity securities, see pages 425–26.
[93] Discussed below at 11.2.6.
[94] For further advantages of listing, see pages 326–27.

specific investors who are planning to hold the securities to maturity and are unlikely to want to trade them in the secondary market.

It will be seen, therefore, that the most onerous disclosure requirements, and therefore the most protection for lenders, comes where retail debt securities are offered to the public (and when none of the exceptions to the requirement for prior publication of a PD prospectus apply) and/or are traded on the GEFIM. The rationale for this seems similar to that for mandatory disclosure in relation to equity securities, namely that investors need information in order to decide whether to purchase the securities, and that mandatory disclosure is the most cost effective method of achieving this.[95] However, where investors are 'sophisticated' (either because they are 'qualified investors' or because the denomination of the securities is high) the disclosure requirements are less onerous.

There seem to be various reasons for this. First, the sophisticated investors are able to make their own enquiries, if they wish, and therefore it is less cost effective to require extensive mandatory disclosure. Second, sophisticated investors are repeat players, and know, better than retail investors, what information is required. Third, sophisticated investors are generally investing large amounts of money, so that it is more cost effective to make their own enquiries. Fourth, large investors can, if there is doubt about the credit-worthiness of the issuer (which will appear from the issuer's rating[96]), put pressure on those drawing up the terms of the securities to include more contractual protection, at least indirectly through indicating what the market will bear. It should be remembered that institutional investors are often pension funds, investment trusts or other asset managers who are investing on behalf of retail investors. Therefore those making the investment decisions are under stringent duties to scrutinise how they invest the institutions' funds.

Given that less protection is needed for such investors, there is a strong argument to reduce the amount of disclosure required, since disclosure is expensive and time-consuming.[97] Bond issues are often put together very quickly, and extensive disclosure requirements where they were not needed would have a very detrimental effect on the market.[98] Thus, the level of regulation should take into account the needs of issuers as well as the protection of the investors. In the end, at least where sophisticated investors are concerned, the optimal extent of regulation is a matter of balance: on whom should the burden of discovering information lie? It may be thought that, in relation to sophisticated investors in debt securities, this is an open question: that is, it does not really matter what the answer is, since the market will find its own equilibrium. However, there is one additional compelling point, made in chapter nine,[99] which probably tips the balance towards at least some mandatory disclosure. This is as regards the benefits of standardisation. This is beneficial for investors, since they are in a better position to compare different

---

[95]   See the argument at 9.3.3.3.

[96]   See pages 32–33 and 11.7.

[97]   The cost of compliance is felt particularly by companies with small market capitalisations, which may deter them from going to capital markets just at the point in their development where they need access to wider pools of capital. The European Commission has estimated that reducing the initial and ongoing disclosure requirements for such companies can be expected to generate overall savings of €173 million every two years. Additional simplification measures addressing other aspects of the regime are expected to create total savings of up to €302 million annually. (See the European Commission's proposal of 23 September 2009 for a directive of the European Parliament and of the Council amending Directives 2003/71/EC and 2004/109/EC).

[98]   Wood, *International Loans, Bonds, Guarantees, Legal Opinions*, n 61, 10–047.

[99]   See page 423.

possible investments. It is also beneficial for both issuers and investors, in that they know that they are on a 'level playing field' with others. Further, it reduces transactions costs, which makes the markets more efficient, and increases transparency, which increases investor confidence.

It should also be borne in mind that there are regulatory ways of protecting investors other than mandatory disclosure per se. When obtaining a rating for an issue of debt securities,[100] the issuer is likely to disclose more to the rating agency than it is compelled to do under the mandatory disclosure rules. This information, then, is distilled for the market through the intermediation of the rating agency. It will only be of benefit to the market if the rating agency gets the rating 'right'.[101] The role played here by the rating agencies raises the question whether such agencies should be regulated: this is discussed below.[102] Further, retail investors often rely on financial intermediaries to advise them in their investments. Mandatorily disclosed information is then used by those intermediaries in giving their advice, so that these intermediaries are also a means of disseminating the information to the actual investors. Thus these intermediaries, too, need to be regulated. As discussed earlier, they are required to be authorised by the FSA.[103]

11.2.3 Information Required in a PD Prospectus

The form of the required prospectus varies according to whether the securities are issued as part of a programme, or as a 'stand-alone' issue. As explained in 7.3.1, plain 'vanilla' issues of securities are usually issued under a programme, where much of the documentation is drafted in advance of the issue, and then specific updated documentation added for each issue. The Prospectus Rules facilitate this, by permitting an issuer of debt securities under a programme to use a 'base prospectus', supplemented, if necessary, by a 'final terms' document.[104] Where there is a 'stand-alone' issue (which tends to be the position where more negotiation of terms is required, for example, for high yield bonds) all the information must be contained either in a composite prospectus, or in a prospectus consisting of separate documents and divided into a registration document, a securities note and a summary.[105]

It will be recalled that, in order to provide useful disclosure to investors in shares, the information in a prospectus must be presented in a comprehensible form which is easy to analyse, and that, to further this aim, a summary must be provided.[106] There is a similar requirement in relation to retail debt securities, but not for wholesale debt securities provided the prospectus is published in connection with an admission to trading (as opposed to a public offer).[107] This is obviously consistent with the policy discussed earlier, in that sophisticated investors are more able to process complicated information, since they have expert analysts at their disposal.

---

[100] This refers to a solicited rating, which is paid for by the issuer, see page 32.
[101] Often an institutional investor will be required to invest in securities of a certain rating, see below, 11.7.
[102] 11.7.
[103] Page 533 above.
[104] PR 2.2.7. A similar structure is permitted where the securities are issued in a 'continuous or repeated manner' by a credit institution.
[105] PR 2.2. A summary is not required for issues of wholesale securities.
[106] See page 426 in relation to shares.
[107] PR 2.1.3; Article 5(2) of the Prospectus Directive.

In terms of actual content of mandatory disclosure, there are, broadly, three levels required in a PD prospectus. The highest level is for an issue of shares, the next highest for retail securities and the least onerous is for wholesale securities. The reasons for this have already been explored: a few examples will now be given to illustrate the point. It needs to be pointed out, however, that there is a considerable degree of overlap between all three regimes, so that, for example, all three share the overriding purpose that the prospectus must contain 'all information necessary to enable investors to make informed assessment of assets and liabilities, financial position, profit and losses and prospects of issuer and any guarantor, and of rights attached to securities'.[108] The differences between the retail and wholesale debt regimes are largely in the amount of detail which must be disclosed in order to comply with this overriding purpose.[109]

For example, one area of difference relates to the disclosure of audited financial information. In the case of shares[110] and retail debt securities,[111] this information must be presented in accordance with International Financial Reporting Standards (IFRS) or an equivalent standard,[112] while for issues of wholesale debt securities, the accounts can be presented in accordance with the issuer's national accounting standards, provided that the prospectus includes a prominent statement that this is the case and a description of the key differences between the accounting standards used and IFRS.[113] At the time of the Prospectus Directive, the requirement to present or restate in accordance with IFRS was onerous for non-EEA issuers. This was one of the main reasons for the retention of the PSM as an exchange-regulated market, to which the Prospectus Rules did not directly apply.[114] It may be expected that as accounting standards around the world converge, the significance of this point diminishes. The information must cover the past three years in the case of a share issue, but only the last two years in the case of a debt issue.

There are considerable areas of disclosure which are required under the retail regime but not at all under the wholesale regime. These include disclosure of selected historical financial information including key figures that summarise the financial condition of issuer,[115] information on trends, uncertainties, demands, commitments or events reasonably likely to have a material effect on the issuer's prospects for at least the current financial year[116] and information about the issuer's board practices.[117] Interestingly, the retail regime also requires disclosure of principal recent and future investments made and to be made by the issuer, and information regarding the anticipated sources of funds needed to fulfil investment commitments.[118] Since investments may generally be funded either from internal cash flows or by issuing new debt or equity securities, the holders of debt securities will be interested to know whether their claims may be diluted by the

---

[108]   FSMA 2000, s 87A(2), implementing Prospectus Directive art 5(1). For shares, see pages 426–27 above.
[109]   It should also be pointed out that a different type of disclosure is required for asset-backed securities: this relates more to the assets themselves than to information about the issuer (see PD Reg Annexes VII and VIII).
[110]   PD Reg Annex I, para 20.1.
[111]   PD Reg Annex IV, para 13.1.
[112]   The disclosure of accounts is discussed at page 427, and the requirements of IFRS are described at pages 477–78.
[113]   PD Reg Annex IX, para 11.1.
[114]   Unless there is an offer to the public (and none of the exceptions apply), which is very unlikely, see pages 541–42 above.
[115]   PD Reg Annex IV, para 3.1.
[116]   PD Reg Annex IV, para 8.2.
[117]   PD Reg Annex IV, para 11.
[118]   PD Reg Annex IV, para 5.2.

company incurring further debt ranking equally with, or ahead of, their own claims.[119] However, the danger of claim dilution can also be addressed through covenants.[120] Although extensive covenants are unlikely to be included in most debt securities, a negative pledge covenant preventing the issue of secured bonds into the same market is very common.[121]

An example of where the regime differs between issues of shares and debt securities is in relation to the disclosure of risk. Where the prospectus relates to an issuer or offer of shares, the issuer must disclose risks which are specific to the issuer or its industry,[122] whereas in the case of both wholesale and retail debt securities, the issuer need only disclose risk factors that may affect the issuer's ability to fulfil its obligations under the securities.[123] This follows logically from the fact that debt is less risky than equity, in the sense that payment of interest is usually an obligation, whereas an investor can only hope for payment of a dividend, and also that holders of debt securities have more effective means of enforcing the repayment obligation owed to them if the company gets into difficulties than shareholders have. Other types of disclosure which are required for shares,[124] but not for debt securities, include more extensive information about the issuer's business,[125] information about its property, plant and equipment,[126] its capital resources,[127] its senior management's remuneration and benefits,[128] and its employees.[129]

11.2.4   Disclosure Required for Listing on the PSM

If debt securities are listed on the PSM but are not offered to the public (or fall within one of the 'public offer' exceptions) then a PD prospectus is not required. Instead, the issuer is required to publish approved 'listing particulars'.[130] The general purpose of disclosure under this regime is the same as under the Prospectus Rules, namely the disclosure of all information 'necessary to enable investors to make informed assessment of assets and liabilities, financial position, profit and losses and prospects of issuer and any guarantor, and of rights attached to securities'.[131] The actual content of the disclosure requirement is generally the same as that under the wholesale regime applicable to a PD prospectus. However, under the Listing Rules regime there is no distinction in the requirements between retail and wholesale securities.[132] Thus an issuer who wishes to issue securities

---

[119]   The danger of claim dilution is discussed at pages 76–77 above.
[120]   See 5.2.1.
[121]   See pages 160–61.
[122]   PD Reg Annex 1, para 4, see pages 427–28.
[123]   PD Reg Annex IV, para 4 (retail debt) and Annex IX, para 3.1 (wholesale debt).
[124]   See pages 427–28.
[125]   Compare Annex 1, paragraph 6 (shares) with Annex IV, paragraph 6 (retail debt) and Annex IX, paragraph 5 (wholesale debt). In the case of shares, the issuer must provide detailed information about its principal markets, with revenues broken down by category of activity and geographically for each year for the period covered by the historical financial information.
[126]   Annex 1, para 8 (shares) (no equivalent for debt securities).
[127]   Annex 1, para 10 (no equivalent for debt securities).
[128]   Annex 1, para 15 (no equivalent for debt securities).
[129]   Annex 1, para 17 (no equivalent for debt securities).
[130]   These are in accordance with the Listing Rules, approved by the UKLA and published (s 79 FSMA). The content requirements for listing particulars are set out in LR 4.
[131]   FSMA 2000, s 80(1).
[132]   LR 4.2.4.

with a denomination of less than €50,000 (in order to access the widest possible number of potential investors[133]) could list the securities on the PSM and avoid the more onerous retail regime applicable on the GEFIM.

11.2.5   Disclosure Requirements Where Securities are Not Listed

If the debt securities are not to be admitted to trading on any market at all, then neither a PD prospectus nor listing particulars are required unless there is an offer to the public, in which case a PD prospectus would be required. Therefore, issuers and their advisers will take care to ensure that the issuer and other persons connected with the financing do not inadvertently make an offer to the public. To achieve this, any hint of a public offer will be strenuously disclaimed in the documents relating to the securities, and 'selling restrictions' will be incorporated into the terms and conditions of the debt securities that are intended to ensure that the offer falls within one of the public offer exemptions.[134] However, even if there is no offer to the public, it is still possible that dissemination of material used for marketing such securities would constitute 'financial promotion' in which case the issuer would need to be authorised, or have the content of the promotion approved by an authorised person, such as an investment bank, so as not to contravene section 21 FSMA.

11.2.6   Restrictions on Financial Promotion

Whether an issue of debt securities is listed or not, there may be materials produced in respect of the issue which are not included in a PD prospectus or listing particulars. There are potentially other restrictions which apply to such materials. If the Prospectus Rules apply, any advertisements must state that a prospectus will be issued, tell the readers where to find the prospectus and make it clear that investment decisions should be based on the prospectus and not on the advertisement.[135] Further, any invitations or inducements to participate in investment activity must be approved by a person authorised under the FSA regime (such as an investment bank) unless one of the exemptions apply.[136] In order to be approved, the material has to comply with various onerous requirements,[137] and borrowers usually take steps to make sure that any materials produced are exempt. It should first be pointed out that 'investments'[138] which fall within 'investment activity' are basically debt and equity securities, and not bank loans. Having said this, the term 'debenture' is included in the definition, under the heading 'instruments creating or acknowledging indebtedness'.[139] There is no definition of 'debenture' in FSMA or any of the statutory

---

[133]   These would have to be qualified investors, in order to fall within the exception to 'offer to the public' in FSMA 2000, s 86(1)(a), see page 539.

[134]   Discussed above at page 539 and pages 425–26.

[135]   PR 3.3.2.

[136]   FSMA 2000, s 21.

[137]   Set out in the FSA's Conduct of Business Sourcebook at COBS 4.

[138]   Defined in Schedule 1 of the Financial Services and Markets Act 2000 (Financial Promotion) Order 2005 SI 2005/1529 (the Financial Promotion Order).

[139]   Ibid, Financial Promotion Order art 15, Sch 1.

instruments issued under it,[140] and there is considerable disagreement whether a loan agreement falls within the term.[141] It makes sense, however, for loans not to be included in the term 'debenture', as this is consistent with the policy of not protecting lenders (as opposed to holders of securities) by regulatory means, but rather expecting them to protect themselves using contractual and other means.[142] Those making loans are usually banks or other large financial institutions who can be expected to look after themselves.[143] The uncertainty about the meaning of 'debenture', however, makes it even more important that borrowers, particularly when soliciting lenders for a syndicated loan, make sure that any information produced, such as an information circular, falls within one of the exemptions to the financial promotion restrictions.

The exemptions are wide ranging:[144] a few relevant ones are highlighted here. Any material required to be produced by the Prospectus Rules and the Listing Rules (except advertisements) is exempt,[145] as is information on how to obtain a prospectus.[146] The justification for this is clear: such material is already regulated by the mandatory disclosure rules discussed earlier.[147] Communications which are made only to investment professionals,[148] to overseas recipients,[149] or to high worth companies, or to unincorporated associations[150] are also exempt.[151] Again, this is consistent with the policy of not protecting those who can take care of themselves.[152] It can be seen that it is very unlikely that the restrictions would apply to the types of finance discussed in this book. Material produced in relation to debt securities will either be limited to sophisticated investors (in which case it will be exempt) or, if distributed to the public, will be in connection with a public offer of securities, which will attract the Prospectus Rules so that required material will be exempt. If material produced in relation to loans is prima facie included, this is very likely to be exempt where the loan is syndicated since those to whom the material is

---

[140]   There is a definition in section 738 of the Companies Act 2006, for the purposes of that statute, which provides that the term includes 'debenture stock, bonds and any other securities of a company, whether or not constituting a charge on the assets of the company'.

[141]   Those who argue that it does include A Berg, 'Syndicated Loans and the FSA' (1991) *International Financial Law Review* 27, who relies on a dictum by Lloyd J in *Slavenburg's Bank NV v Intercontinental Natural Resources Ltd* [1980] 1 All ER 955, 976 and see also G Fuller, *Corporate Borrowing: Law and Practice*, 4th edn (Bristol, Jordan Publishing Ltd, 2009) 17.4 and footnotes thereto. See, however, R Tennekoon, *The Law and Regulation of International Finance* (London, Butterworths, 1991) 124–27, M Hughes, *Legal Principles in Banking and Structured Finance*, 2nd edn (Hayward's Heath, Tottel Publishing Ltd, 2006) 2.2 and A Mugasha, *The Law of Multi-bank Financing* (New York, Oxford University Press, 2007) 11.51, who argue that since the making of the loan gives rise to the debt rather than the agreement, which may precede the loan by some time, the loan agreement is not an instrument which creates or acknowledges indebtedness. It appears that the FSA agrees with the latter view.

[142]   This is discussed below at 11.2.8.

[143]   See Benjamin, n 10, 10.59.

[144]   They are contained in articles 5 to 74 of the Financial Promotions Order.

[145]   Financial Promotion Order, art 70.

[146]   Financial Promotion Order, art 71.

[147]   11.2.3 and 11.2.4.

[148]   Financial Promotion Order, art 19.

[149]   Financial Promotion Order, art 12.

[150]   Financial Promotion Order, art 49.

[151]   For further discussion, see Fuller, *Corporate Borrowing*, n 141, 13.60–13.64.

[152]   Although it is not clear why this argument applies to investors who are overseas: this exception, however, is part of a raft of exemptions which relate to particular types of communication rather than particular types of recipients.

disseminated will be investment professionals and/or high worth companies. In any case, this is unlikely to happen. Borrowers who borrow from a single lender rarely produce promotional material in any event.

11.2.7   Enforcement of the Mandatory Disclosure Regime

11.2.7.1   Claims Against the Issuer

As with the regulation of initial offers of shares, an effective enforcement regime is important if investors are to be protected. Thus the discussion in chapter nine of the aims of enforcement[153] is largely relevant here. There are, however, some crucial differences in relation to enforcement by holders of debt securities. The first is, as mentioned above, that such holders have contractual (and sometimes proprietary) rights against the issuer in respect of the debt itself, and can enforce such rights.[154] Thus a holder of debt securities with a nominal value of £10,000 can sue for £10,000, provided that the obligation to pay has arisen. Holders of equity securities have no such right. All they have is a hope of a dividend or an ultimate surplus. Thus, when faced with misstatements in the prospectus, all they have are common law claims or claims under section 90 FSMA[155] giving rights to damages. Given the strength of the rights of bondholders in respect of the debt, other rights that a bondholder may have against the issuer itself (such as those arising under section 90) are less significant. However, a holder may not wish to enforce the ultimate debt. If an investor buys debt securities which are less valuable that he thought they were, because of inaccurate disclosure, his loss is not the whole value of the debt represented by the securities but the difference in value between what he paid for them and what they are really worth. Thus it is necessary to consider other remedies a holder may have against the issuer.

It should first be noted that, as with claims relating to equity securities, the best claim for an investor against an issuer is likely to be under section 90 FSMA, for the reasons given in chapter nine above.[156] The common law claims are not so straightforward. If the holder buys the securities direct from the issuer, there will be a contract of sale between them, and thus the holder will have a claim under section 2(1) of the Misrepresentation Act 1967.[157] If the holder actually bought from a manager or underwriter, so that the contract of sale was not with the issuer,[158] the position needs more discussion. Section 2(1) provides that there is a remedy 'where a person has entered into a contract after a misrepresentation has been made to him by another party thereto'. The contract here would have to be the debt contract represented by the securities. However, a holder of debt securities is unlikely to be a party to the contract represented by the debt securities: that is likely to be the legal owner of the global bond, who holds the benefit of the contract on

---

[153]   9.5.1.

[154]   The most significant contractual method is probably acceleration and termination of the payment obligation, which arises on an event of default and which is discussed in 5.2.3 above. Enforcement is, of course, often done by a trustee, see pages 345–46.

[155]   See 9.5.2.

[156]   See page 438.

[157]   There is also the possibility of rescission for misrepresentation, see pages 443–44.

[158]   See pages 324–25, and, for a comparison in relation to shares, pages 437–38.

trust for investors or intermediaries as the case may be.[159] Thus it is not at all clear that the holder has an action under section 2(1), although this is unlikely to matter, since it would be able to sue under section 90 FSMA, which, as pointed out in 9.5.2.1, is usually the claim most likely to produce a favourable result.

Were the holder to have an action under section 2(1) (for example, where there is a contract of sale between itself and the issuer), it would be subject to the defence that the issuer had 'reasonable ground to believe and did believe that the facts represented were true'. This reversal of the burden of proof makes a section 2(1) claim much more attractive than a claim based on common law negligence: further, there is a need to establish a duty of care in negligence under *Hedley Byrne & Co Ltd v Heller & Partners Ltd,*[160] which is not always straightforward. If the issuer was fraudulent, there is the possibility of a claim in deceit, although, if the measure of damages under section 2(1) is likely to be the same,[161] there seems little point in taking on the burden of proving fraud. There is also the possibility that the representation has been incorporated into the debt contract, but this is very unlikely. Incorporation would necessitate an intention of the parties that any misstatement would be a breach of contract, potentially giving the right to accelerate and enforce the debt. Given the uncertainty that this would lead to, a court would be very slow to find such an incorporation unless it were express, and, in fact, there is more likely to be a term expressly excluding it. Additionally, the amount of damages would be potentially different from that awarded in a claim for misrepresentation, as the expectation interest would be protected,[162] so again an issuer will try to avoid such liability. It would be possible to include provisions excluding liability for all the common law claims, except for fraud, in the contract between the issuer and the holder, but an exclusion provision would be subject to the reasonableness test under the Unfair Contract Terms Act 1977.[163]

11.2.7.2   Claims Against Other Parties

However, in many cases where a holder has suffered loss because of inaccurate disclosure, the issuer will be insolvent or near insolvent and so a claim against it is useless. In this situation, a holder would wish to sue another person connected with the issue of the securities, preferably one with a deep pocket. Possible contenders are the directors, professionals such as auditors or lawyers, the managers or underwriters of the issue, or the person from whom the holder bought the security (if not the issuer itself).[164] The liability of the seller of the security would be governed by ordinary contract law, and it is very unlikely that the contract of sale would include a warranty that the information in the prospectus or other offering circular was accurate. Further, there would not be a claim under section 2(1) of the Misrepresentation Act unless the seller made the inaccurate statement itself.[165] In relation to the other persons mentioned, the possible causes of

---

[159]   See the discussion in 7.3.2.3.2.

[160]   [1964] AC 465.

[161]   This depends on the status of the decision of the Court of Appeal in *Royscot Trust Ltd v Rogerson* [1991] 2 QB 297, which has been much criticised. See page 443 above.

[162]   See pages 441–42.

[163]   In relation to contractual liability, this would fall under s 3 in relation to negligent misstatement this would fall under s 2(2) and, in relation to misrepresentation, Misrepresentation Act 1967, s 3 would apply.

[164]   See P Wood, *Law and Practice of International Finance* (London, Sweet & Maxwell, 2008) 23–14.

[165]   This is a possibility if the seller were a manager or an underwriter.

action are deceit, negligent misstatement (since these persons are not party to any contract with the holder, so section 2(1) cannot apply) and under section 90 FSMA.

A claim under section 90 FSMA can be brought against anyone responsible for a prospectus or for listing particulars.[166] For debt securities, these are the same as for equity securities,[167] with the exception of the directors. Thus the directors can only be liable if they actually accept responsibility for the content of the prospectus or listing particulars, which is very unlikely to be the case. As pointed out in chapter nine,[168] it is likely that reporting accountants will be liable under section 90, but that other experts are likely to be exempt.[169] Managers and underwriters will only be liable if they assume responsibility in the prospectus.[170]

In order to bring a claim in negligence against any of these persons, the holder will have to establish a duty of care. The relevant case law has been discussed in chapter nine,[171] and it will be seen that the court will look particularly at the purpose for which the statement was made, the knowledge of the maker of the statement and the reliance of the recipient. In relation to statements made by persons other than an issuer in a prospectus or listing particulars, it would seem clear that those who are liable under section 90 because they have assumed responsibility will also owe a common law duty of care. Whether the duty of care is wider than this is open to doubt.[172] However, the facts of each case need to be considered, and an underwriter or manager might be liable for particular statements made, either within the prospectus or otherwise, on the same basis as arranging banks have been liable.[173] The question of whether those buying securities in secondary market would have any claim is also discussed in 9.5.2.2.

Where the prospectus rules apply, the public enforcement measures discussed in 9.5.3 also apply to issues of debt securities.

11.2.8　Comparison of Protection by Regulation for Holders of Debt Securities and Those Making Loans: Disclosure at the Initial Stage

As pointed out earlier,[174] those who provide finance through loans and by asset-based financing (who will be called 'lenders' throughout this section) face a similar credit risk in relation to the borrower to those purchasing debt securities. However, regulatory law

---

[166] PR 5.5 and FSMA 2000 (Official Listing of Securities) Regulations 2001 (SI 2001/2956) reg 6.
[167] See page 441.
[168] Ibid.
[169] PR 5.5.9.
[170] PR 5.5.4(2)(b).
[171] See pages 436–37.
[172] As pointed out at page 437, in one respect the duty of care is narrower than section 90 as it does not cover omissions.
[173] See the discussion in 7.4.3. and Wood, *Law and Practice of International Finance,* n 164, 23–25 and also A Hudson, *The Law of Finance,* (London, Sweet & Maxwell, 2009) 41–14–41–17. There have also been a number of recent cases concerning advice given by banks to clients when selling them investments, where the courts have rejected allegations that the banks owed a duty of care to investors when dealing in investments, both on the grounds that the investors were sophisticated, so that no assumption of responsibility was made (see *JP Morgan Chase Bank (formerly Chase Manhattan Bank) v Springwell Navigation Corp* [2008] EWHC 1186 (Comm)) and on the basis that any agreement between the parties which prevented duties arising or representations being made or relied upon was conclusive (see *Springwell* and also *Titan Steel Wheels Ltd v Royal Bank of Scotland Plc* [2010] EWHC 211 (Comm), David Steel J. Although not strictly on point, these cases demonstrate the unwillingness of the courts to impose liability on banks unless they actually assume responsibility).
[174] See pages 534–35.

provides no protection by mandatory disclosure for these lenders, who have to protect themselves totally by contractual means. This section will compare contractual protection relating to the lender's initial decision whether to lend with that provided to holders of debt securities by the regulatory regime discussed above.

It should first be pointed out that, when deciding whether to lend to a corporate borrower, a certain amount of information about that borrower is likely to be publicly available, and can be used by the lender in making its decision.[175] All companies have to produce annual reports and accounts, and there are more extensive disclosure requirements imposed on public companies, especially quoted companies.[176] Further, if the company's shares are listed on the Main Market, or if it lists retail debt securities on the GEFIM, much more frequent reports will be available.[177] There will also be information about any security interests granted by the company available from the Company Charges Register.[178] However, most lenders will want further information. A single lender is usually able to insist on information being provided by the borrower before it makes the decision to lend, so that it, or those acting on its behalf, can perform a 'due diligence' assessment of risk. Obviously, the amount of information required will vary according to the risk the lender is taking on (the size of the loan), the other protection a lender may have (such as a security or other proprietary interest, guarantees or other credit protection) and, maybe, the ability of the lender to monitor the activities of the borrower closely. The lender can protect itself against inaccuracies in the information provided by insisting that accurate information is a condition precedent of advancing funds,[179] and, in case the inaccuracies are not discovered until after the money is advanced, by requiring continuing warranties so that any inaccuracy, or material change, is an event of default.[180] As well as these contractual rights, the lender would also have the tort remedies of deceit, negligent misstatement and misrepresentation[181] discussed above, which could give rise either to an action in damages or to rescission of the loan agreement.[182] The issue of whether a lender would have an action in tort against any other persons, such as the bank who arranges a syndicated loan, is discussed in 7.4.4 above.

Providing that a lender can insist on obtaining information before it lends, it is in many ways no worse off than an investor protected by mandatory disclosure, and in some senses better off, since it can request the information that is really useful to it, rather than having prescribed information, which may not be ideal (for example, because it is historic[183]). However, there are also benefits in having a baseline of prescribed information, particularly where it is also possible to add to this baseline by negotiation. This is the position where loans are made under standard agreements, including, most obviously, those produced by the Loan Market Association.[184] As pointed out earlier, one of the benefits of regulation by disclosure is standardised information and enforcement rights: the LMA contract shows that this advantage can be obtained by private law means as well as

---

[175] See discussion at pages 166–67.
[176] See 10.3.1.1 for a full discussion.
[177] See 10.3.1.2.
[178] See 6.4.
[179] See page 167.
[180] See page 169.
[181] Under s 2(1) Misrepresentation Act 1967.
[182] 11.2.7.1.
[183] See pages 427–28 for a discussion of these issues in the context of equity securities.
[184] See page 358.

through regulation. There is a particular advantage in standardisation where the loans are to be traded, and the development of the secondary market in loans has meant that there are considerable similarities between the position of lenders and that of holders of debt securities.[185] Given this, it might be thought strange that the regulatory position is so different, even though a similar structure has developed contractually for loans. The differences provide an opportunity for regulatory arbitrage, particularly for well-informed and aggressive participants in the markets, such as hedge funds.[186] There are, however, limits to the use to which hedge funds (and others) can put information disclosed to them at the time of making a loan or purchasing a loan. These limits are imposed by the market abuse regime and are discussed below.[187]

11.3 Ongoing Regulation by Disclosure

11.3.1 Mandatory Ongoing Disclosure

Ongoing disclosure of information to the market is required for debt securities as it is for equity securities. However, the purpose of requiring such disclosure is mainly to protect investors (both existing and potential) and to preserve market integrity:[188] the additional purpose of promoting corporate governance, important in the context of equity securities,[189] is not really relevant here. As pointed out in 3.2.2.4, creditors can play a part in corporate governance, but this is largely through their reaction to breaches of covenants and events of default, and generally the information on which holders of debt securities, or the bond trustee, will act will be contractually required to be provided.[190] Having said this, many bond covenants will only require disclosure of information that is required to be disclosed by the Listing Rules, thus 'piggy-backing' on the statutory requirements,[191] unlike the more 'tailored' contractual requirements in syndicated loan agreements. The more limited role played by ongoing disclosure requirements in relation to debt securities is reflected in the scope of the disclosure required by regulation: material that is only relevant to corporate governance by shareholders is not required to be disclosed. It should be borne in mind, however, that such material will have to be disclosed anyway if the company lists its equity securities on the Main Market, or, to some extent, if it lists them on the AIM,[192] and also that certain material has to be filed at Companies House by every UK company pursuant to the provisions of the Companies Act 2006.[193] The disclosure

---

[185] See 7.4 above for a full comparison.
[186] See Benjamin, n 10, 10.6.
[187] 11.4.2.
[188] See the discussion at 10.2.1.2.
[189] See the discussion at 10.2.2.
[190] See 5.2.2.2. For a sample set of information covenants given to a bond trustee, see G Fuller, *The Law and Practice of International Capital Markets* (London, LexisNexis Butterworths, 2007) 8.106.
[191] Wood, *Law and Practice of International Finance*, n 164, 11–18.
[192] See 10.3 for a discussion of ongoing disclosure obligations. In particular all UK companies are required to file annual reports and accounts (see 10.3.1.1) although the content of these documents varies according to the size and complexity of the company.
[193] See page 477.

requirements applying to issuers which list debt securities on the GEFIM or the PSM are only likely to prove at all onerous to non-UK companies, or to companies whose shares are not listed.

Generally, most of the Disclosure and Transparency Rules ('DTR') apply to debt securities admitted to trading on either the GEFIM[194] or the PSM,[195] although the requirements are slightly different for each. This paragraph will take each category of ongoing disclosure discussed in 10.3.1 in turn. In relation to the first category (periodic reporting)[196] the requirements in DTR 4 of annual financial reports,[197] half yearly reports and interim management statements[198] apply to debt securities trading on the GEFIM unless the issuer only issues wholesale securities.[199] Where an issuer only lists debt securities on the PSM, it need only publish an annual financial report within six months of the relevant financial period.[200]

In relation to ad hoc disclosure requirements, the first category (disclosure of inside information)[201] is required for issuers of all debt securities listed on either market.[202] As regards disclosure of directors' shareholdings,[203] this is required where debt securities are listed on the GEFIM (as a regulated market)[204] but not where they are only listed on the PSM. There is no disclosure requirement equivalent to the disclosure of major shareholdings.[205] This is not surprising given that one of the main purposes of such disclosure is to give information to existing shareholders about possible takeovers. To the extent that the information is also useful to potential investors, it could be said that it was useful to potential bondholders as well as shareholders, but the benefit of this can be seen to be outweighed by the cost of disclosure in situations where it would not be disclosed anyway, that is, where the relevant issuer did not have shares listed on a regulated market in the UK. There is also, at the moment, no disclosure requirement in relation to the acquisition of major holdings of bonds.[206]

Further, none of the disclosure requirements imposed by the Listing Rules only on companies with a premium share listing apply to debt securities. As pointed out, all debt security listings are standard listings.

---

[194]   As a regulated market.
[195]   This is the case even though the PSM is not a regulated market, by virtue of LR 17.3.
[196]   10.3.1.1 and 10.3.1.2.
[197]   10.3.1.1.
[198]   10.3.1.2.
[199]   DTR 4.4.2. For a definition of wholesale securities, see 11.2.1.3 above.
[200]   LR 17.3.4.
[201]   See 10.3.2.1.
[202]   DTR 2, which applies to securities listed on the PSM by virtue of LR 17.3.9.
[203]   See 10.3.2.2.
[204]   DTR 3.
[205]   10.3.2.3.
[206]   There has been considerable discussion as to whether Article 65 of MiFID (Markets in Financial Instruments Directive 2004) should be extended to the bond markets. Initially both the Committee of European Securities Regulators (CESR) (in CESR/07–284b, June 2007) and the European Securities Market Expert Group (ESME) concluded that there was no market failure from lack of transparency and that no action needed to be taken. The CESR has since concluded, in the light of the financial crisis, that post-trade information would be useful to the market (CESR/09–348, July 2009) and has recommended to the European Commission that post-trade transparency for the bond markets should form part of the review of MiFID due to take place in 2011.

11.3.2   Enforcement of Ongoing Disclosure Requirements.

The discussion in 10.4.1.2 in relation to enforcement by investors of investor-focused disclosures applies also in the context of debt securities, both in terms of the common law enforcement and enforcement under section 90A FSMA. Similarly, where ongoing disclosure is required, the public enforcement discussed in 10.4.2 also applies. Since there is no obligation to make governance-based disclosures in relation to debt securities, the section on private enforcement of misstatements in that context[207] does not apply.

11.3.3   Comparison of Protection by Regulation for Holders of Debt Securities and Those Making Loans: Ongoing Disclosure

Most of what was said above[208] also applies to ongoing disclosure. Lenders are usually in a position to bargain for extensive information and monitoring rights, so that financial covenants in loans are usually far more extensive than those in debt securities. Information and financial covenants are discussed above in 5.2.2.2. Obviously, however, the disclosure of this information is for the benefit of those contractually entitled to it, that is, the lender or lenders. There is no general disclosure to the secondary loan market, and so prospective buyers of loans have to obtain the information they require by other means. This will usually entail obtaining at least some information from the seller of the loan. Since this information has been disclosed only to the seller, and may by its nature be sensitive information that has not been disclosed into the public sphere, the borrower requires some protection against disclosure without its consent. Traditionally this has come from the implied duty of confidentiality between bank and customer, so that the original lender, bound by such a duty, would need the borrower's consent to disclose information,[209] and a recipient bank would be under a similar duty of confidentiality.[210] However, now that so many non-banks such as hedge funds have entered the secondary loan market, an express confidentiality clause has been introduced into the LMA standard leveraged loan agreement[211] setting out when and to whom information can be disclosed, and providing that disclosure to transferees must be on condition that they enter into a confidentiality agreement.[212] How much information is actually required to be disclosed to the buyer by the seller of the loan does, of course, depend on the terms of the transfer agreement. A clause in a loan transfer agreement providing that a seller was not obliged to disclose certain information, and was not liable for any non-disclosure was held by the Court of Appeal to satisfy the test of reasonableness under section 2(2) of the Unfair Contract Terms Act,[213] on the grounds that the parties were of equal bargaining power and that such clauses promoted certainty. On this reasoning, it would seem that almost

---

[207]   10.4.1.1.

[208]   Pages 550–52.

[209]   Such consent was usually given in advance in the loan agreement, but on limited terms (Clause 29.8 of the pre-2008 LMA Leveraged Loan agreement).

[210]   K Meloni, 'Lender Confidentiality Undertakings: Recent Changes to LMA Facility Documentation' (2008) 24 *Journal of International Banking and Financial Law* 558.

[211]   Clause 42.

[212]   E Katz, 'Disclosure of Non-public Information in Loan Secondary Market Trading' (2008) 23 *Journal of International Banking and Financial Law* 585.

[213]   *National Westminster Bank v Utrecht-America Finance Company* [2001] EWCA Civ 658, [59]–[62].

any clause restricting a seller's liability in relation to the transfer of a syndicated loan would be likely to be held to be reasonable, since it would be seen as an agreed apportionment of the risks of purchase.

The dissemination of sensitive information in the secondary loan market also gives rise to concerns about market abuse, which will be discussed in the next section.

11.4   Regulation of Market Abuse

11.4.1   Application of the Market Abuse Rules to the Debt Securities Markets

Market abuse is just as possible in relation to the trading of debt securities as in relation to equity securities. As might be expected, both the criminal regime[214] and the regulatory regime[215] described in 10.5 apply to both debt securities markets discussed here, and little more needs to be said in this chapter about the substantive law or the policy arguments.

It should be pointed out, however, that the regulatory regime does not just apply to trades which actually take place on the market, but also to trades which take place over the counter ('OTC') which is the way a large amount of debt security trading takes place.[216] This appears to be so as to ensure a level playing field for the whole market: fairness would seem to require that all who trade in listed debt securities abide by the same standards, even though the trades are not technically on the market. Further, if OTC trades were not regulated, it would be very easy for those trading debt securities to avoid the market abuse regime altogether. In contrast, the criminal offence set out in part V of the Criminal Justice Act 1993[217] is limited to where dealing takes place on a regulated market[218] or where the person dealing relies on a professional intermediary or is himself acting as a professional intermediary.[219] The offence is primarily aimed at trading on formal markets, and the extension to cover dealings involving professional intermediaries was to cover deliberate attempts to avoid the scope of the legislation, rather than to cover all trading.[220]

---

[214] Criminal offence of insider dealing: The Insider Dealing (Securities and Regulated Markets) Order 1994 SI 1994/187 Reg 4 provides that Part V of the Criminal Justice Act 1993 (which creates the criminal offence of insider dealing) applies to any security which is admitted to trading on a regulated market. A regulated market is defined as any market which is established under the rules of a specified investment exchange (Reg 8), which includes the London Stock Exchange. Criminal offence of market manipulation under FSMA 2000 s 397: this applies to misleading statements or conduct in relation to 'investments' which are defined to include debt as well as equity securities (s 397(13)).

[215] The regulatory offence of market abuse (section 118 FSMA) applies to all 'prescribed markets' which includes the GEFIM and the PSM, as markets established under the rules of a UK recognised investment exchange (see Financial Services and Markets Act 2000 (Prescribed Markets and Qualifying Investments) Order 2001 (SI 2001/996), art 4). Qualifying investments are defined in art 5 of the same statutory instrument, and include all transferable securities including debt securities. See 10.5.2.3.

[216] See page 35 above. This is made clear by the FSA factsheet on market abuse, (June 2008).

[217] 10.5.2.1.

[218] This includes the PSM, see n 215 above.

[219] Criminal Justice Act 1993, s 52(3).

[220] PL Davies, *Gower & Davies' Principles of Modern Company Law*, 8th edn, (London, Sweet & Maxwell, 2003) 30–10.

There is one exception to the application of the market abuse rules, which is particularly important in the context of debt securities. This is in relation to the practice of stabilisation, which is described in chapter seven above.[221] The practice of stabilisation is seen as beneficial to the market by increasing confidence in the market pricing,[222] and so is seen as worthy of protection from constituting an offence by falling within two 'safe harbours'. Without these safe harbours stabilisation could constitute either of the criminal offences or the regulatory offence discussed in chapter ten.[223] One safe harbour applies to securities admitted to trading on the GEFIM,[224] provided that there is full disclosure to the market,[225] and that the stabilisation takes place within a limited time period and within a limited price.[226] The other safe harbour applies to debt securities admitted to trading on the PSM.[227] The requirements are similar to that pertaining to the regulated market, except that the public disclosure requirements are less rigorous.[228]

11.4.2   Application of the Market Abuse Rules to the Making and Transfer of Loans

The market abuse regime discussed above and in chapter ten does not apply to the secondary loan market itself, as it is not a regulated market nor is it subject to the FSMA regime. Thus those buying and selling loans in that market can make use of whatever information they wish, and any liability for misinformation will be contractual or tortious, and can be contractually excluded.[229] However, it is possible that a lender or a buyer may obtain information in the course of making a loan, buying a loan or as the owner of a traded loan, which has not been publicly disclosed to the debt and equity markets, and which that lender or buyer could use when entering those markets in a way contrary to the market abuse rules. For example, the purchaser of a loan to a private company may obtain non-public information about that company, and then, when the company makes an IPO of shares, may wish to subscribe for some of those shares.[230] This could count as insider dealing, contrary to section 118 of FSMA,[231] or potentially, even the criminal offence.[232] Similar problems could arise where a lender was given non-public information about a company when deciding whether to make the loan, and then wished to buy equity or debt securities which were already trading on a prescribed market.[233]

---

[221]   See page 326.

[222]   EU Stabilisation Regulation No 2273/2003 recital (11), set out in MAR 2.1.5.

[223]   See page 464 above.

[224]   Or any regulated market. The rules apply to equity securities as well, but stabilisation is particularly common in relation to Eurobonds, see Fuller, n 141, 13.71.

[225]   Usually via the RIS (Regulated Information Service), see page 482.

[226]   The details of the rules are set out in MAR 2.3, reproducing the terms of the EU Stabilisation Regulation, articles 8, 9 and 10.

[227]   These rules would also apply to other prescribed markets, and any listed in MAR 2 Annex 1.

[228]   The requirements of the EU Stabilisation are modified in MAR 2.4.

[229]   This would be subject to the Unfair Contract Terms Act, but it is likely that most exclusions would be held to be reasonable, see page 554 above.

[230]   For discussion of a similar example, see S Bowles and D Fox, 'Credit Markets and Market Abuse' (2007) 22 *Journal of International Banking and Financial Law* 209.

[231]   10.5.2.3.1.

[232]   10.5.2.1.3.

[233]   A prescribed market is a market to which the market abuse regime applies: here the Main Market for equities, and the GEFIM or PSM for debt securities.

There are various steps that can be taken to avoid lenders[234] being liable for market abuse in this way. One possibility, where the lender is a large organisation, is for a Chinese Wall to be set up between the part of the organisation dealing with lending or buying loans, and the part trading on the public markets.[235] Where the lender is smaller, this may not be possible, and the lender must either refrain from trading on the public markets, or limit the information it obtains qua lender to that which is publicly disclosed.[236] Requests by lenders for information provided to be 'scrubbed' of non-public information can be potentially very difficult for a borrower, and a practice has now developed whereby the lender agrees that a nominated third party will receive non-public information on their behalf.[237] Obviously, the more information that is disclosed publicly by the borrower, the less this question is a problem for the lender.[238]

11.5 Accepting Deposits

As mentioned above,[239] accepting deposits by way of business is a regulated activity under FSMA, and can only be carried out by an authorised (or exempt) person.[240] This is potentially relevant for debt finance, since the definition of 'deposit' is very wide and could include corporate loans or debt securities. However, there are a number of exclusions to the definition[241] which will usually mean that this form of regulation does not apply in the area considered by this book. The accepting of deposits is only a regulated activity if the money received by way of deposit is lent to others, or is used to finance the activities of the person accepting the deposit.[242] The first limb of this criterion clearly refers to the financing of banks and financial institutions, but the second limb could potentially refer to any type of corporate debt finance.[243]

A 'deposit' is defined as a sum of money paid on terms that satisfy both limbs of the following test.[244] First, the money is to be repaid on demand or at an agreed time and second, the payment of the money is not referable to the provision of property, services or the giving of security. The words 'giving of security' in the second part of that test do not mean that money received by way of a secured loan is not a deposit. Rather, what is envisaged is that the money is paid by way of 'security' for the performance of a

---

[234] The term 'lender' here includes those who purchase loans, such as hedge funds, as well as those who originate them, such as banks.

[235] Wood, n 164, 10–10.

[236] E Katz, 'Disclosure of Non-public Information in Loan Secondary Market Trading', (2008) 23 *Journal of International Banking and Financial Law* 585.

[237] A new clause has been inserted into the LMA Leveraged Loan agreement to this effect, see cl 32.13 and see further, E Katz, 'Disclosure of Non-public Information in Loan Secondary Market Trading' (2008) 23 *Journal of International Banking and Financial Law* 585.

[238] S Bowles and D Fox, 'Credit Markets and Market Abuse', (2007) 22 *Journal of International Banking and Financial Law* 209.

[239] See page 533.

[240] FSMA 2000 ss 19 and 22; Financial Services and Markets Act 2000 (Regulated Activities) Order 2001 (SI 2001/544) ('Regulated Activities Order') art 5. For details of the authorisation regime, see Benjamin, n 10, 10.2.

[241] Regulated Activities Order, arts 6–9.

[242] Ibid, art 5(1).

[243] Fuller, n 141, 10.9.

[244] Regulated Activities Order, art 5(2).

contract,[245] such as when a percentage of the purchase price is paid on exchange of contracts for the purchase of a house, which will be forfeit if the purchaser fails to complete, and returned if the seller fails to convey the property.[246] So, a secured loan or debenture can still be a 'deposit'. Indeed, the definition is so broad that, as Lewison J pointed out when considering the scope of the definition in *FSA v Anderson (No 1)*, 'to call something a loan is not inconsistent with its being a deposit'.[247]

However, most debt finance considered in this book will fall within one of the exceptions to the definition of 'deposit'. Sums received as consideration for the issue of debt securities are generally exempted,[248] as are sums paid by authorised financial institutions,[249] which means that most loans to companies will not be included.

11.6 Convertible Debt Securities

So far the discussion in this chapter of the regulation of listed securities has concentrated on debt securities. However, it will be recalled that securities can start life as debt securities and be convertible into equity securities, or can be exchangeable for equity securities.[250] The regulation of such securities reflects their hybrid nature, and is discussed in this section.

Convertible debt securities are generally regulated as if they were equity securities of the issuer. For example, the rules on pre-emption apply to them.[251] They may only be admitted if the equity securities into which they are convertible are already, or will become at the same time, listed securities.[252] Where convertible debt securities are to be offered to the public or are themselves to be admitted to trading on the GEFIM (so that a PD prospectus is required), the content requirements are the same as for equity securities.[253] If they are not offered to the public and only admitted to trading on the PSM, then the content requirements for the necessary listing particulars follow the wholesale debt regime.[254] If the convertible debt securities are neither to be offered to the public nor admitted to trading on the GEFIM themselves, but it is intended that the equity securities into which they convert are to be admitted to trading on the Main Market, then a PD prospectus is not required provided that the equity securities are of the same class as equity securities of the issuer already admitted to trading on the Main Market.[255]

---

[245] Ibid, art 5(3).

[246] This example is given by Lewison J in *FSA v Anderson* [2010] EWHC 599 (Ch), [44].

[247] Ibid, *FSA v Anderson*, [44].

[248] Regulated Activities Order art 9. Commercial paper with a redemption value of less than £100,000 is not exempted (Regulated Activities Order arts 9(2), 9(3)): commercial paper is a form of short-term debt security, see page 30.

[249] Regulated Activities Order art 6. Inter-company loans and loans from family members are also excluded, art 6(1)(c) and (d).

[250] See page 45.

[251] See 4.3.1 above.

[252] LR 2.2.12.

[253] These requirements are discussed at 9.4.2. In the PR the term 'equity securities' is defined as including convertible securities, see PR App. 1.1.1 applying Prospectus Directive art 2(1)(b).

[254] LR 4.2.4(1).

[255] PR 1.2.3(7).

If exchangeable debt securities are to be offered to the public or are themselves to be admitted to trading on the GEFIM, a distinction is drawn between exchangeable debt securities issued by an affiliate of the company that is the issuer of the relevant equity securities and those that are issued by a company that is not so affiliated. The former are regarded by the Prospectus Directive as equity securities, but the content requirements for the necessary PD prospectus would seem to follow the retail or wholesale debt regime depending on the denomination of the security.[256] The latter are regarded by the Prospectus Directive as non-equity securities,[257] and the content requirements for the necessary PD prospectus follow the wholesale debt regime regardless of the denomination of the security.[258] If exchangeable debt securities are not offered to the public and are to be admitted to trading only on the PSM, then the content requirements for the necessary listing particulars follow the wholesale debt regime regardless of whether the issuer is affiliated or not with the company that is the issuer of the relevant equity securities, and regardless of the denomination of the securities.[259] If the exchangeable debt securities are neither to be offered to the public nor admitted to trading on the GEFIM themselves, then a PD prospectus is not required where the equity securities for which they are exchangeable are to be admitted to trading on the Main Market.[260]

11.7 Regulation of Credit Rating Agencies

As mentioned in chapter two,[261] credit rating agencies ('CRAs') play an important role in capital markets, although until recently they were largely unregulated. Even before the recent global financial crisis, some steps had been taken to regulate CRAs since they had become 'deeply embedded in investor culture'.[262] They had come to be relied on directly and indirectly not only by investors and issuers, but also by regulatory authorities. For example, investment funds[263] are often required by their mandates to invest only in listed securities, and then only in securities that carry an 'investment grade' rating issued by one or more CRAs.[264] As an indicator of asset quality, banks and other lenders often value financial collateral offered to them on the basis of the credit rating assigned to it, so that investment grade bonds have more value as collateral than high yield bonds.

---

[256]   The condition in Article 4(2)(2)(b) of the Prospectus Directive Regulation is not satisfied, so that Article 7 applies instead.

[257]   It might be wondered why this second kind of exchangeable debt security exists. Investment banks often issue debt securities that are exchangeable for shares in unaffiliated companies and which can be acquired by the bank on the market when the time comes to settle the exchange obligation. Such securities are really specialised investment products designed by the bank to cater to the demands of its sophisticated clients, rather than a significant source of finance for general corporate purposes.

[258]   Article 2(1)(b) of the Prospectus Directive.

[259]   LR 4.2.4(1).

[260]   PR 1.2.3(7). This is provided that the equity securities are of the same class as those already admitted to trading on the Main Market.

[261]   Pages 32–33.

[262]   F Partnoy, 'Historical Perspectives on the Financial Crisis: Ivar Kreuger, the Credit-Rating Agencies, and Two Theories about the Function, and Dysfunction, of Markets' (2009) 26 *Yale Journal on Regulation* 431.

[263]   Such as mutual funds and pension funds.

[264]   See pages 32–33 above. 'Investment grade' securities are those with a credit rating of at least 'BBB-'. 'Speculative grade' securities have a rating of BB+ or below.

Maintaining a good credit rating is also a good way for a company to signal its own creditworthiness, not only to potential investors but also to customers and suppliers. For example, a company may persuade the counterparty to a trading arrangement that it should not have to provide security for its obligations because it has an investment-grade rating. Some companies positively target a particular credit rating, and this target is a management policy which is communicated to analysts.[265] Parties can incorporate credit ratings into their private arrangements by attaching consequences to a rating downgrade. In *Hall v Cable & Wireless*,[266] for example, the dispute concerned an issuer's obligation to disclose to the market the fact that it might be required to provide collateral if its own credit rating was downgraded. It is easy to see how such 'ratings triggers' can become a self-fulfilling prophecy, where the downgrade both reflects and contributes to the increased likelihood of default.[267] Credit ratings are also used by regulatory authorities around the world. In most countries, for example, authorities are prepared to accept credit ratings issued by certain CRAs when determining the risk weighting to apply to assets for the purpose of the capital adequacy requirements imposed on banks and other financial institutions.[268] Securities with the safest ratings carry a low risk weighting and do not need to be funded by equity to the same extent as more risky securities.[269]

Before the recent financial crisis, it was considered satisfactory that CRAs were regulated by the market. It was assumed that CRAs that failed to supply accurate ratings would eventually be excluded by normal market forces, and that there was, therefore, no need for more intrusive regulation.[270] However, as a result of the financial crisis, questions have been raised about the role of credit rating agencies. In particular, their expertise, in rating corporate securities proved insufficient when rating the complicated asset-based securities issued in the period before the crisis.[271] The mathematical models used to rate these new products failed adequately to appreciate the risk and significance of correlated default.[272] Concerns were also raised that there was a conflict of interest problem, in that CRAs were paid by investment banks sponsoring a securitisation, yet the ratings were relied on by investors of varying levels of expertise.[273] The CRAs became involved in designing the securities themselves, so that the arranger's rating objectives could be satisfied.

---

[265] See Financial Services Authority FS09/01, *Insurance Risk Management: The Path to Solvency II* (May 2009) para 5–37.

[266] [2009] EWHC 1793 (Comm).

[267] Such use of ratings triggers is widespread. According to a survey by Moody's, out of 771 US corporate issuers rating Ba1 or higher, only 12.5% reported no triggers, while the remaining 87.5% reported a total of 2,819 rating triggers. See Moody's Investors Service, *The Unintended Consequence of Rating Triggers* (December 2001).

[268] See pages 25–26 above.

[269] A useful cross-country comparison is found in A Estrella et al, 'Credit Ratings and Complementary Sources of Credit Quality Information', Basel Committee on Banking Supervision Working Papers (No 3 August 2000).

[270] S Phillips and A Rechtschaffen, 'International Banking Activities: The Role of the Federal Reserve Bank in Domestic Capital Markets' (1998) *21 Fordham International Law Journal* 1754, 1762. Indeed, even in the aftermath of the global financial crisis, the Financial Stability Forum, the European Securities Market Experts Group and Committee of European Securities Regulation argued that binding regulation was not required.

[271] See pages 35–36.

[272] FSA, *The Turner Review: A Regulatory Response to the Global Banking Crisis*, March 2009, 44, 76.

[273] T Hurst, 'The Role of Credit Rating Agencies in the Current Worldwide Financial Crisis' (2009) 30 *Company Lawyer* 61.

As a result of these concerns, Europe has introduced new regulations for CRAs. The EU Regulation on Credit Rating Agencies,[274] which came into force in full December 2010, has been implemented in the UK.[275] All CRAs are required to register and submit to FSA supervision.[276] There are also detailed requirements intended to address the problems discussed in the previous paragraph. For example, CRAs cannot provide consultancy or advisory services to entities they rate, but can provide so-called 'ancillary services' provided that the nature and extent of these is prominently disclosed.[277] Further, the ratings methodologies and key ratings assumptions must also be open to public scrutiny.[278]

Whether these regulatory developments will be beneficial, and the extent to which they will actually have any effect on the CRAs' business practices, remains to be seen. It could be argued, for example, that requiring CRAs to register and submit to supervision will simply contribute to the problem of over-reliance by private investors on regulatory supervision. Such investors may believe that the ratings are more reliable because they are issued by regulated entities, rather than relying on their own expertise and due diligence.

11.8 Conclusion

The application of regulatory rules to the debt side of corporate finance is complicated and patchy. The chief inconsistency, on one view, is that, while the issuing and trading of debt securities attracts considerable disclosure requirements, and some other types of regulation, there is little regulation of the making of loans, whether single lender loans or those involving multiple lenders. One reason for this could be said to be the identity of those providing the finance. Loans are usually made by banks, and they can be expected to look out for themselves.[279] However, given that most investors in debt securities are institutions of one sort or another, it is hard to see why this is a considerable point of difference. Another reason is that lenders can negotiate considerable contractual (and proprietary) protection, while those purchasing debt securities take them on terms that are already fixed.

However, this is not necessarily as strong a point of difference as it might appear at first, especially as regards syndicated loans. First, many banks and other financial institutions buy loans which are already made as well as making loans themselves: there is an active secondary loan market. Second, debt securities are issued on the terms which the market will bear, and those who are large and repeat players in the market are thus able to influence the terms generally, even if not in particular. Yet another reason for the difference in regulatory treatment is the ability of lenders to investigate the borrower before lending, while it is much less cost effective (or really possible) for those buying debt

---

[274] Regulation (EC) No 1060/2009 of the European Parliament and of the Council of 16 September 2009 on credit rating agencies.

[275] Credit Rating Agencies Regulations 2010 SI 2010/906.

[276] Regulation (EC) No 1060/2009 Title III.

[277] Regulation (EC) No 1060/2009 Annex 1, section B.4.

[278] Regulation (EC) No 1060/2009 Annex 1, section E, I.5. Amendments to the EU Regulation were proposed in June 2010 which would transfer regulatory oversight from national authorities to the new European Securities Marekt Authority (ESMA), but these amendments have not yet been adopted.

[279] Benjamin, n 10, 10.2.4.

securities to do so. However, at least in relation to a syndicated loan, the lenders are given standardised disclosure in the form of the information memorandum, in the same way that potential buyers of debt securities are given a prospectus or offering circular. There are considerable similarities between debt securities issued under a programme and a syndicated loan, and it is certainly arguable that the regulatory regimes should be more similar.

As regards the regulatory regime for debt securities, this can be seen to have been influenced partly by a desire to provide some protection for investors in the market, in a way similar to the regulation of the equity markets, and partly by a desire to attract issuers of debt securities from all over the world to issue and list in the UK. This balance has led to a complex system, riddled with exceptions and distinctions. Given that most investors in debt securities have in the recent past been sophisticated investors, the approach of only requiring limited disclosure appears to be justified. If the market opened up to more individual retail investors, then this might have to change.[280] There is, however, another justification for the difference between the debt securities and the equity securities regimes. This is the inherent difference between debt and equity: debt holders have an ultimate right to sue for the amount due to them, while shareholders merely have a hope of gain, thus necessitating greater regulatory protection.

---

[280]   See pages 31–32 for the possibility of more retail bonds in the future.

12

Takeovers

12.1 Introduction

A takeover bid is an offer by a bidder (usually a company) for shares in the target, in exchange for cash, or for securities of the bidder, or a mixture of the two. The offer is, therefore, made by the bidder company to the shareholders in the target company, not to the directors of the target. There is therefore no obvious act of the target company upon which company law can fasten. As a result many countries leave takeovers to be dealt with by way of securities regulation. In the UK, as this chapter will examine, takeover regulation has been developed within both company law and securities law. The core transaction is therefore between the bidder and the target company's shareholders, and potentially only between the bidder and a proportion of the target company's shareholders large enough to give the bidder control. However, a takeover will have implications for others in the company because the purpose of the takeover is generally not merely a transfer of shares to the bidder but also, crucially, a transfer of control. Depending on the nature of the company, a takeover can have significant implications for the directors of the company, the minority shareholders in the target and for other stakeholders in the target, such as employees. The takeover may also have implications for the shareholders in the bidder company.

A takeover may be contrasted with other scenarios in which control passes to new shareholders in a company, for example as a result of the company issuing or re-purchasing shares, or where the company merges with another company, such as via a scheme of arrangement.[1] In these scenarios a corporate decision is always involved, ie the directors take a decision for the company which is then voted on by the shareholders. Regulation of these corporate transactions takes place by means of general company and securities law measures which regulate directors' behaviour, such as directors' duties, and provide shareholders with oversight of the directors' actions. These devices will be familiar to anyone who has studied corporate law. It is the absence of a corporate decision, and the fact that the bidder makes its offer to the target shareholders, that makes takeovers unique, and justifies their separate treatment.

This chapter will consider the regulatory structure in place in the UK to deal with takeovers and will analyse the substantive law governing takeovers in the UK. As with other chapters in this book, the task of this chapter will also be to assess the effectiveness of the current UK regime. However, in order to assess the success of the regime, some consideration must first be given to what the regime is trying to achieve.

---

[1] Schemes of arrangement are discussed in detail in chapter 13.

12.1.1   The Objectives of Takeover Regulation

One possible goal would be to optimise the number of takeovers that occur. However, academic economists have not been able to establish that takeovers are necessarily a 'good thing'. Indeed there is considerable debate about whether takeovers are value maximising or efficient in a general sense. While empirical studies generally show that target share-holders gain significantly from takeovers,[2] it is less clear whether the bidder shareholders gain as a result of the takeover.[3] Some commentators suggest that the gains to the target shareholders are a result of a redistribution of wealth of some kind, perhaps from the bidder shareholders, or from the other stakeholders in the target firm, such as long-term customers, suppliers and employees, rather than any generation of wealth as a result of the takeover.[4] Therefore the issue of whether takeovers are broadly wealth maximising remains unclear.

These concerns have not, to date, formed an explicit role in determining regulatory objectives in the UK. It is specifically stated in the City Code on Takeovers and Mergers that (the City Code) it 'is not concerned with the financial or commercial advantages or disadvantages of a takeover'.[5] In the wake of the successful takeover of Cadbury by Kraft in 2010, Lord Mandelson, the then Business secretary, suggested a number of changes to the takeover regime. These would, in his words, throw some 'extra grit' into the system, on the basis that the existing rules too often failed to create value for people other than advisers and short-term investors.[6] However, the Takeover Panel reiterated its view that the City Code is not concerned with the financial or commercial advantages or disadvantages of a takeover, and that these are matters for the company and its shareholders.[7]

Instead, takeover regulation in different jurisdictions seems to pursue and advance objectives other than value-enhancement. Specifically, takeover regimes observable in different jurisdictions often appear to be based on different responses to the agency conflicts that arise in those jurisdictions.[8] Quite distinct issues arise where the sharehold-ings in the target company are concentrated in the hands of a few shareholders prior to the takeover as compared with companies in which the shareholdings are dispersed.[9] It is now

---

[2]   For a general discussion of the empirical evidence see R Romano, 'A Guide to Takeovers: Theory, Evidence and Regulation' in KJ Hopt and E Wymeersch (eds), *European Takeovers: Law and Practice* (London, Butter-worths, 1992) and, more recently, M Burkart and F Panunzi, 'Takeovers' ECGI Finance Working Paper No 118/2006.

[3]   Eg K Fuller, J Netter and M Stegemoller, 'What Do Returns to Acquiring Firms Tell Us? Evidence from Firms That Make Many Acquisitions' (2002) 57 *Journal of Finance* 1763.

[4]   For discussion see eg JC Coffee, 'Regulating the Market for Corporate Control: A Critical Assessment of the Tender Offer's Role in Corporate Governance' (1984) 84 *Columbia Law Journal* 1145. This is discussed further in the context of stakeholders in the target company at 12.3.3.

[5]   City Code on Takeovers and Mergers (City Code), Introduction, A1.

[6]   Lord Mandelson, speech at the annual Trade and Industry dinner, Mansion House, 1 March 2010. The suggested changes included raising the required level of shareholder support for a takeover from 50% to two-thirds; lowering the requirement for disclosure of share ownership during a bid from 1% to 0.5% and requiring greater transparency on advisors' fees and incentives.

[7]   Panel Statement 2010/6, Consultation on Aspects of the Takeover Code; City Code, Introduction, A1.

[8]   See eg R Kraakman et al, *The Anatomy of Corporate Law,* 2nd edn (Oxford, Oxford University Press, 2009) 8.6.

[9]   Ibid, chapter 8.

well understood that dispersed shareholdings are more common in the US and the UK,[10] and block-holdings tend to be the norm elsewhere.[11]

In a company with concentrated ownership control lies with the blockholder. Therefore the sale of shares following from a successful takeover offer will effect a control shift between the seller and the acquirer. The decision whether the takeover bid is successful lies de facto with the controlling shareholder and the primary issue for takeover regulation to determine is the need for, and extent of, any protection for the minority shareholders in the target. A detailed discussion of these issues lies outside the remit of this book.[12] By contrast, in a dispersed shareholding scenario such as that prevalent in most UK publicly traded companies, prior to the takeover de facto control of the company is likely to be with the board of directors. Consequently the takeover results in a control shift from a third party (the directors) to the acquirer, not from the seller to the acquirer.

This disjunction creates a significant difficulty as a result of two factors. First, the incumbent directors face potentially severe conflicts of interest where a takeover offers gains to the existing shareholders but threatens their own position. The control shift consequent upon a takeover means that often incumbent directors will be affected personally. In many scenarios a successful takeover will result in the directors losing their jobs, an outcome they are likely to be more or less happy about depending on the size of the compensation package available to them. In a Management Buy Out (MBO) the directors will keep their jobs, but they are equally personally interested in the outcome of the bid. Second, the target directors are in a position to promote the bid to the shareholders, if it is an MBO for example, or to take action to defend their position and to try to frustrate the bid. As a result of these factors, one of the key issues to be resolved in a system of dispersed share ownership, such as that in the UK, is whether to give the decision-making power in a takeover situation to the shareholders alone (since it is their shares that will be transferred), sidelining the target directors whose control will be transferred, or whether that decision should be taken by a combination of the directors and shareholders.

Another problem that arises in companies with dispersed share ownership is the fact that the bidder can potentially exploit the position of small, dispersed shareholders. The bidder can 'divide and conquer', exploiting the coordination problems that inevitably arise in such scenarios. Left to its own devices, the bidder could enter into preferential deals with some shareholders, in order to gain de facto control. The bidder could then put pressure on the remaining shareholders to accept a reduced offer, the alternative for the shareholders being to remain as minority shareholders in the company, with the acquirer now in charge. Consequently, another issue for takeover regulation is whether, and to what extent, to step in and regulate the relationship between the bidder and the target shareholders.[13]

---

[10] This is primarily true of publicly traded companies. Takeovers can occur in companies whose shares are not traded, but they occur much more readily in companies whose shares are publicly traded and as a result it is takeovers of these companies which will provide the focus for this chapter.

[11] Eg R La Porta, F Lopez de Silanes and A Shleifer, 'Corporate Ownership Around the World' (1999) 54 *Journal of Finance* 471.

[12] For an overview of these issues see Kraakman et al, *The Anatomy of Corporate Law,* n 8, 8.3.

[13] In companies with concentrated share ownership similar issues exist for the minority shareholders, and the question arises whether they should have a right of exit when a takeover leads to a control shift, and if so, at what price.

These two issues, namely the amount of interference allowed by target directors in the outcome of the bid and the amount of freedom allowed to the bidder when dealing with the target shareholders, are regarded as the two core issues for UK takeover regulation to determine, though other issues do exist. These issues could be left to the general law (contract law, company law and securities law) to address. However, as will be discussed in this chapter, a significant layer of takeover regulation has been put in place to supplement the general law relating to these issues. In the UK, the first issue is resolved resoundingly in favour of the shareholders: one of the primary aims of the UK regime is to put the shareholders in the target company in control of the bid. The target directors are sidelined in this decision. The resolution of the second issue is also shareholder driven, as the UK takeover regime aims to ensure that the bidder treats all of the shareholders in the target company equally.

12.1.2   Comparative Aspects

Although the focus of this chapter, in common with the rest of this book, is on the UK position, a comparison with other jurisdictions is particularly helpful in this context to understand why the UK system of takeover regulation is shaped as it is, and to assess the success of this model. In recent years, the adoption of the EC Takeover Directive[14] has meant that there has been significant focus on comparing UK takeover regulation with that in Continental Europe. The implementation of the Takeover Directive has resulted in a situation in which Europe is largely harmonised as to the second of the core issues identified above, namely the amount of freedom given to the bidder when dealing with the target shareholders. Despite the directive needing to provide rules for one dispersed shareholding system (the UK) and many blockholding systems, the harmonised rules on this issue in the directive are based on the pre-existing UK model.[15]

More divergence exists on the first of the core issues identified above, as a consequence of the compromises adopted within the directive which were required before the directive could be adopted.[16] Some Member States follow the UK model and give the decision whether to accept the bid to the shareholders. Others, most notably Germany and the Netherlands, retain a significant role in the decision-making process for the directors. These differences are interesting, and important. However, given that the focus of this chapter is an assessment of UK takeover law based on an assessment of how well it addresses the agency issues which arise in this context, a more useful comparison for assessing the UK regime is the US. A comparison between the takeover regimes in the US and UK is particularly apt because they are the two major jurisdictions which display dispersed share ownership patterns within their publicly traded companies. The fact that

---

[14]   2004/25/EC.

[15]   The minority shareholders in companies with concentrated ownership are in a similar position to the dispersed shareholders in UK public companies as regards this issue, although some of the solutions (eg the mandatory bid rule) have different consequences and costs when used in a concentrated ownership system. As a result many European countries have found ways to adjust the impact of these rules. These issues fall outside the remit of this chapter. For discussion see Kraakman, n 8, ch 8.

[16]   For discussion see eg R Skog, 'The Takeover Directive: An Endless Saga' (2002) 13 *European Business Law Review* 301.

some US states (most notably Delaware) have adopted quite different responses to that agency conflict from those adopted in the UK helps us to reflect on the value of the choices adopted in the UK.

There are likely to be a number of reasons why such a strong shareholder-centric model has been adopted in the UK. The UK system of company law has always been strongly shareholder-centric, particularly when compared to the position in the US, where central-ised management has been the norm. The free transferability of a shareholder's shares is regarded as an important aspect of their rights in the UK and this principle is a core tenet of the regulation of listed company shares in the UK.[17] In the UK, the board's powers have traditionally been seen as deriving from the shareholders. Shareholders have, for example, traditionally had the right to remove directors at any time by ordinary resolution.[18] The other significant corporate governance rights held by UK shareholders are discussed at 10.2.2 and again can be contrasted markedly with the position in the US. In addition, the development of the system of takeover regulation in the UK coincided with a rise in institutional shareholder power. This contrasts markedly with the development of the takeover regime in the US, and it may well be that these differences help to explain the marked contrasts in approach observable within the two systems today.[19] The next section will therefore discuss the development of takeover regulation in the UK, in order to help explain the regulation that has been put in place in the UK. The following sections will then examine the substance of UK takeover regulation, comparing it, where relevant, to other jurisdictions, in particular the US.

12.2   The Regulatory Structure of Takeover Regulation in the UK

In the UK, takeovers are regulated by the City Code, a body of rules that is written and administered by the Panel on Takeovers and Mergers (the Takeover Panel).[20] For many years the Takeover Panel was an independent, self-regulating body set up by the main City institutions and organisations with an involvement in public company takeovers.[21] This

---

[17]   FSA Handbook, Listing Rules, LR 2.2.4. For Companies listed on AIM see London Stock Exchange, *AIM Rules for Companies*, February 2010, rule 32.

[18]   For the current incarnation of this rule see Companies Act 2006, s 168.

[19]   J Armour and DA Skeel Jr, 'Who Writes the Rules of Hostile Takeovers, and Why? – The Peculiar Divergence of US and UK Takeover Regulation' (2007) *Georgetown Law Journal* 1727; G Miller, 'Political Structure and Corporate Governance: Some Points of Contrast between the United States and England' (1998) *Columbia Business Law Review* 51.

[20]   See, now, Companies Act 2006, Part 28.

[21]   This self-regulatory model was undoubtedly developed in the face of clear threats of government intervention, should that be necessary, and has therefore been referred to as 'coerced self-regulation': J Black, 'Constitutionalising Self-Regulation' (1996) 59 *Modern Law Review* 24. For discussion see J Armour and DA Skeel, 'Who Writes the Rules of Hostile Takeovers, and Why? – The Peculiar Divergence of US and UK Takeover Regulation' [2007] *Georgetown Law Journal* 1727, 1756–65 esp 1764.

system has now been underpinned by statute as a consequence of the UK's implementation of the Takeover Directive,[22] but this has been designed with the express objective of maintaining the prior self-regulatory approach of the UK's takeover regulation to the greatest extent possible. To understand the current position regarding takeover regulation in the UK it is necessary to appreciate the historical development of this system.

12.2.1   Historical Development

The regulation of takeovers in the UK developed separately to the regulation of the securities markets.[23] The first set of rules was published in 1959,[24] followed by the first City Code on Takeovers and Mergers in 1968. These rules were drawn up in response to a wave of hostile takeovers which took place in the early 1950s. Takeovers were considered sharp practice at that time and they outraged both directors and the City establishment, who believed that takeovers were harmful for industry.[25] However, the first set of rules, drawn up in 1959, was not initiated or controlled by directors, but by a committee comprising representatives of merchant banks, institutional investors, the largest commercial banks and the London Stock Exchange. As a result it is not surprising that the focus for these rules was not securing the position of directors and managers, but safeguarding the interests of the shareholders.

The 1959 guidelines were brief by modern City Code standards, but nevertheless firmly established at their centre shareholder primacy, the core principle of modern UK takeover regulation. The guidelines emphasised that there should be no interference with the free market for shares, and that it was for shareholders themselves to decide whether to sell. Shareholders were also to be given enough information and time to make an informed decision.[26]

These guidelines were well received, and were revised and improved in 1963.[27] However a significant weakness in these guidelines was the lack of any mechanism for adjudication and enforcement. This was remedied in 1968. In addition to a new, and far more comprehensive, set of takeover rules (now the City Code on Takeovers and Mergers), a new body was established with the task of adjudicating disputes about the application of the rules: the Takeover Panel. Until 2006 the Takeover Panel had no statutory authority and relied for its authority on the fact that its membership represented the main parties

---

[22]   Directive 2004/25/EC (for analysis see J Rickford, 'The Emerging European Takeover Law from a British Perspective' [2004] *European Business Law Review* 1379). Since May 20, 2006 both the Takeover Panel and the City Code have been given a legal underpinning as part of the UK's implementation of the Takeover Directive 2004/25/EC.

[23]   Takeover regulation in the UK developed before the statutory regulation of the securities markets (described in chapters 9 and 10).

[24]   Issuing Houses Association, *Notes on Amalgamation of British Businesses* (1959). For discussion see A Johnston, *The City Takeover Code* (Oxford, Oxford University Press, 1980) ch 3.

[25]   For a discussion of the history of UK takeover regulation see A Johnston, 'Takeover Regulation: Historical and Theoretical Perspectives on the City Code' [2007] *Cambridge Law Journal* 422; J Armour and DA Skeel, 'Who Writes the Rules of Hostile Takeovers, and Why? – The Peculiar Divergence of US and UK Takeover Regulation' [2007] *Georgetown Law Journal* 1727, 1756–65.

[26]   Issuing Houses Association, *Notes on Amalgamation of British Businesses* (October 1958).

[27]   Issuing Houses Association, *Revised Notes on Amalgamation of British Businesses* (October 1963).

with a material interest in takeovers.[28] The Takeover Panel's success as a regulator therefore depended to a large extent on the recognition which those involved in takeovers gave to it.[29] At this time 'the City of London prided itself upon being a village community, albeit of a unique kind, which could regulate itself by pressure of professional opinion'.[30]

This short historical overview is helpful in understanding two aspects of the way in which UK takeover regulation developed. First, it helps to explain the shareholder-focused rather than management-focused approach that is in evidence in the UK. The code that emerged in 1968 was significantly longer and more specific than the guidelines drawn up in 1958, but at its core the 1968 Code retained the concept of shareholder choice, and supplemented that with a general ban on frustrating actions by directors. This has formed the basis for the City Code ever since. It is no coincidence that this shareholder-friendly model was drawn up by City institutions, and, importantly, by institutional investors who have a clear interest in rules that maximise expected gains to shareholders.[31]

By contrast, institutional investors have played a much smaller role in the development of US takeover regulation.[32] In the US takeover regulation is only minimally the product of federal law[33] and therefore US takeover regulation is to a large extent the product of state legislatures. Commentators have demonstrated that state takeover legislation is a fertile ground for lobbyists in the managerial cause.[34] This is in sharp contrast to the UK position, where manager-friendly groups have had little or no part to play in the development of takeover regulation. Managers appear to have had a politically stronger and more influential role in the development of US takeover law than is observable in the UK and this seems likely to have influenced the development of the two systems, with the US system developing in a more manager-friendly direction and the UK more shareholder-focused.

Second, it helps to explain the self-regulatory model adopted in the UK, and the relative informality of the approach adopted by the Takeover Panel. From the first, the Takeover Panel's members included representatives from the Stock Exchange, the Bank of England, the major merchant banks, and institutional investors. A decision was taken early in the Takeover Panel's existence that proactive involvement in takeover bids was better than an ex post judicial approach.[35] This was in keeping with the fact that the Takeover

---

[28] In addition to the Chairman and Deputy Chairmen, the Panel consists of up to 20 members appointed by the Panel and individuals appointed by representative bodies of those involved in takeovers: The City Code, Introduction, A8.

[29] If the Panel's decisions had been ignored, or not given full effect, it is certain that Parliament would have stepped in to replace the City Code and the Takeover Panel with some other form of statutory regulation which might have been less attractive to market participants. Knowledge of this possibility was undoubtedly a factor in the recognition accorded to the Takeover Panel prior to 2006 when it had no statutory authority. Therefore some commentators suggest that the model in place should not be regarded as 'self-regulation' but as 'coerced self-regulation': J Black, 'Constitutionalising Self-Regulation' (1996) 59 *Modern Law Review* 24.

[30] *R v Panel of Takeovers and Mergers ex p Datafin plc* [1987] QB 815, 835 per Sir John Donaldson MR.

[31] Institutional investors have also been active in other areas of corporate law in drawing up pro-shareholder rules: see 10.2.2.2.

[32] J Armour and DA Skeel, 'Who Writes the Rules of Hostile Takeovers, and Why? – The Peculiar Divergence of US and UK Takeover Regulation' [2007] *Georgetown Law Journal* 1727, 1767–76.

[33] Eg 1968 Williams Act, 82 Stat 454, codified at 15 USC §§78m(d)–(e) and 78n(d) – (f), adding new §§ 13(d), 13(e) and 14(d) – (f) to the Securities Act 1934.

[34] LA Bebchuk and A Ferrell, 'Federalism and Corporate Law: The Race to Protect Managers from Takeovers' (1999) 99 *Columbia Law Review* 1168.

[35] The Panel on Takeovers and Mergers, Report on the year ended 31st March 1969, 4.

Panel constituted primarily business people rather than lawyers, and that the staff consisted mainly of business and financial experts. Speed and efficiency have been at the centre of the Takeover Panel's regulatory regime, with a clear timetable for bids established from an early stage. It has also been fundamental to the operation of the Takeover Panel that it should address takeover issues as they arise in real time, imposing little or no delay on the progress of the bid.

This contrasts with the position in the US, where takeover regulation is administered by the Securities and Exchange Commission and by the courts. Far more takeover regulation is left to general corporate and fiduciary law principles in the US[36] than in the UK where, as will be seen in 12.3, a significant amount of specialised takeover regulation has been put in place to supplement general corporate law principles. A consequence of the US position is that many of the rules that regulate takeovers in the US are judge-made rather than developed by a regulator like the Takeover Panel. It has been suggested that the fact that the US rules are largely judge-made has made it easier for a pro-management approach to emerge.[37] In addition, in the US if a takeover bidder is unhappy with some aspect of the bid (for example the target directors' response to the bid), they will generally take the matter to the courts, resulting in a number of weeks of delay, longer if the matter is then appealed. In the UK, a hostile bidder unhappy with the behaviour of the target's directors will lodge a protest with the Takeover Panel, which will then issue a ruling as appropriate (eg requiring the target board to remove its interference with a bid).[38] The speed and efficiency of the manner in which the Takeover Panel deals with bids is regarded as a significant advantage of the UK system.

The advantages of the UK's system of takeover regulation when compared to traditional top-down regulation seem clear. The Takeover Panel is able to react quickly to perceived abuses, and the changes made to the City Code over time reveal the Takeover Panel's ability to deal flexibly and responsively to changing circumstances.[39] The nature of the regime, in particular its self-regulatory origins, also means that it has commanded the broad assent of those who are regulated by the Takeover Panel.

Given the perceived advantages of the UK system, the requirement to harmonise UK takeover regulation with that of Europe, via implementation of the Takeover Directive,[40] was a potential concern. The next section will consider the implementation of the Takeover Directive into UK law and explain that the implementation has not undermined any of the perceived advantages of the UK system.

---

[36] Federal law (eg the 1968 Williams Act) and state law (eg Delaware puts in place some rules governing squeeze-out mergers) do create some specific takeover rules.

[37] J Armour and DA Skeel, 'Who Writes the Rules of Hostile Takeovers, and Why? – The Peculiar Divergence of US and UK Takeover Regulation' [2007] *Georgetown Law Journal* 1727, 1793.

[38] A party unhappy with a ruling from the Panel's Executive can appeal to the Panel's Hearings Committee (see The City Code, Introduction, A7–A10). A party to a hearing before the Hearing Committee may appeal to the Takeover Appeal Board, an independent body whose chairman and deputy chairman will usually have held high judicial office and whose members are experienced in takeovers. This was broadly the system in place before the Companies Act 2006 and s 951 of the 2006 Act preserves this system.

[39] For discussion see A Johnston, 'Takeover Regulation: Historical and theoretical perspectives on the City Code' [2007] *Cambridge Law Journal* 422, 442–48.

[40] Dir 2004/25, [2004] OJ L142/12.

12.2.2   The Implementation of the Takeover Directive

The Takeover Directive was eventually adopted in 2004 and required implementation by May 2006. The implementation of the directive in the UK is achieved via the Companies Act 2006.[41]

Many of the substantive measures contained in the directive were heavily influenced by the UK's existing takeover regulation provisions. This was because the UK had the greatest experience of takeovers, particularly hostile ones. Prior to the implementation of the directive a number of different takeover regimes were observable throughout Europe. This is unsurprising given that takeover regulation appears to respond to the different agency conflicts observable in different regimes.[42] As might be expected, these differences were particularly acute when comparing the UK with other European jurisdictions.[43] For some time these differences threatened to prevent agreement being reached on the final form of the directive. However, a compromise was finally reached, allowing Member States to opt out of certain substantive provisions of the directive.[44] These opt-outs allowed Member States to customise the implementation of the takeover directive to some extent. From the UK's perspective the combination of these opt-outs, together with the fact that most of the compulsory aspects of the directive were based on the existing UK regime, meant that the implementation of the directive led to very few *substantive* changes to UK takeover regulation.[45] Certainly the implementation of the regime has not interfered with the strong shareholder-centric model of takeover regulation in place in the UK prior to implementation. A consideration of the substance of UK takeover regulation will take place in 12.3.

The remainder of this section will consider the effect of the Takeover Directive on the *procedural* aspects of the UK's takeover regime and will assess the extent to which the self-regulatory model in evidence prior to implementation has survived. Perhaps the most important elements in retaining the benefits of the existing regime were to preserve the role and status of the Takeover Panel to the extent possible and to preserve the existing position regarding tactical litigation.

12.2.3   Role and Status of the Takeover Panel

The UK Government did have concerns about the effect of some of the directive's provisions on the UK's regulatory regime, and in particular on the role and status of the Takeover Panel.[46] Amendments to the directive were therefore made during the drafting process in order to try to allay these fears and to allow the UK to retain the Takeover Panel in its existing role and status to the extent possible after the directive was implemented.

---

[41]   It was always intended that this implementation should be achieved via the Companies Act 2006, but as the timetable for the 2006 Act slipped it was necessary to put in place interim regulations (the Takeovers Directive (Interim Implementation) Regulations 2006 (SI 2006/1183)) to cover the gap between May 20 2006 and the coming into force of Part 28 of the Companies Act 2006 on 6 April 2007.

[42]   See the discussion in 12.1.

[43]   As discussed in 12.1 the UK generally has dispersed shareholdings within its public companies whereas on Continental Europe blockholdings are more common.

[44]   Takeover Directive, Dir 2004/25, [2004] OJ L142/12, arts 9, 11.

[45]   For discussion see DTI, *Company Law Implementation of the European Directive on Takeover Bids*, January 2005, URN 05/11.

[46]   Ibid.

The implementation of the directive has brought changes to the UK's takeover regulation, principally the fact that the Takeover Panel and the City Code are now on a statutory footing.[47] However, the role and function of both remain largely unchanged. As regards the City Code, prior to implementation it had a wide remit, wider indeed than the directive.[48] This wide remit has been retained. As a result the City Code applies to public offers to the holders of securities on a regulated market, such as the LSE's Main Market, and exchange-regulated markets, such as AIM, and indeed to all public companies, whether they have securities traded on a public market or not.[49] It also applies to other transactions which are analogous to public offers, such as schemes of arrangement.[50]

As regards the Takeover Panel, its status and composition remain unchanged by the implementation of the directive.[51] It retains its two core functions, namely rule-making (writing and keeping up to date the City Code)[52] and a judicial function (giving rulings on the interpretation, application or effect of the rules).[53] However the Companies Act 2006 adds a new power. The Takeover Panel now also has the right to require disclosure of information where this is 'reasonably required in connection with the exercise by the Panel of its functions'.[54] However, given that the Takeover Panel had managed to survive without this power perfectly well for almost 40 years prior to the Companies Act 2006, it is not likely that this will make a major difference to the Takeover Panel's operation.

The sanctions available to the Takeover Panel have been changed slightly by the implementation of the directive. Prior to 2006, the self-regulatory nature of the Takeover Panel was evident in the sanctions it had available to it to ensure compliance with the City Code. These were primarily of an informal nature: private reprimand or public censure and a requirement that the institutions represented on the Takeover Panel withdraw the

---

[47]   Companies Act 2006, ss 942–965. The Takeover Directive, art 4.1 specifically permits the supervisory authority to be a private body, such as the Takeover Panel, although that private body needs to be 'recognised by national law', hence the need for the Takeover Panel to be put on a statutory footing. These provisions do not seek to regulate the constitution of the Takeover Panel (cf the position in relation to the FSA: FSMA, Sch 1). Under these provisions the Panel's Code Committee is empowered to write the City Code and the Panel's Hearings Committee is empowered to give binding rulings on its application.

[48]   The scope of the City Code is wider than the scope of the Takeover Directive 2004/25/EC which applies only to public offers to the holders of securities in the target company where those securities are traded on a regulated market in the EEA and where the objective of the offer is to secure control of the target company: Directive 2004/25/EC, arts 1(1) and 2(1)(a). For discussion of situations where the Takeover Directive requires jurisdiction over a bid to be shared between different jurisdictions see P Davies (ed), *Principles of Modern Company Law*, 8th edn (London, Sweet & Maxwell, 2008) 980–82.

[49]   City Code, Introduction, A3–A5. Some private companies are also within the remit of the City Code if, in the previous decade, their securities have been traded in a public or semi-public manner, or a prospectus has been issued in relation to them.

[50]   City Code, Introduction, A3–A7. For schemes of arrangement see Appendix 7 (for discussion see PCP 2007/1, *Schemes of Arrangement*). The use of schemes of arrangement as an alternative to a takeover offer is discussed further in chapter 13.

[51]   The Companies Act 2006 does not seek to regulate the constitution of the Panel. This is left to the City Code: Introduction, A8.

[52]   The Panel's powers to make rules are very widely formulated: s 943(2)(3); s 944(1). Responsibility for the rules is assigned to a Code Committee of the Panel: The City Code, Introduction, A9–A10. This body keeps the substance of the City Code under review. See Panel Statement 2010/6, *Consultation on Aspects of the Takeover*.

[53]   Companies Act 2006, s 945. The Panel also has the power to make directions to ensure compliance with the rules: s 946. As a result of the introduction of the Human Rights Act 1998 the Panel's judicial and rule making functions have been separated (for example membership of the Panel's Code Committee and Hearings Committee do not overlap: City Code, Introduction, A10).

[54]   Companies Act 2006, s 947(3). See generally Companies Act 2006, ss 947–949 and Sch 2.

facilities of the securities market from the offender. In some circumstances the Takeover Panel also required individuals to make compensation payments. In 1989, for example, the Takeover Panel required Guinness plc to pay compensation of around £85 million to former shareholders of the Distillers Company for breaches of the City Code in failing to make a cash alternative available to them at the level required by the City Code.[55] The power of these sanctions is evident in the fact that defiance of the Takeover Panel's rulings was almost unheard of.

Subsequently these sanctions were bolstered by regulations made under FSMA, which allowed the Takeover Panel to report conduct to the FSA. The FSA could then decide whether those persons were also in breach of the FSA's rules. If the bidder company had behaved in breach of the City Code, the FSA's powers included the ability to suspend the listing of a company, but this could impact on the (innocent) shareholders of the bidder rather than the (wrongdoing) controllers who caused the breach of the City Code. The FSA generally does not have direct sanctions against the directors of the bidder available to it because the takeover itself is not an activity requiring FSA authorisation. However, the FSA does have oversight of the advisers to the bidder, most notably the investment banks, who need the FSA's authorisation in order to carry on their professional activities within the financial services sector. FSMA therefore introduced a 'cold-shouldering' provision which enables the FSA to target bidders and their directors indirectly via their advisers.[56] Cold-shouldering involves advisers within the scope of the FSA's powers being required not to deal with those who are likely not to observe the City Code. As a result companies who act, or are likely to act, in breach of the City Code, can be denied the facilities of the City of London in relation to takeover bids.[57]

The Companies Act 2006 has retained these sanctions and has placed them on a statutory footing,[58] as well as adding some new enforcement mechanisms. For instance, the Takeover Panel has a new power to apply to the court where a person has contravened, or is reasonably likely to contravene, a requirement imposed by or under the City Code, or has failed to comply with a disclosure requirement.[59] A new criminal offence is also created by the Act for a person who knew (or was reckless as to the fact) that offer documentation did not comply with the City Code's requirements and failed to take reasonable steps to ensure compliance.[60]

It can be seen that, following implementation of the directive, the Takeover Panel retains its central role in the supervision of takeover bids in the UK. Despite it now being on a statutory footing, the Takeover Panel's status and role are otherwise largely unchanged.

---

[55]   See Panel Statement 1989/13 (The Distillers Company plc, 14 July 1989). This power is now contained in Companies Act 2006, s 954 (and see The City Code, Introduction, A19).

[56]   FSA Handbook, Code of Market Conduct, MAR 4.3.

[57]   Cold shouldering orders are rare. For a recent example see Takeover Appeal Board Statement 2010/1. The previous cold shoulder order was in 1992 (Panel Statement 1992/09).

[58]   Companies Act 2006, s 952 (and see City Code, Introduction, A20–21).

[59]   Ibid, s 955.

[60]   Ibid, s 953. This offence only applies to offers for target companies whose voting securities are quoted on a regulated market: s 953(1).

12.2.4 Tactical Litigation

The ability of the Takeover Panel to make decisions in real time in relation to a bid is preserved post-2006. As discussed, the Takeover Panel's ability to give speedy, binding rulings in the course of the bid is regarded as one of the advantages of the UK system. The opportunities for the bid to be slowed down, or frustrated entirely, by tactical litigation have traditionally been very small.[61] Because there is a clear timetable laid down within which bids are to occur within the UK, as discussed in 12.3.1, delays caused by tactical litigation could effectively cause a bid to fail without the shareholders having had the chance to decide for themselves. Before the implementation of the directive there was a system of internal speedy appeal within the Takeover Panel itself. This system is retained[62] so that decisions of the Takeover Panel Executive, giving rulings in the course of a bid, can be appealed to a Hearings Committee of the Takeover Panel in the first instance.[63]

In addition, it has been recognised for the past twenty years that the Takeover Panel's decisions themselves are subject to judicial review.[64] However, the courts have established narrow limits within which any judicial review of a Takeover Panel decision will operate.[65] It is expected that parties will still have to abide by Takeover Panel rulings, even if they have indicated an intention to seek judicial review.[66] Crucially, the courts to date have been content to carry out a retrospective review of the Takeover Panel's decisions. The courts will only intervene after a bid has been concluded and will only act to provide guidance as to how the Takeover Panel should proceed in future cases, or to relieve

---

[61]   The Panel has made it clear that in general litigation designed to frustrate an offer is not acceptable. In the decision in relation to Consolidated Gold Fields plc (Panel notice 1989/7, Consolidated Gold Fields plc, 2 May 1989) the Panel ruled that the target directors should not continue litigation in the US to restrain the bid.

[62]   Companies Act 2006, s 951.

[63]   City Code, Introduction, A12–A16. There is then the possibility of appeal to the Takeover Appeal Board, an independent body, whose chairman and deputy chairman will usually have held high judicial office and whose other members will be experienced in takeovers (City Code, Introduction, A16–A17). The Government considered and rejected the idea of setting up a bespoke judicial mechanism to hear issues arising from takeover proceedings: DTI, *Company Law Implementation of the European Directive on Takeover Bids: A Consultation Document* (January 2005, URN 05/11). Such a bespoke system was not required by the Directive. As far as the Takeover Directive is concerned, judicial review is required 'in appropriate circumstances' (preamble para 7) but Art 4(6) leaves it to Member States to decide whether and under what circumstances the parties to a bid are entitled to bring proceedings. Article 4 also provides that the directive will not affect the power which the courts have in Member States to decline to hear legal proceedings and to decide which legal proceedings affect the outcome of the bid.

[64]   *R v Panel on Takeovers and Mergers ex p Datafin* [1987] QB 815. The main basis for this decision was the fact that in the court's opinion the Panel was performing a public function. Broadly, if the Panel was not fulfilling this function the Government would have to step in and create an equivalent body (for discussion see P Cane, 'Self Regulation and Judicial Review' [1987] *Civil Justice Quarterly* 324).

[65]   In *Datafin* (ibid) the court established narrow parameters for a judicial review of the Panel. It was stated that 'there is little scope for complaint that the panel has promulgated rules which are ultra vires, provided only that they do not clearly violate the principle proclaimed by the panel of being based upon the concept of doing equity between one shareholder and another. This is a somewhat unlikely eventuality' (at 841 per Sir John Donaldson MR). When it comes to interpreting its own rules, the Panel 'must clearly be given considerable latitude' (at 841), primarily because, as legislator, it could change the rules at any time. Even where the court felt there was legitimate cause for complaint the Court of Appeal in *Datafin* felt that the most appropriate response would be for the court to declare the true meaning of the rule, leaving it to the Panel to promulgate a new rule accurately expressing its intentions. Challenges to the Panel's power to grant dispensation from its rules are likely to be successful only in 'wholly exceptional' circumstances (at 841). Finally, in relation to the Panel's exercise of its disciplinary powers, the court would be 'reluctant to move in the absence of any credible allegation of lack of bona fides' (at 841). See also *Re Expro International Group plc* [2008] EWHC 1543 (Ch).

[66]   *R v Panel on Takeovers and Mergers ex p Datafin* [1987] QB 815, 840–41.

individuals of disciplinary sanctions. Importantly, the courts have not interfered in the course of an existing bid.[67] On this basis there is very little to be gained by a party making use of litigation in the course of a takeover.

Although the judicial and appeal structure in the UK was left effectively unchanged as a result of the implementation of the Directive, there was nevertheless a concern that the implementation, and in particular the new statutory footing for the City Code and the Takeover Panel, might lead to an increase in tactical litigation. Various measures have been put in place to try to prevent this outcome. To counteract any possibility of a new breach of statutory duty claim arising from the fact that the Takeover Panel is now a statutory body, the Companies Act 2006 specifically excludes this possibility.[68] The Takeover Panel is also given immunity from liability in damages akin to that which exists for the FSA.[69] The Act also addresses the possibility that parties may try to challenge a takeover after the event and seeks to prevent this from occurring by providing that any contravention of any rule-based requirement does not render a transaction void or unenforceable.[70]

One further concern which has been raised relates to the grounds for judicial review. Prior to the directive, the courts had stated that arguments based on the view that the Takeover Panel had propounded rules that were ultra vires were unlikely to succeed. Might the movement to placing the Takeover Panel on a statutory footing alter this approach? To a large extent the wording of the Companies Act 2006 seeks to avoid future ultra vires actions by providing the Takeover Panel with very wide powers. The Takeover Panel may 'do anything that it considers necessary or expedient for the purposes of, or in connection with, its functions'.[71] As long as the courts continue to apply the same line in judicial review cases that they have maintained to date, ie not to overturn a Takeover Panel decision or otherwise interfere in the course of a bid, then it seems likely that tactical litigation will remain of little value to the parties to a bid. Nothing in the directive requires the courts to alter their existing policy in this regard[72] and there is no reason to believe that the courts will adopt a different approach in the future. This was the aim of the Government when implementing the directive.[73]

---

[67]   See *Ex p Datafin*, ibid; *R v Panel of Takeovers and Mergers ex p Guinness plc* [1990] 1 QB 146; *R v Panel of Takeovers and Mergers ex p Fayed* [1992] BCC 524. These cases could be regarded as being at odds with the decision of the House of Lords in *Re Spectrum Plus Ltd* [2005] UKHL 41; [2005] 2 AC 680 in which their Lordships accepted the general retrospective effect of court decisions and stated that in general rulings should not be prospective only. However, in the cases involving judicial review of Panel decisions, a distinction needs to be drawn between the courts deciding what the law was on the day that the Panel made its decision (and therefore whether the Panel was in breach on the day in question) and the courts' decision whether to nullify the resulting act. These cases are retrospective in the former sense.

[68]   Companies Act 2006, s 956(1).

[69]   Companies Act 2006, s 961 (as regards the Panel); FSMA, s 102 (regarding the FSA). This immunity does not extend to situations where the Panel is in bad faith or where there is a claim against it for breach of s 6(1) Human Rights Act 1998 (Companies Act 2006, s 961(3)).

[70]   Ibid, s 956(2). It is intended that transactions can only be unravelled after the event for misrepresentation or fraud, as was the case prior to the Companies Act 2006.

[71]   Companies Act 2006, s 942(2). See also ss 943, 944(1) and 945.

[72]   See Takeover Directive 2004/25/EC, art 4(6) which permits the British courts to retain their existing stance in this regard.

[73]   DTI, *Company Law Implementation of the European Directive on Takeover Bids*, n 63, para 2.38.

12.2.5 Summary

Despite the implementation of the Takeover Directive, which caused the Takeover Panel and the City Code to be put on a statutory footing, the self-regulatory regime put in place in 1968 is still very much in evidence in the UK's takeover regime. The Takeover Directive did not require any significant changes to the provisions of the City Code. Indeed many of the provisions of the directive were modelled on the provisions of the City Code, and the composition and discretion of the Takeover Panel is left largely unchanged by the implementation of the Directive. The Government's goal of producing a situation in which the Takeover Panel could carry on much as before does appear to have been achieved.

This discussion of the development of the UK regime helps to explain two key features of the UK system. First, and most importantly, it helps to explain the shareholder-centric approach adopted by UK takeover regulation which stands in sharp contrast to the US regime. The strong influence of shareholder-friendly groups in the development of the UK regime contrasts with the influence of manager-friendly lobby groups in the US. The shareholder focus of the UK regime, and the consequences of adopting that approach, will be discussed in the next section. The second feature is the speed of decision-making in the UK regime and the absence of tactical litigation which might otherwise be used to frustrate a bid.

The speed of decision-making is regarded as one of the significant practical benefits of the UK system and it has survived the implementation of the Takeover Directive. The absence of tactical litigation is also an important adjunct to the shareholder-focus of the UK model. The no frustration principle discussed at 12.3.2.2 below, provides one of the foundation stones of the UK regime, and is intended to ensure that the decision on the bid is taken by the target shareholders. To allow tactical litigation which has the practical effect of frustrating the bid would significantly undermine that principle.

12.3 The Substance of Takeover Regulation in the UK

Having discussed the regulatory structure of the UK takeover regime in the previous section, this section will now examine the substance of the UK regime.[74] As discussed, the UK regime is strongly shareholder-focused and operates under the twin principles that the decision-making in a bid should be left to the target shareholders, and the target directors should be sidelined (the 'no frustration principle') and that the bidder should treat all of the target shareholders equally. The origins of this shareholder-focused model appear to lie in the historical development of the regime and in particular in the role played by institutional investors in drafting the City Code and developing the regulatory system, as explained in the previous section. The consequences of the shareholder-focused approach will be examined in this section.

---

[74] The substance of the regime, in the shape of the City Code, is kept under review by the Code Committee, see 12.2.3.

12.3.1   The Procedure of a Bid

12.3.1.1   Initial Approach

Perhaps the two dominant policies at work regarding the procedure of a bid in the UK are, first, the desire to allow the shareholders of the target to have the decision-making role and for that decision to be as undistorted as possible and, second, that the target should not be subject to a bid or bid speculation for an excessive period of time.[75]

It may therefore seem surprising that the City Code provides that the offer from the bidder is put forward in the first instance not to the shareholders of the target but to the target board or its advisers.[76] This is in order to enable the board to advise the shareholders on the bid, and to obtain independent advice on the bid, both of which the board is required to do by the City Code.[77] It also allows bidders to make an informal approach,[78] or to request more information about the company before finalising the details of the offer.[79] There is an obvious danger in this period, before a bid has been publicly announced, of insider dealing by those aware that a bid may be about to occur.[80] The City Code attempts to deal with this issue by insisting on 'absolute secrecy' before a bid announcement,[81] and requiring an announcement where secrecy cannot be assured.[82] However, despite these measures, a recent study commissioned by the FSA into the cleanliness of the UK's market reported significant levels of unusual price movements prior to takeover announcements for UK listed firms.[83]

12.3.1.2   Formal Offer

Once a 'firm intention' announcement is made, the bidder becomes obliged to proceed with the bid and to post a formal offer document to the shareholders within 28 days of the announcement.[84] The formal offer must provide shareholders with a significant amount of information about the bid, the intention being that '[s]hareholders must be given sufficient information and advice to enable them to reach a properly informed decision as

---

[75] City Code, GP 6 provides that '[a]n offeree company must not be hindered in the conduct of its affairs for longer than is reasonable by a bid for its securities'.

[76] City Code, rule 1(a).

[77] Ibid, rule 25.1 and rule 3.1 respectively. At the time of writing the Code Committee of the Takeover Panel is also considering whether the target shareholders should themselves receive independent advice: Code Committee of the Takeover Panel, *Review of Certain Aspects of the Regulation of Takeover Bids*, PCP 2010/2, 1 June 2010, section 6.

[78] The target can request the Panel to set a time limit within which the bidder must either make an announcement of a firm intention to make an offer or to state that it does not intend to make a bid ('put up or shut up'): rule 2.4.

[79] Nothing in the City Code or in the general law requires the board to provide the potential bidder with this information.

[80] UK regulation of insider dealing is discussed in 10.5, specifically 10.5.2.1 and 10.5.2.3.

[81] City Code, rule 2.1.

[82] Ibid, rule 2.2.

[83] N Moneiro, Q Zaman and S Leittersdorf, 'Updated Measures of Market Cleanliness' FSA Occasional Paper No 25 (2007). Share movements ahead of such announcements may reflect insider trading, although it is possible that other factors, such as good guesswork by sophisticated investors, are also relevant.

[84] City Code, rules 2.7, 30.1.

to the merits or demerits of an offer'.[85] The City Code sets out in detail the financial and other information which must be made available to the shareholders in order to put them in this position.[86]

As with prospectuses,[87] there is a danger that any profit forecasts included in the information will prove unreliable. Thus, the City Code takes particular care to ensure that the bidder is constrained as to what it can provide, and that shareholders are clear about the assumptions contained in the forecast.[88] Similar issues arise regarding the valuation of assets to be given in connection with an offer.[89] As a general principle, all documents and statements made during the course of an offer 'must be prepared with the highest standards of care and accuracy and the information given must be adequately and fairly presented'.[90] Misstatements in these documents are capable of giving rise to a negligent misstatement claim at common law on the part of the target shareholders, to whom these documents are clearly addressed,[91] or the Takeover Panel has the power to award compensation.[92] Any advertisements connected with an offer which may be used to persuade shareholders to accept the offer made to them are also subject to regulation by the City Code.[93] The City Code attempts to keep high pressure salesmanship techniques that otherwise might be employed by the bidder to a minimum. However, the bidder will do what it can to encourage the shareholders to accept the offer. One common technique employed by bidders is to hold meetings with institutional shareholders, financial journalists and analysts to explain their position.[94]

---

[85]   Ibid, rule 23.

[86]   Ibid, rules 24, 25. The Code Committee of the Takeover Panel is currently consulting on the scope and content of these disclosures, to determine whether the bidder needs to disclose more about, eg, the way in which it plans to finance the bid: Code Committee of the Takeover Panel, *Review of Certain Aspects of the Regulation of Takeover Bids*, n 77. As regards the need for a bidder to comply with the FSA's prospectus requirements on a share-exchange offer see FSA Handbook, Prospectus rules, PR 1.2.2(2) and 1.2.3(3).

[87]   See 9.4.2.

[88]   City Code, rule 28.

[89]   Ibid, rule 29.

[90]   Ibid, rule 19.1.

[91]   *Caparo Industries plc v Dickman* [1990] 2 AC 605. The Court of Appeal in *Morgan Crucible Co plc v Hill Samuel & Co Ltd* [1991] Ch 295 refused to strike out a claim by the bidder against the directors of the target that inaccurate statements by the target company during the course of the bid had been intended to cause the bidder to raise its bid, which indeed the bidder had done. However in *Partco Group Ltd v Wragg* [2002] EWCA Civ 594; [2002] 2 BCLC 323 on similar facts the Court of Appeal expressed doubt that the directors could be said to be liable since in making the relevant statements they had acted for the company (now owned by the bidder) and not personally. However, it seems clear that, in principle, bid documentation can give rise to a claim for negligent misstatement if the claimant can establish that the maker of the statement assumed responsibility for it, and made the statement knowing that it would be made available to a particular person who would rely on it for a particular type of transaction which is known (or ought to be known) to the maker of the statement (see eg *Galoo Ltd v Bright Grahame Murray* [1994] 1 WLR 1360 where the target company auditors sent the accounts to a potential bidder, a purpose that was known to the auditors).

[92]   See Companies Act 2006, s 954 which allows the Panel to award compensation for a breach of a rule. More generally, s 952 gives the Takeover Panel power to develop a range of penalties akin to those of the FSA (for discussion see 9.5.3.2). The FSA's powers are not available in this context since the bid documentation, even in relation to a share-for share exchange, does not amount to a prospectus: PR 1.2.2(2) and 1.2.3(3).

[93]   City Code, rule 19.4. This rule attempts to regulate not only advertisements in the press, on television, radio, video etc but also those circumstances in which shareholders are contacted by representatives of the bidder to try to persuade them to accept the offer (rule 19.5 and see also rule 4.3 regarding approaches to private individuals or small corporate shareholders).

[94]   These are allowed, despite the potential breach of rule 20.1 of the City Code (which provides that '[i]nformation about parties to an offer must be made equally available to all offeree company shareholders and persons with information rights as nearly as possible at the same time and in the same manner') providing that no new material is disclosed and no significant new opinions are expressed (see City Code, Notes on rule 20.1).

The City Code imposes significant restrictions on the ability of the bidder to impose conditions on the offer since one aim of the City Code is that the shareholders should have a clear proposition to accept or reject.[95] However, one condition that will always be present in a bid, because it is required by the City Code, is that an offer for voting securities will be conditional on acceptances being secured by the bidder sufficient to give it, together with securities already held, 50 per cent of the voting rights in the target.[96] An important stage in any bid is therefore when it becomes 'unconditional as to acceptances', which means that it has satisfied all of its conditions (including passing the 50 per cent hurdle — or such higher hurdle as the bidder has imposed on the bid) and the bid has effectively succeeded. Once the formal offer documents have been posted to the shareholders, the bid is open to acceptance by the shareholders to whom it is addressed. The offer must be kept open for acceptance for at least 21 days.[97]

Once the offer period is underway, there is a danger that a false market in the target company's shares may be created, a danger that is specifically recognised within the City Code.[98] In addition to the possibility of insider dealing, for example where the bidder comes to believe that its offer will not succeed and therefore seeks to sell its shares at the inflated price caused by the announcement of a bid, there are concerns about market manipulation. For example, the bidder could attempt to rig the market by causing a fall in the target share price, in order to make the offer look more attractive. The bidder could seek to achieve this by selling its own shares in the target. Of course, the usual rules governing insider dealing, market manipulation and market abuse apply to govern these issues.[99] In addition, the City Code provides some rules to try to prevent such occurrences. For example the City Code provides that the bidder, and those acting in concert with it, must not sell any securities in the target during the offer period without the consent of the Takeover Panel.[100] The concept of 'acting in concert' is an important one, as the City Code attempts to capture not only single bidders acting alone, but also situations where two or more persons cooperate to obtain or consolidate control of a company.[101]

One common feature in many bids is the need for a bidder to revise its initial offer to the shareholders, either because its original offer proves unattractive to the shareholders or

---

[95]   See City Code, rule 13. Rules 13.1 and 13.3, for example, make it clear that the bidder must not make an offer unless financing is already in place (and see also GP 5). However, one exception to this is that the bidder may make the offer conditional on the obtaining of shareholder approval from its own shareholders to allow a fresh issue of shares in the bidder to be used to fund the bid (see City Code, Notes on rules 13.1 and 13.3).

[96]   City Code, rule 10. The bidder can make the offer conditional on a higher level of acceptances than 50%. At the time of writing the Code Committee of the Takeover Panel is consulting on whether to raise this figure to, say, 60% or two thirds of the voting rights of the target company, as part of their consideration whether it should be harder for hostile bids to succeed. A further point being considered by the Code Committee in this document is whether shares acquired during the offer period should be disenfranchised for some purposes, so that they might not count towards this acceptance provision, in order to reduce the possible influence of short-term investors, although this idea does run into potential difficulties with the equality of treatment provision in GP1. See *Review of Certain Aspects of the Regulation of Takeover Bids*, n 77.

[97]   Ibid, rule 31.1 (this can subsequently be extended). The maximum length of time that the offer may remain open for acceptance is until the 60th day after the offer was posted: rule 31.6.

[98]   City Code, GP 4 states that '[f]alse markets must not be created in the securities of the offeree company, of the offeror company or of any other company concerned by the bid in such a way that the rise or fall of the prices of the securities becomes artificial and the normal functioning of the markets is distorted'.

[99]   For discussion see 10.5.

[100]   City Code, rule 4.2. In addition during the offer period there are stricter than usual rules in place governing disclosure (see, for example, City Code, rule 8).

[101]   For the definition of 'acting in concert' for these purposes see City Code, Definitions section (reflecting Takeover Directive 2004/25/EC, art 2(1)(d)).

to take account of an offer from a rival bidder. At this point the City Code provides that the revised offer must be kept open for a further period of at least 14 days[102] and any shareholders who had accepted the original offer are entitled to the revised consideration.[103]

12.3.1.3   Squeeze-out

In some circumstances the bidder will want to acquire total control of the target. This is particularly common in private equity transactions, where bidders generally want to use the target's assets to secure the loans made to the bidder to finance the bid.[104] One possibility is for the bidder to effect the takeover via a scheme of arrangement which requires a special resolution of the target shareholders, but once approved will bind all of the shareholders, including the dissenting minority, to sell their shares.[105] The squeeze-out rules can also help in this situation.[106] They provide that, where a single class of shares has been bid for, the offeror is entitled to acquire compulsorily the shares of the non-acceptors if the offer has been accepted by at least 90 per cent in value of the shares to which the offer relates.[107] If the shares are voting shares the acceptances also have to represent at least 90 per cent of the voting rights carried by those shares.[108] Where more than one class is bid for, the 90 per cent test is applied to each class separately.[109] A takeover offer is defined for these purposes as one to acquire all of the shares[110] of the company (or all of the shares of a class) which on the date of the offer the bidder does not already hold and to do so on the same terms for all of the shares (or all of the shares of a particular class).[111]

The successful bidder triggers the squeeze-out procedure by giving notice to the non-accepting shareholders, accompanied by a statutory declaration of its entitlement to do so,[112] within three months of the last day on which the offer could be accepted.[113] The effect of the notice is that the bidder becomes entitled and bound to acquire the shares on

---

[102]   City Code, rule 32.1.

[103]   Ibid, rule 32.3.

[104]   Private equity is discussed further in chapter 14.

[105]   Schemes of arrangement are discussed in detail in chapter 13.

[106]   Squeeze-out rules have been present in companies legislation since 1929. The current rules are located in Companies Act 2006, Part 28 Ch 3. These rules also implement article 15 of the Takeover Directive 2004/25/EC which required some amendments to the existing law governing takeovers. For discussion of the reforms in the 2006 Act see also the Company Law Review Steering Group, *Modern Company Law for a Competitive Economy: Final Report* (July 2001) URN 01/942–3, 282–300.

[107]   Companies Act 2006, s 979(2)(a). Note that the 90% figure does not relate to the total number of shares of the class, some of which may be held by the bidder before the bid is launched and which are therefore excluded from the calculation. This includes all shares which the bidder has already contracted to acquire unconditionally: s 975(1). As for conditional acceptances, these do not count towards the 90% except where the promise by the existing holder is to accept the offer when and if it is made (ie an irrevocable undertaking) and the undertaking is given for no significant consideration beyond the promise to make the offer (s 975(1)(2) and see *Modern Company Law for a Competitive Economy*, n 106, paras 13.26–13.42). In addition s 977(1) excludes from the definition of 'shares to which the offer relates' shares acquired by the bidder after the date of the offer but outside the bid where the bidder offers more than the final offer price for those shares.

[108]   Ibid, s 979(2)(b).

[109]   Ibid, s 979(3)(4).

[110]   For the definition of 'shares' for this purpose see s 974(4).

[111]   Companies Act 2006, s 974(2)(3). A concession is made as regards the need for the offer to be on the same terms for all shares by s 978, which provides for circumstances in which offers may not be communicated to target shareholders who are foreign residents (see also *Re Joseph Holt plc* [2001] 2 BCLC 604).

[112]   Ibid, s 979(4)–(8). The bidder must also send the documents to the target company: s 980(4)–(8).

[113]   Ibid, s 980(2)–(3). Where the offer is not governed by the City Code, so that there is no fixed closing date for the offer, the period is six months from the date of the offer.

the final terms of the offer.[114] From the bidder's point of view the squeeze-out right is valuable as it prevents the minority exploiting their hold up power in circumstances where the bidder has good reasons to move to 100 per cent ownership. It can therefore be regarded as an incentive to bidders.

The effect of the squeeze-out provision is to allow for an expropriation of the shares of the minority, albeit at a fair price, and it is not surprising that the squeeze-out rule is found in legislation rather than the City Code.[115] Non-accepting shareholders can appeal to the court, objecting to the bidder's right to acquire their shares, or asking for the terms of the acquisition to be amended.[116] The expropriatory nature of these provisions has meant that the courts have tended to construe them strictly when determining whether the bidder has met the requirements for a squeeze-out to occur.[117] However, once it is clear that the bidder does fulfil the requirements, it is for the petitioner to demonstrate that there should be no acquisition or that the terms of the offer (eg the offer price) should be amended.[118] On this latter point, if 90 per cent of the shareholders have accepted an offer this will normally be taken by the court as evidence that the offer is fair. However, the courts may be prepared to amend the offer, or to refuse compulsory acquisition completely, if it can be shown that the 90 per cent acceptances should not be taken as an indication of the fairness of the compulsory acquisition offer to the remaining 10 per cent. Examples that emerge from the cases are where the 90 per cent acceptors were not independent of the bidder, or were not given sufficient information on which to make their decision.[119]

12.3.1.4 Sell-out

The squeeze-out right is now mirrored by a sell-out right, which allows the last 10 per cent of shareholders to leave the company rather than to remain as minority shareholders.[120] Shareholders can therefore refuse the offer initially with the understanding that if the bidder achieves the 90 per cent threshold, then the shareholder can accept the offer at that

---

[114] Ibid, s 981(2). If the final offer gave the shareholders alternative choices of consideration then these must also be made available to the non-accepting shareholders in the squeeze-out. If the alternative is no longer available (eg a non-cash consideration that cannot now be provided either by the bidder or by a third party) then a cash equivalent must be offered: s 981(5) (and see *Re Carlton Holdings Ltd* [1971] 1 WLR 918). One problem arises where the non-accepting shareholders cannot be traced; s 982 provides a solution to this situation.

[115] One consequence is that the Companies Act 2006 has a slightly different ambit from that of the City Code, so that the squeeze-out provisions apply to all companies within the meaning of the Act, including both public and private companies: Companies Act 2006, s 974 and see *Fiske Nominees Ltd v Dwyka Diamond Ltd* [2002] EWHC 770; [2002] 2 BCLC 123.

[116] Companies Act 2006, s 986(1).

[117] Eg *Re Chez Nico (Restaurants) Ltd* [1992] BCLC 192 where Browne-Wilkinson VC construed the actions of the directors of a company as an invitation to the shareholders to offer to sell their shares to them rather than an 'offer' within the terms of the squeeze-out rules and therefore held that the squeeze-out provisions did not apply.

[118] Companies Act 2006, s 986(4).

[119] *Re Bugle Press Ltd* [1961] Ch 270; *Re Chez Nico (Restaurants) Ltd* [1992] BCLC 192; *Fiske Nominees Ltd v Dwyka Diamond Ltd* [2002] EWHC 770; [2002] 2 BCLC 123.

[120] Note however, that the calculation of the 90% threshold operates somewhat differently in squeeze-out and sell-out. In squeeze-out the test is whether there has been a 90% level of acceptances of the offer. In sell-out, by contrast, the test is whether the bid has left the bidder holding 90% of the shares (s 983(1)).

point.[121] The bidder must give each non-accepting shareholder notice of their entitlement to be bought out within one month of the end of the offer period and shareholders then have three months to take up this right.[122] The effect of the notice is that the bidder is bound to acquire the shares on the final terms of the offer.[123] Either the bidder or a non-accepting shareholder may apply for the court to determine the terms of the offer.[124]

In practice the sell-out remedy is not used a great deal, since the City Code requires the bidder to keep the offer open for a further 14 days once the offer has become unconditional as to acceptances,[125] and this gives shareholders an opportunity to change their mind and accept the offer, without the need to demonstrate that the bidder has reached the 90 per cent threshold and without the possibility of court intervention. There are strong reasons to have a squeeze-out right in place. It allows the bidder to achieve a 100 per cent shareholding in the target without exploitation of the last 10 per cent. It also prevents the minority shareholders exploiting their position where the bidder has good reasons to move to 100 per cent ownership. However, the reasons for the sell-out right are less clear.[126] Perhaps the best explanation for it is that it is seen as 'a fair counterpart for the squeeze-out right conferred on the majority shareholders and a component of the proportionality of the squeeze-out solution'.[127]

12.3.1.5   Further Offers

Where an offer has not been successful, ie where it has not become wholly unconditional within the bid timetable, or has been withdrawn or has lapsed, neither the bidder, nor any person in concert with it, may make another offer for the target company within the next 12 months.[128] Further, if a person or concert party holds 50 per cent or more of the voting rights, it must not, within six months of the closure of the offer, make a second offer or acquire any shares from the shareholders on better terms than those under the previous offer.[129]

---

[121]   Companies Act 2006, ss 983–985. This is now a requirement of EC law: Takeover directive 2004/25/EC, art 16. For a discussion of the sell-out rule in the European context see *Report of the High Level Group of Experts (the Winter Group) on Issues Related to Takeover Bids* (January 2002) 63.

[122]   Ibid, s 984(1)–(4). There are criminal sanctions for the bidder and any officer in default: s 984(5)–(7).

[123]   Ibid, s 985.

[124]   Ibid, s 986.

[125]   City Code, rule 31.4.

[126]   The Winter Group suggested three possible explanations for the sell-out right: protection of minority shareholders against abuse by the new controller; protection for the minority given the illiquid nature of the market for selling their shares; and promotion of undistorted choice by the shareholders (see 12.3.4 for further discussion of these issues): *Report of the High Level Group of Experts on Issues Related to Takeover Bids*, Brussels, January 2002. However, Professor Davies has doubted whether any of these explanations holds water: P Davies, 'The Notion of Equality in European Takeover Regulation' in J Payne (ed), *Takeovers in English and German Law* (Oxford, Hart Publishing, 2002) 21.

[127]   *Report of the High Level Group of Experts on Issues Related to Takeover bids*, ibid, 62.

[128]   City Code, rule 35.1. This includes neither the bidder nor a concert party of which it is a member acquiring 30% or more of the shares of the target in that period (ie triggering the mandatory bid rule). The bidder is also prevented from making any statement that might raise the possibility that an offer might be made.

[129]   Ibid, rule 35.3.

12.3.2   The Relationship Between the Target Directors and the Target Shareholders

One of the fundamental decisions which any system of takeover regulation needs to address is whether the decision to accept the bid should be left to the target shareholders alone, or whether the decision is one for both the target shareholders and target directors. As discussed above, the UK has from the outset given the decision to the target shareholders. The Takeover Directive gave Member States the option of opting out of the principle that shareholders should be the decision-makers on the bid. Unsurprisingly, given the UK's long adherence to this principle, the UK did not take up this opportunity.[130]

The current incarnation of this principle is found in the City Code at General Principle 3 (GP 3) and rule 21.[131] This is sometimes referred to as the 'no frustration' principle. It states, in general terms, that the directors of the target cannot take any actions which constrain the freedom of the shareholders as a whole from deciding whether to accept the offer. The general principles set out at the front of the City Code are all taken directly from the Takeover Directive.[132] The general principles are expressed in broad terms. GP 3, for example, states that '[t]he board of an offeree company must act in the interests of the company as a whole and must not deny the holders of securities the opportunity to decide on the merits of the bid'. The general principles in the City Code are supplemented by more detailed rules, such as rule 21, which puts the meat onto the bones of GP 3.

Before moving on to discuss the detail of these provisions, a number of points should be noted. First, the provisions in the City Code provide that the no frustration principle applies only where the 'board has reason to believe that a bona fide offer might be imminent'.[133] A distinction therefore has to be drawn between the period prior to this point, when ordinary principles of company law apply to govern the situation, and the situation when a bid is imminent, or has actually been made, in which case takeover regulation applies on top of the usual rules.[134] These scenarios will be discussed separately next.

---

[130]   See *Company Law Implementation of the European Directive on Takeover Bids*, n 63, para 3.12. The Takeover Directive 2004/25/EC was a very long time in the making. Part of the problem was the fact that very different systems of takeover regulation are in evidence within Europe. For example, the UK's system (where decision-making in a bid is given to the shareholders) is quite different from that of other Member States, such as Germany (which does not apply a board neutrality principle). The drafters found it impossible to get all Member States to agree on a single system of takeover regulation for the EU and therefore hit upon a compromise solution which allows Member States to opt out of certain aspects of the Directive. These include article 9 of the directive (which gives the decision-making role in a bid to the shareholders) and article 11 (the breakthrough rule).

[131]   The Panel's Code Committee can make changes to the Rules, after public consultation: City Code, Introduction, A9. The Rules are interpreted by the Panel purposively so that the sprit as well as the letter of the rules must be observed (Introduction, A2).

[132]   Takeover directive 2004/25/EC, art 3. The six General Principles currently in place in the Code replaced the previous ten General Principles, when the directive was implemented.

[133]   City Code, rule 21.1.

[134]   Cf D Kershaw, 'The Illusion of Importance: Reconsidering the UK's Takeover Defence Prohibition' (2007) 56 *International Comparative Law Quarterly* 267 who argues that pre-bid and post-bid approvals of defensive tactics by shareholders are functionally equivalent (so that the no frustration principle in the Code adds little or nothing to UK company law).

Second, the allocation of the decision on the bid has a number of consequences, including, potentially, corporate governance implications. These are discussed at 12.3.2.2.2 below.

12.3.2.1   Pre-bid Defences

The City Code does not apply before the point where a bid is 'imminent'. There are two good reasons why this is the case. First, the no frustration principle involves a significant interference in normal company law principles. In general the UK operates a system of centralised management, at least in public companies. The courts recognise that as a general rule they should not interfere with the way in which the board exercises its discretion to run the company,[135] subject only to upholding general fiduciary principles. Shareholders in UK companies have control of the board, via their ability to remove directors, as well as some potentially important corporate governance rights,[136] but in general once directors are in place significant powers of management are delegated to them.[137] The no frustration rule prevents the directors from taking actions which are within the usual scope of the board's powers of management. The curtailment of these powers can be justified once a bid is imminent, but to allow this infringement before that point would constitute a significant constraint on the directors' power of management at all times. This would be problematic not only for directors, but also for shareholders, who get the benefit of the existing system of centralised management.

Second, one of the justifications for changing the rules once a bid is imminent is that in addition to the usual agency problem that exists between directors and shareholders in a typical UK public company, which general company law principles address, there is the added problem that if a bid succeeds the target directors stand to lose their jobs. This increases the chance they will behave in a self-serving manner. When a bid is imminent, the particularly acute nature of the agency problem justifies the imposition of the no frustration rule; pre-bid, this justification falls away. The general company law rules governing the agency problem between directors and shareholders are felt to be enough to deal with the pre-bid situation, in combination with the other constraints that exist for directors at this point, discussed below.

As a result, boards have significant freedom, in theory, pre-bid to put in place measures that could prevent a future bid from succeeding. Broadly these measures consist of two types: those designed to make the company less attractive to the bidder, and those which attempt to make it more difficult for the bidder to succeed in the bid. However, these are not mutually exclusive categories and a measure of overlap is possible. An example of the first type of measure is the classic poison pill which provides that the existing shareholders of a company, excluding the bidder, will receive a large amount of equity rights (shares, options etc) at a very substantial discount if one shareholder obtains a specified stake in the company, generally in the region of 10 to 20 per cent of the target's existing voting shares, without the approval of the target's management. Issuing discounted equity rights in this way not only destroys the hostile bidder's voting majority but also significantly

---

[135]   Eg *Automatic Self-Cleansing Filter Syndicate Co Ltd v Cuninghame* [1906] 2 Ch 34.

[136]   For discussion see 10.2.2.

[137]   See eg Model Articles for Public Companies, art 3: The Companies (Model Articles) Regulations 2008 (SI 3229/2008), Sch 3).

dilutes the bidder's investment.[138] Another possibility is to agree that there will be a return of cash to existing shareholders by way of a special dividend or repurchase of shares, which will have an impact on the gearing of the company and may make it less attractive to a bidder.

Other options are for the directors to agree to sell certain assets of the company to a third party should a bid be successful (the crown jewels defence). The specified assets are ideally those of most interest to a potential hostile bidder. Alternatively, the directors could enter into contracts which place the desired assets of the company outside the control of the shareholders in some other way. The directors could alternatively agree to make a significant acquisition in order to make the target more expensive for the bidder.[139] Another possibility is to give certain shareholders significantly enhanced voting rights in the event of a takeover bid. The effect of this measure is to ensure that although the bidder might acquire the majority of the shares in the company, if it does not hold the shares carrying the enhanced voting rights then it will still not acquire control of the management of the target. Another mechanism for achieving much the same end, is to alter the articles of the company in order to raise significantly the requisite majority for shareholder resolutions.[140]

In practice, there tend to be far fewer possibilities of the second type of pre-bid defences, ie those designed to make it more difficult for the bidder to succeed in the bid. One example, however, might involve placing restrictions in the articles of the company so that share transfers are restricted thereby giving the directors control of share transfers.

Directors' ability to make use of these defensive tactics pre-bid in the UK is by no means unconstrained. A number of different constraints exist in practice, namely the need to take account of their directors' duties, to take account of the general requirements imposed by companies and securities legislation, and to take account of the views of the shareholders, particularly the institutional shareholders. These constraints will be considered next.

12.3.2.1.1   Directors' Duties

There are two relevant duties that might operate as a constraint on directors considering defensive tactics in the pre-bid situation: the duty to promote the success of the company in section 172 of the Companies Act 2006 and the requirement that directors must exercise their powers for a proper purpose, now found in section 171 of the Companies Act 2006.

The directors' duty to promote the success of the company in section 172 is a subjectively assessed obligation[141] to act 'for the benefit of its members as a whole'.[142] However, in doing so, the director is required to have regard to a number of factors, such as the likely long-term consequences of the decision, and the interests of a number of

---

[138]   A twist on this defensive tactic is to issue shares to a friendly third party who wishes to see the target remain independent.

[139]   An extreme form of this latter defence that can only be put in place post-bid is the 'Pacman' defence whereby the target makes an offer to acquire the bidder.

[140]   A variation on this idea is to include a provision which restricts the voting rights of certain shareholders (eg the bidder) in the event of a successful bid.

[141]   A director must act 'in the way he considers, in good faith, would be most likely to promote the success of the company . . .' (Companies Act 2006, s 172(1)). See 3.2.1.3.1.

[142]   Companies Act 2006, s 172(1).

different stakeholder groups, including the company's employees and customers.[143] The interests of these other stakeholder groups do not override the interests of the shareholders but are intended to help the director to judge the long-term interests of the shareholders as a whole.[144]

When putting in place any pre-bid defences, the directors will need to ensure that they are acting to promote the success of the company in the manner specified in section 172. However, this could introduce interesting problems in the context of a takeover. Usually shareholders will be interested in the long-term health of the company, and will want to see the company grow over time, since this will entail the best possible income and capital growth for the shareholders, as well as being beneficial to the other stakeholders in the company. Aligning the shareholders with other stakeholders in order to ensure that the directors act in the long-term interests of the shareholders makes sense. However, in the takeover context the shareholders' interests may be much shorter term. They are primarily interested in the cash on the table. This leaves directors in a difficult position if the offer is a good one (in the sense of the amount of cash offered) but the directors believe that the bidder will act in a way that is deleterious to other stakeholder groups, for example by sacking a significant number of employees, or to the company itself, such as where the bidder's plan is to extract synergies from the acquisition by ending the company's ability to carry on business independently. The current formulation of this duty in section 172, and the emphasis on the long-term interests of the members, suggests that the directors are not concerned solely with maximising the amount of the offer and that they should take account of a broader range of issues.

Second, directors are required to exercise their powers for a proper purpose.[145] The proper purpose test is objective, ie even if the directors have acted honestly they may be in breach of this duty if they have exercised their powers for a purpose outside those for which their powers were conferred upon them.[146] The courts will construe the company's articles in order to determine whether a particular purpose is proper.[147] However, the courts have acknowledged that there might be a range of purposes associated with a particular action of the directors.[148] In this case the test is applied to the dominant or primary purpose of the directors' actions.[149] As long as the directors can satisfy the court that the purpose of the action was proper, they will not be in breach of this duty, even if the incidental, and desired, result of the particular action is to secure the directors' control of the company. This is an important restriction on the application of the proper purposes rule. It is for the claimant to demonstrate that the primary purpose of the board's action is to retain control of the company. If some other purpose exists that can be said to be the 'primary' purpose, for example where the action can be said to be primarily referable to the board's general task of managing the company, then they will not be in breach of their

---

[143]   Ibid, s 172(1)(a)–(f).

[144]   See 3.2.1.3.1.

[145]   Companies Act 2006, s 171(b). This reflects the prior common law position (see eg *Howard Smith Ltd v Ampol Petroleum Ltd* [1974] AC 821.

[146]   [1974] AC 821, 834; *Punt v Symons& Co Ltd* [1903] 2 Ch 506.

[147]   *Re Smith and Fawcett Ltd* [1942] Ch 304, 306.

[148]   Section 171(b) provides that a director must 'only exercise powers for the *purposes* for which they are conferred' (emphasis added).

[149]   *Hirsche v Sims* [1894] AC 654.

fiduciary duty. The ambit of the proper purposes rule is therefore narrow. However, where directors are found to have acted for an improper purpose, their act is voidable by the company.[150]

In *Howard Smith Ltd v Ampol Petroleum Ltd,*[151] a majority shareholder (Ampol) in a company (Millers) made an offer to acquire the remaining shares in Millers. The directors of Millers preferred a takeover offer from Howard Smith that could not succeed as long as Ampol retained its majority shareholding. The directors therefore issued new shares to Howard Smith to reduce Ampol to a minority position. Ampol claimed that this issue of new shares involved the directors acting for an improper purpose. The court rejected the idea that the only purpose of an issue of new shares was to raise new capital for the company when it needed it. There could be other, proper, purposes involved in a share issue. For example, where a competitor seeks to acquire shares in a company purely in order to run that company down and reduce competition, it may be a proper issue of the directors' powers to issue further shares in order to maintain their control of the company.[152] In *Howard Smith v Ampol,* however, no such alternative, proper, purpose was in evidence. The only purpose of the issue was to block the bid by Ampol. Therefore, even though the directors in that case were not acting self-interestedly, and indeed believed they were acting in the best interests of the company in attempting to block the bid, they were held to have been acting in breach of the proper purpose rule.

However, it does not seem to be the case that directors who exercise their powers to attempt to promote or defeat a takeover offer will always fall foul of the proper purpose rule. Whilst any such attempt post-bid will fall foul of the City Code,[153] measures put in place pre-bid may not. In *Criterion Properties plc v Stratford UK Properties LLC*[154] the board of Criterion were concerned that a particular company was increasing its shareholding in Criterion and would seek to acquire control. To try to prevent this Criterion amended a joint venture agreement it had entered into with Stratford to allow Criterion to buy out Stratford at either the market value of its interest or a sum calculated to give Stratford a 25 per cent per annum return on its investment, whichever was the greater. This was freely referred to by the parties as a poison pill, intended to act as a disincentive to any takeover of Criterion. Criterion later sought to rescind the variation agreement on the basis, inter alia, that it involved the directors acting for an improper purpose.

At first instance, Hart J accepted that a poison pill agreement of this sort was an improper exercise by the claimant's directors of their powers.[155] Particularly problematic was the fact that this poison pill was not limited to preventing a takeover by a particular unsavoury predator, but would be triggered by any takeover, even a wholly beneficial one. This poison pill seemed designed primarily to entrench the existing directors rather than to protect the company. Also problematic was the fact that the variation exposed Criterion to 'a serious contingent liability'[156] designed to 'poison' the company and therefore could

---

[150] *Howard Smith Ltd v Ampol Petroleum Ltd* [1974] AC 821.
[151] Ibid.
[152] *Cayne v Global Natural Resources plc,* unreported, 12 August 1982 per Megarry J.
[153] City Code, GP 3 and rule 21 discussed below at 12.3.2.2.1.
[154] [2002] EWHC 496 (Ch), [2002] 2 BCLC 151 (Ch); [2002] EWCA Civ 1883, [2003] 1 WLR 2108 (CA); [2004] UKHL 28; [2004] 1 WLR 1846.
[155] [2002] EWHC 496 (Ch); [2002] 2 BCLC 151.
[156] *Criterion Properties plc v Stratford UK Properties LLC* [2002] EWHC 496 (Ch); [2002] 2 BCLC 151, [21] per Hart J.

not be regarded as something which was of benefit to the company as an economic unit. Hart J relied on the line of cases represented by *Howard Smith Ltd v Ampol Petroleum Ltd*,[157] extending this line of argument from its context of directors' share issues to that of poison pill agreements. The Court of Appeal similarly had no difficulty finding that the directors in the instant case had acted for an improper purpose,[158] but left open the possibility that a more limited form of poison pill, targeted at a particular predator genuinely believed to pose a threat to the company, where the measure implemented did not itself cause significant damage to the company, could be permissible.[159]

However, the House of Lords preferred to analyse this as turning solely on whether the managing director of Criterion, who had signed the agreement on behalf of Criterion, acted within the actual or apparent scope of his authority. It was not established that the contract in question had been entered into by persons with authority to bind the promisor. Since those issues had not been properly addressed by counsel or the courts below, and because their resolution seemed likely to turn on contested questions of fact, the House affirmed the Court of Appeal's conclusion that this was not a suitable case for the entry of summary judgment. The consequence of the House of Lords' decision is that the question whether directors are entitled to exercise their powers to deter a takeover by signing a poison pill agreement can be subsumed within the authority issue. Directors acting for an improper purpose can be assumed to lack actual authority to bind the company to an agreement, although it may still be possible for the third party to bind the company on the basis of apparent authority.[160]

Lord Scott acknowledged that this case raised an 'issue of considerable public importance', namely whether it was 'open to a board of directors of a public company to authorise the signing on the company's behalf of a "poison pill" agreement intended to deter outsiders from making offers to shareholders to purchase their shares . . .where, as here, the deterrence consists of a contingent divesting of company assets'.[161] However, his Lordship refused to commit himself as to the validity of such devices, simply observing that the agreement in this case went beyond deterring unwanted predators to deterring desirable predators and entrenching the positions of the managing director and chairman.[162] However, he did state that if actual or apparent authority did exist then he could see no reason why the agreement would not be enforceable.[163]

One difficulty of using these fiduciary duties to regulate pre-bid defensive measures is the fact that these duties are owed to the company and therefore the company is the correct claimant in any action against the directors.[164] Directors of a company owe no general fiduciary duties to the shareholders.[165] However, 'in appropriate and specific circumstances' a director can have a fiduciary duty to a shareholder,[166] and takeovers are

---

[157]   [1974] AC 821.

[158]   However the Court of Appeal came to a different conclusion to Hart J – and allowed the appeal – on other grounds.

[159]   [2002] EWCA Civ 1883, [2003] 1 WLR 2108 (CA).

[160]   For discussion see DD Prentice and J Payne, 'Company Contracts and Vitiating Factors: Developments in the Law on Directors' Authority' [2005] *Lloyd's Maritime and Commercial Law Quarterly* 447.

[161]   [2004] UKHL 28; [2004] 1 WLR 1846, [29].

[162]   Ibid, [29].

[163]   Ibid, [30].

[164]   *Foss v Harbottle* (1843) 2 Hare 461 and see now Companies Act 2006, Part 11.

[165]   *Percival v Wright* [1902] 2 Ch 421; *Peskin v Anderson* [2001] 1 BCLC 372 (CA).

[166]   *Peskin v Anderson* [2000] 2 BCLC 1 (Ch), 14 per Neuberger J.

one of those situations where fiduciary duties have sometimes been said to arise.[167] To date the types of scenarios in which a duty has arisen have involved the directors buying shares from the shareholders where the directors know a takeover is about to occur, and the takeover will have a positive impact on the share price. In these situations courts have held that the directors are under a duty to disclose that information to the shareholders.[168] These cases have not, however, acknowledged that individual shareholders can bring an action against the directors for breach of the proper purpose doctrine.

12.3.2.1.2 Share Transfer Restrictions

The management of a company can retain control if they can prevent ownership of the shares being transferred. Thus, if they can impose a restriction on the transfer of shares (by including such a restriction in the company's articles, for example) then they will make the company less vulnerable to a hostile takeover. However, the Stock Exchange's Listing Rules prevent constraints being imposed on the free transferability of shares. The Listing Rules state that fully paid shares have to be free from any restrictions on the right of transfer.[169]

12.3.2.1.3 Removal of Directors and Staggered Boards

Some measures that are in use in other jurisdictions are not possible in the UK due to existing companies or securities legislation. For example, boards could try to make a takeover less attractive by putting in place a staggered board structure whereby those responsible for the management of the company are appointed for fixed terms, with a number expiring and being renewed every year. The potential difficulties caused by a delay between a bidder acquiring a controlling interest and being able to implement management changes could make a hostile bid less attractive. However in the UK it is impossible to limit the ability of shareholders to remove directors from office at any time by ordinary resolution[170] and so staggered boards of this kind cannot be implemented.[171]

A possible alternative is for the directors to include provisions in their service contracts which provide for substantial compensation in the event of a termination of employment following a takeover bid. If these provisions are substantial enough they may deter a bid. Provisions of this kind may be justified by the need to employ or retain certain individuals but excessive or disproportionate payments will not be justifiable in this way. In relation to all companies in the UK directors' service contracts have to be available for inspection.[172] For quoted companies a copy of the directors' remuneration report including details of termination payments to directors must be sent to the shareholders, and an ordinary

---

[167] *Peskin v Anderson* [2001] 1 BCLC 372, [34] per Mummery LJ (although no such duty arose on the facts of that case); *Coleman v Myers* [1977] 2 NZLR 225 (Sup Ct NZ).

[168] Eg, *Coleman v Myers,* ibid.

[169] FSA Handbook, Listing Rules, LR 2.2.4. For companies listed on AIM see London Stock Exchange, *AIM Rules for Companies,* February 2010, rule 32.

[170] Companies Act 2006, s 168.

[171] Similarly, although it would be possible to include in the articles of association a provision giving only particular shareholders the right to appoint directors (in order to prevent the bidder from being able to do so) these rights would not override the right of the general body of shareholders to remove all of the directors so appointed.

[172] Companies Act 2006, s 228. Shareholders also have the right to request a copy of the contract be sent to them (s 229).

resolution approving the report must be passed by the shareholders in general meeting,[173] although this vote is advisory only and does not affect the validity of the payment.[174]

Where the agreement to pay particular compensation to directors is made after a bid becomes imminent then shareholder approval will be required.[175] A payment made without shareholder approval will be treated as held on trust by the recipient for those who have sold their shares as a result of the offer.[176] This provision also applies where the obligation to make the payment is entered into pre-bid, but 'for the purposes of, in connection with or in consequence of' the takeover.[177] Arrangements entered into in the face of a bid will therefore require specific shareholder approval, although compensation packages entered into at an earlier stage, before a specific takeover is in contemplation, are regulated only by the more general company law provisions.

12.3.2.1.4   The Role of Shareholders, Particularly Institutional Investors

Many of the types of pre-bid defensive measures described above could only be put in place with the consent or agreement of the shareholders. The provisions regarding compensation payments to directors for loss of office have already been discussed. Significant transactions, involving the sale of the company's assets or the acquisition of assets (as in *Criterion*) may well trigger the need for shareholder consent.

Any alteration of the articles, to introduce non-voting shares or to include enhanced voting rights, for example, requires a shareholders' vote.[178] It is possible for measures of this kind to be put in place in the UK, but very rare. Institutional investors have traditionally been hostile towards the introduction of non-voting shares.[179] As regards enhanced voting rights, in the dispersed shareholding structure which exists for most UK publicly traded companies it is not clear how shareholders would benefit from such provisions and what incentive they would have to approve them. Such provisions do, however, exist in other Member States. Article 11 of the Takeover Directive, known as the 'breakthrough' rule, deals with this issue. Broadly Article 11 allows a bidder to over-ride certain shareholder blocking rights. In effect it provides a 'one share, one vote' rule in

---

[173] Companies Act 2006, ss 420–421, 439. This obligation relates only to quoted companies but the Financial Services Act 2010, s 4 contains a power for the Treasury to extend this obligation to companies more generally.

[174] Ibid, s 439(5).

[175] Ibid, s 219(1) (and see also ss 217–218). These provisions are broadly drafted to include payments made to compensate loss of management positions as well as loss of directorships: s 215(1). They also include payments made by 'any person' (s 219(1)). Compensation is defined to include benefits other than cash (s 215(2)). There is a de minimis exception for payments that do not exceed £200 (s 221).

[176] Ibid, s 222(3).

[177] Ibid, s 220(3) which introduces a 'takeover' exception to the general principle that payments to directors 'in discharge of an existing legal obligation' are excluded (s 220(1)(a) and see *Taupo Totaro Timber Co v Rowe* [1978] AC 537).

[178] An alteration of articles requires a special resolution: Companies Act 2006, s 21 (if the alteration involves the variation of a class right then see Companies Act 2006, s 630). However the inclusion of a supermajority clause (which increases the requisite majority for shareholder resolutions in order to make it harder for the bidder to achieve control) requires unanimity: Companies Act 2006, s 22(2)(b).

[179] See J Franks, C Mayer and S Rossi, 'Spending Less time with the Family: The Decline of Family Ownership in the UK' [2004] European Corporate Governance Institute Working Paper No 35/2004, 5.

relation to a range of shareholder measures that could be used to entrench the incumbent management.[180] Article 11, like Article 9, was made optional and the British Government did opt out of Article 11.[181]

Any pre-bid measure involving the issue of shares will also require the consent of the shareholders. In public companies, shareholder authorisation is needed for decisions by the directors to issue shares or to grant rights to subscribe for or convert any security into shares.[182] Although in principle shareholders can provide the directors with authorisation to issue shares up to five years in advance,[183] in practice institutional investors are unwilling to provide the directors with this kind of blank cheque. In addition, if the directors plan to issue shares other than pro rata to all of the existing shareholders, and in practice this will be the case where the bidder is already a shareholder, as otherwise this form of poison pill would be ineffective to reduce the incentives for the bid, then pre-emption rights will need to be disapplied.[184] Again, in principle, pre-emption rights can be disapplied for periods of up to five years, which would give the directors considerable discretion in relation to share issues.

However, in practice institutional investors prevent such wide discretion being given to the directors. A Statement of Principles drawn up by the Stock Exchange Pre-Emption Group[185] provides guidance on the circumstances in which certain institutional investors should vote in favour of a resolution to disapply pre-emption rights.[186] For example, requests by a company to issue not more than five per cent of its issued share capital non-preemptively in any given year are likely to be regarded as 'routine'.[187] A discount of more than five per cent is not likely to be regarded as routine.[188] Whilst the Statement of Principles does not have the force of law, this document represents the views of the majority of major UK institutional investors. In practice, it is the Statement of Principles rather than the statutory pre-emption provisions that creates the significant restriction on companies, at least listed companies, raising capital.[189] It is also this document that gives shareholders, particularly institutional investors, a level of control over the issue of new shares, which constrains directors' ability to introduce certain poison pills in the pre-bid situation.

---

[180]   Eg, the breakthrough rule would apply on any shareholder vote to approve a post-bid defensive measure and would apply at a general meeting called after a successful bid for the purpose of installing the bidder's nominees as directors of the company. For discussion see J Rickford, 'Emerging European Takeover Law from a British Perspective' [2004] *European Business Law Review* 1379.

[181]   See *Company Law Implementation of the European Directive on Takeover Bids*, n 63, para 3.9. However Article 12 of the Takeover Directive 2004/25/EC requires Member States who opt out to permit opting back in on a company by company basis (see Companies Act 2006, Part 28, Chapter 2).

[182]   Companies Act 2006, s 551. Cf the stricter position once the bid is imminent: City Code, Rule 21.

[183]   Ibid, s 551(3)(b). See 4.3.1.

[184]   Ibid, ss 570–571.

[185]   The Pre-Emption Group comprises representatives of institutional investors, investment banks and listed companies.

[186]   See www.pre-emptiongroup.org.uk/principles/index.htm. This Statement of Principles was formerly known as the Pre-Emption Guidelines. For discussion see *A Study by Paul Myners into the Impact of Shareholders' Pre-emption Rights on a Public Company's Ability to Raise New Capital*, February 2005, URN 05/679, available at www.dti.gov.uk/cld/report_pdfs/02–08-final-report.pdf, chapter 3.

[187]   Pre-Emption Group, *Statement of Principles*, available at www.pre-emptiongroup.org.uk/principles/index.htm, Principle 8.

[188]   Ibid, Principle 11.

[189]   See generally Myners, n 186.

12.3.2.1.5   Summary

Although the City Code does not regulate directors' ability to put in place defensive measures before a bid is imminent, it is certainly not the case that directors are unconstrained in this period. General company law principles, particularly directors' duties, combined with securities legislation and the powerful position of institutional investors in the UK place, significant constraints on directors in this period. It is no surprise that the incidence of poison pills and other types of pre-bid defensive measures is very low in the UK. This contrasts with the position in the US, where poison pills are ubiquitous: 'every public company either has adopted a pill or can adopt one if a hostile offer is made'.[190] These devices work very effectively to repel hostile bids: pills are so poisonous to bidders that no bidder ever swallows a pill.[191]

One common tactic of US bidders is to combine a takeover offer with a proxy contest, whereby the bidder attempts to pass a shareholders' resolution to remove the incumbent directors from the board, replacing them with their own directors. Since pills can generally be redeemed by the directors, combining a hostile takeover with a successful proxy contest enables the pill to be disabled and the bid to proceed.[192] However, the incidence of 'staggered boards' in the US, which limits the number of directors that can be removed at any one time (typically a third), significantly reduces the efficacy of this scheme. Poison pills therefore remain effective devices for repelling an initial hostile takeover offer.[193] However, poison pills in the US are generally regarded as providing an opportunity for negotiation between the bidder and the target directors. Rather than preventing a hostile bid entirely they are commonly seen as a mechanism to allow the target directors to negotiate a higher price for the shareholders.[194] Perhaps it is because these devices are so common, and are regarded as working so effectively, that other forms of takeover defence in the US are relatively rare.[195]

12.3.2.2   Post-bid Defences

12.3.2.2.1   The No Frustration Principle

As discussed, once a bid is imminent or has actually been made, GP 3 and rule 21 of the City Code put in place a strong no frustration rule that is intended to give the decision-making role to the target shareholders and not the target directors. This is now

---

[190] R Gilson, 'Unocal Fifteen Years Later (and What We Can Do About It)' (2001) 26 *Delaware Journal of Corporate Law* 491, 501.

[191] It is key to the success of these devices as effective defensive tactics for the directors that they can be put in place without shareholder approval and that the courts have accepted that it is not a breach of directors' duties if the directors adopt such a scheme, or do not remove the poison pill in the face of a bid (discussed further at 12.3.2.2 below).

[192] See eg LA Bebchuk, JC Coats and G Subramanian, 'The Powerful Antitakeover Force of Staggered Boards: Theory, Evidence and Policy' (2002) 54 *Stanford Law Review* 887.

[193] Some commentators have suggested that one way to counteract the role of poison pills as a defensive tactic in the US is through the use of compensation packages for managers which are triggered by a transfer of control, thereby giving managers an incentive not to invoke the poison pill: eg L Bebchuk and J Fried, *Pay Without Performance: The Unfulfilled Promise of Executive Compensation* (Cambridge MA, Harvard University Press, 2004) 89–91.

[194] JN Gordon, 'An American Perspective on Anti-Takeover Laws in the EU: The German Example' in G Ferrarini, KJ Hopt, J Winter and E Wymeersch (eds), *Reforming Company and Takeover Law in Europe* (Oxford, Oxford University Press, 2004) 548.

[195] Ibid, 551.

also the position at European level as a result of Article 9 of the Takeover Directive.[196] The target board 'must not, without the approval of the shareholders in general meeting . . .take any action which may result in any offer or bona fide possible offer being frustrated or in shareholders being denied the opportunity to decide on its merits . . .'.[197] This rule is strictly applied. It is irrelevant whether the target directors had this purpose in mind in taking a particular action.[198] If the effect of their action may result in the frustration of the bid then they are in breach of the no frustration principle.

However, GP 3 and rule 21 do not require passivity on the part of the directors. The board of the target do have an important role in the bid: they must circulate their opinion on the offer to the shareholders.[199] Directors must obviously act in accordance with their fiduciary duties when providing this opinion, but the City Code goes further in attempting to deal with the potential conflict of interest that can arise. Any directors with a particular conflict of interest, for example those who will have a continuing role with the bidder company if the bid is successful, must not join with the rest of the board in expressing a view on the offer.[200] In addition, the board is required to obtain independent advice on any offer and the substance of that advice must be made known to the shareholders.[201]

Some, limited, defensive tactics are open to the directors. First, they can try to persuade the shareholders that their future would be better if they retained the existing management rather than accepting the offer from the bidder company. This is one of the primary weapons available to the target directors. The bidder will claim that its offer represents a fair price and a premium to the trading value of the target's shares. The target's board will assert that the offer is inadequate and fails properly to reflect the true value of the target's shares.[202] The bid will be defeated only if the shareholders of the target are convinced that the value they will enjoy by retaining their shares is such that the price offered by the bidder is insufficient.

Second, directors can buy shares in the target in order to try to block the bid. However, directors are required to disclose their purchase of shares[203] and there is a more general obligation to disclose once the shareholding reaches the three per cent level.[204]

---

[196]   However, Article 12.1 of the Takeover Directive 2004/25/EC allows Member States to opt out of Article 9 of the directive. Even if a Member State does opt out, a company must be given the right to opt in to the no frustration principle: art 12.2. For discussion see J Rickford, 'The Emerging European Takeover Law from a British Perspective' [2004] *European Business Law Review* 1379.

[197]   City Code, rule 21.1. Prior to the implementation of the Takeover Directive this statement was found in a General Principle (GP 7).

[198]   This may be compared to the operation of the proper purpose rule at common law, discussed above at pages 586–87.

[199]   City Code, rule 25.1. If the board of the target is split in its views then the minority view should also be circulated: Note 2 to rule 25.1.

[200]   Rule 25.1, Note 3 and Note 4. This can cause difficulties in a management buy out situation where all, or substantially all, of the board will continue to have a role in management if the bid is successful (see rule 20.3 as part of the attempt to deal with this situation). This is discussed further in chapter 14, regarding private equity transactions (see particularly 14.5.2).

[201]   City Code, rule 3.1.

[202]   Any profit forecasts and asset valuations must be reported on by the target's auditors and financial adviser and to confirm that the target's board has compiled the forecast after 'due care and consideration': City Code, rule 28.1.

[203]   Market Abuse Directive, art 6(4) implemented into UK law via DTR 3. For discussion see 10.3.2.2.

[204]   Transparency Directive, art 9(1) implemented into UK law via DTR 5.1. For discussion see 10.3.2.3.

Third, GP 3 and rule 21 seem to be restricted to internal corporate action[205] and therefore do not prevent the directors making use of external options to try to frustrate the bid, such as lobbying the competition authorities, at national or EU level, to take action to prohibit the bid or to subject it to conditions unacceptable to the bidder.

Fourth, the directors can seek a 'White Knight', ie a more favourable alternative bidder, although there is no duty on them to do so. The motivation may be to encourage an auction in order to ensure that the highest price is received by the shareholders. It may also be to find a bidder whose plans offer a better outcome for the other stakeholders, or to find a bidder who will treat the incumbent management more favourably. In the UK the practice of seeking a White Knight is generally accepted, as it is seen as giving more choice to the target shareholders.[206] Some academics question this, suggesting that allowing directors to seek White Knights raises the costs of a successful bid, which has the effect of reducing the number of bids that will be launched, ultimately therefore reducing shareholder choice.[207] However, the empirical evidence seems to favour the view that competing bids are wealth-enhancing for the target shareholders.[208] By channelling more wealth to the target shareholders, facilitating competing bids can be regarded as a mechanism for ensuring that the gains generated by the takeover are shared between the bidder and the target shareholders.

The principal concern of any White Knight will be to avoid a bidding war with the original bidder. However, in the UK there is relatively little that can be done to protect the White Knight from a subsequent higher offer by the original bidder. In the US it is common for the White Knight to be issued shares or options in the target in order to enable it to protect its position, but the rules governing share issues, described above, generally put these matters under the control of the shareholders rather than the directors. A break fee arrangement can be put in place, whereby the target company will pay the White Knight's costs should the White Knight's bid be unsuccessful.[209] However the maximum break fee allowed by the City Code is an amount equal to one per cent of the value of the offer,[210] a sum which is low enough to be unlikely to act as a deterrent to the original bidder. Another potential difficulty with a break fee arrangement of this kind is that, where the target is a public company, the arrangement may constitute financial assistance.[211] The fee is only payable if the bid fails, but the agreement for the fee could be regarded as entered into for the purpose of the acquisition. The view of financial

---

[205]   See the list provided within rule 21 of situations in which shareholder approval is required: City Code, rule 21.1(b).

[206]   The Takeover Directive 2004/25/EC also makes it clear that seeking an alternative bidder is not caught by the no frustration principle: art 9(2).

[207]   FH Easterbrook and DR Fischel, 'The Proper Role of a Target's Management in Responding to a Tender Offer' (1981) 94 *Harvard Law Review* 1161; R Romano, 'A Guide to Takeovers: Theory, Evidence and Regulation' (1992) 9 *Yale Journal on Regulation* 119.

[208]   J Franks and R Harris, 'Shareholder Wealth Effects of Corporate Takeovers 1955–1985' in S Peck and P Temple (eds), *Mergers and Acquisitions: Critical Perspectives on Business and Management* (London, Routledge, 2008).

[209]   At the time of writing inducement fees of this kind are under review by the Code Committee of the Takeover Panel: *Review of Certain Aspects of the Regulation of Takeover Bids*, n 77, section 9.

[210]   City Code, rule 21.2. The board and its financial adviser must also confirm in writing to the Takeover Panel that they believe the fee arrangement to be in the best interests of the target shareholders, and the break fee arrangement must be disclosed. By contrast break fees (unregulated by specific takeover rules) are common in the US.

[211]   Companies Act 2006, ss 677–680. See 4.4.4.

assistance adopted by the Court of Appeal in *Chaston v SWP Group plc*[212] certainly seems wide enough to include an agreement to pay a break fee within it. However, it is arguable that this form of assistance will be regarded as unlawful only if the net assets of the company are reduced 'to a material extent'[213] and the one per cent limit on break fees means that these fall below that level.

If the directors hold shares in the target themselves, then they may be able to enter into irrevocable undertakings with the White Knight (or any other bidder) to sell those shares to that bidder in order to demonstrate their support for a particular bid.[214] In *Heron International Ltd v Lord Grade*[215] there were two competing bids for a company. The target directors held 50 per cent of the shares. In addition, and unusually for a public company, the directors' consent was required for the transfer of shares. The directors gave irrevocable undertakings to accept what turned out to be the lower bid, and stood by those undertakings. As a result the higher bid was defeated.

The Court of Appeal held that the directors could not separate their position as shareholders from their position as directors. The court held that the duty of the directors was to obtain the best price for the company and, further that '[t]he directors should not commit themselves to transfer their own voting shares to a bidder unless they are satisfied that he is offering the best price reasonably obtainable'.[216] The idea that director-shareholders are constrained as to how they may exercise their shareholder rights is out of step with the general company law view that a share is a piece of property belonging to the shareholder and that shareholders do not owe fiduciary duties as to how they exercise their shareholder rights.[217] It is also notable that the City Code is silent on this issue. It does not impose an obligation on directors to deal with their shares in the target in any particular manner, and therefore leaves them free to act qua shareholder in a self-interested way if they wish.

A preferable view on this issue was expressed by Hoffmann J in *Re a Company*.[218] The facts were somewhat different. *Re a Company* involved a small private company and the issue arose in the context of an unfair prejudice petition. Nevertheless, Hoffmann J was required to consider whether directors can separate their obligations as directors of a target company when competing offers are made, from their rights as shareholders in the target. Hoffmann J did not accept that directors are under a positive duty to recommend and take all steps within their power to facilitate the highest offer, and neither did he accept that this obligation could restrict their freedom of action in relation to their own shares. The extent of their duty was an obligation, when giving advice to the shareholders under rule 25.1, to act in accordance with their fiduciary duties, and not to exercise their

---

[212] [2002] EWCA Civ 1999; [2003] 1 BCLC 675.

[213] Companies Act 2006, s 677(1)(d). This is on the basis that a break fee arrangement would fall within the definition of 'any other financial assistance given by a company' in s 677(1)(d).

[214] These undertakings need to be given by deed since there is no consideration and no mutual exchange of promises. Note that irrevocable undertakings are treated as shares belonging to the bidder for the purposes of the squeeze-out rule (Companies Act 2006, s 979(2) which is a change from the previous law found in Companies Act 1985, s 428).

[215] [1983] BCLC 244.

[216] Ibid, 265 per Lawton LJ.

[217] Some incursions have been made into this principle, both judge made (eg *Allen v Gold Reefs of West Africa Ltd* [1900] 1 Ch 656) and created by statute (eg Companies Act 2006, s 239) but the general principle still holds good.

[218] [1986] BCLC 382.

powers to prevent other shareholders accepting the higher offer. However directors should be free qua shareholder to accept whichever bid they liked, and to give irrevocable undertakings in advance if that is what they wish to do.

The possibility of the directors seeking a White Knight means that the initial bidder might want to try to persuade the target directors to agree not to do so. It is clear that the directors cannot commit to non-cooperation with a competing bidder, should one come forward. The City Code is clear that once competing bids have arisen, the same information must be provided to each bidder by the target board, even if one of the offers is less welcome than the other(s).[219] However, a more difficult issue arises as to whether the directors can agree not to seek an alternative bidder and, further, to recommend the original bid. It might be that the directors are acting in the best interests of the target shareholders in entering into such an agreement, for instance if the bidder would not make the bid at all without such an agreement, and if the directors genuinely believe that no other bidder will come forward. However, the more significant problem is whether the directors can fetter their discretion in this way.

Section 173(2) of the Companies Act 2006 provides that the duty to exercise independent judgment is not infringed by a director acting 'in accordance with an agreement duly entered into by the company that restricts the future exercise of discretion by its directors'. This is in tune with the decision of the Court of Appeal in *Fulham Football Club Ltd v Cabra Estates plc*,[220] a decision taken prior to the Companies Act 2006. In this case the Court of Appeal held that directors can bind themselves as to the future exercise of their fiduciary powers in some circumstances. However, this decision did not arise in the context of a standard takeover bid scenario; the facts involved the directors fettering their own discretion whereas in the standard takeover context the directors are effectively attempting to restrict the shareholders' future choices. The Court of Appeal stopped short of overruling earlier decisions which did cast doubt on the directors' ability to fetter their discretion in this way.[221] More significantly, section 173(2) does not override the directors' obligation to act in accordance with section 172. This suggests that directors can only bind themselves to act in the future in a way which is consistent with their duty under section 172. Should a subsequent offer emerge which the directors judge to be better than the earlier bid (taking into account the long-term interests of the shareholders) then they would presumably be under an obligation to recommend that bid, irrespective of whatever agreement they had entered into with the original bidder. This seems to be in accordance with the spirit of the City Code.

---

[219]   City Code, rule 20.2. This applies both to the information made available by the board and to the terms on which it is made available (eg the imposition of confidentiality agreements).

[220]   [1994] 1 BCLC 363.

[221]   Eg *Dawson International plc v Coats Paton plc* [1991] BCC 278, although on the facts of that case it was held that the agreement not to seek, cooperate with or recommend a competing bid, was not to be construed as intended to be legally binding by the parties. See also *John Crowther Group Ltd v Carpets International plc* [1990] BCLC 460 in which the board undertook to use 'all reasonable endeavours' to secure the consent of the shareholders. When a higher bid emerged the directors recommended that bid and the initial bidder sued for breach of the agreement. The court held that 'all reasonable endeavours' did not require the directors to act contrary to their fiduciary duty.

12.3.2.2.2 Consequences of the UK's Adoption of the No Frustration Principle

In summary, the UK position does not require passivity on the part of the directors, but it does require that directors take no action to frustrate the bid once the bid is imminent or the offer has actually been made. This is an attempt to put the decision regarding the bid into the hands of the shareholders, sidelining the target board to the greatest extent possible.

This stands in considerable contrast to the approach adopted in the US, where the decision-making role is allocated to the target board, in addition to the shareholders.[222] The bid cannot succeed without the consent of the shareholders, but the shareholders will not have the opportunity to decide whether to accept the offer unless the directors allow the offer to be put to them. In *Unocal Corp v Mesa Petroleum Co*[223] the Supreme Court of Delaware formulated a two stage test to determine the legality of defensive tactics adopted by the target board. First, did the directors have reasonable grounds for believing that the takeover endangered corporate policy and effectiveness? Second, were the defensive measures adopted by the directors reasonable in relation to the threat posed? In applying this test the courts have given considerable latitude to the target directors. The first limb of the test will be satisfied where the target board can demonstrate that the takeover threatens one of the board's existing business policies, which will be the case in the vast majority of hostile bids. If the threat is held to justify defensive action, then preventing the takeover will generally be the best way of heading off the threat, so in practice the second limb has not provided a significant constraint on directors either. In practice the *Unocal* test has been applied in such a way as to put the decision-making power in a takeover first and foremost into the remit of the target board.[224] Sole decision-making is given to the shareholders only if the target board's response to the threat is to take the decision to sell the company or to dispose of its assets.[225]

It is interesting to contrast the US and UK responses to this issue. The US model gives significant power to the target board to determine whether a proposed takeover (and the consequent change of control) will take place. The board are therefore in a position to act on behalf of the shareholders to prevent opportunistic behaviour by the acquirer. It is sometimes suggested that a sale process controlled by the directors on behalf of the shareholders is likely to result in a higher premium than an uncontrolled auction.[226] If this is correct, the danger of the UK system is that uninformed or uncoordinated shareholders may sell their shares for less than they are worth. Set against this view is the strong belief in

---

[222]   This position is not exclusive to the US. Some European states, eg Germany, provide some form of joint decision-making in relation to takeover decisions (see eg §33(1) Übernahmegesetz by which shareholders can authorise directors to take specified types of defensive measures in advance of a hostile offer).

[223]   493 A 2d 946 (Delaware, 1985). For discussion see R J Gilson, 'Unocal Fifteen Years Later (And what we can do about it)' (2001) 26 *Delaware Journal of Corporate Law* 491 and M Lipton and PK Rowe, 'Pills, Polls and Professors: A Reply to Professor Gilson' (2002) 27 *Delaware Journal of Corporate Law* 1.

[224]   Eg *Paramount Communications Inc v Time Inc*, 571 A 2d 1140 (Delaware, 1990); *Unitrin Inc v American General Corporation*, 651 A 2d 1361 (Delaware, 1995). For discussion see M Kahan, 'Jurisprudential and Transactional Developments in Takeovers' in K Hopt et al (eds), *Comparative Corporate Governance: The State of the Art and Emerging Research* (Oxford, Oxford University Press, 1998).

[225]   *Revlon Inc v MacAndrews & Forbes Holdings Inc*, 506 A 2d 173 (Delaware, 1986); *Paramount Communications v QVC Network*, 637 A 2d 34 (Delaware, 1994).

[226]   M Kahan and EB Rock, 'Corporate Constitutionalism: Antitakeover Charter Provisions as Precommitment' (2003) 152 *University of Pennsylvania Law Review* 473, 477; cf eg LA Bebchuk, 'The Case Against Board Veto in Corporate Takeovers' [2002] *University of Chicago Law Review* 973.

shareholder sovereignty which exists in the UK, ie that shareholders alone should be able to decide whether or not to sell their shares. It might also be expected that, in the bid context, collective action problems will be less acute as shareholders have strong incentives to determine whether the offer price is appropriate. It is also notable that, if the issue is that the directors have superior information which allows them to determine that the offered price is insufficient, that information can still be communicated to the shareholders. Indeed in the UK directors are required to give the shareholders their opinion of the bid.[227] More recent studies have also contested the fact that a sale process controlled by directors results in a higher premium at all, and suggest that the bid premia in the US and UK are very similar.[228]

A second benefit that is sometimes ascribed to the US system is that the bidder deals primarily with the board rather than the dispersed shareholders which lessens the danger of the bidder 'dividing and conquering' the numerous dispersed shareholders, ie the US model appears to face fewer collective action problems regarding the target shareholders decision-making. On this view, the US model can better promote undistorted choice by the shareholders in their decision-making. It is certainly correct that the UK no frustration principle leaves target shareholders open to potential abuse and that the UK model needs to deal separately with the need to protect the target shareholders from opportunistic behaviour by the bidder. The UK model does put such protections in place, as discussed below at 12.3.4, and in fact deals comprehensively with this issue. By contrast, although US shareholders stand in less need of protection, they are given much less protection, for example there is no mandatory bid rule in either federal law or in Delaware, and therefore they are arguably worse off than their UK counterparts in this regard.[229]

Third, it is sometimes suggested that the US model also provides the directors with the opportunity to determine whether the takeover is in the best interests of the company as a whole, including stakeholder interests separate to those of the shareholders. This is discussed further below at 12.3.3. However, this model will have value in practice only if the directors use their position solely to defeat opportunistic bids, and not merely to entrench their own position. The UK no frustration principle effectively controls the acute agency problem generated by the bid, preventing the directors acting self-interestedly by sidelining them from the decision-making process. By contrast, the present application of the *Unocal* test effectively allows the board to adopt defensive tactics to preserve their own business strategy, and thereby to entrench themselves.[230]

Finally, one of the benefits sometimes ascribed to takeovers is as a mechanism for corporate accountability.[231] The operation of the market for corporate control stems from the same principles as the capital market price function.[232] The target management's

---

[227]   City Code, rule 25.1.
[228]   JC Coates, 'M&A Break Fees: US Litigation vs US Regulation' Harvard Public Law Working paper No 09–57 available at www.ssrn.com/abstract=1475354, Table 1.
[229]   See eg LA Bebchuk, 'The Pressure to Tender: An Analysis and a Proposed Remedy' (1987) 12 *Delaware Journal of Corporate Law* 911.
[230]   For a strong argument against the existence of board veto in the US, see LA Bebchuk, 'The Case Against Board Veto in Corporate Takeovers' (2002) 69 *University of Chicago Law Review* 973.
[231]   Eg HG Manne, 'Mergers and the Market for Corporate Control' (1965) 73 *Journal of Political Economy* 110. For discussion of these issues see J Coffee, 'Regulating the Market for Corporate Control: A Critical Assessment of the Tender Offer's Role in Corporate Governance' (1984) 84 *Columbia Law Review* 1145.
[232]   Discussed at 10.2.1. However, since the operation of the market for corporate control stems from the same principles under which the capital market functions, it is inevitable that it is subject to the same inefficiencies.

laziness or self-dealing may lead the market to discount the price of the target company's shares. The precipitation for this discount may be a bid by one company which is seen by the market as a value-decreasing takeover offer. The drop in share price allows a bidder (or a second bidder in the latter scenario) to come in, purchase control of the company, remove the lazy or self-dealing directors and put the company's assets to more profitable use.[233] On this view the potential ability of a third party to deal directly with the shareholders, sidelining the directors, to facilitate a control shift and thereby get rid of lazy or self-seeking managers, is regarded as one benefit of hostile takeovers. The potential benefits are said to extend further, however, since the threat of a takeover may discourage the lazy or self-seeking behaviour in the first place.

If this is correct, a regulatory environment needs to be conducive to the successful mounting of takeover bids (including hostile bids) in order to enable takeovers to bridge the gap between ownership and control in a large, dispersed company.[234] On this analysis the US model is potentially at a disadvantage to the UK model.[235] Studies have shown that the number of successful hostile bids in the US in the 1990s, for example, were considerably fewer than in the UK, once the relative size of the two economies is taken into account.[236] The UK model potentially provides a mechanism for addressing the agency problem that exists between directors and shareholders in a dispersed shareholding scenario, incentivising directors to prioritise the shareholders' position even when a bid is not imminent.

However, a note of caution need to be added here. First, it is not clear that takeovers necessarily provide a good corporate governance tool. There may be reasons for a bidder to make a bid other than that existing managers are lazy or self-serving, such as where the purpose of the takeover is to exploit synergies between the bidder and target company.[237] In addition, this view of takeovers fails to explain Management Buy Outs (MBOs), in which the top management are part of the acquiring team and stay in control of the company. It might also be noted that takeovers can operate as a corporate governance tool only at a very late stage in the day, when things have already gone badly wrong for the company. Takeovers are likely to serve only as a remedy of last resort where there have been massive managerial failures. Corporate acquisitions involve considerable costs and

---

[233] See eg HG Manne, 'Mergers and the Market for Corporate Control' [1965] *Journal of Political Economy* 110.

[234] Eg FH Easterbrook and DR Fischel, *The Economic Structure of Corporate Law* (Cambridge MA, Harvard University Press, 1991).

[235] In the US a bidder can try to achieve the same effect by using a proxy fight to attempt to remove the directors by a decision in general meeting. This can be particularly powerful when combined with a takeover bid since it is generally within the power of the directors to redeem the poison pill and thereby allow the bid to proceed. However, this is a considerably slower process (especially if the board is staggered, as is common in the US) and far less attractive to the bidder. See eg L Bebchuk and O Hart, 'Takeover bids vs Proxy Fights in Contests for Corporate Control' (2001) ECGI Finance Working Paper No 04/2002; Harvard Law and Economics Discussion Paper No 336 available at www.ssrn.com/abstract=292883; LA Bebchuk, JC Coates and G Subramanian, 'The Powerful Antitakeover Force of Staggered Boards: Theory, Evidence and Policy' (2002) 54 *Stanford Law Review* 887.

[236] Eg C Kirchner and RW Painter, 'European Takeover Law – Towards a European Modified Business Judgment Rule for Takeover Law' (2000) 2 *European Business Organization Law Review* 353, 377.

[237] For a discussion of the variety of reasons to explain why takeovers occur see R Romano, 'A Guide to Takeovers: Theory, Evidence and Regulation' (1992) 9 *Yale Journal on Regulation* 119.

there is no guarantee that the premium available to the bidder, in taking on the under-performing company and putting the corporate assets to better use, will outweigh the total cost of the acquisition.[238]

Other, earlier-operating, more nuanced mechanisms for aligning directors' interests with those of the shareholders might well be more appropriate for incentivising directors, such as managerial compensation schemes, in particular those that result in the directors holding a significant shareholding, which can help align the interests of directors and shareholders.[239] It is unclear why the abstract possibility of a takeover is likely to operate more effectively than, say, performance related pay, in aligning director and shareholder interests. There are also better, earlier-operating, mechanisms for detecting and dealing with management failure.

The link between poorly performing managers and hostile takeovers does not appear to be made out in the UK. Empirical studies have concluded that in the UK '[t]he market for corporate control does not . . . function as a disciplinary device for poorly performing companies'.[240] The role of takeovers as a corporate governance tool appears, therefore, at best, limited.[241] Instead shareholders in the UK, particularly institutional shareholders, have an important role in monitoring management failure.[242] Franks et al have noted the key role that new equity issues appear to play in board restructurings,[243] ie in removing poorly performing managers. As noted previously, institutional shareholders have significant control over new equity issues via pre-emption rights, which generally need to be disapplied before new shares can be issued. The constraints placed upon this process by the law, and more particularly by guidelines drawn up by the institutional investors themselves, means that directors of public companies must enter into a dialogue with shareholders before any new issue takes place.[244] In practice this enables shareholders to express their views on issues, such as the effectiveness of current managers, and a positive relation between UK rights issues and managerial change has been found to exist.[245] It is not at all clear that hostile takeovers are necessarily the best or most cost effective mechanism for ensuring corporate accountability in the UK.

---

[238] Eg J Coffee, 'Regulating the Market for Corporate Control: A Critical Assessment of the Tender Offer's Role in Corporate Governance' (1984) 84 *Columbia Law Review* 1145.

[239] WG Lewellen, C Loderer and A Rosenfeld, 'Merger Decisions and Executive Stock Ownership in Acquiring Firms' (1985) 7 *Journal of Accounting and Economics* 209; DJ Denis, DK Denis and A Sarin, 'Agency Problems, Equity Ownership and Corporate Diversification' (1997) 52(1) *Journal of Finance* 135. For a UK perspective see A Cosh and A Hughes, 'Managerial Discretion and Takeover Performance' ESRC Centre for Business Research, University of Cambridge Working Paper No 216 (2001).

[240] J Franks and C Mayer, 'Hostile Takeovers in the UK and the Correction of Managerial Failure' (1996) 40 *Journal of Financial Economics* 163, 180. See also B Clarke, 'Articles 9 and 11 of the Takeover Directive (2004/25) and the Market for Corporate Control' [2006] *Journal of Business Law* 355.

[241] See also J Coffee, 'Regulating the Market for Corporate Control: A critical assessment of the Tender Offer's Role in Corporate Governance' (1984) 84 *Columbia Law Review* 1145.

[242] The role of shareholders is likely to be more pronounced in countries in which concentrated ownership structures are common, in which case the role of takeovers as a form of corporate governance is likely to be consequently less significant in those jurisdictions: S Grundmann, 'The Market for Corporate Control: The Legal Framework, Alternatives and Policy Considerations' in KJ Hopt et al, *Corporate Governance in Context: Corporations, States, and Markets in Europe, Japan, and the US* (Oxford, Oxford University Press, 2005) 421.

[243] J Franks, C Mayer and L Renneboog, 'Who Disciplines Management in Poorly Performing Companies?' [2001] *Journal of Financial Intermediation* 209.

[244] Discussed at 4.3.1.

[245] J Franks, C Mayer and L Renneboog, 'Who Disciplines Management in Poorly Performing Companies?' [2001] *Journal of Financial Intermediation* 209; D Hillier, SC Linn and P McColgan, 'Equity Issuance, CEO turnover and Corporate Governance' (2005) 11 *European Financial Management* 515.

Second, it should be emphasised that the UK takeover regulation model is not designed to maximise the number of takeovers that occur. Although the approach taken on this first issue (ie the sidelining of directors in the decision-making) will potentially increase the number of takeovers when compared to another jurisdiction which allows directors to entrench themselves, the approach adopted by the UK regime regarding the relationship between the bidder and the target shareholders, discussed below at 12.3.4, has the effect of making bids more expensive, potentially decreasing the number of offers made.

12.3.3   The Relationship Between the Target Directors and Other Stakeholders in the Target

One consequence of creating a shareholder-centric system of takeover regulation is that other stakeholders in the target may not be sufficiently protected in the bid process. The difficulties for stakeholders in a shareholder-centric model exist for company law generally, but the problems are more acute in the event of a takeover. In general, the long-term interests of the shareholders are aligned with the interests of other stakeholders, as a result of section 172 of the Companies Act 2006. When determining the directors' duty to promote the success of the company, section 172 requires the directors to act 'for the benefit of its members as a whole' and in doing so the directors are required to have regard to a number of factors, including the interests of a number of different stakeholder groups, such as the employees.[246] Section 172 envisages that the duty of management is a duty to promote the success of the *business venture* in order to benefit the members. However, these other stakeholder groups are not provided with any remedy under section 172. The only possible litigants are the board, the shareholders,[247] or a liquidator acting on behalf of an insolvent company. Non-shareholder stakeholders do not have any self-standing duties owed to them by the directors; their interests are subsumed generally into the directors' duty to promote the success of the company.[248]

Takeover regulation in the UK does not supplement the common law by giving any decision rights to these groups in the event of a takeover, or by creating any right of action for them. The UK position can be contrasted with that of other European jurisdictions, such as Germany and the Netherlands. In these jurisdictions employee rights are accorded

[246]   Cf Companies Act 1985, s 309 which stated that the matters to which directors were to have regard in the performance of their functions 'include the interests of the company's employees in general, as well as the interests of its members' (although enforcement was by or on behalf of the company under s 309(2), ie the employees had no special rights of enforcing this provision). There is no direct equivalent of this section in the 2006 Act – the reference to employees' interests in section 172 comes closest.

[247]   Either the majority shareholders could bring a claim, or the minority shareholders may be able to bring an action under Companies Act 2006, Part 11 (derivative action), although the latter claim is by no means straightforward.

[248]   See 3.2, esp 3.2.1.3.1. The case of *Re Welfab Engineers Ltd* [1990] BCLC 833 is sometimes cited as an example of a case in which the directors were allowed to prefer the interests of the employees. In that case the company was in financial difficulties. Its principal asset was its freehold premises. The directors received two offers to purchase the company and accepted the lower offer, which involved the purchaser retaining the company's workforce, rather than the higher offer which just purchased the land, and would involve the liquidator being called in straight away. Hoffmann J held that the directors had not breached their duty to the company in accepting the lower offer. However, once the costs associated with accepting the higher offer were factored in (such as the need to pay wages in lieu of notice and to make redundancy payments) then the distance between the two offers was not as great as suggested. On this analysis it is possible to regard the directors as having acted in the interests of the company when reaching their decision.

more recognition by company law generally. In Germany, for instance, employee representatives sit on the supervisory board.[249] This provides employees, though not other stakeholders, with increased protection in the event of a takeover, as it is more likely that employee interests can be taken into account in the takeover decision. In these jurisdictions takeover regulation also supplements the general company law provisions with additional protections for employees in the event of a takeover.[250]

In a takeover situation the shareholders may have a much shorter term focus than usual. They may only be interested in the cash that the bidder can offer them, not the future of the company, and therefore the wellbeing of other stakeholders, once they have accepted the offer, and exited the company. A recent theoretical debate regarding the role of stakeholders in general, and employees in particular, has questioned the value of the no frustration principle. It is suggested that the ban on defensive measures by the target board has a deleterious effect on the company's relationship with its key stakeholders, and that hostile takeovers should be regarded as rent seeking rather than value enhancing. Some commentators have suggested that the managerialist system of company law can encourage employees to specialise their skills and to make investments of firm-specific human capital.[251]

Where implicit contracts are put in place to encourage employees to invest in a company in this way[252] then it has been suggested that employees can in some sense be regarded as residual claimants of the company alongside the shareholders. Similar arguments can be made in relation to other stakeholders of the company, such as suppliers. Indeed the Company Law Review acknowledged that adopting a strong shareholder-centric approach could lead to increased risks for 'employees, suppliers and others, on whom the company depends for factors of production' particularly in a takeover scenario.[253] In a hostile takeover, a change of managers allows these implicit contracts to be breached, enabling a wealth transfer[254] between employees and shareholders to take place.[255]

In the wake of the successful bid by Kraft for Cadbury in 2010, these issues were again discussed in the UK. Lord Mandelson, the then Business Secretary, said: 'it is hard to ignore the fact that the fate of the company with a long history and many tens of thousands of employees was decided by people who had not owned the company a few weeks earlier, and probably had no intention of owning it a few weeks later'.[256] Lord

---

[249]   Aktiengesetz §§ 96, 101, 103–104.

[250]   For discussion see Kraakman et al, n 8, 8.5.

[251]   MM Blair, *Ownership and Control: Rethinking Corporate Governance for the Twenty-First Century* (Washington DC, The Brookings Institution, 1995).

[252]   Implicit contracts are non-binding social arrangements which are typically enforced through market forces (see eg MA O'Connor, 'Restructuring the Corporation's Nexus of Contracts: Recognizing a Fiduciary Duty to Protect Displaced Workers' (1990) 69 *North Carolina Law Review* 1189). Examples of implicit contracts include career ladders and remuneration structures that reward seniority.

[253]   Company Law Review Steering Group, *Modern Company Law for a Competitive Economy: The Strategic Framework* (February 1999) URN 99/654, 42.

[254]   Some commentators have estimated that as much as 14% of total wages and benefits paid to employees of corporations in the US may represent a return to firm-specific human capital: Blair, *Ownership and Control*, n 251, 266.

[255]   A Shleifer and LH Summers, 'Breach of Trust in Hostile Takeovers' in AJ Auerbach (ed), *Corporate Takeovers: Causes and Consequences* (Chicago, University of Chicago Press, 1988). This could be cured in part by the use of legally binding contracts and paying employees more in the present in return for increased uncertainty about future payments.

[256]   Lord Mandelson, Speech at the annual Trade and Industry dinner, Mansion House, 1 March 2010.

Mandelson suggested a number of measures designed to tighten up the takeover rules, including raising the threshold for a successful bid from a 50 per cent minimum to a two-thirds minimum, lowering the requirement to disclose share ownership during a bid from one per cent to 0.5 per cent, giving the bidding company less time to tie up the deal, forcing bidders to reveal how they intend to finance a takeover and requiring greater transparency on advisers fees and incentives. Following the Kraft takeover the Takeover Panel launched a consultation on the City Code. However, tellingly, in the Panel Statement launching the consultation the Takeover Panel reiterated that

> [t]he Code is not concerned with the financial or commercial advantages or disadvantages of a takeover. These are matters for the company and its shareholders. Nor does the Code deal with issues, such as competition policy, which are the responsibility of government and other bodies.[257]

The Code Committee of the Takeover Panel published a detailed consultation document to examine these issues.[258] In general the purpose of this consultation paper is to consider whether it is too easy for a hostile bidder to obtain control of more than 50 per cent of the voting rights of a target company, and whether the outcomes of takeover bids, particularly hostile bids, are unduly influenced by the actions of 'short-term' investors ie those investors who become interested in the shares of the target company only after the possibility of an offer has been publicly announced. The interests of these 'short-term' investors may be set against the non-shareholder stakeholders in a company, but could equally be regarded as being in potential conflict with the long-term shareholders in a company.

In the consultation paper a number of different issues are considered, including whether the minimum acceptance condition threshold for a successful takeover offer should be raised, perhaps to 60 per cent or two-thirds of the voting rights in the target company; whether voting rights should be withheld from shares in a target acquired during the course of an offer period so that those shares are 'disenfranchised' for the purposes of a takeover bid; and whether the one per cent trigger threshold for the disclosure of dealings and positions in relevant securities should be reduced to 0.5 per cent. The paper also considers whether bidders should be required to provide more information in relation to the financing of takeover bids and their implications and effects, and, further, whether the boards of target companies should be required to set out their views on the bidder's intentions for the target company in greater detail. Further, it considers whether shareholders in a target company should be given independent advice on an offer, separate from that given to the target company's board of directors; and whether bidder companies need more protection. Finally it asks whether inducement fees and/or other deal protection measures should be either prohibited or otherwise restricted as a matter of principle; and whether safeguards should be re-introduced by the Takeover Panel in relation to substantial acquisitions of shares. These changes, if introduced, could have a significant impact on UK takeover regulation, and many of them would have the

---

[257]   Panel Statement 2010/6, Consultation on Aspects of the Takeover Code.
[258]   *Review of Certain Aspects of the Regulation of Takeover Bids*, n 77. See also House of Commons, Business, Innovation and Skills Select Committee –Ninth Report (session 2009–10), *Mergers, Acquisitions and Takeovers: The Takeover of Cadbury by Kraft*, March 2010 and *Government Response to the Business, Innovation and Skills Committee's Report on 'Mergers, Acquisitions and Takeovers: The Takeover of Cadbury by Kraft'* Cm 7915, July 2010.

effect of making it less likely that bids would be successful. The outcome of this consultation will be important for the future direction of UK takeover regulation.

The 'expropriation' explanation of hostile takeovers is not uncontested.[259] However, if it is correct, then takeover regulation should arguably contain some protection for non-shareholder stakeholder groups.[260] Some US commentators have suggested that this can be done by providing a degree of entrenchment for incumbent target directors, and freedom from shareholder control in the takeover scenario.[261] However, this would be entirely contrary to the no frustration principle of the City Code, and there seems little likelihood of this principle being overturned, or scaled back, in the near future. Of course, where the board is given a significant role in the takeover process, such as in the US, it is possible for the target directors to further the interests of these other stakeholder groups. Indeed, it is common in the US for statutes to expand the range of interests that directors are entitled, but not bound,[262] to take account of in responding to a takeover bid beyond those of the shareholders.[263] However, the value of this strategy depends upon the directors actually acting protectively towards these groups in the event of a takeover and not using their position to act in a purely self-interested way. In general it can be expected that non-shareholder stakeholder groups will be protected only to the extent that their interests coincide with those of the directors.[264]

The City Code does make one concession to one category of non-shareholder stakeholders. The bidder is required to disclose his intentions for the future of the company including 'its strategic plans for the offeree company, and their likely repercussions on employment…' and 'its intentions with regard to the continued employment of the employees and management of the offeree company and of its subsidiaries, including any material change in the conditions of employment'.[265] When the target board gives its advice to the target shareholders regarding the bid it is required to include its views, and the reasons for those views, on the implications of the bid for the employees.[266] These documents must be made available to the employees' representatives or, in their absence, to the employees themselves.[267] However, as discussed previously, none of these provisions provides the employees with any formal say in the bid decision.[268]

---

[259]   Eg, Romano, n 2.

[260]   Some commentators suggest that protection of stakeholder interests should be left principally to the contracts between them and the company: R Daniels, 'Stakeholders and Takeovers: Can Contractarianism be Compassionate' (1993) 43 *University of Toronto Law Journal* 315.

[261]   MM Blair and LA Stout, 'A Team Production Theory of Corporate Law' (1999) 85 *Virginia Law Review* 247 but see D Millon, 'New Game Plan or Business as Usual? A Critique of the Team Production Model of Corporate Law' (2000) 86 *Virginia Law Review* 1001.

[262]   A prescription to directors to take the interests of all constituencies into account 'is essentially vacuous, because it allows management to justify almost any action on the grounds that it benefits some group': O Hart, 'An Economist's View of Fiduciary Duties' (1993) 43 *University of Toronto Law Journal* 299, 303.

[263]   Eg, New York Business Corporation Law, §717(b).

[264]   Eg, MJ Roe, *Political Determinants of Corporate Governance: Political Context, Corporate Impact* (Oxford, Oxford University Press, 2002) 45. The increase in the use of director compensation schemes and performance related pay means that directors are more likely to be aligned with shareholder interests (since they hold a significant part of their wealth in the form of shares and options) than bondholders or employees (since the directors will have less of their wealth tied to bondholder or employee wealth).

[265]   City Code, rule 24.1.

[266]   Ibid, rule 25.1(b).

[267]   Ibid, rule 26, 32.7.

[268]   However, in some circumstances the bidder and target may need to consult employee representatives on the employment consequences of the bid or of defensive measures: Information and Consultation of Employees Regulations 2004 (SI 2004/3426) reg 20.

No other non-shareholder stakeholder group is provided with any protection by UK takeover regulation. Instead, protection is left to the contracts between the stakeholders and the company, and more specialist regulation, such as employment law.[269] One other group requires brief mention here, namely the creditors. Changes to the company's risk profile consequent upon a successful takeover, perhaps as a result of the bid being highly leveraged, may well have a significant impact on the company's creditors. As discussed in chapters four, five and six, many creditors will be in a position to protect themselves against risks of this kind in their contract, either via security, or other contractual provisions such as covenants requiring the company to maintain certain debt-equity ratios. The latter type of contractual protection might also provide some protection for non-adjusting creditors, as they may be able to free ride on the protection put in place by the adjusting creditors.

12.3.4   The Relationship between the Bidder and the Target Shareholders

The effect of the no frustration principle, discussed above at 12.3.2, means that when the bidder makes an offer for the target company, the bidder deals not with the target board but with the target shareholders. In the UK, where dispersed share ownership is the common pattern in public companies, the bidder tends to deal with the target shareholders as a class, in contrast to the position where the target company has a concentrated ownership structure, in which case the bidder will deal first and foremost with the controlling shareholders.

In the two previous categories, namely the relationship between the target directors and target shareholders, and the relationship between target directors and other stakeholders in the company, general company law principles govern these relationships and provide a base on top of which takeover regulation can be added. As discussed, a more significant top up of general company law principles occurs in the UK in relation to the first of these two relationships. By contrast, general company law has nothing to say about the relationship between the bidder and the target shareholders. In the absence of takeover regulation the relevant principles governing this relationship are found in contract law.

The bidder deals with each target shareholder separately. In the absence of specific takeover regulation, bidders could offer different deals to different shareholders, or make offers with very short periods for acceptance. Bidders would have the opportunity to 'divide and conquer', skewing the offer in order to acquire the company at the cheapest possible price. For example, the bidder could offer one price to those who accept the offer quickly, up until the bidder acquires control, and then could reduce the offer, leaving the remaining shareholders with the choice of accepting the lower offer or of staying in the company now under the bidder's control. Shareholders would find it hard to obtain reliable information about the offers made to their fellow shareholders, and about whether their fellow shareholders intended to accept the bid. The collective action problems faced by the target shareholders potentially increase the bargaining strength of the bidder at the

---

[269]   For example, where a highly leveraged bid for a target company is successful, one of the consequences may be that the risk that the company will default on its obligations under its occupational pension scheme may increase. In these circumstances the Pensions Regulator has the power to require the bidder to make extraordinary payments into the fund, in order to secure the position of the employees. If the bidder refuses to do so the offer will not proceed. See Pensions Act 2004, ss 43–51.

target shareholders' expense. In the anonymous market which exists for public securities, it may be that the shareholder is not even aware that they are dealing with someone who is attempting to obtain control of the company.

However, UK takeover regulation intervenes to regulate the relationship between the bidder and the target shareholders.[270] Indeed, to a large extent these principles are now enshrined in the Takeover Directive so that throughout Europe takeover regulation intervenes in this relationship, although there remains some variation between Member States as to how these principles within the directive operate in practice.[271] The directive provides that 'all holders of the securities of an offeree company of the same class must be afforded equivalent treatment; moreover, if a person acquires control of a company, the other holders of securities must be protected'.[272] This statement is repeated verbatim in General Principle 1 of the City Code, although this same principle was also found in the City Code prior to the implementation of the directive. The principle of equality of treatment between the shareholders in the target is an idea that has been entrenched in the City Code from its inception. Broadly, this principle provides that the consideration paid by the bidder to acquire the target should be shared equally between shareholders of the same class and proportionately between shareholders of different classes.

Before considering how the UK has regulated this issue, it is important to understand why this principle is enshrined in takeover regulation. After all, the idea of equality amongst shareholders in a bid situation is in contrast to general UK company law principles, in which shareholders must be treated fairly, but not necessarily equally.[273] Indeed it is generally accepted that controlling shares in a company are worth more than non-controlling ones,[274] which contradicts the idea of all shareholders being paid rateably in a takeover scenario. The pursuit of equality amongst shareholders for its own sake does not seem to justify the imposition of the equality rules that are put in place during a takeover. Some other principle(s) must be at work to explain the imposition of these rules.

Indeed there seem to be two principal concerns at work in this context: the need to ensure that the decision taken by the shareholders is as undistorted as possible and a desire to protect the minority/non-controlling shareholders from abuse.[275] These will be considered in turn.

12.3.4.1   Undistorted Choice

First, it is clear that the bidder can use the tactics described above to put pressure on the shareholders to accept a particular offer, even if the shareholders do not think that the offer is in their interests. If the best offer is available only to those that accept quickly, there

---

[270]   For a comparison of the protection put in place for the shareholders in a takeover effected via a scheme of arrangement see chapter 13 and J Payne, 'Schemes of Arrangement, Takeovers and Minority Shareholder Protection' [2011] *Journal of Corporate Law Studies* (forthcoming), available at www.ssrn.com/abstract =1600592.

[271]   For a comparative discussion of the concept of equality in the takeover context in the UK, Austria, France, Germany, Switzerland and Italy, see Davies, 'The Notion of Equality in European Takeover Regulation', n 126.

[272]   Takeover Directive 2004/25/EC, article 3, General principle 1.

[273]   Eg *Mutual Life Insurance Co of New York v Rank Organisation Ltd* [1985] BCLC 11.

[274]   *Short v Treasury Commissioners* [1948] AC 534.

[275]   A third argument that can be made is a desire to equalise the position of those shareholders who are close to the market (typically institutional shareholders) and those not close to the market (typically individual shareholders): Davies, n 126, 18–20. However, on the whole the concerns in this context can be seen as aspects of the two principal concerns discussed in the text.

is clear pressure on the shareholders to accept, particularly where they cannot determine the intentions of their fellow shareholders.[276] However, if the decision on the outcome of the bid is given primarily to the shareholders rather than the target board, as it is in the UK, it is crucial that the shareholders' decision-making should be as undistorted as possible.[277] A result of the pressure to tender might be that the bidder will succeed in gaining control over a target even if the value-maximising course of action for the target shareholders would be to reject the bid. The undistorted choice argument is therefore an allocative efficiency argument. Efficiency requires that corporate assets be put to their most productive use. While the acquisition of some companies would produce efficiency gains, perhaps from an improvement in management, the assets of other companies are best left under existing management. A target company should be acquired if, and only if, a majority of its shareholders view the offered acquisition price as higher than the independent target's value.[278] As a result 'ensuring undistorted choice is desirable from the perspectives of both target shareholders and society'.[279]

There are a number of provisions within the City Code which can be seen as promoting undistorted choice amongst the target shareholders. First, within a class of shareholders, such as the class of equity voting shares, the offer must be the same to all those within the class.[280] However, the City Code goes further and requires an equality of protection not only within a class, but also between classes, at least in relation to equity share capital.[281] When a target company has more than one class of equity share capital, a 'comparable' offer must be made for each class, whether it carries voting rights or not.[282] The City Code has rules in place to try to prevent the bidder offering disguised enhanced deals to only some of the shareholders.[283]

However, the definition of class for these purposes has been determined strictly. In the Eurotunnel takeover, for example, some shareholders had certain travel privileges. When a share for share offer was made to the Eurotunnel shareholders by a bidder company, the

---

[276] The need to protect the shareholders' undistorted choice in making this decision is not based on an entitlement argument. The entitlement argument would assert that ensuring undistorted choice is necessary to protect the property rights that a target's shareholders have in the assets that they own. The shareholders, it would be argued, should not be put in a position that would lead them to sell their assets for an acquisition price that they judge to be lower than the value to themselves of retaining their assets: L Bebchuk, 'Toward an Undistorted Choice and Equal Treatment in Corporate Takeovers' (1985) 98 *Harvard Law Review* 1693, 1764 fn 154. However, UK company law seems to regard shareholders being protected by a liability rule rather than a property rule in relation to their shares, ie expropriation of shares is allowed providing a fair price is paid for those shares (see discussion at pages 67–69).

[277] Even in systems which interpose the target board between the bidder and the target shareholders, such as the US, undistorted decision-making is important for those occasions on which the directors allow (or are required by the court to allow) the target shareholders to consider the bid.

[278] See eg L Bebchuk, 'Toward an Undistorted Choice and Equal Treatment in Corporate Takeovers' (1985) 98 *Harvard Law Review* 1693; L Bebchuk, 'The Pressure to Tender: An Analysis and a Proposed Remedy' (1987) 12 *Delaware Journal of Corporate Law* 911.

[279] L Bebchuk, 'The Pressure to Tender: An Analysis and a Proposed Remedy' (1987) 12 *Delaware Journal of Corporate Law* 911, 913. The independent target's value refers to the value that the target will have if it remains, at least for the time being, independent; this value of the independent target obviously includes the value of the prospect of receiving higher acquisition offers in the future.

[280] City Code, GP 1.

[281] Ibid, rule 14.1. As regards classes of non-equity shares, in a voluntary bid, no offer is required, unless the shares are convertible into equity shares (City Code, rule 15). On a mandatory bid, an offer must be made for non-equity securities carrying voting rights, although these are rare in practice: rule 9.1.

[282] Ibid, rule 14.

[283] Ibid, rule 16.

offer included the term that those shareholders accepting the offer would lose their travel privileges. This offer was made to all shareholders, whether they held travel privileges or not. The bidder argued that, in accordance with GP 1, it had treated all of the shareholders equally. The shareholders with travel privileges argued that they were a separate class and that the offer did not take proper account of the value of their travel privileges. The Takeover Panel Executive ruled that there was no breach of the City Code since these rights were personal rights only. No class rights existed in the articles of Eurotunnel and therefore the bidder had behaved properly. This decision was upheld on appeal by the Takeover Appeal Board.[284]

These rules are important, as they prevent the bidder skewing the consideration it offers by, for example, offering enhanced deals to some shareholders, such as the first to accept. They thereby help to prevent a pressure to accept arising amongst those to whom the offer is made. The City Code goes even further however in promoting equality of treatment between shareholders within the bid. If the offer is subsequently increased by the bidder then even those who accepted the original offer are entitled to the new, higher price.[285]

However, the City Code requires not only equality of treatment of shareholders within the bid, but also equality as between offerees and sellers outside the bid.[286] Prior to the introduction of the City Code it was common practice for bidders to enter into deals with some shareholders outside the formal offer at a higher price than that offered to the shareholders in the general bid. If allowed, this would clearly undermine the equality of treatment principle that the City Code tries to protect. It is therefore unsurprising that the City Code seeks to prevent the bidder from doing favourable deals with a few selected shareholders, either before the offer period[287] or during the offer period.[288] The City Code achieves this by providing that, if the bidder makes a favourable offer to a shareholder outside the bid in this way, the bidder must raise the level of the general offer made to shareholders of that class in order to match the favourable offer, made to the select few.[289]

However, the bidder could also seek to put pressure on the shareholders by engaging in a campaign of buying up shares in the target prior to the offer, at a higher price than the general offer it makes subsequently. The shareholders dealing with the bidder prior to the bid would feel under pressure to accept if they knew or suspected that the subsequent general offer would be lower, while the shareholders faced with the general offer might find that the bidder already has de facto control of the target.[290] As a result, the City Code

---

[284] The Takeover Panel Appeal Board's decision in Eurotunnel available at www.thetakeoverappeal board.org.uk/statements.html.

[285] City Code, rule 32.3.

[286] See Davies, n 126.

[287] City Code rule 6.1, which specifies a period of three months before the offer period, but the Panel can extend the period if it believes it is necessary to give effect to GP 1. The Panel can relax this rule if it thinks appropriate.

[288] City Code, rule 6.2.

[289] Distinctions are drawn in City Code, rule 6 between purchases before the offer period begins and those made after a firm intention to make an offer have been announced. In relation to the latter, if the favourable deal to select shareholders is a cash offer, so must be the general offer made under rule 6.2. However the rules are more relaxed in relation to pre-offer period purchases (see rule 6.1), unless rule 11.1 applies.

[290] One issue is how easy it will be to determine whether the bidder is buying shares in the target prior to making a bid, particularly where the bidder is acting via a nominee. Of course there is an obligation on shareholders to declare their interest in shares which is triggered when a shareholder holds three per cent of the total voting rights in the company, and at every one per cent thereafter (FSA Handbook, Disclosure and Transparency Rules, DTR 5.1 discussed at 10.3.2.3). These provisions are intended to make the interests of shareholders transparent even where the bidder is acting via a nominee. In addition, Companies Act 2006, s 793

regulates this scenario, providing that in some circumstances purchases made by the bidder prior to the offer will impact on the required level of consideration offered by the bidder in the general offer. However, limits are set on this principle. It is not all prior purchases by the bidder which will per se have this effect, only those where the bidder, and any persons acting in concert with it, have acquired for cash shares in the target which carry at least 10 per cent of the voting rights in the 12 months prior to the offer.[291] In these circumstances the subsequent offer must be in cash or be accompanied by a cash alternative at the highest level paid outside the offer.[292] Where the initial offer is of securities, the bidder must also offer the same number of securities to the target shareholder in the general offer,[293] although generally it will be the cash alternative which will be most attractive to the target shareholders.

Perhaps the strongest expression of the equality principle at work in the City Code is the mandatory bid rule.[294] The essence of this rule is that, once a person, together with anyone with whom he is acting in concert, acquires 30 per cent of the shares carrying voting rights, or holds between 30 and 50 per cent and acquires additional shares carrying voting rights, then a mandatory bid is required.[295] In other words the mandatory bid rule is triggered when control of a company is secured, assumed for these purposes to occur when 30 per cent of the voting shares are secured, or when control is consolidated by further acquisitions above the 30 per cent level. In general it is the first of these limbs that is most important. After all, in most cases the second limb will not be reached unless the 30 per cent threshold has been passed.[296] Once the mandatory bid is triggered, that person must extend offers to the holders of any class of equity share capital (voting or non-voting) and also to the holders of any other class of transferable securities carrying voting

provides that a public company (whether its shares are traded on a public market or not) may serve notice on a person whom it knows, or has reasonable cause to believe, to have been at any time in the preceding three years interested in the voting shares of the company.

[291] The Panel can exercise its discretion to trigger this requirement even where the 10% threshold has not been reached, if the equality principle requires this: rule 11.1(c). The Panel has indicated that an appropriate case might be where the vendors are the directors of the target: note 4 to rule 11.

[292] City Code, rule 11.1.

[293] Ibid, rule 11.2. This is a weaker protection than rule 11.1 since it is only triggered if the prior acquisitions occurred in the three months before the bid cf rule 11.1 which includes prior acquisitions in the twelve months before the bid.

[294] City Code, rule 9.1. The mandatory bid rule is now required by Takeover Directive 2004/25/EC, art 5. Implementation of this article required some minor amendments to rule 9, although the mandatory bid rule in the City Code remains tougher than that required by the Directive.

[295] Ibid, rule 9.1. The concept of 'acting in concert' in the context of the mandatory bid rule requires particular thought. When a group of persons act in concert to acquire control of a company then rule 9.2 places an obligation to make a general offer on the person who takes the group's shareholding over the threshold, and also on the 'principal members' of the group, if the triggering acquirer is not such a member. If, when the group decide to act, they already hold 30% of the voting shares, then the mandatory bid rule is not triggered when the group make their agreement, but any subsequent acquisition of shares by any of them will trigger the requirement (rule 9.1 note 1). This includes institutional investors who come together to exercise their rights as shareholders although no mandatory bid will be triggered if the shareholders are not seeking 'board control'. Even if the shareholder coalition is seeking to change the whole of the board it will not be regarded as seeking 'board control' if there is no relationship between the institutional shareholders and the proposed new directors (see rule 9.1. note 2).

[296] There may be occasions when the mandatory bid is only triggered by the second limb, such as where the Panel waived the mandatory bid when the 30% level way passed, or where a concert party reached agreement at a time when they already hold 30% of the shares between them (see n 295).

rights.[297] The offer must be a cash offer, or with a cash alternative, and at the highest price paid by the offeror or a member of his concert party within the 12 months prior to the commencement of the offer.[298] The mandatory bid must not contain any conditions other than that it is dependent on acceptances resulting in the bidder holding 50 per cent of the voting rights.[299]

The mandatory bid rule can be seen as having an impact on the issue of undistorted shareholder choice. Without the mandatory bid rule it may be that a shareholder will be more inclined to accept the offer, fearing that once the bidder has control it will be stuck in the target company and the value of its shares may have declined since the bidder will have no obligation to make a general offer at that point.[300] However, another aim of the mandatory bid rule is the protection of minority shareholders, and it will be discussed further in this context below at 12.3.4.2.

Another two aspects of the City Code that are intended to promote undistorted choice are the need for the target shareholders to have adequate information upon which to make a decision, and the need for them to have enough time within which to reach a decision. An initial offer must be open for acceptance for at least 21 days[301] and revised offers for 14 days.[302] These rules reflect General Principle 2, which states that '[t]he holders of the securities of an offeree company must have sufficient time and information to enable them to reach a properly informed decision on the bid'. They are intended to prevent the bidder putting undue pressure on the target shareholders by keeping offers open for a very short period, which does not allow shareholders time to properly assess the merits of the bid. It has been pointed out that, from an individual shareholder's perspective, there are three outcomes of an offer: the offer is rejected, the offer is accepted by the majority of shareholders, including the individual, and the offer is accepted by the majority not including the individual.[303] The shareholder may prefer the first outcome, but be so nervous about the possibility of the third outcome that he

---

[297]   City Code, rule 9.1. The Panel may exercise its discretion to waive the requirement of a mandatory bid in some circumstances, either entirely, or subject to the agreement of the majority of the target shareholders. This will generally occur where the 30% threshold is breached inadvertently (and the error rectified quickly) or where the acquisition of 30% does not confer control (eg where another shareholder holds 50% of the shares). One scenario when the Panel will generally waive the requirement is where the actions of the company (eg redeeming or repurchasing its shares) take a shareholder over the 30% boundary without having acted itself. In these circumstances the Panel will normally waive the bid obligation provided it is consulted in advance, the independent shareholders of the target agree and the procedure set out in Appendix 1 of the City Code is followed: rule 37.

[298]   City Code, rule 9.5. The Panel can agree to an adjusted price.

[299]   Ibid, rule 9.3.

[300]   Bebchuk has argued that this rule falls short of attaining undistorted choice: '[u]nder the rule, a buyer will succeed in gaining control whenever it is willing to pay a per-share acquisition price that exceeds the independent target's value in the view of a sufficiently large plurality of the shareholders. According to the undistorted choice objective, however, the buyer should gain control only if such a view is held by a *majority* of the shareholders' (L Bebchuk, 'Toward an Undistorted Choice and Equal Treatment in Corporate Takeovers' (1985) 98 *Harvard Law Review* 1693, 1801).

[301]   City Code, rule 31.1.

[302]   Ibid, rule 32.1.

[303]   LA Bebchuk, 'Toward an Undistorted Choice and Equal Treatment in Corporate Takeovers' (1985) 98 *Harvard Law Review* 1693; LA Bebchuk, 'The Pressure to Tender: An Analysis and a Proposed Remedy' (1987) 12 *Delaware Journal of Corporate Law* 911, 922–31. Bebchuk's suggested solution is that shareholders can indicate if they approve a takeover and a bidder can only purchase a controlling interest if it attracts the required number of 'approving' tenders or it can proceed only if the bid gains approval in a prior separate vote of the shareholders.

feels pressured to accept the offer. Keeping the offer open for this further period avoids this pressure to accept.[304]

In summary, therefore, undistorted choice is a crucial aspect of UK takeover regulation. In a jurisdiction such as the UK where the target board have effectively been sidelined, and so cannot act as the shareholders' representative when dealing with the bidder, and yet the shareholders are dispersed and therefore face significant coordination problems, these rules are key. Indeed, as a result of the Takeover Directive, many of these principles are now common throughout Europe.[305] By contrast, the position in the US gives the target directors a significant role in determining the outcome of the takeover decision and therefore provides the potential for the directors to protect the target shareholders from opportunistic behaviour on the part of the bidder. Accordingly, the need for specific regulation to protect the target shareholders from exploitation by the bidder is less obvious, and in practice fewer protections are put in place to deal with this issue. Two tier offers are allowed in the US, for example.[306] However, the protection of the target shareholders in the US depends upon the directors actually exercising their protective role.

12.3.4.2   *Protection of Minority Shareholders*

As discussed above, the mandatory bid rule can be seen as having an impact on undistorted choice. However, a further aim of this rule is the protection of minority shareholders. The mandatory bid rule prevents the bidder acquiring control over the whole of the company's assets by purchasing only a proportion of the shares. Of course, the sell-out rule, discussed above, allows the last 10 per cent of shareholders to exit the company at a fair price where the bidder has acquired the other 90 per cent where that percentage has been reached as a result of a general offer,[307] but the mandatory bid rule clearly goes very much further.[308] As a result it is unsurprising that the mandatory bid rule is bolstered in the UK by a general antipathy towards partial offers, ie offers for only part of a class (say, 50 per cent of the equity voting shares),[309] since allowing bidders to launch

---

[304]   Bebchuk points out that this provision can also cause difficulties as it could encourage shareholders to adopt a 'wait and see' approach. A shareholder who would like the bid to proceed might decide not to tender in the 'first round'. If the bid is going to succeed regardless of his decision, then his tender decision will not matter, since shareholders who tender in the 'first round' and those who will tender in the 'second round' will be equally treated. If the bid is going to fail regardless of his decision, the shareholder will be somewhat better off holding out: since the City Code requires failing bidders to return all tendered shares, tendering would lead only to unnecessary transaction costs. The outcome of bids might consequently be distorted *against* bidders: a bid might well fail even if a majority of the shareholders would prefer it to succeed: LA Bebchuk, 'Toward an Undistorted Choice and Equal Treatment in Corporate Takeovers' (1985) 98 *Harvard Law Review* 1693, 1797–98.

[305]   Takeover Directive 2004/25/EC, art 3(1)(a) provides that 'all holders of the securities of an offeree company of the same class must be afforded equivalent treatment; moreover, if a person acquires control of a company, the other holders of securities must be protected' (repeated verbatim at City Code, General Principle 1).

[306]   For a discussion of the pressure that can be put on US shareholders see eg LA Bebchuk, 'Pressure to Tender: An Analysis and a Proposed Remedy' (1987) 12 *Delaware Journal of Corporate Law* 911.

[307]   Companies Act 2006, ss 983–85 discussed at 12.3.1.4.

[308]   According to the Winter Group, one of the reasons for putting a sell-out remedy in place is prevention of abuse for minority shareholders ie the same reasoning as the mandatory bid rule (the other reasons being the promotion of undistorted choice and protection against an illiquid market for the company's shares): *Report of the High Level Group of Experts on Issues Related to Takeover Bids*, Brussels, January 2002, 63. However, all three of these reasons have been doubted by Professor Davies who suggests that the more likely explanation for the sell-out right is that it is regarded as a fair counterpart to the squeeze-out rule: Davies, n 126, 21.

[309]   Partial offers are general offers, and therefore allow all shareholders to dispose of the same proportion of their shares.

partial bids without restriction would quickly allow the mandatory bid rule to be undermined. The starting point in the City Code is that partial offers will not be allowed.[310] In general a bidder will have to make an offer to acquire the whole of the equity share capital of a company if it wishes to obtain control through a takeover.

The need to provide minority shareholders with protection in this scenario requires some thought. Equal treatment of shareholders for its own sake, perhaps based on 'widely held notions of fairness',[311] does not per se justify the mandatory bid rule. Company law in the UK seeks to treat shareholders fairly, but not necessarily equally,[312] and accepts that in general a controlling stake in a company is worth more than a non-controlling stake, which runs contrary to the pro rata sharing of consideration which lies at the heart of the concept of equal treatment of shareholders in a takeover. Of course, this disjunction is not readily apparent in most UK companies involved in a takeover since dispersed share ownership will be the norm in this scenario. Nevertheless, the pursuit of equality amongst shareholders for its own sake is not a goal found elsewhere in company law and merely citing 'fairness' as a justification is not satisfactory. An analysis of the substantive justifications for the concept of equality is required. To the extent that equal treatment of shareholders contributes to undistorted choice, this issue has been dealt with above at 12.3.4.1.

There are two arguments that can be made in favour of providing minority shareholders with this additional protection in a bid situation. The first is that the bidder, once successful and in control of the target, may engage in oppressive acts towards the minority, and that the minority need protection from that potential oppression. The second is that shareholders should be entitled to a right of exit when a change of control occurs following a takeover.

12.3.4.2.1   Prevention of Oppression

Although it is sometimes suggested that the mandatory bid rule is needed in order to prevent oppression of the minority by the bidder, two points can be made against this suggestion. First, the effect of the mandatory bid rule is to give the minority shareholders a remedy on the basis that they may suffer oppression in the future, not on the basis that they have indeed suffered oppression at the hands of the new controller. However, the mere fact that a company has a new controller does not usually lead to a prediction that the new controller will behave oppressively, and it is not clear why a different approach should be followed in the context of a takeover.[313] In general remedies in company law are provided to minority shareholders on the basis that they have suffered actual abuse, and a

---

[310]   City Code, rule 36. The Panel will usually consent to partial offers which would result in the offeror holding less than 30% of the voting rights in the target company: rule 36.1. Consent will not normally be given if the offer could result in the offeror being interested in shares carrying 30% or more of the voting rights in the target company: rule 36.1, but see rules 36.2–36.8 which deal with partial offers where the offeror could obtain more than 30%, (in which case the partial offer is dependent, inter alia, on the bidder obtaining shareholder approval from 50% of the target shareholders: rule 36.5).

[311]   LA Bebchuk, 'Toward an Undistorted Choice and Equal Treatment in Corporate Takeovers' (1985) 98 *Harvard Law Review* 1693, 1707.

[312]   Eg *Mutual Life Insurance Co of New York v Rank Organisation Ltd* [1985] BCLC 11.

[313]   The exception might be where the bidder has a history of acting oppressively towards the minority of target shareholders.

remedy is likely to be denied to a minority shareholder who relies on merely the potential for abuse to occur in the future.[314] It is not clear why the position should be so markedly different in relation to takeovers.

Second, company law already provides remedies for minority shareholders faced with actual abuse. The justification for the mandatory bid rule in this context must therefore be that the remedies provided generally by company law are inadequate to protect the minority shareholders following a change of control in a takeover situation, and that takeover regulation needs to step in in order to bridge the gap. The primary remedy available to shareholders provided by company law is found in section 994 of the Companies Act 2006. This provision allows minority shareholders to petition the court in the event of unfairly prejudicial conduct, the usual remedy being that, if unfairly prejudicial conduct has occurred, the court will order the buy out of the petitioner's shares.[315] The unfairness contemplated by section 994 'may consist in a breach of the rules or in using the rules in a manner which equity would regard as contrary to good faith'.[316] In other words, a section 994 petition can be based on an infringement of the petitioner's legal rights, such as a breach of the articles, or in the unfair use of power which abuses the enjoyment of legal rights. Section 994 petitions generally involve small quasi-partnership companies where the abuse falls into the second category, a typical fact pattern being that the majority are seeking to remove the minority shareholder from their position as director. The appropriate procedure has been followed[317] but the removal is said to be in breach of some informal agreement that the minority remain a director.

In the context of large publicly traded companies, which is the usual scenario in which takeovers occur, while unfair prejudice petitions are possible, successful petitions are extremely rare. Indeed, the view of the courts is generally that allowing unfair prejudice petitions in public companies is a 'recipe for chaos'.[318] There are good reasons for this view. If legal rights are infringed then a section 994 petition in the public company context is certainly possible;[319] however the sort of oppression that seems to be contemplated following a takeover, for example changes to the company's business strategy, a reduction in the payment of dividends, or the sale of the company's assets, is unlikely to involve such an infringement.

This leaves the second category of unfairness. However, the sorts of informal arrangements that can give rise to a successful section 994 action in small private companies[320] are unlikely to arise in the public company context, and indeed should have no place in this context: '[i]f the market in a company's shares is to have any credibility members of the public dealing in that market must it seems to me be entitled to proceed on the footing

---

[314]   See eg *Re Astec (BSR) plc* [1998] 2 BCLC 556 (involving an unfair prejudice petition under s 459 Companies Act 1985, now restated as s 994, Companies Act 2006) where the perceived premature nature of the petition was a contributory factor in the dismissal of the petition.

[315]   Companies Act 2006, s 996 provides the court with a very wide discretion as to the remedy which it can award. Buy out of the petitioner's shares is by no means the only possibility, although it is the most common.

[316]   *O'Neill v Phillips* [1999] 1 WLR 1092, 1099 per Lord Hoffmann.

[317]   Ie an ordinary resolution has been passed: Companies Act 2006, s 168.

[318]   *Re Astec (BSR) plc* [1998] 2 BCLC 556, 589 per Jonathan Parker J.

[319]   The decision of the Court of Appeal in *Clark v Cutland* [2004] 1 WLR 783 suggests that s 994 petitions can also be used by minority shareholders to bring an action based on a breach of duty to the company in order to seek a remedy for the company. It is possible that this could arise in the public company context, although again this would be unusual (for discussion see J Payne, 'Sections 459–461 Companies Act 1985 in Flux: The Future of Shareholder Protection' [2005] *Cambridge Law Journal* 647, 674–75).

[320]   See eg *O'Neill v Phillips* [1999] 1 WLR 1092 albeit that the petition was unsuccessful in that case.

that the constitution of the company is as it appears in the company's public documents, unaffected by any extraneous equitable considerations and constraints'.[321] Of course, it is possible for unfair prejudice to be felt by all members of a company[322] so that 'universal expectations'[323] can form the basis for a petition. However, it can be difficult for judges to determine whether unfair prejudice has occurred in the absence of a clear guideline (such as an informal arrangement between the shareholders) and they have to date been reluctant to do so in the public company context.[324]

Of course, the other reason for unfair prejudice petitions being rare in the context of publicly traded companies is because an active market for the company's shares exists which gives unhappy shareholders immediate access to the remedy which is most often awarded following a successful petition, namely a buy out of the petitioner's shares at a fair price. In a publicly traded company a fair price will generally be the market price of the shares and therefore presumably a minority shareholder would wish to argue that the market price was not fair, and perhaps that the bid price (if higher) is a better assessment of the 'fair' price for the minority's shares.

12.3.4.2.2   An Exit Right

The second argument in favour of the mandatory bid rule is based on the idea that shareholders should be entitled to a right of exit when a change of control occurs following a takeover. This argument is based not on the view that the new controllers will behave oppressively or illegally, or have the potential to do so, but rather on the idea that the position of shareholders in a company depends to a significant extent on the identity of the controllers of a company. Even if the new controllers are not per se oppressive towards the minority, nevertheless the change of control has the potential to affect the minority shareholders adversely. For example, the new controller may implement a new, and less successful, business strategy. This argument is made more strongly in relation to equity shareholders, whose return from the company is more closely associated with the decisions taken by the controllers of the company, than non-equity shareholders. Take the situation where the successful bidder is part of a group of companies so that the previously independent target now also becomes part of a group. Decisions may be taken at group level which impact negatively on the target company, and its minority share-holders.

However, more controversially, the mandatory bid rule not only provides an exit for shareholders (after all shareholders in a public company can always sell their shares in the market), it provides an exit for the shareholders at the bid price. In the UK, the City Code does not just provide exit rights for minority shareholders but provides that they have a right to exit on the same terms as all other shareholders. This is controversial for two reasons. First, in other areas of company law it is accepted that the holders of a majority stake in a company should obtain a premium on the sale of their shares since they are selling control of the company.[325] No such control premium exists in a takeover situation.

---

[321]   *Re Astec (BSR) plc* [1998] 2 BCLC 556, 589 per Jonathan Parker J. Similar sentiments are expressed by Vinelott J in *Re Blue Arrow plc* [1987] BCLC 585.
[322]   Companies Act 2006, s 994(1).
[323]   See E Boros, *Minority Shareholders' Remedies* (Oxford, Clarendon Press, 1995) 137.
[324]   See J Payne, 'Section 459 and Public Companies' [1999] *Law Quarterly Review* 368.
[325]   *Short v Treasury Commissioners* [1948] AC 534.

All of the shareholders receive exactly the same payment in the offer. In a system of dispersed share ownership such as that observable in UK publicly traded companies, this is not particularly significant, but where shareholdings are concentrated, this aspect of the mandatory bid rule is more difficult to justify. Where there is an existing controlling shareholder in the company the existence of the mandatory bid rule makes it less likely that they will sell to the bidder since the existing controlling shareholder may be deprived of the premium for their existing control.[326] Second, requiring the bidder to offer for the whole share capital of the company and requiring the bidder to pay the same price for all of the shares, including those bought after control is obtained, and even for the 'rump' 10 per cent under the squeeze-out and sell-out rules, means that takeover offers are more expensive than they would otherwise be if bidders were free to make bargains with individual shareholders free from the constraints of takeover regulation. Making bids more expensive is likely to reduce the number of bids made overall.[327] If the facilitation of takeovers is desirable, for example for corporate governance reasons, then this is potentially problematic.

However, changes of control can occur in a number of ways, and other events which trigger a change of control could result in changes of policy, such as a change in the company's business activities, and could also have a detrimental effect on the minority shareholders.[328] If this argument is a good one then it might be expected that minority shareholders would have the right to exit on any change of control, however it comes about. That is not what we see, however. Other events causing a change of control do not lead to additional protection for the minority shareholders over and above general company law principles. This is not surprising. To provide the shareholders with a right of exit at a price above that which they can obtain in the market has an obvious cost attached to it. However, developments which result in a change of control within the company can be beneficial to a company's development and it does not seem justifiable to inhibit these potentially beneficial developments in this way. Even without a change of control the existing controllers might implement measures, such as deciding to embark upon a new and less successful business strategy, which can adversely affect the minority shareholders. The question then arises whether a right of exit on a change of control following a takeover can be justified.

There is one difference in the way that takeovers operate in the UK, as compared to the other scenarios outlined, that might justify the different treatment of this particular form of change of control. This is that takeovers can create a controlling shareholder where none existed before. Typically in UK publicly traded companies the shareholding is

---

[326]   In jurisdictions dominated by controlling blockholders, such as exist on the Continent (see eg M Becht and A Röell, 'Blockholding in Europe: An International Comparison' (1999) 43 *European Economic Review* 1049) it is common to see the mandatory bid rule being designed in a way that avoids these difficulties, in order to allow the controlling blockholder to retain some control premium. See Davies, n 126, 27–28.

[327]   FH Easterbrook and DR Fischel, 'The Proper Role of a Target's Management in Responding to a Tender Offer' (1981) 94 *Harvard Law Review* 1161, 1174–80; LA Bebchuk, 'Toward an Undistorted Choice and Equal Treatment in Corporate Takeovers (1985) 98 *Harvard Law Review* 1693, 1740–42.

[328]   See chapter 13 for a discussion of how a change of control can be effected via a scheme of arrangement, and what minority protection is put in place in that instance. See also J Payne, 'Schemes of Arrangement, Takeovers and Minority Shareholder Protection' [2011] *Journal of Corporate Law Studies* (forthcoming) available at www.ssrn.com/abstract=1600592.

dispersed, and there is no single shareholder with control of the company.[329] However, as a result of a successful takeover the bidder acquires control of the company. This may be compared to the situation in which there is an existing controlling shareholder in the target which sells its shares to the bidder,[330] in which case the minority was subject to a controlling shareholder even before the successful takeover. However, it will still be possible for the minority shareholders to sell their shares on the open market, unless the majority has delisted the shares or taken the company private in the interim. Whether this can justify the imposition of the mandatory rule, with its attendant costs, it remains a fact that mandatory bid rules are now quite widespread outside the US.[331]

12.3.5 The Relationship Between the Bidder Directors and Bidder Shareholders

In contrast to the relationship between the target directors and the target shareholders, and the bidder company with the target shareholders, the relationship between the bidder directors and shareholders is largely unregulated by takeover rules. Rule 23 of the City Code requires the bidder to provide its own shareholders with information about the bid and rule 3.2 requires the board of the bidder to obtain independent legal advice on an offer (and to make that advice known to the bidder shareholders where that offer is a reverse takeover or when the directors are faced with a conflict of interest). Otherwise this relationship is left to general company law and securities regulations. This does mean that if the transaction is particularly large it may be necessary for the bidder directors to obtain shareholder consent for the transaction.[332]

This lack of takeover regulation may seem surprising when it is considered that the empirical evidence suggests that, while takeovers are generally wealth enhancing for the target shareholders, the position of the bidder shareholders post-takeover is at best equivocal, with a number of studies suggesting that the bidder shareholders lose out in some scenarios.[333] There are a number of reasons why this might be the case. The takeover might be carried out for reasons other than maximising the wealth of the bidder, for example because of managerial self-interest, or the bidder directors may have overpaid for the target company, or the financial structure of the bid may be deleterious to the bidder shareholders, such as where the bidder ends up highly leveraged as a result of significant

---

[329] A number of institutional shareholders may, between them, have control of the company: J Franks and C Mayer, 'Governance as a Source of Managerial Discipline' available at www.nbb.be/doc/ts/publications/WP/WP31En.pdf.

[330] Ie the typical UK scenario involves an acquisition of control by the bidder and not just a transfer of control: Davies, n 126, 25.

[331] Kraakman et al, n 8, 8.2.5.4.

[332] See FSA Handbook, Listing Rules, LR 10.

[333] Eg K Fuller, J Netter and M Stegemoller, 'What Do Returns to Acquiring Firms Tell Us? Evidence from Firms That Make Many Acquisitions' (2002) 57 *Journal of Finance* 1763 which suggests that in the US bidder shareholders gain when buying a closely held company but lose when purchasing a public company. One major UK study, which looked at all successful UK domestic takeovers with a bid value of over £10 million for the period 1984–92, showed that the post-takeover performance of UK companies undertaking large domestic acquisitions is, on average, negative in the long-term, irrespective of the benchmark used: A Gregory, 'An Examination of the Long Run Performance of UK Acquiring Firms' (1997) 24 *Journal of Business Finance and Accounting* 971. See also M Martynova and L Renneboog, 'Mergers and Acquisitions in Europe' (2006) available at www.ssrn.com/abstract_id=880379). For a discussion of these points see A Kouloridas, *The Law and Economics of Takeovers: An Acquirer's Perspective* (Oxford, Hart Publishing, 2008) ch 1.

debt taken on to fund the acquisition, or it may even be that takeover regulation itself, so keen to protect the target shareholders, introduces rules that secure benefits for the target shareholders at the expense of the bidder shareholders.

However, despite these potential risks faced by the bidder shareholders, this transaction is regarded as an ordinary corporate transaction from the bidder's point of view, with none of the added potential for abuse by directors of the target company towards their shareholders (resulting from the potential loss of job for the director). As a result there is felt to be no justification for overturning the usual board-shareholder relationship which is put in place by general company law principles to deal with this situation.[334]

This issue is under review at the time of writing. In the consultation document published by the Code Committee of the Takeover Panel in June 2010 the position of the bidder shareholders was raised as a topic for discussion. In particular this document considers the suggestion that some protections similar to those afforded by the City Code to target company shareholders should be afforded to shareholders in a bidder company.[335] It is too soon to say whether any changes will be implemented as a result of this review, but it is worth noting that the Code Committee surveyed 16 overseas jurisdictions and found little or no evidence in those jurisdictions for equivalent levels of protection for bidder and target shareholders.[336]

12.4 Conclusion

The UK takeover model is dominated by the decisions taken in relation to two key issues: who should take the decision whether to accept the takeover and how much regulation should be put in place to deal with the bidder's relationship with the target shareholders. The decisions taken in the UK in relation to both of these questions are resoundingly shareholder-focused. Accordingly once a bid is imminent the target directors are sidelined and takeover regulation operates as a significant constraint on their ability to frustrate the bid. Although takeover regulation does not operate in the period before the bid is imminent, a combination of general company law, securities law and the influence and role of institutional shareholders in the UK means that in practice pre-bid defensive measures are very uncommon in the UK. In the bid itself, takeover regulation operates to ensure that the bidder must treat all target shareholders equally, even though this equality is likely to come at a significant cost in terms of the number of takeover offers made. The

---

[334] For a discussion of the position of the bidder shareholders, including some suggestions as to ways in which the position of bidder shareholders could and should be better protected in a takeover, see Kouloridas, *The Law and Economics of Takeovers*, ibid.

[335] *Review of Certain Aspects of the Regulation of Takeover Bids*, n 77, section 7.

[336] The Code Committee surveyed whether, in those 16 jurisdictions, there was either a requirement (legal or regulatory) for the board of a bidder company to obtain independent advice in relation to a takeover bid for the protection of shareholders in the bidder company. The review found that there was a requirement for the board of a bidder to obtain independent advice in only one of those jurisdictions (Hong Kong), and that requirement applied only in the case of a 'reverse takeover'. In a small number of other jurisdictions (most notably the US and, to a lesser extent, Canada) the Code Committee found that the boards of bidder companies might, in practice, choose to obtain a fairness opinion, albeit that there was no requirement for them to do so: Takeover Panel, PCP 2010/2, n 77, 63.

shareholder-focus of the UK regime also has implications for the other stakeholders in the target company. As discussed at 12.3.3 above, there is little attention given to these groups within the UK takeover regime.

The decisions adopted by the UK in relation to these issues has been contrasted with that of other regimes, mostly notably that of the US, since that is the other major regime with dispersed shareholdings as the common feature of its publicly traded companies. As discussed, in US States such as Delaware that allow the use of poison pills, directors are effectively given the power to frustrate a bid and the limited constraints placed upon them by decisions such as *Unocal* mean that they can use that power to entrench themselves. If takeover regimes are designed to address agency issues then the UK model seems more appropriately to address the twin agency problems that face dispersed shareholders in target companies. The UK model is more in tune with the UK approach of shareholder primacy, as compared to the US belief in centralised management, and is a preferable response to these agency issues.

13

Schemes of Arrangement

13.1 Introduction

Schemes of arrangement are an extremely valuable tool for manipulating a company's capital. A scheme of arrangement involves a compromise or arrangement between a company[1] and its creditors, or any class of them, or its members, or any class of them.[2] As discussed in 13.2, schemes of arrangement can be used in a wide variety of ways. Nothing in the Companies Act 2006 prescribes the subject matter of a scheme. In theory a scheme could be a compromise or arrangement between a company and its creditors or members about anything which they can properly agree amongst themselves. A company can therefore use a scheme to effect almost any kind of internal reorganisation, merger or demerger, as long as the necessary approvals have been obtained. Four of the most obvious uses of a scheme will be discussed in 13.2, namely, use of a scheme as an alternative to a takeover offer, to effect a merger between one company and another, to reorganise the share capital within a company, and, finally, to effect an arrangement between the company and its creditors, either when the company is solvent or insolvent, and either alongside or as an alternative to a winding up.

It is important to note from the outset that a scheme of arrangement is an act of the company, and therefore stands in contrast to takeovers, discussed in the previous chapter.[3] Takeovers do not involve the target company, but are an arrangement between the bidder and the target shareholders first and foremost. The consequences of this difference are discussed in 13.2.1 below. Second, the effect of a scheme of arrangement is to enable those who promote the scheme to impose those proposals on a minority of the creditors or shareholders, as the case may be. As long as the requisite majorities are obtained and the court sanctions the scheme, then it will bind all of the relevant creditors or members within the ambit of the scheme. This can be extremely valuable, as in some circumstances opposition to a proposal may be based on ignorance or some interest other than that of the class to which the dissentient belongs. However, it does raise the possibility of abuse of the minority. Minority protection devices are built into the mechanics of a scheme and will be discussed in 13.3 below.

---

[1] For the definition of 'company' for these purposes see Companies Act 2006, s 895(2).
[2] Companies Act 2006, s 895(1).
[3] See also J Payne, 'Schemes of Arrangement, Takeovers and Minority Shareholder Protection' [2011] *Journal of Corporate Law Studies* (forthcoming), available at www.ssrn.com/abstract=1600592.

13.2 Uses of Schemes of Arrangement

As noted in 13.1, schemes of arrangement can be used to effect a wide variety of changes within a company. The phrase 'a compromise or arrangement' within section 895 of the Companies Act 2006 has been construed very widely by the courts. The word 'compromise' offers few difficulties of interpretation: all that is required is some difficulty or dispute which the scheme seeks to resolve.[4] By contrast, the concept of 'arrangement' is wider than that of 'compromise' and is not limited to something analogous to a compromise.[5]

The courts have not sought to provide a definition of the term 'arrangement' for these purposes, limiting it only to the extent that the arrangement must have the features of give and take and not simply amount to a surrender or confiscation.[6] For example, in a scheme between a company and its members, if the members are simply giving up their rights, or their rights are being expropriated, without any sort of compensating advantage for those members, then there is no 'arrangement' between the company and its members for these purposes.[7] A further limitation is that the company must be a party to the arrangement: section 895 does not apply to arrangements between the creditors or members not involving the company. However, subject to these limitations, the courts have deliberately avoided giving the term a narrow meaning. The courts have been prepared to sanction arrangements where the rights of shareholders or creditors as against the company are varied, or where rights are varied between creditors or shareholders, or where those groups give up rights against third parties (such as under guarantees).[8] The breadth of the term 'arrangement' was recently endorsed by the Court of Appeal in *Re Lehman Brothers International (Europe) (in administration) (No 2)*.[9]

As a result, a wide range of circumstances have been held to fall within the concept of a scheme of arrangement. These will be discussed in this section, together with an analysis of why a scheme of arrangement might prove more valuable in certain circumstances than the alternatives that might be available. However, it should be emphasised that the following is not a closed list and provides only examples of how a scheme can be used in practice.

13.2.1 As an Alternative to a Takeover

One very common use of schemes of arrangement is as an alternative to a takeover offer. Takeovers were dealt with in detail in chapter twelve. Indeed, in recent years schemes of

---

[4] *Sneath v Valley Gold Ltd* [1893] 1 Ch 477; *Re NFU Development Trust Ltd* [1972] 1 WLR 1548.
[5] No element of compromise needs to be shown in order for an arrangement to fall within s 895: *Re National Bank Ltd* [1966] 1 WLR 819, 829 per Plowman J; *Re T & N Ltd* [2006] EWHC 1447 (Ch); [2007] 1 BCLC 563, [46]–[50] per David Richards J.
[6] *Re Savoy Hotel Ltd* [1981] Ch 351, 359–61 per Nourse J.
[7] *Re NFU Development Trust Ltd* [1972] 1 WLR 1548.
[8] *Re Lehman Brothers (Europe) International* [2009] EWCA Civ 1161; [2010] BCC 272, [65]. The requirement that a scheme is between the company and its creditors and/or members, can also involve third parties, provided that the arrangement with the third parties is an integral part of the operation of the scheme and is part of a single proposition involving all the parties: *T & N (No 3)* [2006] EWHC 1447 (Ch); [2007] 1 All ER 851.
[9] [2009] EWCA Civ 1161; [2010] BCC 272, [74].

arrangement have become the structure of choice for recommended bids. If a scheme is to be used in this way then, typically, the shareholders of the target agree to the cancellation of their shares in the target company. The reserve created in the target company as a result of this arrangement is then used by the target to pay for new shares which are issued to the offeror. The shareholders of the target then receive, in exchange for their cancelled shares, cash or shares in the offeror company. This is sometimes known as a 'reduction scheme' as it combines a scheme with a reduction of capital. An alternative is a 'transfer scheme' whereby all of the shares of the target not already owned by the bidder are transferred to the bidder. Reduction schemes are more common because they require no transfer of shares and therefore no stamp duty is payable.[10] Reduction schemes do require the target company to comply with the steps to effect the reduction of capital.[11] However, the reduction is fictitious in the sense that the credit arising in the company's accounts following the reduction is immediately applied in paying up new shares in the company, so that no creditor protection issue arises. This is discussed further in 13.3.2.1. The rules of the Takeover Panel apply to takeovers effected via schemes of arrangement, whichever of these mechanisms is adopted.[12] This use of schemes of arrangement is particularly common in private equity transactions.[13]

However, although takeovers and schemes of arrangement can be used to achieve the same end, namely a shift of control of the target company, they operate quite differently and acquirers will need to consider carefully which mechanism is likely to suit them best. First, and most fundamentally, a takeover is an offer by the bidder to the target shareholders without an action by the target company being involved,[14] whereas a scheme of arrangement is an action by the company whereby the target directors ask the target shareholders to vote in favour of the change of control.

Second, a scheme of arrangement will involve the offeror acquiring 100 per cent of the target, unlike a takeover offer which could involve the offeror acquiring less than 100 per cent, and indeed the offer will be successful once the bidder reaches the minimum acceptance condition (which must be at least 50 per cent).[15] If it is important for the offeror to acquire the entire company, then a scheme of arrangement will look more attractive. It is common in private equity transactions, for example, for the offeror to want to use the target company's assets to secure the loans made to the bidder to finance the bid, and for this reason it is important for the offeror to acquire all of the target's shares. It

---

[10] A court will not, however, permit a scheme to be used purely to avoid stamp duty: *Rylands-Whitecross Ltd* (1973), unreported.

[11] This requires either a shareholder resolution to approve the reduction (the meeting to pass this resolution is generally held immediately after the court approved meeting to approve the scheme) and a court order (which can be given at the same time that the court sanctions the scheme) (see Companies Act 2006, ss 645–649) or, now, for private companies the reduction can be supported by a solvency statement (Companies Act 2006, ss 642–644). For discussion see 4.4.3.

[12] For a detailed discussion of the way in which the Takeover Panel regulates takeovers, see chapter 12, especially 12.2. Although the Takeover Panel has always applied its rules to takeovers effected via a scheme of arrangement, the practice of using schemes to effect this result has now become so common that the Panel introduced a new Appendix (Appendix 7) to the City Code on Takeovers and Mergers to deal specifically with this issue.

[13] For discussion see chapter 14.

[14] See chapter 12.

[15] City Code on Takeovers and Mergers (City Code), rule 10. The bidder can make the offer conditional on a higher level of acceptance than 50%. The Code Committee of the Takeover Panel is consulting on whether to raise the level of acceptances above this level: Code Committee of the Takeover Panel, *Review of Certain Aspects of the Regulation of Takeover Bids*, PCP 2010/2, 1 June 2010. For discussion see 12.3.1.

is not impossible to achieve this result using a takeover, though it is more difficult. The squeeze-out provisions do allow an offeror to mop up the last of the minority shareholders, but these provisions only operate once an offeror has acquired 90 per cent in value of the shares to which the offer relates.[16] For this reason some takeover offers, where the acquisition of 100 per cent of the shares is key, will set the minimum level of acceptances at 90 per cent.

It follows from this that, if the scheme is approved,[17] and sanctioned by the court, then all of the shareholders in the target are bound, even those that dissent. As we saw in chapter twelve,[18] in a takeover a number of measures are put in place to protect minority shareholders, in particular the mandatory bid rule,[19] and the sell out rule, which allows a minority shareholder who is left in the 10 per cent rump to have the right to be bought out at the same price paid for the other shares within the offer.[20] By contrast, in a scheme, the protection in place for shareholders consists of the requirement for a vote in favour by a majority in number representing three-fourths in value of the members (or class thereof), and the fact that the court must then sanction the scheme before it becomes binding on all of the members.[21]

Concerns have been voiced that the minority can effectively be bound by a lower percentage of the members in a scheme (a majority in number representing 75 per cent in value of the members present and voting) than in a takeover (where the minority could not be forced to sell their shares unless 90 per cent of the other shareholders had already accepted the offer). It has been suggested that approving a scheme of arrangement in such circumstances should require a very high standard of proof.[22] However, the current approach of the courts is that whether a company proceeds by way of a scheme of arrangement or a takeover is a matter of choice.[23] Courts have rejected the argument that where a scheme is used as an alternative to a takeover the court should insist on a 90 per cent approval of the scheme by shareholders.[24] On this view the lower threshold in a scheme is countered by the fact that the court needs to sanction the scheme.[25] Minority protection should therefore be ensured at that stage in the proceedings. However, if this is correct it means that it will be important for courts to take seriously their role at the sanctioning stage.

It is also important to consider the different purposes of minority protection in a scheme and in a takeover situation. As discussed in chapter twelve, minority protection is needed in relation to takeovers in order to ensure undistorted choice, and in order to prevent oppression of the minority, although the first is a far stronger justification for the minority protection devices put in place than the second.[26] By contrast, because a scheme

---

[16]   Companies Act 2006, s 979(2)(a) and for discussion see 12.3.1.3.

[17]   Approval is by 75% of the shareholders in value plus a majority of the shareholders present and voting in person or by proxy at the relevant meetings: Companies Act 2006, s 899(1).

[18]   See 12.3.4.

[19]   See pages 609–10.

[20]   Companies Act 2006, ss 983–985 and for discussion see 12.3.1.3.

[21]   For discussion see 13.3.3.

[22]   *Re Hellenic and General Trust* [1976] 1 WLR 123.

[23]   *Re BTR plc* [1999] 2 BCLC 675, affirmed [2000] 1 BCLC 740; *Re TDG plc* [2008] EWHC 2334 (Ch); [2009] 1 BCLC 445.

[24]   *Re National Bank* [1966] 1 WLR 819; *Re TDG plc* [2008] EWHC 2334 (Ch); [2009] 1 BCLC 445.

[25]   See 13.3.2.

[26]   See 12.3.4.

involves a decision of the company, taken by the shareholders, there is no opportunity for the bidder to divide and conquer. The concerns regarding distorted choice therefore do not arise in the context of a scheme. The issue in a scheme is simply one of minority protection. Here again, though, it is important to differentiate the position regarding takeover offers. There is no need to worry about the minority shareholders needing a right of exit since all shareholders are bound to transfer their shares to the bidder, following a successful scheme. The bidder acquires 100 per cent of the shares and there is therefore no possibility of any shareholders being left behind who might wish to exit the target company post-bid. The possibility of oppression only arises as regards the fact that the majority decision (to sell their shares at a particular price) will bind the minority, who must also sell at that price. This form of potential oppression is therefore most akin to the position of the rump shareholders who are required to sell their shares in a squeeze-out following a successful takeover.[27] This issue is discussed further at 13.3.3.[28]

As a scheme of arrangement is a corporate action of the target, the process is controlled by the target rather than the bidder. It is the target and its directors that are responsible for the scheme, and it will only be completed if it is recommended by the target directors. In contrast to a takeover offer, there can therefore be no such thing as a hostile scheme of arrangement.[29] In the case of a hostile offer, a bidder will opt for an offer rather than a scheme. A scheme of arrangement requires a friendly target board in order to succeed. Where the acquisition is likely to require a significant amount of due diligence by the acquirer before the offer can be made, this can only occur following the establishment of friendly relations with the target directors, which in turn tends to promote an acquisition via a scheme rather than a hostile takeover. This is another of the reasons why many private equity transactions involving the purchase of a public company have proceeded by way of a scheme.[30]

The fact that it is the target rather than the bidder that is in control of the process in a scheme of arrangement has an important consequence for the offeror regarding the terms of the offer. In a takeover offer it is the bidder who is in control and it is relatively easy for the bidder to change the terms of the bid during the offer process, for example to respond to a competing bid that arises. It is more difficult for the offeror to change the terms of a scheme of arrangement and therefore if a competing bid is possible or likely it may be that a takeover offer will be more suitable than a scheme.

Of course, one other important difference between a takeover offer and a scheme is the involvement of the court in the latter. This has an impact on the timetable for a scheme. It is usual for a scheme to take seven to eight weeks from posting. Takeover offer timetables are more fluid. They can be a lot quicker than a scheme (the minimum time period from posting an offer to declaring the offer unconditional is 21 days) but it could be a lot longer, if complications arise.

Finally, the bidder will need to consider whether a prospectus is required. As discussed in chapter nine, broadly the Prospectus Rules and section 85 FSMA state that a prospectus is required if a company offers shares to the public in the UK or seeks admission of

---

[27]   See 12.3.1.3.

[28]   See also J Payne, 'Schemes of Arrangement, Takeovers and Minority Shareholder Protection' [2011] *Journal of Corporate Law Studies* (forthcoming) available at www.ssrn.com/abstract=1600592.

[29]   However, even if the directors recommend the scheme initially it is possible that they might withdraw their recommendation at a later stage eg for fiduciary reasons.

[30]   See chapter 14.

securities to trading on a regulated market in the UK. Most practitioners consider that a scheme of arrangement will not normally involve an offer to the public to buy or subscribe for securities, since the transaction is effected through a court procedure under which the members or creditors of the company vote on and approve the arrangement, which then becomes effective once sanctioned by the court and registered at Companies House. This view is one which the FSA has been inclined to accept.[31] However, in December 2009, the FSA announced that where the scheme involves a shareholder being able to elect a preferred combination of cash and shares (a mix and match facility) then, because the shareholder is making an investment decision, a prospectus should be produced.[32]

13.2.2   To Effect a Merger

One possible use of a scheme of arrangement is to effect a merger between two or more companies.[33] Section 900 of the Companies Act 2006 deals specifically with schemes of arrangement 'proposed for the purposes of, or in connection with, a scheme for . . .the amalgamation of any two or more companies' and involving the transfer of the undertaking or property of one company involved in the scheme to another.[34] Where a scheme of arrangement amounts to a reconstruction or an amalgamation the court then has certain powers to facilitate the scheme.[35]

Mergers effected via a scheme of arrangement can take various forms. One company can absorb all of the assets and liabilities of the other, which is then dissolved (which might be described as a merger). Alternatively, the second company could be retained as a wholly-owned subsidiary (which might more accurately be described as a takeover). Takeovers effected by way of a scheme of arrangement were discussed in 13.2.1. The shareholders of the absorbed company will usually receive shares in the merged company. Another possibility is that a new company is formed and both companies transfer all of their assets etc to that new company, with the shareholders receiving shares in the new company. Schemes of arrangement can also be used to effect a division or demerger of one company into two or more companies. The assets and liabilities of the original company are then divided up between the new entities.

However, it is relatively rare for mergers of companies to be carried out by means of a scheme of arrangement in the UK. This is for a number of reasons. First, a scheme of arrangement effects a merger by means of a transfer of the undertaking, ie the assets and liabilities of one or more companies are transferred to another company. This has consequences for third parties who deal with a company. As a starting point, those who contract with company A, whose assets and liabilities are then transferred by way of a scheme to company B, will still retain their relationship with company A. The terms of the

---

[31]   UKLA List! Issue 10, 2005. However, a scheme of arrangement constitutes an offer for the purposes of the City Code on Takeovers and Mergers so that, for example, rule 2.1 and rule 2.2 apply. For details of the application of the City Code to schemes of arrangement see City Code, Appendix 7.

[32]   UKLA List! 23 Dec 2009.

[33]   Where the merger involves companies located in different Member States see now the Cross Border Mergers Directive 2005/56/EC, discussed in P Davies, *Gower and Davies: Principles of Company Law*, 8th edn, (London, Sweet & Maxwell, 2009) 1073–79.

[34]   Companies Act 2006, s 900(1). This section also facilitates reconstructions of a company by way the transfer of its undertaking or property to another company.

[35]   Companies Act 2006, s 900.

contract may give the third party the right to terminate the contract or to insist on different terms in these circumstances. A scheme may well involve a negotiation with third parties, therefore, to agree a transfer of the contract to B. Where control of a company is effected by a transfer of shares (as, for example in a takeover) then this issue does not arise from the structure of the transaction, though restrictions in the contract between company A and the third party can mimic the situation regarding a transfer of the undertaking.[36]

Second, as we will see in 13.3, schemes of arrangement involve various stages: an arrangement is proposed, then meetings of those impacted by the scheme are held, whether that is creditors or members of classes thereof, and if these meetings vote in favour of the scheme the court has discretion whether to sanction it.[37] The structure of this process potentially provides more opportunities for the merger to be vetoed than in a takeover. In a transfer of shares by way of a takeover, the group determining whether the transfer will be successful is the shareholders, as discussed in chapter twelve. By contrast, in a scheme of arrangement, all those impacted by the scheme,[38] whether they are members or creditors, also have an opportunity to veto it, since they will need to meet to approve the scheme. Creditors do not have the same opportunity to interfere with the outcome of a takeover.[39] There may be good reasons for the creditors in the transferor company to object, if they feel that competing with the creditors in the transferee company for the assets of the merged entity after the scheme is effected will put them at a disadvantage. In addition, at the stage when the court sanctions the scheme, even if the meetings have approved it, it is open to any creditor to object to the scheme, and the court may take that objection into account in determining whether to sanction it.[40]

A further level of uncertainty regarding the success of a scheme is the fact that the court has discretion whether to sanction the scheme, even if the members and creditors (as relevant) have approved it. Again, this uncertainty does not exist in the context of takeovers, where the court has no equivalent role in determining the success of the bid. These additional levels of uncertainty may make a transfer by way of an undertaking less attractive than a transfer by way of shares. Of course, in a transfer by way of shares (a takeover), this can also be effected by way of a scheme, as discussed at 13.2.1, in which case these same procedural difficulties will arise, but a takeover need not be effected in this way, as discussed in chapter twelve.

Another reason why the use of a scheme to effect a merger might appear unattractive is the fact that in certain cases of mergers and divisions of public companies additional requirements are imposed by the Companies Act 2006[41] in order to meet the requirements

---

[36]   See, in relation to loan contracts, page 158.

[37]   The mechanics of a scheme of arrangement are discussed in detail at 13.3.

[38]   *Re Tea Corporation Ltd* [1904] 1 Ch 12, discussed at 13.3.2.1.

[39]   See chapter 12, in particular 12.3.4.

[40]   See 13.3.3.

[41]   Companies Act 2006, Part 27. First, at least one month before the class meetings are held, a draft scheme has to be drawn up by the boards of all the companies involved (including the transferee company), a copy of which is then delivered to the Registrar who publishes notice of receipt (ss 905–906, 920–921); second, additional information is required in the board's circular (ss 908, 910, 923, 925); third, there have to be separate written reports on the scheme to the members of each company by an independent expert appointed by that company or, if the court approves, a single joint report of all companies by an independent expert appointed by all of them (ss 909, 924, 935–937) although this requirement for an independent report can be dispensed with if all of the members agree (s 918A).

of the Third and Sixth company law directives.[42] However, these additional requirements do not apply where a scheme is used to effect a takeover because the bidder and target remain separate companies after the scheme has been effected. Broadly, the legislation envisages three scenarios falling within these provisions: merger where the undertaking, property etc of a public company is transferred to another public company which has not been specifically formed for the purpose;[43] merger where the undertaking, property etc of two or more public companies is transferred to a new company (not necessarily a public company) specially formed for that purpose;[44] and division of the undertaking, property etc of a public company to two or more companies of which either is a public company or has been formed for the purpose of the scheme.[45] A number of scenarios fall outside this list, such as a reconstruction of a single public company, and a transfer to a new company (public or private) by a single public company. The legislation is also limited in other ways so that, for example, it covers situations where the consideration for the transfer is or includes shares in the transferee, but excludes, therefore, mergers for purely cash consideration.[46]

These are all good reasons why changes of control of companies, particularly public companies, are often effected by means of a takeover rather than a transfer of undertaking via a scheme of arrangement. In some circumstances the takeover may itself be effected via a scheme (see 13.2.1) since even though some of the disadvantages set out above do apply (eg the courts' involvement) others do not. In particular the additional requirements regarding mergers of public companies do not apply.

For smaller companies wishing to effect a merger other options apply that may be more attractive than a scheme under the Companies Act 2006. In particular a company may decide to make use of section 110 of the Insolvency Act 1986. This section enables a solvent winding up to be used to achieve the transfer or sale of the whole or part of a company's business or property to another company. This is done in exchange for shares, policies, or other interests in the second company, to be distributed amongst the members of the liquidating company. Nominally the transferor company remains liable for its debts and commitments, and the creditors of the transferor remain entitled to prove in its liquidation,[47] but in practice the transferee meets the liabilities of the liquidating company as they become due pursuant to an indemnity given to the liquidator as part of the consideration for the transfer. The commercial effect is therefore to transfer the business of the company. Alternatively, this process can be used to effect a merger between two or more companies. This process can also be used to reorganise a single company, in which case a transferee company is incorporated with a capital structure different from that of the liquidating/transferor company.

In order to effect a merger in this way, a special resolution must be passed to commence the winding up. This can be either a members' or a creditors' voluntary liquidation.[48] If it

---

[42]   Directives 78/855/EEC and 82/891/EEC.
[43]   Companies Act 2006, ss 904(1)(a) and 902(2)(b).
[44]   Ibid, ss 904(1)(b) and 902(2)(a).
[45]   Ibid, ss 919 and 902(2).
[46]   Ibid, s 902(1)(c).
[47]   *Pulsford v Devenish* [1903] 2 Ch 625. However, the sale of the undertaking is binding on the creditors, who therefore cannot follow the assets transferred into the transferee company.
[48]   A members' voluntary liquidation is one in which the directors have made a 'declaration of solvency' declaring that all the company's debts will be paid in full within 12 months (see Insolvency Act 1986, s 89). For the distinction between a members' and creditors' voluntary liquidation see Insolvency Act 1986, s 90.

is a members' voluntary liquidation, a further special resolution will be required sanction-ing the scheme, and in the case of a creditors' voluntary liquidation the sanction of either the court or the liquidation committee is required.[49] The sale then becomes binding on all members of the company.

The advantage of using section 110 of the Insolvency Act is that, as long as a members' voluntary liquidation is used, no confirmation by the court is required. This is a significant advantage over a scheme under the Companies Act. However, in a members' voluntary liquidation, any dissenting shareholder can require the liquidator to abstain from carrying the special resolution into effect, or to purchase his interest at a price to be determined by agreement or by arbitration.[50] Two significant differences between section 110 (consequent on a members' winding up) and a scheme under section 895 of the Companies Act 2006 are worth mentioning. First, under section 110 (consequent on a members' winding up) the company must be solvent, whereas a scheme under the Companies Act 2006 can involve either a solvent or insolvent company. Second, whereas under a Companies Act scheme of arrangement dissenters are bound once the court has sanctioned the scheme, under section 110 following a members' winding up the dissenters are not bound by the scheme proposed, but are entitled to exit the company in exchange for an agreed or arbitrated cash price for their shares.

Use of section 110 is a popular means of reconstructing private or family controlled companies as an alternative to a scheme under the Companies Act.[51] However, what can be achieved by means of section 110 is relatively limited. The ability of dissenting minorities in a members' voluntary winding up to serve notice on the liquidator means that, although members' rights can be varied using this form of arrangement, it will not generally be possible to make them significantly less attractive. If a number of the members elect to be bought out, the reorganisation under section 110 may well become prohibitively expensive.

In summary, although schemes of arrangement can be used to effect a control shift by way of a transfer of undertaking, in practice they are relatively rarely used for this purpose. For small companies it may be preferable to use section 110 of the Insolvency Act and for larger companies, particularly public companies, a takeover (effected by way of a scheme or otherwise) will often be a preferable way to structure the transaction.

13.2.3   To Effect an Arrangement Between the Company and its Shareholders

In 13.2.1 and 13.2.2 schemes of arrangement were envisaged as operating between two or more companies to effect a merger or to mimic the effect of a takeover. However, it is possible for a scheme to have effect purely within one company, and this could involve an arrangement between the company and its shareholders (discussed in this section) or an arrangement between a company and its creditors (discussed in 13.2.4).

---

[49]   Insolvency Act 1986, s 110(3). The sanction of the court or liquidation committee is unlikely to be given in relation to a creditors' voluntary liquidation unless the creditors are paid in full.

[50]   Insolvency Act 1986, s 111. The Company Law Review (CLR) recommended that the arbitration procedure found within s 111 should be modernised (CLR, *Modern Company Law for a Competitive Economy: Completing the Structure*, URN 00/1335, November 2000, 208–9) but these proposals have not been imple-mented.

[51]   See *Completing the Structure*, ibid, 208.

Since a scheme encompasses an arrangement 'between a company and its . . . members, or any class of them'[52] this mechanism can be used within a company to reorganise the company's share capital by, for example, consolidating different classes of shares or dividing the existing shares into different classes. However, if the rights attached to the shares appear in the company's articles, as they commonly will, it will generally be far simpler for the share capital to be reorganised by altering the articles by special resolution.[53] Further, it is no longer necessary to use a scheme to alter class rights since a simplified statutory procedure now applies to all such rights: essentially class rights can be altered as long as 75 per cent of the class consent.[54] In general therefore these forms of reorganisations will not be carried out via a scheme. However, there may be circumstances in which a scheme becomes useful, for example where there are a number of untraceable shareholders who must be bound by the scheme.[55]

Schemes are sometimes used in combination with a reduction of capital, in which case the statutory procedures for a reduction, discussed in chapter four, must also be followed.[56] A scheme cannot, therefore, be used to effect an unauthorised reduction. One reason to combine a scheme with an authorised reduction is where the reduction involves treating one class of equity shares differently from another.[57] Alternatively, by using a reduction of capital and a scheme of arrangement it is possible to change shares into redeemable shares, something that could not be managed using other statutory procedures, without the addition of a scheme. In this case, the scheme cancels the old shares, thereby creating a reserve that can be capitalised by the issue of redeemable shares.[58]

Schemes can be useful in some instances in order to achieve reorganisations of the share capital that could not otherwise be effected. For example, it is possible for companies to structure a return of capital to shareholders using a scheme of arrangement that would not otherwise be possible. This route involves a reconstruction of the company, with a new holding company being inserted between a company and its shareholders. As part of the process the shareholders will receive ordinary shares in the new holding company and either a cash payment or new 'B' shares in the new holding company. If the latter, the B shares can then be redeemed, bought back or cancelled by way of a reduction of capital. The benefit of this form of scheme for a company with low distributable reserves is that it facilitates the creation of additional distributable reserves. It is therefore a mechanism for unlocking previously undistributable reserves for return to the shareholders.

These forms of schemes can be very useful to companies. However, this has not been the primary use of schemes in recent years. Much greater use has been made of schemes to reorganise a company's debt, as discussed in the next section.

---

[52]   Companies Act 2006, s 895(1).

[53]   Ibid, s 21. It may also be necessary to obtain the consent of the separate classes of shareholders if class rights are being altered: Companies Act 2006, s 630.

[54]   Ibid, ss 630–635.

[55]   Eg *Re BAT Industries plc*, unreported, 3 September 1998.

[56]   See Companies Act 2006, Part 17, Chapter 10 for the court approval mechanism (public and private companies) and the solvency statement mechanism (private companies only) discussed at 4.4.3.

[57]   *Re Stephen (Robert) Holdings* [1968] 1 WLR 552.

[58]   If the company is to provide financial assistance for the purchase of its shares under the proposed scheme then the provisions of the Companies Act 2006 will not apply so long as the scheme has been approved by the court.

13.2.4   To Effect an Arrangement between the Company and its Creditors

When schemes of arrangement were first introduced in 1870[59] they applied only to arrangements between a company and its creditors, and only to arrangements proposed by companies in the course of being wound up. Both of these constraints were subsequently dropped,[60] but it remains a common use of schemes of arrangement to effect a compromise between the company and its creditors. Both solvent and insolvent schemes are common.

It is possible for an arrangement between a company and its creditors to be effected via informal consensual arrangements between the parties. The difficulty with this mechanism is that all of the creditors would have to agree. In general, the position regarding creditors is therefore distinct from that regarding shareholders. As described in 13.2.3 above, for shareholders, if the rights are in the articles, the 75 per cent majority shareholders can in principle bind the minority.[61] As regards creditors the usual position is that a single dissenting creditor, even one holding only a very small percentage of the company's debts, can prevent the compromise.[62] By contrast, in a successful scheme the majority creditors are able to bind the minority, as discussed in the next section.[63] There are other statutory processes that can be used to effect arrangements between a company and its creditors, but a scheme of arrangement is the most common.[64] One of the particular advantages of a scheme over a company voluntary arrangement (CVA), for example, is the ability to bind all creditors, including secured creditors, in a scheme, whereas secured creditors fall outside CVAs.[65]

The term 'creditor' is not defined by statute for the purpose of a scheme of arrangement.[66] The courts have tended to construe this term widely.[67] A creditor has been held to consist of anyone who has a monetary claim against the company which, when payable,

---

[59]   Joint Stock Companies Arrangement Act 1870.

[60]   The Companies Act 1907 extended schemes to companies not in liquidation and the Companies (Consolidation) Act 1908 extended schemes to arrangements between a company and its members or any class of them.

[61]   Companies Act 2006, s 21 (regarding alterations of articles). This is subject to the common law principle that the majority must act bona fide in the best interests of the company: *Allen v Gold Reefs of West Africa Ltd* [1900] 1 Ch 656.

[62]   However, this position can be varied by contract. In deeds of debt securities, for example, it is common to provide that the trustee can take action against a corporate borrower with the approval of a specified majority less than 100%. See 7.3.3. As with shareholders' ability to alter the articles, there are common law restrictions on the ability of the majority to exercise its voting power in these situations for an improper purpose: *British America Nickel Corporation v O'Brien* [1927] AC 369 (see pages 341–42). These can obviously only bind the parties to the contract whereas a scheme can bind other creditors.

[63]   See 13.3.

[64]   For example, a creditors' voluntary arrangement is possible, under Insolvency Act 1986, ss 1–7 (see eg V Finch, *Corporate Insolvency Law*, 2nd edn (Cambridge University Press, 2009) ch 11). It may even be possible to make use of Insolvency Act 1986, s 110, discussed above at 13.2.2 (which involves the disposal of the company's business to another company in exchange for shares or other interests in the transferee company).

[65]   Insolvency Act 1986, ss 1–7 (see eg Finch, *Corporate Insolvency Law*, ibid, ch 11).

[66]   For a discussion of the definition of 'creditor' where a bond issue is represented by a global note see pages 342–43.

[67]   *Re Alabama, New Orleans, Texas, and Pacific Junction Railway Co* [1891] 1 Ch 913, 236–37; *Re Midland Coal, Coke and Iron Co* [1895] 1 Ch 267, 277.

will constitute a debt.[68] This has been held to include secured creditors[69] so that schemes can, and frequently do, involve the removal or modification of security. Further, a creditor for these purposes is not limited to someone who has an immediately provable debt. It has been accepted that a person with a contingent claim against the company qualifies as a creditor under a scheme of arrangement: 'the word "creditor" is used [in this context] in the widest sense, and…includes all persons having any pecuniary claims against the company'.[70] The holders of share options are therefore regarded as creditors by virtue of their contingent claims against the company.[71] Neither is the word limited to those who would have a provable claim in the winding up of the company.[72] In *Re T & N Ltd (No 2)*[73] future tort claimants in respect of asbestosis damage claims were held to be creditors for this purpose, on proof of exposure to asbestos, even though the judge held that they had no provable debt in the winding up.[74] In that case David Richards J regarded contingent liability for these purposes as being liability arising by reason of something done by the company (in this case the use or distribution of asbestos) which would necessarily arise if certain future events were to occur (ie the onset of asbestos-related conditions in those exposed to asbestos by the company).

One of the recognised purposes of a scheme of arrangement is to facilitate the financial rehabilitation of the company and this is a strong policy reason to give the interpretation of 'creditor' as wide a meaning as possible. However, as David Richards J recognised in *Re T & N Ltd*, there may be dangers with defining the term too widely since a scheme is a mechanism 'whereby an arrangement may be imposed on dissenting or non-participating members of the class and [therefore] such a power is not to be construed as extending so as to bind persons who cannot properly be described as "creditors"'.[75]

This issue was raised recently in the decision in *Re Lehman Brothers International (Europe)(in administration)(No 2)*.[76] In that case the administrators of a company proposed a scheme the effect of which was to modify the rights held by clients of the company. The clients held property rights under trusts of which the company was the trustee. The question for the court was whether the clients could be regarded as creditors for the purpose of the scheme. There was no dispute that to the extent that these clients also held pecuniary claims against the company, for example in respect of claims against the company for equitable compensation for breach of trust, they could be regarded as (unsecured) creditors. The question was whether the court had jurisdiction to sanction a scheme insofar as it compromised or removed their rights over the trust property.

---

[68]   *Re Lehman Bothers International (Europe)(in administration)* [2009] EWCA Civ 1161; [2010] BCC 272, [58].

[69]   *Re Empire Mining Co* (1890) 44 Ch D 402, 409; *Re Alabama, New Orleans, Texas and Pacific Junction Railway Co* [1891] 1 Ch 213, 246.

[70]   *Re Midland Coal, Coke & Iron Co* [1895] 1 Ch 267, 277 per Lindley LJ.

[71]   *Re Compania de Electricidad de la Provincia de Buenos Aires Ltd* [1980] Ch 146.

[72]   *Re T & N Ltd (No 2)* [2005] EWHC 2870 (Ch); [2006] 1 WLR 1728.

[73]   [2005] EWHC 2870 (Ch); [2006] 1 WLR 1728.

[74]   The court's decision in *T & N Ltd* that future asbestos claims were not provable debts for the purpose of winding up prompted the Insolvency Rules 1986 to be changed to provide that a liability in tort was a debt provable in a winding up if either the cause of action had accrued at the date on which the company went into liquidation or all the elements necessary to establish the cause of action existed at that date except for actionable damage: Insolvency Rules 1986, r 13.12(2).

[75]   [2005] EWHC 2870 (Ch); [2006] 1 WLR 1728, [40].

[76]   [2009] EWCA Civ 1161; [2010] BCC 272.

The Court of Appeal held that the concept of creditor did not extend to those whose relationship is not that of a debtor/creditor at all, and a proprietary claim to trust property is not a claim in respect of a debt or liability of the company. The concept of 'creditor' for these purposes is not limitless. The position of a beneficiary under a trust was held not to be analogous to the position of a secured creditor (whose rights can be amended via a scheme):

> In the case of a secured creditor, the security is an incident of the debt…as section 895 enables a scheme which varies the debt, then it must follow that the variation must, as it were, be followed through to the security. No such argument can be mounted in relation to trust property held in the name of the company, which also happens to have a debt to the beneficiary, even if the debt arises out of the trustee-beneficiary relationship.[77]

This must be correct. The Court of Appeal was also asked to consider the argument that if a creditor of the company held some pecuniary claims against the company, and therefore could properly be regarded as a creditor in relation to those claims, that they could be regarded as a creditor under section 895 of the Companies Act 2006 for all purposes, so that the scheme can then extend to any property or interest of that person. This argument was dismissed by the Court of Appeal. Unless a person's claim renders him a creditor of the company, then the subject matter of that claim cannot be covered by a scheme of arrangement. The mere fact that a beneficiary happens also to be a creditor of a company does not entitle the company, or its liquidators or administrators, to include that property in a scheme when they would not otherwise be allowed to do so. The arrangement must be made with creditors in their capacity as creditors and must concern their position as creditors. Again, this must be the correct approach.

Schemes can be used by both solvent and insolvent companies in order to effect an arrangement between a company and its creditors.

13.2.4.1   *Arrangements with Creditors Involving Solvent Companies*

Although many schemes do involve companies in financial distress, a scheme can also be used to alter the rights of creditors in a solvent company. One use that is commonly made of schemes, for example, is to convert debt into equity.[78]

Another use of schemes, which has been developed recently, relates to solvent run-offs of insurance companies.[79] Schemes can be particularly helpful to insurance companies wanting to deal with incurred but not yet reported (IBNR) obligations. This is particularly important for insurance offered in relation to issues such as asbestos, where exposure to the harm occurs during the period covered by the policy, but the personal injury resulting from that exposure might only manifest itself years or even decades later. From time to time, insurance companies elect to stop writing certain types of coverage, and go into 'run-off', meaning that the company ceases to provide that type of coverage, but it continues to remain bound by its pre-existing contractual commitments under the policies it has already issued. As long as claims continue to be presented and the company

---

[77]   At [82] per Lord Neuberger, MR.
[78]   See eg the Telewest scheme of arrangement: *Re Telewest Communications plc* [2004] EWHC 924 (Ch); [2004] BCC 342; [2004] EWCA Civ 728; [2005] BCC 29 (the first court hearing) and [2004] EWHC 1466 (Ch); [2005] BCC 36 (the sanctioning hearing).
[79]   It is also possible to use schemes to deal with insolvent run-offs. This is discussed below at 13.2.4.2.

remains solvent, the claims will continue to be met in full. Notably, run-off does not mean the company is insolvent, merely that it declines to write new business. Run-off of insurance policies of this kind can take a long time to administer because claims may be presented for many years to come.

If a company wants to expedite this process, it could offer to commute its obligations to its policyholders, exchanging early payout for cancellation of the insurer's future obligation to pay claims as they arise in the ordinary course of business. Commutations are frequently based on actuarial calculations of the present value of future claims, determined in accordance with historical claims experience. An insured may be willing to accept a commutation of its policy rights if the amount of the early payout is sufficient, but only if the insurer is in a formal statutory winding up or liquidation procedure can it compel the policyholder to enter into a commutation. A policyholder with IBNR claims might refuse to commute its policy because of the extraordinary difficulty it would face in reaching agreement with the issuer about the value of its claim.

To expedite the run-off process and terminate their longstanding contractual commitments to their policyholders without entering into a formal insolvency or liquidation proceeding, and without having to enter into formal commutation with each policyholder, a number of solvent UK insurance companies have proposed schemes of arrangement.[80] These schemes can allow wholly solvent companies to manage their IBNR liabilities. The effect of a scheme in such a situation is to enable the company to achieve finality in relation to these claims, thus enabling a release of capital to the shareholders that had previously been held against the possibility of future claims, or perhaps allowing the company to move into a new area of operation.

There are potential disadvantages to such schemes, of course, not least the fact that the claims are estimated and therefore some policyholders or creditors will receive less (or more) than they would have received had the scheme not been implemented. The problems of estimation are obviously far more acute for IBNR claims than for those claims that have already matured. Also problematic is the fact that, in order to achieve finality, a scheme may introduce a bar date by which point creditors must submit their claims. Any creditor failing to submit a claim by this date may not receive payment under the scheme. Issues of creditor protection will therefore be important. These issues are discussed in 13.3.3.

13.2.4.2   Arrangements with Creditors Involving Financially Distressed Companies

There are numerous different ways to make use of a scheme where a company is financially distressed. For example, where existing creditors of a company in financial difficulties seek to encourage the provision of new venture capital by a third party they may have to agree to convert their debt or a portion of it into equity, or at least subordinate their debt to that of the prospective new lender. In other circumstances the creditors might decide between themselves to enter into a new credit agreement whereby they postpone or forgive some of their debt.

---

[80]   Eg *British Aviation Insurance Co Ltd* [2005] EWHC 1621 (Ch); [2006] BCC 14.

Often the scheme of arrangement will operate alongside a winding up[81] of the company. The addition of the scheme of arrangement into the mix will be used where it is felt that the company's assets can be got in and distributed more quickly and effectively via the scheme than via the winding up. However, in other circumstances a scheme can operate as an alternative to the winding up.[82]

Schemes are regarded as having a number of distinct advantages when dealing with actually or potentially insolvent companies. A scheme can be used to try to rehabilitate or rescue such a company. There is significant flexibility in the arrangement that can form the basis of a scheme. One advantage of schemes of arrangement, of particular relevance to rescue scenarios, is that, because schemes can be formulated and approved without the requirement of impending insolvency, early attention to corporate difficulties can be instituted. Where the scheme is intended to be in force for some reasonably lengthy period the scheme will generally contain provisions to ensure the adequate flow of information to creditors. A further possible advantage is that a scheme is an arrangement between the company and its creditors, and does not involve an insolvency practitioner in formulating or implementing the scheme. The directors therefore stay in control of the company.[83] Schemes also bind all the relevant creditors, once the requisite approvals and the sanction of the court has been obtained, including secured creditors. This is a very significant advantage and is in contrast to other forms of voluntary arrangements, such as company voluntary arrangements (CVAs).[84] Finally, schemes can be used to reorganise corporate groups. Debt can be exchanged for equity and schemes can provide for the transfer of shares or assets between companies or even for the amalgamation of companies.

Reconstruction schemes of this kind will invariably need to involve the creditors accepting a moratorium on the enforcement of their claims against the company in order to give the company the opportunity to effect the rescue plan. However, one of the main disadvantages of a scheme over other insolvency arrangements is that it offers no moratorium at the present time. For a financially distressed company wishing to be freed from its most pressing claims, so as to be able to trade back into solvency, a scheme alone will therefore be of limited assistance.[85] This weakness in the scheme procedure was

---

[81] Since the Enterprise Act 2002 there can now be distributions in administration and therefore administration can act as an alternative to winding up. As a result it is also now common for schemes to also operate alongside administrations.

[82] The courts have upheld a scheme *after* a liquidation to effect a compromise with creditors in preference to that which would arise under the Insolvency Act 1986 (*Re Trix Ltd* [1970] 1 WLR 1422). See also *Re Anglo American Insurance Ltd* [2001] 1 BCLC 755 in which the judge (Neuberger J) upheld a scheme which was binding on the liquidator and after a liquidation but which involved a departure from normal insolvency principles (in that instance Insolvency Act 1986, r 4.90), although the judge suggested that this was an exceptional case (at 770).

[83] This could be a disadvantage of course if the directors lack the will or ability to deal with the company's difficulties.

[84] Insolvency Act 1986, ss 1–7, discussed in Finch, n 64, ch 11.

[85] Insolvency Law and Practice, *Report of the Review Committee*, (Cmd 8558, 1982) (the Cork Report) para 406 criticised schemes of arrangement as a debtor restructuring regime on this basis. Schemes of arrangement cannot be invoked quickly (see 13.3 for a discussion of the mechanics of a scheme of arrangement): at least eight weeks are generally necessary between the formulation of the scheme and the eventual court order sanctioning the scheme. This is too long a period for the company to be unprotected from creditor enforcement procedures. In all likelihood during this period a creditor would sue the company and petition for its winding up.

highlighted in *Sea Assets Ltd v PT Garuda Indonesia*.[86] In that case the court was forced to exercise its discretion to grant a stay of execution in order to protect a scheme of arrangement that was being put together.

Schemes are therefore often coupled with administration orders in order to secure this protection. This difficulty, which arises from the fact that schemes of arrangement lack a moratorium, has been recognised for some time. It was raised by the Cork Report,[87] and the Company Law Review acknowledged that it was an issue requiring review, but stated that, as an insolvency law issue, it fell outside its terms of reference.[88] This issue was finally tackled by the Insolvency Service in its consultation document on Corporate Rescue, in 2009, in which it was suggested that the moratorium be extended to schemes of arrangement implemented under the Companies Act.[89] More detailed proposals for a restructuring moratorium were then put forward by the Insolvency Service in July 2010.[90] It is envisaged that this restructuring moratorium would potentially be available to companies seeking a contractual compromise, or which are preparing a statutory compromise proposal, either a CVA or a scheme of arrangement. The proposed moratorium would initially last for three months, providing company directors with a protected breathing space in which to negotiate with the company's creditors. In order to help safeguard creditors' interests, the directors' application for a moratorium would be sanctioned at a court hearing, at which any creditor of the company could appear and object to the moratorium on specified grounds. The consultation document also envisages the appointment of an insolvency practitioner (known as a 'monitor') who would have a role at certain key stages of the application process and would help to safeguard creditors' interests once the moratorium was in force. So, one use of schemes of arrangement is to effect some form of rehabilitation of the company. A good example of this can be seen in *In Re Cape plc*.[91] Cape was not insolvent but was faced with a present and future liability of enormous and unknowable proportions from the claims of employees exposed to asbestos dust. Under the proposed scheme a subsidiary, CCS Ltd, would be created for the purpose of meeting the claims, and all asbestos claims would then only be enforceable against CCS Ltd. CCS Ltd would be funded by an initial payment of £40 million from the parent company, Cape, and would be in receipt of future funding as necessary to meet the cost of future claims. The scheme would therefore be subject to future revision, as those future claims arose.[92] In this way, Cape could meet its current asbestos liabilities and hoped to trade out of its future difficulties. The court's approval of this scheme effectively allowed

---

[86]   27 June 2001, unreported (2001 WL 1251844) discussed in G Moss, 'Scheme of Arrangement: a Recent Example' (2003) 16(1) *Insolvency Intelligence* 6.

[87]   *Cork Report*, n 85, para 406.

[88]   See *Completing the Structure*, n 50, para 13.11.

[89]   Insolvency Service, *Encouraging Company Rescue – A Consultation*, June 2009. There was widespread support for this suggestion: Insolvency Service, *Encouraging Company Rescue – Summary of Responses*, November 2009 paras 24–26.

[90]   Insolvency Service, *Proposals for a Restructuring Moratorium- A Consultation*, July 2010.

[91]   [2006] EWHC 1316 (Ch); [2006] 3 All ER 1222. For discussion see J Townsend, 'Schemes of Arrangement and Asbestos Litigation: *In re Cape plc*' [2007] *Modern Law Review* 837.

[92]   It is important to note that in this case, therefore, the court was prepared to sanction a scheme even though it was subject to amendment by an internal decision-making process. This was despite policy arguments to the contrary, along the lines that this scheme would have the effect of excluding the court's supervisory role, and that 'clarity and certainty' are the touchstones for court-sanctioned schemes of arrangement (*In re NRMA* (2000) 33 ACSR 595, 647 per Santow J). However on the facts of this case the judge, rightly, saw a 'clear case for flexibility' (at [69] per David Richards J).

both the company and the asbestos claimants to reach a collaborative solution to this situation. Without this scheme it was likely that both present and future asbestos victims would have been prejudiced in their attempts to recover compensation by the likely insolvency of Cape. Liquidation was not a realistic alternative to the scheme in this case as present and future liabilities could not be met in any insolvency. The scheme therefore protected Cape from the asbestos victims, and also protected the asbestos victims from each other. If they had been able to enforce their individual or group claims, the insolvency of Cape would have been to their collective detriment, as insufficient compensation would be recoverable in liquidation.

A second common use of schemes in this context is to enable a more efficient and effective run-off of the liabilities of the company and collection of its assets than may be possible within a liquidation. In general the use of a scheme can introduce an element of flexibility to the proceedings which can prove helpful. For example, the liquidator is constrained to apply the mandatory set-off rules in rule 4.90 of the Insolvency Rules 1986.[93] However, a court may allow these rules to be set aside in some instances under a scheme.[94] Use of a scheme can also be beneficial to the process of collection of a company's assets. This exercise can be complex in a liquidation. Generally, the liquidator will concentrate on gathering in and realising the company's assets before considering in any detail the claims of the creditors. In long-tail businesses such as insurance companies the process of ascertaining the company's assets and then considering the creditors' claims can take years. Schemes have therefore been used in the past decade or so to provide an alternative to liquidation for such companies, since they can provide a much more flexible (and quicker) way of collecting the company's assets, agreeing its liabilities and returning funds to creditors.

Another benefit of using a scheme as an alternative to a winding up can be seen in *T & N Ltd (No 3)*.[95] In that case the administrators of a company (T) and its associated companies, proposed to make a scheme of arrangement with those employees and former employees of T and its associated companies, or their dependants, who had, or might have, claims for damages for personal injuries arising out of exposure to asbestos covered by employers' liability insurance. The insurers had denied liability for asbestos-related claims, and sought to avoid the policies. The administrators had brought proceedings against the insurers, and the proposed scheme of arrangement embodied a compromise of that litigation. The outline of the scheme was that the scheme companies and actual or potential claimants would not assert claims against the insurers, and instead the insurers would establish a fund to be held on trust to pay a dividend on such claims as and when they were established. All rights of claimants would be assigned to the trustees. The scheme covered personal injury claims by employees and their dependants and contribution claims by other employers outside the T group. The scheme in this case therefore involved the creditors of the company giving up their rights against a third party, the insurers. This was nevertheless held to be an arrangement between T and its creditors because the creditors' claims against the insurers were closely connected to their rights

---

[93] The equivalent provision for administration is Insolvency Rules 1986, r 2.85. For discussion see 5.2.4.6.
[94] *Re Anglo American Insurance Ltd* [2001] 1 BCLC 755.
[95] [2006] EWHC 1447 (Ch); [2007] 1 All ER 851.

against the company.[96] The fact that the scheme here was held to be capable of extending to and varying the rights of the creditors against a third party means that this was not an arrangement that could have been facilitated by making use of any of the available insolvency procedures.

In terms of the disadvantages of using schemes to effect arrangements between a company and its creditors, one has been mentioned already, namely that at the present time schemes do not involve a moratorium of the creditors' claims against the company. The other major disadvantage of a scheme as compared to other insolvency arrangements is more general and relates, predominantly, to the complexity of implementing a scheme. The procedure is said to be too long, drawn out and inflexible,[97] and it is not always straightforward for those promoting a scheme to identify appropriate classes of creditors. This is discussed further in 13.3 below.

13.2.5   Summary

A scheme of arrangement can be a very valuable tool for effecting any number of arrangements between a company and its creditors or members, as discussed in this section. In practice however, schemes are predominantly used in two ways: as an alternative to a takeover, and to effect an arrangement between a company and its creditors, often, but not exclusively, where the company is financially distressed. For a company, one of the distinct advantages of a scheme is that, once approved, it will bind all of the affected creditors and members, even if they dissent. Schemes therefore raise the possibility of minority oppression. As will be discussed in the next section it is predominantly the court's role to determine how much minority protection should be put in place. More minority protection will mean that more schemes will potentially fail, reducing their value as a tool for the company, but too little minority protection also raises difficulties. The level of minority protection created by the court will be explored in the next section.

13.3   The Mechanics of a Scheme of Arrangement

There are three main steps involved in implementing a scheme of arrangement. First, a compromise or arrangement is proposed between the company and its members or creditors.[98] A scheme will often be proposed by the board on behalf of the company.[99] An application must then be made to court under section 896 of the Companies Act 2006 for an order that a meeting or meetings be summoned. Second, meetings of the members or

---

[96]   This reasoning was approved in *Re Lehman Brothers (Europe) International* [2009] EWCA Civ 1161; [2010] BCC 272, although the decision in *Re T & N Ltd (No 3)* on this point was said to be 'near the outer limits of the scope of section 895' (at [83] per Lord Neuberger, Master of the Rolls).

[97]   See *Completing the Structure*, n 50, 207.

[98]   Companies Act 2006, s 895(1).

[99]   It is also possible for the general meeting to propose a scheme on behalf of a company (see eg *Re Savoy Hotel Ltd* [1981] Ch 351).

creditors will be held to seek approval of the scheme by the appropriate majorities. Third, the scheme must be sanctioned by the court.[100] As Chadwick LJ said in *Re Hawk Insurance Co Ltd*:

> It can be seen that each of those stages serves a distinct purpose. At the first stage the court directs how the meeting or meetings are to be summoned. It is concerned, at that stage, to ensure that those who are to be affected by the compromise or arrangement proposed have a proper opportunity of being present (in person or by proxy) at the meeting or meetings at which the proposals are to be considered and voted upon. The second stage ensures that the proposals are acceptable to at least a majority in number, representing three-fourths in value, of those who take the opportunity of being present (in person or by proxy) at the meeting or meetings. At the third stage the court is concerned (i) to ensure that the meeting or meetings have been summoned and held in accordance with its previous order, (ii) to ensure that the proposals have been approved by the requisite majority of those present at the meeting or meetings and (iii) to ensure that the views and interests of those who have not approved the proposals at the meeting or meetings (either because they were not present or, being present, did not vote in favour of the proposals) receive impartial consideration.[101]

These three different stages will now be examined in detail.

13.3.1   Application to the Court for Meetings to be Summoned

Once the proposed scheme has been formulated, an application must then be made to the court by (or on behalf of) the company[102] for the court to order meetings of the creditors or the members, or classes thereof, to be summoned.[103] The court will also generally give directions about the length of notice, the forms of proxy etc.[104] The court has a wide discretion to order these meetings on such terms as it thinks fit.[105] The court is not concerned with the merits or fairness of the scheme at this stage.[106] Instead, one of the key issues at this stage is deciding whether the members or creditors should be split into separate classes for the purpose of voting on the scheme.[107] The substantive issues regarding different classes of creditors and members are discussed at 13.3.2 below.

Until 2001, the court would offer no guidance to the company on the issue of class meetings at this stage, and would only consider the issue at the sanctioning stage, when the only option for the court, if the wrong class meetings had been held, would be to refuse to sanction the scheme. This practice was criticised by the Company Law Review,[108] and,

---

[100]   Companies Act 2006, s 899.
[101]   [2001] EWCA Civ 241; [2002] BCC 300, [12].
[102]   The application can be made by the company, any member or creditor, or, if the company is being wound up or is in administration, by the liquidator or administrator: Companies Act 2006, s 896(2).
[103]   Companies Act 2006, s 896(1).
[104]   The right to vote by proxy is specified by the Companies Act: s 899(1).
[105]   See eg *Re T & N Ltd (No 2)* [2005] EWHC 2870 (Ch); [2006] 1 WLR 1728.
[106]   *Re Telewest Communications plc* [2004] EWHC 924 (Ch); [2004] BCC 342.
[107]   Of course the same facts can be argued both as to the existence of a separate class and as to the merits of the scheme. In practice, if the distinction is not considered to merit a separate class meeting then it is unlikely to be regarded as unfair (see eg *Re Telewest Communications plc* [2004] BCC 342).
[108]   CLR, *Completing the Structure*, n 50, 207. The Company Law Review also proposed other changes to the procedure at this stage (see CLR, *Modern Company Law for a Competitive Economy: Final Report*, URN 01/942, July 2001, paras 13.6–13.7) which have not been implemented. In particular the Company Law Review suggested that the court should have a general discretion to determine the appropriate classes at this point when asked to do so by the company, and that if it exercised its discretion it should be bound by it at the sanctioning stage. It

subsequently, by Chadwick LJ in *Re Hawk Insurance Co Ltd*.[109] A Practice Statement has now been issued, designed to produce substantive consideration of classes of creditors at this stage.[110] The onus is still on the applicant company to identify the correct classes, but it must now draw to the court's attention any potential problems at the initial application. All relevant creditors should be notified of the scheme unless there are very good reasons for not doing so. Where an issue of identifying classes is brought to the court's attention in this way, the court will then consider whether to postpone the meeting so as to resolve the issue and/or to allow any objectors to apply to vary or discharge any order summoning the meetings. If creditors only object at the later sanctioning hearing, the court will expect them to show good reason why the issue was not raised at the earlier stage. The position in relation to classes of members was not dealt with in this Practice Statement, but the criticisms of the Company Law Review and *Hawk Insurance* apply equally to that situation. Where difficult issues arise regarding the composition of classes of members, there seems to be no reason why these same principles should not apply to those classes.

Any notice sent out summoning the meetings must be accompanied by a statement explaining the effect of the arrangement and in particular stating any material interests of the directors and the effect of those interests on the scheme.[111] It is also common for a notice to be given by way of advertisement, since that may be the only way to notify certain groups, such as the holders of bearer bonds, although these are now very uncommon.[112]

The purpose is to provide all of the information necessary to enable recipients to determine how to vote.[113] In general the courts have applied strict standards of disclosure to this circular: 'in dealing with disclosure or nondisclosure of material interests of directors in the context of [schemes of arrangement], the court must for obvious reasons of public policy approach the matter strictly and can only tolerate nondisclosure in a case where it is satisfied that it is essentially of a de minimis nature'.[114] However, the courts have been prepared to apply a more relaxed standard where it is felt that no reasonable shareholder would have changed their decision on the scheme had the information been disclosed.[115] The court is also prepared to take into account the level of sophistication of the recipients in determining whether the information provided is adequate. For example, where a scheme is being proposed as an alternative to liquidation and all of the known creditors are sophisticated institutions, the fact that the scheme documents did not spell

---

also suggested that the court should have the discretion to sanction the scheme even if appropriate class meetings had not been held, provided the court felt that the composition of the meetings had not had a substantive effect on the outcome.

[109]   [2001] EWCA Civ 241; [2002] BCC 300.

[110]   *Practice Statement (Ch D: Schemes of Arrangement with Creditors)* [2002] 1 WLR 1345. Although a creditor can still challenge the way the meetings were convened at the sanctioning stage, the court will expect them to show good reason why they did not raise the issue at the earlier stage.

[111]   Companies Act 2006, s 897. Where the scheme affects the rights of debenture holders the statement must give a similar explanation regarding the interests of any trustees for the debenture holders: s 897(3).

[112]   See Companies Act 2006, ss 897(1)(b), 897(4).

[113]   *Re Dorman Long & Co Ltd* [1934] Ch 635, 657 per Maugham J.

[114]   *Re Jessel Trust Ltd* [1985] BCLC 119, 127 per Slade J. In that case the information was correct when sent but altered subsequently. Slade J refused to sanction the scheme despite the fact that there were substantial majorities in favour and no one appeared in court to oppose the petition.

[115]   *Re Minster Assets plc* [1985] BCLC 200.

out every instance where the scheme differed from what would happen in a liquidation did not of itself prevent the scheme from being sanctioned.[116]

13.3.2   Meeting(s) of the Members or Creditors

13.3.2.1   Who Needs to Consider the Scheme?

It is only necessary for the proposed scheme to be considered and voted on by those groups affected by it. In both creditors' schemes and members' schemes it is the person who is the legal rather than the beneficial owner of the economic interest who will be party to the scheme. In the case of a members' scheme, therefore, it will be the person on the register of members, and as regards rights attached to debt securities, the person who is the legal owner.[117]

However it will not necessarily be the case that all legal owners of the company's securities will be affected by a scheme. In *Re Tea Corporation Ltd*[118] a scheme was proposed for the sale of assets of a hopelessly insolvent company. The court directed meetings to be held of the debenture holders, the unsecured creditors, the preference shareholders and the ordinary shareholders. The first three groups voted in favour of the scheme, but the last did not. However, the court sanctioned the scheme despite this lack of consent. The fact that the company was insolvent meant that the ordinary shareholders had no interest in the scheme,[119] and their assent to the scheme was not, therefore, required.[120] This principle has also been used to exclude a group of deferred creditors,[121] and a group of mezzanine lenders where the value of the assets of the company was significantly and demonstrably less than the value of the senior debt.[122]

However care should be taken with this principle. The mere fact that a company is insolvent does not necessarily mean that these low-ranking groups in the insolvency will have no interest in the scheme. A distinction should be drawn between those companies whose plight is hopeless (as it was, for example, in *Re Tea Corporation Ltd*) and those where there is a reasonable chance that the company's fortunes can be revived.[123] In the latter scenario it would be wrong to assert that the shareholders, or perhaps low-ranking creditors such as subordinated creditors, have no real interest in the scheme and that their consent can be dispensed with. Where the scheme is geared towards the rescue of the company, even if the company is insolvent at the time, it could be dangerous to exclude these groups.[124]

---

[116]   *Re Telewest Communications plc* [2004] EWHC 924 (Ch); [2004] BCC 342.
[117]   See pages 342–43.
[118]   [1904] 1 Ch 12.
[119]   For discussion see chapter 3.
[120]   This principle was affirmed in *Re Oceanic Steam Navigation Co Ltd* [1939] Ch 41.
[121]   *Re British & Commonwealth Holdings plc (No 3)* [1992] BCLC 323.
[122]   *Re Bluebrook Ltd* [2009] EWHC 2114 (Ch); [2010] BCC 209.
[123]   See eg *Re Neath and Brecon Railway Co Ltd* [1892] 1 Ch 349 in which the court accepted that the preference shareholders were interested in the scheme even though there were several categories of prior-ranking debenture holders and there had never been sufficient profits to pay even the first group of debenture holders their full entitlement.
[124]   Schemes may be contrasted with CVAs on this issue since CVAs must involve a meeting of the shareholders even though a shareholder veto is not binding (though the shareholders can still apply to court to challenge the CVA on the grounds of unfair prejudice): Insolvency Act 1986, s 4A.

In other circumstances it may be that the creditors as a whole could be said to have no interest in the scheme. If the scheme is between the company and its shareholders then in some circumstances the consent of the creditors might well be unnecessary. This will be the case where the scheme is being used to effect a takeover, for example. Even those takeovers effected via 'reduction' schemes will not require creditor involvement or approval as the reduction is fictitious in the sense that the credit arising in the company's accounts following the reduction is immediately applied in paying up new shares in the company, so that no creditor protection issue arises. However, if the company is on the verge of insolvency at the time of the reorganisation then there would be a strong argument for regarding the company's creditors as having an interest in the scheme.[125]

13.3.2.2   *Separate Class Meetings: General*

Once it is determined which groups are interested in the scheme, and therefore whose consent is required, the next question is whether those groups should meet and vote to approve the scheme at a single meeting, or at separate meetings. The general test to determine whether members or creditors should meet as a whole or as separate classes is relatively easily stated, although it has proved difficult to apply in practice. The accepted test was set out by Bowen LJ in *Sovereign Life Assurance Co v Dodd*:

> It seems plain that we must give such a meaning to the term 'class' as will prevent the section being so worked as to result in confiscation and injustice, and that it must be confined to those persons whose rights are not so dissimilar as to make it impossible for them to consult together with a view to their common interest.[126]

A balancing act is required. A class with genuinely different rights requires the protection of a separate meeting, but if too many artificial distinctions are drawn then the scheme will be at the mercy of a veto by any one of the separate meetings that are held. It is easy to see that the fewer meetings held, the more schemes will be approved, but this has potential consequences for the protection of minorities. In recent years, there has been a shift of emphasis in applying this test, away from overzealous distinctions which give minorities strong veto rights. As Nourse J has commented: 'if one gets too picky about potential different classes, one could end up with virtually as many classes as there are members of a particular group'.[127] Clearly, the composition of class meetings cannot be allowed to operate in a way that permits majority oppression either. As Bowen LJ said of schemes in *Sovereign Life*:

> It makes the majority of the creditors or of a class of creditors bind the minority; it exercises a most formidable compulsion upon dissentient, or would-be dissentient, creditors; and it therefore requires to be construed with care, so as not to place in the hands of some of the creditors the means and opportunity of forcing dissentients to do that which it is unreasonable to require them to do, or of making a mere jest of the interests of the minority.[128]

---

[125] Other issues might also arise at this point in time, depending on the nature of the reorganisation (see eg the wrongful trading provisions in the Insolvency Act 1986, s 214).
[126] [1892] 2 QB 573, 583 per Bowen LJ.
[127] *Re Anglo American Insurance Ltd* [2001] 1 BCLC 755, 764.
[128] [1892] 2 QB 573, 582–83.

In *Re Hawk Insurance Ltd*[129] Chadwick LJ refined the test set out in *Sovereign Life*. That test, he said, must be applied in the context of the question 'with whom is the compromise or arrangement to be made?':

> In each case the answer to that question will depend upon analysis (i) of the rights which are to be released or varied under the scheme and (ii) the new rights (if any) which the scheme gives, by way of compromise or arrangement, to those whose rights are to be released or varied. It is in the light of that analysis that the test formulated by Bowen LJ in order to determine which creditors fall into a separate class — that is to say, that a class 'must be confined to those persons whose rights are not so dissimilar as to make it impossible for them to consult together with a view to their common interest' — has to be applied.[130]

Although *Hawk Insurance* involved creditors, this statement must apply equally to schemes involving shareholders.

The approach suggested by Chadwick LJ has been criticised[131] but it has subsequently been applied by the courts.[132] The question for the court in determining the issue of class meetings is therefore whether the groups in question are really so dissimilar that they cannot consult together. Of course, it is not difficult to distinguish between the class of shareholders and the class of creditors. More difficult is distinguishing divisions within those classes. This is discussed in more detail next. Before this analysis, however, it is worth making one general point about the shift in emphasis instituted by Chadwick LJ's approach. This approach tends to reduce the number of class meetings that are held. This has a consequential effect of reducing minority protection at this stage in the procedure. Minorities will, as a result, be more reliant on the court's scrutiny function at the sanctioning stage, discussed at 13.3.3 below.

13.3.2.3 *Separate Meetings for Shareholders*

As far as shareholders are concerned, an obvious division is that based on different class rights. Ordinary and preference shareholders, for example, will typically have different rights to income and capital,[133] and many reorganisations of share capital within the company will impact differently on these groups such that they should meet in separate meetings. However, in other circumstances even different classes of shareholders might be regarded as having the same rights for the purposes of a scheme. For example, where the company is hopelessly insolvent all classes of shareholders might be regarded as having the same, non-existent, rights.

However, the division of shareholders into meetings for the purposes of a scheme will not necessarily be organised purely along the lines of class. First, the mere fact that the rights of members, or indeed creditors, prior to the scheme are identical does not necessarily mean that they should be treated as one class for the purposes of the scheme. If

---

[129] [2001] EWCA Civ 241; [2002] BCC 300.

[130] Ibid, [30].

[131] See eg CLR, *Final Report*, n 108, para 13.8; R Sykes, 'Schemes of Arrangement: The Hawk that Muddied the Waters' (2001) 12(5) *Practical Law Company* 6.

[132] Eg *Re Equitable Life Assurance Society* [2002] BCC 319; *Re Telewest Communications plc* [2005] 1 BCLC 752, affirmed [2005] BCC 29; *Re Mytravel Group plc* [2005] BCC 457.

[133] See the discussion in chapter 2.

the scheme itself proposes to treat different groups of members within a particular class differently, then it may well be that there will need to be separate meetings of these groups.[134]

Second, in some cases the courts have regarded shareholders within a class as having sufficiently different rights to justify separate meetings. For example, the distinction between fully paid and partly paid shares within a class has been held sufficient to establish two separate classes.[135] However, some care needs to be taken in this regard. The attitude of the courts on this issue has changed, and narrowed, over time.

Re Hellenic and General Trust Ltd[136] concerned a scheme that was effecting a takeover. The court in that case regarded it as necessary to separate the ordinary shareholders into two classes. Templeman J held that one shareholder in the target company which was a wholly owned subsidiary of the bidder needed to be treated as a separate class from the other shareholders in the target. Although the rights held by all of the shareholders were identical (all of the shares in the target were identical), their interests in the scheme were different. The wholly owned subsidiary had a community of interest in the bidder company which the other shareholders did not. According to Templeman J these different interests meant that they should meet separately.

However, in a more recent case, *Re BTR plc*, Jonathan Parker J restricted the decision in *Hellenic* to deciding only that a subsidiary's shares should be discounted.[137] This was on the basis that the financial position of the parties was the same whether or not the subsidiary accepted the offer. He rejected the proposition that members with different *interests*, rather than different *rights*, could form a separate class:

> Shareholders with the same rights in respect of the shares which they hold may be subject to an infinite number of different interests and may therefore, assessing their own personal interests (as they are perfectly entitled to do), vote their shares in the light of those interests. But that in itself, in my judgment, is simply a fact of life: it does not lead to the conclusion that shareholders who propose to vote differently are in some way a separate class of shareholders entitled to a separate class meeting. Indeed a journey down that road would in my judgment lead to impracticality and unworkability.[138]

Differences between the interests of the shareholders will not, as a result, be taken into account at the meeting stage but might be relevant at the court sanctioning stage. Applying this analysis, one issue that has arisen in practice is whether shareholders giving irrevocable undertakings to a bidder should be treated differently to other shareholders. Dicta in *Re BTR plc* suggests that while the giving of irrevocable undertakings will not affect the ability of those target shareholders to vote at the class meeting where they have the same rights as the other shareholders, nevertheless where they have special interests as a result of giving those irrevocable undertakings this might lead the court to exercise its discretion, and refuse to sanction the scheme.[139] There are clear statements in the recent authorities that the existence of different motives among shareholders does not give rise to separate classes. As Chadwick LJ commented in *Re BTR plc*: 'it is a fact of life that

[134] *Re Anglo American Insurance Ltd* [2001] 1 BCLC 755.
[135] *Re United Provident Assurance Co Ltd* [1910] 2 Ch 477.
[136] [1976] 1 WLR 123.
[137] [1999] 2 BCLC 675.
[138] Ibid, 682–83.
[139] (Leave to Appeal) [2000] 1 BCLC 740, 746.

shareholders having shares which confer the same rights under the company's constitution and under the scheme may, nevertheless, be motivated to vote in different ways . . . It is quite impossible, in my view, to accommodate an approach of that nature within the structure of [section 895]'.[140] Irrevocable undertakings limited to voting for the scheme are unlikely to be problematic, although even this view is not universally held. However, if breach of the undertaking involves the payment of a break fee, for example, this might well suggest that the giver of the undertaking has a different interest to that of other shareholders.

One advantage of the *Re BTR* approach is that the rights of the members (or creditors) will generally be easier for the company to apply in the scheme context than their interests. It will generally be difficult for the company to assess the different interests of its members without requiring a considerable amount of personal information from them. Requiring that type of information would lead to 'a wholly unworkable, and highly undesirable, situation'[141] A consequence of this approach however is that fewer class meetings are likely to be held, and there is less chance of a veto of the scheme by the minority at this stage. This change must be read in conjunction with the shift in emphasis in applying the *Sovereign Life* test which was discussed above. As discussed there, the potential reduction in minority protection at this point means that the court's role in scrutinising the scheme prior to sanctioning it becomes more important.

One other point should be raised about the sanctioning stage. As we shall see,[142] one of the issues of interest to the court at the sanctioning stage is whether the decision taken by the meeting was representative of the class as a whole.[143] The court's sanction can be refused if the votes necessary to secure the approval were cast in order to promote a special interest of some shareholders that was not shared by the class as a whole.[144] Where separate class meetings are held according to the interests of the members then the possibility of members voting other than in the interests of the class is reduced, if not completely eliminated. However, the decision in *Re BTR*, to move away from *Hellenic* and to emphasise the separation of groups based on rights rather than interests, means that there is a possibility that shareholders within a group might vote other than in the interests of the group. It will therefore be of greater importance post-*Re BTR* for the court to consider this issue with care at the sanctioning stage.

13.3.2.4   Separate Meetings for Creditors

The proper division of creditors poses even more difficulties than the proper division of shareholders. In large part this is because the variations in the types of creditors are so much greater than the variations in the types of shareholders a company is likely to have. This was discussed in chapter two. Following the more stringent approach set down by Chadwick LJ in *Re Hawk Insurance*, the question for the court is whether the creditors are so clearly different as to their rights before and after the scheme that they cannot consult together.

---

[140]   Ibid, 747.
[141]   *Re BTR plc* [1999] 2 BCLC 675, 683.
[142]   See 13.3.3.2.
[143]   *Re Alabama, New Orleans, Texas & Pacific Junction Railway Co* [1891] 1 Ch 213, 245 per Bowen LJ.
[144]   *Re BTR plc* [1999] 2 BCLC 675.

The decision in *Re Hawk Insurance* itself is instructive as an example of how this approach will be applied in practice. *Hawk Insurance* involved the question whether different types of unsecured creditors, some with vested claims and some with contingent claims, should be treated as being part of the same class for the purposes of voting on a proposed scheme. At first instance Arden J held that these creditors should be treated as comprising different classes.[145] Those with vested claims should be treated as being in the same class as other unsecured creditors, since they all had an accrued claim against the company which they had an immediate right to sue for in full. By contrast those with contingent claims had no such immediate right and the structure of the scheme was such that those whose claims had not yet accrued would have those claims scaled down to proportions less than 100 per cent. Although these creditors would rank equally on insolvency (as they were all unsecured creditors) these differences, in Arden J's opinion, meant that they should not all be treated as one class for scheme purposes.

The Court of Appeal in *Hawk Insurance* disagreed with this approach. Applying the re-stated *Sovereign Life* test set out above, Chadwick LJ held that all of the creditors, including therefore those with contingent rights and those with vested rights, could be treated as a single class for this purpose. Chadwick LJ quoted with approval the following passage:

> It is appropriate that creditors who share an interest vis-à-vis the company which places them in a position distinct from that of other creditors and so dissimilar as to make it impossible for them to consult together with a view to their common interest should be allowed to make a separate decision. To break creditors up into classes, however, will give each class an opportunity to veto the scheme, a process which undermines the basic approach of decision by a large majority, and one which should only be permitted if there are dissimilar interests related to the company and its scheme to be protected. The fact that two views may be expressed at a meeting because one group may for extraneous reasons prefer one course, while another group prefers another is not a reason for calling two separate meetings.[146]

As discussed above in the context of the *Re BTR* decision, this approach shifts minority protection away from this stage in the procedure of a scheme. According to Chadwick LJ, the danger is that too generous an interpretation of rights, leading to an increased number of separate class meetings, could provide a veto for minority groups and could open up the possibility of oppression by the minority. On this analysis the proper safeguard from oppression does not arise at this stage, but at the later court sanctioning stage, since at that point the court is not bound by the decision at the meetings, but can nevertheless refuse to sanction the scheme on the ground of minority oppression.[147]

According to Chadwick LJ all of the creditors here had the same rights. Since the company was insolvent the correct approach was to consider the position on the basis of their relevant rights on a winding up. On a winding up they would all have the same right, namely to submit their claims in the winding up, and to have those claims accepted or rejected. The only difference would be that those with contingent claims held debts

---

[145] [2001] 2 BCLC 480.
[146] *Nordic Bank plc v International Harvester Australia Ltd* [1982] 2 VR 298, 301 per Lush J, quoted at [2001] 2 BCLC 480, [32].
[147] For discussion see 13.3.3.

without a certain value, and therefore those debts would be subject to an estimate. However, in Chadwick LJ's view this did not mean that they should be treated as a separate class for scheme purposes.

The effect of the *Hawk Insurance* decision will therefore tend to reduce the number of separate class meetings. Again, it is the rights of the creditors and not their interests that will be key. However, *Hawk Insurance* makes it clear that even those with different rights might be able to meet as a single class in some circumstances. There is little doubt that the vested and contingent creditors have different rights in one sense, for example they clearly had different rights to distribution, as Arden J pointed out, and yet their interests were not so different as to make it impossible for them to consult together in their common interest. It may be that reducing the number of separate class meetings in this way does not unduly reduce the protection available to creditors. When the Cork Committee examined schemes of arrangement, it noted the difficulties associated with determining different classes.[148] It is notable that, as a result, this Committee did not recommend that separate class meetings be required for the purposes of company voluntary arrangements.[149]

The other point of interest raised by Chadwick LJ is that where a company is insolvent, the starting point for determining separate classes will be the rights of those creditors on winding up. Clearly some groups, such as secured creditors, and preferred creditors, should therefore meet separately. In addition, where subordinated creditors have an interest in the company which could be affected in a different way from other creditors, they will constitute a separate class.[150] This might arise, for example, in different tranches of a securitised bond issue[151] or in a leveraged buy out.[152] In such cases it is the rights of creditors on an insolvent liquidation which will be relevant in determining whether they should meet as a separate class.[153] Even within these categories it may be necessary to make further differentiations. While *Hawk Insurance* suggests that all unsecured creditors will generally be treated as one class, other classes may admit further division. For example, within the category of secured creditors, further division will generally be required, on the basis of differing securities. A creditor whose claim is protected by a fixed charge is far less vulnerable than one whose security is a floating charge.[154] Even creditors whose claims are secured over the same property may have divergent interests. A scheme that proposes the sale of a security and a transfer of the rights of the secured creditors to a substituted security might be acceptable to the first, but not the second chargee. We would therefore expect to see secured creditors, unsecured creditors, preferred creditors and subordinated creditors being treated as separate classes.

By contrast, where a company is solvent the rights of the creditors on insolvency may not be accurate comparators.[155] In *Re British Aviation Insurance Co Ltd*, for example,

---

[148] See *The Cork Report*, n 85, para 400 et seq.
[149] Insolvency Act 1986, ss 1–7.
[150] *Re British and Commonwealth Holdings plc (No 3)* [1992] BCC 56; *Soden v British and Commonwealth Holdings plc (in administration)* [1995] BCC 531; *Re Mytravel Group plc* [2004] EWHC 2741 (Ch); [2005] 1 WLR 2365.
[151] See pages pages 209–10 and pages 403–4.
[152] For discussion see chapter 14.
[153] *Re Telewest Communications plc* [2004] EWHC 924 (Ch); [2004] BCC 342.
[154] See chapter 6 for discussion.
[155] *Re British Aviation Insurance Co Ltd* [2005] EWHC 1621 (Ch); [2006] BCC 14; *Re Sovereign Marine and General Insurance Co Ltd* [2006] EWHC 1335; [2007] 1 BCLC 228.

Lewison J held that the appropriate comparator in that case was a continuing solvent run-off.[156] This will often have an impact on the decision of the court as to the appropriate number of class meetings to be held. In *British Aviation*, where the company was solvent, liquidation was not a realistic alternative to the scheme. The valuation and immediate satisfaction of contingent claims under the solvent scheme in *British Aviation* involved a clear variation of the claimants' rights to prove in liquidation. In contrast to *Hawk Insurance*, the creditors did therefore need to be separated into different classes.

Identifying different classes of creditors is particularly challenging in the insurance industry because some creditors may have matured claims (which might be established as to liability and quantum, or liability might have been admitted but damages as yet unquantified, or an actionable condition, such as asbestosis, may have arisen, but liability and damages have yet to be established) or the condition may have been incurred but not reported (IBNR). In asbestos claims, for example, a policyholder's exposure to asbestos may have occurred during the policy coverage years, but the resulting personal injury claim will generally only arise some time later. In *British Aviation* creditors with matured and contingent claims were grouped separately from those with IBNR claims and it was determined that separate meetings should be held for these classes. As a result of these difficulties (amongst other issues) Lewison J did not sanction the scheme in *British Aviation*.

Some claimants against the company may be excluded from the scheme altogether. Where the claim for the return of money from the company is on the basis that the claimant is a beneficiary under a trust then the basis of the claim is ownership by the claimant. As the Court of Appeal held recently in *Re Lehman Brothers* the concept of a creditor for the purposes of a scheme of arrangement does not extend to those whose relationship is not that of a debtor/creditor at all, and a proprietary claim to trust property is not a claim in respect of a debt or liability of the company.[157] A similar argument can be made in relation to those who supply goods subject to retention of title clauses.[158] However, this casts no doubt on the position of secured creditors under a scheme since the security is an incident of the debt, and, since section 895 enables a scheme which varies the debt, then it follows that the variation must be followed through to the security.[159]

13.3.2.5   Approval at the Class Meetings

The company needs to obtain the approval of all members or creditors, or classes thereof, who will be affected by the scheme. There is no quorum requirement for a vote on a scheme, and the vote is on a poll rather than by way of a show of hands. The level of approval required at the meeting is a majority in number, representing three-fourths in value[160] of its creditors or members present and voting in person or by proxy.[161] Non-voting shareholders, and those that do not turn up at the meeting, are therefore excluded for the purposes of calculating the majority. To this extent it is a much lower

---

[156]   *Re British Aviation Insurance Co Ltd* [2005] EWHC 1621 (Ch); [2006] BCC 14, [88].
[157]   [2009] EWCA Civ 1161; [2010] BCC 272.
[158]   2.3.4.3.4.
[159]   [2009] EWCA Civ 1161; [2010] BCC 272, [82] per Lord Neuberger, MR.
[160]   In the case of shares, each share has a nominal value. In the case of creditors, it will depend upon the value of the debt: *Re British Aviation Insurance Co Ltd* [2005] EWHC 1621 (Ch); [2006] BCC 14.
[161]   Companies Act 2006, s 899(1).

majority than is required on an offer. A creditors' scheme will have to work out in advance the amount (or a formula) in respect of which each creditor will be allowed to vote.

The Company Law Review criticised the 'majority in number' requirement as being 'irrelevant and burdensome'[162] and it is a requirement that is not found elsewhere in the Companies Act.[163] A review of the Corporations and Markets Advisory Committee (CAMAC) in Australia recently recommended the removal of the headcount test for the approval of schemes, leaving only the voted shares test, namely 75 per cent of the shares voted on the resolution, to bring this decision-making vote into line with decisions on other fundamental corporate matters, such as changes to the company's constitution.[164] While the test might be seen as adding some protection for small shareholders, it has the potential to result in a scheme being blocked even where the holders of the overwhelming number of shares in a company have voted in favour. It is difficult to see why this issue should be treated differently to other decisions on fundamental corporate issues which are determined by means of shares voted, rather than the number of shareholders. Small shareholders have other protections, such as the duties of directors when proposing the scheme, and, ultimately, the fact that the court has to sanction the scheme, discussed at 13.3.3 below. Nevertheless this test remains in place for schemes of arrangement in the UK for the present time.

13.3.2.6   Summary

At the first court hearing, the predominant concern is to determine whether the members and/or creditors should be split into different classes for the purposes of voting on the scheme. As this section has discussed, this is by no means a simple matter to determine. Two separate but linked trends in the approach taken by the court have resulted in a reduction of the number of separate meetings that are held in practice. These are, first, the redefinition of the *Sovereign Life* test by Chadwick LJ in *Hawk Insurance* and, second, the shift from defining classes for this purpose by reference to the interests of the shareholders/creditors and instead focusing on their rights.

As noted previously, the number of class meetings held is potentially significant in two regards. First, it affects the likely success of the scheme, since the more class meetings that are held, the greater the chance that the scheme will fail to obtain the consent of one or more of those classes. Second, a reduction in the number of class meetings potentially reduces the amount of minority protection available at this stage. Consequently, minority protection becomes more focused on the exercise of the court's discretion at the sanctioning stage. This issue is discussed in the next section.

13.3.3   The Sanction of the Court

Following the approval of the scheme in the separate class meetings, described above, application is made to the court for approval of the scheme.[165] This application can be opposed by members and creditors who object to the scheme. The court will be concerned

---

[162] CLR, *Completing the Structure*, n 50, 207.
[163] This is also a problem for bondholders where the issue is represented by a global note: page 342.
[164] CAMAC, *Members' Schemes of Arrangement*, December 2009, 77–94, available at www.camac.gov.au.
[165] Companies Act 2006, s 899(2). The application may be from the company, any member or creditor, or, if appointed, a liquidator or administrator.

with three matters at this point.[166] The first is to see that the statutory provisions have been complied with. The second is that the majority fairly represented the class. The third is that the scheme is one which a reasonable person would approve. Of course, the court will not sanction a scheme the provisions of which fall outside the general law. It should be clear, for example, that the court has no jurisdiction to sanction a scheme which involves an act which is ultra vires.[167]

13.3.3.1   *Have the Statutory Provisions Been Complied With?*

The court will want to ensure that the explanatory statement provided in relation to the scheme was adequate. If not, or if it is defective in some way, the court will not sanction the scheme. In addition, the court will want to see that the resolutions at the class meetings are passed by the statutory majority of each class. If this has not occurred then the court cannot approve the scheme, even if the court considers it to be fair and the scheme would, otherwise, have been approved.[168] As discussed above, the somewhat peculiar way in which approval must be obtained at these meetings, ie the majority in number, representing three-fourths in value of its creditors or members present and voting in person or by proxy,[169] makes this task more complicated than it might otherwise be.

In principle the court can refuse to sanction the scheme if there has been a failure to obtain the appropriate consent at court convened meetings of each separate class of creditors and/or members. If the court decides at the sanctioning hearing that the correct meetings of creditors/members have not been held, then that can result in the court refusing to sanction the scheme.[170] However, as discussed above, following the 2002 Practice Statement, issues regarding the composition and summoning of class meetings should be resolved at an earlier stage in proceedings. This Practice Statement states that creditors (or members) who feel unfairly treated can still raise objections to the scheme at the sanctioning stage, but the court will expect them to show good reason why they did not raise any concerns (eg regarding the composition of classes) at the earlier stage. It is nevertheless still possible for creditors to raise these issues at the sanctioning stage even though they were not raised at the first court hearing.[171] In any case, the court has acknowledged that it might not always be possible to provide creditors (or members) with full details of the scheme (including details of class constitution) before the first court hearing, in which case it will not be reasonable to expect creditors to raise objections at the first court hearing.[172]

As a result it is still possible for the court to refuse to sanction a scheme on the basis that the classes were incorrectly constituted. However, as discussed above, the effect of the restatement of the *Sovereign Life* test in *Hawk Insurance* has had the effect of diminishing

---

[166]   *Re Anglo Continental Supply Co Ltd* [1922] 2 Ch 723, 733; *Re National Bank Ltd* [1966] 1 WLR 819.
[167]   *Re Oceanic Steam Navigation Company Limited* [1939] Ch 41.
[168]   *Re Neath and Brecon Railway* [1892] Ch 349.
[169]   Companies Act 2006, s 899(1).
[170]   See eg *Re British Aviation Insurance Co Ltd* [2005] EWHC 1621 (Ch); [2006] BCC 14, where the court did just that, and refused to sanction a scheme where the court convened a single meeting for the scheme's creditors when the court at the sanctioning stage held that the creditors should properly have been separated into two classes for this purpose.
[171]   *Re British Aviation Insurance Co Ltd* [2005] EWHC 1621 (Ch); [2006] BCC 14.
[172]   *Re Marconi Corporation plc v Marconi plc* [2003] EWHC 663 (Ch).

the likely number of separate meetings that will need to be held. As a result it is less likely that a creditor or member will be able to object that insufficient meetings were held.

13.3.3.2   Did the Majority Fairly Represent the Class?

In addition to these practical issues, the court will be concerned to ensure that the decision taken by the meeting was representative of the class as a whole.[173] The court's sanction can be refused if only a tiny minority of the class actually attended and voted, or if the votes necessary to secure the approval were cast in order to promote a special interest of some shareholders or creditors that was not shared by the class as a whole.[174] Lewison J in *Re British Aviation Insurance Co Ltd* stated that, while a low turnout at the meeting is not itself a valid reason for a court refusing to sanction the scheme, the size of turnout might be relevant in considering whether the result of the vote could have been affected by collateral factors, ie by those members or creditors with special interests.[175]

This test presupposes that the class (or classes) of creditors/members has been correctly identified. Yet the cases emphasise that the court is not required simply to endorse the majority vote. If the court considers that the meeting is unrepresentative, or that those voting at the meeting have done so with a special interest to promote which differs from the interest of the ordinary independent and objective creditor/member, then the court can refuse to sanction the scheme. Consequently, the votes of the majority are not treated by the court as conclusive. Bowen LJ has explained the reasoning behind this requirement as follows:

> [A]lthough in a meeting which is to be held under this section it is perfectly fair for every man to do that which is best for himself, yet the Court, which has to see what is reasonable and just as regards the interests of the whole class, would certainly be very much influenced in its decision, if it turned out that the majority was composed of persons who had not really the interests of that class at stake.[176]

This test seems to be akin to the requirement that shareholders vote bona fide in the best interests of the company when voting to change the articles of the company.[177] However, in some circumstances the courts have been prepared to sanction a scheme even where such a conflict of interest exists, provided full disclosure is made to the rest of the class.[178]

An interesting variation on this theme arose in a recent Hong Kong case, *Re PCCW Ltd*[179] which involved the issue of share splitting. Generally, transfers of shares by a person holding a large block of shares to a number of different recipients are unlikely to cause a court concern. This will be so even though the transfers increase the number of members who may attend the meeting (and may therefore affect whether a majority in number vote in favour of the scheme) and even if the share recipients are known to be inclined to vote the shares in favour of the scheme. However, the Court of Appeal in Hong Kong noted that share splitting could be used to distort the vote, which could be characterised as a

---

[173]   *Re Alabama, New Orleans, Texas & Pacific Junction Railway Co* [1891] 1 Ch 213.

[174]   *Re BTR plc (Leave to appeal)* [2000] 1 BCLC 740.

[175]   *Re British Aviation Insurance Co Ltd* [2005] EWHC 1621 (Ch); [2006] BCC 14.

[176]   *Re Alabama, New Orleans, Texas & Pacific Junction Railway Co* [1891] 1 Ch 213, 244.

[177]   See *Allen v Gold Reefs of West Africa Ltd* [1900] 1 Ch 656; *Citco Banking Corp NV v Pusser's Ltd* [2007] UKPC 13; [2007] 2 BCLC 483 (PC).

[178]   *Goodfellow v Nelson Line (Liverpool) Ltd* [1912] 2 Ch 324. The court in that case also allowed the votes of the conflicted class member to be counted.

[179]   [2009] HKCA 178 (Hong Kong Court of Appeal).

form of dishonesty, or coercion, where the wishes of the minority were overridden by those holding a majority of the shares. The court stated that the burden was on the applicant to satisfy the court that the majority's decision was representative of the class entitled to vote at the meeting, and if the applicant fails to discharge that burden then the court should not exercise its discretion to sanction the scheme.[180]

The role of the court in this regard can operate as an important protection for minority creditors and shareholders. In the previous section it was noted that developments in the courts in recent years has led to a reduction in the amount of minority protection available at the first stage of the court's review making this second, sanctioning, stage all the more important. For example, the decision in *Re BTR* to move away from *Hellenic*, and to emphasise the separation of groups based on rights rather than interests, increases the possibility that shareholders or creditors within a group might vote other than in the interests of the group. This means that the court's scrutiny of whether the majority have fairly represented the class on a vote in a meeting under a scheme, will be potentially important as a protective device for minorities within that class.

Courts are prepared to refuse to sanction a scheme if they believe that the majority has not voted in the interests of the class as a whole and so this hurdle can operate as a real protection for minorities. In *Re NFU Development Trust Ltd*[181] Brightman J refused to sanction the scheme even though it had been passed by the requisite majority of the members. The scheme there involved the members surrendering their membership rights. Brightman J therefore held that this was not an 'arrangement' for these purposes, since there was no element of give and take,[182] however he went on to say that a further problem with the scheme was that 'no member voting in the interests of members as a whole' could reasonably approve it.[183] More recent discussion on this issue, by Lewison J in *British Aviation Insurance Co Ltd* indicates that this is an issue which the courts take seriously, and, in appropriate circumstances, will cause them to refuse to sanction the scheme in question.[184]

13.3.3.3   Would a Reasonable Person Approve the Scheme?

Providing the court is satisfied as to these first two matters, the court's role is then to determine 'whether the proposal is such that an intelligent and honest man, a member of the class concerned and acting in respect of his interest, might reasonably approve'.[185] The court has emphasised that its role is not to usurp the views of those who have properly voted in its favour, and the court will be strongly influenced if there is a substantial majority vote in favour of the scheme.[186] The test is not 'is this a reasonable scheme?' but rather 'could the class of creditors/members reasonably have approved it?' However, neither will the court automatically confirm it if all of the formal elements of the scheme

---

[180]   Ibid, [71], [76], [150].
[181]   [1972] 1 WLR 1548.
[182]   See 13.2.
[183]   [1972] 1 WLR 1548, 1555.
[184]   [2005] EWHC 1621 (Ch); [2006] BCC 14, [118]–[123].
[185]   *Re Dorman Long & Co Ltd* [1934] Ch 635, 657 per Maugham J.
[186]   *Re Equitable Life Assurance Society* [2002] EWHC 140 (Ch); [2002] BCC 319; *Re TDG plc* [2008] EWHC 2334; [2009] 1 BCLC 445.

are correct. The court's sanction is therefore not simply a rubber stamping exercise, once it has determined that the proper approvals of the meetings have been obtained.[187]

The court will consider the full commercial and factual context of the scheme. The central issue will be whether the scheme is fair between the various interests involved and so could reasonably have been approved at the meetings.[188] However, the court may also consider the effect on third parties.[189] In *BAT Industries plc* a scheme sought only the consent of the members but Neuberger J allowed prospective litigants against the company to object to the scheme.[190] The judge held that there were no statutory restrictions on whom the court could hear or what it could take into account in deciding whether to sanction a scheme.[191] However, providing the scheme is fair and equitable the court will not itself judge its commercial merits.

The consequences of the application of this reasonable man test is, however, that it will be extremely rare for the court to exercise its discretion to refuse to sanction a scheme which has been approved by the correct majority of members/creditors, where the classes are completely constituted and there is no suggestion that the majority did not represent the class. Lewison J considered this issue in *British Aviation Insurance Co Ltd*:

> Where, as here, those who voted in favour of the scheme are large and sophisticated corporations, the rigid application of this test as the sole criterion would rarely, I think, enable the court to refuse to sanction a scheme. It is also not entirely clear to me how the rigid application of this test sits with statements that the court has an unfettered discretion.
>
> Be that as it may, none of the very experienced counsel in the case was able to show me a case in this jurisdiction in which the court, having decided that it had jurisdiction to sanction a scheme, nevertheless refused, as a matter of discretion, to do so. There is one possible exception in the shape of *Re Canning Jarrah Timber Co (Western Australia) Ltd* [1900] 1 Ch. 708 where Cozens-Hardy J. refused to sanction a scheme; but after the scheme had been amended it was ultimately sanctioned by the Court of Appeal.[192]

The fact that there are no cases in which a court has exercised its discretion to refuse to sanction a scheme where all of the hurdles, discussed above, have been passed, must call into question the value of this test as a minority protection device.

13.3.3.4   *Effect of the Scheme*

Once the court has sanctioned the scheme it then becomes binding on the company (including the liquidator/administrator if the company is in liquidation/administration)[193] and on all the relevant members and creditors. Crucially, therefore, the scheme also binds any dissentients. The court could set aside the scheme subsequently

---

[187]   See eg *Re BTR plc* [2000] 1 BCLC 740, 747 per Jonathan Parker J; *Re TDG plc* [2008] EWHC 2334; [2009] 1 BCLC 445.

[188]   *Re Cape plc* [2006] EWHC 1316 (Ch); [2006] 3 All ER 1222.

[189]   *Re RAC Motoring Services Ltd* [2000] 1 BCLC 307.

[190]   Unreported, 3 September 1998.

[191]   The court has complete discretion as to whether to award costs for or against an objector or to make no costs order at all: Civil Procedure Rules, r 44.3.

[192]   [2005] EWHC 1621 (Ch); [2006] BCC 14, [75]–[76].

[193]   Companies Act 2006, s 899(3). The courts have rejected the argument that a scheme that satisfies the requirements of the Act might nevertheless amount to a deprivation of possessions contrary to Article 1 of the First protocol of the European Convention on Human Rights: *Re Equitable Life Assurance Society* (No 2) [2002] EWHC 140 (Ch); [2002] BCC 319; *Re Waste Recycling Group plc* [2003] EWHC 2065 (Ch); [2004] 1 BCLC 352.

only on very limited grounds, for example if the consent has been obtained by fraud. The order sanctioning the scheme takes effect once a copy is delivered to the Registrar of Companies.[194]

13.4 Conclusion

It was discussed, in 13.3.2 above, that various recent decisions of the courts have had the practical effect of diminishing the minority protection available in the first court hearing stage of schemes of arrangement. It has been suggested that this diminution in protection should not be a concern if the court is prepared to scrutinise schemes properly at the second court hearing, and if necessary to exercise its discretion to refuse to sanction a scheme where minority protection issues exist. However, as the discussion above has demonstrated, the amount of minority protection at this second court hearing may not be as significant as it appears.

Courts will check that the statutory provisions have been complied with, and this may include refusing to sanction the scheme if the court determines that the incorrect meetings were held. However, the 2002 Practice Statement aims to encourage these issues to be dealt with at the earlier court stage, where possible, and, even if these issues are raised at the second court hearing, the effect of the *Hawk Insurance* decision is to diminish the chances of the dissenting creditors/members succeeding on this ground. It is also possible for the dissenting members/creditors to argue that the majority did not fairly represent the class, and the operation of this requirement does seem to form a minority protection rule, as the courts do, on occasion, refuse to sanction schemes on this basis. The catch-all test, which provides that even if the classes are correctly formulated and the majority did not fairly represent the class, the court can still refuse to sanction the scheme if the class of creditors/members could not reasonably have approved it, has the potential to be developed as a powerful minority protection device by the courts. However, as discussed, this has not occurred to date and there are no instances of the courts ultimately refusing to sanction a scheme on this basis.

The question, of course, is whether this relatively low level of minority protection should be a cause for concern. In general, the courts retain a wide discretion to refuse to exercise their discretion to sanction should they feel the need to do so. It is also important to consider the need for minority protection, which will be dependent on the specific factual circumstances of the scheme in question. In schemes which effect takeovers, for example, it has already been noted that the level of protection required by minority shareholders is relatively low, certainly lower than the level of protection required by minority shareholders in a takeover by way of an offer.[195] In a scheme, the purpose of minority protection is not to ensure that the shareholders' choice is undistorted. Since the bidder deals with the company and not with individual shareholders, the collective action problem that arises in relation to takeovers does not exist. There is also no need to provide

---

[194]   Companies Act 2006, s 899(4). If the order amends the company's articles or any constitutional resolution or agreement, a copy of the amended articles/resolution/agreement must then be sent to the registrar: s 901.

[195]   See 13.2.2 and for a fuller discussion J Payne, 'Schemes of Arrangement, Takeovers and Minority Shareholder Protection' (2011) *Journal of Corporate Law Studies* (forthcoming), available at www.ssrn.com/abstract=1600592.

an exit right to minority shareholders or to protect them against oppression should they remain as a minority in the target company, since the outcome of a successful scheme is that the bidder will hold 100 per cent of the shares. Instead the danger is that the minority shareholders will be bound by the decision of the majority to sell their shares and this might, in some circumstances, be oppressive.

In most circumstances it is proper for the minority to be bound by the majority decision, even if the result is that the minority will be required to sell their shares to the bidder. In fact, the possibility of oppression facing the minority shareholders in a scheme is most akin to the position of the rump shareholders facing a squeeze-out by the bidder in a takeover. Seen in this light the level of minority protection provided in both situations is remarkably similar. In both instances the court will allow the expropriation at the price accepted by the majority unless the minority can demonstrate that there was some additional element of unfairness, such as the fact that the majority shareholders are not independent of the bidder. This seems appropriate. A shareholder has no intrinsic right to retain its shares and expropriation should be allowed if the price is fair. In general the fact that the remainder of the shareholders have accepted the price will be a good indication of fairness. Only in exceptional circumstances, where this is not the case, should the court interfere.

These issues are slightly different in relation to creditor schemes. As discussed a creditor's relationship with the company is contractual and it would be usual to expect that that relationship could not be altered without the consent of the creditor. However, a scheme, if approved in the class meetings and sanctioned by the court, will bind dissenting creditors and alter their rights against the company. The need for minority protection is therefore more significant in the context of creditor schemes than shareholder schemes. However the levels of protection for creditors described in this chapter need not be a cause for concern. A distinction needs to be drawn between solvent and insolvent schemes. In terms of defining the correct classes of creditor for the purposes of agreeing to a scheme it is crucial to use the correct comparator. Where the correct comparator is a winding up, it will be more appropriate to define the classes of creditors, particularly the unsecured creditors who are unlikely to receive a significant amount on the winding up in any case, in broad terms. This is what we see in *Hawk Insurance*, for example, which was a case in which the correct comparator was a winding up. A cram down of the creditors in such a case might be entirely proper, and of course the court still retains a broad discretion at the second stage to refuse to sanction the scheme if it believes that some of the creditors are being prejudiced in some way. By contrast, where the correct comparator is a solvent run-off the courts have been quicker to separate the creditors into different classes in order to ensure that their rights are protected.

14

Private Equity

14.1 Introduction

Private equity grew enormously in the UK in the period until 2008, to the point where it was said to rival the public markets as a source of financing. In the first half of 2006, for example, UK-based private equity fund managers raised £11.2 billion of capital, compared to just £10.4 billion of funds raised via IPOs on the London Stock Exchange in the same period.[1] The reach of private equity was also extended at this time, to the point where, in 2007, Alliance Boots was the first FTSE 100 company to be purchased by a private equity firm. However, these developments also raised concerns, most notably regarding the lack of disclosure and transparency to which private equity-backed companies were subject, compared to public companies, and the position of non-shareholder stakeholders, particularly employees, within private equity-backed companies.[2] These developments prompted a flurry of reports in the UK,[3] and the European Commission is also developing plans to regulate the private equity industry.[4] The recession, and in particular the contraction of the market for debt prompted by the collapse of Lehman Brothers in September 2008, has had a significant impact on the private equity sector. Since 2008, the number and value of private equity deals has substantially reduced. However, the calls to regulate this industry have not diminished. If anything the impact of the recession on private equity funds has heightened calls for private equity to be regulated.

This chapter will examine the development of private equity transactions in the UK, will analyse the nature of these transactions, and will then consider whether the concerns raised in relation to private equity are justified. First, though, a definition is required. The term 'private equity' actually encompasses a number of different types of transactions, the unifying theme being that the capital involved has been raised privately and will not be deployed by investing in publicly traded equity securities. These transactions include the provision of venture capital or development capital to young or emerging companies,

---

[1] FSA, *Private Equity: A Discussion of Risk and Regulatory Engagement*, Discussion paper 06/6, November 2006, 3.

[2] It was estimated in 2006 that 8% of the UK workforce was employed in private equity owned firms: House of Commons Treasury Committee, tenth report of session 2006–07, *Private Equity*, 30 July 2007, HC 567-I, 7.

[3] Eg *Private Equity: A Discussion of Risk and Regulatory Engagement*, n 1; D Walker, *Disclosure and Transparency in Private Equity, Consultation Document* (July 2007) and *Final Report* (November 2007).

[4] At the time of writing there are two competing texts in existence for a new directive to regulate Alternative Investment Funds (AIF), a term which includes private equity, and Alternative Investment Fund Managers (AIFM). These competing texts are serving as the basis for negotiations at a series of 'trilogue' meetings, which are taking place between representatives of the Parliament, Council and European Commission, with a view to adopting a single compromise text: Council of the European Union, 7500/10 (Presse 64)18 May 2010. This is discussed further at 14.6.5 below.

which typically does not involve the private equity firm obtaining a majority stake, and buy outs, where the private equity firm buys majority control of an existing or mature firm. A variation on this latter type of funding is the buy out of a publicly owned company which is then taken private. In recent years the term 'private equity' has come to be most closely associated with the buy out transaction.

14.2   Historical Development

The core concept and model of modern private equity originated in the US. Private equity began to develop there in the 1970s,[5] following the founding of the buy out firm Kohlberg Kravis Roberts (KKR) and the development of the leveraged buy out (LBO) model.[6] This model involves buying a business by borrowing money from a third party (often a bank). The company's cash flows are used to make the loan repayments and, together with the company's assets, to provide security for the lenders until the debt is repaid. Often the aim is to buy the greatest amount of assets for the smallest amount of equity investment, ie to leverage the purchase to the greatest extent possible. There are a number of explanations why private equity developed in the US from the 1970s onwards, but one important factor was undoubtedly the rise of high yield ('junk') bonds[7] which provided firms such as KKR with a highly liquid market for available debt. Over time other forms of LBO model emerged in the US, including 'break-up' LBOs where the assets of the purchased company were seen as the main vehicle for repaying the debt, and 'strategic' LBOs where a number of single entities (perhaps loss making) were consolidated into a more attractive whole before being offered for sale.

The number of private equity firms in the US gradually increased, as did the amount of capital available to them. In addition to a liquid debt market, the firms found that a number of investors (notably the US state pension funds) wanted to make equity investments into this sector. By 1989 the sector had grown to the point where KKR was able to make a $31 billion hostile takeover of the US listed foods and tobacco company RJR Nabisco/Borden. The 1990s saw the continued growth of the market, and the development of a wider variety of private equity formats, but no deals of a size to match the takeover of RJR Nabisco/Borden. Private equity in the US had a quiet period in 2001–2004, corresponding to a downturn in the global economy in that period. However, the recovery of the economy, together with low interest rates and increasing levels of cheap debt, fuelled another surge in private equity activity after 2004. As of February 2007, eight of the ten largest public to private buy outs of all-time had occurred in 2006 or 2007, and the record set by KKR in 1989 was finally beaten.[8] The availability of cheap debt, together

---

[5]   However, the US private equity industry existed much earlier, see eg the formation of the American Research and Development Corporation in Boston in 1946: HM Treasury, *Myners Review of Institutional Investment in the UK* (2001) para 12.30.

[6]   GP Baker and GD Smith, *The New Financial Capitalists: Kohlberg Kravis Roberts and the Creation of Corporate Value* (Cambridge, Cambridge University Press, 1998).

[7]   See 2.3.3.3.

[8]   'The Top Ten Buyouts', cited by B Cheffins and J Armour, 'The Eclipse of Private Equity' (2008) 33 *Delaware Journal of Corporate Law* 1, 3–4. The record fell in July 2006 when KKR beat its own record when

with the impact of the Sarbanes-Oxley Act, which arguably made private equity even more attractive than public companies, helped to fuel this increase. The private equity market has slowed down in the period since, as a result of the financial crisis and the consequent contraction of the debt market. However the US remains the most important global centre for private equity transactions.

Private equity was slower to develop in the UK. Although private equity in some form has existed in the UK for more than 70 years,[9] it only really started to develop in the late 1980s. At this point private equity in the UK still only comprised venture capital, ie private equity was being used to provide funding to start-up businesses. It is also notable that in this period the transactions were management-led, ie the managers of a company would identify an opportunity which they wished to pursue and they would then take their business plan to private equity organisations (then called venture capitalists) in order to obtain backing in the deal. These deals were therefore quite unlike the more dynamic LBO model in existence in the US at this time. It can fairly be said that at this point private equity in the UK 'operated at the fringes of corporate finance and corporate activity'.[10]

However, the following fifteen years saw an enormous expansion and development of this industry in the UK. In 1984 the members of the British Venture Capital Association (BVCA) invested £190 million in 479 companies. In 2007, members of the BVCA invested £31.6 billion in more than 1,600 companies worldwide.[11] As the market developed, the deals tended not to be initiated by the management team but by the private equity funds themselves, as they sought deals to finance. This change from deals being management-led to investor-led impacted on the nature of the deals themselves. Whereas in the 1980s it was common for management to hold the majority of the shares in the private equity-backed firm, this changed so that the private equity fund would hold the majority and the management would hold the minority. Today it is uncommon for the management to hold more than 25 per cent of the equity in the company. The consequential effect of this change has been to put the company under the control of the fund rather than the management. The language used to describe these deals has also changed. Instead of referring to the transactions as 'management buy outs' or 'management buy ins' (where the management team joined the business at the time of the acquisition) it has become more common to refer to them as 'leveraged buy outs', in the US style, or 'institutional buyouts'. The general term 'private equity' is used today to cover all those transactions where investment funds managed by private equity funds are invested in private companies (or public companies which have been taken private). Although venture capital and growth capital funding are still an important aspect of private equity activity in the UK, in terms of the scale of transactions buy out activity is now the largest part of the industry and it is this form of funding which has become synonymous with the term private equity in recent years.

---

buying HCA, a hospital chain, and fell again in November 2006 when the Blackstone Group, another leading private equity firm, agreed to buy Equity Office Properties.

[9] Venture capital in the UK can trace its origins back to the 1930s at least, with the founding of Charterhouse and the identification of the 'equity gap' for smaller unquoted companies by the Macmillan Report in 1931: HM Treasury, *Myners Review of Institutional Investment in the UK*, n 5, para 12.23.

[10] C Hale in C Hale (ed), *Private Equity: A Transactional Analysis,* 2nd edn (London, Globe Law and Business, 2010) 5.

[11] British Venture Capital Association, *Private Equity and Venture Capital Report on Investment Activity 2008*, July 2009.

The amount of money invested by UK-based private equity firms grew steadily in this period, reaching a peak in 2007. As in the US, this growth was fuelled by the availability of large amounts of cheap debt coupled with a desire from increasing numbers of investors, particularly institutional investors, to invest in this market. During this period the size of funds also increased in size, and private equity funds were prepared to cooperate on single transactions ('club deals'). In consequence even the largest public companies became possible targets for private equity funds. The deal which perhaps best exemplified the new reach of private equity funds was the purchase of Alliance Boots, a FTSE 100 company, by a KKR led consortium for £10.6 billion in 2007.

As in the US, the financial crisis, and the accompanying contraction of the debt market, has had a significant impact on private equity in the UK, with the overall money invested by UK-based firms dropping substantially, and reductions in the numbers of companies receiving private equity backing.[12] Research conducted by the Centre for Management Buy-out and Private Equity Research at Nottingham University found that there were 31 UK private equity deals in the three months to September 2009, the lowest level since 1984,[13] although 2010 has seen a recovery from these very low levels.[14] The principal problem is not the absence of equity. There are funds available within private equity firms. Rather, the difficulty revolves around the continuing absence of cheap available debt in the market. The private equity model depends on a high percentage of debt in the deal. Although the debt:equity ratios in private equity deals have fallen from their pre-financial crisis levels (where ratios of 70:30 or more were common) it would be very unusual for a deal to be done with less than 40–50 per cent debt. Without available debt therefore, deals will not occur.

The nature of the private equity deals being done post-recession has also changed. They are smaller on the whole: even the largest deals done in 2009, such as the purchase of Gatwick Airport by Global Infrastructure Partners for £1.5 billion in December 2009, look small in comparison to some of the pre-2008 deals, and the vast majority of post-2008 private equity deals are much smaller than this transaction. As discussed, the deals are also less highly leveraged than before. This will be considered further in the next section.

Private equity activity appears to experience boom and bust cycles.[15] After the boom in the early part of this century which came to an end in 2008, at the time of writing the industry is experiencing one of its cyclical downturns. Private equity has suffered a significant setback as a result of the contraction of the debt markets following the financial crisis, but the expectation within the private equity industry is that it will continue to play an important role in the capital markets, albeit that private equity might have to take on a 'leaner, less leveraged form'.[16]

[12] *Private Equity and Venture Capital Report on Investment Activity 2008*, ibid.
[13] Centre for Management Buy-Out and Private Equity Research, Nottingham University, Press release, 5 October 2009.
[14] Ibid, Press releases 11 May 2010, 28 June 2010.
[15] SN Kaplan and P Strömberg, 'Leveraged Buyouts and Private Equity' (2009) 23 *Journal of Economic Perspectives* 121.
[16] Ben Jenkins, co-head of Blackstone's corporate private equity business in Asia, in a speech at the International Financial Law Review (IFLR)'s Private Equity Forum, September 2009.

14.3   Private Equity Funds

14.3.1   Structure of a Typical Private Equity Fund

Funds can vary enormously in terms of their size and the sorts of investments into which they will enter. Some may specialise in providing venture capital funding or buy out funding. Some may specialise in the types of company in which they will invest. However, the structure of the fund itself will generally be the same. The typical structure of a UK private equity fund is an English limited partnership,[17] although limited partnerships from other jurisdictions (eg, Guernsey, Jersey, Scotland and Delaware) may also be used. A limited partnership lacks legal personality.[18] In a limited partnership there must be one or more partners with unlimited liability. These partners are called 'general partners'. In a private equity fund the general partner will generally be a separate vehicle, usually either an English limited company or a limited partnership, owned by the private equity firm. In theory the general partner makes the investment decisions on behalf of the limited partnership.[19] In practice, however, the fund will usually be managed by a separate vehicle to the general partner, the fund manager. The fund manager then provides the limited partnership with investment advice and makes investment decisions on behalf of the limited partnership and is regulated by the FSA.[20]

The general partner will usually invest equity into the fund. This ensures that the interests of the general partner are aligned with the interests of the fund investors.[21] However, the size of this investment will generally be small: the general partner's return is primarily generated from its fees. The general partner will receive an annual management fee,[22] commonly 1.5–2.5 per cent of funds committed,[23] and a share (or 'carry') of profits

---

[17]   See Limited Partnership Act 1907. In 2008 the Government announced plans to repeal this Act and to introduce new provisions into the Partnership Act 1890 by way of a legislative reform order, to be implemented from 1 October 2009 (see BERR, *Reform of Limited Partnership Law: Legislative Reform Order to Repeal and Replace the Limited Partnership Act 1907: A Consultative Document*, August 2008 available at www.berr.gov.uk/files/file47577.pdf). These proposals are on hold at the time of writing.

[18]   The Law Commission recommended a change to the law in this regard *(Limited Liability Partnerships: A Joint Consultation Paper* (Law Com. Consultation Paper No 161); *Partnership Law: A Joint Report* (Law Com. Report No 283, 2003) but this change has not been taken up by the Government in its reform proposals (BERR, *Reform of Limited Partnership Law*, ibid, para 92).

[19]   The Limited Partnership fund will usually be an unregulated Collective Investment Scheme (CIS) under Financial Services and Markets Act 2000, s 235. Establishing and operating a CIS is a regulated activity.

[20]   This structure means that a private equity firm can establish different general partners for each private equity fund, but needs only one vehicle, the fund manager, to be authorised by the FSA.

[21]   This alignment of interests may break down, however, if staff investment is not fully aligned with that of the investors eg if staff are able to under or over commit to specific transactions – effectively cherry picking: FSA, *Private Equity: A Discussion of Risk and Regulatory Engagement*, n 1, para 4.60. Alternatively a conflict may arise where a fund manager acts for several different private equity funds.

[22]   These fees may be taken as a share of profits in order to avoid paying VAT on them.

[23]   These percentages have remained consistent for many years, despite the size of funds increasing dramatically. This has caused some concern since the effect can be to incentivise private equity firms to set up bigger and bigger funds. In a fund of £100 million the fee will be 10 times that of a fund of £10 million, but the workload is unlikely to be ten times as great. However, these figures may be changing. The recession has had a number of consequences for private equity firms, one of which is that limited partners in funds are fighting for reduced management fees in light of the changed market conditions.

made by the fund as a whole (commonly 20 per cent) although this latter payment will be subject to a minimum hurdle level of return to investors, usually about eight per cent.[24]

The other partners are the 'limited partners' and they contribute to the partnership assets a specified amount in money or money's worth, and enjoy immunity from liability beyond the amount contributed. However, it is an essential condition of this immunity that a limited partner shall not take part in the management of the business, and has no power to bind the firm.[25] A limited partner may inspect the books and may consult with the other partners as to the state and prospects of the business, but must not go beyond this. If the limited partner does so, even if inadvertently, or in ignorance of the law, or at the urgent request of the general partners, then he forfeits his immunity from liability.[26] The main document governing the relationship between the general partner and the limited partner investors is therefore the partnership agreement, which will be carefully negotiated and which will generally specify the types of investment which may be made by the fund, as well as specifying the management fees and other commercial terms. The limited partners will also expect to receive regular and detailed updates from the general partner on the investments made by the fund.

One issue that has arisen in relation to the use of the limited partnership structure for private equity firms is the extent of the involvement that is possible by the limited partners without them becoming liable to forfeit their limited liability status. There is a concern that by engaging in overseeing the investment activity of the general partner the limited partners could be deemed to be managing the partnership.[27] The Government's current proposals for the reform of limited liability partnerships include a provision that there should be a list of activities that limited partners are allowed to undertake without jeopardising the limitation of their liability. This is intended to provide greater assurance to limited partners that they are able to monitor their investments in a normal way, for example by receiving financial information regarding the progress of their investments and exercising voting rights, without exposing themselves to unlimited liability.[28]

One of the significant considerations when structuring a private equity fund is to ensure that it is tax efficient. English limited partnerships are tax transparent. As a result, the limited partners are treated for tax purposes as if they owned the shares in the portfolio companies directly. Since these limited partnerships are not bodies corporate and do not have legal personality separate to that of their partners, the limited partnership is afforded the same treatment elsewhere and overseas investors should therefore be treated in their home jurisdictions as receiving dividends, interest and capital gains as if they were the direct owners of the relevant shares, and be taxed accordingly. There is no tax charge at the limited partnership level and there is no liability to tax when the limited partnership distributes its assets to its partners.

---

[24] An additional limited partner may be created as a carry vehicle for the executives in the private equity firm. To date the carry has been taxed as a capital gain and has not been subject to income tax, but this tax regime is under threat, particularly in the US, and it is not clear how long this tax position will continue.

[25] Limited Partnership Act 1907, s 6(1).

[26] Ibid.

[27] See *Myners Review*, n 5, para 12.103. Paul Myners also raised another problem with limited partnerships, namely the fact that they were subject to a 20 partner limit. However, this limit was abolished in 2002: Regulatory Reform (Removal of the 20 Member Limit in Partnerships etc) Order 2002 (SI 2002/3203).

[28] BERR, *Reform of Limited Partnership Law*, n 17, August 2008, paras 20.111–20.112.

Before leaving this section, it is worth contrasting the position of private equity funds, described here, and hedge funds.[29] In some ways these two forms of investment are similar. Both types of funds are managed by a team of skilled investment professionals that solicit investors directly, rather than through general advertising or a public offering. Both are commonly organised by way of limited partnerships. In both cases a management company, which acts as an investment adviser, will hold the general partnership interest of the limited partnership, and in both cases the investors (the limited partners) usually consist of high net-worth individuals and families, pension funds, endowments, banks, and insurance companies. However, traditionally the investment strategies and partnership terms of these two types of investment have been quite distinct.

Unlike the typical private equity fund described above, hedge funds have traditionally been open-ended, with no specified duration. This means that hedge fund managers have a quasi-permanent source of capital to be invested at their discretion, in contrast to private equity funds which must keep raising money via new funds. Hedge fund managers are typically subject to far fewer limitations than private equity fund managers on the types of product into which they can invest. This means they are able to invest in equity, debt with equity-like characteristics, pure debt, structured products and derivatives.

Hedge funds have typically sought absolute returns, but within that framework managers tend to have wide discretion as to the investment strategies they may adopt, being able to take both long and short positions in securities as they judge appropriate. Significantly, hedge funds have traditionally been regarded as a liquid investment, providing investors with the opportunity to enter and leave over the life of the fund. For example, it is generally possible for investors to be offered quarterly liquidity, with a 90 day notice period. As a result managers of hedge funds have tended to be short-term investors in relatively liquid instruments (such as public company shares) in order to be able to meet any redemption requests as they arise. Management fees, which have tended to be somewhat higher than private equity fees, are taken at regular intervals. Typically hedge fund managers earn two per cent management fees and 20 per cent performance fees based on regular (current) valuations of the fund with no hurdle rate and with all fees being payable in the year they are earned.

However, hedge funds are evolving. Some hedge funds have broadened their investment strategies to encompass typical private equity style investments and in some instances hedge funds have invested in private equity transactions, usually by providing part of the debt component of the transaction, as discussed below at 14.4.3. This can present challenges to the hedge fund model which permits investor redemptions on a periodic basis. One method which hedge funds have evolved to deal with this issue is to include 'side pockets' in a fund, ie different classes of shares within the hedge fund that are subject to a different (lesser) liquidity profile. Lock up periods, during which time the investor cannot dispose of its investment, are used for this purpose, and gates, which place an upper limit on the absolute amount of money that can be redeemed at any one time, can be added. By contrast, some private equity firms, at least pre-2008, started to add hedge funds to their product lines. To some extent the distinction between hedge funds and private equity may be becoming less obvious, although differences in the partnership structures do continue to exist and differences in the nature and risk profile of the

---

[29] See generally J Bevilacqua, 'Convergence and Divergence: Blurring the Lines Between Hedge Funds and Private Equity Funds' (2006) 54 *Buffalo Law Review* 251.

investments undertaken are still observable. There are also different systemic risk issues at work which may justify different regulatory treatment of private equity and hedge funds. This is discussed further at 14.6.5.

14.3.2   Sources of Funding for Private Equity Funds

As described in 14.2 above, private equity is cyclical in nature and the precise form of private equity at any one time will depend on the availability and cost of funding, particularly debt funding. The issues described here are intended to provide a sense of the parameters within which private equity operates, and to explain the pressures which affect the precise shape of private equity at any given point.

As discussed, from the 1980s until 2008, there was a significant increase in the amount of money invested in private equity funds. The advent of the recession has seen levels fall off from that high. Initially, many private equity organisations were wholly owned subsidiaries of large financial institutions. These organisations, known as 'captives', therefore obtained their funding from the parent institution. More recently, many of these organisations have become independent, or at least semi-captive, and therefore raise some or all of their funding from external sources.[30]

The principal sources of capital for independent or semi-captive private equity firms are institutional investors, which account for well over half of the total investment in private equity funds.[31] These include pension funds, charities, not-for-profit organisations and insurance companies. Other sources of funding include sovereign wealth funds and endowments and wealthy individuals who may participate in the fund as a limited partner.[32] Of the money invested into UK private equity, a significant percentage comes from overseas sources, in particular overseas pension funds. For example, in 2008 76 per cent of funding came from outside the UK, with 45 per cent of that coming from the US.[33] The effect of the financial crisis has been felt here, also, although the impact has not been evenly spread, hitting institutional investors most heavily, but leaving many sovereign wealth funds relatively untouched. Nevertheless the financial crisis has meant that there have been reductions in the amount of money being raised for new funds. For the immediate future, therefore, it is likely that funds will be smaller, with fewer investors.

There is usually a relatively high minimum subscription for new private equity fund offerings, often £5–10 million for mid to large cap funds.[34] Even in the funds which specialise in the UK smaller cap market, which are usually smaller funds, minimum subscriptions may still be in the region of £500,000. These high minimum subscriptions have a number of consequences. First, they reduce the number of investors with whom a fund manager needs to deal. This helps reduce administrative costs. Second, it helps to ensure that the investor base is professional/expert and helps to avoid direct retail investment. Indeed, marketing limited partnerships to individuals in the UK is highly

---

[30]   In early 2010 it was reported that in the US President Barack Obama plans to limit financial risk taking could force banks to shed parts of their private equity operations, which would put an end to captive institutions: Reuters, 22 January 2010.

[31]   *Myners Review*, n 5, paras 12.6–12.75.

[32]   See J Bevilaqua, 'Convergence and Divergence: Blurring the Lines between hedge Funds and Private Equity Funds' (2006) 54 *Buffalo Law Review* 251.

[33]   *Private Equity and Venture Capital Report on Investment Activity 2008*, n 11.

[34]   *Private Equity: A Discussion of Risk and Regulatory Engagement*, n 1, 23.

regulated by the FSA[35] and if investment in private equity by individuals other than by sophisticated or high net worth individuals is to take place this will generally occur via a publicly listed vehicle such as an investment trust or venture capital trust. This is in contrast to investment in public companies when members of the public can invest directly in those companies very easily, with a very meagre investment level, if that is what they choose. This has regulatory implications. As we saw in chapters nine and ten, where securities are offered directly to the public, for example in an IPO, the need for investor protection has led to the development of a significant regulatory apparatus in that regard. This contrasts with the light, almost non-existent, regulatory regime affecting private equity at the time of writing although, as discussed in 14.6.5, this is changing.

One of the key features of a private equity investment, certainly when compared to an investment in public company shares, is its illiquidity. The asset held by the limited partners is their stake in the fund. Private equity funds are typically raised with an expected life of around ten years, a term that is established in the partnership agreement at the outset. The typical hold period for individual portfolio companies purchased by the fund is therefore shorter. Typically three-five years after which time the aim will be to exit that company, usually by way of a flotation, a trade sale, or a sale to another private equity fund.[36] A fourth exit option, which has become much more prevalent post-2008, is exit by means of a liquidation. There is a limited secondary market for the stakes of limited partners in private equity funds, but this does not materially detract from the view that assets held by limited partners are illiquid.

In contrast to this traditional model of private equity, some private equity houses have also looked to the public markets for funding. There are a number of private equity funds listed on the London Stock Exchange including buyout funds, development capital funds, general funds, turnaround/restructuring funds, venture capital funds, and funds of funds. In addition, some private equity firms have themselves floated on the public markets. As a result the public are able to invest in the private equity firm, and thereby invest indirectly in the funds run by those private equity houses.

14.3.3   Why have Investors Wanted to Invest in Private Equity Funds?

The reason why investors have been keen to invest in private equity funds is simple: they believe they will receive superior returns compared to alternative available investment opportunities.[37] For example, Paul Myners's report for the Treasury in 2001 on institutional investment, including the private equity industry, noted that the net returns per annum to investors in UK-managed private equity funds raised between 1980 and 1995

---

[35]   The provision of management, advisory and arranging services to a fund or its investors in or from the UK constitutes a regulated activity for the purposes of FSMA, s 19, and the Financial Services and Markets Act 2000 (Regulated Activities) Order 2001.

[36]   For a comparison with publicly listed companies see 14.6.4.

[37]   Some doubt has been cast on whether superior returns do actually result: L Phallipou and O Gottschalg, 'The Performance of Private Equity Funds' (2009) *The Review of Financial Studies* 1747 who find that the performance of private equity funds as reported by industry associations and previous research is overstated. They find an average net-of-fees fund performance of three per cent per year below that of the S&P 500.

outperformed public equity market comparators over one, three, five and ten year periods and that over the ten year period to 2001 private equity as a whole outperformed UK equities as an investment class.[38]

However, these numbers mask wide variations between the performances of different funds. Over the ten years to 2001, for example, the Myners Report noted that while the performance of the better funds (the top 10th percentile of private equity) had been outstanding (46.8 per cent per year), across private equity funds in the bottom 10th percentile the figures were significantly lower (6.6 per cent per year).[39] In the same period, ten-year annual returns from the FTSE All-Share stood at 14.9 per cent and UK bonds at just over 10 per cent.[40] In his comments to the House of Commons Treasury Committee on Private Equity Paul Myners commented that 'on average private equity funds have produced inferior returns to public equity funds over most periods . . . The best private equity funds have produced very good returns; a significant number have disappointed, some very badly'.[41] There has traditionally been no obligation on private equity firms to disclose the information which would help an investor to distinguish between the good and not so good. The issue of transparency and disclosure is discussed at 14.6.5.

14.4 The Capital Structure of a Typical Private Equity Transaction

In general a new company (Newco), or more likely a series of Newcos, will be incorporated to provide the structure for the private equity acquired company. Tax is often a significant driver regarding the structuring of these new companies. This section will concentrate on how the financing of a typical private equity transaction is structured. Generally the financing will comprise a combination of equity, quasi-equity (either subordinated loan notes from the private equity fund or, less often, redeemable preference shares) and debt.

A typical buyout structure will contain a number of tiers of Newcos. The equity investment portion of the financing (which comes from the private equity fund and the managers of the target company who are participating in the private equity deal) will be done at the Newco 1 level. Newco 1 will then hold 100 per cent of Newco 2 and the debt part of the financing flowing from the private equity fund (the loan notes) will be put in at the Newco 2 level. Newco 2 will then hold 100 per cent of Newco 3 and the debt financing from investors other than the managers and private equity fund, such as the banks, will be put in at Newco 3 level. Newco 3 will then acquire the shares in the target. If the tranching of debt described below in 14.4.3 involves structural rather than contractual subordination, it is possible that there may also additional Newcos in the structure, ie the mezzanine debt would go in at Newco 3 and the senior and second lien debt at Newco 4 (which would then become the bid company). This structure is partly tax driven but is also driven by the

---

[38] *Myners Review,* n 5, para 12.50.
[39] Ibid, para 12.55.
[40] Ibid, para 12.59.
[41] *Private Equity,* n 2, 12–13.

need to structurally subordinate the loan made by the private equity fund from the loans made by the banks and other external investors.

However, as described above, private equity funding models are sensitive to the existence of funding, particularly debt, in the market and therefore the nature of a private equity funding model varies over time.[42] One common feature of the funding model is the high level of debt in the package, but this can vary from levels at or around the 50 per cent level (which are the typical levels at the time of writing this book) up to 70 per cent or even more in periods when debt is readily and cheaply available. The sources of the financing also vary over time. For example, in early models much of the equity financing came from the management of the company, whereas at the time of writing the majority tends to come from the private equity firm. Even greater changes are observable on the debt financing side, as discussed below. Therefore there is no such thing as a 'typical' private equity transaction. Nevertheless this section will examine the most common models, and explain the variables that tend to arise over time.

14.4.1   Equity Financing

As described, the equity financing part of the funding occurs at the Newco 1 level of the typical buy out structure. In the five year period prior to 2008 it was common to see about 30 per cent of the capital to finance a private equity transaction being provided by equity financing, although in the period immediately pre-recession the levels could sometimes be much lower than this figure. After 2008 the lack of available debt has meant that the percentage of equity in the deal has increased to somewhere around the 50 per cent level. The number of investors putting equity into the company will be small whatever the economic conditions: generally just the private equity fund and the management team. Typically only ordinary shares will be used to fund the company.[43]

A key feature of private equity has always been the involvement of management in the transaction. This has not been affected by changes in economic conditions. However, in contrast to the early days of private equity deals in the UK, which were management-led and saw management taking the majority equity stake in the company, today it is the private equity fund which invariably leads the transaction and takes the majority share. The management team will be expected to invest in the company to a significant extent, perhaps several hundred thousand pounds of their own money. In return they will receive a significant minority stake in the company (often referred to as 'sweet equity').[44]

---

[42]   For a discussion of the cyclical nature of funding in this context see P Gomper and J Lerner, *The Venture Capital Cycle*, 2nd edn (Cambridge MA, Massachussetts Institute of Technology Press, 2004); SN Kaplan and P Strömberg, 'Leveraged Buyouts and Private Equity' (2009) 23 *Journal of Economic Perspectives* 121.

[43]   In the past preference shares were often issued for tax reasons, but the abolition of advanced corporation tax in 1997 meant that preference shares largely ceased to be a feature in private equity transactions. Preference shares may also have been used to provide the minority private equity investor with protection from, and priority over, the management team. However, since the private equity investor is invariably in a majority position today the need for this form of protection has dropped away.

[44]   It is called 'sweet equity' because the amount of return the management can receive on their investment can be disproportionate to the amount invested. This is because the investment by the private equity fund is by way of loan note as well as equity. The loan note, naturally, has a fixed return. Once the bank loan and loan note have been paid off the value of the business is shared equally among the equity owners. The capital gains made by the management can therefore be disproportionate to the amount of money they put in as a percentage of the cost of acquiring the business.

Generally the private equity fund will hold more than 75 per cent of the equity and voting rights in the company, and the management will take the remainder. The amount that the private equity fund invests will usually be calculated by reference to the amount that the management can contribute. If the management have £100,000 for a 10 per cent stake in the business, the private equity fund will invest £900,000 in ordinary shares and any remaining investment will be by way of a loan note (see 14.4.2). Consequently the fund has control of the company. This has meant that the articles of association of a private equity-backed company are far simpler than they used to be in management-led MBOs, when complex provisions were inserted into the articles to protect the position of the private equity investor.

Following the private equity acquisition, the management team will be in day to day charge of running the company. However the fund will expect to have considerable oversight of this process. The investment agreement between the private equity fund and the management team will specify the (substantial) amount of financial and other information which the fund will expect to receive from the management team, including regular accounts (generally quarterly) and monthly board packs (including, for example, the latest balance sheet, profit and loss figures, latest cash position and cash flow forecast) in advance of monthly board meetings. The private equity fund will generally be under an obligation to keep this information confidential. In addition, the private equity fund will usually have at least one representative on the board of the company, and may also suggest some non-executive directors from outside the private equity fund to provide additional expertise on the board.

It is notable, therefore, that the shareholding structure of a private equity-backed company, with its small number of shareholders, and single controlling blockholder, looks more like a small family-owned private company than a large public company.

14.4.2   Quasi Equity

As discussed, the private equity fund will also generally invest (in Newco 2 in the above structure) via a loan note. Indeed it has become common for the majority of the fund's investment to be in this format. The reasons for this are two fold. First, the scale of the fund's investment in ordinary shares in the company is usually limited by the amount of the management's investment. As described above, if the management have £100,000 available to invest in a 10 per cent stake then the maximum investment that the fund can make in ordinary shares is £900,000. Presuming that the fund wants to invest more than £900,000 then it must do so in some other way. It could decide to invest via preference shares, and indeed in private equity transactions in the 1990s this was relatively common since the private equity investor could reclaim the advanced corporation tax paid on these dividends, which made them more valuable. Since the abolition of advanced corporation tax[45] it has become more common for funds to invest the remainder of their investment by way of a (subordinated) loan note. In the tiered Newco structure described above, this loan note ranks ahead of the equity financing not only because debt ranks ahead of equity

---

[45]   The abolition of advanced corporation tax was announced in 1997 and came into effect on 6 April 1999, for discussion see HMRC, *A Modern System for Corporation Tax Payments, A Consultative Document*, 1998, available at www.hmrc.gov.uk.

in a winding up but also because of the structural subordination in place. This debt is also structurally subordinated to the debt financing described in 14.4.3 below.[46]

A loan note has a number of significant advantages over preference shares for this purpose.[47] There are tax advantages to the company since the interest is tax deductible whereas dividends are not. There are also advantages from the fund's point of view. Whilst preference shares can be seen as a form of fixed interest security akin to debt, the position of a preference shareholder will generally be inferior to that of the company's creditors in certain crucial respects.[48] Unlike interest payments, the preferential dividend entitlement is not a debt until declared, and therefore cannot be guaranteed.[49] Even if the articles specify that the dividend does not need to be declared and specifies the due date, the payment will still be subject to distributable profits being available.[50] The preference shareholder has less security of capital than the company's creditors, who may have a charge on the assets of the company, although, the loan note will be subordinated to the other lenders to the company. The loan note will rank ahead of the shareholders claims qua shareholder in a winding up,[51] but will be subordinated to the bank debt in order to ensure that in the event of insolvency the bank receives its repayment prior to the loan note being repaid.[52]

14.4.3   Debt Financing

The use of debt finance is a key tool in private equity transactions. As described above, the debt financing element will generally be inserted at Newco 3 (the bid company) although it is possible for the different tranches of debt discussed below to be structurally subordinated and therefore for there to be additional Newcos inserted into the structure representing different tranches of debt.

As discussed, there is no such thing as a typical debt:equity ratio in a private equity-backed company. This level rarely drops below 50:50 but in certain economic conditions (when debt is plentiful and cheap) it can rise to levels of 70:30 or higher. There are a number of reasons why high levels of debt are found in private equity deals. It is cheaper than equity, particularly because the interest is tax deductible. It does not interfere with the ownership structures put in place in the Newco, and while preference shares could perform the same function, they are generally less attractive to both the company and the investor for the reasons given above. Debt is also a far more flexible financing tool than equity, as discussed in chapter two. As this section will discuss, a wide variety of debt financing techniques have evolved in this context, which can be customised to fit the requirements of each deal. Finally, on a practical level, debt financing can often be put in

---

[46]   For a description of structural subordination see 5.4.3.1.4.

[47]   For a general discussion of preference shares see 3.2.1.2.

[48]   See 3.2.1.2.

[49]   *Bond v Barrow Haematite Steel Co* [1902] 1 Ch 353.

[50]   See Companies Act 2006, ss 830–831. See 3.2.1.

[51]   Insolvency Act 1986, s 74(2)(f) and see 3.3.1.2.5.

[52]   In addition, for a period of time there were tax advantages to providing the investment via a loan note which made this option attractive. In essence, if the loan note was structured correctly, the company could claim tax deductability for the interest payments due on the loan note even when the cash interest payment was deferred to a future date. Most loan note instruments would provide for payment at a future date, the idea being that both accrued interest and the capital sum would be repaid from the sale proceeds of the company on the funds exit from the investment. However these advantages have now been removed.

place more speedily than equity financing and this can be key in private equity transactions which are often run on a very tight timetable.

In the years prior to 2008 the debt available to private equity funds increased significantly. It is estimated that in 2006, for example, $302 billion of leverage loans were made to US and European borrowers owned by private equity sponsors.[53] The availability of this amount of debt was one of the drivers of the rapid expansion of the private equity market in the early years of this century. The withdrawal of this pool of debt following the financial crisis has also been the chief reason for the significant decrease in the number of private equity deals done after the crisis.

Two other developments in debt financing helped to fuel the boom in private equity transactions prior up to 2008. First, although historically the majority of debt finance was provided by the major commercial and investment banks, in this period debt funding became potentially available from a greater variety of sources, including a wider range of banks, investment funds and even hedge funds. Second, the variety of debt instruments on offer to fund private equity investments also developed, particularly the use of subordinated finance. It became common in large transactions to supplement the debt financing with the issuance of high yield bonds or other forms of debt.[54] In addition, for all but the smallest private equity transactions there were likely to be two or more layers of debt, typically senior debt and mezzanine debt and, possibly, sandwiched between them, second lien debt. Each of these layers could in turn comprise a number of different tranches with slightly different lending terms and interest rates attached to them.[55]

One effect of these additional layers in the capital structure is to adjust the relative proportions of equity, subordinated debt and senior debt in capital structures. In particular it can adjust the debt/equity ratio as the innovative debt tranches, with more flexible repayment mechanisms, allow companies to carry a larger debt burden. In a survey carried out by the FSA, for example, it emerged that amongst the banks they surveyed, the proportions of senior debt: subordinated debt: equity in banks' five largest LBO transactions during the 12 months to June 2006 were on average 57:22:21,[56] ie an even lower percentage of equity financing that the 30 per cent traditionally associated with private equity transactions. In transactions of this type, the subordinated debt element of the package, which has some equity characteristics, replaces the equity component of private equity financing transactions to some extent. A further, general, issue is that in any but the smallest transactions, syndication of the debt is very likely.[57]

Many of these issues have been affected by the recession. Some of these forms of debt financing, for example, have all but disappeared in the post-2008 period.

14.4.3.1   Senior Debt

This is the first ranking layer of debt which forms the core part, and invariably the largest part, of the debt finance structure. This debt will be unsubordinated and will be inserted at the bid company level (Newco 3 or Newco 4 depending on whether structural subordination is used to separate the tranches of external debt financing) and secured on

---

[53]   Standard & Poor's Leveraged Commentary and Data, 2006.
[54]   See 2.3.3.3.
[55]   For a discussion of tranching in the context of securitisation see pages 403–4.
[56]   FSA, *Private Equity*, n 1, 35.
[57]   For further discussion see 7.4.

a first ranking basis. Generally the senior debt will be used to purchase the target company, to provide the company with the working capital it needs following the acquisition, and perhaps also to provide financing for any capital expenditure that the company needs to engage in following acquisition. The debt will comprise different forms including several term loans and revolving credit facilities.[58] For example, the working capital will generally be provided under a revolving credit facility, often by way of an overdraft facility, whereas any capital expenditure financing will usually be provided by way of a secured term loan.

The financing required to purchase the target will generally be the largest proportion of the senior debt and may be split into different tranches, depending on the amount of financing required and the sophistication of the package put together by the lender. Different tranches of debt may have different pricing and different repayment profiles. Some of the tranches will be amortising (ie repayable in regular, fixed amounts), others will provide for a single lump sum at maturity (sometimes called a bullet payment). Non-amortising debt has the benefit of allowing a company to use debt finance without having to eat into its short-term cash flow in order to make large debt repayments. A lack of amortisation therefore allows companies to bear a higher amount of debt financing than they might otherwise have been able to afford.

All of the debt in a private equity transaction (senior, second lien and mezzanine) will invariably be supported by guarantees[59] and the taking of security.[60] Guarantees will generally be given by the Newcos and may also be given by the target group (subject to possible issues of financial assistance). In terms of security, this will encompass both fixed and floating charges. The Newcos will generally be shelf companies without any assets (other than, in the case of the Newco which bids for and purchases the target, the shares it acquires in the target) against which the lenders could have recourse in the event of insolvency or receivership. Security will be taken over all, or substantially all, of the assets and shareholdings of the Newco group. This structure will give the lenders an element of control over any restructuring as they will be able to appoint an administrator if they hold a floating charge over all, or substantially all, of the assets of the company.[61] Where the debt is syndicated, a security trustee (often the senior lender) will usually be appointed to hold the security on trust on behalf of all the syndicate lenders.[62]

Given that the Newco structure described above involves an off the shelf shell company with no assets of its own, other than the target company which it acquires, it can be important for the lender to ensure the credit-worthiness of the target company post-acquisition. It is therefore common to see significant covenants in senior debt agreements, which are then usually repeated in the mezzanine debt and the second lien debt, if any. Some of these covenants will be of a general nature, and will restrict the company from changing its business, will restrict the creation of further security (a negative pledge clause), will restrict the company from disposals, mergers, joint ventures or issuing further

---

[58] See 2.3 esp 2.3.2.

[59] See 5.3.1.3.

[60] See chapter 6.

[61] Insolvency Act 1986, Sch B1 paras 14–21. Although the insolvent company can also appoint an administrator, it must notify the secured creditors holding a qualifying floating charge (ie a floating charge over all, or substantially all, of the assets of the company) which may, in turn, appoint an administrator of their choice. This is discussed at 6.3.3.

[62] For further discussion of this issue see 7.4.

debt, and will prohibit the payment of dividends or any other payments to the equity investors.[63] It is also usual for the lenders to receive an agreed package of regular financial information which will allow the lenders to monitor the performance of the target company.[64] In addition, specific financial covenants will commonly be put in place, requiring the company to operate within certain financial ratios, such as the ratio of total debt to earnings before interest, taxes, depreciation and amortisation (EBITDA) and the ratio of cash flow to total funding costs.[65] These financial covenants may well change over time, as the level of leverage in the company decreases. Failure to meet a financial covenant will lead to an event of default being triggered, which allows the lender to terminate and accelerate the loan.[66]

However, one development that emerged during the 2004–2007 period in the UK, when there were very extensive levels of debt available to private equity firms, was 'covenant lite' financing deals. This development arose not only from the abundance of debt (leading to borrower-friendly market) but also because it made the loans operate much more like bonds, which have very light covenants. Some of the newer investor types in that period, such as hedge funds, were comfortable with the covenant-lite package in place in bonds. In this period the market in syndicated loans also developed so that the lenders thought they could exit at the first sign of trouble (they still kept enough information covenants to enable them to do this).[67] In these deals the covenants are only tested when an event occurs rather than being continuously tested. These types of covenant-lite financing deals have disappeared in the wake of the recession.

14.4.3.2 Second Lien Debt

Second lien debt developed in the US in the late 1990s, and began to be utilised in the UK in 2003. The abundance of debt available to private equity funds in the early part of this century facilitated the development of this additional layer of debt, which can be used as an alternative to mezzanine debt or in conjunction with it, to form a distinct third layer sandwiched between senior and mezzanine debt. One significant difference between senior debt and second lien debt is the identity of the providers of this finance. In contrast to senior debt which is typically provided by the traditional lending banks, second lien debt was originally dominated by hedge funds, although subsequently all kinds of institutional investors became involved in providing this form of financing, and even the banks got involved and started lending in this category as well. In essence second lien debt forms part of the senior debt, but is subordinated to the rest of the senior debt and is secured on a second-ranking basis. It is generally contractually subordinated to the senior debt.[68] In contrast to senior debt, it generally comprises just a single term loan and is non-amortised, being repayable only at maturity. However, since 2008 this form of debt has all but disappeared.

---

[63]   See 5.2.1.
[64]   See 5.2.2.
[65]   Ibid.
[66]   5.2.3.
[67]   M Campbell and S Hughes, 'Leveraged Finance – Financial Covenants Under Stress' (2007) 22 *Journal of International Banking and Financial Law* 353; J Markland, 'Cov-lite – the New Cutting Edge in Acquisition Finance' (2007) 22 *Journal of International Banking and Financial Law* 379.
[68]   See 5.3.4.1.3.

14.4.3.3   *Mezzanine Debt*

Mezzanine debt ranks after the senior debt and any second lien debt and is secured on a second (or third) ranking basis. It is subordinated to the senior debt and second lien debt (if any), usually by way of contractual subordination (although it can also be structurally subordinated by the insertion of an additional Newco into the Newco tiered structure described above), but it will rank ahead of any loan notes provided by the private equity fund, and of course it ranks ahead of the equity invested into Newco.[69] To compensate the lenders for this increased risk profile (as compared to the senior debt, for example), mezzanine lenders receive a higher interest rate than senior lenders. In addition mezzanine lenders have traditionally received some kind of performance-related reward, such as warrants to subscribe for shares in Newco at some point in the future, for example on the private equity fund's exit via a sale or listing (known as an 'equity kicker'). However, during periods when there has been significant liquidity in the debt markets it has not always been necessary for private equity funds to offer warrants of this kind in order to secure mezzanine financing.

Mezzanine debt usually comprises just a single, non-amortised, term loan. It generally follows the terms of the senior debt (in terms of covenants, events of default etc). If the mezzanine debt is of a sufficient size then it will be syndicated in the same way as the senior debt, either by the same arranger or by a separate arranging bank. A mezzanine lender may have the right to appoint a director to the board of the company in order to represent the interests of that lender, which could differ from the interests of the senior lender. If so, this lender could perform an important corporate governance function, especially as such lenders generally have less security than the senior lender and so may be incentivised to monitor more closely. However, where the mezzanine debt is syndicated this may reduce the likelihood of monitoring as a result of coordination difficulties.[70]

14.5   Public to Private Transactions

Public to private transactions involve the use of private equity to purchase a listed public company and then to take it into private ownership. In the ten years to 2008 these transactions became more common in the UK, to the point where the term 'private equity' became almost synonymous with this type of transaction. As with many other aspects of private equity transactions, the advent of the recession has had an impact, and has significantly reduced this aspect of private equity.

A public to private transaction is more heavily regulated than a standard private equity transaction, involving the purchase of a private company. There are two principal mechanisms for these transactions: a takeover offer and a scheme of arrangement. Although takeovers may be thought to be the more usual mechanism by which to acquire a public company, schemes of arrangement have also been a popular tool for public to private transactions. There are two main reasons for this. First, in general lenders will only commit the very significant sums of debt financing involved in these highly leveraged

---

[69]   Insolvency Act 1986, s 74(2)(f), for discussion see 3.3.1.2.5.
[70]   The corporate governance role of debt in private equity transactions is discussed further at 14.6.2 below.

transactions if the private equity fund has carried out significant levels of due diligence on the target company. Due diligence of any depth and detail will require the cooperation of the target board and consequently (friendly) schemes of arrangement rather than hostile takeovers have been the norm. Second, it is often crucial for the fund to purchase 100 per cent of the target in order to put in place the funding structures it requires and a successful scheme of arrangement guarantees this outcome, whereas a takeover offer can only guarantee this outcome if the minimum acceptance condition is set at 90 per cent.[71]

Where either of these mechanisms is used to purchase a public company, the City Code on Takeovers and Mergers (the City Code) will apply in order to regulate the purchase. It is the nature of the target and not the bidding entity which determines whether the City Code applies. Takeover offers were discussed extensively in chapter twelve and Schemes of Arrangement in chapter thirteen, including a comparison of these two techniques as mechanisms for acquiring a company.[72] However, public-to-private transactions bring with them a specific set of issues and concerns and therefore the application of takeover regulation to these transactions does merit some analysis.

14.5.1   Financial issues

Two issues regarding the financial aspects of the deal differ when the transaction is a public to private deal rather than a purely private transaction. First, the City Code requires that the bidder is permitted to announce an offer only after it has ensured that it can fulfil all of its obligations under the offer.[73] This means that the bidder must have made all of the arrangements regarding financing (particularly its debt financing) before the offer is made. The lending banks will therefore have to commit to making the debt facilities available subject only to a very limited set of conditions. Many of the usual funding conditions will therefore have to be satisfied before the offer is made.

Second, financial assistance has traditionally been a tricky issue in private equity transactions.[74] It is common for the private equity fund to consider using cash in the acquired company to finance the offer. This has traditionally run into difficulties with the ban on the giving of financial assistance.[75] Indeed it is strongly arguable that the main reason for the introduction of the financial assistance provisions in the first place was to prevent leveraged buyouts from occurring,[76] although there is little evidence that the financial assistance rules have actually had this effect.[77] Prior to the Companies Act 2006 it was possible for private companies to use a whitewash procedure in order to avoid the financial assistance provisions.[78] The Companies Act 2006 abolished the ban on financial

---

[71]   For discussion see chapter 13.

[72]   See 13.2.1.

[73]   City Code on Takeovers and Mergers (City Code), General Principle 5 and rule 2.5(c), which requires a third party to confirm that the bidder will have resources available to satisfy full acceptance of the offer.

[74]   See generally, E Ferran, 'Regulation of Private Equity-backed Leveraged Buyout Activity in Europe' ECGI Law Working Paper 084/2007 May 2007 available at www.ssrn.com/abstract=989748.

[75]   Discussed at 4.4.4.

[76]   J Armour, 'Share Capital and Creditor Protection: Efficient Rules for a Modern Company Law' (2000) 63 *Modern Law Review* 255, 378, discussed at 4.4.4.

[77]   L Enriques, 'EC Company Law Directives and Regulations: How Trivial Are They?' in J Armour and JA McCahery (eds), *After Enron: Improving Corporate Law and Modernising Securities Regulation in Europe and the US* (Oxford, Hart Publishing, 2006).

[78]   Companies Act 1985, ss 153–155.

assistance for private companies, although it is retained for public companies.[79] Therefore although funding a purchase of a private company in this way is now acceptable, cash resources in a target in a public to private transaction can only be extracted once the offer is completed and the company has been re-registered as a private company.[80]

14.5.2   Recommendation by the Directors

Whenever an offer is made under the City Code the target board is required to provide its opinion on the offer to the target shareholders[81] in addition to obtaining competent independent advice on the offer which will then be made known to the target shareholders.[82] This latter requirement relates to all bids but the City Code states that this requirement is particularly important in the event of a management buy out or similar transaction.[83]

   This recommendation by the target board creates a number of specific issues in the context of private equity transactions. The increase in the number of private equity bids for public companies has led to a degree of scepticism among institutional shareholders regarding the willingness of target directors to recommend these bids. It is well known that private equity funds will not enter transactions unless they have identified a profit to be made, and therefore there is a general concern that target boards are too quick to recommend offers which may be too low. The fact that the competent independent advice supports the views of the directors does not seem to have provided institutional shareholders with a great deal of comfort, and indeed recent empirical work suggests that one of the major reasons for the wealth gains that flow from public to private transactions is the undervaluation of the pre-transaction target firm. These results suggest that the target shareholders' scepticism may be justified.[84]

   However, a more particular difficulty arises in relation to many private equity transactions, namely that since the majority of private equity bids involve some form of management buy out, the management of the target will face a significant conflict of interest when providing this advice. Of course directors are subject to their normal fiduciary duties at this time, including the obligation to act in the best interests of the target, but the City Code goes further and specifically regulates this issue. Rule 25.1 provides that directors with a conflict of interest should not normally take part in the recommendation process. Participants in a management buy out are regarded as having a conflict for these purposes.[85] Indeed any director, executive or non-executive, who will

---

[79]   Companies Act 2006, ss 677–683.

[80]   Alternatively, if the acquisition is by way of a scheme of arrangement, any actions that would otherwise be prevented by the financial assistance provisions could be approved by the court as part of the scheme. Schemes of Arrangement are discussed in detail in chapter 13.

[81]   City Code rule 25.1.

[82]   Ibid, rule 3.1.

[83]   Ibid, rule 3.1, note 1.

[84]   L Renneboog, T Simons and M Wright, 'Why Do Public Firms Go Private in the UK? The Impact of Private Equity Investors, Incentive Realignment and Undervaluation' (2007) 13 *Journal of Corporate Finance* 591. However, other studies suggest that in fact bids from companies with diffuse ownership structures (typically, public companies) pay *too much* for the companies they bid for: LL Bargeron, FP Schlingemann, RM Stulz and CJ Zutter, 'Why Do Private Acquirers Pay So Little Compared to Public Acquirers?' (2008) 89 *Journal of Financial Economics* 375.

[85]   City Code, rule 25.1, note 4.

have a continuing interest in the target or the bidder after a successful offer is likely to be regarded as conflicted. Where a management buy out occurs the target board will need to constitute an independent committee of directors, comprising those directors who do not have a conflict of interest. In some circumstances this committee may not contain any members of the existing target board, if they are all conflicted. It is this independent committee that will provide its opinion on the offer to the target shareholders. Similarly it is this independent committee which becomes the public face of the target as far as the offer is concerned, and therefore it is this committee with which the bidder will negotiate.

14.5.3 Equality between Bidders

One of the potential difficulties that can arise in a management buy out scenario is ensuring that equal information is provided to all bidders. Under Rule 20.2 of the City Code any information generated by the target that is provided to the management buy out team (whether the management team, the bidder associated with such a bid, or the private equity house backing the bid) must, on request, be provided by the target to other competing bidders. However the competing bidder cannot simply ask for all of the information provided to earlier bidders and must make specific requests for information. Similarly any information generated by the management team, or the bidder with which they are associated, and provided to potential financiers (in particular potential lenders) must be provided to the independent committee of the target if they request it.[86]

14.5.4 Equality of Treatment of Shareholders

As we saw in chapter twelve, equality of treatment of the target shareholders is one of the key aims of the City Code.[87] Particular issues arise in the context of a management buy out because special deals may be offered to certain shareholders, namely the managers of the target who also hold shares in the company. The bidder may wish to incentivise and involve members of the target board by rolling over their target shares, but it may wish to pay cash to all of the other shareholders. Special deals of this kind are generally prohibited, and this prohibition has been interpreted to cover both the quantum and the form of consideration.[88] However there are two important exceptions to this principle.

First, just as this rule does not apply to a single bidder who already holds shares in the target, it does not apply to parties who are joint bidders.[89] Accordingly, where a consortium of private equity funds come together to purchase a public company, a consortium member could be classified as a joint bidder and therefore be subject to a special deal. More significantly, the City Code provides an exemption for special deals for management in certain circumstances.[90] The Takeover Panel recognises that there may be a legitimate commercial interest for permitting the management of the target to remain financially involved in the business. However, a number of conditions are put in place before this can

---

[86] City Code, rule 20.3.
[87] See particularly 12.3.4.
[88] City Code, rule 16.
[89] The City Code does not contain a definition of joint bidder but the Takeover Panel sets out a non-exhaustive list of criteria they will consider in this context at Panel Statement 2003/25.
[90] City Code, rule 16.2.

occur.[91] First, the Takeover Panel must be consulted in all cases where a special deal will be offered to management, and its consent obtained. The Panel will be particularly keen to ensure that the management are not insulated from the risks of the business. Option arrangements that guarantee the original offer price as a minimum, for example, are unlikely to be acceptable. Second, the independent competent adviser under rule 3 of the City Code must state publicly that these arrangements are fair and reasonable. Third, these arrangements must be approved at a general meeting of the target shareholders, in a vote taken by the independent shareholders.

14.5.5   Market Abuse

As we saw in chapter ten, the prevention of market abuse is a key aim of the regulation of the capital markets. The dangers of market abuse are regarded as arising particularly keenly in the context of public to private transactions, due to the complexity of these transactions and the number of parties that tend to be involved.[92] The private equity firm will generally approach the directors of the target company and enter into talks with them about a possible purchase; the target company's advisors might then approach other private equity managers to ascertain their level of interest; each interested private equity fund will then approach numerous debt providers in order to set up the complex debt financing for the transaction. This may well be done via a tendering process so that a large number of potential debt providers will receive information about the possible purchase: 'Clearly, the more parties involved in putting together the finance, the more potential there is for leakage and misuse of price sensitive information. Typically several hundred individuals will be aware of a deal, rising to over a thousand in the case of larger deals'.[93]

The FSA has acknowledged that the implications for market confidence of this enhanced market integrity risk in the context of private equity are significant and merit ongoing scrutiny from regulators, and enhanced vigilance and preventative action from market participants.[94] It is clear that fears that markets may not be clean can damage market efficiency by discouraging trading.[95]

14.6   A Comparison of Private Equity and Public Company Structures

14.6.1   Ownership Structures

A number of important differences exist between the ownership structures in most private equity companies and most UK publicly listed companies. The first relates to the size of

---

[91]   Ibid.
[92]   *Private Equity*, n 1, paras 4.43–4.57.
[93]   Ibid, para 4.47.
[94]   Ibid, para 4.57.
[95]   See chapter 10, in particular 10.2.1.3 and 10.5, for discussion.

the investing group. Typically UK publicly traded companies have a dispersed shareholding structure. Most large listed companies will have a significant element of institutional investment, but there remains a substantial percentage of most listed companies that is held by private individuals.[96] By contrast, there are far fewer shareholders in a private equity-backed company. Usually the private fund will hold a significant percentage of the shares (eg 75 per cent) and the managers of the company will hold the remaining shares. Of course, this does not present the whole picture because the fund here is acting as a proxy for the underlying investors in the private equity fund. However, even if these investors are taken into account, the picture looks quite different from the pattern of investment typical in a publicly listed company, and the main reason for this difference is the high minimum investment that is required to invest in a private equity fund. A private equity fund with a focus on medium to large-scale acquisitions might typically have some 150 limited partners, in sharp contrast with the average of some 150,000 shareholders for a FTSE 100 company in the UK.[97]

Second, investors in publicly traded companies come in all shapes and sizes, including both institutional investors and small retail investors. The latter, in particular, are generally unsophisticated and need the assistance of the law to ensure that they receive from the company a minimum package of standardised information about what they are buying (particularly at the IPO stage) and to enable them to monitor their investment thereafter.[98] In general, the limited partners in private equity firms, the underlying investors in the private equity-backed companies, are in a strong position, via their contractual arrangements with the general partners in the private equity firm, to insist upon extensive disclosure obligations regarding the businesses in which the private equity fund invests. The reviews of the private equity industry that have been carried out in recent years have found that the information provided by the general partners to the investors in the fund is satisfactory.[99]

One consequence of the fact that private equity investors tend to be wholesale investors is that retail investors have only limited direct access to the private equity market via venture capital trusts (which arguably offer access to one of the riskier parts of this market) and a small number of private equity trusts. Indirect access is further limited as few UK pension funds or insurance companies have committed significant capital to private equity.[100] A risk therefore arises that retail consumers are not getting sufficient access to investment products which might form a beneficial component of a balanced investment portfolio. This risk of insufficient access to private equity is, however, counterbalanced against the risk that any enhancement of access to private equity potentially exposes investors to an asset class and risk return environment that they may not be able to fully understand.

A third significant difference between the ownership models is that the stakes held by investors in UK publicly listed companies are, on the whole, small and liquid. Even institutional investors typically hold no more than a five per cent stake, and often only two

---

[96] See 10.2.2, especially 10.2.2.1.
[97] D Walker, *Guidelines for Disclosure and Transparency in Private Equity*, November 2007, 8.
[98] These issues are discussed in detail in chapters 9 and 10.
[99] Eg, Walker, *Disclosure and Transparency in Private Equity, Consultation Document*, n 3, 6; *Private Equity*, n 2, para 78.
[100] For discussion see FSA, *Private Equity*, n 1, 13.

to three per cent.[101] By contrast, the private equity fund holds a very large stake in the private equity-backed company which cannot be regarded as liquid, and indeed the issue of exit will be a significant issue for the fund. Within the private equity fund, the stakes held by limited partners are also, in principle, illiquid, subject to the existence of a small secondary market in private equity investments described above. Exit is not generally an option for the investors in the fund. Voice therefore becomes a much more compelling corporate governance tool.

It has been suggested that private equity-backed companies can resolve one of the central weaknesses of large public corporations, namely the separation of ownership and control and the agency problems between the shareholders and directors that arise as a result.[102] In a traditional UK publicly listed company there is dispersed public ownership, professional managers without substantial equity holdings (although the increase in share-based remuneration means that they are likely to have some equity holdings) and a board of directors dominated by management-appointed outsiders. The problems associated with the separation of ownership and control are well understood.[103] The central problem of corporate governance for UK publicly quoted companies is how to hold managers accountable to the shareholders.[104]

A number of techniques have been discussed in this book so far to deal with this difficulty in UK public companies. One possibility is to try to include oversight of the directors from within the board, using board structure or, in the UK context, the appointment of non-executive directors. This is achieved in the UK via the UK Corporate Governance Code.[105] However the 'idea that outside directors with little or no equity stake in the company could effectively monitor and discipline managers who selected them has proven hollow at best'.[106] There is no evidence that the existence of non-executive directors in the UK results in the directors of poorly performing companies being disciplined.[107] This is discussed further at 14.6.3.

A second possibility is to rely on the shareholders in the company to discipline the management. As discussed in chapter ten, shareholders in UK companies have a number of governance entitlements.[108] For example, shareholders have the right to remove the directors at any time by ordinary resolution;[109] shareholders have a role in approving certain categories of transactions, such as substantial property transactions,[110] and, in listed companies, related party transactions and large transactions involving the company

---

[101]   J Franks and C Mayer 'Governance as a Source of Managerial Discipline' available at www.nbb.be/doc/ts/publications/WP/WP31En.pdf.

[102]   See eg MC Jensen, 'Eclipse of the Public Corporation' (1989) 67 *Harvard Business Review* 61 revised edition available at www.ssrn.com/abstract=146149 (1997). Citations in this chapter are for the 1997 version.

[103]   Eg MC Jensen and WH Meckling, 'Theory of the Firm: Managerial Behavior, Agency Costs and Ownership Structure' (1976) 3 *Journal of Financial Economics* 305.

[104]   R Kraakman et al, *The Anatomy of Corporate Law: A Comparative and Functional Approach*, 2nd edn (Oxford, Oxford University Press, 2009) ch 3.

[105]   Financial Reporting Council, *UK Corporate Governance Code*, June 2010, available at www.frc.org.uk.

[106]   Jensen, 'Eclipse of the Public Corporation', n 102, 6.

[107]   J Franks, C Mayer and L Renneboog, 'Who Disciplines the Management in Poorly Performing Companies?' (2001) 10 *Journal of Financial Intermediation* 209.

[108]   See 10.2.2.

[109]   Companies Act 2006, s 168(1).

[110]   Ibid, ss 190–196.

need to be put to a shareholder vote.[111] In general, dispersed shareholders do not take an active, monitoring role in UK plcs. Small retail investors tend to be rationally apathetic, and to use their 'exit' rather than their 'voice' if they are unhappy with the way in which a company is being run.[112] Institutional investors have the potential to have a more significant role, and there is little doubt that they have had an important role in developing a generally shareholder-friendly regime in the UK for public companies.[113] Particular examples of this include their influence in the development of the UK Corporate Governance Code, in the introduction of pre-emption rights and the development of the Pre-Emption Guidelines, and the development of the Takeover Code.[114] However on the whole they have not used their 'voice' (ie their vote in shareholders' meeting) as a tool of corporate governance.[115]

There is one important exception to this, however. Managers of poorly performing companies may be disciplined by shareholders (particularly the institutional investors) in circumstances where financial distress leads to capital restructuring being required. In order to issue new shares the directors will generally need to disapply pre-emption rights, and therefore get the consent of 75 per cent of the shareholders. This provides a specific occasion for a dialogue between the shareholders, particularly the institutional investors, and the management of a company. This provides a focal point for shareholders to engage with the company and potentially provide a monitoring role. As discussed previously in this book, a positive relation between UK rights issues and managerial change has been found to exist.[116]

A third possible form of corporate governance is the market for corporate control. This envisages takeovers operating as a form of discipline for poorly performing managers. On this analysis, given that a takeover offer in the UK involves the acquirer dealing directly with the target shareholders and sidelining the target directors, there is the potential for a takeover to facilitate a control shift and thereby to get rid of any lazy or self-seeking managers. Indeed the threat of a takeover occurring might even discourage the directors from being lazy and self-serving in the first place. This is sometimes seen as one of the benefits of hostile takeovers.[117] However, it is not clear that takeovers necessarily operate as a good corporate governance tool. There are reasons why takeover bids might be made, other than the fact that the management are performing poorly; takeovers tend to operate only as an instrument of last resort when massive management failures have already occurred; and there are better, earlier operating tools for aligning the interests of directors

---

[111]   See FSA Handbook, Listing Rules, LR 10 (transactions with a value of 5–25% of the company's business require disclosure to the shareholders, transactions in excess of 25% require disclosure plus a shareholder vote); LR 11 (related party transactions require disclosure plus a shareholders vote). See 10.3.2.4.

[112]   See 10.2.2.1. For a discussion of rational apathy amongst dispersed shareholders in public companies see AA Berle and GC Means, *The Modern Corporation and Private Property* (New York, Macmillan, 1932) although it was Robert Clark who actually coined the phrase 'rational apathy': RC Clark, 'Vote Buying and Corporate Law' (1979) 29 *Case Western Reserve Law Review* 776, 779.

[113]   See 10.2.2.2.

[114]   This is discussed at 12.2.

[115]   Discussed at 10.2.2.2. For a discussion of the position in the US see M Kahan and E Rock, 'Hedge Funds in Corporate Governance and Corporate Control' (2007) 155 *University of Pennsylvania Law Review* 1021.

[116]   J Franks, C Mayer and L Renneboog, 'Who Disciplines Management in Poorly Performing Companies?' (2001) 10 *Journal of Financial Intermediation* 209; D Hillier, SC Linn and P McColgan, 'Equity Issuance, CEO turnover and Corporate Governance' (2005) 11 *European Financial Management* 515. For discussion see 4.3.1.

[117]   See eg HG Manne, 'Mergers and the Market for Corporate Control' (1965) *Journal of Political Economics* 110.

and shareholders, such as performance related pay.[118] Further, the empirical evidence does not support a link between takeovers and the disciplining of poorly performing directors in the UK.[119]

A fourth possible form of corporate governance is the use of debt as a disciplinary tool.[120] Given the highly leveraged form of private equity companies, if debt is a good tool in this regard, it might be expected that private equity-backed companies would be particularly well regulated. A discussion of the use of debt in this context takes place in the next section, where the position and role of creditors in a private equity company is discussed.

The private equity ownership model can effectively resolve the owner-manager conflict. In a typical private equity-backed company the private equity firm will hold at least 75 per cent of the ordinary shares and will control the board, and the remaining ordinary shares will all be held by managers, each of whom will have a substantial equity stake in the company, far larger than will be the case under the equity-based compensation schemes in place in public companies. The deal is that managers 'may be asked to put a few hundred thousand of their own money into the business and then, if they are successful, they can walk away in three years' time with many millions of pounds'.[121] The management team obtains a significant equity stake in the private equity company.[122] Directors will be able to participate in the upside of the company (and this will be exacerbated by remuneration packages heavily weighted towards share options and performance related pay) but will also participate in any downside. The fact that private equity companies are highly leveraged allows the directors to acquire relatively large equity stakes for a relatively modest investment. The illiquidity of these equity stakes reduces the directors' incentive to manipulate short-term performance. Directors will only realise the value of their equity when the scheduled exit transaction occurs, whether that is via an IPO or a sale.

As regards the equity investors which the general partner in the private equity fund represents, again the numbers are small, with 150 being the average for a medium to large sized fund. As a result the 'chain of ownership and communication is relatively short'.[123] As discussed, recent studies suggest that these investors receive extensive information about their investment, ie about the companies in which the fund is invested. These investors are also relatively sophisticated and are motivated to make use of their voice as a corporate governance tool. They can therefore have a meaningful role in directing the actions of the private equity fund vis-à-vis the company.

There are a number of benefits to this structure. In particular, in a recent study, it was concluded that the closer alignment of director and shareholder interests, and the most

---

[118]   See 12.3.2.2.2.

[119]   J Franks, C Mayer and L Renneboog, 'Who Disciplines Management in Poorly Performing Companies?' (2001) 10 *Journal of Financial Intermediation* 209; J Franks and C Mayer, 'Hostile Takeovers in the UK and the Correction of Managerial Failure' (1996) 40 *Journal of Financial Economics* 163, 180. See also B Clarke, 'Articles 9 and 11 of the Takeover Directive (2004/25) and the Market for Corporate Control' [2006] *Journal of Business Law* 355.

[120]   For discussion see 3.2.2.4 and 14.6.2.2.

[121]   *Private Equity*, n 2, para 14, quoting Professor Tim Jenkinson.

[122]   For figures as to the position in the US see SN Kaplan and P Stromberg, 'Leveraged Buyouts and Private Equity' (2009) 23 *Journal of Economic Perspectives* 121, 131 and for Europe see VV Acharya, M Hahn and C Kehoe, 'Corporate Governance and Value Creation: Evidence from Private Equity' (2010) available at www.ssrn.com/abstract=1354519.

[123]   *Private Equity*, n 2, para 17, quoting the Treasury.

concentrated ownership structure, within private equity-backed companies were two of the reasons why public to private transactions generated wealth.[124]

14.6.2 Debt vs Equity Levels

Private equity-owned companies typically have far higher levels of debt than public companies. As discussed above, the level of debt in a private equity deal will vary according to the availability of debt in the market, so that levels may range from 50 per cent up to 70 per cent plus. In one notorious deal in 2006, Allianz sold the Four Seasons Nursing Homes to a Qatari sovereign wealth fund for £1.4 billion, of which £1.3 billion was borrowed. By contrast the debt-equity ratio for public companies is typically 30:70. Higher levels of debt to earnings are also typical in private equity-backed companies compared to public companies.[125]

As we discussed in chapter two, there is no ideal mix of debt and equity which will apply to all companies.[126] The amount of leverage that will suit each company will vary according to a number of factors. In the UK, the tax system favours debt over equity as a form of company funding since although there is tax deduction for interest there is no such favourable treatment for dividends.[127] One common criticism of private equity is that it makes money for its investors by making use of the tax advantages of debt rather than by creating operational or economic value in the private equity company. This is discussed at 14.6.6.

Increasing the amount of debt increases the risks to which the company is exposed. As the proportion of debt in the company increases, it becomes more likely that the company will default and enter into insolvency. Financial distress and insolvency are costly, in terms of the direct costs of lawyers, courts and insolvency practitioners, as well as the reduction in the value of the company associated with insolvency. There are also the indirect costs attached to the difficulties of running a company while going through insolvency.[128] Even if the company avoids insolvency it will still face the costs of financial distress, for example, suppliers may demand more protection, creditors may charge more and employees may leave and look for other jobs. In addition, more highly geared companies are felt to be more at risk in a recession that less highly geared companies.

The recent financial crisis has clearly caused problems for private equity-backed companies. It is estimated that, at the global level, more than $500 billion of leveraged loans and high-yield bonds needed to be refinanced between 2008 and 2010.[129] A report by Moody's, the rating agency, in November 2009, concluded that in the US about 19.4 percent of companies bought by the 14 largest private equity firms from January 2008 to September 2009 had defaulted, slightly more than the 18.6 percent default rate for

---

[124] L Renneboog, T Simons and M Wright, 'Why Do Public Firms Go Private in the UK? The Impact of Private Equity Investors, Incentive Realignment and Undervaluation' (2007) 13 *Journal of Corporate Finance* 591.

[125] Eg Bank of England, *Financial Stability*, April 2007, Issue No 21, 19.

[126] For discussion see 2.6.

[127] See 2.6.

[128] JB Warner, 'Bankruptcy Costs: Some Evidence' (1977) 32 *Journal of Finance* 337–348; LA Weiss, 'Bankruptcy Resolution: Direct Costs and Violation of Priority of Claims' (1990) 27 *Journal of Financial Economics* 285; EI Altman, 'A Further Investigation of the Bankruptcy Cost Question' (1984) 39 *Journal of Finance* 1067; G Andrade and SN Kaplan, 'How Costly is Financial (Not Economic) Distress? Evidence from Highly Leveraged Transactions that Became Distressed' (1998) 53 *Journal of Finance* 1443.

[129] European Central Bank, Financial Stability Review, December 2008.

similarly rated companies without private equity backing. However, the picture is much starker when it comes to big deals. According to Moody's, the 10 largest companies bought by private equity companies in the US were performing worse than similar stand-alone companies or smaller private equity deals. Indeed of the 10, Moody's found that four had already defaulted and the fifth was expected to default in the near future.[130] In the UK, the position is more equivocal.[131]

The trade off theory of capital structure recognises that investors will look for an enhanced return to compensate them for the increased risk of having to absorb these costs of financial distress. The addition of debt to a company's capital structure is beneficial, but only up to the point where the tax savings resulting from the debt are outweighed by the insolvency costs. The theoretical optimum is reached when the present value of the tax saving is just offset by increases in the value of the costs of financial distress.

Other relevant factors for a company will be the availability of internal funds (retained profits) as a source of financing, and the cost and availability of debt financing available to it. These principles apply to all UK companies, not just private equity-backed companies, but for some reason these rules have impacted differently on private equity companies and public companies, such that the ratios of debt:equity raised by each are consistently very distinct, with private equity firms taking on consistently more debt than equity.

There are felt to be two explanations why private equity-backed companies tend to be much more highly leveraged than public companies. First, Professor Jenkinson has suggested that the pattern of returns which shareholders in public companies expect, ie stable predictable dividends,[132] make it very hard for public companies to be more highly leveraged because it is 'very difficult…to maintain a constant dividend stream or a constant growth of dividends if you have a very highly-leveraged structure because, by its very nature, the residual profits tend to go up and down a lot with interest rates and with changes in the economy'.[133]

On this view, the leverage levels in UK public companies are inefficiently low and should be increased. In other words, the effect of taking a company private is that private equity fund managers are simply transforming the companies they back into capital efficient operations. Public to private transactions can therefore make the most of the generous tax treatment and flexible financing options associated with debt capital. A study carried out by Professor Williams and others demonstrated that if the debt:equity ratios of the FTSE 100 companies were changed from 30:70 to 70:30 the effect would be to increase the volatility of returns to equity, but would result in higher returns at least during upswings in the economy, albeit that the model also suggests that public company shareholders would receive poorer returns during downturns.[134]

The second explanation for the higher leverage levels in private equity-backed companies is that the investors in private equity firms are more comfortable with higher levels of debt than shareholders in public companies: 'a single shareholder who has spent millions of pounds understanding the potential of a company and put great resources into

---

[130]   Moody's Global Corporate Finance Report, November 2009.
[131]   Centre for Management Buy-Out Research, Nottingham University Business School, Press releases 2009–10.
[132]   For discussion see 2.5.
[133]   *Private Equity*, n 2, para 27, quoting Professor Tim Jenkinson.
[134]   Ibid, para 45 quoting from research by J Froud, S Johal, A Leaver and K Williams, Centre for Research on Socio-Cultural Change, University of Manchester.

exploiting it is very well placed to decide where the efficient frontier is'[135] as compared to many shareholders in public companies. In the theoretical model described above whereby ideal debt:equity ratios for a company are determined, the attitude of the shareholders to debt is crucial, since it is the shareholders' need to be compensated for the increased risks of insolvency associated with debt which generally increase the costs of financing, and counterbalance the tax advantages of debt. If the shareholders are comfortable with higher levels of debt (and the increased risk of insolvency that this brings) because they have carefully analysed the risks and potential of the target company, then it will be cost effective to have higher debt levels, as compared to a company where the shareholders do demand that compensation.

This is all well and good, but it does not take account of the other stakeholders in the company who are exposed to greater risks as a result of the increased debt levels in private equity companies. Two groups in particular will be considered, namely the employees and the creditors, although other stakeholders may also be affected.

14.6.2.1 The Employees

Two concerns tend to be voiced about the position of employees in private equity-backed companies. The first concern is that one of the ways in which private equity firms generate wealth is via wealth transfers from stakeholders, such as employees, to the shareholders, ie that private equity companies will cut jobs and reduce wages in order to produce gains for the investors. The second concern is that, because private equity firms are higher risk, the employees in these companies are at greater risk of losing their jobs. Given the number of employees in the UK workforce now employed by private equity-backed companies,[136] these concerns are significant. This latter concern was lent some credence in 2006 by the FSA which stated that jobs in 'overleveraged' private equity companies looked 'increasingly precarious'.[137] To date, little additional protection has been granted to the employees of these companies. However, concerns regarding the position of employees in private equity-backed companies has been one of the major drivers behind the creation of new disclosure obligations in the UK, discussed at 14.6.5 below. While this regime offers employees the opportunity to discover more about some private equity funds, it provides them with nothing more concrete. Employees must look to the protection of employment law for direct rights.

14.6.2.2 The Creditors

Generally, in solvent companies, the creditors' interests are subsumed beneath the interests of the shareholders. Section 172 of the Companies Act 2006 requires directors of a solvent company to act 'in the way he considers, in good faith, would be most likely to promote the success of the company for the benefit of its members as a whole' whilst also having regard to other stakeholders although not, crucially, creditors.[138] The ordinary shareholders are the residual claimants and they have the greatest interest in monitoring the

---

[135] Ibid, para 27, quoting Philip Yea of 3i.
[136] It was estimated by the British Venture Capital Association (BVCA) in 2005 that 19% of the private sector workforce were employed by companies that had received private equity backing: BVCA, *Economic Impact of Private Equity*, 2005.
[137] *Private Equity,* n 1, para 4.22.
[138] Companies Act 2006, s 172(1). See 3.2.1.3.1.

company in this period since they will take the lion's share of the loss if things go wrong (and the lion's share of the gain if the company succeeds).[139] The creditors, who are fixed claimants, are, in general, protected by the directors' shareholder-focused duties, as long as the company remains a profitable going concern. This will change of course once the company starts to run into financial difficulties and directors' duties become creditor-regarding once the company is insolvent, or on the verge of insolvency.[140] To make the directors creditor-regarding at an earlier stage would generally have the effect of making directors too risk averse, since creditors are primarily interested in low risk projects which ensure that they are repaid.

However, in the private equity model the private equity fund takes a large equity stake in the company but only a relatively small stake in the private equity-backed company's debt and the directors in the company typically hold none of the debt. This could lead to high-risk management gambles by the directors of the private equity company which are tolerated by the director-shareholders. If the gamble succeeds the directors and the private equity fund will reap the rewards; if they fail the creditors will bear the costs. The private equity scenario is therefore a more extreme version of the usual scenario in place for creditors of all companies, because the highly leveraged nature of the company in this instance creates a greater potential for the shareholder-focused directors to use the creditors' money to fund the shareholders' (potential) gains. In most companies this conflict only becomes clearly apparent in the twilight period just prior to insolvency, when there is a possibility that the directors might gamble with the creditors' money in order to benefit the shareholders. Measures have been put in place to deal with the conflict which arises at this point.[141] This conflict has the potential to arise earlier in time in a private equity company, when no specific measures are put in place by the law to deal with this conflict.

Of course it might be expected that the banks and other major lenders in a private equity transaction will put in place contractual and proprietary measures to protect themselves, or at least will ensure that they are properly compensated for the risks which they take (and they are in a good position to assess accurately the level of risk which they are taking to ensure that the bargained for compensation does adequately cover the risk undertaken). All of the major lenders (senior, second lien and mezzanine) will take security and guarantees in order to protect themselves. The lower ranked lenders will expect their return to reflect the increased risk which they take. It is also notable that it is standard for these loans to include specific financial covenants, requiring the company to operate within certain financial ratios, such as the ratio of total debt to earnings before interest, taxes, depreciation and amortisation (EBITDA) and the ratio of cash flow to total funding costs.

Whilst it is open to the major lenders to put in place security packages and financial covenants in order to protect themselves, the non-adjusting creditors[142] are not in a position to do so, and are left potentially exposed. It is sometimes suggested that debt can operate as a corporate governance tool, ie the monitoring of certain lenders can have a

---

[139]   See 3.2.
[140]   See 3.3.
[141]   Ibid.
[142]   See 3.2.2.1 for a discussion of non-adjusting creditors.

disciplinary effect on directors such that all stakeholders in the company, including therefore the non-adjusting creditors, can benefit.

There is a general disciplining effect that can be said to flow from debt, in that, while returns to shareholders are in the discretion of directors (dividend payments, for example, only become a debt if the company has distributable profits and after the directors have declared the dividend, whatever the articles say),[143] contracted-for interest and capital payments must be met by the directors, otherwise the company can potentially be declared insolvent. The existence of debt in a company therefore can meet Professor Jensen's concerns that public companies are inefficient because directors do not distribute the free cash flow that exists in the company. Debt can be seen as a mechanism for forcing managers to disgorge cash, albeit to the creditors rather than to the shareholders. Where most of the free cash flow is committed to debt repayments, directors are forced to adhere to strict results-orientated financial projections.[144] Set against this analysis are two aspects of the way that private equity companies operate in practice. First, as discussed above, private equity companies solve the owner-manager dilemma such that shareholders can force the directors to distribute free cash flows to them if they so wish, so that the 'waste' of free cash flow that Jensen envisages in public companies does not tend to arise in the private equity context. Second, in recent years it has become common for many private equity debt repayments to be payable as a single bullet payment at the end of the term, such that there is little disciplining effect on a month to month basis within the company.

Major lenders can have a significant corporate governance role both by monitoring corporate activity and influencing it, largely using the contractual rights they have in the loan agreement. This is discussed at 3.2.2.4.

A number of aspects of the way that debt financing operates in private equity transactions in practice reduces the likelihood of this monitoring effect. First, where covenant-lite financing has occurred, the covenants are only tested when an event occurs rather than being continuously tested. This will clearly diminish the potential monitoring role of the debt, however, covenant-lite deals have been relatively little used to date, and therefore this is not, at present, a significant concern.

Second, and of more significance, is the fact that, certainly prior to 2008, most of the larger private equity transactions were syndicated, which reduced the potential governance role of the lender.[145] Third, these loans are generally transferred by the original lender.[146] The FSA found that, in the period pre-2008, on average banks distributed 81 per cent of their exposures to their largest transactions within 120 days of finalising the deal.[147] In smaller transactions the debt finance is often kept within the banking community, but in larger, more complex transactions it might be sold to participants in the institutional debt market, such as hedge funds or institutional investors. This has the effect that the ownership of the risks being under taken in this highly leveraged system is not always clear.[148] Although the diversification of the debt market results in a reduction of individual exposure, it also reduces the capacity for monitoring and controlling the underlying risks.

---

[143] *Bond v Barrow Haematite Steel Co* [1902] 1 Ch 353. For discussion see page 58 and page 61.
[144] K Palepu, 'Consequences of Leveraged Buyouts' (1990) 27 *Journal of Financial Economics* 247.
[145] For discussion see pages 81–82 and chapter 7.
[146] See pages 86–87.
[147] *Private Equity,* n 1, 3–4.
[148] *Private Equity,* n 1, 10.

A final mechanism whereby debt can operate as a corporate governance tool is via the use of security. This is discussed at 6.6.2. Certainly the senior lender in a private equity transaction will take security and will be in a position to use that security to discipline the directors, in particular by performing a monitoring role.

14.6.3 Board/Management Structures

In terms of UK publicly listed companies, board structure is now heavily influenced by the UK Corporate Governance Code.[149] The Code advocates that, except for smaller companies (ie those below the FTSE 350 throughout the year immediately prior to the reporting year), at least half the board, excluding the chairman, should comprise non-executive directors determined by the board to be independent. A smaller company should have at least two independent non-executive directors.[150] The non-executive directors are regarded as having a key role in monitoring the performance of the company's executive directors. As a result the Code envisages that they will have a role in setting the company's strategy.[151] The Code also provides that there should be committees of the board to deal with certain specific matters, such as audit, remuneration and appointments, on which the non-executive directors should be the only or the majority of the members.[152] In order to enable the non-executive directors to fulfil their role, the Code provides that they should have access to appropriate outside professional advice and to internal information from the company. Finally, the Code provides that in principle, the CEO and the chair of the board should not be the same person.[153] The UK Corporate Governance Code is a classic example of 'soft law': it is not obligatory for companies to follow these rules but companies must state in their annual report whether they have complied, and explain any areas of non-compliance.[154]

Two significant differences emerge therefore regarding the board structure of private equity-backed firms as compared to public companies. The first relates to the number and type of directors on the board. Typically boards of UK publicly listed companies are large, with perhaps between 12 and 20 members, containing a significant number of external directors. In contrast, in a private equity firm, the number of people on the board tends to be much smaller.[155] Generally the board will consist of representatives of the general partner of the fund (who are invariably members of the private equity firm), the directors who were part of the buy out team, and possible one or two external experts brought in by the private equity fund in order to provide specialist advice and assistance to the other directors. Empirical evidence also suggests that the boards of private equity companies

---

[149] *UK Corporate Governance Code*, n 105. For discussion see P Davies, 'Board Structure in the UK and Germany: Convergence or Continuing Divergence' (2009) available at www.ssrn.com/abstract=262959.

[150] Ibid, B.1.2. Independent for these purposes means 'independent in character and judgement' and that there are no 'relationships or circumstances which are likely to affect, or could appear to affect, the director's judgement' (ibid, B.1.1).

[151] Ibid, A.4.

[152] Ibid, B.2.1 (appointment committee), C.3.1 (audit committee), D.2.1 (remuneration committee).

[153] Ibid, A.2.1.

[154] FSA Handbook, Listing Rules, LR 9.8.6(5)–(6).

[155] F Cornelli and O Karakas, 'Private Equity and Corporate Governance: Do LBOs Have More Effective Boards?' Working paper, February 2008, available at www.ecgi.org. Studies of public companies suggest that smaller boards are more effective: D Yermack, 'Higher Market Valuation of Companies with a Small Board of Directors' (1996) 40(2) *Journal of Financial Economics* 185.

have more formal meetings and many more informal contacts than their public company counterparts.[156] It is also significant, of course, that the private equity fund will have a sufficient equity stake to remove any director, by ordinary resolution, who is performing poorly.

The second significant difference relates to the role of the directors. The board of a plc is perceived as having two functions: to lead and to control the company. The latter role falls in the main to the non-executive directors. However, although the idea is that these non-executive directors will provide a disciplining function on the executive directors, in practice the empirical evidence does not suggest that this occurs.[157] Instead the focus of the non-executive directors tends to be on compliance issues and committee duties. As we discussed in chapters nine and ten the burdens placed on the directors of public companies by the regulatory system are significant. The general view is that the directors of public companies spend a great deal of time engaged in communicating with their shareholders, in investor relations and in periodic reporting.

By contrast, a private equity-backed company is freed from these burdens. It is not subject to the obligations of the UK Corporate Governance Code regarding the composition and structure of the board, and nor is it subject to the same array of disclosure obligations that is imposed upon public companies. It is notable, in particular, that private equity-backed companies are under no legal obligation to publish six monthly earnings statements,[158] and their annual report only needs to be published nine months after the year end.[159] As a result of a new set of voluntary guidelines discussed below at 14.6.5, some of the largest public equity-backed companies are now expected to comply with some, but not all, of the same disclosure obligations faced by public companies. However, most private equity-backed companies fall outside even this voluntary scheme. In contrast to publicly listed companies, the directors of private equity-backed companies have only one function, not two: they can focus on trading and strategy and do not have to concern themselves with compliance and control. If they supplement the board with outside directors at all, this will not be for the purposes of control, but because these outside directors will enhance the expertise and strategic thinking of the board. Typically private equity firms will supplement the board by recruiting directors with expertise in the relevant industrial sector, or the management of business more generally.

As discussed above, another difference between the directors of publicly listed companies and private equity companies is the level of equity they hold. Although equity-based compensation schemes are becoming more common in the UK for directors of listed companies, typically directors will still hold a far lower level of equity than is common in private equity-backed companies. The remuneration of directors in private equity-backed companies is therefore far more closely related to the performance of the company. In studies carried out in the US it was found that the salary of the typical private

---

[156]   VV Acharya, M Hahn and C Kehoe, 'Corporate Governance and Value Creation: Evidence from Private Equity' (2010) NYU Working Paper No. FIN-08–032 available at www.ssrn.com/abstract=1354519.

[157]   J Franks, C Mayer and L Renneboog, 'Who Disciplines Management in Poorly Performing Companies?' (2001) 10 *Journal of Financial Intermediation* 209.

[158]   This obligation only attaches to companies whose shares are admitted to trading (and whose Home State is the UK): FSA Handbook, Disclosure Rules and Transparency Rules, DTR 4.3.

[159]   Companies Act 2006, s 442(2)(a), cf public companies which must publish within six months: s 442(2)(b).

equity-backed company director was significantly more sensitive to the performance of the company than that of a typical public company director.[160]

14.6.4   Period of Investment

The usual 'hold' period for an investment in a company by a private equity firm is three to five years, at which point an exit will be organised, usually by way of a sale or an IPO. Private equity investments are not, therefore, made on an open-ended basis. By contrast, investments in public companies have no built in exit. However, some studies have revealed that on average institutional investors hold shares in publicly traded companies for only 2.5 years.[161] On this view, the investment of a private equity fund allows for a *longer* term view of the company's prospects to be taken, without necessarily having to have regard to the short-term earnings performance of the company, than might occur in a public company.

Nevertheless, various groups have expressed concern that this three to five year period encourages private equity-backed companies to be too short-term in their approach, being likely to look less favourably on investments that would deliver outside this time frame.[162] However, in order for the private equity firm to be able to exit its investment and to get a good price for the company, it will have to create a company which has good long-term prospects.[163] The directors who are running the company will know that there is a guarantee of future liquidity occurring by way of an unbiased valuation event, in which they will participate because of their equity stakes, and therefore they have a significant incentive to add value to the company in order to sell or float at a good price. Similarly, the private equity partners running a particular fund know that they must dispose of all of the assets in the fund within a fixed period and they are therefore strongly motivated to move swiftly to get portfolio companies into shape for an advantageous sale.

14.6.5   Transparency and Disclosure Issues

Traditionally, relatively little information has been available regarding the private equity industry. Many in the industry believed that 'private means private' to the point of secretiveness.[164] However, the growth in the private equity market, particularly the development of public to private transactions, has put pressure on this state of affairs. As we saw in chapters nine and ten, a significant amount of regulation is put in place in relation to public companies, and the contrast between this position, and that relating to private equity-backed companies is particularly stark when a FTSE 100 company such as Alliance Boots is taken private.

It is not lack of transparency to investors in the private equity fund that is felt to be the problem. In general, private equity fund investors are kept well informed about the

---

[160]   S Kaplan, 'The Effects of Management Buyouts on Operating Performance and Value' (1989) *24 Journal of Financial Economics* 217; MC Jensen and KJ Murphy, 'Performance Pay and Top Management Incentives' (1990) 98 *Journal of Political Economy* 225.

[161]   *Private Equity*, n 2, para 21.

[162]   Ibid.

[163]   Ibid, para 22, quoting Professor Tim Jenkinson.

[164]   See Walker, *Disclosure and Transparency in Private Equity: Consultation Document*, n 3, 3.

performance of the businesses in their fund. Not only is the amount of information given to the investors extensive,[165] but because private equity is predominantly a wholesale rather than a retail market, the investors are far better able to assess the information given to them by the funds in which they have invested, or in which they plan to invest. Reporting arrangements between the private equity firms (the general managers in a fund) and the investors (the limited partners in the fund) are felt to be satisfactory.[166] Indeed it is generally accepted that private equity fund investors frequently receive far more extensive and detailed disclosures than investors in public companies. Albeit that this information is not usually standardised in form, the fact that these are sophisticated wholesale investors means that they have the appropriate skills to assess this information and to determine whether to invest in a fund, and then to monitor the performance of that fund on an ongoing basis.

Rather it is lack of transparency to non-shareholder stakeholders in public equity-backed companies that is felt to be problematic:

> the difference [between the reporting requirements for private equity backed companies and public companies] is logical—it is rooted in the distinction between keeping a small group of private shareholders informed, and reporting to markets as a whole. Nevertheless, large businesses, and particularly those in the public eye, have a wider responsibility to engage with the community in which they operate and to meet the legitimate interests of stakeholders, both employees and the wider public, in how their operations affect them. As the private equity sector has grown and as some major companies have moved from transparent public to opaque private markets, this need has become more acute.[167]

On this view, reporting by listed companies performs a dual function, not just to inform the shareholders of the company about the business, but also to address the legitimate interest in the company's policies and performance of stakeholder groups such as employees, suppliers and customers, as well as the public interest more widely. However, the law creates no provision whereby non-investors in private equity might determine this information. The private equity industry came to understand—and accept—that the growth in the volume and size of private equity transactions introduced a wider stakeholder base into the equation who may well have a legitimate interest in the nature of the private equity firm acquiring the company. As a result, in February 2007 the British Venture Capital Association asked Sir David Walker to undertake a review of the adequacy of disclosure and transparency in private equity with a view to recommending a set of voluntary guidelines.

The Walker Review agreed that there was a 'major transparency and accountability gap to be filled',[168] although it did not suggest that the full array of reporting obligations imposed on public companies should also be imposed on private equity-backed companies. Instead the Review suggested a set of voluntary guidelines, regulated on a comply or explain basis. These guidelines are intended to tackle the transparency and accountability gap, and are

---

[165] *Private Equity*, n 2, para 78.
[166] Walker, *Disclosure and Transparency in Private Equity: Consultation Document*, n 3, 6.
[167] Speech by the then Economic Secretary to the Treasury, Ed Balls MP, to the London Business School, March 2007.
[168] Walker, *Disclosure and Transparency in Private Equity: Consultation Document*, n 3, 6.

largely aimed at providing more information about the private equity-backed company, and the private equity firm behind it, to the non-shareholder stakeholders and to the wider public, rather than to the investors.[169]

The Walker guidelines[170] do not apply to all private equity-backed companies but only those that were acquired in one of two ways. The first involves the company being acquired by one or more private equity firms in a public to private transaction, where the market capitalisation together with the premium for acquisition of control was in excess of £300 million, more than 50 per cent of revenues were generated in the UK and UK employees totalled in excess of 1,000 full-time equivalents. The second way involves the company being acquired by one or more private equity firms in a secondary or other non-market transaction where enterprise value at the time of the transaction was in excess of £500 million, more than 50 per cent of revenues were generated in the UK and UK employees totalled in excess of 1,000 full-time equivalents. Only the largest companies are therefore captured by the guidelines. At the time that the Walker Guidelines were published, it was estimated that 65 companies would fall within these criteria.[171]

A Guidelines Monitoring Group has subsequently been established to review the private equity industry's conformity with the Walker Guidelines.[172] This Group has recommended changes to the definition of a portfolio company, which broaden the definition and therefore bring more portfolio companies within the disclosure regime, though the numbers are still relatively small.[173]

Additional reporting requirements are imposed on these companies. The Walker guidelines recommend that they should file their annual report and financial statements on their company website[174] within six months of year end rather than the nine months as otherwise provided by companies' legislation for private companies.[175] That report should include information regarding the identity of the private equity fund or funds that own the company, the senior managers or advisers who have oversight of the fund or funds, and details on the composition of its board.[176] It should also include a business review that substantially conforms to the provisions of section 417 of the Companies Act 2006, including an indication of main trends and factors likely to affect the future development, performance and position of the company's business and to include information on the

---

[169] The guidelines do not have much to say about the need for private equity firms reporting obligations to their investors, beyond noting that private equity firms should, in their reporting to limited partners, follow established guidelines, such as those published by European Venture Capital Association (EVCA) and should commit to follow established guidelines in the valuation of their assets (see eg Walker, *Guidelines for Disclosure and Transparency in Private Equity, Final Report*, n 3, 9).

[170] Ibid, n 3, 24–28.

[171] Ibid, 16.

[172] Guidelines Monitoring Group, *Update Report*, April 2009.

[173] For example, the guidelines Monitoring Group estimated that a further 23 portfolio companies would be brought within the guidelines' disclosure regime as a result of the changes it proposed in April 2009 (although approximately 14 of those 23 portfolio companies already complied on a voluntary basis): Guidelines Monitoring Group, *Update Report*, April 2009.

[174] Generally companies legislation only places an obligation on quoted companies to make annual reports and accounts available on the company website: Companies Act 2006, s 430.

[175] Companies Act 2006, s 442(2)(a). Public companies are generally required to file their reports within six months: s 442(2)(b).

[176] None of the other corporate governance requirements regarding the composition of the board which apply to publicly listed companies are required to be adopted by private equity companies.

company's employees, environmental matters and social and community issues.[177] Finally, it should also include a financial review to cover risk management objectives and policies in the light of the principal financial risks and uncertainties facing the company, including those relating to leverage. These companies should publish a summary mid-year update no later than three months after mid-year giving a brief account of major developments in the company, but the guidelines do not place them under an obligation to comply with the quarterly reporting requirements that are imposed on quoted companies.[178]

The Walker guidelines also envisage more information being provided regarding the private equity firms that are backing these particular private equity companies. Accordingly, they recommend that such private equity firms publish certain information about themselves either by way of an annual review or through regular updating of their websites. The information required includes a description of the firm's structure and investment approach, a description of the UK companies in its portfolio, an indication of the leadership of the firm in the UK and confirmation that arrangements are in place to deal with conflicts of interest, and a categorisation of its limited partners by geography and by type. The guidelines also require firms to publish a statement of their commitment to conform to the guidelines on a comply or explain basis. The Guidelines Monitoring Group is intended to ensure conformity with the guidelines.[179]

It can be seen that these guidelines are fairly limited in scope, both as to the number of private equity-backed companies that fall within their remit, and as to the nature of the disclosure required of these companies. Nevertheless these voluntary guidelines do appear to have quietened the call for legislative intervention in the UK.

By contrast, the European Commission has announced its intention to regulate the private equity industry despite attempts by the European private equity industry to avert mandatory regulation by proposing a unified code of conduct.[180] In April 2009 the European Commission published a proposal for a Directive on Alternative Investment Fund Managers (AIFM),[181] which included regulation of the private equity industry, as well as hedge funds, commodity funds, infrastructure funds and others. The remit of this directive is wider than the remit of the Walker guidelines. In addition to issues of transparency and investor protection the objectives of the draft directive also include the control of systemic risks. This is perhaps unsurprising given the occurrence of the financial crisis and ensuing recession that intervened between the publication of these two different proposals:

> While AIFM were not the cause of the crisis, recent events have placed severe stress on the sector. Many AIFM have experienced liquidity problems as they struggle to manage the mismatch between the degree of liquidity promised to investors and the illiquidity of their investments. In some cases, adverse impacts have been felt by the wider market. For example, the abrupt

---

[177]   See Companies Act 2006, s 417 which otherwise only applies to quoted companies. For discussion see pages 479–80.

[178]   See 10.3.1.2 for discussion of half yearly and quarterly reporting requirements for quoted companies.

[179]   For the role and remit of the Guidelines Monitoring Group see www.walker-gmg.co.uk.

[180]   European Venture Capital Association, *Private Equity and Venture Capital in the European Economy: An Industry response to the European Parliament and European Commission*, Brussels, 25 February 2009 available at www.evca.eu.

[181]   Proposal for a Directive of the European Parliament and of the Council on Alternative Investment Fund Managers, Brussels, 30.4.2009, COM(2009) 207 final.

unwinding of large, leveraged positions by hedge funds in response to tightening credit conditions and investor redemption requests has had a procyclical impact on declining markets and may have impaired market liquidity.[182]

This draft directive has been one of the most rigorously debated pieces of financial regulation ever to emerge from the EU, with over 1,000 amendments tabled by MEPs. At the time of writing the final form of the directive remains to be settled, and indeed there are two competing versions of the directive in play, as the European Parliament and Council each adopted their own versions of the AIFM Directive, on 17 and 18 May 2010 respectively. These competing texts are serving as the basis for negotiations at a series of 'trilogue' meetings, which are taking place between representatives of the Parliament, Council and European Commission, with a view to adopting a single compromise text.[183] A great deal will depend on the compromises reached during this process as significant differences remain between these two versions.

As originally drafted the directive includes provisions designed to enhance the transparency of AIFM and the funds they manage towards supervisors, investors and other key stakeholders. The requirement of transparency to investors is uncontroversial and is something which occurs already in private equity funds[184] and the provision of information to non-shareholder stakeholders is reasonably minimal.[185] It is the requirement to provide information to a financial regulator which marks these proposals out from existing UK practice.[186]

The original draft directive includes provisions designed to ensure that all regulated entities be subject to appropriate governance standards and have robust systems in place for the management of risks, liquidity and conflicts of interest. It is these provisions which will, if implemented, result in the greatest changes in the UK. The directive as originally drafted provides that in order to operate in the European Union, all AIFM be required to obtain authorisation from the competent authority of their home Member State.[187] To ensure that the risks associated with AIFM activity are effectively managed on an ongoing basis, the AIFM would be required, inter alia, to satisfy the competent authority of the robustness of internal arrangements with respect to risk management, in particular liquidity risks and additional operational and counterparty risks associated with short selling; the management and disclosure of conflicts of interest; the fair valuation of assets; and the security of depository/custodial arrangements.[188] It is also notable that the level at which these provisions would apply is set very low in the draft: they apply to funds of 100 million euros, where the assets were acquired through the use of debt, or 500 million euros, where no leveraging was used.[189]

As stated, numerous amendments to this draft have been suggested. The version adopted by the Council differs in a number of important respects from the original draft

---

[182]　Executive Summary of the Impact Assessment of the Proposed Directive, Brussels, 29.4.09, SEC (2009) 577, 3.

[183]　Council of the European Union, 7500/10 (Presse 64) 18 May 2010.

[184]　Proposal for a Directive of the European Parliament and of the Council on Alternative Investment Fund Managers, Brussels, 30.4.2009, COM(2009) 207 final, Article 20.

[185]　Ibid, Article 19.

[186]　Ibid, Article 21.

[187]　Ibid, Article 4.

[188]　See generally articles 4–18.

[189]　Ibid, Article 2.

and the version of the directive adopted by the European Parliament takes a different line on many of these issues.[190] One of the major concerns of the European private equity industry, for example, is that the risks addressed by this directive are mainly prompted by the activities of the hedge fund sector, since it is there that the mismatch between the degree of liquidity promised to investors and the illiquidity of their investments is felt particularly strongly. Private equity funds are illiquid investments during the life of the fund and therefore this mismatch does not arise.[191] However the original draft directive applies equally to all AIFMs, leading the private equity industry to call the regulations contained in the draft directive 'inappropriate, irrelevant or disproportionate'[192] in so far as they relate to that industry. In the version of the directive adopted by the European Parliament, funds such as private equity and investment trusts would be more lightly regulated than hedge funds and some other types of alternative investment funds would be completely exempted.

Until the details of this directive are settled it is impossible to say exactly what impact it will have on the private equity industry. All that can be said for certain is that the directive will be approved in some form and that it will have an impact, potentially a significant impact, on that industry.

14.6.6   Summary

There are a number of explanations put forward to explain the increase in the number of public to private transactions prior to 2008. One practical reason for the increase during the early years of this century is likely to have been a result of an increase in the size of private equity funds and of the cheap debt available to funds, coupled with a reduction in the opportunities in the private arena, as that market became saturated. However, these deals would not be done unless they were perceived as presenting opportunities to the private equity firms, and a number of reasons have been suggested as to why this is likely to be the case.[193]

The first explanation is that a public to private transaction involves tax savings. As discussed, a public company will carry less debt than most private equity-backed companies. Since debt is cheaper than equity (because of the tax saving that is made on interest payments) purchasing a public company, taking it private and leveraging it more highly could involve tax savings, and therefore result in gains to the company and its shareholders.[194]

A second explanation is that the value arises from a reduction of agency costs. This reduction could be due to aligning the incentives of the directors and shareholders more closely (since the directors in private equity companies typically all have substantial equity

---

[190]   The Council of the European Union published an issues note setting out the differences between the positions of the Council and the European Parliament as at January 2010: www.register.consilium.europa.eu/pdf/en/10/st05/st05164.en10.pdf.

[191]   See 14.3.1.

[192]   EVCA, *Response to the Proposed Directive of the European Parliament and Council on Alternative Investment Fund Managers*, Brussels, 26 June 2009, available at www.evca.eu, 2.

[193]   See generally, Centre for Management Buy-out Research (CMBOR), *UK Quarterly Reports* which analyse the trends and report on activity in the UK private equity industry, available at www.nottingham.ac.uk/business/cmbor.

[194]   This is often suggested to be one of the significant gains in US public to private transactions eg SN Kaplan, 'Management Buyouts: Evidence on Taxes as a Source of Value' (1989) 44 *Journal of Finance* 611.

stakes in the company, compared to directors in public companies who tend to have significantly smaller equity stakes). Alternatively it could be because there are fewer shareholders in private equity companies, and those shareholders, particularly the private equity fund, are interested in monitoring the activities of the directors closely, and tend to have the knowledge and experience to do so, in sharp contrast to the position regarding the dispersed shareholders in a public company. The reduction in agency costs could also be due to the fact that private equity companies can solve the free cash problem identified by Professor Jensen, whereby directors in public company hang onto the 'free cash' in a company rather than distributing it to the shareholders.[195] Free cash flow is defined for these purposes as cash flow in excess of that required to fund all investment projects with positive net present values when discounted at the relevant cost of capital. Directors have incentives to retain cash in this way because cash reserves increase their autonomy as regards the capital markets. This can lead to waste and inefficiency, or it might mean that the directors use the cash inappropriately, such as on self-promoting acquisitions. In a private equity company the higher levels of debt mean that the directors are likely to be contractually bound to distribute the free cash (to the creditors) and the shareholders in a private equity company are in a position to force the directors to transfer to them any free cash that remains, should they so wish.

A third possible reason for these transactions is that they generate wealth as a result of wealth transfers from stakeholders to shareholders. This is an issue which has received some attention recently in the context of takeovers.[196] Fourth, these transactions could generate gains for the private equity fund because of reductions in transaction costs, ie the fact that regulatory and other burdens are lower, and therefore cheaper, for private companies. Fifth, the target companies may be undervalued prior to purchase by the private equity fund, ie private equity funds manage to buy the companies cheaply. The gain is therefore their exploitation of their ability to price the company more accurately than the market.

If the gains arise because of tax breaks, or because the company was under priced, or because of wealth transfers between the stakeholders and shareholders, then private equity transactions would not appear to add any particular operational value to the company. By contrast, if the value arises as a result of financial, governance or operational changes in the target company then private equity transactions could be said to create economic value. A recent empirical study has found that, of the various explanations put forward for public to private transactions, support can be found for the view that an important source of expected shareholder wealth gains is the undervaluation of the target firms' share prices over a one-year period prior to the first public to private announcement. However the study also concluded that aligning the directors and shareholders' interests was a relevant factor in the resulting gains, as was the concentration of control among a few shareholders.[197] There was found to be no support for the free cash flow analysis put forward to explain public to private transactions.[198]

---

[195]   See eg MC Jensen, 'Eclipse of the Public Corporation' (1989) 67 *Harvard Business Review* 61 revised version available at www.ssrn.com/abstract=146149 (1997).

[196]   See 12.3.3.

[197]   L Renneboog, T Simons and M Wright, 'Why do Public Firms go Private in the UK? The Impact of Private Equity Investors, Incentive Realignment and Undervaluation' (2007) 13 *Journal of Corporate Finance* 591.

[198]   Ibid.

Other studies have investigated whether private equity transactions increase shareholder wealth via operating and efficiency gains and have concluded that modest operating improvements do result from public to private transactions.[199] Further studies have considered whether the gains to private equity investors come at the expense of stakeholders such as employees and conclude that, on the whole, employment levels continue to increase post-buy out, but at slower levels than other firms in the industry,[200] or that employment grows at an equivalent rate but with slower wage increases.[201] These results are not consistent with concerns about job destruction and indeed seem more consistent with the view that private equity companies create some value by operating more efficiently, since low levels of wage cuts and job reductions are consistent with gains in productivity and operating improvements. Whilst the picture emerging from these studies is by no means clear cut it does at least appear that private equity transactions do add some economic value, although this accounts for only part of the gains made: 'It has been said that private equity made its money by leverage in the 1980s, by price/earnings arbitrage in the 1990s and since then by genuinely changing companies. In fact all three components have always played their part'.[202]

14.7 Conclusion

In the period until 2008, private equity began to be seen as a threat to the public markets and indeed some commentators even suggested that private equity might eventually become the dominant corporate organisational form.[203] The FSA noted in its 2006 analysis of the private equity industry that 'UK equity market capitalisation shrank by a net £46.9 billion in the first half of 2006 and has not grown since the last quarter of 2004. This reflects (in addition to share price movements) the impact of public to private transactions, widespread share buy-backs/payment of special dividends (sometimes as part of a defence against a private equity bid) and reduced capital flows from the private market'.[204] One concern was therefore that the growth of private equity could threaten the public markets by reducing their overall size.

A second concern was that the private equity market could expand to the point where publicly traded companies would be either very mature, stable, cash generative but slow growth companies or highly volatile, perhaps politically sensitive, companies that private equity funds would not consider backing. On this view all (stable) high growth potential

---

[199] Eg C Weir, P Jones and M Wright, 'Public to Private Transactions, Private Equity and Performance in the UK: An Empirical Analysis of the Impact of Going Private' (2008) available at www.ssrn.com/abstract=1138616 (for a UK study) and similar results emerge in a US study: S Guo, E Hotchkiss and W Song, 'Do Buyouts (Still) Create Value?' (2009) available at www.ssrn.com/abstract=1009281.

[200] Eg SN Kaplan, 'The Effects of Management Buyouts on Operating Performance and Value' (1989) 24(2) *Journal of Financial Economics* 217; S Davis, J Haltiwanger, R Jarmin, J Lerner and J Miranda 'Private Equity and Employment' (2008) at www.ssrn.com/abstract=1107175.

[201] K Amess and M Wright, 'The Wage and Employment Effects of Leveraged Buyouts in the UK' (2007) *International Journal of the Economics of Business* 179.

[202] Hale, *Private Equity: A Transactional Analysis*, n 10, 8.

[203] MC Jensen, 'Eclipse of the Public Corporation' (1989) 67 *Harvard Business Review* 61 revised version available at www.ssrn.com/abstract=146149 (1997).

[204] *Private Equity*, n 1, 4.

companies would be privately owned.[205] In addition, the growth potential of those companies that did go public may already have been fully exploited. If this occurred then the quality, size and depth of the public markets could be damaged by the expansion of the private equity market.

However, there is no evidence of this happening in practice. While private equity as a model has a great deal to offer, it does not undermine the value of the public markets. Publicly traded companies perform a very valuable function. They enable a large number of individuals to purchase shares and allow the risk to be borne by investors without requiring them to manage the companies which they own. For very minimal stakes any individual is able to participate in the public market:

> The public corporation is a social invention of vast historical importance. Its genius is rooted in its capacity to spread financial risk over the diversified portfolios of millions of individuals and institutions and to allow investors to customize risk to their unique circumstances and predilections.[206]

After a period of significant public to private transactions, there was a diminution in the number of transactions even prior to 2008, perhaps as the market recognised that one of the main gains for private equity funds in these transactions had been the under valuation of the company.[207] It is likely that private equity investors in the future will acquire public companies only where they can prove that they can add real value that could not be achieved in the public markets.

---

[205]   Ibid, 68.
[206]   Jensen, n 102, 5.
[207]   Once this was recognised, shareholders got better at rejecting the initial offer made by private equity firms, forcing the cost of transactions up and thereby reducing the likely gains to private equity investors.

Index